Contemporary authors, new revision series : ... -- Detroit, MI : Gale Research, c2001.
1 v. ; 29 cm.

1. Authors - Dict. 2. Literature - Bio-bibl. 3. Biography - Dict. 4. Authors, American. 5. U.S. - Bio-bibl.

Contemporary Authors®

NEW REVISION SERIES

ISSN 0275-7176

Contemporary Authors®

A Bio-Bibliographical Guide to Current Writers in Fiction, General Nonfiction, Poetry, Journalism, Drama, Motion Pictures, Television, and Other Fields

NEW REVISION SERIES volume 98

Library of Congress Catalog Card Number 62-52046
ISBN 0-7876-4607-5
ISSN 0275-7176
Printed in the United States of America

10 9 8 7 6 5 4 3 2 1

Contents

Indexing note: All *Contemporary Authors* entries are indexed in the *Contemporary Authors* cumulative index, which is published separately and distributed twice a year.

As always, the most recent Contemporary Authors cumulative index continues to be the user's guide to the location of an individual author's listing.

Preface

Contemporary Authors (*CA*) provides information on approximately 100,000 writers in a wide range of media, including:

- Current writers of fiction, nonfiction, poetry, and drama whose works have been issued by commercial publishers, risk publishers, or university presses (authors whose books have been published only by known vanity or author-subsidized firms are ordinarily not included)

- Prominent print and broadcast journalists, editors, photojournalists, syndicated cartoonists, graphic novelists, screenwriters, television scriptwriters, and other media people

- Authors who write in languages other than English, provided their works have been published in the United States or translated into English

- Literary greats of the early twentieth century whose works are popular in today's high school and college curriculums and continue to elicit critical attention

A *CA* listing entails no charge or obligation. Authors are included on the basis of the above criteria and their interest to *CA* users. Sources of potential listees include trade periodicals, publishers' catalogs, librarians, and other users.

How to Get the Most out of *CA*: Use the Index

The key to locating an author's most recent entry is the *CA* cumulative index, which is published separately and distributed twice a year. It provides access to *all* entries in *CA* and *Contemporary Authors New Revision Series* (*CANR*). Always consult the latest index to find an author's most recent entry.

For the convenience of users, the *CA* cumulative index also includes references to all entries in these Gale literary series: *Authors and Artists for Young Adults, Authors in the News, Bestsellers, Black Literature Criticism, Black Literature Criticism Supplement, Black Writers, Children's Literature Review, Concise Dictionary of American Literary Biography, Concise Dictionary of British Literary Biography, Contemporary Authors Autobiography Series, Contemporary Authors Bibliographical Series, Contemporary Dramatists, Contemporary Literary Criticism, Contemporary Novelists, Contemporary Poets, Contemporary Popular Writers, Contemporary Southern Writers, Contemporary Women Poets, Dictionary of Literary Biography, Dictionary of Literary Biography Documentary Series, Dictionary of Literary Biography Yearbook, DISCovering Authors, DISCovering Authors: British, DISCovering Authors: Canadian, DISCovering Authors: Modules* (including modules for Dramatists, Most-Studied Authors, Multicultural Authors, Novelists, Poets, and Popular/Genre Authors), DISCovering Authors 3.0, *Drama Criticism, Drama for Students, Feminist Writers, Hispanic Literature Criticism, Hispanic Writers, Junior DISCovering Authors, Major Authors and Illustrators for Children and Young Adults, Major 20th-Century Writers, Native North American Literature, Novels for Students, Poetry Criticism, Poetry for Students, Short Stories for Students, Short Story Criticism, Something about the Author, Something about the Author Autobiography Series, St. James Guide to Children's Writers, St. James Guide to Crime & Mystery Writers, St. James Guide to Fantasy Writers, St. James Guide to Horror, Ghost & Gothic Writers, St. James Guide to Science Fiction Writers, St. James Guide to Young Adult Writers, Twentieth-Century Literary Criticism, 20th Century Romance and Historical Writers, World Literature Criticism,* and *Yesterday's Authors of Books for Children.*

A Sample Index Entry:

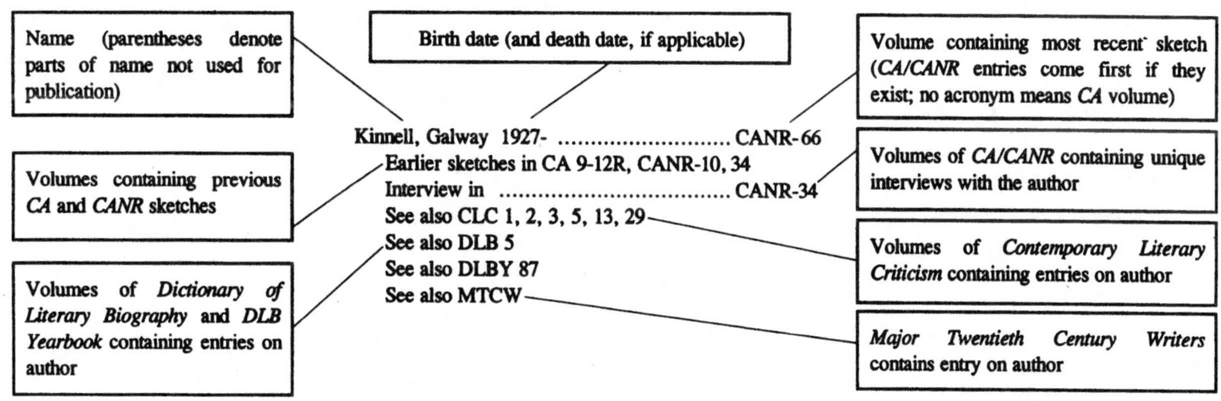

How Are Entries Compiled?

The editors make every effort to secure new information directly from the authors; listees' responses to our questionnaires and query letters provide most of the information featured in *CA*. For deceased writers, or those who fail to reply to requests for data, we consult other reliable biographical sources, such as those indexed in Gale's *Biography and Genealogy Master Index,* and bibliographical sources, including *National Union Catalog, LC MARC,* and *British National Bibliography.* Further details come from published interviews, feature stories, and book reviews, as well as information supplied by the authors' publishers and agents.

An asterisk (*) at the end of a sketch indicates that the listing has been compiled from secondary sources believed to be reliable but has not been personally verified for this edition by the author sketched.

What Kinds of Information Does An Entry Provide?

Sketches in *CA* contain the following biographical and bibliographical information:

- **Entry heading:** the most complete form of author's name, plus any pseudonyms or name variations used for writing

- **Personal information:** author's date and place of birth, family data, ethnicity, educational background, political and religious affiliations, and hobbies and leisure interests

- **Addresses:** author's home, office, or agent's addresses, plus e-mail and fax numbers, as available

- **Career summary:** name of employer, position, and dates held for each career post; resume of other vocational achievements; military service

- **Membership information:** professional, civic, and other association memberships and any official posts held

- **Awards and honors:** military and civic citations, major prizes and nominations, fellowships, grants, and honorary degrees

- **Writings:** a comprehensive, chronological list of titles, publishers, dates of original publication and revised editions, and production information for plays, television scripts, and screenplays

- **Adaptations:** a list of films, plays, and other media which have been adapted from the author's work

- **Work in progress:** current or planned projects, with dates of completion and/or publication, and expected publisher, when known

- **Sidelights:** a biographical portrait of the author's development; information about the critical reception of the author's works; revealing comments, often by the author, on personal interests, aspirations, motivations, and thoughts on writing

- **Interview:** a one-on-one discussion with authors conducted especially for *CA*, offering insight into authors' thoughts about their craft

- **Autobiographical essay:** an original essay written by noted authors for *CA*, a forum in which writers may present themselves, on their own terms, to their audience

- **Photographs:** portraits and personal photographs of notable authors

- **Biographical and critical sources:** a list of books and periodicals in which additional information on an author's life and/or writings appears

- **Obituary Notices** in *CA* provide date and place of birth as well as death information about authors whose full-length sketches appeared in the series before their deaths. The entries also summarize the authors' careers and writings and list other sources of biographical and death information.

Related Titles in the *CA* Series

Contemporary Authors Autobiography Series complements *CA* original and revised volumes with specially commissioned autobiographical essays by important current authors, illustrated with personal photographs they provide. Common topics include their motivations for writing, the people and experiences that shaped their careers, the rewards they derive from their work, and their impressions of the current literary scene.

Contemporary Authors Bibliographical Series surveys writings by and about important American authors since World War II. Each volume concentrates on a specific genre and features approximately ten writers; entries list works written by and about the author and contain a bibliographical essay discussing the merits and deficiencies of major critical and scholarly studies in detail.

Available in Electronic Formats

GaleNet. *CA* is available on a subscription basis through GaleNet, an online information resource that features an easy-to-use end-user interface, powerful search capabilities, and ease of access through the World-Wide Web. For more information, call 1-800-877-GALE.

Licensing. *CA* is available for licensing. The complete database is provided in a fielded format and is deliverable on such media as disk, CD-ROM, or tape. For more information, contact Gale's Business Development Group at 1-800-877-GALE, or visit us on our website at www.galegroup.com/bizdev.

Suggestions Are Welcome

The editors welcome comments and suggestions from users on any aspect of the *CA* series. If readers would like to recommend authors for inclusion in future volumes of the series, they are cordially invited to write the Editors at *Contemporary Authors*, Gale Group, 27500 Drake Rd., Farmington Hills, MI 48331-3535; or call at 1-248-699-4253; or fax at 1-248-699-8054.

Contemporary Authors Product Advisory Board

The editors of *Contemporary Authors* are dedicated to maintaining a high standard of excellence by publishing comprehensive, accurate, and highly readable entries on a wide array of writers. In addition to the quality of the content, the editors take pride in the graphic design of the series, which is intended to be orderly yet inviting, allowing readers to utilize the pages of *CA* easily and with efficiency. Despite the longevity of the *CA* print series, and the success of its format, we are mindful that the vitality of a literary reference product is dependent on its ability to serve its users over time. As literature, and attitudes about literature, constantly evolve, so do the reference needs of students, teachers, scholars, journalists, researchers, and book club members. To be certain that we continue to keep pace with the expectations of our customers, the editors of *CA* listen carefully to their comments regarding the value, utility, and quality of the series. Librarians, who have firsthand knowledge of the needs of library users, are a valuable resource for us. The *Contemporary Authors* Product Advisory Board, made up of school, public, and academic librarians, is a forum to promote focused feedback about *CA* on a regular basis. The five-member advisory board includes the following individuals, whom the editors wish to thank for sharing their expertise:

- **Barbara C. Chumard,** Reference/Adult Services Librarian, Middletown Thrall Library, Middletown, New York.

- **Eva M. Davis,** Teen Services Librarian, Plymouth District Library, Plymouth, Michigan.

- **Adam Janowski, Jr.,** Library Media Specialist, Naples High School Library Media Center, Naples, Florida.

- **Robert Reginald,** Head of Technical Services and Collection Development, California State University, San Bernadino, California.

- **Barbara A. Wencl,** Media Specialist, Como Park High School, St. Paul, Minnesota.

International Advisory Board

Well-represented among the 100,000 author entries published in *Contemporary Authors* are sketches on notable writers from many non-English-speaking countries. The primary criteria for inclusion of such authors has traditionally been the publication of at least one title in English, either as an original work or as a translation. However, the editors of *Contemporary Authors* came to observe that many important international writers were being overlooked due to a strict adherence to our inclusion criteria. In addition, writers who were publishing in languages other than English were not being covered in the traditional sources we used for identifying new listees. Intent on increasing our coverage of international authors, including those who write only in their native language and have not been translated into English, the editors enlisted the aid of a board of advisors, each of whom is an expert on the literature of a particular country or region. Among the countries we focused attention on in 2000 are Mexico, Puerto Rico, Germany, Luxembourg, Belgium, the Netherlands, Norway, Sweden, Denmark, Finland, Taiwan, Singapore, and Japan, as well as England, Scotland, Wales, Ireland, Australia, and New Zealand. The nine-member advisory board includes the following individuals, whom the editors wish to thank for sharing their expertise:

- **Lowell A. Bangerter,** Professor of German, University of Wyoming, Laramie, Wyoming.

- **David William Foster,** Regent's Professor of Spanish, Interdisciplinary Humanities, and Women's Studies, Arizona State University, Tempe, Arizona.

- **Frances Devlin-Glass,** Associate Professor, School of Literary and Communication Studies, Deakin University, Burwood, Victoria, Australia.

- **Hosea Hirata,** Director of the Japanese Program, Associate Professor of Japanese, Tufts University, Medford, Massachusetts.

- **Linda M. Rodríguez Guglielmoni,** Associate Professor, University of Puerto Rico—Mayagüez, Puerto Rico.

- **Sven Hakon Rossel,** Professor and Chair of Scandanvian Studies, University of Vienna, Vienna, Austria.

- **Steven R. Serafin,** Director, Writing Center, Hunter College of the City University of New York, New York City.

- **Ismail S. Talib,** Senior Lecturer, Department of English Language and Literature, National University of Singapore, Singapore.

- **Mark Williams,** Associate Professor, English Department, University of Canterbury, Christchurch, New Zealand.

CA Numbering System and Volume Update Chart

Occasionally questions arise about the *CA* numbering system and which volumes, if any, can be discarded. Despite numbers like " 29-32R," " 97-100" and " 189," the entire *CA* print series consists of only 215 physical volumes with the publication of *CA* Volume 190. The following charts note changes in the numbering system and cover design, and indicate which volumes are essential for the most complete, up-to-date coverage.

***CA* First Revision**

- 1-4R through 41-44R (11 books)
  Cover: Brown with black and gold trim.
  There will be no further First Revision volumes because revised entries are now being handled exclusively through the more efficient *New Revision Series* mentioned below.

***CA* Original Volumes**

- 45-48 through 97-100 (14 books)
  Cover: Brown with black and gold trim.
  101 through 190 (90 books)
  Cover: Blue and black with orange bands.
  The same as previous *CA* original volumes but with a new, simplified numbering system and new cover design.

***CA* Permanent Series**

- *CAP*-1 and *CAP*-2 (2 books)
  Cover: Brown with red and gold trim.
  There will be no further Permanent Series volumes because revised entries are now being handled exclusively through the more efficient *New Revision Series* mentioned below.

***CA* New Revision Series**

- CANR-1 through CANR-98 (98 books)
  Cover: Blue and black with green bands.
  Includes only sketches requiring significant changes; **sketches are taken from any previously published CA, CAP, or CANR volume.**

If You Have:	You May Discard:
CA First Revision Volumes 1-4R through 41-44R and *CA Permanent Series* Volumes 1 and 2	*CA* Original Volumes 1, 2, 3, 4 Volumes 5-6 through 41-44
CA Original Volumes 45-48 through 97-100 and 101 through 190	**NONE:** These volumes will not be superseded by corresponding revised volumes. Individual entries from these and all other volumes appearing in the left column of this chart may be revised and included in the various volumes of the *New Revision Series.*
CA New Revision Series Volumes *CANR*-1 through *CANR*-98	**NONE:** The *New Revision Series* does not replace any single volume of *CA*. Instead, volumes of *CANR* include entries from many previous *CA* series volumes. All *New Revision Series* volumes must be retained for full coverage.

A Sampling of Authors and Media People Featured in This Volume

John Crowley

Crowley is consistently lauded for his thoughtful, finely wrought works of science fiction and fantasy, which include the novels *The Deep, Ægypt, Love and Sleep,* and *Dæmonomania.* Critics are quick to point out that his fiction rises above mere genre trappings, challenging the accepted perceptions of things and offering multi-layered mysteries for his characters—and his readers—to explore. Crowley is the winner of two World Fantasy Awards, for *Little, Big* in 1982 and *Great Work of Time* in 1990.

Vine Deloria, Jr.

A Standing Rock Sioux lawyer and educator, Deloria is perhaps the most prominent spokesman in the U.S. for Native American nationalism. He gained reknown in 1969 with the publication of his first book, *Custer Died for Your Sins: An Indian Manifesto,* which is a scathing indictment of white America's treatment of Indians and an articulation of the goal of Indian activists, an existence that is culturally but not economically separate. Deloria has, in addition to serving as executive director of the National Congress of American Indians and chair of the Institute for the Development of Indian Law, written several books decrying the effects of racism and colonialism and advocating a strong Indian nationalism.

Laurie Garrett

A veteran science reporter who has examined a wide range of health topics, Garrett focuses her research on deadly diseases and the global threat they pose in the twenty-first century. Her books, which include *The Coming Plague: Newly Emerging Diseases in a World out of Balance* and *Betrayal of Trust: The Collapse of Global Public Health,* warn readers that new, deadly diseases are threatening humans, that some microbes are becoming resistant to antibiotics, and that governments have become dangerously complacent about public health. Garrett has won many honors for her journalism, including a George Foster Peabody Award, a Polk Award, and the Pulitzer Prize.

Lynn Johnston

Johnston is the creator of the "For Better or for Worse" comic strip, which has been collected in many volumes, including *Things Are Looking Up* and *Sunshine & Shadow.* Her drawings of the fictional Patterson family are seen in hundreds of newspapers in the United States and Canada, and "For Better or for Worse," which developed out of many of Johnston's real life situations and concerns, has consistently been voted as one of the top five strips in reader polls. Johnston has received a Reuben Award, a National Cartoonists Society Category Award for best comic strip, an Inkpot Award, and numerous other honors.

Stanley Kunitz

Kunitz became the tenth Poet Laureate of the United States in the autumn of 2000. Although ninety-five years old at the time, he was still actively publishing and promoting poetry to new generations of readers. Kunitz's first volume of poetry, *Intellectual Things,* was published in 1930 and he has continued to publish consistently throughout the greater part of the twentieth century, exerting a subtle but steady influence on such major poets as Theodore Roethke, W. H. Auden, and Robert Lowell. Through his teaching, he has provided encouragement to hundreds of younger poets as well. In 1959 Kunitz received a Pulitzer Prize for his third poetry collection, *Selected Poems, 1928-1958.*

Chaim Potok

Potok is familiar to many readers as the author of best-selling novels like *The Chosen* and *The Promise.* Less well known, though equally important to Potok, is his devotion to Judaism: he is an ordained rabbi and scholar of Judaic texts. Potok's personal attempts to reconcile these disparate commitments have enriched his fiction, as many of his works explore the ways in which characters learn to deal with cultural conflict. Potok was honored with a National Book Award nomination for *The Chosen* and a Jewish National Book Award for *The Gift of Asher Lev.*

W. G. Sebald

German-born literary and theatrical scholar Sebald, who immigrated to England in 1966, is widely known in the German-speaking world for his genre-crossing works of creative prose, as well as for his literary criticism. His novels, including *Vertigo, The Emigrants,* and *The Rings of Saturn,* were published in English during the 1990s to nearly universal acclaim. Joining that list is his novel

Austerlitz, published in 2001. Sebald has received a number of international awards honoring his works, including a Berlin Literature Prize, *Jewish Quarterly* Literary Prize for fiction, *Los Angeles Times* Book Prize for Fiction, and Heinrich Böll Preis.

Banana Yoshimoto

Yoshimoto took Japan by storm in 1988 with her premier work, *Kitchen,* comprised of two novellas about life and death in contemporary Japan. *Kitchen,* of particular appeal to young adults, sold over two million copies in Japan and won several literary awards. Four years later Yoshimoto's audience expanded to the United States when an English translation of *Kitchen* made its way onto best-seller lists. Yoshimoto's 2000 novel *Asleep* is a collection of three novellas, "each telling a somewhat mystical tale of haunted slumber," according to Kathleen Hughes in *Booklist.*

Acknowledgments

Grateful acknowledgment is madc to those publishers, photographers, and artists whose work appear with these authors' essays. Following is a list of the copyright holders who have granted us permission to reproduce material in this volume of *CA*. Every effort has been made to trace copyright, but if omissions have been made, please let us know.

Photographs/Art

Malcolm Bradbury: Bradbury, photograph. © Jerry Bauer. Reproduced by permission.

Barbara Taylor Bradford: Bradford, photograph by Deborah Feingold. Reproduced by permission of Bradford Enterprises.

Rosellen Brown: Brown, photograph. © Jerry Bauer. Reproduced by permission.

Jackie Collins: Collins, photograph. AP/Wide World Photos. Reproduced by permission.

Vine Deloria, Jr.: Deloria, photograph. The Library of Congress.

Jacques Derrida: Derrida, photograph. Archive Photos, Inc. Reproduced by permission.

Howard Fast: Fast, photograph. AP/Wide World Photos. Reproduced by permission.

Tony Harrison: Harrison, photograph. Mark Gerson. Reproduced by permission.

Lynn Johnston: Johnston, photograph. Reproduced by permission.

Stanley Kunitz: Kunitz, photograph. © Jerry Bauer. Reproduced by permission.

Colleen McCullough: McCullough, photograph. AP/Wide World Photos. Reproduced by permission.

Sharon Olds: Olds, photograph. Reproduced by permission of author.

Thomas Neilson Paulin: Paulin, photograph. Mark Gerson. Reproduced by permission.

Chaim Potok: Potok, photograph. © Jerry Bauer. Reproduced by permission.

Carol Shields: Shields, photograph. AP/Wide World Photos. Reproduced by permission.

A

** Indicates that a listing has been compiled from secondary sources believed to be reliable, but has not been personally verified for this edition by the author sketched.*

AFKHAMI, Mahnaz 1941-

PERSONAL: Born January 18, 1941, in Kerman, Iran; dual citizen of Iran and the United States; daughter of Majid and Ferdows (Naficy) Ebrahimi; married Gholam R. Afkhami (a scholar), 1959; children: Babak. *Ethnicity:* "Iranian." *Education:* University of Colorado, M.A. and doctoral study. *Religion:* Muslim.

ADDRESSES: *Home*—3101 Cummings Lane, Chevy Chase, MD 20815. *Office*—Women's Learning Partnership for Rights, Development, and Peace, 4343 Montgomery Ave., Suite 201, Bethesda, MD 20814; fax: 301-654-2775. *Agent*—Edite Kroll, Edite Kroll Literary Agency, 12 Grayhurst Park, Portland, ME 04102. *E-mail*—wlp@learningpartnership.org.

CAREER: *Abstracts of English Studies,* Boulder, CO, assistant editor, 1965-66; University of Colorado, Colorado Springs, lecturer, 1966-67; National University of Iran (also known as Melli University), Teheran, assistant professor of English, 1967-68, department head, 1968-70; Women's Organization of Iran, secretary general, 1970-79, chair of board of trustees of School of Social Work, 1973-79; consultant on women and development, 1979-81; Foundation for Iranian Studies, executive director and publisher of *Iran Nameh,* 1981—. Oral History of Iran Archives, founder, 1982, director, 1982—; Sisterhood Is Global Institute, vice-president, 1989-92, executive director, 1992-96, president, 1996-99; Women's Learning Partnership for Rights, Development, and Peace, founder and president, 2000—. Human Rights Watch, member of advisory committee on women, 1991—; World Movement for Democracy, member of steering committee, 1999—; Harvard University, John F. Kennedy School of Government, member of steering committee of Women Waging Peace Initiative, Women and Public Policy Program, 1999—. National Blood Transfusion Organization of Iran, founding member, 1974; Government of Iran, member of High Council for Welfare, 1974-79, and High Council for Family Planning, 1975-79, minister of state for women's affairs and prime minister's deputy for South Teheran Urban Development and Welfare Project, both 1976-78; Sixth National Development Plan of Iran, chair of Quality of Life Planning Committee, 1977; Organization for Exceptional Children (of Iran), member of board of directors and chair of executive committee, 1977-79. International Council of Women, head of Iranian delegations, 1972-75; United Nations General Assembly, adviser to Iranian delegation, later organizer of a panel on global feminism, 1993; Global Fund for Women, member of advisory board, 1998—; Parliamentarians for Global Action, member of steering committee for Women in Legislation League project, 1999—; World Water Vision, member of gender advisory committee, 1999—. Maryland Public Television, member of advisory committee for Women's Global Film Project, 1994—; guest on television and radio programs in the United States and abroad, including presentations of Voice of America, National Public Radio, and Radio Free Iran. Member of board of trustees, Kerman University, 1976-79, and Farah University for Women, 1977-79.

MEMBER: Middle East Studies Association, Association of Women in Development (member of international advisory group, 1998—).

AWARDS, HONORS: Shared One Hundred Heroines Award, Sisterhood Is Global Institute, 1998.

WRITINGS:

(With Charlotte Albright) *Iran: A Pre-collegiate Handbook,* Foundation for Iranian Studies, 1992.

Women in Exile, University Press of Virginia (Charlottesville, VA), 1994.

(Editor, with Erika Friedl) *In the Eye of the Storm: Women in Post-revolutionary Iran,* Syracuse University Press (Syracuse, NY), 1994.

(Editor and author of introduction) *Women and the Law in Iran, 1967-1978* (in Persian), Foundation for Iranian Studies, 1994.

Faith and Freedom: Women's Human Rights in the Muslim World, Syracuse University Press (Syracuse, NY), 1995.

(With Haleh Vaziri) *Claiming Our Rights: A Manual for Women's Human Rights Education in Muslim Societies,* Sisterhood Is Global Institute (Bethesda, MD), 1996.

(Contributor) Diane Bell and Renate Klein, editors, *Radically Speaking: Feminism Reclaimed,* Spinifex Press, 1996.

(Editor, with Erika Friedl) *Muslim Women and the Politics of Participation: Implementing the Beijing Platform in Muslim Societies,* Syracuse University Press (Syracuse, NY), 1997.

(With Vaziri and Greta H. Nemiroff) *Safe and Secure: Eliminating Violence against Women and Girls in Muslim Societies,* Sisterhood Is Global Institute (Bethesda, MD), 1998.

(Contributor) Marjorie Agosin, editor, *A Map of Hope,* Rutgers University Press (New Brunswick, NJ), 1999.

(Contributor) Courtney Howland, editor, *Religious Fundamentalisms and the Human Rights of Women,* St. Martin's Press (New York, NY), 1999.

Also editor, with Goli Emami, of *Readings in Feminist Theory: An Anthology* (in Persian), 1995. Work represented in other anthologies, including *Sisterhood Is Global: The International Women's Movement Anthology,* edited by Robin Morgan, 1984; *Women, Culture, and Society: A Reader,* Kendall/Hunt, 1994; and *Women in Iran from Medieval Times to the Islamic Republic,* edited by Guity Nashat, 1994. Contributor to periodicals, including *Ms.* Afkhami's writings have been published in Bulgarian, German, Spanish, Arabic, Azeri, Bangla, Hindi, Malay, Russian, Urdu, Uzbek, and Turkish.

BIOGRAPHICAL/CRITICAL SOURCES:

PERIODICALS

New York Times, December 29, 1996, Barbara Crossette, "A Manual on Rights of Women under Islam."

OTHER

Sisterhood Is Global Institute, http://www.sigi.org/ (September 14, 2000).

Women's Learning Partnership, http://www.learningpartnership.org/ (May 22, 2001).

* * *

AHLBERG, Allan 1938-

PERSONAL: Born June 5, 1938, in England; married Janet Hall (an illustrator), July, 1969 (died, 1994); children: Jessica. *Education:* Sunderland College of Education, certificate in education, 1966.

ADDRESSES: Home and office—20 Nether Hall Ln., Birstall, Leicester LE4 4DT, England. *Office*—c/o Penguin Books Ltd., 27 Wrights Ln., London W8 5TZ, England.

CAREER: Worked as letter carrier, grave digger, soldier, plumber's helper, and teacher; full-time children's writer, 1975—.

AWARDS, HONORS: Commendation, British Library Association, 1977, for *Burglar Bill;* Kate Greenaway Medal, British Library Association, 1979, citation, Notable Children's Book Committee of the Association for Library Service to Children, 1979, and citation on honor list for illustration in Great Britain, International Board on Books for Young People, 1980, all for *Each Peach Pear Plum;* Other Award, Children's Rights Workshop, 1980, for *Mrs. Plug the Plumber;* Best Books of the Year award, *School Library Journal,* 1981, and Silver Paint Brush award (Holland), 1988, both for *Funnybones;* citation, Notable Children's Book Committee of the Association for Library Service to Children, 1981, and Best Book for Babies award, *Parents* magazine, 1985, both for *Peek-a-Boo!;* commendation, British Library Association, 1982, Best Books of the Year award, *School Library Journal,* 1983, Children's Books of the Year award, Library of Congress, 1983, Teacher's Choice award, National Council of Teachers of English, 1983, and citation, Notable Children's Book Committee of the Association for Library Service to Children, 1983, all for *The Baby's Catalogue;* Emil/Kurt Mashler Award, British Book Trust, commendation, British Library Association, and award, Federation of Children's Book Groups, all 1986, Golden Key (Holland), 1988, and Prix du Livre pour la Jeunesse (France), all for *The*

Jolly Postman; or, Other People's Letters; Signal Poetry Award, 1990, for *Heard It in the Playground;* Kate Greenaway Medal, British Library Association, 1991, for *The Jolly Christmas Postman;* runner-up, British Book Awards, 1989, 1991.

WRITINGS:

CHILDREN'S BOOKS; WITH WIFE, JANET AHLBERG

Here Are the Brick Street Boys (part of "Brick Street Boys" series), Collins, 1975.
A Place to Play (part of "Brick Street Boys" series), Collins, 1975.
Sam the Referee (part of "Brick Street Boys" series), Collins, 1975.
Fred's Dream (part of "Brick Street Boys" series), Collins, 1976.
The Great Marathon Football Match (part of "Brick Street Boys" series), Collins, 1976.
The Old Joke Book, Kestrel, 1976, Viking, 1977.
The Vanishment of Thomas Tull, Scribner, 1977.
Burglar Bill, Greenwillow, 1977.
Jeremiah in the Dark Woods, Kestrel, 1977, Viking, 1978.
Cops and Robbers (verse), Greenwillow, 1978.
Each Peach Pear Plum: An "I Spy" Story (verse), Kestrel, 1978, Viking, 1979.
The One and Only Two Heads, Collins, 1979.
Two Wheels, Two Heads, Collins, 1979.
Son of a Gun, Heinemann, 1979.
The Little Worm Book, Granada, 1979, Viking, 1980.
Funnybones, Greenwillow, 1980.
Peek-a-Boo! (verse), Viking, 1981, published in England as *Peepo!,* Kestrel, 1981.
The Ha Ha Bonk Book, Penguin, 1982.
The Baby's Catalogue (see also below), Little, Brown, 1982.
Yum Yum (part of "Slot Book" series), Viking (London, England), 1984, Viking (New York, NY), 1985.
Playmates (part of "Slot Book" series), Viking (London, England), 1984, Viking (New York, City), 1985.
The Jolly Postman; or, Other People's Letters, Little, Brown, 1986.
The Cinderella Show, Viking (New York, NY), 1986.
The Clothes Horse and Other Stories, Viking (London, England), 1987, Viking (New York, NY), 1988.
Starting School, Viking (New York, NY), 1988.
Bye-Bye, Baby: A Sad Story with a Happy Ending, Little, Brown, 1989, published as *Bye-Bye, Baby: A Baby without a Mommy in Search of One,* 1990.
The Jolly Christmas Postman, Little, Brown, 1991.
The Bear Nobody Wanted, Viking, 1992.
It Was a Dark and Stormy Night, Viking, 1993.
The Jolly Pocket Postman, Little, Brown, 1995.
See the Rabbit, Doll and Teddy, Baby Sleeps, and *Blue Pram* (board books adapted from *The Baby's Catalogue*), Little, Brown, 1998.

"HAPPY FAMILIES" SERIES

Mr. Biff the Boxer, illustrated by Janet Ahlberg, Puffin, 1980, published in "Wacky Families" series, Golden Press (New York, NY), 1982.
Mr. Cosmo the Conjuror, illustrated by Joe Wright, Puffin, 1980.
Miss Jump the Jockey, illustrated by Andre Amstutz, Puffin, 1980.
Master Salt the Sailor's Son, illustrated by A. Amstutz, Puffin, 1980, published in "Wacky Families" series, Golden Press (New York, NY), 1982.
Mrs. Plug the Plumber, illustrated by J. Wright, Puffin, 1980, published in "Wacky Families" series, Golden Press (New York, NY), 1982.
Mrs. Wobble the Waitress, illustrated by J. Ahlberg, Puffin, 1980, published in "Wacky Families" series, Golden Press (New York, NY), 1982.
Miss Brick the Builder's Baby, illustrated by Colin McNaughton, Puffin, 1981, published in "Wacky Families" series, Golden Press (New York, NY), 1982.
Mr. Buzz the Beeman, illustrated by Faith Jaques, Puffin, 1981, published in "Wacky Families" series, Golden Press (New York, NY), 1982.
Mr. and Mrs. Hay the Horse, illustrated by C. McNaughton, Puffin, 1981, published in "Wacky Families" series, Golden Press (New York, NY), 1982.
Mr. Tick the Teacher, illustrated by F. Jaques, Puffin, 1981.
Mrs. Lather's Laundry, illustrated by A. Amstutz, Puffin, 1981, published in "Wacky Families" series, Golden Press (New York, NY), 1982.
Master Money the Millionaire, illustrated by A. Amstutz, Puffin, 1981.
Master Bun the Baker's Boy, illustrated by Fritz Wegner, Puffin, 1988.
Miss Dose the Doctor's Daughter, illustrated by F. Wegner, Puffin, 1988.
Mr. Creep the Crook, illustrated by A. Amstutz, Puffin, 1988.
Mrs. Jolly's Joke Shop, illustrated by C. McNaughton, Viking (New York, NY), 1988.
Miss Dust the Dustman's Daughter, illustrated by Tony Ross, Viking, 1996.
Mrs. Vole the Vet, illustrated by Emma Chichester-Clark, Viking, 1996.

Ms. Cliff the Climber, illustrated by F. Wegner, Viking, 1997.

Master Track's Train, illustrated by A. Amstutz, Viking, 1997.

"HELP YOUR CHILD TO READ" SERIES

Bad Bear (also see below), illustrated by Eric Hill, Granada, 1982.

Double Ducks (also see below), illustrated by E. Hill, Granada, 1982.

Fast Frog (also see below), illustrated by E. Hill, Granada, 1982.

Poorly Pig (also see below), illustrated by E. Hill, Granada, 1982, Rand McNally, 1984.

Rubber Rabbit (also see below), illustrated by E. Hill, Granada, 1982.

Silly Sheep (also see below), illustrated by E. Hill, Granada, 1982.

Hip-Hippo-Ray, illustrated by A. Amstutz, Granada, 1983, Rand McNally, 1984.

King Kangaroo, illustrated by A. Amstutz, Granada, 1983.

Mister Wolf, illustrated by A. Amstutz, Granada, 1983.

Spider Spy, illustrated by A. Amstutz, Granada, 1983.

Tell-Tale-Tiger, illustrated by A. Amstutz, Granada, 1983.

Travelling Moose, illustrated by A. Amstutz, Granada, 1983.

Fast Frog and Friends: Help Your Child to Read Collection (first six volumes of series), illustrated by E. Hill, Dragon, 1984.

"DAISYCHAINS" VERSE SERIES

Ready Teddy Go, illustrated by J. Ahlberg, Heinemann, 1983.

Summer Snowmen, illustrated by J. Ahlberg, Heinemann, 1983.

That's My Baby!, illustrated by J. Ahlberg, Heinemann, 1983.

Which Witch, illustrated by J. Ahlberg, Heinemann, 1983.

Monster Munch, illustrated by A. Amstutz, Heinemann, 1984.

The Good Old Dolls, illustrated by A. Amstutz, Heinemann, 1984.

Rent-a-Robot, illustrated by A. Amstutz, Heinemann, 1984.

Clowning About, illustrated by A. Amstutz, Heinemann, 1984.

One True Santa, illustrated by J. Ahlberg, Heinemann, 1985.

"FOLDAWAYS" SERIES; ILLUSTRATED BY C. MCNAUGHTON

Families, Granada, 1984.

Monsters, Granada, 1984.

Zoo, Granada, 1984.

Circus, Granada, 1984.

"RED NOSE READERS" SERIES; ILLUSTRATED BY C. MCNAUGHTON

Jumping, Walker, 1985.

So Can I, Walker, 1985.

Big Bad Pig, Random House, 1985.

Bear's Birthday, Walker, 1985.

Help!, Random House, 1985.

Fee Fi Fo Fum, Random House, 1985.

Happy Worm, Random House, 1985.

Make a Face, Walker, 1985.

One Two Flea!, Walker, 1986.

Tell Us a Story, Walker, 1986.

Blow Me Down, Walker, 1986.

Look out for the Seals!, Walker, 1986.

Shirley Shops, Random House, 1986.

Me and My Friend, Random House, 1986.

Crash, Bang, Wallop!, Random House, 1986.

Push the Dog, Random House, 1986.

Who Stole the Pie, Walker, 1996.

Put on a Show!, Walker, 1996.

"FUNNYBONES" SERIES; ILLUSTRATED BY A. AMSTUTZ

The Pet Shop, Greenwillow, 1990.

The Black Cat, Greenwillow, 1990.

Mystery Tour, Greenwillow, 1991.

Dinosaur Dreams, Greenwillow, 1991.

Bumps in the Night, Greenwillow, 1991.

Give the Dog a Bone, Greenwillow, 1991.

Skeleton Crew, Greenwillow, 1992.

The Ghost Train, Greenwillow, 1992.

"FAST FOX, SLOW DOG" SERIES; ILLUSTRATED BY A. AMSTUTZ

Chicken, Chips, and Peas, Viking, 1999.

Fast Fox Goes Crazy, Viking, 1999.

The Hen House, Viking, 1999.

Slow Dog Falling, Viking, 1999.

Slow Dog's Nose, Viking, 2000.

OTHER

The History of a Pair of Sinners: Forgetting Not Their Ma Who Was One Also (verse), illustrated by John Lawrence, Granada, 1980.

Ten in a Bed (fiction), illustrated by A. Amstutz, Granada, 1983.

Please, Mrs. Butler (verse), illustrated by F. Wegner, Kestrel Books, 1983.

Woof! (fiction), illustrated by F. Wegner, Viking (New York, NY), 1986.

The Mighty Slide (verse), illustrated by Charlotte Voake, Viking (New York, NY), 1988.

Heard It in the Playground (verse), Viking (New York, NY), 1989.

Mrs. Butler Song Book (based on poems from *Please, Mrs. Butler* and *Heard It in the Playground*), music by Colin Matthews, illustrated by F. Wegner, Viking, 1992.

The Giant Baby, illustrated by F. Wegner, Viking, 1994.

The Better Brown Stories, illustrated by F. Wegner, Viking, 1995.

Janet's Last Book: Janet Ahlberg 1944-1994 (biography), Penguin, 1997.

The Mysteries of Zigomar, illustrated by J. Lawrence, Walker, 1997.

Mockingbird, illustrated by Paul Howard, Walker, 1998.

Monkey Do!, illustrated by A. Amstutz, 1998.

The Bravest Ever Bear, illustrated by Paul Howard, Walker, 1999.

My Brother's Ghost, illustrated by F. Wegner, Viking, 2000.

The Snail House, illustrated by Gillian Tyler, Candlewick Press (Cambridge, MA), 2001.

The Man Who Wore All His Clothes, illustrated by Katharine McEwen, Candlewick Press (Cambridge, MA), 2001.

Treasure Hunt, illustrated by Gillian Tyler, Candlewick Press (Cambridge, MA), in press.

The Woman Who Won Things, illustrated by Katharine McEwen, Candlewick Press (Cambridge, MA), in press.

Also author of the stage play, *The Giant's Baby.*

ADAPTATIONS: A number of Allan and Janet Ahlberg's books are available on audiocassette, including *A Place to Play, Fred's Dream,* and *Each Peach Pear Plum.*

SIDELIGHTS: Allan Ahlberg is an award-winning British writer of children's stories, verse, picture books, and short novels. He is known for his irreverent wit and unfailing ability to make the commonplace quite extraordinary. Ahlberg manages to imbue simple reading books with a tongue-in-cheek humor that keeps kids turning the pages. In series such as the "Red Nose Readers," "Funnybones," and the ever-popular and zany "Happy Families," Ahlberg sets nonsense rhymes at play and teases inspiration out of academic reading schemes. Reviewing the "Happy Families" series, Jeff Hynds of *Books for Keeps* wondered: "How was it that Allan Ahlberg could write books like those in reading schemes and yet, unlike the schemes be so entertaining?" Hynds answered his own question, "This is Ahlberg in satirical vein—Ahlberg the arch-parodist. . . . 'Happy Families' is not a reading scheme but a wonderful parody of one."

From the outset of his writing career, in collaboration with his wife, Janet, an illustrator, Ahlberg enjoyed such self-referential parodies. His first series, the "Brick Street Boys," was a send-up of the old "Dick and Jane" readers, in comic book style. Since the mid-1970s, Ahlberg has worked with his wife and other illustrators, including Andre Amstutz, Eric Hill, Colin McNaughton, and Fritz Wegner, to create hundreds of titles, each bearing the distinctive Ahlberg humor, light-heartedness, and exaggeration. Such a formula has obviously worked; his "Happy Families" series has sold two and a half million copies in the United Kingdom in the twenty years since it was first published. Ahlberg has also won such prestigious awards as the Kate Greenaway Medal for his seemingly effortless labors.

Born in 1938, Ahlberg was educated at Sunderland Teacher Training College in England where he met his future wife, Janet Hall. In 1969 the two married and Ahlberg went on to work at a variety of jobs, including teaching. His wife, meanwhile, was pursuing a career in the graphic arts. By the mid-1970s they had set up a collaborative effort producing picture books, a joint effort that began with the "Brick Street Boys," and carried them through twenty years and over forty titles, including the popular and award-winning *Each Peach Pear Plum* and the "Jolly Postman" books.

Ahlberg created numerous picture books during the years of collaborative effort with his wife, and since her death in 1994 from cancer has continued to blend his sardonic humor and often-times wacky view of the world with the illustrations of a wide range of talented artists. The "Happy Families" series, twenty books strong and growing, features the antics of a variety of families from *Mr. Biff the Boxer,* the first title in 1980, to *Ms. Cliff the Climber,* in 1997. "To the uninitiated," remarked Hynds, "they might seem like simple stories in simple language, but those who think like this are missing the parody and underestimating the linguistic tricks that Ahlberg plays continually with his readers." There are silly jokes and puns galore, and parodies of the prescribed word repetition for beginning readers, as well as a "consistently excellent interplay . . . between text and illustrations," according to Hynds. Some of the stories also involve rather complex themes, such as the competing needs of work and family when divorce breaks up a family as in *Mrs. Vole the Vet.* Liz Waterland, reviewing the classroom use of the "Happy Families" books in *Books for Keeps,* noted that "sophisticated and mature readership skills" were needed for these books, despite their simple vocabulary. Waterland went on to call the series a "delight," offering "little gems of entertainment." Reviewing *Master Bun the Baker's Boy* and *Miss Dose the Doctor's Daughter, Growing Point*'s Margery Fisher concluded, "Simple jokes and expressive, dramatically active coloured pictures should confirm the popularity of a favourite series, conducted with the utmost expertise in word and line." Reviewing several titles in the series, including *Miss Dose the Doctor's Daughter,* a writer for *Books for Keeps* commented on Ahlberg's "resourceful and ambitious" female character who saves her whole town. The same reviewer concluded, "I have no idea how the Ahlbergs do it but everything they do is magic and these . . . books by Allan Ahlberg are winners all over again." Jill Bennett, writing in *Books for Keeps,* praised a 1997 addition to the series, *Master Track's Train,* as a "homage to Oscar Wilde which will amuse adult readers in this multi-layered story which is told through many voices." In this tale, young Toby gives chase to would-be train robbers, the Creeps, who also have their own book in the series.

Another popular series from Ahlberg, working with illustrator Colin McNaughton, is the "Red Nose Readers," a "brilliant . . . collaboration," according to Pat Triggs in *Books for Keeps.* In a *School Library Journal* review of four early titles in the series, *Big Bad Pig, Fee Fi Fo Fum, Happy Worm,* and *Help!,* Louise L. Sherman described this quartet as "zany word and concept books whose bright droll illustrations and amusing situations will tickle the funnybones of children just beginning to read." A writer for *Junior Bookshelf* noted that Ahlberg's *One Two Flea!* "appeals to the irreverence which lurks within the best behaved infants," and presents nursery reading "which is neither condescending nor over-earnest." Reviewing the same title as well as seven others in the series, a contributor for *Books for Keeps* noted that the series "has a lot of young fans" and employs "jokey illustrations and bubble talk." The same reviewer concluded that the "Red Nose Readers" "are a good bet for school bookshops and very good value . . . ." Some of the most popular scenes from the series are collected in two 1996 titles, *Who Stole the Pie?* and *Put on a Show!,* welcome revisitings of these "zany" stories, according to a *Books for Keeps* reviewer. "Both books present words in imaginative ways likely to amuse children of infant age," commented a writer for *Junior Bookshelf.*

Yet another popular series is "Funnybones," featuring a cast of skeletons in the usual crazy and downright silly situations that are the Ahlberg trademark. Reviewing the first two in the series, *The Black Cat* and *The Pet Shop,* Ruth Smith of *School Library Journal* described the books with their "cartoonlike layout, repetitive language, and situational humor" as a "good choice for beginning readers." Reviewing *Dinosaur Dreams* and *Mystery Tour* in *School Library Journal,* Leslie Barban remarked that these "crazy and wacky" books are "more funnier-than-spooky entries for an audience often looking for good material in this genre." A *Books for Keeps* contributor, reviewing reprints of *Mystery Tour* and *The Black Cat,* noted that "few beginning readers can resist the sheer silliness of these stories and few teachers can resist the brilliance with which Allan Ahlberg writes stories which are full of repetition, so easy to read and yet are quirky, witty and original."

Ahlberg maintains such brilliance, as well as his witty and quirky storylines in his stand-alone picture books and verse for younger readers. Working with his wife, Janet, Ahlberg created some amusing and charming fairy tale pastiches with *Jeremiah in the Dark Woods, Each Peach Pear Plum,* and the "Jolly Postman" books. Working with Amstutz, he wrote *Ten in a Bed,* about a little girl who finds a different fairy tale character in her bed each night: the Three Bears, the Big Bad Wolf, and the Cat from "Hey Diddle, Diddle," among others. Each time, the girl is able to get rid of the intruder by telling her own version of the fairy tale they inhabit. Critiquing this title in *Books for Your Children,* J. Tweedie commented, "The stories are ideal for children at the stage when fantasy and reality are still interchangeable." Tweedie concluded that the stories "are racy and humorous and bound to become familiar favourites." More postmodern wit is presented in *The Bravest Ever Bear* in which well known fairy tale characters such as Red Riding Hood and the Big Bad Wolf tell their stories from their own perspective and create new endings for old tales. The characters also encounter each other as their tales overlap in a sort of tag-team narrative structure. A *Publishers Weekly* reviewer felt this was a "kid-tickling, episodic narrative that mixes familiar and never-before-seen characters . . . , plot twists and hustling watercolors and pencil art into a silly and satisfying stew."

Writing expressly for middle grader readers, Ahlberg has turned his humorous talents to novels with *Woof!* and *The Giant Baby,* and to short stories with *The Better Brown Stories.* With *Woof!,* Ahlberg creates a Kafkaesque scenario when young Eric Banks suddenly turns into a Norfolk terrier one morning. Eric gets a dog's eye view of things until he becomes Eric once more, but he never knows when this change will occur again. Kathleen Brachman noted in *School Library Journal* that the book "is told in an understated manner with delightfully quiet, tongue-in-cheek humor." A reviewer for *Books for Keeps* called the novel a "good book . . . thoroughly recommended for mid-juniors."

With *The Giant Baby,* Ahlberg again pushes the bounds of reality when a giant baby arrives on Alice's doorstep one day. Though the young girl longs for a baby brother, this is rather too much for her at first. But soon, she and her parents become attached to the large infant and they get into all sorts of predicaments trying to keep the foundling out of foster families. "Fast-paced, tightly plotted, and packed with excitement and humor, this tale is destined to take its place with the very best novels for this age group," wrote Ruth Semrau in a *School Library Journal* review of *The Giant Baby.* Comparing Ahlberg's prose to that of Roald Dahl, Semrau further commented that Ahlberg's "wry wit makes his book as appealing to adults as to children." A contributor to *Books for Keeps* concluded, "Humour, huge attention to the practical and emotional implications, an instinctive interest in any abandoned baby, plus Ahlberg's personal writing style make this absolutely riveting."

Ahlberg presents characters who rebel against their creator in *The Better Brown Stories.* Miffed with the stories that are shaping their lives, the members of the Brown family seek out the writer responsible and give him a piece of their communal mind. Christina Dorr, writing in *School Library Journal,* called the book a "clever collection of short stories that's sure to be a hit." *Booklist*'s Hazel Rochman concluded that if American readers did not quite get the British references, "everyone will enjoy the mischief and the wry characters that suddenly move from the mundane to the marvelous." A writer for *Books for Keeps* remarked, "Picking up a book by Allan Ahlberg is always exciting, for children and adults. There is a feeling that one is going to be both entertained and challenged, and this new title certainly lives up to that expectation."

With *The Mysteries of Zigomar,* Ahlberg presents something of a hybrid, part story collection and part verse collection. *Books for Keeps* contributor Annabel Gibb wrote that she "very much preferred the poems to the prose pieces," and indeed Ahlberg has written a variety of popular poetry collections for young readers, including *Cops and Robbers, Each Peach Pear Plum,* and *Peepo!* in collaboration with his wife, and other humorous volumes, including *Please, Mrs. Butler, Heard It in the Playground,* illustrated by Wegner, *Mockingbird,* with illustrations from Paul Howard, and *Monkey Do!,* illustrated by Amstutz. *Heard It in the Playground* serves up "serious situations for the young . . . treated lightly but shrewdly in rhymed stanzas or freer verse-lines," according to Fisher in *Growing Point.* Fisher went on to conclude, "A judicious and expert mixture of real life and that eternal wish-dream when school momentarily becomes really entertaining."

In *Mockingbird,* Ahlberg plays off the old song lyrics, "Hush little baby don't say a word / Mama's gonna buy you a mockingbird." In this adaptation, an adoring family and friends promise the baby in question all sorts of presents. "Ahlberg's variation on a familiar theme turns that beloved old nursery song . . . into a newly realized birthday lullaby," wrote Janice M. Del Negro in a *Bulletin of the Center for Children's Books* review. Valerie Coghlan, reviewing the same title in *Books for Keeps,* felt the book would "undoubtedly appeal to a market for nostalgia with its almost familiar words and the careful details of Howard's pictures." *Booklist*'s Carolyn Phelan urged, "Even if you have every other picture-book version of the song, make room for this beguiling edition." In *Monkey Do!* an adventurous and rather mischievous monkey escapes from the zoo and its exploits are recounted in rhyming verse by Ahlberg. Pat Mathews noted in *Bulletin of the Center for Children's Books* that "there are plenty of monkey shenanigans in this picture-book offering." A reviewer for *Magpies* featured the book in a roundup of picture books, calling it a "cheeky story told with great flair and perfect to read aloud." Linda Perkins, writing in *Booklist,* concluded, "this appealing story will tickle and delight."

Whether producing whimsical series readers or stand-alones with tongue-in-cheek wit, Ahlberg has proven to be one of the most popular picture book authors on either side of the Atlantic. Collaborating with his wife and with other illustrators, Ahlberg has created a body of work that has won awards, critical acclaim, and legions of readers in the United States and his native Great Britain. Yet the author is supremely understated about his achievement. "It's play," he once told Victoria Neumark in the *Times Literary Supplement.* "It's farce, it's the neatness of the plot."

BIOGRAPHICAL/CRITICAL SOURCES:

BOOKS

Children's Books and Their Creators, edited by Anita Silvey, Houghton Mifflin, 1995.

Children's Literature Review, Volume 18, Gale (Detroit, MI), 1989.

St. James Guide to Children's Writers, 5th edition, edited by Sara Pendergast and Tom Pendergast, St. James Press (Detroit, MI), 1999.

PERIODICALS

Booklist, May 1, 1994, p. 1606; January 1, 1996, Hazel Rochman, review of *The Better Brown Stories,* p. 832; December 1, 1997, p. 61; April, 1998, Linda Perkins, review of *Monkey Do!,* p. 1328; September 15, 1998, Carolyn Phelan, review of *Mockingbird,* p. 228; January 1, 1999, p. 784.

Books for Keeps, January, 1988, Pat Triggs, "Editor's Page," p. 3; January, 1988, review of *Woof!,* p. 17; May, 1988, review of *One Two Flea!,* p. 12; September, 1988, review of *Miss Dose the Doctor's Daughter,* p. 8; March, 1993, review of *Mystery Tour,* p. 10; July, 1996, review of *The Giant Baby,* p. 12; November, 1996, Jeff Hynds, "Master Allan the Ahlberg," pp. 4-5; November, 1996, Liz Waterland, review of "Happy Families," p. 5; November, 1996, review of *Who Stole the Pie?,* p. 8; January, 1997, review of *The Better Brown Stories,* p. 23; September, 1997, Jill Bennett, review of *Master Track's Train,* p. 21; January, 1998, Annabel Gibb, review of *The Mysteries of Zigomar,* p. 19; January, 1999, Valerie Coghlan, review of *Mockingbird,* p. 18.

Books for Your Children, spring, 1991, J. Tweedie, review of *Ten in a Bed,* p. 17.

Bulletin of the Center for Children's Books, April, 1998, Pat Mathews, review of *Monkey Do!,* pp. 272-73; October, 1998, Janice M. Del Negro, review of *Mockingbird,* p. 51.

Carousel, summer, 2000, Pat Tate, review of *My Brother's Ghost,* p. 25.

Growing Point, September, 1988, Margery Fisher, review of *Master Bun the Baker's Boy* and *Miss Dose the Doctor's Daughter,* p. 5049; January, 1990, M. Fisher, review of *Heard It in the Playground,* p. 5283.

Horn Book, July-August, 1993, p. 456; September-October, 1996, pp. 590-91; May-June, 1999, p. 354.

Junior Bookshelf, August, 1987, review of *One Two Flea,* p. 158; April, 1996, review of *Who Stole the Pie?,* pp. 64-65.

Magpies, May, 1998, review of *Monkey Do!,* p. 5.

New York Times Book Review, April 10, 1977; April 22, 1979; April 29, 1979; May 20, 1979; March 1, 1981.

Observer (London), July 19, 1981; December 6, 1981; December 7, 1997, p. 17.

Publishers Weekly, November 2, 1990, p. 73; August 9, 1991, p. 56; January 25, 1993, p. 87; February 28, 1994, p. 88; November 27, 1995, p. 70; October 13, 1997, p. 75; January 31, 2000, review of *The Bravest Ever Bear,* p. 106.

School Library Journal, April, 1986, Louise L. Sherman, review of *Big Bad Pig,,* p. 67; February, 1987, Kathleen Brachman, review of *Woof!,* p. 76; March, 1991, Ruth Smith, review of *The Black Cat,* p. 166; July, 1991, Leslie Barban, review of *Dinosaur Dreams,* p. 52; July, 1995, Ruth Semrau, review of *The Giant Baby,* p. 76; February, 1996, Christina Dorr, review of *The Better Brown Stories,* p. 100.

Teacher Librarian, November, 1998, pp. 42, 44.

Times Educational Supplement, November 23, 1979; January 18, 1980; March 7, 1980; June 20, 1980; November 21, 1980; January 2, 1981; July 24, 1981; November 20, 1981; November 19, 1982; March 11, 1983; June 3, 1983; September 30, 1983; November 7, 1997, p. 2; December 5, 1997, p. 17; January 2, 1998, p. 23; November 20, 1998, p. 10; March 19, 1999, p. 25.

Times Literary Supplement, June 20, 1980, Victoria Neumark, "A Marriage of Words and Pictures," p. 42.*

* * *

ALLSOPP, (Harold) Bruce 1912-2000

PERSONAL: Born July 4, 1912, in Oxford, England; died February 22, 2000; son of Henry (a poet and historian) and Elizabeth May (Robertson) Allsopp; married Cyrilla Woodroffe (an artist), December 29, 1935; children: Roger Henry, Christopher John. *Education:* University of Liverpool, B.Arch. (first class honors), 1933, Dip.C.D., 1935. *Religion:* Quaker. *Avocational interests:* Painting, drawing, gardening, poetry, walking, music.

CAREER: Architectural assistant in Chichester and London, 1934-35; Leeds College of Art, Leeds, England, lecturer in history and design, 1935-40; University of Durham, Durham, England, lecturer, 1946-55, senior lecturer in history and design, 1955-63; University of Newcastle upon Tyne, Newcastle upon Tyne, England, senior lecturer, 1963-65, director of architectural studies, 1965-69, senior lecturer in architectural history, 1969-73, reader in history of architecture, 1973-77; Oriel Press Ltd., Stocksfield, England, director and chair, 1962-85; Routledge & Kegan Paul, Ltd., London, director, 1974-86. Photographer and book illustrator. *Military service:* Royal Engineers, 1940-46; became captain.

MEMBER: Society of Architectural Historians of Great Britain (founder member; chair, 1959-65), Royal Institute of British Architects (fellow; associate), Society of Antiquaries of London (fellow), Royal Town Planning Institute, Art Workers Guild (master, 1970), Independent Publishers Guild (chair, 1971-73), Northern Federation of Art Societies (president, 1980-83), Athenaeum.

WRITINGS:

Decoration and Furniture, Pitman, Volume I: *The English Tradition,* 1952, Volume II: *Principles of Modern Design,* 1953.
Art and the Nature of Architecture, Pitman, 1952.
A General History of Architecture, Pitman, 1955.
Style in the Visual Arts, Pitman, 1956.
A History of Renaissance Architecture, Pitman, 1959.
The Future of the Arts, Pitman, 1959.
Possessed, R. Hale, 1961.
The Naked Flame, R. Hale, 1962.
(With Ursula Clark) *Architecture of France,* Oriel, 1963.
(With Clark) *Architecture of Italy,* Oriel, 1964.
(With Clark) *Architecture of England,* Oriel, 1964.
To Kill a King, R. Hale, 1965.
A History of Classical Architecture: From Its Origins to the Emergence of Hellenesque and Romanesque Architecture, Pitman, 1965.
(With Clark) *Photography for Tourists,* Oriel, 1966.
(With H. W. Booton and Clark) *The Great Tradition of Western Architecture,* A. & C. Black, 1966.
Historic Architecture of Newcastle upon Tyne (also see below), Oriel, 1967.
(With Clark) *Historic Architecture of Northumberland* (also see below), Oriel, 1969.
Civilization: The Next Stage, Oriel, 1969.
(Editor) *Modern Architecture of Northern England,* Oriel, 1970.
The Study of Architectural History, Studio Vista, 1970.
Inigo Jones on Palladio, Oriel, 1970.
Romanesque Architecture, Arthur Barker, 1971.
The Garden Earth: The Case for Ecological Morality, Morrow, 1972, published as *Ecological Morality,* Muller (London), 1972.
Towards a Humane Architecture, Muller, 1974, Transatlantic, 1975.
Return of the Pagan, Routledge & Kegan Paul, 1974.
Cecilia, Scorpio, 1975.
Inigo Jones and the Lords a'Leaping, Scorpio, 1975.
A Modern Theory of Architecture, Routledge & Kegan Paul, 1976.
(With Clark) *Historic Architecture of Northumberland and Newcastle upon Tyne* (a combined revision of *Historic Architecture of Newcastle upon Tyne* and *Historic Architecture of Northumberland*), Oriel, 1977.
(With Clark) *English Architecture: An Introduction to the Architectural History of England from the Bronze Age to the Present Day,* Oriel, 1979.
Appeal to the Gods, Oriel, 1980.
Social Responsibility and the Responsible Society, Oriel, 1985.
The Country Life Companion to British and European Architecture, Larousse, 1985.

Also author of *Should Man Survive?,* 1982. Editor of "Oriel Guides." Presenter for television films on environmental and art subjects. Contributor to *Encyclopedia Americana, Didaskalos, Oxford International Symposia,* and to art and architectural journals. Allsopp's books have been translated into Hungarian, German, and Portuguese.

SIDELIGHTS: A novelist in addition to being a scholar of architectural history and one of the founder members of the Society of Architectural Historians of Great Britain, Bruce Allsopp was especially noted for his books *A History of Classical Architecture: From Its Origins to the Emergence of Hellenesque and Romanesque Architecture* and *The Study of Architectural History.*

In *A History of Classical Architecure,* Allsopp presents a look at the beginnings of Western architecture and traces its development in both Greece and Rome. A reviewer for *Choice* found that "the account of the earlier and less well represented periods is the best, and Allsopp's architectural eye stands him in good stead." J. A. Gaertner, reviewing the book for *Classical World,* noted that "wherever Allsopp speaks about architecture proper, he is marvelously informing."

Allsopp's *The Study of Architectural History* is divided into two parts: "The Relationship between Architectural History and Practice" and "The Nature of Architectural

History." The study caused Lincoln Kirstein, writing in the *Nation,* to describe Allsopp as "a well-known English teacher and historian, with a cool, clear artist's eye." David Gebhard, in his review of the book for *Library Journal,* called it "an important and valuable contribution to architectural theory."

Allsopp once told *CA:* "Writing is difficult; writing about one's own work is very difficult! As a writer I want to say something and explore something. I can admire writing which is simply beautiful in itself but for me writing is a practical activity. In almost all I have written there is an element of discovery, just as much in a text book of architectural history as in a novel or a philosophical work like *Ecological Morality.* . . . In my early historical novels I was finding out about people, about personality under the constraint of slavery in particular, and reading between the lines of ancient chronicles to discover the truth beyond the limitations of academically acceptable history. My later novels, though more entertaining, have really been about the human mind in the context of nature. Imagination is an important part of my life and I think it is a faculty which our society undervalues, to its detriment as a civilization.

"Two activities strongly affect my work as an author: drawing and gardening. When I am writing I often help visualisation by drawing. I admire concision in writing and often I would prefer drawing to description as the better method of communicating visual images. I would like to do a book which is a combination of writing and drawing, but it has not come yet and it would be hard to publish. I paint pictures and in recent years have had one-man shows in London and other places in England. I nearly always have more than one job in hand and often I deliberately balance an academic or philosophical work, where the emphasis is on knowledge or thinking, with something more imaginative in writing, painting or illustration.

"Gardening provides me with many analogies and it is creative within the inexorable disciplines of nature. In art one has to find one's own disciplines if anything is to be achieved. Whatever the medium, I divide my work into two categories, that which I do for myself and that which I intend to communicate to other people. Often the latter follows from the former but I don't expect what I do for myself to be of value to other people though it may be. I believe it is important for artists of all kinds to make this distinction and to be realistic about recognition.

"I became a publisher in 1962 when I founded Oriel Press to produce short-run books by off-set lithography, which was then considered only suitable for long runs, and explore ways of relating photography and writing. The 'Oriel Guides,' still in print, were the first fruit. Now, as a director of a major publishing house, I understand more about the author/publisher love/hate relationship without knowing how to reconcile it! As an author I still think publishers can be stupid, unimaginative, and occasionally rapacious, but as a publisher I see that the public, upon which publication depends, will only buy and read what it wants to read and therefore gets a little better than it deserves because there are still some publishers with a soul."

BIOGRAPHICAL/CRITICAL SOURCES:

PERIODICALS

Choice, October, 1966, review of *A History of Classical Architecture,* p. 624.
Classical World, January, 1967, J. A. Gaertner, review of *A History of Classical Architecture,* p. 211.
Library Journal, January 1, 1971, David Gebhard, review of *The Study of Architectural History,* p. 66.
Nation, December 21, 1970, Lincoln Kirstein, review of *The Study of Architectural History,* p. 663.
New Humanity, April, 1985.
New Society, February 28, 1985.
Schmaefilm, April, 1961.
Schweizer Industrieblatt, March 11, 1961.
Time and Tide, May 13, 1957.
Times Literary Supplement, January 1, 1959.

OBITUARIES:

PERIODICALS

Times (London), March 22, 2000.*

* * *

ANVIC, Frank
See SHERMAN, Jory (Tecumseh)

* * *

AUGER, C(harles) P(eter) 1931-

PERSONAL: Born November 6, 1931, in Birmingham, England; son of Charles (an accountant) and Margaret Ivy (Wilmott) Auger; married Jean Margaret, September 4, 1954. *Education:* Attended grammar school in Birmingham, England. *Avocational interests:* Cricket, growing flowers.

ADDRESSES: Home—82 Malvern Rd., Redditch, Worcestershire B97 5DP, England.

CAREER: Lucas Industries, Solihull, England, research manager, 1957-88; Peter Auger Research Services, Redditch, England, information consultant, 1988—; writer.

MEMBER: Library Association (fellow).

WRITINGS:

Engineering Eponyms, LA Publishing (Franklin, VA), 1975.

Use of Reports Literature, Butterworths (Markham, Ontario, Canada), 1975.

Information Sources in Grey Literature, Bowker (New Providence, NJ), 2nd edition, 1989, 4th edition, 1998.

(Editor) *Information Sources in Patents,* Bowker (New York, NY), 1992.

A History of the Bureau of Engineer Surveyors, Institution of Plant Engineers, 1992.

WORK IN PROGRESS: Continuing research on developments in grey literature.

SIDELIGHTS: C. P. Auger told *CA:* "All writing is hard work, but writing nonfiction is harder because opinions, statements, facts, and other data all need to be backed by sources and references, which take time to locate and verify. Furthermore it is well known that experts do not usually agree with each other. In consequence, on publication, challenges may have to be met and rebuffed. The reward is not monetary, but is simply the satisfaction of seeing one's work in print."

B

BACKSCHEIDER, Paula R(ice) 1943-

PERSONAL: Born March 31, 1943, in Brownsville, TN; daughter of Valentine S. (a cotton buyer) and Catherine (an accountant; maiden name, Currie) Rice; married Nickolas Andrew Backscheider (a systems analyst), January 18, 1964; children: Andrea Gayle, Nickolas Andrew. *Education:* Purdue University, B.A. (with honors), 1964; Southern Connecticut State College, M.S., 1967; Purdue University, Ph.D., 1972. *Politics:* Democrat. *Religion:* Presbyterian.

ADDRESSES: *Home*—1930 Canary Dr., Auburn, AL 36830. *Office*—Department of English, Auburn University, Auburn, AL 36849.

CAREER: Rollins College, Winter Park, FL, assistant professor, 1973-75; University of Rochester, Rochester, NY, assistant professor, 1975-78, associate professor, 1978-87, vice provost for academic concerns, 1981-82, professor of English, 1987—, Roswell Burrows Professor of English, beginning 1991; Auburn University, Auburn, AL, Stevens-Philpott Eminent Scholar, 1992—. Associated with University of Edinburgh's Institute for Advanced Studies, 1980—.

MEMBER: Modern Language Association, American Society for Eighteenth-Century Studies (vice president, 1991—; president, 1992).

AWARDS, HONORS: Fellowship from William Andrews Clark Library at University of California at Los Angeles, 1974; grants from American Philosophical Society, 1975, 1980, and 1986; fellowships from National Endowment for the Humanities, 1983, American Antiquarian Society, 1987, and Guggenheim Foundation, 1991; prize for best humanities book from British Council, 1990, for *Daniel Defoe: His Life.*

WRITINGS:

NONFICTION

(With Felicity Nussbaum and Philip Anderson) *An Annotated Bibliography of Twentieth-Century Studies of Women and Literature, 1660-1800,* Garland, 1977.

A Being More Intense: The Prose Works of Bunyan, Swift, and Defoe, AMS Press, 1984.

Daniel Defoe: Ambition and Innovation, University Press of Kentucky, 1986.

Daniel Defoe: His Life, Johns Hopkins University Press, 1989.

Spectacular Politics: Theatrical Power and Mass Culture in Early Modern England, Johns Hopkins University Press, 1993.

Reflections on Biography, Oxford University Press, 1999.

EDITOR

Probability, Time, and Space in Eighteenth-Century Literature, AMS Press, 1979.

The Plays of Charles Gildon, Garland, 1979.

The Plays of Elizabeth Inchbald, two volumes, Garland, 1980.

(With Douglas Howard) *The Plays of Samuel Foote,* three volumes, Garland, 1983.

Dictionary of Literary Biography, Volume 80: *Restoration and Eighteenth-Century Dramatists, First Series,* Gale (Detroit), 1989.

Dictionary of Literary Biography, Volume 84: *Restoration and Eighteenth-Century Dramatists, Second Series,* Gale, 1989.

Dictionary of Literary Biography, Volume 89: *Restoration and Eighteenth-Century Dramatists, Third Series,* Gale, 1989.

Moll Flanders: The Making of a Criminal Mind, G. K. Hall, 1990.

(With Timothy Dykstal) *The Intersections of the Public and Private Spheres in Early Modern England,* F. Cass (Portland, OR), 1996.

(With John J. Richetti) *Popular Fiction by Women, 1660-1730: An Anthology,* Oxford University Press, 1996.

(With Hope D. Cotton) Frances Brooke, *The Excursion,* University Press of Kentucky (Lexington), 1997.

Selected Fiction and Drama of Eliza Haywood, Oxford University Press, 1999.

Revising Women: Eighteenth-Century "Women's Fiction" and Social Engagement, Johns Hopkins University Press (Baltimore), 2000.

Also editor of Daniel Defoe's *A Journal of the Plague Year,* Norton. Editor of "Eighteenth-Century Drama" series, sixty-nine volumes, Garland, 1979-83.

OTHER

Contributor to *Eighteenth-Century Correspondences,* edited by Alan T. McKenzie. Contributor to periodicals, including *Modern Language Review, Modern Language Studies, Modern Philology, Novel, Philological Quarterly, South Atlantic Review, Studies in English Literature, Eighteenth-Century Fiction, Theatre Journal,* and *Studies in the Literary Imagination.*

WORK IN PROGRESS: "Fighting Fashion," a book on eighteenth-century women's poetry and their adaptations of traditional poetic forms.

SIDELIGHTS: Paula Backscheider is an authority on eighteenth-century English literature, particularly that of renowned novelist Daniel Defoe. Although Backscheider has published a range of works within her field, she is probably best known for *Daniel Defoe: His Life,* a widely encompassing biography of the distinguished British writer. Backscheider's book details Defoe's dramatic, occasionally obscure life, including his journalism career, and she provides background and analysis of Defoe's greatest works, including the long poems "True Born Englishman" and "Jure Divino," the satire *Shortest Way with Dissenters,* and the books *Robinson Crusoe* and *Journal of the Plague Year.*

Backscheider's *Daniel Defoe: His Life* is recognized as an accomplished, exhaustive consideration of its subject. *Washington Post Book World* reviewer John Kenyon, who described the writing of a Defoe biography as an "intimidating project," hailed Backscheider's book as "a very considerable work of scholarship." Pat Rogers wrote in the *New York Times Book Review* that with *Daniel Defoe: His Life,* Backscheider had realized a "considerable achievement," while Bruce Redford, in his *Washington Times* review, lauded the biography as a "true magnum opus." Redford added that *Daniel Defoe: His Life* is destined to be "the standard scholarly guide" on its subject. Among Backscheider's other writings on Defoe are *A Being More Intense: The Prose Works of Bunyan, Swift, and Defoe* and *Daniel Defoe: Ambition and Innovation.* In addition, she has edited editions of Defoe's *Moll Flanders* and *Journal of the Plague Year.*

In her study *Reflections on Biography,* Backscheider examines the choices a biographer must make and how those choices shape the completed manuscript. Her insights into the craft of biography are aimed at giving readers a better understanding of their limitations and possibilities while increasing the enjoyment that reading a biography can bring. Backscheider begins with four chapters detailing such considerations as the biographer's tone of voice and choice of subject, moves on to an evaluation of particular biographies and why they are successful, and concludes with looks at the current state of biography in Great Britain and the United States and its possible future. Writing in the *London Review of Books,* Inga Clendinnen called *Reflections on Biography* "a practical guide to the novice biographer" which is written in "a fluent, good-humoured, often humorous prose."

BIOGRAPHICAL/CRITICAL SOURCES:

PERIODICALS

Albion, spring, 1995, review of *Spectacular Politics,* p. 123.

American Journalism, summer, 1990, pp. 180-181.

Bloomsbury Review, January/February, 1990, p. 27.

Choice, June, 1994, review of *Spectacular Politics,* p. 1592; October, 1997, review of *Popular Fiction by Women,* p. 300.

Eighteenth-Century Studies, fall, 1995, p. 117.
London Review of Books, March 16, 2000, review of *Reflections on Biography,* pp. 9-10.
Modern Language Review, April, 1995, p. 414.
New York Times Book Review, January 14, 1990, Pat Rogers, review of *Daniel Defoe,* pp. 11-12.
Smithsonian, March, 1990, pp. 152-153.
Studies in English Literature, summer, 1990.
Times Literary Supplement, May 4, 1990, p. 469; May 13, 1994, review of *Spectacular Politics,* p. 22; March 21, 1997, review of *Popular Fiction by Women,* p. 8.
Tribune Books (Chicago), November 5, 1989, p. 6.
Virginia Quarterly Review, spring, 1990, p. 56.
Washington Post Book World, December 10, 1989, John Kenyon, review of *Daniel Defoe,* p. 15.
Washington Times, September 18, 1989, Bruce Redford, review of *Daniel Defoe,* pp. E7, E10.
Yearbook of English Studies, 1992, pp. 302-304.

* * *

BAKER, T(homas) Lindsay 1947-

PERSONAL: Born April 22, 1947, in Cleburne, TX; son of Garnell A. and Mary Lois (Miller) Baker; married Julie Philips. *Ethnicity:* "White." *Education:* Texas Tech University, B.A., 1969, M.A., 1972, Ph.D., 1977.

ADDRESSES: Home—Rio Vista, TX. *Office*—P.O. Box 507, Rio Vista, TX 76093. *E-mail*—TLBAKER@hill-college.cc.tx.us.

CAREER: Texas Tech University, Lubbock, lecturer in history, 1970-75; Technical University of Wroclaw, Wroclaw, Poland, Fulbright lecturer, 1975-77; Texas Tech University, lecturer in history and program manager of history of engineering program, 1977-79; Panhandle-Plains Historical Museum, Canyon, TX, curator of science and technology, 1978-87; Fort Worth Museum of Science and History, Fort Worth, TX, curator of history, 1987-89; Baylor University, curator of Governor Bill and Vara Daniel Historical Village, Strecker Museum, 1989-92, director of academic programs and graduate studies, Department of Museum Studies, 1992-98. Director, Texas Heritage Museum, Hill College, Hillsboro, Texas, 1998—. Consultant to museums and historical agencies.

MEMBER: International Molinological Society (member of council, 1992-2000), American Association of Museums, American Historical Association, National Trust for Historic Preservation, American Association for State and Local History, Polish American Historical Association, Association for Living Historical Farms and Agricultural Museums, Western History Association, Society of Southwest Archivists, Texas Archaeological Society, Texas State Historical Association (fellow), Texas Association of Museums, Texas Folklore Society, Gamma Theta Upsilon.

AWARDS, HONORS: Scholarship recipient from Kosciuszko Foundation, 1973-74 and 1977; Coral H. Tullis Award from Texas State Historical Association and Elizabeth Broocks Bates Award from Daughters of the Republic of Texas, both 1979, for *The First Polish Americans;* Coke Wood Award from Westerners International, 1986, for *The Survey of the Headwaters of the Red River, 1876;* Ralph Coats Roe Medal from American Society of Mechanical Engineers, 1987, for "contributions to a better understanding of the role of engineers in contemporary society"; Texas Award for Preservation of Historic Architecture from Texas Historical Commission, 1987, and Award for Excellence, Society for Technical Communication, 1988, both for *Building the Lone Star;* certificate of commendation, American Association for State and Local History, and citation from San Antonio Conservation Society, both 1993, for *Lighthouses of Texas.* Certificate of Commendation, American Association for State and Local History, 1998, for *Till Freedom Cried Out.*

WRITINGS:

(With Steven R. Rae) *Information Summaries: Sixty Sites of Historic Engineering Works in Arizona, Colorado, New Mexico, Texas, and Utah,* Water Resources Center, Texas Tech University (Lubbock, TX), 1972.

(With Rae, Joseph E. Minor, and Seymour V. Connor) *Water for the Southwest: Historical Survey and Guide to Historic Sites,* American Society of Civil Engineers (New York City), 1973.

(Developmental editor) *Poles in Texas Resource Guide,* Ethnic Heritage Studies Program, Southwest Educational Development Laboratory, 1975.

The First Polish Americans: Silesian Settlements in Texas, Texas A & M University Press (College Station, TX), 1979.

Historia najstarszych polskich osad w Ameryce, Zaklad Narodowy im. Ossolinskich, 1981.

The Polish Texans, Institute of Texan Cultures, 1982.

The Reverend Leopold Moczygemba: Patriarch of Polonia, Polish American Priests Association, 1984.

A Field Guide to American Windmills, University of Oklahoma Press (Norman), 1985.

(Editor) *The Survey of the Headwaters of the Red River, 1876,* Panhandle-Plains Historical Society, 1985.

(With Billy R. Harrison) *Adobe Walls: The History and Archeology of the 1874 Trading Post,* Texas A & M University Press, 1986.

Building the Lone Star: An Illustrated Guide to Historic Sites, Texas A & M University Press, 1986.

Ghost Towns of Texas, University of Oklahoma Press, 1986.

Lighthouses of Texas, Texas A & M University Press, 1991.

Blades in the Sky: Windmilling through the Eyes of B. H. "Tex" Burdick, Texas Tech University Press, 1992.

(Editor with Julie P. Baker)*The WPA Oklahoma Slave Narratives,* University of Oklahoma Press, 1996.

(Editor with Julie P. Baker) *Till Freedom Cried Out: Memories of Texas Slave Life,* Texas A & M University Press, 1997.

North American Windmill Manufacturers' Trade Literature: A Descriptive Guide, University of Oklahoma Press, 1998.

The Texas Red River Country: The Official Surveys of the Headwaters, 1876, Texas A & M University Press, 1998.

The 702 Model Windmill: Its Assembly, Installation, and Use, American Wind Power Center, 1999.

Contributor to history journals. Editor and publisher of *Windmillers' Gazette.*

SIDELIGHTS: T. Lindsay Baker once told *CA:* "I am an active participant in the 'living history interpretation' of the experiences of the people who lived in the American West. I have served as one of the founders of living history groups that portray the lives of traders on the Santa Fe Trail in the 1840s and buffalo hide hunters in Kansas in the 1870s. I also built and lived for eighteen months in a turn-of-the-century-style sod house.

"James S. French, the individual whom I portray in many of the living history presentations, was an actual person who lived on the southwestern frontier in the 1870s. A one-time whisky peddler among the Cheyenne Indians, among whom he lived for two years, he later became the camp cook and a skinner for a buffalo hide hunting crew headed by William Dixon, and as such he participated in the Battle of Adobe Walls on June 27, 1874.

"The living history programs, given alone or in company with colleagues, are usually presented at historic sites and museums on the southern Great Plains. In these programs the presenters dress in authentic historic attire and recreate a lived-in camp of the type used in the past by the people who are portrayed. The presentations are based on original research into primary source materials from the time periods portrayed, such as diaries and journals, business records, reminiscences, letters, and transcripts of interviews.

"The reason for my construction of the sod house was to give myself a better understanding of what day-to-day life on the agricultural frontier actually was like. I lived in the one-room earthen structure for eighteen months, drinking and washing in hauled water, heating and cooking with wood as fuel, lighting with kerosene, and living on a dirt floor. My nearest neighbor was two miles away and my company each evening as I drifted off to sleep was the singing of coyotes in the distance. Through such experiences I gained insights into life on the fringe of settlement that I never would have achieved in a lifetime of studying written sources."

Baker more recently told *CA:* "Today I live on an historic cotton farm beneath the live oak trees about halfway between Fort Worth and Waco in the middle of nowhere. The place is one that my great grandparents purchased as poor cotton farmers in 1900, and the office in which I write is the same room in the wood-frame farmhouse in which the wake was held for my great grandfather in 1914. When I began structural restoration of the dwelling, it was a derelict hulk half-filled with mouldy hay and a few dead animals. After a very strict two-year structural restoration, today it looks about the way that it did in 1910. Although the home does have electricity, it is heated mostly with wood fires (including a wood-burning range in the kitchen for cooking as well) and has no central heating or air conditioning. Who could ask for an atmosphere more conducive to writing? You're either melting or shivering."

BIOGRAPHICAL/CRITICAL SOURCES:

PERIODICALS

AB Bookman's Weekly, March 8, 1999.

Accent West, January, 1982.

American Historical Review, April, 1980.

Biography, fall, 1997.

Chronicles of Oklahoma, winter, 1997-98; summer, 2000.

Farm Collector, January, 2000.

Great Plains Quarterly, spring, 1998; fall, 1998.

Journal of American History, September, 1986.

Journal of Southern History, May, 1997.

PolAmerica, summer, 1978.

South Dakota History, fall, 1985.

Western Historical Quarterly, April, 1986; winter, 1996; summer, 1998; spring, 2000.

* * *

BALL, Ann (E. Bolton) 1944-

PERSONAL: Born May 13, 1944, in Dallas, TX; daughter of Julian Henry (in public relations with a local electric company) and Ora Louise (a teacher; maiden name, Ervin) Bolton; married Eldon Ray Ball (a journalist), 1964 (divorced, 1981); children: Joanna, Samuel, Raul Quintero (foster son). *Education:* Attended Lon Morris Junior College, Jacksonville, TX, 1962-63; attended University of Texas, Austin, 1962-64; University of Houston, B.S.ed, 1973. *Politics:* Republican. *Religion:* Catholic. *Avocational interests:* Reading, herb gardening, crafts.

ADDRESSES: Home—4726 Creekbend, Houston, TX 77035. *Office*—All State Guard Service, Inc., P.O. Box 22551, Houston, TX 77227-2551; fax: 713-863-1771. *E-mail*—Annalert@aol.com.

CAREER: Teacher in parochial and public elementary, middle, and high schools in Texas and California, 1964-78; Marian Christian High School, Houston, TX, teacher, 1980-85; Security Guard Services, Houston, private investigator, 1981; M. Herman and Associates, Houston, private investigator, 1981; All State Guard Service, Inc., Houston, president and owner, 1981—.

MEMBER: Association of Security Services and Investigators of the State of Texas (state secretary, 1984-88, Houston president, 1997-99).

WRITINGS:

Modern Saints, Their Lives and Faces, Tan Books (Rockford, IL), 1983.

A Litany of Mary, Our Sunday Visitor Press (Huntington, IN), 1988.

Heroes of God: A Coloring Book for Children, Regina Press (New York), 1989.

Modern Saints, Their Lives and Faces, Book II, Tan Books, 1990.

The Holy Names of Jesus, Our Sunday Visitor Press, 1990.

The Persecuted Church, Magnificat Press (Avon, NJ), 1990.

Handbook of Catholic Sacramentals, Our Sunday Visitor Press, 1991.

A Litany of Saints, Our Sunday Visitor Press, 1993.

Catholic Traditions in Cooking, Our Sunday Visitor Press, 1993.

Catholic Book of the Dead, Our Sunday Visitor Press, 1995.

Blessed Miguel Pro: 20th Century Mexican Martyr, Tan Books, 1996.

Catholic Traditions in Crafts, Our Sunday Visitor Press, 1997.

Catholic Traditions in the Garden, Our Sunday Visitor Press, 1998.

Faces of Holiness: Modern Saints in Photos and Words, Our Sunday Visitor Press, 1998.

A Saint for Your Name: Saints for Boys, revision of the work by Albert Nevins, Our Sunday Visitor Press, 2000.

A Saint for Your Name: Saints for Girls, revision of the work by Albert Nevins, Our Sunday Visitor Press, 2000.

Modern Saints, Their Lives and Faces and *Modern Saints, Their Lives and Faces, Book II* have been translated into Polish, and a Spanish translation is being considered.

Also contributor of articles to such periodicals as *Our Sunday Visitor, Catholic Digest, Catholic Parent, Christian Beginnings, Today's Catholic Teacher, Catholic Heritage, Texas Law Enforcement Monthly,* and *The Blues.* Columnist for *Catholic Heritage* magazine, 1991—; editor of *A.S.S.I.S.T. Update,* 1992—.

WORK IN PROGRESS: Faces of Holiness Volume 2, Our Sunday Visitor Press; *A Saints Guide to Joy and Laughter,* Servant Publications; *The Encyclopedia of Catholic Devotions,* Our Sunday Visitor Press.

SIDELIGHTS: Ann Ball told *CA:* "Curiosity may kill the cat, but it sometimes fills the cash box. I'd like to say I write because of some esoteric or high-minded motive, but I have to admit the work, especially the articles, greatly improves the cash flow. A single mom with two children in Catholic schools can rarely get by on a single job, and my writing helped support a number of nasty habits like eating and paying the house note. Besides, at heart I'm basically a curious person. That's the same way I got into the security field; when teaching and writing still weren't enough, I wound up with a third job as a private investigator, too. I'm not only excessively curious, but also just flat nosy!

"My first book was a hobby that got out of hand. I once showed a photograph of St. Therese Lisieux to a group of students and was stunned at their reaction. They couldn't accept the wan, sick girl in the wheelchair; saints were pretty plaster statues in church. When I discovered that many Catholic adults had the same idea, I started collecting photos of modern saints. One day in the midst of a pile of saintly countenances scattered about the dining room floor, I decided my picture collection should get published. The publisher wouldn't do that unless I wrote something about them, so I did.

"As an adult convert, I was curious about a lot of the strange-seeming Catholic customs. All of my books published by Our Sunday Visitor Press stem from my curiosity about the church; if I keep writing a book every two years or so, I figure by the time I'm ninety I might really know a little about my religion.

"To be honest, I always was a writer. I remember getting up in the middle of the night as a child to scribble down a poem or story. To my horror and my children's amusement, at my mother's death we discovered a rather large puddle of this early work going back to about the age of eight. Ouch!

"I still love poetry and it's not unusual for me to be hammering out a poem at three or four in the morning. These are written because they are inside of me demanding to get out and frankly they pick some pretty screwy times to call for release. The poems, written for friends and loved ones, are never offered for publication; I couldn't afford the expensive books that will publish them for free, anyway.

"As an idealistic journalism student at the University of Texas in the '60s, I had happy notions of being a Pulitzer Prize-winning world correspondent. Didn't happen. Got an Mrs. instead of a B.J. and a twenty-year break from writing.

"What would I tell aspiring young writers? If you want to write, then write. Study the market and develop the ability to slash up your own work so the editor doesn't have to work so hard. Most of all, never give up. I was inspired by the story of the famous writer who decided that he would write and submit things so fast that the editors couldn't possibly reject them all. I still have every rejection slip I ever received, and one day I really will paper the bathroom with them. If you want to be a writer, don't give up! I know. After fifteen books, I've been there, done that, got the T-shirt."

* * *

BANTA, Trudy W.

PERSONAL: Born in Roanoke, VA; daughter of John Gay Webb and Gertrude Cundiff Carigan Webb; married John Lancaster Banta (deceased); children: Holiday Wellington, John Logan Lancaster. *Ethnicity:* "Caucasian." *Education:* Received B.A. and M.A. from University of Kentucky and Ed.D. from University of Tennessee.

ADDRESSES: *Home*—6530-D Meridian Parkway, Indianapolis, IN 46220. *Office*—Indiana University-Purdue University Indianapolis, 355 North Lansing St., AO 140, Indianapolis, IN 46202-2896. *E-mail*—tbanta@iupui.edu.

CAREER: University of Tennessee, Knoxville, special assistant to the chancellor, 1979-82, began as assistant professor, became professor of education, 1979-92, research professor at Learning Research Center, 1986-89, director of National Assessment Resource Center, 1986-89, founding director of Center for Assessment Research and Development, 1989-92; Indiana University-Purdue University Indianapolis, professor of higher education and vice chancellor for planning and institutional improvement, 1992—. Bryn Mawr Summer Institute for Women in Higher Education Administration, guest faculty member; conference speaker and workshop presenter in the United States and abroad, including China, Hong Kong, England, the Netherlands, France, Germany, Spain and South Africa. State of Tennessee, past director of State-wide Nutrition Education Evaluation and State-wide Career Education Evaluation; consultant to the National Research Council, the Educational Commission of the States and National Center for Education Statistics. United Way of Indiana, member of board of directors, Community Service Council, 1994—; Ruth Lilly Health Education Center, member of board of directors and executive committee, 1994—.

MEMBER: European Association for Institutional Research, American Educational Research Association, Association for the Study of Higher Education, American Association for Higher Education, Phi Beta Kappa, Phi Kappa Phi, Phi Delta Kappa, Phi Alpha Theta, Pi Lambda Theta, Kappa Delta Pi.

AWARDS, HONORS: Grant from W. K. Kellogg Foundation, 1981-83; award from National Council on Measurement in Education, 1984; grants from Fund for the Improvement of Postsecondary Education, 1986-89 and 1989-92; American Association for Higher Education, award, 1988, grant, 1990; grant from National Intramural and Recreational Sports Association, 1990-92.

WRITINGS:

(Editor and contributor) *Performance Funding in Higher Education: A Critical Analysis of Tennessee's Experience,* National Center for Higher Education Management Systems, 1986.

(Editor and contributor) *Implementing Outcomes Assessment: Promise and Perils,* Jossey-Bass (San Francisco, CA), 1988.

(Coeditor) *Making a Difference: Outcomes of a Decade of Assessment in Higher Education,* Jossey-Bass (San Francisco, CA), 1993.

(Editor with V. M. H. Borden, and contributor) *Using Performance Indicators to Guide Strategic Decision Making,* Jossey-Bass (San Francisco, CA), 1994.

Assessment in Practice: Putting Principles to Work on College Campuses, Jossey-Bass (San Francisco, CA), 1996.

(With Catherine Palomba) *Assessment Essentials,* Jossey-Bass (San Francisco, CA), 1998.

Contributor to books, including *Continuous Quality Improvement: Making the Transition to Education,* edited by D. L. Hubbard, Prescott (Maryville, MO), 1993; *Quality in Higher Education,* edited by B. D. Ruben, Transaction Books (New Brunswick, NJ), 1995; and *Better Teaching and Learning in College: Using Scholarship to Improve Practice,* edited by M. Weimer and R. Menges, Jossey-Bass (San Francisco, CA), 1995. Contributor of about two hundred articles to professional journals. Editor, *New Directions for Higher Education,* 1988, and *Assessment Update;* member of editorial board, *Journal of General Education,* 1990-94, and *Assessment and Evaluation in Higher Education,* 1995—.

SIDELIGHTS: Trudy W. Banta once told *CA:* "I enjoy writing and editing. I have always felt an obligation to contribute to the literature of my field, and I spend most of my spare time doing the reading and study that prepares me to do so. I also like to promote the work of others. Thus, my books have been edited collections of interesting perspectives and case studies prepared by my colleagues. I perceive my task to be drawing and presenting generalizations and implications from their contributions."

* * *

BARNES, Kim 1958-

PERSONAL: Born May 22, 1958, in Lewiston, ID; daughter of Arthur Oneil (a logger and truck driver) and Claudette Keasling (an office worker) Barnes; married Robert Wrigley (a poet and college professor), July 20, 1983; children: Jordan, Jace; stepchildren: Philip. *Education:* Lewis-Clark St. College, B.A. (English), 1983; Washington State University, M.A., 1985; University of Montana, M.F.A. (creative writing), 1995. *Politics:* Democrat. *Avocational interests:* Backpacking, fishing, gardening.

ADDRESSES: Home—Moscow, ID. *Office*—University of Idaho, Moscow, ID 83843. *Agent*—Sally Wofford-Girard, Elaine Markson Agency, 44 Greenwich Ave., New York, NY 10011. *E-mail*—barneswrig@aol.com.

CAREER: Washington State University, Pullman, lecturer in English, 1983-85; University of Idaho, Moscow, lecturer in English, 1985-90; Lewis-Clark State College, Lewiston, ID, lecturer, 1991-97, assistant professor of English, 1997-2000; University of Idaho, assistant professor of English, 2000—. University of Montana, lecturer, 1994-95; also taught at Ocooch Writers Retreat, University of Wisconsin-Richland Center, 1993, Summer Writers' Workshop, University of Nevada, Reno, 1996, Writers at Work, Park City, UT, 1997, and Western Writers Conference, 1998.

AWARDS, HONORS: Fellow, Idaho Commission on the Arts, 1991 and 2001; Academy of American Poets Prize, University of Montana, 1995; Jerard Fund Award for a work in progress by an emerging female writer, International PEN, 1995, for *In the Wilderness: Coming of Age in Unknown Country;* finalist for Martha Albrand Award, 1997; Award for Excellence in Teaching, Lewis-Clark State Foundation, 1997; Pacific Northwest Booksellers Association Award, and finalist for Pulitzer Prize for autobiography or biography, both 1997, both for *In the Wilderness: Coming of Age in Unknown Country;* fellow, Heekin Group Foundation, 1998.

WRITINGS:

(Editor, with Mary Clearman Blew, and contributor) *Circle of Women: An Anthology of Contemporary Western Women Writers,* Penguin (New York, NY), 1994.

In the Wilderness: Coming of Age in Unknown Country, Doubleday (New York, NY), 1996.

Hungry for the World: A Memoir, Random House, 2000.

Works represented in anthologies, including *Idaho Unbound,* West Bound Books, *Tumblewords,* University of Nevada Press (Reno, NV), and *Women on Hunting,* Ecco Press (New York, NY). Contributor to periodicals, including *Shenandoah, Georgia Review, Cimarron Review, Northern Lights,* and *Manoa.* Poetry editor, *Northwest Review,* 1991.

WORK IN PROGRESS: Goodnight, Irene, a novel; *Family Travel,* essays; *Out of the Fire,* a memoir.

SIDELIGHTS: A Pulitzer Prize finalist for her 1996 memoir *In the Wilderness: Coming of Age in Unknown Country,* Kim Barnes has become known for her ability to turn painful childhood memories into dramatic reading. Her second work of autobiography, *Hungry for the World: A Memoir,* details events from her young adulthood during the years prior to her enrolling in college and studying creative writing. Barnes subsequently became a lecturer and English professor.

Barnes grew up in Idaho during the 1970s, the daughter of a logger turned truck driver. After enjoying a life close to the land during her early years, she was forced to adapt to a dramatically different existence when her family moved to the mill town of Lewiston. Her parents had converted to the Pentecostal Christian faith, adopting a radically different lifestyle in which most worldly pleasures were forbidden. Her father, who said that God had told him to leave logging, seemed to her to metamorphose into a distant, forbidding figure of authority. Declared a healer at age eleven, Barnes at first followed her parents' faith, but rebelled against it in adolescence, when the appeal of her peers' more hedonistic lifestyle became too powerful to resist. At the time of her graduation from high school—when her father told her that she could not attend a graduation party—Barnes left home and began an abusive relationship with an older man. After their breakup, she turned to college as a refuge. Barnes later married one of her professors, became a writer, and settled in a home in rural Idaho with her family.

Many of these experiences are recounted in *In the Wilderness,* which received considerable critical attention. A *Kirkus Reviews* commentator referred to the book as a "sad and beautiful memoir" that provides "the kind of bold, perspective-wrenching joy that is the province of real literature" and "forces reconsideration of the form." Donna Seaman of *Booklist* applied the epithet "unique" to the volume, and spoke of its "healing intensity," while a *Publishers Weekly* reviewer called the book "nonjudgmental and generous" and "deeply moving." *Salon* contributor Maud Casey asserted that Barnes's "memoir has a mythic feel," praised the author's eye for detail, and declared: "Barnes charms her way out of cliché, turning typical angst into something a little stranger."

The events of *In the Wilderness* are summarized in the first seventy-five pages of *Hungry for the World,* which goes on to recount Barnes's experiences from the age of eighteen to age twenty-one. The book is dominated by her relationship with a Vietnam veteran who is old enough to be her father, and who rather resembles her father in his interests and attitudes. As Barnes reveals, she submitted to his degrading sexual demands and listened to his threats of future violence, having previously been taught that women want to be hurt by men. The account ends with the author's partial reconciliation with her parents, her marriage and parenthood, and her first work as a writer of poems, stories, and memoirs.

Hungry for the World generated mixed reviews, some of which offered commendation for her writing style and honesty, while other reviewers felt that Barnes failed to generate the same kind of resonance found in *In the Wilderness.* Writing for *Library Journal,* Gina Kaiser remarked that some of the details unhappily resembled stories from *True Romance.* While she found the section reprising *In the Wilderness* to be "lyrical and engaging," the critic judged that overall Barnes "fails to draw deep parallels among her life choices" and that it was hard to be sympathetic to "problems that she seems to bring on herself." In a review for the *Salt Lake Tribune,* Martin Naparsteck found a similar imbalance, calling the book "a memoir of degradation and redemption—a lot of degradation, the redemption tacked on at the end." Roberta Bernstein, who reviewed the book for the *New York Times,* suggested that the author fell short of recreating the impact of her first memoir, saying "she relies, less effectively, on an almost documentary recitation of events intercut with overblown emotional summations." Bernstein concluded that "honesty makes [Barnes's] story effective."

More positive responses included a *Publishers Weekly* review that called the book a "well-crafted memoir" in which "Barnes explores the complicities of an abusive relationship that eerily echoes the patriarchal domination of family and church she sought to escape." Donna Seaman, in *Booklist,* called the work "candid but dignified" and "profoundly disturbing." Seaman remarked, "Barnes tells [her story] with consummate skill, courage, and generosity, transforming her pain into an antidote for others." In the *Decatur Daily* Vivian K. Moore enthused, "Beginning with the first paragraph, I had the sensation that the author was sitting across the room telling me, personally, of these events. A pure, almost poetic style of prose had me dog-earing corners and reaching for a pen."

Prior to the success of her first memoir, Barnes had been known primarily as the co-editor of *Circle of Women: An Anthology of Contemporary Western Women Writers,* which was published in 1994. That collection, which *Publishers Weekly* reviewer Maria Simson labeled "evocative," expanded the range of the literary West, going beyond rugged cowboy-style individualism to express a sense of community and connectedness found in the work of many female writers. Among the thirty-five writers whose fiction, nonfiction, and poems were selected for the anthology were Mailynne Robinson, Tess Gallagher, Terry Tempest Williams, Melanie Rae Thon, Gretel Ehrlich, Cyra McFadden, and the two editors themselves. Lynn Cothern, reviewing the volume for *Western American Literature,* called it "an important contribution to the literature of the American West," and Cheryl L. Conway, recommending the book to readers of *Library Journal,* noted themes that included "growing up, painful or strained family relationships, love for men and friends, and the West itself."

BIOGRAPHICAL/CRITICAL SOURCES:

PERIODICALS

American Library Book Review, February, 1995, p. 21.

Booklist, July, 1994, pp. 1915, 1929; May 1, 1996, p. 1485; March 1, 2000, Donna Seaman, review of *Hungry for the World,* p. 1187.

Decatur Daily, June 4, 2000, Vivian K. Moore, "A Woman's Struggle against Subservience."

Kirkus Reviews, May 15, 1994, p. 674; February 15, 1996, p. 269.

Kliatt, January, 1995, p. 23.

Library Journal, June 1, 1994, Cheryl L. Conway, review of *Circle of Women,* p. 106; April 1, 2000, Gina Kaiser, review of *Hungry for the World,* p. 109.

New York Times, March 16, 2000, Christopher Lehmann-Haupt, review of *Hungry for the World;* April 2, 2000, Roberta Bernstein, review of *Hungry for the World.*

Publishers Weekly, June 6, 1994, Maria Simson, review of *Circle of Women,* p. 61; April 15, 1996, p. 58; February 21, 2000, review of *Hungry for the World,* p. 78.

Salt Lake Tribune, May 21, 2000, Martin Naparsteck, "The West under Cover."

Western American Literature, summer, 1995, Lynn Cothern, review of *Circle of Women,* pp. 218-219.

OTHER

Salon, http://www.salon.com/ (March 30, 2001), Maud Casey, review of *In the Wilderness.*

* * *

BARON, Naomi S(usan) 1946-

PERSONAL: Born September 27, 1946, in New York, NY; daughter of Leonard and Ruth Joan (Josephson) Baron; married; children: Aneil. *Education:* Brandeis University, B.A. (magna cum laude), 1968; Stanford University, Ph.D., 1972.

ADDRESSES: *Office*—Asbury Bldg., American University, Washington, DC 20016-8045. *E-mail*—nbaron@american.edu.

CAREER: Brown University, Providence, RI, assistant professor, 1972-78, associate professor of linguistics, 1978-85, associate dean of the college, 1981-83; American University, Washington, DC, professor of linguistics, 1987—, associate dean for undergraduate affairs, 1987-92, associate dean for curriculum and faculty development, 1992-94, chair of Department of Language and Foreign Studies, 1996-2000. Rhode Island School of Design, visiting faculty member, 1982-83; Emory University, visiting National Endowment for the Humanities chair, 1983-84; University of Texas at Austin, visiting scholar, 1984-85; Southwestern University, Brown Visiting Chair, 1985-87.

MEMBER: Linguistic Society of America, Semiotic Society of America (vice president, 1985-86; president, 1986-87), Phi Beta Kappa (president of Zeta chapter, 1998-2000).

AWARDS, HONORS: Grants from Bureau of Education for the Handicapped, 1976-84, American Council of Learned Societies, 1977, and National Endowment for the Humanities, 1979-81; Guggenheim fellow, 1984-85; *Computer Languages: A Guide for the Perplexed* was selected by *Library Journal* as one of the best one hundred science and technology books of 1986; high commendation from competition for Duke of Edinburgh English Language Award, English-speaking Union, 2000.

WRITINGS:

Language Acquisition and Historical Change, North-Holland (New York, NY), 1977.
Speech, Writing, and Sign, Indiana University Press (Bloomington, IN), 1981.
Computer Languages: A Guide for the Perplexed, Doubleday (New York, NY), 1986.
Pigeon-Birds and Rhyming Words: The Role of Parents in Language Learning, Prentice-Hall (Englewood Cliffs, NJ), 1990.
Growing Up with Language: How Children Learn to Talk, Addison-Wesley (Reading, MA), 1992.
Alphabet to E-mail: How Written English Evolved and Where It's Heading, Routledge (New York, NY), 2000.

Contributor to *Encyclopedia of Language and Linguistics* and *Encyclopedic Dictionary of Semiotics.* Contributor to periodicals, including *Semiotica, Liberal Education, Computers and Translation, Language and Communication,* and *Journal of Creole Studies.* Coeditor, *Semiotica,* Volume XXVI, numbers 3-4, 1979; member of editorial board, *Visible Language* and *Language Sciences.*

SIDELIGHTS: In her book, *Alphabet to E-mail: How Written English Evolved and Where It's Heading,* linguist Naomi S. Baron writes about the historical differences between spoken and written English and speculates on the possible effects that e-mail—a medium of neither quite spoken nor written communication—might have on the future development of the English language. Kevin Jackson in the London *Times,* while faulting Baron for her own use of the English language, found that, "to be scrupulously fair, a good deal of the book is adequately interesting." The critic for *Publishers Weekly* described *Alphabet to E-mail* as "thorough, yet not in the least pedantic."

Baron once told *CA:* "Computers, language acquisition, language in social context, writing systems, the history and future of higher education—all of these threads make up my field of inquiry. The threads often interconnect in my work, as when I look at the effects of computers on written and spoken language, and when I study how new disciplines (including linguistics) find their way into the academy.

"My next project is to learn Japanese. The relationship between language structure and the social web is radically different in Japan than in societies speaking Indo-European languages. I also want to understand how the intricate writing system in Japan affects the development of literacy."

BIOGRAPHICAL/CRITICAL SOURCES:

PERIODICALS

Bloomsbury Review, September, 1992, review of *Growing Up with Language,* p. 9.
Publishers Weekly, May 29, 2000, review of *Alphabet to E-mail,* p. 73.
Times (London), February 20, 2000, Kevin Jackson, review of *Alphabet to E-mail,* "Culture," p. 44.

* * *

BARRETT, Tracy 1955-

PERSONAL: Born March 1, 1955, in Cleveland, OH; daughter of Richard Sears (a psychologist and consultant) and Shirley Irene (a teacher; maiden name, Peters) Barrett; married Gregory Giles (a telephone interconnect owner), November, 1983; children: Laura Elizabeth, Patrick Walter. *Education:* Attended Intercollegiate Center for Classical Studies, Rome, Italy, 1974-75; Brown University, A.B. (classics), 1976; University of California, Berkeley, M.A. (Italian), 1979, Ph.D. (Italian), 1987. *Politics:* Democrat.

ADDRESSES: *Office*—Department of French and Italian, Vanderbilt University, Box 6312-B, Nashville, TN 37235. *E-mail*—scbwi.midsouth@juno.com.

CAREER: Writer and educator. Vanderbilt University, Nashville, TN, from lecturer in Italian to senior lecturer in Italian, 1984—.

MEMBER: National Women's Book Association, Authors Guild, American Association of Teachers of Italian, Society of Children's Book Writers and Illustrators (regional advisor), Tennessee Writers Alliance, Tennessee Foreign Language Teachers Association.

AWARDS, HONORS: National Endowment for the Humanities grant; Best Books for Young Adults, American Library Association (ALA), Quick Picks for Reluctant Readers, ALA, Books for the Teen Age, New York Public Library, and Texas Lone Star Reading List, all for *Anna of Byzantium.*

WRITINGS:

NONFICTION; FOR CHILDREN

Nat Turner and the Slave Revolt, Millbrook Press (Brookfield, CT), 1993.
Harpers Ferry: The Story of John Brown's Raid, Millbrook Press (Brookfield, CT), 1994.
Growing Up in Colonial America, Millbrook Press (Brookfield, CT), 1995.
Virginia, Benchmark Books (New York, NY), 1997.
Kidding around Nashville: What to Do, Where to Go, and How to Have Fun in Nashville, John Muir Publications (Santa Fe, NM), 1998.
Tennessee, Benchmark Books (New York, NY), 1998.
Kentucky, Benchmark Books (New York, NY), 1999.
The Trail of Tears: An American Tragedy, Perfection Learning (Des Moines, IA), 2000.

FICTION; FOR CHILDREN

Anna of Byzantium (novel), Delacorte (New York, NY), 1999.

Also author of five children's stories for the educational series "Reading Works," 1975.

OTHER

Instructor's Manual and Testing Program to Accompany Insieme: An Intermediate Italian Course, McGraw-Hill (New York, NY), 1994.
(Translator and author of introduction) *Cecco, as I Am and Was: The Poems of Cecco Angiolieri,* Branden Publications (Boston, MA), 1994.

Contributor of articles to *Medieval Perspectives, Diacritics, Quilt World, Quaderni d'italianistica,* and *Feminist Issues.* Editorial assistant, *Romance Philology,* 1978-79, and *Kidney International,* 1984.

SIDELIGHTS: Tracy Barrett has published both nonfiction for children and the young adult novel *Anna of Byzantium.* Among Barrett's nonfiction efforts are two books concerned with important events just before America's Civil War began. *Nat Turner and the Slave Revolt,* published as part of the "Gateway Civil Rights" series, tells the story of an African-American slave and preacher who came to believe that God wanted him to free the slaves. Based on his visions, Turner led a group of slaves in a bloody revolt that took the lives of over 260 people. The book begins with Turner's court conviction in 1831, traces his upbringing and education, and concludes with the famous revolt. In a review for *Booklist,* Janice Del Negro praised Barrett's objectivity, stating that she "attempts to place the event in its historical context in a concise, noninflammatory text." Barrett's next book was *Harpers Ferry: The Story of John Brown's Raid,* published as part of the "Spotlight on American History" series. The book profiles John Brown, an abolitionist who took weapons during a raid on the United States arsenal at Harpers Ferry, West Virginia, in 1859. Reviewing several books in the series for *School Library Journal,* George Gleason noted that they "cover their subjects well and occasionally include unusual tidbits of information."

The novel *Anna of Byzantium* is based on the real-life story of Princess Anna Comnena, a member of the Byzantine nobility of the eleventh century. Anna is expected to someday assume the throne, but the birth of her younger brother changes the line of succession. The rivalry between the two siblings leads to an attempted murder, political turmoil, and eventual exile. A reviewer for *Horn Book* called the novel "a fascinating mix of history, mystery, and intrigue." "The author's precise use of detail," Ilene Cooper noted in *Booklist,* "helps re-create Anna's world." In her review of the book for *Bulletin of the Center for Children's Books,* Elizabeth Bush concluded that *Anna of Byzantium* was "a gripping saga of alliances, intrigues, deceits, and treacheries worthy of a place among the tragic myths."

Barrett told *CA:* "I grew up outside of New York City in a town where many authors live, so it never seemed like an unusual kind of job to have. I liked writing and got good grades in English, but I never thought of being a writer because whenever I read a really good book I'd get discouraged and think, 'I could never write something like that.' It wasn't until after I grew up that I realized I didn't have to write a book like *Charlotte's Web* or *A Wrinkle in Time* because someone else had already done that. What I wrote would be something new, and there was no point in trying to write like someone else.

"I started by writing nonfiction because in graduate school I had learned how to do research and I loved doing it. While I was doing research for something to do with my teaching, I came across the story of the Byzantine princess Anna Comnena, and she interested me so much that I decided to see if I could write a story based on her life. What interested me so much about her was that there are many stories about children who are rich and powerful and wish they could just be ordinary kids. I never believed that! I always thought that most people with a lot of money and power like it just fine and would never trade with a poor person. And I also was intrigued at the strong sibling rivalry between Anna and her brother John. It seemed to me that this was something that lots of kids could relate to. So I just started writing, and with the encouragement of my writing group, I finished the book about a year later. *Anna of Byzantium* has been my most successful book so far, although *Growing Up in Colonial America* has done quite well too, especially for nonfiction."

BIOGRAPHICAL/CRITICAL SOURCES:

PERIODICALS

Booklist, August, 1993, Janice Del Negro, review of *Nat Turner and the Slave Revolt,* pp. 2051-2052; December 15, 1995, review of *Growing Up in Colonial America,* p. 700; April 1, 1999, Ilene Cooper, review of *Anna of Byzantium,* p. 1425.

Bulletin of the Center for Children's Books, April, 1993, Betsy Hearne, review of *Nat Turner and the Slave Revolt,* p. 240; July, 1999, Elizabeth Bush, review of *Anna of Byzantium,* p. 377.

Globe and Mail (Toronto), review of *Anna of Byzantium,* p. D13.

Horn Book Guide, spring, 1994, review of *Nat Turner and the Slave Revolt,* pp. 156, 169; fall, 1999, review of *Anna of Byzantium,* p. 302.

Horn Book Magazine, July, 1999, review of *Anna of Byzantium,* p. 460.

Kirkus Reviews, April 15, 1999, review of *Anna of Byzantium,* p. 626.

Kliatt, July, 1999, review of *Anna of Byzantium,* p. 6.

Publishers Weekly, June 28, 1999, review of *Anna of Byzantium,* p. 80.

School Library Journal, January, 1994, George Gleason, review of *Harpers Ferry,* p. 118; December, 1995, review of *Growing Up in Colonial America,* p. 112; June, 1997, review of *Virginia,* p. 130; July, 1999, review of *Anna of Byzantium,* p. 92.

BARTHELME, Steve(n) 1947-

PERSONAL: Born July 7, 1947, in Houston, TX; son of Donald, Sr. (an architect) and Helen L. (a teacher; maiden name, Bechtold) Barthelme. *Education:* Attended Boston College, 1965-66; University of Texas at Austin, B.A., 1972; Johns Hopkins University, M.A., 1984.

ADDRESSES: Office—Department of English, University of Southern Mississippi, Southern Station, Box 5144, Hattiesburg, MS 39406. *Agent*—Andrew Wylie, 250 West 57th St., Suite 2106, New York, NY 10107.

CAREER: Texas Observer, Austin, review editor, 1972-73; copywriter for advertising agencies in Austin and Houston, TX, 1973-83; Northeast Louisiana University, Monroe, instructor, 1984-86; University of Southern Mississippi, Hattiesburg, associate professor of English, 1986—.

AWARDS, HONORS: Transatlantic Review Award for Fiction, 1984; awards from PEN Syndicated Fiction Project, 1985, 1986, and 1987; Short Story Award, Texas Institute of Letters, 1988, for "Zorro"; Hemingway Short Story Award, 1990; Pushcart Prize, 1993.

WRITINGS:

And He Tells the Little Horse the Whole Story (poetry and stories), Johns Hopkins University Press (Baltimore, MD), 1987.

Nineball (novel), Random House (New York, NY), 1992.

(With brother, Frederick Barthelme) *Double Down: Reflections on Gambling and Loss* (memoir), Houghton (Boston, MA), 1999.

Contributor of articles and stories to periodicals, including *Boulevard, Massachusetts Review, North American Review, Yale Review, Los Angeles Times, New York Times Magazine, Texas Observer, Elle Decor, New York Times,* and *Washington Post.*

SIDELIGHTS: Steve Barthelme's first book, *And He Tells the Little Horse the Whole Story,* is a collection of poetry and seventeen stories in which the author "recounts a string of adulteries from different points of view and throws in a rape and a murder for good measure," reported Jim Spencer in a *Chicago Tribune* review. Barthelme's stories are populated by characters such as a cat with insight on the human condition, a market analyst who pretends to be a professional football player, a phony psychologist who murders a boring patient, and a man who takes his wife to a restaurant to meet his lover. Often pessimistic or darkly humorous, Barthelme's stories "accomplish one of the things that short stories have always done best," remarked *Studies in Short Fiction* contributor Gerald Locklin: "They trace the subcutaneous, prelingual capillaries of the self's relationship with others and with itself (or its selves)." Although some critics considered the collection to be of uneven quality, others proclaimed the author's talent. Spencer asserted that "you have to accept occasional excesses to enjoy the usually intriguing twists and turns of a great creator. And Barthelme is just that."

Barthelme teamed with his brother, fellow writer and University of Southern Mississippi professor Frederick Barthelme, to produce a memoir, *Double Down: Reflections on Gambling and Loss.* The memoir is, according to Tom De Haven in *Entertainment Weekly,* "a brutally candid, unflattering self-portrait of two successful middle-aged men" who behaved "like 'overage children.'" "*Double Down* is also an unsentimental, even edgy meditation on . . . the often crazy-making trauma of being orphaned in midlife," continued De Haven. Following the death of their father, the brothers received "an inheritance that totaled about $300,000," reported De Haven, and "they blew it. Every penny. And then some." Steve and Frederick developed a gambling addiction that escalated with the death of their parents. They favored the slot machines and blackjack tables of Mississippi riverboat casinos. In November of 1996, while at their regular spot at the Grand Casino in Gulfport, Mississippi, the brothers were accused of conspiring with a dealer to cheat. Jim Hanas reported in *Salon* that "widely publicized criminal charges loomed over them for nearly two years." After they finished writing *Double Down,* Hanas added, the charges against the Barthelmes were dropped, because "prosecutors announced they had found no evidence of impropriety on the bothers' part."

After speaking of the brothers' lifestyle and addiction, *Newsweek* contributor David Gates remarked of the Barthelmes and *Double Down* that "their redemption is the book itself, in which shell shock is transfigured by literary grace." *Double Down* shifts "fluently between an account of the brothers' fall into addiction and their memories of . . . family life," commented a *Publishers Weekly* reviewer who predicted that readers would be drawn "into the intimacy of their self-deception." In the book, Steve and Frederick Barthelme, who take responsibility for their actions and addiction, try to pierce the surface of their conduct, analyzing the reasons for their behavior. "Together, as in the book's first-person-plural narration, the two complete each other's thoughts, each offering his own perspective on their common obsessions," observed Hanas. *Library Journal* critic Marty Soven "enthusiastically recommended" *Double Down* as "mesmerizing" and a "work of high art." The work "[beautifully evokes] the gamblers' addition," praised Soven. *Double Down* is "by turns dazzlingly canny and achingly abject," stated the reviewer for *Publishers Weekly.* Frank Caso, in *Booklist,* described the book as "simultaneously intoxicating and chilling," although at "other times, however, their tone is somewhat disingenuous."

Steve and Frederick Barthelme are also brothers of the late Donald Barthelme, a critically acclaimed writer.

BIOGRAPHICAL/CRITICAL SOURCES:

PERIODICALS

Booklist, October 15, 1999, Frank Caso, review of *Double Down,* p. 409.

Chicago Tribune, January 12, 1988, Jim Spencer, review of *And He Tells the Little Horse the Whole Story.*

Entertainment Weekly, November 12, 1999, Tom De Haven, "Roll Play: In the Engrossing *Double Down,* Two Southern Writers Set Aside Literary Fiction to Confront Their Gambling Addiction," p. 72.

Library Journal, September 1, 1999, Marty Soven, review of *Double Down,* p. 202.

Los Angeles Times, December 15, 1987.

New York Review of Books, March 9, 2000, A. Alvarez, "High Rollers," p. 24.

New York Times Book Review, December 20, 1987, review of *And He Tells the Little Horse the Whole Story,* p. 8.

Newsweek, December 6, 1999, David Gates, "Losing Hand: On Grief and Gambling," p. 85.

Publishers Weekly, October 4, 1999, review of *Double Down,* p. 53.

Studies in Short Fiction, spring, 1988, Gerald Locklin, review of *And He Tells the Little Horse the Whole Story,* p. 160.

OTHER

Salon, http://www.salon.com/ (December 1, 1999), Jim Hanas, "Games People Play."*

BEACHAM, Richard C. 1946-

PERSONAL: Born March 28, 1946, in Washington, DC; son of Lowrie M. and Margaret (Thorne) Beacham. *Education:* University of Hamburg, Teaching Certificate, 1967; Yale University, B.A., 1968, M.F.A., D.F.A., 1972.

ADDRESSES: Office—School of Theatre Studies, University of Warwick, Coventry CV4 7AL, England. *E-mail*—tsrai@titanic.csv.warwick.ac.uk.

CAREER: Yale University, New Haven, CT, visiting lecturer in theater studies, 1970-72; Hiram College, Hiram, OH, assistant professor of theater studies and chairperson of department, 1972-74; University of Warwick, Coventry, England, began as lecturer, became professor in theater studies, 1976—. Yale University, dramaturg at Yale Repertory Theatre, 1969-72, resident fellow and visiting professor, 1979, and 1982-83; University of California, Santa Barbara, visiting professor, 1989; American Institute for Foreign Study, lecturer; Museum Scholar, Getty Center for the History of Art and Humanities; head of THEATRON (Theater History in Europe: Architectural and Textual Resources Online) Project. BBC World Service, German-language broadcaster.

MEMBER: International Federation for Theatre Research, Society for the Promotion of Roman Studies, American Society for Theatre Research, British Society for Theatre Research, Yale Elizabethan Club.

AWARDS, HONORS: National Endowment for the Humanities grant for research in Pompeii; Nuffield Foundation grant for research in Greece; grants from British Universities Film Council, British Academy, Consortium for Drama and Media in Higher Education, Warwickshire County Council, Stanley Thomas Johnson Foundation, *Pro Helvetia,* Dr. Radcliffe Trust, and Swiss Science Foundation.

WRITINGS:

Adolphe Appia, Theatre Artist, Cambridge University Press, 1987.

(Editor) Adolphe Appia, *Essays, Scenarios, and Designs,* UMI Research Press, 1989.

The Roman Theatre and Its Audience, Harvard University Press, 1991.

(Editor) Appia, *Texts on Theatre,* Routledge & Kegan Paul, 1993.

Adolphe Appia: Artist and Visionary of the Modern Theatre, Harwood (Philadelphia, PA), 1994.

Spectacle Entertainments of Early Imperial Rome, Yale University Press (New Haven, CT), 1999.

Author and presenter of the films *Staging Greek Tragedy: Insights on Sites* (also co-producer), *Staging Roman Comedy: Pompeian Painting and Plautus, The Italian Renaissance Stage: The Idea and Image of Antiquity, Revolution and Rebirth: Modern Theatrical Reform and Its Debt to Antiquity,* and *Gluck's "Orpheus and Eurydice": A Production Inspired by Appia and Dalcroze's 1913 Staging at Hellerau.* Work represented in anthologies, including *Living Greek Theatre,* edited by Michael Walton, Greenwood Press, 1987; *Themes in Drama,* Volume 13, edited by J. Redmond, Cambridge University Press, 1991; and *Theatre in the Roman World,* edited by E. J. Jory, Cambridge University Press, 1993. General editor of "Ancient Theatre and Its Legacy," a series of video study packages. Contributor of numerous articles and reviews to scholarly journals and newspapers. Associate editor, *Yale/Theatre,* 1969-72.

WORK IN PROGRESS: Editing *Theatre in the Roman World: A Documentary History,* for Cambridge University Press; translating several ancient plays for publication by Johns Hopkins University Press.

SIDELIGHTS: Richard C. Beacham, a drama professor who specializes in ancient theater, has written extensively about early twentieth-century playwright Adolphe Appia and about the theatrical presentations of ancient Rome. Beacham's study *Adolphe Appia, Theatre Artist* records Appia's rejection of traditional theatre and exploration of new possibilities. Because of the rise of cinema in the early twentieth century, Appia was among those playwrights who questioned the role of theatrical productions when film presentations could do so much more. Appia envisioned a theatre focused upon the actor, with the stage cleared of everything else. He also theorized about the new possibilities offered by electric light in stage productions, including the use of spotlights to highlight particular scenes or actions. Hans-Jurgen Syberberg, in his review of the book for the *New Republic,* called Appia "one of those revolutionaries whom you simultaneously push to the side and start curiously taking nibbles at, the heritage of whose experiment will produce great new riches."

In *Spectacle Entertainments of Early Imperial Rome* Beacham describes the various public entertainments—including animal hunts, gladiator battles, and chariot races—with which imperial Rome amused itself. Tracing the development of entertainment forms from the late Republic to the reign of the emperor Nero, Beacham relates the political climate to the popular entertainment of the time. "Erudite, exemplary, and well written," according to D. B. Wilmeth in *Choice,* "this study . . . will be welcomed by serious students and specialists."

BIOGRAPHICAL/CRITICAL SOURCES:

PERIODICALS

Choice, January, 2000, D. B. Wilmeth, review of *Spectacle Entertainments of Early Imperial Rome,* p. 941.

New Republic, October 3, 1988, Hans-Jurgen Syberberg, review of *Adolphe Appia, Theatre Artist,* p. 32.

Times Literary Supplement, December 14, 1990, p. 1352.*

* * *

BEGLEY, Louis 1933-

PERSONAL: Born Ludwik Begleiter, October 6, 1933, in Stryj, Poland; immigrated to United States, 1948; naturalized U.S. citizen, 1953; son of Edward David (a physician) and Frances (Hauser) Begley; married Sally Higginson, February 11, 1956 (divorced May, 1970); married Anne Muhlstein Dujarric dela Riviere (a writer), March 30, 1974; children: (first marriage) Peter, Amey B., Adam C. *Education:* Harvard University, A.B. (summa cum laude), 1954; LL.B. (magna cum laude), 1959. *Politics:* Democrat.

ADDRESSES: Home—925 Park Ave., New York, NY 10022. *Office*—Debevoise & Plimpton, 919 Third Ave., New York, NY 10022. *Agent*—Georges Borchardt, 136 East 57th St., New York, NY 10022.

CAREER: Admitted to the Bar of New York State, 1961; Debevoise & Plimpton (law firm), New York City, associate, 1959-67, partner, 1968—; writer; lecturer. Senior visiting lecturer at University of Pennsylvania, 1985 and 1986. *Military:* U.S. Army, 1954-56.

MEMBER: Association Bar of City of New York, Council on Foreign Relations, Century Association, American Phi.

AWARDS, HONORS: Irish Times-Aer Lingus International Fiction Prize, 1991; National Book Award nomination, 1991; National Book Critics' Circle Award nomination, 1991; *Los Angeles Times* Book Prize nomination, 1991; PEN/Ernest Hemingway First Fiction Award, 1992; Prix Medicis Etranger, 1992, for *Wartime Lies;* Harold U. Ribalow Prize, 1992; Award in Literature, American Academy of Arts and Letters, 1995; Jeanette Literatur Preis, 2000; Chevalier de l'Ordre des Arts et Lettres.

WRITINGS:

Wartime Lies (novel), Knopf (New York, NY), 1991.

The Man Who Was Late (novel), Knopf (New York, NY), 1993.

As Max Saw It (novel), Knopf (New York, NY), 1994.

About Schmidt (novel), Knopf (New York, NY), 1996.

Mistler's Exit (novel), Knopf (New York, NY), 1998.

Schmidt Delivered (novel), Knopf (New York, NY), 2000.

Contributor to periodicals, including *New York Times Book Review.*

WORK IN PROGRESS: A novel.

SIDELIGHTS: Louis Begley, a prominent attorney specializing in international corporate law, won substantial acclaim with his literary debut, *Wartime Lies.* Since then Begley has become well known for his novels that feature "the emotional landscape of the detached, aging businessman-aesthete," to quote Vanessa V. Friedman in *Entertainment Weekly.* In the tradition of the novel of manners, Begley writes domestic dramas about the wealthy—"an unblinking bird's-eye view of a tiny world plagued by excess leisure and the demanding upkeep of luxury," as Daphne Merkin put it in the *New York Times Book Review.* Merkin added: "Armed with insider information about the controlling familial maneuvers and byzantine financial stratagems of the wealthy, Begley imparts a bracingly sour wisdom to his descriptions of the conclaves where the moneyed and powerful meet and share their avarice, need and obsessive anxiety about gift versus estate taxes."

Himself a refugee from Nazi atrocities in Poland, Begley creates characters with identity problems and grim cynicism about the vagaries of fate. According to Victoria N. Alexander in the *Antioch Review,* one of the author's recurring themes is "the idea of divine capriciousness which can reward the undeserving and punish the good." The critic further noted that Begley "also examines the implications of divine justice's secular analogue, poetic justice." In the *New York Times Book Review,* Jack Miles stated that "the falsification of the self" is a prevailing interest of Begley's, most notably in his first two novels but also present throughout his oeuvre. Miles explained: "Self-deception at any point in a lifetime is like a dream in that the playwright and the audience are one, and the action can only be carried out under a certain anesthesia. That anesthesia, that strange numbness, has been the haunted and haunting mood around all of Begley's . . . work." *Denver Post* correspondent Paul Kafka-Gibbons likewise found Begley to be adept at revealing "men struggling, in midlife, to take possession of their own experience." Many critics have praised Begley's work for its precise, even understated, prose. As Phyllis Rose noted in the *New York Times Book Review,* the author's "exceptional literary intelligence is always in control, making me wonder if more novelists shouldn't develop the virtues of lawyers as writers: accuracy, economy, abjuring the language of emotion."

Begley's debut novel, *Wartime Lies,* was published when the author was in his late fifties. Having never written fiction before, Begley has said that this award-winning work took only three months to complete. The novel recounts the experiences of a six-year-old orphan, Maciek, and his hearty aunt, Tania, as they struggle to survive in war-torn Poland during World War II. Maciek and Tania adopt false identities, using these "wartime lies" to avoid persecution as Jews. Recalling his childhood decades later, Maciek likens his memories to the very lies he promoted to survive during that time. Judith Grossman observed in the *New York Times Book Review:* "The final perspective on little Maciek is given to the man in mid-life, who . . . speaks an epitaph consigning his childhood self to the realm of *vanitas*—the emptiness of lies." She added that this resolution remains "faithful to the dark ironies of Maciek's fate, which it is Louis Begley's great achievement to have confronted and sustained."

Wartime Lies won praise as an incisive, compelling account of suffering and survival. Grossman wrote in the *New York Times Book Review* that Begley's novel is "masterly." *Newsweek* reviewer James N. Baker described the book as "melancholy" and added that it "shows us that survival can have too high a price." And *Times Literary Supplement* reviewer Bryan Cheyette, who perceived *Wartime Lies* as Begley's "bid to recapture his lost childhood," noted that the novel "is as much about the psychological consequences of this loss as anything else."

Although critics such as Cheyette have explicitly linked Begley's life with that of Maciek in *Wartime Lies,* Begley himself has been less precise on the subject. "It is no secret," he acknowledged in the *New York Times Book Review,* "that I am a Jew, that I was born in Poland in the same year as Maciek, that I lived in Poland during the war and that the name I bear is not the one that was written in my first birth certificate." But he noted that any memoir he might produce would prove much less dramatic than his novel. "I can only trust my recollection of feelings I had, and of the general tone of those years," he wrote in the same *New York Times Book Review* piece. "Any memoir I wrote would have to be scrupulously truthful. I would have written a very short and—in all likelihood—a rather boring book." And to the *New York Times* he explained: "Reality is really not very interesting, except colossal events or if you have a special interest. If there's no intrinsic interest you have to rework it so there's a structure, and then your imagination gets involved."

Victoria Alexander wrote: "Where exactly *Wartime Lies* stands between life and art, truth and lies, no one, not even Begley, I am sure, can say. If the novel had more obvious artistic designs than it has, extraordinary designs that could not be explained in terms of probable natural, social, or psychological factors, then these might be the parts of the novel that we could easily identify as its 'lies.'" However, Alexander concluded that "in this instance . . . I find myself agreeing with [other reviewers] that Maciek of *Wartime Lies* is strongly grounded in biographical fact."

Begley's 1993 novel, *The Man Who Was Late,* is the story of Ben, a fiercely self-made man, as told by his closest friend, Jack. Jack pieces the facts of Ben's life together from his own memory and from the personal papers that come into his possession as executor of Ben's will. One prominent element of the narrative is the revealing of Ben's tumultuous love affair with Jack's cousin Veronique, a woman whose dazzling beauty masks darkness and disquiet. In recounting the story, Jack comes to understand why Ben believed himself to be "late in the major matters of existence." Once again, some critics found close parallels between the suicidal Ben and his creator. Alexander wrote: "Like his author, Ben, a Central European Jew who has somehow missed the train to Auschwitz, redefines himself, somewhat guiltily among the leisured rich in America. . . . The narrator's vivid familiarity with Ben's anguish is authoritative."

R. Z. Shepard, in his *Time* assessment of *The Man Who Was Late,* called Begley "a fine technician," praising the author's ability to "reveal the hidden flaws in an outwardly flawless character." *Washington Post Book World* contributor Paul Buttenwieser lauded the narrative's "urbanity and wit and filigree elegance." "With *The Man Who Was Late* the organization is as sophisticated as the content," declared Gabriele Annan in *New York Review of Books.* The reviewer concluded: "It is a very elegant, and readable novel, and very serious as well." In her *New York Times Book Review* piece on the novel, Eva Hoffman concluded: "The damage wrought upon the survivor's and refugee's psyche—the alienation of carrying unshareable memories, the obscure shame often felt by those who have been exposed to cruelty, the anesthesia of denial and forgetting—this, I believe, is the thematic substratum of 'The Man Who Was Late.'"

As Max Saw It introduces another curiously detached narrator who ultimately must come to terms with his humanity. Max, a Harvard law professor, finds emotional engagement as well as heightened anxiety in his friendship with Charlie Swan and Charlie's lover, Toby. When Toby falls ill, presumably with AIDS, Max is torn between his desire to remain distant from the reality of the sickness and his sense of responsibility to his friends and family. In his *New York Times Book Review* essay on the novel, Bruce Bawer contended that the work underscores "the perennial failure of human beings to recognize their connection to and responsibility for one another." The critic added that *As Max Saw It* "points up the brutal consequences of dishonesty and self-deception in supposedly private matters. It is a consummately beautiful—and major—work of literary art."

About Schmidt has been called "a novel of bad manners" by R. Z. Sheppard in *Time* magazine. The protagonist, Albert Schmidt, is a wealthy, retired WASP attorney who has recently lost his wife and who, to his dismay, is about to gain an unprincipled—and Jewish—son-in-law. From his home in the Hamptons, Schmidt contemplates his future and quarrels with his daughter who accuses him of anti-Semitism. According to Phyllis Rose, Begley "is too fastidious to make Schmidt likable, as though to elicit sympathy for him would then be too easy. How much greater the literary accomplishment to make us pity, understand, even identify with someone we have permission to write off." Indeed, as the novel progresses, Schmidt is seen to have been an indifferent father and constant womanizer, someone who makes decisions based on tax consequences rather than emotional ties. A transformation begins, however, when Schmidt commences an affair with a Puerto Rican waitress who is younger than his daughter. Rose declared: "This book exists at a point where the dry probity of a certain high-WASP temperament and the dry secular spirit in Judaism meet. It resolutely refuses transcendence. The temperature never goes up. The pitch never varies. You never feel you are being manipulated into a falsely emotional response." A *Kirkus* reviewer called *About Schmidt* "an elegant, precise, droll novel," adding: "It's one of the pleasures of Begley's . . . narrative that he both reveals Schmidt's . . . shortcomings and makes him nonetheless a fascinating character." Likewise, in his *Bookpage* online review, Charles Flowers concluded that the work is "a grimly witty, credible examination of a flawed, disappointed prince of privilege." Flowers further commended Begley for "finding moral weight within the vanities of the well-to-do."

Another wealthy and successful WASP faces a reckoning in *Mistler's Exit.* Thomas Mistler is in the process of selling his New York advertising firm for a huge profit when he discovers that he has inoperable liver cancer. Faced with the knowledge that he has only months to live, he travels to Venice, "the one place on earth where nothing irritated him." There he has a short, bitter sexual encounter with one woman and a reunion with another, an old flame from college. As with Schmidt before him, Mistler is hardly a sympathetic protagonist. If he eventually comes to see that his life has been "bought and sold on the auction block of success," as Vern Wiessner put it in a *Bookreporter* online review, he nevertheless meets his destiny with few regrets. A *Publishers Weekly* reviewer concluded of Begley: "Once again he has created a sinister, highly ambiguous protagonist in a haunting, ambivalent work of art."

Schmidt Delivered continues Begley's examination of the moral flaws of the wealthy in modern America. "Schmidtie" returns in this novel, and although he seems to have been vindicated in his opinion of his son-in-law, he cannot emerge completely triumphant. Charlotte, his daughter, continues to demand money and dole out criticism, and Carrie, the Puerto Rican mistress, refuses his offer of marriage, seeking new relationships instead. A new neighbor named Michael Mansour injects an aura of disquiet into the proceedings when he brings his *nouveau riche* manners into the stuffy confines of the Hamptons. Schmidt continues to nurse his prejudices and delusions but, as Merkin observed, "In Begley's adroitly conceived variation on the novel of manners, it's left purposely ambiguous whether all's well that doesn't end quite well—or whether, in fact, the thinness of the ice Schmidt walks on will crack under future pressures." Merkin added that Begley has written "a richly nuanced concoction, cut by a lethally dry wit. . . . The book's singular achievement . . . is to quietly nudge the novel of manners in a more provocative direction." In her *New York Times* review, Janet Maslin concluded: "Mr. Begley places his hero at a fine vantage point to see how few of the black-and-white distinctions he once valued make sense anymore and where his own place in this changing social cosmos lies. Schmidt is delivered by discovering shades of gray."

BIOGRAPHICAL/CRITICAL SOURCES:

PERIODICALS

Antioch Review, summer, 1997, Victoria N. Alexander, "Louis Begley: Trying to Make Sense of It."

Booklist, April 1, 2000, Karen Harris, review of *Wartime Lies,* p. 1481.

Boston Globe, March 16, 1993, p. 1.

Economist (US), October 7, 2000, review of *Schmidt Delivered,* p. 101.

Entertainment Weekly, September 18, 1998, Vanessa V. Friedman, review of *Mistler's Exit,* p. 82.

Kirkus Reviews, March 1, 1994, review of *As Max Saw It;* July 1, 1996, review of *About Schmidt.*

Los Angeles Times, January 24, 1993, p. 3.

Newsweek, July 29, 1991, p. 51.

New York Review of Books, June 13, 1991, p. 16; January 28, 1993; November 5, 1998, Gabriele Annan, review of *Mistler's Exit,* p. 44.

New York Times, October 6, 1991, section LI, p. 10; January 15, 1993, Michiko Kakutani, "Closing Gates, to the Past and Others," p. 25; December 14, 2000, Janet Maslin, "The Geezer Has a Kitten (A Young Girlfriend, Too)."

New York Times Book Review, May 5, 1991, pp. 1, 27; August 16, 1992, pp. 1, 22-23; January 31, 1993, Eva Hoffman, "The Soul He Threw Away"; April 24, 1994, Bruce Bawer, "Henry James in the Age of AIDS"; September 22, 1996, Phyllis Rose, "An Ordinary Bigot," p. 13; September 20, 1998, Jack Miles, "Death in Venice," p. 10; December 17, 2000, Daphne Merkin, "Retirement Benefits."

Publishers Weekly, July 6, 1998, review of *Mistler's Exit,* p. 49; September 11, 2000, review of *Schmidt Delivered,* p. 66.

Sunday Times (London) January 17, 1993.

Time, May 27, 1991, p. 69; February 1, 1993, p. 70; September 16, 1996, R. Z. Sheppard, "Comedy of Bad Manners: Lawyers, Anti-Semitism, the Hamptons—Yikes!"

Times Literary Supplement, August 16, 1991, p. 23.

Vanity Fair, February, 1993.

Washington Post Book World, January 10, 1993, p. 1.

OTHER

Bookpage, http://www.bookpage.com/9809bp/ (September, 1996), Charles Flowers, review of *About Schmidt;* (September, 1998), Charles Flowers, review of *Mistler's Exit.*

Bookreporter, http://www.bookreporter.com/ (November 6, 2000), Vern Wiessner, review of *Mistler's Exit.*

Canoe, http://www.canoe.ca/JamBooksReviewsA/ (November 3, 1996), Heather Mallick, "In Praise of Older Men: Louis Begley's Startling New Novel Shows Us the Humanity beneath the Pinstriped Suit."

Denver Post, http://www.denverpost.com/books/ (September 13, 1998), Paul Kafka-Gibbons, review of *Mistler's Exit.*

* * *

BERG, Elizabeth 1948-

PERSONAL: Born December 2, 1948; daughter of Arthur and Jeanne Hoff; married Howard Berg (a marketing director), March 30, 1974 (divorced); children: Julie, Jennifer. *Education:* Attended University of Minnesota; St. Mary's College, A.A.S.

ADDRESSES: Home—Near Boston, MA. *Office*—1131 Lake Street, #160, Oak Park, IL 60301. *Agent*—Lisa Bankoff, International Creative Management, 40 West 57th St., New York, NY 10019.

CAREER: Writer. Worked variously as a waitress, chicken washer, singer, information clerk, and registered nurse. Taught a writing workshop at Radcliffe College.

AWARDS, HONORS: American Booksellers Book of the Year finalist, for *Talk before Sleep;* New England Book Award for fiction, 1997, for body of work.

WRITINGS:

NOVELS

Durable Goods, Random House (New York, NY), 1993.

Talk before Sleep, Random House (New York, NY), 1994.

Range of Motion, Random House (New York, NY), 1995.

The Pull of the Moon, Random House (New York, NY), 1996.

Joy School (sequel to *Durable Goods*), Random House (New York, NY), 1997.

What We Keep, Random House (New York, NY), 1998.

Until the Real Thing Comes Along, Random House (New York, NY), 1999.

Open House, Random House (New York, NY), 2000.

Never Change, Pocket Books (New York, NY), 2001.

OTHER

Family Traditions: Celebrations for Holidays and Everyday (nonfiction), Reader's Digest (Pleasantville, NY), 1992.

Escaping into the Open: The Art of Writing True (nonfiction), HarperCollins (New York, NY), 1999.

Contributor to periodicals, including *Good Housekeeping, Ladies' Home Journal, New York Times Magazine, Parents, Redbook,* and *Woman's Day.*

ADAPTATIONS: Range of Motion was made into a original movie of the same name by the Lifetime network, 2000.

SIDELIGHTS: Elizabeth Berg, author of *Durable Goods*, "specializes in plots of a female confronting a life transition," informed Gilbert Taylor in a complimentary *Booklist* review of the author's fifth novel, *Joy School.* "Berg always takes on the big issues: living, loving and loss," summarized Ruth Coughlin in *People Weekly.* "Berg's impeccable prose gives voice to that element in our psyche that enables us to cope with the impossible," commented Donna Seaman in her *Booklist* assessment of *Range of Motion.* Although reviews of Berg's work vary between complimentary and critical, critics have often made sweeping, positive assessments of her work. One *Publishers Weekly* critic assessment of *Range of Motion* stated, "Once again, Berg . . . has orchestrated the voices of women with no-holds-barred honesty." "Berg's writing is . . . measured, delicate, and impossible to walk away from until [its] . . . completion," exclaimed Kate Wilson in an *Entertainment Weekly.* Berg manages "to deliver a story that tugs at the heartstrings while largely avoiding canned sentiment," remarked Kim Hubbard in a *People Weekly* review of *Joy School.* The author characteristically "refreshes a well-worn plot with knowing domestic detail, an understanding of familiar—sometimes conflicting—female emotions and an infectious sentimental optimism. Neither deep nor complex," attested a *Publishers Weekly* critic about Berg's eighth novel, *Open House,* the story of a women finding life after her husband leaves their twenty-year marriage.

Berg's debut as a novelist came with the publication of *Durable Goods.* This 1993 release recounts the trials and tribulations of Katie, a Texas adolescent who expects to relocate, as in the past, whenever her father's Army career dictates. With her mother dead from cancer, Katie shares quarters with her sister and an abusive father. She has great "emotional durability," as one *Publishers Weekly* contributor stated, shows potential as a poet, and longs to leave home. Similarly, Patrick T. Reardon, writing in Chicago *Tribune Books,* described Katie as "strong enough, solid enough, flexible enough to make it through the rough handling of life—and still remain a 12-year-old like any other." Berg's rendering of Katie's plight in *Durable Goods* is executed with "sensitivity rather than sentimentality," judged Reardon. A *Publishers Weekly* critic called the novel an "understated and promising fiction debut." "Hope and sorrow mingle at the close of this finely observed, compassionate book," praised a *Kirkus Reviews* contributor.

Three books and four years later, Berg released a sequel to *Durable Goods* titled *Joy School.* The 1997 publication follows Katie through her family's move to Missouri and into her first romantic fantasies and relationship. A *Publishers Weekly* reviewer called the work a "painfully accurate tale of first love in the days of princess phones and circle pins." "If books were food," asserted a *Kirkus Reviews* contributor, "[then *Joy School*] might be a Twinkie. . . . A pleasant between-meals snack of the kids-are-great genre: teary, funny, Hallmarkian wise, its true space waiting among the [young adults.]"

Berg's second novel, *Talk before Sleep,* was declared "another perfectly constructed and tender novel" by *Booklist* reviewer Donna Seaman, who described the story as a "sensitive coming-to-terms-with-death tale." In stark contrast, a *Kirkus Reviews* critic considered *Talk before Sleep* "a sappy tale. . . . sentimental, disappointing." The story tells of struggles with marriage and family, life, and death. Ann, the narrator, is a nurse who withdrawals from her daily life to care for her best friend, Ruth, an artist dying of cancer. Ruth, like Ann, has a child and is unhappily married. Ruth, unlike Ann, confronts her fear and leaves her husband—a decision Ann first envies. "The weakness of these women, in a book that purports to be about women offering each other strength, proves too unbelievable," maintained the *Kirkus Reviews* critic. A *Publishers Weekly* contributor differed, saying *Talk before Sleep* contains "accurately observed details and honest descriptions . . . intensely real characterizations, outrageous black humor and graceful prose." "The narrative [is] griping and immediate," praised the *Publishers Weekly* reviewer.

In *What We Keep* Berg addresses mother-daughter relations between a pair that have not seen each other in thirty-five years. Some critics gave unflattering assessments of the 1998 novel, while others praised it. "The plot fails to seem plausible or compelling," said a *Kirkus Reviews* writer, calling *What We Keep* "an unremarkable visit to that overworked territory where mothers and daughters visit to blame and explain." "Berg's customary skill in rendering domestic details is intact, but the story seems stitched together," judged a *Publishers Weekly* reviewer, who stated that "crucial scenes feel highlighted rather than fleshed out." In contrast, Caroline M. Hallsworth's *Library Journal* review applauded Berg as an author who "excels at writing novels about the close personal relationships between women."

Berg tackles "the now familiar girl-loves-gay-guy plot" with *Until the Real Thing Comes Along,* remarked Nancy Pearl in *Booklist.* Patty loves Ethan, her childhood sweetheart who broke their engagement and announced that he was gay. They remain friends, but Patty still hopes for a family life with Ethan. He agrees to father her child. Patty wonders if her family will accept her choice to be a single mother and thinks about the possibility of more sexual relations with Ethan. Pearl claimed that the story lacks "any of the emotion depth and tones of Berg's *Talk before Sleep.*" Also comparing the 1999 novel with *Talk before Sleep, Library Journal* contributor Beth Gibbs described *Until the Real Thing Comes Along* as "light and fluffy, unlike her amazingly powerful earlier work." A *Publishers Weekly* writer, however, asserted that *Until the Real Thing Comes Along* is a "sparkling and witty . . . poignant and clever tale" with a "zestful combination of commercial and literary appeal."

Among Berg's nonfiction titles is *Escaping into the Open: The Art of Writing True. Booklist* contributor GraceAnne A. DeCandido described the 1999 publication as "a really good book about how to write." "Berg is completely charming and no-nonsense," related DeCandido.

BIOGRAPHICAL/CRITICAL SOURCES:

PERIODICALS

Booklist, April 15, 1994, Donna Seaman, review of *Talk before Sleep,* p. 1514; August, 1995, Donna Seaman, review of *Range of Motion,* p. 1928; April 1, 1996, Joanne Wilkinson, review of *The Pull of the Moon,* p. 1342; March 1, 1997, Gilbert Taylor, review of *Joy School,* p. 1108; May 15, 1998, Nancy Pearl, review of *What We Keep,* p. 1593; June 1, 1999, GraceAnne A. DeCandido, review of *Escaping into the Open: The Art of Writing True,* p. 1770; July, 1999, Nancy Pearl, review of *Until the Real Thing Comes Along,* p. 1920.

Entertainment Weekly, September 15, 1995, Kate Wilson, review of *Range of Motion,* p. 100; June 7, 1996, Suzanne Ruta, review of *The Pull of the Moon,* p. 55.

Hollywood Reporter, December 4, 2000, Marilyn Moss, "Range of Motion," p. 23.

Kirkus Reviews, February 15, 1993, review of *Durable Goods;* March 1, 1994, review of *Talk before Sleep;* March 1, 1996, review of *The Pull of the Moon;* February 1, 1997, review of *Joy School;* April 15, 1998, review of *What We Keep.*

Library Journal, November 15, 1998, Joyce Kessel, review of *Range of Motion,* p. 111; May 1, 1998, Caroline M. Hallsworth, review of *What We Keep,* p. 135; May 15, 1999, Beth Gibbs, review of *Until the Real Thing Comes Along,* p. 123.

New Yorker, July 12, 1993, p. 103.

New York Times Book Review, October 24, 1993, p. 22.

People Weekly, October 23, 1995, Ruth Coughlin, review of *Range of Motion,* p. 30; April 21, 1997, Kim Hubbard, review of *Joy School,* p. 35.

Publishers Weekly, February 22, 1993, review of *Durable Goods,* p. 81; February 21, 1994, review of *Talk Before Sleep,* p. 232; July 3, 1995, review of *Range of Motion,* p. 49; February 26, 1996, review of *The Pull of the Moon,* p. 82; February 10, 1997, review of *Joy School,* p. 66; April 6, 1998, review of *What We Keep,* p. 59; May 24, 1999, review of *Until the Real Thing Comes Along,* p. 62; May 22, 2000, review of *Open House,* p. 70.

Tribune Books (Chicago), June 21, 1993, Patrick T. Reardon, review of *Durable Goods,* p. E5.

OTHER

Book, http:///www.bookmagazine.com/ (September-October, 1999), Cara Jespen and Mimi O'Connor, "Elizabeth Berg's Writing Life—How Sweet It Is."

Bookreporter, http://www.bookreporter.com/ (August 18, 2000), interview with Elizabeth Berg.*

* * *

BERLIN, Ira 1941-

PERSONAL: Born May 27, 1941, in New York, NY; son of Louis and Sylvia Toby (Lebwohl) Berlin; married Martha L. Chait, August 31, 1963; children: Lisa Jill, Richard Aaron. *Education:* University of Wisconsin—Madison, B.A., M.A., and Ph.D., 1970.

ADDRESSES: Office—Department of History, University of Maryland, College Park, MD 20742; fax: 301-314-9399. *E-mail*—ib3@umail.umd.edu.

CAREER: I. B. Alan, Inc., New York, NY, vice president, 1967-69; *Wisconsin Magazine of History,* Madison, WI, book review editor, 1969; University of Illinois at Chicago Circle, Chicago, instructor in history, 1970-72; Federal City College, Washington, DC, assistant professor of history, 1972-74; Princeton University, Princeton, NJ, fellow at Davis Center for Historical Studies, 1975; University of Maryland, College Park, associate professor of history, 1976—, director, Freedman and Southern Society Project, former dean of undergraduate studies, and acting dean of the College of Arts and Humanities. Fulbright Bicentennial Professor, University of Paris. Project editor for National Archives. Presidential appointee, National Council on the Humanities, 2000—.

MEMBER: International Sociological Association, American Historical Association, Organization of American Historians, Southern Historical Association, Columbia University Economic Seminars.

AWARDS, HONORS: Younger humanist fellow, National Endowment for the Humanities, 1971; Ford Foundation fellow; Best First Book Prize, National Historical Society, 1975, and Bancroft Prize, Columbia University, both for *Slaves without Masters: Free Negroes in the Antebellum South;* Jefferson Prize, Society for History in Federal Government, 1987, for *The Destruction of Slavery,* and 1991, for *The Wartime Genesis of Free Labor: The Lower South;* J. Franklin Jameson Prize, American Historical Association, for *The Black Military Experience;* Lincoln Prize (cowinner), Gettysburg College, 1994, for *Free at Last: A Documentary History of Slavery, Freedom, and the Civil War;* Frederick Douglass Prize, Gilder Lehrman Center, 1999, for *Many Thousands Gone: The First Two Centuries of Slavery in North America.*

WRITINGS:

NONFICTION

Slaves without Masters: Free Negroes in the Antebellum South, Pantheon (New York, NY), 1975.

(With others) *Slaves No More: Three Essays on Emancipation and the Civil War* (includes the introductory essays from the first four volumes of *Freedom: A Documentary History of Emancipation, 1861-1867*), Cambridge University Press (New York, NY), 1992.

Many Thousands Gone: The First Two Centuries of Slavery in North America, Belknap Press of Harvard University (Cambridge, MA), 1998.

Contributor to journals.

EDITOR

(With associate editors Joseph P. Reidy and Leslie S. Rowland) *Freedom: A Documentary History of Emancipation, 1861-1867,* Cambridge University Press (New York, NY), Volume 1: *The Destruction of Slavery,* 1985, Volume 2: *The Black Military Experience,* 1982, reprinted as *The Wartime Genesis of Free Labor: The Upper South,* 1993, Volume 3, *The Wartime Genesis of Free Labor: The Lower South,* 1990.

(With Ronald Hoffman) *Slavery and Freedom in the Age of the American Revolution,* University Press of Virginia (Charlottesville, VA), 1983.

Herbert G. Gutman, *Power and Culture: Essays on the American Working Class,* Pantheon (New York, NY), 1987.

(With Philip D. Morgan) *The Slaves' Economy: Independent Production by Slaves in the Americas,* Frank Cass (Portland, OR), 1991.

(With others) *Free at Last: A Documentary History of Slavery, Freedom, and the Civil War,* New Press (New York, NY), 1992.

(With Morgan) *Cultivation and Culture: Labor and the Shaping of Slave Life in the Americas,* University Press of Virginia (Charlottesville, VA), 1993.

(With Rowland) *Families and Freedom: A Documentary History of African-American Kinship in the Civil War Era,* New Press (New York, NY), 1997.

(With Reidy and Rowland) *Freedom's Soldiers: The Black Military Experience in the Civil War,* Cambridge University Press (New York, NY), 1998.

(With Marc Favreau and Steven F. Miller) *Remembering Slavery: African Americans Talk about Their Personal Experience of Slavery and Freedom* (with cassette) New Press (New York, NY), 1998.

(General editor) *Records of Southern Plantations from Emancipation to the Great Migration* (selections from the Rare Book, Manuscript, and Special Collections Library at Duke University), University Publications of America (Bethesda, MD), 2001.

WORK IN PROGRESS: Social Structure of Nineteenth-Century Southern Cities.

SIDELIGHTS: During the 1980s and 1990s, Ira Berlin "resolutely transformed the ways by which we understand early American slavery," lauded Graham Russell Hodges in an *America* review of *Many Thousands Gone: The First Two Centuries of Slavery in North America.* Berlin, specified Hodges, "has painstakingly moved attempts to comprehend the conditions of enslavement from a monolithic, timeless portrayal to specific examination of when and where slavery existed." "The culmination of his efforts," analyzed Hodges, is *Many Thousands Gone,* a 1998 publication that "represents a profound redirection of all early U.S. social history." In the "rich and well-written narrative," praised Kenneth Maxwell in *Foreign Affairs,* "Berlin restores historical depth and a human face to a field usually mired in . . . narrow quantification." *Many Thousands Gone* is "a major contribution to the study of slavery in the United States," declared *Library Journal* contributor Anthony O. Edmonds. The book contains "serviceable [prose]" and "[impressive] economic and historical research," observed a *Publishers Weekly* critic, claiming that "what gives the book an additional dimension is its deftly employed social insights." "Throughout this fascinating book, Berlin deftly outlines the human negotiations that went on even in so unequal a relationship as mater-slave," concluded Vanessa Bush in a *Booklist* review. Hodges judged *Many Thousands Gone* to be an "authoritative, original, beautifully organized and composed . . . state-of-the-art achievement."

According to Hodges, Berlin is "a masterful historian" who is "best known as the general editor of the multi-volume, award-winning documentary series . . . on the African-American experiences in the Civil War and Reconstruction," the *Freedom: A Documentary History of Emancipation, 1861-1867* collection. Although designated the second volume in the series, *The Black Military Experience,* which is based mainly on documents written by black soldiers during the Civil War, was the first of the *Freedom* series to be released. When this volume was published in 1982, Herbert Mitgang of the *New York Times* called the book "the kind of book that Civil War historians dream about." Mitgang went on to praise the editors for using "facts derived from original sources" and avoiding the current vogue for "revisionist historical psychobabble." Historian C. Vann Woodward, writing for the *New York Times Book Review,* added his praise for the "weighty enterprise" undertaken by the Freedmen and Southern Society Project of the University of Maryland and for the chief editor Berlin.

This second volume of *Freedom: A Documentary History of Emancipation, 1861-1867* is regarded as a landmark in historical accounts of black American life and the Civil War. Chiefly edited by Berlin, with associate editors Joseph P. Reidy and Leslie S. Rowland, *The Black Military Experience* uses National Archives source materials neglected for over a century. The editors examined "perhaps two million documents," explained historian Eric Foner in the *New York Times Book Review.* They "first selected about forty thousand for possible publication, and then whittled that group down to the four thousand or so that will appear in print. (The remainder will be made available on microfilm, along with a guide and index.)" Foner believes that "the result is a series that will transform the way historians think about slavery, the Civil War, and emancipation." The importance of "the *Freedom* documents," said Foner, is that they "present the statements of black soldiers and their families, as well as black ministers, educators, and political leaders" thereby "demonstrat[ing] both the possibility of writing history 'from the bottom up,' and the capacity of anonymous people to express their beliefs with eloquence and conviction."

The first volume of the *Freedom* series, *The Destruction of Slavery,* was published in 1985 to equally high critical acclaim. William S. McFeeley of the *Washington Post Book World* explained: "this is a book not only about people seeking their emancipation, but about [black] civilians caught between warring armies." He encourages both lay and scholarly readers to "open the book" because "you will have before you rich sources for the understanding of the complex and inspiring story of how black Americans—who still must struggle to give the word meaning—achieved their freedom." Leon F. Litwack of the *New York Times Book Review* stated that *The Destruction of Slavery* "examines the evolution of Federal policy and the revolutionary process by which black men and women helped to subvert both the

Confederacy and the system of slave labor on which it was based." George M. Fredrickson of the *Times Literary Supplement* stated that the volume's basic thesis is that "the slaves were 'the prime movers in securing their own liberty,'" contributing to "their own emancipation by deserting their masters when Union troops approached, by their willingness to provide labour for the invading forces, and by their eagerness to fight for the North's cause. By their own actions they made themselves—and their freedom—a decisive factor in the war."

Berlin has edited and written publications outside of the *Freedom* documentary series. With Ronald Hoffman, Berlin coedited *Slavery and Freedom in the Age of the American Revolution.* John White of the *Times Literary Supplement* explained that the essays collected in this work "demonstrate conclusively the centrality of the Revolution in the development of slave and free black communities, and the emergence of a single Afro-American society in which social divisions turned on status (free or slave) rather than on degrees of acculturation (creole or African)."

In 1988, Berlin edited another contribution to American economic history—a collection of essays by Herbert G. Gutman titled *Power and Culture: Essays on the American Working Class.* Social historian Nell Irvin Painter, writing for the *Washington Post Book World,* calls Gutman "a pioneer of social history," a "founder and leader of what is sometimes termed the 'new labor history.'" *Power and Culture* contains many of Gutman's previously unpublished essays. Painter observed that "Berlin's long, thoughtful introduction provides a sharply-focused picture of Gutman the man—lively, energetic, deeply and perpetually engaged—with a careful tracing of Gutman's own history." In addition, the critic stated: "Berlin probes the connections between Gutman's two major fields of inquiry, free/wage workers and enslaved workers . . . and explains Gutman's growing preoccupation with the totality of workers' lives."

Berlin's editing, with Marc Favreau and Steven F. Miller, of the 1998 publication *Remembering Slavery: African Americans Talk about Their Personal Experience of Slavery and Freedom,* is, as the title suggests, an account of "slavery as the ex-slaves remember and choose to tell it," indicated Randall M. Miller in a *Library Journal* assessment. Miller claimed that he was extremely impressed with the book, which he stated "brings slavery to life as few recent books have done." The work is a combination of sound recordings and transcripts. The text of more than one hundred interviews conducted in the 1920s and 1930s with former slaves is presented alongside an audio tape of various other interviews with, and statements from, ex-slaves. "This project will enrich every American home and classroom," determined a *Publishers Weekly* reviewer who found "the tapes particularly . . . riveting." The words of those interviewed describe slaves' daily life and the culture in which they lived. "The editors' interpolations are kept to a minimum and are used strictly to tie themes together, without disrupting the [interviewees'] accounts," observed *Booklist*'s Vanessa Bush. A *Publishers Weekly* contributor lauded Berlin as "a master of allowing the natural drama of history to unfold." In contrast to more traditional historical accounts, Berlin's *Remembering Slavery* presents the history and stories of people enslaved in the United States in a more lively manner, assessed Bush, who remarked; "these stories and occurrences . . . are rendered far more memorable by the ex-slaves' own words."

BIOGRAPHICAL/CRITICAL SOURCES:

PERIODICALS

African American Review, fall, 2000, review of *Many Thousands Gone: The First Two Centuries of Slavery in North America,* p. 515.

America, April 24, 1999, Graham Russell Hodges, "Colonial Servitude," p. 17.

American Historical Review, April, 1984, p. 512.

Booklist, August, 1998, Vanessa Bush, review of *Remembering Slavery: African Americans Talk about Their Personal Experience of Slavery and Freedom,* p. 1918; January 1, 1999, review of *Remembering Slavery,* p. 778.

Book Report, September, 1987, p. 48.

Choice, May, 1983, p. 1357; July, 1992, p. 1748.

Christian Science Monitor, February 7, 1986, p. B1; October 15, 1998, Neal M. Rosendorf, review of *Many Thousands Gone,* p. B6; October 15, 1998, Walter Robinson, review of *Remembering Slavery,* p. B6.

Commonweal, December 3, 1982, p. 661.

Foreign Affairs, November, 1998, Kenneth Maxwell, review of *Many Thousands Gone,* p. 159.

Journal of American Ethnic History, summer, 2000, review of *Many Thousands Gone,* p. 98.

Journal of American History, June, 1984, p. 119; September, 1999, J. Matthew Gallman, review of *Freedom's Soldiers,* p. 782.

Journal of American Studies, April, 1985, p. 126.

Journal of Economic History, September, 1992, p. 722.
Journal of Social History, spring, 1987, p. 568.
Journal of Southern History, February, 1984, p. 135; May, 1984, p. 304.
Library Journal, September 1, 1998, Randall M. Miller, review of *Remembering Slavery,* p. 198; September 15, 1998, Anthony O. Edmonds, review of *Many Thousands Gone,* p. 90.
New Yorker, March 21, 1983, p. 132.
New York Review of Books, March 1, 1984, p. 37; December 3, 1998, Edmund S. Morgan, review of *Many Thousands Gone,* p. 14.
New York Times, July 9, 1983, p. 11; February 21, 1994, "Back to the Library, for an Award," p. B2; July 18, 1998, Paul Lewis, "A Closer Look at Slavery's Many Stages, p. A13.
New York Times Book Review, February 13, 1983, p. 9; September 14, 1986, p. 34; January 17, 1988, p. 39; October 4, 1998, George M. Fredrickson, review of *Many Thousands Gone,* p. 9; April 4, 1999, Johanna Berkman, review of *Remembering Slavery,* p. 16.
Publishers Weekly, August 24, 1998, review of *Many Thousands Gone,* p. 40; August 31, 1998, review of *Remembering Slavery,* p. 59.
Reviews in American History, March, 1984, pp. 31, 40.
School Library Journal, April, 1999, Pamela Cooper-Smuzynski, review of *Remembering Slavery,* p. 162.
Times Literary Supplement, September 30, 1983, p. 1066; January 9, 1987, p. 31.
Washington Post, January 24, 1988.
Washington Post Book World, February 23, 1986, p. 1; January 17, 1988, p. 5.
William and Mary Quarterly, January, 1985, p. 144; October, 1992, p. 712.*

* * *

BILL, J(ohn) Brent 1951-

PERSONAL: Born May 11, 1951, in Columbus, OH; son of John H. (a maintenance supervisor) and JoAnn (a homemaker; maiden name, Shields) Bill; married Sharon Deming, March 6, 1971 (divorced 1988); married Nancy Elizabeth Pierson Ragan, April 2, 1989; children: John Benjamin, Timothy Alan; step-children: Michele Tridle, Laura LaPorte, Lisa Peterson, Christopher Ragan. *Ethnicity:* "White." *Education:* Chatfield College, A.A., 1977; Wilmington College, Wilmington, OH, A.B. (magna cum laude), 1978; Earlham College, M.A., 1980; also attended Trinity Lutheran Seminary, Young Life's Institute of Youth Ministry, Henry County Academy for Community Leadership, and United Way of America's National Academy of Volunteerism. *Politics:* Independent.

ADDRESSES: Home—3812 North Redding Road, Muncie, IN 47304. *Office*—Earlham School of Religion, 228 College Ave, Richmond, IN 47374. *E-mail*—billbr@earlham.edu; brentbil@ecicnet.org.

CAREER: Recorded minister of Society of Friends (Quakers), 1980; Young Life of Central Ohio, Columbus, staff representative, 1972-76; associate minister of United Methodist church in Hillsboro, OH, 1976-79; pastoral minister of Jericho Friends Meeting in Winchester, IN, 1979-81; Western Yearly Meeting of Friends, Plainfield, IN, director of Christian education, 1981-88; pastoral minister, Friends Memorial Church, Muncie Indiana, 1987—; Earlham School of Religion, Richmond, IN, instructor in religious creative writing, 1987—; director, The Ministry of Writing (annual colloquium), Richmond, IN, 1987—. Executive director, United Way of Henry County, IN, 1989-91; staff member, Indiana Association of United Ways, 1991-97.

MEMBER: Friends World Committee for Consultation (section of the Americas), Quaker Hill Conference Center Foundation, Delaware County Ministerial Association (member of executive committee), Friends of Muncie Public Library.

WRITINGS:

David B. Updegraff: Quaker Holiness Preacher, Friends United Press, 1983.
(Contributor) Arlo Reichter, editor, *The Group Retreat Book,* Group Books, 1983.
Rock and Roll: Proceed With Caution, Fleming Revell, 1984.
Stay Tuned: A Christian Look at TV Land, Fleming Revell, 1985.
The First Day of High School and Other Teenage Nightmares, Fleming Revell, 1986.
Counselor-In-Training Course, Western Yearly Meeting, 1986.
Faith and Practice: A Study Guide, Western Yearly Meeting, 1986.
How to be a Friend in an Unfriendly World, Friends United Press, 1987.
Lunch is My Favorite Subject, Fleming H. Revell, 1987.
(Contributor) *The Youth Group Meeting Guide,* Group Publishing, 1988.

Cruisin' and Choosin', Fleming H. Revell, 1989.
Stuff Your Guidance Counselor Never Told You, Fleming H. Revell, 1990.
(Contributor) *The Youth Study Bible,* Group Publishing, 1991.
(Contributor) *Creative Worship Ideas,* Group Publishing, 1993.
The Secret Junior High Survival Guide, Fleming H. Revell, 1993.
(Contributor) *Quaker Lite,* The Lite Company, 1998.

Author of "Top 40," a monthly column in *Group.* Contributor to magazines, including *Christian Century, Parenting Today's Teen, Muncie Star Press, Youth Update, Quaker Life, Evangelical Friend, Christianity Today, Fruit of the Vine,* and *Friends Journal.*

WORK IN PROGRESS: The Silver Star, a novel; *The Unfriendly Persuasion: Death at the Pastor's Conference,* a murder mystery; *Publishers of Truth: Modern Quaker Writers,* an anthology of twentieth-century Quaker writing; *Ocean of Darkness,* a novel.

SIDELIGHTS: J. Brent Bill once told *CA:* "I got my start writing book reviews for *Quaker Life* and the *Evangelical Friend.* The reviews gave me the confidence to move on to articles. My first book, *David B. Updegraff,* grew out of my master's thesis. I chose Updegraff as a subject because, though he was quite influential in shaping what modern Quakerism looks like, nothing had been written about him since 1895, a year after his death. I felt people should know why.

"My media books, *Rock and Roll* and *Stay Tuned,* grew out of the conviction that there is nothing wrong with the mediums of entertainment—it's what we do with them. So my books present objective looks at rock music and television and teach readers how to best use them.

"I feel that writing is a way to discover what we believe about faith and the world. To that end, I teach courses at Earlham School of Religion (a Quaker seminary) in writing as a form of public ministry. I am now concentrating on writing fiction—both novel length and short story."

* * *

BLAKESLEE, Sandra 1943-

PERSONAL: Born July 24, 1943, in Flushing, NY; daughter of Alton Lauren (a writer) and Virginia (a community volunteer; maiden name, Boulden) Blakeslee; married Kenneth Lyell Stallcup (a computer software developer), June, 1971; children: Matthew Jeremy, Abi. *Education:* Attended Northwestern University, 1961-63; University of California, Berkeley, B.A., 1965.

ADDRESSES: Home and office—Santa Fe, NM. *Agent*—Carol Mann, 55 Fifth Ave., New York, NY 10003. *E-mail*—blakes@nytimes.com.

CAREER: New York Times, New York, NY, science correspondent, 1968—. Science adviser to Foundation for American Communications.

MEMBER: National Association of Science Writers.

AWARDS, HONORS: Westinghouse Award, American Association for the Advancement of Science, 1971; Howard Blakeslee Award, American Heart Association, 1987.

WRITINGS:

(With Laurian Gillespie) *You Don't Have to Live With Cystitis,* Rawson, Wade (New York, NY), 1986.
(Editor) *Human Heart Replacement: A New Challenge for Physicians and Reporters,* Gannett Foundation (Rochester, NY), 1986.
(With Judith S. Wallerstein) *Second Chances: Men, Women, and Children a Decade After Divorce,* Ticknor & Fields (New York, NY), 1989.
(With Wallerstein) *The Good Marriage: How and Why Love Lasts,* Houghton (Boston), 1995.
(With V. S. Ramachandran) *Phantoms in the Brain: Probing the Mysteries of the Human Mind,* Morrow (New York, NY), 1998.
(With Wallerstein and Julia Lewis) *The Unexpected Legacy of Divorce: A 25 Year Landmark Study,* Hyperion (New York, NY), 2000.

Contributor to magazines.

SIDELIGHTS: Sandra Blakeslee is a science correspondent for the *New York Times* and other periodicals. She specializes in neuroscience but has also written on numerous topics pertinent to physical and mental health. In 1999 Blakeslee teamed with V. S. Ramachandran to publish *Phantoms in the Brain: Probing the Mysteries of the Human Mind,* a study of the brain's circuitry and how it performs both in healthy and pathological circumstances. In the work, the authors describe

Ramachandran's "experiences with patients whose clinical problems provide insight into the workings of the brain," wrote *New York Times Book Review* correspondent Michael E. Goldberg. The authors explore science's effort, Goldberg continued, "to understand why brain damage can make a young man think his parents are impostors, or a woman with a stroke laugh uncontrollably; how a man with a stroke can be unaware that his left side is paralyzed, or why certain types of epileptic patients have intense religious experiences." The book is intended for general audiences—one reviewer even felt that teens would find it interesting. *Library Journal* contributor Laurie Bartolini found it "absorbing and enlightening," and a *Publishers Weekly* review deemed it "entertaining, tip-of-the-neurological-iceberg sleuthing." In a review published at New York University's Web site, Susan Hurley praised *Phantoms in the Brain* as "a pleasure to read and [a] valuable contribution to popular science." Hurley added that the work is enriched by its "wealth of clinical details, the lucidity of [Ramachandran's] theorizing, and the ease with which he moves between them."

Blakeslee is better known for her long-standing collaboration with Judith Wallerstein, a research psychologist who has studied the effects of divorce on children. More than thirty years ago, Wallerstein began charting the social and emotional development of a select group of children from divorced households. She followed these same children as they grew into adulthood, noting their particular vulnerabilities. While Wallerstein and Blakeslee have been careful not to draw conclusions from the study, due to its size and the lack, early on, of a control group, their books do indicate that children of divorce suffer the consequences of their parents' actions well into adulthood. As Blakeslee told *Publishers Weekly,* "The big surprise, by following them into their 20s and 30s and 40s, was that there were these whole bunch of feelings no one could have predicted."

The first Blakeslee-Wallerstein collaboration was *Second Chances: Men, Women, and Children a Decade After Divorce.* More recently they have published (with Julia Lewis) *The Unexpected Legacy of Divorce: A 25 Year Landmark Study,* and in between those two they coauthored a book on successful marriage titled *The Good Marriage: How and Why Love Lasts.* While all of these works state that children are best served emotionally by the presence of both parents within the home, they neither condemn divorce out of hand nor advocate remaining in a bad marriage for the sake of the children. As Margaret Talbot noted in the *New York Times Book Review,* the notion that children quickly rebound from the trauma of divorce "has . . . begun to seem more self-serving than truthful—and for this dawning recognition we owe a great deal to the work of the psychologist Judith Wallerstein. She, more than anyone else, has made us face the truth that a divorce can free one or both parents to start a new and more hopeful life and still hurt their children."

While Wallerstein is the acknowledged scientist behind *Second Chance, The Good Marriage,* and *The Unexpected Legacy of Divorce,* reviewers have duly noted Blakeslee's abilities as a science writer. In a *New York Times Book Review* piece about *Second Chances,* Carol Tavris wrote: "Many books in popular psychology are a melange of the author's comments, a dollop of research, and stupefyingly dull transcriptions from interviews. This is the first book-length study I've read in a long time that avoids this formula, undoubtedly because of the skill of the co-author, Sandra Blakeslee. . . . The research findings, clinical interpretations and interviews are interwoven beautifully. The case studies are believable and compelling, and benefit enormously from the Rashomon effect of hearing from all members of a family." Tavris concluded that the book "is a beautiful piece of writing, full of insights that will prove indispensable to people contemplating divorce as a necessary evil." In a similar vein, *Atlantic Monthly* reviewer Barbara Dafoe Whitehead commended *The Good Marriage* for its "modesty." Whitehead explained: "It doesn't pretend to offer a philosophy or even a lecture on marriage. It takes no position on the ideologically charged issues of women's marital roles and status. . . . It is refreshingly free of 'rights' talk and therapy talk. Indeed, [the authors place] much more emphasis on the development of good judgment and a moral sense than on the acquisition of effective communication or negotiation skills."

Blakeslee once told *CA:* "I am captivated by neuroscience, molecular biology, and other life sciences. These topics are endlessly fascinating. My goal is to captivate readers and to instill in them a sense of discovery about ideas that matter."

BIOGRAPHICAL/CRITICAL SOURCES:

PERIODICALS

Atlantic Monthly, September, 1995, Barbara Dafoe Whitehead, "The Moral State of Marriage."

Booklist, September 15, 1998, William Beatty, review of *Phantoms in the Brain: Probing the Mysteries of the Human Mind,* p. 181.

Christian Century, January 31, 1996, Trudy Bush review of *The Good Marriage: How and Why Love Lasts,* p. 109.

Commentary, January, 2001, Claudia Winkler, review of *The Unexpected Legacy of Divorce: A 25 Year Landmark Study,* p. 76.

Library Journal, October 15, 1998, Laurie Bartolini, review of *Phantoms in the Brain: Probing the Mysteries of the Human Mind,* p. 94.

National Review, October 9, 2000, James Q. Wilson, "Marriage Matters."

New York Times, February 11, 1989, Caryn James, "Sins of the Fathers and Mothers," p. A16; February 27, 1989.

New York Times Book Review, February 26, 1989, Carol Tavris, "A Remedy but Not a Cure," p. 13; January 17, 1999, Michael E. Goldberg, "Gone Haywire," p. 16; October 1, 2000, Margaret Talbot, "The Price of Divorce."

Publishers Weekly, August 3, 1998, review of *Phantoms in the Brain: Probing the Mysteries of the Human Mind,* p. 65; July 17, 2000, review of *The Unexpected Legacy of Divorce: A 25 Year Landmark Study,* p. 181; August 14, 2000, Bridget Kinsella, "Parents Split; the Kids Can't Commit," p. 201.

OTHER

New York University Web site, http://www.nyu.edu/gsas/philo/courses/consciousness/papers/GAZZRAMA.html (September 24, 2000), Susan Hurley, "Making Up Minds."*

* * *

BLUMENTHAL, John 1949-

PERSONAL: Born January 5, 1949, in Middletown, NY; son of Fritz F. and Marianne (Leiter) Blumenthal; married Ingrid Van Eckert (a commercial producer), June 20, 1982; children: Julia, Elizabeth. *Education:* Tufts University, B.A. (cum laude), 1971.

ADDRESSES: Home—2821 Rainfield Ave., Thousand Oaks, CA 91362. *Agent*—Lynn Seligman, 400 Highland Ave., Upper Montclair, NJ 07043. *E-mail*—jbautog@aol.com.

CAREER: Playboy, Chicago, IL, assistant editor, 1974-75, associate editor, 1975-77, associate West Coast editor, 1978-80, contributing editor, 1981-85; freelance writer.

MEMBER: Writers Guild of America.

WRITINGS:

The Official Hollywood Handbook, Simon & Schuster (New York, NY), 1983.

(With Barry Golson) *Love's Reckless Rash,* St. Martin's (New York, NY), 1984.

The Case of the Hard-Boiled Dicks (novel), Simon & Schuster (New York, NY), 1986.

The Tinseltown Murders (novel), Simon & Schuster (New York, NY), 1986.

(Coauthor) *Foxworth* (television pilot), American Broadcasting Co. (ABC-TV), 1986.

(Coauthor) *Smith and Watson* (television pilot), American Broadcasting Co. (ABC-TV), 1986.

(Coauthor) "Simon & Simon & Associates" (episode of the series *Simon & Simon*), Columbia Broadcasting System (CBS-TV), 1988.

Hollywood High: The History of America's Most Famous Public School, Random House (New York, NY), 1988.

(With Michael Berry) *Short Time* (screenplay), Twentieth Century-Fox, 1990.

(With Berry and Steve Carpenter) *Blue Streak* (screenplay), Tristar, 1999.

What's Wrong with Dorfman? (novel), Farmer Street Press (Thousand Oaks, CA), 2000.

Contributor to periodicals, including *Oui, National Lampoon, Punch, Esquire,* and *Special Reports.*

SIDELIGHTS: In his humorous novel, *What's Wrong with Dorfman?,* John Blumenthal tells of forty-year-old Martin Dorfman, a hypochondriac screenwriter who develops a mysterious disease. When his doctors are stumped by his ailment, Dorfman begins to explore bizarre alternative medical treatments. Meanwhile, he is also trying to get his latest screenplay through what he calls Hollywood Development Hell.

As someone who has written both books and screenplays, Blumenthal explained to Rebecca of *RebeccasReads.com:* "I like writing books better because nobody changes the writing. In movies, your original script is changed a lot. . . . But what I really like about books is the interior dialogue which you can't do that much in films."

BIOGRAPHICAL/CRITICAL SOURCES:

OTHER

RebeccasReads.com, http://www.rebeccasreads.com/interviews (July 2, 2000).

BONNER, John Tyler 1920-

PERSONAL: Born May 12, 1920, in New York, NY; son of Paul Hyde (an author) and Lilly Marguerite (Stehli) Bonner; married Ruth Anna Graham, July 11, 1942; children: Rebecca, Jonathan Graham, Jeremy Tyndall, Andrew Duncan. *Education:* Phillips Exeter Academy, graduate, 1937; Harvard University, B.S. (magna cum laude), 1941, M.A., 1942, Ph.D., 1947.

ADDRESSES: Home—52-A Patton Ave., Princeton, NJ 08540. *Office*—Department of Ecology and Evolutionary Biology, Princeton University, Princeton, NJ 08544. *E-mail*—jtbonner@princeton.edu.

CAREER: Princeton University, Princeton, NJ, assistant professor, 1947-50, associate professor, 1950-58, professor, 1958-66, George M. Moffett Professor of Biology, 1966—, chairman of department, 1965-77, 1983-84, 1987-88. Special lecturer at Marine Biology Laboratory, Woods Hole, MA, 1951-52, University of London, winter, 1956, and Brooklyn College of the City University of New York, spring, 1966. Trustee, *Biological Abstracts,* 1958-63; advisory editor, Dodd, Mead & Co., 1962-69; member of editorial board, Princeton University Press, 1964-68, 1971, trustee, 1975. *Military:* U.S. Army Air Forces, 1942-46; became first lieutenant.

MEMBER: American Academy of Arts and Sciences (fellow), National Academy of Sciences, American Society of Naturalists, Society for Developmental Biology, American Philosophical Society, Mycological Society of America, Phi Beta Kappa, Sigma Xi.

AWARDS, HONORS: Sheldon traveling fellow in Panama and Cuba, Harvard University, 1941; Rockefeller traveling fellow in Paris, 1953; Selman A. Waksman Award, Theobald Smith Society, 1955, for contributions to microbiology; Guggenheim fellow in Edinburgh, Scotland, 1958, 1971-72; National Science Foundation senior postdoctoral fellow in Cambridge, England, 1963; D.Sc., Middlebury College, 1970.

WRITINGS:

Morphogenesis: An Essay on Development, Princeton University Press (Princeton, NJ), 1952.

Cells and Societies, Princeton University Press (Princeton, NJ), 1955.

The Evolution of Development, Cambridge University Press (New York, NY), 1958.

The Cellular Slime Molds, Princeton University Press (Princeton, NJ), 1959, 2nd edition, 1966.

(Editor) D'Arcy Wentworth Thompson, *On Growth and Form,* abridged edition, Cambridge University Press (New York, NY), 1961.

The Ideas of Biology, Harper (New York, NY), 1962.

Size and Cycle: An Essay on the Structure of Biology, Princeton University Press (Princeton, NJ), 1965.

The Scale of Nature, Harper (New York, NY), 1969.

On Development: The Biology of Form, Harvard University Press (Cambridge, MA), 1974.

The Evolution of Culture in Animals, Princeton University Press (Princeton, NJ), 1980.

(Editor) *Evolution and Development,* Dahlem Workshop on Evolution and Development (Berlin, Germany), 1981, Springer (New York, NY), 1982.

The Evolution of Complexity by Means of Natural Selection, Princeton University Press (Princeton, NJ), 1988.

Researches on Cellular Slime Moulds: Selected Papers of J. T. Bonner, Indian Academy of Sciences (Bangalore, India), 1991.

Life Cycles: Reflections of an Evolutionary Biologist, Princeton University Press (Princeton, NJ), 1993.

Sixty Years of Biology: Essays on Evolution and Development, Princeton University Press (Princeton, NJ), 1996.

First Signals: The Evolution of Multicellular Development, Princeton University Press (Princeton, NJ), 2000.

Also author, with T. A. McMahon, of *On Life and Size,* 1983. Contributor to books, including *Developmental Biology,* W. C. Brown (Dubuque, IA), 1966; *Chemical Ecology,* Academic Press (New York, NY), 1970; and *The Process of Biology: Primary Sources,* Addison-Wesley (Reading, MA), 1970.

Contributor to *Science Digest, Scientific American, Natural History,* and other periodicals. Member of editorial board, *Growth,* 1955—, *American Naturalist,* 1958-60, 1966-68, *Journal of General Physiology,* 1962-69, *Oxford Surveys in Evolutionary Biology,* 1982—; associate editor of two sections, *Biological Abstracts,* 1957—; associate editor, *American Scientist,* 1961-69, and *Differentiation,* 1976—.

The Ideas of Biology has been translated into Italian, Danish, Portuguese, German, Arabic, and Norwegian.

BIOGRAPHICAL/CRITICAL SOURCES:

PERIODICALS

American Anthropologist, September, 1981, p. 708.
Best Sellers, October 15, 1970, p. 294.
Catholic World, December, 1969, p. 134.
Library Journal, May 1, 1969, p. 1887.
Los Angeles Times Book Review, September 21, 1980, p. 12.
Nature, November 17, 1988, p. 269.
New Yorker, August 11, 1980, p. 90.
New York Review of Books, January 21, 1981, p. 42.
Science and Technology, November, 1988; October, 1990.
Times Literary Supplement, September 19, 1980, p. 1014.

* * *

BOSTDORFF, Denise M. 1959-

PERSONAL: Born March 25, 1959, in Bowling Green, OH; daughter of James F. (a farmer) and Nancy (a secretary; maiden name, Spitler) Bostdorff; married Daniel J. O'Rourke III (a professor), July 25, 1987; children: Morgan, Devin. *Education:* Bowling Green State University, B.S., 1982; University of Illinois at Urbana-Champaign, M.A., 1983; Purdue University, Ph.D., 1987. *Politics:* Independent. *Religion:* Unitarian-Universalist.

ADDRESSES: Home—1425 Fox Lake Rd., Wooster, OH 44691. *Office*—103 Wishart Hall, College of Wooster, Wooster, OH 44691. *E-mail*—dbostdorff@acs.wooster.edu.

CAREER: Purdue University, Lafayette, IN, visiting assistant professor, 1987-88, assistant professor, 1988-93, associate professor of communication, 1994; College of Wooster, Wooster, OH, assistant professor of communication, 1994-95, associate professor, 1997—, chair of communication, 1998—. National Communication Association, Central States Communication Association, Center for the Study of the Presidency.

MEMBER: Member of Nature Conservancy, Southern Poverty Law Center, and Unitarian Universalist Fellowship of Wayne County.

AWARDS, HONORS: Moody grant from Lyndon Baines Johnson Foundation, 1988-89; B. Aubrey Fisher Outstanding Article Award from Western States Communication Association, 1992, for "Vice-Presidential Comedy and the Traditional Female Role: The Rhetorical Characteristics of the Vice-Presidency"; Outstanding Professor, National Speakers Association, 2000.

WRITINGS:

The Presidency and the Rhetoric of Foreign Crisis, University of South Carolina Press (Columbia, SC), 1994.

Work represented in anthologies, including *The Clinton Presidency: A Communication Perspective,* 1995 and *The 1996 Presidential Campaign,* 1998. Contributor to communication journals and other scholarly periodicals.

WORK IN PROGRESS: A study of Richard Nixon's rhetoric during the opening of China; an examination of Ku Klux Klan's recruitment efforts on the Internet.

* * *

BOURDAIN, Anthony 1956-

PERSONAL: Born 1956, in Leonia, NJ; son of Pierre (a record executive) and Gladys (an editor for the *New York Times*) Bourdain; married Nancy Putkoski. *Education:* Attended Vassar College and Culinary Institute of America.

ADDRESSES: Office—Brasserie Les Halles, 411 Park Ave. S., New York, NY 10016.

CAREER: Brasserie Les Halles, New York, NY, executive chef, 1998—. Former chef at Supper Club and later at Vince & Linda at One Fifth, both New York, NY.

WRITINGS:

Bone In the Throat: A Novel of Death and Digestion, Villard Books (New York, NY), 1995.
Gone Bamboo, Villard Books (New York, NY), 1997.
Kitchen Confidential: Adventures in the Culinary Underbelly, Bloomsbury (New York, NY), 2000.
Typhoid Mary: An Urban Historical, Bloomsbury (New York, NY), 2001.

SIDELIGHTS: Anthony Bourdain has spent more than twenty-five years in the restaurant industry, most recently as the executive chef at Manhattan's Brasserie Les Halles. Few people know more than Bourdain about the process of planning and preparing gourmet restaurant fare, so when Bourdain began to publish exposés about the restaurant industry, both insiders *and* their customers paid close attention. After the *New Yorker* printed his article, "Don't Eat before Reading This," in 1999, Bourdain was invited to address the realities of behind-the-scenes preparation of *haute cuisine* for a full-length book. The resulting title, *Kitchen Confidential: Adventures in the Culinary Underbelly,* became a bestseller that put the hard-living, Hunter Thompsonesque Bourdain on the literary map. According to Jerry Adler in *Newsweek, Kitchen Confidential* is "a gonzo memoir of what's really going on behind those swinging doors." Adler added: "In the annals of chef memoirs, *Kitchen Confidential* by Anthony Bourdain is unique, and not only because he fails to provide a single recipe. . . . Instead of food, Bourdain writes about restaurants: cooking in them, eating in them, and certain other things that go on in them about which, until now, the less said the better."

Bourdain began working in restaurants as a teenager, and he admired the bravado and freewheeling behavior exhibited by the chefs. After briefly attending Vassar College, he enrolled at the Culinary Institute of America and completed its demanding program for gourmet chefs. During his early years in the business, he fueled himself for fourteen-hour, stress-laden work days by taking drugs. "I was the last person you'd want to employ in any capacity," he told *People* magazine. Nevertheless, while he worked he observed, and his book reveals "cooking and the kitchen and the human circus of moral degenerates, dopeheads, thieves, drunks and psychopaths it attracts," to quote Margaret Sheridan in *Restaurants & Institutions.* Bourdain told the *Knight-Ridder Tribune News Service:* "I wanted very much for this book to have a sense of paranoia, and tunnel vision, and a colloquial twisted, dysfunctional view that a chef has on a Saturday night at 8 p.m."

Among its other revelations, *Kitchen Confidential* warns readers not to order fish on Mondays (because it has probably been sitting around since Friday), and to avoid Sunday brunch and well-done meats. Bourdain declares that any restaurant with a dirty bathroom has an even filthier kitchen, that bread and butter are recycled from customer to customer, and that strong sauces sometimes mask the odors of old meat. The book also details Bourdain's own personal journey through a career as a top chef, using the same strong language he employs when managing a busy kitchen. "Bourdain pulls no punches in this memoir," a *Publishers Weekly* reviewer wrote. The reviewer nevertheless felt that the author "has a tender side, and when it peeks through . . . the wall of four-letter words he constructs, it elevates this book to something more than blustery memoir." In an online review for *BookBrowser,* Terry Mathews noted: "*Kitchen Confidential* did not disappoint. I laughed all the way through the book and learned a lot along the way. . . . I learned the restaurant business isn't for the faint of heart."

Bourdain has also written several novels in which murder and mayhem are interwoven with the culinary arts. He cast the hero of *Bone In the Throat: A Novel of Death and Digestion,* his 1995 comic thriller, as a New York chef. The hero, Tommy Pagano, does not join the mob—much to the disappointment of certain members of his extended family—but instead trains as a chef. Nonetheless, Pagano becomes involved in brutal *Cosa Nostra* activities when he gets a job at a restaurant in Little Italy. He soon discovers that the FBI has created the restaurant as part of an operation to sting a mob loan shark.

A reviewer for *Entertainment Weekly* called the plot of *Bone in the Throat* "a dumbed-down version of *The Godfather,*" and a *Library Journal* contributor offered a similarly negative assessment. But in the *New York Times Book Review,* Marilyn Stasio praised Bourdain's "clever narrative" and characterized his "comic vision" as "deliciously depraved." A *Publishers Weekly* contributor deemed the book "a perfect sendup of macho mobsters and feebs alike."

In *Gone Bamboo,* a freelance assassin and one of his surviving victims—a mafioso turned government witness—find themselves living as neighbors on a Caribbean island. In short order the erstwhile enemies discover that they have both been targeted for death by the same mob leader. A *Publishers Weekly* correspondent described the book as "a stylish mix of irony, snappy dialogue and amoral verve," declaring Bourdain to be "a new master of the wiseass crime comedy."

Bourdain wrote *Kitchen Confidential,* and his novels as well, in the early morning hours before beginning his day's duties as a chef. "Writing is harder than cooking," he told *Restaurants & Institutions.* "In the restaurant I know how to do 300 covers, know how much we spend and take in. I've got figures. [With writing] you never know, you're never sure or satisfied."

BIOGRAPHICAL/CRITICAL SOURCES:

PERIODICALS

Booklist, September 1, 1997, David Pitt, review of *Gone Bamboo,* p. 62; June 1, 2000, review of *Kitchen Confidential,* p. 1827.
Entertainment Weekly, August 4, 1995, p. 53.
Knight-Ridder Tribune News Service, June 12, 2000, Elizabeth DeGivenchy, "Les Halles' Chef Anthony Bourdain Pens Book on Restaurant Industry," p. K6930.
Library Journal, June 1, 1995, p. 158.
Newsweek, May 15, 2000, Jerry Adler, "The Cook-And-Tell Chef," p. 54.
New York Times, April 12, 1995, p. B4.
New York Times Book Review, August 6, 1995, p. 23.
People Weekly, August 14, 2000, "Reality Bites: New York City Chef Anthony Bourdain's Spicy Memoir Serves Up Real Dish about Big-League Kitchens," p. 81.
Publishers Weekly, May 15, 1995, p. 56; July 28, 1997, review of *Gone Bamboo,* p. 54; April 24, 2000, review of *Kitchen Confidential,* p. 74.
Restaurant Business, September 1, 1999, Meredith Petran, "Anthony Bourdain," p. 38.
Restaurants & Institutions, August 15, 2000, Margaret Sheridan, "On Life in the Kitchen and the Wages of Fame," p. 23.
U.S. News & World Report, May 29, 2000, Linda Kulman, "This Tell-All Chef Gives an Inside Look at Dining Out," p. 65.

OTHER

BookBrowser, http://www.bookbrowser.com/ (September 24, 2000), Terry Mathews, review of *Kitchen Confidential.*

* * *

BRADBURY, Malcolm (Stanley) 1932-2000

Malcolm Bradbury

PERSONAL: Born September 7, 1932, in Sheffield, England; died following a long illness and heart problems, November 27, 2000, in Norwich, England; son of Arthur and Doris Ethel (Marshall) Bradbury; married Elizabeth Salt, October, 1959; children: Matthew, Dominic. *Education:* University College, University of Leicester, B.A. (first class honors), 1953; Queen Mary College, University of London, M.A., 1955; attended Indiana University, 1955-56, University of Manchester, 1956-58, Yale University, 1958-59; University of Manchester, Ph.D., 1962.

CAREER: University of Hull, Hull, England, staff tutor in literature and drama in department of adult education, 1959-61; University of Birmingham, Birmingham, England, lecturer in English language and literature, 1961-65; University of East Anglia, Norwich, England, lecturer, 1965-67, senior lecturer, 1967-69, reader in English, 1969-70, professor of American studies, 1970-95, professor emeritus, 1995-2000. Teaching fellow, Indiana University, 1955-56; junior fellow, Yale University, 1958-59; fellow, Harvard University, 1965-66; visiting professor, University of California, Davis, 1966; visiting fellow, All Souls College, Oxford University, 1969; visiting professor, University of Zurich, 1972; Fanny Hurst Professor of Writing, Washington University, 1982; Davis Professor, University of Queensland, and visiting professor, Griffith University, 1983; Senior Visiting Research Fellow, St. John's College, Oxford, 1994; Wells Professor, Indiana University, 1997. Chair of British Council English Studies Seminar, 1976-84; Booker-McConnell Prize for Fiction, chair of judges, 1981, member of management committee, 1984-91;

member of management committee, Book Trust, 1987-89; judge of Royal Television Society Drama Awards, 1993; judge for British Academy of Film and Television Arts, 1995, 1998; chair of judges, Whitbread Prize, 1997. Founding director of Radio Broadland (independent radio station), 1984-96; director, East Anglian Radio, 1990-96.

MEMBER: British Association of American Studies, Society of Authors, PEN (executive committee, 1973-75), Royal Society of Literature (fellow).

AWARDS, HONORS: British Association of American Studies junior fellow in United States, 1958-59; American Council of Learned Societies fellow, 1965-66; Heinemann Prize, Royal Society of Literature, 1975, for *The History Man;* named among twenty best British writers by Book Marketing Council, 1982; shortlisted for Booker-McConnell Prize for Fiction, 1983, for *Rates of Exchange;* International Emmy Award, 1987, for *Porterhouse Blue;* Decorated Commander of the Order of the British Empire, 1991; Silver Nymph award for best screenplay for a series, Monte Carlo Television Festival, 1991, for *The Gravy Train;* Writers' Guild Macallan Award nomination, best drama serial for television, 1993, for *The Gravy Train Goes East;* best film made for television award, Banff Film Festival, 1995, for *Cold Comfort Farm;* Edgar Award nomination for best television feature, Mystery Writers of America, 1997, for "An Autumn Shroud," episode of television series *Dalziel and Pascoe;* D. Litt., University of Leicester, 1987, Birmingham University, 1989, University of Hull, 1994, and Nottingham University, 1996.

WRITINGS:

Eating People Is Wrong (novel), Secker & Warburg (London, England), 1959, Knopf (New York, NY), 1960.

Phogey!; or, How to Have Class in a Classless Society (also see below), Parrish, 1960.

All Dressed Up and Nowhere to Go: The Poor Man's Guide to the Affluent Society (also see below), Parrish, 1962.

Evelyn Waugh (critical study), Oliver & Boyd, 1962.

Stepping Westward (novel), Secker & Warburg, 1965, Houghton, 1966.

(With Allan Rodway) *Two Poets* (verse), Byron Press, 1966.

What Is a Novel?, Edward Arnold, 1969.

The Social Context of Modern English Literature (criticism), Schocken, 1971.

Possibilities: Essays on the State of the Novel, Oxford University Press, 1972.

The History Man (novel), Secker & Warburg, 1975, Houghton, 1976.

Who Do You Think You Are?: Stories and Parodies, Secker & Warburg, 1976.

The Outland Dart: American Writers and European Modernism, Oxford University Press, 1978.

Saul Bellow (critical study), Methuen, 1982.

All Dressed Up and Nowhere to Go (contains revised versions of *Phogey!* and *All Dressed Up and Nowhere to Go*), Pavilion, 1982.

Rates of Exchange (novel), Knopf, 1983.

The Modern American Novel (criticism), Oxford University Press, 1983, revised edition, Viking, 1993.

Why Come to Slaka?, Secker & Warburg, 1986.

Cuts: A Very Short Novel (novella), Harper, 1987.

My Strange Quest for Mensonge, Penguin (New York, NY), 1988, also issued as *Mensonge: Structuralism's Hidden Hero.*

No, Not Bloomsbury (collected essays), Columbia University Press, 1988.

Unsent Letters: Irreverent Notes from a Literary Life, Penguin, 1988.

The Modern World: Ten Great Writers (criticism), Penguin, 1989.

(With Richard Ruland) *From Puritanism to Postmodernism: A History of American Literature* (criticism), Viking, 1991.

Doctor Criminale (novel), Viking, 1992.

The Modern British Novel (criticism), Penguin, 1994.

Dangerous Pilgrimages: Trans-Atlantic Mythologies and the Novel (criticism), Secker & Warburg, 1995.

To the Hermitage (novel), Picador (London), 2000.

Contributor of more than 1,500 articles and reviews to periodicals, including *Punch, New Yorker, New York Times, Times* (London), *Times Literary Supplement, New York Review of Books, Spectator,* and *New Republic.*

DRAMA

(With David Lodge and James Duckett) *Between These Four Walls* (stage revue), first produced in Birmingham, England, 1963.

(With Lodge, Duckett, and David Turner) *Slap in the Middle* (stage revue), first produced in Birmingham, England, 1965.

(With Chris Bigsby) *The After Dinner Game* (television play), British Broadcasting Corporation (BBC), 1975.

(With Bigsby) *Stones* (television play), BBC, 1976.

Love on a Gunboat (television play), BBC, 1977.

The Enigma (television play; based on a story by John Fowles), BBC, 1980.

Standing In for Henry (television play), BBC, 1980.

Congress (radio play), BBC, 1981.

The After Dinner Game: Three Plays for Television, Arrow Books, 1982, revised edition, 1989.

Rates of Exchange (television series; based on Bradbury's novel of the same title), BBC, 1985.

Blott on the Landscape (television series; adapted from novel by Tom Sharpe), BBC, 1985.

Porterhouse Blue (television series; adapted from the novel by Tom Sharpe), Channel 4, 1987.

Imaginary Friends (television series; adapted from the novel by Alison Lurie), Thames, 1987.

The Green Man (television series; adapted from the novel by Kingsley Amis), BBC, 1990.

Cold Comfort Farm (television series; adapted from the novel by Stella Gibbons), BBC, 1996.

Cold Comfort Farm (screenplay; based on the novel by Stella Gibbons), BBC, 1996.

Inside Trading: A Comedy in Three Acts (drama; produced at the Norwich Playhouse, November-December, 1996), Methuen Drama, 1996.

In the Red (television series; adapted from the novel by Mark Tavener), BBC2, 1998.

Author of plays *Scenes from Provincial Life,* based on the novel by William Cooper, and *Pemberton Billing and the Little Black Book.* Author, with wife, Elizabeth Bradbury, of radio play *This Sporting Life,* 1974-75. Author of six episodes of series *Anything More Would Be Greedy,* Anglia, 1989; four episodes of *The Gravy Train,* Channel 4, 1991; and four episodes of *The Gravy Train Goes West,* Channel 4, 1992. Adaptor of works by Reginald Hill, including "An Autumn Shroud," BBC1, 1996, for the series *Dalziel and Pascoe.* Also author or adaptor of episodes of television series *A Touch of Frost, Kavanagh QC, Dalziel and Pascoe,* and *Inspector Morse.* Literary advisor for South Bank Show television series *The Modern World: Ten Great Writers,* LWT, 1988.

EDITOR

E. M. Forster: A Collection of Critical Essays, Prentice-Hall, 1965.

Mark Twain, *"Pudd'nhead Wilson" and "Those Extraordinary Twins,"* Penguin, 1969.

E. M. Forster, A Passage to India: A Casebook, Macmillan, 1970.

(With David Palmer) *Contemporary Criticism,* Edward Arnold, 1970, St. Martin's, 1971.

(With Eric Mottram and Jean Franco) *The Penguin Companion to American Literature,* McGraw, 1971, published as *The Penguin Companion to Literature, Volume III: U.S.A.,* Allen Lane (London), 1971, published as *The Avenal Companion to English and American Literature,* Avenal, 1981.

(With Palmer) *Metaphysical Poetry,* Indiana University Press, 1971.

(With Palmer) *The American Novel and the Nineteen Twenties,* Edward Arnold, 1971.

(With Palmer) *Shakespearean Comedy,* Edward Arnold, 1972.

(With James McFarlane) *Modernism: A Guide to European Literature, 1890-1930,* Penguin, 1976, revised edition, 1990.

The Novel Today: Contemporary Writers on Modern Fiction, Rowman & Littlefield, 1977, revised edition, 1991.

(With Palmer) *Decadence and the 1890s,* Edward Arnold, 1979.

(With Palmer) *The Contemporary English Novel,* Edward Arnold, 1979.

(With Palmer) *Contemporary Theatre,* Holmes & Meier, 1979.

(With Howard Temperley) *An Introduction to American Studies,* Longman, 1980, revised edition, 1997.

Stephen Crane, *The Red Badge of Courage* (critical edition), Dent, 1983.

(With Palmer) *Shakespearean Tragedy,* Holmes & Meier, 1984.

(With Sigmund Ro) *Contemporary American Fiction,* E. Arnold, 1987.

The Penguin Book of Modern British Short Stories, Penguin, 1988.

(With Judy Cooke) *New Writing,* Heinemann, 1992.

(With Andrew Motion) *New Writing 2,* Heinemann, 1993.

Washington Irving, *The Sketch Book of Geoffrey Crayon, Gent.,* J. M. Dent, 1993.

Present Laughter: An Anthology of Modern Comic Fiction, Weidenfeld & Nicolson, 1994.

Class Work: An Anthology of University of East Anglia Stories (anthology), Sceptre, 1995.

The Atlas of Literature, D'Agostini (New York, NY), 1996.

Henry James, *The American,* Everyman, 1997.

(And author of introduction and notes) E. M. Forster, *A Room with a View,* Penguin, 2000.

General editor, "Stratford-upon-Avon Studies" series, Edward Arnold, 1970-81, and "Contemporary Writers" series, Methuen. Associate editor, Leicester University literary magazine, *Luciad,* 1952-53, Indiana University literary magazine, *Folio,* 1955-56; joint editor of *Yale Penny Poems,* Yale University, 1958-59; advisory and guest editor to several literary magazines.

ADAPTATIONS: The History Man was adapted as a four-part television series by Christopher Hampton, BBC, 1979.

SIDELIGHTS: Malcolm Bradbury was a highly regarded English novelist and critic. Considered among England's preeminent scholars, Bradbury was also esteemed for his critically lauded satirical novels, including *Eating People Is Wrong, The History of Man, Doctor Criminale,* and *To the Hermitage.* In addition to novels and literary criticism, Bradbury also authored short stories, stage revues, teleplays and dramas, and worked on many well-known television series in Great Britain, including *A Touch of Frost* and *Inspector Morse.* Bradbury was professor emeritus at the University of East Anglia, where he taught from 1965 until his death in 2000.

Herbert Burke in *Library Journal* called Malcolm Bradbury's first novel, *Eating People Is Wrong,* "a novel . . . about how weary academic life is in the English Midlands of the '50s—but this is not a weary novel. Often truly comic, its satire has many barbs and they often draw blood. . . . If seriousness of intent—a sociology of the British establishment of the times as seen through the microcosm of the academy—gets in the way of hearty satire, bawdiness is not lacking." According to Martin Tucker in *New Republic,* the author wrote "a first novel that is sloppy, structurally flabby, occasionally inane, frequently magnificent and ultimately successful. It is as if [Charles] Dickens and Evelyn Waugh sat down together and said 'Let's write a comic novel in the manner of Kingsley Amis about a man in search of his lost innocence who finds it.' The result is one of the most substantial and dazzling literary feasts this year." Not all reviewers were so generous in their appraisal of the book, however. In *New York Herald Tribune Book Review,* Patrick Dennis wrote: "While Malcolm Bradbury's first novel is brilliant, witty, sensitive, adult, funny and a lot of other pleasant and desirable things, it is not a good novel. And I know why: Mr. Bradbury has been so busy entertaining himself with his brilliance, wit, etc., that he has quite forgotten about those less gifted people who are expected to buy, read and enjoy his book. . . . While his knaves and fools are elegantly written, his 'sympathetic' characters are so feckless or so grotesque that one has almost no feeling for them." And a *New Yorker* critic found that "there are no funny situations, and the few comic episodes that occur are much too light, and perhaps also too tired, to stand up against the predominant, tragic predicament that is [the main character's] life . . . and even if this spectacle were more richly decorated than it is with jokes and puns and so on, it would not be good enough. Mr. Bradbury has created a serious and very human character, and has obscured him with jugglers."

Stepping Westward, Bradbury's second novel, also about university life, was hailed by a *Times Literary Supplement* reviewer as "a *vade mecum* for every youthful or aspiring first visitor to the United States. Every situational joke, every classic encounter is exactly and wittily exploited. The dialogue is often marvellously acute, the tricks of American speech expertly 'bugged.'" On the other hand, however, Rita Estok in *Library Journal* wrote that "the school, faculty and students do not ring true; in fact, it is almost a travesty on university life. James Walker, the principal character, never becomes believable and remains unsympathetic throughout the story. *Stepping Westward,* be it a travesty or satire on university life, fails to hit the mark as either." And Bernard McCabe in *Saturday Review* wrote: "Within this very funny book Mr. Bradbury proposes a serious novel about freedom and community and friendship's inevitable failures. The result is interesting, but too schematic and analytical to be really successful. The comedy works, though, thanks to Bradbury's artful writing. I leave to some future scholar the precise significance of the recurrent buttocks-motif and ear-motif. . . . [The author's] exaggerated versions of [university life] work by lending a British ear and eye to the oddities of the American scene."

Robert Nye commented in *Christian Science Monitor* that Bradbury, in his third novel, *The History Man,* achieved "some charming comic efforts—and not a few cruel ones. Bradbury has a baleful eye for human weakness. He describes with skill and obvious relish. The result is a clever, queer, witty, uncomfortable sort of book—a book whose prose possesses considerable surface brilliance but with a cutting edge concealed beneath." Margaret Drabble in *New York Times Book Review* called the book "a small narrative masterpiece," and felt that "one of the reasons why this novel is so immensely readable is its evocation of physical reality; it may be a book about ideas, but the ideas are embodied in closely observed details. . . . A thoroughly civilized writer, [Bradbury] has written a novel that raises some very serious questions about the nature of civilization without for a moment appearing pretentious or didactic—a fine achievement."

Bradbury's fourth novel, *Rates of Exchange,* was published in 1983 to praise from critics such as *New York Times Book Review* contributor Rachel Billington, who labeled it "an astonishing tour de force." The tale of a linguist traveling to a fictive Eastern bloc country, *Rates of Exchange* takes on the subject of language itself and "manages to be funny, gloomy, shrewd and silly all at once," according to Joel Conarroe in the *Washington Post Book World.* Bradbury's inventive use of language—both the locals' fractured English and their native Slakan, a hybrid of several European languages—is a highlight for many reviewers. Noted Anatole Broyard in the *New York Times:* "Bradbury is in such virtuoso form that he can even make you enjoy an entire book in which the majority of the characters speak various degrees of broken English." Although some critics took issue with the book's pacing, characterization, and sometimes uneasy mixture of humor and seriousness, many valued its wit and pungent observations on travel. Wrote *Los Angeles Times* reviewer Elaine Kendall, "Hilarious and accurate, deepened by the author's concern for subtle political and social factors, *Rates of Exchange* turns tour de force into an unequivocal compliment, elevating the genre to a major literary category."

In the 1992 novel, *Doctor Criminale,* Bradbury returned to the intellectual circuit for a satirical look at the charming and worldly Dr. Criminale, a fictional "superpower of contemporary thought." The doctor's shadowy past contributes to his mysterious appeal; students, scholars, and virtually all available members of the female gender are dazzled by his social, political, economic, philosophical, and literary wisdom. When a young journalist lands the job of researching the doctor's life for a TV documentary, the hunt for the *real* Criminale begins. This is, according to Michiko Kakutani of the *New York Times,* "an ambitious novel about large, unwieldy ideas. Mr. Bradbury raises questions about Criminale's past to examine the meaning of political commitment, the relationship between moral responsibility and esthetic principles, and the consequences of ethical pragmatism in an individual's public and private lives. . . . The . . . novel," she concluded, "is provocative and smart but also somehow bloodless." Other reviewers also felt that the character of Dr. Criminale needed fleshing out. "The eponymous subject is meant to be absolutely intriguing, but he is so 'elusive' that we have to attend instead to a thwarted narrator, in whom we're allowed no interest at all," asserted Mick Imlah in the *Times Literary Supplement.*

"In alternating chapters, our narrator, an unnamed British novelist, describes two journeys to St. Petersburg," wrote Hugo Barnacle in *New Statesman* about Bradbury's 2000 novel, *To the Hermitage.* "One is his own, made as part of a slightly mysterious international junket in October 1993. The other is a visit paid by the French encyclopedist and philosopher [Denis] Diderot to the court of Catherine the Great in the 1770s." The novel, inspired in part by Laurence Stern's *Tristram Shandy,* is the story of the narrator's trip to a conference called the Diderot Project, the goal of which is to track down Diderot's papers after "his library had been bought by the Empress Catherine the Great, who also bought the philosopher himself as librarian," noted Brian Martin in the *Financial Times.* "In counterpoint to the shenanigans of the Project taking place in 1993," summarized Martin, "Bradbury tells the 1773 story of Diderot journeying to St. Petersburg and passing endless afternoons in philosophical and political discussions with the legendary tsarina."

"The book has its faults," found David Horspool in the London *Daily Telegraph,* "which are less to do with the intended lack of focus than the occasional relaxation of control. . . . But these are stray brushstrokes on a very broad canvas. The novel is a sweeping, engrossing and overwhelmingly impressive piece of work." Other critics had a similar reaction. "*To the Hermitage* is delightfully stimulating," argued Martin. "As readers, we watch and admire Bradbury's intellectual fireworks display." Barnacle, however, felt that if "the novel were roughly a third shorter, the amount of wit and ideas on display would fill it nicely. As it is, it feels rather padded." David Coward in the *Times Literary Supplement* cautioned that there is "no drama, no urgency, no characters to love or hate," but nonetheless concluded, "Ultimately it is his [Bradbury's] teasing, winking Shandyism which gives a centre to what may not be a story but is a wise and engaging entertainment."

In 1994, Bradbury's sweeping literary survey, *The Modern British Novel,* was published to mixed reviews. *Times Literary Supplement* critic Peter Kemp listed several instances in which the names of characters and the titles of books under discussion are cited incorrectly; furthermore, he called the author's accounts of various literary movements "little more than reaccumulations of the hackneyed. . . . As original critical analysis, [this book] is virtually non-existent." But, Kemp conceded, "where it does briefly spark into life is as polemic. . . . Bradbury stirs into energetic and eloquent defence of the twentieth-century British novel's variety, versatility, and vitality. With comic regularity, he demonstrates, jeremiahs throughout the century have been announcing the death of the novel, only to be elbowed aside by the emergence of vigorous new practitioners of the genre."

Dangerous Pilgrimages: Trans-Atlantic Mythologies and the Novel, Bradbury's 1996 look at the reciprocal influence of British and American literary content and style, is generally regarded as an impressive and much-needed addition to the study of literary history. The book focuses largely on about a dozen American novelists and a half dozen Europeans (a couple of French writers along with British heavyweights of the last three centuries) and concludes that myths, rather than mimicry, have fueled the rich flow of ideas that make up "trans-Atlantic fiction." John Sutherland proclaimed in the *Times Literary Supplement:* "Academic criticism of American literature is currently densely theorized, introverted and, for anyone not professionally obliged to work with it, repugnant. This book is clearly a tool for the scholar but is generously accessible to any generally literate reader."

Bradbury also wrote numerous stage revues and television mini-series and teleplays, including the original television series *Anything More Would Be Greedy, The Gravy Train,* and *The Gravy Train Goes East.* In addition to writing original episodes for well-known television series, including *A Touch of Frost, Kavanagh QC, Dalziel and Pascoe,* and *Inspector Morse,* Bradbury adapted numerous works as teleplays. Bradbury's adaptation of Tom Sharpe's *Porterhouse Blue* garnered an International Emmy award; his adaptation of Stella Gibbons' *Cold Comfort Farm,* later released as a full-length motion picture directed by John Schlesinger that was based on the screenplay by Bradbury, received the best film-made-for-television award at the Banff Film Festival.

Bradbury once commented: "As a novelist, I achieved four novels (and a volume of short stories) in twenty-five years. It may seem a slow record, but then I have been a critic, reviewer, and professor of American studies too, as well as a regular writer for television. I believe the writer has a responsibility for literary study, and this belief has gone into my teaching of creative writing and my editorship of series like Methuen's "Contemporary Writers," where I and my fellow editor Chris Bigsby have sought to show that we live in a major period of literary creation very different from that of the earlier part of the century. I believe in fact we live in a remarkable international age of fiction, and this has affected my own writing. Though I started with provincial themes and in a relatively realistic mode I have grown vastly more international in preoccupation and far more experimental in method. Looking back over my books, they now seem to me to follow the curve of the development of British fiction from the 1950s: from the comic social realism of the postwar period through to a much harsher, more ironic vision which involves the use of fictiveness and fantasy—though always, in my case, with an edge of tragic commentary on the world we live in as this dark century moves to its end. I think I have grown far more exact as a writer, more concerned to deal with major themes, to escape provincial limitations, and to follow the fate of liberal hopes through the many intellectual, moral, and historical challenges it has now to face. As I said earlier: 'Serious writing is not an innocent act; it is an act of connection with the major acts of writing achieved by others. It is also . . . a new set of grammars, forms, and styles for the age we live in.'

"My books have been widely translated and are set-texts in schools and universities, and two—*The History Man* and *Rates of Exchange*—have been made into British Broadcasting Corporation television series. This has done a good deal to free me of the unfortunate label of being a 'university novelist,' since my aims are wider. I have myself been considerably influenced by writing for television, and I think the imagery and grammar of film and television has brought home new concepts of presentation and perception to the novel. I have also been influenced by (and perhaps also have influenced) younger writers like Ian McEwan and Clive Sinclair who have been in my creative writing classes at the University of East Anglia. I have fought for a view of the novel in Britain as a serious and experimental form, and I believe it has increasingly become so. I believe in our great need for fiction; in *Rates of Exchange,* set in Eastern Europe, I have tried to relate our awareness of an oppressive modern reality forged by the fictions of politicians and the structures of ideology to our need for true fictions that can challenge them. My basic themes, though, remain the same: the conflict between liberal humanism and the harsh systems and behaviorisms of the modern world, and the tragic implications, which, however, I believe must be expressed in comic form. In an age when the big ideologies grow tired, I think we need the abrasive vision of the writer, and in some of our great contemporaries of the novel, from Saul Bellow to Milan Kundera, I think we find that. So the novel is what gives me hope, and lasting pleasure."

BIOGRAPHICAL/CRITICAL SOURCES:

BOOKS

Bigsby, Christopher, and Heide Ziegler, editors, *The Radical Imagination and the Liberal Tradition: Interviews with English and American Novelists,* Junction Books, 1982.

Contemporary Literary Criticism, Volume 32, Gale (Detroit, MI), 1985.

Dictionary of Literary Biography, Volume 14: *British Novelists since 1960,* Gale, 1983.

Morace, Robert A., *The Dialogic Novels of Malcolm Bradbury and David Lodge,* Southern Illinois University Press, 1989.

PERIODICALS

Atlantic, November, 1992, p. 162.

Booklist, April 15, 1960; July, 1996, p. 1796; December 15, 1996, review of *The Atlas of Literature,* p. 745.

Books and Bookmen, April, 1983.

California, October, 1988.

Christian Science Monitor, February 18, 1976.

Commentary, September, 1989.

Commonweal, April 22, 1960.

Daily Telegraph (London), May 20, 2000, David Horspool, review of *To the Hermitage.*

Economist (US), July 15, 2000, review of *To the Hermitage,* p. 13.

Financial Times, June 10, 2000, Brian Martin, review of *To the Hermitage,* p. 4.

Globe and Mail (Toronto), September 12, 1987; August 20, 1988.

Library Journal, March 1, 1960; June 1, 1966; May 15, 1988; June 15, 1988; January, 1989; November 15, 1991.

Literary Review, October, 1983.

London Review of Books, September 24, 1992, p. 18; November 18, 1993, p. 23.

Los Angeles Times, October 21, 1983; December 9, 1988.

Los Angeles Times Book Review, October 18, 1987; September 25, 1988.

Mother Jones, October, 1987.

National Review, May 2, 1960; June 17, 1996, p. 57.

New Leader, January 11, 1988, pp. 20-21.

New Republic December 14, 1987; May 27, 1996, pp. 28-29.

New Statesman, October 31, 1959; April 17, 1987; August 28, 1987; May 29, 2000, Hugo Barnacle, review of *To the Hermitage,* p. 54.

New Statesman and Society, October 12, 1990.

Newsweek, October 24, 1983.

New Yorker, July 16, 1960; May 3, 1976.

New York Herald Tribune Book Review, May 22, 1960.

New York Times, April 10, 1960; October 1, 1983; November 7, 1987; January 30, 1989.

New York Times Book Review, February 8, 1976; November 20, 1983; October 18, 1987; September 25, 1988; December 16, 1991; October 6, 1992, Michiko Kakutani, review of *Doctor Criminale,* p. C15; October 25, 1992, Joel Conarroe, review of *Doctor Criminale;* August 9, 1996, Michiko Kakutani, review of *Dangerous Pilgrimages;* September 22, 1996, Robert M. Adams, review of *Dangerous Pilgrimages.*

People Weekly, May 27, 1996, p. 19.

Publishers Weekly, September 11, 1987; May 27, 1988; November 18, 1988; July 20, 1992, p. 220; June 10, 1996, p. 80.

San Francisco Chronicle, April 26, 1960.

Saturday Review, April 9, 1960; May 21, 1966.

Spectator, September 12, 1992, p. 37; October 30, 1993, p. 29; April 15, 1995, p. 35.

Time, June 3, 1966; November 14, 1983; July 18, 1988, p. 70.

Times (London), April 7, 1983; January 14, 1988; May 12, 1988; June 4, 1988.

Times Literary Supplement, November 13, 1959; August 5, 1965; November 7, 1975; September 3, 1982; April 8, 1983, February 22, 1985; October 24, 1986; June 12, 1987; November 12, 1987; May 13, 1988; September 11, 1992, p. 23; November 12, 1993, p. 24; April 28, 1995, p. 21; May 19, 2000, David Coward, review of *To the Hermitage,* p. 22.

Tribune Books (Chicago), August 28, 1988.

Washington Post, October 14, 1987.

Washington Post Book World, November 20, 1983; July 3, 1988; October 25, 1992, p. 5.

OBITUARIES:

PERIODICALS

Independent (London), November 29, 2000, p. 6.

New York Times, November 29, 2000, p. C25.

Washington Post, December 2, 2000, p. B5.*

* * *

BRADFORD, Barbara Taylor 1933-

PERSONAL: Born May 10, 1933, in Leeds, Yorkshire, England; dual United States and British citizenship; daughter of Winston (an industrial engineer) and Freda (a children's nurse and nanny; maiden name, Walker) Taylor; married Robert Bradford (a movie producer), December 24, 1963. *Education:* Studied in private schools, England.

ADDRESSES: *Home*—Manhattan, NY. *Office*—Bradford Enterprises, 450 Park Ave., New York, NY 10022-2605. *Agent*—Morton Janklow, Janklow & Nesbit Associates, 445 Park Ave., New York, NY 10022.

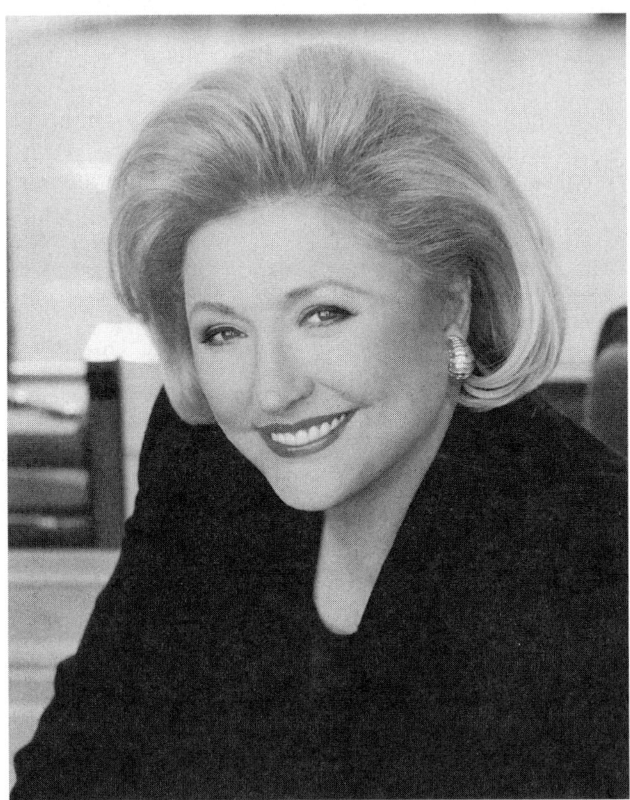

Barbara Taylor Bradford

CAREER: Author of fiction and nonfiction. *Yorkshire Evening Post,* Yorkshire, England, reporter, 1949-51, Women's Page editor, 1951-53; *Women's Own,* London, fashion editor, 1953-54; *London Evening News,* London, columnist, 1955-57; *London American,* London, executive editor, 1959-62; *Today Magazine,* columnist, 1962-63; National Design Center, New York City, editor-in-chief, decorating and design magazines, 1965-69; *Newsday,* Long Island, NY, syndicated columnist, 1966-70; *Chicago Tribune/New York News* syndicate, New York City, columnist, 1970-75; *Los Angeles Times* syndicate, columnist, 1975-81. March of Dimes, ambassador, 1999; also associated with other charities, among them City-Meals-On-Wheels and the Susan G. Koman Breast Cancer Foundation. Member of board, Police Athletic League (charity for underprivileged children) and Girls Inc. (national charity for underprivileged girls). Also associated with various charities in the United Kingdom, several of them in Yorkshire.

MEMBER: Authors Guild of America (member of council, 1989—), National Society of Interior Designers, American Society of Interior Designers.

AWARDS, HONORS: Distinguished Editorial Award, 1969, and National Press Award, 1971, National Society of Interior Designers; Dorothy Dawe Award, American Furniture Mart, 1970 and 1971; National Press Award, 1971; Matrix Award, New York chapter of Women in Communications, 1985; Editorial Award for Writing, American Society of Interior Designers, 1985; D. of Letters, 1990, Leeds University; special jury prize for body of literature, Festival of American Film, Deauville, France, 1994; Spirit of Life Award and establishment of the Barbara Taylor Bradford Research Fellowship in Pediatric Leukemia, City of Hope, 1995; She Knows Where She's Going Award, Girls Inc., 1995; "Gala 12" Woman of Distinction Award, Birmingham-Southern College, Alabama, 1995; D. of Letters, University of Bradford, 1995; Woman of the Year Award, Police Athletic League, 1995; D. of Humane Letters, Teikyo Post University, Waterbury, CT, 1996; Spirit of Achievement Award, Albert Einstein College of Medicine, 1996; Award of Achievement for outstanding accomplishments in the field of literature, Five Towns Music and Art Foundation, 1997; British Excellence Award (given aboard the *QE2*), 1998; inducted into Matrix Hall of Fame, 1998. Novels have all achieved international bestseller status; Bradford's image was used on postal stamps in St. Vincent and the Grenadines and Grenada, 2000, and she was celebrated in the postage stamp series *Great Writers of the 20th Century.*

WRITINGS:

JUVENILE; EDITOR EXCEPT AS NOTED

(Author) *Children's Stories of the Bible from the Old Testament,* illustrated by Laszlo Matulay, Lion Press (New York, NY), 1966.

Children's Stories of Jesus from the New Testament, Lion Press (New York, NY), 1966.

Samuel Nisenson, *The Dictionary of One Thousand and One Famous People: Outstanding Personages in the World of Science, the Arts, Music, and Literature,* Lion Press (New York, NY), 1966.

(Author) *A Garland of Children's Verse,* Lion Press (New York, NY), 1968.

Childrens' Stories of the Bible from the Old and New Testament, Crown (New York, NY), 1988.

NONFICTION

The Complete Encyclopedia of Homemaking Ideas, Meredith (New York, NY), 1968.

How to Be the Perfect Wife: Etiquette to Please Him, Essandess, 1969.

How to Be the Perfect Wife: Entertaining to Please Him, Essandess, 1969.

How to Be the Perfect Wife: Fashions That Please Him, Essandess, 1970.

Easy Steps to Successful Decorating, Simon & Schuster (New York, NY), 1971.

How to Solve Your Decorating Problems, Simon & Schuster (New York, NY), 1976.

Decorating Ideas for Casual Living, Simon & Schuster (New York, NY), 1977.

Making Space Grow, Simon & Schuster (New York, NY), 1979.

Luxury Designs for Apartment Living, Doubleday (New York, NY), 1981.

NOVELS

A Woman of Substance (alternate selection of Doubleday Book Club and Literary Guild), Doubleday (Garden City, NY), 1979.

Voice of the Heart (main selection of Literary Guild and Doubleday Book Club), Doubleday (Garden City, NY), 1983.

Hold the Dream: The Sequel to A Woman of Substance (main selection of Literary Guild and Doubleday Book Club; also see below), Doubleday (Garden City, NY), 1985.

Act of Will (main selection of Literary Guild and Doubleday Book Club; also see below), Doubleday (Garden City, NY), 1986.

To Be the Best (main selection of Literary Guild and Doubleday Book Club; also see below), Doubleday (New York, NY), 1988.

The Women in His Life (main selection of Literary Guild and Doubleday Book Club), Random House (New York, NY), 1990.

Remember (main selection of Literary Guild and Doubleday Book Club), Random House (New York, NY), 1991.

Barbara Taylor Bradford: Three Complete Novels (contains *Hold the Dream, To Be the Best,* and *Act of Will*), Wings (New York, NY), 1992.

Angel (main selection of Literary Guild and Doubleday Book Club), Random House (New York, NY), 1993.

Everything to Gain (main selection of Literary Guild and Doubleday Book Club; also see below), HarperCollins (New York, NY), 1994.

Dangerous to Know (main selection of Literary Guild and Doubleday Book Club), HarperCollins (New York, NY), 1995.

Love in Another Town (main selection of Literary Guild and Doubleday Book Club; also see below), HarperCollins (New York, NY), 1995.

Her Own Rules (main selection of Literary Guild and Doubleday Book Club), HarperCollins (New York, NY), 1996.

A Secret Affair (main selection of Literary Guild and Doubleday Book Club; also see below), HarperCollins (New York, NY), 1996.

Power of a Woman (main selection of Literary Guild and Doubleday Book Club), HarperCollins (New York, NY), 1997.

A Sudden Change of Heart (main selection of Literary Guild and Doubleday Book Club), Doubleday (New York, NY), 1999.

Where You Belong (main selection of Literary Guild and Doubleday Book Club), Doubleday (New York, NY), 2000.

Barbara Taylor Bradford—Three Complete Novels: Love in Another Town, Everything to Gain, A Secret Affair, Wings (New York, NY), 2000.

The Triumph of Katie Byrne (main selection of Literary Guild and Doubleday Book Club), Doubleday (New York, NY), 2001.

OTHER

Also author of *Hold the Dream* and *Voice of the Heart,* television miniseries adaptations of her novels; editor-in-chief, *Guide to Home Decorating Ideas;* creator/author of "Designing Woman," a syndicated column that appeared three times a week, was award winning, and was published for twelve years in nearly two hundred U.S. newspapers; contributor to periodicals, among them *Writer.*

Bradford's works have been translated into thirty-nine languages; author archive held in the Brotherton Collection of the Brotherton Library at the University of Leeds.

ADAPTATIONS: Ten of Bradford's novels have been adapted as television miniseries and movies of the week, earning award nominations and airing in various countries; eight of the miniseries were produced by Robert Bradford; those novels adapted are: *A Woman of Substance* (Portman/Artemis Productions), *Hold the Dream* (Bradford/Portman Productions), *Voice of the Heart* (Bradford/Portman Productions), *Act of Will* (Bradford/Portman Productions), *To Be the Best* (Robert Bradford Production/Bradford Entertainment), *Remember* (H.R. Productions, List/Estrin Productions, Gemmy/Bradford Productions with NBC Productions), *Everything to Gain* (Adelson Entertainment/Bradford Entertainment for the CBS Network), *Love in Another Town* (Adelson

Entertainment/Bradford Entertainment for the CBS Network), *Her Own Rules* (Adelson Entertainment/ Bradford Entertainment for the CBS Network), and *A Secret Affair* (Adelson Entertainment/Bradford Entertainment for the CBS Network). The *Women in His Life* was adapted and aired as a radio play by BBC Radio Drama. All of Bradford's books are on audio cassette.

SIDELIGHTS: Best-selling author Barbara Taylor Bradford has earned a wide readership with her mainstream fiction featuring strong women who succeed against all odds. As a *Contemporary Popular Writers* essayist stated: "It is in capturing the complexities within women that Barbara Taylor Bradford succeeds. Truly a commercial storyteller, Bradford adds class to a genre that receives little respect." "Bradford's novels allow her audience to glimpse the glamorous lives and enjoy the exotic playgrounds of the rich and famous while developing characters who engage the reader's interest and emotions," reported a *Twentieth-Century Romance & Historical Writers* essayist.

Prior to her 1979 best-selling debut as a novelist, Bradford published several books for juveniles and a number of nonfiction works, among them *The Complete Encyclopedia of Homemaking Ideas, How to Be the Perfect Wife: Etiquette to Please Him,* and *Easy Steps to Successful Decorating.* A former journalist covering everything from crime to show business, Bradford expressed great satisfaction over the turn her writing career has taken since 1980. "If anyone asks me whether I like being a popular writer," she told the *New York Times,* "I ask them whether they think I'd rather be an unpopular writer." Bradford's works have been translated into more than thirty-nine languages and published in more than eighty-nine countries, selling more than sixty-three million copies. Ten of her novels have been adapted as television miniseries and movies of the week. Before the turn of the twenty-first century fifteen of Bradford's novels became major international bestsellers.

Bradford grew up in the north of England, an imaginative youngster who had read all the works of Charles Dickens and the Brontë sisters by the time she was twelve. When she was ten years old she sold her first short story to a British children's magazine for seven shillings and sixpence. Determined to become a writer, Bradford left school at sixteen to work as a typist at the *Yorkshire Evening Post.* Six months later she was a cub reporter, then a reporter, and within two years she was promoted to women's page editor, at eighteen the youngest in the whole of England. When she was twenty, Bradford went to London as fashion editor of a weekly magazine, *Woman's Own.* But she missed newspapers, and after a year joined the *London Evening News* as a feature writer and columnist. Later she was an editor on *Today Magazine,* before becoming executive editor of the *London American,* a weekly newspaper.

In 1963 Barbara married Robert Bradford, an American movie producer, and moved to the United States, where she continued her career as a journalist. After writing a best-selling book on interior design, the *Newsday* syndicate offered her a column. "Designing Woman" covered lifestyle and interior design topics; Bradford also wrote a number of books on interior design, including *Easy Steps to Successful Decorating, How to Solve Your Decorating Problems,* and *Luxury Designs for Apartment Living.*

Between 1969 and 1976 Bradford started but did not finish four novels. Having never lost sight of her childhood dream to be a novelist, she was determined to complete a work of fiction. She did so when she delivered *A Woman of Substance* to Doubleday. Started in 1976, the novel was completed two years later. The debut novel sold 25,000 copies in hardcover. But it was the paperback edition that broke records. *A Woman of Substance* stayed on the paperback bestseller lists for more than a year, including fourteen months on the *New York Times* Bestseller List. More than three-and-a-half million copies of the book were sold in that time in the United States.

Today *A Woman of Substance* has become a classic, and it has sold over nineteen million copies world wide. The book begins the saga of Emma Harte, a Yorkshire woman who rises from obscurity to found a great retail empire and family dynasty and to enact revenge on the family of a young man who seduced and abandoned her when she was a girl. In the *New York Times,* Bradford characterized Emma as "a powerful woman who started with nothing but acquired dignity and polish." Bradford added that she strove to make Emma—and her other female characters as well—"tough but not hard." She wrote two sequels to *A Woman of Substance; Hold the Dream* and *To Be the Best* form the trilogy which began with her first novel.

Some of Bradford's subsequent novels, such as *The Women in His Life,* feature male protagonists, but she remains best known for her strong heroines. In *Everything to Gain,* she presents the story of a woman with a seemingly idyllic life, who in an instant loses everything that matters to her. Bradford portrays her charmed early years, then her subsequent journey from the brink of suicide to a renewed love of life. A writer for *Kirkus Reviews* commented: "The sunshine half of this novel is a fun glide through Beautiful Living, and the dark stuff has a weepier potential for the susceptible." The reviewer rated *Everything to Gain* as "stronger" than some of Bradford's more intricately plotted books. A *Publishers Weekly* contributor dismissed it as a "maudlin saga about a woman's struggle to go on," but a *Booklist* writer assured: "Bradford's fans won't be disappointed."

While a strong female lead is almost a given in Bradford's novels, her books are far from formulaic. Many illuminate interesting or little-known aspects of history. For example, *Her Own Rules* explores the British practice of exiling children in orphanages, who were often not orphans, to the far corners of the empire—a practice that continued even after World War II. Other books simply offer enjoyable entertainment. For example, *Love in Another Town* details a complicated May-September romance, and *A Secret Affair* is the story of an illicit affair that plunges into mystery.

Bradford does not classify her books as romances, but *Los Angeles Times Book Review* correspondent Judith Moore felt that the author "makes tasteful, intelligent use of the romance genre." Moore continued: "In [Bradford's] hands this maligned category takes on plausibility and a heft more than the book's weight." Moore also suggested that Bradford's characters reveal a 1980s brand of emotional complexity. Her heroes, wrote Moore, "reflect the changes in relations between men and women. They encourage women's careers. They cook dinner and clean up the mess. . . . The heroines are also new. . . . more autonomous, as motivated by work as by love."

Bradford herself seems highly motivated by the work ethic. Her writing days begin at six in the morning and can last ten to twelve hours—she adapted her novel, *Hold the Dream,* for television in just five weeks. Although she often emphasizes how much she loves her work, she also pointed out to *Atlanta Journal-Constitution* writer Don O'Briant that "there's nothing glamorous about it." She went on to describe writing novels as "the hardest work I've ever done." Yet she told *Writers Digest* that she derives tremendous satisfaction from her labors. "I *need* it," she reflected. "If I didn't write fiction, they'd take me away in a straitjacket, because I have all this . . . *stuff* going on in my head. I have to get it out."

Asked by *Writer* for advice to aspiring novelists, Bradford replied, "Don't lose your nerve. Keep going." She also suggested that novice writers always "start with an outline," a practice she always follows. Bradford went on to say: "You must have what I call the six D's: 'D' for *desire,* the desire to sit down in the first place to do it; 'D' for *discipline,* 'D' for *drive, dedication,* and *determination.* If you don't have all those qualities or traits when you start to write a novel, you are never going to finish it, because it is hard. . . . You have to want to write that novel more than you want to do anything else." She concluded, "The last 'D' is for *distraction,* which means that you have to want to write that novel more than you want to go to the movies, the theater, out to dinner, or have some free time. For me, it is a long process. I keep very long hours. You need a lot of physical stamina to be able to keep those hours, but the rewards are wonderful."

Bradford put her six D's to the test when creating her 2000 novel, *Where You Belong.* After completing 250 pages and nearing her publishing deadline, she suddenly decided to switch narrative perspectives. She related in a *Writer* article that the voice of Val, her protagonist, "was coming through . . . so strongly—consistently and insistently" that she finally attended to the voice, revising her third-person draft into the novel's existing first-person format. Although she had written two earlier novels—*Everything to Gain* and *Dangerous to Know*—in the first person, she remained slightly uneasy about the style. As she stated in *Writer,* "Writing a novel in the first person is terribly difficult, probably the hardest way to write fiction. . . . The novelist cannot move away from the actual in order to get into the heads, hearts, minds, and souls of the other characters." Bradford stated that she was glad she changed perspectives and was pleased with the final storytelling.

In *Where You Belong,* readers follow Val, an American photojournalist who leaves her Paris home and enters Kosovo to document the conflict of war, accompanied by Tony, her colleague and lover. The pair, along with Jake, an American photojournalist, are caught in an ambush and wounded, and Val's lover eventually dies. After the two survivors return to Paris, Jake professes his love for Val, as she is trying to redefine her life and career. Bradford described Val's personal struggles in *Writer:* "Val takes [readers] with her when she goes to make peace with an estranged sibling, when she uncovers the mystery of her unhappy childhood, and confronts her mother and her painful past. [Readers] are by her side when she finally accepts where she belongs in life and with whom. Her journey is fascinating."

BIOGRAPHICAL/CRITICAL SOURCES:

BOOKS

Contemporary Popular Writers, St. James Press (Detroit, MI), 1997.

Twentieth-Century Romance and Historical Writers, third edition, St. James Press (London, England), 1994.

PERIODICALS

Atlanta Journal, June 8, 1979.

Atlanta Journal-Constitution, November 24, 1991, p. N11; July 13, 1995, p. C1.

Architectural Digest, December, 1994, p. 176; July, 1998, Barbara Taylor Bradford, "A Writer's New York Narrative: Barbara Taylor Bradford Brings a European Flair to Her East Side Apartment," p. 162.

Booklist, July 15, 1979; July, 1994, p. 1893; January 1, 1999, Kathleen Hughes, review of *A Sudden Change of Heart,* p. 791; February 1, 2000, Kristin Kloberdanz, review of *Where You Belong,* p. 995; April 15, 2000, Leah Sparks, review of audio version of *A Sudden Change of Heart,* p. 1562; August, 2000, Nancy Spillman, review of *Where You Belong,* p. 2163.

Boston Globe, August 16, 1995, p. 81.

Broadcasting & Cable, November 24, 1997, Joe Schlosser, "Columbia TriStar Unveils New Productions," p. 88

Chicago Tribune, September 18, 1995, section 5, p. 5.

Columbus Dispatch, July 8, 1979.

Cosmopolitan, October, 1994, p. 250.

Daily Messenger, June 11, 1979.

Detroit News, May 19, 1985.

Entertainment Weekly, June 28, 1996, Rhonda Johnson, review of *Her Own Rules,* p. 101.

Globe and Mail (Toronto), November 3, 1984.

Good Housekeeping, June, 1993, p. 189.

Guardian, July 22, 1995, Megan Tresidder, "A Woman Worried by Good Reviews," p. 29.

Independent, July 29, 1995, John Walsh, "She's a Friend of Norman Mailer and Is the Richest Englishwoman after the Queen. Her Name Is Barbara Taylor Bradford," p. S3.

Kirkus Reviews, July 1, 1994, p. 861-862.

Knight-Ridder/Tribune News Service, October 21, 1993, Ron Miller, "When Her Stories Are Changed for TV, Barbara Taylor Bradford Understands."

Ladies Home Journal, November, 1995, p. 270.

Library Journal, September 15, 1969, p. 3229; January, 1992, p. 198; September 1, 1995, p. 206; December, 1995, p. 180; April 15, 1998, Catherine Swenson, review of *Power of Woman,* p. 134; February 1, 1999, Bettie Alston Shea, review of *A Sudden Change of Heart,* p. 118; March 15, 2000, Shea, review of *Where You Belong,* p. 124; May 1, 2000, Nancy R. Ives, review of audio version of *A Sudden Change of Heart,* p. 170.

Los Angeles Times Book Review, March 20, 1983; August 10, 1986; June 19, 1988.

Maclean's, March 8, 1999, "The Bradford Take on Writing," p. 55.

McCall's, September, 1998, Sophia Dembling, "The Last Words on Romance," p. 53.

Naples Daily News, July 29, 1979.

New York Times, November 10, 1981; October 26, 1986; May 6, 1992, Ester B. Fein, "$20 Million for Bradford," p. B3; May 20, 1992, Fein, "Winning an Author," p. B4; July 31, 1992, John J. O'Connor, "To Be the Best," p. B2; June 16, 1993, Sarah Lyall, "Falling 'Angel,'" p. B6.

New York Times Book Review, September 9, 1979; August 3, 1980, Ray Walters, "People," p. 25; April 17, 1983, "End of the Fiction Doldrums?," p. 34; April 24, 1983, Mel Watkins, "Voice of the Heart," p. 16; March 4, 1984, review of *Voice of the Heart,* p. 34; June 9, 1985, Kiki Olson, "Hold the Dream," p. 22; July 20, 1986, Andrew Postman, "Act of Will," p. 18; July 31, 1988, Joyce Cohen, "To Be the Best," p. 18.

People, June 13, 1983.

People Weekly, October 14, 1996, "Barbara Taylor Bradford's Everything to Gain," p. 20; February 22, 1999, Francine Prose, review of *A Sudden Change of Heart,* p. 44; April 17, 2000, Lan N. Nguyen, review of *Where You Belong,* p. 47.

Publishers Weekly, October 28, 1968, pp. 59-60; December 6, 1991, p. 44; May 3, 1993, p. 38; June 27, 1994, p. 55; July 10, 1995, p. 45; October 9, 1995, p. 77; January 1, 1996, p. 39; April 8, 1996, p. 55; May 19, 1997, Paul Nathan, "Trio," p. 23; September 1, 1997, Judy Quinn, "Ah, More HarperCollins Transitions," p. 20; January 4, 1999, review of *A Sudden Change of Heart,* p. 75; February 28, 2000, review of *Where You Belong,* p. 58; February 26, 2001, review of *The Triumph of Katie Byrne,* p. 57.

School Library Journal, February 1997, Katherine Fitch, review of *Her Own Rules,* p. 134.

Spectator, November 16, 1996, David Sexton, review of *A Secret Affair,* p. 48.

St. Louis Post-Dispatch, June 24, 1979.

Tribune Books (Chicago), November 24, 1991; June 27, 1993, p. 4; August 27, 1995, p. 6.

Times, January 3, 1995, "Model for a Woman of Substance," p. 11.
Variety, July 27, 1992, p. 63.
Wall Street Journal, September 10, 1986, Joanne Kaufman, "Heft and Heavy Breathing," p. 30; February 11, 2000, "Barbara Taylor Bradford," p. W2.
Washington Post, June 12, 1979; May 17, 1985.
Washington Post Book World, April 3, 1983; July 6, 1986; June 6, 1993, p. 10.
Writer, March, 1986; May, 1996, pp. 7-10; October, 2000, Barbara Taylor Bradford, "In Whose Voice?," p. 7.
Writer's Digest, June, 1987.

OTHER

Barbara Taylor Bradford Web site, http://www.barbarataylorbradford.com (May 24, 2001).

* * *

BRAND, Alice Glarden 1938-

PERSONAL: Born September 8, 1938, in New York, NY; daughter of Alfred (a watch maker and importer) and Claire (an artist and volunteer; maiden name, Rindner) Glarden; married Ira Brand (an educator), April 10, 1960; children: Kerry Dhunna, Janice Kaylor, Jonathan Brand. *Education:* Attended University of Rochester, 1956-58; City College of New York, B.A. (cum laude), 1960; Rutgers University, Ed.M., 1973, Ed.D., 1979. *Ethnicity:* "Caucasian." *Politics:* Liberal Democrat. *Religion:* Jewish. *Avocational interests:* Travel, archaeology, geography, architecture.

ADDRESSES: *Home*—1235 North Astor St. #2, Chicago, IL 60610. *Office*—State University of New York (SUNY) at Brockport, Brockport, NY 14420. *E-mail*—abrand@brockport.edu.

CAREER: Taught English and creative writing in New York and New Jersey Public Schools, 1960-78; writing instructor at Rutgers University, Middlesex County College, Somerset County College, and Rider College, 1978-80; University of Missouri-St. Louis, assistant professor, 1980-86, director of communications programs and program director of the Gateway Writing Project, 1980-87, associate professor of English, 1987; Clarion University of Pennsylvania, associate professor of English and director of writing, 1987-89; State University of New York (SUNY) at Brockport, associate professor, 1989-91, director of composition, 1989-93, professor of English, 1992-99. Visiting scholar, University of California, Berkeley, 1982-83. Director of community writing programs in New Jersey, including New Jersey State Teen Arts Festival and Highland Park and East Brunswick Poet in the Schools, 1977-80; editor of the *Journal of the Assembly for Expanded Perspectives on Learning;* reviewer for publishers including Prentice Hall, Houghton Mifflin, Harper & Row, Simon & Schuster, and Macmillan; reader for *Journal of Advanced Composition, College English,* and *College Composition and Communiction.* Has served on editorial and advisory boards for textbooks, anthologies, and composition journals. Has presented workshops, readings, and lectures, and served on panels on writing throughout the United States, Canada, and Australia.

MEMBER: Phi Beta Kappa, Kappa Delta Pi, Modern Language Association, Academy of American Poets, Poetry Society of America, National Council of Teachers of English, Poets & Writers (New York), SUNY Council on Writing.

AWARDS, HONORS: Contest winner, *New Jersey Poetry Monthly,* 1978; winner of poetry festival sponsored by *English Journal,* 1979; New Jersey State Council on the Arts fellowship in poetry, 1981; cited as Woman of Promise by the Feminist Writers' Guild, 1981; first prize for feature article, Missouri Writers' Guild, 1981; first prize, Wednesday Club of St. Louis poetry contest, 1981 and 1986; first prize, St. Louis Writers' Guild short fiction contest, 1982; first place in Midwest Regional Poetry Society of America contest, 1985; first prize, *Sing Heavenly Muse!* poetry contest, 1986; writing residencies at Yaddo Artist's Colony, 1986, 1987, and 1991; finalist in *Iowa Woman* poetry contest, 1987; Wildwood Poetry Prize, 1988; poetry finalist, Roberts Writing Awards, 1991; second place, Rochester Poetry Society Prize, 1991; honorable mention, National Writers' Union National Poetry Competition, 1993; honorable mention, *Mulberry Press* annual poetry contest, 1994.

WRITINGS:

Therapy in Writing: A Psycho-Educational Enterprise, D.C. Health (Washington, DC), 1980.
as it happens (poetry), Wampeter Press (Green Harbor, MA), 1983.
Studies on Zone (poetry), BkMk Press (Kansas City, MO), 1989.
The Psychology of Writing: The Affective Experience, Greenwood Press (New York, NY), 1989.

(Editor with Richard L. Graves) *Presence of Mind: Writing and the Domain Beyond the Cognitive,* Heinemann (Portsmouth, NH), 1994.

Court of Common Pleas, Edwin Mellen Press, 1996.

Writing in the Majors: A Guide to Disciplinary Faculty, SUNY (Brockport, NY), 1998.

Contributor of poems and articles to anthologies, including *Twentieth Century Literary Criticism,* Gale, 1983; *Dreaming of Wings,* 1984; *First Inago Anthology of Poetry,* 1984; *First Anthology of Missouri Women Writers,* 1987; *Anthology of Magazine Verse & Yearbook of American Poetry,* 1988; *The Palanquin Sampler,* 1989; *The Helicon Nine Reader,* 1990; *Rhetoric and Composition: A Sourcebook for Teachers and Writers,* third edition, 1990; *Acts Anthology,* 1994; *Colors of a Different Horse: Rethinking How We Teach Creative Writing,* 1994; *Rhetoric Review,* 1998; and *Writing and Healing: Toward an Informed Practice,* 1999.

Also contributor of poems, articles, and short stories to periodicals, including *New York Times, Anthologist, New Jersey Poetry Monthly, Wisconsin Review, English Journal, New Kent Quarterly, Outerbridge, A Different Drummer, Berkeley Poetry Review, Woman: A Journal of Liberation, Salome, Panhandler, Blue Unicorn, Northeast Journal, Confrontation, River Styx, Kalliope, Midwest Arts and Literature, Iowa Woman, Poetry Society of America Bulletin, Kansas Quarterly, Helicon Nine, California State Poetry Quarterly, Nimrod, South Florida Poetry Review, Croton Review, Sing Heavenly Muse! Collages and Bricolages, Pig Iron Press, Minnesota Review, New Delta Review, Heartlands Today, ACTS: Havens for Creatives, Widener Review, Rohwedder, Phoebe, Pleiades, Wordsmith, blueLINE, Footwork: The Paterson Literary Review,* and *Midwest Quarterly.*

SIDELIGHTS: Alice Glarden Brand has devoted her academic career to the study of the writing process. As well as teaching composition and creative writing to many students, both youngsters and adults, she has written or edited important titles on the process of writing. These include *Therapy in Writing: A Psycho-Educational Enterprise* (1980), *The Psychology of Writing: The Affective Experience* (1989), and an editorial collaboration with Richard L. Graves titled *Presence of Mind: Writing and the Domain Beyond the Cognitive* (1994). Brand is also a poet and an author of short fiction and literary nonfiction, however, and her poetry collections include *as it happens, Studies on Zone,* and *Court of Common Pleas.* She has made many contributions of her work to academic and literary periodicals, and has garnered several national and regional prizes for her efforts. In 1994, Brand collaborated with Jill Gussow on an exhibition in poetry and photographs called "Lessons on Being Female." With Richard L. Graves, Brand is the co-founder of the Assembly for Expanded Perspectives on Learning, a special interest group of the National Council of Teachers of English.

In *The Psychology of Writing,* Brand turns her attention and analysis to the emotional aspects of the writing process. Though she makes the point that emotions have been ignored in favor of promoting cognitive procedures in writing—and concentrates on the role of emotion in writing in her book—she does not argue for the primacy of emotion. Rather, Brand advocates a combination of cognitive and emotional approaches in writing classes. As writing expert Peter Elbow observed in his foreword to *The Psychology of Writing,* "she explicitly invites collaboration with writing specialists of the cognitive persuasion." He further noted that Brand "has made important progress into territory the profession has neglected, and if her research serves to mobilize some portion of the considerable research energies that now exist in our field, the results will be very happy indeed." Reviewers of the volume praised it as well. A *Health* magazine contributor lauded the book because it "dispels the notion of the misery of writing"; Walter S. Minot in *Rhetoric Review* declared that "Brand's careful, thoughtful work deserves a careful reading from the profession. Even those who disagree with her approach will benefit from grappling with new and challenging ideas."

Presence of Mind, which Brand edited with Graves, is a collection of essays by several authors concerned with the ways of knowing beyond what is traditionally considered the cognitive domain. These authors, with Brand, are part of a special interest group called the Assembly for Expanded Perspectives on Learning, which is affiliated with the National Council of Teachers of English. The book is divided into parts, entitled "Silence," "Wisdom of the Unconscious," "Wisdom of the Body," "Images," "Emotions," and "The Open Door." Again, Brand's own writing in the book advocates a blend of both cognitive and emotional methods: "Clearly," she announces, "the best way of teaching and learning embody both intellectual and nonintellectual strategies."

In 1998-99, Brand completed a campus publication resulting from over twenty years in the field of writing and rhetoric and seven years of faculty training titled *Writing in the Majors: A Guide for Disciplinary Faculty.* It includes sections on the composing process, disciplinary products (such as a case study or lab report) and teaching activties.

Brand's work as a poet has received much praise from reviewers, as well. Diane Elaine Shuey, critiquing *as it happens* in *Small Press Review,* asserted that Brand's poetry "talks about life," and "is so true, so universal, and so personal, that the reader is at once sympathetic and awed." Subjects in the volume include fear of mediocrity, fear of anti-Semitism, worries about adolescent children, and white liberal guilt. *Studies on Zone,* her 1989 volume, explores the ways in which people have developed from hunter-gatherer tribes into more complex civilizations, and questions whether the transition has been a good one. Gunvor Skogsholm, reviewing the volume in *Poetry Forum Newsletter,* hailed it as "gripping and thought provoking," and added that "one gets the most pleasure . . . out of this work by reading it slowly and by listening to the melody the words create all by themselves." Phebe Davidson in *Palanquin* decreed that *Studies on Zone* "is a volume well worth the purchase price, and then some."

BIOGRAPHICAL/CRITICAL SOURCES:

BOOKS

Brand, Alice Glarden, and Richard L. Graves, editors, *Presence of Mind: Writing and the Domain Beyond the Cognitive,* Heinemann, 1994.

Brand, Alice Glarden, *The Psychology of Writing: The Affective Experience,* foreword by Peter Elbow, Greenwood Press, 1989.

PERIODICALS

Health, July, 1989, p. 13.

Palanquin, July, 1990.

Poetry Forum Newsletter, July, 1989.

Rhetoric Review, fall, 1991, pp. 171-174.

Small Press Review, August, 1984, p. 10.

* * *

BRAYBROOKE, David 1924-

PERSONAL: Born October 18, 1924, in Hackettstown, NJ; dual citizen of the United States and Canada; son of Walter Leonard (a civil engineer) and Netta Rose (Foyle) Braybrooke; married Alice Boyd Noble, December 31, 1948 (divorced, 1982); married Margaret Eva Odell, 1984 (divorced, 1994); married Michiko Gomyo, 1994; children: (first marriage) Nicholas, Geoffrey, Elizabeth Page. *Ethnicity:* "Caucasian." *Education:* Hobart College, student, 1941-43; Harvard University, B.A., 1948; Cornell University, M.A., 1951, Ph. D., 1953; Oxford University, postgraduate study, 1952-53, postdoctoral study, 1959-60. *Politics:* Independent.

ADDRESSES: *Home*—6045 Fraser St., Halifax, Nova Scotia, Canada B3H 1R7; 1500 Scenic Dr. #300, Austin, TX 78703. *Office*—Philosophy Department, Dalhousie University, Halifax, Nova Scotia, Canada B3H 3J5; Department of Government, University of Texas at Austin, Austin, TX 78712-1087; fax: 512-479-8963, 512-471-1061, or 512-466-3660. *E-mail*—braeburn@mail.la.utexas.edu.

CAREER: Hobart College (now Hobart and William Smith Colleges), Geneva, NY, instructor in history and literature, 1948-50; instructor in philosophy at University of Michigan, Ann Arbor, 1953-54, and Bowdoin College, Brunswick, ME, 1954-56; Yale University, New Haven, CT, assistant professor of philosophy, 1956-63; Dalhousie University, Halifax, Nova Scotia, Canada, associate professor, 1963-65, professor of philosophy and politics, 1965-90, professor emeritus, 1990—; University of Texas, Austin, professor of government and philosophy, 1990—. Visiting professor of philosophy at University of Pittsburgh, 1965, 1966, University of Toronto, 1966-67, Bowling Green State University, 1982, and University of Waterloo, 1984; visiting professor of political science, University of Minnesota, Twin Cities, 1971, and University of Chicago, 1984; visiting professor, School of Social Sciences, University of California, Irvine, 1980. Visiting fellow, Wolfson College, Cambridge, 1985-86. Research assistant, Committee on the Study of Political Behavior, Social Science Research Council, summers, 1957, 1958; part-time dean of liberal arts, Bridgeport Engineering Institute, 1961-63; external examiner, College of Social Studies, Wesleyan University, 1961-64, 1967, 1970. Member of academic advisory panel to the Canada Council, 1968-71; member of the Council for Philosophical Studies, 1974-79. Chairman, Town Democratic Committee, Guilford, CT, 1961-62. *Military service:* U.S. Army, 1943-46.

MEMBER: American Philosophical Association, American Society for Political and Legal Philosophy, American Political Science Association (vice president, 1981-82), Canadian Philosophical Association (president, 1971-72), Canadian Political Science Association, Royal Institute of Public Administration, Canadian Association of University Teachers (member-at-large of national executive committee, 1970-71; president, 1975-76), Royal Society of Canada (fellow, 1980—), Amnesty International, Phi Beta Kappa.

AWARDS, HONORS: Rockefeller Foundation grant in legal and political philosophy, Oxford University, 1959-60; Guggenheim fellow, 1962-63; leave fellowships, Social Sciences and Humanities Research Council of Canada, 1978-79, and 1985-86; Royal Society of Canada fellow, 1980.

WRITINGS:

(With Charles E. Lindblom) *A Strategy of Decision: Policy Evaluation as a Social Process,* Free Press, 1963.

(Editor) *Philosophical Problems of the Social Sciences,* Macmillan, 1965.

Three Tests for Democracy: Personal Rights, Human Welfare, Collective Preference, Random House, 1968.

Traffic Congestion Goes through the Issue-Machine, Routledge & Kegan Paul, 1974.

Ethics in the World of Business, Rowman & Allanheld, 1983.

Meeting Needs, Princeton University Press, 1987.

Philosophy of Social Science, Prentice-Hall, 1987.

(With P. K. Schotch and Bryson Brown) *Logic on the Track of Social Change,* Clarendon Press, 1995.

(Editor) *Social Rules,* Westview, 1996.

Moral Objectives, Rules, and the Forms of Social Change, University of Toronto Press, 1998.

Natural Law Modernized, University of Toronto Press, 2001.

CONTRIBUTOR

Carl J. Friedrich, editor, *The Public Interest,* Atherton, 1962.

Nelson W. Polsby, Robert A. Dentler, and Paul A. Smith, editors, *Politics and Social Life,* Houghton, 1963.

Nicholas Rescher, editor, *Studies in Moral Philosophy,* Basil Blackwell, 1968.

Kurt Baier and Nicholas Rescher, *Values and the Future,* Free Press, 1969.

Howard E. Kiefer and Milton K. Munitz, editors, *Mind, Science, and History,* State University of New York Press, 1970.

J. R. Pennock and J. W. Chapman, editors, *Participation in Politics,* Lieber-Atherton, 1975.

C. A. Hooker and others, editors, *Foundations and Applications of Decision Theory,* Reidel, 1978.

T. Regan, editor, *Just Business,* Random House, 1984.

R. Benjamin and S. Elkins, editors, *The Democratic State,* Kansas Universities Press, 1985.

J. Fishkin and P. Laslett, editors, *Justice Between Generations,* Yale University Press, 1992.

G. Brock, editor, *Necessary Goods,* Rowman & Littlefield, 1998.

L. Becker and C. Becker, *Encyclopedia of Ethics,* Garland, 1992, new edition, 2000.

Routledge Encyclopedia of Philosophy, Routledge & Kegen Paul, 1998.

Contributor of articles and reviews to *Analysis, Ethics, Journal of Philosophy, Philosophical Review, Review of Metaphysics, Dialogue, American Philosophical Quarterly, History and Theory, Social Research, Canadian Journal of Philosophy, Nous, Midwest Journal of Philosophy,* and *Philosophical Studies.* Member of board of editors of *American Political Science Review,* 1970-72, *Philosophical Studies,* 1972-76, *Dialogue,* 1974-78, and 1980—, and *Ethics,* 1979—. Editor, *Philosophy in Canada,* 1973-78.

WORK IN PROGRESS: A book on the theory of absurdities with applications to U.S. politics; a book on repairs and renovations to utilitarianism.

SIDELIGHTS: David Braybrooke told *CA:* "The practical effect of many philosophical inquiries—not to speak of their practical importance—is hard to see. I am ready, even so, to defend carrying them on and to do so vigorously. Yet I am glad that I was trained in a style of philosophy—ordinary language analysis—that works within the reach of unsophisticated serious minds. I am glad, too, that I have been specially concerned with topics—concepts important to social choices—on which philosophy, both in this style and in a more formalistic one, has its best chance to promote human happiness. I would now add to this statement simply an expression of surprise and gratification that my flow of ideas has continued so late in life. Because it has continued, I don't feel that it is so late."

* * *

BRETT, John Michael
See TRIPP, Miles (Barton)

* * *

BRETT, Michael
See TRIPP, Miles (Barton)

BROWN, Rosellen 1939-

Rosellen Brown

PERSONAL: Born May 12, 1939, in Philadelphia, PA; daughter of David H. and Blossom (Lieberman) Brown; married Marvin Hoffman (a teacher), March 16, 1963; children: Adina, Elana. *Education:* Barnard College, B.A., 1960; Brandeis University, M.A., 1962. *Religion:* Jewish.

ADDRESSES: *Agent*—Virginia Barber Literary Agency, Inc., 353 West 21st St., New York City 10011.

CAREER: Writer. Tougaloo College, Tougaloo, MS, instructor in English and American literature, 1965-67; Bread Loaf Writer's Conference, Middlebury, VT, member of fiction staff, summer, 1974; Goddard College, Plainfield, VT, instructor in creative writing, 1976; Boston University, Boston, visiting professor of creative writing, 1977-78; University of Houston, Houston, associate professor of creative writing, 1982-85, instructor in English and American literature, 1989—. School of the Art Institute of Chicago, instructor in the graduate creative writing program; Northwestern University, Center for the Writing Arts, writer-in-residence; c. 2000; has also participated in poets-in-the-schools programs and writing workshops.

AWARDS, HONORS: Woodrow Wilson fellow, 1960; Howard Foundation grant, 1971-72; National Endowment for the Humanities creative writing grants, 1973-74 and 1981-82; Radcliffe Institute fellow, 1973-75; Best First Novel, Great Lakes College Association, 1976, for *The Autobiography of My Mother;* Guggenheim fellow, 1976-77; Janet Kafka award, 1984, for *Civil Wars;* co-named women of the year, *Ms. Magazine,* 1984; American Academy and Institute of Arts and Letters award, 1987; Ingram-Merrill grant, 1989-90; fellowship, Bunting Institute.

WRITINGS:

Some Deaths in the Delta and Other Poems, University of Massachusetts Press, 1970.

(Editor, with husband, Marvin Hoffman, and Martin Kushner, Philip Lopate, and Sheila Murphy) *Whole World Catalog,* Teachers and Writers Collaborative, 1972.

Street Games (stories), Doubleday (New York City), 1974.

The Autobiography of My Mother (novel), Doubleday, 1976.

Cora Fry (poems), Norton (New York City), 1977.

Tender Mercies (novel), Knopf (New York City), 1978.

(Adaptor with Laurie MacGregor) *The Secret Garden* (play; adapted from the novel by Frances Hodgson Burnett), produced in New York City, 1983.

Civil Wars (novel), Knopf, 1984.

Before and After, Farrar, Straus (New York City), 1992.

A Rosellen Brown Reader: Selected Poetry and Prose, University Press of New England (Hanover, NH), 1992.

Cora Fry's Pillow Book (poetry), Farrar, Straus, 1994.

Half a Heart, Farrar, Straus, 2000.

Editor, *Men Portray Women, Women Portray Men,* 1978. Contributor to anthologies, including *O. Henry Prize Stories,* 1972, 1973, 1976; *Best American Short Stories,* 1975 and 1979; and *Pushcart Prizes.* Contributor of poems and stories to magazines, including *Ms., Atlantic,* and *Hudson Review.* Associated with Catherine Gourley's *Beryl Markham: Never Turn Back,* 1997.

ADAPTATIONS: *Before and After* has been adapted into a major motion picture.

SIDELIGHTS: Rosellen Brown's *The Autobiography of My Mother* is the story of two women: Gerta Stein, a well-known civil-rights lawyer, and her daughter,

Renata. The novel opens with Renata, a former Haight-Ashbury flower-child, returning home to her mother's Upper-West-Side New York apartment with her infant daughter who was born out of wedlock in California. The two women have not seen each other in eight years, and the book is filled with tension as they try to readjust to living together. As Laurie Stone explains in the *New York Times Book Review,* "Gerta and Renata cannot stop judging one another by the opposing standards that have made of each of their lives, in its way, a suffocating and dead-ended half-life."

Anatole Broyard, in a *New York Times* review, complains that although "Brown's book raises a number of interesting questions . . . it is part of the complacency of some modern novelists to believe that they need only ask interesting questions—no answers are required." "Answer may be too strong a word," qualifies Broyard, continuing: "A novel need not give us answers, but it should, perhaps, question the questions until they bleed a little. The main trouble with *The Autobiography of My Mother* lies in the fact that Gerta is monolithic and Renata is, well, mononucleotic. Larger than life and smaller than life—that is the way they strike me. One gives me agoraphobia with her abstractions, and the other makes me feel claustrophobic inside her narrow egoism." Stone, however, compares Brown's novel to the work of Grace Paley, stating that both authors have "a talent for writing the things that very intelligent people say and think when they are slowly going crazy." Stone concludes that *The Autobiography of My Mother* "is a bitter, funny, stringently unsentimental novel of rare merit. Rosellen Brown's strength lies in the steady but often dazzling accumulation of facts and details. She writes with great candor and ease, never retreating for one moment from her conviction that family is an accident from which the victims can never recover. That they try to, nevertheless, is what makes this novel dramatic and even hopeful."

Brown's next novel, *Tender Mercies,* is an "intense and challenging" book, in which "some recognizable contemporary themes are reworked with rough imaginative power," according to Chicago *Tribune Books* reviewer Bruce Allen. He finds *Tender Mercies* to be "a truly radical portrayal . . . of the subjection of women by men—self-contained creatures who're unable to understand what they've done, and must be educated in suffering." The novel involves Laura Sturrock, an intellectual girl from Boston, who marries Dan Courser and becomes paralyzed when Dan mismanages the tiller of a boat and causes an accident that results in her breaking her neck. She spends a year in a rehabilitation institute, trying to learn to adjust to her new physical limitations, then Dan brings her home to their house in New Hampshire. The bulk of the book deals with their readjustment to each other.

Carole Horn states in the *Washington Post Book World* that "for the quadriplegic, every simple act of living becomes perilous, fraught with danger, and Brown skillfully conveys the awkwardness and desperation of the untrained person, however loving and well-meaning, trying to deal with these problems for the first time." The point-of-view in the novel shifts between Dan, presented as third-person narrative, and Laura, in the form of first-person sequences that Horn calls monologues. "Uncanny, sometimes brilliant," she writes, "those interior monologues drift from present to past, from reality into dreams. . . . Reading them is scary, and it is moving." And Joyce Carol Oates, writing in the *New York Times Book Review,* maintains that *Tender Mercies* is "a haunting novel, as successful in its own way as *The Autobiography of My Mother.* If the earlier novel is more immediately appealing, this novel, re-read, gives forth small astonishing gems. The virtuoso passage in which poor Laura, totally paralyzed, strives to move a single finger—unfortunately too long to be quoted here, and it would have to be quoted completely—contains prose as masterful, and as moving, as any being written today. And there are many such passages, most of them Laura's, in this fine book."

Brown's third novel, *Civil Wars,* features the Carlls, Teddy and Jessie, and their two children. Teddy, describes *Time* reviewer John Skow, is "an idealistic white Mississippian . . . a hero of the civil rights marches of the 1960s" who, unlike many former activists, has maintained his ideological stance, in his case, by "living as virtually the only whites in a black development in Jackson." But through the years, the attitude of the other residents toward their white neighbors has changed, and, writes a *Newsweek* reviewer, "thievery, vandalism and threatening phone calls late at night make Jessie think it's time to move." Teddy, however, remains determined to stay; his life as a traveling textbook salesman is given meaning only because he believes he is still a vital part of an active civil rights campaign. Living in a predominantly black neighborhood is his only remaining ideological statement.

The conflict is resolved when Teddy's sister and her husband, both virulent racists, are suddenly killed in an automobile accident. To the Carlls' surprise, they are named in the wills as guardians of two surviving children: a boy, eight, and a girl, thirteen, budding racists in their own right. With the increased space requirements of the household, the issue of whether or not to stay in the old house is settled as the Carlls move to larger quarters in a white, middle-class neighborhood. Here, notes Skow, the focus of the novel shifts from Teddy's civil rights ideology to "Jessie's desperate efforts to stabilize her in-laws' children at some workable level of sanity and racial tolerance." Also crucial at this point, states Elaine Kendall in the *Los Angeles Times,* is "the developing relationship among the [four] children," who all have many adjustments to make. Surprisingly, "there is no explosion; all goes more smoothly than anyone could have hoped. [The boy] is young enough to be responsive and resilient; [the girl] seems remarkably self-contained, her secret diary the only outlet for her anguish."

"Anyone who's discouraged by the reams of contemporary fiction about dull men and women engaged in the grim modern hobby of endless self-examination couldn't do better than to read this fine, new novel. . . . *Civil Wars* is a fascinating story about serious people dealing with the kinds of serious human problems that make reading fiction fun and worthwhile," writes Howard Frank Mosher in *Tribune Books.* He adds, "In its rich, authentic detailing of the textures of everyday (and not so everyday) family life, *Civil Wars* reminds me of [Judith Guest's] *Ordinary People.* Yet Brown's novel ranges well beyond the Carlls' own ups and downs to reflect much of the recent history of the South and any number of people who live there. It is an important story." Kendall states that "though Brown's concerns are deep and abiding, she can be a witty and aphoristic writer." Lynne Sharon Schwartz concludes in the *New York Times Book Review,* "Any work so clearly of the heart and spirit takes immense risks, this one particularly. It dares to be about ideals and the perils awaiting those committed to them, and it dares to dwell on the most quotidian of matters, with critical scenes taking place in the kitchen and the family car. It directly confronts the sorely ambivalent position of a white family enmeshed in the fight for black people's rights. At a time when fiction by women seems perversely misunderstood, one can only hope that *Civil Wars* will be recognized as a brave and fine work."

In 1992's *Before and After,* Brown "addresses, more than anything else, the cherished concept of personal independence," according to *New York Times Book Review* contributor Michael Dorris. Are families free to create their own rules, or are they linked to the community they inhabit? Do an individual's accomplishments over many years transcend a temporary run of bad luck or erase it, thus redefining his being? In the novel, Carolyn, a pediatrician, and her husband, sculptor Ben Reiser, live in rural New Hampshire and lead a quiet life with their two teenagers, Jacob and Judith. Their quiet life is destroyed after a young woman who was last seen with their son, Jacob, is found brutally murdered. The accusation transforms both the Reiser family and the community wherein they live. Specifically, as Dorris reveals, "Ben assumes the mantle of an almost Old Testament paternity while Carolyn, the scientist, strives to maintain a clinical analysis of the situation. Jacob . . . wrenchingly communicates the wider context of the crime, and Judith, staggered by the collapse she witnesses in every direction, retreats into herself."

Calling *Before and After* "a superior novel" and, "for all its pain and sadness,. . . [Brown's] most affirmative book," *Washington Post Book World* contributor Howard Frank Mosher notes that the novel's central dilemma "is how in the world the Reisers will deal with the truth [of their son's actions], as each member of the family sees it, and still maintain their love for one another." However, *Nation* reviewer Stacey D'Erasmo finds the work less satisfactory due to the lack of consequences meted out in response to Jacob's crime. "*Before and After* ends with an image of the family literally adrift, all four Reisers in a boat, floating aimlessly down a river," comments D'Erasmo. "Closed in on themselves, yoked together, at a tremendous distance from one another, they're stranded between a personal order they can't leave and a social order they can't ignore. It's one of the more insidiously dismal visions of the family . . . just kind of drifting. This vision is very right in one way, but, still, I closed this novel unsatisfied." As *Contemporary Novelist* contributor Jill Franks describes Brown's characters this way: "adults, teenagers, and children alike—[they] are living on the edge, from the beginning to the end of her novels." Characterizing Brown's overall theme as one of angst, Franks concludes, "Reading Rosellen Brown is a highly personal experience; hers isn't the angst for everybody."

With *Half a Heart,* Brown once again explores racial tensions, and, among other issues, mother-daughter relations. The story alternates between the perspective of Miriam—a white, Jewish, wealthy, married, mother of three living in suburban Houston—and Ronnee, the hidden product of a love affair Miriam had with a black professor she knew while teaching at a Mississippi college eighteen years earlier. Out of touch since full custody of the very young child was given to her father, Miriam succumbs to her continual longing for connection with Ronnee and contacts her. Ronnee, who, unknown to Miriam, needs money to pay her Stanford tuition, goes against her father's wishes and agrees to a reunion with her mother. Ronnee's father, who believes

Ronnee is just being used as a black poster-child for Stanford, is very cynical.

"Ronnee's presence poses a critical question for Miriam: how to introduce a daughter, and one of mixed race besides, of whom none of her friends have ever heard," writes Paul Gray in *Time.* Gray writes, "The situation is an intriguing one rendered all the more so by Brown's skillful and sympathetic handling of her two central characters." *Booklist* contributor Kristine Huntley, however, complains that *Half a Heart* is uneven, specifying that in the segments where Ronnee is at Miriam's home Brown includes "a few too many clichés and stereotypical characters." The "interesting and entertaining" story, contends Huntley, is best when Brown addresses the feelings between mother and daughter. Reba Leiding, judging *Half a Heart* to be one of Brown's weaker novels, states in *Library Journal* that "here her prose is overwrought, and it's difficult to care about this batch of unsympathetic . . . soap opera-like characters." A *Publishers Weekly* critic maintained, however, that the 2000 novel is "surely one of Brown's most challenging, intelligent and masterful accomplishments." As in her past works, summarizes the critic, Brown "tackles timeless, yet timely, moral issues with . . . insight and gravity." Gray lauds, "*Half a Heart* not only keeps its eventual outcome engagingly in doubt but also accomplishes a remarkably evenhanded treatment of its racially charged subject. . . . Brown is writing very close to the bone."

BIOGRAPHICAL/CRITICAL SOURCES:

BOOKS

Contemporary Novelists, sixth edition, St. James (Detroit), 1996.

Contemporary Literary Criticism, Volume 32, Gale (Detroit), 1985.

PERIODICALS

Atlantic, July, 1976, p. 94.

Booklist, February 15, 1994, Karen Harris, review of sound recording version of *Before and After,* p. 1100; February 15, 2000, Kristine Huntley, review of *Half a Heart,* p. 1050.

Kirkus Reviews, July 1, 1992, review of *Before and After.*

Library Journal, March 15 2000, Reba Leiding, review of *Half a Heart,* p. 124.

Los Angeles Times, May 22, 1984, Elaine Kendall, review of *Civil Wars.*

Nation, September 28, 1992, Stacey D'Erasmo, review of *Before and After,* pp. 335-336.

Newsweek, May 28, 1984, review of *Civil Wars.*

New York Times, May 26, 1976; November 24, 1978.

New York Times Book Review, June 20, 1976; December 10, 1978; May 6, 1984; August 23, 1992, p. 1; April 3, 1994, p. 28; December 31, 1995, p. 16.

Publishers Weekly, August 29, 1994, review of *Cora Fry's Pillow Book,* p. 67; March 13, 2000, review of *Half a Heart,* p. 62.

Time, April 30, 1984, John Skow, review of *Civil Wars;* May 8, 2000, Paul Gray, review of *Half a Heart,* p. 95.

Tribune Books (Chicago), November 5, 1978; April 22, 1984; July 19, 1992, p. 9.

Washington Post Book World, November 18, 1978; August 30, 1992, pp. 3, 6.*

* * *

BROWN, Wesley 1945-

PERSONAL: Born May 23, 1945, in New York, NY. *Education:* State University of New York at Oswego, B.A. (history and political science), 1968; City College of the City University of New York, M.A. (literature and creative writing), 1976.

ADDRESSES: *Office*—Murray Hall 047, Rutgers University, Newark, NJ 08901. *E-mail*—langston@rci.rutgers.edu.

CAREER: Writer. Taught at York College, Hunter College, and Sarah Lawrence College during the late 1970s; Rutgers University, Newark, NJ, professor of literature and creative writing, 1979—.

WRITINGS:

Tragic Magic (novel), Random House (New York, NY), 1978.

Early Intervention Regulation: Annotation and Analysis of Part H (legislation), LRP Publications, 1990.

(Editor, with Amy Ling) *Imagining America: Stories from the Promised Land,* Persea (New York, NY), 1991.

(Editor, with Ling) *Visions of America: Personal Narratives from the Promised Land,* Persea (New York, NY), 1992.

Darktown Strutters (novel), Cane Hill (New York, NY), 1994.

(Editor) *The Teachers & Writers Guide to Frederick Douglass,* Teachers & Writers Collaborative (New York, NY), 1996.

Also, co-author and co-narrator (with Toni Cade Bambara, Amiri Baraka, and Thulani Davis) of *W.E.B. DuBois: A Biography in Four Voices* (video recording; series of documentary short stories), produced in association with Scribe Video Center, 1996. Work represented in anthologies, including *Poetry* and *We Be Word Sorcerers.* Contributor of poems and short stories to *Essence, Harper's, Black Creation,* and other periodicals.

SIDELIGHTS: Wesley Brown's first novel, *Tragic Magic,* is the story of Melvin Ellington, a well-educated young black man, who returns to his Queens, New York, neighborhood after serving two years in prison as a conscientious objector to the Vietnam War. The narrative covers the events of Ellington's first day home, interspersed with recollections of prison life and college days. Trying to get all the pieces of his life back together, Melvin rejoins his family for dinner, and later in the evening goes out with a high school friend on a nighttime excursion that turns catastrophic.

Tragic Magic won the attention and praise of many critics. They particularly admired Brown's ability to evoke urban black America and his sensitivity to the search for meaning and identity in life. "Wesley Brown has a careful eye for the details and nuances of urban black existence," remarked a *Choice* contributor, who then hailed Brown as "a gifted writer, capable of exploring a wide range of human emotions" and judged *Tragic Magic* "an impressive first novel." Likewise, a *New Yorker* contributor assessed Brown's portrait of Ellington as "effective and original" and lauded the author's recording of "the provocative, singsong slang of the street and prison." In *Village Voice,* Lin Rosechild Harris complimented Brown for creating "a wonderful addition to the pantheon of heroic young initiates," while also observing that "the book sings with images and rhythms of urban black America." Alan Cheuse, writing in *New York Times Book Review,* described *Tragic Magic* as a "jaunty prose version of the urban blues" that "deserves an attentive audience."

In later work, Brown joined forces with Amy Ling to edit two collections of short stories which focus on America's multiculturalism. The volumes, which were published in the early 1990s, present tales of twentieth-century immigrants from all over the world and include stories of the Native American experience. *Visions of America: Personal Narratives from the Promised Land* is a "rich and diverse collection [in which] three dozen 20th-century writers muse about their experiences in and observations of America," stated a *Publishers Weekly* review. *Imagining America: Stories from the Promised Land* is a "compilation [that] demonstrates what a tangy stew simmers in the American melting pot," wrote a reviewer for *Publishers Weekly. Imagining America* includes "In the Land of the Free," in which a young Chinese family arriving in San Francisco is separated when a customs agent seizes their "unofficial" newborn. Other stories tell of a Jewish German refugee learning English, and a Native American denied his heritage because he lacks a Bureau of Indian Affairs registration number. Of *Imagining America, Washington Post Book World* contributor Richard Lipez noted that "in their brief, deft introduction, the editors point out that the 'Multiculturalism' of American life constitutes a whole thing that can best be known 'through its quarrelsome parts.'" Lipez judged *Imagining America* to be a "vibrant book about a multiplicity of struggling people forming and re-forming a nation."

An Irish immigrant, Jack Diamond, plays a notable part in Brown's second novel, *Darktown Strutters.* In a story set across several decades surrounding the American Civil War, Brown presents the life experience of Diamond's would-be friend and fellow performer, Jim Crow, a black slave navigating his way through nineteenth-century American life via the entertainment world. A *Kirkus Reviews* critic felt that Brown, at times, "shoehorn[s] [history] awkwardly into the narrative." Of the author's "use of the historical facts," Thomas Fleming noted in *New York Times Book Review* that Brown is "freewheeling." "Brown's focus is on personal identity, black and white. . . . Mr. Brown attempts, with less success, to explore some of the mysteries of sexual identity," asserted Fleming, who concluded, "Combining the simple prose of a folk tale with the meta-psychology of a philosopher, Wesley Brown has created a vivid, disturbing work of the historical imagination." In contrast, a *Kirkus Reviews* critic described *Darktown Strutters* as "uneven" and maintained that the 1994 release was weakened because its author did not "[stick] closer to Jim's point of view and [did not vary] the gibe-and-riposte pattern of his dialogue."

However, Brad Hooper applauded *Darktown Strutters* in *Booklist,* calling it an "absorbing tale of Jim Crow." Leased to Tom Rice, a homosexual man who owns a minstrel show, Crow becomes the only black person in an otherwise all-white ensemble that performs in black masks. Crow's "dancing feet unleash all sorts of wild impulses in his audiences," remarked Fleming. While his white colleagues refuse to travel in the same train car with him, they later come to rescue him when a group of white people attempt to kill him. After Crow's boss, Rice, is violently killed, Crow joins an all-black troupe led by two homosexual sisters. The lives of many in this minstrel show are brutally ended. This fate is "a bit too predictable" according to Fleming, who nevertheless lauded *Darktown Strutters* and its "powerful and ominous [images]."

BIOGRAPHICAL/CRITICAL SOURCES:

PERIODICALS

African American Review, spring, 1997, Eric Lott, review of *Darktown Strutters,* p. 169.
American Book Review, summer, 1979.
Booklist, December 15, 1992, Roland Wulbert, review of *Visions of America,* p. 703; February 15, 1998, Brad Hooper, review of *Darktown Strutters,* p. 979.
Choice, February, 1979; April, 1992.
Kirkus Reviews, December 15, 1993, review of *Darktown Strutters.*
Library Journal, November 15, 1991, Janet Ingraham, review of *Imagining America,* p. 109; December, 1992, Ingraham, review of *Visions of America,* p. 142; January, 1994, David Keymer, review of *Darktown Strutters,* p. 158.
Nation, December 29, 1979; November 16, 1992, Robert S. Fogarty, review of *Imagining America,* p. 588.
New York, February 19, 1997, John Leonard, review of *W.E.B. DuBois: A Biography in Four Voices,* p. 115.
New Yorker, October, 1978, review of *Tragic Magic.*
New York Times Book Review, February 11, 1979, Alan Cheuse, review of *Tragic Magic;* March 6, 1994, Thomas Fleming, "Hit the Ground Dancing."
New York Times Magazine, September 10, 1989.
Publishers Weekly, December 20, 1991, review of *Imagining America,* p. 74; November 23, 1992, review of *Visions of America,* p. 59.
School Library Journal, June, 1992, review of *Imagining America,* p. 152; November, 1997, Rob Tench, review of *W.E.B. DuBois: A Biography in Four Voices,* p. 66.
Utne Reader, March-April, 1993, Lynette Lamb, review of *Visions of America,* p. 118.
Village Voice, November 20, 1978, Lin Rosechild Harris, review of *Tragic Magic.*
Washington Post Book World, January 26, 1992, Richard Lipez, review of *Imagining America,* pp. 1, 11.*

* * *

BUCHEISTER, Patt 1942-
(Patt Parrish)

PERSONAL: Surname is pronounced "boo-eye-ster"; born March 27, 1942, in Waterloo, IA; daughter of David M. and Elaine (Sandberg) Fluharty; married Raymond C. Bucheister (retired), January 14, 1961; children: Scott, Todd; grandchildren: Gillian, Tyler, Priscilla. *Education:* Graduated from high school in Clear Lake, IA. *Religion:* Protestant.

ADDRESSES: *Home*—901 Shady Hollow Lane, Virginia Beach, VA 23452. *Agent*—Joyce A. Flaherty, 816 Lynda Court, St. Louis, MO 63122.

CAREER: Chamber of Commerce, Clear Lake, IA, secretary, 1959-60; artist; romance writer.

MEMBER: Romance Writers of America, National Society of Tole and Decorative Painters, Tidewater Decorative Painters (second vice president, 1983-84).

AWARDS, HONORS: Silver Palette Award, Tidewater Decorative Painters, 1985.

WRITINGS:

ROMANCE NOVELS

Night and Day, Bantam (New York, NY), 1986.
The Dragon Slayer, Bantam (New York, NY), 1987.
Touch the Stars, Bantam (New York, NY), 1987.
Two Roads, Bantam (New York, NY), 1987.
The Luck o' the Irish, Bantam (New York, NY), 1988.
Flynn's Fate, Bantam (New York, NY), 1988.
Time Out, Bantam (New York, NY), 1988.
Near the Edge, Bantam (New York, NY), 1989.
Fire and Ice, Bantam (New York, NY), 1989.
Elusive Gypsy, Bantam (New York, NY), 1989.
Once Burned, Twice As Hot, Bantam (New York, NY), 1990.

The Rogue, Bantam (New York, NY), 1990.
Relentless, Bantam (New York, NY), 1990.
Tropical Heat, Bantam (New York, NY), 1990.
Tropical Storm, Bantam (New York, NY), 1991.
Hot Pursuit, Bantam (New York, NY), 1991.
Island Lover, Bantam (New York, NY), 1992.
Mischief and Magic, Bantam (New York, NY), 1992.
Struck by Lightning, Bantam (New York, NY), 1992.
Tilt at Windmills, Silhouette (New York, NY), 1992.
Stroke by Stroke, Bantam (New York, NY), 1993.
Tame a Wildcat, Bantam (New York, NY), 1993.
Strange Bedfellows, Bantam (New York, NY), 1994.
Unpredictable, Silhouette, 1994.
Hot Southern Nights, Bantam (New York, NY), 1995.
Instant Family, Silhouette, 1995.
Wild in the Night, Bantam (New York, NY), 1995.
Gypsy Dance, Bantam (New York, NY), 1997.
Below the Salt, Shady Hollow, 1999.

ROMANCE NOVELS; UNDER PSEUDONYM PATT PARRISH

Make the Angel Weep, R. Hale (London, England), 1979, published as *His Fierce Angel,* Bantam (New York, NY), 1983.
Summer of Silence, R. Hale (London, England), 1980, published as *A Gift to Cherish,* Bantam (New York, NY), 1985.
Feather in the Wind, R. Hale (London, England), 1981, Bantam (New York, NY), 1982.
The Sheltered Haven, R. Hale (London, England), 1981, Bantam (New York, NY), 1982.
The Amberley Affair, R. Hale (London, England), 1983.
Lifetime Affair, Harlequin (Tarrytown, NY), 1985.
Escape the Past, Walker & Co. (New York City), 1985.

OTHER

Contributor of articles and stories to magazines. Editor of newsletter *Brushstrokes.*

WORK IN PROGRESS: Hannah.

SIDELIGHTS: Patt Bucheister told *CA:* "I began to write seriously in 1976 while living in Chesham, England. So far away from familiar art exhibits, my painting took a backseat to writing once I had my first book published in 1979 in England.

"My novels are based on the relationship between a man and a woman. They usually have interesting occupations and are warm, likable characters with a sense of humor and traditional values. My characters have a few problems in their lives and their relationships, but there is always a happy ending.

"I write six days a week from 8:00 A.M. until 6:00 P.M., occasionally working in the evenings. I try to write at least ten pages a day. My main purpose in writing novels is to entertain the reader. I don't try to solve any major universal situation; I leave that to those who are more qualified.

"Due to my husband's former career as a naval officer I have resided in various places, including Hawaii and California, and I spent four years in England. I am able to use a variety of locations in my novels from personal knowledge of the areas."

* * *

BUCKEYE, Donald A(ndrew) 1930-

PERSONAL: Born March 12, 1930, in Lakewood, OH; son of Andrew M. (a pattern maker) and Elizabeth (Wagner) Buckeye; married Nancy R. O'Neill, June 16, 1962; children: Pamela Jean, Karen Ann. *Ethnicity:* "Slovak." *Education:* Ashland College, B.S. Ed., 1953; Indiana University, M.A., 1961, Ed.D., 1968.

ADDRESSES: Home—1823 Witmire Blvd., Ypsilanti, MI 48197. *Office*—Department of Mathematics, Eastern Michigan University, Ypsilanti, MI 48197. *E-mail*—mth_buckeye@online.emich.edu.

CAREER: High school teacher, 1953-54; math instructor, Army Education Center, Sendai, Japan, 1954-56; high school mathematics teacher in public schools in Lakewood, OH, 1957-65; Eastern Michigan University, Ypsilanti, professor of mathematics, 1968-2000 (retired). Teaching assistant at Ohio State University, 1962-65; teaching associate at Indiana University, 1966-68. *Military service:* U.S. Army, 1954-56.

MEMBER: National Council of Teachers of Mathematics, Michigan Council of Teachers of Mathematics, Ohio Council of Teachers of Mathematics, Cleveland Council of Teachers of Mathematics (vice president, 1960-61; president, 1962-63), Math Association of America, Michigan section, Phi Delta Kappa.

WRITINGS:

Experiments in Probability and Statistics, Midwest Publications (Troy, MI), 1969.

(With William A. Ewbank and John L. Ginther) *Downpour of Math Lab Experiments,* Midwest Publications (Troy, MI), 1969.

Experiments and Puzzles in Logic, Midwest Publications (Troy, MI), 1970.

Creative Geometry Experiments, Midwest Publications (Troy, MI), 1970.

Creative Experiments in Algebra, Midwest Publications (Troy, MI), 1971.

(With Ginther) *Creative Mathematics,* Canfield Press, 1971.

(With Ginther) *Creative Mathematics Laboratory Manual,* Canfield Press, 1971.

(With Ewbank and Ginther) *Cloudburst of Math Lab Experiments,* five volumes, Midwest Publications (Troy, MI), 1971.

N.R. Math Activities, Midwest Publications (Troy, MI), Volume 1, 1972, Volume 2, 1973, Volume 3, 1974.

Experiments in Fractions, Midwest Publications (Troy, MI), 1972.

Introducing the Metric System with Activities, Midwest Publications (Troy, MI), 1972.

Primary Activities in Mathematics, Midwest Publications (Troy, MI), 1972.

(With Ewbank and Ginther) *Cheap Math Lab Equipment,* Midwest Publications (Troy, MI), 1972.

I'm OK, You're OK, Let's Go Metric, 1974.

(With others) *School Math,* eight volumes, Rand McNally (Chicago, IL), 1974.

Basic Math Amusements, Midwest Publications (Troy, MI), 1976.

Bottle Cap Mathematics, Midwest Publications (Troy, MI), 1976.

Cheap Metric Equipment: Activities and Games, Midwest Publications (Troy, MI), 1976.

(With Karen Buckeye) *Problem Solving Using Computers,* three volumes, Midwest Publications (Pacific Grove, CA), 1984.

(With Ginther) *Cloudburst of Creative Mathematics Activities,* two volumes, Midwest Publications (Pacific Grove, CA), 1989.

Problem Solving Using Bingo Chips, two volumes, Tricon, 1995.

(With others) *Mathematics Activities* (CD-ROM), Great Lakes Collaborative, 1995.

Magic Patterns, Tricon Publishing (Mt. Pleasant, MI), 1995.

Problem Solving Using Cryptarithm, 2 volumes, Huron Valley Imaging, 1998.

The Adventures of a High School Mathematics, Huron Valley Imaging, 2000.

The Adventures of a University Mathematics Professor, Huron Valley Imaging, 2000.

BIOGRAPHICAL/CRITICAL SOURCES:

PERIODICALS

Booklist, October 15, 1974, p. 224.

Science Books & Films, December, 1971, p. 201.

*   *   *

BUCKLEY, Anthony D. 1945-

PERSONAL: Born July 3, 1945, in Castleford, Yorkshire, England; son of John K. (a printer) and Kathleen (a teacher; maiden name, Beaumont) Buckley; married Linda J. Roberts (a university teacher), July 8, 1966; children: Thomas John, Benjamin David, Samuel James Edgar, Daniel Robert Francis. *Education:* University of York, B.A. (with honors), 1967; University of Leicester, M.A., 1968; attended University of Ibadan, 1969-71, and Queen's University, Belfast, 1973-75; University of Birmingham, Ph.D., 1982. *Religion:* Atheist.

ADDRESSES: *Home*—4 Church Ave., Holywood, County Down, Northern Ireland. *Office*—Ulster Folk and Transport Museum, Cultra Manor, Holywood, County Down, Northern Ireland; fax: +44 2890 428428. *E-mail*—A.D.Buckley@Talk21.com.

CAREER: History teacher at school in Isle of Sheppey, Kent, England, 1971-73; Ulster Folk and Transport Museum, Holywood, Northern Ireland, research anthropologist, 1975—. Organizer of museum exhibitions in Northern Ireland, "Brotherhoods in Ireland," 1986, and "Remembering 1690," 1990.

MEMBER: Royal Anthropological Institute, Association of Social Anthropologists, Anthropological Association of Ireland (chair, 1994—).

AWARDS, HONORS: Leverhulme scholar in Nigeria, 1969-71; Dr. John Kirk Essay Prize from Society for Folklife Studies, 1985, for article "The Chosen Few: Biblical Texts in the Regalia of an Ulster Secret Society"; Amaury Talbot Prize for African Anthropology from Amaury Talbot Trust, 1985, for *Yoruba Medicine.*

WRITINGS:

A Gentle People: A Study of a Peaceful Community in Northern Ireland, Ulster Folk and Transport Museum, 1982.

Yoruba Medicine, Oxford University Press, 1985.

(With M. C. Kenney) *Negotiating Identity: Rhetoric and Social Drama in Northern Ireland,* Smithsonian Institution Press (Washington, DC), 1995.

(Editor) *Symbols in Western Ireland,* Institute of Irish Studies, Queen's University of Belfast (Belfast, Ireland), 1998.

Contributor to anthropology, folklore, and sociology journals.

WORK IN PROGRESS: Research on the fraternal societies, the religious life, and the social structure of Northern Ireland.

SIDELIGHTS: Anthony D. Buckley once told *CA:* "My book *Yoruba Medicine* arose from research I did in Nigeria, where I spent two years discussing the opinions of a small handful of traditional healers. I found that these men employed a germ theory to explain the ailments of the body, as well as elaborate pharmacopeia to kill the germs and drive them from the body. Whereas European theory regards germs as harmful agents waiting to invade the body, Yoruba thought sees them as beneficial until, because of the bad habits of their owner, 'they overflow the bag [in the body] where God has placed them.' Though Yoruba herbalists do have 'magical' practices, their work is primarily an attempt to cure diseases that is based upon a rational understanding of the human body.

"Since 1975, I have been an anthropologist at the Ulster Folk and Transport Museum. Here I have made studies of both Protestant and Catholic communities, as well as studies of unofficial healing, fundamentalist religion, the marching tradition, and secret and fraternal societies.

"I have been struck with the way that even the most serious elements in everyday Ulster life are permeated by playfulness. This is true, for example, in the rituals of the Orange and Black Institutions which express through biblical imagery the political and religious concerns of many modern Ulster Protestants. In this strife-torn country, I have been led to doubt the reality of its so-called 'two cultural traditions.' And I have found it necessary to try to explain the paradoxical co-existence of bitter sectarian hostility with friendly good-neighborliness often across the 'sectarian divide.'"

Buckley more recently told *CA* that his book *Negotiating Identity: Rhetoric and Social Drama in Northern Ireland,* written jointly with M. C. Kenney, "concerns the way that individuals describe and dramatize their identities through social drama including play, secular and religious ritual, rioting, etc."

BIOGRAPHICAL/CRITICAL SOURCES:

PERIODICALS

Times Literary Supplement, January 10, 1986.

C

CALVIN, William H(oward) 1939-

PERSONAL: Born April 30, 1939, in Kansas City, MO; son of Fred Howard (an insurance executive) and Agnes (Leebrick) Calvin; married Katherine Graubard (a neurobiologist), September 1, 1966. *Education:* Northwestern University, B.A., 1961; graduate study at Massachusetts Institute of Technology, 1961-62; University of Washington, Seattle, Ph.D., 1966.

ADDRESSES: *Home*—1543 17th Ave. E., Seattle, WA 98112. *Office*—NJ-15, University of Washington, Seattle, WA 98195. *Agent*—John Brockman, 2307 Broadway, New York, NY 10024. *E-mail*—WCalvin@U.Washington.edu.

CAREER: University of Washington School of Medicine, Seattle, instructor, 1967-69, assistant professor, 1969-73, associate professor of neurological surgery, 1974-86, affiliate associate professor of biology, 1986-92, affiliate professor of psychiatry and behavioral sciences, 1992—. Visiting professor of neurobiology at Hebrew University of Jerusalem, 1978-79.

MEMBER: International Association for the Study of Pain, International Brain Research Organization, American Physiological Society, American Civil Liberties Union of Washington (state president, 1973-74), Biophysical Society, Society for Neuroscience.

AWARDS, HONORS: Travel grants from National Academy of Sciences, 1966 and 1971; National Institutes of Health grants, 1971-84, senior fellow, 1978-79.

WRITINGS:

(With George A. Ojemann) *Inside the Brain,* New American Library, 1980.

The Throwing Madonna: From Nervous Cells to Hominid Brains (essays), McGraw, 1983, revised with a new preface, Bantam (New York, NY), 1991.

The River That Flows Uphill: A Journey from the Big Bang to the Big Brain, Macmillan, 1986.

The Cerebral Symphony: Seashore Reflections on the Structure of Consciousness, Bantam (New York, NY), 1990.

The Ascent of Mind: Ice Age Climates and the Evolution of Intelligence, Bantam (New York, NY), 1991.

(And photographer) *How the Shaman Stole the Moon: In Search of Ancient Prophet-Scientists: From Stonehenge to the Grand Canyon,* illustrated by Malcolm Wells, Bantam (New York, NY), 1991.

(With Ojemann) *Conversations with Neil's Brain: The Neural Nature of Thought and Language,* Addison-Wesley (Reading, MA), 1994.

How Brains Think: Evolving Intelligence, Then and Now ("Science Masters" series), Basic Books (New York, NY), 1996.

The Cerebral Code: Thinking a Thought in the Mosaics of the Mind, MIT Press (Cambridge, MA), 1996.

(With Derek Bickerton) *Lingua ex Machina: Reconciling Darwin and Chomsky with the Human Brain,* MIT Press (Cambridge, MA), 2000.

Member of editorial board of *Journal of Theoretical Neurobiology,* 1982—.

WORK IN PROGRESS: Cool, Crash, and Burn: The Once and Future Climate for Human Evolution.

SIDELIGHTS: In *The Throwing Madonna: From Nervous Cells to Hominid Brains,* neurobiologist William H. Calvin presents seventeen essays about the structure and function of the brain. Writing in the *New York Times*

Book Review, Maya Pines was impressed by the author's success in making his complex subject matter accessible: "Mr. Calvin writes in the tradition of scientists who offer readers a great deal of information in bite-sized essays that are easy to read." Beginning with the title essay, which unfolds the author's intricate theory on the role that women played in the brain's evolution, Calvin discusses a wide variety of subjects involving the brain. One article considers how the law can deal with a brain-damaged, emotionally unstable president; another compares the workings of the computer to the functioning of neurons in the brain, a discussion Pines praised as "unusually vivid." Pines concluded, "For anyone interested in biology and evolution, this book will prove appealing."

In *The River That Flows Uphill: A Journey from the Big Bang to the Big Brain,* Calvin "takes as his subject virtually everything that a neurobiologist . . . might muse upon while rafting through the Grand Canyon in Arizona," wrote Dennis Drabelle in the *Washington Post.* As he journeys down the Colorado River, the author ponders not only the nature of the brain but also such diverse topics as the evolution of birds' feathers and flight, the ecological effects of nuclear war, and philosophical questions, such as the meaning of consciousness, that attracted him to the study of neurobiology. "Calvin retains a child's wonder at the world," Lee Dembart said in the *Los Angeles Times.* "He writes of scientific puzzles and human puzzles, and his most frequent thought is *Why?*" Drabelle also noted that the author "conveys not only scientific concepts but the verve of thinking them through."

Calvin's *The Ascent of Mind: Ice Age Climates and the Evolution of Intelligence* is his proposal that the human brain, which has grown to four times the size of that of the apes from which it evolved, has done so because of climate change, as it adapted to environment. Calvin studies increased throwing ability by the early hunters who depended on their aim and power to kill their food. As the number of neurons in the brain increased over time, throwing ability improved, increasing the chance of early man's survival. Robert Kanigel wrote in the *New York Times Book Review* that "whatever the scientific merits of Mr. Calvin's 'proposal,' it needs editorial work. It is hopelessly episodic, rambling, and repetitive. Part of the problem stems from the author's sheer literary ambition. He is not content to make his case clearly and simply, but rather weaves into the main text what amounts to a second book, a kind of ecological travelogue." However, a *Publishers Weekly* reviewer felt Calvin's subject to be compelling in view of current concerns over global climate changes. The critic called *The Ascent of Mind* "good science and good writing, a study that harmonizes strong echoes from the past and future of our species."

In *How the Shaman Stole the Moon: In Search of Ancient Prophet-Scientists from Stonehenge to the Grand Canyon* Calvin theorizes on the ways in which ancient forecasters predicted seasonal changes and solar events such as lunar eclipses. He camped in Arizona, New Mexico, and on England's Salisbury Plain as he contemplated the possible relationships between religion and science, as practiced by prophets, shamans, and "prophet-scientists." A contributor to *Kirkus Reviews* wished Calvin "had spent as much time exploring the significance of archaeoastronomers as he does in persuading us of their probable existence. Still, lively and literate science for the nonscientist." A *Publishers Weekly* reviewer called the book "somewhat technical" but said "some individual sections sparkle."

Calvin wrote *Conversations with Neil's Brain: The Neural Nature of Thought and Language* with neurosurgeon George A. Ojemann. Neil, an engineer whose epilepsy resulted from a car crash, is a composite of several epileptic patients, and it is through him that the authors view research on memory and language and learning disabilities, and study the connection between brain damage and various disorders, including depression and schizophrenia. A *Publishers Weekly* reviewer called this exercise "a model of lucid scientific exposition." The book is a first-person account, beginning with Calvin and Ojemann preparing to drill into Neil's head in an attempt to determine the root cause of his epilepsy. They stimulate the cerebral cortex and map the regions that control brain functions. The book contains illustrations and thirty-five pages of notes. Other case examples in the book include President Woodrow Wilson and author Virginia Woolf. *Booklist* reviewer William Beatty called *Conversations with Neil's Brain* "informative and lucid."

Calvin wrote *How Brains Think: Evolving Intelligence, Then and Now* for the "Science Masters" series aimed at nonprofessional readers. Calvin describes intelligence, its evolution, and its physiology. *Booklist* reviewer Gilbert Taylor said Calvin "hits his stride" as he explains nerve cell anatomy and bundling and the firing of electric impulses. "Still partially a mystery," wrote Taylor, "intelligence's nature . . . gets a consummately clear summary in Calvin's hands." Marcia Bartusiak wrote in the *New York Times Book Review* that *How Brains Think* "offers an exquisite distillation of his key ideas. He's a member of that rare breed of scientists who can translate the arcana of their fields into lay language, and he's one of the best. . . . Calvin, so lyrical and imaginative in his presentation, draws you into his world of neural Darwinism and inspires you to read more."

Calvin and linguist Derek Bickerton explore opposing theories in *Lingua ex Machina: Reconciling Darwin and Chomsky with the Human Brain.* The book focuses on syntax, or how words are combined in creating sentences. Chomsky proposed that syntax, or language, is an innate capacity of the human mind. Darwinians, however, believe that language evolved by accident or as a mutation. Paul Bloom wrote in the *New York Times Book Review* that Calvin and Bickerton "believe both Chomsky and Darwin are right, and try to integrate this idea with modern neuroscience to provide a plausible account of how language evolved." The authors propose that language may have first consisted of short phrases with no grammatical structure used to communicate while hunting or foraging, activities necessary to the survival of early hominids, and that from this early form, the more complex syntax developed.

The authors wrote the book while at a conference in Bellagio, Italy, and make frequent references to their surroundings and breakfasts with Susan Sontag. Bloom called *Lingua ex Machina* "an intellectual tour de force; few other scholars possess the knowledge and confidence to integrate neuroscience, linguistics, and evolution so skillfully. I should add that I don't believe a word of it. . . . They present a complicated narrative with great authority but fail to make a persuasive case for almost all their claims." Conversely, *Booklist* reviewer Bryce Christensen felt the authors' speculations "reflect a theoretical daring that defies ideological rigidity and invites cross-disciplinary debate."

BIOGRAPHICAL/CRITICAL SOURCES:

PERIODICALS

Astronomy, October, 1992, Dave Bruning, review of *How the Shaman Stole the Moon,* p. 88.

Booklist, April 1, 1994, William Beatty, review of *Conversations with Neil's Brain,* p. 1406; September 1, 1996, Gilbert Taylor, review of *How Brains Think,* p. 50; April 1, 2000, Bryce Christensen, review of *Lingua ex Machina: Reconciling Darwin and Chomsky with the Human Brain,* p. 1422.

Kirkus Reviews, October 1, 1991, review of *How the Shaman Stole the Moon;* March 15, 1994, review of *Conversations with Neil's Brain.*

Library Journal, November 15, 1989, Mark L. Shelton, review of *The Cerebral Symphony,* p. 103; November 1, 1991, Elizabeth Salt, review of *How the Shaman Stole the Moon,* p. 125; April 15, 1994, Carol R. Glatt, review of *Conversations with Neil's Brain,* p. 105.

Los Angeles Times, January 13, 1987.

New York Times Book Review, August 21, 1983, December 14, 1986; January 6, 1991, Robert Kanigel, "Brained by the Fastball"; April 12, 1992, Chet Raymo, review of *How the Shaman Stole the Moon,* p. 17; September 11, 1994, Steven Rose, "Who Is at Home in Our Heads?"; November 17, 1996, Marcia Bartusiak, "The Mechanics of the Soul"; April 16, 2000, Paul Bloom, "From Grunting to Grammar."

Publishers Weekly, November 24, 1989, review of *The Cerebral Symphony,* p. 64; November 9, 1990, review of *The Ascent of Mind,* p. 52; October 4, 1991, review of *How the Shaman Stole the Moon,* p. 76; April 4, 1994, review of *Conversations with Neil's Brain,* p. 64; March 27, 2000, review of *Lingua ex Machina,* p. 59.

Scientific American, January, 1992, Philip Morrison, review of *How the Shaman Stole the Moon,* p. 147.

Washington Post, December 15, 1986.

Whole Earth Review, spring, 1991, Howard Rheingold, review of *The Ascent of Mind,* p. 63.

OTHER

University of Washington Web site, http://faculty.washington.edu/ (May 12, 2001), biography of William H. Calvin.

William H. Calvin Web site, http://www.WilliamCalvin.com (May 12, 2001).*

* * *

CAMP, John (Roswell) 1944-
(John Sandford, a pseudonym)

PERSONAL: Born February 23, 1944, in Cedar Rapids, IA; son of Roswell Sandford and Anne (Barron) Camp; married Susan Lee Jones, December 28, 1965; children: Roswell Anthony, Emily Sarah. *Education:* State University of Iowa, B.A., 1966, M.A., 1971. *Religion:* Roman Catholic. *Avocational interests:* Painting, archaeology.

ADDRESSES: *Home*—Near St. Paul, MN. *Agent*—Esther Newberg, International Creative Management, 40 West 57th St., New York, NY 10019. *E-mail*—js@johnsandford.org.

CAREER: Miami Herald, Miami, FL, reporter, 1971-78; *St. Paul Pioneer Press,* St. Paul, MN, reporter and columnist, 1978-89; writer. *Military service:* U.S. Army, 1966-68, served in Korea.

AWARDS, HONORS: Pulitzer Prize nomination, 1980, for series of articles on Native Americans in *St. Paul Pioneer Press Dispatch;* Pulitzer Prize for Feature Writing, 1986, for series of articles on a farming family in *Pioneer Press Dispatch;* Distinguished Writing Award, American Society of Newspaper Editors, 1986.

WRITINGS:

The Eye and the Heart: The Watercolors of John Stuart Ingle, Rizzoli (New York, NY), 1988.
Plastic Surgery: The Kindest Cuts (nonfiction), Holt (New York, NY), 1989.
The Fool's Run (novel), Holt (New York, NY), 1989.
The Empress File (novel), Holt (New York, NY), 1991.
(Under pseudonym John Sandford) *The Night Crew,* Putnam (New York, NY), 1997.
(Under pseudonym John Sandford) *The Devil's Code,* Putnam (New York, NY), 2000.

UNDER PSEUDONYM JOHN SANDFORD; "LUCAS DAVENPORT" SUSPENSE NOVELS

Rules of Prey, Putnam (New York, NY), 1989.
Shadow Prey, Putnam (New York, NY), 1990.
Eyes of Prey, Putnam (New York, NY), 1991.
Silent Prey, Putnam (New York, NY), 1992.
Winter Prey, Putnam (New York, NY), 1993.
Night Prey, Putnam (New York, NY), 1994.
Mind Prey (also see below), Putnam (New York, NY), 1995.
Sudden Prey (also see below), Putnam (New York, NY), 1996.
Secret Prey (also see below), Putnam (New York, NY), 1998.
Certain Prey, Putnam (New York, NY), 1999.
Easy Prey, Putnam (New York, NY), 2000.
Three Complete Novels: Mind Prey, Sudden Prey, Secret Prey, Putnam (New York, NY), 2000.
Chosen Prey, Putnam (New York, NY), 2001.

ADAPTATIONS: Rules of Prey was adapted for film by Adam Greenman and released as *Mind Prey,* Jaffe/Braunstein, Ltd., 1999.

WORK IN PROGRESS: More "Lucas Davenport" novels.

SIDELIGHTS: Pulitzer Prize-winning journalist John Camp is a versatile writer who has distinguished himself as an author of both nonfiction and mysteries. He is best known under the pseudonym John Sandford for his "Lucas Davenport" novels, a series of thrillers that all feature the word "Prey" in their titles. Throughout the 1990s and into the first decade of the twenty-first century, Camp—as John Sandford—has published *Prey* novels at a rate of almost one per year. A *Publishers Weekly* contributor noted the "vast popularity" of the titles and credited it to the author's "clever plotting, sure pacing and fully rounded villains." The reviewer went on to commend the *Prey* novels as "a series with long, muscular legs."

As far back as high school, Camp knew he had a talent for writing. After earning a bachelor's degree from the University of Iowa in 1966, he entered the United States Army, and it was there that he began to train as a journalist. Upon completion of his military service, he returned to the University of Iowa, where he earned a master's degree in journalism. He began his career as a newspaper reporter, eventually earning a Pulitzer Prize for a lengthy investigative series in the *St. Paul Pioneer Press* about the difficulties facing one farm family in Minnesota.

Camp's experiences as a reporter inform his earliest books, both fictional and nonfictional. He once told *Publishers Weekly* that "most of the hard information in my books comes from a series I did in a newspaper." That series, in fact, was based on a group of incarcerated murderers who had formed a computer corporation in prison. Camp has since said that the opportunity to interview nearly fifty intelligent men serving life sentences was central to his ability to develop villains for his thrillers.

Camp's first book, *The Eye and the Heart: Watercolors of John Stuart Ingle,* is a catalog of Ingle's works seen in a touring exhibition in the late 1980s. Included in the book, which features an essay by Camp, are more than forty color reproductions of the contemporary painter's meticulously realistic works. Camp's next nonfiction publication, *Plastic Surgery: The Kindest Cut,* relates his insights about cosmetic and restorative surgery. Camp's observations derive from his time spent with surgeon Bruce Cunningham, who allowed Camp operating-room access. Critics found the book to be an engrossing and frank look at plastic surgery.

Camp began publishing fiction in 1989 with *The Fool's Run,* a suspense novel about an eccentric computer criminal hired to undermine a defense contracter. Kidd, the narrator and hero, is a painter, martial arts student, and occult dabbler who possesses considerable computer wizardry. He is hired to disable an aerospace company's information system. Accordingly, he wreaks havoc on the company's computer programs, but in so doing he also discovers the existence of a formidable foe. Critics praised Camp's first fictional effort, and several described *The Fool's Run* as fast-paced, suspenseful, and engaging. A second novel, *The Empress File,* finds Kidd embroiled in racial conflict. His employer, a black activist, engages him to sabotage a band of racist, corrupt officials in Mississippi. Kidd and his lover/accomplice Luellen, a skilled burglar, soon manage to infiltrate the group and draw them into a scheme designed to result in their downfall. The officials, however, eventually discover that their operation risks exposure, and they retaliate with violence.

Both *The Fool's Run* and *The Empress File* were published by Henry Holt under the author's real name, John Camp. When Camp's agent sold the first Lucas Davenport novel, *Rules of Prey,* to Putnam, that publisher wanted to print it under a pseudonym. Putnam felt that the *Prey* books would become bestsellers, and the company reportedly did not want Holt to cash in on the success by riding the *Prey* books' coattails. Camp cooperated, choosing his great-grandfather's name, Sandford, as a pseudonym. That name is so widely recognized now that Camp is even using it on sequels to *The Fool's Run* and *The Empress File.*

Rules of Prey, the first novel written by Camp as Sandford, presents Lucas Davenport, a resourceful Minneapolis detective determined to apprehend a particularly vicious killer, Maddog, who preys on young women. At the scene of each crime Maddog leaves a note relating his rules for murder. "Never kill anyone you know," reads one message. "Never carry a weapon after it has been used," reads another. Determined to jar Maddog's sense of gamesmanship, Davenport engages the psychopath in a dangerous cat-and-mouse contest, one with potentially fatal repercussions. *Washington Post Book World* contributor Daniel Woodrell, in his assessment of *Rules of Prey,* deemed it "a big, suspenseful thriller."

In *Shadow Prey,* the next Lucas Davenport novel, the detective opposes a terrorist network operated by local Native Americans avenging themselves against their white oppressors. Davenport discovers that one of the group's intended victims is a loathsome FBI director who molests Native American children. The ensuing action builds to a violent climax. Another Lucas Davenport novel, *Eyes of Prey,* involves a murderous, drug-addicted hospital pathologist, Michael Bekker, and a disfigured actor, Carlo Druze. The two men commit murders for each other, with Bekker killing Druze's theater manager and Druze killing Bekker's wife. By working together, Bekker and Druze are also able to conveniently provide alibis for each other. It is left to Davenport, who is fighting depression and is involved in a rocky love relationship, to apprehend these criminals.

Subsequent *Prey* titles have built upon their predecessors without becoming dependent upon one another. Lucas Davenport is always present in each story, but in some of them he plays a smaller role. Critics have commended the author for creating, in Davenport, a character whose career choice simultaneously stimulates and depresses him—like an addict, the detective cannot extricate himself from his work no matter how grisly the killings become, not even when they tear apart his relationships with women. It is the author's villains, however, who draw the most praise in the reviews. In *Booklist,* Wes Lukowsky suggested that the series has been sustained "most of all" by its plethora of "great villains." A *Publishers Weekly* correspondent likewise noted that the people Davenport vies against in his labors "are shrewdly conceived originals, cut from fabric way at the back of the bin."

In recent years Camp, as Sandford, has taken temporary leave of his *Prey* series to write independent thrillers featuring other heroes. He has brought back Kidd in the novel *The Devil's Code,* a work described by a *Kirkus* reviewer as "computer skullduggery on an epic scale." He has also introduced Anna Batory, a video freelancer who speeds around Los Angeles looking for footage of murder and mayhem that she can sell to the television stations. Batory finds herself a target for violence in *The Night Crew,* a thriller that Pam Lambert commended in *People* magazine as "tough, fiercely intelligent and irresistible."

Camp returned to the "Prey" series in 2001 with the publication of *Chosen Prey,* the twelfth novel in the series. Deputy Police Chief Lucas Davenport decides to take matters in his own hands when a serial killer begins murdering young women in Wisconsin and Minnesota. Though distracted with sudden changes in his personal life, Davenport gradually links the dead women with a prominent art professor at a local university, James Qatar. However, wrapping up the case before Qatar strikes again proves to be a daunting challenge for Davenport, one that nearly claims his life. The author "is in top form here," claimed a *Publishers Weekly* contributor, "his wry humor . . . lighting up the dark of another grisly investigation."

In an interview first published on Microsoft Network's Books & Reading Forum—and subsequently made available on *The Official John Sandford Website*—the author differentiated between his two major protagonists. Davenport, he said, "is an amalgam of cops I've known, a couple of movie stars, and the characters in any number of thrillers I've read in the past." He added: "There really aren't any cops like Davenport, because he's just too much like Sherlock Holmes, he's a little over the top." Kidd is hardly less extravagant. His creator described Kidd as "a criminal who does industrial espionage to support his watercolor painting habit."

Camp told *Publishers Weekly* that he plans to continue writing books featuring his two popular protagonists, Kidd and Davenport, as well as contemplating a new pseudonym under which to write mainstream novels of a more literary nature. "Those are the kind of strategies that you have to think about," he remarked, adding: "I like to write books that have real stories in them, but I don't know whether a person who writes thrillers, as I do, *can* write literary books; whether critics will accept them."

This is not to suggest that Camp doesn't see his thrillers as legitimate literature. In his online interview, he said: "What I do is really pretty hard, and I appreciate it when people take my effort with some degree of seriousness, as well as enjoying the stories." He concluded: "Readers are the other half of the essential storytelling partnership. What writers do is create the skeleton of a dream, which is dreamt in full by the readers."

BIOGRAPHICAL/CRITICAL SOURCES:

BOOKS

Sandford, John, *Rules of Prey,* Putnam (New York, NY), 1989.

PERIODICALS

Booklist, March 15, 1996, Wes Lukowsky, review of *Sudden Prey,* p. 1220; March 1, 1997, Emily Melton, review of *The Night Crew,* p. 1069; March 15, 1998, Wes Lukowsky, review of *Secret Prey,* p. 1180; April 15, 1999, Jenny McLarin, review of *Certain Prey,* p. 1484; March 1, 2000, Wes Lukowsky, review of *Easy Prey,* p. 1148.

Globe and Mail (Toronto), April 27, 1991, p. C7.

Kirkus Reviews, August 1, 2000, review of *The Devil's Code,* p. 1067.

Library Journal, April 1, 2000, Jo Ann Vicarel, review of *Easy Prey,* p. 132; April 15, 2000, Michael Adams, review of *Certain Prey,* p. 141.

New York Times Book Review, June 7, 1998, Marilyn Stasio, review of *Secret Prey,* p. 47.

People Weekly, March 31, 1997, Pam Lambert, review of *The Night Crew,* p. 39.

Publishers Weekly, June 29, 1990, pp. 83-84; April 1, 1996, review of *Sudden Prey,* p. 54; March 10, 1997, review of *The Night Crew,* p. 49; April 20, 1998, review of *Secret Prey,* p. 47; April 19, 1999, review of *Certain Prey,* p. 60; March 20, 2000, review of *Easy Prey,* p. 68; September 4, 2000, review of *The Devil's Code,* p. 79; April 23, 2001, review of *Chosen Prey,* p. 49.

Tribune Books (Chicago), July 2, 1989, p. 4.

Washington Post Book World, July 16, 1989, p. 6.

Writer, September, 2000, Lewis Burke Frumkes, "A Conversation with . . . John Sandford," p. 26.

OTHER

John Sandford Interview, http://www.goldengate.net/ (October 9, 2000).

The Official John Sandford Web Site, http://www.johnsandford.org/ (May 7, 2001).*

* * *

CARLE, Eric 1929-

PERSONAL: Born June 25, 1929, in Syracuse, NY; son of Erich W. (a civil servant) and Johanna (Oelschlaeger) Carle; married Dorothea Wohlenberg, June, 1954 (divorced, 1964); married Barbara Morrison, June, 1973; children: (first marriage) Cirsten, Rolf. *Education:* Graduated from Akademie der bildenden Künste, Stuttgart, Germany, 1950.

ADDRESSES: Home—P.O. Box 485, Northampton, MA 01060.

CAREER: U.S. Information Center, Stuttgart, Germany, poster designer, 1950-52; *New York Times,* New York City, graphic designer, 1952-56; L. W. Frohlich & Co.,

New York City, art director, 1956-63; freelance writer, illustrator, and designer, 1963—. Guest instructor, Pratt Institute, 1964. *Military service:* U.S. Army, 1952-54.

MEMBER: Authors Guild.

AWARDS, HONORS: New York Times Ten Best Illustrated Books of the Year award, 1969, for *The Very Hungry Caterpillar,* and Outstanding Children's Books of the Year selection, 1974, for *My Very First Library;* Deutscher Jugendpreis, for *1, 2, 3 to the Zoo!* and *The Very Hungry Caterpillar,* both 1970, and 1972, for *Do You Want to Be My Friend?;* first prize for picture books, International Children's Book Fair, 1970, for *1, 2, 3 to the Zoo!,* 1972, for *Do You Want to Be My Friend?,* and for *Papa, Please Get the Moon for Me;* Children's Book of the Year awards, Child Study Association, 1977, for *Do You Want to Be My Friend?, The Very Busy Spider,* and *The Very Lonely Firefly;* American Institute of Graphic Arts (AIGA) awards, both 1970, for *Pancakes, Pancakes* and *The Very Hungry Caterpillar;* Selections du Grand Prix des Treize, 1972, for *The Very Hungry Caterpillar,* and 1973, for *Do You Want to Be My Friend?* and *Have You Seen My Cat?,*; Nakamori Reader's Prize, 1975, for *The Very Hungry Caterpillar;* AIGA certificate of excellence, 1981, for *The Honeybee and the Robber;* silver medal from the city of Milan, Italy, 1989, for *The Very Quiet Cricket;* Heinrich-Wolgast prize, German Education and Science Union, 1996, for *My Apron;* Medallion award, University of Southern Mississippi, 1997; best book award, 1997, for *From Head to Toe,* and platinum book award, 1999, for *You Can Make a Collage,* both from Oppenhein Toy Portfolio; Regina Medal, Catholic Library Association, 1999; Literary Lights for Children award, Boston Public Library, 2000; Japan Picture Book Awards translation winner, 2000, for *Hello, Red Fox.* Recipient of numerous other awards, including awards from New York Art Directors Show, New York Type Directors Show, Society of Illustrators Show, Best Book Jacket of the Year Show, the Carnegie Award for Excellence in Video for Children, and Bratslavia Biennial of Illustration gold medal.

Notable citations including Child Study Association citation, 1970, for *Pancakes, Pancakes;* American Library Association (ALA) notable book, for *The Very Busy Spider,* and 1971, for *Do You Want to Be My Friend?;* One Hundred Titles for Reading and Sharing selection, for *The Very Quiet Cricket,* and Gift List selections, 1971, for *Do You Want to Be My Friend?,* and 1972, for *Secret Birthday Message,* all from New York Public Library; Brooklyn Museum of Art citation, 1973, for *The Very Hungry Caterpillar;* Outstanding Science Trade Book for Children, *A House for Hermit Crab;* National Children's Trade Book in the field of social studies, 1977, for *The Grouchy Ladybug;* Children's Choices award, Children's Book Council/International Reading Association, for *The Very Lonely Firefly,* 1984, for *Brown Bear, Brown Bear* and 1987, for *Papa, Please Get the Moon for Me;* Parents Choice award, 1986, for *Papa, Please Get the Moon for Me,* and 1988, for *The Mixed-up Chameleon* (paperback); Jane Addams Children's Book Honorary Award, 1987, for *All in a Day;* ALA/Booklist Children's Editor's Choices award, for *Animals, Animals,* and Best Books of the '80s pick, for *The Very Busy Spider,* both 1989; *Parenting Magazine* certificate of excellence, 1989, for *Animals, Animals;* California Children's Book and Video award, 1990, for *The Very Quiet Cricket* (picture book category); *Redbook* Top Ten Children's Books of the Year, 1989, for *Animals, Animals,* and 1990, for *The Very Quiet Cricket; Parents Magazine* Best Kid's Books award, 1989, for *Animals, Animals,* and 1995, for *The Very Lonely Firefly;* Buckeye Children's Book Award, Ohio Council of the International Reading Association, 1993, for *The Very Quiet Cricket;* Association of Booksellers Children Bookseller's Choices award, 1995, for *The Very Hungry Caterpillar* board book; David McCord Children's Literature citation, Framingham State College and Nobscot Reading Council of the International Reading Association, 1995; National Parenting Publications award, 1998, for *You Can Make a Collage;* Bank Street College Best Books award, 1998, for *Hello, Red Fox;* numerous titles selected for American Bookseller's Pick of the List. Additional awards for *The Very Busy Spider* include Library of Congress advisory committee recommended title; Best Books for Children selection, R.R. Bowker and Co.; Children's Editor's choice, *Booklist*; *Horn Book* Fanfair title; California Reading Initiative title. *The Very Hungry Caterpillar* named Book of the Year, California Reading Initiative, and was among England's best books in 1971. *The Very Lonely Firefly* named a Kansas City Reading Circle selection, 1996.

WRITINGS:

SELF-ILLUSTRATED

The Say-with-Me ABC Book, Holt, 1967.
1, 2, 3 to the Zoo, World Publishing, 1968.
The Very Hungry Caterpillar, World Publishing, 1969.
Pancakes, Pancakes, Knopf, 1970.
The Tiny Seed, Crowell, 1970, published as *The Tiny Seed and the Giant Flower,* Nelson (London), 1970.

Do You Want to Be My Friend?, Crowell, 1971.

The Rooster Who Set out to See the World, F. Watts, 1972, published as *Rooster's Off to See the World,* Picture Book Studio, 1987.

The Secret Birthday Message, Crowell, 1972.

The Very Long Tail (folding book), Crowell, 1972.

The Very Long Train (folding book), Crowell, 1972.

Walter the Baker: An Old Story Retold and Illustrated, Knopf, 1972.

Have You Seen My Cat?, F. Watts, 1973.

I See a Song, Crowell, 1973, Scholastic, 1996.

My Very First Library, Crowell, 1974.

All about Arthur (an Absolutely Absurd Ape), F. Watts, 1974.

The Mixed-up Chameleon, Crowell, 1975.

Eric Carle's Storybook: Seven Tales by the Brothers Grimm, F. Watts, 1976.

The Grouchy Ladybug, Crowell, 1977, published as *The Bad-Tempered Ladybird,* Hamish Hamilton (London), 1977.

(Reteller) *Seven Stories by Hans Christian Andersen,* F. Watts, 1978.

Watch Out! A Giant!, Philomel, 1978.

Twelve Tales from Aesop: Retold and Illustrated, Philomel, 1980.

The Honeybee and the Robber: A Moving Picture Book, Philomel, 1981.

Catch the Ball, Philomel, 1982, Scholastic, 1998.

Let's Paint a Rainbow, Philomel, 1982, Scholastic, 1998.

What's for Lunch?, Philomel, 1982, Scholastic, 1998.

The Very Busy Spider, Philomel, 1985.

All around Us, Picture Book Studio, 1986.

Papa, Please Get the Moon for Me, Picture Book Studio, 1986.

A House for Hermit Crab, Picture Book Studio, 1987.

Treasury of Classic Stories for Children, Orchard Books, 1988.

Animals, Animals, edited by Laura Whipple, Philomel, 1989.

The Very Quiet Cricket, Philomel, 1990.

Dragons, Dragons, edited by Whipple, Philomel, 1991.

Draw Me a Star, Philomel, 1992.

Today Is Monday, Philomel, 1993.

My Apron: A Story from My Childhood, Philomel, 1994.

The Very Lonely Firefly, Philomel, 1995.

Little Cloud, Philomel, 1996.

The Art of Eric Carle, Philomel, 1996.

The Very Special World of Eric Carle, Penguin Putnam, 1996.

From Head to Toe, HarperCollins, 1997.

Flora and the Tiger: Nineteen Very Short Stories from My Life, Philomel, 1997.

Hello, Red Fox, Simon & Schuster, 1998.

You Can Make a Collage, Klutz, 1998.

The Eric Carle Library, HarperCollins, 1998.

The Very Clumsy Click Beetle, Putnam, 1999.

Does a Kangaroo Have a Mother, Too?, HarperCollins, 2000.

Dream Snow, Putnam, 2000.

"MY VERY FIRST LIBRARY" SERIES; SELF-ILLUSTRATED

My Very First Book of Colors, Crowell, 1974.

My Very First Book of Numbers, Crowell, 1974.

My Very First Book of Shapes, Crowell, 1974.

My Very First Book of Words, Crowell, 1974.

My Very First Book of Food, Crowell, 1986.

My Very First Book of Growth, Crowell, 1986.

My Very First Book of Heads and Tails, Crowell, 1986.

My Very First Book of Homes, Crowell, 1986.

My Very First Book of Motion, Crowell, 1986.

My Very First Book of Sounds, Crowell, 1986.

My Very First Book of Tools, Crowell, 1986.

My Very First Book of Touch, Crowell, 1986.

ILLUSTRATOR

Sune Engelbrektson, *Gravity at Work and Play,* Holt, 1963.

Engelbrektson, *The Sun Is a Star,* Holt, 1963.

Bill Martin, *If You Can Count to Ten,* Holt, 1964.

Aesop's Fables for Modern Readers, Pauper Press, 1965.

Louise Bachelder, editor, *Nature Thoughts,* Pauper Press, 1965.

Lila Perl, *Red-Flannel Hash and Shoo-Fly Pie: America's Regional Foods and Festivals,* World Publishers, 1965.

Samm S. Baker, *Indoor and Outdoor Grow-It Book,* Random House, 1966.

Bachelder, editor, *On Friendship,* Pauper Press, 1966.

Martin, *Brown Bear, Brown Bear, What Do You See?,* Holt, 1967, 1992.

Carl H. Voss, *In Search of Meaning: Living Religions of the World,* World Publishers, 1968.

Nora Roberts Wainer, *The Whale in a Jail,* Funk, 1968.

William Knowlton, *The Boastful Fisherman,* Knopf, 1970.

Martin, *A Ghost Story,* Holt, 1970.

Eleanor O. Heady, *Tales of the Nimipoo from the Land of the Nez Pierce Indians,* World Publishing 1970.

Aileen Fisher, *Feathered Ones and Furry,* Crowell, 1971.

George Mendoza, *The Scarecrow Clock,* Holt, 1971.

Vanishing Animals (posters), F. Watts, 1972.

Fisher, *Do Bears Have Mothers Too?,* Crowell, 1973, published as *Animals and Their Babies,* Hamish Hamilton, 1974.

Isaac Bashevis Singer, *Why Noah Chose the Dove,* translated by Elizabeth Shub, Farrar, Straus, 1974.

Norma Green, reteller, *The Hole in the Dike,* Crowell, 1975.

Norton Juster, *Otter Nonsense,* Philomel, 1982.

Hans Baumann, *Chip Has Many Brothers,* Philomel, 1983.

Richard Buckley, *The Foolish Tortoise,* Picture Book Studio, 1985.

Buckley, *The Greedy Python,* Picture Book Studio, 1985.

Alice McLerran, *The Mountain That Loved a Bird,* Picture Book Studio, 1985.

Mitsumasa Anno, *All in a Day,* Dowaya (Tokyo, Japan), 1986.

Arnold Sundgaard, *The Lamb and the Butterfly,* Orchard Books, 1988.

Martin, *Polar Bear, Polar Bear, What Do You Hear?,* Holt, 1991.

Peter Martins, *Tributes,* Morrow, 1998.

Glassman, Peter, editor, *Oz: The Hundredth Anniversary Celebration,* HarperCollins, 2000.

SIDELIGHTS: Eric Carle "is one of the most beloved illustrators of children's books," according to *Booklist*'s Ilene Cooper. The author/illustrator of over seventy books, most of them bestsellers and many award winners, Carle has had his work translated into more than thirty languages with sales in the millions. Known as a pioneer of the novelty book, Carle has developed innovative picture books for very young readers which include pages that grow larger as a ladybug meets ever larger animals, which have holes in them bored by a ravenous caterpillar, or which contain computer chips that provide the chirping of a cricket and the flashing lights of a firefly—books which bridge the gap between touchable book and readable toy. As Ethel Heins noted in *Horn Book,* "Almost from the start [Carle] has worked in collage—brilliantly painted tissue paper, cut and layered for nuances in color and texture." Even as a child, Carle was fascinated by drawing, and he first displayed this playfully artistic approach to picture books with his 1969 *The Very Hungry Caterpillar,* a book that is still in print around the world and as popular as ever. Carle blends simple, primary-colored cut-paper art depicting mostly small animals and insects with direct and repetitive text, a winning formula for his legion of very young readers.

"Until I was six years old I lived in Syracuse, New York, where I went to kindergarten. I remember happy days with large sheets of paper, bright colors and wide brushes!" the author once commented. Just after Carle started first grade, his family moved to Stuttgart, Germany, his father's original home. There Carle grew up in Hitler's Germany, a country gearing for war. His strict schooling was counterpoised with encouragement from an art teacher who praised the young boy's drawings. He also quickly made friends and was made to feel secure in the warm circle of a large extended family. But when war came in 1939, Carle's world changed. His father was absent from the family for eight years—first in the German army and then in a Soviet prisoner of war camp. Along with other children his age, Carle was a loyal German citizen, following news of the war and each of Hitler's victories. When the fortunes of war began to change, Carle and his family would spend nights in the local air raid shelter. Finally he was removed to the country to be safe from the bombing raids.

With the end of the war, Germany slowly recovered. Carle's father returned to his family in 1947; Carle entered the fine arts academy and was soon designing posters for the American information center in Stuttgart. Finally, in 1952, Carle felt confident enough in his art to take his portfolio and return to the United States. Soon after arriving, however, he was drafted into the U.S. Army and was stationed back in Stuttgart, where he met his first wife. After Carle's discharge the couple moved back to New York; they eventually had two children together, but separated in 1964. During this time, Carle worked as a designer and art director. In 1963, Carle quit his full-time company job to begin working as a freelance artist. As he related in his *Something about the Author Autobiography Series* (SAAS) essay, "I had come to the conclusion that I didn't want to sit in meetings, write memos, entertain clients, and catch commuter trains. I simply wanted to create pictures."

Carle first became interested in children's literature when he was asked to do illustrations for a book by Bill Martin. "I found Bill's approach to the world of the preschool and first grade child very stimulating; it reawakened in me struggles of my own childhood," Carle commented to Delores R. Klingberg in *Language Arts.* Remembering his difficult early schooldays in Germany, Carle added that the conflicts from that time "remained hidden until the opportunity and insight presented themselves. Through my work with Bill Martin, an unfinished area of my own growing up had been touched."

"I didn't realize it clearly then, but my life was beginning to move onto its true course," Carle said in the *SAAS* essay. "The long, dark time of growing up in wartime Germany, the cruelly enforced discipline of my school years there, the dutifully performed work at my jobs in advertising—all these were finally losing their rigid grip on me. The child inside me—who had been so suddenly and sharply uprooted and repressed—was beginning to come joyfully back to life."

"It was then that I met Ann Beneduce (then editor with World), and with her kind help and understanding I created my first two books: *1, 2, 3 to the Zoo* and *The Very Hungry Caterpillar,*" Carle once commented. "A mixture of negative and positive influences had led to a fruitful expression." Both of Carle's first books contain bold, collage pictures and feature many different animals. The author recalled in a *Books for Keeps* article that his early years with his father taught him about nature. "We used to go for long walks in the countryside together, and he would peel back tree bark to show me what was underneath it, lift rocks to reveal the insects. As a result, I have an abiding love and affection for small, insignificant animals."

1, 2, 3 to the Zoo was published in 1968 and follows several animals on their train trip to live in a zoo, with a tiny mouse observing each car. The book is full of "superb paintings of animals, bold, lively, handsome, spreading over big double-spread pages," Adele McRae of the *Christian Science Monitor* wrote. "His elephant is all magnificent power, his giraffes a precision of delicacy, his monkeys a tangle of liveliness. This is a book to grow with its owner. The tiny mouse lurking in every picture may remain invisible to the smallest reader and, as the title implies, the book is waiting to teach the art of counting." Carle's award-winning book *The Very Hungry Caterpillar* was published in 1969. "I was just playfully punching holes in a stack of paper," the author told Molly McQuade of *Publishers Weekly,* "and I thought to myself, 'This could've been done by a bookworm.' From that came a caterpillar." *The Very Hungry Caterpillar* "tells the story of a caterpillar's life-cycle, from egg to butterfly," as John A. Cunliffe described it in *Children's Book Review.* The caterpillar "eats through a great many things on the way—one apple on Monday, two pears on Tuesday, and so on, to a list of ten exotic items on Saturday." Cunliffe went on to note "the book's delight, and originality, lie in the way in which these cumulative items are shown. . . . The text is brief and simple, and has a satisfying cumulative effect that neatly matches the pictures, which are large and bold, in brilliant colours and crisp forms set against the white page, mainly achieved by the use of collage."

Not only does *Caterpillar* contain brightly colored shapes designed to appeal to young children, it also has holes in the pages that match the path of the caterpillar. As Carle explained in *Books for Your Children,* the holes in *Caterpillar* "are a bridge from toy to book, from plaything, from the touching to understanding. . . . In the very young child the thought travels mightily fast from fingertips to brain. This book has many layers. There is fun, nonsense, colour, surprise. There is learning, but if the child ignores the learning part, let him, it's OK. Someday he'll hit upon it by himself. That is the way we learn." Carle's approach in *Caterpillar* has proved so popular that the book has sold millions of copies and been translated into over thirty languages.

Do You Want to Be My Friend? is another innovative picture book filled with bright and colorful animals. The only words in the story are the title question "Do you want to be my friend?" spoken by a lonely mouse, and a joyful "yes" from the new friend he finally discovers. Calling it "a perfect picture book for a small child," *Washington Post Book World* contributor Polly Goodwin added that *Do You Want to Be My Friend?* "offers a splendid opportunity for a pre-reader, with a little initial help, to create his own story based on the brilliantly colored, wonderfully expressive pictures." *The Rooster Who Set out to See the World,* later published as *Rooster's Off to See the World,* is another "brilliantly colored picture story that does double duty as a counting book," Lillian N. Gerhardt said in *Library Journal.* The story follows a rooster who decides to travel and see the world. As he travels, he adds friends in twos, threes, fours, and fives. "The sums are presented pictorially in the corners of the page," Marcus Crouch of *Junior Bookshelf* noted, but this doesn't distract from Carle's "exquisitely drawn coloured pictures. Mr. Carle is still the best of all artists for the very young," Crouch concluded.

Carle introduced another innovation in his 1977 book *The Grouchy Ladybug:* the pages grow in size as larger and larger animals appear on them. The story follows a bad-tempered ladybug as she challenges different creatures, starting with other insects and ending with the whale whose cutout tail slaps her back to her home leaf. While Carle presents such instructive concepts as time and size, "this book is chiefly a pleasure to read and to look at," Caroline Moorhead wrote in the *Times Educational Supplement,* "with its cross and good-natured ladybirds . . . and its deep-toned illustrations of animals."

The Very Busy Spider follows a spider that spends her day spinning a web, which grows larger with each page. Although she is interrupted by a number of farm animals, the spider continues her work until the web is finished and she catches the fly that has been bothering the other animals. Because the web and fly are raised above the page so that they can be felt, the book "is obviously of value to the visually handicapped," as Julia Eccleshare commented in the *Times Literary Supplement.* Denise M. Wilms agreed, writing in *Booklist* "this good-looking picture book has just the ingredients" to become an "instant classic."

More of these "Very" insect books have followed. *The Very Quiet Cricket* tells the tale of a cricket who wants to find someone to talk to. He desperately wants to be able to rub his wings together and make a sound to return the greetings of other insects, and finally, after much labor, he gets his wish. The cricket's sound is reproduced via a battery-aided computer chip on the final page of the book. "Carle has created yet another celebration of nature," declared Starr LaTronica in a *School Library Journal* review of the book. LaTronica further noted, "Typical of Carle's style, the language is simple, with rhythm, repetition, and alliteration to delight young listeners. Painted collage illustrations are lavish and expressive." A *Books for Keeps* reviewer called the same book "perfect," remarking that "the lyrical text illustrated in Carle's individual and immediately recognisable style, moves to a moment of pure astonishment that touches every young reader."

The Very Lonely Firefly presents another lovable insect in search of love, a firefly that goes out into the night in search of others like itself. In its quest for illuminated buddies, it mistakes headlights, fireworks, even a flashlight for other fireflies before it finally finds its own kind on the final page of the book, with battery-powered twinkling lights. Roger Sutton, writing in *Bulletin of the Center for Children's Books,* noted that "toddlers will appreciate the predictability and rhythm of the text and the bold shapes of the firefly and other figures set against the streaky blue-black sky." Reviewing this supposed final book in the series, Christina Dorr concluded in *School Library Journal,* "This is a compelling accomplishment that will leave readers and listeners alike wishing Carle would turn the quartet into a quintet. A guaranteed winner as a read-aloud or read-alone." In the event Dorr, and thousands of young fans, were rewarded with a fifth entrant in the series in 1999, *The Very Clumsy Click Beetle,* about this peculiar insect which must learn to jump in the air in order to move once it has fallen on its back. Julie Corsaro called the book a "winning addition to Carle's oeuvre," in a *Booklist* review.

Carle has produced another series of books that deal with numbers, letters of the alphabet, tools, and a plethora of other activities and subjects for the very young. The "My Very First Book" series is designed in a "Dutch-door" style, each page split in half with separate illustrations on top and bottom halves so that the young reader can mix and match images. Again, such images are designed from brilliantly vibrant bits of collage tissue paper. Additionally, Carle has also written his own versions of familiar children's works, such as Grimm's fairy tales, Aesop's fables, and Hans Christian Andersen's stories. Reviewing *Treasury of Classic Stories for Children,* a compilation of his retellings, LaTronica noted in *School Library Journal* "Carle's distinctive style of bright watercolor and collage illustration provides an excellent complement to the lively text."

Poems for young readers—from haiku to Kipling—were adapted for two popular picture books for the young reader, *Animals, Animals* and *Dragons, Dragons.* Susan Schuller, reviewing the first named in *School Library Journal,* observed, "Carle's distinctive tissue paper collages bring brilliance and verve to this excellent anthology of poems which conveys the wonder and diversity of the animal world." Betsy Hearne commented in the *Bulletin of the Center for Children's Books* that *Animals* provided a "splendid showcase for Carle's dramatic double image." Reviewing *Dragons, Dragons,* a contributor to *Kirkus Reviews* called it a "well-chosen, gorgeously illustrated collection of poetry."

Carle has also produced many stand-alone titles that both delight and educate very young readers. *Today Is Monday* takes the young reader on a song-journey through the days of the week and the foods eaten every day. "Lovely to look at; delightful to know," concluded Trevor Dickinson in a *Books for Keeps* review. In *Little Cloud,* Carle tells of the "whimsical world of ever-changing shapes in the sky," according to Kathy Mitchell in *School Library Journal.* The cloud in mention delights in changing its shape into a lamb or airplane or shark, finally joining the others in one large rain cloud. "Children will enjoy the simple text and the colorful illustrations," Mitchell concluded. Dickinson, reviewing *Little Cloud* in the *School Librarian,* felt that the book was a "delight in its own artistic right," and would "encourage close and interested observation of the wider world."

Carle's 1997 *From Head to Toe* presents animals and multiethnic children demonstrating various body movements. "Keeping both text and graphics to a minimum, Carle proves once again just how effective simplicity can be," wrote a reviewer for *Publishers Weekly.* The same contributor concluded that children will "eagerly clap, stomp, kick and wriggle their way through these pages from start to finish." *Booklist*'s Cooper observed, "Carle's signature strong collages are put to good use in this book about movement." In *Hello, Red Fox,* "Carle asks readers to engage in optical illusions to view his illustrations for a story that becomes an unforgettable lesson in complementary colors," according to a *Kirkus Reviews* critic. After staring at a picture of the fox in green, for ten seconds, the reader then shifts focus to a pure white facing page and the fox appears in red as an after image. A reviewer for *Publishers Weekly* felt that Carle once again proved the old adage that "Less is more" with a "straightforward, repetitive text and minimalist cut-paper art." *Booklist*'s Linda Perkins commented that this "playful starting point for science discussions at home or at school" would be "sure to intrigue children."

Carle has used his childhood in Germany for several other books, including his award-winning *Draw Me a Star,* the autobiographical *My Apron: A Story from My Childhood,* and his only book for older readers, *Flora and Tiger: Nineteen Very Short Stories from My Life.* In *Draw Me a Star,* he harks back to memories of his German grandmother and links it to a dream that parallels the story of Creation. A reviewer for *Books for Keeps* called this a "splendid book for its colour, its richness and its potential for thought and imagination." *School Library Journal*'s Eve Larkin thought *Draw Me a Star* was an "inspired book in every sense of the word." *My Apron: A Story from My Childhood* tells of a young boy whose aunt makes him an apron so that he can help his uncle plaster the chimney. In this novelty book, a child-size apron is included for young readers. *Flora and Tiger: Nineteen Very Short Stories from My Life* presents "spare autobiographical vignettes that take place from [Carle's] childhood to the present," according to *Booklist*'s Hazel Rochman. Jane Claes noted in *School Library Journal* that these "sketches are sometimes moving, sometimes funny, and sometimes uplifting" and are a "super addition to any study of Carle or his work."

Such work continues into the new millennium. With his 2000 title, *Does a Kangaroo Have a Mother, Too?,* Carle asks this question about ten other animals, to show that all animals have mothers. Reviewing the title in *Booklist,* Tim Arnold noted, "Almost no author/illustrator over the past 30 years has played a more prominent role in the literary lives of preschoolers than Eric Carle." Arnold further commented, "His large, inviting graphic animals have consistently delighted and taught children during early stages of development. This latest effort is no exception." Whatever their topic, all of Carle's works are educational tools that interest children with their bold, imaginative drawings and whimsical presentations. "We underestimate children," Carle said in a 1982 *Early Years* interview. "They have tremendous capacities for learning." Such a belief in the inquisitiveness of the child has not altered in Carle over the years. In his Web page, the author/illustrator responds to frequently asked questions about himself. Under "hobbies" he notes, "I would have to say my work is my hobby. And my hobby is my work. Even when I'm not working in my studio, I might be thinking about future books. I will probably never retire from creating books."

Carle devotes a multi-layered artistic sensibility to this "hobby." As Donnarae MacCann and Olga Richard claimed in *Wilson Library Bulletin,* "Eric Carle is like a half dozen creative people rolled into one." Because of Carle's skill in writing for pre-schoolers, his "innovativeness and artistic discipline," and his ability to turn a book into a toy, the critics concluded, "a child reared on such books will blossom into a confirmed bibliophile."

BIOGRAPHICAL/CRITICAL SOURCES:

BOOKS

Children's Books and Their Creators, edited by Anita Silvey, Houghton Mifflin, 1995.

Children's Literature Review, Volume 10, Gale (Detroit, MI), 1986.

Famous Children's Authors, edited by Shirley Norby and Gregory Ryan, Denison, 1988.

Something about the Author Autobiography Series, Volume 6, Gale (Detroit, MI), 1988.

St. James Guide to Children's Writers, 5th edition, edited by Sara Pendergast and Tom Pendergast, St. James Press (Detroit, MI), 1999.

PERIODICALS

Booklist, June 1, 1985, Denise M. Wilms, review of *The Very Busy Spider,* p. 1398; September 15, 1996, Ilene Cooper, review of *The Art of Eric Carle,* p. 253; April 15, 1997, I. Cooper, review of *From Head to Toe,* p. 1431; December 15, 1997, Hazel Rochman, review of *Flora and Tiger,* p. 692; April, 1998, Linda Perkins, review of *Hello, Red Fox,* p. 1329; October 1, 1999, Julie Corsaro, review of

The Very Clumsy Click Beetle, p. 360; January 1, 2000, Tim Arnold, review of *Does a Kangaroo Have a Mother, Too?,* p. 930.

Books for Keeps, May, 1985, Eric Carle, "Authorgraph No. 2: Eric Carle," pp. 14-15; November, 1987, p. 4; May, 1994, Trevor Dickinson, review of *Today Is Monday,* p. 33; March, 1995, p. 25; July, 1995, review of *Draw Me a Star,* p. 6; December, 1996, p. 82; January, 1997, p. 18; March, 1997, p. 7; June, 1997, p. 352; November, 1997, review of *The Very Quiet Cricket,* pp. 5-6; January, 1998, p. 156.

Books for Your Children, spring, 1978, Eric Carle, "From Hungry Caterpillars to Bad Tempered Ladybirds," p. 7.

Bulletin of the Center for Children's Books, October, 1989, Betsy Hearne, review of *Animals, Animals,* p. 47; November, 1990, p. 56; July-August, 1995, Roger Sutton, review of *The Very Lonely Firefly,* pp. 379-80.

Children's Book Review, February, 1971, John A. Cunliffe, review of *The Very Hungry Caterpillar,* p. 14.

Christian Science Monitor, May 1, 1969, Adele McRae, "Crayoned Morality Plays," p. B2.

Early Years, April, 1982, "Eric Carle's Children's Books Are to Touch," p. 23.

Horn Book, March-April, 1997, Ethel Heins, review of *The Art of Eric Carle,* pp. 215-16.

Junior Bookshelf, October, 1972, Marcus Crouch, review of *The Rooster Who Set Out to See the World,* pp. 301-02; January, 1994, p. 14; June, 1994, p. 93; October, 1995, p. 167.

Kirkus Reviews, July 1, 1989, p. 988; July 15, 1991, review of *Dragons, Dragons,* p. 940; June 1, 1995, p. 778; August 1, 1996, p. 1159; April 1, 1997, p. 551; February 1, 1998, review of *Hello, Red Fox,* p. 194.

Language Arts, April, 1977, Delores R. Klingberg, "Eric Carle," p. 447.

Library Journal, June 15, 1973, Lillian N. Gerhardt, review of *The Rooster Who Set out to See the World,* pp. 1992-93.

Los Angeles Times Book Review, April 11, 1999, p. 6.

Magpies, July, 1996, p. 26.

Publishers Weekly, September 29, 1989, Molly McQuade, "Ballyhooing Birthdays: Four Children's Classics and How They Grew," pp. 28-29; February 17, 1997, review of *From Head to Toe,* p. 219; January 26, 1998, review of *Hello, Red Fox,* p. 91; October 18, 1999, p. 86; January 10, 2000, p. 66.

School Arts, May, 1999, p. 18.

School Librarian, August, 1997, p. 130; November, 1997, Trevor Dickinson, review of *Little Cloud,* p. 184; autumn, 1998, p. 129.

School Library Journal, April, 1988, Starr LaTronica, review of *Eric Carle's Treasury of Classic Stories for Children,* p. 94; November, 1989, Susan Schuller, review of *Animals, Animals,* p. 101; December, 1990, S. LaTronica, review of *The Very Quiet Cricket,* p. 72; October, 1992, Eve Larkin, review of *Draw Me a Star,* p. 80; November, 1992. p. 133; April, 1993, p. 109; November, 1994, p. 73; February, 1995, p. 126; August, 1995, Christina Dorr, review of *The Very Lonely Firefly,* pp. 120-21; May, 1996, Kathy Mitchell, review of *Little Cloud,* p. 85; December, 1996, p. 46; April, 1997, p. 120; February, 1998, Jane Claes, review of *Flora and Tiger,* p. 113; July, 1998, p. 71; November, 1999, p. 112.

Times Educational Supplement, February 3, 1978, Caroline Moorhead, "Animal/Animal, Animal/Human," p. 45.

Times Literary Supplement, March 29, 1985, Julia Eccleshare, "Following the Thread," p. 351.

Washington Post Book World, Part II, May 9, 1971, Polly Goodwin, review of *Do You Want to Be My Friend?,* p. 4.

Wilson Library Bulletin, January, 1989, Donnarae MacCann and Olga Richard, "Picture Books for Children," pp. 90-91.

OTHER

The Official Eric Carle Web site, http://www.eric-carle.com/ (August 9, 2000).

* * *

CHEATHAM, Karyn Follis 1943-

PERSONAL: Born January 30, 1943, in Oberlin, OH; daughter of Benjamin Curtis (U.S. Air Force) and Elizabeth (a secretary; maiden name, Blackburn) Follis; married Eugene C. Cheatham, July 17, 1965 (divorced, December, 1994); children: Nisah (son), Onika (daughter). *Education:* Attended Ohio State University, 1960-66. *Religion:* "Native American." *Avocational interests:* Art (water colors, pen and ink), music, soccer, and equestrian events.

ADDRESSES: Home—Helena, MT. *Agent*—c/o Lucent Books, Box 289011, San Diego, CA 92128-9011. *E-mail*—agk@Kaios.com.

CAREER: Battelle Memorial Institute, Columbus, OH, research analyst, 1965-69; University of Michigan, Ann Arbor, administrative secretary at Environmental Simulation Laboratory, 1969-70; K & S Radiology, Nashville, TN, research assistant, 1978-80; Athlon Sports Communications, Nashville, TN, assistant editor, 1995-98. Tutor and counselor for Prevent High School Drop Outs (Raleigh, NC), 1975-76; lecturer on Blacks in the West and Native American history; adviser on Indian recruitment for colleges and universities.

MEMBER: Western Writers of America, Women Writing the West, Nashville Writers Alliance.

AWARDS, HONORS: Notable children's trade book citation from National Council on Social Studies Children's Book Council, 1983, for *The Best Way Out;* Spur Award finalist, 1998, for *Dennis Banks: Native American Activist.*

WRITINGS:

Spotted Flower and the Ponokomita, Westminster (Philadelphia, PA), 1977.

(Contributor) Jane B. Katz, editor, *I Am the Fire of Time: The Voices of Native American Women,* Dutton (New York, NY), 1977.

Life on a Cool Plastic Ice Floe, Westminster (Philadelphia, PA), 1978.

Bring Home the Ghost, Harcourt (New York, NY), 1980.

The Best Way Out, Harcourt (New York, NY), 1982.

Dennis Banks: Native American Activist, Enslow Publishing, 1998.

The Adventures of Elizabeth Fortune, Blue Heron (Grand Rapids, MI), 2000.

The Crocodile, Lucent Books (San Diego, CA), 2001.

Also author of *Murder in Sumner County, Where Night Stands Waiting, Child of Mist* and *Daughter of the Stone.* Author of a review column in *Carolina Indian Voice,* 1975-1976. Poetry published in *Art/Life, Conditioned Response, Panhandler, Crosscurrents, Sojourner, West Wind Review, Spectrum, Phoenix,* and *Kalliope.* Contributor to periodicals, including *American Cowboy* and *Knoxville Magazine.* Contributor to and editor of newsletters for various organizations, including American Indians Unlimited, Ann Arbor, MI, 1971-72, American Red Cross, Nashville TN, 1978, Franklin Photo Club, Franklin, TN, 1994-97, and Wakina Sky Learning Circle and Library, Helena, MT, 2000—. Volunteer tutor at Wakima Sky Learning Circle and Library, Helena, MT.

WORK IN PROGRESS: New edition of *Spotted Flower and the Ponokomita,* Mountain Press, Missoula, MT, 2001; essays and short stories; an action mystery set in post-civil war Indian Territory; several poetry chapbooks.

SIDELIGHTS: Karyn Follis Cheatham writes: "I consider myself a communicator to children and other free beings, one who harmonizes with creation and expresses this through writing. I have wanted to be a professional writer since I was six, but never gained that status until I was thirty-three. Perhaps it took that long to establish an order to my own mind so that I could clearly express things to others.

"For me, writing is just a natural extension of the verbal and mental communication I have with all things around me. Much of my writing has been to convey information to my readers they have overlooked, ignored, or of which they have been deprived. My first book developed because I learned that most people believe the horse has always been a part of this country and were ignorant of the culture of indigenous peoples who have populated this hemisphere for countless centuries. The book tells how the Blackfeet Nation (the strongest part of my own heritage) first encountered this new animal in 1736.

"That was the beginning of my interest in historical fiction. Not only did I feel right about what I was communicating, but I also enjoyed the research that included re-remembering old stories I had heard, and reading new materials to give the story and characters vivid imagery.

"Not all of my writing is about history, but even in these other manuscripts I have tried to give realism to people's inner spirit, fears, and momentum. I hope that good characterization can give others greater insight into their own lives, and produce a better understanding of all things around them.

"The ability to see all aspects of the environment is a necessity not only to my writing, but to any true communication. Communication requires both a giver and a receiver. I receive from my surroundings and at the same time am giving. Like musical notes, this communication works best when the giver and receiver are in harmony. Therefore each occurrence and being I experience is a part of my learning to harmonize. Each moment I can remember, translate, decipher, and live is another note in my communication and I continually remember that everything on this Earth is unique. Through my writing I hope that others may read my thoughts and blend them with their own life experiences to lead them toward their own holistic identity, just as I am growing toward mine."

In recent years, Cheatham has incorporated another hobby, photography, into her writing. She began supplying photographs with her articles and her work has since then appeared in several periodicals, including *Pro Rodeo World, Bloodlines, American Cowboy, Tempo, The Roundup, Armed Force Publication* and in books such as *Sacajewea* by Alana White. She was a finalist in the 1993 *Photographers Forum* spring contest. Over the past few years, Cheatham has increasingly merged her photography with her writing, now specializing in rural industry and domestic animal enterprises to produce and design flyers, brochures, Web advertisements and pages for her clients.

The Adventures of Elizabeth Fortune fulfills Cheatham's goal of creating historical fiction based on "that which is not told in normal history books." In an author's statement on *Amazon.com,* Cheatham noted that her historical research is aimed at information that "falls between the cracks—especially regarding Blacks in the American West." The heroine of *The Adventures of Elizabeth Fortune* is a mixed-race young woman who, disowned by her wealthy grandfather, must make her way along the Santa Fe Trail in search of her soldier father. Elizabeth Fortune is able to pass as a white teenaged boy, but she is very proud of her African American and Native American heritage. When circumstances force her to dress as a man and spend months in the most rugged terrain, pursued by outlaws, she still maintains a sense of herself and a vision of what she wants to become. In the *Bloomsbury Review,* Susan G. Butruille commended Cheatham for creating "a woman who has the unique breadth of wisdom born of her multicultural heritage." Butruille also noted of *The Adventures of Elizabeth Fortune:* "Readers looking for a hard-to-find good western yarn will discover it right here. This novel has it all: the lonesome western landscape, the good guys, bad guys, suspense, intrigue, brawls, gunfights, an ambush, a showdown, romance." In *Roundup Online Magazine,* Doris Meredith likewise praised the novel as "an exciting, carefully researched historical novel with one of the most likable and well-drawn characters in years."

Cheatham, who lives in Helena, Montana, shares her time with two horses and a dog.

BIOGRAPHICAL/CRITICAL SOURCES:

PERIODICALS

Bloomsbury Review, July/August, 2000, Susan G. Butruille, review of *The Adventures of Elizabeth Fortune.*

Christian Century, September 24, 1975.

Kirkus Reviews, August 1, 1977.

Nashville Banner, May 2, 1973.

Review for Religious, September, 1975.

Social Education, April, 1978.

OTHER

Karyn Folio Cheatam Web site, http://Kaios.com(October 1, 2000).

Roundup Online Magazine, http://www.westernwriters.org/ (October 1, 2000), Doris Meredith, review of *The Adventures of Elizabeth Fortune.*

Scanner, http://www.teleport.com/ (October 1, 2000), review of *The Adventures of Elizabeth Fortune.*

* * *

CIRESI, Rita 1960-

PERSONAL: Born September 29, 1960, in New Haven, CT; daughter of Salvatore (a food distributor) and Maria Saveria (a nurse) Ciresi. *Education:* New College, B.A., 1981; University of Iowa, M.A., 1983; Pennsylvania State University, M.F.A., 1988. *Religion:* Roman Catholic. *Avocational interests:* Playing classical piano.

ADDRESSES: Office—Department of English, University of South Florida, Tampa, FL 33634. *Agent*—Geri Thoma, Elaine Markson Literary Agency, 44 Greenwich Ave., New York, NY 10011. *E-mail*—rciresi@hotmail.com.

CAREER: Pennsylvania State University, University Park, science writer and editor for department of agriculture, 1989-92; Hollins College, Roanoke, VA, assistant professor of English, 1992-95; University of South Florida, Tampa, began as assistant professor, became associate professor of English, 1995—.

MEMBER: American Italian Historical Association, Associated Writing Programs, Italian American Writers Association.

AWARDS, HONORS: Honorable mention, Chester H. Jones National Poetry Competition, 1986; Academy of American Poets contest, honorable mention, 1986, first prize, 1987; Edwin Erle Sparks liberal arts fellowship, Pennsylvania State University, 1987; first prize in poetry, Central Pennsylvania Festival of the Arts, 1988; master fellowship, Pennsylvania Council on the Arts,

1989; first prize, *Connecticut Writer* poetry contest, 1990; honorable mention, *Kingfisher* fiction contest, 1991; award for best agribusiness article, Pennsylvania Agricultural Industries Council, 1991; Flannery O'Connor Award for short fiction, University of Georgia Press, 1991, for *Mother Rocket;* finalist for Art Seidenbaum Award for first fiction, *Los Angeles Times Book Award,* 1993, for *Mother Rocket;* teaching fellow at Wesleyan Writers Conference, 1995; William Faulkner Prize for best novel, 1997, for *Pink Slip.*

WRITINGS:

Mother Rocket (short stories), University of Georgia Press (Athens, GA), 1993.
Blue Italian (novel), Ecco Press (Hopewell, NJ), 1996.
Pink Slip (novel), Delacorte (New York, NY), 1999.
Sometimes I Dream in Italian (short stories), Delacorte (New York, NY), 2000.

Work represented in anthologies, including *Chester H. Jones Foundation Anthology,* 1986. Contributor to periodicals, including *Alaska Quarterly Review, California Quarterly, Embers, Connecticut Writer, Hawaii Pacific Review, Italian Americana, Kingfisher, Library Journal, Northern Review, New Oregon Review, Penn State Agriculture, Pleiades, Poet Lore, Prairie Schooner, South Carolina Review, Worcester Review,* and *Yellow Silk.*

WORK IN PROGRESS: Remind Me Again Why I Married You, a novel, publication by Delacorte (New York, NY) expected in 2002; *How Long Do You Have to Live,* a novel, Delacorte (New York, NY).

SIDELIGHTS: Rita Ciresi has won a Flannery O'Connor Award and a William Faulkner Prize for her candid portraits of Italian American families and the tension between generations as children grow up, pursue careers, and get married outside the ethnic community. Born and raised in New Haven, Connecticut, Ciresi often uses her hometown in her novels and stories. She has received critical praise for her wit and humor, as well as for her depth of understanding for young, middle-class women who find themselves at a crossroads between their parents' values and their own blossoming sense of self. According to a *Publishers Weekly* contributor, Ciresi has established herself as a "resonant voice chronicling the lives of Italian-Americans."

Ciresi's first story collection, *Mother Rocket,* features characters who are "propelled by the inexorable and inexplicable force of their passions," according to Ralph Sassone in the *New York Times Book Review.* Ciresi writes about intense, forlorn individuals impulsively striving for even modest personal satisfaction. Among the notable tales in *Mother Rocket* are "Lifelines," in which a teenage girl struggles to assert herself against her emotionally hardened mother, and "Resurrection," in which a teenage boy becomes infatuated with a significantly older woman. Sassone proclaimed that, for the most part, the tales in *Mother Rocket* are "artfully balanced . . . and often funny." The book won the 1991 Flannery O'Connor Award for short fiction.

Blue Italian, Ciresi's debut novel, is a bittersweet story of an interfaith marriage. Italian Catholic Rosa Salvatore falls in love with Jewish law student Gary Fisher. Their tragically short union brings together Rosa's artless mother and Gary's wealthy but dysfunctional Long Island parents. In the *New York Times Book Review,* Elinor Lipman praised the novel for its "cranky heroine" and noted the presence of "a sure hand and a keen eye reporting from the two ethnic camps." A *Publishers Weekly* reviewer cited the book for its "smooth prose, snappy pace and clever, if nasty, repartee." The reviewer concluded that readers will find "real substance in this tragicomic story of two people with smart mouths and starved hearts." In *Booklist,* Joanne Wilkinson called *Blue Italian* "a remarkably accomplished debut."

Ciresi won the prestigious William Faulkner Prize for her second novel, *Pink Slip,* which also features a witty and sharp-tongued heroine. Lisa Diodetto takes her cousin's advice and cuts her ties to Manhattan by taking a job at a large pharmaceutical manufacturer outside the city. Once there she commits the biggest *faux pas* of the corporate world by falling in love with her straitlaced Jewish boss. Their subsequent relationship is threatened not only by their respective positions within the company, but also by the secrets they have kept from one another about their pasts. In *Library Journal,* Beth Gibbs pronounced the novel "a wonderful read, a warm and romantic love story that is also sharp and funny." *Booklist* correspondent Toni Hyde likewise declared the work a "deliciously risque and unconventional story that runs the gamut from hilarious to bittersweet." *New York Times Book Review* contributor Barbara Quick admired the "tongue-in-cheek" narrative, observing: "It's refreshing to find a female narrator with an authentically lusty voice."

Ciresi returned to the short story form in *Sometimes I Dream in Italian.* The series of interrelated stories reveals the relationship between sisters Angel and Lina, who are growing up in an Italian American family in

New Haven. Angel, the narrator, struggles to come to terms with sibling rivalry and with her parents' immigrant values. "Each of these 12 linked stories offers new insight into Angel's difficult reckoning with her mixed feelings and her colorful family and heritage," noted a *Publishers Weekly* reviewer. GraceAnne A. DeCandido described the work in *Booklist* as "a bitter olive of a collection" in which "Ciresi gets the details horribly right." And Gibbs, in her *Library Journal* piece, found *Sometimes I Dream in Italian* to be "a stirring novel about the pull of the past and the force of the future." A *Kirkus Reviews* critic declared the book "classic Italian-American fiction: characters and situations rendered with such skill and honesty . . . that they are instantly and universally recognizable."

BIOGRAPHICAL/CRITICAL SOURCES:

PERIODICALS

Booklist, September 1, 1996, Joanne Wilkinson, review of *Blue Italian,* p. 60; December 1, 1998, Toni Hyde, review of *Pink Slip,* p. 650; September 1, 2000, GraceAnne A. DeCandido, review of *Sometimes I Dream in Italian,* p. 63.

Kirkus Reviews, November 1, 1998, review of *Pink Slip;* August 15, 2000, review of *Sometimes I Dream in Italian,* p. 1133.

Library Journal, October 15, 1998, Beth Gibbs, review of *Pink Slip,* p. 95; August, 2000, Beth Gibbs, review of *Sometimes I Dream in Italian,* p. 152.

Los Angeles Times, September 5, 1993, p. 6.

New York Times Book Review, October 31, 1993, Ralph Sassone, "University Presses: Antic Longing," p. 37; September 22, 1996, Elinor Lipman, "Love Story," p. 34; March 21, 1999, Barbara Quick, review of *Pink Slip,* p. 21.

Publishers Weekly, August 12, 1996, review of *Blue Italian,* p. 65; August 14, 2000, review of *Sometimes I Dream in Italian,* p. 324.

* * *

CLINTON, Catherine 1952-

PERSONAL: Born April 5, 1952, in Seattle, WA; daughter of Fletcher Allen and Claudene (an executive) Johnson; stepfather's name, George W. Clinton; married Daniel Lee Colbert (an architect), June 20, 1982; children: Drew, Ned. *Education:* Harvard University, B.A., 1973; University of Sussex, M.A., 1974; Princeton University, Ph.D., 1980. *Politics:* "Feminist."

ADDRESSES: Agent—Kris Dahl, International Creative Management, 40 West 57th St., New York, NY 10019; Rosemary Sandberg, 6 Bayley St., London WC1B 3HB, England. *E-mail*—redhead2@mail.idt.net.

CAREER: University of Benghazi, Benghazi, Libya, lecturer in history, 1974; Union College, Schenectady, NY, assistant professor of history, 1979-83; Harvard University, Cambridge, MA, assistant professor of history, 1983-88; Brandeis University, Waltham, MA, visiting professor of history, 1988-90; Harvard University, W. E. B. DuBois Institute, visiting fellow, 1993-97; Brown University, Providence, RI, visiting professor of history, 1993; Douglas Southall Freeman Distinguished Visiting Chair of History, University of Richmond, 1997-98; Lewis Jones Distinguished Visiting Chair of History, Wofford College, 1998-99; Weissman Visiting Chair of History, Baruch College, City University of New York, 1999-2001; Mark Clark Chair of History, the Citadel, 2001-2002. Charles Warren Center Affiliate, Harvard University, 1998-99; Gilder Lehrman Center Affiliate, Yale University, 1999—. Member of Pulitzer Prize jury for history, 1986, Francis Parkman Prize committee, 1991, Pulitzer Prize jury for biography, 1993, and Lincoln Prize jury, 1995. Consultant to television corporations, stations, and production companies, including the Arts & Entertainment Channel, History Channel, Disney Channel, WGBH (Boston, MA), and Greystone Productions.

MEMBER: Organization of American Historians, Southern Historical Association, Southern Association of Women Historians (president, 1997-98), Society of American Historians, Screen Writer's Guild East.

AWARDS, HONORS: Isobel Briggs traveling fellowship; Bank Street Poetry Prize, Bank Street College, 1998, for *I, Too, Sing America: Three Centuries of African American Poetry.*

WRITINGS:

The Plantation Mistress: Woman's World in the Old South, Pantheon (New York, NY), 1982.

The Other Civil War: American Women in the Nineteenth Century, Hill & Wang (New York, NY), 1984, revised edition, 1999.

(Compiler, with G. J. Barker-Benfield) *Portraits of American Women,* St. Martin's Press (New York, NY), 1991.

(Editor, with Nina Silber) *Divided Houses: Gender and the Civil War,* Oxford University Press (New York, NY), 1992.
(Editor) *Half Sisters of History: Southern Women and the American Past,* Duke University Press (Durham, NC), 1994.
Tara Revisited: Women, War and the Plantation Legend, Abbeville (New York, NY), 1995.
Life in Civil War America, Eastern National Park and Monument Association (Conshohocken, PA), 1996.
(Editor, with Michele Gillespie) *The Devil's Lane: Sex and Race in the Early South,* Oxford University Press (New York, NY), 1997.
We the People (kindergarten through sixth grade textbook series), Houghton (Boston, MA), 1997.
(Editor, with Gillespie) *Taking off the White Gloves: Southern Women and Women Historians,* University of Missouri Press (Columbia, MO), 1998.
Civil War Stories, University of Georgia Press (Athens, GA), 1998.
(Editor) *I, Too, Sing America: Three Centuries of African American Poetry,* illustrations by Stephen Alcorn, Houghton (Boston, MA), 1998.
Public Women and the Confederacy, Marquette University Press (Milwaukee, WI), 1999.
The Scholastic Encyclopedia of the Civil War, Scholastic (New York, NY), 1999.
(Editor) *Southern Families at War: Loyalty and Conflict in the Civil War South,* Oxford University Press (New York, NY), 2000.
The Black Soldier: 1492 to the Present, Houghton (Boston, MA), 2000.
(With Christine Lunardini) *The Columbia Guide to American Women in the Nineteenth Century,* Columbia University Press (New York, NY), 2000.
Fanny Kemble's Civil Wars, Simon & Schuster (New York, NY), 2000.
(Editor and author of introduction) *Fanny Kemble's Journals,* Harvard University Press (Cambridge, MA), 2000.

Also associate editor of *American National Biography,* Oxford University Press.

WORK IN PROGRESS: (Coeditor) *Black Women's Autobiographies,* for Oxford University Press; (series editor) three volumes in the "Viewpoints on American Culture" series, *Native American Women, Race on Trial,* and *Votes for Women Revisited,* for Oxford University Press; a biography of Harriet Tubman.

SIDELIGHTS: Catherine Clinton once told *CA:* "I spend a lot of time and energy on women's history. The field is growing, and respect for this important aspect of our past is increasing as well. I travel in the South whenever possible to renew my acquaintance with the region I study. I try to be accessible in my writing, as well as my career as an educator. My interest in students as our future in the United States is enormous."

In the 1990s Clinton established herself as a specialist on the roles of American women in the nineteenth century, with emphasis on the South. Her work seeks to challenge stereotypes that have been perpetuated through fiction and racial prejudice, from that of the submissive female slave "Mammy" to that of the pampered, apolitical Southern "belle." In works such as *Tara Revisited: Women, War and the Plantation Legend,* Clinton has demonstrated that Southern women exerted an enormous responsibility in plantation management both before and during the Civil War, and that they sometimes resented their dependency on men. As for Southern women of color, Clinton has proven that they resisted slavery in the antebellum years and quietly supported Union efforts during the war. In her *New York Times Book Review* assessment of *Tara Revisited,* Joan E. Cashan concluded: "Ms. Clinton has written a subtle essay on some extremely complex questions about collective memory. The 'mammy,' the 'belle' and the 'Lost Cause' have all proved to have an enduring national appeal, and, as she observes, they cry out for investigation."

Clinton's interests lie far afield of the standard, male-authored Victorian histories of the Civil War, and her research has led her to the oral histories, diaries, letters, and other original documents women of that era have left behind. *Civil War Stories* presents essays based on these primary sources and was described by Edward McCormack in his *Library Journal* review as "enlightening . . . enjoyable, useful, and informative." In a *Pif Magazine* online review of Clinton's *The Other Civil War: American Women in the Nineteenth Century,* Abby Arnold commended the work as "a tremendous achievement, as relevant today, when women's history courses are a part of the college curriculum, as it was when it was first published in 1984 and women's studies barely existed." Arnold went on to characterize *The Other Civil War* as "lively and energetic, crammed with valuable, important and entertaining information, and an excellent place to begin to understand the events and assumptions that still shape the lives of American women today."

One nineteenth-century woman who left behind a wealth of written observation was Fanny Kemble. A British stage actress whose diaries and published writings reveal a strong abolitionist bent based upon her own observations as a Georgia plantation mistress, Kemble is the subject of Clinton's biography *Fanny Kemble's Civil Wars.* The biography traces Kemble from her days as a matinee idol, through her disappointing marriage, to her emergence as a writer who influenced Britain's political stand on the Civil War. *Fanny Kemble's Journals,* a volume of Kemble's writings edited by Clinton, was released simultaneously with the biography. In his *New York Times Book Review* essay on both works, David Walton wrote: "Read together, the biography and journals tell a remarkable story, the journals supplying color and atmosphere and Kemble's distinctive voice, the biography clarifying the domestic turmoil that shadowed each stage of their publication—the 'civil wars' of Clinton's title." A *Publishers Weekly* reviewer noted that the distinguished Kemble "has long awaited a biographer that can match her," and that Clinton "is Kemble's equal—this biography is every bit as sharp, evocative and eloquent as Kemble's *Journal.*"

BIOGRAPHICAL/CRITICAL SOURCES:

PERIODICALS

Booklist, September 15, 2000, Gilbert Taylor, review of *Fanny Kemble's Civil War,* p. 213, and Carolyn Phelan, review of *The Black Soldier: 1492 to Present,* p. 233.

Kirkus Reviews, June 15, 2000, review of *Fanny Kemble's Civil War,* pp. 852-853.

Library Journal, September 15, 1998, Edward McCormack, review of *Civil War Stories,* p. 92; July, 2000, Theresa McDevitt, review of *Southern Families at War: Loyalty and Conflict in the Civil War South,* p. 116; August, 2000, Randall M. Miller, review of *Fanny Kemble's Civil War,* p. 124.

New York Times Book Review, May 7, 1995, Joan E. Cashin, "The War between the Women," p. 37; September 10, 2000, David Walton, "Fearless Fanny."

Publishers Weekly, November 9, 1998, review of *I, Too, Sing America: Three Centuries of African American Poetry,* p. 74; July 10, 2000, review of *Fanny Kemble's Civil Wars,* p. 51.

School Library Journal, May, 2000, Peg Glisson, review of *The Scholastic Encyclopedia of the Civil War,* p. 85.

Washington Post, January 12, 1983.

OTHER

Pif Magazine,(September 2, 2000), Abby Arnold, review of *The Other Civil War: American Women in the Nineteenth Century.**

COCKS, Geoffrey (Campbell) 1948-

PERSONAL: Born November 13, 1948, in New Bedford, MA; son of James Fraser (a tax accountant) and Lillias Brown (a homemaker; maiden name, Campbell) Cocks; married Sarah Rogers (a legal secretary), August 28, 1971; children: Emily Anne. *Ethnicity:* "Caucasian." *Education:* Occidental College, A.B., 1970; University of California, Los Angeles, M.A., 1971, Ph.D., 1975. *Politics:* Social Democratic.

ADDRESSES: Home—1002 South Locust Lane, Albion, MI 49224. *Office*—Department of History, Albion College, 611 East Porter St., Albion, MI 49224. *E-mail*—gcocks@albion.edu.

CAREER: Occidental College, Los Angeles, CA, instructor in history, 1974-75; Albion College, Albion, MI, assistant professor, 1975-82, associate professor, 1983-87, professor of history, 1987—, Royal G. Hall Professor of History, 1994—. Visiting assistant professor of history at University of California, Los Angeles, 1980.

MEMBER: American Historical Association, Conference Group for Central European History, Group for the Use of Psychology in History.

AWARDS, HONORS: Fellowships from German Academic Exchange Service (DAAD), 1973-74 and 1985, National Endowment for the Humanities, 1980, 1988-89, Fulbright, 1988, IREX, 1988, and National Library of Medicine Publication Grant, 1991-92; *New York Times* Notable Book of the Year, 1985, for *Psychotherapy in the Third Reich.*

WRITINGS:

Psychotherapy in the Third Reich: The Göring Institute, Oxford University Press (New York, NY), 1985, 2nd edition, Transaction Publishers (New Brunswick, NJ), 1997.

(Editor with Travis L. Crosby) *Psycho/History: Readings in the Method of Psychology, Psychoanalysis, and History,* Yale University Press (New Haven, CT), 1987.

(Editor with Konrad H. Jarausch) *German Professions, 1800-1950,* Oxford University Press (New York, NY), 1990.

(Editor) *The Curve of Life: Correspondence of Heinz Kohut, 1923-1981,* Chicago University Press (Chicago, IL), 1994.

(Editor with Maufred Berg) *Medicine and Modernity: Public Health and Medical Care in Nineteenth-and Twentieth-Century Germany,* Cambridge University Press (New York, NY), 1996.

Treating Mind and Body: Essays in the History of Science, Professions, and Society under Extreme Conditions, Transaction Publications (New Brunswick, NJ), 1998.

Contributor to periodicals, including *American Historical Review, Journal of Modern History, Psychoanalytic Review, Isis, Psychohistory Review, American Imago, Central European History, Psyche, Journal of the History of Behavioral Sciences, Extrapolation, Political Psychology,* and *Social Science and Medicine.*

WORK IN PROGRESS: Sick Heil: A Social History of Illness in Nazi Germany; a novel, *The Institute,* based on *Psychotherapy in the Third Reich; The Wold at the Door: Stanley Kubrick and the Germans;* co-editor, *Kubrick: A Critical Assessment.*

SIDELIGHTS: Geoffrey Cocks examines how Nazi totalitarianism affected the practice of psychotherapy in Germany between 1933 and 1945 in *Psychotherapy in the Third Reich: The Goering Institute.* The author contends that German psychotherapy was allowed to organize professionally despite repressive Nazi sociopolitical doctrines. "Psychotherapy underwent a process of Aryanization, disguised its psychoanalytical character, and manifested a preparedness to respond obediently to the State's requirements," explained Sidney Bloch in a review for the *Times Literary Supplement.* "So long as psychotherapy could be demonstrated as useful to the Reich, and its practitioners were prepared to meet the Reich's requirements," the critic elaborated, "it could continue to operate, even in a quasi-psychoanalytical fashion." In his study Cocks also reveals how the German Institute for Psychological Research and Psychotherapy maintained a mutually convenient relationship with the Nazi regime and provided for a continuity of professional development into both postwar German successor states.

Reviewing *Psychotherapy in the Third Reich* for the *Los Angeles Times Book Review,* Harvey Mindess called it "objective and careful," a scholarly, detailed study "that will serve as a reference work for students of the period." *New York Times* critic John Gross commended Cocks's "solid research and sound judgment" as well, thankful that "a neglected chapter in the history of the Nazi era . . . has at last received the attention it deserves." Bloch deemed the book "a fascinating account of [an] unsavoury chapter in the history of psychotherapy" that alerts practitioners to "the ease with which they can relinquish their autonomy and become subordinate to social, political and ideological forces contrary to the interests of their patients."

Cocks told *CA:* "I have long been interested in the relationships between academia and political authority—how ideas, theories, and professional practices are realized in the 'real' world. This interest underlies my continuing research into the history of medical psychology in Germany. My interest in German history has been lifelong, since I was born when the world was still perceptibly quivering from the thankfully failed assertion of German power. I have expanded this interest to include the study of how Germans across the social spectrum dealt with illness as experienced and defined by themselves and by various agencies of the Nazi regime. More recently, I have been studying the surprising and subtle impact of the history of Nazi Germany and the Holocaust on the films of Stanley Kubrick."

BIOGRAPHICAL/CRITICAL SOURCES:

PERIODICALS

Los Angeles Times Book Review, January 13, 1985, Harvey Mindess, review of *Psychotherapy in the Third Reich.*

New York Times, July 3, 1984; January 18, 1985, John Gross, review of *Psychotherapy in the Third Reich.*

Times Literary Supplement, October 4, 1985, Sidney Bloch, review of *Psychotherapy in the Third Reich.*

* * *

COLE, Joanna 1944-
(Ann Cooke)

PERSONAL: Born August 11, 1944, in Newark, NJ; daughter of Mario and Elizabeth (Reid) Basilea; married Philip A. Cole (an artist and retired psychotherapist), October 8, 1965; children: Rachel Elizabeth. *Education:* Attended University of Massachusetts at Amherst and Indiana University—Bloomington; City College of New York (now of the City University of New York), B.A., 1967.

ADDRESSES: Office—c/o Scholastic, Inc., 555 Broadway, New York, NY 10012-3999.

CAREER: New York City Board of Education, New York, NY, elementary school librarian and instructor, 1967-68; *Newsweek,* New York, NY, letters correspondent, 1968-71; Scholastic, Inc., New York, NY, associate editor of See-Saw Book Club, 1971-73; Doubleday & Co., Garden City, NY, senior editor of books for young readers, 1973-80; full-time writer, 1980—.

MEMBER: Authors Guild, Authors League of America, Society of Children's Book Writers and Illustrators, American Association for the Advancement of Science.

AWARDS, HONORS: All of Cole's science books have been named Outstanding Science Trade Books for Children, National Science Teachers Association/Children's Book Council; Child Study Association of America's Children's Books of the Year, 1971, for *Cockroaches,* 1972, for *Giraffes at Home* and *Twins: The Story of Multiple Births,* 1973, for *My Puppy Is Born* and *Plants in Winter,* 1974, for *Dinosaur Story,* 1975, for *A Calf Is Born,* and 1985, for *Large as Life: Daytime Animals, Large as Life: Nighttime Animals,* and *The New Baby at Your House;* Children's Book Showcase selection, Children's Book Council, 1977, for *A Chick Hatches;* New York Academy of Sciences Children's Science honor book, 1981, and Children's Choice selection, International Reading Association Children's Book Council (IRA/CBC), 1982, both for *A Snake's Body;* Golden Kite Honor Book Award, Society of Children's Book Writers and Illustrators, and Notable Children's Book selection, Association for Library Service to Children, both 1984, both for *How You Were Born;* Irma Simonton Black Award for Excellence in Children's Literature, 1986, for *Doctor Change; Boston Globe-Horn Book* Honor Book for Nonfiction, 1987, for *The Magic School Bus at the Waterworks;* IRA/CBC Children's Choice award, 1990, for *The Magic School Bus inside the Earth;* Eva L. Gordon Award, American Nature Study Society, 1990, for body of science and nature writing; *Washington Post*/Children's Book Guild Award for Nonfiction, 1991, for body of work; David McCord Children's Literature Citation, Framingham (MA) State College and the Nobscot Council of the International Reading Association, 1994, for significant contribution to excellence in children's literature.

Recipient of state children's book awards, including Colorado Children's Choice Award and Washington State Children's Choice Award, both 1989, both for *The Magic School Bus at the Waterworks,* and the Garden State Award for nonfiction, 1992, for *The Magic School Bus inside the Human Body,* and 1993, for *The Magic School Bus Lost in the Solar System.* Many of Cole's books have received best or notable book citations from the American Library Association, *Horn Book,* and *School Library Journal.*

WRITINGS:

NONFICTION FOR CHILDREN

Cockroaches, illustrated by Jean Zallinger, Morrow, 1971.

(Under pseudonym Ann Cooke) *Giraffes at Home,* illustrated by Robert Quackenbush, Crowell, 1972.

(With Madeleine Edmondson) *Twins: The Story of Multiple Births,* illustrated by Salvatore Raciti, Morrow, 1972.

Plants in Winter, illustrated by Kazue Mizumura, Crowell, 1973.

Fleas, illustrated by Elsie Wrigley, Morrow, 1973.

Dinosaur Story, illustrated by Mort Kunstler, Morrow, 1974.

Saber-toothed Tiger and Other Ice-Age Mammals, illustrated by Lydia Rosier, Morrow, 1977.

Cars and How They Go, illustrated by Gail Gibbons, Crowell, 1983.

How You Were Born, Morrow, 1984, revised edition, photographs by Margaret Miller, 1994.

The New Baby at Your House, photographs by Hella Hammid, Morrow, 1985, revised edition with photographs by Miller, Morrow, 1998.

Cuts, Breaks, Bruises, and Burns: How Your Body Heals, illustrated by True Kelly, Crowell, 1985.

Large as Life: Daytime Animals, illustrated by Kenneth Lilly, Knopf, 1985.

Large as Life: Nighttime Animals, illustrated by Lilly, Knopf, 1985, published as *Large as Life Animals in Beautiful Life-Size Paintings,* 1990.

A Dog's Body, photographs by Jim and Ann Monteith, Morrow, 1985.

Hungry, Hungry Sharks: A Step Two Book, illustrated by Patricia Wynne, Random House, 1986.

The Human Body: How We Evolved, illustrated by Walter Gaffney-Kessell and Juan Carlos Barberis, Morrow, 1987.

Evolution, illustrated by Aliki, Crowell, 1987.

Asking about Sex and Growing Up: A Question-and-Answer Book for Boys & Girls, illustrated by Alan Tiegreen, Morrow, 1988.

A Gift from Saint Francis: The First Creche, illustrated by Michele Lemieux, Morrow, 1989.
Your New Potty, illustrated by Miller, Morrow, 1989.
Your Insides, illustrated by Paul Meisel, Putnam, 1992.
You Can't Smell a Flower with Your Ear!: All about Your Five Senses, illustrated by Mavis Smith, Putnam, 1994.
(With Stephanie Calmenson) *Crazy Eights and Other Card Games,* illustrated by Tiegreen, Morrow, 1994.
My New Kitten, photographs by Miller, Morrow, 1995.
Spider's Lunch: All about Garden Spiders, illustrated by Ron Broda, Grosset and Dunlap, 1995.
Riding Silver Star, photographs by Miller, Morrow, 1996.
(With Calmenson) *The Rain or Shine Activity Book: Fun Things to Make or Do,* illustrated by Tiegreen, Morrow, 1997.
(With Calmenson) *The Any Day Book,* Morrow, 1997.
(With Calmenson and Michael Street) *Marbles: 101 Ways to Play,* illustrated by Tiegreen, Morrow, 1998.
(With Calmenson and Street) *Fun on the Run: Travel Games and Songs,* illustrated by Tiegreen, Morrow, 1999.
Potty Book about a Boy, Morrow, 1999.
My Big Girl Potty, Morrow, illustrated by Maxie Chambliss, 2000.
My Big Boy Potty, Morrow, illustrated by Chambliss, 2000.
Card Games, Morrow, 2000.
Hopscotch and Sidewalk Game, Morrow, 2000.
When You Were inside Mommy, illustrated by Chambliss, HarperCollins, 2001.

NONFICTION FOR CHILDREN; PHOTOGRAPHS BY JEROME WEXLER

My Puppy Is Born, Morrow, 1973, revised edition, photographs by Miller, 1991.
A Calf Is Born, Morrow, 1975.
A Chick Hatches, Morrow, 1976.
A Fish Hatches, Morrow, 1978.
(With Wexler) *Find the Hidden Insect,* Morrow, 1979.
A Frog's Body, Morrow, 1980.
A Horse's Body, Morrow, 1981.
A Snake's Body, Morrow, 1981.
A Cat's Body, Morrow, 1982.
A Bird's Body, Morrow, 1982.
An Insect's Body, photographs by Wexler and Raymond A. Mendez, Morrow, 1984.

"MAGIC SCHOOL BUS" NONFICTION SERIES; ILLUSTRATED BY BRUCE DEGEN

The Magic School Bus at the Waterworks, Scholastic, 1986, special edition, Scholastic/New York City Department of Environmental Protection, 1990.
The Magic School Bus inside the Earth, Scholastic, 1987.
The Magic School Bus inside the Human Body, Scholastic, 1989.
The Magic School Bus Lost in the Solar System, Scholastic, 1990.
The Magic School Bus on the Ocean Floor, Scholastic, 1992.
The Magic School Bus in the Time of the Dinosaurs, Scholastic, 1994.
The Magic School Bus inside a Hurricane, Scholastic, 1995.
The Magic School Bus Gets Baked in a Cake, Scholastic, 1995.
The Magic School Bus Plants Seeds, Scholastic, 1995.
The Magic School Bus Briefcase, Scholastic, 1995.
The Magic School Bus Meets the Rot Squad, Scholastic, 1995.
The Magic School Bus Hello out There, Scholastic, 1995.
The Magic School Bus in the Haunted Museum, Scholastic, 1995.
The Magic School Bus Hops Home, Scholastic, 1995.
The Magic School Bus Gets All Dried Up, Scholastic, 1996.
The Magic School Bus Wet All Over, Scholastic, 1996.
The Magic School Bus inside a Beehive, Scholastic, 1996.
The Magic School Bus out of This World, Scholastic, 1996.
The Magic School Bus Gets Eaten, Scholastic, 1996.
The Magic School Bus Blows Its Top, Scholastic, 1996.
The Magic School Bus Ups and Downs, Scholastic, 1997.
The Magic School Bus and the Electric Field Trip, Scholastic, 1997.
The Magic School Bus Goes Upstream, Scholastic, 1997.
The Magic School Bus Gets Planted, Scholastic, 1997.
The Magic School Bus Shows and Tells: A Book about Archaeology, Scholastic, 1997.
The Magic School Bus in a Pickle, Scholastic, 1997.
The Magic School Bus Plays Ball, Scholastic, 1998.
The Magic School Bus in the Arctic, Scholastic, 1998.
The Magic School Bus in the Rain Forest, Scholastic, 1998.
The Magic School Bus Explores the Senses, Scholastic, 1999.
The Magic School Bus Sees Stars, Scholastic, 1999.
The Magic School Bus Answers Questions, Scholastic, 1999.
The Magic School Bus Taking Flight, Scholastic, 1999.
The Magic School Bus Going Batty, Scholastic, 1999.

The Magic School Bus Gets Ants in Its Pants, Scholastic, 1999.

Ms. Frizzle's Adventures in Egypt, Scholastic, 2000.

FICTION FOR CHILDREN

Cousin Matilda and the Foolish Wolf, A. Whitman, 1970.

The Secret Box, Morrow, 1971.

Fun on Wheels, illustrated by Whitney Darrow, Morrow, 1976.

The Clown-Arounds, illustrated by Jerry Smath, Parents Magazine Press, 1981.

The Clown-Arounds Have a Party, illustrated by Smath, Parents Magazine Press, 1982.

Golly Gump Swallowed a Fly, illustrated by Bari Weissman, Parents Magazine Press, 1982.

Get Well, Clown-Arounds!, illustrated by Smath, Parents Magazine Press, 1982.

The Clown-Arounds Go on Vacation, illustrated by Smath, Parents Magazine Press, 1983.

Aren't You Forgetting Something, Fiona?, illustrated by Ned Delaney, Parents Magazine Press, 1983.

Bony-Legs, illustrated by Dirk Zimmer, Four Winds, 1983.

Sweet Dreams, Clown-Arounds, illustrated by Smath, Parents Magazine Press, 1985.

Monster Manners, illustrated by Jared Lee, Scholastic, 1986.

This Is the Place for Me, illustrated by William Van Horn, Scholastic, 1986.

Doctor Change, illustrated by Donald Carrick, Morrow, 1986.

Monster Movie, illustrated by Lee, Scholastic, 1987.

Norma Jean, Jumping Bean, illustrated by Lynn Munsinger, Random House, 1987.

Mixed-Up Magic, illustrated by Kelly, Scholastic, 1987.

(With husband, Philip Cole) *Hank and Frank Fix up the House,* illustrated by Van Horn, Scholastic, 1988.

Animal Sleepyheads: One to Ten, illustrated by Jeni Bassett, Scholastic, 1988.

The Missing Tooth, illustrated by Marilyn Hafner, Random House, 1988.

(With P. Cole) *Big Goof and Little Goof,* illustrated by M. K. Brown, Scholastic, 1989.

Who Put the Pepper in the Pot?, illustrated by R. W. Alley, Parents Magazine Press, 1989.

It's Too Noisy!, illustrated by Kate Duke, Crowell, 1989.

Buster Cat Goes Out, illustrated by Rose Mary Berlin, Western Publishing, 1989.

Bully Trouble: A Step Two Book, illustrated by Hafner, Random House, 1989.

Monster Valentines, illustrated by Lee, Scholastic, 1990.

Don't Call Me Names!, illustrated by Munsinger, Random House, 1990.

Don't Tell the Whole World!, illustrated by Duke, Crowell, 1990.

How I Was Adopted: Samantha's Story, illustrated by Chambliss, Morrow, 1995.

(With Stephanie Calmenson) *The Gator Girls,* illustrated by Munsinger, Morrow, 1995.

Monster and Muffin, illustrated by Karen Lee Schmidt, Grosset and Dunlap, 1996.

(With Calmenson) *Rockin' Reptiles,* illustrated by Munsinger, Morrow, 1997.

(With Calmenson) *Bug in a Rug: Reading Fun for Just Beginners,* illustrated by Alan Tiegreen, Morrow, 1996.

I'm a Big Brother, illustrated by Chambliss, Morrow, 1997.

I'm a Big Sister, illustrated by Chambliss, Morrow, 1997.

(With Calmenson) *Get Well, Gators!,* illustrated by Munsinger, Morrow, 1998.

Liz Sorts It Out, Scholastic, 1998.

Liz Looks for a New Home, Scholastic, 1998.

(With Calmenson) *Gator Halloween,* Morrow, 1999.

Jump Rope Rhymes, Morrow, 2000.

Street Rhymes, Morrow, 2000.

When Mommy and Daddy Go to Work, illustrated by Chambliss, HarperCollins, 2001.

EDITOR OF CHILDREN'S ANTHOLOGIES

(And author of introduction) *Best-loved Folktales of the World,* illustrated by Jill K. Schwarz, Doubleday, 1982.

A New Treasury of Children's Poetry: Old Favorites and New Discoveries, illustrated by Judith Gwyn Brown, Doubleday, 1983.

(With Calmenson) *The Laugh Book,* illustrated by Hafner, Doubleday, 1986.

(With Calmenson) *The Read-aloud Treasury: Favorite Nursery Rhymes, Poems, Stories & More for the Very Young,* illustrated by Ann Schweninger, Doubleday, 1988.

Anna Banana: 101 Jump Rope Rhymes, illustrated by Tiegreen, Morrow, 1989.

(With Calmenson) *Miss Mary Mack: And Other Children's Street Rhymes,* illustrated by Tiegreen, Morrow, 1990.

(With Calmenson) *Ready . . . Set . . . Read! The Beginning Reader Treasury,* illustrated by Anne Burgess, Doubleday, 1990.

(With Calmenson) *The Scary Book,* illustrated by Chris Demarest, Morrow, 1991.

(With Calmenson) *The Eentsy, Weentsy Spider: Fingerplays and Action Rhymes,* illustrated by Tiegreen, Morrow, 1991.

(With Calmenson) *Pat-a-Cake and Other Play Rhymes,* illustrated by Tiegreen, Morrow, 1992.

(With Calmenson) *Pin the Tail on the Donkey and Other Party Games,* illustrated by Tiegreen, Morrow, 1993.

(With Calmenson) *Six Sick Sheep: One Hundred Tongue Twisters,* illustrated by Tiegreen, Morrow, 1993.

(With Calmenson) *Give a Dog a Bone: Stories, Poems, Jokes, and Riddles about Dogs,* illustrated by John Speirs, Scholastic, 1994.

(With Calmenson) *Why Did the Chicken Cross the Road?: And Other Riddles Old and New,* illustrated by Tiegreen, Morrow, 1994.

(With Calmenson) *A Pocketful of Laughs: Stories, Poems, Jokes, and Riddles,* illustrated by Hafner, Doubleday, 1995.

(With Calmenson) *Ready, Set, Read—and Laugh!: A Funny Treasury for Beginning Readers,* Doubleday, 1995.

(With Calmenson) *Yours Till Banana Splits: 201 Autograph Rhymes,* illustrated by Tiegreen, Morrow, 1995.

OTHER

The Parents' Book of Toilet Teaching, Ballantine, Morrow, 1983.

(With Calmenson) *Safe from the Start: Your Child's Safety from Birth to Age Five,* Facts on File, 1990.

(With Wendy Saul) *On the Bus with Joanna Cole: A Creative Autobiography,* Heinemann, 1996.

Also contributor of articles to *Parents.*

ADAPTATIONS: An animated series for PBS-TV based on the "Magic School Bus" books began in 1994 and features the voices of Lily Tomlin as Ms. Frizzle, Robby Benson, Carol Channing, and Malcolm-Jamal Warner; the series is also available in a CD-ROM version by Microsoft Home and Scholastic, Inc. The "Magic School Bus" series was used as the basis of the American Library Association's 1994 reading program, "Reading Is a Magic Trip." Cassette recordings have been made of *Bony-Legs,* Random House, 1985, and *Monster Movie* and *Dinosaur Story,* both Scholastic, 1989.

SIDELIGHTS: Joanna Cole is the author of over one hundred children's books on subjects as varied as any young reader's interests. Cole's fertile imagination has produced first readers with jokes and puzzles, humorous tales of the Clown-Around family, retellings of folk tales and myths, and books about science that dazzle, inspire, and inform. The winner of numerous awards from the American Library Association, the National Science Teachers Association/Children's Book Council, and various state reading associations, Cole follows her own widespread interests to write about the life cycle of an insect, to field questions on sex, to talk about potty training, or to take a trip to the stars in a Magic School Bus. Cole has introduced the fascinating world of science to young readers in her stand-alone titles and in several series, including the hugely popular "Magic School Bus" books, the latter of which has spawned a television spin-off. A thorough researcher, the author has been praised by critics for her scientific accuracy, but her books are most effective because of her humor and frank and easily understood explanations that bring complicated, technical subjects within reach of younger audiences.

Cole first discovered the pleasures of writing when she was in grade school. "I discovered in the fifth grade what I liked to do; write reports and stories, make them interesting and/or funny and draw pictures to go along with the words," she once commented. "Except for the pictures, I still do that. I remember grade school very clearly when I sat at my desk, happily interested in whatever subject I was writing about. Science was my favorite. Our teacher, Miss Bair, would assign us to read a science trade book every week. And each week, she would choose one student to do an experiment and report on it to the class. I would have done an experiment every week if she had let me. Grade school was very important to me, much more influential than my later education. Maybe that's why as an adult I ended up writing books for children."

After receiving her bachelor's degree from the City College of New York, Cole pursued her interest in books by working variously as a librarian, teacher, and editor. It was during her first job at an elementary school that she was inspired by an article about cockroaches in the *Wall Street Journal.* Realizing that this was a subject she had never read about in school, Cole decided to write about it herself. The first publisher she submitted her manuscript to rejected the idea, but the author had more luck when she sent her book to the publishing house of William Morrow, where editor Connie C. Epstein helped Cole hone her skills in science writing. Since the time of that debut book, Cole has written both nonfiction and fiction books for younger readers, and in 1980, after a decade of editing children's books, she went full time as a writer.

Many of Cole's nonfiction works focus on the life sciences. In her series, "Animal Bodies," Cole introduces young readers to the anatomy of such animals as horses, frogs, dogs, birds, cats, and snakes. Reviewing *An Insect's Body* in *Horn Book,* Sarah S. Gagne commented, "If it is possible for Joanna Cole to improve on the unparalleled series of books about animal bodies that she has written over the years, she has now done so." Using the cricket as a representative insect, Cole examined its body structure and how this corresponds to its environment. *Booklist*'s Ilene Cooper, reviewing the same title, remarked, "Anyone whose curiosity is intact cannot help but be captivated by this fascinating work." This series concludes with *The Human Body: How We Evolved,* which explains how archaeologists have pieced together the evolutionary history of mankind and how human anatomy compares to that of apes, chimpanzees, gorillas, and others of our primate cousins. Cooper called this volume a "fine introduction to evolution that will go a long way toward answering children's questions about their origins," while Jason R. Taylor, writing in *Science Books and Films,* felt that it was "an excellent, extremely well-researched book."

In her science writing, Cole has always been aware of how children's feelings affect their reactions to factual material. In her series on animals' births, which includes *A Calf Is Born, My Puppy Is Born, How You Were Born,* and *My New Kitten,* the author explains the physiology of birth with candor and accuracy, and is careful to include the gentle care baby mammals need to grow, which mirrors children's own experience. Reviewing a revised edition of *How You Were Born,* Denise L. Moll noted in *School Library Journal* that "Cole relates the process of conception and birth in a personalized manner," and that while several other titles on the same subject are available, "Cole's book continues to set the standard." That standard was upheld in *My New Kitten,* a book that "promotes warm, fuzzy feelings and at the same time gives youngsters just a peek at the creatures' developmental stages," according to Margaret Chatham writing in *School Library Journal.*

Similarly, a number of Cole's books focus on child development. These titles—*The New Baby at Your House, Your New Potty, Asking about Sex and Growing Up, I'm a Big Brother, I'm a Big Sister,* and *How I Was Adopted: Samantha's Story*—help families share facts and feelings about key issues in children's lives. The first title deals with all topics involving the arrival of a new infant, including sibling rivalry. Martha Topol of *School Library Journal* felt that *The New Baby at Your House* "gives honest, practical advice on helping youngsters prepare for and cope with a new arrival." Such advice is furthered in the companion volumes *I'm a Big Brother* and *I'm a Big Sister.* Dina Sherman, reviewing the books in *School Library Journal,* felt, "Familiar situations, as well as positive reinforcement of individuality and importance as part of the family, are good reasons to put this book into the hands of children who will soon be older siblings." Cole employs a question and answer format for her 1988 title on sex education for pre-teens, *Asking about Sex and Growing Up,* an "invaluable" book, according to a writer for *Kirkus Reviews,* and one that is "brief and to the point," as *Booklist*'s Denise M. Wilms pointed out, with "lots of information at a level younger children will appreciate." Adoption gets the Cole treatment in *How I Was Adopted: Samantha's Story,* about a young girl who tells her own story. A contributor for *Publishers Weekly* felt that this book presented a "cheerful, informative approach" to the subject. Stephanie Zvirin, writing in *Booklist,* noted, "Cole expertly negotiates a middle course that provides children with some excellent, age-appropriate background on adoption."

Of all her science books, however, it is her popular "Magic School Bus" series for which Cole is best known. All the books in the series combine science and imaginative fun into stories that have been warmly received by critics and readers alike. As a writer for *Children's Books and Their Creators* put it, "In recent years [Cole] has given the term nonfiction new meaning with the 'Magic School Bus' series. A masterly combination of scientific facts, humor, and fantasy, these books turn science class into story hour." Each book takes a class of school children led by their eccentric teacher, Ms. Frizzle, on some new adventure of discovery. The humorous illustrations by Bruce Degen and the unlimited possibilities for travel in a bus that can dig through the earth, shrink to microscopic size, or blast off into space result in lively reading. Each page is a combination of fact-and fun-filled text blending with and sometimes competing for room with Degen's artwork. "Just as 'Sesame Street' revolutionized the teaching of letters and numbers by making it so entertaining that children had no idea they were actually learning something, so the 'Magic School Bus' books make science so much fun that the information is almost incidental," wrote Katherine Bouton in the *New York Times Book Review.* Bouton declared that these books offer "the freshest, most amusing approach to science for children that I've seen." Andrea Cleghorn, writing in *Publishers Weekly,* commented, "'The Magic School Bus' books serve science with a sizzle," and further noted that specialists in the field check all the books in the series for accuracy.

Cole based the character of the teacher, Ms. Frizzle, on her own favorite science teacher, Miss Bair, although, the author once commented, "Miss Bair did not dress at all like Ms. Frizzle!" The kids in the "Magic School Bus" books may grumble a bit about the adventures they experience, but in their hearts they love Ms. Frizzle and are proud to be in her class. "In 'The Magic School Bus' books I use the same criteria as I do in all my science books," Cole explained. "I write about ideas, rather than just facts. I try to ask an implicit question—such as, How do our bodies get energy from the food we eat? or How do scientists guess what dinosaurs were like? Then I try to answer the question in writing the book." The success of Cole's "Magic School Bus" books, which have sold in the millions worldwide, has carried over to television, where PBS has turned them into an animated series; Cole and illustrator Degen serve as consultants.

Adventures on the school bus take the students and Ms. Frizzle, as well as Mr. Wilde, the assistant principle, inside the human body, down to the waterworks, inside a dog's nose or beehive or hurricane, and back in time to the world of the dinosaurs or through space to the stars. "Climb aboard," John Peters encouraged readers in a *School Library Journal* review of *The Magic School Bus in the Time of the Dinosaurs,* "there's never a dull moment with 'the Friz' at the wheel!" Reviewing the 1999 addition to the series, *The Magic School Bus Explores the Senses,* Christine A. Moesch remarked in *School Library Journal* that it was "another fun, fact-filled adventure in the series." Commenting on *The Magic School Bus and the Electric Field Trip,* Blair Christolon noted in *School Library Journal* that the book "makes a complex subject fun to read about and simple to understand." The same could be said for all the titles in the series, books that mix a sense of humor with lucid explanations of scientific facts.

Although Cole is more often recognized for her science books, she is also the author of a number of stories for children, has compiled anthologies of children's literature, and has written books for adults on parenting and child development. Early in her career Cole wrote a series of amusing easy-readers featuring the Clown-Arounds, a silly family who sleep in shoes and generally approach life from a goofy angle. Popular retellings of folk tales from Cole include *Bony-Legs,* "a bang-up read," according to Nancy Palmer writing in *School Library Journal,* and *Don't Tell the Whole World!,* an example of "fine storytelling," as a *Publishers Weekly* contributor noted.

Working with Stephanie Calmenson, Cole has produced both nonfiction anthologies as well as popular fiction titles, including "The Gator Girls" series. Together the two have dealt with riddles, card games, rhymes, and brainteasers. In their 1995 *Ready, Set, Read—and Laugh: A Funny Treasury for Beginning Readers,* Cole and Calmenson have compiled a combination of stories, poems, jokes, and games that, according to *Booklist*'s Hazel Rochman, "will turn readers on to the fun of books." Rochman concluded, "Kids will delight in the word play and the nonsense, and they'll want to read more." Other popular titles include *Give a Dog a Bone, The Rain or Shine Activity Book, Marbles: One Hundred One Ways to Play,* and *Bug in a Rug.* With their "Gator Girls" series, they present best reptilian friends Allie and Amy Gator in adventures from going to summer camp to getting over an illness. In the debut volume, *The Gator Girls,* the two girls want to cram all their summertime activities into the few days they have before going off to camp. *Booklist*'s Mary Harris Veeder thought that in this beginning chapter book "the joys of true-blue friendship are humorously realized." *Get Well, Gators!* sees the duo fighting swamp fever in time to take part in a local street fair. "Give this one to chapter-book readers looking for a funny book," advised Kay Weisman in a *Booklist* review. And in *Gator Halloween,* the girls "are up to their old tricks," according to Stephanie Zvirin in *Booklist,* determined to win the best costume prize in the local Halloween parade. Zvirin called the book "fun, with a dash of over-the-top comedy and wonderful illustrations."

Whether sharing the antics of Ms. Frizzle and her dauntless crew in search of scientific knowledge, or having fun with rhymes and jokes, or making everyday developmental activities into a meaningful experience, Cole has proven that she has what it takes to hook a young reader and bring him or her back for more. "Always keeping mind the emotional level of her audience, Joanna Cole presents her information in a reassuring, caring tone, with great respect for children," concluded the critic for *Children's Books and Their Creators.* For Cole, being able to write for children is the fulfillment of a childhood dream; for her legions of contented readers it is a windfall.

BIOGRAPHICAL/CRITICAL SOURCES:

BOOKS

Authors of Books for Young People, 3rd edition, Scarecrow Press, 1990.

Children's Books and Their Creators, edited by Anita Silvey, Houghton Mifflin, 1995.

Children's Literature Review, Volume 5, 1983, Volume 40, Gale (Detroit, MI), 1996.

PERIODICALS

Appraisal: Science Books for Young People, spring, 1973; spring, 1975; spring, 1978; winter, 1980; winter, 1981; winter, 1982.

Booklist, June 15, 1984, Ilene Cooper, review of *An Insect's Body,* p. 1482; September 1, 1987, I. Cooper, review of *The Human Body,* p. 61; June 15, 1988, Denise M. Wilms, review of *Asking about Sex and Growing Up,* pp. 1733-34; April 15, 1995, Mary Harris Veeder, review of *The Gator Girls,* p. 1497; August, 1995, Stephanie Zvirin, review of *How I Was Adopted,* p. 1955; October 1, 1995, Hazel Rochman, review of *Ready, Set, Read—and Laugh!,* p. 329; October 15, 1997, p. 408; March 1, 1998, p. 1138; November 15, 1998, Kay Weisman, review of *Get Well, Gators!,* p. 590; September 1, 1999, S. Zvirin, review of *Gator Halloween,* p. 145; November 1, 1999, p. 534; January 1, 2000, p. 928; February 1, 2001, Kathy Broderick, reviews of *My Big Boy Potty* and *My Big Girl Potty,* p. 1055.

Bulletin of the Center for Children's Books, July-August, 1986; November, 1986; February, 1987; January, 1988; March, 1988; June, 1988; December, 1992, p. 108; October, 1994, p. 40; October, 1996, p. 52; June, 1995, p. 340.

Horn Book, October, 1980; February, 1982; October, 1984, Sarah S. Gagne, review of *An Insect's Body,* p. 627; May-June, 1986, p. 347; September-October, 1986, p. 609; May-June, 1995, p. 348; January-February, 1998, p. 90; July-August, 1999, p. 480.

Kirkus Reviews, March 1, 1988, review of *Asking about Sex and Growing Up,* p. 361.

Los Angeles Times Book Review, March 22, 1987; February 28, 1988; July 30, 1989; December 17, 1989; September 30, 1990.

New York Times, April 23, 1999, p. E39.

New York Times Book Review, February 7, 1988, Katherine Bouton, p. 28.

Publishers Weekly, October 12, 1990, review of *Don't Tell the Whole World!,* p. 63; January 25, 1991, Andrea Cleghorn, "Aboard the Magic School Bus," pp. 27-28; April 18, 1994, p. 27; July 4, 1994, p. 63; October 2, 1995, review of *How I Was Adopted,* p. 74; August 23, 1999, p. 61.

School Library Journal, December, 1971; February, 1973; January, 1980; May, 1982; December, 1983, Nancy Palmer, review of *Bony-Legs,* p. 79; March, 1987, pp. 113-115; November, 1992, p. 38; December, 1992, p. 95; April, 1993, Denise L. Moll, review of *How You Were Born,* p. 110; September, 1994, John Peters, review of *The Magic School Bus in the Time of the Dinosaurs,* pp. 206, 226; April, 1995, Margaret Chatham, review of *My New Kitten,* p. 123; March, 1996, p. 1881; October, 1996, p. 111; April, 1997, Dina Sherman, review of *I'm a Big Brother* and *I'm a Big Sister,* pp. 96-97; November, 1997, Blair Christolon, review of *The Magic School Bus and the Electric Field Trip,* p. 106; April, 1998, Martha Topol, review of *The New Baby at Your House,* p. 114; May, 1998, p. 130; February, 1999, Christine A. Moesch, review of *The Magic School Bus Explores the Senses,* p. 96; October, 1999, p. 166; November, 2000, Jane Marino, review of *My Big Boy Potty,* p. 112.

Science Books and Films, January-February, 1988, Jason R. Taylor, review of *The Human Body,* pp. 174-75.

OTHER

Riding the Magic School Bus with Joanna Cole and Bruce Degen (videotape), Scholastic, 1993.*

* * *

COLLINS, Jackie 1941-

PERSONAL: Born 1941, in England; daughter of Joseph (a theatrical agent) and Elsa (a dancer); married Wallace Austin, 1959 (divorced, 1963); married Oscar Lerman, 1966 (died, 1992); children: Tracy (first marriage), Tiffany, Rory.

ADDRESSES: *Home*—Los Angeles, CA. *Agent*—Morton Janklow, Janklow & Nesbit, 445 Park Ave., New York, NY 10022.

CAREER: Novelist and screen actress. Producer of television mini-series and specials for CBS-TV, including *Hollywood Kids* and *Sexual Secrets of Men,* 1995—.

WRITINGS:

NOVELS

The World Is Full of Married Men, World Publishing (New York City), 1968.

The Stud, W. H. Allen (London), 1969, World Publishing, 1970.

Jackie Collins

Sunday Simmons and Charlie Brick, W. H. Allen, 1971, published as *The Hollywood Zoo,* Pinnacle Books (New York City), 1975.
Lovehead, W. H. Allen, 1974, published as *The Love Killers,* Warner Books (New York City), 1975.
The World Is Full of Divorced Women, W. H. Allen, 1975.
Lovers and Gamblers, W. H. Allen, 1977, Grosset (New York City), 1978.
The Bitch, Pan Books (London), 1979.
Chances, Warner Books, 1981.
Hollywood Wives, Simon & Schuster (New York City), 1983.
Sinners, Pan Books, 1984.
Lucky, Simon & Schuster, 1985.
Hollywood Husbands, Simon & Schuster, 1986.
Rock Star, Simon & Schuster, 1988.
Lady Boss, Simon & Schuster, 1990.
American Star: A Love Story, Simon & Schuster, 1993.
Hollywood Kids, Simon & Schuster, 1994.
Vendetta: Lucky's Revenge, HarperCollins (New York City), 1996.
Thrill!, Simon & Schuster, 1997.
Dangerous Kiss, Simon & Schuster, 1999.
Lethal Seduction, Simon & Schuster, 2000.

ADAPTATIONS: The World is Full of Married Men was released as a feature film. *Chances, Lucky, Hollywood Wives,* and *Hollywood Kids* were produced as television mini-series. *Lady Boss* was produced as a television feature, 1992.

SIDELIGHTS: Novelist Jackie Collins has crafted more than a dozen international best-sellers loosely based upon her own experiences and discoveries as a Hollywood insider. The sister of diva Joan Collins—and an actress and producer in her own right—Collins has been uniquely positioned to observe the lives of the wealthy and famous, and then to fictionalize them in sensational stories that combine steamy sex, intrigue, romance, and revenge. "One does not . . . pick up a novel by Jackie Collins expecting something even approaching what is loosely defined as literature," wrote Joy Fielding in the Toronto *Globe & Mail.* Instead, she noted, readers turn to Collins for "sex-drenched, best-selling sleaze." Collins's novels regularly feature rich, ambitious people in competition for money and power. "Some of them get involved with drugs and sex and crime (the bad people)," declared *Washington Post* contributor Bruce Van Wyngarder. "Some of them get involved with drugs and sex and love (the good people)." In *Booklist,* Ilene Cooper gave Collins credit for knowing her audience's tastes "and feeding . . . them with no pretense that what she's serving is anything but candy."

Although some reviewers have dismissed Collins's novels as tasteless and excessive, others, such as Leola Floren in the *Detroit News,* have defended the books for their occasional valuable insights. Floren's review of *Hollywood Wives* stated: "It would be easy to self-righteously label this book trashy and worthless—but it's not entirely either. Jackie Collins has a talent for titillation and a knack for wooing the most reluctant of readers into a plot that spends 15 percent of the time peeking at people in the sack and the other 85 percent daydreaming about it." Collins is able to woo her readers, according to Eve Babitz in *Los Angeles Magazine,* because of the special quality that her novels possess. "It's the *clef*—the sense that her characters and even their most outrageous erotic adventures come from an insider's knowledge of real life in the jet set—that makes her novels so seductive." Floren found a deeper level in Collins's novels. "Deliberately or not," maintained the reviewer, "[Collins] speaks eloquently of emptiness through the lives of people who would seem to have *everything:* French poodles, Mexican maids, American Express." *Los Angeles Times* contributor Judy Bass believed that Collins's novels are among the most enjoyable of their genre. She concluded: "Jackie Collins caricatures the life styles of the rich and famous with devastating accuracy. She spoofs every nuance of their attire, speech and relationships, never allowing tedium or predictability to dilute the reader's fun."

Born in London in 1941, Collins was encouraged to enter show business by her father, a theatrical agent. Blessed with beauty and talent, both she and her sister, Joan, soon found their way to Los Angeles. While Joan Collins made her name in films and television dramas, Jackie became a listener who drew celebrities out about their secrets and then turned them into fiction. In an online interview with *CNN Interactive,* Collins said: "I'm very accepted [in Hollywood], and people like telling me the stories. I guess that it's fun for me. Because I'll be sitting at a dinner party, I'll have a producer on one side, and a famous director on the other, and they will be telling me all the stories from the set, the real stories." Incredibly, Collins has said that the "real stories" are often more steamy and bizarre than her plots.

In her 1988 novel, *Rock Star,* Collins turns her insider's eye from its usual quarry, the movie industry, to its cousin—the music business. Both her Hollywood novels and *Rock Star,* Terrence Rafferty suggested in the *New Yorker,* "are straight forward success-and-failure stories with naughty bits thrown in." Through the lives, sex lives, and rocky careers of Kris Phoenix, a British singer and guitarist, Bobby Mondella, an African-American soul man, and Rafealla, a blues songstress of mixed heritage, Collins reveals the world of contemporary music as seamy and steamy. It is true, observed Victoria Balfour in the *New York Times Book Review,* that "like Ms. Collins's other novels . . . 'Rock Star' is stuffed with sex scandals, drugs, mobsters and stretch limos." But, in Balfour's opinion, "She is clearly not as comfortable or as confident exposing the music business as when she is taking on the movie industry."

American Star: A Love Story is another rags-to-celebrity story. This time, Collins follows three young people from the same small town in Kansas as they struggle to make their way in show business. Nick Angelo seeks fame as an actor. His half sister, Cyndra, hopes to make it in Las Vegas as a singer. One of Nick's high school flames, Lauren, is drawn to New York and the world of modeling. "*American Star* is classic Collins," noted Richard Rouilard in *Los Angeles Times Book Review,* "chock full of all the expected plot twists, fabulous clichés about stardom and Hollywood, and enough unprotected sex, sex, sex to make the caveat [at the beginning of the novel urging readers to practice safe sex] seem like a promotional gimmick." John Sutherland conceded in his *London Review of Books* piece that Collins has an insider's knowledge of these worlds of celebrity, but he credited her with scant insight into her characters' modest origins. "She is profoundly vague about the details of growing up a young man in small-town America. The best she can manage is a kind of low-budget film-set illusionism." However, as Rouilard suggested, readers of Collins are not looking for Americana. "A good Jackie Collins novel is like a thoughtfully prepared bowl of vanilla pudding—tasty and comfortingly predictable," he stated. "And this is a good Collins novel. All the flashier ingredients of the Jackie recipe are not included."

After *Hollywood Wives* and *Hollywood Husbands,* it was inevitable that Jackie would pen *Hollywood Kids.* Having probed the lives of self-centered parents who have too much, Collins found stories just as rich among their children, who have "too much, too soon"—money, cars, and access to the best restaurants and parties. As Eve Babitz explained in *Los Angeles Magazine,* "The book braids three strands: AIDS in the background like the Plague; the impulse to be sexy and fabulous; and the practical plodding of life, where days have to be filled somehow, if not by work then trouble." Collins's Hollywood kids include Jordanna, the daughter of a producer, and her four friends, sons and daughters of movie stars and television executives. Each is wrapped up in some kind of mischief and lurking in the wings is a killer bent on eliminating the young witnesses who testified against him in a murder trial. "Plot, though suspenseful, offers few surprises" wrote a contributor to *Kirkus Reviews.* "Still, it's a Porscheload of fun."

Some critics cannot resist reviewing Collins with tongue in cheek. Joe Queenan, writing in the *New York Times Book Review,* offered a humorous assessment of *Hollywood Kids:* "Readers impervious to nuance will be tempted to dismiss *Hollywood Kids* as just another trashy novel about a serial killer," he began, ". . . . But if we can look beyond Ms. Collins's glitzy, gory, grubby scaffolding, we can see that the real subject of *Hollywood Kids* is the death of the American family." Queenan concluded: "In its own perverse way, *Hollywood Kids* is an admirable, ambitious dissection of the horrible times we live in." Not to be outdone, Michiko Kakutani disguised herself as film character Austin Powers when she reviewed Collins's *Dangerous Kiss* in the *New York Times.* "First up, baby, let me tell you why I dig Jackie Collins's Hollywood," she quipped. ". . . . To me, Jackie's Hollywood is the '60s with money. . . . My bag exactly! And the babes are all so groovy: they've all got big hair and tiny frocks, and they all shag like minxes."

Collins has created a number of recurring characters for her novels, the best known of them the beautiful and powerful Lucky Santangelo who has appeared in *Lucky, Chances, Lady Boss, Vendetta: Lucky's Revenge,* and

Dangerous Kiss. A film studio owner with more than her share of moxie, Lucky has survived mob violence and multiple marriages and skillfully wreaks vengeance on those who would harm her or her loved ones. The "Lucky" novels typically feature "a Hollywood setting; a rich, gorgeous heroine; a generous sprinkling of movie stars, studio bosses, tycoons, socialites, scheming relatives and hangers-on; and a sex scene (or two) per chapter," to quote Jill Gerston in the *New York Times Book Review. Booklist* correspondent Catherine Sias called Lucky "a calm, cool center for the whirlwind of recklessness, murder, and deceit that surrounds her." Collins has said that she was inspired to create Lucky—as well as her other assertive heroines—by the lack of such female characters in the books she read as a child. She told *CNN Interactive* that it is these characters, in turn, that spark the steamy sex in her plots. "It's the characters that drive the books, not the sex," she explained. "The sex happens because it happens in life and I'm writing about life."

While reviewers continue to debate the value of Collins' novels, few have argued that her work is dull. A *Publishers Weekly* contributor observed of *Dangerous Kiss:* "Believable? Not for a minute. Entertaining? Of course." *People* critic Joanne Kaufman likewise characterized *Vendetta: Lucky's Revenge* as "embarrassing to pick up, impossible to put down."

Collins has sold more than 200 million copies of her novels.

BIOGRAPHICAL/CRITICAL SOURCES:

PERIODICALS

Atlanta Constitution, May 3, 1988, p. F1.
Booklist, July 1985, p. 1474; December 15, 1996, p. 691; December 15, 1997, Ilene Cooper, review of *Thrill!,* p. 667; April 15, 1999, Catherine Sias, review of *Dangerous Kiss,* p. 1451.
Chicago Tribune, December 4, 1979; October 1, 1990, sec. 5, p. 1; October 5, 1990, sec. 5, p. 5; October 7, 1990, sec. 11, p. 3.
Detroit News, September 11, 1983.
Entertainment Weekly, February 14, 1997, p. 56.
Esquire, July, 1989, p. 82.
Globe & Mail (Toronto), September 7, 1985; November 22, 1986.
Interview, November, 1990, p. 152.
Kirkus Reviews, August 1, 1994, p. 1005.
London Review of Books, May 13, 1993, pp. 23-24.
Los Angeles, November, 1988, p. 178; September, 1994, p. 96.
Los Angeles Times, August 25, 1981; October 29, 1985; August 23, 1987, sec. 6, p. 1.
Los Angeles Times Book Review, January 4, 1987; December 28, 1986, p. 5; April 17, 1988, p. 10; October 7, 1990, p. 14; July 21, 1991, p. 10; April 11, 1993, p. 15.
New Yorker, June 20, 1988, p. 90.
New York Times, June 15, 1999, Michiko Kakutani, "Those Lips! Those Eyes! That Mojo's Working!"
New York Times Book Review, June 21, 1970; June 12, 1988, p. 22; August 20, 1989, p. 12; September 30, 1990, Jill Gerston, "Tell Me about It, Lucky," p. 37; March 28, 1993, p. 25; October 9, 1994, p. 14.
Observer, April 24, 1988, p. 41; October 7, 1990, p. 61.
People, January 12, 1987, pp. 80-82; May 23, 1988, p. 31; November 5, 1990, p. 39; September 5, 1994, pp. 110-112; February 3, 1997, Joanne Kaufman, review of *Vendetta: Lucky's Revenge,* p. 33.
Premiere, July, 1994, p. 95.
Publishers Weekly, July 5, 1985, p. 54; June 6, 1986, p. 66; June 19, 1993, p. 12; February 6, 1995, p. 22; December 16, 1996, p. 42.
Quill and Quire, November, 1983, p. 28.
Rapport, June-July, 1993, p. 26.
Time, October 15, 1990, p. 86; October 9, 1995, p. 25.
Times Literary Supplement, February 10, 1978; May 28, 1993, p. 7.
Tribune Books (Chicago), October 9, 1990, p. 3; March 19, 1997, p. 3.
USA Today, June 23, 1988, p. D6; October 4, 1990, p. D3; October 5, 1990, p. D3; June 30, 1993, p. D7.
Vanity Fair, April, 1995, p. 126.
Voice Literary Supplement, July, 1988, p. 3.
Washington Post, August 26, 1985; October 6, 1990, p. C1.
Washington Post Book World, October 16, 1994, p. 8.

OTHER

CNN Interactive, http://www.cnn.com/ (March 23, 1998), interview with Collins.
Simon Says, http://www.simonsays.com/ (September 2, 2000), interview with Collins.*

* * *

COOK, Thomas H. 1947-

PERSONAL: Born September 19, 1947, in Ft. Payne, AL; son of Virgil Richard (in management) and Myrick (a secretary; maiden name, Harper) Cook; married Susan Terner (a writer for radio), March 17, 1978; children: Justine Ariel. *Education:* Georgia State College, B.A., 1969; Hunter College, City University of New York, M.A., 1972; Columbia University, M.Phil., 1976.

ADDRESSES: Home—New York, NY. *Agent*—Jim Seldes, Russell & Volkening, 50 West 29th St., New York, NY 10017.

CAREER: U.S. Industrial Chemicals, New York City, advertising executive, 1970-72; Association for Help of Retarded Adults, New York City, clerk and typist, 1973-75; Dekalb Community College, Clarkston, GA, teacher of English and history, 1978-81; contributing editor and book review editor of *Atlanta* magazine, 1978-82; full-time writer, 1981—.

MEMBER: Authors Guild, Authors League.

AWARDS, HONORS: Nominated for Edgar Allan Poe Award, Mystery Writers of America, 1981, for *Blood Innocents,* 1988, for *Sacrificial Ground,* and 1992, for *Blood Echoes: The True Story of an Infamous Mass Murder and Its Aftermath,* and award winner, 1996, for *The Chatham School Affair;* Hammett Prize, International Association of Crime Writers, 1995, for *Breakheart Hill.*

WRITINGS:

NOVELS

Blood Innocents, Playboy Press (Chicago, IL), 1980.
The Orchids, Houghton (Boston, MA), 1982.
Tabernacle, Houghton (Boston, MA), 1983.
Elena, Houghton (Boston, MA), 1986.
Sacrificial Ground, Putnam (New York, NY), 1988.
Flesh and Blood, Putnam (New York, NY), 1989.
Streets of Fire, Putnam (New York, NY), 1989.
The City When It Rains, Putnam (New York, NY), 1991.
Evidence of Blood, Putnam (New York, NY), 1991.
Night Secrets, Putnam (New York, NY), 1990.
Mortal Memory, Putnam (New York, NY), 1993.
Breakheart Hill, Bantam (New York, NY), 1995.
The Chatham School Affair, Bantam (New York, NY), 1996.
Instruments of Night, Bantam (New York, NY), 1998.
Places in the Dark, Bantam (New York, NY), 2000.

OTHER

Early Graves: A Shocking True-Crime Story of the Youngest Woman Ever Sentenced to Death Row, Dutton (New York, NY), 1990.

Blood Echoes: The True Story of an Infamous Mass Murder and Its Aftermath, Dutton (New York, NY), 1992.

Contributor to periodicals, including *New York Times Book Review.*

SIDELIGHTS: Thomas H. Cook is a popular author of both novels and true-crime books. In both areas, the author is known for his meticulous attention to character development and setting. Cook's murder mysteries are often set in rural areas of the southern United States, where the author himself was raised. His fiction has been well received, with critics highlighting Cook's successful evocation of small-town life in the rural South and the often painful process of remembering the past. While Cook has occasionally been faulted for overworking his simple stories, he has also been cited among the mystery genre's most accomplished storytellers. As Robert Dahlin remarked in a review in *Publishers Weekly,* Cook knows "how to spin out a tale in an artful fashion." Cook, who is "often described as a dean of 'literary suspense,'" related to Dahlin that "physical atmosphere of place" and "reflective content" are important elements in his novels. The plots of a number of Cook's mysteries hinge on memory as well as murder, and some reviewers highlighted the author's expert rendering of the process of recollecting painful memories as an essential element of his success. While Cook himself has characterized these police procedurals as mere money-makers which enable him to write more literary fare, his attention to details of character and setting, as well as his skills as a storyteller, have earned him a respected place among successful mystery writers. For *The Chatham School Affair,* Cook was awarded the Mystery Writers of America's coveted Edgar Allan Poe Award for best novel in 1996.

Cook's first publication, *Blood Innocents,* was written while the author was in graduate school. A police procedural set in New York City, the novel is "essentially . . . about the capacity of a man to hold to his goodness while pursuing a rather squalid labor—police work," Cook once explained to *CA.* "My scheme, if I may call it that, is to write solid and artistically sound police procedurals like *Blood Innocents* and *Tabernacle* in order to buy the time needed to write such literary efforts as *The Orchids* and *Elena.*" *The Orchids,* a literary novel that followed *Blood Innocents,* was warmly received by critics such as S. L. Stebel who, in a *Los Angeles Herald Examiner* review, found Cook's language "imbued with the kind of image and metaphor present in our very best poetry." And in *Literary Boston*

Lee Grove deemed *The Orchids* "a Holocaust novel that will blow you away . . . Cook wants you to be both comfortable and uncomfortable—and he succeeds, perfectly. You'll feel as cozy as a razor blade in a Halloween apple. You'll see just how easy it is for a brilliant, powerful, sensitive intellect to go bad, to weld itself to corruption. This novel, however, will never go bad and is anything but corrupt."

"In my literary novels I would like to help bring back what I think of as the 'meditative novel,'" Cook once revealed to *CA,* "that is, the work with a quiet, reasoned, and highly reflective voice. I prefer novels that depart somewhat from strictly linear forms of action and narrative as well as works that have taken on greater themes, rather than yet more books about middle-class or academic angst or restrictively autobiographical works, those that never venture beyond the usually rather limited experience of the novelist. In *The Orchids,* for example, I tried to render the density and precision of the German language into English, and to create a narrative voice that could convey the horrors of Langhof's experience without resorting to sensationalism of any kind. In *Elena* the narrative voice is that of a brother talking of his sister's life, a method by which not only a woman's life can be portrayed, but that of a man as well, so that the two genuinely merge into a single narrative tone."

Cook's detective novels of the 1990s, including *Breakheart Hill, Evidence of Blood,* and *Blood Echoes: The True Story of an Infamous Mass Murder and Its Aftermath,* have been judged by some critics in terms similar to those the author uses himself for his more literary efforts. In particular, the avoidance of linear structures and the inclusion of "greater themes" have brought Cook critical acclaim.

In *Evidence of Blood* Cook's protagonist, Jackson Kinley, returns to his hometown in rural Georgia for the funeral of his oldest friend, and stays on to solve a thirty-year-old murder case his late friend had been working on at the time of his death. The victim, a teenage girl, was never found, but a man was quickly arrested, convicted, and put to death. Decades later the condemned man's daughter convinces first Kinley's friend and then Kinley himself to try and find the real murderer. "Cook knows this terrain, both in locale and in disquiet," remarked Steven Slosberg in the *New York Times Book Review.* Although Jon L. Breen, writing in the *Armchair Detective,* had a few "procedural quibbles" regarding Cook's rendering of transcripts from other cases Kinley looks into, Slosberg concluded: "*Evidence of Blood* is a highly satisfying story, strong in color and atmosphere, intelligent and exacting." A *Kirkus Reviews* contributor promoted *Evidence of Blood* as a "gripping southern drama. . . . One of the better Cooks to date," and referred to the author as "lush-languaged Cook."

As with *Evidence of Blood,* Cook's novel, *Mortal Memory,* focuses on the long-term effects of a violent crime. In this work, a boy visiting friends for the afternoon returns home to find that his mother and siblings have been gruesomely killed, and his father, the presumed murderer, has run away. Years later, the young man's powerful emotions are brought to the surface again when a woman researching a book on fathers who kill their families contacts him. *Atlanta Constitution* contributor William A. Henry praised *Evidence of Blood* for its surprising plot twists and satisfying conclusion, but singled out for special praise the author's mode of storytelling, which relies on "repetition and insight" as the protagonist revisits his memory of the time of the murders from different perspectives, "almost as though he were on a Freudian analyst's couch." The result "gradually elevates a sordid personal history to mythic proportions—a 'Medea' for the middle class," Henry concluded.

Like *Evidence of Blood,* the murder at the center of *Breakheart Hill*—that of a high school girl—continues to affect her survivors decades after the crime. In this case, Ben Wade, now the town doctor but once secretly in love with the murdered girl, Kelli Troy, continues to carry the guilt of Kelli's death with him twenty-five years later. Although a reviewer for the *Washington Post Book World* faulted Cook's execution of the scenario, and *New York Times Book Review* critic Marilyn Stasio found the author's "painstaking variations on his theme and the delicacy of his writing" somewhat wearying, a reviewer for *Publishers Weekly* maintained that Cook's "expert storytelling" redeems his simple story. *Breakheart Hill* is "a haunting evocation that gains power and resonance with each twist of its spiral-like narration," the *Publishers Weekly* reviewer concluded.

In 1996 Cook gave readers his award-winning *The Chatham School Affair.* In this novel, Cook takes readers back to the mid-1920s, and the arrival of the beautiful Elizabeth Channing in a small Massachusetts town. Hired as a teacher of a local prep school, Channing quickly finds a fan in young Henry Griswald, who is assigned to assist the new teacher during her first year at the school. Tragically, Channing's growing relationship with a married fellow teacher ends in murder, suicide, and a mystery that haunts Henry throughout his adult life. Noting Cook's knack for building suspense, a *Kirkus* reviewer commented that "reading [*The Chatham School Affair*] is like watching an . . . avalanche in agonizing, exquisite slow-motion."

Cook followed *The Chatham School Affair* with the 1998 novel *Instruments of Night,* "an excellent psychological thriller" according to David Pitt in *Booklist.* Not all reviewers were as complimentary as Pitt, however. *Library Journal* contributor Roland C. Person maintained that Cook's "Gothic, even melodramatic, prose style . . . will often seem repetitious and jarring to contemporary readers." Still, Person acknowledged that the novelist's style effectively promotes both the story's "mood and setting." A *Publishers Weekly* critic heralded *Instruments of Night* as "equal" to its prize-winning predecessor, and described *Instruments of Night* as "a beautifully composed tale with . . . [satisfying] plot twists." Although noting that Cook employed some "classic [genre] device[s]" in his novel, the *Publishers Weekly* contributor concluded that the novelist's ability to create "harrowing situations" in his "indelibly haunting tale . . . demonstrates that he is among the best in the business."

Cook's 2000 novel, *Places in the Dark,* is set on the rocky coast of Maine, and takes place during the Great Depression of the 1930s. Explained his choice of setting to a *Mystery Guild* interviewer, Cook revealed part of his technique in plotting his novels: "Coastal Maine . . . struck me as a place of extremity, not only in terms of its warm summers and very cold winters, but as a place where water battles stone. For me, time and place are never calculated as things separate from the story. I set the story in a particular place and time at the moment I begin to imagine it, and with one exception, I don't remember ever having changed either." The hardest part of novel writing? "Work[ing] out the 'surprise'," Cook admitted to the *Mystery Guild* interviewer. With each new novel ". . . . readers get more savvy about your tricks and harder to fool."

BIOGRAPHICAL/CRITICAL SOURCES:

PERIODICALS

Armchair Detective, summer, 1989, p. 238; summer, 1991, p. 293; spring, 1992, p. 247; fall, 1992, p. 505; winter, 1992, p. 36; spring, 1993, p. 12; fall, 1993, p. 115; spring, 1995, p. 204.

Atlanta Journal, October 17, 1982.

Atlanta Journal-Constitution, January 6, 1991, p. N10; March 3, 1991, p. N11; November 4, 1991, p. N10; March 22, 1992, p. N12; May 8, 1994, p. N11.

Booklist, January 1, 1986, p. 658; March 1, 1988, p. 1097; January 1, 1989, p. 753; June 1, 1989, p. 1673; April 15, 1990, p. 1585; November 1, 1990, p. 485; December 15, 1990, p. 804; September 15, 1991, pp. 123, 131; February 15, 1992, p. 1070; July, 1995, p. 1858; September 1, 1998, David Pitt, review of *Instruments of Night,* p. 69.

Book Watch, May, 1992, p. 1.

Boston Globe, December 29, 1991, p. A15.

Chicago Tribune, April 18, 1993, sec. 14, p. 6.

Christian Science Monitor, August 4, 1989, p. 13.

Kirkus Reviews, November 1, 1985, p. 1147; March 1, 1988, p. 325; November 15, 1988, p. 1639; July 1, 1989, p. 953; May 1, 1990, p. 610; October 1, 1990, p. 1365; December 1, 1990, p. 1640; August 15, 1991, review of *Evidence of Blood,* p. 1028; January 1, 1992, p. 28; February 15, 1993, p. 185; July 15, 1996, review of *The Chatham School Affair.*

Library Journal, January, 1986, p. 100; March 1, 1988, p. 79; January, 1989, p. 104; August, 1989, p. 162; October 1, 1990, p. 102; January, 1991, p. 147; February 1, 1992, p. 111; July, 1995, p. 118; October 1, 1998, Roland C. Person, review of *Instruments of Night,* p. 131.

Literary Boston, December, 1982.

Los Angeles Herald Examiner, February 13, 1983.

Los Angeles Times, November 17, 1991, p. 12.

Los Angeles Times Book Review, March 13, 1988, p. 13; January 1, 1989, p. 9; September 10, 1989, p. 10; January 13, 1991, p. 8; November 17, 1991, p. 12; April 11, 1993, p. 8.

New York Times Book Review, October 31, 1982; January 5, 1986, p. 23; February 19, 1989, p. 23; September 24, 1989, p. 29; June 24, 1990, p. 22; January 20, 1991, p. 27; June 9, 1991, p. 22; October 20, 1991, p. 47; January 26, 1992, p. 24; August 6, 1995, p. 23.

Observer (London), January 17, 1993, p. 49.

People, August 20, 1990, p. 29.

Publishers Weekly, November 1, 1985, p. 56; January 15, 1988, p. 82; October 21, 1988, p. 51; July 7, 1989, p. 50; May 4, 1990, p. 51; December 14, 1990, p. 52; August 9, 1991, p. 42; January 27, 1992, p. 81; May 18, 1992, p. 66; November 16, 1992, p. 60; February 15, 1993, p. 197; February 22, 1993, p. 90; May 1, 1995, p. 44; September 7, 1998, review of *Instruments of Night,* p. 88; October 19, 1998, Robert Dahlin, "Stretching the Mystery Envelope," p. 43; April 17, 2000, review of *Place in the Dark,* p. 55.

Punch, December 9, 1988, p. 72.

School Library Journal, August, 1993, p. 205; February, 1996, p. 131.
Southern Living, April, 1992, p. 112.
Tribune Books (Chicago), April 18, 1993, p. 6.
Washington Post, March 7, 1992, p. B3; August 27, 1995, p. 4.
Washington Post Book World, November 6, 1983; February 2, 1986, p. 8; March 22, 1992, p. 12; August 27, 1995, p. 4.
West Coast Review of Books, April, 1989, p. 29.
Wilson Library Bulletin, December, 1980, p. 295.

OTHER

Mystery Guild Web site, http://www.mysteryguild.com/ (May 19, 2001), interview with Thomas H. Cook.*

* * *

COOKE, Ann
See COLE, Joanna

* * *

CRAWFORD, John W(illiam) 1936-

PERSONAL: Born September 2, 1936, in Ashdown, AR; son of John C. and Allie B. (Phillips) Crawford; married Kathryn Bizzell, June 17, 1962; children: Jeffry Wayne, Sonja Rene. *Ethnicity:* "Anglo-Native American." *Education:* Ouachita Baptist College (now University), B.A., B.S.E. (with honors), 1959; Drake University, M.S.E., 1962; Oklahoma State University, Ed.D. (with honors), 1968. *Politics:* Independent. *Religion:* Methodist.

ADDRESSES: *Home*—1813 Walnut, Arkadelphia, AR 71923. *Office*—Department of English, Henderson State University, Arkadelphia, AR 71999. *E-mail*—crawford@hsu.edu.

CAREER: English teacher in public schools in Iowa, 1959-62; Clinton Community College, Clinton, IA, instructor in English, 1962-66; Henderson State University, Arkadelphia, AR, assistant professor, 1967-68, associate professor, 1968-73, professor of English, 1973-1997, chairman of department, 1977-1986, professor emeritus, 1997—.

MEMBER: National Education Association, College English Association, South Central Modern Language Association, South Central College English Association, Poets' Roundtable of Arkansas, Arkansas Philological Association, Missouri Poetry Society, Phi Delta Kappa, Kappa Delta Pi, Phi Sigma Kappa, Theta Alpha Phi.

AWARDS, HONORS: Poetry awards from *Mentor* (magazine) summer contests, 1964, 1965, 1966, Iowa Poetry Association contest, 1965, 1966, Southwest Literary Festival, 1969, Kentucky Poetry Society, 1970, 1979, South and West Literary Arts Festival, 1970, Arkansas Writers Conference, 1971, 1972, 1973, 1974, Arkansas Poetry Day, 1971-75, 1980, Mississippi Poetry Society, 1971, New Mexico Poetry Society, 1972, and Deep South Writer's Conference, 1975; Sybil Nash Abrams Prize, 1982, 1995; Merit Award, Poets' Roundtable of Arkansas, 1988; Arkansas Haiku Society Award, 1998.

WRITINGS:

Shakespeare's Comedies: A Guide, privately printed, 1968.
Shakespeare's Tragedies: A Guide, privately printed, 1968.
Steps to Success: A Study Skills Handbook, Kendall/Hunt, 1976, revised edition, 1978.
Discourse: Essay on English and American Literature, Rodopi (Amsterdam), 1978.
Romantic Criticism of Shakespearean Drama, [Salzburg], 1978.
Early Shakespeare Actresses, Peter Lang (New York, NY), 1984.
Making the Connection (poetry), Mellen Press, 1989.
The Learning, Wit, and Wisdom of Shakespeare's Renaissance Women, Mellen Press, 1997.
I Have Become Acquainted with the Rain (poetry), Mellen Press, 1997.

Work is anthologized in *American Poetry,* edited by Jeanne Holleyfield, 1965, *Lyrical Iowa,* edited by Ruth Peterson, 1965, 2nd edition, 1966, *Counterpoint,* edited by H. M. Rosenberg, 1966, *America Sings,* edited by Dennis Hartmann, 1967, *Poems by Arkansas Poets' Roundtable,* edited by Arkansas Poets' Roundtable, 1969, *Contemporary Poets of Arkansas,* edited by Sue Abbot Boyd, 1969, 2nd edition, 1971, and *American Poets,* edited by Stella Croft Tremble, 1969. Contributor of poems and articles to numerous magazines, including *Bardic Echoes, Mississippi Poetry Journal, Victorian Poetry, Seventeenth Century News, Roundtable, University of Dayton Review, Missouri English Bulletin, Rendezvous, Southern Quarterly, Explicator, Publications of APA,* and *CEA Critic.*

WORK IN PROGRESS: A volume of verse titled *White Knights and Gumdrop Sights;* a volume of verse titled *Vieux Carpé Cuisine.*

SIDELIGHTS: John W. Crawford to *CA:* "I have always written critical essays and poetry for self-satisfaction. I like to get my ideas before the public. I have written a lot on Shakespeare's work because I grew to enjoy his plays in high school. My favorite poet in high school was Robert Frost, so his influence on my poetry is strong. Now that I teach part-time only, I spend most of my writing time with poetry."

* * *

CROSBY, Faye J. 1947-

PERSONAL: Born July 12, 1947, in Bethesda, MD; daughter of Robert and Andree Newman; married Travis Crosby, September 5, 1970; children: Matthew, Timothy. *Education:* Wheaton College, B.A., 1969; Boston University, Ph.D., 1976.

ADDRESSES: Office—Department of Psychology, Room 379, Social Sciences 2, University of California, Santa Cruz, CA 95064. *E-mail*—fjcrosby@cats.ucsc.edu.

CAREER: Yale University, New Haven, CT, assistant professor, 1977-82, associate professor of psychology, 1982-85; Smith College, Northampton, MA, professor of psychology, 1985-97; University of California, Santa Cruz, currently professor of psychology.

WRITINGS:

Relative Deprivation and Working Women, Oxford University Press (New York, NY), 1982.
(Editor) *Spouse, Parent, Worker,* Yale University Press (New Haven, CT), 1987.
(Co-editor) *Affirmative Action in Perspective,* Springer-Verlag (New York, NY), 1989.
Juggling: The Unexpected Advantages of Balancing Career and Home for Women and Their Families, Free Press (New York, NY), 1991.
(With Susan D. Clayton) *Justice, Gender, and Affirmative Action,* University of Michigan Press (Ann Arbor, MI), 1992.
(Editor, with Karen Fraser Wyche) *Women's Ethnicities: Journeys through Psychology,* Westview (Boulder, CO), 1996.
(With Richard F. Tomasson and Sharon D. Herzberger) *Affirmative Action: The Pros and Cons of Policy and Practice,* American University Press (Washington, DC), 1996.
(Contributor) *Off White: Readings on Society, Race, and Culture,* Routledge (New York, NY), 1997.
(Editor, with Audrey J. Murrell and Robin J. Ely) *Mentoring Dilemmas: Developmental Relationships within Multicultural Organizations,* Lawrence Erlbaum (Hillsdale, NJ), 1999.
(Editor, with Cheryl VanDeVeer) *Sex, Race, and Merit: Debating Affirmative Action in Education and Employment,* University of Michigan Press (Ann Arbor, MI), 2000.

Contributor to *Journal of Social Issues, Psychology of Women Quarterly, Journal of Applied Social Psychology,* and other periodicals.

SIDELIGHTS: Faye J. Crosby is "a leading authority on affirmative action," according to Jennifer McNulty in *Currents.* A professor of psychology, Crosby's writings focus on such topics as the role of women in business, affirmative action, and multicultural organizations. In her book *Juggling: The Unexpected Advantages of Balancing Career and Home for Women and Their Families,* Crosby argues that the busy schedules of contemporary women who have both families to raise and careers to pursue are actually beneficial to them. In *Women's Ethnicities: Journeys through Psychology,* Crosby and co-editor Karen Fraser Wyche present a collection of essays examining how ethnic groups approach such issues as educating their children, achieving business success, and raising their families in startlingly different ways. *Affirmative Action: The Pros and Cons of Policy and Practice,* edited by Crosby, Richard F. Tomasson, and Sharon D. Herzberger, analyzes how the concept of affirmative action is practiced in America today, as well as the benefits and drawbacks of the policy.

Crosby turned her attention to the role of mentoring in today's multicultural organizations in *Mentoring Dilemmas: Developmental Relationships within Multicultural Organizations,* edited with Audrey J. Murrell and Robin J. Ely. Because studies have shown that people from similar backgrounds can establish mentoring relationships most easily, multicultural organizations face special problems when attempting to establish fruitful mentoring programs. *Mentoring Dilemmas* examines the problem and offers possible solutions. According to Mark L. Lengnick-Hall in *Personnel Psychology,* the book "offers a rich mix of articles" on its subject and "does an excellent job of stimulating thought and developing ideas of interest."

Crosby once told *CA:* "An interest in working women prompted me to look at the conditions which allow women to function in the face of sexual discrimination."

BIOGRAPHICAL/CRITICAL SOURCES:

PERIODICALS

Library Journal, October 1, 1991, Linda Beck, review of *Juggling,* p. 125.

Personnel Psychology, spring, 2000, Mark. L. Lengnick-Hall, review of *Mentoring Dilemmas,* p. 224.

OTHER

Currents, http://www.ucsc.edu/oncampus/currents/ (April 12, 1999), Jennifer McNulty, "Successful Corporate Mentoring Programs Depend on Clarity and Purpose, Says Psychologist."

* * *

CROWLEY, John 1942-

PERSONAL: Born December 1, 1942, in Presque Isle, ME; son of Joseph B. (a doctor) and Patience (Lyon) Crowley; married Laurie Block, 1984; children: two daughters. *Education:* Indiana University, B.A., 1964.

ADDRESSES: Home—Box 395, Conway, MA 01341.

CAREER: Photographer and commercial artist, 1964-66; fiction writer and freelance writer for films and television, 1966—. Yale University, visiting professor of creative writing.

AWARDS, HONORS: American Book Award nomination, 1980, for *Engine Summer;* Hugo Award nomination, Nebula Award nomination, and World Fantasy Award, all 1982, all for *Little, Big;* American Film Festival Award, 1982, for *America Lost and Found;* World Fantasy Award, 1990, for *Great Work of Time;* American Academy of Arts and Letters Award for literature; *Locus* award, for short story "Gone."

WRITINGS:

NOVELS

The Deep, Doubleday (New York, NY), 1975.

Beasts, Doubleday (New York, NY), 1976.

Engine Summer, Doubleday (New York, NY), 1979.

Little, Big, Bantam (New York, NY), 1981.

Ægypt (first novel in tetralogy), Bantam (New York, NY), 1987.

Great Work of Time (novella), Bantam (New York, NY), 1991.

Love and Sleep (second novel in tetralogy), Bantam (New York, NY), 1994.

Three Novels, Bantam (New York, NY), 1994.

Dæmonomania (third novel in tetralogy), Bantam (New York, NY), 2000.

The Translator, Avon, 2002.

OTHER

Novelty (short stories), Bantam (New York, NY), 1989.

Antiquities: Seven Stories, Incunabula (Seattle, WA), 1993.

Work represented in anthologies, including *Shadows,* Doubleday (New York, NY), 1977; and *Elsewhere,* Ace Books (New York, NY), 1981. Author of television scripts for *America Lost and Found* and *No Place to Hide,* Public Broadcasting System. Contributor to periodicals, including *Omni.*

SIDELIGHTS: Author John Crowley has been praised by critics for his thoughtful, finely wrought works of science fiction and fantasy, which include the novels *The Deep, Ægypt, Love and Sleep,* and *Dæmonomania.* A successful television writer who has never pandered to popular tastes, Crowley infuses his genre writings with literary quality and "mind-catching philosophical musings," according to a *Publishers Weekly* reviewer of *Dæmonomania.* Suzanne Keen reported in *Commonweal* that his characters "are psychologically convincing, an accomplishment that makes the historical and fantastic elements of his [novel *Love and Sleep*] all the more thrilling." Whether his work visits far planets or local neighborhoods, some critics have suggested, Crowley always challenges the accepted perceptions of things and offers multi-layered mysteries for his characters—and his readers—to explore. As a *Kirkus Reviews* contributor explained it in a review of *Dæmonomania,* "Crowley's work is a taste well worth acquiring, but you have to work at it."

In a *New York Times Book Review* piece on Crowley's first novel, *The Deep,* Gerald Jonas declared that "paraphrase is useless to convey the intensity of Crowley's prose; anyone interested in the risk-taking side of modern science fiction will want to experience it firsthand."

Jonathan Dee noted, also in the *New York Times Book Review,* that Crowley "is an abundantly gifted writer, a scholar whose passion for history is matched by his ability to write a graceful sentence." Some reviewers observed that with his third novel, *Engine Summer,* Crowley had begun developing more complex plots and characters, and his themes reflected the influence of the fantasy genre. Charles Nicol wrote in *Saturday Review:* "A lyric adventure as concerned with the meaning of actions as with the actions themselves, [*Engine Summer*] presents a meditative world that should appeal to lovers of the great fantasies. Crowley has published some science fiction previously; here he has gone beyond his genre into that hilly country on the borderlands of literature." Similarly, the Nebula and Hugo Award nominee *Little, Big* was described by John Clute in the *Washington Post Book World* as a "dense, marvelous, magic-realist family chronicle about the end of time and the new world to come."

Novelist Carolyn See, in a review for the *Los Angeles Times,* commented that Crowley's fifth novel, *Ægypt,* contains "some extraordinary storytelling." Incorporating fantasy, satire, and philosophical romance, the novel centers on Pierce Moffett, a professor of Renaissance history whose desire to write a book about finding the meaning in life leads him to a mythical area and a mysterious woman. *Washington Post Book World* contributor Michael Dirda remarked that *Ægypt* "is clearly a novel where thought speaks louder than action, where people, places and events are at once actual and allegorical. . . . Crowley wants readers to appreciate his foreshadowings, echoes, bits of odd lore, multiple voices—in the evolution of complex pattern is his art." Dirda also noted, however, that Crowley's narrative is so complex that it can occasionally be confusing. Commenting on this complexity, John Clute, in a review for the *New York Times Book Review,* suggested that *Ægypt* provides "a dizzying experience." *Ægypt* is the first novel in an ambitious tetralogy centering upon the intellectual and personal journey of Moffett.

In *Love and Sleep,* Crowley continues the tale begun in *Ægypt.* While *Ægypt* tells of Moffett's life during the 1960s and 1970s, *Love and Sleep* frames that period, returning to the 1950s and allowing readers a glimpse of Moffett's Kentucky childhood, a time full of "minor incidents and wonders," according to *Washington Post Book Review* critic Lawrence Norfolk, before leaping ahead of *Ægypt* in true sequel fashion. In the novel, Norfolk explained, Crowley hangs his plot upon the speculation that "between the old world of things as they used to be, and the new world of things as they would be instead, there has always fallen a sort of passage time, a chaos of unformed possibilities in which all sorts of manifestations could be witnessed." It has "an interim feel, a sense of its author treading water while the players are maneuvered into position" for the proposed third and fourth segments of the series, Norfolk continued. "As it stands, *Love and Sleep* is a collection of strange episodes, of hints and premonitions. The ultimate worth of this strange, teasing book hangs on the two yet to be written." Jonathan Dee agreed in his assessment of the work for the *New York Times Book Review:* while the first section of *Love and Sleep* "generates a true, expansive sense of human mystery . . . the novel's own vision, so crystal clear in that opening section, grows woollier and more diffuse" as Moffett's saga continues. Chicago *Tribune Books* contributor Robert Chatain maintained that the author's mixture of realism and fantasy "is not for every reader," yet the critic added: "to dislike fantasy is not to dismiss Crowley; he's one of the few writers who successfully crosses the razor-thin but definite line between genre fiction and literary fiction." Citing the author's "metaphysical conceits," Chatain concluded of Crowley, "there is no temptation to confuse [his novels] with other fictions; there's really nothing like them."

Dæmonomania continues the Pierce Moffett saga, as magic seeps further into the lives of Moffett and his acquaintances in Faraway Hills, New York. The title refers to a possible case of demonic possession, but the book portends even more massive shifts in what appears to be reality. For his part, Moffett comes to understand that magic once worked, that science has only temporarily halted the potency of magic, and that a "secret history," shared by a select few, actually directs the course of human actions. A *Kirkus Reviews* critic, while noting that the book will mean more to those who have read its two predecessors, called it "[d]eeply atmospheric, impressively learned, endlessly suggestive."

Crowley told *Publishers Weekly* writer Robert K. J. Killheffer that the tetralogy he began with *Ægypt* may ultimately be his life's work. "I find myself appalled every once in a while that I have committed myself to this thing that will take up a large part of what I realize to be a not-infinitely-long creative life," Crowley said. Nevertheless, he denied that he feels trapped by the work: "Pierce's story continues to show me new things; it keeps staying alive and interesting."

BIOGRAPHICAL/CRITICAL SOURCES:

BOOKS

Contemporary Literary Criticism, Volume 57, Gale (Detroit, MI), 1990.

Dictionary of Literary Biography Yearbook 1982, Gale (Detroit, MI), 1983.

PERIODICALS

Analog: Science Fiction/Science Fact, June, 1977; August, 1987; December, 1989.
Atlantic Monthly, September, 1994, review of *Love and Sleep,* p. 112.
Berkshire Sampler, September 13, 1981.
Commonweal, December 2, 1994, Suzanne Keen, review of *Love and Sleep,* p. 26.
Extrapolation, spring, 1990.
Kirkus Reviews, June 15, 1994, review of *Love and Sleep;* June 15, 2000, review of *Dæmonomania,* p. 815.
Locus, August, 1991; September, 1991; May, 2001, pp. 4-5, 66-67.
Los Angeles Times, May 4, 1987, Carolyn See, review of *Ægypt.*
Magazine of Fantasy and Science Fiction, April, 1980; December, 1987; January, 1992.
New Statesman, November 20, 1987.
New York Times Book Review, November 21, 1976, Gerald Jonas, review of *The Deep;* March 27, 1977; May 20, 1979; March 2, 1986; October 12, 1986; May 3, 1987, pp. 9, 11, John Clute, review of *Ægypt;* August 14, 1988; May 21, 1989; July 5, 1992; February 6, 1994, review of *Antiquities,* p. 22; September 4, 1994, Jonathan Dee, review of *Love and Sleep,* p. 9; September 17, 2000, Jeff Waggoner, review of *Dæmonomania,* p. 25.
Publishers Weekly, February 20, 1987; April 14, 1989; August 29, 1994, Robert K. J. Killheffer, "John Crowley: 'I Still Owe a Debt of Gratitude,'" p. 53; July 3, 2000, review of *Dæmonomania,* p. 53.
Saturday Review, April 14, 1979, article by Charles Nicol.
Science Fiction and Fantasy Book Review, January-February, 1982.
Times Literary Supplement, May 28, 1982; November 20-26, 1987, p. 1274.
Tribune Books (Chicago), October 18, 1981; June 18, 1989, p. 6; September 11, 1994, Robert Chatain, review of *Love and Sleep,* pp. 1, 13.
Voice Literary Supplement, September, 1994, p. 31.
Washington Post Book World, March 23, 1980; July 26, 1981, article by John Clute; October 4, 1981; April 19, 1987, pp. 1, 7, Michael Dirda, review of *Ægypt;* March 19, 1989; December 6, 1992, review of *Little, Big,* p. 4; November 28, 1993, review of *Antiquities,* p. 8; July 10, 1994; August 14, 1994, Lawrence Norfolk, review of *Love and Sleep,* p. 5.*

* * *

CUNNINGHAM, E. V.
See FAST, Howard (Melvin)

CUNO, Kenneth M. 1950-

PERSONAL: Born January 4, 1950, in Syracuse, NY; son of Ernest A. (a labor relations consultant) and Dortha D. (a secretary; maiden name, Cunningham; present name, Wade) Cuno; married Marilyn L. Booth (a scholar and translator), December 11, 1986; children: Paul Cuno-Booth, Carrie Cuno-Booth. *Education:* Lewis and Clark College, B.A., 1972; University of California, Los Angeles, M.A., 1977, Ph.D., 1985.

ADDRESSES: Office—Department of History, University of Illinois, 309 Gregory Hall, 810 South Wright St., Urbana, IL 61801.

CAREER: American University, Cairo, Egypt, visiting assistant professor of history, 1985-90; University of Illinois at Urbana-Champaign, assistant professor, 1990-96, associate professor of history, 1996—. Visiting lecturer at the University of California, Santa Barbara, 1985; has conducted extracurricular discussions on Middle Eastern topics, and has presented papers at seminars and conferences.

MEMBER: American Historical Association, Middle East Studies Association of North America, American Research Center in Egypt, Center for Middle Eastern Studies (University of Chicago).

AWARDS, HONORS: Center for Arabic Studies Abroad fellowship, 1979-80; Fulbright-Hays Dissertation Research Abroad fellowship, 1980-81; Social Science Research Council International Doctoral Research fellowship, 1981-82; Albert Hourani Book Prize competition, Middle East Studies Association, honorable mention, 1993, for *The Pasha's Peasants: Land, Society, and Economy in Lower Egypt, 1740-1858;* American Research Center (Egypt) fellowship, 1994; Center for Advanced Study fellowship, University of Illinois at Urbana-Champaign, 1994; Fulbright fellowship, 1998-99; Social Sciences Research Council fellowship, 1999.

WRITINGS:

(Contributor) *Land Tenure and Social Transformation in the Near East,* edited by Tarif Khalidi, American University of Beirut (Beirut, Lebanon), 1984.
The Pasha's Peasants: Land, Society, and Economy in Lower Egypt, 1740-1858, Cambridge University Press (Cambridge, MA), 1992.

(Contributor) *The Modern Middle East: A Reader,* edited by Albert Hourani, Philip Khoury, and Mary Wilson, University of California Press (Berkeley, CA), 1994.

(Contributor) *Agriculture in Egypt from Pharaonic to Modern Times,* edited by Alan Bowman and Eugene Rogan, British Academy (Oxford, England), 1999.

(Contributor) *Imagining the Twentieth Century,* edited by Charles Stewart and Peter Fritzsche, University of Illinois Press (Urbana, IL), 1997.

(Contributor) *Reform or Modernization: Egypt under Mohammad Ali,* edited by Rauf Abbas, Supreme Council for Culture (Cairo, Egypt), 2000.

Contributor of articles and reviews to periodicals, including *Islamic Law and Society, British Journal of Middle Eastern Studies, Studia Islamica, Annales Islamologiques, Islamic and Mediterranean Women's History Network Newsletter, International Journal of Middle East Studies, Journal of the American Research Center in Egypt, Turkish Studies Association Bulletin, American Ethnologist, Jusur, International Journal of African Historical Studies, History of Education Quarterly, Middle East Studies Association Bulletin,* and *Middle East Journal.*

WORK IN PROGRESS: Families in Transition: Egypt in the Long Nineteenth Century.

SIDELIGHTS: "Kenneth M. Cuno's work on land tenure and rural society in early nineteenth-century Egypt has been known to specialists for some time," declared Nathan Brown in the *Middle East Studies Association Bulletin.* In 1992, however, Cuno issued his first full-length book on the subject, *The Pasha's Peasants: Land, Society, and Economy in Lower Egypt, 1740-1858.* With this, remarked Brown, Cuno's "cautious arguments, built on exhaustive research, are helping to develop a more nuanced and complex understanding of Egyptian social and economic history."

In *The Pasha's Peasants* Cuno surveys a period of Egyptian history not usually studied as a unit. Most scholars in the field have used the rule of nineteenth-century Egyptian leader Muhammad Ali to mark the beginning of Egypt's modernization, but by also examining many decades previous to this, and utilizing difficult-to-access archival records of land transactions and court proceedings, Cuno has changed the older perception. As Robert L. Tignor observed in the *Middle East Journal,* "Cuno demonstrates that Egypt had lively markets, a monetized economy, and land-holding inequities in the [century preceding Ali's rule]." Tignor went on to predict that "these and other insights will establish *The Pasha's Peasants* as a standard in the social and economic history of modern Egypt." Murat Cizakca in the *Journal of Economic History* offered praise for the volume as well, hailing it as "a most original and important book, one that should be read by everybody interested in the economic and social history of Egypt as well as by those whose main interest is broader." Although Cizakca noted that in *The Pasha's Peasants* "Cuno tends to concentrate too narrowly on Egypt itself, seemingly oblivious to the fact that the country was, after all, an Ottoman province," he credited Cuno with providing "a superb service" to Egyptian historical scholarship.

BIOGRAPHICAL/CRITICAL SOURCES:

PERIODICALS

American Historical Review, October, 1994.

Asian and African Studies, Volume 26, 1992, pp. 263-273.

Digest of Middle East Studies, winter, 1994.

Journal of Economic History, June, 1994, Murat Cizakca, review of *The Pasha's Peasants,* pp. 463-464.

Middle East Journal, spring, 1994, Robert L. Tignor, review of *The Pasha's Peasants,* pp. 374-375.

Middle East Studies Association Bulletin, December, 1993, Nathan Brown, review of *The Pasha's Peasants,* p. 264.

* * *

CURRIE, Edwina 1946-

PERSONAL: Born October 13, 1946, in Liverpool, England; married Ray Currie (an accountant), 1972 (divorced, 2001); married John Benjamin Paul Jones (a police detective), 2001; children: (first marriage) Deborah, Susannah. *Education:* St. Anne's College, Oxford, M.A., 1972; London School of Economics and Political Science, M.Sc., 1972.

ADDRESSES: E-mail—edwina@currie.co.uk.

CAREER: British Parliament, London, England, Conservative member of House of Commons for Derbyshire, 1983-97, minister, Department of Health, 1986-

88. British Broadcasting Corp., host of the program *Late Night Currie* on BBC-Radio. Conservative Group for Europe, chair, 1995-97; European Movement, vice-chair of British branch, 1995-99. Birmingham City Council, past member; Central Birmingham Health Authority, past chair.

AWARDS, HONORS: Named Speaker of the Year, Association of Speakers Clubs, 1990, and Campaigner of the Year, *Spectator,* 1994.

WRITINGS:

Lifelines (nonfiction), Sidgwick & Jackson (London, England), 1989.
What Women Want (essays), Sidgwick & Jackson (London, England), 1990.
Three-Line Quips (humor), ABE, 1991.

NOVELS

A Parliamentary Affair, Hodder & Stoughton (London, England), 1994.
A Woman's Place, Hodder & Stoughton (London, England), 1996.
She's Leaving Home, Little, Brown (London, England), 1997, Warner Books (New York, NY), 1998.
The Ambassador, Little, Brown (London, England), 1999, Warner Books (New York, NY), 2000.
Chasing Men, Little, Brown (London, England), 2000, Warner Books (New York, NY), 2001.
This Honourable House, Little, Brown (London, England), 2001.

SIDELIGHTS: Edwina Currie served as a conservative member of the British Parliament from 1983 to 1997, and now works as the host of a British radio program. She has also written several successful novels—"notorious and bestselling," according to Liz Thomson in *Books*—which feature healthy helpings of political machination and sexual escapade.

In *A Parliamentary Affair,* her first novel, Currie tells the story of a female member of Parliament who has an affair with a colleague. "I wanted to write about really authentic characters in an authentic background," Currie explained to John Russell of *Books.* She further noted: "Insofar as I am highly critical of the way in which this place [Parliament] works and the pressure that it puts on the people in it, I am making a profound political point."

For *She's Leaving Home,* Currie drew on her own family background, telling the story of a young Jewish girl in the 1960s who goes to college and falls in love with an American gentile pilot. Their relationship is harshly opposed by her Orthodox family. As Thomson remarked, *She's Leaving Home* "shatters expectations" for a Currie novel.

Although she has left politics, Currie still has opinions on the political scene. She explained in an interview for BBC-Radio that voters "should be much more sophisticated, and we shouldn't be demanding that politicians make promises that are probably off the wall, and that they cannot keep. [Voters should] be much more realistic about what politicians can and should deliver."

BIOGRAPHICAL/CRITICAL SOURCES:

PERIODICALS

Books, January, 1994, John Russell, review of *A Parliamentary Affair,* p. 6; October, 1997, Liz Thomson, review of *She's Leaving Home,* p. 4.
New Scientist, February 20, 1999, review of *The Ambassador,* p. 47.
Observer (London), February 13, 1994, review of *A Parliamentary Affair,* p. 20; January 21, 1996, review of *A Woman's Place,* p. 16.
Spectator, March 27, 1999, review of *The Ambassador,* p. 31.
Times Literary Supplement, September 26, 1997, review of *She's Leaving Home,* p. 24.
Woman's Journal, September, 1997, review of *She's Leaving Home,* p. 16.

OTHER

BBC Online, http://www.ftp.bbc.co.uk/ (September 7, 2000).
Edwina Currie Web site, http://edwina.currie.co.uk/ (May 25, 2001).

D

DAMASIO, Antonio R. 1944-

PERSONAL: Born February 25, 1944, in Lisbon, Portugal; immigrated to United States, 1975; naturalized U.S. citizen; married; wife's name, Hanna. *Education:* University of Lisbon, M.D., 1969, D.M.S., 1974.

ADDRESSES: *Office*—Department of Neurology, University of Iowa, Iowa City, IA 52242; University of Iowa Hospitals and Clinics, PET Imaging Center, 0911-Z JPP, 200 Hawkins Dr., Iowa City, IA 52242-1009. *E-mail*—antonio-damasio@uiowa.edu.

CAREER: University of Iowa, Iowa City, associate professor, 1976-80, chief of division of behavioral neurology and cognitive neuroscience, 1977—, professor of neurology, 1980—, head of department, 1986—, M. W. Van Allen Distinguished Professor, 1989—. Adjunct professor at Salk Institute, 1989—.

MEMBER: American Academy of Neurology (fellow), American Neurological Association, National Academy of Science, Institute of Medicine, Society for Neuroscience, Behavioral Neurology Society, European Academy of Arts and Sciences, Belgium Royal Society of Medicine, Academy Aphasia.

AWARDS, HONORS: Distinguished Professor Award, University of Southern California, 1985; Dr. William Beaumont Award, American Medical Association, and Association of American Publications award, both 1990, for *Lesion Analysis in Neuropsychology;* Pessoa Prize, Government of Portugal, 1992; Golden Brain Award, Minerva Foundation, 1995; *Los Angeles Times Book Review* award for *Descartes's Error.*

WRITINGS:

(With wife, Hanna Damasio) *Lesion Analysis in Neuropsychology,* Oxford University Press (New York, NY), 1989.

Descartes's Error: Emotion, Reason, and the Human Brain, Putnam (New York, NY), 1994.

(Editor, with Hanna Damasio and Yves Christen) *Neurobiology of Decision-making,* Springer (New York, NY), 1996.

The Feeling of What Happens: Body and Emotion in the Making of Consciousness, Harcourt (New York, NY), 1999.

(Editor, with others) *Unity of Knowledge: The Convergence of Natural and Human Science,* New York Academy of Sciences (New York, NY), 2001.

Contributor to *The Scientific American Book of the Brain,* Lyons Press (New York, NY), 1999; also contributor to periodicals. Member of editorial boards for *Trends in Neurosciences,* 1986-91, *Behavioral Brain Research,* 1988—, *Journal of Neuroscience,* 1990, and *Cerebral Cortex,* 1990—. *Descartes's Error* has been translated into nine languages.

SIDELIGHTS: Antonio R. Damasio is a prominent neuroscientist who has taught neurology at the University of Iowa since 1976. His *Descartes's Error: Emotion, Reason, and the Human Brain* was described by Steven Rose in the *New York Times Book Review* as a work that seeks "to explain aberrant behavior, cognition, affect and perception in terms of the workings of the brain." According to Damasio, whom Rose ranked "among the world's leading neurologists," Descartes's dictum "I think, therefore I am" is more accurate when reversed: "I am, therefore I think." Damasio explains in *Descartes's Error* that feelings are themselves linked to the complex thought process and that the process itself can generate feelings as a means of making determinations and projections.

Damasio distinguishes between primary emotions, including motivations and fears, and secondary emotions, which he characterizes as the cognitively formulated feelings. He thus relates that feeling and thought are, within the process of normal cognition, inextricably linked. Daniel C. Dennett, writing in the *Times Literary Supplement,* lauded the success with which Damasio transforms his argument "into a vision of the brain and its parts that really makes sense, biologically, psychologically and philosophically."

Upon its publication in 1994, *Descartes's Error* was hailed as a significant and impressive study. *Natural History* reviewer Michael S. Gazzaniga affirmed that Damasio "is to be congratulated for presenting us with a clear view of how reason and emotions interact to produce our decisions, our beliefs, our plans for action." Keith Ferrell, meanwhile, asserted in *Omni* that *Descartes's Error* "is a serious popular book in the best sense of both of those words. It is accessible, graceful, and provocative." *New York Times Book Review* contributor Steven Rose declared that the book "should be crucial reading not only for neuroscientists and philosophers but for lay readers too."

In *The Feeling of What Happens: Body and Emotion in the Making of Consciousness,* Damasio examines the nature of human consciousness, trying to unlock just what subjective awareness is and where its biological sources may be. Drawing on medical cases he has personally dealt with in his own practice, Damasio fashions a theory that human consciousness exists on two levels, a core level and a public level, which interact with one another via memory and dream. According to William H. Calvin in the *New York Times Book Review, The Feeling of What Happens* is a "must-read book" that proves Damasio "has one of the best brains of the decade." Andrew Crumey, in his review for *Scotland on Sunday,* found *The Feeling of What Happens* to be a "rewarding if demanding book" and believed that the reader "comes away with a deepened awareness." "Damasio's spirited writing style and scientific rigor," wrote Laurie Bartolini in *Library Journal,* "will make a conscientious reading well worthwhile."

BIOGRAPHICAL/CRITICAL SOURCES:

PERIODICALS

Booklist, September 15, 1999, Donna Seaman, review of *The Feeling of What Happens: Body and Emotion in the Making of Consciousness,* p. 199.

Library Journal, September 1, 1999, Laurie Bartolini, review of *The Feeling of What Happens,* p. 229.

Natural History, February, 1995, Michael S. Gazzaniga, review of *Descartes's Error,* pp. 68-71.

Nature, November 17, 1994, p. 287; October 28, 1999, Raymond J. Dolan, review of *The Feeling of What Happens.*

New Scientist, November 5, 1994, p. 42.

New York Times Book Review, September 11, 1994, Steven Rose, review of *Descartes's Error,* p. 38; October 24, 1999, William H. Calvin, review of *The Feeling of What Happens,* p. 8.

Omni, November, 1994, Keith Ferrell, review of *Descartes's Error,* p. 10.

Publishers Weekly, July 26, 1999, review of *The Feeling of What Happens,* p. 70.

Scotland on Sunday, January, 2000, Andrew Crumey, review of *The Feeling of What Happens.*

Time, October 18, 1999, J. Madeleine Nash, review of *The Feeling of What Happens.*

Times Literary Supplement, August 25, 1995, Daniel C. Dennett, review of *Descartes's Error,* pp. 3-4.*

* * *

DAYAN, Yaël 1939-
(Yael Dayan)

PERSONAL: Born February 12, 1939, in Nahalal, Palestine (now Israel); daughter of Moshe (a former foreign minister of Israel and general in the Israeli Army) and Ruth (Schwartz) Dayan; married Tat-Aluf Dov Sion (a colonel in the Israeli Army), July 22, 1967; children: Dan, Raheli. *Education:* Attended Hebrew University of Jerusalem and the Open University of Israel.

ADDRESSES: *Home*—Tel Aviv, Israel. *Office*—c/o Knesset, Kiryat Ben-Gurion, 91950 Jerusalem, Israel. *E-mail*—edayan@knesset.gov.il.

CAREER: Journalist and novelist. Former public relations worker for the Israeli Government Tourist Office; assistant to Greek film director Michael Cacoyannes, 1964; correspondent in the Sinai during Six-Day War, 1967, and in Vietnam; elected member of Israeli Knesset, 1992—. *Military service:* Israeli Army, 1956-58; became lieutenant. Israeli Army Reserves, 1967; morale officer during Six-Day War.

WRITINGS:

New Face in the Mirror (autobiographical novel), World Publishing, 1959.

Envy the Frightened (novel), World Publishing, 1961.

Dust (novel), World Publishing, 1963.

Death Had Two Sons (novel), McGraw (New York, NY), 1967.

Israel Journal: June, 1967 (diary), McGraw, 1967, published as *A Soldier's Diary: Sinai, 1967,* Weidenfeld & Nicolson (London, England), 1967.

Three Weeks in October (autobiographical novel), Delacorte (New York, NY), 1979.

My Father, His Daughter, Farrar (New York, NY), 1985.

Also author of a travel book. Contributor of articles to Israeli and international newspapers.

SIDELIGHTS: Daughter of renowned Israeli general and politician Moshe Dayan, Yaël Dayan became a world famous author when her first novel, *New Face in the Mirror,* was published in 1959. Written during her compulsory two years in the military service, *New Face* is autobiographical, tracing the life of a young Israeli woman who often reveals herself to be an "arrogant, able, independent Israeli woman soldier." Since 1992 Dayan has served in the Israeli Knesset, the country's parliament, and she has also written the books *Death Had Two Sons, Israel Journal, Three Weeks in October,* and *My Father, His Daughter.*

New Face in the Mirror is narrated by Ariel Ron, a young Israeli woman who rebels against the discipline of army life despite the fact that her father is a general in the army. While Anzia Yezierska in the *New York Times* found "an honesty and a compulsive intensity" in the story, other critics sometimes faulted Dayan's novel. For example, Dorothy Nyren, writing in the *Library Journal,* noted that "Dayan's naive, professional prose is unable to bring this story to life." But a critic for the *Times Literary Supplement* concluded: "Because it comes from the heart, her novel is good in spite of many crude faults."

Critics reviewing Dayan's novel, *Death Had Two Sons,* were reminded of the Bible story of Abraham, who was asked by God to sacrifice his son Isaac. In her novel, however, Dayan replaces Abraham with Haim Kalinsky, a Polish Jew who is forced by the Nazis to choose between his two sons for the sacrifice. Ironically, Daniel, the son who was chosen for death, survives and grows up on an Israeli kibbutz. Father and son are finally reunited through the efforts of an Israeli social agency which has traced Haim to a Beer-Sheba hospital where he lies dying of lung cancer.

A critic from *Books and Bookmen* found *Death Had Two Sons* to be "too one-sided . . . and its picture of life in Israel with its differing ideologies, overheated emotional climate and casual sex encounters is clearer than its view of life outside, which is sketched too hazily, like the faintest childhood memory." However, a *Harper's* critic observed, "Dayan writes with involvement and a passion for life, of death and guilt and the tragedy inherent in human choices. And she writes with riveting and beautiful intensity of the geography and physical feel of the country."

Published in 1967, some months after *Death Had Two Sons, Israel Journal* is Dayan's personal account of the Six-Day War from her position in the Sinai. Assigned to General Ariel Sharon's division for one month, Dayan was both war correspondent and army officer, whose duties often included cooking. The book is a record of how "Sharon, outmanned and outranked, swept out of the Negev, cracked the Egyptian main line of resistance at Um-Katef, and opened the route to the Suez Canal for Israeli armor," the critic for the *New York Times Book Review* noted.

After twelve years, Dayan wrote another novel, *Three Weeks in October.* Like *New Face in the Mirror,* it is also autobiographical and, like *Israel Journal,* it deals with another Arab-Israeli war—the Yom Kippur War in 1973. *Three Weeks in October* tells the story of Amalia and her disintegrating marriage which is somehow revived during the war. For Amalia the war is particularly painful for she is forced to remember her lover who died in battle in a previous war. She longs to be young again and free. A *New Yorker* critic commented, "The power of personal and national devotion, and the ways in which one may inspire or undermine the other, are Yaël Dayan's concern, and she describes with luminous precision the charged atmosphere bending these impassioned people."

In 1985 Dayan wrote *My Father, His Daughter,* a memoir of her father. Moshe Dayan served as leader of the Israeli military forces during the victorious Six-Day War of 1967 and is considered by some a hero in Israel. But Dayan's memoir tells of the real man, including his sometimes painful flaws. When writing of her father's love affairs, Dayan notes: "I am not class-conscious, but there is a matter of good taste. Most of his women were outright vulgar." According to Andrea Chambers in *People,* Dayan's memoir reveals her "honesty at any cost, outspokenness and the Dayan bravado." The critic for *Time* called the book a "tense, embittered account."

In a *McCall's* article Dayan talked about what the "Good Life" meant for Israelis. In a country scarred by war and ever on guard for terrorist attacks, "the Good

Life is simply *life itself.* It is not having to pay the top price of one's life for the most elementary rights—the right to have a home and to bring up children without wondering whether they will reach their twentieth birthday."

Dayan speaks French, Hebrew, Greek, and English, and writes all her novels in English. She has traveled in Europe, South America, Africa, and the Far East.

BIOGRAPHICAL/CRITICAL SOURCES:

BOOKS

Authors in the News, Volume I, Gale (Detroit, MI), 1976.

PERIODICALS

Best Sellers, December 1, 1967, C. M. Siggins, review of *Israel Journal,* p. 344.
Books and Bookmen, May, 1967.
Harper's, January, 1968.
Jewish Quarterly, winter, 1967-1968.
Library Journal, July, 1959, Dorothy Nyren, review of *New Face in the Mirror,* p. 2210; November 15, 1967, David Shavit, review of *Israel Journal,* p. 4147.
McCall's, January, 1970.
National Observer, November 20, 1967.
Newsweek, November 20, 1967, Howard Junker, review of *Israel Journal,* p. 112.
New Yorker, April 23, 1979.
New York Times, August 16, 1959, Anzia Yezierska, review of *New Face in the Mirror,* p. 4; November 2, 1967.
New York Times Book Review, December 17, 1967, Saul Maloff, review of *Death Had Two Sons,* p. 23; December 31, 1967, review of *Israel Journal,* p. 14; March 11, 1979; November 3, 1985, Alison Knopf, review of *My Father, His Daughter.*
People, November 11, 1985, Andrea Chambers, review of *My Father, His Daughter,* p. 69.
Observer Review, December 10, 1967.
Time, November 17, 1967, review of *Israel Journal,* p. 116; November 11, 1985, review of *My Father, His Daughter,* p. 10.
Times Literary Supplement, July 10, 1959, review of *New Face in the Mirror,* p. 409; May 25, 1967.
Washington Post, March 5, 1979.

OTHER

The Knesset Website, http://www.knesset.gov/ (May 21, 2001), biography of Yaël Dayan.*

* * *

DELORIA, Vine (Victor), Jr. 1933-

PERSONAL: Born March 26, 1933, in Martin, SD; son of Vine Victor (a minister) and Barbara (Eastburn) Deloria; married Barbara Jeanne Nystrom, June 14, 1958; children: Philip, Daniel, Jeanne Ann. *Education:* Iowa State University, B.S., 1958; Lutheran School of Theology, Rock Island, IL, M.Th., 1963; University of Colorado, J.D., 1970. *Politics:* Republican. *Religion:* "Seven Day Absentist."

ADDRESSES: Office—Department of History, University of Colorado, Campus Box 234, Boulder, CO 80309 and c/o Fulcrum Publishing, 16100 Table Mountain Parkway, Golden, CO 80403.

CAREER: United Scholarship Service, Denver, CO, staff associate, 1963-64; National Congress of American Indians, Washington, DC, executive director, 1964-67; Institute for the Development of Indian Law, Golden, CO, chair, 1970-76; University of Arizona, Tucson, professor of political science, 1978-90, chairman of American Indian studies, 1979-82; University of Colorado, Boulder, professor of history, 1990-2000; retired. Lecturer at Western Washington State College (now University), 1970-72, and University of California at Los Angeles, 1972-74. Member, Board of Inquiry on Hunger and Malnutrition in the United States, 1967-68, executive council of Episcopal Church, 1969-70, and National Office for the Rights of the Indigent. Consultant to U.S. Senate Select Committee on Aging. *Military service:* U.S. Marine Corps Reserve, 1954-56.

AWARDS, HONORS: Anisfield-Wolf Award, 1970, for *Custer Died for Your Sins: An Indian Manifesto;* D.H. Litt., Augustana College, 1971; Indian Achievement Award from Indian Council Fire, 1972; D.H.L., Scholastica College, 1976, and Hamline University, 1979; Distinguished Alumni Award, Iowa State University, 1977, and University of Colorado School of Law, 1985; D.H.L., Northern Michigan University, 1991; Lifetime Achievement Award, Mountains and Plains Booksellers Association, 1996; Lifetime Achievement Award, Native Writers of America, 1996; Spirit of Excellence Award, American Bar Association, 2001.

Vine Deloria, Jr.

WRITINGS:

Custer Died for Your Sins: An Indian Manifesto, Macmillan, 1969, with new preface by Deloria, 1988.

We Talk, You Listen: New Tribes, New Turf, Macmillan, 1970.

(Compiler) *Of Utmost Good Faith,* Straight Arrow Books, 1971.

God Is Red, Grosset, 1973, 2nd edition published as *God Is Red: A Native View of Religion,* North American Press, 1992.

Behind the Trail of Broken Treaties: An Indian Declaration of Independence, Delacorte, 1974.

The Indian Affair, Friendship, 1974.

A Better Day for Indians, Field Foundation, 1976.

Indians of the Pacific Northwest: From the Coming of the White Man to the Present Day, Doubleday, 1977.

The Metaphysics of Modern Existence, Harper, 1979.

(With Clifford M. Lytle) *American Indians, American Justice,* University of Texas Press (Austin), 1983.

(With Lytle) *The Nations Within: The Past and Future of American Indian Sovereignty,* Pantheon, 1984.

Indian Education in America: Eight Essays by Vine Deloria, Jr., American Indian Science and Engineering Society, 1991.

Red Earth, White Lies: Native Americans and the Myth of Scientific Fact, Scribner (New York City), 1995.

For This Land: Writings on Religion in America, Routledge (New York City), 1998.

Singing for a Spirit: A Portrait of the Dakota Sioux, Clear Light, 1999.

Spirit and Reason: The Vine Deloria, Jr., Reader, edited by Barbara Deloria, Kristen Foehner, and Sam Scinta, Fulcrum (Golden, CO), 1999.

(With David E. Wilkins) *Tribes, Treaties, and Constitutional Tribulations,* University of Texas Press, 1999.

(With Raymond DeMallie) *Documents of American Indian Diplomacy*, University of Oklahoma Press, 2000.

(With Daniel Wildcat) *Power and Place: Essays in American Indian Education*, Fulcrum, 2001.

EDITOR

(And author of introduction) Jennings Cooper Wise, *The Red Man in the New World Drama: A Politico-Legal Study with a Pageantry of American History,* Macmillan, 1971.

(With Sandra L. Cadwalader) *The Aggressions of Civilization: Federal Indian Policy since the 1880s,* Temple University Press, 1984.

A Sender of Words: Essays in Memory of John G. Neihardt, Howe Brothers, 1984.

American Indian Policy in the Twentieth Century, University of Oklahoma Press, 1984.

Frank Waters: Man and Mystic, Swallow Press, 1993.

Also editor of *A Ballad of the West: Seekers of the Fleece,* by Bobby Bridger, 2nd edition, published by Augustine. Contributor to books, including *Native American Testimony: An Anthology of Indian and White Relations,* by Peter Nabokov, HarperCollins, 1984; *Keepers of the Animals: Native American Stories and Wildlife Activities for Children,* by Michael Caduto, Fulcrum Publishing, 1991; *The Dream Seekers: Native American Visionary Traditions of the Great Plains,* by Lee Irwin, University of Oklahoma Press, 1994; contributor of introduction to new edition of *Speaking of Indians* by Ella Deloria, originally published 1944, new edition by University of Nebraska Press, 1998; and compiler, with Raymond J. DeMallie and Daniel K. Inouye, of *Documents of American Indian Diplomacy: Treaties, Agreements, and Conventions, 1775-1979,* University of Oklahoma Press, 1999.

WORK IN PROGRESS: Research on Indian legends concerning the creation of mountains, rivers, and other natural phenomena; research on Indian treaties, social problems, and political history.

SIDELIGHTS: "Among his people, Vine Deloria, Jr., has achieved a status somewhat similar to that of Sitting Bull's leadership of the Sioux tribes a century ago," wrote Dee Brown in the *New York Times Book Review.* A Standing Rock Sioux lawyer and educator, Deloria is perhaps the most prominent spokesman in the country for Native American nationalism. He first came to the public's attention in 1969 with the publication of his first book, *Custer Died for Your Sins: An Indian Manifesto.* Deloria, said Douglas N. Mount of *Publishers Weekly,* "wants to be the red man's Ralph Nader." To that end, Deloria has, in addition to serving as executive director of the National Congress of American Indians and chairman of the Institute for the Development of Indian Law, written several books decrying the effects of racism and colonialism and advocating a strong Indian nationalism.

Custer Died for Your Sins: An Indian Manifesto is both a scathing indictment of white America's treatment of Indians and an articulation of the goal of Indian activists: an existence that is culturally but not economically separate. J. A. Phillips of *Best Sellers* noted that if this book "is indicative of Deloria's methods, he's more interested in results than in being tactful. Nauseated by the traditional Indian image, he asserts the worth if not the dignity of the red man and blasts the political, social, and religious forces that perpetuate the Little Big Horn and wigwam stereotyping of his people." A *Time* critic declared that what Deloria really wants to talk about, aside from the origins of scalping and the differences between Black and Indian nationalism, is something "few white Americans know anything about—termination and tribalism." Termination is a government policy designed to cut federal aid to Indians, close down reservations, and blend all remaining Indians into the American economic and cultural mainstream. The *Time* critic opined that in Deloria's opinion, "the termination policy, which implies integration of Indians, is a loser's game."

Deloria sees tribalism—whereby people, land, and religion form a single covenantal relationship that gives each community a unique character—as the key to the whole Indian struggle, but adds that it may also be Indians' greatest liability. In an interview with Mount, he describes tribalism as "a way of life, a way of thinking, . . . a great tradition which is timeless, which has nothing to do with the sequence of events. This creates a wonderful relaxing atmosphere, a tremendous sense of invulnerability." But he cautions that it also fosters the impression that the white man will just go away and leave the Indian alone.

Custer Died For Your Sins became a seminal text for anthropologists, exposing both deep flaws in their typical methods of studying tribal peoples as well as possible new approaches to such field work. Much new thinking in anthropology, including decisions to return human remains and sacred artifacts, often held in museums, to the tribes from which they had been taken, can be traced to Deloria's critique in his first book. His arguments were so influential that in 1989, the American Anthropological Association sponsored a panel at which were presented ten essays inspired by his thinking. These were published in *Indians and Anthropologists: Vine Deloria, Jr., and the Critique of Anthropologists,* which also contains his response to the essays. In reviewing the volume for *Journal of the Royal Anthropological Institute,* Paula L. Wagoner pointed out that "most North American anthropologists trained after 1969 have benefited from Vine Deloria Jr.'s critique of social science's invasion into Indian country." She added that the essays Deloria inspired "are particularly useful in challenging contemporary anthropologists to ferret out biases that sometimes stubbornly persist even as we accuse our intellectual predecessors." In his response, Deloria writes that "as long as anthropology and anthropologists focus on Indians and other tribal peoples and report back to their own society about the quaint and sometimes romantic people they are studying, there is no respect for tribal peoples. . . . If, however, anthropologists and other social scientists begin to speak critically to the shortcomings of their own society using knowledge derived from observations of tribal peoples, that will be a signal that something of real value is contained within the tribal context."

Tribalism is also the subject of Deloria's second book, *We Talk, You Listen: New Tribes, New Turf.* Examining what he considers to be the deteriorating core of contemporary technological society, Deloria attacks the corporate patterns of American life, advocates a return to tribal social organization, and describes the tribal characteristics he perceives in American minority groups. Cecil Eby of *Book World* commented that in this book, as well as in *Custer Died for Your Sins,* Deloria "describes the thrust of the Red-Power movement without anointing himself as its oracle or its official spokesman . . . [He] brings into focus the moods and habitat of the contemporary Indian as seen by a Standing Rock Sioux, not by a research anthropologist or a jobber in the basketry trades. He peels away layers of tinsel and feathers heaped upon the Indian by misinformed whites. . . . and he reveals an uncanny ability for impaling them on the fine points of their own illogic." However, N. Scott Momaday, writing in the *New York Review of Books,* considered Deloria's portrayal of the contemporary Indian weak: "Deloria is a thoughtful man, and he is articulate as well; but [*Custer Died for Your Sins* and *We Talk, You Listen*] are disappointing in one respect: they tell us very little about Indians, after all. In neither book is there any real evocation of that spirit and mentality which distinguishes the Indian as a man and as a race. . . . This seems all the more regrettable in view of the fact that he really knows something about the subject by virtue of blood as well as experience."

In *God Is Red,* Deloria, the son of an Indian Episcopalian clergyman and himself seminary-trained, not only attempts to evoke that spirit and mentality which is unique to the Indian but argues that its theological basis in tribal religions seems to be "more at home in the modern world than Christian ideas and Western man's traditional concepts." Asserting that Christianity inculcates and justifies imperialism, rootlessness, and ecocide, Deloria maintains that America can survive only if there is a revolution in theological concepts. Peter Mayer claimed in *Best Sellers* that "Deloria could have made his point—that Indian religious practices are far more in accord with the necessities of contemporary life than are Christian—without dredging up the many failures of the sons of the Church upon the earth. . . . But read the book; I found it hard to put down." A later book on spirituality, *For This Land: Writings on Religion in America,* focuses more specifically on the relationship between Indian spirituality and sacred land. A collection of Deloria's shorter essays and articles, the book suggests that disputes over treaty rights and other legal matters are for Indians as much a religious as a political concern, and that common ground between them and other Americans cannot be found until mainstream culture acknowledges the intrinsic sacredness of the land.

Serving as an Indian treaties expert, Deloria was the first witness for the defense in the Wounded Knee trial of 1974, held in St. Paul, Minnesota. His book, *Behind the Trail of Broken Treaties,* "is not only the best account yet written of events leading to Wounded Knee 1973," commended Dee Brown in the *New York Times Book Review,* but "it is also a compelling argument for a reopening of the treaty-making procedure between Indian tribes and the U.S. Government." L. A. Howard of *Best Sellers* echoed Brown's assessment: "Step by step, argument by argument, [Deloria] refutes those who would label treaty-making as an implausible way at best for the United States to conduct its relations with the American Indians." L. E. Oliva of *Library Journal* noted that Deloria does not consider this proposal "as a panacea but simply as a necessary first step" to insure the survival of Indian tribes, their lands, and their ways of life. What Deloria hopes for is a new treaty relationship which will give Indian tribes the status of quasi-international independence, with the United States acting as protector.

In *Red Earth, White Lies,* Deloria seeks to discredit Western scientific theories on the human and animal population of the Western hemisphere and how they came to be. Proposed as the first of a series examining Western science, religion, and government, the title received mixed reviews. While acknowledging the negative response of the scientific community to Deloria's proposals, Mary B. Davis in *Library Journal* felt that Deloria's argument "echoes a cry heard through Native American communities"; and a *Publishers Weekly* reviewer suggested that Deloria's theories "should provoke more evaluation." But a critic for *Kirkus Reviews* found Deloria's text "unconvincing . . . because of his seeming lack of even the most basic understanding of the subject." Calling the book "historical nonsense," Brian Fagan in the *New York Times Book Review* concluded that Deloria "treats both scientific research and Native American sources with equal disrespect," and accuses him of using "marginal and usually long-discredited scientific sources to bolster his arguments."

Deloria's more recent works return to historical concerns. With David E. Wilkins, he wrote *Tribes, Treaties, and Constitutional Tribulations,* a study of the treatment of Indians under American constitutional law. *Library Journal*'s Steve Anderson considered it a "shocking indictment" of the ways in which the Supreme Court has failed to support Indian rights. Calling the book a "much-needed historical work," Anderson added that the study isn't as thorough as it could be in analyzing "the many U.S. Supreme Court decisions that have stripped away even the slimmest constitutional guarantees." *Documents of American Indian Diplomacy: Treaties, Agreements, and Conventions, 1775-1979,* on which Deloria collaborated with Raymond J. DeMallie, is a compilation of legal documents. And *Singing for a Spirit: A Portrait of the Dakota Sioux,* is a reworking of traditional Dakota Sioux stories, legends, and biographical sketches that Deloria had learned from his grandfather, Chief Tipi Sapa.

BIOGRAPHICAL/CRITICAL SOURCES:

BOOKS

Biolsi, Thomas, and Larry J. Zimmerman, *Indians and Anthropologists: Vine Deloria, Jr., and the Critique of Anthropology,* University of Arizona Press, 1997.
Contemporary Literary Criticism, Volume 21, Gale, 1982.
Deloria, Vine, Jr., *Custer Died for Your Sins: An Indian Manifesto,* Macmillan, 1969.
Deloria, Vine, Jr., *God Is Red,* Grosset, 1973.
Gridley Marian E., *Contemporary American Indian Leaders,* Dodd, 1972.
Gridley, Marian E., editor, *Indians of Today,* I.C.E.P., 1971.
Native North American Literature, Gale, 1994.
Warrior, Robert Allen, *Tribal Secrets: Recovering American Indian Intellectual Traditions,* University of Minnesota Press (Minneapolis), 1994.
Who's Who in Writers, Editors and Poets, United States and Canada, 1992-1993, December Press (Highland Park, IL), 1992.

PERIODICALS

America, March 16, 1974, pp. 198-200; May 22, 1976, pp. 456-457.
American Anthropologist, Volume 73, number 4, 1971, pp. 953-955; Volume 77, number 1, 1975, p. 109.
American Political Science Review, December, 1976, pp. 1306-1307.
Best Sellers, October 15, 1970, pp. 281-82; November 15, 1973, p. 363; September 1, 1974, p. 254.
Bloomsbury Review, March/April 2000.
Booklist, September 1, 1977, p. 38; March 1, 1999, p. 1128.
Book World, October 4, 1970, p. 4.
Choice, December, 1974, p. 1508; April, 1975, p. 256.
Christian Century, February 18, 1970, p. 213; March 7, 1984, pp. 256-257.
Christian Science Monitor, February, 26, 1970; January 2, 1974, p. F7.
Commonweal, February 6, 1970, p. 515.
Ethics, January, 1985, pp. 398-399.
Harper's, November, 1970, p. 134.
Journal of the Royal Anthropological Institute, March 1999, p. 131,
Kirkus Reviews, August 15, 1995, p. 1155.
Library Journal, September 15, 1995, p. 80; February 15, 2000, p. 181.
Mademoiselle, April, 1971.
Nation, January 26, 1970, pp. 86-88; February 9, 1974, pp. 186-187.
New Yorker, October 24, 1970, p. 76.
New York Review of Books, April 8, 1971.
New York Times Book Review, November 9, 1969, p. 46; September 13, 1970, pp. 8, 10; November 24, 1974; April 11, 1993, p. 22; November 26, 1995, p. 18.
Pacific Historical Review, November, 1970, pp. 553-554.
Progressive, April, 1990, p. 24.
Publishers Weekly, December 1, 1969; August 7, 1995, p. 448; January 11, 1999, p. 67.
Saturday Review, October 4, 1969, pp. 39-41, 80-81.
School Library Journal, April, 1977, p. 76.
Southwest Review, autumn, 1985, pp. 550-551.
Time, October 10, 1969, p. 102.
Village Voice, January 29, 1970, pp. 8, 33, 48.
Western American Literature, spring, 1985, pp. 79-80.
Western Historical Quarterly, October, 1984, pp. 451-452; January, 1986, pp. 77-78.

* * *

DENVER, Walt
See SHERMAN, Jory (Tecumseh)

* * *

DERRIDA, Jacques 1930-

PERSONAL: Born July 15, 1930, in El Biar, Algeria; son of Aime and Georgette (Safar) Derrida. *Education:* Attended Ecole Normale Superieure, 1952-56; University of Paris, Sorbonne, Licence es Lettres, 1953, Licence de Philosophie, 1953, Diplome d'Etudes Superieures, 1954; received Certificat d'Ethnologie, 1954, Agregation de Philosophie, 1956, Doctorat en Philosophie, 1967, Doctorat d'Etat es Lettres, 1980; graduate study at Harvard University, 1956-57.

ADDRESSES: Home—Paris, France. *Office*—Ecole des Hautes Etudes en Sciences Sociales, 54 bis Raspail, 75006 Paris, France; c/o University of Chicago Press, 5801 South Ellis Ave., Chicago, IL 60637.

CAREER: Philosopher and educator. Professeur de lettres superieures at Lycee du Mans, 1959-60; University of Paris, Sorbonne, Paris, France, professor of phi-

Jacques Derrida

losophy, 1960-64; Ecole Normale Superieure, Paris, professor of philosophy, 1964-84; Ecole des Hautes Etudes en Sciences Sociales, Paris, director, 1984—. College International de Philosophie, member of planning board, 1982-83, director, 1983-84, member of administrative council, 1986. Visiting professor and lecturer at numerous universities in Europe and the United States, including Johns Hopkins University, Yale University, University of California at Irvine, Cornell University, and City University of New York.

MEMBER: Institut des Textes et Manuscrits Modernes (member of steering committee, 1983-86), Groupe de Recherches sur l'Enseignement Philosophique (president), Association Jan Hus (vice president), Fondation Culturelle Contre l'Apartheid, American Academy of Arts and Sciences (foreign honorary member), Modern Language Association of America (honorary member), Academy for the Humanities and Sciences (honorary member).

AWARDS, HONORS: Prix Cavailles from Societe des Amis de Jean Cavailles, 1964, for translation into French and introduction of Edmund Husserl's *Origin of Geometry;* named to Liste d'Aptitude a l'Enseignement Superieur, 1968; Chevalier, 1968, Officier, 1980, des Palmes Academiques; Commandeur des Arts et des Lettres, 1983; Prix Nietzsche from Association Internationale de Philosophie, 1988; Chevalier de la Legion d'Honneur, 1995. Honorary doctorates from Columbia University, 1980, University of Louvain, 1983, University of Essex, 1987.

WRITINGS:

(Translator and author of introduction) Edmund Husserl, *L'Origine de la geometrie,* Presses Universitaires de France (Paris), 1962, translation by John P. Leavy published as *Edmund Husserl's "Origin of Geometry": An Introduction,* Nicolas-Hays (York Beach, ME), 1977.

La Voix et le phenomene: Introduction au probleme du signe dans la phenomenologie de Husserl, Presses Universitaires de France, 1967, translation by David B. Allison published as *Speech and Phenomena and Other Essays on Husserl's Theory of Signs,* Northwestern University Press (Evanston, IL), 1973.

L'Ecriture et la difference, Editions du Seuil (Paris), 1967, translation by Alan Bass published as *Writing and Difference,* University of Chicago Press (Chicago, IL), 1978.

De la grammatologie, Minuit, 1967, translation by Gayatri Chakravorty Spivak published as *Of Grammatology,* Johns Hopkins University Press (Baltimore, MD), 1976.

La Dissemination, Editions du Seuil, 1972, translation by Barbara Johnson published as *Dissemination,* University of Chicago Press, 1981.

Marges de la philosophie, Minuit, 1972, translation by Alan Bass published as *Margins of Philosophy,* University of Chicago Press, 1982.

Positions: Entretiens avec Henri Ronse, Julia Kristeva, Jean-Louis Houdebine, Guy Scarpetta (interviews), Minuit, 1972, translation by Alan Bass published as *Positions,* University of Chicago Press, 1981.

Glas, Galilée, 1974, translation by John P. Leavey, Jr., and Richard Rand published as *Glas,* University of Nebraska Press (Lincoln, NE), 1986.

L'Archeologie du frivole (first published as introduction to Etienne de Condillac, *L'Essai sur l'origine des connaissances humaines,* Galilée, 1973), Editions Denoel, 1976, translation by John P. Leavey, Jr., published as *The Archaeology of the Frivolous: Reading Condillac,* Duquesne University Press (Atlantic Highlands, NJ), 1980.

Eperons: Les Styles de Nietzsche, Flammarion (Paris), 1976, translation by Barbara Harlow published as *Spurs: Nietzsche's Styles,* University of Chicago Press, 1979.

Limited Inc: abc, Johns Hopkins University Press, 1977.

La vérité en peinture (title means "Truth in Painting"), Flammarion, 1978.

La carte postale: De Socrate a Freud et au-dela, Flammarion, 1980, translation by Alan Bass published as *The Post Card: From Socrates to Freud and Beyond,* University of Chicago Press, 1987.

L'Oreille de l'autre: Otobiographies, transferts, traductions; textes et debats, VLB (Montreal), 1982, translation by Peggy Kamuf published as *The Ear of the Other: Otobiography, Transference, Translation,* Schocken (New York City), 1985.

D'un ton apocalyptique adopte naguere en philosophie, Galilée, 1983.

Feu la cendre/Cio'che resta del fuoco, Sansoni (Florence), 1984, published as *Feu la cendre,* Editions des Femmes, 1987.

Signeponge/Signsponge (French and English text; English translation by Richard Rand), Columbia University Press (New York City), 1984, revised, Editions du Seuil, 1988.

Otobiographies: L'Enseignement de Nietzsche et la politique du nom propre, Galilée, 1984.

Droit de regards, Editions de Minuit (Paris), 1985.

La faculté de juger, Editions de Minuit, 1985.

Parages, Galilée, 1986.

De l'esprit: Heidegger et la question, Galilée, 1987, translation by Geoffrey Bennington and Rachel Bowlby published as *Of Spirit: Heidegger and the Question,* University of Chicago Press, 1989.

Psyche: Inventions de l'autre, Galilée, 1987.

Memoires: Pour Paul de Man, Galilée, 1988, translation by Cecile Lindsay, Jonathan Culler, and Eduardo Cadava published as *Memoires: Lectures for Paul de Man,* Columbia University Press, 1986.

Le probleme de la genese dans la philosophie de Husserl, Presses Universitaires de France, 1990.

De droit a la philosophie, Galilée, 1990.

Memoires de'aveugle, L'autoportrait et autres ruins, Reunion des musees nationaux, 1990, translation by Pascale Ann Brault and Michael Nass published as *Memoirs of the Blind, the Self-Portrait and Other Ruins,* University of Chicago Press, 1993.

Donner le temps, 1, Fausse monnai, Galilée, 1991, translation by Peggy Kamuf published as *Given Time, 1: Counterfeit Money,* University of Chicago Press, 1992.

L'autre cap; suivre de la democratie ajournaee, Editions de Minuit, 1991, translation by Pascale-Anne Brault and Michael Naas published as *The Other Heading: Reflections of Today's Europe,* Indiana University Press (Bloomington, IN), 1992.

A Derrida Reader: Between the Blinds, edited by Peggy Kamuf, Columbia University Press, 1991.

Cinders, translation by Ned Lukacher, University of Nebraska Press, 1991.

(With Geoffrey Derrida) *Jacques Derrida,* Editions du Seuil, 1991.

Prejuges, Edition Passagen, 1992.

Acts of Literature, edited by Derek Attridge, Routledge (London), 1992.

Donner la mort, Seuil, 1992, translation by David Wells published as *The Gift of Death,* University of Chicago Press, 1995.

Passions, Galilée, 1993.

Khora, Galilée, 1993.

Apories: mourir-s'attendre aux "limites de la vérite," Galilée, 1993, translation by Thomas Dutoit published as *Aporias: Dying-Awaiting (One Another at) the "Limits of Truth,"* Stanford University Press (Stanford, CA), 1993.

Spectres de Marx: l'état de la dette, le travail du deuil et la nouvelle internationale, Galilée, 1993, translation by Peggy Kamuf published as *Spectres of Marx, State of the Debt, the Work of Mourning, and the New International,* Routledge, 1994.

Force de loi; le "fondement mystique de l'autorité," Galilée, 1994.

On the Name, edited by Thomas Dutoit, translated by David Wood and others, Stanford University Press, 1995.

Politiques de l'amitié, Galilée, 1994, translation by George Collins published as *The Politics of Friendship,* Verso, 1997.

Mal d'archive, une impression freudienne, Galilée, 1995, translation by Eric Predowitz published as *Archive Fever: A Freudian Impression,* University of Chicago Press, 1996.

Deconstruction and Philosophy: The Texts of Jacques Derrida, translation by David Wells, University of Chicago Press, 1995.

Deconstruction and Pragmatism, 1996.

Résistances, de la psychanalyse, Galilée, 1996, published as *Resistances of Psychoanalysis,* Stanford University Press, 1998.

La monolinguisme de l'autre, ou La prothèse d'origine, Galilée, 1996, translation by Patrick Mensa published as *Monolingualism of the Other; or, The Prosthesis of Origin,* Stanford University Press, 1998.

Passions de la littaerature: avec Jacques Derrida, Galilée, 1996.

(With Bernard Stiegler) *Echographies de la télévision,* Galilée, 1996.

(With Peter Eisenman) *Chora L Works,* Monacelli Press, 1997.

Deconstruction in a Nutshell: A Conversation with Jacques Derrida, edited by John D. Caputo, Fordham University Press (Bronx, NY), 1997.

(With Paule Thevenin) *Secret Art of Antonin Artaud,* translation by Mary AnnCaws, MIT Press (Cambridge, MA), 1997.

Cosmopolites de tous les pays, encore un effort, Galilée, 1997.

Adieu à Emmanuel Lévines, Galilée, 1997, translation by Pascale-Anne Brault and Michael Naas published as *Adieu to Emmanuel Levinas,* Stanford University Press, 1999.

Sur Parole: Instantanés philosophiques, Aube (La Tour d'Aigues), 1999.

Le Toucher, Jean-Luc Nancy/Jacques Derrida: Accompagné de travaux de lecture de Simon Hantai, Galilée, 1999.

(With Catherine Malabou) *Jacques Derrida: La contre-allée,* Quinzaine litteraire-Louis Vuitton (Paris), 1999.

De l'hospitalité/Anne Duformantelle invite Jacques Derrida à répondre, Calmann Levy, 1997, translation by Rachel Bowlby published as *Of Hospitality: Anne Dufourmantelle Invites Jacques Derrida To Respond,* Stanford University Press, 2000.

The Instant of My Death, translated by Elizabeth Rottenberg, Stanford University Press, 2000.

(With Safaa Fathy) *Tourner les mots: Au bord d'un film,* Galilée, 2000.

Also author of *Moscou aller-retour,* Aube.

CONTRIBUTOR

Tableau de la litterature francaise, Gallimard, 1974.

Mimesis, Aubier-Flammarion, 1976.

Politiques de la philosophie, Grasset, 1976.

Qui a peur de la philosophie?, Flammarion, 1977.

Les États Generaux de la philosophie, Flammarion, 1979.

Deconstruction and Criticism, Seabury Press (New York City), 1979.

Philosophy in France Today, Cambridge University Press (Cambridge, England), 1983.

Joseph H. Smith and William Kerrigan, editors, *Taking Chances: Derrida, Psychoanalysis, and Literature,* Johns Hopkins University Press, 1984.

Text und Interpretation, Fink, 1984.

Post-structuralist Joyce, Cambridge University Press, 1984.

La faculté de juger, Minuit, 1985.

Qu'est-ce que Dieu?, [Brussels], 1985.

Difference in Translation, Cornell University Press (Ithaca, NY), 1985.

Genese de Babel, Joyce et la creation, Editions du CNRS, 1985.

Paul Celan, Galilée, 1986.

La grève des philosophes: école et philosophie, Editions Osiris, 1986, published as *Raising the Tone of Philosophy,* edited by Peter Fenves, Johns Hopkins University Press, 1993.

La case vide, Achitectural Association (London), 1986.

Pour Nelson Mandela, Gallimard, 1986.

Romeo et Juliette, Papiers, 1986.

OTHER

Co-director of the collection, *La Philosophie en effet.* Member of editorial boards of *Critique, Structuralist Review, Contemporary Studies in Philosophy and the Human Sciences,* and *Revue senegalaise de philosophie.* Associated with *Tel Quel* during 1960s and 1970s.

SIDELIGHTS: French philosopher Jacques Derrida is the leading light of the post-structuralist intellectual movement that has significantly influenced philosophy, the social sciences, and literary criticism in recent years. By means of a "strategy of deconstruction," Derrida and other post-structuralists seek to reveal the play of multiple meanings in our cultural products and expose the tacit metaphysical assumptions that they believe underlie much of contemporary social thought. The deconstructionist project has ignited intense controversy among intellectuals in Europe and the United States, with detractors dismissing it as a particularly insidious form of nihilism, while its advocates argue that deconstructive practice allows the possibility of creating new values amid what they see as cynicism and spiritual emptiness of postmodern society.

Derrida first outlined his seminal ideas in a lengthy introduction to his 1962 French translation of German philosopher Edmund Husserl's *Origin of Geometry.* The strategy of deconstruction is rigorously delineated in Derrida's difficult masterwork, *Of Grammatology,* but the philosopher explains some of his basic concepts in more accessible terms in a 1972 collection of interviews called *Positions.* Derrida's thought builds on a variety of so-called subversive literature, including the writings of German philosophers Friedrich Nietzsche and Martin Heidegger, who both sought to overturn established values and depart from the traditional approach to the study of metaphysics; the political, social, and cultural insights of political economist Karl Marx and psychologist Sigmund Freud, who postulated underlying contradictory phenomena beneath the surface of everyday social life; and the linguistic analysis of the Swiss linguist Ferdinand de Saussure, who posited that language functions in a self-referential manner and has no "natural" relation to external reality. Many of Derrida's texts are subtle analyses of the writings of these thinkers and the literature of the modern structuralist movement, another strong influence on the philosopher. While accepting the structuralist notion, derived from Saussure, that cultural phenomena are best understood as self-referential systems of signs, Derrida denies the existence of a common intellectual structure capable of unifying the diverse cultural structures.

In the *New York Times Magazine,* Colin Campbell wrote: "'Post-structuralism' is a term that lumps together various French and other thinkers who write as though they want to overthrow oppressive philosophic structures by subverting language. Deconstruction was invented by Jacques Derrida . . . and Derrida is still the movement's leading theoretician." Campbell added: "In 1966, Derrida delivered his first lectures in the United States. The movement has been upsetting people and texts since."

Derrida's insistence on the inadequacy of language to render a complete and unambiguous representation of reality forms the basis for his deconstructivist strategy of reading texts. Campbell stated: "To 'deconstruct' a text is pretty much what it sounds like—to pick the thing carefully apart, exposing what deconstructors see as the central fact and tragic little secret of Western philosophy—namely, the circular tendency of language to refer to itself. Because the 'language' of a text refers mainly to other 'languages' and texts—and not to some hard, extratexual reality—the text tends to have several possible meanings, which usually undermine one another. In fact, the 'meaning' of a piece of writing—it doesn't matter whether it's a poem or a novel or a philosophic treatise—is indeterminate."

In reading, Derrida studies texts for the multiple meanings that underlie and subvert the surface meaning of every piece of writing. To do this, he scrutinizes seemingly marginal textual elements such as idiosyncrasies of vocabulary and style, and subverts what appear to be simple words and phrases with a battery of puns, allusions, and neologisms. He illuminates the continual play of differences in language—a movement he calls "differance." As he wrote in *Positions,* differance prevents any simple element of language from being "*present* in and of itself, referring only to itself." Rather, every element contains differences and spaces within itself and *traces* of other elements that interweave to transform one text into another. There is, in Derrida's famous phrase, "nothing outside the text," that is, no clear and simple meaning represented by words, but only the play of differance and the multiplication of meanings in the deconstructive project. Although a deconstructive reading is never definitive, it is also not arbitrary, and the textual transformations can be followed systematically and even subjected to a structural analysis. Derrida's own deconstructive analyses of philosophical and literary texts include *Margins of Philosophy, Dissemination,* and *Spurs: Nietzsche's Styles.* "Derrida, in a typically bold and outrageous way, has gone so far as to say that writing is more basic than speaking, that speaking is only a form of writing," Campbell related. "But there's more. Because all writing is said to be metaphorical, working by tropes and figures, it follows that trained deconstructors should be able to interpret texts of all sorts, not just 'literature.'"

Given his devotion to textual analysis, Derrida has strongly influenced literary criticism, particularly in France and in the United States. J. Hillis Miller and the late Paul de Man of Yale University are the best-known American deconstructivists, but younger critics in many universities have also adopted the method. Derrida himself, meanwhile, has attempted to deconstruct the distinction between criticism and creative writing in his books such as *Glas* and *The Post Card.* The first work is considered one of the most unusual books ever printed. The pages of *Glas* are divided into two columns, one being a philosophical, psychological, and biographical portrait of the German philosopher G. W. F. Hegel, and the other a critical analysis of the writings of French playwright Jean Genet. The columns are, in turn, fractured within themselves into sub-columns and boxes. Both texts begin and end in mid-sentence and appear at first to be completely independent from each other—indeed, they can be read that way. But the reader can also create his or her own text by uncovering the textual traces that link the two columns and illuminate their differences. In fact, there is a virtually infinite number of ways to read and interpret *Glas,* which stoutly resists any total understanding. "The disorderly philosophical conduct of this work is so magnificent that it defies linear exposition," Geoffrey H. Hartman remarked in his critical study *Saving the Text: Literature/Derrida/Philosophy.* "Not since *Finnegans Wake* has there been such a deliberate and curious work: less original . . . and mosaic than the *Wake,* even flushed and overreaching, but as intriguingly, wearyingly allusive." *New York Times Book Review* contributor John Sturrock noted that *Glas* "is so made as to impose a certain vagrancy on the eyes and attention of whoever reads it and to break us of our nasty linear habits."

Derrida's strategy of deconstruction has implications far beyond literary criticism in the postmodern age, in the opinion of some moral philosophers. At a time when both religion and secular humanist ideologies have failed for many people, the post-structuralist celebration of difference offers an escape from alienated individualism. The metaphysical search is nostalgic and totalizing—seeking origin and end—while the deconstructive project recognizes no permanence and subverts all hierarchies. Dismissed by some readers and critics as nihilistic, this radical insistence on difference, incompleteness, and ephemerality impresses others as a positive grounding for social tolerance, mutual respect, and open discourse as the world enters the twenty-first century.

It is in the fields of philosophy, political philosophy, and literary criticism, however, that Derrida's impact has been felt most strongly. "Jacques Derrida is a philosopher from whom many of us have learned what we judge to be important and seductive truths about the nature of language," Sturrock declared, "and it would be good to go on learning from him." Also in the *New York Times Book Review,* Perry Meisel observed: "In fact, literary study in America has never been in better shape. Enriched by a variety of European methodologies since the early 1970s, it has grown into a vast, synthetic enterprise characterized by powerful continuities rather than by disjunctions. Feminism, deconstruction, 'reader-response,' 'New Historicism,' 'postcolonialism'—all share similar ends and similar ways of getting there in a momentous collaboration."

BIOGRAPHICAL/CRITICAL SOURCES:

BOOKS

Behler, Ernst, *Confrontations: Derrida/Heidegger/ Nietzsche,* Stanford University Press (Stanford, CA), 1991.

Caputo, John D., *The Prayers and Tears of Jacques Derrida: Religion without Religion,* Indiana University Press (Bloomington, IN), 1997.

Collins, Jeff, *Introducing Derrida,* Totem Books, 1997.

Contemporary Literary Criticism, Volume 24, Gale (Detroit, MI), 1983.

Garver, Newton, *Derrida and Wittgenstein,* Temple University Press (Philadelphia, PA), 1994.

Gasche, Rodolphe, *The Train of the Mirror: Derrida and the Philosophy of Difference,* Harvard University Press (Cambridge, MA), 1986.

Hartman, Geoffrey H., *Saving the Text: Literature/ Derrida/Philosophy,* Johns Hopkins University Press (Baltimore, MD), 1981.

Harvey, Irene E., *Derrida and the Economy of Difference,* Indiana University Press, 1986.

Llewelyn, John, *Derrida on the Threshold of Sense,* Macmillan (New York City), 1986.

Lucy, Niall, *Debating Derrida,* Melbourne University Press, 1995.

Magliola, Robert R., *Derrida on the Mend,* Purdue University Press (West Lafayette, IN), 1984.

Megill, Allan, *Prophets of Extremity,* University of California Press (Berkeley, CA), 1985.

Norris, Christopher, *Derrida,* Harvard University Press, 1987.

Staten, Henry, *Wittgenstein and Derrida,* University of Nebraska Press (Lincoln, NE), 1984.

Sturrock, John, editor, *Structuralism and Since: From Levi-Strauss to Derrida,* Oxford University Press (Oxford, England), 1979.

PERIODICALS

Contemporary Literature, spring, 1979.

Critical Inquiry, summer, 1978.

Criticism, summer, 1979; winter, 1993.

New Literary History, autumn, 1978.

New Republic, April 16, 1977.

New York Review of Books, March 3, 1977; January 14, 1993; June 25, 1998, Mark Lilla, "The Politics of Jacques Derrida," pp. 36-41.

New York Times Book Review, February 1, 1987; September 13, 1987, John Sturrock, "The Book Is Dead, Long Live the Book!" p. 3; May 28, 2000, Perry Meisel, "Let a Hundred Isms Blossom."

New York Times Magazine, February 9, 1986, Colin Campbell, "The Tyranny of the Yale Critics," p. 20.

Partisan Review, number 2, 1976; number 2, 1981.

Times Literary Supplement, February 15, 1968; September 30, 1983; December 5, 1986.

Virginia Quarterly Review, winter, 1992.*

* * *

DEWHURST, Eileen (Mary) 1929-

PERSONAL: Born May 27, 1929, in Liverpool, England. *Education:* St. Anne's College, Oxford, B.A., 1951, M.A., 1958. *Avocational interests:* The fine arts (particularly pictures and furniture), friendships, painting, animals.

ADDRESSES: Office—c/o Gregory & Radice, 3 Barb Mews, London W6 7PA, England.

CAREER: Writer.

MEMBER: Society of Authors, Crime Writers Association, Oxford Society.

WRITINGS:

CRIME NOVELS

Death Came Smiling, R. Hale (London, England), 1975.
After the Ball, Macmillan (London, England), 1976.
Curtain Fall, Macmillan (London, England), 1977, Doubleday (New York, NY), 1982.
Drink This, Collins Crime Club (London, England), 1980, Doubleday (New York, NY), 1981.
Trio in Three Flats, Doubleday (New York, NY), 1981.
Whoever I Am, Collins Crime Club (London, England), 1982, Doubleday (New York, NY), 1983.
The House That Jack Built, Collins Crime Club (London, England), 1983.
There Was a Little Girl, Collins Crime Club (London, England), 1984, Doubleday (New York, NY), 1986.
Playing Safe, Collins Crime Club (London, England), 1985, Doubleday (New York, NY), 1987.
A Private Prosecution, Collins Crime Club (London, England), 1986, Doubleday (New York, NY), 1987.
A Nice Little Business, Doubleday (New York, NY), 1987.
The Sleeper, Doubleday (New York, NY), 1988.
Dear Mr. Right, Doubleday (New York, NY), 1990.
The Innocence of Guilt, Doubleday (New York, NY), 1991.
Death in Candie Gardens, Piatkus (London, England), 1992.
Now You See Her, Severn House (London, England), 1995.
The Verdict on Winter, Severn House (London, England), 1996.
Alias the Enemy, Severn House (London, England), 1997.
Roundabout, Severn House (London, England), 1998.
Death of a Stranger, Severn House (London, England), 1999.
Double Act, Severn House (London, England), 2000.
Closing Stages, Severn House (London, England), 2001.

OTHER

Contributor of short stories to anthologies, including *Northern Blood* and several anthologies of the Crime Writers Association. Contributor to periodicals, including *Ellery Queen's Mystery.*

SIDELIGHTS: Eileen Dewhurst is a British crime writer who has enjoyed modest success in the United States as well. As with many crime writers, she uses a recurring cast of characters in her books, including an actress-sleuth named Phyllida Moon and a married, crime-fighting couple, Neil and Cathy Carter. Dewhurst's stories often feature small town or seaside settings and are occasionally set in the theater and television world. She also enjoys creating plots in which one or more characters conceal their identities, sometimes even by cross-dressing. "Few, if any, contemporary crime novelists can be as preoccupied as Dewhurst with questions of identity," wrote Martin Edwards on the *TW Books* Web site. Edwards expressed disappointment that Dewhurst remains relatively unknown, especially in America. "Although her work is variable in quality, that is largely because she does not write to a formula," he stated, "and at her best, she is very good indeed . . . she is a writer of distinct talent."

Dewhurst told *CA:* "As a crime writer I have of course portrayed a variety of violent deaths, but always contain them within an overall structure which tends toward the triumph of good. Perhaps in fact, I feel at home in the crime genre because its basic theme is the disclosing and routing of the bad!

"Despite writing crime fiction exclusively (apart from journalistic articles and a few plays which have been produced by amateur companies in England), my chief concern is human relationships and everyday life—out of which the frightening, the suspenseful, the mysterious can arise with peculiar shock."

BIOGRAPHICAL/CRITICAL SOURCES:

PERIODICALS

Booklist, December 1, 1984.
Library Journal, September 1, 2000, Rex Klett, review of *Double Act,* p. 255.
Publishers Weekly, August 14, 2000, review of *Double Act,* p. 332.
Times (London), August 7, 1986.
Tribune Books (Chicago), February 23, 1986.
Washington Post Book World, June 21, 1981.
Wilson Library Bulletin, January, 1985.

OTHER

TW Books, http://www.twbooks.co.uk/crimescene/ (October 1, 2000), Martin Edwards, "Eileen Dewhurst."

DIRINGER, David 1900-1975

PERSONAL: Born June 16, 1900, in Tlumacz, East Galicia (now Ukraine); died February 13, 1975, in Cambridge, England; son of Jacob (a town clerk) and Mina Diringer; married, December 1, 1927; children: Kedma. *Education:* University of Florence, D.Litt., 1927, diploma, 1929. *Religion:* Jewish.

CAREER: University of Florence, Florence, Italy, lector, 1931-34, assistant professor, 1934-38; Cambridge University, Cambridge, England, 1948-75, began as lecturer in Semitic epigraphy, became professor emeritus; University of Florence, assistant professor, beginning 1952. Scientific secretary of Conference on Etruscan Studies, 1926, International Congress on Etruscan Studies, 1928, and Congresses of Colonial Studies, 1931, 1934, and 1937, all held in Florence. Alphabet Museum, Cambridge, founder, 1959.

MEMBER: Society of Old Testament Studies, Royal Institute of Anthropology, Institute of Archaeology, Association of University Teachers, Palestine Exploration Society, Anglo-Israel Archaeological Society, Near Eastern Society (president).

AWARDS, HONORS: Awards for oriental studies from Royal Academy of Italy, Royal Geographical Society of Italy, University of Florence, and Bollingen Foundation; M.A., Cambridge University, 1948.

WRITINGS:

Le Iscrizioni antico-ebraiche palestinesi, Le Monnier Felice, 1934.

L'Alfabeto nella storia della civilta, G. Barbera Editore, 1937, translation published as *The Alphabet: A Key to the History of Mankind,* two volumes, Philosophical Library (New York, NY), 1948, 3rd edition (with Reinhold Regensburger), Funk (New York, NY), 1968.

The Hand-produced Book, Philosophical Library (New York, NY), 1953.

(With N. Freeman) *The Staples Alphabet Exhibition,* Staples Press, 1953.

The Illuminated Book: Its History and Production, Philosophical Library (New York, NY), 1958, 3rd edition (with Regensburger), Praeger (New York, NY), 1967.

The Story of the Aleph Beth, Philosophical Library (New York, NY), 1958.

Writing, Praeger (New York, NY), 1962.

(With H. Freeman) *A History of the Alphabet throughout the Ages and in All Lands,* Unwin Brothers, 1977.

Contributor of over 450 articles in fields of archaeology, philology, epigraphy, Biblical studies, ancient history, and allied fields to encyclopedias, magazines, and learned journals.

SIDELIGHTS: An expert on the history of writing and printing, David Diringer wrote a number of books on such topics as the rise and development of written communication and the early forms of printed books. In *The Alphabet: A Key to the History of Mankind* Diringer traces the development of such forms of writing as ideograms, hieroglyphics, syllabaries, and the many alphabets used in the modern world. He argues that the creation of the Semitic alphabet was the first true alphabet, an assertion to which several critics took exception. The critic for the *Times Literary Supplement,* for example, called this argument "the most serious defect in an otherwise excellent and staggeringly erudite work." Other critics praised the depth of Diringer's knowledge of the history of written communication. G. R. Driver in the *Spectator* found Diringer's book to be "the fruit of an encyclopedic knowledge," while E. A. Speiser in the *Saturday Review of Literature* called it "an excellent exposition of a significant and fascinating subject."

Diringer approached the same topic in his book *Writing,* in which he chronicled the history of writing and printing for a general readership. Called "a triumph of humane popularization" by the *New Yorker* critic, the book was described as "an oddity [but] most fascinating" by H. G. Porteus in the *Spectator.* Porteus suggested that Diringer was sometimes misleading in his explanations, but the critic for the *Times Literary Supplement* praised Diringer for his "immensely wide knowledge" of his subject, while the reviewer for *Booklist* concluded that *Writing* was "a well-written, comprehensive volume."

In *The Illuminated Book: Its History and Production* and *The Hand-produced Book,* Diringer examines two phases in the history of book printing. *The Illuminated Book* looks at the history of lavishly illustrated books painted by hand. The illuminated book was first developed by the ancient Egyptians, came into prominence in Europe during the Middle Ages, and essentially disappeared by the seventeenth century. The critic for the *Times Literary Supplement* explained that "the work contains a vast mass of information and a wealth of illustration and it constitutes what is virtually an encyclopedia of illumination." The reviewer for *Catholic World* noted that "this work by a highly competent authority in the field will serve to enlighten the cultured layman."

Diringer's *The Hand-produced Book* examines the materials and methods used to create and bind early books. As in his other works, Diringer draws on examples from all parts of the world to give a detailed world history of the subject. "The writer is learned," noted the critic for the *Times Literary Supplement,* "and where points are uncertain he offers a variety of authoritative opinions." "Diringer's new book," wrote the *Spectator* reviewer, "is a remarkable work of synthetic scholarship, a history of 'the book' from scratchings in prehistoric caves to the invention of printing." Howard Winger in his review for *Library Quarterly* called it "a valuable guide to the oldest known examples of book production."

BIOGRAPHICAL/CRITICAL SOURCES:

PERIODICALS

Booklist, September 1, 1948, review of *The Alphabet,* p. 6; September 1, 1962, review of *Writing,* p. 15.

Book World, February 9, 1969.

Catholic World, September, 1958, review of *The Illuminated Book,* p. 479.

Library Quarterly, October, 1954, Howard Winger, review of *The Hand-produced Book,* p. 406; April, 1959, F. R. Horlbeck, review of *The Illuminated Book,* p. 136.

Manchester Guardian, April 20, 1948, H. J. Fleure, review of *The Alphabet,* p. 3; November 27, 1953, F. Taylor, review of *The Hand-produced Book,* p. 8.

New Statesman, July 19, 1958, review of *The Illuminated Book,* p. 94.

New Yorker, August 25, 1962, review of *Writing,* p. 108.

Saturday Review of Literature, August 28, 1948, E. A. Speiser, review of *The Alphabet,* p. 32.

Spectator, May 14, 1948, G. R. Driver, review of *The Alphabet,* p. 592; November 20, 1953, review of *The Hand-produced Book,* p. 616; June 8, 1962, H. G. Porteus, review of *Writing,* p. 757.

Times Literary Supplement, July 17, 1948, review of *The Alphabet,* p. 406; January 15, 1954, review of *The Hand-produced Book,* p. 48; June 6, 1958, review of *The Illuminated Book,* p. 310; November 23, 1962, review of *Writing,* p. 928.*

DOLLIMORE, Jonathan 1948-

PERSONAL: Born July 31, 1948. *Education:* University of Keele, B.A. (with first class honors), 1974; University of London, Ph.D., 1984.

ADDRESSES: *Office*—Department of English, York University, Heslington, York Y010 5DD, England.

CAREER: Farm worker, 1962-64; engineering apprentice in automobile factory, 1963-64; freelance journalist and correspondent, 1964-69; University of Sussex, Brighton, England, professor at Humanities Research Centre; York University, York, England, professor elect; writer. Visiting fellow at Humanities Research Centre, Canberra, Australia, 1988; scholar-in-residence at the University of Maryland, 1991-92; visiting fellow at Human Sciences Research Council of South Africa, 1996; visiting professor at University of British Columbia, 1997.

AWARDS, HONORS: Mellon fellowship, 1988-89.

WRITINGS:

(Editor, with Alan Sinfield) *The Selected Plays of John Webster,* Cambridge University Press, 1983.

(Author of introduction) J. W. Lever, *The Tragedy of State,* 1987.

Radical Tragedy: Religion, Ideology, and Power in the Drama of Shakespeare and His Contemporaries, University of Chicago Press, 1984, 2nd edition, Harvester Wheatsheaf, 1989.

(Editor, with Sinfield) *Political Shakespeare: New Essays in Cultural Materialism,* Cornell University Press, 1985, 2nd edition, 1994.

Sexual Dissidence: Augustine to Wilde, Freud to Foucault, Oxford University Press (New York, NY), 1991.

Death, Desire, and Loss in Western Culture, Routledge (New York, NY), 1998.

Sex, Literature, and Censorship, Polity Press (Malden, MA), 2001.

CONTRIBUTOR

James Redmond, editor, *Drama and Mimesis,* Cambridge University Press, 1980.

Alan Sinfield, editor, *Society and Literature: The Context of English Literature,* Methuen, 1983.

H. Abelove, editor, *The Lesbian and Gay Reader,* Routledge (New York, NY), 1993.

Peter Brooker and Peter Widdowson, editors, *A Practical Reader in Contemporary Literary Theory,* Prentice Hall/Harvester Wheatsheaf (London, England), 1996.

Margreta de Grazia and others, editors, *Subject and Object in Renaissance Culture,* Cambridge University Press, 1996.

John Drakakis, editor, *Alternative Shakespeares,* Methuen, 1985.

R. Porter, *Rewriting the Self,* Routledge (New York, NY), 1996.

Andrew Miller and James Adams, editors, *Sexualities in Victorian Britain,* Indiana University Press, 1996.

Michael Eubel, editor, *Back to the Raft: Race and the Subject of Masculinities,* Duke University Press, 1997.

A. Medhurst and S. Munt, editors, *Lesbian and Gay Studies: A Critical Introduction,* Cassell, 1997.

Martin Orkin and Ania Loomba, editors, *Alternative Shakespeares 3,* Routledge (New York, NY), 1998.

Also contributor to *Essays and Studies,* edited by Inga-Stina Ewbank, 1980. Contributor of articles to periodicals, including *Critical Quarterly, Literature Teaching Politics, Oxford Literary Review, Radical, Renaissance Drama,* and *Radical.*

OTHER

Work represented in anthologies, including *Futures of English,* C. MacCabe, editor, Manchester University Press, 1987; *Renaissance Drama as Cultural History,* Mary Beth Rose, editor, Northwestern University Press, 1989; *Studying Shakespeare,* John Russell Brown, editor, Macmillan (New York, NY), 1990; *Camp: A Reader,* edited by Fabio Cleto, Edinburgh University Press, 1999; and *Literary Theories: A Reader and Guide,* edited by Julian Wolfreys, Edinburgh University Press, 1999.

SIDELIGHTS: Jonathan Dollimore is an English professor and writer, with publications on such subjects as William Shakespeare, gender, and Renaissance culture. Born in 1948, he interrupted his education in his mid-teens to find work as a laborer, subsequently working in a factory and on a farm. After also working as a freelance journalist, he became a student at the University of Keele, from which he graduated with honors in 1974. He later studied at the University of London, where he earned a doctorate in 1984.

Dollimore began his teaching career at the University of Sussex, where he was professor at the Humanities Research Center. He eventually left Sussex and became professor elect at York University. In addition to stints at Sussex and York universities, Dollimore has been a visiting scholar at universities and research centers around the world, including the University of Maryland, the University of British Columbia, the Humanities Research Centre in Canberra, Australia, and the Human Sciences Research Council of South Africa.

Dollimore's publications include *Radical Tragedy: Religion, Ideology, and Power in the Drama of Shakespeare and His Contemporaries,* which appeared in 1984. Among Dollimore's other books on Shakespeare is *Political Shakespeare: New Essays in Cultural Materialism,* which he edited with Alan Sinfield. In addition, Dollimore contributed to both *Alternative Shakespeares,* which was edited by John Drakakis, and *Alternative Shakespeares 3,* which was edited by Martin Orkin and Ania Loomba.

Aside from his Shakespeare studies, Dollimore has also produced writings on various aspects of gender, including *Sexual Dissidence: Augustine to Wilde, Freud to Foucault, in 1991.* He has also provided essays to several publications, including *The Lesbian and Gay Reader,* edited by H. Abelove, and *Lesbian and Gay Studies: A Critical Introduction,* edited by A. Medhurst and S. Munt.

Among Dollimore's other publications is *Death, Desire, and Loss in Western Culture,* which analyzes the relationship between death and desire in the works of figures such as Shakespeare, Sigmund Freud, Karl Marx, and Richard Wagner. In the book, Dollimore traces death and desire as they have been perceived in art and philosophy since the time of ancient Greece, and he includes a study on these themes as they have existed in the arts since the rise of AIDS.

Since its publication in 1998, *Death, Desire, and Loss in Western Culture* has been praised as an impressive work. *Library Journal* reviewer David Gordon called Dollimore's book a "brilliant study" and added that it is an "immensely wide-ranging account." Another reviewer, Michael Spinella, wrote in *Booklist* that *Death, Desire, and Loss in Western Culture* constitutes an "engaging study" and a "marvelous, enrapturing, and accessible work." A *Publishers Weekly* critic, meanwhile, described Dollimore's volume as a "prodigiously intelligent, deeply challenging and ultimately rewarding book."

Dollimore has also published such works as *The Selected Plays of John Webster,* which he edited with Alan Sinfield, and has contributed to such volumes as *Society and Literature: The Context of English Literature,* edited by Sinfield; *Drama and Mimesis,* edited by James Redmond; and *Subject and Object in Renaissance Culture,* edited by Margreta de Grazia and others. Anthologies reprinting Dollimore's writings include *Futures of English,* edited by C. MacCabe; *Renaissance Drama as Cultural History,* edited by Mary Beth Rose; *Studying Shakespeare,* edited by John Russell Brown; and *Camp: A Reader,* edited by Fabio Cleto.

BIOGRAPHICAL/CRITICAL SOURCES:

PERIODICALS

Booklist, September 15, 1998, Michael Spinella, review of *Death, Desire, and Loss in Western Culture.*

Library Journal, October 15, 1998, David Gordon, review of *Death, Desire, and Loss in Western Culture,* p. 74.

Publishers Weekly, August 31, 1998, review of *Death, Desire, and Loss in Western Culture,* p. 60.

Shakespeare Studies, annual 2000, Mario DiGangi, review of *Death, Desire, and Loss in Western Culture,* p. 308.

Theological Studies, December, 1999, W. W. Meissner, review of *Death, Desire, and Loss in Western Culture,* p. 766.

Times Literary Supplement, August 17, 1984.*

* * *

DONELSON, Kenneth L(avern) 1927-

PERSONAL: Born June 16, 1927, in Holdrege, NE; son of Lester Homer Irving (a meatcutter) and Minnie Irene (Lyons) Donelson; married Virginia J. Watts, May 11, 1948 (divorced October, 1969); married Annette E. Whetton (a legal secretary), June 5, 1970 (divorced January, 1983); married Marie Elizabeth Smith (English teacher and librarian), May 29, 1983; children: Sheryl Lynette Donelson George, Kurt Allen, Jenny Patrick (stepdaughter). *Ethnicity:* "Caucasian." *Education:* University of Iowa, B.A., 1950, M.A., 1951, Ph.D., 1963. *Politics:* Democrat.

ADDRESSES: *Home*—53809 West Kesler Lane, Chandler, AZ 85226. *Office*—English Department, Arizona State University, Tempe, AZ 85287-0302. *E-mail*—Ken.Donelson@asu.edu.

CAREER: High school English teacher in Glidden, IA, 1951-56, and in Cedar Rapids, IA, 1956-63; Kansas State University, Manhattan, assistant professor of English and education, 1963-65; Arizona State University, Tempe, assistant professor, 1965-67, associate professor, 1967-70, professor of English, 1970—. *Military service:* U.S. Navy, 1945-46.

MEMBER: American Civil Liberties Union, National Council of Teachers of English (executive committee member, 1974-76), Conference on English Education (executive committee member, 1974-77; national chairman, 1974-76), Freedom to Read Foundation, Arizona English Teachers Association.

WRITINGS:

The Students' Right to Read, National Council of Teachers of English (Urbana, IL), 1972.

(With Dwight Burton, Bryant Fillion, and Beverly Haley) *Teaching English Today,* Houghton (Boston, MA), 1975.

(Editor) *Books for You,* National Council of Teachers of English (Urbana, IL), 1976.

Teaching Guide to E. L. Doctorow's 'Ragtime,' Bantam (New York, NY), 1976.

(With Alleen Pace Nilsen) *Literature for Today's Young Adults,* Scott Foresman, 1980, sixth edition, 2000.

(With Sam Sebesta) *Inspiring Literacy: Literature for Children and Young Adults,* Transaction Press, 1993.

Writer of column, "Ruminating and Rambling," in *English Journal,* 1973-74. Contributor of more than five hundred articles to journals, including *English Journal, Media and Methods, School Library Journal, Voice of Youth Advocates,* and *Dime Novel Roundup.* Editor, *Arizona English Bulletin,* 1967-76, 1988-1992; editor, with Alleen Pace Nilsen, *English Journal,* 1980-87.

WORK IN PROGRESS: Two books, one on significant young adult books from 1830 to 1967, the other on a commonplace book of quotations for secondary English teachers.

SIDELIGHTS: Kenneth L. Donelson told *CA:* "I write for at least a couple of reasons. Sometimes I think I have something to say somebody else might like to hear. Mostly it's because I am an English teacher, the only game I've known most of my life and still the best one in town. I believe every teacher ought to write if he is to have any understanding of the difficulties his students face in finding words to match thoughts and stringing them together to make attractive sense. Teachers who don't write to prove their literacy but who ask students to write are hypocrites or intellectual frauds, nothing more.

"I write what I write because I'm committed to English teaching and English teachers, and I continue to worry about pretty much what worried me when I taught high school thirteen years ago. That means I write a lot about censorship (still a big worry for teachers and getting worse as teachers try to lead or push communities into the twentieth century some eighty years late), adolescent literature and film (still unexplored territories for too many teachers), and composition (more art than science but the frustrating and important work any teacher can do). I've been told I worry too much about things I can directly affect but little, and that's probably true. Occasionally, I tell my classes that when I'm buried, I'd like the headstone to read simply, 'He gave a damn.' Most students think I'm joking. I'm not.

"As for my avocations, traveling leads all the rest. When my wife Marie and I were younger (and more often broke than not) we went camping a lot. Other traveling was fun; camping was essential and kept us sane. And no effete stuff for us—we camped on the ground and cooked our meals on our faithful Coleman burner. Our favorite place was Bandelier National Monument about 40 or 50 miles north by northwest of Santa Fe, new Mexico. It still is, even if we don't camp, one of my most favored spots, and whenever we get to Santa Fe, which is often, we never miss the chance to return to Bandelier. It's the one place we both find an inner peace that we find no place else, as close to heaven as I expect to get. For the last ten or so years, we've traveled a lot, mostly to Europe. London is my favorite place—for theatre and music and opera and second-hand books and CDs I can't find over here. Paris is Marie's favorite place, though she's as fond of British theatre as I am. We love going to St. Petersburg, just as we love leaving it. Both of us love Hungary and Norway and Finland and lots of other places in between. We try to spend a couple of weeks in London each year and try to go to places we've not yet seen at other times."

* * *

DURBAN, (Rosa) Pam 1947-

PERSONAL: Surname is pronounced Dur-*ban;* born March 4, 1947, in Aiken, SC; daughter of Frampton Wyman (a real estate appraiser) and Maria (a homemaker; maiden name, Hertwig) Durban; married Frank H. Hunter (a photographer), June 18, 1983. *Education:* University of North Carolina at Greensboro, B.A., 1969; University of Iowa, M.F.A., 1979.

ADDRESSES: Home—Atlanta, GA. *Office*—Department of English, Georgia State University, Atlanta, GA 30303. *Agent*—Gail Hochman, Brandt & Brandt Literary Agents, Inc., 1501 Broadway, New York, NY 10036.

CAREER: Atlanta Gazette, Atlanta, GA, editor and writer, 1974-75; State University of New York at Geneseo, visiting assistant professor of creative writing, 1979-80; Murray State University, Murray, KY, assistant professor of creative writing, 1980-81; Ohio University, Athens, associate professor of creative writing, 1981-86; Georgia State University, Atlanta, GA, professor of English and creative writing, founding editor of *Five Points* literary magazine, 1986—.

AWARDS, HONORS: Fiction award from *Crazyhorse,* 1982, for "In Darkness"; James Michener Fellowship from University of Iowa, 1982-83; Rinehart Award in Fiction from Rinehart Foundation, 1984, for collected work; fellowships from Ohio Arts Council, 1983-84 and 1986-87; Whiting Writer's Award, 1987; Creative Writing Fellowship, National Endowment for the Arts, 1998.

WRITINGS:

All Set about with Fever Trees, and Other Stories, David Godine (Boston, MA), 1985.

(Contributor) George E. Murphy, editor, *The Editor's Choice: New American Stories,* Volume II, Bantam (New York, NY), 1986.

(Contributor) Stanley Lindberg and Stephen Corey, editors, *Necessary Fictions,* University of Georgia Press (Athens, GA), 1986.

(Contributor) Charles East, editor, *New Writers of the South,* University of Georgia Press (Athens, GA), 1987.

(Contributor) *New Stories from the South: The Year's Best 1988,* Algonquin (Chapel Hill, NC), 1988.

The Laughing Place (novel), Scribner (New York, NY), 1993.

(Contributor) *Best American Short Stories 1997,* edited by E. Anne Proulx, Houghton Mifflin (Boston, MA), 1997.

(Contributor) *Best American Short Stories of the Century,* edited by John Updike, Houghton Mifflin (Boston, MA), 1999.

So Far Back (novel), Picador (New York, NY), 2000.

Contributor to periodicals, including *Ohio Review, Georgia Review, Tri-Quarterly, Epoch, Southern Review,* and *New Virginia Review.*

SIDELIGHTS: Pam Durban is a South Carolina native, currently based in Georgia, whose fiction at once reflects and transcends its Southern setting. Although her novels have been well received, it is as a short story writer that Durban has made her mark. In a *New York Times Book Review* piece, Robb Forman Dew praised Durban's *All Set about with Fever Trees, and Other Stories,* noting: "Throughout this collection the reader is privy to an uncanny visual intelligence—a perception recreated through language of the image the eye takes in." Ellen Lesser of the *Village Voice* also traced the collection's appeal to Durban's careful rendering of scenes and characters. "Durban's stories," she wrote, "rely on language and imagery more than startling turns of plot; their power builds with the accumulation of detail, insight, and atmosphere." Durban, who grew up in South Carolina, sets all of these stories in the South, and Lesser noted that much of their detail has a flavor distinctly of that region, "a Southern kind of ampleness, generosity."

But more important than the stories' setting, claimed Dew, is the "dangerous emotional territory" they explore. In "This Heat," a mill worker named Ruby Clinton faces the sudden death of her teenage son. The protagonist of the title story contemplates the impact her grandmother's life has had upon her own. Lesser concluded that all seven stories "align themselves" along "poles" of "death and survival, loss and love, disillusionment and desire," and that in each narrative Durban "works through her characters toward a larger vision." Dew cited Durban for a "voice . . . that has power and integrity."

Durban's longer fiction has earned the high regard of critics as well. *The Laughing Place,* her debut novel, was praised by Jack Sullivan in the *New York Times Book Review* as an "evocative" exploration of "the continuing conflict between the Old and New South." The story's action unfolds when a young widow returns to her former home in South Carolina, where her mother—also recently widowed—is in need of emotional support. Durban portrays the stifling mother-daughter relationship against a background of Christian fundamentalism and old-fashioned Southern formalism. Sullivan concluded that with *The Laughing Place,* Durban "emerges as a forceful novelist."

So Far Back examines an older woman's attempts to come to terms with her wealthy family's legacy of slavery. Cleaning out the family mansion after her mother's death, Louisa Hilliard Marion discovers a diary kept by one of her ancestors in 1830—a diary that reveals high levels of cruelty to slaves. A *Kirkus Reviews* critic observed that *So Far Back* concerns itself with "ancestral guilt, racial conflict, and the call of the unlived life," concluding that the tale proves to be "generally absorbing and eventually very moving." In *Booklist,* Mary Ellen Quinn declared that the novel "combines well-drawn characters with a deft evocation of both the old and the new Charleston."

Durban told *CA:* "I began writing fiction after working for a year or so in an urban textile mill community in Atlanta, Georgia, interviewing people who lived there. Their voices stuck in my mind and I continued to think about their lives for years afterward. One of my first published stories, 'This Heat,' came out of that experience, and I believe that the time I spent in that place also helped me see that I was most interested in who people are and how they got to be that way, and what makes them or allows them to go on living in the face of everything that happens to them.

"I don't consider myself a Southern writer in the sense that my *subject* is Southernness or that I deal with people in my work as *representatives* of any region. In fact, the whole issue has gotten so tiresome to me that I prefer not to talk about it at all. Why doesn't anyone get asked if he or she is a New England writer or a Great Plains writer or a Northwestern writer?"

BIOGRAPHICAL/CRITICAL SOURCES:

BOOKS

Contemporary Literary Criticism, Volume 39, Gale (Detroit, MI), 1986.

PERIODICALS

Booklist, July, 2000, Mary Ellen Quinn, review of *So Far Back,* p. 2006.

Kirkus Reviews, August 1, 2000, review of *So Far Back,* p. 1058.

New York Times Book Review, October 13, 1985, Robb Forman Dew, "Family Ties, Family Perils," p. 13; August 29, 1993, Jack Sullivan, review of *The Laughing Place.*

Village Voice, December 3, 1985.

DUTTON, Geoffrey (Piers Henry) 1922-1998

PERSONAL: Born August 2, 1922, in Anlaby, Kapunda, Australia; died September 17, 1998; son of Henry Hampden and Emily (Martin) Dutton; married Ninette Trott (an enameler), July 31, 1944 (divorced); married Robin Lucas (a writer), April 4, 1985; children: (first marriage) Francis, Teresa, Sam. *Education:* Attended University of Adelaide, 1940-41; Magdalen College, Oxford, B.A., 1949.

CAREER: Writer in Europe and Australia, 1949-54; University of Adelaide, Adelaide, South Australia, Australia, lecturer, 1954-58, senior lecturer in English, 1958-62; Penguin Books Ltd., Melbourne, Victoria, Australia, editor, 1961-65; writer and farmer, beginning 1962; Sun Books Ltd., Melbourne, co-founder, 1966, editorial director. Editor, *Bulletin Literary Supplement,* Sydney, 1980-85; *Australian Literary Quarterly,* 1985-88, and *Sydney Morning Herald Literary Supplement,* 1988. Commonwealth Lecturer in Australian Literature at University of Leeds, 1960; visiting professor at Kansas State University, 1962. Member, Australian Council for the Arts, 1968-70, Commonwealth Literary Fund Advisory Board, 1972-73, Australian Literature Board, beginning 1973, and Australian National University. Has appeared on television. *Military service:* Royal Australian Air Force, pilot, 1941-45; became flight lieutenant.

AWARDS, HONORS: Weickhardt Prize, 1978, for *White on Black: The Australian Aborigine Portrayed in Art.*

WRITINGS:

POETRY

Nightflight and Sunrise, Reed & Harris (Melbourne), 1944.
Antipodes in Shoes, Edwards & Shaw (Sydney), 1955.
Flowers and Fury, F. W. Cheshire (Melbourne), 1962.
On My Island: Poems for Children, F. W. Cheshire, 1967.
Poems Soft and Loud, F. W. Cheshire, 1967.
Findings and Keepings: Selected Poems, 1940-70, Australian Letters (Adelaide), 1970.
New Poems to 1972, Australian Letters, 1972.
A Body of Words, Edwards & Shaw, 1977.
Selective Affinities, Angus & Robertson (Sydney), 1985.

Also author of *Night Fishing,* Australian Letters.

FICTION (NOVELS EXCEPT AS NOTED)

The Mortal and the Marble, Chapman & Hall (London), 1950.
Andy, Collins (Sydney), 1968.
Tamara, Collins, 1970.
Queen Emma of the South Seas, St. Martin's (New York City), Macmillan (Melbourne), 1976.
The Wedge-tailed Eagle (stories), Macmillan, 1980.
The Eye Opener, University of Queensland Press (St. Lucia), 1982.

BIOGRAPHIES

Founder of a City: The Life of William Light, F. W. Cheshire, 1960.
The Hero as Murderer: The Life of Edward John Eyre, F. W. Cheshire, 1967, published as *Edward John Eyre: The Hero as Murderer,* Penguin (London), 1977.
Australia's Last Explorer: Ernest Giles, Barnes & Noble (New York City), 1970.
In Search of Edward John Eyre, Macmillan, 1982.
Kenneth Slessor, Ashton Scholastic (Gosford, New South Wales), 1987.
Arthur Streeton 1867-1943: A Biographical Sketch, Oz (Brisbane), 1987.
Tom Roberts 1856-1931, A Biographical Sketch, Oz, 1987.
Henry Lawson, Ashton Scholastic, 1988.
Kanga Creek: Havelock Ellis in Australia, Pan (Sydney), 1989.
Russell Drysdale 1912-1981: A Biographical Sketch, Mallard Press (Moorebank, New South Wales), 1989.
Kenneth Slessor: A Biography, Viking, 1991.

TRAVEL AND HISTORY

A Long Way South, Chapman & Hall, 1953.
Africa in Black and White, Chapman & Hall, 1956.
States of the Union, Chapman & Hall, 1958.
Australia since the Camera: 1901-1914, F. W. Cheshire, 1971, published as *From Federation to War,* Longman (London), 1972.
Swimming Free: On and below the Surfaces of Lake, River, and Sea, St. Martin's, 1972.
A Taste of History: Geoffrey Dutton's South Australia, Rigby (Adelaide), 1978.
The Australian Heroes, Angus & Robertson (Sydney), 1981.

Patterns of Australia, photographs by Harri Peccinotti, Macmillan, 1981.

Impressions of Singapore, photographs by Harri Peccinotti, Macmillan, 1981.

Country Life in Old Australia, O'Neill (South Yarra, Victoria), 1982.

Sun, Sea, Surf, and Sand: The Myth of the Beach, Oxford University Press (New York City), 1985.

The Squatters: An Illustrated History of Australia's Pastoral Pioneers, O'Neill, 1985.

The Book of Australian Islands, Macmillan, 1986.

Waterways of Sydney: A Sketchbook, Dent (Melbourne), 1988.

Images of Melbourne: A Sketchbook, illustrated by Kay Stewart, Houghton Mifflin (Ferntree Gully, Victoria), 1989.

JUVENILES

Tisi and the Yabby, Collins, 1965.

Seal Bay, Collins, 1966.

Tisi and the Pageant, Rigby, 1968.

The Prowlers, Collins, 1982.

LITERARY AND ART CRITICISM

Patrick White, Landsdowne Press (Melbourne), 1961, 4th edition, Oxford University Press, 1971.

(Author of introduction and commentaries) *Paintings of S. T. Gill,* Rigby, 1962.

Russell Drysdale, Thames & Hudson (London), 1964, revised edition published as *Russell Drysdale: A Biographical and Critical Study,* Angus & Robertson, 1969.

Whitman, Grove, 1971 (published in England as *Walt Whitman,* Oliver & Boyd, 1971).

White on Black: The Australian Aborigine Portrayed in Art, Macmillan, 1974.

S. T. Gill's Australia, Macmillan, 1981.

Snow on the Saltbush: The Australian Literary Experience, Viking (Ringwood, Victoria), 1984.

The Australian Collection: Australia's Greatest Books, Angus & Robertson, 1985.

The Innovators: The Sydney Alternatives in the Rise of Modern Art, Literature, and Ideas, Macmillan, 1986.

Famous Australian Art: Frederick McCubbin, Oz, 1987.

EDITOR

The Literature of Australia, Penguin, 1964, revised edition, 1976.

Modern Australian Writing, Fontana (London), 1966.

Australia and the Monarchy, Sun Books (Melbourne), 1966.

(With Max Harris) *The Vital Decade: Ten Years of Australian Art and Letters,* Sun Books, 1968.

(With Harris) *Australia's Censorship Crisis,* Sun Books, 1970.

(With Harris) *Sir Henry Bjelke: Don Baby and Friends,* Sun Books, 1971.

The Australian Uppercrust Book, Sun Books, 1971.

Australian Verse from 1805, Rigby, 1976.

Republican Australia?, Sun Books, 1977.

The Illustrated Treasury of Australian Stories, Nelson (Melbourne), 1986.

The Australian Bedside Book: A Selection of Writings from the Australian Literary Supplement, Macmillan, 1987.

The Poetic Language: An Anthology of Great Poems of the English-speaking World, Macmillan, 1987.

TRANSLATOR

(With Igor Mezhakoff-Koriakin) Evgenii Aleksandrovich Evtushenko, *The Bratsk Station and Other Poems,* Sun Books, 1966, Doubleday, 1967.

(With Mezhakoff-Koriakin) Bella Akhmadulina, *Fever and Other Poems,* Sun Books, 1968, Morrow, 1969.

Robert Ivanovich Rozhdestvenskii, *A Poem on Various Points of View and Other Poems,* Sun Books, 1968.

Evtushenko, *Bratsk Station, The City of Yes and the City of No, and Other Poems,* Sun Books, 1970.

Andre Andreevich Voznesenskii, *Little Woods,* Sun Books, 1972.

(With Eleanor Jacka) Evtuschenko, *Kazan University and Other New Poems,* Sun Books, 1973.

OTHER

Editor, *Australian* (literary magazine); co-founder, *Literary Quarterly, Australian Letters,* 1957, and *Fortnightly Australian Book Review,* 1962. Dutton's manuscript collection is housed at the Australian National Library, Canberra.

SIDELIGHTS: In a writing, editing, and publishing career that spanned nearly five decades, Australian Geoffrey Dutton produced an impressive quantity and variety of work. His credits include ten books of poetry, five novels, a collection of stories, and dozens of nonfiction works that encompass biography, travel, history, and literary and artistic criticism. Dutton also edited numerous anthologies of Australian literature and helped to translate modern Russian poets Yevtushenko, Akhmadulina, and Voznesensky into English. The son of one of South Australia's pioneer colonists, Dutton was educated in England at Oxford University, served in the Australian Air Force during World War II, and traveled extensively during his life, including several sojourns to Russia where he developed close ties with its poetic community.

Discussing Dutton's poetry in the *Reference Guide to English Literature,* Garth Clucas felt the author's wartime experiences played a significant role in shaping its vision. Clucas was not referring to the subject matter of Dutton's poems but rather to the viewpoint they embody: "the lone pilot among the clouds pondering the meaning of existence, the freshness and intensity of his perceptions of the world below enriched by a grateful return to base." The result, according to Clucas, is a poetry that provides "a rare marriage of delicate observation and abstract discourse." Citing poems such as "Abandoned Airstrip, Northern Territory," "Night Fishing," and "Russian Journey," Clucas praised the diversity of emotion and experience to be found in Dutton's work as well as its evocative power. In contrast, *Contemporary Poets* essayist Bruce Beaver, judging Dutton to be underrated by the majority of critics, felt that "intrinsic light-heartedness" is the most significant quality in his verse. Beaver continued, singling out some of the same poems as Clucas: "Despite the light-heartedness, this poet is capable of extended lyrical meditations of a uniquely beautiful nature." Beaver also commented positively on the descriptive powers of Dutton's travel poetry, his satiric works that poke fun at "the tasteless and the chauvinistic in modern Australia," and protest poems concerning the Vietnam War.

Discussing his own poetry, Dutton told *Contemporary Poets* that his studies of Walt Whitman in the 1960s influenced him "towards attempting a more complex human response to my own country." He also remarks that his exposure to Russian poets both gave him valuable insights into the modern world and "helped shore up my technical beliefs" regarding "the importance of rhyme and rhythm."

Like his poetry, Dutton's novels also present considerable variety in subject matter and intent. In his comments to *Contemporary Novelists,* Dutton contended that despite the diversity of characters and settings, his first three novels explore "the same theme, that of Australian innocence as against the experience of 'older' countries." *The Mortal and the Marble,* his first novel, dismissed as "the least considerable" by Clement Semmler of *Contemporary Novelists,* deals with the conflicts engendered by an Anglo-Australian marriage. His second novel, *Andy,* based on Dutton's own experiences as a pilot, is described by Semmler as the "picaresque tale of a devil-may-care flying instructor." Semmler compared the book to the work of Saint-Exupery in terms of its portrayal of "the sheer beauty and exhilaration of flying," also praising it highly as "an enduring portrait of a born leader" and "a shrewdly observed and often disturbing account of the excesses and follies of war." Dutton's next novelistic outing, *Tamara,* again turns to the author's life experiences for inspiration. Dutton describes it as dealing with "the impact on an intelligent but relatively unsophisticated Australian scientist of the complex world of Soviet Russian poetry." *Tamara* also details an affair between the book's protagonist, Angus James, and the Russian woman poet of the title. According to Semmler: "This is a novel about poets by a poet: in its simplicity, its lyricism, its rich yet economical evocations of Georgia and the Georgians, it is, in the truest sense, a deeply romantic story."

Dutton's fourth novel, *Queen Emma of the South Seas,* marked a change of pace for the author. An historical novel based on the life of a nineteenth-century Samoan-American woman who built a trading empire in the Pacific Ocean, the book is described by Semmler as "exotic and remarkable." Dutton employs shifting viewpoints in the novel, a technique which Semmler felt he handles "deftly . . . in recording Emma's story through narratives by herself, her father, her brother and sisters, traders, missionaries, planters, diplomats and lovers." Discussing Dutton's final novel, Semmler noted that he "has extended his versatility to that of satire in *The Eye-Opener.*" The plot of the book centers on preparations for an annual art festival in the Australian city of Adelaide. Semmler credited it with being "a clever comic creation and a shrewd examination of life in Australia."

BIOGRAPHICAL/CRITICAL SOURCES:

BOOKS

Contemporary Novelists, 5th edition, St. James Press (Detroit), 1991.

Contemporary Poets, 5th edition, St. James Press, 1991.

Reference Guide to English Literature, 2nd edition, St. James Press, 1991.

PERIODICALS

Best Sellers, September, 1978.
Books and Bookmen, June, 1966; March, 1970.
New Statesman, January 12, 1968.
Observer (London), February 1, 1970; December 19, 1976.
Spectator, June 3, 1966; January 17, 1970.
Times Literary Supplement, January 4, 1968; October 2, 1970; August 16, 1974; November 12, 1976.

OBITUARIES:

PERIODICALS

Times (London), October 12, 1998.*

E

EARLE, (Karl Mc)Neil 1947-

PERSONAL: Born February 25, 1947, in Carbonear, Newfoundland, Canada; son of George William (a fisherman and clerical worker) and Frances Katherine (a teacher and homemaker; maiden name, Howell) Earle; married Linda Susan Welch (a secretary), July 23, 1972. *Education:* Memorial University of Newfoundland, B.A. (Education), 1967; Ambassador University, B.A., 1972; Fuller Theological Seminary, M.A., 1978; University of Toronto, M.A., 1992; also attended Simon Fraser University, Regent College (Vancouver, British Columbia) and University of California at Los Angeles, 1998—. *Religion:* Worldwide Church of God. *Avocational interests:* Aerobics, walking, swimming.

ADDRESSES: *Home*—1643 Calle Coronado, Duarte, CA 91010.

CAREER: Teacher of history and English in Newfoundland and Labrador, 1965-68; pastor of churches in Brandon, Manitoba, Calgary, Alberta, Moosomin, Saskatchewan, Toronto, Ontario and Glendora-San Bernardino, CA, 1972-2000; *Plain Truth,* Pasadena, CA, Canadian regional editor, 1992-93, international editor, 1993-95, senior editor, 1995-96. Coordinator of conventions. Director of Calgary Outreach Players, 1982-84, and Toronto Outreach Players, 1986-91. Freelance writer, *Trade Press Services,* 1998—. Editor, *Reconcile* newsletter, 1998—.

MEMBER: Association for Canadian Studies in the United States (ACSUS).

WRITINGS:

The Wonderful Wizard of Oz in American Popular Culture: Uneasy in Eden, Edwin Mellen (Lewiston, NY), 1993.

(Editor) *A History of the Multinational,* [London], 2000.

Contributor to *Journal of Canadian Studies, ACSUS Journal, Church and State,* and *Social Science Journal.*

WORK IN PROGRESS: *The Time of Heroes,* a book on ice hockey in Canadian culture as a reflection of national identity; *Blow the Dust off Your Bible: Herbert Armstrong and American Popular Religion.*

SIDELIGHTS: Neil Earle told *CA:* "I am living proof of the importance of getting an early start in education. I thank my mother and aunt (both teachers) for that excellent start. Early praise is essential for nurturing budding writers. You need that to shield you from the rejections that will surely come. My writing reflects several influences: Winston Churchill for the big picture; Arthur Schlesinger, Jr., for the magisterial touch; William Manchester for narrative flair; Barbara Tuchman, the Bible, and Canada's own E. J. Pratt, the poet, for the oracular mood and for staying serious; Alan Fotheringham and Tom Wolfe for life and verve."

* * *

EDDY, Paul 1944-

PERSONAL: Born December 14, 1944, in England; son of Ernest (an accountant) and Doris (a buyer; maiden name, Zeirsen) Eddy; married Elaine Davenport (a writer), August, 1977; children: (from previous marriage) Nicolas, Simon. *Education:* Attended King Edward VIth School in Stratford-upon-Avon, England.

ADDRESSES: Home—London, England. *Office*—Putnam Publishing Group, 200 Madison Ave., New York, NY 10016. *Agent*—Robert Ducas, 350 Hudson St., New York, NY 10014.

CAREER: Journalist and novelist. *Morning News,* Leamington Spa, England, reporter, 1961-64; East London News Agency, London, England, reporter, 1964-65; freelance writer in Europe, 1965-71; *Sunday Times,* London, investigative reporter, 1971-78, editor, Insight Team, 1978-82, deputy features editor, beginning 1982. Has traveled on assignment to the United States, Europe, Northern Ireland, Hong Kong, the Middle East, Rhodesia, and Israel.

WRITINGS:

(With Bruce Page and Elaine Potter) *Destination Disaster: From the Tri-Motor to the DC-10, the Risk of Flying,* Quadrangle (New York, NY), 1976, published as *Destination Disaster,* Hart-Davis (London, England), 1976.

(With wife, Elaine Davenport, and Mark Hurwitz) *Howard Hughes' Final Years: Based on an Examination of the Hughes Papers,* Ballantine (New York, NY), 1977.

(With wife, Elaine Davenport, and Peter Gillman) *The Plumbat Affair,* Lippincott (Philadelphia, PA), 1978.

(With Peter Gillman, Magnus Linklater, and others) *War in the Falklands,* Harper (New York, NY), 1982, published as *The Falklands War,* Deutsch (London, England), 1982.

(With others) *The DeLorean Tapes,* Collins (London, England), 1984.

(With Hugo Sabogal and Sara Walden) *The Cocaine Wars,* Norton (New York, NY), 1988.

(With Sara Walden) *Hunting Marco Polo: The Pursuit of the Drug Smuggler Who Couldn't Be Caught, by the Agent Who Wouldn't Quit,* Little, Brown (Boston, MA), 1991, published as *Hunting Marco Polo: The Pursuit and Capture of Howard Marks,* Bantam (New York, NY), 1991.

Flint (novel), Putnam (New York, NY), 2000.

ADAPTATIONS: Film rights to *Flint* were sold to Columbia Pictures.

SIDELIGHTS: An investigative journalist well known in his native England, Paul Eddy has drawn on his background to inform his debut novel, *Flint,* which features an undercover investigator. Among the many events Eddy has investigated was the 1974 crash of a Turkish Airlines DC-10 that killed 346 people. Along with collaborators Bruce Page and Elaine Potter, Eddy outlined his findings regarding the crash in his first book, 1976's *Destination Disaster: From the Tri-Motor to the DC-10, the Risk of Flying.* In a *New York Times Book Review* article, Robert Sherrill dubbed the writing team of Eddy and his fellow journalists "another of those magically coordinated—how do three people write a book so perfectly?—London *Sunday Times* teams who attack an event with the relentless gusto of piranha, gobbling up every fact and rumor and anecdote. They handle massive complexities with deceptive tidiness."

Eddy and co-authors Hugo Sabogal and Sara Walden took on an even more complex subject in *The Cocaine Wars.* In this 1988 volume, they attempt to give a comprehensive picture of the rise of international cocaine trafficking and the social, economic, and political disruptions it has caused. Focusing most tightly on events in Colombia, the Bahamas, and Miami, Florida, Eddy and Walden paint "a portrait of those strange inhabitants of the drug world, people who thrive as traffickers, law enforcement officials, informants and sometimes as all three," noted Peter Kerr in his appraisal of *The Cocaine Wars* for the *New York Times Book Review.* Rampant problems within the Miami police department are illustrated through the story of Raul Diaz, who the authors showed slowly metamorphosed from a decorated member of an antidrug task force to a suspect in a drug case, to a private eye working for drug traffickers. *The Cocaine Wars* also presents a thorough account of the rise of the powerful Medellin drug cartel and its domination of the Colombian government. Kerr faulted the book's authors for dwelling "on lurid details while failing to address larger questions, such as why in the late 1970s Americans, including the nation's medical establishment, forgot the damage caused by cocaine just three generations earlier." While also noting that *The Cocaine Wars* "leaves out important chapters, such as the corruption of Panama and the development of crack distribution gangs," Kerr concluded: "This is by no means the definitive work the subject demands, but it is not a bad start."

Eddy and Walden collaborated again on *Hunting Marco Polo: The Pursuit of the Drug Smuggler Who Couldn't Be Caught, by the Agent Who Wouldn't Quit.* "Marco Polo" was the nickname of Howard Marks, a charming, intelligent Briton who made his living laundering drug money and running a worldwide distribution network for marijuana and hashish. He was finally apprehended and given a thirty-year prison sentence due to the efforts of Craig Lovato, a tenacious agent of the U.S. Drug Enforcement Agency. "The authors present the contest between the two men as a highly dramatic chess game," advised Genevieve Stuttaford in her *Publishers Weekly* review. Stuttaford went on to call the book "fast-paced, riveting reading."

Eddy's reporting on international crime provided him with plenty of background for his first novel, *Flint.* The title character, Grace Flint, is a British undercover officer who has been physically and emotionally scarred while in the line of duty. After a traumatic incident in which she was almost killed, she is shuffled off to a desk job for a time, only to be called back into active service on a counterfeit case. Along the way, Flint becomes involved in a search for the person who attempted to kill her. "What Flint uncovers in her search for her would-be killer leads to an international conspiracy intricate and ambitious even by the standards of spy fiction," remarked a writer for *Kirkus Reviews.* A *Publishers Weekly* reviewer called Flint "an engaging and thoroughly sympathetic heroine, wrestling her doubts and fears as she moves through an utterly amoral world. Eddy . . . keeps his story fast and seamless, expertly ratcheting up the tension in a breathlessly complex web of intrigue that keeps the reader guessing about loyalties and betrayals right up to the end."

Eddy once explained that his aim is "to investigate complex affairs and write about them in a way that the largest possible number of people will find . . . understandable and interesting. It seems to me that in a world that is increasingly bureaucratic and polarised we need to understand what is really going on around us. One way of assisting in that process is to take events, exhaustively investigate them, and place them in a context and a perspective that people can readily understand. Obviously, this can become a fairly depressing vocation because we tend to concentrate on the less attractive sides of life—war, corruption, accidental slaughter and so on—and so in my spare time I like to 'escape' by traveling widely and, particularly, by sailing. My ability to speak foreign languages is pathetic but I have a passion to learn."

BIOGRAPHICAL/CRITICAL SOURCES:

PERIODICALS

Kirkus Reviews, July 1, 2000, review of *Flint,* p. 904.

New York Times, November 16, 1976.

New York Times Book Review, October 10, 1976; August 21, 1988, Peter Kerr, "The Scourge of Choice," p. 19.

Publishers Weekly, April 5, 1991, Genevieve Stuttaford, review of *Hunting Marco Polo: The Pursuit of the Drug Smuggler Who Couldn't Be Caught by the Agent Who Wouldn't Quit,* p. 131; July 3, 2000, review of *Flint,* p. 48.

Sunday Times (London), February 4, 2001, John Dugdale, "Danger Man."

Time, August 21, 2000, Paul Gray, "Say Hello to Our Woman Flint: A British Journalist Creates a Spunky Thriller Heroine," p. 76.

Times Literary Supplement, May 13, 1983.

Washington Post Book World, October 17, 1976.*

* * *

EMERSON, Kathy Lynn 1947-
(Kaitlyn Gorton)

PERSONAL: Born October 25, 1947, in Liberty, NY; daughter of William Russell and Theresa Marie (Coburg) Gorton; married Sanford Merritt Emerson (in law enforcement), May 10, 1969. *Education:* Bates College, A.B., 1969; Old Dominion University, M.A., 1972.

ADDRESSES: Home—P.O. Box 156, Wilton, ME 04294.

CAREER: Tidewater Community College, Virginia Beach, VA, instructor in English, 1972-73; tutor and counselor in Franklin County Community Action Program, 1974-75; language arts teacher at Wilton Academy, 1975-76; University of Maine at Farmington, library assistant, 1979-85, lecturer, 1985-87; freelance writer, 1976—.

MEMBER: Mystery Writers of America, Novelists, Inc., Romance Writers of America, Sisters in Crime.

WRITINGS:

ROMANTIC SUSPENSE NOVELS

Winter Tapestry (historical), Harper (New York, NY), 1991.

Echoes and Illusions (contemporary), Harper (New York, NY), 1993.

Firebrand (historical), Harper (New York, NY), 1993.

The Green Rose (historical), Harper (New York, NY), 1994.
Unquiet Hearts (historical), Harper (New York, NY), 1994.

ROMANCE NOVELS

Sleepwalking Beauty, Bantam, 1997.
Relative Strangers, Bantam, 1997.
Love Thy Neighbor, Bantam, 1997.
Sight Unseen, Bantam, 1998.
Tried and True, 1998.
That Special Smile, Bantam, 1998.

"CHRONICLE OF LADY APPLETON" MYSTERY SERIES

Face Down in the Marrow-Bone Pie, St. Martin's Press (New York, NY), 1997.
Face Down upon an Herbal, St. Martin's Press (New York, NY), 1998.
Face Down among the Winchester Geese, St. Martin's Press (New York, NY), 1999.
Face Down beneath the Eleanor Cross, St. Martin's Press (New York, NY), 2000.
Face Down under the Wych Elm, St. Martin's Press (New York, NY), 2000.
Face Down before the Rebel Hooves, St. Martin's Press (New York, NY), 2001.

ROMANCE NOVELS; UNDER PSEUDONYM KAITLYN GORTON

Cloud Castles, Silhouette Books (New York, NY), 1989.
Hearth, Home, and Hope, Silhouette Books (New York, NY), 1995.
Separated Sisters, Silhouette Books (New York, NY), 1997.

NOVELS; FOR CHILDREN

The Mystery of Hilliard's Castle, Down East (Camden, ME), 1985.
Julia's Mending, Orchard Books (New York, NY), 1987.
The Mystery of the Missing Bagpipes, Avon, 1991.

NONFICTION

Wives and Daughters: The Women of Sixteenth-Century England, Whitston (Troy, NY), 1984.
Making Headlines: A Biography of Nellie Bly (juvenile), Dillon Press (Minneapolis, MN), 1989.
The Writer's Guide to Everyday Life in Renaissance England, Writer's Digest Books (Cincinnati, OH), 1996.

OTHER

Columnist, "Kathy's Corner," for *Mainely Romance* (newsletter of Maine chapter of Romance Writers of America), 1995—. Contributor to anthologies, including *Murder Most Medieval,* Cumberland House, and *More Murder They Wrote,* Berkley. Contributor of articles and stories to periodicals, including *D.A.R. Magazine, First Person Female American, Highlights for Children, Medieval Chronicle, Mystery News, Notes on Teaching English, Primary Treasure,* and *Renaissance Papers.*

SIDELIGHTS: Kathy Lynn Emerson is a well-established writer of popular and historical romances, but her greatest success has probably come since the mid-1990s, when she wrote the first entry in her "Chronicles of Lady Appleton" series, *Face Down in the Marrow-Bone Pie.* The story begins in 1559, when Lord Robert Appleton leaves England for France, where he is to serve as an ambassador for Queen Elizabeth. His wife Susanna—an intelligent, independent woman—remains behind, fully aware that her husband will be unfaithful to her while he is gone. When the steward of the Appleton estate dies a mysterious death, Susanna sets out to solve the mystery. Toby Bromberg, a reviewer for *Romantic Times,* called Susanna a "shrewdly likeable" character, and called *Face Down in the Marrow-Bone Pie* a "sparkling" mystery.

Face Down upon an Herbal continued Susanna's adventures. In this mystery, Lady Appleton has published an herbal manual. At the command of Queen Elizabeth, she travels to Madderly Castle to assist Lady Madderly, who is also working on herbals. When Susanna arrives, however, she learns that a visiting Scottish nobleman has died while visiting Madderly Castle, and that he was found dead clutching a copy of Susanna's book. Once again she determines to sort out the mysterious characters and events that envelop her. A reviewer for *The Mystery Reader* found the plot "intricate," yet complained that it was difficult to care about the characters in the story. A more enthusiastic review of *Face Down upon an Herbal* was offered by Harriet Klausner in *Bookbrowser.* Klausner stated that "any person interested in the intrigues, politics, and lifestyles of the Elizabethan era will want to devour *Face Down upon an Herbal.* Kathy Lynn Emerson's impeccable and detailed research is on every page, making the period seem alive. . . . This is one of the best historical mystery series on the market."

Emerson's sixth entry in the series, *Face Down under the Wych Elm,* finds Susanna defending a mistress of her deceased husband. Constance Crane, accused of being a witch, must rely on Susanna to discover who actually poisoned her supposed victim and why. By story's end, the sleuth realizes that the accusation of witchcraft actually hides an intricate web of greed and lust. Noting that the author "creates an Elizabethan atmosphere by using archaic words . . . and describing plants and herbal remedies," a *Publishers Weekly* contributor stated that the volume "begins slowly but ends with an exciting rush." Reviewing *Face Down under the Wych Elm* in *Booklist,* GraceAnne A. DeCandido called the work "another intriguing story of the resourceful Susanna and her equally plucky servant and friend, Jennet."

Emerson once told *CA:* "I alternate between writing contemporary and historical fiction with an occasional nonfiction project for variety. My favorite historical period is the sixteenth century, in which I have set several adult novels. The 1880s have provided background for *Julia's Mending* and a biography of Nellie Bly, both for young readers. I frequently use family stories as the basis for plot development. *Julia's Mending* incorporates many of the adventures my grandfather had as a young boy. If there is any single theme running through my work, it concerns the dangers of jumping to conclusions about people. My protagonists frequently must learn to be more open-minded and fight unintentional prejudices they discover within themselves."

BIOGRAPHICAL/CRITICAL SOURCES:

PERIODICALS

American Libraries, February, 1999, review of *Face Down upon an Herbal,* p. 61.

Armchair Detective, summer, 1997, review of *Face Down in the Marrow-Bone Pie,* p. 362.

Booklist, August, 1996, review of *The Writer's Guide to Everyday Life in Renaissance England,* p. 1874; April 15, 1998, review of *Face Down upon an Herbal,* p. 1381; May 15, 1999, review of *Face Down among the Winchester Geese,* p. 1672; January 1, 2000, review of *Face Down beneath the Eleanor Cross,* p. 883; December 1, 2000, GraceAnne A. DeCandido, review of *Face Down under the Wych Elm,* p. 696.

Kirkus Reviews, February 15, 1997, review of *Face Down in the Marrow-Bone Pie,* p. 257; March 1, 1998, review of *Face Down upon an Herbal,* p. 303; June 1, 1999, review of *Face Down among the Winchester Geese,* p. 837; January 1, 2000, review of *Face Down beneath the Eleanor Cross,* p. 18.

Library Journal, April 1, 1997, review of *Face Down in the Marrow-Bone Pie,* p. 133; December, 1997, review of *Face Down in the Marrow-Bone Pie,* p. 184; June 1, 1999, *Face Down among the Winchester Geese,* p. 184; March 1, 2000, Rex Klett, review of *Face Down beneath the Eleanor Cross,* p. 128; December, 2000, Klett, review of *Face Down under the Wych Elm,* p. 195.

Publishers Weekly, February 9, 1998, review of *Face Down upon an Herbal,* p. 77; May 24, 1999, review of *Face Down among the Winchester Geese,* p. 70; February 21, 2000, review of *Face Down beneath the Eleanor Cross,* p. 68; October 23, 2000, review of *Face Down under the Wych Elm,* p. 61.

Romance Reader, August 24, 1998, review of *Tried and True.*

School Library Journal, February, 1997, review of *The Writer's Guide to Everyday Life in Renaissance England,* p. 37.

Voice of Youth Advocates, December, 1998, review of *Face Down in the Bone-Marrow Pie,* p. 333.

OTHER

Bookbrowser, http://www.bookbrowser.com/ (August 27, 2000), Harriet Klausner, review of *Face Down upon an Herbal.*

Kathy Lynn Emerson Web site, http://www.kathylynnemerson.com/ (May 21, 2001).

The Mystery Reader, http://www.themysteryreader.com/ (August 27, 2000), Lesley Dunlap, review of *Face Down upon an Herbal.*

Romantic Times, http://www.romantictimes.com/ (August 27, 2000), Melinda Helfer, reviews of *Tried and True, Sleepwalking Beauty, Sight Unseen, Relative Strangers,* and *Love Thy Neighbor,* and Toby Bromber, reviews of *Face Down in the Bone-Marrow Pie,* and *Face Down among the Winchester Geese.**

* * *

EMMONS, Shirlee 1923-

PERSONAL: Born August 5, 1923, in Stevens Point, WI; daughter of Myron Frederick (in business) and Irene Evelyn (a homemaker; maiden name, Kortendick) Emmons; married Rollin Baldwin (an educator), November, 1948; children: Hilary Baldwin. *Ethnicity:*

"English/German." *Education:* Lawrence University, Mus.B., 1944; Curtis Institute, diploma, 1945; additional study at Conservatorio Giuseppe Verdi, Milan, Italy, 1950-51. *Politics:* Independent. *Religion:* Episcopalian. *Avocational interests:* Sewing, hiking.

ADDRESSES: Home—12 West 96th St., New York, NY 10025. *E-mail*—voiceperformance@aol.com.

CAREER: Professional singer, speaker, teacher, and writer. Columbia University, Barnard College, adjunct teacher, 1963-66; private studio, 1964—, New York; Princeton University, adjunct teacher, 1966-81; Tanglewood Institute, voice teacher, 1982; American Institute of Musical Studies, Graz, Austria, voice teacher, 1983 and 1985; State University of New York, State University College at Purchase, adjunct teacher, 1980-91; Boston University, associate professor, 1981-87; Rutgers University, adjunct teacher, 1987-90; Queens College, adjunct teacher, 1988—; Hunter College, visiting professor, 1991-2000.

MEMBER: American Academy of Teachers of Singing (chair), National Association of Teachers of Singing (board member, New York chapter), New York Singing Teachers Association (board member), Vocal Arts Society, (Washington, DC; board member).

AWARDS, HONORS: Obie Award, for Distinguished Performance in Leading Operatic Role, 1957, for *The Mother of Us All;* winner of Marian Anderson International Competition; Fulbright scholar to Italy; honorary Doctor of Fine Arts, Lawrence University, 2000.

WRITINGS:

(With Stanley Sonntag) *The Art of the Song Recital,* Schirmer Books (Riverside, NJ), 1979.

Tristanissimo: The Authorized Biography of Heroic Tenor Lauritz Melchior, Schirmer Books (Riverside, NJ), 1990.

(With Alma Thomas) *Power Performance for Singers,* Oxford University Press (New York, NY), 1998.

Contributor of articles to *American Music Teacher, National Association of Teachers of Singing (NATS) Journal, NATS Bulletin,* and *Journal of Voice.*

WORK IN PROGRESS: A dictionary of literary allusions in song literature, with Wilbur Watkin Lewis; a technical book of choral conducting and singing.

SIDELIGHTS: Shirlee Emmons once told *CA:* "My pursuit of a career as a voice teacher stemmed from a strong desire to be a master teacher of vocal technique, able to clear up difficulties, restructure faulty technique, and enable singers to achieve their full potential as artists."

Emmons has written three books that have been enthusiastically received for their contributions to music scholarship. The first, *The Art of the Song Recital,* written with professional accompanist Stanley Sonntag and published in 1979, was praised as a valuable resource for vocal music teachers, students, and performers. Emmons told *CA,* "I wrote *The Art of the Song Recital* because I deplored the decline of the song recital as a musical form and I wanted to be of all possible help to the singers who wished to continue to do recitals, and music lovers who still loved them."

Leland Fox of the *Opera Journal* described *The Art of the Song Recital* as "a practical 'how to' book of clear, methodical, and useful information on every facet of the recital art." Critics noted Emmons's inclusion of advice on how to construct a successful recital program, numerous sample programs, technical discussions of interpretation, learning new music, the singing actor, and resources for constructing further programs and purchasing music. Richard Dale Sjördsma asserted in his review in the *NATS Bulletin: "The Art of the Song Recital* can not be too highly recommended. It is a captivating book. . . . Anyone who has anything at all to do with the art of singing, will find pertinent information of enormous value."

In Emmons's next publication, 1990's *Tristanissimo: The Authorized Biography of Heroic Tenor Lauritz Melchior,* the author presents the life story of twentieth-century operatic tenor Lauritz Melchior, famous for his powerful, resonant voice and eccentric behavior. "*Tristanissimo* was written because I was affronted at the absence of a biography of this great singer, the premier heroic tenor of the twentieth century," Emmons told *CA.* "Having toured with him as a young singer after he left the Metropolitan Opera, I had a personal admiration for him and technical interest in his artistry."

Manuela Hölterhoff commented in the *Wall Street Journal* that *Tristanissimo* "is a perfectly splendid biography, candid, informed, amusing." Emmons draws on her subject's diaries and letters as well as interviews and the public record of Melchior's nearly forty-year singing career to present what critics found to be a scrupulously fair depiction of both the genius and the failings of her subject. The narrative is augmented by numerous photographs, notes, bibliography, a listing of Melchior's professional performances, a discography, and an index. Wrote J. O. Tate in his review in *Chronicles:* "Emmons has succeeded handsomely in doing justice not only to her peerless subject, but to the familial, cultural, and historical contexts of his life. . . . *Tristanissimo* is the best biography I have read in years."

BIOGRAPHICAL/CRITICAL SOURCES:

PERIODICALS

Choice, October, 1990.

Chronicles, November, 1990, J. O. Tate, review of *Tristanissimo.*

NATS Bulletin, May-June, 1979, Richard Dale Sjördsma, review of *The Art of the Song Recital,* pp. 47-48.

Opera Journal, Volume 12, 1979, Leland Fox, review of *The Art of the Song Recital.*

Wall Street Journal, May 31, 1990, Manuela Hölterhoff, review of *Tristanissimo.*

* * *

ERICSON, Walter
See FAST, Howard (Melvin)

* * *

EVANS, Robert C. 1955-

PERSONAL: Born March 1, 1955, in Braddock, PA; son of Charles M. (a laborer) and Emma (a waiter; maiden name, Schall) Evans; married Ruth Dunham (a librarian), May 28, 1978. *Ethnicity:* "White." *Education:* University of Pittsburgh, B.A. (magna cum laude), 1977; Princeton University, Ph.D., 1984.

ADDRESSES: *Office*—Department of English and Philosophy, Auburn University at Montgomery, Box 244023, Montgomery, AL 36124-4023. *E-mail*—litpage@aol.com, bobevans@strudel.aum.edu; fax: 334-244-3740.

CAREER: Auburn University at Montgomery, Montgomery, AL, instructor, 1982-84, assistant professor, 1984-86, associate professor, 1986-94, professor of English, 1994—, Distinguished Research Professor, 1994-97, second university alumni professor, 1997-2000.

MEMBER: Sixteenth-Century Studies Conference, Phi Kappa Phi.

AWARDS, HONORS: Whiting fellowship, 1981-82; G.E. Bentley Prize, 1982; fellow of Newberry Library, 1984, American Council of Learned Societies, 1985, and Folger Shakespeare Library, 1986, 1989, and 1993; Mellon fellow, 1986; fellow of Huntington Library, 1987; grants from National Endowment for the Humanities, 1988 and 1993, and American Philosophical Society, 1988; fellow at Center for Medieval and Renaissance Studies, University of California, Los Angeles, 1989; named CASE Professor of the Year for Alabama, Council for the Advancement and Support of Education, 1989; Auburn University at Montgomery Faculty Excellence Award, 1989; departmental award for collaborative work with students, 1999.

WRITINGS:

Ben Jonson and the Poetics of Patronage, Bucknell University Press (Lewisburg, PA), 1989.

Jonson, Lipsius, and the Politics of Renaissance Stoicism, Longwood (Wakefield, NH), 1992.

(Editor with Barbara Wiedemann) *"My Name Was Martha": A Renaissance Woman's Autobiographical Poem,* Locust Hill Press (West Cornwall, CT), 1993.

Jonson and the Contexts of His Time, Bucknell University Press, 1994.

Habits of Mind: Evidence and Effects of Ben Jonson's Reading, Bucknell University Press, 1995.

(Editor with Anne C. Little) *"The Muses Females Are": Martha Moulsworth and Other Women Writers of the English Renaissance,* Locust Hill Press, 1995.

(Editor with Ann Depas-Orange) *"The Birthday of My Self": Martha Moulsworth, Renaissance Poet,* Critical Matrix (Princeton, NJ), 1996.

(Editor with Anne C. Little and Barbara Wiedemann) *Short Fiction: A Critical Companion,* Locust Hill Press, 1997.

(Editor with Richard Harp) *Frank O'Connor: New Perspectives,* Locust Hill Press, 1998.

(Compiler, with editorial assistance from Kim Barron, Deborah Hill, Ann O'Clair, and Carolyn Young) *Ben Jonson's Major Plays: Summaries of Modern Monographs,* Locust Hill Press, 2000.

(Editor with Harp) *Brian Friel: New Perspectives,* Locust Hill Press, 2001.

Kate Chopin's Short Fiction: A Critical Companion, Locust Hill Press, 2001.

Member of editorial board, *Ben Jonson Journal,* 1993-97, and *Explorations in Renaissance Culture,* 1995—. One of three primary editors, *Ben Jonson Journal,* 1997—; renaissance editor for *Comparative Drama,* 1998—.

Contributor to books, including *Dictionary of Literary Biography: Seventeenth-Century British Non-Dramatic Poets,* edited by M. Thomas Hester, Gale (Detroit, MI), 1992; *Drama and the Classical Heritage: Comparative and Critical Essays,* edited by Clifford Davidson, Rand Johnson, and John H. Stroupe, AMS Press (New York City), 1992; *The Wit of Seventeenth-Century Poetry,* edited by Claude J. Summers and Ted-Larry Pebworth, University of Missouri Press (Columbia, MO), 1994; *Encyclopedia of British Humorists,* edited by Steven Gale, Garland Press, 1996; *Re-presenting Ben Jonson,* edited by Martin Butler, St. Martin's Press, 1999; *The English Civil Wars in the Literary Imagination,* edited by Claude J. Sumers and Ted-Larry Pebworth, University of Missouri Press, 1999; and *Cambridge Companion to Ben Jonson,* edited by Richard Harp and Stanley Stewert, Cambridge Univesity Press, 2000. Contributor of about one hundred and sixty articles and reviews to literary journals.

WORK IN PROGRESS: A book on Thomas Nashe and Elizabethan erotic literature; a book on Flannery O'Connor; a collection of Renaissance documents; a series of books on short fiction; research on Ben Jonson, Kate Chopin, Renaissance women writers, lyric poetry, and critical theory (especially pluralism); commissioned to edit the *Ben Jonson Encyclopedia* for Greenwood Press.

SIDELIGHTS: Robert C. Evans told *CA:* "Most of my work has dealt with Ben Jonson as a representative writer of the English Renaissance. I hadn't originally planned to spend as much time on Jonson as I have, but learning about him has been a great way of learning about the larger period in which he played such a significant role. In particular, tracing his reading has been an education in itself: studying Jonson has encouraged me to explore facets of the classical, medieval, and Renaissance eras that I might otherwise have ignored. At the same time, in dealing with Jonson, I have tried to keep my eye on issues of enduring importance, particularly the ways in which 'literature' intersects with the practicalities of everyday life. Finally, my critical orientation has always favored the close reading of texts. I tell my students that any good literary text is at least as complex and multifaceted as a human being is. I feel almost a moral obligation to explore texts in very close detail and am uncomfortable with interpretations that seem too general or abstract.

"Much of my recent work has been collaborative. In working with colleagues, I have been trying to break free of the assumption (widespread in the humanities) that scholarly work is necessarily private and individual. I have found shared scholarly work to be a wonderful way to achieve a sense of community that has always been very important to me. Similarly, my collaborative work with students has been one of the most satisfying aspects of my career. I began this work partly as a way of overcoming the common view that research and teaching are distinct or even conflicting activities. I've always found that my research has enhanced my teaching, and now I have found a way to integrate the two even more fully. Each project on which I've worked with a different student has taught me something new, about both research and teaching. I have found that students love the idea of making genuine contributions to some lasting body of knowledge, and that they tend to be highly motivated when working on these projects. Although these collaborative projects would often have been finished more easily and quickly if I had simply done them myself, they would rarely have been more rewarding.

"For the last few years, then, I have been in the wonderful position of learning a good deal about education, writing, and life from some really fine students and from some outstanding colleagues. I feel a greater sense of integration in my life than at any time in the past. My teaching, research, and relations with colleagues now often feel like a seamless web.

"In the past decade my work has moved even more firmly in the direction of increased integration of teaching and research. Each book I have published since 1995 has deliberately included work by student contributors, and the extent of that contribution has grown proportionately larger as I have tried to think of new ways to make students (both as individuals and as class members) active participants in legitimate scholarly endeavors. My goal is to help students produce work that is not read just once (by me) but that instead makes a permanent and widely available contribution to knowledge.

"I have now come to believe that it is realistically possible to involve whole classes in serious scholarly projects. Not only do students respond enthusiastically to this kind of challenge, but such work has also brought a new and very satisfying dimension to my own experience of teaching every class at every level. Although much of my students' work has now been published in books or articles, the Internet has also provided a wonderful new means both of sharing and accessing knowledge. I look forward to focusing even more intently on such new possibilities, especially by developing the Litpage Web site (www.litpage.com).

"My interests have also turned increasingly in the direction of pluralist criticism—the view that all interpretation is perspectival, that many perspectives are welcome, but that an interpreter is obligated to use each perspective with rigorous attention not only to developing its potential but also to acknowledge its limits. I've come to believe that this approach to interpretation is not only the most sensible but is also the kind that best permits (or demands) the closest possible attention to the specific details of whatever text is being interpreted. The Internet, I suspect, opens up whole new possibilities for pluralist work, particularly through precise and constant updated annotation of great works.

"I continue to remain very fortunate in my family, friends, colleagues, publishers, and students. In particular, the last decade has helped me appreciate the joys of collaborative learning and has helped remind me of the ideal of always remaining a student, first and foremost."

F

FAST, Howard (Melvin) 1914-
(E. V. Cunningham, Walter Ericson)

PERSONAL: Born November 11, 1914, in New York, NY; son of Barney (an ironworker, cable car gripper, tin factory worker, and dress factory cutter) and Ida (a homemaker; maiden name, Miller) Fast; married Bette Cohen (a painter and sculptor), June 6, 1937 (died November, 1994); married Mimi O'Connor, June 17, 1999; children: (first marriage) Rachel, Jonathan. *Education:* Attended National Academy of Design. *Religion:* Jewish. *Avocational interests:* "Home, my family, the theater, the film, and the proper study of ancient history. And the follies of mankind."

ADDRESSES: Home—55 Tomac Avenue, Old Greenwich, CT 06870. *Agent*—Sterling Lord Agency, 65 Bleeker St., New York, NY 10012.

CAREER: Worked at several odd jobs and as a page in the New York Public Library prior to 1932; writer, 1932—. Foreign correspondent for *Esquire* and *Coronet,* 1945. Taught at Indiana University, 1947; member of World Peace Council, 1950-55; American Labor Party candidate for U.S. Congress, 23rd New York District, 1952; owner, Blue Heron Press, New York, 1952-57; film writer, 1958-67; chief news writer, Voice of America, 1982-84. Has given numerous lectures and made numerous appearances on radio and television programs. *Military service:* Affiliated with U.S. Office of War Information, 1942-44; correspondent with special Signal Corps unit and war correspondent in China-India-Burma theater, 1945.

MEMBER: Century Club, Fellowship of Reconciliation.

Howard Fast

AWARDS, HONORS: Bread Loaf Literary Award, 1937; Schomberg Award for Race Relations, 1944, for *Freedom Road;* Newspaper Guild award, 1947; National Jewish Book Award, Jewish Book Council, 1949, for *My Glorious Brothers;* International Peace Prize from the Soviet Union, 1954; Screenwriters annual award, 1960; annual book award, National Association of Independent Schools, 1962; American Library Association notable book citation, 1972, for *The Hessian;* Emmy Award for outstanding writing in a drama series, American Academy of Television Arts and Sciences, 1975, for episode "The Ambassador," *Benjamin Franklin;* Literary Lions Award, New York Public Library, 1985; Prix de la Policia (France), for books under name E. V. Cunningham.

WRITINGS:

Two Valleys, Dial (New York, NY), 1933.
Strange Yesterday, Dodd (New York, NY), 1934.
Place in the City, Harcourt (New York, NY), 1937.
Conceived in Liberty: A Novel of Valley Forge, Simon & Schuster (New York, NY), 1939.
The Last Frontier, Duell, Sloan & Pearce (New York, NY), 1941, reprinted, North Castle Books (Armonk, NY), 1997.
The Romance of a People, Hebrew Publishing (New York, NY), 1941.
Lord Baden-Powell of the Boy Scouts, Messner (New York, NY), 1941.
Haym Salomon, Son of Liberty, Messner (New York, NY), 1941.
The Unvanquished, Duell, Sloan & Pearce (New York, NY), 1942, reprinted, M. E. Sharpe (Armonk, NY), 1997.
The Tall Hunter, Harper (New York, NY), 1942.
(With wife, Bette Fast) *The Picture-Book History of the Jews,* Hebrew Publishing (New York, NY), 1942.
Goethals and the Panama Canal, Messner (New York, NY), 1942.
Citizen Tom Paine, Duell, Sloan & Pearce (New York, NY), 1943.
The Incredible Tito, Magazine House (New York, NY), 1944.
Tito and His People, Contemporary Publishers (Winnipeg, Manitoba, Canada), 1944.
Freedom Road, Duell, Sloan & Pearce (New York, NY), 1944, new edition with foreword by W. E. B. DuBois, introduction by Eric Foner, M. E. Sharpe (Armonk, NY), 1995.
Patrick Henry and the Frigate's Keel, and Other Stories of a Young Nation, Duell, Sloan & Pearce (New York, NY), 1945.
The American: A Middle Western Legend, Duell, Sloan & Pearce (New York, NY), 1946.
(With William Gropper) *Never Forget: The Story of the Warsaw Ghetto,* Book League of the Jewish Fraternal Order, 1946.
(Editor) Thomas Paine, *Selected Works,* Modern Library (New York, NY), 1946.
The Children, Duell, Sloan & Pearce (New York, NY), 1947.
(Editor) Theodore Dreiser, *Best Short Stories,* World Publishing (New York, NY), 1947.
Clarkton, Duell, Sloan & Pearce (New York, NY), 1947.
My Glorious Brothers, Little, Brown (Boston, MA), 1948, new edition, Hebrew Publications (New York, NY), 1977.
Departure and Other Stories, Little, Brown (Boston, MA), 1949.
Intellectuals in the Fight for Peace, Masses & Mainstream (New York, NY), 1949.
The Proud and the Free, Little, Brown (Boston, MA), 1950.
Literature and Reality, International Publishers (New York, NY), 1950.
Spartacus, Blue Heron (New York, NY), 1951, reprinted with new introduction, North Castle Books (Armonk, NY), 1996.
Peekskill, U.S.A.: A Personal Experience, Civil Rights Congress (New York, NY), 1951.
(Under pseudonym Walter Erickson) *Fallen Angel,* Little, Brown (Boston, MA), 1951.
Tony and the Wonderful Door, Blue Heron (New York, NY), 1952.
Spain and Peace, Joint Anti-Fascist Refugee Committee, 1952.
The Passion of Sacco and Vanzetti: A New England Legend, Blue Heron (New York, NY), 1953.
Silas Timberman, Blue Heron (New York, NY), 1954.
The Last Supper, and Other Stories, Blue Heron (New York, NY), 1955.
The Story of Lola Gregg, Blue Heron (New York, NY), 1956.
The Naked God: The Writer and the Communist Party (memoir), Praeger (New York, NY), 1957.
Moses, Prince of Egypt, Crown (New York, NY), 1958, with new introduction by the author, Pocket Books (New York, NY), 2000.
The Winston Affair, Crown (New York, NY), 1959.
The Howard Fast Reader, Crown (New York, NY), 1960.
April Morning, Crown (New York, NY), 1961.
The Edge of Tomorrow (stories), Bantam (New York, NY), 1961.
Power, Doubleday (New York, NY), 1962.
Agrippa's Daughter, Doubleday (New York, NY), 1964.
The Hill, Doubleday (New York, NY), 1964.
Torquemada, Doubleday (New York, NY), 1966.
The Hunter and the Trap, Dial (New York, NY), 1967.
The Jews: Story of a People, Dial (New York, NY), 1968, Cassell (London), 1960.
The General Zapped an Angel, Morrow (New York, NY), 1970.

The Crossing (based on his play of the same title), Morrow (New York, NY), 1971, New Jersey Historical Society, 1985.

The Hessian, Morrow (New York, NY), 1972, reprinted with new foreword, North Castle Books, 1996.

A Touch of Infinity: Thirteen Stories of Fantasy and Science Fiction, Morrow (New York, NY), 1973.

Mohawk (screenplay; short film), Paulist Productions, 1974.

Time and the Riddle: Thirty-one Zen Stories, Ward Richie Press, 1975.

The Immigrants, Houghton Mifflin (Boston, MA), 1977.

The Art of Zen Meditation, Peace Press (Culver City, CA), 1977.

The Second Generation, Houghton Mifflin (Boston, MA), 1978.

The Establishment, Houghton Mifflin (Boston, MA), 1979.

The Legacy, Houghton Mifflin (Boston, MA), 1980.

The Magic Door (juvenile), Avon (New York, NY), 1980.

Max, Houghton Mifflin (Boston, MA), 1982.

The Outsider, Houghton Mifflin (Boston, MA), 1984.

The Immigrant's Daughter, Houghton Mifflin (Boston, MA), 1985.

The Dinner Party, Houghton Mifflin (Boston, MA), 1987.

The Call of Fife and Drum: Three Novels of the Revolution (contains *The Unvanquished, Conceived in Liberty,* and *The Proud and the Free*), Citadel, 1987.

The Pledge, Houghton Mifflin (Boston, MA), 1988.

The Confession of Joe Cullen, Houghton Mifflin (Boston, MA), 1989.

Being Red: A Memoir, Houghton Mifflin (Boston, MA), 1990.

The Trial of Abigail Goodman: A Novel, Crown (New York, NY), 1993.

War and Peace: Observations on Our Times, M. E. Sharpe (Armonk, NY), 1993.

Seven Days in June: A Novel of the American Revolution, Carol (Secaucus, NJ), 1994.

The Bridge Builder's Story, M. E. Sharpe (Armonk, NY), 1995.

An Independent Woman, Harcourt (New York, NY), 1997.

Redemption, Harcourt (New York, NY), 1999.

Greenwich, Harcourt (New York, NY), 2000.

Masuto Investigates (contains *Samantha* and *The Case of the One-Penny Orange;* also see below), ibooks (New York, NY), 2000.

Author of weekly column, *New York Observer,* 1989-92; also columnist for *Greenwich Time* and *Stamford Advocate.*

PLAYS

The Hammer, produced in New York, NY, 1950.

Thirty Pieces of Silver (produced in Melbourne, 1951), Blue Heron (New York, NY), 1954.

George Washington and the Water Witch, Bodley Head (London, England), 1956.

The Crossing, produced in Dallas, TX, 1962.

The Hill (screenplay; produced for television by A&E, 1999), Doubleday (New York, NY), 1964.

The Hessian, 1971.

David and Paula, produced in New York at American Jewish Theater, November 20, 1982.

Citizen Tom Paine: A Play in Two Acts (produced in Williamstown, MA, then in Washington, DC, at the John F. Kennedy Center for the Performing Arts, 1987), Houghton Mifflin (Boston, MA), 1986.

The Novelist (produced in Williamstown, MA, then Mamaroneck, NY, 1991), published as *The Novelist: A Romantic Portrait of Jane Austen,* Samuel French (New York, NY), 1992.

Also wrote for television series *Benjamin Franklin,* Columbia Broadcasting System, Inc. (CBS), 1974 and *How the West Was Won,* American Broadcasting Companies, Inc.(ABC), 1978-79.

NOVELS; UNDER PSEUDONYM E. V. CUNNINGHAM

Sylvia, Doubleday (New York, NY), 1960, published under name Howard Fast, Carol, 1992.

Phyllis, Doubleday (New York, NY), 1962.

Alice, Doubleday (New York, NY), 1963.

Shirley, Doubleday (New York, NY), 1963.

Lydia, Doubleday (New York, NY), 1964.

Penelope, Doubleday (New York, NY), 1965.

Helen, Doubleday (New York, NY), 1966.

Margie, Morrow (New York, NY), 1966.

Sally, Morrow (New York, NY), 1967, published under name Howard Fast, Chivers, 1994.

Samantha, Morrow (New York, NY), 1967.

Cynthia, Morrow (New York, NY), 1968.

The Assassin Who Gave up His Gun, Morrow (New York, NY), 1969.

Millie, Morrow (New York, NY), 1973.

The Case of the One-Penny Orange, Holt (New York, NY), 1977.

The Case of the Russian Diplomat, Holt (New York, NY), 1978.

The Case of the Poisoned Eclairs, Holt (New York, NY), 1979.

The Case of the Sliding Pool, Delacorte (New York, NY), 1981.

The Case of the Kidnapped Angel, Delacorte (New York, NY), 1982.

The Case of the Angry Actress, Delacorte (New York, NY), 1984.

The Case of the Murdered Mackenzie, Delacorte (New York, NY), 1984.

The Wabash Factor, Doubleday (New York, NY), 1986.

Author of introduction for *Saving the Fragments: From Auschwitz to New York,* by Isabella Leitner and Irving A. Leitner, New American Library (New York, NY), 1985; *Red Scare in Court: New York versus the International Workers Order,* by Arthur J. Sabin, University of Pennsylvania Press (Philadelphia, PA), 1993; and *The Sculpture of Bette Fast,* M. E. Sharpe (Armonk, NY), 1995.

ADAPTATIONS: The film *Rachel and the Stranger,* RKO Radio Pictures, 1948, was based on the novels *Rachel* and *Neighbor Sam; Spartacus* was filmed in 1960 by Universal Pictures, directed by Stanley Kubrick and Anthony Mann, and starred Kirk Douglas, Laurence Olivier, Tony Curtis, Jean Simmons, Charles Laughton, and Peter Ustinov. Other works by Fast have been adapted to film, including *Man in the Middle,* Twentieth-Century Fox, 1964, based on his novel *The Winston Affair; Mirage,* based on a story he wrote under the pseudonym Walter Ericson, Universal, 1965; *Fallen Angel,* based on his novel of the same title; *Sylvia,* Paramount, 1965, based on the novel of the same title; *Penelope,* Metro-Goldwyn-Mayer (MGM), 1966, based on the novel of the same title written under the pseudonym E. V. Cunningham; and *Jigsaw,* Universal, 1968, based on the screenplay for *Mirage* which was based on Fast's novel *Fallen Angel.* Writings by Fast have also been adapted for television, including *The Face of Fear,* CBS, 1971, based on the novel *Sally* written under the pseudonym E. V. Cunningham; *What's a Nice Girl like You . . .?,* ABC, 1971, based on his novel *Shirley; 21 Hours at Munich,* ABC, 1976, based on a story by Fast, *The Immigrants,* syndicated, 1978, based on his novel of the same title; *Freedom Road,* National Broadcasting Corporation (NBC), 1979, based on his novel of the same title; *April Morning,* broadcast as a *Hallmark Hall of Fame* movie, CBS, 1988, based on the novel of the same title; and *The Crossing,* Arts and Entertainment (A&E), 2000, based on his novel of the same name. *The Crossing* was recorded on cassette, narrated by Norman Dietz, Recorded Books, 1988; *The Immigrant's Daughter* was recorded on cassette, narrated by Sandra Burr, Brilliance Corporation, 1991.

SIDELIGHTS: A prolific writer, Howard Fast has published novels, plays, screenplays, stories, historical fiction, and biographies in a career that dates from the early days of the Great Depression. Fast's works have been translated into eighty-two languages and have sold millions of copies worldwide. Some observers have ranked him as the most widely read writer of the twentieth century. *Los Angeles Times* contributor Elaine Kendall wrote: "For half a century, Fast's novels, histories, and biographies have appeared at frequent intervals, a moveable feast with a distinct political flavor." *Washington Post* correspondent Joseph McLellan found Fast's work "easy to read and relatively nourishing," adding that the author "demands little of the reader, beyond a willingness to keep turning the pages, and he supplies enough activity and suspense to make this exercise worthwhile."

The grandson of Ukrainian immigrants and son of a British mother, Fast was raised in New York City. His family struggled to make ends meet, so Fast went to work as a teen and found time to indulge his passion—writing—in his spare moments. His first published novel, *Two Valleys,* was released in 1933 when he was only eighteen. Thereafter Fast began writing full time, and within a decade he had earned a considerable reputation as an historical novelist with his realistic tales of American frontier life. *Dictionary of Literary Biography* contributor Anthony Manousos commented, "As a storyteller, Fast has his greatest appeal: his knack for sketching lifelike characters and creating brisk, action-packed narratives has always insured him a wide readership, despite occasionally slipshod writing."

Fast found himself drawn to the downtrodden peoples in America's history—the Cheyenne Indians and their tragic attempt to regain their homeland (*The Last Frontier*), the starving soldiers at Valley Forge (*Conceived in Liberty: A Novel of Valley Forge*), and African Americans trying to survive the Reconstruction era in the South (*Freedom Road*). In *Publishers Weekly,* John F. Baker called these works "books on which a whole generation of radicals was brought up." A *Christian Science Monitor* contributor likewise noted: "Human nature rather than history is Howard Fast's field. In presenting these harassed human beings without any heroics he makes us all the more respectful of the price paid for American liberty." *Freedom Road* in particular was praised by the nation's black leaders for its depiction of one race's struggle for liberation; the book became a bestseller and won the Schomberg Award for Race Relations in 1944.

During the World War II, Fast worked as a correspondent for several periodicals and for the Office of War

Information. After the conflict ended he found himself at odds with the Cold War mentality developing in the United States. At the time Fast was a member of the Communist Party and a contributor of time and money to a number of anti-fascist causes. His writing during the period addressed such issues as the abuse of power, the suppression of labor unions, and communism as the basis for a utopian future. Works such as *Clarkton, My Glorious Brothers,* and *The Proud and the Free* were widely translated behind the Iron Curtain and earned Fast the International Peace Prize in 1954.

Baker noted that Fast's political views "made him for a time in the 1950s a pariah of the publishing world." The author was jailed for three months on a contempt of Congress charge for refusing to testify before the House Committee on Un-American Activities about his political views. Worse, he found himself blacklisted to such an extent that no publishing house would accept his manuscripts. Fast's persecution seemed ironic to some observers, because in the historical and biographical novels he had already published—like *Conceived in Liberty: A Novel of Valley Forge* and *The Unvanquished*—as well as in his work for the Office of War Information, Fast emphasized the importance of freedom and illuminated the heroic acts that had built American society. As a correspondent for the radio program that would become the Voice of America, he was entrusted with the job of assuring millions of foreigners of the country's greatness and benevolence during World War II.

Fast makes the relatively unknown or forgotten history of the United States accessible to millions of Americans in books like *The Last Frontier,* in which he writes a fictional account of the real-life 1978 rebellion by a tribe of northern Cheyenne Indians. According to *Twentieth-Century Western Writers* reviewer David Marion Holman, "Starved and denuded of pride, the small group of 300 men, women, and children illegally leave the reservation to return to their ancestral homeland. After eluding the U.S. cavalry for weeks . . . part of the tribe is eventually captured. As a result of their unwavering determination not to return to the Oklahoma reservation, the imprisoned Indians suffer from starvation and exposure, and are eventually massacred when they attempt a desperate escape." Because of this tragedy, the Secretary of the Interior eventually grants the rest of the tribe its freedom. Holman concluded, "Throughout the novel, Fast impresses upon the reader the inherent racism of American settlers' treatment of the Indian and points out the irony of double standards of freedom in a democracy."

Fast subsequently learned of Stalin's atrocities and broke his ties with the Communist Party in 1956; but he did not regret the decision he had made in 1944. His experience as the target of political persecution evoked some of his best and most popular works. It also led Fast to establish his own publishing house, the Blue Heron Press. In a discussion of Fast's fiction from 1944 through 1959, *Nation* correspondent Stanley Meisler contended that the "older writings must not be ignored. They document a unique political record, a depressing American waste. They describe a man who distorted his vision of America to fit a vision of communism, and then lost both." Fast published *Spartacus* under the Blue Heron imprint in 1951. A fictional account of a slave revolt in ancient Rome, *Spartacus* became a bestseller after it was made into a feature film in 1960.

Fast went on to publish five books chronicling the fictional Lavette family, beginning with *The Immigrants* in 1977. *The Immigrants* and its sequels represent some of his most popular work. The first book of the series is set mostly in San Francisco, where Dan Lavette, the son of an Italian fisherman, lives through the great earthquake in that city and goes on to build a fortune in the shipping business. The fates of an Irish family and a Chinese family are also entwined with those of the Lavettes. *The Immigrant's Daughter* relates the story of Barbara Lavette—Dan Lavette's daughter—and her political aspirations. Denise Gess in the *New York Times Book Review* called *The Immigrant's Daughter* "satisfying, old-fashioned story-telling" despite finding the novel occasionally "soap-operatic and uneven." Barbara Conaty, reviewing the novel in *Library Journal,* called Fast a "smooth and assured writer." A reviewer for *Publishers Weekly* concurred, commenting that, "smoothly written, fast-paced, alive with plots and subplots, the story reads easily." With the publication of *The Immigrant's Daughter,* the series appeared to reach its conclusion, but in 1997, Fast surprised readers with a sixth installment in the saga, *An Independent Woman.* This book relates the final years of Barbara Lavette's life. Barbara has some things in common with her creator: like him, she is a reporter, a victim of McCarthyism, and a worker for civil rights. The twilight years of her life continue to be dynamic. She battles injustice and cancer, finds romance, and astonishes her family by marrying again. A *Kirkus Reviews* writer called *An Independent Woman* "a muted, somewhat puzzling, addenda to a lively (and successful) series."

Fast published another politically charged novel in 1989, with *The Confession of Joe Cullen.* Focusing on U.S. military involvement in Central America, *The Confession of Joe Cullen* is the story of a C.I.A. pilot who confesses to New York City police that, among other things, he murdered a priest in Honduras, and has been smuggling cocaine into the United States. Arguing that the conspiracy theory that implicates the federal government in drug trafficking and gun running has never been proved, Morton Kondracke in the *New York Times Book Review* had reservations about the "political propaganda" involved in *The Confession of Joe Cullen.* Robert H. Donahugh, however, highly recommended the novel in *Library Journal,* calling it "unexpected and welcome," and lauding both the "fast-moving" storyline and the philosophical probing into Catholicism. Denise Perry Donavin, in *Booklist,* concurred, finding the politics suiting the characters "without lessening the pace of a powerful tale."

Fast focuses on another controversial subject, the issue of abortion, in his 1993 novel, *The Trial of Abigail Goodman.* As a *Publishers Weekly* critic noted, Fast views America's attitude toward abortion as "parochial," and is sympathetic to his protagonist, a college professor who has an abortion during the third trimester in a southern state with a retroactive law forbidding such acts. Critical reaction to the novel was mixed. Ray Olson in *Booklist* argued that "every anti-abortion character" is stereotyped, and that Fast "undermines . . . any pretensions to evenhandedness," and called the novel "an execrable work." The *Publishers Weekly* critic, on the other hand, found *The Trial of Abigail Goodman* "electrifying" and considered Fast "a master of courtroom pyrotechnics." Many critics, including Susan Dooley in the *Washington Post,* viewed the novel as too polemical, failing to flesh out the characters and the story. Dooley argued that Fast "has not really written a novel; his book is a tract for a cause, and like other similar endeavors, it concentrates more on making converts than creating characters." A reviewer for *Armchair Detective* concluded that the novel would have been much stronger if "there were some real sincerity and some well-expressed arguments from the antagonists." A *Rapport* reviewer commented, "Fast is more than capable of compelling character studies. There's a kernel of a powerful trial novel here, but this prestigious writer chooses not to flesh it out."

Fast returned to the topic of the American Revolution in *Seven Days in June: A Novel of the American Revolution.* A *Publishers Weekly* critic summarized: "Fictionalizing the experiences of British commanders, loyalists to the crown and a motley collection of American revolutionaries, Fast . . . fashions this dramatic look at a week of profound tension that will erupt [into] the battle of Bunker Hill." Some critics saw *Seven Days in June* as inferior to Fast's *April Morning,* also a novel about the American Revolution, which was considered by some to be a minor masterpiece. Charles Michaud in *Library Journal* found that *Seven Days* "is very readable pop history, but as a novel it is not as involving as . . . *April Morning.*" A *Kirkus Reviews* critic faulted the novel for repetitiveness and a disproportionate amount of focus on the sexual exploits of the British commanders, concluding that *Seven Days* "has a slipshod, slapdash feel, cluttered with hurried, lazy characterizations." The critic for *Publishers Weekly,* however, argued that the novel "ekes genuine suspense" and lauded Fast's "accomplished storytelling."

The Bridge Builder's Story tells of Scott Waring and his young bride, Martha, who honeymoon in Europe during the Nazi era and find themselves persecuted by Hitler's thuggish minions. After Martha is killed by the Gestapo, Scott makes his way to New York, where his ensuing sessions with a psychiatrist provide much of the narrative. Albert Wilheim, writing in *Library Journal,* thought that the novel tested "the limits of credibility," but praised Fast's "skillful narration." And Alice Joyce, in *Booklist,* opined that in *The Bridge Builder's Story,* "Fast's remarkable prowess for storytelling" results in a "riveting tale, sure to satisfy readers."

Fast's time as a communist in cold war America provided him with an extraordinary story to share in his autobiographical works, which included *Being Red: A Memoir.* Charles C. Nash of *Library Journal* called *Being Red* "indispensable to the . . . literature on America's terrifying postwar Red Scare." Fast explained to Jean W. Ross in an interview for *CA:* "There is no way to imagine war or to imagine jail or to imagine being a father or a mother. These things can only be understood if you live through them. Maybe that's a price that a writer should pay." Fast told Ken Gross in *People Weekly* that he wrote the book at the request of his son Jonathan, who wanted to share the story with his own children. Rhoda Koenig of *New York* magazine remarked that Fast's story is "a lively and gripping one," and that he "brings alive the days of parochial-school children carrying signs that read 'KILL A COMMIE FOR CHRIST.'"

With a critical eye, Ronald Radosh claimed in *Commentary* that *Being Red* contains information and perspectives that contradict portions of Fast's 1957 memoir, *The Naked God: The Writer and the Communist Party.* In Radosh's opinion, *Being Red* was the author's attempt to "rehabilitate" the Communist Party he had admonished in *The Naked God.* "Now, nearly thirty-five years later, it almost sounds as though Fast wants to end his days winning back the admiration of those unreconstructed Communists," Radosh asserted, even calling them "some of the noblest human beings I have ever known."

In 1999 Fast published *Redemption,* a suspense novel featuring Ike Goldman, a character who seems to be the author's alter ego. Goldman is a retired professor, highly intelligent, and the veteran of numerous political and social struggles. Driving through New York City one night, he sees a woman, Elizabeth, about to jump from a bridge. He talks Elizabeth out of her desperate act and, in the weeks that follow, finds himself falling in love with her. The two are planning to wed, when Elizabeth's ex-husband is found dead in suspicious circumstances, making her a suspect. Goldman does all he can to aid in her defense, but as the evidence against her mounts, his own doubts about her innocence increase. "The story moves along sedately in Fast's most relaxed style ever, with the author . . . plainly enjoying and indulging himself in this smoked salmon of romantic fantasy, adding plot dollops to keep the reader alert. . . . Fast's followers won't be disappointed," advised a contributor to *Kirkus Reviews.* The following year, Fast published *Greenwich,* a tale of eight people invited to a high-society dinner party in Greenwich, Connecticut. The comfortable life they enjoy masks an evil undercurrent; Fast suggests that guilt is widespread, and redemption is vital. Although faulting the book as stylistically "bland," a *Kirkus Reviews* writer nevertheless added: "It doesn't have to be a classic if it comes from the heart."

Fast has also published a number of detective novels under the pseudonym E. V. Cunningham, for which he was awarded with a Prix de la Policia. Many of these novels feature a fictional Japanese-American detective named Masao Masuto, who works with the Beverly Hills Police Department. Fast told *Publishers Weekly,* "Critics can't stand my mainline books, maybe because they sell so well, [but] they love Cunningham. Even the *New Yorker* has reviewed him, and they've never reviewed me." In the *New York Times Book Review,* Newgate Callendar called detective Masuto "a well-conceived character whose further exploits should gain him a wide audience." *Toronto Globe and Mail* contributor Derrick Murdoch also found Masuto "a welcome addition to the lighter side of crime fiction." "Functional and efficient, Fast's prose is a machine in which plot and ideals mesh, turn and clash," Kendall concluded, adding, "The reader is constantly being instructed, but the manner is so disarming and the hectic activity so absorbing that the didacticism seldom intrudes upon the entertainment."

Fast's voice has interpreted America's past and present and has helped shape its reputation at home and abroad. One of his own favorites among his novels, *April Morning,* has been standard reading in public schools for generations. The film *Spartacus* has become a popular classic, and *Being Red* offers an account of American history that Americans may never want to forget, whether or not they agree with Fast's perspectives. As Victor Howes commented in *Christian Science Monitor,* if Howard Fast "is a chronicler of some of mankind's most glorious moments, he is also a register of some of our more senseless deeds."

BIOGRAPHICAL/CRITICAL SOURCES:

BOOKS

Authors and Artists for Young Adults, Volume 16, Gale (Detroit, MI), 1995.

Contemporary Authors Autobiograpy Series, Volume 18, Gale (Detroit, MI), 1994.

Contemporary Literary Criticism, Gale (Detroit, MI), Volume 23, 1983, Volume 131, 2000.

Contemporary Novelists, 6th edition, St. James Press (Detroit, MI), 1996.

Contemporary Popular Writers, St. James Press (Detroit, MI), 1997.

Dictionary of Literary Biography, Volume 9: *American Novelists, 1910-1945,* Gale (Detroit, MI), 1981.

MacDonald, Andrew, *Howard Fast: A Critical Companion,* Greenwood (Westport, CT), 1996.

Meyer, Hershel, D., *History and Conscience: The Case of Howard Fast,* Anvil-Atlas (New York, NY), 1958.

St. James Guide to Crime and Mystery Writers, 4th edition, St. James Press (Detroit, MI), 1996.

St. James Guide to Young Adult Writers, 2nd edition, St. James Press (Detroit, MI), 1999.

Twentieth-Century Romance and Historical Writers, 3rd edition, St. James Press (Detroit, MI), 1994.

Twentieth-Century Western Writers, St. James Press (Detroit, MI), 1991.

PERIODICALS

Antioch Review, winter, 1993, review of *Sylvia,* p. 156.

Armchair Detective, spring, 1994, review of *The Trial of Abigail Goodman,* p. 218.

Atlantic Monthly, September, 1944; June, 1970.

Best Sellers, February 1, 1971; September 1, 1973; January, 1979; November, 1979.

Booklist, June 15, 1989, p. 1739; July, 1993, review of *The Trial of Abigail Goodman,* p. 1916; October 1, 1995, review of *The Bridge Builder's Story,* p. 252;

May 1, 1997, review of *An Independent Woman,* p. 1460; February 15, 1999, review of *Redemption,* p. 1003; February 1, 2000, review of *Greenwich,* p. 996.

Book Week, May 9, 1943.

Chicago Tribune, April 21, 1987; January 20, 1991, section 14, p. 7.

Christian Science Monitor, July 8, 1939; August 23, 1972, p. 11; November 7, 1977, p. 18; November 1, 1991, p. 12; August 12, 1999, review of *Redemption,* p. 20.

Commentary, March, 1991, pp. 62-64.

Detroit News, October 31, 1982.

Entertainment Weekly, August 1, 1997, review of *An Independent Woman,* p. 69; July 30, 1999, review of *Redemption,* p. 66.

Globe and Mail (Toronto), September 15, 1984; March 1, 1986; July 17, 1999, review of *Redemption,* p. D14.

Kirkus Reviews, June 15, 1993, review of *The Trial of Abigail Goodman,* p. 739; June 15, 1994, review of *Seven Days in June,* p. 793; July 15, 1995, review of *The Bridge Builder's Story,* p. 968; June 15, 1997, review of *An Independent Woman,* p. 909; May 1, 1999, review of *Redemption,* p. 650.

Library Journal, November 15, 1978; September 15, 1985, p. 92; May 15, 1989, p. 88; October 1, 1990, p. 96; August, 1991, p. 162; July, 1994, review of *Seven Days in June,* p. 126; September 1, 1995, review of *The Bridge Builder's Story,* p. 206; February 1, 1997, p. 112; June 15, 1997, review of *An Independent Woman,* p. 96; May 15, 1999, review of *Redemption,* p. 125.

Los Angeles Times, November 11, 1982; November 11, 1985; November 21, 1988.

Los Angeles Times Book Review, December 9, 1990.

Nation, April 5, 1952; May 30, 1959.

New Republic, August 17, 1942, p. 203; August 14, 1944; November 4, 1978; May 27, 1992.

New Statesman, August 8, 1959.

New York, November 5, 1990, pp. 124-125.

New Yorker, July 1, 1939; May 1, 1943.

New York Herald Tribune Book Review, July 21, 1963.

New York Herald Tribune Books, July 27, 1941, p. 3.

New York Times, October 15, 1933; June 25, 1939; April 25, 1943; February 3, 1952; September 24, 1984; February 9, 1987, p. C16; March 10, 1987; April 21, 1991, pp. 20-21; October 23, 1991, p. C19; November 19, 1993, p. A2.

New York Times Book Review, October 13, 1933; April 25, 1943; February 3, 1952; March 4, 1962; July 14, 1963; February 6, 1966; October 2, 1977, p. 24; October 30, 1977; May 14, 1978; June 10, 1979; September 15, 1985, p. 24; March 29, 1987, p. 22; August 20, 1989, p. 23; February 28, 1993, review of *The Jews: Story of a People,* p. 32; October 22, 1995, review of *The Bridge Builder's Story,* p. 37.

People Weekly, January 28, 1991, pp. 75-79.

Publishers Weekly, August 6, 1979; April 1, 1983; July 19, 1985, p. 48; November 28, 1986, p. 66; July 22, 1988, p. 41; June 30, 1989, p. 84; June 21, 1993, review of *The Trial of Abigail Goodman,* p. 83; July 11, 1994, review of *Seven Days in June,* p. 66; September 4, 1995, review of *The Bridge Builder's Story,* p. 49; May 26, 1997, review of *An Independent Woman,* p. 64; May 17, 1999, review of *Redemption,* p. 54.

Rapport, Number 1, 1994, review of *The Trial of Abigail Goodman,* p. 38.

Reference and Research Book News, November, 1995, review of *Freedom Road,* p. 69; February, 1998, review of *The Unvanquished,* p. 150.

Saturday Review, March 8, 1952; January 22, 1966; September 17, 1977.

Saturday Review of Literature, July 1, 1939; July 26, 1941, p. 5; May 1, 1943; December 24, 1949.

Science and Society, spring, 1993, review of *Being Red,* p. 86.

Time, November 6, 1977.

Times Literary Supplement, November 11, 1939.

Tribune Books (Chicago), February 8, 1987, pp. 6x7.

Washington Post, October 4, 1979; September 26, 1981; September 25, 1982; September 3, 1985; February 9, 1987; March 3, 1987; September 6, 1993, p. C2.

Washington Post Book World, October 23, 1988; November 25, 1990; November 17, 1996, p. 12; August 8, 1999, review of *Redemption,* p. 4.

* * *

FISHER, Leonard Everett 1924-

PERSONAL: Born June 24, 1924, in the Bronx, NY; son of Benjamin M. and Ray M. (Shapiro) Fisher; married Margery M. Meskin (a school librarian), 1952; children: Julie Anne, Susan Abby, James Albert. *Education:* Attended Art Students League, 1941, and Brooklyn College, 1941-42; Yale University, B.F.A., 1949, M.F.A., 1950.

ADDRESSES: Home and office—7 Twin Bridge Acres Rd., Westport, CT 06880. *E-mail*—LeonardoE1@aol.com.

CAREER: Painter, illustrator, author, and educator. Graduate teaching fellow, Yale Art School, 1949-50; Whitney School of Art, New Haven, CT, dean, 1951-

53; faculty member, Paier College of Art, 1966-78, academic dean, 1978-82, dean emeritus, 1982—, visiting professor, 1982-87. Visiting professor, artist, or consultant at various universities and colleges, including Case Western Reserve University, Silvermine Guild School of the Arts, Hartford University School of Art, Fairfield University, and University of California. Designer of U.S. postage stamps for the U.S. Postal Service, 1972-77; design consultant, Postal Agent, Staffa and Bernera Islands, Scotland, 1979-82. Delegate to national and international conferences; member of arts councils and historical societies in Westport, CT, and Greater New Haven, CT; trustee, Westport Public Library Board of Trustees, 1982-85, vice president, 1985-86, president, 1986-89. Lecturer and speaker at art institutes, academic seminars, education workshops and children's book programs nationwide. *Military service:* U.S. Army, Corps of Engineers, 1942-46; became technical sergeant; participated in topographic mapping of major invasion campaigns in European and Pacific areas. *Exhibitions:* Various one-man shows at museums, libraries, galleries, and universities in the United States, including Hewitt Gallery, NY; New Britain Museum of American Art(retrospective), New Britain, CT; Everson Museum, University of Syracuse, NY; Kimberly Gallery, New York, NY; Museum of American Illustration, Society of Illustrators (retrospective), New York, NY; Homer Babbidge Library, University of Connecticut (retrospective); and special mini-exhibitions (including Smithsonian Institution, and Fairview Park Library, OH), 1952—.

Work exhibited at various group shows at galleries, museums, and universities in the United States, including Brooklyn Museum, NY; Rockefeller Center, NY; Seligmann Galleries, NY; Eggleston Galleries, NY; Hewitt Gallery, NY; American Federation of Arts and Emily Lowe Foundation national tours; Whitney Museum, NY; National Academy (Audubon Artists), NY; New York Historical Society, NY; Society of Illustrators, NY; Yale Art Gallery, CT; and many others, 1939—.

Work included in collections of various museums, libraries, and universities, including Library of Congress, Washington, DC; Free Library of Philadelphia, PA; New Britain Museum of American Art, New Britain, CT; Museum of American Illustration, New York, NY; universities of Connecticut, Oregon, Minnesota, Southern Mississippi, and Appalachian State; Fairfield University, Fairfield, CT; Brown University, Providence, RI; Smithsonian Institution, Washington, DC; and other public and private collections in Iowa, Massachusetts, Michigan, Delaware, Hawaii, Maryland, New York, New Jersey, Wisconsin, California, North Carolina, and Oklahoma.

MEMBER: PEN, Society of Children's Book Writers and Illustrators, Authors Guild, Society of Illustrators, Silvermine Guild of Artists (trustee, 1970-74), New Haven Paint and Clay Club (president, 1968-70; trustee, 1968-74), Westport-Weston Arts Council (founding member; director, 1969-76; vice president, 1972-73; president, 1973-74; board chairman, 1975-76).

AWARDS, HONORS: William Wirt Winchester traveling fellowship, Yale University, 1949; Joseph Pulitzer scholarship in art, Columbia University and the National Academy of Design, 1950; American Institute of Graphic Arts outstanding textbooks, 1958, outstanding children's books, 1963; Newbery Honor Award, 1960, for *America Is Born: A History for Peter* with text by Gerald W. Johnson; Spring Book Festival Older Honor Award, 1960, for *America Grows Up: A History for Peter* with text by Johnson; Newbery Honor Award, 1961, for *America Moves Forward: A History for Peter,* with text by Johnson; Ten Best Illustrated Books Award of the *New York Times,* 1964, for *Casey at the Bat;* New Haven Paint and Clay Club, Carle J. Blenner Prize for painting, 1968; premio grafico, Fiera di Bologna, 5a Fiera Internazionale del Libro per l'Infanzia e la Gioventu, Italy, 1968, for *The Schoolmasters;* Mayor's Proclamation: Leonard Everett Fisher Day, Fairview Park, OH, opening National Children's Book Week, November 12, 1978; New York Library Association/School Library Media Section Award for Outstanding Contributions in the Fields of Art and Literature, 1979; Medallion of the University of Southern Mississippi for Distinguished Contributions to Children's Literature, 1979; Christopher Medal for illustration, 1981, for *All Times, All Peoples: A World History of Slavery;* National Jewish Book Award for Children's Literature, and Association of Jewish Libraries Award for Children's Literature, both 1981, both for *A Russian Farewell;* Parenting's Reading Magic Award, Time-Life, 1988, for *Monticello;* Children's Book Guild/*Washington Post* Nonfiction Award, 1989; nominee, Orbis Pictus Award for Outstanding Nonfiction for Children, National Council of Teachers of English, 1989, for *The White House;* Parents' Choice Award, 1989, for *The Seven Days of Creation;* Regina Medal, Catholic Library Association, 1991, for distinguished contributions to children's literature; Kerlan Award, University of Minnesota, 1991, for "singular attainments in the creation of children's literature"; Arbuthnot Honor Lecturer, Association of Library Services to Children of the American Library Association, 1995.

Fisher's books have received numerous awards or special citations from the American Institute of Graphic Arts, the *New York Times, Booklist,* the American Library Association, the National Council of Social Studies, various state library and reading organizations in Utah, Kentucky, Oklahoma, and Texas, and the National Council of Social Studies, including all books in his "Colonial Americans" and "Nineteenth-Century America" series.

WRITINGS:

SELF-ILLUSTRATED CHILDREN'S BOOKS

Pumpers, Boilers, Hooks, and Ladders, Dial, 1961.
Pushers, Spads, Jennies, and Jets, Dial, 1961.
A Head Full of Hats, Dial, 1962.
Two If by Sea, Random House, 1970.
Picture Book of Revolutionary War Heroes, Stockpole, 1970.
The Death of Evening Star: The Diary of a Young New England Whaler, Doubleday, 1972.
The Art Experience, F. Watts, 1973.
The Warlock of Westfall, Doubleday, 1974.
Across the Sea from Galway, Four Winds, 1975.
Sweeney's Ghost, Doubleday, 1975.
Leonard Everett Fisher's Liberty Book, Doubleday, 1976.
Letters from Italy, Four Winds, 1977.
Noonan, Doubleday, 1978, Avon, 1981.
Alphabet Art: Thirteen ABC's from around the World, Four Winds, 1979.
A Russian Farewell, Four Winds, 1980.
Storm at the Jetty, Viking, 1980.
The Seven Days of Creation, Holiday House, 1981.
Number Art: Thirteen 1, 2, 3's from around the World, Four Winds, 1982.
Star Signs, Holiday House, 1983.
Symbol Art: Thirteen Squares, Circles, and Triangles from around the World, Four Winds, 1984.
Boxes! Boxes!, Viking, 1984.
The Olympians: Great Gods and Goddesses of Ancient Greece, Holiday House, 1984.
The Statue of Liberty, Holiday House, 1985.
The Great Wall of China, Macmillan, 1986.
Ellis Island: Gateway to the New World, Holiday House, 1986.
Calendar Art: Thirteen Days, Weeks, Months, and Years from around the World, Four Winds, 1987.
The Tower of London, Macmillan, 1987.
The Alamo, Holiday House, 1987.
Look Around: A Book about Shapes, Viking, 1987.
Monticello, Holiday House, 1988.
Pyramid of the Sun, Pyramid of the Moon, Macmillan, 1988.
Theseus and the Minotaur, Holiday House, 1988.
The Wailing Wall, Macmillan, 1989.
The White House, Holiday House, 1989.
Prince Henry the Navigator, Macmillan, 1990.
Jason and the Golden Fleece, Holiday House, 1990.
The Oregon Trail, Holiday House, 1990.
The ABC Exhibit, Macmillan, 1991.
Sailboat Lost, Macmillan, 1991.
Cyclops, Holiday House, 1991.
Galileo, Macmillan, 1992.
Tracks across America: The Story of the American Railroad, 1825-1900, Holiday House, 1992.
Gutenberg, Macmillan, 1993.
David and Goliath, Holiday House, 1993.
Stars and Stripes: Our National Flag, Holiday House, 1993.
Marie Curie, Macmillan, 1994.
Kinderdike, Macmillan, 1994.
Gandhi, Atheneum, 1995.
Moses, Holiday House, 1995.
William Tell, Farrar, Straus, and Giroux, 1996.
Niagara Falls: Nature's Wonder, Holiday House, 1996.
Gods and Goddesses of Ancient Egypt, Holiday House, 1997.
The Jetty Chronicles, Marshall Cavendish, 1997.
Anasazi, Atheneum, 1997.
To Bigotry No Sanction: The Story of the Oldest Synagogue in America, Holiday House, 1998.
Alexander Graham Bell, Simon & Schuster, 1999.
Gods and Goddesses of the Ancient Maya, Holiday House, 1999.
Gods and Goddesses of the Ancient Norse, Holiday House, 2001.
Sky, Sea, the Jetty, and Me, Marshall Cavendish, 2001.

"COLONIAL AMERICANS" SERIES; SELF-ILLUSTRATED

The Glassmakers, F. Watts, 1964.
The Silversmiths, F. Watts, 1964.
The Papermakers, F. Watts, 1965.
The Printers, F. Watts, 1965.
The Wigmakers, F. Watts, 1965.
The Hatters, F. Watts, 1965.
The Weavers, F. Watts, 1966.
The Cabinet Makers, F. Watts, 1966.
The Tanners, F. Watts, 1966.
The Shoemakers, F. Watts, 1967.
The Schoolmasters, F. Watts, 1967.
The Peddlers, F. Watts, 1968.
The Doctors, F. Watts, 1968.
The Potters, F. Watts, 1969.
The Limners, F. Watts, 1969.
The Architects, F. Watts, 1970.

The Shipbuilders, F. Watts, 1971.
The Homemakers, F. Watts, 1973.
The Blacksmiths, F. Watts, 1976.

"NINETEENTH-CENTURY AMERICA" SERIES; SELF-ILLUSTRATED

The Factories, Holiday House, 1979.
The Railroads, Holiday House, 1979.
The Hospitals, Holiday House, 1980.
The Sports, Holiday House, 1980.
The Newspapers, Holiday House, 1981.
The Unions, Holiday House, 1982.
The Schools, Holiday House, 1983.

ILLUSTRATOR

Geoffrey Household, *The Exploits of Xenophon,* Random House, 1955, revised edition, Shoestring Press, 1989.
Florence Walton Taylor, *Carrier Boy,* Abelard, 1956.
Manley Wade Wellman, *To Unknown Lands,* Holiday House, 1956.
Roger P. Buliard, *My Eskimos: A Priest in the Arctic,* Farrar, Straus, 1956.
Richard B. Morris, *The First Book of the American Revolution,* F. Watts, 1956, revised edition published as *The American Revolution,* Lerner Publications, 1985.
L. D. Rich, *The First Book of New England,* F. Watts, 1957.
Kenneth S. Giniger, *America, America, America,* F. Watts, 1957.
Henry Steele Commager, *The First Book of American History,* F. Watts, 1957.
James C. Bowman, *Mike Fink,* Little, Brown, 1957.
Robert Payne, *The Splendor of Persia,* Knopf, 1957.
Morris, *The First Book of the Constitution,* F. Watts, 1958, revised edition published as *The Constitution,* Lerner Publications, 1985.
Jeanette Eaton, *America's Own Mark Twain,* Morrow, 1958.
Harry B. Ellis, *The Arabs,* World, 1958.
Robert Irving, *Energy and Power,* Knopf, 1958.
Estelle Friedman, *Digging into Yesterday,* Putnam, 1958.
E. B. Meyer, *Dynamite and Peace,* Little, Brown, 1958.
E. M. Brown, *Kateri Tekakwitha,* Farrar, Straus, 1958.
C. Edell, *Here Come the Clowns,* Putnam, 1958.
L. H. Kuhn, *The World of Jo Davidson,* Farrar, Straus, 1958.
Catharine Wooley, *David's Campaign Buttons,* Morrow, 1959.
Maurice Dolbier, *Paul Bunyan,* Random House, 1959.
Edith L. Boyd, *Boy Joe Goes to Sea,* Rand McNally, 1959.
Gerald W. Johnson, *America Is Born: A History for Peter,* Morrow, 1959.
Morris, *The First Book of Indian Wars,* F. Watts, 1959, revised edition published as *The Indian Wars,* Lerner Publications, 1985.
Elizabeth Abell, editor, *Westward, Westward, Westward,* F. Watts, 1959.
Phillip H. Ault, *This Is the Desert,* Dodd, 1959.
Irving, *Sound and Ultrasonics,* Knopf, 1959.
Johnson, *America Moves Forward: A History for Peter,* Morrow, 1960.
Johnson, *America Grows Up: A History for Peter,* Morrow, 1960.
Irving, *Electromagnetic Waves,* Knopf, 1960.
Declaration of Independence, F. Watts, 1960.
Trevor N. Dupuy, *Military History of Civil War Naval Actions,* F. Watts, 1960.
Dupuy, *Military History of Civil War Land Battles,* F. Watts, 1960.
Edward E. Hale, *The Man without a Country,* F. Watts, 1960.
Anico Surnay, *Ride the Cold Wind,* Putnam, 1960.
Natalia M. Belting, *Indy and Mrs. Lincoln,* Holt, 1960.
Belting, *Verity Mullens and the Indian,* Holt, 1960.
Morris, *The First Book of the War of 1812,* F. Watts, 1961, revised edition published as *The War of 1812,* Lerner Publications, 1985.
Emma G. Sterne, *Vasco Nunez De Balboa,* Knopf, 1961.
James Playsted Wood, *The Queen's Most Honorable Pirate,* Harper, 1961.
Harold W. Felton, *A Horse Named Justin Morgan,* Dodd, 1962.
Charles M. Daugherty, *Great Archaeologists,* Crowell, 1962.
Margery M. Fisher, *But Not Our Daddy,* Dial, 1962.
Robert C. Suggs, *Modern Discoveries in Archaeology,* Crowell, 1962.
Paul Engle, *Golden Child,* Dutton, 1962.
Jean L. Latham, *Man of the Monitor,* Harper, 1962.
Johnson, *The Supreme Court,* Morrow, 1962.
Harold W. Felton, *Sergeant O'Keefe and His Mule, Balaam,* Dodd, 1962.
Johnson. *The Presidency,* Morrow, 1962.
Jack London, *Before Adam,* Macmillan, 1962.
Eric B. Smith and Robert Meredith, *Pilgrim Courage,* Little, Brown, 1962.
E. Hubbard, *Message of Garcia,* F. Watts, 1962.
Charles Ferguson, *Getting to Know the U.S.A.,* Coward, 1963.
A. Surany, *Golden Frog,* Putnam, 1963.
Johnson, *The Congress,* Morrow, 1963.

Margery M. Fisher, *One and One,* Dial, 1963.
Andre Maurois, *The Weigher of Souls,* Macmillan, 1963.
London, *Star Rover,* Macmillan, 1963.
Helen Hoke, editor, *Patriotism, Patriotism, Patriotism,* F. Watts, 1963.
Gettysburg Address, F. Watts, 1963.
Johnson, *Communism: An American's View,* Morrow, 1964.
Smith and Meredith, *Coming of the Pilgrims,* Little, Brown, 1964.
Richard Armour, *Our Presidents,* Norton, 1964.
Meredith and Smith, *Riding with Coronado,* Little, Brown, 1964.
Robert C. Suggs, *Alexander the Great, Scientist-King,* Macmillan, 1964.
John F. Kennedy's Inaugural Address, F. Watts, 1964.
Suggs, *Archaeology of San Francisco,* Crowell, 1965.
Martin Gardner, *Archimedes,* Macmillan, 1965.
Florence Stevenson, *The Story of Aida* (based on the opera by Giuseppe Verdi), Putnam, 1965.
Lois P. Jones, *The First Book of the White House,* F. Watts, 1965.
Ernest L. Thayer, *Casey at the Bat,* F. Watts, 1965.
John Foster, *Rebel Sea Raider,* Morrow, 1965.
Surany, *The Burning Mountain,* Holiday House, 1965.
Martha Shapp and Charles Shapp, *Let's Find out about John Fitzgerald Kennedy,* F. Watts, 1965.
Suggs, *Archaeology of New York,* Crowell, 1966.
Clifford L. Alderman, *The Story of the Thirteen Colonies,* Random House, 1966.
Foster, *Guadalcanal General,* Morrow, 1966.
Robert Silverberg, *Forgotten by Time,* Crowell, 1966.
Johnson, *The Cabinet,* Morrow, 1966.
Washington Irving, *The Legend of Sleepy Hollow,* F. Watts, 1966.
Surany, *Kati and Kormos,* Holiday House, 1966.
Surany, *A Jungle Jumble,* Putnam, 1966.
Meredith and Smith, *Quest of Columbus,* Little, Brown, 1966.
Madeleine L'Engle, *Journey with Jonah,* Farrar, Straus, 1967.
L. Sprague and Catherine C. De Camp, *The Story of Science in America,* Scribner, 1967.
Nathaniel Hawthorne, *Great Stone Face and Two Other Stories,* F. Watts, 1967.
Johnson, *Franklin D. Roosevelt,* Morrow, 1967.
George B. Shaw, *The Devil's Disciple,* F. Watts, 1967.
Surany, *Covered Bridge,* Holiday House, 1967.
Surany, *Monsieur Jolicoeur's Umbrella,* Putnam, 1967.
Irving, *Rip Van Winkle,* F. Watts, 1967.
Morris, *The First Book of the Founding of the Republic,* F. Watts, 1968.
Surany, *Malachy's Gold,* Holiday House, 1968.
Bret Harte, *The Luck of Roaring Camp,* F. Watts, 1968.
(With Cynthia Basil) J. Foster, *Napoleon's Marshall,* Morrow, 1968.
Gerald W. Foster, *The British Empire,* Morris, 1969.
Meredith and Smith, *Exploring the Great River,* Little, Brown, 1969.
Surany, *Lora Lorita,* Putnam, 1969.
Julian May, *Why the Earth Quakes,* Holiday House, 1969.
Victor B. Scheffer, *The Year of the Whale,* Scribner, 1969.
Scheffer, *The Year of the Seal,* Scribner, 1970.
Berenice R. Morris, *American Popular Music,* F. Watts, 1970.
Scheffer, *Little Calf,* Scribner, 1970.
Loren Eisely, *The Night Country,* Scribner, 1971.
May, *The Land beneath the Sea,* Holiday House, 1971.
Isaac B. Singer, *The Wicked City,* Farrar, Straus, 1972.
Jan Wahl, *Juan Diego and the Lady,* Putnam, 1973.
Gladys Conklin, *The Journey of the Gray Whales,* Holiday House, 1974.
James E. Gunn, *Some Dreams Are Nightmares,* Scribner, 1974.
E. Thompson, *The White Falcon,* Doubleday, 1976.
Milton Meltzer, *All Times, All Peoples: A World History of Slavery,* Harper, 1980.
Myra Cohn Livingston, *A Circle of Seasons,* Holiday House, 1982.
Richard Armour, *Our Presidents,* revised edition, Woodbridge Press, 1983.
Livingston, *Sky Songs,* Holiday House, 1984.
Livingston, *Celebrations,* Holiday House, 1985.
Livingston, *Sea Songs,* Holiday House, 1986.
Livingston, *Earth Songs,* Holiday House, 1986.
Livingston, *Space Songs,* Holiday House, 1988.
Livingston, *Up in the Air,* Holiday House, 1989.
Alice Schertle, *Little Frog's Song,* Harper, 1992.
Livingston, *If You Ever Meet a Whale,* Holiday House, 1992.
Eric A. Kimmel, editor, *The Spotted Pony: A Collection of Hanukkah Stories,* Holiday House, 1992.
David and Goliath: Retold from the Bible, Holiday House, 1993.
Kimmel, reteller, *The Three Princes: A Tale from the Middle East,* Holiday House, 1994.
Moses: Retold from the Bible, Holiday House, 1995.
Livingston, *Festivals,* Holiday House, 1996.
Kimmel, reteller, *The Two Mountains: An Aztec Legend,* Holiday House, 1999.

ILLUSTRATOR; TEXT BOOKS AND LEARNING MATERIALS

Our Reading Heritage (six volumes), Holt, 1956-58.
Marjorie Wescott Barrows, *Good English through Practice,* Holt, 1956.

Don Parker, editor, *The Multilevel Reading Laboratory* (eight volumes), Science Research Associates, 1957-62.

M. W. Barrows and E. N. Woods, *Reading Skills,* Holt, 1958.

Dolores Betler, editor, *The Literature Sampler* (two volumes), Learning Materials, Inc., 1962, 1964.

How Things Change, Field Enterprise, 1964.

ILLUSTRATOR; AUDIO-VISUAL FILMSTRIPS

Edgar Allan Poe, *Murders in the Rue Morgue,* Encyclopaedia Britannica, 1978.

Robert Louis Stevenson, *Dr. Jekyll and Mr. Hyde,* Encyclopaedia Britannica, 1978.

Bram Stoker, *The Judge's House,* Encyclopaedia Britannica, 1978.

A. B. Edwards, *Snow* (from *The Phantom Coach*), Encyclopaedia Britannica, 1978.

Poe, *The Tell-Tale Heart,* Encyclopaedia Britannica, 1980.

OTHER

Masterpieces of American Painting (for adults), Bison/Exeter, 1985.

Remington and Russell (for adults), W. H. Smith, 1986.

Also illustrator for *Cricket* and *Lady Bug* magazines. Many of Fisher's manuscripts, illustrations, drawings, and correspondence are housed at the Leonard Everett Fisher Archive, University of Connecticut, Storrs, the Kerlan Collection, University of Minnesota, Minneapolis, the de Grummond Collection, University of Southern Mississippi, Hattiesburg, the library of the University of Oregon, Eugene, and at the Postal History Collection, Smithsonian Institution, Washington, DC.

ADAPTATIONS: Filmstrips, all by Anico Surany and all produced by Random House: *The Golden Frog, The Burning Mountain, A Jungle Jumble, Monsieur Jolicouer's Umbrella, Ride the Cold Wind,* and *Lora Lorita.*

SIDELIGHTS: Prolific and diverse are adjectives often used to describe the work of Leonard Everett Fisher, a prominent author/illustrator of both fiction and nonfiction books for children, particularly books of American and world history. On his own, Fisher has published more than eighty books; he has illustrated over one hundred and sixty by authors as diverse as Washington Irving, Madeleine L'Engle, the poet Myra Cohn Livingston, and Eric Kimmel; he has also illustrated nearly twenty textbooks and learning tools.

Fisher's books of nonfiction are targeted at readers in the elementary and middle grades and present cogent and informative introductions to topics from world mythology, as in *The Olympians: Great Gods and Goddesses of Ancient Greece, Gods and Goddesses of Ancient Egypt,* and *Gods and Goddesses of the Ancient Maya,* to great moments in American history as revealed by buildings and institutions, such as *The Statue of Liberty, Ellis Island, The White House, Monticello,* and *Stars and Stripes.* Fisher's two historical series for young readers, "Colonial Americans" and "Nineteenth-Century America," also serve as introductions to the social history of the age, providing "accurate reflections of the period," according to Reba Pinney, writing in *St. James Guide to Children's Writers.* Pinney further noted that these series books "are often witty and amusing" and clearly display Fisher's "desire to connect the reader with the institutions of the past." Fisher has also written numerous biographies, including *Galileo, Gutenberg, Gandhi, Marie Curie, William Tell,* and *Alexander Graham Bell;* short picture books that offer unique perspectives on the works and achievements of such famous people. Natural history gets the Fisher treatment as well, in works such as *Niagara Falls: Nature's Wonder,* and ancient civilization are illuminated by his pen in *Anasazi.*

Fisher is also the author of many works of fiction, several of them inspired by the writer's interest in the immigrant life, as in *Across the Sea from Galway, Letters from Italy,* and *A Russian Farewell.* The weird and fantastical also are deployed by Fisher in novels such as *The Warlock of Westfall, The Death of Evening Star,* and *Sweeney's Ghost,* while his childhood home at Sea Gate in Brooklyn serves as the setting for other tales, such as *The Jetty Chronicles.* In all of his work, Fisher accompanies text with powerful illustrations in a variety of media from pen-and-ink to acrylics. A renowned artist in his own right, Fisher brings to his illustrations the training and insight of a fine arts painter.

Fisher credits his father's love of art with his own decision to become an artist. The elder Fisher was a ship designer and draftsman who painted in his spare time. One of his paintings was still on the easel when two-year-old Leonard got hold of some india ink and a paintbrush and added his own embellishments to his father's work. The result was an unusable mess. But instead of being punished, Fisher was given his own little studio—a converted hall closet—complete with worktable, crayons, paper, and pencils. "I was cozily in business," Fisher recalled in his article for *Something about the Author Autobiography Series* (*SAAS*), "ensconced in my first studio, lit from the ceiling by a naked bulb and about six steps from the kitchen."

While in school, Fisher began to win local art competitions, including several prizes sponsored by department stores. One of these was a float design for the Macy Thanksgiving Day parade. A pencil drawing was exhibited with the works of other high school students at the Brooklyn Museum. In addition to his schoolwork, Fisher also took art classes at Moses Soyer's art studio, at the Art Students' League, and at the Heckscher Foundation. His mother also made sure he visited the art museums of New York. After graduating from high school at the age of sixteen, Fisher studied art and geology at Brooklyn College for a time before entering the Army. He enlisted in 1942 and was assigned to become a mapmaker.

Fisher returned to college after his military service, earning two degrees from Yale University. "The Yale experience was memorable," Fisher explained in his *SAAS* article. "It prepared me for every artistic eventuality. It was up to me to discover those eventualities." Following graduation, Fisher traveled to Europe using money received from two fellowships. He visited the major art museums of London, Paris, Milan, Florence, Venice, Rome, and elsewhere in Italy. "I saw every painting I came to see and more," he remarked in *SAAS.* Returning to the United States, Fisher became dean of the Whitney School of Art. He had his first New York exhibition at the Edwin C. Hewitt Gallery in 1952. Although not one painting was sold, the critical reviews were favorable and Fisher, emboldened by the response, proposed marriage to Margery Meskin, then a systems service representative with IBM. The couple was married later that year and eventually had three children.

Shortly after leaving the Whitney School of Art in 1953, Fisher began to illustrate books for children. His first was *The Exploits of Xenophon,* written by Geoffrey Household, which tells the story of an ancient Greek writer, historian, and military leader. Other projects soon followed, including the six-volume *Our Reading Heritage* and the *Multilevel Reading Laboratory,* an experimental concept in which 150 reading selections were printed with 150 suitable illustrations. Fisher did the illustrations for eight of the "laboratory" packages, more than 3,000 illustrations in all. In addition to illustrating educational materials, Fisher also illustrated a number of children's picture books, working for Holiday House and Franklin Watts. These books included both fiction and nonfiction titles, including many on American history, a subject close to Fisher's heart. "American history," he explained in *SAAS,* "had a strong presence during my growing years. To my parents, one an immigrant, the other the son of immigrants, the United States was heaven-sent."

Fisher has also written his own children's books, his first solo effort appearing in 1961. Many of these works have been about historical subjects. His "Nineteenth-Century America" series for Holiday House describes various aspects of American society, such as the growth of the railroads or the nation's most popular leisure-time activities, and is meant to provide a panoramic picture of the development of nineteenth century America. Fisher explained in *SAAS* that the books also "deal with my determination not to disconnect. In a culture like ours, wherein today's material gratification seems to deny any historical link, knowledge of the past is often and mistakenly brushed aside as irrelevant to our present and future values, much less the course of our nation. I try to say otherwise."

Reviewing the first two titles in the series, *The Factories* and *The Railroads,* Shirley Wilton in *School Library Journal* remarked that the books "are characterized by excellent design, well-spaced, readable type, and Fisher's dramatic black-and-white scratchboard illustrations." Wilton further commented, "Lively writing, startling facts and striking illustrations make these books excellent supplements to standard historical coverage of industrial growth in America." Focusing on the human side of history, Fisher's books on nineteenth-century America follow the fortunes of various men and women who helped to build the country through newspapers, schools, hospitals, unions, and sports. Reviewing *The Sports,* a writer for *Publishers Weekly* noted that Fisher "writes briskly and authoritatively about competitive games and their social implications during American's early days." This same reviewer concluded, "Fisher describes the feats of legendary figures . . . creating an exemplary document on an energetic age."

The "Colonial Americans" series from Franklin Watts (since republished by Marshall Cavendish) consists of nineteen books describing colonial crafts, trades, and professions. Each begins with a brief history of the craft, trade, or profession in question and then proceeds to describe the actual techniques used by colonial craftsmen. Fisher's illustrations for the books were done in a style reminiscent of old-time engravings to give them the proper feeling. The "Colonial Americans" series, according to O. Mell Busbin in the *Dictionary of Literary Biography,* "has received wide use in classrooms throughout the United States, especially in the arts and social sciences." Over 500,000 copies of the series have been sold.

The American experience is also illuminated in Fisher's books about immigrants. *Across the Sea from Galway* tells the story of a group of Irish immigrants who flee famine and oppression in Ireland only to be shipwrecked off the Massachusetts coast. Cynthia Adams, writing in *School Library Journal,* felt the book was a "deft treatment of a survival theme as well as an accurate depiction of Irish life." *Letters from Italy* is the story of several generations of an Italian-American family, beginning with a grandfather who fought with Garibaldi for Italian independence and ending with a grandson who dies in World War II fighting Mussolini. *A Russian Farewell* traces a Jewish-Ukrainian family from their trials under the Czarist government to their decision to leave for America, while *Ellis Island* profiles the famous entry point for many immigrants to the United States. Reviewing *A Russian Farewell* in *School Library Journal,* Jack Forman noted that the tale is "broadly representative of the experiences of thousands of Russian Jews fleeing to the U.S.," and that "the story is given added force by the author's bleak and stark black-and-white sketches."

Other books were inspired by Fisher's childhood on the seashore. *The Death of Evening Star, Noonan, Storm at the Jetty,* and *The Jetty Chronicles* are all based on his recollections of living in the family house at Sea Gate in Brooklyn. Situated on the jetty of land where the Atlantic Ocean waters met the waters of Gravesend Bay, the family house had a magnificent view of passing ships, storms at sea, and the local lighthouse. *Storm at the Jetty* is a descriptive story of how a beautiful August afternoon on the seashore gradually transforms into a violent and ugly thunderstorm at sea. Barbara Hawkins called this "beautifully illustrated vignette of a summer storm" an "ode to the sea," in a *School Library Journal* review. *The Death of Evening Star* concerns a nineteenth-century whaling ship from New England and the many tribulations of its final voyage. *The Jetty Chronicles* is based on Fisher's reminiscences of his life from 1934 to 1939, and is peopled by fictional characters including a geologist, an ex-convict, an Olympic hopeful, and a radical newspaper vendor. "This is a piece of Americana," wrote Marilyn Payne Phillips in *School Library Journal,* "an antidote to Normal Rockwell, portraying a real place and time that no longer exists. A place of power and majesty reclaimed by nature."

Fisher has also commemorated the achievements of mankind around the world in the monuments and buildings of many cultures. He paid tribute to the human spirit in *The Great Wall of China,* an "impressive" book, according to *Booklist*'s Ilene Cooper, with "striking black-and-white acrylic paintings that spread over the pages and surround the text." In *The Tower of London* Fisher "sets a high standard in . . . dramatic nonfiction," according to a reviewer for *Publishers Weekly.* Closer to home, Fisher has taken a look at many of the monuments of American history. *The Statue of Liberty* "offers one of the more eye-catching books on the subject," according to Deborah Vose in *School Library Journal,* while his *Ellis Island: Gateway to the New World* is "profusely illustrated," according to Zena Sutherland writing in *Bulletin of the Center for Children's Books,* offering "a detailed history of the island in Upper New York Bay that eventually came to be called Ellis Island." Fisher's award-winning *Monticello* is, as a *Kirkus Reviews* contributor noted, a "handsomely produced history of the house that Jefferson spent a lifetime working on in his spare time." Betsy Hearne, reviewing *Monticello* in *Bulletin of the Center for Children's Books,* called it a "prerequisite for any young reader's visit to Monticello, and an armchair tour for students who can't make the trip."

Fisher has acted as social and natural historian of the American experience, as well, in illustrated studies of other aspects of the culture and terrain. With the *Anasazi,* he took a look at the ancient culture, which once inhabited the Four Corners region of the Southwest. Darcy Schild remarked in *School Library Journal* that for this title Fisher "created unique and striking monochrome paintings to illustrate his interpretation of a historical event." However Schild found "some of the theories presented . . . no longer considered correct." Fisher's *Stars and Stripes* tells the story of the American flag in a book "that makes every day Flag Day and the Fourth of July," according to Sylvia S. Marantz in *School Library Journal.* Marantz concluded that *Stars and Stripes* would be an "eye-catching addition to any collection." The Touro Synagogue in Newport, Rhode Island, completed in 1763, is the focus for *To Bigotry No Sanction: The Story of the Oldest Synagogue in America,* a book that details the struggle for Jewish religious freedom in America. *Booklist*'s Cooper concluded, "Although some may see this as the story of a particular group, it is also the story of religious freedom in the U.S." And with *Niagara Falls: Nature's Wonder,*

Fisher turned his artist's eye to the natural history and wonders of North America, a blend of photographs old and new and a potpourri of facts and myths about the place.

Famous men and women worldwide provide the focus for a series of biographies from Fisher. His *Galileo* employed "spare prose and bold black-and-white illustrations" to bring that Italian astronomer to life, according to *Booklist*'s Cooper, who also felt that his *Marie Curie* "ably brings Curie to life and highlights the role of women in the sciences in particular and society in general." Kathleen Odean, writing in *School Library Journal,* called *Marie Curie* a "gripping introduction to the remarkable woman . . . ." Gutenberg, Gandhi, and even William Tell have received the Fisher biographical treatment, a mixture of spare text and black-and-white acrylic paintings. In *Alexander Graham Bell,* Fisher tackled the father of the telephone with "warm, story-like text" and "full-and double-page illustrations (in rather dark tones)" which provide, as a reviewer for *Horn Book* commented, "a good introduction to the subject." Carol Fazioli, reviewing *Alexander Graham Bell* in *School Library Journal,* felt that like Fisher's earlier biographies of Galileo and Gutenberg, "this title provides an overview of an individual's life without intimidating young readers."

Mythology, religion, and legend have also acted as catalysts for Fisher in a series of books on Greek, Egyptian, and Mayan deities and myths. Twelve deities of ancient Greece are served up in *The Olympians: Great Gods and Goddesses of Ancient Greece,* "a handsomely designed volume ideally suited for introducing the characters of Greek mythology," as *Booklist*'s Karen Stang Hanley commented. Thirteen gods and goddesses of Egypt appeared in his *Gods and Goddesses of Ancient Egypt,* and in *Gods and Goddesses of the Ancient Maya* Fisher focuses on the principal figures in Mayan mythology. Reviewing the last-named title, *Booklist*'s Susan Dove Lempke called it a "visually striking edition." Fisher has also retold and illustrated individual takes of Greek mythology, including *Theseus and the Minotaur, Jason and the Golden Fleece,* and *Cyclops,* and has adapted tales from the Bible, such as *David and Goliath* and *Moses.* Reviewing *David and Goliath* in *School Library Journal,* Linda Boyles called the book "a vigorous retelling of an ancient story in an exciting picture book."

Collaborative efforts have also explored the world of myths and legends. Working with Eric A. Kimmel, Fisher illustrated *The Spotted Pony: A Collection of Hanukkah Stories, The Three Princes: A Tale from the Middle East,* and *The Two Mountains: An Aztec Legend.* Reviewing *The Two Mountains* a *Publishers Weekly* writer noted, "Fisher's acrylic paintings range from austere, boldly hued portraits of the warriorlike celestial residents to verdant landscapes of both heaven and earth." Such collaborative efforts have taken much of Fisher's creative energy, and some of the most successful blending of text and art occurred in Fisher's work with poet Myra Cohn Livingston. Peter Neumeyer, reviewing *A Circle of Seasons,* their first collaborative effort, in *School Library Journal,* called the teamwork in that book "the perfect blending of poetry and painting." Fisher and Livingston also worked together on *Sky Songs, Celebrations, Sea Songs, Earth Songs, Space Songs, Festivals,* and *Up in the Air.* Additionally, the ever-busy Fisher has led a full career as an artist, creating easel paintings, holding exhibitions of his work, and coordinating efforts to transpose his art into murals for such public buildings as the Washington Monument. In the early the 1970s and 1980s he designed a number of postage stamps for the U.S. Postal Service, including a series of eight stamps on American craftsmen for the Bicentennial.

Writing in *Horn Book* about the place of art in contemporary children's nonfiction, Fisher offered these observations: "We have a tendency in children's nonfiction to respond only to the desires of curriculum and educators and to ignore the other needs. . . . The qualities of high art are hardly ever a factor for the judgment of nonfiction." He continued: "What is important about me is the quality of my thinking, what drives me to do what I am doing; not the facts of my life—but the creative impulse behind that life. I am trying to make an artistic statement logically, and a logical statement to children artistically. I think the time has come for a stronger and more artistically expansive view of nonfiction." Such devotion to craft has made Fisher, as a writer for *Children's Books and Their Creators* summed up, "one of the most multifaceted creators in the field of children's literature."

BIOGRAPHICAL/CRITICAL SOURCES:

BOOKS

Children's Books and Their Creators, edited by Anita Silvey, Houghton Mifflin, 1995, pp. 242-43.

Children's Literature Review, Volume 18, Gale (Detroit, MI), 1989.

Daugherty, Charles M., *Six Artists Paint a Still Life,* North Light, 1977, pp. 10-29.

Dictionary of Literary Biography, Volume 61: *American Writers for Children since 1960: Poets, Illustrators, and Nonfiction Authors,* Gale (Detroit, MI), 1987, pp. 57-67.

Fisher, Leonard Everett, *A Life of Art,* University of Connecticut Dodd Research Center, 1998.

Hopkins, Lee Bennett, *More Books by More People,* Citation, 1971, pp. 159-164, 316.

Munce, Howard, editor, *Magic and Other Realism,* Hastings House, 1979, pp. 56-59.

Something about the Author Autobiography Series, Volume 1, Gale (Detroit, MI), 1986, pp. 89-113.

St. James Guide to Children's Writers, 5th edition, edited by Sara Pendergast and Tom Pendergast, St. James Press (Detroit, MI), 1999, pp. 376-80.

PERIODICALS

American Artist, September, 1966, pp. 42-47, 67-70.

Booklist, October 1, 1984, Karen Stang Hanley, review of *The Olympians,* p. 246; March 15, 1986, Ilene Cooper, review of *The Great Wall of China,* p. 1082; September 1, 1996, p. 71; October 15, 1997, p. 397; November 1, 1997, p. 464; December 1, 1997, p. 618; December 1, 1998, I. Cooper, review of *Galileo* and *Marie Curie,* p. 680; February 1, 1999, I. Cooper, review of *To Bigotry No Sanction,* p. 971; March 15, 1999, p. 1326; October 1, 1999, p. 373; February 1, 2000, Susan Dove Lempke, review of *Gods and Goddesses of the Ancient Maya,* p. 1019; March 15, 2001, Carolyn Phelan, reviews of *The Potters* and *The Hatters,* p. 1397, John Peters, review of *Sky, Sea, the Jetty, and Me,* p. 1403.

Bulletin of the Center for Children's Books, December, 1986, Zena Sutherland, review of *Ellis Island,* pp. 65-66; June, 1988, Betsy Hearne, review of *Monticello,* pp. 203-04; July, 1996, p. 370; April, 1999, p. 279.

Horn Book, May-June, 1988, Leonard Everett Fisher, "The Artist at Work: Creating Nonfiction," pp. 315-323; July-August, 1999, review of *Alexander Graham Bell,* p. 481.

Kirkus Reviews, May 15, 1988, review of *Monticello,* p. 760; March 15, 1996, p. 455; September 15, 1997, p. 1456; January 1, 1999, p. 65.

Language Arts, March, 1982, pp. 224-230.

Publishers Weekly, December 19, 1980, review of *The Sports,* p. 51; February 26, 1982, pp. 62-63; September 25, 1987, review of *The Tower of London,* p. 109; January 18, 1999, p. 340; November 29, 1999, p. 71; February 7, 2000, review of *The Two Mountains,* p. 84.

School Library Journal, January, 1976, Cynthia Adams, review of *Across the Sea from Galway,* pp. 52-53; November, 1979, Shirley Wilton, reviews of *The Factories* and *The Railroads,* p. 76; January, 1981, Jack Forman, review of *A Russian Farewell,* p. 60; October, 1981, Barbara Hawkins, review of *Storm at the Jetty,* p. 128; August, 1982, Peter Neumeyer, review of *A Circle of Seasons,* p. 118; December, 1985, Deborah Vose, review of *The Statue of Liberty,* pp. 86-87; June, 1993, Linda Boyles, review of *David and Goliath,* pp. 95-96; October, 1993, Sylvia S. Marantz, review of *Stars and Stripes,* pp. 117-18; July, 1996, p. 79; October, 1996, p. 132; December, 1996, Kathleen Odean, review of *Marie Curie,* p. 45; November, 1997, p. 106; December, 1997, Marilyn Payne Phillips, review of *The Jetty Chronicles,* p. 123; December, 1997, Darcy Schild, review of *Anasazi,* p. 108; March, 1999, Carol Fazioli, review of *Alexander Graham Bell,* p. 192; December, 1999, p. 149; April, 2000, Daryl Grabarek, review of *The Two Mountains,* p. 121; April, 2001, Martha Topol, review of *Sky, Sea, the Jetty, and Me,* p. 108.

Voice of Youth Advocates, February, 1998, p. 384.

* * *

FOY, George 1952-

PERSONAL: Born December 14, 1952, in Barnstable, MA; son of Louis (a journalist) and Katharine (a concert pianist; maiden name, Schaefer) Foy. *Education:* Attended Institute d'Etudes Politiques, University of Paris, 1970-71; London School of Economics and Political Science, London, B.Sc. (with honors), 1974.

ADDRESSES: Home—P.O. Box 211, Cummaquid, MA 02637. *Agent*—Harvey Klinger, Inc., 301 West 53rd St., New York, NY 10019.

CAREER: Tower Shipping Ltd., London, England, ship's mate, 1947-75; Ocean Ventures, Inc., Orleans, MA, ship's mate, 1975-77; *International Herald Tribune,* Paris, France, assistant to news editor, 1977-78; *Cape Cod Register,* Yarmouth, MA, news editor, 1978-81; freelance journalist, 1981—.

AWARDS, HONORS: National Endowment for the Arts fellow, 1994-95; shortlist, Philip K. Dick Award, Philadelphia Science Fiction Society, 1996, for *The Shift.*

WRITINGS:

(Editor and contributor) *Music in Stone* (nonfiction), Harper (New York, NY), 1984.

Asia Rip, Viking (New York, NY), 1984.
Coaster, Viking (New York, NY), 1986.
Challenge, Viking (New York, NY), 1988.
The Shift, Bantam (New York, NY), 1996.
Contraband, Bantam (New York, NY), 1997.
The Memory of Fire, Bantam (New York, NY), 2000.
The Last Harbor, Bantam (New York, NY), 2001.

Author of "Foy on Fashion," a column in *Style.* Contributor to *Commercial Fisheries News, Rolling Stone,* and *Harper's.*

SIDELIGHTS: George Foy has written several suspense novels set in a near-future world of danger. In *The Shift,* a television writer finds that the fictional serial killer he wrote for a show has entered the real world, while in *The Memory of Fire,* an artist struggles against a tyrannical government which has banned creative expression.

Set in a near-future version of America, *The Shift* tells of Alex Munn's troubles when a serial killer character he has created for a new virtual-reality show comes to life and begins to murder people in the real world. The killer, known as the Fishman, is a Jack the Ripper type who, in Munn's imaginary story, haunted 1850s New York City. When the Fishman murders Munn's estranged wife, however, the television writer finds himself entangled in a nightmare. A critic for *Publishers Weekly* called *The Shift* "an absolutely terrifying adventure filled with plenty of plot twists." Carl Hayes, reviewing the novel for *Library Journal,* called it "fresh and powerfully imagined."

When her South American artists' colony is destroyed by security forces, Soledad MacCrae of *The Memory of Fire* flees to San Francisco to join another colony. But she finds that she has been followed and must now battle a repressive government. A *Publishers Weekly* contributor praised the novel's "finely detailed setting," while Jackie Cassada, writing in *Library Journal,* found *The Memory of Fire* to be "thoughtful and disturbing."

Foy once told *CA:* "My ultimate goal is to write prose so resonant that it could be read as poetry, but in a down-to-earth context of recognizable people, and in the familiar structure of an adventure story. I want to interpret the transcendent in the mundane.

"I am a professional political cartoonist and a licensed ship's captain, as well as a writer. I would like to continue studies in the politics of developing countries, at least as an excuse for returning to Central Africa. I am fluent in German, conversant in Italian and Spanish, and can get by in Swahili, if not pressed.

"The highlights of my years at sea were the days when I finally drew my pay and got off the ship; seafaring, like war, consists mainly of long periods of boredom defined only by instants of panic (such as narrowly averted collisions in the North Sea fog, cargo of rolled steel shifting in storms, and storm waves breaking the gunwales).

"I went to Central Africa as a result of a long-standing interest in this area, where the problems of development meet head on with the cynical or ignorant policies of the developed world.

"My novel *Asia Rip* concerns the struggle of a New England fisherman to avenge the death of a friend who was murdered by the cartel controlling the sale of fresh fish on the East Coast. This outward struggle is reflected within as the fisherman comes to grips with the emotional traumas that have caused him to withdraw from struggles in general."

BIOGRAPHICAL/CRITICAL SOURCES:

PERIODICALS

Booklist, June 1, 1996, Carl Hayes, review of *The Shift,* p. 1682; January 1, 2000, John Mort, review of *The Memory of Fire,* p. 887.
Boston Globe, July 29, 1984.
Cape Cod Times, June 28, 1984.
Dallas Times Herald, July 8, 1984.
Library Journal, January, 2000, Jackie Cassada, review of *The Memory of Fire,* p. 167.
Los Angeles Times Book Review, July 15, 1984.
New York Times Book Review, September 13, 1984.
Publishers Weekly, May 20, 1988, Sybil Steinberg, review of *Challenge,* p. 70; April 29, 1996, review of *The Shift,* p. 68; March 24, 1997, review of *Contraband,* p. 63; December 6, 1999, review of *The Memory of Fire,* p. 57.*

* * *

FRIMAN, Alice 1933-

PERSONAL: Born October 20, 1933, in New York, NY; daughter of Joseph and Helen Pesner; married Elmer Friman, July, 1955 (marriage ended); married Bruce Gentry, 1989; children: (first marriage) Richard, Paul,

Lillian. *Education:* Brooklyn College (now of the City University of New York), B.A., 1954; attended Indiana University—Bloomington, 1964-66; Butler University, M.A., 1971.

ADDRESSES: Home—6312 Central Ave., Indianapolis, IN 46220. *Office*—Department of English, University of Indianapolis, 1400 East Hanna Ave., Indianapolis, IN 46227.

CAREER: University of Indianapolis, Indianapolis, IN, instructor, 1971-74, assistant professor, 1974-81, associate professor, 1981-90, professor of English, 1990-93, professor emerita, 1993—. Indiana and Purdue Universities at Indianapolis, instructor in English, 1971-74; Indiana State University, visiting professor, 1982; Curtin University, Perth, Australia, writer-in-residence, 1989; Ball State University, visiting professor, 1996. Writers' Center of Indianapolis, charter member, 1979—, member of board of directors, 1984-89; gives poetry readings and workshops; judge of poetry contests.

MEMBER: Poets and Writers, Poetry Society of America, Modern Language Association of America, Associated Writing Programs, Society for the Study of Midwestern Literature, Northeast Modern Language Association, Indiana College English Association.

AWARDS, HONORS: Fellow at Dorland Mountain Art Colony, 1983, Virginia Center for the Creative Arts, 1983 and 1984, Ragdale Foundation, 1983 and 1985, and Yaddo Colony, Millay Colony for the Arts, Mary Anderson Center, Leighton Art Colony, Kalani Honua, and Byrdcliffe Writers Colony; National bronze medal from Council for the Advancement and Support of Education, 1987; Poetry Society of America, Consuelo Ford Award, 1988, for "Love in the Time of Drought," Cecil Hemley Memorial Award, 1990, for "Letter to the Children," and Lucille Medwick Memorial Award, 1993, for "The Squirrel"; Gwendolyn Brooks Award, Society for the Study of Midwestern Literature, 1990, for "In This Night's Rain"; Erika Mumford Prize, New England Poetry Club, 1990, for "From the Earth's Book"; first prize, Start with Art Literary Competition, 1992, for "Cardiology"; Pushcart Prize nominations, 1992, 1993; first prize, *Abiko Quarterly* International Poetry Contest, 1994, for "Cherries"; Award of Excellence in Poetry, *Hopewell Review,* 1995, for "The Drawstring"; Firman Houghton Award, New England Poetry Club, 1996, for "From the Lava Papers"; fellow, Indiana Arts Commission, 1996-97; Ezra Pound Poetry Award, Truman State University, 1998, for *Zoo;* Creative Renewal fellowship, Arts Council of Indianapolis, 1999-2000.

WRITINGS:

A Question of Innocence (poetry chapbook), Raintree Press (Bloomington, IN), 1978.

Song to My Sister (poetry chapbook), Writers' Center Press (Indianapolis, IN), 1979.

(Editor) *Loaves and Fishes: Women Poets of Indiana,* Writers' Center Press (Indianapolis, IN), 1983.

Reporting from Corinth (poems), Barnwood (Daleville, IN), 1984.

Insomniac Heart (poetry chapbook), Years Press, 1990.

Driving for Jimmy Wonderland (poetry chapbook), Barnwood (Daleville, IN), 1992.

Inverted Fire (poems), BkMk Press (Kansas City, MO), 1997.

Zoo (poems), University of Arkansas Press, 1999.

Work represented in anthologies, including *The Land-Locked Heart: Poems from Indiana,* 1980; *The Anthology of Magazine Verse and American Poetry,* 1981, 1983, and 1986-87; *The Poet Dreaming in the Artist's House,* edited by Ruth Rosten and Emilie Buchwald, Milkweed Editions, 1984; and *Keener Sounds: Selected Poems from the Georgia Review,* 1987. Contributor of more than one hundred poems, articles, and reviews to magazines, including *Poetry, Prairie Schooner, Beloit Poetry Journal, Georgia Review, Stand, Chelsea, Manoa, New Letters, Field, Boulevard, London Review of Books, Texas Review, Indiana Review, Southern Poetry Review,* and *Shenandoah.* Poetry editor, *Flying Island,* 1993, 1996, 2000.

WORK IN PROGRESS: Tattoo, a collection of poems.

SIDELIGHTS: Alice Friman once told *CA:* "My work itself comes from inner conflict, with memory or nature often serving as the jumping off point. I write about love and its poignant impossibilities. My images are, I imagine, mostly from childhood, and seem to be about *yearning*—the ocean for its beach, the further planets for the sun, the inside to be expressed. As I look back through my work, I see that I use certain symbols—the tattoo for instance—that is yearning consummated; the tattoo is suggestive of the poem itself. Perhaps that is what poetry, then, is for me; the *bridge* between what yearns and the thing wished for, be it love, warmth, meaning, or home. Only in the writing of the poem is the circuit closed between the perpetual 'I want, I want' and the bliss of 'I have, I have.'"

BIOGRAPHICAL/CRITICAL SOURCES:

PERIODICALS

Arkansas Democrat-Gazette, March 5, 2000, Andrea Hollander Budy, "Four Collections with the Power to Offer Sustenance," p. J6.

Arts Indiana, April, 1988, Pat Watson, "Alice Friman: Poet," p. 26; March/April, 1998, Julie Pratt McQuiston, review of *Inverted Fire,* pp. 48-49.

Arts Insight, January, 1982, Edwin F. Casebeer, "Writer's Center Regional Poets No. 2: Alice Friman," p. 20; May, 1985, Barbara Koons, "Alice Friman: Poems from behind the Piano," p. 5.

Calyx, Volume 18, number 2, 1998-99, Helen Frost, review of *Inverted Fire,* pp. 107-108.

Canto, Number 5, 1992, Brooke Horvath, "A Conversation," pp. 57-64.

Cream City Review, Volume 16, number 1, 1992, Cynthia Belmont, review of *Insomniac Heart,* pp. 198-200.

Dusty Dog, June, 1991, Jim Sullivan, review of *Insomniac Heart.*

Indianapolis Star, May 21, 2000, Charlotte Sargeant, "Alice Friman's *Zoo* Is Bestiary of Planet Earth, p. D8.

Indianapolis Woman, April, 1989, Sabrina Ehlert, "G'Day, Alice Friman," p. 70.

Indiana Review, Volume 20, number 2, 1997, Brooke Horvath, review of *Inverted Fire,* pp. 171-173.

Iowa Woman, Volume 11, number 3, 1991, Sandra Witt, "Reading like a River," pp. 45-47.

Northwest Arkansas Times (Fayetteville), May 31, 1998, Paul Bone, "Reigniting the Stars," p. C2; December 12, 1999, Ginny Masullo, "Poet Friman's Work Hailed for Metaphor, Detail," p. G6.

Nuvo Newsweekly, August 12, 1997, Julie Pratt McQuiston, "Rebellious Art: The Cosmological Metaphor of Poet Alice Friman," pp. 15-16; February 3, 2000, Julie Pratt McQuiston, "God's Kitchen," p. 18.

Puerto del sol, Volume 33, number 2, 1998, Gilberto Lucero, "Buttons and Slashers," pp. 235-239.

Small Press Review, March, 1985, Leslie Carper, review of *Reporting from Corinth,* p. 12.

Texas Review, Volume 19, numbers 1-2, 1998, Philip Heldrich, review of *Inverted Fire,* pp. 114-117.

G

GARDNER, Ted
See GARDNER, Theodore Roosevelt II

* * *

GARDNER, Theodore Roosevelt II 1934-
(Ted Gardner)

PERSONAL: Born July 20, 1934, in Allentown, PA; son of Theodore Roosevelt (a judge) and Margaret Schaffer (a homemaker) Gardner; married Virginia Louis Twining (a bookseller); children: Melora Eden, Julia Susan, Abigail. *Education:* University of Southern California, B.A., 1956.

ADDRESSES: *Office*—c/o Allen A. Knoll, Publishers, 200 West Victoria, Santa Barbara, CA 93101. *E-mail*—bookinfo@knollpublishers.com.

CAREER: Writer.

WRITINGS:

The Paper Dynasty (adult fiction), Knoll (Santa Barbara, CA), 1990.
(Under name Ted Gardner) *Off the Wall: The Newspaper Columns of Ted Gardner,* Knoll (Santa Barbara, CA), 1993.
Something Nice to See (children's book), illustrated by Peter J. Hamlin, Knoll (Santa Barbara, CA), 1994.
(Author of text) *Lotusland: A Photographic Odyssey,* Knoll (Santa Barbara, CA), 1995.
The Real Sleeper: A Love Story, Knoll (Santa Barbara, CA), 1996.
Flip Side: A Novel of Suspense, Knoll (Santa Barbara, CA), 1997.
(Author of text) *Nature's Kaleidoscope: The Santa Barbara Botanic Garden,* photographs by Robert Glenn Ketchum, Knoll (Santa Barbara, CA), 1999.
Give Gravity a Chance: A Love Story, Knoll (Santa Barbara, CA), 1999.
(Under name Ted Gardner) *Wit's End,* Knoll (Santa Barbara, CA), 2000.
He's Back, Knoll (Santa Barbara, CA), 2000.

SIDELIGHTS: Theodore Roosevelt Gardner II, a West Coast-based newspaper columnist and book writer, has produced novels in several genres, including suspense, juvenile fiction, and romance. His imagination leads him to experiment with both form and subject matter. In *Flip Side,* for instance, a mystery unfolds as first a prosecution and then a defense each present a murder case featuring a high-profile Hollywood star as defendant. In order to read the defense's presentation, the book must literally be flipped upside down and backwards, a technique more commonly seen in children's picture books. *Give Gravity a Chance: A Love Story* challenges the conventions of romance fiction by featuring two obese protagonists who grow fond of one another after a blind date arranged simply to shock a racist parent. In a *Booklist* review of the novel, Deborah Ryan observed: "These two misfits from different worlds . . . do inspire each other to better themselves, and that qualifies as a happy ending." A *Publishers Weekly* critic likewise commended *Give Gravity a Chance* as "a well intentioned, even sweet-tempered romantic comedy." His novel *He's Back* explores the modern-day ramifications of the return of Jesus Christ.

Gardner once commented: "Vanity, it is said, is the spice of something or other. For me it is the spice of writing. I've written epic novels (*The Paper Dynasty, He's Back*), humorous essays (*Wit's End, Off the Wall*), a children's book (*Something Nice to See*), love stories (*The Real Sleeper, Give Gravity a Chance*), and a suspense novel (*Flip Side*). I am constantly invigorated and excited at each new creation.

"*Flip Side* is a unique book about a high-profile murder case, told from the viewpoint of the prosecution, then by turning the book upside down you get the diametrically opposed defense viewpoint.

"Ideas for stories are all around us—you can't escape them. Ideas are easy. For me writing is also easy and I love it. The hard part is the thinking—the turning of the idea into a gripping story.

"For me the enjoyment is in the process, not the product. The final lines of my children's book, *Something Nice to See,* embody my philosophy: 'Fame and fortune are not my survival / My joy's in the journey, not the arrival.'"

BIOGRAPHICAL/CRITICAL SOURCES:

PERIODICALS

Booklist, November 15, 1998, Deborah Rysso, review of *Give Gravity a Chance: A Love Story,* p. 574.

Horticulture: The Magazine of American Gardening, November, 1996, Christopher Reed, review of *Lotusland: A Photographic Odyssey,* p. 64.

Publishers Weekly, July 14, 1997, review of *Flip Side,* p. 68; October 19, 1998, review of *Give Gravity a Chance: A Love Story,* p. 54.

* * *

GARRETT, Laurie 1951-

PERSONAL: Born September 8, 1951, in Los Angeles, CA; daughter of Banning and Lou Ann (Pierose) Garrett. *Education:* Graduated with honors from University of California at Santa Cruz, 1975; conducted graduate studies at University of California at Berkeley.

ADDRESSES: Office—Newsday, 235 Pinelawn Rd., Melville, NY 11747. *Agent*—Charlotte Sheedy, 65 Bleecker St., New York, NY 10012.

CAREER: Worked at KPFA (radio station), Berkeley, CA, and for California Department of Food and Agriculture; freelance journalist in Southern Europe and East Africa, 1979; freelance reporter for National Public Radio (NPR), British Broadcasting Corp. (BBC), American Broadcasting Co. (ABC), Canadian Broadcasting Corp. (CBC), Pacifica News Service, Pacifica Radio, and other media outlets, c. 1980-88; *Newsday,* science correspondent, 1988—. Visiting fellow, Harvard School of Public Health, 1992-93, and University of California at Berkeley, 1997. Host of five-hour Public Broadcasting System (PBS) series, *Great Minds of Medicine,* 1998. Has made appearances on national television programs, including *Dateline, McNeill/Lehrer Newshour, Talkback, Under Scrutiny,* and *Nightline.*

MEMBER: American Association for the Advancement of Science, National Association of Science Writers (president, 1995-97).

AWARDS, HONORS: George Foster Peabody Broadcasting Award, 1977, for "Science Story"; Edwin Howard Armstrong Broadcast Award, 1978, for "Hard Rain: Pests, Pesticides, and People"; National Press Club Award for Best Consumer Journalism, 1982, for "The VDT Controversy"; Media Alliance Meritorious Achievement Award in Radio, 1983; World Hunger Media Award (first prize), 1987, for "Why Children Die in Africa"; J. C. Penney/Missouri Journalism Certificate of Merit, and Award of Excellence of National Association of Black Journalists (second place), both 1989, both for "AIDS in Africa"; *Newsday* Publishers Award for Best Beat Reporter, 1990 and 1995; Best Beat Reporter, Deadline Club of New York, 1993; first place, New York State AP Writing Contest, Press Club of Long Island, and Society of the Silurians (health and science reporting), all 1994, all for "Breast Cancer"; Bob Considine Award, Overseas Press Club of America, 1995, for "AIDS in India"; Front Page Award from Newswomen's Club of New York, 1995, Pulitzer Prize for explanatory journalism, 1996, and Madeliene Dane Ross Award, 1996, all for "Ebola"; Presidential Citation from American Public Health Association, and Distinguished Achievement Award from Educational Press Association of America, both 1996; Media Health Promotion Award from County of Los Angeles Health Services, "champion of prevention" citation from Centers of Disease Control and Prevention, and Best Beat Reporter citation from Long Island Press Club, all 1997; "Distinguished Leader in the Life Sciences" citation from National Academy of Sciences, and "National Public Health Hero" citation from University of California School of Public Health, both 1998; George C. Polk Award for international reporting, John P. McGovern Award from Medical Library Association, and Newsday Publishers Award for enterprise reporting, all 1998, all for "Collapsed Empire, Shattered Health"; Victor Cohn Prize for Excellence in Medical Reporting, Council for the Advancement of Science Writing, 2000; First Place, International Reporting, New York Association of Black Journalists, for "Orphans of AIDS," 2000; Public Health Hero Award, New York City Department of Health, 2000; *Newsday* Publisher's Award for Outstanding Specialist Reporting, for "AIDS in Africa," 2000; George C. Polk Award, Best Book of 2000, and Madeliene Dane Ross Award for Reporting on the Human Condition, Overseas Press Club of America, both for *Betrayal of Trust: The Collapse of Global Public Health,* both 2000. D.H.L., Illinois Wesleyan University, 1998.

WRITINGS:

The Coming Plague: Newly Emerging Diseases in a World out of Balance, Farrar, Straus (New York, NY), 1994.

Microbes versus Mankind: The Coming Plague, Foreign Policy Association (New York, NY), 1996.

Betrayal of Trust: The Collapse of Global Public Health, Hyperion (New York, NY), 2000.

Contributor to books, including *Aids in the World,* edited by Jonathan Mann, Daniel Tarantola, and Thomas Netter, Oxford University Press, 1993; and *Disease in Evolution: Global Changes and Emergence of Infectious Diseases,* edited by Mary E. Wilson, New York Academy of Sciences, 1994. Also contributor of articles to periodicals, including *Newsday, Omni, Washington Post, Los Angeles Times, Foreign Affairs, Current Issues in Public Health, Vanity Fair,* and *Ladies Home Journal.* Contributor of reports to National Public Radio and other radio programs, including "Science Story," "Hard Rain: Pests, Pesticides, and People," and "Why Children Die in Africa."

ADAPTATIONS: The Coming Plague: Newly Emerging Diseases in a World out of Balance was adapted as a four-hour television special, *The Coming Plague,* by Turner Original Productions, 1997.

SIDELIGHTS: A veteran science reporter who has examined a wide range of health topics, Laurie Garrett focuses her research on deadly diseases and the global threat they pose in the twenty-first century. Her books, *The Coming Plague: Newly Emerging Diseases in a World out of Balance,* and *Betrayal of Trust: The Collapse of Global Public Health,* warn readers that new, deadly diseases are threatening humans, that some microbes are becoming resistant to antibiotics, and that governments have become dangerously complacent about public health. Garrett reached her conclusions while serving as a reporter for *Newsday,* having traveled worldwide to investigate outbreaks of disease and to report on crises in health care. In the process of addressing one of the most important issues facing humankind, Garrett has won almost every prestigious award bestowed by the journalistic community, including a George Foster Peabody Award, a Polk Award, and the Pulitzer Prize.

The Coming Plague alerts readers to both newly mutating viruses, such as the Ebola strains endemic to equatorial Africa, and to the conditions in the modern world that will allow such illnesses to have global impact in the foreseeable future. Such conditions, according to Garrett, include increasingly common travel to and from previously remote areas of the world, and increased commercial development of wilderness regions that once served as geographical buffers against the spread of disease. Garrett examines many specific viruses and disease agents in her book, from such relatively recent developments as AIDS to new, drug-resistant versions of old plagues like cholera and tuberculosis. Reading these sections of *The Coming Plague,* observed *New York Times Book Review* contributor Stephen S. Hall, "is to come away with a perverse admiration for the invisible agents of so much suffering and mortality." Hall commented that "viruses and bacteria do not care about national health reform or the information highway. . . . They thrive in the chop shops of evolution, borrowing or stealing or mutating the biologic tricks that will serve their single reason for being—to find hosts and replicate, to copy their genetic material so they can borrow and steal and mutate another day."

Hall complimented Garrett's thoroughness in *The Coming Plague,* although he cautioned that the sheer volume of material might diminish the book's appeal to a general audience. "Her journalistic instincts are excellent," the critic reported. "She cites the key articles, talks to the right researchers, focuses on the crucial scientific issues." Malcolm Jones, Jr., reviewing Garrett's book in *Newsweek,* praised her thoroughness as well, and termed *The Coming Plague* an "encyclopedic and absorbing study." In the *Journal of the American Medical Association (JAMA),* Stuart M. Polly declared: "*The Coming Plague* is a thoughtful, thought-provoking book. Garrett builds her case carefully, drawing from the social and historical as well as the scientific arenas.

Her case is compelling. This is a book that should be read by anyone with an interest in the survival of society as we know it."

Betrayal of Trust: The Collapse of Global Public Health explores the current and potential crises stemming from a collapse in public health systems, not only in Third World countries but in developed nations such as Russia and the United States. In *Publishers Weekly,* Scott Sherman noted that the book "is at once a nightmarish journey through the shattered landscapes of Zaire, India and the former Soviet Union, and an impassioned call for a robust, comprehensive international public health infrastructure." Sherman also found the work "a sobering antidote to the news media's interminable proclamations about U.S. prosperity."

"There is no question that Garrett has built a compelling case that global public health at the dawn of the 21st century is in many ways far less able to deal with disease and pestilence than it was 100 years ago," observed a *Business Week* reviewer of *Betrayal of Trust.* The reviewer added: "Garrett has done a masterful job of laying out the near-crisis state of public health. After finishing *Betrayal of Trust,* the reader isn't likely to escape the feeling that something must be done urgently." Another *Publishers Weekly* correspondent felt the book to be "on a par with Rachel Carson's *Silent Spring,"* noting further that it "should be taken seriously by leaders and policymakers around the world." In a *New York Times Book Review* piece on *Betrayal of Trust,* Fitzhugh Mullan wrote: "These are lurid, disturbing and well-documented images that are not easily dismissed as alarmist. . . . Garrett is a journalist by profession but a scholar by instinct. She has a nose for both the lurid and the arcane, leading her to tell her stories at great length and document them profusely. . . . Her message . . . is a momentous one that is delivered persuasively."

BIOGRAPHICAL/CRITICAL SOURCES:

PERIODICALS

Booklist, September 1, 1994, p. 13; August, 2000, Mary Carroll, review of *Betrayal of Trust: The Collapse of Global Public Health,* p. 2068.

Business Week, October 2, 2000, review of *Betrayal of Trust: The Collapse of Global Public Health,* p. 29.

Journal of the American Medical Association (JAMA), January 17, 1996, Stuart M. Polly, review of *The Coming Plague: Newly Emerging Diseases in a World out of Balance,* p. 249.

Newsweek, September 19, 1994, p. 63.

New York Times Book Review, October 30, 1994, pp. 13-14, 16; October 22, 2000, Fitzhugh Mullan, "Feeling O.K.? Just Wait."

Publishers Weekly, August 15, 1994, p. 79; July 31, 2000, review of *Betrayal of Trust: The Collapse of Global Public Health,* p. 86; August 21, 2000, Scott Sherman, "Laurie Garrett: Coming Plague, Current Crisis," p. 40.

USA Today, December 2, 1999, Anita Manning, "The Prophet of the 'Plague.'"

OTHER

BookRadio, http://www.bookradio.com/ (October 19, 2000), review of *Betrayal of Trust: The Collapse of Global Public Health.*

Newsday, http://www.newsday.com/ (October 18, 2000), Rita Ciolli, "About Medical Writer Laurie Garrett."

* * *

GASH, Jonathan
See GRANT, John

* * *

GAUNT, Graham
See GRANT, John

* * *

GILES, Molly 1942-

PERSONAL: Born March 12, 1942, in CA; daughter of John Daniel (in business) and Doris (a writer; maiden name, McConnell) Murphy; married Daniel Giles, September 29, 1961 (divorced, 1974); married Richard King (in business), July 22, 1976 (marriage ended); children: Gretchen, Rachel, Devon. *Education:* Attended University of California at Berkeley, 1960-61; San Francisco State University, B.A., 1978, M.A., 1980.

ADDRESSES: Office—c/o Department of English, University of Arkansas, 333 Kimpel Hall, Fayetteville, AR 72701. *Agent*—Ellen Levine, Blassingame, McCauley & Wood, 432 Park Ave. S., New York, NY 10016. *E-mail*—mollyg@comp.uark.edu.

CAREER: San Francisco State University, San Francisco, CA, lecturer in creative writing, 1980-99; University of Arkansas, Fayetteville, associate professor of creative writing, 1999—; writer.

AWARDS, HONORS: Herbert Wilner Prize, 1979; Henfield Prize, 1981; Flannery O'Connor Award for Short Fiction, Boston Globe Award, Bay Area Book Reviewers Award for Fiction, and Pulitzer Prize nomination, all for *Rough Translations;* National Book Critics Circle Citation for Excellence in Book Reviewing, 1991; Small Press Best Fiction/Short Story Award, 1998, for *Creek Walk and Other Stories;* PEN Syndicated Fiction Award; National Endowment for the Arts grant; California Book Award for Fiction.

WRITINGS:

Rough Translations (short stories), University of Georgia Press (Athens, GA), 1985.

Creek Walk and Other Stories, Papier-Maché Press (Watsonville, CA), 1996.

Iron Shoes (novel), Simon and Schuster (New York, NY), 2000.

Contributor of short stories to periodicals, including *North American Review, New England Review, Ascent, Redbook, McCall's, San Francisco Review of Books,* and *Playgirl.*

SIDELIGHTS: Molly Giles's first collection of short stories, *Rough Translations,* touches on issues of loneliness, fear, and despair. The stories of this award-winning collection, told mainly from a woman's point of view, are woven together with recurring characters who experience impediments to communication, warmth, and intimacy. Giles's women attempt to translate their dreams and ideas into reality, only to find that the reality they have created is an imperfect representation of their vision.

Called an "accomplished" writer by Roberta Grant in an article for the *New York Times Book Review,* Giles reveals a unique insight into the human condition through her direct and unsentimental approach to highly emotional situations. Through Ramona, for example, one of the characters from *Rough Translations,* Giles evokes "social panic": Ramona defines such panic as the way she used to feel when her husband wanted her "to give a dinner party for his clients and the guests would arrive and [she'd] still be in [her] slip clutching a bucket of live lobsters." Commenting on the author's realistic character portrayals, Michael J. Carroll remarked in the *Los Angeles Times Book Review* that Giles is "a perceptive writer with a fine ear for the psyche's voice." Keith Cushman, writing for *Studies in Short Fiction,* observed that *Rough Translations* exhibits the universal nature of its author's perspective and "offers an effective, absorbing vision of the perils that are part of being alive."

Giles's second collection, *Creek Walk and Other Stories,* also looks at life from women's viewpoints. While some of the male characters are sympathetic, others are clueless or even menacing, and the stories, as Emily Barton put it in the *New York Times,* "all concern women's struggles to be fully realized and heard." The protagonist of "The Writers' Model" is a woman who bares her life and body to a group of male writers who are (unsuccessfully) trying to understand women and create believable female characters. "Smoke and Mirrors" deals with a woman whose affection for her husband ebbs in the face of her obsession with another, rather peculiar man. In "Talking to Strangers," a woman tells the story of her own murder. These and the other stories in *Creek Walk* show Giles to be "a master of the short story, each segment unique and complete," claimed Susan Kelly in *USA Today.* "Her writer's voice is perceptive and compassionate, the sentiments expressed deeply moving, the language often beautiful." Barton noted that "Giles's stories are unsettling, full of realistic and sometimes rancid details," although "they often seem fettered by their rigid thematic unity and propensity to moralize. . . . But the writing . . . is honest and clean." A *Publishers Weekly* reviewer praised Giles's work as "exquisitely voice-driven stories that bring arch humor to the social and interior lives of their characters," while *Booklist* contributor Whitney Scott defined Giles's achievement as "raising the ordinary, through her craft, to extraordinary levels."

Giles's first novel, *Iron Shoes,* focuses on Kay, an emotionally immature forty-year-old woman whose mother, Ida, is terminally ill. Ida is distant and sometimes cruel; illness has not mellowed her in the least. In dealing with Ida's dying, Kay is able to resolve her feelings toward her mother and to make positive changes in her own disordered life. Barbara Sutton, writing in the *New York Times,* thought Kay an unsympathetic heroine, "too given to self-castigation and self-analysis," but praised Giles's writing as "witty, with keen comic timing and a graceful sense of economy." *Los Angeles Times Book Review* critic Mark Rozzo called *Iron Shoes* a "subtly moving novel" and "as taut as a well-turned short story." Writing in *Publishers Weekly,* a contributor noted that "in spite of the dark terrain this novel navigates, it is a sparkling and witty account of one woman's coming of age."

BIOGRAPHICAL/CRITICAL SOURCES:

BOOKS

Contemporary Literary Criticism, Volume 39, Gale (Detroit, MI), 1985.
Giles, Molly, *Rough Translations,* University of Georgia Press (Athens, GA), 1985.

PERIODICALS

Booklist, January 1, 1997, Whitney Scott, review of *Creek Walk and Other Stories,* p. 818; June 1, 2000, Marlene Chamberlain, review of *Iron Shoes,* p. 1856.
Library Journal, June 15, 2000, Beth E. Anderson, review of *Iron Shoes,* p. 114.
Los Angeles Times Book Review, August 11, 1985; August 20, 2000, Mark Rozzo, review of *Iron Shoes,* p. 10.
New York Times, March 2, 1997, Emily Barton, "From Beyond the Grave"; September 3, 2000, Barbara Sutton, review of *Iron Shoes.*
New York Times Book Review, May 12, 1985.
Publishers Weekly, December 30, 1996, review of *Creek Walk and Other Stories,* p. 54; July 3, 2000, review of *Iron Shoes,* p. 47.
Studies in Short Fiction, summer, 1986.
USA Today, February 19, 1997, Susan Kelly, review of *Creek Walk and Other Stories.*
Voice Literary Supplement, June, 1985.

OTHER

Bookpage, http://www.bookpage.com/ (August, 2000), Alden Mudge, "Short Story Master Tackles the Terrain of the Novel."
Lit, http://www.sfbg.com/lit/ (February 26, 1997), Adam Klein, "Molly-fied: An Interview with Molly Giles."*

* * *

GLASS, Leslie

PERSONAL: Born in Chicago, IL; daughter of Milton (a television producer and investment banker) and Elinor (a children's advocate; maiden name, Loeff) Gordon; married Edmund Glass, 1971; children: Alex, Leslie. *Education:* Sarah Lawrence College, B.A.

ADDRESSES: Office—c/o Dutton, 375 Hudson St., New York, NY 10014. *E-mail*—leslie@mystery-book.com

CAREER: Novelist.

MEMBER: International Association of Crime Writers, Mystery Writers of America (member of board, New York chapter), Sisters in Crime, Screen Writers Guild, Dramatist Guild, Police Foundation (trustee; member, Crime Stoppers Award committee), The Leslie Glass Foundation (founder), Association of Small Foundations, Philanthropy Foundation.

AWARDS, HONORS: Loving Time named one of the best novels of 1996, *Mostly Murder;* nomination for Career Achievement Award in the Female Sleuth category, *Romantic Times,* 2001.

WRITINGS:

Getting away with It (novel), Dutton (New York, NY), 1976.
Modern Love (novel), St. Martin's Press (New York, NY), 1983.
Strokes (play), produced at the American Repertory Theater, Boston, 1984.
The Survivors (one-act play), first produced in 1989.
On the Edge: A Play on Teen Stress (one-act play), first produced at Lincoln Center for the Arts, New York, NY, 1991.

MYSTERY

To Do No Harm, Doubleday (New York, NY), 1992.
Burning Time, Doubleday (New York, NY), 1993.
Hanging Time, Bantam (New York, NY), 1995.
Loving Time, Bantam (New York, NY), 1996.
Judging Time, Dutton (New York, NY), 1998.
Stealing Time, Dutton (New York, NY), 1999.
Tracking Time, Dutton (New York, NY), 2000.

Former writer of *New York* magazine's "Intelligencer" column; contributor to periodicals, including *Cosmopolitan, Redbook,* and *Women's Own. Modern Love* was optioned for film and translated into six languages.

SIDELIGHTS: Writer Leslie Glass is a New York City-based author of detective novels. She has also penned several plays, including *Strokes,* which was staged at

Boston's American Repertory Theater in 1984, and *On the Edge,* a one-act play on teen violence that played at the Lincoln Center for the Performing Arts in New York City. Educated at Sarah Lawrence College, Glass was the first author of the "Intelligencer" column in *New York* magazine. Her first novel, *Getting away with It,* is a workday drama of life at a successful city magazine. Published in 1976, the novel chronicles the disintegrating marriage of an assistant magazine editor and his staff-writer wife. Both are equally promiscuous, and Barrett Martin's scheme to embezzle money from his wealthier wife in order to buy a local newspaper backfires on him in a disastrous way. A *Library Journal* review praised the dialogue and tone in *Getting away with It,* noting that it might have worked even better on the stage. Martin Levin, writing in the *New York Times Book Review,* asserted that Glass's dissection of the marriage was deft, and "the effect is wryly humorous and cautionary."

In her second book, *Modern Love,* Glass creates the character Annie Flood, whose longtime boyfriend has just moved out as the novel opens. This calamitous event, occurring near her thirtieth birthday, is made worse by Flood's mother and sister, who try to convince her to settle down and have children. Flood is a successful stockbroker who resists their arguments; nevertheless, after a series of romantic mishaps she meets the man of her dreams. He is a coworker and literally the boy next door (next-door office, that is), making the novel "a development of plot rather than of character," as a *Publishers Weekly* review noted. Marcia R. Hoffman in *Library Journal* stated that what distinguishes the work "from others like it is the depiction of its three female characters."

With the publication of *Burning Time,* Glass launched her detective-novel series featuring the smart, funny character of Asian-American New York City homicide detective April Woo. As *Burning Time* gets underway, a college student has gone missing and her parents come to Woo for help. The corpse is then discovered on the other side of the country. Complicating matters, a New York psychoanalyst contacts Woo after his wife, an attractive actress, is plagued by harassing letters originating in San Diego. Woo suspects a link between the letters and the murder. She solves the mystery, but Glass provides readers with both gore (the victims are branded, and there are graphic details of torture-murders) and modern-day family values, as the iconoclastic Woo does off-duty verbal battle with her more tradition-minded Chinese mother. Emily Melton, reviewing *Burning Time* in *Booklist,* compared it to the bestseller *Silence of the Lambs,* by Thomas Harris. She praised the author for bringing the plot to a climax which includes a brief interlude in which "Glass stuns her white-knuckled readers into almost believing the good guys may not win."

In Glass's second April Woo mystery, *Hanging Time,* a sales associate in an upscale clothing store is found hanging from the boutique's chandelier, but Woo is certain the death was not a suicide. Her psychoanalyst friend from the first novel, Jason Frank, has a client who believes her own sister is dangerous, and though the two issues proceed independently, Glass eventually ties the pieces together as Woo solves the mystery. She also includes a secondary storyline about strife at the station house: Woo is hoping to advance to the rank of sergeant, but machinations by her colleagues almost keep her from unraveling the murder case. "Deft plotting and strong characterization will leave readers eager for further installments," declared *Library Journal* reviewer Kathy Piehl.

Loving Time, the third in the April Woo series, has the Manhattan detective again teamed with Mike Sanchez on the homicide beat. The two become romantically involved while investigating Clara Treadwell, who runs a well-regarded psychiatric center. Treadwell is being harassed by a mysterious stalker, who may or may not be her former mentor. Early in her career, Dr. Treadwell once tried to "reverse" a man's sexual orientation; several years later the man is found dead, but Woo discerns the cause as other than an apparent suicide. Treadwell and her onetime boss are being sued for causing emotional damage to the man, and the ambitious, self-serving psychiatrist turns on her former cohort, who also turns up dead. Glass won praise for the well-developed characters in this mystery. "In Glass's dark vision, the cops need policing, and the shrinks are in dire need of psychiatric help," concluded a *Publishers Weekly* contributor.

Woo finally earns her promotion as the 1998 novel, *Judging Time,* begins. Woo's latest challenge concerns a former pro athlete suspected of stabbing his wife and a male friend to death. The former football star, Rick Liberty, then vanishes. Woo and Sanchez are still a team on and off the job, but other characters enter to add more tumult to Woo's personal and professional life. There is more interdepartmental drama at the police station, and her mother—who calls Woo "worm daughter"—still pressures her to quit her job. "Glass writes a masterful police procedural," declared *Booklist* reviewer Melton. Like other reviewers, Melton singled out the author's "wonderfully rich portrait of smart, sensible, intrepid, stubborn April Woo."

In the fifth and sixth installments in this series, *Stealing Time* and *Tracking Time,* Glass's strength as an observer of inter-cultural clashes comes to the fore. In *Stealing Time,* Heather Rose Papescu, a Chinese-American woman, is beaten and her adopted infant kidnaped, but the mother refuses to identify her attacker and neither she nor her husband can produce adoption papers. The investigation into the whereabouts of this twice-stolen child is tangentially connected to the novel's other major plot strand, one involving an illegal alien who works in a sweatshop owned by Heather's husband. The array of characters allows Woo and her creator, Glass, to muse upon the varying styles of Chinese assimilation to U.S. culture, from rejection of the traditional culture, which Heather exemplifies, to rejection of American culture, which April's cousin Nanci exemplifies, to a kind of schizophrenic adoption of both cultures, the mode April has adopted. For a critic in *Publishers Weekly,* "While this overpopulated, overschematized story ends on an up beat, it's the themes of shame, guilt and familial obedience that make it work."

Likewise, in *Tracking Time,* Glass captured reviewers' attention less with the workings of her plot than with her insights into protagonist Woo's prickly relations with family members, her lover, and her coworkers, as she attempts to crack her latest case. In this kidnaping adventure, a Manhattan psychoanalyst goes missing after a meeting with a particularly disturbed client who is obsessed by him. Though this makes the patient, Allegra Caldera, the prime suspect for others involved with the case, April discovers that two teenagers from wealthy families have captured both doctor and patient and are torturing them in a cave in Central Park. *New York Times Book Review* contributor Marilyn Stasio remarks: "Leslie Glass gets one thing right in *Tracking Time:* parents and their adolescent offspring do not speak the same language—if, indeed, they speak at all." Similarly, for a reviewer with *Publishers Weekly,* the success of the latest April Woo mystery is separate from the rise and fall of the plot: "The strength of Glass's story lies in her cultivation of themes—broken families, culture clash, ambition and pride—as well as her strong portrayals of secondary characters."

Glass once told *CA:* "The *Time* series are novels of psychological suspense. They feature April Woo, the first Asian-American law enforcement officer in American crime fiction, and Dr. Jason Frank, a New York psychoanalyst. The series explores crime from both a psychiatrist's and cop's point of view. There is quite a bit of precinct and police department politics, procedure, forensics, as well as gender and cultural issues (April's boyfriend Detective Sergeant Mike Sanchez is Mexican-American). My research and writing have opened the door to many other interests, including my foundation work and my involvement as a trustee of the New York City Police Foundation."

BIOGRAPHICAL/CRITICAL SOURCES:

PERIODICALS

Booklist, October 1, 1993, review of *Burning Time,* p. 1257; September 15, 1996, review of *Loving Time,* p. 224; February 1, 1998, pp. 902-903.

Kirkus Reviews, August 1, 1993, review of *Burning Time,* p. 967; August 15, 1995, review of *Hanging Time,* p. 1143; September 1, 1996, review of *Loving Time,* p. 1276; December 17, 1997, review of *Judging Time,* p. 1807; August 1, 2000, review of *Tracking Time.*

Library Journal, October 1, 1976, p. 2085; June 15, 1983, p. 1274; October 1, 1992, review of *To Do No Harm,* p. 118; August, 1993, review of *Burning Time,* p. 150; October 1, 1995, review of *Hanging Time,* p. 119; September 1, 1996, p. 1276.

New York Times Book Review, September 19, 1976, p. 44; October 22, 2000, Marilyn Stasio, review of *Tracking Time.*

Publishers Weekly, July 5, 1976, p. 82; May 6, 1983, p. 85; September 27, 1993, review of *Burning Time,* p. 44; August 14, 1995, review of *Hanging Time,* p. 74; September 9, 1996, review of *Loving Time,* p. 63; November 24, 1997, review of *Judging Time,* p. 55; January 18, 1999, review of *Stealing Time,* p. 330; September 4, 2000, review of *Tracking Time,* p. 80.

Romantic Times, October, 2000, review of *Tracking Time.*

* * *

GOOD, Howard 1951-

PERSONAL: Born November 15, 1951, in New York, NY; son of Samuel (a furrier) and Lillie (a homemaker) Good; married Barbara Mintzer (a public health nurse), 1973; children: Gabriel, Graham, Brittany, Darla. *Education:* Bard College, B.A., 1973; University of Iowa, M.A., 1974; University of Michigan, Ph.D., 1984. *Politics:* Independent. *Religion:* Jewish.

ADDRESSES: Home—155 Grand St., Highland, NY 12528. *Office*—State University of New York, New Paltz, NY 12561. *E-mail*—goodh@newpaltz.edu.

CAREER: Ann Arbor News, Ann Arbor, MI, editor, 1977-78; *Charlotte Observer,* Charlotte, NC, editor, 1978-80; *Grand Forks Herald,* Grand Forks, ND, editor, 1980-83; University of North Dakota, Grand Forks, assistant professor of journalism, 1980-83; State University of New York, New Paltz, NY, associate professor of journalism, 1985-91, professor of journalism, 1992—.

MEMBER: American Journalism Historians Association, American Educators in Journalism and Mass Communication, Highland Central School District Board of Education (president).

WRITINGS:

Acquainted with the Night, Scarecrow Press (Metuchen, NJ), 1986.
Outcasts, Scarecrow Press (Metuchen, NJ), 1989.
The Journalist as Autobiographer, Scarecrow Press (Metuchen, NJ), 1993.
Diamonds in the Dark, Scarecrow Press (Lanham, MD), 1997.
Girl Reporter, Scarecrow Press (Lanham, MD), 1998.
The Drunken Journalist, Scarecrow Press (Lanham, MD), 2000.

WORK IN PROGRESS: Media Ethics Goes to the Movies, for Praeger.

* * *

GORTON, Kaitlyn
See EMERSON, Kathy Lynn

* * *

GRAHAM, Peter W(illiam) 1951-

PERSONAL: Born February 11, 1951, in Manchester, CT; son of Thomas William (an insurance executive) and Marion (Barrows) Graham; married Kathryn Videon (a college teacher), December 28, 1973; children: Thomas Austin, James Dominic. *Education:* Davidson College, A.B. (cum laude), 1973; Duke University, M.A., 1974, Ph.D., 1977.

ADDRESSES: Home—208 Sunset Blvd., Blacksburg, VA 24060. *Office*—Department of English, Virginia Polytechnic Institute and State University, Blacksburg, VA 24061.

CAREER: Virginia Polytechnic Institute and State University, Blacksburg, VA, assistant professor, 1978-84, associate professor, 1984-90, professor of English, 1990—, Clifford A. Cutching III Professor of English, 2000—.

MEMBER: Modern Language Association of America, Phi Beta Kappa. Secretary, Board of Directors, Byron Society of North America.

AWARDS, HONORS: Eli Lilly fellowship, University of Florida, 1977-78, for postdoctoral work in the humanities and the professions; Mellon fellowship, Duke University, 1980-81, for postdoctoral research in English.

WRITINGS:

(Editor) *Byron's Bulldog: The Letters of John Cam Hobhouse to Lord Byron,* Ohio State University Press (Columbus, OH), 1984.
(Editor) *Literature and Medicine,* Volume 4: *Psychiatry and Literature,* Johns Hopkins University Press (Baltimore, MD), 1985.
Don Juan and Regency, University Press of Virginia (Charlottesville, VA), 1990.
(Editor, with Elizabeth Sewell) *Literature and Medicine,* Volume 9: *Fictive Ills: Literary Perspectives on Wounds and Diseases,* Johns Hopkins University Press (Baltimore, MD), 1990.
(With Fritz Oehlschlaeger) *Articulating the Elephant Man: Joseph Merrick and His Interpreters,* Johns Hopkins University Press (Baltimore, MD), 1992.
(Editor, with Lilian Furst) *Disorderly Eaters: Texts in Self-Empowerment,* Pennsylvania State University (University Park, PA), 1992.
(Editor, with Duncan M. Porter) *The Portable Darwin,* Viking (New York, NY), 1993.
Lord Byron, Twayne (New York, NY), 1998.

Member of board of editors of *Literature and Medicine.*

BIOGRAPHICAL/CRITICAL SOURCES:

PERIODICALS

Times Literary Supplement, May 17, 1985.

GRANT, John 1933-
(Jonathan Gash, Graham Gaunt, Jonathan Grant, pseudonyms)

PERSONAL: Born September 30, 1933, in Bolton, Lancastershire, England; son of Peter Watson (a mill worker) and Anne (a mill worker; maiden name, Turner) Grant; married Pamela Richard (a nurse), February 19, 1955; children: Alison Mary, Jacqueline Clare, Yvonne. *Education:* University of London, M.B. and B.S., 1958; Royal College of Surgeons and Physicians, M.R.C.S. and L.R.C.P., 1958; also earned D.Path., D.Bact., D.H. M., M.D., and D.T.M.H. *Avocational interests:* Music ("I play a few instruments; choral music"), history, antiques.

ADDRESSES: Home—Silver Willows, Chapel Lane, West Bergholt, Colchester, Essex CO6 3EF, England. *Agent*—Desmond Elliott Management, 38 Bury St., London SW1Y 6AV, England.

CAREER: General practitioner in London, England, 1958-59; pathologist in London and Essex, England, 1959-62; clinical pathologist in Hannover and Berlin, Germany, 1962-65; University of Hong Kong, Hong Kong, lecturer in clinical pathology and head of division, 1965-68; microbiologist in Hong Kong and London, 1968-71; University of London, School of Hygiene and Tropical Medicine, London, head of bacteriology unit, 1971-88. *Military service:* British Army, Medical Corps; attained rank of major; posted to Germany.

MEMBER: International College of Surgeons (fellow), Royal Society of Tropical Medicine (fellow).

AWARDS, HONORS: Creasy Award, British Crime Writers' Association, 1977, for *The Judas Pair.*

WRITINGS:

"LOVEJOY" MYSTERIES; UNDER PSEUDONYM JONATHAN GASH

The Judas Pair, Harper (New York, NY), 1977.
Gold by Gemini, Harper (New York, NY), 1978.
The Grail Tree, Harper (New York, NY), 1979.
Spend Game, Collins (London, England), 1980, Ticknor & Fields (New Haven, CT), 1981.
The Vatican Rip, Collins (London, England), 1981, Ticknor & Fields (New Haven, CT), 1982.
The Sleepers of Erin, Dutton (New York, NY), 1983.
Firefly Gadroon, St. Martin's Press (New York, NY), 1984.
The Gondola Scam, St. Martin's Press (New York, NY), 1984.
Pearlhanger, St. Martin's Press (New York, NY), 1985.
The Tartan Sell, St. Martin's Press (New York, NY), 1986, published as *The Tartan Ringers,* Collins (London, England), 1986.
Moonspender, St. Martin's Press (New York, NY), 1987.
Jade Woman, St. Martin's Press (New York, NY), 1989.
The Very Last Gambado, St. Martin's Press (New York, NY), 1990.
The Great California Game, St. Martin's Press (New York, NY), 1991.
The Lies of Fair Ladies, St. Martin's Press (New York, NY), 1992.
Paid and Loving Eyes, St. Martin's Press (New York, NY), 1993.
The Sin within Her Smile, Viking (New York, NY), 1994.
The Grace in Older Women, Viking (New York, NY), 1995.
The Possessions of a Lady, Viking (New York, NY), 1996.
The Rich and the Profane, Macmillan (London, England), 1998, Viking (New York, NY) 1999.
A Rag, a Bone, and a Hank of Hair, Viking (New York, NY), 2000.

"DR. CLARE BURTONALL" MYSTERIES; UNDER PSEUDONYM JONATHAN GASH

Different Women Dancing, Viking (New York, NY), 1997.
Prey Dancing, Viking (New York, NY), 1998.

OTHER

(Under pseudonym Jonathan Gash) *Member of Parliament,* M. Joseph (London, England), 1974.
(Under pseudonym Graham Gaunt) *The Incomer,* Doubleday (New York, NY), 1982.
(Under pseudonym Jonathan Grant) *Mehala, Lady of Sealandings,* 1993.

Also author of *Terminus* (play), produced at Chester Festival, England, 1976. Contributor of poems to *Record.*

ADAPTATIONS: Grant's Lovejoy novels were adapted for the television series *Lovejoy,* produced by the British Broadcasting Company (BBC-TV) and starring Ian McShane.

SIDELIGHTS: Novelist John Grant, known to his fans under the nom de plume Jonathan Gash, is the creator of the widely successful Lovejoy mystery series. Grant's experiences of the 1970s, working in the antique stalls of London during his days as a medical student, inspired a lifelong interest in antiques, as well as his budding career as a novelist. Antiques would figure prominently in Grant's Lovejoy, who first appeared in the 1977 novel *The Judas Pair.* Encouraged by the success of that first novel, which won the Crime Writers' Association award, Grant has continued his literary endeavors; among his many novels are *The Rich and the Profane, Possessions of a Lady,* and *A Rag, a Bone, and a Hank of Hair.* The last, published in 2000, was the twenty-first installment in the Lovejoy series.

Lovejoy, an English antiques dealer who serves at the center of the series, is not a typical hero. Newgate Callendar described Lovejoy in the *New York Times Book Review:* "He may be perpetually broke, his private life is always in a mess, he is a liar and pretends to be a coward, his business dealings are unethical, no woman is safe from him, but he responds to antiques the way Mozart responded to the key of D minor. Antiques set up a vibration in him, and all of a sudden this dubious character becomes an artist." In another review, Callendar explained why Lovejoy is an effective hero despite his shortcomings: "He is a genuine hero because, like Don Giovanni or Carmen, he is faithful to himself. In this way, he seeks the truth, the unattainable vision, backed by tremendous knowledge and a rapt love for what he is doing."

In reviewing *The Grace of Older Women,* which finds Lovejoy cavorting with more mature ladies, *Booklist* reviewer Emily Melton commented that Grant "has the formula for success down pat, but he's never repetitive—each story is more outrageously fun and funny than the last." Melton wrote that with *The Possessions of a Lady* "Grant offers up another hilarious tale featuring one of the most appealing eccentrics in crime fiction." In her review of the twentieth Lovejoy mystery, *The Rich and the Profane,* Jenny McLarin noted in *Booklist* that "seemingly thousands of ancillary characters are involved in an astonishing variety of scams, schemes, thefts, and affairs," while a *Publishers Weekly* reviewer called Grant "in top form."

In *A Rag, a Bone, and a Hank of Hair* Lovejoy's research to verify the authenticity of green gemstones leads him to another mystery, as the antiqueing sleuth discovers his old partner has died mysteriously. A *Publishers Weekly* reviewer wrote that "the pace is more than leisurely, with many a detour to natter about antiques. . . . Fans will chuckle all the way." "Lovable rogue Lovejoy has found a permanent home on the shady side of the antiques trade," noted Bill Ott in his *Booklist* appraisal, adding that afficionados of Grant's series "will have a ball this time."

Following his retirement from the practice of medicine in 1988, Grant, still writing as Gash, developed a second series featuring cardiologist Clare Burtonall. In *Different Women Dancing,* published in 1997, Clare's life is one of hospital routine and marriage to a wealthy realtor involved in shady schemes. She witnesses an accident and becomes involved with Bonn, a fellow witness who is a former seminary student-turned-male prostitute, and whose life style is the polar opposite of hers. A *Publishers Weekly* reviewer described Bonn as "a kind of Candide, innocent and charismatic, a rising star in the underworld of sex for hire and the syndicate of which he is a part." *Booklist* reviewer David Pitt compared Grant's new series to the Lovejoy books, noting that the Clare Burtonall books promised to be "a lot rougher." In *Library Journal* contributor Rex E. Klett praised *Different Women Dancing* as "told with the author's accustomed panache."

Clare has become a sometime customer of Bonn, and readers find her drawn into his world of drugs and violence in *Prey Dancing.* A *Publishers Weekly* reviewer noted of the 1998 novel that "in edgy, slangy, and original prose, [Grant] captures his quirky cast and unusual settings to create entertainment of the first rank." *Booklist* reviewer Emily Melton dubbed *Prey Dancing* "brilliantly written, mysterious, menacing, and filled with unforgettable characters . . . another winner in an extraordinary new series."

BIOGRAPHICAL/CRITICAL SOURCES:

PERIODICALS

Booklist, March 15, 1995, Emily Melton, review of *The Grace in Older Women,* p. 1283; August, 1996, Emily Melton, review of *The Possessions of a Lady,* p. 1886; April 15, 1997, David Pitt, review of *Different Women Dancing,* p. 1404; July, 1998, Emily

Melton, review of *Prey Dancing,* p. 1864; February 15, 1999, Jenny McLarin, review of *The Rich and the Profane,* p. 1045; February 15, 2000, Bill Ott, review of *A Rag, a Bone, and a Hank of Hair,* p. 1088.

Kirkus Reviews, April 1, 1994, review of *The Sin within Her Smile;* June 15, 1996, review of *The Possessions of a Lady;* May 1, 1997, review of *Different Women Dancing.*

Library Journal, June 1, 1997, Rex E. Klett, review of *Different Women Dancing,* p. 154.

Listener, January 10, 1980, p. 62; November 13, 1980, p. 665; April 12, 1984, p. 27.

Los Angeles Times Book Review, February 12, 1989, p. 6; August 9, 1992, p. 9.

New Republic, February 16, 1980, p. 37; May 2, 1981, p. 38.

New Statesman, June 27, 1980, p. 975.

New Yorker, September 3, 1979, p. 108; July 9, 1984, p. 95; October 22, 1984, p. 164; April 10, 1989, p. 124.

New York Times Book Review, August 19, 1979, p. 17; August 17, 1980, p. 19; July 19, 1981, p. 18; February 21, 1982, p. 42; May 8, 1983, p. 27; April 29, 1984, p. 26; November 4, 1984, p. 35; June 23, 1985, p. 33; July 6, 1986, p. 21; April 12, 1987, p. 34; March 19, 1989, p. 29; September 9, 1990, p. 39; November 3, 1991, p. 27; September 6, 1992, p. 17; July 18, 1993, Marilyn Stasio, review of *Paid and Loving Eyes,* p. 17; June 29, 1997, Marilyn Stasio, review of *Different Women Dancing,* p. 22; April 4, 1999, Marilyn Stasio, review of *The Rich and the Profane,* p. 20.

Observer (London), August 3, 1980, p. 29; November 22, 1981, p. 27; April 13, 1986, p. 25.

Publishers Weekly, March 13, 1995, review of *The Grace in Older Women,* p. 62; July 1, 1996, review of *Possessions of a Lady,* p. 45; April 7, 1997, review of *Different Women Dancing,* p. 76; July 6, 1998, review of *Prey Dancing,* p. 54; March 15, 1999, review of *The Rich and the Profane,* p. 50; February 14, 2000, review of *A Rag, a Bone, and a Hank of Hair,* p. 177.

Times Literary Supplement, October 2, 1981, p. 1139; May 18, 1984, p. 557; April 5, 1985, p. 394; August 8, 1986, p. 863.

Tribune Books (Chicago), May 23, 1982, p. 4; January 29, 1989, p. 7; September 2, 1990, p. 4; October 6, 1991, p. 6.

Washington Post Book World, June 15, 1980, p. 11; March 19, 1989, p. 8.

OTHER

Lovejoy in Print Web site, http://members-http-3.rwcl.sfba.home.net/unclepj/lovejoy/ (May 19, 2001), biography of John Grant.*

* * *

GRANT, Jonathan
See GRANT, John

* * *

GRIMSHAW, James A(lbert), Jr. 1940-

PERSONAL: Born December 10, 1940, in Kingsville, TX; son of James A. and Maureen (Haley) Grimshaw; married Darlene Hargett, June 10, 1961; children: Courtney Anne, James A. IV. *Education:* Texas Tech University, B.A., 1962, M.A., 1968; Louisiana State University, Ph.D., 1972. *Ethnicity:* "Caucasian."

ADDRESSES: *Home*—248 Country Road 4101, Greenville, TX 75401-4799. *Office*—Department of Literature and Languages, Texas A & M-Commerce, Commerce, TX 75429. *E-mail*—bison@koyote.com; fax: 903-455-2428.

CAREER: U.S. Air Force, career officer, 1963-83, associated with personnel services in Waco, TX, Tan Son Nhut Air Force Base, South Vietnam, and Sacramento, CA, 1963-68, U.S. Air Force Academy, Colorado Springs, Colo., instructor, 1968-69, assistant professor, 1972-74, associate professor, 1974-79, professor of English, 1980-83, retiring as lieutenant colonel; Texas A&M University-Commerce (formerly East Texas State University, Commerce), professor of literature and languages and department head, 1983-1990, regents professor, 1995—. Visiting lecturer at University of Colorado, 1972-73; Flannery O'Connor Visiting Professor of English at Georgia College, 1977; visiting fellow in bibliography at Beinecke Rare Book and Manuscript Library, Yale University, 1979-80; reader in English for Educational Testing Service, 1979-1983.

MEMBER: Association of Teachers of Technical Writing, Society for the Study of Southern Literature, Bibliographical Society of the University of Virginia, South Central Modern Language Association, College Teachers of English (Texas), American Literature Association.

AWARDS, HONORS: Military: Bronze Star. Other: Faculty Senate Distinguished Faculty Award, East Texas State University, 1988, 1995; Editor's Choice Award, *Poet Magazine,* 1992, for poem "When the Cat Calls Your Name"; Editor's Choice Award, National Library of Poetry, 1995, for "Advice from a Father."

WRITINGS:

(General editor) *The United States Air Force Academy's First Twenty-five Years: Some Perceptions,* Dean of Faculty, U.S. Air Force Academy, 1979.

(Editor) *Cleanth Brooks at the United States Air Force Academy,* Department of English, U.S. Air Force Academy, 1980.

The Flannery O'Connor Companion, Greenwood Press, 1981.

Robert Penn Warren: A Descriptive Bibliography, 1922-1979, University Press of Virginia, 1982.

(Contributor) Donald Ahern and Robert Shenk, editors, *Literature in the Education of the Military Professional,* Department of English, U.S. Air Force Academy, 1983.

(Editor) *Robert Penn Warren's "Brother to Dragons": A Discussion,* Louisiana State University Press, 1983.

(Contributor) Matthew J. Bruccoli and C. E. Frazer Clark, editors, *The Concise First Printings of American Authors,* Gale, 1983.

(Editor) *"Time's Glory": Original Essays on Robert Penn Warren,* University of Central Arkansas Press, 1986.

(Editor) *The Paul Wells Barrus Lectures, 1983-1989,* East Texas State University Press, 1990.

(Editor) *Robert Penn Warren/Cleanth Brooks: Friends of Their Youth,* King Library Press (Lexington), 1993.

(Editor) *Cleanth Brooks and Robert Penn Warren: A Literary Correspondence,* University of Missouri Press, 1998,

(Editor with James Perkins) *Robert Penn Warren's* All the King's Men*: Three Stage Versions,* University of Georgia Press, 2000.

Understanding Robert Penn Warren, University of South Carolina Press, forthcoming.

Contributor to *Annual Bibliography of English Language and Literature,* 1974-82. Contributor of articles, poems, and reviews to magazines, including *Southern Review, Daedalus, Southern Literary Journal, Kentucky Review, Shakespeare Quarterly,* and *Explicator.* Founder and editor of *Icarus: A Magazine of Creativity,* 1969-82.

WORK IN PROGRESS: A Robert Penn Warren Bibliography, 1921-1996, with Jon Eller; *The Wednesday Night Carnival,* children's book of beast fables; *Relationships: Ricocheting toward Infinity,* poems; *Clyde Edgerton.*

SIDELIGHTS: James A. Grimshaw told *CA:* "At a recent honors colloquium, I told students that I write because I have a fire in my belly to do so. Writing is still a way of thinking for me, and it helps to clarify my perceptions. It also enhances my teaching. Trying to stay abreast of the changes in audience expectations, in focus, and in trends remains a challenge. As a teacher of writing for more than thirty years, I cannot imagine not being actively involved in the writing process.

"Over the years many influences have affected my writing: life experiences such as two bouts with cancer influence the way I read literature, interact with other people, and write. Academic writing I consider a service to my colleagues and students; it is a way of sharing idea. Although my first interest has remained the works of Robert Penn Warren, who has had a profound influence on my writing, I have made a concerted effort to examine more closely the works of other authors such as Faulkner, Donald Justice, E. A. Robinson, Clyde Edgerton, Flannery O'Connor, and Walt McDonald. Not only what I read but what I teach, then, influences my writing. Philosophy has been a particular focus in the last ten years. Yet another influence in my work has been my teachers, especially the ones with whom I have remained in contact over the years. Last, but far from least, is my wife. Without her support it would not have happened.

"Writing process? I write most things in my head before I ever commit them to paper or, now, to a disk. When I do start to write down those thoughts, I work straight through, from introduction to conclusion, before I begin the rewrite process. Nothing sent to an editor is "first draft" or "off the top of my head." The editors with whom I have been fortunate enough to work have taught me a great deal about writing. Although I do not agree with every change they suggest, I divorce myself from the edited work and try to see it from their perspective. When I separate myself from it, I learn.

"My choice of subjects has been from personal interest. In 1962 I read *All the King's Men* and knew I wanted to know more about Robert Penn Warren, the writer. My interest in his writing has not waned; and when I discover something new, perhaps a new angle or an unpublished piece, I want to share it with others. For example, the correspondence between Cleanth Brooks and Robert Penn Warren over nearly sixty years fascinated me. I asked each of them if they would mind if I edited those letters. Their response was they doubted if there was anything in those letters of much interest. That book of letters came out in 1998, and critics who reviewed the book were appreciative of the relationship that correspondence represents. Among some of the other subjects, I enjoy Edgerton and O'Connor's humor; I appreciate Donald Justice's sense of form in his poetry in an era that is relatively formless; and McDonald depicts relationships that I can relate to in his poetry.

"Changes to my writing are difficult for me to assess. However, I know the direction in which I am heading. My academic writing is slowing down, and I am preparing to spend more time on my creative efforts. My volume of poems is about half filled. After being put aside for a rest, my beast fables are due for revision. And since I have taught fiction, poetry, and drama throughout my teaching career, I want to write at least one book in each genre to see for myself whether I learned anything from the other authors. The ideas for the novel and the play are in my head—the pre-write phase. When you ask about changes, I suppose those goals represent one kind of change in my writing."

* * *

GURA, Philip F(rancis) 1950-

PERSONAL: Born June 14, 1950, in Ware, MA; son of Oswald Eugene and Stephanie R. (Koziara) Gura; married Leslie Ann Cobig, August 4, 1979; children: David Austin, Katherine Blair, Daniel Alden. *Ethnicity:* "Caucasian." *Education:* Harvard University, B.A. (magna cum laude), 1972, Ph.D., 1977.

ADDRESSES: Home—P. O. Box 163, Chapel Hill, NC 27514. *Office*—Department of English, University of North Carolina, Chapel Hill, NC 27599-3520. *E-mail*—gura@email.unc.edu.

CAREER: Middlebury College, Middlebury, VT, instructor in American literature, 1974-76; University of Colorado, Boulder, assistant professor, 1976-80, associate professor of English, 1980-85, director of American studies, 1978-80, director of graduate studies, 1981-85, professor of English, 1985-87; University of North Carolina, Chapel Hill, professor of English and American studies, 1987-2000, William S. Newman Distinguished Professor of American Literature and Culture, 2000—. Fellow, Charles Warren Center for Studies in American History, Harvard University, 1980-81; fellow, Institute of Early American History and Culture, Williamsburg, VA, 1985-86; senior fellow, National Endowment for the Humanities, 1985-86; Peterson fellow, American Antiquarian Society, 1989, 1998.

MEMBER: Modern Language Association of America, Colonial Society of Massachusetts, American Antiquarian Society, Massachusetts Historical Society.

AWARDS, HONORS: Norman Foerster Prize in American Literature, Modern Language Association of America, 1977, for "Thoreau's Maine Woods Indians: More Representative Men"; Frances Densmore Prize, American Musical Instrument Society, 1996.

WRITINGS:

The Wisdom of Words: Language, Theology, and Literature in the New England Renaissance, Wesleyan University Press (Middletown, CT), 1981.

(Editor with Joel Myerson) *Critical Essays on American Transcendentalism,* G. K. Hall (Boston, MA), 1982.

A Glimpse of Sion's Glory: Puritan Radicalism in New England, 1620-1660, Wesleyan University Press (Middletown, CT), 1983.

Early Nineteenth-Century Painting in Rural Massachusetts: John Howe of Greenwich and Enfield, c. 1803-1845, with a Transcription of His "Printer's Book," c. 1832, American Antiquarian Society (Worcester, MA), 1991.

The Crossroads of American History and Literature, Penn State University Press (University Park, PA), 1996.

America's Instrument: The Banjo in the Nineteenth Century, University of North Carolina Press (Chapel Hill, NC), 1999.

Buried from the World: Inside the Massachusetts State Prison, 1829-31, Massachusetts Historical Society, 2001.

Contributor to literature and history journals, including *American Literature, Virginia Quarterly, Yale Review,* and *Sewanee Review.*

SIDELIGHTS: In *The Wisdom of Words: Language, Theology, and Literature in the New England Renaissance,* Philip F. Gura examines the cultural context out of which American literary symbolism emerged in the decades before the Civil War. Gura focuses on religion and language theory in the first section of the book, while in the latter chapters he discusses the works of such writers as Ralph Waldo Emerson, Henry David Thoreau, and Herman Melville. In the *Journal of American History* Robert D. Richardson, Jr. writes that "the integrity of [Gura's] study lies in its fidelity to the issues and judgements of the period about which he is writing. Thus his work is solid and will last, and his readers are free to make their own connections with the present."

Gura continues his examination of New England history in *A Glimpse of Sion's Glory: Puritan Radicalism in New England, 1620-1660.* In this work Gura asserts that the Puritans were not as ideologically homogeneous as some historians have suggested and that there were, in fact, numerous acts of dissent committed by Puritan radicals. Divided into three sections, *A Glimpse of Sion's Glory* catalogs the various types of Puritan dissent, discusses the response of the Puritan establishment to radical thinkers, and provides case studies of three radicals: Anne Hutchinson, Samuel Gorton, and William Pynchon. In the *American Historical Review,* Theodore Dwight Bozeman states that "Gura displays the most thorough and integrated knowledge of New England dissent from 1620 to 1660 yet attained by any historian." Pauline Maier, writing in the *New York Times Book Review,* also offers praise for *A Glimpse of Sion's Glory:* "[Gura's] book is an evocative account of the 17th century; so sustained a work of intelligence and human sensitivity is always a rare achievement."

BIOGRAPHICAL/CRITICAL SOURCES:

PERIODICALS

American Anthropologist, September, 1982, p. 751.

American Historical Review, April, 1985, Theodore Dwight Bozeman, review of *A Glimpse of Sion's Glory,* p. 478.

American Literature, May, 1982, pp. 296-298; May, 1985, p. 326.

Choice, January, 1982, p. 626; January, 1983, p. 704; December, 1984, p. 610.

Journal of American History, June, 1982, Robert D. Richardson, Jr., review of *The Wisdom of Words;* March, 1985, p. 855.

Journal of American Studies, August, 1983, pp. 281-283; December, 1987, p. 453.

Kirkus Reviews, November 15, 1983, p. 1194.

New England Quarterly, March, 1982, pp. 132-134; March, 1985, p. 104.

New York Times Book Review, April 1, 1984, Pauline Maier, review of *A Glimpse of Sion's Glory,* p. 21.

Virginia Quarterly Review, winter, 1985, p. 7.

H

HAHN (GARCES), Oscar (Arturo) 1938-

PERSONAL: Born July 5, 1938, in Iquique, Chile; immigrated to United States, 1974, naturalized citizen; married Nancy Jorquera, 1971; children: one daughter. *Education:* Graduated from University of Chile, 1963; University of Iowa, M.A., 1972; University of Maryland at College Park, Ph.D., 1977.

ADDRESSES: *Office*—Department of Spanish, University of Iowa, Iowa City, Iowa 52240.

CAREER: University of Chile Arica, Santiago, professor of Hispanic literature, 1965-73; University of Maryland at College Park, instructor, 1974-77; University of Iowa, Iowa City, assistant professor, 1977-79, associate professor of Spanish-American literature, 1979—, honorary fellow of International Writing Program, 1972.

MEMBER: Instituto Internacional de Literatura Iberoamericana, Modern Language Association of America.

AWARDS, HONORS: Premio Alerce, 1961, for *Esta rosa negra;* Poetry Award from University of Chile, 1966.

WRITINGS:

Esta rosa negra (poems), Ediciones Alerce (Santiago, Chile), 1961.

Agua final (poems), Ediciones de la Rama Florida (Lima, Peru), 1967.

Arte de morir (poems), Hispamerica (Buenos Aires, Argentina), 1977, 2nd edition, Editorial Nascimento (Santiago, Chile), 1979, translation by James Haggard published as *The Art of Dying,* Latin American Literary Review Press (Pittsburgh, PA), 1987.

El cuento fantástico hispanoamericano en el siglo XIX, Premia Editora (Mexico City, Mexico), 1978.

Mal de amor, Ediciones Ganymedes (Santiago, Chile), 1981, translation by James Hoggard published as *Love Breaks,* Latin American Literary Review, 1991.

Imagenes nucleares, Ediciones America del Sur (Santiago, Chile), 1983.

Texto sobre texto, Coordinacion de Humanidades, Universidad Nacional Autonoma de Mexico, 1984.

Tratado de sortilegios, Hiperion (Madrid, Spain), 1992.

Antología poética, Editorial Universitaria (Santiago, Chile), 1993.

Antología virtual, Fondo de Cultura Economica (Santiago, Chile), 1996.

(With Matias Rivas and Roberto Merino) *Que hacia yo el once de septiembre de 1973?* (collection of reminiscences of Pinochet military coup), LOM (Santiago, Chile), 1997.

Antología retroactiva, Montel Avila Editores (Caracas, Venezuela), 1998.

Verso robados/Stolen Verses and Other Poems (bilingual edition), translated with an introduction by James Hoggard, Northwestern University Press (Evanston, IL), 2000.

Also author of *Flor de enamorados,* F. Zegers (Santiago, Chile). Contributing editor of *Handbook of Latin American Studies.* Contributor to literature journals.

SIDELIGHTS: Considered one of the leading postmodern voices in Chilean poetry, Oscar Hahn escaped political persecution in his native country of Chile by fleeing to the United States in 1974. After finishing graduate work at the University of Maryland, he began a teaching career at the University of Iowa, where he became a professor of Spanish-American literature. He has written or edited several highly respected volumes of poetry, and coedited a collection of reminiscences about the Chilean coup d'etat of 1973.

Hahn, who has been writing poetry since his late teens, was awarded the Premio Alerce for poetry in 1961 for his first book, *Esta rosa negra,* which included poems he wrote between the ages of seventeen and nineteen. He put out another collection, *Agua final,* in 1967. After attending the University of Iowa's International Writing Program in 1971, he returned to Chile. During the 1973 coup that toppled the Allende government, however, Hahn was imprisoned for ten days. Though he has lived in the United States since 1974, he frequently travels to South America and continues to write in Spanish.

Despite the critical success of Hahn's early work, it was *Arte de morir,* published in Buenos Aires in 1977, that catapulted the poet to literary fame. Critics praised the blend of fantastic, ironic, and realistic elements with which Hahn explores the theme of death and which led critics to associate him with postmodernism and surrealism. Reviewing the book's 1988 bilingual edition, *The Art of Dying,* for *Choice,* Marjorie Agosin called it "both a satirical statement on the banality of everyday existence and a celebration of life" that secured Hahn a place among such Chilean luminaries as Nobel-laureate Pablo Neruda and Gabriela Mistral. Indeed, according to *Spanish American Authors* contributor Angel Flores, Hahn considers *Arte de morir* to be the only book he has ever written—the others, he insists, are earlier editions.

Yet Hahn wrote several later books, including *Mal de amor,* which was banned by Chile's military regime. The book, translated by James Hoggard, appeared in English as *Love Breaks.* Hoggard also translated Hahn's *Versos robados/Stolen Verses,* which appeared in a bilingual edition in 2000 and was hailed by a *Kirkus Reviews* contributor as a "work of . . . genius." Hahn, the critic observed, "takes ordinary situations and images and implants within them a kind of surrealist grenade that explodes when least expected—and with striking effect." Also reviewing the English translation, *Booklist* contributor Ray Olson went so far as to call Hahn "a genuine surrealist wizard, capable of rousing uneasiness with memorable imagery that is pregnant with violence and lust," and deemed the collection both powerful and filled with beauty.

BIOGRAPHICAL/CRITICAL SOURCES:

BOOKS

Flores, Angel, *Spanish American Authors: The Twentieth Century,* H. W. Wilson Company (New York, NY), 1992.

PERIODICALS

Bloomsbury Review, March-April, 2000, review of *Stolen Verses and Other Poems.*

Booklist, March 1, 2000, review of *Stolen Verses and Other Poems,* p. 1190.

Kirkus Reviews, February 15, 2000, review of *Stolen Verses and Other Poems,* p. 208.

Publishers Weekly, March 27, 2000, "Recovered Texts," p. 74.

World Literature Today, autumn, 1982.*

* * *

HALVERSON, William H(agen) 1930-

PERSONAL: Born July 28, 1930, in Sebeka, MN; son of Arthur William (a farmer) and Clara (Hagen) Halverson; married Marolyn Sortland, August 25, 1951; children: Lynn, Kay, Beth, Susan, Carol. *Education:* Augsburg College, B.A., 1951, B.Th., 1955; Princeton Seminary, Th.M., 1957; Princeton University, M.A., 1959, Ph.D., 1961. *Politics:* Independent. *Religion:* "None."

ADDRESSES: *Home and office*—2330 Nayland Rd., Columbus, OH 43220.

CAREER: Sherburn High School, Sherburn, MN, teacher of music and English, 1951-52; Princeton Theological Seminary, Princeton, NJ, instructor in philosophy, 1957-59; Augsburg College, Minneapolis, MN, assistant professor, 1959-61, associate professor, 1961-65, professor of philosophy and chair of department, 1959-67; Ohio State University, Columbus, associate dean of University College, 1967-87; freelance writer and translator, 1987—.

MEMBER: American Philosophical Association, Mind Society.

WRITINGS:

A Concise Introduction to Philosophy (college textbook), Random House (New York, NY), 1967, 4th edition, 1981.

A Concise Logic (college textbook), Random House (New York, NY), 1984.

EDITOR AND AUTHOR OF INTRODUCTION

Concise Readings in Philosophy, Random House (New York, NY), 1981.

Edvard Grieg Today, St. Olaf College (Northfield), 1994.

TRANSLATOR

(With Leland B. Sateren) Finn Benestad and Dag Schjelderup-Ebbe, *Edvard Greig: The Man and the Artist,* University of Nebraska Press (Lincoln, NE), 1988.

Finn Benestad and Dag Schjelderup-Ebbe, *Johan Svendsen: The Man, the Maestro, the Music,* Peer Gynt Press (Columbus, OH), 1988.

(Translator of song texts) *Edvard Grieg: Complete Works,* C. F. Peters Verlag (Frankfurt, Germany), Volume 14, 1990, Volume 15, 1991.

(With Sateren) Nils Grinde, *A History of Norwegian Music,* University of Nebraska Press (Lincoln, NE), 1991.

Jon-Roar Bjorkvold, *The Muse Within,* HarperCollins (New York, NY), 1992.

Einar Steen-Nøkleberg, *Onstage with Grieg,* University of Indiana Press, 1997.

Roy Jacobsen, *The New Water,* Peer Gynt Press (Columbus, OH), 1997.

Edvard Grieg, *Letters to Colleagues and Friends,* edited by Finn Benestad, Peer Gynt Press (Columbus, OH), 2000.

(Coeditor, with Finn Benestad, and translator) *Edvard Grieg: Diaries, Articles, Speeches,* Peer Gynt Press (Columbus, OH), 2001.

OTHER

Contributor of articles to theology and philosophy journals, including *Mind, Journal of Religion,* and *Pacific Journal of Philosophy.*

SIDELIGHTS: William H. Halverson told *CA:* "Scholarly writing has been an important part of my life since the beginning of my professional career. As a college professor I always planned my summers around my writing—several articles, to begin with, and then, in the summer of 1965, my first book, which was published in 1967. Upon becoming a university administrator I vowed that I would continue to write, and I did. My pattern for those twenty years was to spend four evenings each week plus Saturday at my writing desk—about twenty hours per week minus unavoidable interruptions. Approximately 100,000 students have been introduced to philosophy through the several editions of *A Concise Introduction to Philosophy.* Since 1987, I have had the luxury of spending the best hours of each day at my writing desk. Meanwhile, the primary focus of my work has changed from writing books on philosophy to, primarily, translating books dealing with Norwegian music.

"My interest in Norwegian music (and the Norwegian language) was initially stimulated by a study trip to Norway in the summer of 1950, when I met the legendary musicologist O. M. Sandvik. That interest, which remained on the back burner throughout much of my career, was revived during extended visits to Norway in 1976 and 1978, and since 1987 I have devoted much of my time to this previously avocational interest."

BIOGRAPHICAL/CRITICAL SOURCES:

PERIODICALS

New York Times Book Review, March 19, 1989, p. 22.

* * *

HAM, Debra Newman 1948-
(Debra Lynn Newman)

PERSONAL: Born August 27, 1948, in York, PA; daughter of Earl Franklin (a machinist) and Eva Pansylee (a seamstress; maiden name, Mitchell; present surname, Owens) Newman; married Lester James Ham (an electronic technician), April 29, 1989; children: Lester James, Jr., Leslyn Jaye. *Ethnicity:* "African American." *Education:* Howard University, B.A., 1970, Ph.D., 1984; Boston University, M.A., 1971. *Politics:* Republican. *Religion:* Baptist. *Avocational interests:* Bible teaching.

ADDRESSES: Home—8613 Magnolia St., Laurel, MD 20707. *Office*—Department of History, Morgan State University, 1700 East Cold Spring Lane, Baltimore, MD 21251; fax: 410-319-4367. *E-mail*—dham@moac.morgan.edu.

CAREER: National Archives, Washington, DC, summer intern, 1970-71, assistant to the black history specialist, 1972-74, project archivist with Industrial and Social branch, 1974-78, African American history specialist in Civil Archives division, 1978-84, archivist, 1984-86; Library of Congress, Washington, DC, African American history and culture specialist, 1986-95; Morgan State University, Baltimore, MD, professor of history, 1995—. Syracuse University, member of Seminar in Kenya and Tanzania, 1973; University of Liberia, member of Liberian Women in Development project, 1981; Northern Virginia Community College, adjunct professor, 1986-88. Opportunities Industrialization Centers, chairperson of archival advisory board, 1986-90.

MEMBER: Association for the Study of Afro-American Life and History (member of executive committee, 1989-96), Society of American Archivists (member of editorial board, 1990-94), Afro-American Historical and Genealogical Society (founding member; past vice president), Association of Black Women Historians (eastern regional director, 1999—), Mid-Atlantic Regional Archives Conference.

AWARDS, HONORS: National Archives citation, 1984, Finding Aid Award from Mid-Atlantic Regional Archives Conference, 1985, and Coker Finding Aid Award from Society of American Archivists, 1985, all for *Black History: A Guide to Civilian Records in the National Archives;* Arlene Custer Award from Mid-Atlantic Regional Archive Conference and Meritorious Service Award from Library of Congress, both 1994, both for *The African-American Mosaic: A Library of Congress Resource Guide for the Study of Black History and Culture.*

WRITINGS:

UNDER NAME DEBRA LYNN NEWMAN

List of Free Black Heads of Families in the 1790 Census, National Archives (Washington, DC), 1973.

List of Black Servicemen Compiled from the War Department Collection of Revolutionary War Records, National Archives, 1974.

Preliminary Inventory of the Records of the Social Security Administration, National Archives, 1976.

Preliminary Inventory of the Records of the Office of Economic Opportunity, National Archives, 1977.

Selected Documents Pertaining to Black Workers among the Records of the Department of Labor and Its Component Bureaus, 1902-69, National Archives, 1977.

Black History: A Guide to Civilian Records in the National Archives, National Archives, 1984.

Contributor to periodicals.

UNDER NAME DEBRA NEWMAN HAM

(Editor) *The African-American Mosaic: A Library of Congress Resource Guide for the Study of Black History and Culture,* Library of Congress (Washington, DC), 1993.

(Editor) *The African American Odyssey,* Library of Congress, 1998.

Contributor to books, including *Black Women in American History,* edited by Darlene Clark Hine, Carlson Publishers (New York City), 1990; *Global Dimensions of the African Diaspora,* edited by Joseph E. Harris, second edition, Howard University Press, 1993; *The Harvard Guide to African-American History,* Harvard University Press, 1995; and *Public History Essays from the Field,* edited by James Gardner and Peter LaPaglia, Krieger Press, 1999. Contributor to history journals. Newsletter editor, Association of Black Women Historians, 1986-90.

WORK IN PROGRESS: Liberia's Women: A Nineteenth-Century Experiment in Colonization; a biography of Lorraine Anderson Williams, the first female vice president of Howard University.

SIDELIGHTS: Debra Newman Ham told *CA:* "My faith in Jesus Christ, my family and friends, and my research and writing have been the supreme joys of my life. They have provided me with fulfillment and satisfaction on my life's journey. I read voraciously as a youth and discovered early that history is a fruitful field for bibliophiles.

"Howard University introduced me to the wonders of African American history and culture, the pursuit of which has become my life's work. My twenty-four-year stint in archival and manuscript repositories seemed to me the odyssey of a historian lost in paradise. I had the pleasure of leafing through manuscripts documenting almost three hundred years of African American history. Through these I learned much about myself and my people. That knowledge provided nurturing roots for me and gave me the security of a tree planted by the water.

"Opportunities to provide guideposts to these historical documents, so that generations of researchers would be able to find what I found, motivated my writing. I sought techniques for writing clearly and concisely, and I labored to reduce complicated procedures to the simplest common denominators. During my senior year at Howard, I worked at the *Washington Post,* where I typed stories as reporters dictated them over the telephone. That year I tried to absorb a journalistic style that conveyed information in the most straightforward manner.

"I love to write, but have never considered myself to be a writer. Classified as an archivist, but trained as a historian, I fancy the title manuscript historian. At the beginning of 1995, I left the dusty documents and became a professor. I find it an exciting adventure. At Morgan State University I hope to guide many others in their tentative explorations of little-known historical terrain."

* * *

Tony Harrison

HARRISON, Tony 1937-

PERSONAL: Born April 30, 1937, in Leeds, Yorkshire, England; son of Harry Ashton (a baker) and Florence (Horner) Harrison; married Rosemarie Crossfield Dietzsch (an artist), January 16, 1960 (divorced); married Teresa Stratas (an opera singer), 1984; children: (first marriage) Jane, Max. *Education:* University of Leeds, B.A. (classics), 1958, postgraduate work in linguistics. *Religion:* None.

ADDRESSES: *Home*—New York City and Newcastle upon Tyne, England. *Agent*—c/o Gordon Dickerson, 2 Crescent Grove, London 7AH, England.

CAREER: Poet, playwright, and translator. Lecturer at Ahmadu Bello University, Zaria, Nigeria, 1962-66, and Charles University, Prague, 1966-67. Northern Arts Fellow in Poetry at Universities of Newcastle and Durham, 1967-68 and 1976-77; United Nations Educational, Scientific, and Cultural Organization (UNESCO) traveling fellow in poetry, 1969; Gregynog Arts Fellow at University of Wales, 1973-74; resident dramatist at National Theatre, London, 1977-79; UK/US Bi-Centennial Fellow, New York, 1979-80.

MEMBER: Writers' Action Group.

AWARDS, HONORS: Cholmondeley Award for Poetry, Society of Authors, 1969; Geoffrey Faber Memorial Prize, 1972, for *The Loiners;* fellow of the Royal Society of Literature, 1984; Faber Memorial Award; U.S. Bicentennial fellowship; European Poetry Translation Prize.

WRITINGS:

POETRY

Earthworks, Northern House, 1964.
Newcastle Is Peru, Eagle Press, 1969.
The Loiners, London Magazine Editions, 1970.

From "The School of Eloquence" and Other Poems, Rex Collings, 1978.

Continuous: Fifty Sonnets from "The School of Eloquence," Rex Collings, 1981.

A Kumquat for John Keats, Bloodaxe (Newcastle upon Tyne, England), 1981.

U.S. Martial, Bloodaxe, 1981.

Selected Poems, Viking, 1984, Random House, 1987.

v. and other poems (contains *v.* [play], first produced in London at Waterman Arts Centre, 1990), Farrar, 1990.

A Cold Coming: Gulf War Poems, Bloodaxe, 1991.

The Gaze of the Gorgon (contains "The Cold Coming"; filmed poems), Bloodaxe, 1992.

The Shadow of Hiroshima and Other Film/Poems, Faber, 1995.

Permanently Bard: Selected Poetry, edited by Carol Rutter, Bloodaxe, 1995.

Laureate's Block, Penguin, 2000.

Also author of *The Common Chorus,* 1992, and *Prometheus* (filmed poem), 1998. Contributor to *Corgi Modern Poets in Focus,* Volume 4, Corgi, 1971, and *Rex Collings Christmas Book,* Rex Collings, 1976. Contributor to periodicals, including *Guardian.*

OTHER

(Adapter with James Simmons) *Aikin Mata* (play; based on Aristophanes' *Lysistrata;* first produced in Zaria, Nigeria, 1965), Oxford University Press, 1966.

(Translator and adapter) *The Misanthrope* (play; based on Moliere's *Le Misanthrope;* first produced in London at National Theatre, February 22, 1973), Rex Collings, 1973, Third Press, 1973.

(Translator and adapter) *Phaedra Britannica* (play; based on Racine's *Phedre;* first produced in London at Old Vic Theatre, September 9, 1975; produced in New York City at CSC Repertory Theater, December, 1988), Rex Collings, 1975.

(Translator) *The Poems of Palladas,* Anvil Press, 1975.

The Passion (play; first produced in London at Cottesloe Theatre, April 21, 1977), Rex Collings, 1977.

Bow Down (play; first produced at Cottesloe Theatre, July 5, 1977), Rex Collings, 1977.

A Source Book of Dinghies, Ward Lock, 1978.

(Translator) *The Bartered Bride* (libretto for opera; based on the work by Bedrich Smetana; first produced in New York City, October, 1978), E. C. Schirmer, 1978.

(With Philip Sharpe) *Looking Up,* Migrant Press, 1979.

(Translator and adapter) *The Oresteia* (play; based on the work by Aeschylus; first produced in London at Olivier Theatre, November 28, 1981), Rex Collings, 1981.

The Mysteries (three plays; first produced in London at National Theatre, December 22, 1984), Faber, 1985.

Dramatic Verse, 1973-1985, Bloodaxe Books, 1985.

The Trackers of Oxyrhynchus: The Delphi Text 1988 (based on Sophocles' *Ichneutae*), Faber, 1988.

Square Rounds, produced at the National Theatre, 1992.

(Translator) Victor Hugo, *Le roi s'amuse/The Prince's Play,* Faber (London), 1996.

Author of lyrics for the film *Bluebird,* 1976. Author of *The Big H,* a television drama broadcast on the BBC, December 26, 1984, and of *Medea: A Sexwar Opera,* produced in 1985. Contributor to British magazines and newspapers.

Also author of *Voortrekker,* 1972; *The Fire Gap,* 1985; *Theatre Works, 1973-1985,* 1986; *Black Daisies for the Bride,* 1993; *Poetry or Bust,* 1993; *A Maybe Day in Kazakhstan,* 1994; and *Plays 3,* 1996. Editor and translator, *Poems of Palladas of Alexandria,* 1973.

SIDELIGHTS: Tony Harrison has enjoyed significant success as a poet, playwright, translator, and screenwriter. According to Simon Armitage in *New Statesman,* Harrison sees himself as a poet, regardless of the format of his writing, which also includes "journalistic pieces." "[H]e sees it all as part of the same task, the task of being a poet," stated Armitage. C. E. Lamb noted in *Dictionary of Literary Biography* that Harrison "has through his work as a poet and translator developed a technical skill of extraordinary brilliance, wit, and vigor, which has recently allowed him to support in his poetry themes of immense personal and historical pain. As a translator, he has enormous range; he has had equal success with Racine, Moliere, and Aeschylus, always rendering the plays completely new while retaining the essential qualities of the originals."

Among other qualities, Armitage is "impressed with the way [Harrison] deals with his upbringing and background in his poems, and more specifically, his accent." "Who'd have thought," remarked Armitage, "that some of t'most moving poems in t'language would have been composed in a form of English normally reserved for sheep-shaggers and colliers?" "Harrison is a distinctly British poet, one whose central poetic concern is with a distinctly British problem," observed Mary Kaiser in a *World Literature Today* review, calling Harrison's 1995 collection *Permanently Bard: Selected Poetry,* "an accessible overview of Harrison's poetry." Harrison has a "predominant fascination with social and class conflict," stated Kaiser, who noted that "throughout his work the dynamic of an overlooked minority resisting an elite and powerful majority plays itself out, whether the context is ancient Greece or Rome, the postwar Leeds of his childhood, or contemporary London."

Born into a Yorkshire working-class family, Harrison's lifelong artistic concerns have been shaped by his efforts to bridge the gap between his working-class origins and his upper-class education. At age eleven, he was one of six working-class boys to win a scholarship to the prestigious Leeds Grammar School, an experience to which his poetry has returned countless times, beginning with "The School of Eloquence." Harrison's work on class has threatened and dismayed some critics while delighting others. Writing in the *Times Literary Supplement,* Patricia Craig summarized the critical confusion surrounding Harrison's work: "Is Harrison a proletarian poet, and if so, what does he mean by displaying all the resources of language and scholarship traditionally denied to the working class? Is his purpose to restore to the verse-drama all the vitality that went out of it earlier in the century, and if it is, why does he allow himself to get diverted into sonnet sequences and the like?" To ask such questions, Craig contended, is to miss the point, for the essence of Harrison's work is to unify widely divergent concerns, styles, and experiences into a coherent, if ironic view, helping the reader to see commonly understood experiences in a new way.

In Harrison's first full-length book of poetry, *The Loiners,* the author explored his relationship with citizens of the working-class community of Leeds, who are known as Loiners. Yet, reflecting Harrison's own experiences of teaching in Nigeria and working in Prague, the book ranges widely in location and topic, from childhood encounters with sex in Leeds to tales of love in Eastern Europe. In a review of *The Loiners, Listener*'s John Fuller concluded, "The sheer vigour and intelligence of Harrison's poetry is as heady as young wine, and should produce great things when it matures."

A pivotal point in Harrison's career came with his translation of Moliere's *Le Misanthrope,* which he undertook at the invitation of London National Theatre director John Dexter. Harrison's previous dramatic work—*Aikin Mata,* a version of *Lysistrata* set in Nigeria—had focused on showing a classic play as a living work. His later dramatic writing continued this pattern: he set *The Misanthrope* in 1966, earning the praise of the London *Observer*'s Robert Brustein, who called it "dazzling, a work of art in its own right, brilliantly witty, clever and conversational . . . the most actable version of Moliere I know." Harrison went on to create a version of *Phedre* set in the British Raj, to create a modern version of the fifteenth-century York mystery plays, and to find other ways of adapting classical works into modern idiom. In 1977, he became the resident dramatist at the National Theatre for two years, during which time he also completed *Bow Down,* an original exploration of traditional and ancient ballads.

Harrison's next full-length book of poetry appeared in 1978. *From "The School of Eloquence" and Other Poems* was a more explicit exploration of class issues than *The Loiners* had been, and as such, provoked more critical controversy. Writing in *Encounter,* Alan Brownjohn found Harrison's insights "hammered into crude containers for heavy irony and his very own brand of chip-on-the-shoulder coarseness," while in the *Spectator,* Emma Fisher found the poems "clever, chewy, good but indigestible like rock buns." In a *Times Literary Supplement* review of *Continuous,* Christopher Reid found Harrison "frequently both touching and funny when he writes about his own role as a poet" and described the book as "splendidly rich . . . , full of wit, tenderness, honesty, intelligence and anger."

"It is [Harrison's] obsession to convey a message—whether personal or political—to the public at large that persuades many fellow poets of Harrison's qualifications as poet laureate," asserted Francis Gilbert, who recognized in *New Statesman and Society* that "Harrison has been tacitly acknowledged as poet laureate of the hard left for many years now." After "almost two decades writing poetry containing his optimistic views on socialism" Harrison turned his attention to "his personal life," reported Gilbert. His optimism declined "by the mid-1980s," but that "his belief in 'unadulterated' socialism remains to this day." "[B]y the nineties, when the revolution Harrison spent so many years preparing still showed no sign of taking place, the poet mined from the class war to his personal life," wrote Gilbert. In a *Times Literary Supplement* article, Tim Kendall recognized that "Harrison's poetry in recent years has become increasingly public and politically engaged." Reviewing *Laureate's Block,* Kendall, who noted the 2000 collection as "poet as controversialist," wrote, "Sending back his rhyming bulletins from Iraq and Bosnia, or pronouncing on the wickedness of the monarchy and the failure of God to exist, Harrison has sought to appal the forces of the establishment." "Watching him breaking butterflies on the wheel of his remorseless pentameters proves an unedifying spectacle," remarked

Kendall, who judged the poetry in *Laureate's Block* as "maddeningly uneven." The work, however, "becomes more successful when Harrison retreats into the private realm."

Critics have generally praised Harrison over the years, finding his work has grown in depth, maturity, and mastery of the language. In a London *Times* review of *Selected Poems,* Robert Nye noted that Harrison "has been hailed as the first genuine working-class poet England has produced this century." Harrison's dramatic work also continues to win critical praise. He is particularly noted for the "actable" quality of his dramatic writing, which led Oswyn Murray, writing in the *Times Literary Supplement,* to name him "our leading theatrical poet" and describe him as "genuinely a poet of the theatre, not a poet attempting to write for the theatre."

In fact, the title poem of *The Gaze of the Gorgon* was written for television and was broadcast on the BBC. "In it," explained Michael Lockwood in *School Library Journal.* "Tony Harrison uses Greek myth and an elaborate narrative concerned with the statutes of German poets to trace the dehumanizing force of war as it has re-emerged in recent conflicts." Concerned primarily with war, the book also includes "The Cold Coming," a poem spoken in the voice of an Iraqi soldier killed at the end of the Gulf War. More of Harrison's works written for the theater and television were published in *The Shadow of Hiroshima and Other Film/Poems.* According to the book's back cover, the purpose of the film/poems is "to confront the major horrors of the twentieth century." *Times Literary Supplement* critic Mick Imlah remarked, "Harrison's effort is not without its moments of strain . . . but the whole casts its dark imprint firmly on the mind." Armitage claimed that "Harrison's achievements in [the] poetic fields [within film and television] have helped to create the opportunity for others, such as me, to have a go."

BIOGRAPHICAL/CRITICAL SOURCES:

BOOKS

Byrne, Sandie, *H, v., & O: The Poetry of Tony Harrison,* Manchester University Press, 1998.

Byrne, editor, *Tony Harrison: Loiner,* Oxford University Press, c. 1997.

Contemporary Literary Criticism, Volume 43, Gale, 1987.

Dictionary of Literary Biography, Volume 40: *Poets of Great Britain and Ireland since 1960,* Gale, 1985.

Tony Harrison: Loiner, Clarendon Press, 1997.

PERIODICALS

Economist, January 23, 1993, p. 83.

Encounter, March, 1979, Alan Brownjohn, review of *From "The School of Eloquence" and Other Poems.*

Honest Ulsterman, September-October, 1970.

Listener, October 8, 1970, John Fuller, review of *The Loiners.*

Los Angeles Times Book Review, November 1, 1987, p. 5.

Nation, January 4, 1993, p. 29.

New Statesman and Society, April 25, 1997, Simon Armitage, "Tony Harrison Is Sixty: Simon Armitage Salutes the Master," p. 45; April 2, 1999, Francis Gilbert, "Tony Harrison: Poet Laureate of the Hard Left, the Bennite Bard Still Awaits the Revolution," p. 18.

New York Times, December 17, 1988.

New York Times Book Review, November 29, 1987, p. 25; November 18, 1990, p. 24.

School Library Journal, February, 1993, p. 37.

Spectator, December 9, 1978; November 28, 1992, p. 51.

Times (London), December 6, 1984; December 22, 1984; January 18, 1985; September 7, 1990.

Times Literary Supplement, January 15, 1982, p. 49; January 4, 1985, p. 10; June 6, 1986, p. 615; November 29, 1991, p. 24; August 11, 1995, p. 18; April 7, 2000, Time Kendall, "Putting the Bulletin," p. 29.

Washington Post Book World, January 31, 1988, p. 4; July 22, 1990, p. 4.

World Literature Today, winter, 1997, Mary Kaiser, "Permanently Bard: Selected Poetry, p. 157.

Village Voice, March 20, 1990, p. 78.

Voice Literary Supplement, March 20, 1990, p. 78.*

* * *

HARRISON, William (Neal) 1933-

PERSONAL: Born October 29, 1933, in Dallas, TX; son of Samuel Scott and Mary Etta (Cook) Harrison; married Merlee Kimsey, February 2, 1957; children: Laurie, Sean, Quentin. *Education:* Texas Christian University, B.A., 1955; Vanderbilt University, M.A., 1959; graduate study at University of Iowa, 1962.

ADDRESSES: *Office*—Department of English, University of Arkansas, Fayetteville, AR 72701. *Agent*—Owen Laster, William Morris Agency, 1325 Avenue of the Americas, New York, NY 10019.

CAREER: University of Arkansas, Fayetteville, member of English department faculty, 1964—.

AWARDS, HONORS: Guggenheim fellowship, 1973-74; National Endowment for the Arts grant, 1977; Christopher Award, 1979, for work in television.

WRITINGS:

Roller Ball Murder, and Other Stories (also see below), Morrow (New York, NY), 1974.

Contributor of short stories to magazines and anthologies.

NOVELS

The Theologian, Harper (New York, NY), 1965.
In a Wild Sanctuary, Morrow (New York, NY), 1969.
Lessons in Paradise, Morrow (New York, NY), 1971.
Africana, Morrow (New York, NY), 1977.
Savannah Blue, Richard Marek (New York, NY), 1981.
Burton and Speke (also see below), Richard Marek (New York, NY), 1982.
Three Hunters, Random House (New York, NY), 1989.
The Buddha in Malibu: New and Selected Stories, University of Missouri Press (Columbia, MO), 1998.
The Blood Latitudes, MacMurray and Beck (Denver, CO), 1999.

SCREENPLAYS

Rollerball (screenplay; based on story "Roller Ball Murder"), United Artists, 1975.
A Shining Season (television screenplay; based on the book by William Buchanan), Columbia Pictures Television, 1979.
(With Bob Rafelson) *Mountains of the Moon* (screenplay; based on *Burton and Speke* and the journals of Sir Richard Francis Burton), TriStar Pictures, 1990.

Author of screenplays for television and film.

SIDELIGHTS: Many of William Harrison's writings focus on the lives of the alienated and the disaffected. The themes of several of his novels and of his screenplay for *Rollerball* concern the struggle of individuals against society and its traditional mores and values. In some of Harrison's novels, such as *The Theologian,* the characters create their own tortured worlds. In other of his works—*Rollerball,* for example—it is the world itself that has gone awry, and the heroes are left to challenge the established powers.

The protagonist of *The Theologian,* Randle Fast, is a seminarian in the rural South. Increasingly obsessed with the occult and with the wife of his mentor, Fast moves further and further from conventional mores until he breaks completely with orthodox religious and moral values. Ultimately, Fast, whose life is "colored by peyote dreams and desperate desires" as Martin Levin observed in the *New York Times Book Review,* emerges as a psychopathic murderer. According to J. S. Phillipson in *Best Sellers,* Fast is "amoral" and thus becomes "in the traditional Judaeo-Christian view, something less than human. . . . Using the standards of an amoral society, [Harrison] has produced another antihero of the sort common in present-day literature."

The four misfit graduate students of *In a Wild Sanctuary* are also at odds with a society that they see as corrupt and unbearable but cannot seem to transcend. The four—"linked not by mutual sympathy so much as by this personal understanding of each other's solitude," as a *Times Literary Supplement* critic commented—make a pact to commit suicide one by one and to leave no clue of the pact or the motive. When three of the four friends begin to waver, they are driven on by Clive, who is "no mere misfit," according to Levin, "but a gaudy psychopath in the Leopold-Loeb tradition." "Yes, it strains the credulity at first," wrote the *New York Times* critic John Leonard, but as the four students "wound one another and drink poisonous abstractions, and fail to connect private despairs with public violence (Vietnam)—the attitudinizing achieves a mad logic of its own." A twist in the plot reveals the finally ordered suicides to not be suicides at all, but rather murders perpetrated by Clive and then discovered by the father of one of the dead students. The final confrontation between Clive and the father is, said Leonard, "a shouting into the wind across a generational, and moral divide, [that turns] suicide into murder, and opens a hole in our conceptual world beyond which ideas have become monsters."

In *Africana,* a man named Leo and his band of mercenaries troop across Africa, crossing countries in societal and political upheaval and fighting wars wherever they can find them, in order to avoid their internal "civilization," or what E. S. Duvall called in *Atlantic,* "the bitter truth . . . , [the] mundanity of spirit [that] lies behind their violent self-assertion." *Africana,* said Robert Brian in *Times Literary Supplement,* is a pastiche of fable, philosophy, poetry, and adventure story in which the crazed, "uncivilized" Leo and his mercenaries are contrasted with such historical figures as United Nations Secretary General Dag Hammerskjold. As the two visions of reality—the uncivilized and the civilized—are brought to confront one another, there is a stalemate. Hammerskjold, Brian noted, dies as he dreams "of ordering chaos in Africa," two of the mercenaries fade into the domesticity of suburban London, and Leo perishes as he machine-guns bathers on a Mombasa beach, unable to find peace in any country or culture. Brian commented, "Violence is set against tameness, the wild against the domestic, war against peace, the individual against the group, man against woman."

Harrison again emphasizes the contrast between the "civilized" and the "uncivilized" in *Savannah Blue,* when he pits American businessmen and the C.I.A. against Quent Clare, second-generation colonialist in Africa. When Clare's mother dies of a disease transmitted by some visiting Americans, Clare becomes "obsessed with the collision of cultures in the modern world [and then] goes on a one-man spree of savage civil disobedience," according to Eric Zorn in *Chicago Tribune Book World. Savannah Blue* pits Clare against not only the American agents sent to apprehend him, but also against "the influences of American ways on the savage purity of African culture," as Zorn observed. This failed to impress *New York Times* critic Anatole Broyard; he found *Savannah Blue* "carelessly, even condescendingly written" and lacking in realistic characters.

The film *Rollerball,* based on Harrison's short story, "Roller Ball Murder," also examines the clash between the individual and society. In *Rollerball, Time* critic Jay Cocks wrote, Harrison "champion[s] nonconformity and the glories of individuality against a faceless state." The film is set in 2018, and the brutal game of rollerball is designed to be "the bloodletter of mankind's aggressive instinct, . . . the cure for war, and the emblem of a unified world that . . . has mysteriously rid [itself] of opinion, poverty, and every foreseeable physical distress," as Penelope Gilliatt commented in the *New Yorker.* The game, meant to demonstrate to spectators that individual effort is futile, succeeds as a cultural pacifier until one rollerball player manages to remain so long in the sport that he becomes a national hero, thus challenging the corporate state's power and authority. "*Rollerball* isn't a movie," according to Arthur Cooper in *Newsweek,* "it's a protest demonstration . . . [against] the increasing sterility of modern life."

The historical novel *Burton and Speke* and its film adaptation, *Mountains of the Moon,* focus on a famous nonconformist of the nineteenth century, Sir Richard Francis Burton, who was a noted explorer and also a rebel against Victorian sexual prudery; he translated erotic literature such as the *Kama Sutra* and *The Perfumed Garden* into English. The story follows the Irish Burton and Englishman John Hanning Speke on their travels through Africa in search of the source of the Nile. It also examines how the issue of credit for discoveries strained their friendship, and makes the case that Speke was a repressed homosexual and in love with Burton. Burton is shown to be open-minded toward African culture, an attitude atypical of Europeans in his time; Desson Howe, reviewing *Mountains of the Moon* for the *Washington Post,* wrote: "In reality Burton had nothing but contempt for Africans." Many other aspects of the film, according to Howe, are historically inaccurate as well; overall, it is "not only factually but dramatically disappointing," nothing more than a "colonial buddy picture." Roger Ebert of the *Chicago Sun-Times,* however, asserted that the movie "is completely absorbing. It tells its story soberly and intelligently, and with quiet style." Although an epic, "it's not a movie about adventure and action, it's an epic about the personalities of the men who endured incredible hardships because of their curiosity, egos, greed or even because of their nobility," Ebert related, adding that *Mountains of the Moon* is certain to make viewers want to learn more about Burton. Another *Washington Post* reviewer, Rita Kempley, deemed the script, "slightly muzzy," but still thought *Mountains of the Moon* was "an epic worth discovering," and "not only touching but irreverent." On the whole, she observed, "this saga has the feel of a traveler's dusty journal, full of hope and terror, exhilaration and despair."

The novel *The Blood Latitudes* is yet another work set in Africa. Buck Hobbs, a young journalist, disappears while on assignment there; his father, Will, a onetime Africa-based correspondent now retired in London, goes in search of him and is caught up in the war between the Hutu and Tutsi tribes in Rwanda. Will sees that Africa has changed greatly over the years, and he finds the war's atrocities appalling, but, as a *Publishers Weekly* critic noted, "must struggle against his temptation to become a killer himself." Also woven into the story is the competition between father and son, and it is not only professional but personal—Will has fallen in love with Buck's wife, Kay. *New York Times Book Review* contributor Jonathan Miles deemed *The Blood Latitudes* "bleakly amoral and rather ugly," but a *Kirkus Reviews* writer called it "Harrison's most deeply pondered work, masterfully restrained in style." The *Publishers Weekly* commentator concluded, "Harrison's suspenseful tale provides a compelling picture of a continent in turbulence and a journalist rediscovering his voice and identity."

BIOGRAPHICAL/CRITICAL SOURCES:

PERIODICALS

Atlantic, June, 1977.
Best Sellers, October 15, 1965; November 1, 1969; July 7, 1977.
Booklist, March 15, 2000, Grace Fill, review of *The Blood Latitudes,* p. 1327.
Chicago Sun-Times, March 23, 1990, Roger Ebert, review of *Mountains of the Moon.*
Chicago Tribune Book World, May 10, 1981.
Commonweal, July 18, 1975.
Kirkus Reviews, February 15, 2000, review of *The Blood Latitudes,* p. 194.
Library Journal, September 1, 1965; January 15, 1970; March 15, 1971; March 1, 1981.
New Republic, July 26, 1975.
Newsweek, November 3, 1969; July 7, 1975.
New Yorker, July 7, 1975.
New York Times, October 30, 1969; February 7, 1981, "Books of the Times," section 2, p. 31.
New York Times Book Review, October 24, 1965; November 30, 1969; July 12, 1998, Paula Friedman, review of *The Buddha in Malibu;* May 7, 2000.
Publishers Weekly, August 11, 1969; October 12, 1970; January 11, 1971; March 7, 1977; December 12, 1980; February 21, 2000, review of *The Blood Latitudes,* p. 63.
Saturday Review, August 9, 1975.
Time, December 19, 1969; July 7, 1975.
Times Literary Supplement, December 11, 1970; December 2, 1977.
Washington Post, March 23, 1990.
Washington Post Book World, November 23, 1982.*

* * *

HAYES, Penny 1940-
A pseudonym

PERSONAL: Born February 10, 1940, in Johnson City, NY. *Education:* State University of New York at Buffalo, B.S., 1969, M.S., 1970. *Avocational interests:* Hiking, mountain climbing, singing, reading, and gardening.

ADDRESSES: Agent—c/o Naiad Press, P.O. Box 10543, Tallahassee, FL 32302.

CAREER: Worked as typist and keypunch operator for six years before attending college; special education teacher, 1970—; writer, 1981—.

MEMBER: Adirondack Forty-sixers (mountain-climbing group), Cayuga Chimes (women's barbershop chorus; vice president).

WRITINGS:

LESBIAN FEMINIST NOVELS

The Long Trail, Naiad Press (Tallahassee, FL), 1986.
Yellowthroat, Naiad Press (Tallahassee, FL), 1988.
Montana Feathers, Naiad Press (Tallahassee, FL), 1990.
Grassy Flats, Naiad Press (Tallahassee, FL), 1992.
Kathleen O'Donald, Naiad Press (Tallahassee, FL), 1994.
City Lights, Country Candles, Naiad Press (Tallahassee, FL), 1998.
Omaha's Bell, Naiad Press (Tallahassee, FL), 1999.

Contributor to anthologies, including *Of the Summits,* Adirondack Forty-Sixers, 1991; *The Erotic Naiad,* Naiad Press (Tallahassee, FL), 1992; *The Romantic Naiad,* Naiad Press (Tallahassee, FL), 1992; and *The Mysterious Naiad,* Naiad Press (Tallahassee, FL), 1994.

SIDELIGHTS: Penny Hayes told *CA:* "I have taught special education for twenty-four years with four and a half of those years spent in West Virginia schools, deep in the coal mining areas. There coal dust collected so quickly and so thick overnight that it was necessary to dust chairs, desks and tables before the children and I could begin our school day.

"I've always been interested in writing, but it wasn't until I was thirty-nine—with the full intention of being published by the time I was forty—that I took my quest seriously. A great motivating factor in disciplining myself for writing came from watching athletes on television. It took a couple of years to decide that if those men and women could drive themselves day after day, year after year, to gain what they wanted, I could do the same. It wasn't easy to sit down daily the first few months. It took every bit of discipline I had. Five years passed before my first manuscript was accepted for publication. Writing is now something that I must do. It has become an important part of my daily routine and my life.

"Originally, there were no major circumstances surrounding the creation of my plots. My purpose for writing a book was the enjoyment of spinning a good old yarn; nothing necessarily political, nothing deep or earth shaking; just a little interesting bit of history characterizing the way things were and the way they might have been for women at that time. Other purposes were to depict strong women, mostly lesbian feminists, presenting how they might have adjusted to and overcome difficulties they encountered.

"I've since made modifications in my philosophy of writing, having picked up important views from friends and critics. Heeding their advice has made each book I've completed more meaningful, more challenging and much more difficult than when I first began writing.

"I like to add historical information to my narratives, making them as factual as possible. I use antique dictionaries, newspapers, magazines, encyclopedias, and authors from yesteryear. I also glean information from modern-day writers. Films, talk shows and notes from people who live or once lived areas in which the story takes place may become part of the plot or background. I am uncomfortable sending out any manuscript without first having visited the locale of each novel.

"I write twelve months of the year—seven days a week during the winter months and four or five during the more pleasant weather. Some days I will write for only a couple of hours; other days I may spend as many as ten or twelve hours writing. There are times when it is extremely difficult to compose because the day's school activities have left me with little energy. However, a book was never completed without its author helping it along."

* * *

HENLEY, Virginia 1935-

PERSONAL: Born December 5, 1935, in Bolton, Lancashire, England; daughter of Thomas (a steelworker) and Lillian (Bleakley) Syddall; married Arthur Howard Henley (an architect), July 7, 1956; children: Sean, Adam. *Education:* Attended University of Toronto, 1966-67. *Religion:* Anglican.

ADDRESSES: Home—Beamsville, Ontario, Canada, and St. Petersburg, Florida. *E-mail*—VIRHENLEY@aol.com.

CAREER: Steel Co. of Canada, Hamilton, Ontario, Canada, executive secretary, 1953-56; Labatts Brewery, London, Ontario, Canada, assistant buyer, 1956-61; writer, 1977—.

WRITINGS:

HISTORICAL ROMANCE NOVELS

The Irish Gypsy, Avon (New York, NY), 1982, published as *Enticed,* Island Books (New York, NY), 1994.

Bold Conquest, Avon (New York, NY), 1983.

A Skulk of Foxes, Avon (New York, NY), 1984.

The Raven and the Rose, Dell (New York, NY), 1987.

The Hawk and the Dove, Dell (New York, NY), 1988.

The Falcon and the Flower (first book in "Plantagenet" trilogy), Dell (New York, NY), 1989.

The Pirate and the Pagan, Dell (New York, NY), 1990.

The Dragon and the Jewel (second book in "Plantagenet" trilogy), Dell (New York, NY), 1991.

Wild Hearts, Avon (New York, NY), 1993.

Tempted, Dell (New York, NY), 1993.

Seduced, Dell (New York, NY), 1994.

Desired, Dell (New York, NY), 1995.

Enslaved, Island Books (New York, NY), 1995.

(With Brenda Joyce, Fern Michaels, and Jo Goodman) *A Gift of Joy,* Zebra Books (New York, NY), 1995.

Dream Lover, Delacorte (New York, NY), 1997.

A Year and a Day, Delacorte (New York, NY), 1998.

(With Katherine Kingsley, Rebecca Paisley, and Stephanie Mittman) *A Christmas Miracle,* Island Books (New York, NY), 1998.

A Woman of Passion, Delacorte (New York, NY), 1999.

The Marriage Prize, Delacorte (New York, NY), 2000.

The Border Hostage (third book in "Plantagenet" trilogy), Delacorte (New York, NY), 2001.

Henley's works have been translated into other languages, including Spanish, French, Cantonese, German, and Italian.

WORK IN PROGRESS: The Lion's Share, a novel set in the Regency period, for Signet.

SIDELIGHTS: Author Virginia Henley once commented: "After my mother died of cancer in 1976, I desperately needed an outlet. She had been deeply interested in the occult and was a voracious reader. The books I gave her had to become lighter in subject matter, and we both started to enjoy historical romances. I decided I could write them as well as read them.

"Women need a romantic escape from everyday realities. I don't want women to read me to raise their consciousness! I want them to derive pure pleasure and escape. A romantic novel is a small luxury, like chocolates or perfume, with which a woman can indulge herself. If just one woman can put her feet up after she puts the kids to bed and lose herself in a book I have written, I will be satisfied. All of us at times meet situations we think we cannot face, but somehow we manage to cope, as my heroines do. I hope that between the first and last pages of any of my novels my heroine grows as a woman and as a human being, but that is all I require of her."

Reviewers note that Henley's heroines are also frequently strongminded and physically passionate. For example, Elizabeth Hardwick, the protagonist of *A Woman of Passion,* is "comfortable with her own highly erotic nature and force of will," reports Melanie Duncan in *Booklist.* This character, based on an historical figure, is an oft-married noblewoman and friend of Queen Elizabeth I of England. Political rivalries and intrigues figure importantly in this novel, but the romance takes priority. This is a consistent pattern in Henley's work; she has noted that while she tries to give readers a large helping of accurate history, her primary aim is to provide them with a lusty, romantic tale. Her body of work has brought her a "reputation for bold, bawdy storytelling," as a *Publishers Weekly* contributor observes in a review of *Desired.* Her novels are more sexually explicit than many in the romance genre; a *Kirkus Reviews* critic relates that in *Dream Lover,* her first hardcover, "she titillates with sex talk, incorporates common parlance for intercourse, and calls some sex organs by their less-exalted names." *A Year and a Day* contains "graphic sex" and "occasionally unorthodox sexual fantasies," reports Kristin Ramsdell in *Library Journal.*

Henley's stories are usually set in the British Isles, and many, like *A Woman of Passion,* feature historical personages. *A Year and Day,* which takes place in medieval Scotland, is the fictional love story of an unconventional young woman with healing powers and an English lord desperate for an heir, but in the background are historical figures such as Scottish king Robert the Bruce and independence fighter William Wallace. The Plantagenet rulers of England play key roles in the trilogy consisting of *The Falcon and the Flower, The Dragon and the Jewel,* and *The Marriage Prize.* Some of Henley's work touches on more than one historical period; *Enslaved* has a frustrated eighteenth-century British aristocrat time-traveling back to the era of the Roman Empire to meet the man who can arouse her passions.

Some critics find Henley's dialogue occasionally anachronistic, with modern phrases such as "cut to the chase," and are less than impressed with her writing style in general, feeling that action takes precedence over character development. In *Dream Lover,* "some characters are inconsistent . . . as suits the tale," says a *Publishers Weekly* reviewer. In *A Woman of Passion,* according to another *Publishers Weekly* commentator, the portrayal of Elizabeth Hardwick is "stifled . . . by the confines of the romantic fiction genre." Still, several critics think Henley produces quality work within romance fiction's conventions. In a *Booklist* review of *A Year and a Day,* Patty Engelmann observes that the expected happy resolution of the lovers' problems comes "with humor, wit, and lusty encounters." A *Publishers Weekly* contributor remarks of the same book, "Steamy sex and bloody battles are vividly detailed in a nicely paced narrative that uses genre stereotypes without apology and to good effect." And *Desired,* in the opinion of a *Publishers Weekly* writer, is a hard-to-put-down volume that will have readers "intrigued by the adventure, mesmerized by the pageantry and stunned by the book's ribaldry."

BIOGRAPHICAL/CRITICAL SOURCES:

PERIODICALS

Booklist, January 1, 1997, Melanie Duncan, review of *Dream Lover,* p. 820; February 1, 1998, Patty Engelmann, review of *A Year and a Day,* p. 899; May 1, 1999, Melanie Duncan, review of *A Woman of Passion,* p. 1581.

Kirkus Reviews, December 1, 1996; January 1, 1998, review of *A Year and a Day.*

Library Journal, February 15, 1998, Kristin Ramsdell, review of *A Year and a Day,* p. 129; March 1, 2000, review of *The Marriage Prize,* p. 85.

Publishers Weekly, June 25, 1982; July 22, 1988, p. 53; July 21, 1989, p. 54; October 26, 1990, p. 64; January 2, 1995, review of *Desired,* p. 70; January 6, 1997, review of *Dream Lover,* p. 65; December 1, 1997, review of *A Year and a Day,* p. 43; June 14, 1999, review of *A Woman of Passion,* p. 49; June 12, 2000, "Love Stories," p. 56.

OTHER

Virginia Henley's Home Page, http://www.geocities.com/Athens/Atlantis/3504 (May 16, 2001).*

* * *

HERRING, George (C.) 1936-

PERSONAL: Born May 23, 1936, in Blacksburg, VA; son of George and Gordon (Saunders) Herring; married Nancy W. Herring, March 15, 1958 (divorced, May 7, 1991); married Dorothy A. Leathers, August 5, 1995; children: John Waltan, Lisa Herring Harris. *Education:* Roanoke College, B.A., 1957; University of Virginia, M.A., 1962, Ph.D., 1965. *Avocational interests:* Tennis.

ADDRESSES: *Home*—828 Cahaba Rd., Lexington, KY 40502. *Office*—Department of History, University of Kentucky, Lexington, KY 40506. *E-mail*—gherrin@pop.uky.edu.

CAREER: Ohio University, Athens, OH, assistant professor of history, 1965-69; University of Kentucky, Lexington, KY, associate professor then professor, 1969—, chair of Department of History, 1973-76, 1988-91, 1992-96, Hallam Professor of History, 1985-87. Department of State historical advisory committee, member, 1990-96; Kentucky Humanities Council, member of board of advisors, 1990-96; United States Military Academy, visiting professor, 1993-94. *Military service:* U.S. Navy, 1958-60.

MEMBER: Society for Historians of American Foreign Relations (president, 1989).

AWARDS, HONORS: Fellowship, National Endowment for the Humanities, 1976-77; Moncado Prize for Excellence in the Writing of Military History, 1983; advanced research grant, U.S. Army Military History Institute; travel grant, Lyndon Baines Johnson Foundation; distinguished professor, University of Kentucky, 1988; Fulbright Award, 1991; William B. Sturgill Award for Outstanding Contribution to Graduate Teaching, 1995; Guggenheim fellowship, 1997-98.

WRITINGS:

LBJ and Vietnam: A Different Kind of War, University of Texas Press, 1994.

America's Longest War: The United States and Vietnam, 1950-1975, second edition, Knopf, 1985, third edition, McGraw, 1995.

(Editor, with Kenneth M. Coleman) *The Central American Crisis: Sources of Conflict and the Failure of U.S. Policy,* Scholarly Resources, 1985, revised edition, 1991.

The Secret Diplomacy of the Vietnam War: The Negotiating Volumes of the Pentagon Papers, University of Texas Press, 1983.

The Diaries of Edward R. Stettinius, Jr., 1943-1946, New Viewpoints, 1975.

Aid to Russia, 1941-1946: Strategy, Diplomacy, the Origins of the Cold War, Columbia University Press, 1973.

Editor, *Diplomatic History,* 1982-86. Contributor of articles to periodicals, including *Journal of American History, Political Science Quarterly, Diplomatic History, Virginia Quarterly Review,* and *Military Affairs.*

WORK IN PROGRESS: A volume on foreign relations, for Oxford University Press "History of the United States Series."

* * *

HEYEN, William 1940-

PERSONAL: Born November 1, 1940, in Brooklyn, NY; son of Henry Jurgen (a cabinet maker) and Wilhelmina (Woermke) Heyen; married Hannelore Greiner, July 7, 1962; children: William, Kristen. *Education:* State University of New York College at Brockport, B.S.Ed., 1961; Ohio University, M.A., 1963, Ph.D., 1967.

ADDRESSES: *Home*—142 Frazier St., Brockport, NY 14420. *Office*—Department of English, State University of New York College, Brockport, NY 14420. *E-mail*—WHeyen1@aol.com.

CAREER: Springville High School, New York, 1961-62; State University of New York College at Cortland, instructor in English, 1963-65; State University of New York College at Brockport, assistant professor, 1967-70, associate professor, 1970-73, professor of English and poet-in-residence, 1973-2000. Fulbright lecturer to Germany, 1971-72; visiting professor, University of Hawaii, Honolulu, spring, 1985.

AWARDS, HONORS: Borestone Mountain award, 1966; National Endowment for the Arts fellowship, 1974 and 1984; Guggenheim fellowship, 1977; *Ontario Review* award, 1977; Eunice Tietjens memorial prize from *Poetry* magazine, 1978; Fairchild Award, and Small Press Book Award, both 1997, both for *Crazy Horse in Stillness;* American Academy Witter Bynner prize, 1982.

WRITINGS:

(With William Taggart) *What Happens in Fort Lauderdale* (nonfiction), Grove (New York, NY), 1968.

The Mower, privately printed, 1970.

Depth of Field (poetry), Louisiana State University Press (Baton Rouge, LA), 1970.

(Editor) *A Profile of Theodore Roethke,* C. E. Merrill (Columbus, OH), 1971.

The Fireman Next Door, Slow Loris Press (Buffalo, NY), 1971.

The Train, Valley Press (Rochester, NY), 1972.

The Trail beside the River Platte, Sceptre Press (Rushden, Northamptonshire, England), 1973.

The Pigeons, Perishable Press (Mount Horeb, WI), 1973.

Noise in the Trees: Poems and a Memoir, Vanguard Press (New York, NY), 1974.

Mermaid, Rook Press (Derry, PA), 1975.

The Pearl, Slow Loris Press (Pittsburgh, PA), 1976.

Cardinals, Rook Press (Derry, PA), 1976.

Of Palestine: A Meditation, Abattoir (Omaha, NE), 1976.

Pickerel, Rook Press (Derry, PA), 1976.

Dusk, Rook Press (Derry, PA), 1976.

Eighteen Poems and a Story, Rook Press (Derry, PA), 1976.

The Trench, Rook Press (Derry, PA), 1976.

The Carrie White Auction at Brockport, May 1974, Rook Press (Derry, PA), 1976.

(Editor) *American Poets in 1976,* Bobbs-Merrill (Indianapolis, IN), 1976.

XVII Machines, Rook Press (Derry, PA), 1976.

Ars Poetica, Rook Press (Derry, PA), 1976.

Mare, Rook Press (Derry, PA), 1976.

(Editor) *I Would Also Like to Mention Aluminum: A Conversation with William Stafford,* Slow Loris Press (Buffalo, NY), 1976.

Darkness, Rook Press (Derry, PA), 1977.

Fires, Croissant (Athens, OH), 1977.

The Elm's Home, Scrimshaw Editions (Derry, PA), 1977.

The Swastika Poems, Vanguard Press (New York, NY), 1977.

Son Dream/Daughter Dream, Rook Press (Ruffsdale, PA), 1978.

From This Book of Praise: Poems and a Conversation with William Heyen, Street Press (Port Jefferson, NY), 1978.

The Ash, Banjo Press (Potsdam, NY), 1978.

Witness, Rara Avis Press (Madison, WI), 1978.

Lord Dragonfly, Scrimshaw (Ruffsdale, PA), 1978.

Brockport's Poems, Challenger Press (Brockport, NY), 1978.

The Descent, Sceptre Press (Rushden, Northamptonshire, England), 1979.

The Children, Sceptre Press (Rushden, Northamptonshire, England), 1979.

Long Island Light: Poems and a Memoir, Vanguard Press (New York, NY), 1979.

Evening Dawning, Ewert (Concord, NH), 1979.

The Snow Hen: Sections 1-7 of The Chestnut Rain, a Poem in Progress (also see below), Ewert (Concord, NH), 1979.

Abortion, Stefanik (Ruffsdale, PA), 1979.

The Descent, Sceptre Press (Rushden, Northamptonshire, England), 1979.

Mantle, Ewert (Concord, NH), 1979.

The City Parables, Croissant (Athens, OH), 1980.

The Shy Bird, Rosemary Duggan (Concord, NH), 1980.

Our Light, Tamarack (Syracuse, NY), 1980.

My Holocaust Songs, wood engraving by Michael McCurdy, Ewert (Concord, NH), 1980.

1829-1979: The Bells, Challenger Press (New York, NY), 1980.

December 31, 1979: The Candle, Martin Booth (Knotting, England), 1980.

The Ewe's Song: Sections 8-18 of The Chestnut Rain, a Poem in Progress (also see below), Ewert (Concord, NH), 1980.

Auction, Ewert (Concord, NH), 1981.

Bean, South Congregational Church (Concord, NH), 1981.

Blackberry Light: Sections 19-32 of "The Chestnut Rain," a Poem in Progress (also see below), Ewert (Concord, NH), 1981.

The Eternal Ash, Tamarack (Syracuse, NY), 1981.

The Bees, Tamarack (Syracuse, NY), 1981.

The Trains, Metacom Press (Worcester, MA), 1981.

Lord Dragonfly: Five Sequences, Vanguard Press (New York, NY), 1981.

The Berries, Ewert (Concord, NH), 1982.

Jesus: Three Poems, Tamarack (Syracuse, NY), 1983.

Along This Water, Tamarack (Syracuse, NY), 1983.

Ram Time, Stone House Press (Roslyn, NY), 1983.

Ensoulment, Ewert (Concord, NH), 1983.

The Numinous, Scarab Press (Salisbury, MD), 1983.

(Editor) *The Generation of 2000: Contemporary American Poets,* Ontario Review Press (Princeton, NJ), 1984.

Erika, Poems of the Holocaust, Vanguard Press (New York, NY), 1984.

Wenzel/The Ghost (also see below), Ewert (Concord, NH), 1984.

Winter Letter to Dave Smith, Palaemon Press (Winston-Salem, NC), 1984.

Eight Poems for Saint Walt, with wood engravings by John De Pol, Stone House Press (Roslyn, NY), 1985.

The Cabin, Ewert (Concord, NH), 1985.

The Spruce in Winter, Ewert (Concord, NH), 1985.

At West Hills, Long Island, Stone House Press (Roslyn, NY), 1985.

The Trophy, Ewert (Concord, NH), 1986.

The Chestnut Rain (includes *The Snow Hen, The Ewe's Song, Blackberry Light,* and *Wenzel/The Ghost*), Ballantine (New York, NY), 1986.

Vic Holyfield and the Class of 1957: A Romance (novel), Available Press (New York, NY), 1986.

Brockport Sunflowers, Ewert (Concord, NH), 1986.

The Amber, New England Reading Association (Manchester, NH), 1986.

The Bells, Ewert (Concord, NH), 1987.

Mother and Son, Northouse & Northouse (Dallas, TX), 1987.

What Do You Have to Lose?, Ewert (Concord, NH), 1987.

Four from Brockport, Northouse & Northouse (Dallas, TX), 1988.

Brockport, New York: Beginning with "and" . . . , Northouse & Northouse (Dallas, TX), 1988.

Americans, Ewert (Concord, NH), 1989.

(Editor, with Elizabeth Spires) *The Pushcart Prize Fifteen: 1990-1991, Best of the Small Presses,* Pushcart Press (Wainscott, NY), 1990.

(With L. D. Brodsky) *Falling from Heaven: Holocaust Poems of a Jew and a Gentile,* Timeless Press (St. Louis, MO), 1991.

Pterodactyl Rose: Poems of Ecology, Time Being Books (St. Louis, MO), 1991.

The Shore, with wood engravings by John DePol, Stone House Press (Roslyn, NY), 1991.

Ribbons: The Gulf War, Time Being Books (St. Louis, MO), 1992.

The Tower, Magpie Press (Drayton, England), 1993.

The Host: Selected Poems 1965-1990, Time Being Books (St. Louis, MO), 1994.

With Me Far Away: A Memoir, Stone House Press (Roslyn, NY), 1994.

Crazy Horse in Stillness (poetry), BOA Editions (Brockport, NY), 1996.

Diana, Charles, and the Queen (poetry), BOA Editions (Rochester, NY), 1998.

Pig Notes and Dumb Music: Prose on Poetry, BOA Editions (Rochester, NY), 1998.

Contributor of poems, articles, and essays to periodicals, literary magazines, and newspapers, including *Poetry, New Yorker, American Scholar, Prose, Southern Review, Nation, Texas Studies in Literature and Language, Prairie Schooner, New York Times, Quarterly Review of Literature,* and *Saturday Review.*

SIDELIGHTS: William Heyen is a respected American poet whose work has led many reviewers to compare him to one of his spiritual forefathers, Walt Whitman. Heyen has professed his deep indebtedness to Whitman; he subscribes to the earlier poet's belief that "the poet's art is not to chart but to voyage," and that "poetry is an activity of mind and heart that explores, embraces, and reconciles," according to *Dictionary of Literary Biography* essayist William B. Thesing. Thesing further noted that "Heyen's lyre has basically seven thematic strings—memory, nature, perception, disintegration, death, the past in Long Island and Germany, and the present community in Brockport [where he makes his home]." Heyen's first collection, *Depth of Field,* inspired John T. Irwin to declare in *Poetry:* "This book is a 'must,' and . . . its author seems destined to be an important poet."

Heyen focuses closely on his Long Island memories in *Long Island Light.* The volume is reminiscent of Whitman and also Thoreau, in the opinion of an essayist for *Contemporary Poets,* who advised that "Heyen stays at home and descends within himself into various layers of the past." Like *Leaves of Grass, Long Island Light* is "ever-expanding," commented the writer. "The depth of Heyen's emotional and spiritual commitment, the steady growth of his technical skills, and the intensification of his vision has elevated the people and places of his Long Island past—the farmer Wenzel, Gibbs Pond, Lake Ronkonkoma, Short Beach, St. James Harbor, Nesconset, even the Jericho Turnpike—to the status of myth."

Heyen has shown a persistent concern over his family's German roots and the horrors of the Nazi Holocaust, which was fully expressed in his collection, *The Swastika Poems.* He used a variety of voices and perspectives to try and come to terms with both the victims and perpetrators of Nazi atrocities. It is a difficult but rewarding group of poems, in the opinion of numerous reviewers. The *Contemporary Poets* writer called *The Swastika Poems* "a courageous undertaking, and to read it, to feel its cumulative power is a painful but memorable experience." Other commentators noted the challenges faced by a poet writing about the Holocaust, especially a poet who was not an eyewitness, since, in the words of Sandra McPherson in *American Poetry Re-*

view, "a bare prose account by any survivor of the death camps is so strong that a poet who wasn't there faces a very hard task indeed." Yet Heyen met the challenges well, in the estimation of *Georgia Review* writer Peter Stitt. He declared: "Heyen's book ultimately is as fine and important as it is courageous. These are not poems to be read and reread endlessly for the sheer pleasure of it; they are much too painful for that. I am sure there are many people, in fact, who will not be able to look these poems in the face. And how much harder must they have been to write? . . . This book will not—cannot—be forgotten; it shows decency and human love triumphant over the darkest side of the human spirit, and we cannot ask for much more than that."

Heyen's 1996 collection, *Crazy Horse in Stillness,* is a poetic exploration of the spiritual aspects of George Custer and Crazy Horse, two prominent figures in nineteenth-century American history and the battle between Native Americans and the people of the United States. George Wallace, in *Academic Library Book Review,* wrote that Heyen is "respectful of the complexity of his subject . . . instead of handing us a straightforward plot, with its inevitable distillations and oversimplifications, the poet offers us hundreds of rapid-fire, multi-angled, randomly organized moments. Each is complete, telling, and epigrammatically crystallized detail." Other reviewers found *Crazy Horse in Stillness* to be a great accomplishment. "[Heyen's] ability to maintain the reader's sense of surprise and wonder through an avalanche of poems both surreally plain ('Footnoted') and plainly surreal ('Custer in Cyberspace') is an amazing achievement in itself, enriching our sense of the past with a singular sense of the present," according to Fred Muratori of *Small Press.*

In *Pig Notes and Dumb Music: Prose on Poetry,* Heyen proved that his writing talent extended to prose as well as poetry. Each of the brief pieces in the collection "posits some thought or scene that is rich enough to cause reflection and resonate harmoniously like some beautifully struck bell," commented a *Booklist* reviewer. "Heyen demonstrates sensitivity and playful curiosity while remaining steady in a pursuit of inspiration."

Collections of Heyen's poetry are held at Mugar Memorial Library, Boston University Library, Ohio University—Athens Library, and the University of Rochester Library, New York.

Heyen told *CA:* "[The following] brief prose piece, 'History,' may serve as a sort of parable of what I've been up to in several of my books:

"Evening. I sat at the dining room table, working with tongs, sorting a shoebox of German stamps that had reached me a few months before from Switzerland after an Internet auction.

"I found dozens of glassines thickly packed with issues ranging from the 1850s to my own century's end. Below the glassines, too, were a few inches of loose stamps, used & mint. Thousands of *Briefmarken* in my horde. As I sorted, I was excited, alive. I realized that my American dollars had gone a long way.

"Sorting, I remembered as a boy spending much time with my stamps. But another childhood memory kept crowding in until I wondered why: hour after hour, I'm at my microscope, tilting its mirror to catch the indoor or outdoor light, eyedroppering pondwater onto slides, staring, surprised by the dimensions I can keep focusing into view. Just when I think I've located every organism in a particular drop, another amoeba or paramecium appears, or a grotesque & fearsome hydra that startles me. . . .

"Time passed quickly. I was tonging various stamps into various groups. I mounted some in my albums, placed others in stockbooks, others in new glassines that I arranged in numerical Michel catalogue order in my files. There were the shield varieties of the early confederation, & many Germanias of the early empire, and a great many of the inflation issues of the 1920s, but I am most interested in the issues of the Third Reich.

"I found several of the death's mask Reinhardt Heydrich, the 'Blond Beast' whose assassination led to the annihilation of a village in Czechoslovakia, Lidice, & most of its inhabitants. But of all the propaganda stamps from this period, the greatest quantity were those of variously -sized & -colored Hitler heads. . . .

"As I grew tired & my eyes began to cross, I hoped to at least organize all the stamps in this particular series, but it seemed no matter how long I sorted through the glassines & then the loose stamps at the bottom of the shoe box—all this history emanating from the center of Europe—there was always another right-facing profile of the Fuhrer. Each time he appeared, he seemed smug, enriddled, immortal, not at all surprised to have reached light again, to have made his way even to America. Each time he appeared, I realized I'd never be able to isolate & bring into focus all the animals in this pond."

BIOGRAPHICAL/CRITICAL SOURCES:

BOOKS

Contemporary Authors Autobiography Series, Volume 9, Gale (Detroit, MI), 1989.

Contemporary Literary Criticism, Gale, Volume 13, 1980, Volume 18, 1981.

Contemporary Poets, St. James Press (Detroit, MI), 1996.

Dictionary of Literary Biography, Volume 5: *American Poets since World War II,* Gale (Detroit, MI), 1980.

Heyen, William, *From This Book of Praise: Poems and a Conversation with William Heyen,* Street Press (Port Jefferson, NY), 1978.

Magill, Frank N., editor, *Critical Survey of Literature,* Salem Books (Pasadena, CA), 1992.

Magill, Frank N., editor, *Critical Survey of Poetry,* Salem Press (Englewood Cliffs, NJ), 1983.

PERIODICALS

Academic Poetry Review, summer, 1996, George Wallace, review of *Crazy Horse in Stillness.*

American Poetry Review, November, 1977, Sandra McPherson, review of *The Swastika Poems,* pp. 31-32; January, 1978, Stanley Plumly, "Chapter and Verse"; March, 1980, Dave Smith, "One Man's Music."

Bellingham Review, summer, 1998, John Hoppenthaler, review of *Diana, Charles, and the Queen,* pp. 114-118.

Black Dirt, spring-summer, 1998, pp. 119-167.

Booklist, January 1, 1996, Elizabeth Millard, review of *Crazy Horse in Stillness,* p. 778; January 1, 1998, review of *Pig Notes and Dumb Music,* p. 766.

Bulletin of Bibliography, summer, 1979; October, 1979, Ernest Stefanik, "William Heyen," pp. 157-176.

Choice, October, 1977; March, 1980, Dave Smith, review of *Long Island Light,* pp. 40-43.

Georgia Review, winter, 1977, Peter Stitt, review of *The Swastika Poems,* pp. 957-959; spring, 1980, Peter Stitt, "The Sincere, the Mythic, the Playful," pp. 202-212.

Hudson Review, winter, 1979-80, Vernon Young, review of *Long Island Light,* pp. 621-634.

Library Journal, March 1, 1981, Robert Peters, review of *The City Parables,* p. 562; September 1, 1984, review of *The Generation of 2000,* p. 1676; February 15, 1998, Frank Allen, review of *Diana, Charles, and the Queen,* p. 145.

Manassas Review, summer, 1978, Kenneth MacLean, "Animate Mystique," pp. 70-79; Hayden Carruth, review of *The Swastika Poems,* pp. 97-98.

Modern Poetry Studies, Volume 9, number 2, 1978, Pamela S. Rasso, review of *The Swastika Poems,* pp. 158-60.

New York Times Book Review, October 2, 1977; July 27, 1986, Richard Goodman, review of *Vic Holyfield and the Class of 1957,* p. 18; November 11, 1990, Robert von Hallberg, review of *The Chestnut Rain,* p. 42; November 11, 1990, p. 60; November 29, 1992, Gardner McFall, review of *Ribbons,* p. 18.

Ontario Review, spring-summer, 1975, Tom Marshall, review of *Noise in the Trees,* pp. 90-91; spring, 1980, John R. Reed, review of *Long Island Light,* pp. 81-82.

Parnassus, spring, 1982, Michael McFee, "The Harvest of a Quiet Eye."

Partisan Review, Volume 47, number 2, 1980, Robert Phillips, review of *The Swastika Poems,* pp. 317-318.

Poetry, September, 1971, John T. Irwin, review of *Depth of Field,* pp. 352-353; July, 1975; May, 1983, Bonnie Costello, review of *Lord Dragonfly,* p. 106.

Prose, spring, 1972.

Publishers Weekly, July 13, 1984, *The Generation of 2000,* p. 42; October 26, 1984, review of *Erika,* p. 93; May 2, 1986, review of *Vic Holyfield and the Class of 1957,* p. 72; March 28, 1994, review of *The Host,* p. 89; December 22, 1997, review of *Pig Notes and Dumb Music,* p. 50.

Small Press, September-October, 1997, Fred Muratori, review of *Crazy Horse in Stillness.*

Tar River Poetry, fall, 1996, Elizabeth Dodd, review of *Crazy Horse in Stillness.*

Virginia Quarterly Review, summer, 1977.

Western Humanities Review, summer, 1969, "The Individual Voice: A Conversation with William Heyen," pp. 223-233.

* * *

HEYWOOD, Joe T.
See HEYWOOD, Joseph (T.)

* * *

HEYWOOD, Joseph (T.) 1943-
(Joe T. Heywood)

PERSONAL: Born 1943, in Rhinebeck, NY; son of Edwin T. (a U.S. Air Force officer) and Wilma C. (Hegwood) Heywood; married Sandra V. Phillips, August 21, 1965; children: Timothy Brian, Todd Allan, Troy Joseph, Trevor Michael, Tara Lynne. *Education:* Michigan State University, B.A., 1965; graduate study at Western Michigan University, 1973-75. *Avocational interests:* Reading, cartooning, painting, photography, fishing, coaching ice hockey and soccer.

ADDRESSES: *Home*—1603 Edington, Portage, MI 49002. *Agent*—Betsy Nolan, 50 West 29th St., Suite 9W, New York, NY 10001.

CAREER: Upjohn Co., Kalamazoo, MI, executive director of worldwide public relations, beginning in 1970—; writer. *Military service:* U.S. Air Force, navigator, 1965-70; served in Vietnam; received Distinguished Service Medal and Air Medal with six oak leaf clusters.

WRITINGS:

(Under name Joe T. Heywood) *Taxi Dancer* (novel), Berkley Publishing (New York, NY), 1985.

The Berkut (novel), Random House (New York, NY), 1987.

The Domino Conspiracy (novel), Random House (New York, NY), 1992.

The Snowfly (novel), Lyons, 2000.

Ice Hunter: A Woods Cop Mystery, Lyons, 2001.

ADAPTATIONS:

The Berkut has been optioned for adaptation as a screenplay.

SIDELIGHTS: Joseph Heywood has combined his success as a public relations executive with an impressive sideline as a best-selling novelist. Heywood received a journalism degree from Michigan State University in 1965, but, following a five-year stint in the U.S. Air Force as a navigator, he joined the public relations staff of the Upjohn Company. Writing at night and on weekends, he published his debut novel, *Taxi Dancer,* in 1985. The story of fighter pilots in Vietnam, the book sold more than 70,000 copies.

Heywood followed *Taxi Dancer* with *The Berkut,* a thriller based on the premise that Nazi leader Adolf Hitler survived World War II. Facing defeat in 1945, Hitler is believed to have shot himself in an underground Berlin bunker and left instructions that his remains be incinerated. In *The Berkut,* however, Heywood suggests that an imposter was killed and burned in the bunker, while Hitler, disguised as a refugee, escaped from his enemies. Named for a small Russian eagle that preys on wolves, the novel traces Soviet special agent Vasily Petrov's hunt for Hitler, now known as Herr Wolf. *The Berkut* achieved best-seller status and attracted considerable critical attention. Michael J. Bandler, writing in Chicago *Tribune Books,* deemed the novel a "sizzling thriller" and praised Heywood's "unfailingly compelling" blend of history and fiction. And while *Washington Post* reviewer Richard Harwood called into question the believability of the events portrayed in the book, he nevertheless conceded, "The action is relentless," and added, "There is tension and suspense from beginning to end."

Heywood once told *CA:* "I don't believe in Muses or divine inspiration. Writing is a relatively straightforward process once a story has percolated, scut work in pursuit of a higher order. I write every night, year-round, and start each night by hacking up what I wrote the previous night, which then puts me into the flow of the new material. I write first drafts in longhand with a fountain pen; all subsequent revisions go onto the word processor. I need a 'governor,' and longhand serves that purpose; writing an original on the word processor tends to make it too easy to fly. While a story may be intended to put the reader into a jet stream, the crafting needs to be carefully measured. In car terms, the novel is a hand-built Indy car, not an off-the-production-line model. There's an anachronistic element to my approach as well, a link to times past when virtually all writers hand-wrote their manuscripts, and I relish that connection.

"I work in a dark basement at an oak roll-top desk without a desktop lamp, a television above me (which is on and loud all the time), and surrounded by dusty, musty gewgaws. I need stimuli (sound) to write, but I tend to edit and revise in stone silence. Over the years I've probably heard bits and pieces of several thousand movies. From time to time mice come to check my progress. One year I bought traps to kill them but couldn't handle the reality of it.

"When I'm working, ten or twelve hours can pass in a snap. It's quite extraordinary what happens to time when your nose is down. I have no real advice for aspiring writers other than to write every day and everywhere. I firmly believe that good work will eventually find light, but you have to do the work. For me, it's the work that's good, not the collateral activities related to publishing. My high comes when the first draft is done, not when there are books on shelves. Writing excites rather than depresses—even revisions. Many people have talents for all sorts of endeavors, but few have the discipline to do the work and stay at it. No writer is ever as good as he wants to be, which is where the continuity comes from—the endless drive to do it better, cleaner, more efficiently—this being the contest with yourself, one that ultimately cannot be won. I've always got ten more novels in mind. The world presents me with new ideas virtually every day. I thank it for such generosity."

BIOGRAPHICAL/CRITICAL SOURCES:

BOOKS

Heywood, Joseph, *The Berkut,* Random House, 1987.

PERIODICALS

Booklist, September 1, 1992, Eloise Kinney, review of *The Domino Conspiracy,* p. 36; September 1, 2000, Dennis Dodge, review of *The Snowfly,* p. 65.

Detroit Free Press, March 18, 1987.

Kirkus Reviews, August 15, 2000, review of *The Snowfly,* p. 1135.

Library Journal, August, 1992, Jo Ann Vicarel, review of *The Domino Conspiracy,* p. 149; August, 2000, Fred M. Gervat, review of *The Snowfly,* p. 156.

Los Angeles Times Book Review, September 6, 1987.

New Yorker, September 28, 1987, review of *The Berkut,* p. 98.

New York Times Book Review, November 29, 1987, Stewart Kellerman, review of *The Berkut,* p. 20.

Publishers Weekly, July 10, 1987, Sybil Steinberg, review of *The Berkut,* p. 57; June 15, 1992, review of *The Domino Conspiracy,* p. 82; August 7, 2000, review of *The Snowfly,* p. 76.

Tribune Books (Chicago), September 13, 1987, Michael J. Bandler, review of *The Berkut.*

Washington Post, September 28, 1987, Richard Harwood, review of *The Berkut.*

* * *

HIGGINS, Kathleen M(arie) 1954-

PERSONAL: Born October 15, 1954, in Jacksonville, FL; daughter of Eugene Anthony (in U.S. Navy and Social Security Administration) and Kathryn Ann (a homemaker; maiden name, Merz) Higgins; married Robert Charles Solomon (a professor of philosophy), February 17, 1990. *Education:* University of Missouri at Kansas City, B.A., 1977; Yale University, M.A., 1978, M.Phil., 1979, Ph.D., 1982. *Politics:* Democrat. *Religion:* Roman Catholic.

ADDRESSES: Office—Department of Philosophy, Waggener Hall 408A, University of Texas at Austin, Austin, TX 78712-1180. *E-mail*—plac645@utxvms.cc.utexas.edu.

CAREER: University of Texas at Austin, instructor, 1982-83, assistant professor, 1983-89, associate professor, 1989-95, professor of philosophy, 1995—. University of California, Riverside, visiting assistant professor, 1986-87; University of Auckland, New Zealand, visiting senior lecturer, summers, 1989-92.

MEMBER: North American Nietzsche Society, American Society for Aesthetics (member of board of trustees, 1991-94), American Philosophical Association.

AWARDS, HONORS: Nietzsche's Zarathustra was named an Outstanding Academic Book by *Choice,* 1988-89.

WRITINGS:

Nietzsche's Zarathustra, Temple University Press (Philadelphia, PA), 1987.

(Editor, with husband, Robert C. Solomon) *Reading Nietzsche,* Oxford University Press (New York, NY), 1988.

The Music of Our Lives, Temple University Press (Philadelphia, PA), 1991.

(Editor, with Solomon) *The Philosophy of (Erotic) Love,* University Press of Kansas (Lawrence, KS), 1992.

(Editor, with Lee Bowie and Meredith Michaels) *Thirteen Questions in Ethics,* Harcourt (Fort Worth, TX), 1992, revised edition published as *Thirteen Questions in Ethics and Social Philosophy,* 1998.

(Editor, with Solomon) *The Age of German Idealism,* Routledge (New York, NY), 1993.

(Editor, with Solomon) *From Africa to Zen: An Invitation to World Philosophy,* Rowman & Littlefield (Lanham, MD), 1993.

(Editor, with Solomon) *World Philosophy: A Text with Readings,* McGraw (New York, NY), 1995.

(Editor, with Bernd Magnus) *The Cambridge Companion to Nietzsche,* Cambridge University Press (New York, NY), 1996.

Aesthetics in Perspective, Harcourt (Fort Worth, TX), 1996.

(With Solomon) *A Short History of Philosophy,* Oxford University Press (New York, NY), 1996.

(With Solomon) *A Passion for Wisdom: A Very Brief History of Philosophy,* Oxford University Press (New York, NY), 1997.

Comic Relief: Nietzsche's Gay Science, Oxford University Press (New York, NY), 2000.

(With Solomon) *What Nietzsche Really Said,* Schocken (New York, NY), 2000.

SIDELIGHTS: Kathleen M. Higgins is a professor of philosophy who has written and edited many books in her field, frequently working with Robert C. Solomon, who is her husband and a colleague at the University of Texas at Austin. Among their collaborative efforts is *A Passion for Wisdom: A Very Brief History of Philosophy.* Compressing the history of philosophy into a 132-page volume might seem to be an impossible task, but according to *Library Journal* reviewer Terry C. Skeats, Higgins and Solomon have done an admirable job. Skeats notes that other short histories usually suffer from at least one of three common defects: they ignore significant philosophers or movements; they give nothing more than a simplistic overview; or they focus solely on the Western tradition. Higgins and Solomon avoid "all three pitfalls," claims Skeats. They "keep their history clear and understandable, and the newcomer should have no difficulty tracing its development." *Booklist* commentator Gilbert Taylor also finds *A Passion for Wisdom* to have surprising depth, considering its length. He comments that "the authors . . . deliver an interesting narrative that, if given to Philo 101 students, might turn some of them into majors. . . . A cogent summary capable of exciting reader interest."

Higgins and Solomon took on a more specific subject in their book *What Nietzsche Really Said.* In it, they address the common perception of Nietzsche as "one of the main villains in the story of American decline," as a *Publishers Weekly* reviewer puts it. Many believe that the intellectual and moral standards of the United States have dropped precipitously in the last decades, largely because of "a relativism, skepticism and godlessness that can be traced to the baleful influence of Nietzsche." The coauthors vigorously defend the philosopher, and "in brisk, forthright prose," they "debunk widely accepted myths and rumors about Nietzsche: he was not a German nationalist, not an anti-Semite, did not hate women and plainly opposed everything the Nazis would later stand for," concludes the *Publishers Weekly* writer. Bryce Christensen, a contributor to *Booklist,* remarks: "Their analysis dispels numerous misreadings simply by identifying Nietzsche not as an abstract philosopher but as a literary artist, one who crafted his metaphors and aphorisms with profound psychological insight and shrewd irony."

BIOGRAPHICAL/CRITICAL SOURCES:

PERIODICALS

Booklist, March 15, 1997, Gilbert Taylor, review of *A Passion for Wisdom: A Very Brief History of Philosophy,* p. 1207; January 1, 2000, review of *What Nietzsche Really Said,* p. 836.

Library Journal, September 1, 1993, Terry Skeats, review of *The Age of German Idealism,* p. 187; November 15, 1995, Leon H. Brody, review of *A Short History of Philosophy,* p. 78; April 1, 1997, review of *A Passion for Wisdom: A Very Brief History of Philosophy,* p. 97.

New York Times, February 17, 2000, Christopher Lehmann-Haupt, "A High-End Top 30 List: Myths about Nietzsche, p. B13.

Publishers Weekly, January 10, 2000, review of *What Nietzsche Really Said,* p. 53.*

* * *

HILL, Samuel S(mythe, Jr.) 1927-

PERSONAL: Born October 25, 1927, in Richmond, VA; son of Samuel Smythe (a minister) and Mary L. (Brown) Hill; married Claire Cohen, August 22, 1958 (divorced, 1984); married Helen Louise Thompson, June 29, 1984; children: (first marriage) Sarah, Charles. *Education:* Georgetown College, Georgetown, KY, A.B., 1949; Vanderbilt University, M.A., 1952; Southern Baptist Theological Seminary, B.D., 1953; Cambridge University, postgraduate study, 1955-56; Duke University, Ph.D., 1960. *Politics:* Democrat. *Religion:* Episcopalian. *Avocational interests:* Travel, cycling, mountain hiking.

ADDRESSES: Home—1644 Northwest 10th Ave., Gainesville, FL 32605. *Office*—c/o Department of Religion, University of Florida, Gainesville, FL 32611.

CAREER: Educator and author. Pastor of Baptist church in Burlington, KY, 1953-55; Stetson University, De Land, FL, assistant professor of religion, 1959-60; University of North Carolina, Chapel Hill, assistant professor, 1960-64, associate professor, 1964-67, professor of religion, 1967-72, then chair of department, 1961-70; University of Florida, Gainesville, professor of religion, 1972-94, chair of department, 1972-77. Member of panel, National Endowment for the Humanities, 1978-93, and Mellon Fellowship in Humanities, 1983-92.

MEMBER: American Academy of Religion (regional president, 1973-74; associate director, 1981-83), Society for the Scientific Study of Religion, American Society of Church History, Southern Historical Association.

AWARDS, HONORS: Tanner Award for undergraduate teaching, University of North Carolina, 1964; postdoctoral fellowship from Society for Religion in Higher

Education, 1964-65; excellence in teaching award, University of Florida, 1983; Ring Professorship, University of Florida, 1991.

WRITINGS:

NONFICTION

(With Robert G. Torbet) *Baptists North and South,* Judson (Valley Forge, PA), 1964.

Southern Churches in Crisis, Holt (New York, NY), 1967, revised edition, published under name Samuel S. Hill as *Southern Churches in Crisis Revisited,* University of Alabama Press (Tuscaloosa, AL), 1999.

(With Edgar T. Thompson and others) *Religion and the Solid South,* Abingdon Press (Nashville, TN), 1972.

The South and the North in American Religion, University of Georgia Press (Athens, GA), 1980.

(With Dennis E. Owen) *The New Religious-Political Right in America,* Abingdon Press (Nashville, TN), 1982.

One Name but Several Faces: Variety in Popular Christian Denominations in Southern History, University of Georgia Press (Athens, GA), 1996.

OTHER

(Editor) *Religion in the Southern States: An Historical Study,* Mercer University Press (Macon, GA), 1983.

(Editor) *On Jordan's Stormy Banks: Religion in the South: A Southern Exposure Profile* (revised and expanded edition of article first published in *Southern Exposure,* Vol. 4, no. 3), Mercer University Press (Macon, GA), 1983.

(Editor) *Encyclopedia of Religion in the South,* Mercer University Press (Macon, GA), 1984, revised edition, 1997.

(Author of revised introduction, conclusion, and bibliography) John Lee Eighmy, *Churches in Cultural Captivity: A History of the Social Attitudes of Southern Baptists,* University of Tennessee Press (Knoxville, TN), 1987.

(Editor) *Varieties of Southern Religious Experience,* Louisiana State University Press (Baton Rouge, LA), 1988.

(Reviser) Frank S. Mead, *Handbook of Denominations in the United States,* Abingdon Press (Nashville, TN), 8th edition, 1985, 10th edition, 1995.

Contributor of numerous articles and reviews to periodicals.

SIDELIGHTS: "If the subject is southern religion and if Samuel S. Hill's name accompanies it, look closely—it merits attention," declared Walter B. Shurden in *Christian Century.* That endorsement has been echoed by many reviewers of Hill's books. He has written and contributed to more than a dozen volumes, all concerned with the subject of religion in the American South, among them *Baptists North and South, Southern Churches in Crisis,* and *The New Religious-Political Right in America.* C. H. Lippy, a contributor to *Choice,* credited 1967's *Southern Churches in Crisis* with having "launched the study of religion in the South as a disciplinary endeavor," and hailed its revised edition, *Southern Churches in Crisis Revisited,* as "a seminal work." In that book, Hill proposes that by the mid-twentieth century religion in the southern states was in the grip of a vicious racism that was destroying it from within. In the updated edition, Hill provides historical perspective on his original thesis and comments on a newer threat to southern religion: an obsession with rigidly pure doctrine which stifles the churches' ability to nurture souls and aid in the cause of social justice.

Reviewing Hill's 1984 work *Encyclopedia of Religion in the South,* Mel Piehl in *Library Journal* stated: "This hefty reference work reflects the growth of studies in Southern religion, and satisfies the need for an accessible compendium of current knowledge of the subject." Piehl called the biographies contained in the encyclopedia "brief and solid," and noted that "the denominational and institutional descriptions are admirably succinct and informative." A *Booklist* reviewer concurred: "The editor and his contributor have succeeded in providing a useful summary of facts and scholarly interpretation relative to this broad and important subject." *Encyclopedia of Religion in the South* was revised by Hill in 1997.

BIOGRAPHICAL/CRITICAL SOURCES:

PERIODICALS

Booklist, June 15, 1985, review of *Encyclopedia of Religion in the South,* p. 1441.

Choice, March, 1985, J. R. Kennedy, review of *Encyclopedia of Religion in the South,* p. 962; January, 2000, C. H. Lippy, review of *Southern Churches in Crisis Revisited.*

Christian Century, May 31, 1967; December 14, 1988, Walter B. Shurden, review of *Varieties of Southern Religious Experience,* p. 1160.

Encounter, summer, 1967.

Journal of American History, September, 1989, review of *Varieties of Southern Religious Experience,* p. 570.

Library Journal, April 15, 1982, review of *The New Religious-Political Right in America,* p. 799; January, 1985, Mel Pichl, review of *Encyclopedia of Religion in the South,* p. 74.

South Atlantic Quarterly, winter, 1968.*

* * *

HITCHINS, Keith 1931-

PERSONAL: Born April 2, 1931, in Schenectady, NY. *Education:* Union College, A.B., 1952; Harvard University, A.M, 1953, Ph.D., 1964; attended University of Paris, 1957-58, University of Bucharest, 1960-61, and University of Cluj, 1961-62.

ADDRESSES: Office—Department of History, 309 Gregory Hall, 810 South Wright St., University of Illinois at Urbana-Champaign, Urbana, IL 61801. *E-mail*—khitchin@uiuc.edu; fax: 217-333-2297.

CAREER: Wake Forest University, Winston-Salem, NC, instructor in history, 1958-60 and 1962-1964, assistant professor, 1964-65; Rice University, Houston, TX, assistant professor, 1966-67; University of Illinois at Urbana-Champaign, Urbana, associate professor, 1967-69, professor of history, 1969—. Council for the International Exchange of Scholars, member of advisory committee, 1970-79; International Research and Exchange Board, member of East European screening committee, 1972-75, residential fellow for Hungary, 1973; American Council of Learned Societies, Joint Committee on Eastern Europe, 1982-89.

AWARDS, HONORS: American Council of Learned Societies research fellow in Hungary and Romania, 1969-70; International Research and Exchanges Board, residential fellow in Hungary, 1973; member, Romanian Academy, 1991; Doctor honoris causa, or D.H., University of Cluj, 1991, and University of Sibiu, 1993.

WRITINGS:

The Rumanian National Movement in Transylvania, 1780-1849, Harvard University Press (Cambridge, MA), 1969.

Rumanian Studies, Brill (Leiden, Netherlands), Volume I, 1970, Volume II, 1971-72, Volume III, 1973-75, Volume IV, 1976-79, Volume V, 1980-86.

Orthodoxy and Nationality: Andreiu Saguna and the Rumanians of Transylvania, 1846-1873, Harvard University Press, 1977.

Hungarica 1961-1974: Literaturbericht über Neuerscheinungen zur Geschichte Ungarns von den Arpaden bis 1970, Oldenburg (Munich), 1981.

Studies on Romanian National Consciousness, Nagard (Pelham, NY), 1983.

The Idea of Nation: The Romanians of Transylvania, 1691-1849, Editura stiintifica si enciclopedica (Bucharest), 1985.

(Associate editor) *Great Historians from Antiquity to 1800,* Greenwood Press (New York, NY), 1989.

(Associate editor) *Great Historians of the Modern Age,* Greenwood Press, 1991.

Biserica Ortodoxa Romana in secolul XVIII, Sibiu, 1991.

Constiinta nationala si actiune politica la Romanii din Transilvania, Editura Dacia (Cluj), Volume I: *1700-1868,* 1987, Volume II: *1868-1918,* 1992.

Rumania: 1866-1947, Clarendon Press (Oxford), 1994.

The Romanians, 1774-1866, Clarendon Press, 1996.

Mit si realitate in istoriografia romaneasca, Editura Enciclopedica (Bucharest), 1997.

A Nation Discovered: Romanian Intellectuals in Transylvania and the Ida of Nation, 1700-1848, Editura Enciclopedica, 1999.

A Nation Discovered: The Romanian National Movement in Transylvania, 1860-1914, Editura Enciclopedica, 1999.

Also author of *The Nationality Problem in Austria-Hungary,* published in 1974, and editor of an ongoing series titled "Studies in East European Social History," Brill, 1977—; contributor to periodicals including *American Historical Review, Journal of Modern History, Slavic Review,* and *Slavonic and East European Review;* consulting editor for caucasian studies and contributor to *Encyclopaedia Iranica;* editor of *Journal of Kurdish Studies,* 1995—.

WORK IN PROGRESS: Southeastern Europe, 1350-1800, to be published by Oxford University Press; *The Balkans in the Twentieth Century,* to be published by Oxford University Press; a book on the Tajiks for the Hoover Institution's "Series on Nationalities."

SIDELIGHTS: As a scholar, Keith Hitchins is concerned with the study of Romania, particularly the country's political history. In between earning advanced degrees, including a Ph.D. in history from Harvard University, Hitchins began his academic career at Wake Forest University. He then taught at Rice University in Texas before joining the faculty of the University of Illinois at Urbana-Champaign in 1969. Since then, Hitchins has written a number of books on Romania and its history, including *The Rumanian National Movement in Transylvania, 1780-1849, Orthodoxy and Nationality: Andreiu Saguna and the Rumanians of Transylvania, 1846-1873,* and *Studies on Romanian National Consciousness.* Among his most comprehensive tomes on the subject is 1994's *Rumania: 1866-1947.* In this work, Hitchins examines political aspects of the small, mountainous nation's modern history, especially its period of constitutional monarchy.

Hitchins's *Rumania* focuses on how the country's constitution was adopted and a German prince invited to become head of state. The tome chronicles what some observers characterize as the arbitrary way in which Romania was governed for many decades—a process termed constitutional monarchy but one that failed to appease the country's opposing factions. Such practices led eventually to an authoritarian rule in the years prior to World War II. Hitchins explains the division, within Romania, between the country's more conservative, tradition-minded political factions and those who looked toward Western Europe as a role model. According to the author this divergence of opinion and sentiments proved troublesome for the country at the onset of World War II, when Romania found itself caught between warring Nazi Germany and the Soviet Union. *Rumania* examines these years as well as their aftermath, and interprets the circumstances that eventually resulted in the post-war authoritarian regime of Nicolae Ceausescu that ended with his death in 1989.

In reviewing *Rumania* for *Times Literary Supplement,* critic Dennis Deletant faulted the author for not looking more deeply into the problems of nationalism in Romania, a country with an established Hungarian minority that has long charged both official and unofficial discrimination. Deletant asserted that "Hitchins focuses too exclusively on the Romanians themselves," and observed that "given the theme of the book, this presents a curious imbalance." Yet the critic remarked: "Hitchins's history . . . will long stand as a work of reference. It is meticulously researched and has invaluable chapters on the social and economic, as well as the political, history of the Romanians."

Hitchins's study of nationalism and nation building extends beyond his interest in Romania to include research and examination of the Caucasus, Central Asia, and the Middle East. Recent academic work has focused on the Azerbaijani novel, the Kazakh epic, modern Tajik literature, and the Kurdish national movement.

BIOGRAPHICAL/CRITICAL SOURCES:

PERIODICALS

Times Literary Supplement, July 22, 1994, p. 26.

* * *

HOCKNEY, David 1937-

PERSONAL: Born July 9, 1937, in Bradford, Yorkshire, England; immigrated to the United States, 1964; son of Kenneth and Laura Hockney. *Education:* Attended Bradford College of Art, 1953-57; Royal College of Art, graduated (with gold medal), 1962.

ADDRESSES: Office—7508 Santa Monica Blvd., West Hollywood, CA 90046-6407.

CAREER: Artist. Maidstone College of Art, England, instructor, 1962; University of Iowa, Iowa City, lecturer, 1963-64; University of Colorado, Boulder, lecturer, 1965; University of California at Los Angeles, lecturer, 1966, honorary chair of drawing, 1980; University of California at Berkeley, lecturer, 1967. Work exhibited in solo shows at Kasmin Gallery, Ltd., London, 1963-89; Museum of Modern Art, 1964 and 1968; Alan Gallery, New York City, 1964-67; Stedlijk Museum, Amsterdam, Netherlands, 1966; Whitworth Gallery, Manchester, England, 1969; (retrospective) Whitechapel Art Gallery, London, 1970; Andre Emmerich Gallery, New York City, 1970 and 1972—; Galerie Springer, Berlin, Germany, 1970; Kunsthalle Bielefeld, 1971; Musee des Arts Decoratifs, Paris, France, 1974; Michael Walls Gallery, New York City, 1974; Galerie Claude Bernard, Paris, 1975; in "Travels with Pen, Pencil, and Ink," on tour of U.S. cities, 1978-80, and at Tate Gallery, London, 1980; "Paper Pools," Andre Emmrich Gallery and Warehouse Gallery, London, 1979; (retrospective) Hayward Gallery, London, 1983; Museo Tamayo, Mexico City, 1984; L.A. Louvre, 1986 and 1989-90; Nishimura Gallery, Tokyo, Japan, 1986 and 1989; Metropolitan Museum of Art, 1988; Los Angeles County Museum of Art, 1988; and Tate Gallery, 1988. Designer for stage productions, including *Ubu Roi,* Royal Court Theater, London, 1966; *Rake's Progress,*

Glyndebourne, England, 1975; *Magic Flute,* Glyndebourne, 1978; Parade Triple Bill, Stravinsky Triple Bill, Metropolitan Opera House, New York City, 1980-81; *Tristan and Isolde,* Los Angeles Music Center Opera, 1987; *Turandot,* Chicago Lyric Opera, 1992; *Die Frau ohne Schatten,* Covent Garden, 1992, and Los Angeles Music Center Opera 1993; and San Francisco Opera, 1993. Worked at a hospital as an alternative to military service, prior to 1959.

AWARDS, HONORS: Guinness Award and first prize for etching, 1961; Graphic prize, Paris Biennale, 1963; first prize, Eighth International Exhibition of Drawings, Lugano, Italy, 1964; first prize, John Moores Exhibition, Liverpool, England, 1967; German award of excellence, 1983; Kodak photography book award, 1984, for *Cameraworks;* first prize, International Center of Photography, New York City, 1985; honorary degree, University of Aberdeen, 1988; Praemium Imperiale, Japan Art Association, 1989.

WRITINGS:

David Hockney by David Hockney (autobiography), edited by Nikos Stangos, Thames & Hudson, 1976, 2nd edition, with introduction by Henry Geldzahler, Abrams (New York City), 1977.

Paper Pools, edited by Stangos, Abrams, 1980.

David Hockney: Looking at Pictures in a Book, Petersburg Press (New York City), 1981.

Cameraworks (includes essay "True to Life" by Lawrence Weschler), Knopf (New York City), 1984.

Martha's Vineyard: My Third Sketchbook from the Summer of 1982 (facsimile reproduction), Abrams, 1985.

Hockney on Photography: Conversations with Paul Joyce, Harmony Books (New York City), 1988.

Picasso, Hanuman Books, 1990.

Hockney's Alphabet, written contributions edited by Stephen Spender, Random House (New York City), 1991.

That's the Way I See It (autobiography), Chronicle Books (San Francisco, CA), 1993.

(Author of introduction) Jeffery Camp, *Draw: How to Master the Art,* Dorling Kindersley, 1994.

(Author of introduction) *Making It New: Collected Essays and Writings of Henry Geldzahler,* Turtle Point Press, 1994.

(Contributor) *Stamberg Aferiat,* photographs by Paul Warchol, Rizzoli International (New York City), 1997.

David Hockney, dialogue avec Picasso, Reunion des musees nationaux (Paris, France), 1999.

(Contributor of commentary) *A Degas Sketchbook,* J. Paul Getty Museum (Los Angeles), 2000.

Hockney on "Art": In Conversation with Paul Joyce, Little, Brown (Boston, MA), 2000.

ILLUSTRATOR

David Posner, *A Rake's Progress: A Poem in Five Sections,* Lion and Unicorn Press (London, England), 1962.

Six Fairy Tales from the Brothers Grimm, Petersburg Press, 1970.

William Hogarth, *A Rake's Progress,* translated into German by Alfred Hrdlicka, Oesterreichisches Museum für Angewandte Kunst (Vienna, Austria), 1971.

Wallace Stephens, *The Man with the Blue Guitar,* Petersburg Press, 1977.

Tor Seidler, *The Dulcimer Boy,* Viking (New York City), 1979.

Stephen Spender, *China Diary,* Abrams, 1982.

Horst Bienek, *Selected Poems: 1958-1988,* Unicorn Press, 1989.

COLLECTIONS

Seventy-two Drawings Chosen by the Artist, J. Cape, 1971.

Eighteen Portraits by David Hockney, photographs by Malcolm Lubliner and Sidney B. Felsen, Gemini G.E.L. (Los Angeles, CA), 1977.

David Hockney Prints, 1954-77, Petersburg Press, 1979.

Pictures by David Hockney, selected and edited by Stangos, Thames & Hudson, 1979, 2nd edition, Abrams, 1979.

David Hockney, Twenty-three Lithographs, Tyler Graphics (New York City), 1980.

David Hockney Photographs, Petersburg Press, 1982.

Hockney's Photographs, Arts Council of Great Britain, 1983.

Kasmin's Hockneys: Forty-five Drawings, Knoedler Gallery (London), 1983.

David Hockney fotografo, Alinari (Florence, Italy), 1983.

David Hockney in America, introduction by Christopher Finch, W. Beadleston (New York City), 1983.

Hockney Posters, Harmony Books, 1983.

Photographs by David Hockney, edited by B. J. Bradley, Art Services International, 1986.

David Hockney: Etchings and Lithographs, text by Marco Livingstone, Thames & Hudson (New York City), 1988, new edition, 1996.

David Hockney: Graphics, Distributed Art Publishers, 1992.

Off the Wall, Pavilion Books (London), 1994, published as *David Hockney: Poster Art,* Chronicle Books, 1994.

David Hockney: Retrospektive Photoworks, text by Jochen Pötter and others (includes interview with Hockney), edited by Reinhold Misselbeck, Edition Braus (Heidelberg, Germany), 1998.

David Hockney's Dog Days, Bulfinch Press (Boston), 1998.

EXHIBIT CATALOGS

Paintings, Prints, and Drawings, 1960-1970 (Whitechapel Art Gallery exhibit, 1970), Boston Book and Art, 1970.

David Hockney: tableau et dessins: Musee des arts decoratifs, Palais du Louvre, Pavillon de Marsan, 11 Octobre-9 Decembre 1974, Petersburg Press, 1974.

David Hockney: dessins et gravures, Galerie Claude Bernard, Paris, Avril 1975, introduction by Marc Fumaroli, Galerie Claude Bernard, 1975.

David Hockney: Prints and Drawings Circulated by the International Exhibits Foundation, Washington, D.C., 1978-1980, International Exhibits Foundation, 1978.

Travels with Pen, Pencil, and Ink, introduction by Edmund Pillsbury, Petersburg Press, 1978.

David Hockney: Sources and Experiments: An Exhibition Held at the Sewall Gallery, Rice University, September 7 to October 15, 1982, text by Esther de Vecsey, Sewall Art Gallery, 1982.

David Hockney: Frankfurter Kunstverein, Steinernes Haus am Romerberg, Frankfurt am Main, 15.3.-24.4. 1983, introduction by Peter Weiermair, Der Verein (Frankfurt, Germany), 1983.

Hockney Paints the Stage, text by Martin Friedman with contributions by John Cox and others, Walker Art Center (Minneapolis, MN), 1983.

Photographs by David Hockney: Organized and Circulated by the International Exhibitions Foundation, Washington, D.C., 1986-88, introduction by Mark Haworth-Booth and essay by Hockney, International Exhibits Foundation, 1986.

David Hockney: A Retrospective, Los Angeles County Museum of Art, 1988.

David Hockney: Fax Cuadros, Centro Cultural/Arte Contemporaneo (Mexico), 1990.

David Hockney: Paintings and Photographs of Paintings, Museum Boymans-van Beuningen (Rotterdam, Netherlands), 1996.

SIDELIGHTS: "No other English artist has ever been as popular in his own time, with as many people, in as many places, as David Hockney," Robert Hughes asserted in *Time.* Throughout Hockney's career, his reputation as a serious artist has depended on the attention of critics, but his versatility and willingness to reveal his artistic processes have earned him admirers around the world. Like Pablo Picasso, Hockney refuses to limit himself to a single discipline or style and has continually expanded his practice to include engraving, painting, illustration, photography, graphic design, and stage design. Hockney has also filled the role of critic and theorist, and his writings have found a significant readership. It is Hockney's desire to engage his audience in narrative, both as a visual artist and writer, that underscores his success. Unlike the work of many of his counterparts, Hockney's art is primarily figurative (that is, representational). Hockney's narratives, then, begin in pictures which tell stories and are continued in the artist's ready explanation of his intentions. The demonstrative relationship between image and narrative is characteristic of Hockney's most highly regarded work. Hockney, the artist, captures his viewer's imagination as a storyteller.

Hockney was born in Bradford, Yorkshire, England, in 1937. He attended Bradford Grammar School and as a teenager entered the Bradford College of Art. When Hockney became a student at the progressive Royal College of Art in London, his skills as a draftsman were already firmly established. During these student years, Hockney experimented with the most visible styles of the time, abstract expressionism (which demanded nonrepresentational, purely visual expression) and pop (which appropriated the imagery and reproduction techniques of mass media). In 1960 Hockney viewed his first Picasso retrospective, and in the same year, according to Kay Larson in *New York,* invented his singular manner of drawing. Larson described the typical Hockney drawing as "a cross between Saul Steinberg and Dr. Seuss, though the more common references are Francis Bacon, English Pop, and modern magazine illustration." Hockney's early influcnccs also included classmates from the Royal College who later gained considerable reputations, including the American painter R. B. Kitaj.

In 1961 Hockney was chosen to participate in an exhibit titled "Young Contemporaries." The show was immediately recognized as a turning point in contemporary British art and is today viewed as something of a landmark. Hockney and several of the artists selected were still students when the show was mounted. Nearly thirty years later, *Nation* critic Arthur C. Danto opened his review of a major Hockney retrospective with an analysis of a painting included in "Young Contemporaries." "The Most Beautiful Boy" combines obscure imagery at the canvas margins, such as an Alka Seltzer label, with a rough portrait of a figure wearing what appears to be a woman's nightclothes. As is usual in early Hockney, text is also forced into the space surrounding the figure, adding an articulate layer of meaning to the work. Danto noted that in 1961 British critic Lawrence Alloway declared that Hockney's imagery was fundamentally urban and likened his use of text to graffiti. "The Most Beautiful Boy" and its companion paintings were presumed to demonstrate a new concern for the depiction of the city.

Without denying the presence of the urban environment in these works, Danto contended that "The Most Beautiful Boy," and Hockey's art in general, is more personal. The sexual ambiguity of the boy is taken as reference to Hockney's homosexuality (an issue the artist has dealt with frankly in other works), while the symbolism and the alternating crude and delicate aspects of the portrait are understood as expressions of desire. "It is a witty and confessional piece of work," Danto proclaimed, "a declaration of love, and sexually explicit, . . . and it engages the viewer in the artist's own emotional affairs, as if he wore his heart on his canvas." This was unique in 1961, according to Danto, because Hockney's work was neither abstract nor pop but full of people he had actually seen, interiors he observed, and landscapes that might be located on a map. As a result, Hockney communicated something about the world, as well as something about his relationship to the objects of his affection. "Hockney's art is to be found between the work and its viewers," Danto declared, "a space curiously filled by the artist himself."

Upon graduating from the Royal College in 1962, Hockney became a popular personality, sporting large round-rimmed glasses and playboy clothes. In 1963 Hockney traveled to Los Angeles; he became a resident of the city a year later. During this period Hockney turned his attention to his new surroundings, and his paintings of the Los Angeles landscape are often credited with establishing the iconography of the city. While Hockney's observation of the intense light of Southern California was not always accurate, wrote Hughes, "he fixed other things—those pastel planes, insouciant scraggy palms, blank panes of glass, and blue pools full of wreathing reflections and brown bodies." Hockney's most frequently seen works from this period are paintings of swimming pools, where the surface of the water is treated as if it held spiritual implications for the culture of Los Angeles. Hockney evoked meaning from these oases of water in the middle of the desert and depicted the swimming pool as a representation of the California lifestyle.

"A Bigger Splash," painted in 1967, utilizes the pool and the pool deck as a landscape. A diving board cantilevers from the front of the picture into the scene and out over the pool, where the surface of the water has just been broken, the splash and spray frozen in the air. With the exception of the taut energy of the splash, the scene is curiously still: the light is intense and uninflected, an empty deck chair faces the pool, and the diving board is flat, without indication of the shock of the implied dive. Noting the importance of this work, *Time*'s Hughes called *A Bigger Splash* "the quintessential L.A. painting . . . a radiant acceptance of Now—an eye blink, picture perfect."

"Portrait of an Artist (Pool with Two Figures)," painted in 1972, is among the most naturalistic of the pool paintings. In addition to the quality of the rendering, the ten foot by seven foot canvas lends a certain life-size authority to the figures. In the painting a man swims underwater, from left to right, arms ahead of him and body fully extended, toward the edge of a pool. The second figure, also male, stands at the pool edge fully clothed, facing the swimmer and peering down into the pool. In the background the green hillsides of Southern California momentarily frame the scene, then overlap into the distance. In a *Film Comment* article, David Thomson asserted that the painting's power springs from the visual relationship of the figures: the standing figure waits unnoticed, that is, unseen. The painting depicts the moment before the revelatory moment when the swimmer surfaces and confronts the watcher. "That is how it is such a study of yearning," Thomson concluded, "that is why there is a feeling of fragility or danger in this secluded Eden up above L.A."

"American Collectors (Fred and Marcia Weisman)," from 1968, presents another facet of Hockney's study of Los Angeles. Here two figures stand on opposite sides of a courtyard containing a few outdoor pieces from their art collection. Fred is presented in profile, staring intently in the direction of Marcia, who faces the viewer. Thomson pointed out the similarity of this situation to the setup in "Portrait of an Artist (Pool with Two Figures)," but here "one figure has turned to look at the other, while the other resolutely fails to notice the attention." In his comments on "American Collectors," Hughes noted that Marcia's features are slightly distorted to resemble a totem in the background and that paint is dribbling from Fred's hand, as if the couple have actually become artifacts in the process of collecting art.

Hockney continued to paint into the 1970s, but in the second half of the decade his production dropped precipitously. During this period Hockney was approached by the Glyndebourne Opera about doing stage design for a production of Igor Stravinsky's *The Rake's Progress.* "To begin with, the music seemed very difficult," Hockney recalled in his 1993 book, *That's the Way I See It.* "I listened and there was probably very little I got. . . . But slowly the music came to me. The more I listened, the more beautiful it became, and I saw how exciting it was." Hockney proposed a sequence of sets inspired by the engravings of William Hogarth, the eighteenth-century originator of *The Rake's Progress* and a series of prints with the same title that Hockney had done in the early sixties. Cross-hatching became the central motif of the designs, a stylized version of the technique Hogarth employed in his engravings. The production received wide acclaim, and Hockney has continued to design sets for a variety of opera companies in England and the United States.

It was during his sabbatical from painting that Hockney began to explore photography as a vehicle for his art. In Lawrence Weschler's essay "True to Life" (originally published in *New Yorker* and later as a preface to Hockney's 1984 volume *Cameraworks*), Weschler illuminated Hockney's practice of using photographs as an aid to memory while painting. Some of these photographs had even been assembled for an exhibition at the Pompidou Center in Paris in 1982. Despite its value as a recording device, Hockney maintained what he characterized as an ambivalent relationship to photography. "It's not that I despised photography *ever,*" Hockney told Weschler, "it's just that I distrusted the claims that were made on its behalf—claims as to its greater reality or authenticity." That suspicion of the limitations of photography launched Hockney on a series of photographic experiments that resulted in the photo-collages presented in *Cameraworks.*

Initially, Hockney combined dozens of Polaroid photos in a grid; the individual photos created a composite image, with several points of view and locations in time represented. As the work progressed, the grids gave way to compositions which adapted to the forms of the subject matter: sprawling collages of the Grand Canyon, strongly vertical arrangements showing a telephone pole bursting from the ground in Los Angeles, portraits which present several views and facial expressions. "There is, in some of these collages, as in some of Hockney's finest pencil drawings, a remarkable psychological acuity at work," Weschler declared. "In the [Stephen] Spender combine, for example, the face itself develops out of six squares—three tall and two wide—those aspects to the left are alert, inquisitive and probing; to the right, they are tired, weary, resigned. Spender, Hockney seems to be suggesting, is both." In another collage, "The Scrabble Game" from 1983, Hockney incorporates an element from his earlier work, creating a fragmented narrative with the words played on the Scrabble board.

According to Larson in *New York,* Hockney's photography allowed him to resume painting with a new sense of perspective that avoided the "claustrophobic intimacy" of some of his earlier paintings. Larson found Hockney's narratives more "systematic" following the photographic experiments as well and pointed to the mural "Mulholland Drive: The Road to the Studio" as evidence. The intense colors used to depict the vegetation of the California hills are reminiscent of the Fauvist landscapes painted by Derain and Matisse, while the road is a sinuous line running up the center of the composition. In *That's the Way I See It* Hockney offered this insight on the painting: "When you look at *Mulholland Drive*—and drive is not the name of the road, but the act of driving—your eye moves around the painting at about the same speed as a car drives along the road." Despite the stylization of images in the painting, Hockney maintained that the work is the result of intense observation and that the presentation of the vegetation and color, especially, are more realistic than they might initially seem.

Since he resumed painting, Hockney has continued to experiment with perception and has explored Cubism as well as other styles. While his concerns have changed since the early days of his celebrity, most notably with respect to naturalism, Hockney continues to challenge audiences with works of dedicated craftsmanship. Hockney's reflections on his work and his interests in new technology, such as photo reproduction, are collected in *That's the Way I See It.* This "lively, unpretentious memoir," as a *Publishers Weekly* reviewer described it, presents the text of recorded and unrecorded conversations between David Hockney and Nikos Stangos. Much of this book is devoted to Hockney's "break with naturalism," as well as his explorations of spatial perception and new printing or reproduction techniques, which include faxing and laser color printing. During the five years of discussions between Stangos and Hockney presented in *That's the Way I See It,* Hockney recalls his travels through China and Egypt, reflects about the death of his father, and expresses his thoughts about his own loss of hearing. Hockney also explains the production of his acclaimed opera sets for *Tristan and Isolde* and *The Magic Flute*. Throughout the book, drawings, paintings, and collages illustrate Hockney's creative process.

While Stephen Galloway in the *Los Angeles Times Book Review* found the work to be repetitive at times, he felt that "it is impossible not to be drawn" to Hockney and concluded that the artist's "endless questioning and genuine delight in all the processes of creation make it difficult not to admire him." In the *Times Literary Supplement,* Rosemary Hill asserted that *That's the Way I See It* is "the friendliest and most enjoyable book about art since *David Hockney by David Hockney* appeared in 1976." "Readers are in for an insightful journey," exclaimed *Booklist*'s Alice Joyce.

In *That's the Way I See It,* Hockney touches the subject of AIDS as he discusses death. "The first friend of mine to die was Joe MacDonald. . . . He was the first person I knew to become ill with AIDS, just after 1981." Hockney went on to describe MacDonald's death of pneumonia and related, "Then there were more deaths, each person dying in a different way." In the early 1990s, Hockney contributed his talent and reputation to an AIDS fund-raising project with editor Stephen Spender. The result, *Hockney's Alphabet,* is a "picture book for adults of the highest order" as Ray Olson in *Booklist* described it. Each of the twenty-six letters of the alphabet is rendered in Hockney's unique style and accompanied by short literary pieces written by respected contemporary writers, including Joyce Carol Oates, John Updike, Patrick Leigh Fermor, Susan Sontag, and Ian McEwan. Hockney's letters, according to David Bryant in *Library Journal,* are "bright, cheery, surprising mini-artworks." One hundred percent of the net proceeds of *Hockney's Alphabet* were promised to the fight against AIDS.

While Hockney continues to live in the Los Angeles area, his reputation as an artist reaches around the world. He has also worked in variety of locations, particularly as a stage designer, and his travels are a source of inspiration and influence. Hockney's willingness to experiment, his craftsmanship, and his unfailing ability to evoke narrative through the image, have expanded the importance of the figure, especially the human figure, in contemporary art. Hockney expressed his commitment to the figure in the form of a question posed to Weschler: "Cezanne's apples are lovely and very special," Hockney confessed, "but what finally can compare to the image of another human being?"

BIOGRAPHICAL/CRITICAL SOURCES:

BOOKS

Contemporary Artists, 4th edition, St. James Press, 1996.

Contemporary Photographers, 3rd edition, St. James Press, 1996.

Contemporary Theater, Film, and Television, volume 17, Gale (Detroit), 1997.

Encyclopedia of World Biography, 2nd edition, Gale, 1998.

Gay and Lesbian Biography, St. James Press, 1997.

Hockney, David, *Cameraworks,* introduction by Lawrence Weschler, Knopf, 1984.

Hockney, David, *That's the Way I See It,* Chronicle Books, 1993.

Newsmakers, Gale, 1998.

PERIODICALS

Booklist, February 1, 1992, Ray Olson, review of *Hockney's Alphabet,* p. 1001; January 1, 1994, Alice Joyce, review of *That's the Way I See It,* p. 799.

Book News, August 1, 1994, review of *That's the Way I See It.*

Contemporary Review, September, 2000, Geoffrey Heptonstall, "Hockney Talks about Hockney," p. 184.

Film Comment, July-August 1989, article by David Thomson, pp. 53-65.

Library Journal, March 15, 1992, David Bryant, review of *Hockney's Alphabet,* p. 86; September 15, 1993, p. 38.

Los Angeles Times Book Review, December 26, 1993, Stephen Galloway, review of *That's the Way I See It,* p. 9.

Nation, July 30-August 6, 1988, review by Arthur C. Danto, pp. 104-7.

New York, June 20, 1988, article by Kay Larson, pp. 62-63.

New Yorker, January 31, 2000, Lawrence Weschler, "The Looking Glass," pp. 64-75.

Publishers Weekly, February 5, 1988, p. 80; October 11, 1993, review of *That's the Way I See It,* p. 76.

School Arts, September, 1999, Diane Mark-Walker, "One Landscape, Many Views," p. 31; January, 2001, Maureen Albano, "Prints and Patterns," p. 43.

Time, June 20, 1988, article by Robert Hughes, pp. 76-79.

Times Higher Education Supplement, June 16, 2000, Elaine Williams, "An Optical Disillusion," p. 17.

Times Literary Supplement, November 22, 1991, p. 19; November 19, 1993, Rosemary Hill, review of *That's the Way I See It,* p. 8; April 7, 2000, James Hall, "Variety Shows," p. 13.

U.S. News and World Report, September 25, 1989, p. 18.*

* * *

HODGINS, Bruce W(illard) 1931-

PERSONAL: Born January 29, 1931, in Kitchener, Ontario, Canada; son of Stanley Earl (a teacher) and Laura Belle (Turel) Hodgins; married Carol Edith Creelman (a physiotherapist), July 24, 1958; children: Shawn Prescott, Geoff Stanley (sons). *Education:* University of Western Ontario, B.A., 1953; Queen's University at Kingston, M.A., 1955; Duke University, Ph.D., 1965. *Politics:* New Democrat.

ADDRESSES: Home—7 Engelburn Pl., Peterborough, Ontario, Canada. *Office*—Department of History, Trent University, Peterborough, Ontario, Canada.

CAREER: Prince of Wales College (now University of Prince of Wales), Charlottetown, Prince Edward Island, instructor in history, 1955-58, 1961-62; University of Western Ontario, London, assistant professor of history, 1962-65; Trent University, Peterborough, Ontario, assistant professor, 1965-67, associate professor, 1967-72, professor of history, 1972—. Australian National University, fellow in history, 1970. Camp Wanapitei, Temagami, Ontario, director. New Democrat Party, candidate for Parliament, 1968; former member of Ontario provincial council.

MEMBER: Canadian Historical Association (member of council, 1961-64), Royal Commonwealth Society, United Nations Association of Canada (member of national policy council, 1965-72; president of national administrative council, 1967-69), Ontario Confederation of University Faculty Associations (member of executive board, 1971-72), Ontario Historical Society.

AWARDS, HONORS: Centenary Medal of Canadian Government, 1967; Cruikshank Award, Ontario Historical Society, 1968.

WRITINGS:

John Sandfield Macdonald: 1812-1872, University of Toronto Press (Toronto, Ontario, Canada), 1971.

(Editor, with Richard P. Bowles, Hanley, and George A. Rawlyk) *The Indian: Assimilation, Integration, or Separation,* Prentice-Hall (Englewood Cliffs, NJ), 1972.

Canadiens, Canadians, and Quebeçois, Prentice-Hall (Englewood Cliffs, NJ), 1974.

Paradis of Temagami, 1848-1926, Highway Bookshop, 1976.

(Editor, with Benidickson and Rawlyk) *The Canadian North: Source of Wealth or Vanishing Heritage,* Prentice-Hall (Englewood Cliffs, NJ), 1977.

(With Wright and Heick) *Federalism in Canada and Australia: The Early Years,* Wilfrid Laurier Press, 1978.

(Editor, with Robert Page) *Canadian History since Confederation: Essays and Interpretations,* 2nd edition, Irwin-Dorsey (Georgetown, Ontario, Canada), 1979.

(With Bowles and Rawlyk) *Regionalism in Canada: Flexible Federalism or Fractured Nation?,* Prentice-Hall of Canada (Scarborough, Ontario, Canada), 1979.

(Editor, with Margaret Hobbs) *Nastawgan: The Canadian North by Canoe and Snowshoe; A Collection of Historical Essays,* Betelgeuse Books (Toronto, Ontario, Canada), 1985.

(With Jamie Benidickson) *The Temagami Experience: Recreation, Resources, and Aboriginal Rights in the Northern Ontario Wilderness,* University of Toronto Press (Buffalo, NY), 1989.

(Coeditor) *Federalism in Canada and Australia: Historical Perspectives, 1920-1988,* Frost Centre for Canadian Heritage and Development Studies, Trent University (Peterborough, Ontario, Canada), 1989.

(With Shawn Heard and John S. Milloy) *Co-existence? Studies in Ontario-First Nations Relations,* Frost Centre for Canadian Heritage and Development Studies, Trent University (Peterborough, Ontario, Canada), 1992.

(With Gwyneth Hoyle) *Canoeing North into the Unknown: A Record of Canoe Travel, 1874-1974,* Natural Heritage/Natural History (Toronto, Ontario, Canada), 1994.

(Editor, with Kerry A. Cannon) *On the Land: Confronting the Challenges to Aboriginal Self-determination in Northern Quebec and Labrador,* Betelgeuse Books, 1995.

(Editor, with John Jennings and Doreen Small) *The Canoe in Canadian Cultures,* Natural Heritage/Natural History (Toronto, Ontario, Canada), 1999.

Other writings include *The Pre-Confederation Premiers: Ontario Government Leaders, 1841-1867,* 1984. Member of editorial board, *Alternatives,* 1971—.

SIDELIGHTS: With his wife and children, Bruce W. Hodgins drove from Ireland to Ceylon, via Turkey, Iran, Afghanistan, and India, thence by boat to Perth and overland from Perth to Canberra, 1969-70. He has traveled more than 8,000 miles by canoe in the Canadian north, frequently with his wife.

BIOGRAPHICAL/CRITICAL SOURCES:

PERIODICALS

Beaver: Exploring Canada's History, October-November, 1987, J. M. Bumstead, review of *Nastawgan,* p. 61; April-May, 1991, Bumstead, review of *The Temagami Experience,* p. 55.

Books in Canada, winter, 2000, Brian Brett, "Canonizing Canada's Canoe," pp. 38-39.

Canadian Geographic, April-May, 1986, James Raffan, review of *Nastawgan,* p. 76; October-November, 1989, Margaret Mironowitz, review of *The Temagami Experience,* p. 92.

Canadian Historical Review, September, 1984, review of *The Pre-Confederation Premiers,* p. S8; December, 1987, Janet Foster, review of *Nastawgan,* p. 669; June, 1990, James Morrison, review of *The Temagami Experience,* p. 303.

Nature Canada, fall, 1990, Paul R. Martin, review of *The Temagami Experience,* p. 58.

OTHER

All about Canoes, http://www.canoe.ca/ (October 18, 2000).*

* * *

HOOTON, Joy 1935-

PERSONAL: Born January 13, 1935, in Harrogate, England; daughter of Charles (a bank employee) and Lizzie (a teacher; maiden name, Braithwaite) Freeman; married Vivian Hooton; children: Judith, Guy, Fiona. *Education:* Attended University of Leeds, 1952-54; University of London, B.A., 1963, M.Phil., 1974.

ADDRESSES: Home and office—P.O. Box 1269, Batenaw Bay, New South Wales 2536, Australia. *E-mail*—hooton@act.net.au.

CAREER: Teacher in Hong Kong, 1954-58; librarian, 1964-70; research assistant, 1970-76; Australian Defence Force Academy, Campbell, lecturer, 1977-87, senior lecturer, 1987-90, associate professor of English, 1990-95; Australian National University, Canberra, currently visiting professor.

MEMBER: Association for the Study of Australian Literature, Australasian Drama Studies Association.

AWARDS, HONORS: New South Wales Premier's Award, 1986, and A. A. Phillips Award, Association for the Study of Australian Literature, 1987, both for *The Oxford Companion to Australian Literature.*

WRITINGS:

A. D. Hope, Oxford University Press (New York, NY), 1981.

(With William H. Wilde and Barry G. Andrews) *The Oxford Companion to Australian Literature,* Oxford University Press (New York, NY), 1985, 2nd edition, 1994.

(Editor) *Studies in Prose Literature,* Faculty of Military Studies, University of New South Wales (Kensington, Australia), 1985.

Stories of Herself When Young: Autobiographies of Childhood by Australian Women, Oxford University Press (Melbourne, Australia), 1990.

(With H. P. Heseltine) *Annals of Australian Literature,* 2nd edition, Oxford University Press (New York, NY), 1992.

(With Kay Walsh) *Australian Autobiographical Narratives: An Annotated Bibliography,* National Library of Australia (Canberra, Australia), Volume I: *To 1850,* 1993, Volume II: *1850-1900,* 1998.

(Editor, with David Headon and Donald Horne) *The Abundant Culture: Meaning and Significance in Everyday Australia,* Allen & Unwin (St. Leonards, Australia), 1995.

(Editor) *Ruth Park: A Celebration,* Friends of the National Library of Australia (Canberra, Australia), 1996.

(Editor) *Australian Lives: An Oxford Anthology,* Oxford University Press (Melbourne, Australia), 1998.

(Editor) *Rosemary Dobron,* National Library of Australia (Canberra, Australia), 2000.

SIDELIGHTS: Joy Hooton once told *CA:* "I am interested in neglected areas of Australian literature, especially women's writing, both contemporary and past. I am studying the ways in which increased knowledge of these areas modifies ideas about Australian culture. I am interested in contributing to basic bibliographical and editorial work in the field, and I have a continuing interest in Australian and international autobiography."

BIOGRAPHICAL/CRITICAL SOURCES:

PERIODICALS

Choice, January, 2000, W. Comins-Richmond, review of *Australian Lives,* p. 913.
Times Literary Supplement, May 8, 1987.

* * *

HOPKINS, David 1948-

PERSONAL: Born September 11, 1948, in Salisbury, Wiltshire, England; son of Clifford (a schoolmaster) and Marjorie (a schoolmistress; maiden name, Gay) Hopkins; married Sandra Harmer (a university continuing education tutor), July 31, 1971; children: Kate, James. *Education:* St. Catharine's College, Cambridge, B.A., 1969, M.A., 1973; University of Leicester, Ph.D., 1979.

ADDRESSES: Home—89 Hill View, Henleaze, Bristol, Avon BS9 4QQ, England. *Office*—Department of English, University of Bristol, 3/5 Woodland Rd., Bristol, Avon BS8 1TB, England. *E-mail*—david.hopkins@bris.ac.uk.

CAREER: University of Bristol, Bristol, England, lecturer in English, 1977—, reader in English poetry, 1993—.

WRITINGS:

(Author of introduction) John Wilson, *Specimens of the British Critics,* Scholars' Facsimiles and Reprints (Delmar, NY), 1979.
(Editor with Thomas Mason) *The Beauties of Dryden,* Bristol Classical Press (Bristol, England), 1982.
John Dryden, Cambridge University Press (Cambridge, England), 1986.
(Editor) *English Poetry: A Poetic Record, from Chaucer to Yeats,* Routledge (London, England), 1990, revised edition published as *The Routledge Anthology of Poets on Poets: Poetic Responses to English Poetry from Chaucer to Yeats,* 1994.
(Editor with Charles Martindale) *Horace Made New,* Cambridge University Press (New York, NY), 1993.
(Editor with Tom Mason) *The Story of Poetry,* Broadcast Books, 1993.
(Editor with Tom Mason) *Abraham Cowley: Selected Poems,* Carcanet Press (Manchester, England), 1994.
(Editor) *John Dryden: Selected Poems,* Dent/Everyman (London, England), 1998.
(Editor) *Homer: Selected Verse from the "Iliad" and the "Odyssey", Translated by Alexander Pope,* Dent/Everyman (London, England), 1999.
(Editor with Hammond) *John Dryden: Tercentenary Essays,* Clarendon Press, 2000.
(Editor with Paul Hammond) *The Poems of John Dryden,* Volume Three: *1686-1693,* Longman/Pearson, 2000.
(Editor with Hammond) *The Poems of John Dryden,* Volume Four: *1693-1696,* Longman/Pearson, 2000.
(Editor with Sandra Hopkins) *Women in Love: Heroines in Verse,* Dent/Everyman (London, England), 2000.

Contributor to books, including *Ovid Renewed: Ovidian Influences on Literature and Art from the Middle Ages to the Twentieth Century,* edited by Charles Martindale, Cambridge University Press (New York, NY), 1998, and *The Oxford Guide to Literature in English Translation,* edited by Peter France, Oxford University Press (New York, NY), 2000. Contributor to periodicals, including *Modern Language Review, Review of English Studies, Yearbook of English Studies, Notes and Queries, Comparative Literature, Translation and Literature,* and *Cambridge Quarterly.* Member of editorial board, *Translation and Literature.*

WORK IN PROGRESS: Monograph on John Dryden for the British Council/Northcote House "Writers and Their Work" series; editor with Paul Hammond, *The Poems of John Dryden,* Volume 5.

SIDELIGHTS: In *John Dryden,* David Hopkins explains that Dryden's poetry has been neglected primarily because of late Victorian judgments. Though Dryden's reputation is based mainly upon a few of his satires, Hopkins claims that Dryden's genius is more evident in his translations of such authors as Virgil, Juvenal, Chaucer, and Boccaccio. He takes a somewhat dim view of Dryden's plays, and sees Dryden's shift from playwriting to religious and philosophical verse as an important point in the poet's career. *John Dryden* has "the virtues of energy and clarity," wrote David Nokes for the *Times Literary Supplement,* adding that Hopkins's "enthusiasm" for his subject "is refreshing."

Hopkins once told *CA:* "My research and teaching are motivated by a desire to communicate the pleasure and power of English literature (particularly English poetry). I wish to explain literature's capacity, in the words of Samuel Johnson, 'to enable readers better to enjoy life, or better to endure it.' Since I believe English literature is the birthright of all, not merely the preserve of the academy, I try to work on assumptions and employ arguments that might have an appeal for any serious readers of the works I discuss—not merely for 'students' or 'scholarly specialists.'

"My main aims are first, to present the work of certain neglected (or misunderstood) English poets of the past in ways that make them intelligible and attractive to modern readers, and second, to explore the relations between English poetry (especially that of the seventeenth and eighteenth centuries) and that of classical Greece and Rome."

BIOGRAPHICAL/CRITICAL SOURCES:

PERIODICALS

Times Literary Supplement, August 8, 1986, David Nokes, review of *John Dryden.*

* * *

HORWITZ, Richard P(aul) 1949-

PERSONAL: Born October 12, 1949, in New Britain, CT; son of Sydney Jonas (a dentist) and Shirley (a homemaker; maiden name, Brander) Horwitz; married Ilona Rifkin (a physical therapist), August 24, 1969; children: Carl Allen. *Education:* University of Pennsylvania, B.A. (cum laude), 1971, M.A., 1972, Ph.D., 1975. *Politics:* "Left-of-center." *Religion:* Jewish.

ADDRESSES: Home—3431 480th St., S.W., Iowa City, IA 52240. *Office*—American Studies Department, 202 Jefferson Building, University of Iowa, Iowa City, IA 52242; fax: 319-335-0314. *E-mail*—richard-horwitz@uiowa.edu.

CAREER: Colby College, Waterville, ME, assistant professor of history and American studies, 1975-76; University of Minnesota, Minneapolis, assistant professor of American studies, 1976-77; University of Iowa, Iowa City, assistant professor, 1977-81, associate professor, 1981-87, professor of American studies, 1987—, director of undergraduate program in American studies, 1982-86, chair of undergraduate program in American studies, 1986-90, director of graduate studies in American studies, 1993—, director of public outreach, 2000—. Hired hand, Stutsman Farms, Johnson County, Iowa, 1977-96; visiting scholar in the Republic of China, Republic of Korea, Japan, and India, 1984-85, and distinguished senior lecturer for Netherlands American Commission for Educational Exchange, 1990-91. Speaker at conventions, conferences, and workshops, field researcher and consultant for public, educational, scientific, policy, arts, and humanities agencies.

MEMBER: American Anthropological Association, American Studies Association, Organization of American Historians, American Folklore Society, Popular/American Culture Association, Mid-America American Studies Association (president, 1992-93), Heartland Folklorists.

AWARDS, HONORS: Old Gold summer fellowship, 1980, 1981; U.S.I.S. and Fulbright grants to Japan, India, and Republic of Korea, 1985, Switzerland, 1990, Denmark, Finland, Germany, the Netherlands, and Portugal, 1991, People's Republic of China, 1999-2000; fellowship from National Science Council, 1984-85; University House interdisciplinary research grant, 1987; fellow, National Endowment for the Humanities, 1990, 1992; development assignment, University of Iowa, 1990-91; Lingnan Foundation award, 1995-96; Smithsonian Institution folklife research grant, 1995, 1996; New Technology in the Learning Environment award, 1997.

WRITINGS:

Anthropology toward History: Culture and Work in a Nineteenth-Century Maine Town, Wesleyan University Press (Middletown, CT), 1978.

The Strip: An American Place, photographs by Karin E. Becker, University of Nebraska Press (Lincoln, NE), 1985.

(Editor and contributor) *Exporting America: Essays on American Studies Abroad,* Garland Publishing (New York City), 1993.

(Contributor) *Iowa Folklife: Our People, Communities, and Traditions* (learning guide for teachers, students, and senior citizens), Smithsonian Institution, 1997.

Hog Ties: Pigs, Manure, and Mortality in American Culture, St. Martin's Press, 1998.

(Editor and contributor) *Roots of American Studies,* Scholarly Resources (Wilmington, DE), in press.

Also contributor to books, including *Exploring Society Photographically,* edited by Howard S. Becker, Mary & Leigh Block Gallery, Northwestern University (Chicago, IL), 1981; *When They Read What We Write: The Politics of Ethnography,* edited by Caroline B. Brettell, Bergin & Garvey (Westport, CT), 1993; *The Fulbright Difference, 1948-1992,* edited by Richard T. Arndt and David L. Rubin, Transaction (New Brunswick, NJ), 1993; and *Multiculturalism and the Canon of American Culture,* edited by Hans Bak, VU University Press (Amsterdam), 1993.

Contributor of articles and reviews to *American Studies, American Studies International, American Quarterly, Ethnohistory, Journal of the Society for the Humanities and Technology, North Dakota Quarterly,* and *Winterthur Portfolio.*

WORK IN PROGRESS: Interpretation of cultures of the U.S. interdisciplinary method, everyday life in nineteenth- and twentieth-century America, fieldwork, ethnographic writing, and cultural relations across national and occupational boundaries; research on contemporary American folklife, especially in rural areas and small towns; assessing the implications of recent developments in natural, medical, policy and applied sciences for the quality of life in America; challenging the cultural, ethical, and institutional barriers to the development of understanding of the U.S. at home and abroad.

SIDELIGHTS: Richard P. Horwitz researched *Anthropology toward History: Culture and Work in a Nineteenth-Century Maine Town* by living in Winthrop, Maine, for three years. He perused the local records for material that would reveal to him what life had been like in the town between 1820 and 1850, years during which Winthrop changed from a farming village to a mill town. "By piling up . . . instances of vivid, ordinary language," a reviewer for the *New York Times Book Review* said, "Professor Horwitz produces a basic and apparently objective picture of the past in one place."

Horwitz carefully researches the subjects of his anthropological work. For instance, he once told *CA:* "With the help of photographer and journalism professor Karin Becker I spent more than three years cruising for burgers and chatting with strip-side workers to assess roadside commerce for *The Strip.*" More recently, Horwitz commented: "I have spent fifteen years working part-time as a hired hand on a 2,000-acre hay-grain-cattle farm in Iowa, a source and resource for my latest obsession."

BIOGRAPHICAL/CRITICAL SOURCES:

PERIODICALS

New York Times Book Review, March 19, 1978.

* * *

HUBBARD, Susan (Mary) 1951-

PERSONAL: Born September 6, 1951, in Syracuse, NY; daughter of Middleton John Schwartz and Dorothy Katherine Long; married J. T. W. Hubbard, June 16, 1979 (divorced, August, 1994); married Robley Wilson, June 17, 1995; children: (first marriage) Katherine Ada, Clare Adrian. *Education:* Syracuse University, B.A. (with honors), 1974, M.F.A., 1984.

ADDRESSES: *Home*—P.O. Box 4009, Winter Park, FL 32798. *Office*—Dept. Of English, University of Central Florida, P.O. Box 161346, Orlando, FL 32816-1346. *E-mail*—shubbard@pegasus.cc.ucf.edu

CAREER: *Instructor Magazine,* Dansville, NY, editorial intern, 1973; *Evening Press,* Binghamton, NY, reporter, 1974-76, business columnist, 1974-75, general columnist, 1975-76; *Evening Sentinel,* Ansonia, CT, reporter and columnist, 1976-78; *Journal-Courier,* New Haven, CT, investigative reporter, 1978; *Herald-Journal,* Syracuse, NY, reporter, 1979-80; Syracuse University, Syracuse, instructor in English, 1984-88, project editor at Educational Resources Information Center, 1986-87; State University of New York College of Environmental Science and Forestry, Syracuse, instructor in English, 1988; Cornell University, Ithaca, NY, senior lecturer in engineering communications, 1988-95, faculty adviser, *Cornell Engineer,* 1991-95; University of Central Florida, associate professor of English, 1995—. Writer-in-residence, Pitzer College, Claremont, CA, 1995,

Yaddo, 1999, Djerassi Resident Artists' Program, 2000, Virginia Center for Creative Arts, 2000, and Cill Rialaig, 2001. Quadrant Research Associates, co-founder and partner, 1980—.

MEMBER: Authors' Guild, Poets and Writers, Associated Writing Programs (executive board member, 1999—; vice president, 2000—), Florida College English Association (executive secretary, 1998-2000).

AWARDS, HONORS: Stephen Crane Prize for Fiction, 1983; Norris B. Taylor Prize, Aspen Writers Conference, 1987; Short Fiction Prize, Associated Writing Programs, 1989, for *Walking on Ice;* Special Merit Award, Syracuse University, 1988, "for exceptional contributions in teaching and service to the Writing Program"; Dean's Prize for Excellence and Innovation in Teaching, Cornell University, 1991; Award for Excellence in Undergraduate Teaching, University of Central Florida, 1999; South Atlantic Administrators of Departments of English teaching award, 2000.

WRITINGS:

Walking on Ice (stories), University of Missouri Press, (Columbia, MO), 1990.

Blue Money (short fiction), University of Missouri Press (Columbia, MO), 1999.

(Editor, with Robley Wilson) *One hundred Percent Pure Florida Fiction,* University Press of Florida (Gainesville, FL), 2000.

Also author of an Internet chapbook, located at http://webdelsol.com. Contributor of articles and stories to periodicals, including *TriQuarterly, North American Review, Mississippi Review, Ploughshares, America West,* and *Passages North.* Associate editor, *Epoch,* 1990.

BIOGRAPHICAL/CRITICAL SOURCES:

PERIODICALS

Booklist, March 1, 1999, Brian McCombie, review of *Blue Money,* p. 1151.

Ploughshares, fall, 1991, Henry DeWitt, review of *Walking on Ice,* pp. 281-282.

Publishers Weekly, February 15, 1999, review of *Blue Money,* p. 89.

OTHER

Web del Sol, http://www.webdelsol.com/LITARTS/Susan_Hubbard/ (May 20, 2001).

I-J

IVINS, Mary Tyler 1944-
(Molly Ivins)

PERSONAL: Born August 30, 1944, in Monterey, CA; daughter of Jim and Margo Ivins. *Education:* Received B.A. from Smith College, and M.A. from Columbia University; attended Institute of Political Science, Paris, France.

ADDRESSES: *Office*—Creators Syndicate, 5777 West Century Blvd., Suite 700, Los Angeles, CA 90045.

CAREER: Worked as a reporter for the *Chronicle,* Houston, TX, and the *Star Tribune,* Minneapolis, MN; *Texas Observer,* Austin, reporter, 1970-76; *New York Times,* New York, NY, reporter, 1976-77, Rocky Mountain bureau chief in Denver, CO, 1977-80; *Dallas Times Herald,* Dallas, TX, columnist, 1980—. National News Council, former board member. Member of Pulitzer Prize jury, 1992.

MEMBER: Amnesty International, Reporter's Committee for Freedom of the Press.

AWARDS, HONORS: Named Outstanding Alumna, Columbia University's School of Journalism, 1976; Headliner's Award, 1991, for best Texas column; Lifetime Achievement Award, National Society of Newspaper Columnists, 1994; finalist for three Pulitzer Prizes.

WRITINGS:

Molly Ivins Can't Say That, Can She?, Random House, 1991.

Nothin' But Good Times Ahead, Random House, 1993.

(Contributor) *Old Dogs Remembered,* edited by Bud Johns, Carroll & Graf (New York, NY), 1993.

You Got to Dance with Them What Brung You: Politics in the Clinton Years, Random House, 1998.

(With Lou Dubose) *Shrub: The Short But Happy Political Life of George W. Bush,* Random House, 2000.

Author of introduction to *The Edge of the West and Other Stories,* by Bryan Woolley, Texas Western Press, 1990, and to *The Betrayal of America: How the Supreme Court Undermined the Constitution and Chose Our President,* by Vincent Bugliosi, Thunder Mouth's Press, 2001. Contributor to periodicals, including *Nation, New York Times Book Review, Mother Jones, Ms.,* and *Progressive.*

SIDELIGHTS: Known for her sharp wit and irreverent style, columnist Mary Tyler Ivins, who writes under the name Molly Ivins, has gained a reputation as an insightful political commentator. A writer for the *Dallas Times Herald* and a regular contributor to magazines such as the *Progressive, Nation,* and *Mother Jones,* Ivins reached an even larger audience with the publication of her first book, *Molly Ivins Can't Say That, Can She?,* a collection of essays and articles that became a best-seller in 1991. Ivins, a native Texan, often lampoons Texas politics in her column: she once commented that if a state representative's "IQ slips any lower, we'll have to water him twice a day." Some members of the Dallas business community, offended by Ivins's remark, attempted to pressure the *Times Herald* into censuring Ivins by withdrawing their advertisements from the newspaper. But the *Times Herald* did not reproach Ivins; instead, the publication covered Dallas billboards with the question, "Molly Ivins Can't Say *That,* Can She?"

In addition to Texas politics, which she once described in the *Nation* as the "finest form of free entertainment ever invented," Ivins covers a range of topics in her essays, including national politics, government scandals, the sanctity of football in Texas, country music, a group called Debutantes for Christ, feminism, and the idiosyncrasies that make Texans different from other Southerners and Southerners different from other Americans. Politicians are among her favorite targets. Ivins was quoted by *People* as saying that America's forty-first president, George Bush, "spends more money on military bands than he does on Head Start [a preschool program for poor children]. . . . Personally, I think he's further evidence that the Great Scriptwriter in the sky has an overdeveloped sense of irony."

Ivins's humor and straight talk have earned her many loyal admirers, including former Texas Governor Ann Richards who, according to *People,* deemed *Molly Ivins Can't Say That, Can She?* "more fun than riding a mechanical bull and almost as dangerous." Allen Lacy, writing in *New York Times Book Review,* remarked that "Molly Ivins proves that keen intelligence and a Southern accent are real good buddies. She is a canny observer of the political and cultural scene at both the local level . . . and the national level. And she expresses her opinions firmly, with brio and a lot of irreverence." *Women's Review of Books* contributor Judith Beth Cohen applauded Ivins's "love of exaggeration, her delight in vernacular speech and her fascination with what's left of the frontier," and added, "Now women writers working on political humor have an iconoclastic model of their own."

In typical Ivins fashion, she titled her 1998 book *You Got to Dance with Them What Brung You:* an old saying that underscores the idea that special-interest money fuels the political system. *Dance* is a collection of newspaper essays that takes on all manner of national and Texas politics, including such 1990s touchstones as NAFTA, welfare reform, and budget battles. Nor are individuals spared: High-profile personalities like Bob Dole, Newt Gingrich, and George W. Bush are in line for their lumps. But throughout the book, suggested a *Kirkus Reviews* article, Ivins is to be credited for maintaining a friendly tone: "Unlike many of her conservative peers, Ivins actually likes people, even the politicians she has made a career of skewering."

As the United States presidential race of 2000 heated up, Ivins and coauthor Lou Dubose took on one of the front-runners in *Shrub: The Short but Happy Political Life of George W. Bush.* As might be expected from a Texas liberal, *Shrub* seeks to shed light on the Lone Star Republican's record, and Ivins makes her views clear in the introduction: "If, at the end of this short book, you find W. Bush's political resume a little light, don't blame us. There's really not much there. We have been looking for six years." The governor's privileged upbringing and blue-blooded heritage (son of President George Bush; grandson of Senator Prescott Bush; thirteenth cousin, once removed, of England's Queen Elizabeth) have been the subject of some scrutiny. Bush, "an aristocrat," as *New York Review of Books* contributor Lars-Erik Nelson called him, is a man whose "successes are in one way or another a direct consequence of his name and family, and he has been exempt from the normal competition—academic, financial, professional, political—that confronts most Americans and sorts them on life's ladder." Accordingly, Ivins and Dubose dissect Bush's actual accomplishments and find them lacking. Worse, they note, the authors find their subject "punitive toward welfare recipients and oblivious of children's health needs" in Texas, as Nelson related. In the same review, Nelson reported that Ivins and Dubose "are adept at sorting through the intricacies of Bush's oil deals, the Texas Rangers transactions, and the power balance between Texas's weak governorship and powerful legislation."

However, *Shrub* provides some balance in its perspective. The authors credit the governor's record on education; his wooing of the Hispanic vote, which led to higher voter registration; and his ability to bridge the gap between the Christian far right and the more centrist members of the Republican party."

As for Ivins's distinctive writing style, she "has both a penetrating mind and a light touch, but some of her mannerisms—like repeatedly writing about the 'oil bidness'—become cloying, even to her," said Nelson. "She defends the spelling of 'bidness' in a footnote by informing us that this is how the word is actually pronounced. Yes, and Texans also tell us that they have let Chrahst into thur horts, but we need not beat it to death." Likewise, *Christian Science Monitor* critic James Thurman compared reading *Shrub* to "sucking salsa through a straw. When Ivins writes, there has to be a jalapeno in every line." Nevertheless, "her bluntness on Bush's vagueness is funny: 'If you think his daddy had trouble with "the vision thing," wait till you meet this one.'"

BIOGRAPHICAL/CRITICAL SOURCES:

PERIODICALS

Christian Science Monitor, February 17, 2000, "Molly Ivins Is Still Shooting Fish in a Barrel," p. 15.

Library Journal, March 1, 2000, Michael A. Genovese, review of *Shrub: The Short But Happy Political Life of George W. Bush,* p. 110.
Nation, June 7, 1986, pp. 786-787.
National Review, April 17, 2000, Charlotte Hays, "This Bush Has Thorns."
New York Review of Books, February 24, 2000, Lars-Erik Nelson, "Legacy," pp. 4-6.
New York Times Book Review, October 20, 1991, p. 13.
People, December 9, 1991, pp. 100-102.
Publishers Weekly, February 7, 2000, review of *Shrub: The Short But Happy Political Life of George W. Bush,* p. 79.
Women's Review of Books, December, 1991, pp. 8-9.*

* * *

IVINS, Molly
See IVINS, Mary Tyler

* * *

JOHNSON, Chalmers (Ashby) 1931-

PERSONAL: Born August 6, 1931, in Phoenix, AZ; son of David F., Jr., and Katherine (Ashby) Johnson; married Sheila Knipscheer, May 25, 1957. *Education:* University of California, Berkeley, A.B., 1953, M.A., 1957, Ph.D., 1961.

ADDRESSES: Office—Japan Policy Research Institute, 2138 Via Tiempo, Cardiff, CA 92007. *E-mail*—chaljohnson@jpri.org.

CAREER: United Nations, intern, 1958; University of California, Berkeley, began as associate professor, became professor of political science, 1962-88, chair of Center for Chinese Studies, 1967-72; University of California, San Diego, professor at Graduate School of International Relations and Pacific Studies, 1988-92; Japan Policy Research Institute, Cardiff, CA, co-founder and president, 1994—. Former adviser to the Central Intelligence Agency. *Military service:* U.S. Navy, 1953-55; became lieutenant junior grade.

MEMBER: Association for Asian Studies, American Academy of Arts and Sciences.

AWARDS, HONORS: Ford Foundation fellowship for Japan, 1961-62; Social Science Research Council fellowship for Hong Kong, 1965-66.

WRITINGS:

Freedom of Thought and Expression in China: Communist Policies toward the Intellectual Class, Union Research Institute (Hong Kong, China), 1959.
Peasant Nationalism and Communist Power: The Emergence of Revolutionary China, 1937-1945, Stanford University Press (Stanford, CA), 1962.
An Instance of Treason: Ozaki Hotsumi and the Sorge Spy Ring, Stanford University Press (Stanford, CA), 1964, expanded edition, 1990.
Revolution and the Social System, Hoover Institution (Stanford, CA), 1964.
Revolutionary Change, Little, Brown (Boston, MA), 1966, second edition, Stanford University Press (Stanford, CA), 1982.
(Editor and contributor) *Change in Communist Systems,* Stanford University Press (Stanford, CA), 1970.
Conspiracy at Matsukawa, University of California Press (Berkeley, CA), 1972.
Autopsy on People's War, University of California Press (Berkeley, CA), 1973.
(Editor) *Ideology and Politics in Contemporary China,* University of Washington Press (Seattle, WA), 1973.
Japan's Public Policy Companies, American Enterprise Institute for Public Policy Research (Washington, DC), 1978.
MITI and the Japanese Miracle: The Growth of Industrial Policy, 1925-1975, Stanford University Press (Stanford, CA), 1982.
(Editor) *The Industrial Policy Debate,* ICS Press (San Francisco, CA), 1984.
(Editor, with Laura D'Andrea Tyson and John Zysman) *Politics and Productivity: The Real Story of Why Japan Works,* Ballinger (Cambridge, MA), 1989.
History Restarted: Japanese-American Relations at the End of the Century, Peace Research Centre, Research School of Pacific Studies, Australian National University (Canberra, Australia), 1992.
Japan, Who Governs: The Rise of the Developmental State, Norton (New York, NY), 1995.
(Editor) *Okinawa: Cold War Island,* Japan Policy Research Institute (Cardiff, CA), 1999.
Blowback: The Costs and Consequences of American Empire, Metropolitan Books (New York, NY), 2000.

Contributor to books. Contributor to professional journals.

SIDELIGHTS: Chalmers Johnson is a veteran observer of Asian economics and politics. He explained the planned nature of Japan's economy in *Japan, Who Gov-*

erns: The Rise of the Developmental State, and, in the words of *Nation* contributor Patrick Smith, "forced late-McCarthyist America to acknowledge the treasonous truth that the Chinese Communists enjoyed immense popularity in the years leading up to the revolution" in *Peasant Nationalism and Communist Power: The Emergence of Revolutionary China, 1937-1945.* Smith related that *Peasant Nationalism and Communist Power* is among several of Johnson's books that "have turned out to subvert the orthodoxy." Another is *MITI and the Japanese Miracle: The Growth of Industrial Policy, 1925-1975,* which led to a new view of Japan's economics. Smith quoted Johnson as saying that his research for that 1982 book "would lead me to see clearly for the first time the shape of the empire that I had so long uncritically supported." The empire he refers to is the United States, and Johnson critiques it in *Blowback: The Costs and Consequences of American Empire.* He contends that the United States has clung to Cold War policies even after the breakup of the Soviet Union and that this stance will have disastrous results—which he calls "blowback," using the Central Intelligence Agency term for unintended consequences. The nation's military, he asserts, has resisted budget cuts and overseas base closings, even though host countries often (justifiably, in Johnson's view) resent the presence of these bases. Johnson also deplores massive United States arms sales around the world, seeing them as an invitation to war.

"*Blowback* is expansive thinking," Smith opined. "It arrives just as our national conversation begins to suggest we're waking up from a dream. The book does much to articulate this change—and will do much to advance it further." He also lauded Johnson's "plain diction," and Edward N. Luttwak, a contributor to *World & I,* praised the author's "learned cultural insight" and "elegant prose." Luttwak noted that while many of Johnson's criticisms of U.S. policy echo those made by the far left "in order to demoralize Americans and encourage [America's] enemies, Johnson's purpose is exactly the opposite: He denounces excesses because he believes they damage American long-term interests." *New York Times* reviewer Richard Bernstein, however, suggested that Johnson showed a "strong but unsubstantiated conviction that the United States all along has been little better than any other imperial power, including the Soviet Union." Bernstein found the book "a useful and timely alert by a man with robustly contrarian views" but "marred by an overriding, sweeping and cranky one-sidedness." In *Time International,* Bruce W. Nelan deemed *Blowback* "more a scattershot polemic than an academic analysis. It suffers from its contradictions and overstatements, as well as its lack of evidence for some accusations." A *Business Week* writer expressed concern that "Johnson finds malice in U.S. policies fostering free markets around the world"; the writer granted that on military topics, Johnson raises reasonable questions, but "few may take him seriously when he comes off like a street-corner preacher with a sign proclaiming 'Repent—the world will end tomorrow!'"

Luttwak noted that while he "acknowledg[ed] the validity" of Johnson's examples of U.S. misconduct around the world, "this reviewer must disagree with a general premise of the book: I believe that there is no global American empire, only a facade behind which there is more impotence than power." This is because "the United States enjoys a divided government designed to limit rather than enhance executive power." Smith, on the other hand, remarked that one of Johnson's points is that the military is "under scant civilian control, while we have assumed a militarized consciousness we seem not even to notice in ourselves." He allowed that there is "plenty to contest" in *Blowback,* but predicted that the arguments the book will generate would be useful ones. "It gives us back what our newspapers and our academic specialists have declined to supply since the late forties: a framework in which we can understand where we've come from, who we've made of ourselves and where we're headed." Nelan, even while noting that "Johnson's denunciations are debatable and not all of his predictions are probabilities," admitted that "if self-absorbed America goes on ignoring the world, some of them might come true."

BIOGRAPHICAL/CRITICAL SOURCES:

PERIODICALS

Business Week, April 10, 1995, review of *Japan, Who Governs,* p. 19; March 27, 2000, "A Shrill Sermon Against U.S. Globalism," p. 19.

Foreign Affairs, November-December, 1995, Donald Zagoria, review of *Japan, Who Governs,* p. 140.

Nation, August 7, 2000, Patrick Smith, "'Manifest Duplicity,'" p. 37.

New York Times, March 29, 2000, Richard Bernstein, "Another Evil Empire, This One in the Mirror."

New York Times Book Review, March 19, 1995, Adam Smith, "Japan Inc. Is Still in Business," p. 6.

Time International, May 29, 2000, Bruce W. Nelan, "A Jeremiad at Work: A One-Time 'Spear Carrier for Empire' Takes a Swipe at Modern-Day American Imperialism," p. 73.

Whole Earth Review, winter, 1990, Charles Sweet, review of *MITI and the Japanese Miracle,* p. 30.

World & I, July, 2000, Edward N. Luttwak, "What American Empire?," pp. 261-264.

OTHER

Japan Policy Research Institute, http://www.jpri.org/ (March 12, 2001).

* * *

JOHNSON, Joan J. 1942-

PERSONAL: Born September 8, 1942, in Norwalk, CT; daughter of John Lincoln (a corporation president) and Edith (a homemaker; maiden name, Wood) Irving; divorced; children: Jedidiah Lincoln David, Nathan Azariah Jacob. *Education:* Bethany College (Bethany, WV), B.A., 1964; University of Pennsylvania, graduate study, 1964-65; Fairfield University, M.A., 1983. *Politics:* Independent.

ADDRESSES: Home—Norwalk, CT. *Office*—Darien High School, School Lane, Darien, CT 06820.

CAREER: High school English teacher, Ipswich, MA, 1966-70; Stauffer Chemical Co., Westport, CT, assistant records administrator, 1978-79; Darien High School, Darien, CT, teacher of English and of talented and gifted students, 1979—.

WRITINGS:

YOUNG ADULT

The Cult Movement, F. Watts (New York, NY), 1984.

America's War on Drugs, F. Watts (New York, NY), 1989.

Kids without Homes, F. Watts (New York, NY), 1991.

Teen Prostitution, F. Watts (New York, NY), 1992.

Children of Welfare, Holt (New York, NY), 1996.

JUVENILE

Justice, F. Watts (New York, NY), 1985.

JOHNSTON, Lynn (Beverley) 1947-

PERSONAL: Born May 28, 1947, in Collingwood, Ontario, Canada; daughter of Mervyn (a jeweler) and Ursula (an artisan; maiden name, Bainbridge) Ridgway; married first husband (a cameraman), c. 1975 (divorced); married John Roderick Johnston (a dentist and pilot), February 15, 1977; children: (first marriage) Aaron Michael; (second marriage) Katherine Elizabeth. *Education:* Attended Vancouver School of Arts, 1964-67. *Religion:* Unitarian-Universalist. *Avocational interests:* Travel, doll collecting, playing the accordion, copiloting and navigating aircraft.

ADDRESSES: Home—North of North Bay, Ontario, Canada. *Office*—c/o Andrews McMeel Publishing, 4520 Main St., Kansas City, MO 64111.

CAREER: McMaster University, Hamilton, Ontario, Canada, worked as a medical artist, 1968-73; freelance commercial artist and writer, 1973—; author and illustrator of "For Better or for Worse" cartoon strip syndicated by Universal Press Syndicate, 1979—. President, Lynn Johnston Productions, Inc.

AWARDS, HONORS: Reuben Award, National Cartoonists Society, 1986, for outstanding cartoonist of the year; named member of the Order of Canada, 1992; Reuben Award finalist, National Cartoonists Society, 1995, for outstanding cartoonist of the year; National Cartoonists Society Category Award for best comic strip; Quill Award, National Association of Writing Instrument Distributors; Inkpot Award, San Diego Comics Convention; EDI Award; two honorary degrees.

WRITINGS:

SELF-ILLUSTRATED CARTOON BOOKS

David! We're Pregnant!, Potlatch Publications, 1973, published as *David! We're Pregnant!: 101 Cartoons for Expecting Parents,* Meadowbrook, 1977, revised edition, 1992.

Hi, Mom! Hi, Dad!: The First Twelve Months of Parenthood, P. M. A. Books, 1975, revised edition, Meadowbrook, 1977.

Do They Ever Grow Up?, Meadowbrook, 1978, published as *Do They Ever Grow Up?: 101 Cartoons about the Terrible Twos and Beyond,* 1983.

Lynn Johnston

"FOR BETTER OR FOR WORSE" COMIC COLLECTIONS

I've Got the One-More-Washload Blues, Andrews & McMeel, 1981.

Is This "One of Those Days," Daddy?, Andrews & McMeel, 1982.

It Must Be Nice to Be Little, Andrews & McMeel, 1983.

More Than a Month of Sundays: A For Better or for Worse Sunday Collection, Andrews & McMeel, 1983.

Our Sunday Best: A For Better or for Worse Sunday Collection, Andrews & McMeel, 1984.

Just One More Hug, Andrews & McMeel, 1984.

The Last Straw, Andrews & McMeel, 1985.

Keep the Home Fries Burning, Andrews & McMeel, 1986.

It's All Downhill from Here, Andrews & McMeel, 1987.

Pushing 40, Andrews & McMeel, 1988.

A Look Inside—For Better or for Worse: The Tenth Anniversary Collection, Andrews & McMeel, 1989.

It All Comes Out in the Wash (contains reprints from previous books), Tor Books, 1990.

If This Is a Lecture, How Long Will It Be?, Andrews & McMeel, 1990.

For Better or for Worse: Another Day, Another Lecture (contains reprints from previous books), Tor Books, 1991.

What, Me Pregnant?, Andrews & McMeel, 1991.

For Better or for Worse: You Can Play in the Barn, But You Can't Get Dirty (contains reprints from previous books), Tor Books, 1992.

For Better or for Worse: You Never Know What's around the Corner (contains reprints from previous books), Tor Books, 1992.

Things Are Looking Up, Andrews & McMeel, 1992.

For Better or for Worse: It's a Pig-Eat-Chicken World (contains reprints from previous books), Tor Books, 1993.

For Better or for Worse: Shhh—Mom's Working! (contains reprints from previous books), Tor Books, 1993.

But, I Read the Destructions!: For Better or for Worse, T. Doherty Associates, 1993.

"There Goes My Baby!": A For Better or for Worse Collection, Andrews & McMeel, 1993.

It's the Thought That Counts—: For Better or for Worse Fifteenth Anniversary Collection, Andrews & McMeel, 1994.

Starting from Scratch, Andrews & McMeel, 1995.

Love Just Screws Everything Up, Andrews & McMeel, 1996.

Remembering Farley: A Tribute to the Life of Our Favorite Cartoon Dog, Andrews & McMeel, 1996.

Growing Like a Weed: A For Better or for Worse Collection, Andrews & McMeel, 1997.

Middle Age Spread: A For Better or for Worse Collection, Andrews & McMeel, 1998.

The Lives behind the Lines: 20 Years of For Better or for Worse, Andrews & McMeel, 1999.

Sunshine & Shadow: A For Better or for Worse Collection, Andrews & McMeel, 1999.

The Big 5-0: A For Better or for Worse Collection, Andrews & McMeel, 2000.

Isn't He Beautiful?, Andrews & McMeel, 2000.

Isn't She Beautiful?, Andrews & McMeel, 2000.

ILLUSTRATOR

Bruce Lansky, editor, *The Best Baby Name Book in the Whole Wide World,* Meadowbrook Press, 1979.

Vicki Lansky, *The Taming of the C.A.N.D.Y. Monster,* revised edition, Book Peddlers, 1988.

Vicki Lansky, *Practical Parenting Tips for the First Five Years,* revised and enlarged edition, Meadowbrook Press, 1992.

OTHER

Has also contributed one story and a cover illustration to *Canadian Children's Annual.*

ADAPTATIONS: Ottawa's Funbag Animation Studios produced a weekly animated series based on "For Better or for Worse," 2000.

SIDELIGHTS: A precious, tiny baby and the family dog are sharing a moment. They are both on the floor, happily munching on the canine's food. When a parent discovers them, they look up from their feast with smiles—and dog food—on their faces. This scene of family disarray comes courtesy of Lynn Johnston, the creator of the "For Better or for Worse" comic strip, where this tableau graced the cover of her book, *Things Are Looking Up.* When it comes to chronicling the problems and phobias of the typical North American family, no one does it like Johnston. Her drawings of the fictional—but believable—Patterson family are seen in hundreds of newspapers in the United States and Canada, and "For Better or for Worse" has consistently been voted as one of the top five strips in reader polls.

"For Better or for Worse" developed out of many of Johnston's real life situations and concerns. The strip is populated by the Patterson family: two parents, two children, and a family dog. In this slice-of-life strip, there is a harried mother named Elly, and her nice and slightly bumbling husband, John. Elly was named after one of Johnston's friends, who died in high school from a tumor. Her friend Elly also wore her hair in the same way that Elly Patterson now does.

There are more similarities, too. Both the Johnstons and the Pattersons are Canadian. Johnston is married to Rod, who, like his fictional counterpart John, is a tall, affable dentist who is also a pilot. The two Patterson children, Michael and Elizabeth, are near in age to the Johnston children, Aaron and Katie, whose middle names have become the first names of the cartoon characters. The Johnstons even had an English sheep dog named Farley, who passed away, as the dog in the comic strip did. The Johnstons now own a black spaniel named Willie. Finally, Elly's brother Phil is a wayward trumpet player just like Johnston's brother, Alan Philip Ridgway.

And there are yet more subtle, more emotional similarities. Johnston herself has admitted that both she and Elly want to be rescuers. They both feel motivated to try to fix everyone and everything in their family. Rod Johnston admitted to Jeanne Malmgren in the *St. Petersburg Times Floridian* that "their insecurities are similar. They both worry about saying the wrong thing and offending somebody. Lynn also overworks like Elly. She gets exhausted, trying to please everybody all the time. And the losing weight thing. They both do that."

Johnston's emotional closeness to her characters has made them very real to her. Rod has said: "You can ask her what Elly's wearing today, and she'll tell you. If you ask about their house, she'll describe the sun room at the back and the driveway and all the junk in the garage."

At a certain point, though, the parallels end. "I find that somehow the characters develop their personalities independently of me," Johnston told Janice Dineen in the *Toronto Star.* Husband Rod has also noted the differences, telling Malmgren that Lynn has more polish than her fictional character, and that she "is much more of a businessperson. And she's more in charge of our family than Elly is." Johnston's children "both look very, very different from the characters in the strip, and their lives are very different," Johnston commented in an interview for *Authors and Artists for Young Adults.* Her son once said: "'I don't want Michael to wear glasses, I want him to be as separate from me as he can be,' and so Elizabeth got the glasses, which was great for my daughter who does not wear glasses."

The addition of daughter April also signals a departure for Johnston. While she grappled with her feelings of wanting another baby, she worked out this issue on paper instead of in reality. "I brought the baby into the strip," Johnston remarked to Dineen, "because for a while I really wanted another baby. I thought about adopting but instead, in the end, I made my baby up."

April is a very unique character in the strip, since she is the only one who is totally fictional and not based on one of Johnston's family members. "I can have a lot more fun with her and reveal a lot more about her private life because in reality she doesn't exist, so it's not as though I'm opening up a closet that no one has a right to see in," Johnston once related.

The suburban and slightly idyllic life of the Patterson family is somewhat removed from Johnston's own beginnings. Johnston, a self-described angry child, used drawing and art as an outlet for her emotions. "I drew lots when I was mad," she recalled in a *People* article by Ned Geeslin. "It helped me vent my anger. I was really an angry girl, even in elementary school. I wanted to be grown up. I'd fantasize and draw a picture of what I'd look like when I was old and what my husband would look like."

Sometimes this tendency for fantasizing would land her in difficulties in school, like the time where she doodled all over her math exam. "It was often hard for me to take anything seriously and even though I enjoyed school, there were times, especially during math class, when I would rather draw than take part," she told *Authors and Artists for Young Adults.* But things weren't always so dire—"I remember . . . getting an 'A' for the doodles and a 'D' for the exam," Johnston quipped.

The child of a watchmaker and a self-taught calligrapher and illustrator, one of Johnston's early memories was of her mother correcting her posture. "My mum was a real stickler for posture," Johnston said to Malmgren. "She made me walk around with a book on my head and stand against the wall to make sure my shoulders were back." As an adult, her rebellion against this teaching comes out in her work—Elly Patterson has an almost perpetual slouch. "So whenever I draw that slouch," she added, "it's almost a direct way of getting back at my mother."

Her parents' artistic sensibilities were to greatly influence Johnston in her later career. "My mother had tremendous talent when it came to painting and craft work. She was always making hooked rugs and all that sort of thing, but she was a calligrapher for my grandfather who had a stamp dealership." She spent a lot of time with her father, who was one of the greatest influences on her artistic talent. "My dad was a closet cartoonist. More than drawing cartoons, he appreciated cartoons. We would pour over these illustrations one at a time and he would point out the drawings and what made them funny. He just loved comics; he just loved cartoons."

More than simply appreciate cartoons and movies, Johnston's father would encourage her to analyze the humor in them, see how timing and setting played an important part in the humor of a piece. This was great training for the work Johnston would later do in her strip, where timing was essential. "He wouldn't just take you to a movie. He would talk about the comedy as it was timed and as it was set up and how difficult it was to set up these pratfalls. So comedy for me was not just a matter of sitting down and enjoying it, it was a matter of analyzing it as well. That went for both cartoons in the paper and cartoon behavior on live film."

For a short while, Johnston was enrolled in the Vancouver School of Art. She quit, however, and took jobs in animation and illustration. Marrying a cameraman named Doug, she moved to Ontario because of the better job opportunities. But Johnston found herself missing the mountains of British Columbia. Still, the move proved to be the right decision when she found a job in the city of Hamilton. "I got a wonderful job as a medical artist for McMaster University. . . . They trained me to do medical illustration. I did first year medical school and went to all the anatomy courses and did dissection and everything with the medical students," she once said. "It was a great time of learning and a whole new career and I loved it." Soon, her son Aaron was born. Unfortunately, Johnston and her husband soon separated and Doug moved back to Vancouver.

After her divorce, Johnston started to do freelance work out of her home and soon found her business booming. Oddly enough, it was her obstetrician who started a chain of events that would eventually lead to her being offered a contract for a comic strip. Knowing that she was a comic artist, he challenged her to come up with some cartoons to be put on the ceiling above his examining tables. "I was the type of person that liked a challenge, and if somebody I admired gave me a challenge, I went through that open door. That challenge was enough to make me do eighty drawings for him." With her friend's help, she found a publisher for the illustrations, eventually completing enough material for three books.

Submissions editors at Universal Press Syndicate had seen Johnston's first book, *David! We're Pregnant!,* and they were impressed with the quality and humor in her drawings. They were searching for a comic strip that could compete with the family-oriented "Blondie" and "Hi and Lois" and thought Johnston might be a shoo-in for that position. She was contacted and asked if she could produce in a four-frame format.

Johnston was both excited and nervous about the proposition. She had never written in a daily format, but was willing to give it a try. Shortly after Universal Press's offer, she sent them samples of a strip she had developed based loosely on her own family life. To her surprise, they accepted her submissions and offered her a daily, syndicated strip. She received a one-year development contract with which she was allowed to work on her strip for a year before it was published. After the year, she was offered a twenty-year contract.

"When I got the contract, I was totally blown out of the water," she told Malmgren. "It was the opportunity of a lifetime, but at the same time, it was terrifying. I never thought I would be able to come up with funny gags 200 or 300 times a year." She turned to her friend Cathy Guisewite, the creator of the very successful "Cathy" comic strip, for some friendly advice. Guisewite suggested that before doing the art she should write all the dialogue down as if she were doing script. "I had a tremendously good relationship with her on the phone," Johnston once remarked. "She gave me lots of hints on how she worked and then I went from there."

Over 150 papers signed on to carry "For Better or for Worse," even before the strip began to officially run. "It's hard to sell a new feature to papers, and many new cartoonists only start with about fifty papers, and maybe they never get past that," the cartoonist said. "I know now some young people who are struggling and they cannot seem to get past their fifty papers. So for me to start with 150 was quite an exciting thing. But then it was one of the first of the family strips that was not done by a man and also was done in a contemporary style. So I was breaking new ground in a way. . . . I was very fortunate."

As her comic career was developing, another story had been brewing as well. A few years before, while driving along with her young son, she happened to spot a small plane flying overhead. She loved flying and small aircraft, so on a whim she drove to the airport to see the plane land. "This nice young fellow jumped out of the plane and walked over and we had a conversation. He invited me to fly with him to the next airport for a hamburger," she told *Authors and Artists for Young Adults.* Shortly afterward, the two realized that they were pretty compatible, except for one thing. He wanted to move north, and she wanted to stay in southern Canada. Overlooking this slight obstacle she and Rod Johnston were married in 1976. He adopted her son and they had a daughter of their own shortly afterward.

Rod's graduation from dental school and their move to the north coincided with Johnston's proposal for Universal Press Syndicate. She found herself packing boxes for an income while trying to land the job with Universal. Shortly afterward, they moved to northern Manitoba, where Rod became a flying dentist.

Johnston cites some of her husband's qualities as being helpful to her career. "We [cartoonists] are very difficult people to live with," she once remarked. "In order to maintain a career that's based on fantasy, you have to live with someone who is very down to earth, who is very reassuring." Rod has provided her with this stability, as well as something else equally essential. "He's also very funny. He's one of the funniest people I know."

The move to northern Canada proved to be fortuitous in many ways. First, Johnston got to have a remarkable adventure and meet new and different people. Second, it helped ease her adjustment to the fame she was getting. "It was good for me because the publicity was something that I didn't know how to handle. I'm a ham; I'm a frustrated actor as it probably shows in the work that I do. And so if I had more access to the city, I probably would have been a bigger jerk than I was. It was a very good thing that I lived in isolation for six years and I learned how to handle the publicity and not be such a ham."

Johnston works almost every day. In the studio of the big log house they own on the edge of a lake in northern Ontario, where they moved after Manitoba, she produces her strip. "I like to sit in a corner with my feet up and a cup of coffee and a couple of pads of paper and I like to just write before I do anything." It takes her about one or two days to write the dialogue for one week of her comic strip, a task that is especially trying for her. "There's a fine line between what makes something funny and what makes something just barely amusing. I think it takes a sort of acting ability to be able to set up a scene, get the expressions and then bring it to a punch line. All in four frames. It's a knack that's taken me a long time to develop," she confided to Malmgren. Johnston feels that over the course of a week, one or two strips will be significantly funny, while the rest just build the story line.

After the writing process, she sets to work creating the art. "I waste almost no paper. I draw it in pencil, then I go over it with India ink pens, and then I put on the Lettra film, with the little dots that gives you the gray tones," she told Malmgren. "You have to be the characters as you are drawing," Johnston told Dineen. "You have to feel what the character is feeling. Even Farley the dog: as he stretches, I feel that." In this way, her feelings of being a frustrated actor have benefited her drawing. In her career, Johnston has drawn close to five thousand "For Better or for Worse" sketches. "It's like writing little sitcoms all the time and I'm playing all the roles and controlling all the camera angles," she told Dineen.

Johnston's early comics were very simple sketches of the Pattersons. Their two children were tiny, and they acquired a small puppy also, who was to grow into the massive Farley. They dealt with the normal grind of a family growing up together—parents and kids fighting, exhaustion and mess, and so on. But as the Patterson family has grown and grown up, Johnston has tackled more complex and controversial issues in her strip.

At one point, Elly has to deal with the problem of her friend, who gave birth to a baby with six fingers on both hands. Later on, the Pattersons discover their own feelings on race relations as an Asian family moves into the house across the street. In a 1992 story line, Mike Patterson finds out that his friend, Gordon, is being abused by his father. Johnston admitted that the strip was taken from an incident that had happened to a friend of her daughter. She told John Przybys in the *Las Vegas Review-Journal:* "It was an experience I had and it bothered me. And, sometimes, when experiences bother you, you know how you tend to dream about them? For me, the dreaming came out on paper."

Johnston tackled another difficult topic in a 1993 strip series. In it, family friend Lawrence Poirier admits to his family that he is gay. Unfortunately, his parents react badly, denying the news and eventually kicking him out of the house. This topic choice was partly inspired by Johnston's brother-in-law, Ralph, who is gay. Ralph revealed his feelings to the family years before, but the admission of his homosexuality changed her family forever. "What happens when you hear this news is you change," Johnston told John Tanasychuk of the *Detroit Free Press.* "You change because your point of view is shattered. You think one thing about the person and then this comes along. Then you realize that they haven't changed. It's you."

Johnston was a catalyst for family healing when this situation happened. By writing a series of strips about a gay character, the cartoonist hoped to reach her readers with this same sort of information and sharing she had discovered. However, because of the controversial topic, forty papers took alternate material and nineteen cancelled the strip outright. About this reaction, Johnston commented to Tanasychuk, "It surprises me in today's environment that people would want to [keep] something like that out of a newspaper. I think that the readers should be able to decide for themselves whether they want to read that."

Johnston received more than three thousand letters after the strips were published, two thirds of which praised her for having the courage to address the issue. However, there was also a significant amount of vicious, negative comments on the strip that could only be described as "hate mail." "What happens when something like this hits the paper," Johnston once stated, "is that the very angry people and generally very religious people unite first because they are used to crusading against something that they feel is threatening to their beliefs. The very angry, angry letters came first, the very angry response, and then, as soon as the angry response was visible, the thinking, caring people and especially people who work with families . . . started to write."

"I took a chance. I knew there would be some controversy," Johnston concluded. "And I didn't intend it to be quite as overwhelming as it was. Nonetheless it's a subject that horrifies, terrifies people. They're so afraid of it and so unwilling to learn about it, and that's why it's taking so long for acceptance and understanding to happen." Johnston has turned all the letters over to the sociology department of her local university, where they will be sorted and studied. "People were outraged that I would allow this word to enter their home. That it would be something that they would see on the comics page. . . . It was a really amazing situation. Not something I would want to engineer again." She later added, however, that a "great deal of good was done despite the emotional roller coaster ride we all endured!"

In general, Johnston receives a lot of positive feedback from her more controversial strips. "If I do something of a serious nature, I'll get one letter against and 20 letters for," she told Przybys. "People are really comfortable reading about (serious) stuff as long as I'm careful to treat it with dignity and in a light way, because it *is* an entertainment medium and people do read comics for fun." The problem with confronting a controversial issue is that other special interest groups have sometimes requested that Johnston give equal time to their causes: A "lot of people want me to go further: 'Oh gosh, if she's willing to talk about child abuse, let's have her champion the abortion issue.' It's dangerous, when you do realistic things, turning the strip into a soapbox and people wanting you to champion their cause. You can't do that."

Asked whether she would enter into such a controversial area again, Johnston answered: "I often find myself writing and being surprised by the twists or the conversation that has just shown up. So I don't know what's going to happen. I certainly don't plan on shying away from controversy, but I don't intend to cause such concern for editors again. It was a difficult time for them because they were damned if they did and damned if they didn't." She feels that pretty much any topic is fair game as long as it fits her strip. "I don't think I betrayed the style of work that I do."

The cartoonist's willingness to take on just about any issue in her strip is sometimes bemoaned by her family because they realize that she will agonize for weeks until the story has run. With her children, Johnston knows that she can't use anything too personal from their lives. "I think the fact that neither of my kids reads my work is not an insult. It's a compliment in that they trust me, they know that they don't have to read it and watch over my shoulder to make sure that I'm not invading their privacy."

However, with her husband sometimes the issue is a little different. There was once a strip that ran where John breaks a foot by having a huge frozen turkey fall on it. Although this didn't really happen to him, he could not live it down. "I took tremendous abuse for that," he told Malmgren. "Everywhere I went, people were asking 'Where's the cast?'" On the other hand, Johnston finds that her husband is "probably my very best editor," as she related to *Authors and Artists for Young Adults.* He has provided essential editing advice and suggestions on what works and what is funny. "At one point though, he was saying 'Gosh, John always ends up a bit of a buffoon and I don't like that.' I was impressed by that, and yet at the same time, he said 'But if it's funny, it's awfully hard not to let it go.'. . . So I try not to make John look like a twit, I try to give them equal twit billing."

Johnston has won numerous awards and accolades throughout her career. In 1986, she won the prestigious Reuben Award for outstanding cartoonist of the year from the National Cartoonists Society, making her the first female and the youngest person ever to win. At the time, Johnston felt a little cowed by winning the award. "I felt at the time that it was too much, too soon. I really felt that I hadn't earned it yet," she once confessed. "I was afraid of the statue. It's a huge, heavy thing. I brought it home and hid it. I didn't want to look at it because I didn't feel that I could live up to it."

The award literally changed her life. "The morning after I got home from the award ceremony, I walked into my studio and everything looked different, just the whole room had a different meaning to it. It was terrifying. And the one person I knew who would understand was Charles M. Schulz, so I sat down and started to write him a letter. As I was sealing the letter in the envelope, the phone rang. It was [Schulz], and he said, 'Hi, when you walked into your studio this morning, did everything look different?'" That moment not only helped Johnston get over her fear, but she knew she had found a good friend in the creator of the famous "Peanuts" comic strip.

Johnston has cited the camaraderie among her fellow cartoonists as one of the benefits of her career. "There are times when you feel drained. The deadlines get you down and you can't think of anything. You feel pressured . . . and it's great to call each other. We're very supportive of each other. Even though there is competition for space in magazines and on comic pages, there's a tremendous amount of camaraderie." She was heartened by the strong backing she received from other cartoonists when the backlash from her Lawrence story was becoming evident.

Johnston also admits she likes to visit her fellow cartoonists and peek into their studios. "The first thing you want to do is see the studio because it's sort of a shrine," she once said. "It's one of those jobs that requires almost no equipment. I mean, most of us don't even have anything as expensive as a word processor. It's all pens and paper, which are very easy to obtain. The rest all comes from you. So there's a certain magic to that corner and that old wooden drafting table. You want to stand in that place that's so full of fantasy."

In comic strip popularity polls held by many newspapers in the early 1990s, Johnston's "For Better or for Worse" consistently placed in the top five, and, even more consistently, the top two spots. Johnston's strip was picked number one by readers of such newspapers as the *Detroit Free Press,* the *Oregonian,* the *Toronto Star,* the *L.A. Life Daily News,* the Denver *Rocky Mountain News,* the Norfolk *Virginian Pilot,* the *Cincinnati Enquirer,* and the Monterrey County, California, *Herald.*

But these statistics aren't surprising, considering the almost universal appeal of Johnston's work. She is barraged by fan mail from people who claim that the cartoonist is drawing from their experience. "I'm . . . surprised by how many people read the strip then tell me, 'My daughter said that exact thing,' or 'That happened to me yesterday,'" Johnston admitted to Dineen. One woman who was confined to a body cast wrote to tell Johnston that although things were going poorly, she had laughed at one of Johnston's strips. Johnston was so touched that she sent the original of the strip to the woman.

When asked about the reasons for the popularity of her strips, Johnston replied, "I think because people can identify with it, and I try to be very true to life. I enjoy what I do and I think it shows. The letters I get tend to tell me that people trust me and want to confide in me. They feel that I'm talking about their family and that it's the truth."

Johnston readily admits that she loves her job, telling Dineen, "I wouldn't trade it for anything. It keeps me in touch with people and their lives. I get to make people laugh." She knows that her cartooning is not only a profession, but a means of self-expression. "This is my way of communicating. Some people use music or dance or literature. I use cartooning." Her husband has mused that perhaps, with the Patterson family aging in the strip, Johnston will eventually write her way out of a job. But she disagrees, believing that there will always be a story line for her fictional family. In the final analysis, the strip is more than just work for Johnston. "I research a lot of my feelings through the strip. My personal philosophy comes out in it. The strip is what I do best."

BIOGRAPHICAL/CRITICAL SOURCES:

BOOKS

Authors and Artists for Young Adults, Volume 12, Gale (Detroit, MI), 1994.

Encyclopedia of World Biography Supplement, Volume 18, Gale (Detroit, MI), 1998.

PERIODICALS

Chatelaine, February, 1987; June, 1989.

Detroit Free Press, March 17, 1993, John Tanasychuk, "Gay Teen Comes Out in 'For Better or for Worse'"; August 8, 1993, pp. 1J, 4J.

Editor & Publisher, April 3, 1993, David Astor, "Comic With Gay Character Is Dropped By Some Papers: But Most 'For Better or For Worse' Clients Decide to Publish the Sequence, Which Runs Until April 24," p. 32; April 10, 1993, David Astor, "More Papers Cancel Controversial Comic," p. 34; March 11, 1995, p. 40; September 13, 1997, David Astor, "'For Better' Creator Explains Her Move," p. 36; February 20, 1999, David Astor, "'Better' Bests Competitors in Survey of Major Papers," p. 37; December 4, 2000, David Astor, "'Better' Creator in the Canadian Club of Celebrity," p. 45.

Las Vegas Review-Journal, May 31, 1992, John Przybys, "Getting Serious."

Los Angeles Times Book Review, November 26, 1989; September 13, 1992.

Maclean's, November 6, 2000, "For Better, Not Worse," p. 83.

People, September 15, 1986, Ned Geeslin, "For Better or Worse, Canadian Cartoonist Lynn Johnston Draws Her Inspiration from Reality."

St. Petersburg Times Floridian, February 1, 1989, Jeanne Malmgren, "It's Getting 'Better.'"

Toronto Star, October 9, 1992, Janice Dineen, "Better Than Ever."

Variety, January 1, 1986.

Washington Post, April 7, 1996, Charles Truehart, "In Lynn Johnston's Drawing Room," p. F1.

K

KAHIN, Audrey R. 1934-

PERSONAL: Born May 18, 1934, in Newcastle upon Tyne, England; immigrated to the United States, 1963, naturalized citizen, 1982; daughter of Charles J. (in insurance) and Florence (a homemaker; maiden name, Anderson) Richey; married George M. Kahin (a professor), March 8, 1967. *Education:* University of Nottingham, B.A., 1955; Cornell University, M.A., 1976, Ph.D., 1979. *Politics:* Democrat.

ADDRESSES: *Home*—1017 Cayuga Heights Rd., Ithaca, NY 14850.

CAREER: Longmans, Green, and Co., Ltd. (publisher), London, England, editorial assistant, 1956-58; Interpreters School, Bergamo, Italy, teacher, 1958-60; Cornell University, Ithaca, NY, administrative and research assistant, 1963-66; worked at American University, 1966-67; Cornell University, editor of Modern Indonesia Project, 1979-95, and Southeast Asia Program, 1986-95.

MEMBER: Association for Asian Studies, League of Women Voters.

AWARDS, HONORS: Fulbright awards, 1975-76 and 1984-85; grants from Social Science Research Council, 1981-82 and 1995.

WRITINGS:

(Editor, with Benedict Anderson) *Interpreting Indonesian Politics,* Modern Indonesia Project, Cornell University (Ithaca, NY), 1982.

(Editor and contributor) *Regional Dynamics of the Indonesian Revolution,* University of Hawaii Press (Honolulu, HI), 1985.

(Translator) Leon Salim, *Prisoners at Kota Cane,* Cornell University Modern Indonesia Project, Cornell University (Ithaca, NY), 1986.

(With George M. Kahin) *Subversion as Foreign Policy: The Secret Eisenhower and Dulles Debacle in Indonesia,* New Press (New York, NY), 1995.

Rebellion to Integration: West Sumatra and the Indonesian Polity, 1926-1998, Amsterdam University Press (Amsterdam, Netherlands), 1999.

Editor of the journal *Indonesia.*

SIDELIGHTS: Audrey R. Kahin, a scholar of Indonesia, looks critically at U.S. policy toward that nation in *Subversion as Foreign Policy: The Secret Eisenhower and Dulles Debacle in Indonesia,* written with her husband, George M. Kahin. In 1957, fearing that Indonesia's President Sukarno was too sympathetic to communism, U.S. President Dwight Eisenhower, along with Secretary of State John Foster Dulles and his brother, Central Intelligence Agency chief Allen Dulles, began secretly aiding anti-Sukarno rebels from outside Java, the center of Indonesia's political and economic power. After much bloodshed by both soldiers and civilians, the rebellion failed, and Sukarno adopted a more dictatorial style of governing. A *Publishers Weekly* reviewer terms the Kahins' account "a disturbing, scholarly exposé" of events that "paved the way for the Indonesian army's massacre of half a million people in 1965-66 with Washington's support."

Kahin's next book, *Rebellion to Integration: West Sumatra and the Indonesian Polity, 1926-1998,* examines the West Sumatrans' resentment of centralized power in Java, especially in the aftermath of the crushed 1950s rebellion, and also explores their role in Indonesia's winning of independence from the Netherlands in 1949. The Minangkabau people of West Sumatra, she asserts, have a far different vision of the ideal Indonesian state than do the Javanese. Where West Sumatra favors decentralization and egalitarianism, she writes, Java wants centralized power and hierarchy. *Times Literary Supplement* contributor Margaret Scott agreed that Kahin "is right that the clash between a unitary and a more democratic view of the nation is one of Indonesia's central themes" and "that the triumph of centralized power has led to a cycle of authoritarian rule and rebellion." Scott, though, disagreed that cultural differences are at the root of Indonesia's problems. She noted that many others besides the Minangkabau have opposed centralized power. "Yet understanding the role of culture and history does matter," Scott added, "and Kahin's contribution is in showing how many nationalists from Minangkabau—none more than Mohammed Hatta, Sukarno's co-independence leader and Indonesia's first vice-president—pushed for a decentralized, democratic state."

BIOGRAPHICAL/CRITICAL SOURCES:

PERIODICALS

Journal of American History, June, 1996, p. 283.
Publishers Weekly, March 27, 1995, review of *Subversion as Foreign Policy,* p. 68.
Times Literary Supplement, May 24, 1996, p. 30; July 21, 2000, Margaret Scott, "Beyond the Dirty Wars?," pp. 26-27.

* * *

KALETA, Kenneth C. 1948-

PERSONAL: Born April 11, 1948, in Chicago, IL; son of Charles J. (a lawyer) and Wanda (a homemaker; maiden name, Wiercioch) Kaleta; married Jane Green (a travel agent), November, 1969. *Ethnicity:* "Polish-American." *Education:* Villanova University, B.A., 1967, M.A., 1975; New York University, Ph.D., 1986. *Politics:* Republican. *Religion:* Roman Catholic. *Avocational interests:* Seal-point Siamese cats, travel.

ADDRESSES: Office—Rowan University, 201 Mullica Hill Rd., Glassboro, NJ 08028; fax 856-256-4344. *E-mail*—kaleta@rowan.edu.

CAREER: Rowan University, Glassboro, NJ, professor of cinema studies, 1977—.

MEMBER: U.S. Diving Association, University Film and Video Association.

WRITINGS:

Asphodel, Blackbird Press, 1989.
Occasional Papers, Glassboro College Press (Glassboro, NJ), 1993.
David Lynch, Twayne (New York, NY), 1993.
Hanif Kureishi: Postcolonial Storyteller, University of Texas Press (Austin, TX), 1997.

WORK IN PROGRESS: Hal Hartley: True Fiction Pictures; writing a play; researching haute couture and the 1960s.

SIDELIGHTS: Kenneth C. Kaleta once told *CA:* "The power of film as an international language is evident to me. I investigate it daily in teaching my film courses. It is equally evident in my everyday film-going. I am particularly interested in the dynamics of literature and film. Writing and its place in filmmaking is fascinating, as is the influence of film on contemporary writing. F. Scott Fitzgerald, my favorite author, wrote about and for the movies about sixty years ago. David Lynch, about whom I wrote a book, is a screenwriter, as is the subject of an upcoming book, filmmaker Hal Hartley. I was first drawn to his screenplays, and then to the breadth of his filmmaking in direction, music and editing for digital video and film pieces."

Kaleta added: "I have been fortunate to have written books about artists who interest me, and I have enjoyed changes in the process of crafting my books. For example, most recently I spent extensive time with filmmaker Hal Hartley. In my most recent project, I worked with a research assistant, Michael Johnston, who has made my investigation of and with Hal Hartley at True Fiction Pictures an exhilarating experience. From journeys to Austria and London to journeys into the aesthetics of Jean Cocteau and Robert LePage, the research has been a learning process for me. As long as I continue to learn from my writing, I will continue to write."

* * *

KANFER, Stefan 1933-

PERSONAL: Born May 17, 1933; son of Allen (a teacher) and Violet (a scriptwriter; maiden name, Leonard) Kanfer; married May Markey (a teacher), 1956; children: Lilian, Ethan. *Education:* New York University, B.A., 1953, graduate study, 1955-57.

ADDRESSES: Agent—Kathy Robbins, The Robbins Office, 405 Park Ave., New York, NY 10020. *E-mail*—kanfer1@aol.com.

CAREER: New York Herald Tribune, New York City, copy boy, 1951-53; television writer for *The Patty Duke Show* in the early 1960s and for Victor Borge and Allen Funt, 1964-65; *Time,* New York City, show business writer, cinema critic, essay anchor man, and book review editor, 1967-75, senior editor, 1975-88; *New Leader,* theatre critic, 1990—. *Military service:* U.S. Army, 1953-55.

MEMBER: Writers Guild of America, Dramatists Guild.

AWARDS, HONORS: J. C. Penney-University of Missouri Journalism Award, 1975; named Literary Lion of the New York Public Library, 1988; Westchester Writers Prize, 1995, 2000.

WRITINGS:

NONFICTION

A Journal of the Plague Years, Atheneum (New York, NY), 1973.

A Summer World: The Attempt to Build a Jewish Eden in the Catskills from the Days of the Ghetto to the Rise of the Borscht Belt, Farrar, Straus (New York, NY), 1989.

The Last Empire: De Beers, Diamonds, and the World, Farrar, Straus (New York, NY), 1993.

Serious Business: The Art and Commerce of Animation in America from Betty Boop to Toy Story, Scribner (New York, NY), 1997.

Groucho: The Life and Times of Julius Henry Marx, Knopf (New York, NY), 2000.

(Editor and author of introduction) *The Essential Groucho: Writings by and for Groucho Marx,* Vintage (New York, NY), 2000.

NOVELS

The Eighth Sin, Random House (New York, NY), 1978.

Fear Itself, Putnam (New York, NY), 1981.

The International Garage Sale, Norton (New York, NY), 1985.

PLAYS

I Want You (two-act musical), first produced Off-Broadway at Maidman Playhouse, 1958.

The Coffee Lover (two-act comedy), first produced in eastern United States at summer stock theaters, 1964.

Author of short stories. Contributor of articles and reviews to publications, including *Atlantic, New York Times Magazine, Harper's,* and *New Republic.* Contributing editor, *City Journal.*

SIDELIGHTS: Stefan Kanfer has produced a diverse selection of books, encompassing satirical and serious novels as well as chronicles of diamond mining in South Africa and the life of famed comedian Groucho Marx. His first book, *Journal of the Plague Years,* is an account of the "blacklisting and persecution" in the entertainment industry during the McCarthy era. Convinced that such a plague could again afflict the United States, Kanfer warns that complacency in such matters "is extremely ill-advised." The author offers another admonition in his second book, *The Eighth Sin,* where the sin of the title refers to forgetting about the Nazi Holocaust.

The Eighth Sin tells the story of Benoit, a gypsy survivor of the Auschwitz prison camp where the rest of his family has died. He is adopted by an American and his wife in England and then moves with his new family to New York City. His talent for painting is obscured by a penchant for shoplifting, a term in prison, and later a troubled marriage and alcoholism. In addition to his personal problems, Benoit carries with him the haunting memory of prison camp life. As Richard Freedman pointed out, "Benoit cannot and will not forget; the memory of the horror blights his life. . . . Ultimately Benoit must seek revenge on Elezar Jassy, a gypsy who collaborated with the Nazis while protecting the boy when he was in Auschwitz."

Some critics saw *The Eighth Sin* as a flawed but powerful work. It is an "alert but wobbly first novel," advised Ross Feld. Freedman, meanwhile, objected to the "factual 'Items'" that "obstruct the fictional flow, suggesting cool authorial research rather than genuine remembrance of nightmares past. This only slightly mars an absorbing narrative otherwise compounded of hot rage and ribald humor." And Curt Leviant viewed the gypsy motif as "bookish and contrived," while regarding some scenes as a betrayal "to the impassioned honesty of the rest of the book." That honesty is "Kanfer's eloquent cry . . . Do not forget! The Germans, he says, not only destroyed the dead, they destroyed—marked forever—those who survived; among them is the lonely, anguished Benoit."

A subsequent novel, *The International Garage Sale,* is lighter in tone but still has serious points to make. Its protagonist is Alex Lessing, a television journalist covering the World Body, an organization resembling the United Nations. He finds a surreal environment where lies, bribery, and even murder are accepted means of managing world affairs. He is "the sane, principled character in a world lacking a common moral denominator," explained Eugene J. McCarthy in the *New Republic.* McCarthy had high praise for the novel: "The book is very close to what Evelyn Waugh might have written were he living and observing, as Kanfer does, the United Nations, network television, and today's sexual, social, and family mores." *People* reviewer Campbell Geeslin also applauded the work, calling it "an elaborate, carefully crafted book that has too much truth in its outrageous plot."

The Last Empire: De Beers, Diamonds, and the World is a study of the Oppenheimer family, controllers of two huge South African companies, De Beers and Anglo American, involved in diamond and gold mining and many other enterprises. The Oppenheimers have been not only successful capitalists but strong voices of opposition to South Africa's apartheid system, which was finally dismantled in the 1990s. "They have also been inevitably accused of hypocrisy for criticizing the repressive policies of South African governments while continuing to exploit cheap black labor," reported Peter Foster in a review of Kanfer's book for *Canadian Business.* "Nevertheless, one of the first people Nelson Mandela wanted to see on his release from prison . . . was Harry Oppenheimer, son of Ernest, the founder of the De Beers/Anglo American empire." Foster thought highly of *The Last Empire*'s telling of the Oppenheimer saga, saying, "Kanfer deals well with the enormous complexities of South African history in particular with the evolution of the frequently testy relationship between commercial adventurers such as [Cecil] Rhodes and [Ernest] Oppenheimer and the local farmers of Dutch origin, the Boers." A *Publishers Weekly* critic, though, opined that Kanfer "focuses more clearly on history than on analysis" and lamented the absence of information about the role of De Beers and Anglo in constructing a post-apartheid South Africa and what reforms in the nation would mean for the companies.

In other works, Kanfer has dealt with various aspects of show business, and one of its icons is the subject of *Groucho: The Life and Times of Julius Henry Marx.* Kanfer chronicles the launching of the Marx Brothers' career by their ambitious mother, Minnie; their success in vaudeville, on Broadway, and in films; Groucho's development into the most famous member of the act, with his wisecracking, mustachioed, cigar-chomping persona; and his personal failings, including mistreatment of his wives and children. *New York Times Book Review* commentator Gary Giddins described the book as "a vivid, cleanly written biography," and he observed that Kanfer "stays away from facile psychology and moves his story along at a clip." However, he found that Kanfer had made several factual errors, something that "undermines his authority," and he deplored the dearth of primary research on Kanfer's part. Groucho's grandson, Andy Marx, reviewing the book for *Variety,* noted that "there's very little that hasn't appeared somewhere else," but "Kanfer has managed the Herculean task of synthesizing the material into a thorough, all-encompassing, though sometimes heavy-handed" account of Groucho and his brothers. Still, Marx found the book lacking in drama: "While Groucho's career was certainly fascinating, he didn't lead a life teeming with explosive secrets. . . . Sure, he was married three times, a modest number by Hollywood standards. And, yes, he was abusive to the people around him, including his wives and children, and was a narcissistic parent. But these traits aren't exactly rare in the entertainment industry. And the profile of the comedian with the dark, sad persona is as old as the history of clowns."

BIOGRAPHICAL/CRITICAL SOURCES:

PERIODICALS

Canadian Business, April, 1994, Peter Foster, review of *The Last Empire,* p. 94.

Nation, June 17, 1978.

New Republic, February 17, 1986, Eugene J. McCarthy, review of *The International Garage Sale,* p. 40.

New Yorker, August 19, 1985, p. 89; August 16, 1993, p. 95.

New York Times, June 11, 1973; May 11, 1978.

New York Times Book Review, July 8, 1973; April 30, 1978; December 24, 1989, p. 24; August 8, 1993, p. 10; June 18, 2000, Gary Giddins, review of *Groucho.*

People, September 16, 1985, Campbell Geeslin, review of *The International Garage Sale,* p. 23.

Publishers Weekly, November 3, 1989, p. 79; July 5, 1993, review of *The Last Empire,* p. 54; March 3, 1997, p. 56; March 20, 2000, p. 77.

Saturday Review, May 13, 1978.
Time, June 11, 1973; May 15, 1978; August 20, 1979.
Variety, May 1, 2000, Andy Marx, review of *Groucho,* p. 39.
Washington Post Book World, June 3, 1973; May 21, 1978.
World, June 19, 1973.

* * *

KAY, Susan 1952-

PERSONAL: Born June 24, 1952, in England; daughter of Donald Jackson and Joyce (a homemaker; maiden name, Martyn) Hodgson; married Norman Kay (a salesperson), July 6, 1974; children: Tristan, Sarah. *Education:* Mather College of Education, B.Ed. (honors).

ADDRESSES: *Home*—Cheshire, England. *Agent*—Heather Jeeves, 235/241 Regent St., London W1A 2JT, England.

CAREER: Primary school teacher, Manchester, England, 1974-78; writer.

AWARDS, HONORS: Historical Novel Prize in Memory of Georgette Heyer, Bodley Head and Transworld Publishers, and Betty Trask Prize, Society of Authors (United Kingdom), both 1985, both for *Legacy;* Boots/Romantic Novelists' Association award, 1991, for *Phantom.*

WRITINGS:

Legacy, Random House (London, England), 1985, Crown (New York, NY), 1986.
Phantom, Doubleday (London, England), 1990, Delacorte (New York, NY), 1991.

SIDELIGHTS: Susan Kay parlayed her knowledge of Elizabethan England into the award-winning historical novel *Legacy,* about the life and loves of Queen Elizabeth I, who ruled England from 1558 to 1603. The author's fascination with Elizabeth began when Kay was only a schoolgirl. Fifteen years after Kay started the novel, *Legacy* came off the presses to largely positive reviews. *Legacy* focuses not only on the political events of Elizabeth's reign but on her relationships with the men around her, among them Thomas Seymour, William Cecil, and especially Robert Dudley, Earl of Leicester.

"Susan Kay has woven a powerful tale of Elizabeth's turbulent life," wrote Linda Cahill in the Toronto *Globe and Mail.* "Skillfully blending history and an imaginative re-creation of the Queen's life, particularly her love for Robert Dudley . . . , Kay evokes the monarch and the woman. It is a masterful job for the most part." Though Susan Dooley of the *Washington Post Book World* felt the plot lagged in spots, Merle Rubin, critic for the *New York Times Book Review,* remarked: "The narrative is detailed, yet fast-paced. Susan Kay . . . has a knack of summarizing complex problems in a neat paragraph or two." "*Legacy* reads like a thriller, holding the reader for every one of its 647 pages," added Cahill. Barbara Cartland called *Legacy* "amazing, exciting, and unusual." In the *Spectator,* she wrote: "I have never before read anything which made Elizabeth so human, and at the same time so inspiring. Every word that Susan Kay writes creates an unforgettable picture which one finds oneself remembering long after the book is finished." Cahill concluded that *Legacy* "is a worthy addition to the Elizabeth canon and an excellent novel."

With *Phantom,* Kay embellishes the story of *The Phantom of the Opera,* published in 1910 by French novelist Gaston Leroux. "What Susan Kay has tried to do," explained Chris Morgan in an essay for *St. James Guide to Horror, Ghost, and Gothic Writers,* "is to take the Leroux story and extend it to cover the complete life of Erik, the Phantom, instead of only his last few months. The result is a big book (over 500 pages) and more than 65 years of events. But there are few surprises; given the character of Erik at the end of his life, his childhood, youth and earlier exploits are slightly more cliched than one would hope but otherwise as expected. Kay has followed the Leroux line in steering clear of the supernatural; the horror here is physical and psychological."

Kay uses six different narrators to tell Erik's story, and the reader witnesses the different stages of his young life. Erik is introduced as an alienated, deformed child prodigy who displays a talent for architecture and music. A runaway at age nine, he is taken in by Gypsies who put him on display in a freak show. Erik escapes and makes his way to Rome, where he becomes a stonemason's apprentice, and he later tours Russia as a magician and even designs a palace for the Shah of Persia. At twenty-five Erik settles in Paris and collaborates on the building of a new opera house, where he creates a unique suite of rooms—a subterranean living quarters for himself, complete with a mirrored "torture chamber" and secret passageways. "The non-supernatural but gothic atmosphere of the opera house is one of the best aspects of the novel," wrote Morgan.

Morgan noted that "Kay has researched her period and her countries, yet one still feels disappointed at a lack of interesting detail. Perhaps it is Erik's failure to interact with other characters for so much of his life that has removed a certain spark from the book. While the terrible nature of Erik's disfigurement is always present, while his behaviour is often unpleasant, and while his spying is sinister, this is not really a novel to be read for its horror content. Nevertheless, it won an award as the best romantic novel of its year, and no doubt is capable of giving pleasure to many readers." In *Publishers Weekly,* Sybil Steinberg recommended the book more enthusiastically: "Haunting and unforgettable, this is a book to be savored."

BIOGRAPHICAL/CRITICAL SOURCES:

BOOKS

St. James Guide to Horror, Ghost, and Gothic Writers, St. James Press (Detroit, MI), 1998.

PERIODICALS

Globe and Mail (Toronto), February 15, 1986, Linda Cahill, review of *Legacy.*

New York Times Book Review, May 11, 1986, Merle Rubin, review of *Legacy.*

Publishers Weekly, March 1, 1991, Sybil Steinberg, review of *Phantom,* pp. 57-58.

Spectator, October 5, 1985, Barbara Cartland, review of *Legacy.*

Times (London), October 24, 1985.

Times Literary Supplement, February 21, 1986.

Washington Post Book World, May 19, 1986, Susan Dooley, review of *Legacy.**

* * *

KAYE, Evelyn 1937-

PERSONAL: Born October 1, 1937, in London, England; naturalized U.S. citizen; married Christopher Sarson (a TV producer), March 25, 1963; children: Katrina, David. *Education:* Educated in England.

ADDRESSES: *Office*—c/o Blue Panda Publications, 3031 Fifth St., Boulder, CO 80304. *E-mail*—ekaye@amexol.net.

CAREER: Elek Books Ltd., London, England, secretary and publicity assistant, 1957-58; general reporter in England for *Southend Times, Willesden Citizen,* and East London News Agency, 1958-61; worked as an economist's editorial assistant in Jerusalem, Israel, 1959-60; Reuters News Agency, Paris, France, staff reporter, 1961-62; *Guardian,* Manchester, England, reporter and feature writer, 1962-63; freelance writer in Boston, MA, 1963-68; Action for Children's Television, Newtonville, MA, co-founder and president, 1969-71, executive director, 1971-73, publications director, 1973-74; freelance writer and journalist, 1974—. Speaker and media consultant on children's television.

MEMBER: American Society of Journalists and Authors, Publishers Marketing Association, Small Publishers Association of North America, Boulder Media Women, Colorado Independent Publishers Association.

AWARDS, HONORS: Colorado Independent Publishers Association, Gold First Prize, cover and interior design, 1994, for *Family Travel: Terrific New Vacations for Today's Families,* Nonfiction Award, 1995, for *Amazing Traveler, Isabella Bird: The Biography of a Victorian Adventurer,* and Travel Book Award, 1996, for *Free Vacations and Bargain Adventures in the USA;* National Media Award, Best Travel Book, 1992, and Midwest Independent Publisher Association, Award of Merit, Best Travel Book, 1993, both for *Travel and Learn.*

WRITINGS:

(Editor) *Action for Children's Television,* Avon (New York, NY), 1971.

The Family Guide to Children's Television, Pantheon (New York, NY), 1974.

(With Bernice Chesler) *A Guide to Cape Cod: What to Do When You Don't Want to Do What Everyone Else Is Doing,* Barre Publications (Barre, MA), 1976.

The ACT Guide to Children's Television: or How to Treat TV with T.L.C., Beacon Press (Boston, MA), 1979.

Crosscurrents: Children, Families, and Religion, C. N. Potter (New York, NY), 1980.

(With Ann Loring) *Write and Sell Your TV Drama,* Alek (Englewood, NJ), 1984.

(With Nick Stinnett and James Walters) *Relationships in Marriage and the Family,* Macmillan (New York, NY), 1984.

The Hole in the Sheet: A Modern Woman Looks at Orthodox and Hasidic Judaism, Lyle Stuart (Secaucus, NJ), 1987.

(With Janet Gardner) *The Parents' Going-away Planner,* Dell (New York, NY), 1987.

(With Gardner) *College Bound: The Student's Handbook for Getting Ready, Moving in, and Succeeding on Campus,* College Entrance Examination Board (New York, NY), 1988.

Travel and Learn, Blue Penguin (Leonia, NJ), 1990, third edition, 1994.

Eco-Vacations: Enjoy Yourself and Save the Earth, Blue Penguin (Leonia, NJ), 1991, revised edition published as *Free Vacations and Bargain Adventures in the USA,* Blue Penguin (Boulder, CO), 1995, new edition, Blue Panda (Boulder, CO), 1998.

Family Travel: Terrific New Vacations for Today's Families, Blue Penguin (Boulder, CO), 1993.

Amazing Traveler, Isabella Bird: The Biography of a Victorian Adventurer, Blue Penguin (Boulder, CO), 1994, second edition, Blue Panda (Boulder, CO), 1999.

Active Woman Vacation Guide: True Stories by Women Travelers, Plus 1,001 Exciting Adventure Tips, Blue Panda (Boulder, CO), 1997.

Adventures in Japan: A Literary Journey in the Footsteps of a Victorian Lady, Blue Panda (Boulder, CO), 2000.

Contributor to *Boston Globe, New York Times, Denver Post, McCall's, Travel and Leisure, Glamour, Ladies' Home Journal, New York* magazine and other periodicals.

SIDELIGHTS: Evelyn Kaye has written on a variety of subjects, but she is perhaps best known as a travel writer. She is particularly fond of "adventure" travel, which calls for travelers to engage in athletic pursuits such as mountain hiking, river rafting, horseback riding, and snorkeling, and she wishes to encourage and assist other women participating in adventure tours. Toward this end she put together the *Active Woman Vacation Guide: True Stories by Women Travelers, Plus 1,001 Exciting Adventure Tips,* which contains her interviews with contemporary women adventurers and accounts of historical ones, plus advice on preparing for adventure travel and a list of tour operators. The book has "a delightful balance between entertaining travel stories of others and resources to plan your own trip," said *Library Journal* contributor Melinda Stivers Leach.

Also among Kaye's travel writings are *Amazing Traveler, Isabella Bird: The Biography of a Victorian Adventurer,* and an account of going over one of the routes traveled and described by Bird, *Adventures in Japan: A Literary Journey in the Footsteps of a Victorian Lady. Library Journal*'s Kathleen Shanahan deemed the latter "uninspiring," while Robert Francis in the *Monterey County Post* dubbed it "a lively and entertaining narrative" and "a must read."

BIOGRAPHICAL/CRITICAL SOURCES:

PERIODICALS

Booklist, September 15, 1993, review of *Family Travel: Terrific New Vacations for Today's Families,* p. 135; April 15, 1994, review of *Travel and Learn,* p. 1554.

Library Journal, June 15, 1980, Priscilla Richards, review of *Crosscurrents: Children, Families, and Religion,* p. 1397; September 1, 1990, review of *Travel and Learn,* p. 246; June 1, 1993, Elizabeth Loftus, review of *Family Travel: Terrific New Vacations for Today's Families,* p. 174; October 15, 1994, Caroline Mitchell, review of *Amazing Traveler, Isabella Bird: The Biography of a Victorian Adventurer,* p. 76; June 15, 1997, Melinda Stivers Leach, review of *Active Woman Vacation Guide: True Stories by Women Travelers, Plus 1,001 Exciting Adventure Tips,* p. 88; June 1, 2000, Kathleen Shanahan, review of *Adventures in Japan: A Literary Journey in the Footsteps of a Victorian Lady,* p. 176.

Monterey County Post, June 29, 2000, Robert Francis, review of *Adventures in Japan.*

Publishers Weekly, January 15, 1980, review of *Crosscurrents: Children, Families, and Religion,* p. 334.

* * *

KAYE, Harvey J(ordan) 1949-

PERSONAL: Born October 9, 1949, in Englewood, NJ; son of Murray N. (a contractor) and Frances A. (a sales clerk; maiden name, Sehres) Kaye; married Lorna C. Stewart, May 5, 1973; children: Rhiannon, Fiona. *Education:* Attended National University of Mexico, 1970; Rutgers University, B.A., 1971; University of London, M.A., 1973; Louisiana State University, Ph.D., 1976. *Politics:* "Democratic socialist." *Religion:* Jewish.

ADDRESSES: Home—523 Larscheid St., Green Bay, WI 54302. *Office*—Department of Social Change and Development, University of Wisconsin—Green Bay, Green Bay, WI 54301.

CAREER: Louisiana State University, Baton Rouge, instructor in social science and assistant director of summer school in Mexico City, 1974, 1975; St. Cloud State University, St. Cloud, MN, assistant professor of social science, 1977-78; University of Wisconsin—Green Bay, assistant professor, 1978-83, associate professor, 1983-85, professor of social change and development, 1985-88, Rosenberg Professor of Social Change and Development, 1990—, chair of department of social change and development, 1985-88, director of Center for History and Social Change, 1990—. Visiting fellow at Institute for Advanced Research in the Humanities, University of Birmingham, 1986-87. Executor of George Rude's literary estate, 1993—.

MEMBER: American Historical Association, Organization of American Historians, American Studies Association, Wisconsin Labor History Society (vice president, 1984-86).

AWARDS, HONORS: Lilly Endowment fellow, 1978-79; Wisconsin Humanities Council grant, 1979-80; National Endowment for the Humanities fellow, 1981, 1983; Isaac Deutscher Memorial Prize, 1993, for *The Education of Desire: Marxists and the Writing of History.*

WRITINGS:

The British Marxist Historians: An Introductory Analysis, Basil Blackwell/Polity Press (Oxford, England), 1984.

(Editor and author of introduction) *Selected Writings of V. G. Kiernan,* Volume 1: *History, Classes and Nation-States,* Basil Blackwell/Polity Press (Oxford, England), 1988, Volume 2: *Poets, Politics, and the People,* Verso (New York, NY), 1989, Volume 3: *Imperialism and Its Contradictions,* Routledge & Kegan Paul (New York, NY), 1995.

(Editor and author of introduction) *The Face of the Crowd: Selected Essays of George Rude,* Humanities (Atlantic Highlands, NJ), 1988.

(Editor, with Keith McClelland, and contributor) *E. P. Thompson: Critical Perspectives,* Temple University Press (Philadelphia, PA), 1990.

The Powers of the Past: Reflections on the Crisis and the Promise of History, University of Minnesota Press (Minneapolis, MN), 1991.

The Education of Desire: Marxists and the Writing of History, Routledge & Kegan Paul (New York, NY), 1992.

(Editor, with Mari Jo Buhle and Paul Buhle, and contributor) *The American Radical,* Routledge & Kegan Paul (New York, NY), 1994.

(Editor) George Rude, *Ideology and Popular Protest,* University of North Carolina Press (Chapel Hill, NC), 1995.

"Why Do Ruling Classes Fear History?" and Other Questions, St. Martin's Press/Macmillan (New York, NY), 1996.

Thomas Paine: Firebrand of the Revolution (young adult biography), Oxford University Press, 2000.

(Editor) George Rude, *Revolutionary Europe,* Blackwell (Cambridge, MA), 2000.

Are We Good Citizens?: Affairs Political, Literary, and Academic, Teachers College Press (New York, NY), 2001.

Contributor to books, including *After the End of History,* edited by J. Gardner, Collins & Brown (London, England), 1992; *Protest and Survival: Essays for E. P. Thompson,* edited by J. Rule and R. Malcolmson, New Press (New York, NY), 1993; and *Writing and Reading Arguments: A Rhetoric and Reader,* edited by R. P. Bateiger, Allyn & Bacon (Boston, MA), 1994. Contributor to encyclopedias. Editor with Elliott J. Gorn of "American Radicals" series, Routledge & Kegan Paul, 1994—. Contributor to numerous periodicals, including *Politics and Society, Canadian Review of Sociology and Anthropology, Times Higher Education Supplement, Chronicle of Higher Education, Radical History Review, Contemporary Sociology,* and *American Historical Review.* Member of editorial board, *Marxist Perspectives,* 1978-80, *Wisconsin Sociologist,* 1985-87, 1991-93, and *Review of Education, Pedagogy, and Cultural Studies,* 1993—.

The British Marxist Historians: An Introductory Analysis has been published in Japanese, Spanish, and Chinese.

WORK IN PROGRESS: The Prophetic Memory of American Democracy.

SIDELIGHTS: Harvey J. Kaye once told *CA:* "All of my writings are concerned with history: historical perspective, historical consciousness, and historical imagination. I attribute this to the influence of my grandfather, a lawyer and student of history. The words of Antonio Gramsci well state the feeling for the past he instilled in me: 'I think you must like history as I did when I was your age, for it deals with men and women as they unite together in society and work and struggle and make a bid for a better life.' Remembrance can contribute to liberation.

"My interest in the British Marxist historians—Maurice Dobb, Rodney Hilton, Christopher Hill, Eric Hobsbawm, George Rude, E. P. Thompson, and Victor Kiernan (along with others)—can be understood in these terms: they have contributed more than any other group of historians to the development of the approach to studying the past known as history from below or from the bottom up; recovering the lives, struggles, and aspirations of the common people, peasants, and workers."

Kaye more recently added: "Increasingly, I find myself exploring the American radical tradition. Co-editing *The American Radical,* for which I wrote the chapter on Tom Paine, I was impressed by the diversity and pluralism which have characterized the history of American radicalism. And I have come to understand America's revolutionaries, rebels and reformers as 'the prophetic memory of American democracy.' Truly a 'tradition,' every generation of American radicals has found inspiration in the struggles and aspirations of its predecessors, and this experience, or process, has regularly transcended lines of race, ethnicity, and gender. That is the subject of my next writing project."

BIOGRAPHICAL/CRITICAL SOURCES:

PERIODICALS

Booklist, January 1, 1996, Mary Carroll, review of *"Why Do Ruling Classes Fear History?" and Other Questions,* p. 759; March 1, 2000, Carolyn Phelan, review of *Thomas Paine,* p. 1235.

History Today, February, 1996, Brian Dooley, review of *The American Radical,* p. 58; August, 1996, David Washbrook, review of *Imperialism and Its Contradictions,* p. 56.

Library Journal, April 1, 2000, Thomas A. Karel, review of *Thomas Paine,* p. 117.

New Republic, February 10, 1986.

School Library Journal, April, 2000, Marilyn Long Graham, review of *Thomas Paine,* p. 150.

Times Literary Supplement, May 23, 1986.

* * *

KAZIN, Michael 1948-

PERSONAL: Born June 6, 1948, in New York, NY; son of Alfred Kazin (a writer and teacher) and Carol Bookman (in advertising); married Beth Carrie Horowitz (a physician), August 24, 1980; children: Daniel, Maia. *Education:* Harvard University, B.A., 1972; Stanford University, Ph.D., 1983. *Politics:* "Democratic socialist, but also a Democrat." *Religion:* Jewish. *Avocational interests:* Running, baseball (fan of the San Francisco Giants), reading fiction.

ADDRESSES: Home—4113 Leland St., Chevy Chase, MD 20815. *Office*—Department of History, Georgetown University, Washington, DC 20057.

CAREER: San Francisco State University, San Francisco, CA, lecturer in history, 1978-82; Stanford University, Stanford, CA, visiting assistant professor of history, 1983-85; American University, Washington, DC, 1985—, began as assistant professor, became professor of history; Georgetown University, Washington, DC, professor of history, 1999—.

MEMBER: American Historical Association, Organization of American Historians, American Studies Association, Democratic Socialists of America, American Civil Liberties Union.

AWARDS, HONORS: Fellow of Smithsonian Institution, 1988-89; Herbert Gutman Prize from University of Illinois Press, 1988; Fulbright fellow, 1996; National Endowment for the Humanities fellow, 1998-99; Woodrow Wilson Center fellow, 1998-99.

WRITINGS:

Barons of Labor: The San Francisco Building Trades and Union Power in the Progressive Era, University of Illinois Press (Urbana, IL), 1987.

The Populist Persuasion: An American History, Basic Books (New York, NY), 1995, revised edition, Cornell University Press (Ithaca, NY), 1998.

(With Maurice Isserman) *American Divided: The Civil War of the 1960s,* Oxford University Press (New York, NY), 1999.

Sports columnist for *Berkeley Barb,* 1978-80. Contributor of articles and reviews to magazines and newspapers, including *New York Review of Books, Nation, New Republic,* and *Mother Jones.* Member of editorial board of *Radical America,* 1976—, and *Socialist Review,* 1978-83; book editor of *San Francisco Bay Guardian,* 1982-84, and *Tikkun,* 1987-96; member of editorial board, *Dissent,* 2000—.

SIDELIGHTS: Michael Kazin's books offer in-depth social and political analysis of American society. They also reflect his decidedly liberal stance; Kazin began his writing career as a journalist on an underground newspaper during the 1960s, and has described himself as a former member of a "revolutionary youth collective." In *The Populist Persuasion: An American History,* he takes a look at the meaning of the term "populist" throughout the history of the United States. It is a broad term with an ever-shifting meaning, one that has at various times encompassed both right-and left-wing viewpoints. It is sometimes used to describe a peculiarly American tradition of political thought, one that includes "a nostalgia for an agrarian society, coupled with a hostility toward urban and industrial civilization; an obsession with economic panaceas, . . . a conspiratorial interpretation of politics, and an enthusiasm for various forms of direct democracy," according to *New Republic* writer Michael Lind. It is also used as a synonym for egalitarianism. Lind called *The Populist Persuasion* "a rich and thoughtful account of the evolution of populist rhetoric on the left and the right in American politics in the past century—an account that can only increase skepticism about the ability of conventional liberals to counter the populism of conservatives with a populism of their own." Adds Wilson Carey McWilliams in *Commonweal,* "Kazin does an admirable job of tracing the transformations of the populist 'persuasion,' ending with its recent 'capture' by the Right." *Nation* reviewer Thomas Bender found the commentary on the recent usage of the populist label by right-wing politicians to be the most vital part of this "splendid and timely book."

Kazin and co-author Maurice Isserman provide a history of one of America's most turbulent periods in *America Divided: The Civil War of the 1960s.* They begin by drawing a parallel between the 1960s and the Civil War that took place in the United States one hundred years earlier. Sol Stern, reviewing the book in *Commentary,* criticized the authors for introducing this parallel but failing to support it throughout the rest of the book. He rated *America Divided* as a "mindless celebration of the 1960s as marking an emancipatory break with the dead past," and accused Kazin and Isserman of failing to analyze the negative effects brought about by the culture of drugs and sexual freedom introduced in the 1960s. Stern concluded: "By avoiding every genuine controversy raised by the 1960's, Isserman and Kazin have taken the path of safety—for which they may be rewarded by the polite applause of their fellow tenured radicals—at the price of a book that is at once flimsy and irrelevant."

America Divided drew high praise, however, from other reviewers, including Tom Engelhardt in *Nation.* While he commented on a certain lack of balance, noting that it "seems overweighted by the civil rights movement, and, similarly, overwhelmed by the Vietnam War," he nevertheless stated that there is "much to recommend" in this "strange, divided book" that reveals "the confounding problems national history faces in capturing the forces that rule our present world." *Library Journal* contributor Scott H. Silverman identified the authors' most important accomplishment as "demonstrating the rise not only of a New Left but a new and persistent Right," and Mary Carroll in *Booklist* concluded: "*America Divided* . . . resists easy generalizations, elucidating a confusing time in all its complexity."

Kazin once told *CA:* "My involvement in the New Left during the 1960s and 1970s continues to motivate me intellectually. While I have changed some of my perspectives about the 'revolutionary' politics of that time, I continue to be fascinated by the rise and fall of social movements and by the many ways, cultural as well as political, that they shape history."

BIOGRAPHICAL/CRITICAL SOURCES:

PERIODICALS

American Annals of the American Academy of Political and Social Science, Volume 545, 1996, review of *The Populist Persuasion: An American History,* p. 197.

American Historical Review, April, 1988, Bruno Ramirez, review of *Barons of Labor: The San Francisco Building Trades and Union Power in the Progressive Era,* p. 511.

American Spectator, July, 1995, review of *The Populist Persuasion: An American History,* p. 73.

Booklist, January 1, 1995, review of *The Populist Persuasion: An American History,* p. 797; November 1, 1999, review of *America Divided: The Civil War of the 1960s,* p. 506.

Commentary, February, 2000, review of *America Divided: The Civil War of the 1960s,* p. 67.

Commonweal, June 2, 1995, Wilson Carey McWilliams, review of *The Populist Persuasion: An American History,* p. 24.

Electronic News, September 4, 1995, Robert Sobel, review of *The Populist Persuasion: An American History,* p. 25.

Journal of American History, September, 1988, Shelton Stormquist, review of *Barons of Labor: The San Francisco Building Trades and Union Power in the Progressive Era,* p. 643; March, 1996, review of *The Populist Persuasion: An American History,* p. 1594.

Labor Studies Journal, winter, 1988, Lois S. Gray, review of *Barons of Labor: The San Francisco Building Trades and Union Power in the Progressive Era,* p. 82.

Library Journal, February 1, 1995, review of *The Populist Persuasion: An American History,* p. 90; October 15, 1999, Scott H. Silverman, review of *America Divided: The Civil War of the 1960s,* p. 84.

Nation, April 25, 1987, Joshua B. Freeman, review of *Barons of Labor: The San Francisco Building Trades and Union Power in the Progressive Era,* p. 550; March 13, 1995, Thomas Bender, review of *The Populist Persuasion: An American History,* p. 350; December 13, 1999, Tom Engelhardt, review of *America Divided: The Civil War of the 1960s,* p. 13.

New Republic, September 4, 1995, Michael Lind, review of *The Populist Persuasion: An American History,* p. 37.

New York Times Book Review, June 7, 1987, Julia Gilden, review of *Barons of Labor: The San Francisco Building Trades and Union Power in the Progressive Era,* p. 31; February 12, 1995, review of *The Populist Persuasion: An American History,* p. 14; January 16, 2000, Brent Staples, "Blaming Nixon: The Authors Conduct a Post-Mortem on the Flower-Power and How It Went Wrong," p. 10.

Publishers Weekly, December 5, 1994, review of *The Populist Persuasion: An American History,* p. 62; October 4, 1999, review of *America Divided: The Civil War of the 1960s,* p. 52.

Society, January, 1997, Louis Filler, review of *The Populist Persuasion,* p. 92.

* * *

KEITH, Michael C(urtis) 1945-

PERSONAL: Born 1945, in Albany, NY; son of Margaret McKenna and Fred Keith; divorced; children: Marlo. *Education:* University of Rhode Island, B.A. (with honors), 1975, M.A., 1977, and Ph.D. *Avocational interests:* Collecting vintage radio receivers, cinema history, media analysis.

ADDRESSES: Office—c/o Department of Communication, Lyons Hall 215, Boston College, Chestnut Hill, MA, 02467-3804. *Agent*—Michael Robins, Shapiro-Lichtman Agency. *E-mail*—keithm@bc.edu.

CAREER: Roger Williams College, Bristol, RI, adjunct instructor in communications, 1977-78; Dean Junior College, Franklin, MA, associate professor of communications and director of radio and television program, 1978-90, chairperson of department of humanities and communication arts, 1988-89; Emerson College, Boston, MA, adjunct professor in communications, 1989-90; George Washington University, Washington, DC, visiting professor of communications, 1990-92; Museum of Broadcast Communications, Chicago, IL, chair of education, 1992-93; Marquette University, Milwaukee, WI, visiting professor of communications, 1992-93; Boston College, Boston, senior lecturer of communications, 1993—. Partner, Halper & Keith Associates. Instructor at School of Medical Secretarial Science, 1978. Worked for a dozen broadcast stations as account executive, news reporter, production director, announcer, promotion director, and copywriter, 1966-83. Lecturer at conferences. *Military service:* U.S. Army, served in Korea.

MEMBER: American Association of University Professors, Broadcast Educators Association, Antique Wireless Association, Popular Culture Association, Society to Preserve and Encourage Radio Drama, Variety, and Comedy, Massachusetts Broadcasters Association, Intercollegiate Broadcasting System, Old Time Radio National Archive Foundation, Broadcast Pioneers Library, Library of American Broadcasting (Academic Advisory Board Member).

AWARDS, HONORS: Finalist for Electronic Media Book of the Year Award, National Association of Broadcasters and Broadcast Education Association, 1987, for *Radio Programming: Consultancy and Formatics;* Distinguished Scholar Honoree, Marquette University, 1992; Distinguished Research Award nominee, Boston College; Distinguished Lecture Series speaker, Newbury College, 1999.

WRITINGS:

Production in Format Radio Handbook, University Press of America (Lanham, MD), 1984.

The Radio Station, Focal Press (Boston, MA), 1986, 5th edition, 2000.

Radio Programming: Consultancy and Formatics, Focal Press (Boston, MA), 1987.

Broadcast Voice Performance, Focal Press (Boston, MA), 1989.

Radio Production: Art and Science, Focal Press (Boston, MA), 1990.

(With Robert Hilliard) *The Broadcast Century and Beyond,* Focal Press (Boston, MA), 1990, 2nd edition, 1997, 3rd edition, 2001.

Selling Radio Direct, Focal Press (Boston, MA), 1992.

Signals in the Air: Native Broadcasting in America, Praeger (Westport, CT), 1995.

Global Broadcasting Systems, Focal Press (Boston, MA), 1996.

Voices in the Purple Haze: Underground Radio and the Sixties, Praeger (Westport, CT), 1997.

The Hidden Screen: Low-Power Television in America, M. E. Sharpe (Armonk, NY), 1999.

(With Hilliard) *Waves of Rancor: Tuning in the Radical Right,* M. E. Sharpe (Armonk, NY), 1999.

Talking Radio: An Oral History of American Radio in the Television Age, M. E. Sharpe (Armonk, NY), 2000.

(With Ed Shane) *Disconnected America: The Consequences of Mass Media in a Narcissistic World,* M. E. Sharpe (Armonk, NY), 2000.

(With Phyllis Johnson) *Queer Airwaves: Gay and Lesbian Broadcasting in America,* M. E. Sharpe (Armonk, NY), 2001.

Sounds in the Dark: All Night-Radio in American Culture, Iowa State University Press, in press.

Contributor to periodicals, including *RadioActive, Feedback, Signals, Rhode Island, Journal of College Radio, Radio Waves, Journal of Radio Studies, Media Ethics Journal, Media Studies Journal, Radio Ink, Broadcasting and Cable,* and *E.M.E.X.* Contributor to anthologies, including *Radio: The Forgotten Medium,* Transaction Press (New Jersey), 1995. Author of entry "Radio Broadcasting" in *Focal Guide to Electronic Media,* edited by Christopher H. Sterling, Focal Press (Boston, MA), 1997; of entries "Native American Broadcasting" and "Underground Radio" in *Historical Dictionary of American Radio,* edited by David G. Godfrey and Frederic A. Leigh, Greenwood Press (Westport, CT), 1997; and of foreword and study guides to *Electronic Media Sales,* written by Ed Shane, Focal Press (Boston, MA), 1999.

Editor of books and journals, including series coeditor, *Media, Communication, and Culture in America,* M. E. Sharpe (Armonk, NY); consulting editor, *Radio Encyclopedia,* Museum of Broadcast Communications (Chicago, IL); radio editor, *World Book Encyclopedia* (Chicago, IL); features and forum editor, *Journal of Radio Studies;* and radio editor, *Communication Booknotes Quarterly.*

WORK IN PROGRESS: The Dream of Motion: A Memoir; Vision Great—Allen B. Dumont and the Making of Television; Libido Ethereal: Sex and American Radio; From Red to Amber Waves: The Ideological Battle between Russian Broadcasters in the United States; Dirty Discourse: Polluting the Air and Net; six children's books.

SIDELIGHTS: Michael C. Keith has written numerous books on the history and practice of radio broadcasting. His works are frequently used as textbooks in communications courses at the university level, and Keith is himself a professor of communications. In *Talking Radio: An Oral History of American Radio in the Television Age,* the author uses interviews with many radio personalities and authorities to examine what has happened to the radio industry since the end of World War II. It was then that radio reached its peak of popularity, only to rapidly decline as television came to the fore. He traces the medium's "transformation from a source of drama and news to an outlet for music, the advent of FM and transistor radios, discrimination in broadcasting, and the future of the medium," claimed a *Publishers Weekly* reviewer. His conversational partners include Walter Cronkite, Dick Clark, Paul Harvey, Studs Terkel, and the cofounder of National Public Radio, William Siemering.

Keith has collaborated more than once with another communications professor, Robert L. Hilliard. In their book, *Waves of Rancor: Tuning in the Radical Right,* they explore the phenomenon of "hate media" in what *Library Journal* reviewer Donna L. Schulman termed an "intriguing but ultimately uneven book." As with *Talking Radio,* interviews are the foundation of *Waves of Rancor,* which categorizes the wide variety of radical right groups who use radio, television, and the Internet to further their causes. *Waves of Rancor* also provides brief sketches of some of the leading purveyors of "hate media," as the authors describe it, including Rush Limbaugh, David Duke, and Chuck Harder.

Keith once told *CA:* "Ernest Hemingway suggested writing one true sentence. He also recommended writing on subjects with which you are most familiar. Following his advice has allowed me to start a project and complete it. Be focused, organized, and disciplined."

BIOGRAPHICAL/CRITICAL SOURCES:

PERIODICALS

Journal of Broadcasting & Electronic Media, summer, 1988, Lynne Gross, review of *Radio Programming: Consultancy and Formatics,* p. 367; winter, 1988, review of *Radio Programming: Consultancy and Formatics,* p. 126; summer, 1989, review of *Broadcast Voice Performance,* p. 34.

Library Journal, May 15, 1999, Donna L. Schulman, review of *Waves of Rancor: Tuning in the Radical Right,* p. 110.

Publishers Weekly, November 22, 1999, review of *Talking Radio: An Oral History of American Radio in the Television Age,* p. 53.*

* * *

KIMBALL, Michael 1949-

PERSONAL: Born November 25, 1949, in Worcester, MA; son of Harold Arthur (in sales) and Lois (a volunteer worker; maiden name, Crossman) Kimball; married Glenna Pope (an outreach worker), June 22, 1969; children: Jesse Russell, Sarah Alix. *Education:* Worcester State College, B.A., 1974.

ADDRESSES: Home and office—RFD 1, Box 350, Coopers Mills, ME 04341. *Agent*—Howard Morhaim Literary Agency, 175 Fifth Ave., New York, NY 10010. *E-mail*—mikimba999@aol.com.

CAREER: Baratta Advertising, Worcester, MA, darkroom technician, 1969-71; Hillcrest Dairy, Worcester, milkman, 1971-72; teacher of music at public schools in Maine, 1974-85; writer, 1986—. Director of Migrant Summer Education Project in Monmouth, ME, 1982; member of Maine Governor's Task Force on Unwanted Teenage Pregnancy and Parenting, 1986.

MEMBER: Maine Writers and Publishers Alliance.

AWARDS, HONORS: Fresh Talent Award, W. H. Smith; Ten Most Intriguing People in Maine, *Portland Monthly.*

WRITINGS:

NOVELS

Firewater Pond, Putnam (New York, NY), 1985.

Undone, Avon (New York, NY), 1996.

The Way the Family Got Away, Four Walls Eight Windows, 2000.

Mouth to Mouth, Avon (New York, NY), 2000.

OTHER

(Contributor) *Ten Years of CoEvolution Quarterly—News That Stayed News,* North Point Press (Berkeley, CA), 1986.

Tales of the Extraordinary, Yankee Books (Dublin, NH), 1986.

(With Richard C. Kennedy) *Choosing the Right Camp 1993-94 Edition: The Complete Guide to the Best Summer Camp for Your Child,* Random House (New York, NY), 1992.

Author of screenplays. Contributor of articles to *Yankee* magazine.

WORK IN PROGRESS: A book about milkmen and military contractors, tentatively titled either *Strikepoint* or *Dead Ringers.*

SIDELIGHTS: Michael Kimball's first novel, *Firewater Pond,* is the story of a Maine campground which, according to Vic Sussman in his *Washington Post* review, is inhabited by "a congregation of aging hippies, motorcycle goons and surreal misfits so weird they make Fellini's street people look wholesome." The pond at Camp Wind in the Pines is polluted, and local officials, hoping to buy up the land so they can open a money-making resort, constantly threaten to close down the camp. Meanwhile, con man Larry Jones attempts to turn Wind in the Pines into a carnival-like sideshow. This sets the stage for a battle over the park's ownership.

Reviewing *Firewater Pond* for the *Boston Globe,* Amanda Heller commended Kimball for his sometimes "black" and sometimes "blue" humor, delivered at a "whiz-bang slapstick pace that leaves us alternately laughing, squirming and gasping for breath." Bob Kerr, writing in the Providence *Journal,* called the book "a whole lot of fun," adding that it "lacerates so many of the tacky excesses of the '80's with such fine precision." Christine Kassel, however, declared in the *Detroit News* that *Firewater Pond* "would be better were [Kimball] to try less hard to fracture funny bones." Sussman admitted that Kimball's humor was sometimes excessive, noting that he "uses . . . loonies to assault readers with mondo bizarro explosions of graphic and gratuitous violence" and that the book "overflows its banks with sex, drugs, brain-damaged animals, mistaken identities, sociopathic children and naughty words." Nonetheless, Sussman added, Kimball "handles dialogue and detail skillfully, has a flair for creating original characters and is genuinely funny when he's not overwhelming us with his theater of cruelty slapstick." Kassel added, "Kimball has an undeniable talent for plotting, for characterization, even for comedy."

Kimball created a taut, psychological thriller with his 1996 novel, *Undone.* It is a bizarre story of Bobby Swift's attempt to make a new life for himself by faking his own death in order to avoid repaying a $2 million loan. But when his wife and a co-conspirator fail to dig up his coffin, Bobby meets a grisly end. Readers are drawn into a complex mystery regarding multiple schemes and double-crosses. Like *Firewater Pond, Undone* is set in rural Maine. A *Publishers Weekly* writer noted that Kimball "skillfully juggles the murderous motives of varied suspects. . . . The characters, briefly drawn but compelling, vivify the passions that lurk beneath the placid surface of a rural community and that, here, resolve dramatically in a keen-edged climax." *Booklist* contributor Liz Rifken was also enthusiastic about the book, calling it "completely unpredictable" and praising Kimball as "extremely creative," yet she cautioned that the author "fails to imbue the characters with enough mental and emotional depth to sustain the frenetic pacing as the novel reaches its gripping conclusion."

Murder and betrayal are again at the fore in *Mouth to Mouth.* In this story, teenaged Neal Chambers reenters the lives of his Uncle Scott and Aunt Ellen, thirteen years after his father committed suicide because of Scott's affair with Neal's mother. The youth seems helpful and eager to forget the past, but he is really a disturbed individual with sinister motives. A *Publishers Weekly* writer found *Mouth to Mouth*'s one weakness to be an unbelievable naiveté on the part of Ellen, but stated that nonetheless, the book has much to recommend it: "Intelligently crafted plot twists come at top speed, revealing interlocking family secrets, deaths to be avenged, hidden patterns to be discovered. The denouement is one gripping cliffhanger after another, a chilling melange of vengeance and obsession that will keep readers glued to the page." *Booklist* contributor George Needham observed: "This is a dark, nasty story with a serpentine plot; intriguing but thoroughly revolting characters; and a stunning finale. Highly recommended, but not as bedtime reading."

Kimball uses an unusual narrative device in *The Way the Family Got Away.* This novel is narrated by two extremely young children, who are swept along in a strange odyssey as their grief-stricken parents attempt to escape the pain of an infant's death. The family's possessions are sold off to raise traveling money, and when the parents finally reach the home of a relative, they abandon the surviving children. A reviewer for *Publishers Weekly* found the book innovative but flawed, stating: "The notion that young children's thoughts contain a poeticism and profundity destroyed by the pressure to conform to adult society is presented with a heavy hand. Despite the presence of some genuine stylistic flair and a consistent tone, the tale feels underdeveloped, yet overworked." Still, the reviewer praised Kimball for his "undeniable feel for the cadences of children's speech." Calling the book "A difficult but compelling novel," *Booklist* critic George Needham claimed that the author "pulls off a remarkable feat: by filtering everything through the child's eyes, the reader is kept off balance, never sure what is real and what is a child's interpretation of unfamiliar and frightening events."

Kimball once told *CA:* "The best thing I ever did was to write about farting for *CoEvolution Quarterly*—now the *Whole Earth Review*—in the summer issue of 1982. Although I felt a bit guilty researching and writing it (I was underemployed with my family on food stamps), the piece brought me a lot of luck. It was reprinted in the *Frying Pan,* the *Utne Reader,* the book *Ten Years of CoEvolution Quarterly—News That Stayed News,* and in a German-English language primer. Best of all, Stephen King loved it and decided he'd read my *Firewater Pond* manuscript. He liked it as well and sent it to his editor at Putnam's. That's how I got my novel published."

BIOGRAPHICAL/CRITICAL SOURCES:

PERIODICALS

Booklist, October 15, 1992, Denise Perry Donavin, review of *Choosing the Right Camp 1993-1994 Edition: The Complete Guide to the Best Summer Camp for Your Children,* p. 392; September 15, 1996, Liz Rifken, review of *Undone,* p. 221; December 1, 1999, George Needham, review of *Mouth to Mouth,* p. 687; May 1, 2000, Needham, review of *The Way the Family Got Away,* p. 1652.

Boston Globe, January 12, 1986.

Detroit News, February 9, 1986.

Journal (Providence), January 13, 1986.

Library Journal, October 15, 1992, Jennifer Langlois, review of *Choosing the Right Camp 1993-1994 Edition: The Complete Guide to the Best Summer Camp for Your Child,* p. 79; September 15, 1996,

Holly M. Ward, review of *Undone,* p. 96; November 15, 1999, Jane Jorgenson, review of *Mouth to Mouth,* p. 98; June 1, 2000, Rebecca Stuhr, review of *The Way the Family Got Away,* p. 198.

Los Angeles Times, December 11, 1985.

New York Times Book Review, February 9, 1986, Albert Mobilio, review of *Firewater Pond,* p. 24; Marilyn Stasio, "Crime," March 5, 2000, p. 34.

Publishers Weekly, November 8, 1985, Sybil Steinberg, review of *Firewater Pond,* p. 54; July 15, 1996, Paul Nathan, "Sixties, Fifties, 100," p. 23; September 16, 1996, review of *Undone,* p. 71; November 22, 1999, review of *Mouth to Mouth,* p. 40; March 13, 2000, review of *The Way the Family Got Away,* p. 60.

Washington Post, January 13, 1986. Vic Sussman, review of *Firewater Pond.**

* * *

KIPP, Rita Smith 1948-

PERSONAL: Born April 4, 1948, in Wilburton, OK; daughter of Ernest (a postal clerk) and LaVell (a cashier and receptionist) Smith; married Richard D. Kipp (a financial planner), August 24, 1969; children: Nathan Smith, Sarah Storms, Jesse Lucas. *Ethnicity:* "Caucasian." *Education:* Attended Eastern Oklahoma State College, 1965-66; University of Oklahoma, B.A., 1968; University of Pittsburgh, Ph.D., 1976. *Politics:* Democrat.

ADDRESSES: Home—20245 Zion Rd., Gambier, OH 43022. *Office*—Department of Anthropology, Kenyon College, Gambier, OH 43022. *E-mail*—kipp@kenyon.edu.

CAREER: University of Pittsburgh at Johnstown, Johnstown, PA, instructor, 1971-72; Kenyon College, Gambier, OH, professor of sociology and anthropology, 1976-2000, Rob Oden Professor of anthropology, 2000-2005. Archaeological Tours, lecturer, 1987-90.

MEMBER: American Anthropological Association, Association for Asian Studies, ASIANetwork (member of board of directors, 1993-96), Midwest Conference on Asian Affairs (president, 1988-89; member of advisory board, 1992—; chairperson of Indonesian Studies Committee, 1992—).

AWARDS, HONORS: Fellow, National Endowment for the Humanities, 1980-81; senior Fulbright researcher, 1986; Best Academic Books citation, *Choice,* 1994, for *Dissociated Identities.*

WRITINGS:

(Editor with husband, Richard D. Kipp) *Beyond Samosir,* Ohio University Press (Athens, OH), 1983.

(Editor with Susan Rodgers) *Indonesian Religions in Transition,* University of Arizona Press (Tucson, AZ), 1987.

The Early Years of a Dutch Colonial Mission, University of Michigan Press (Ann Arbor, MI), 1990.

Dissociated Identities, University of Michigan Press (Ann Arbor, MI), 1993.

Assistant editor, *Journal of Asian Studies,* 1990-92; series co-editor, "Politics, Meaning and Memory: Southeast Asia," University of Michigan Press, 1999—.

WORK IN PROGRESS: A book on Indonesia's Christian minority.

SIDELIGHTS: Rita Smith Kipp once told *CA:* "My oldest sister used to accuse me of always having my nose in a book. Because we lived in the country, and because I was not close in age to my two older sisters, I spent a great deal of time alone. Barefoot all summer, I read and imagined my way through many long, hot afternoons on the front porch, counting the days until school started.

"Early on, I decided to be a writer. I planned to attend college and then drift from one small town to another, finding whatever manual labor presented itself while collecting images, characters, and stories to fill my nights with writing. I was not sure whether I wanted to be a novelist or a journalist. I had never heard of anthropology.

"When it came time to transfer to the University of Oklahoma, I was forced to declare a major. I had loved almost everything I studied in my first two years of college, from art history to zoology. This would not be an easy decision. Thumbing through the university's course catalog, I got stuck on several pages where every single course sounded wonderful: human evolution, archaeology of North America, people and cultures of the Pacific. I discovered that all these and more were part of something called anthropology. It was a revelation. My unwieldy loves and curiosities, which I had supposed to be totally idiosyncratic, actually had a name. This would be perfect training for a writer, I thought, studying how people have lived in other times and places. Before I had finished my first semester, I knew that I would become an anthropologist, and the romance of being a struggling writer quickly faded from view.

"As a young anthropologist in the making, I wrote countless academic papers, but I did not think much about the art of writing until I began to teach at Kenyon College. Was it the teacher's chore of having to critique and correct student papers, or was it working where the *Kenyon Review* had been born in the 1940s and where, during my early years there, the periodical was reborn?

"Recently it occurred to me that my adolescent dreams had not been that far off the mark after all. Aiming to be a writer who incidentally knew something about anthropology, I have become instead an anthropologist who is trying, incidentally, to be a credible writer."

BIOGRAPHICAL/CRITICAL SOURCES:

PERIODICALS

Antara Kita, June, 1991.
Asian Folklore Studies, May, 1988.
International Bulletin of Missionary Research, October, 1992.

* * *

KIRKPATRICK, Sidney D(ale) 1955-

PERSONAL: Born October 4, 1955, in New York, NY; son of Sidney Dale (a travel executive) and Audrey (Neuman) Kirkpatrick; married Thelma Jeane Vickroy, November 25, 1983 (marriage ended); companion of Nancy Webster Thurlbeck (a writer); children: Nicholas Austin, Alexander Turner. *Education:* Hampshire College, B.A., 1977; New York University, M.F.A., 1982. *Avocational interests:* Collecting grave rubbings.

ADDRESSES: Home—Pasadena, CA. *Agent*—Tim Seldes, 50 West 29th St., New York, NY 10001.

CAREER: Writer. Associate producer of television special *The Indomitable Teddy Roosevelt,* American Broadcasting Company (ABC), 1986. Affiliated with Paramount Studios, 1987—. Producer of literary events, including one at Pasadena Public Library, Pasadena, CA, 1997.

MEMBER: Writers Guild, Saint Andrew's Society, London County Guild of Change Ringers.

AWARDS, HONORS: Blue ribbon, American Film Festival, 1981, for *My Father the President;* award for "best small event of 1997," *Events,* for a literary presentation at Pasadena Public Library.

WRITINGS:

A Cast of Killers, Dutton (New York, NY), 1986.
(With Peter Abrahams) *Turning the Tide: One Man against the Medellin Cartel,* Dutton (New York, NY), 1991.
Lords of Sipan: A Tale of Pre-Inca Tombs, Archaeology, and Crime, Morrow (New York, NY), 1992.
One Deadly Summer, Viking (New York, NY), 1999.
Edgar Cayce: An American Prophet, Riverhead Books (New York, NY), 2000.

Author and director of the documentary film *My Father the President,* c1982.

SIDELIGHTS: Sidney D. Kirkpatrick is the author of *A Cast of Killers,* an account of Hollywood film director King Vidor's investigation into the 1922 murder of fellow filmmaker William Desmond Taylor. Vidor, long intrigued by the crime, had conducted his own investigation in the 1960s hoping eventually to turn the events into a film. After presumably identifying Taylor's actual killer, however, Vidor decided not to proceed with his film version for fear of offending individuals still living. After Vidor's death in 1982, Kirkpatrick planned a biography of the distinguished director, whose films include *Duel in the Sun, Stella Dallas, The Fountainhead,* and *War and Peace.* In examining Vidor's belongings, Kirkpatrick discovered the director's research and consequently produced *A Cast of Killers.*

The Taylor murder had been one of considerable scandal in its time. Taylor was a prominent Paramount director whose wide-ranging sexual proclivities were a source of consternation to studio executives eager to conceal both his homosexuality and his affairs with young starlets. Among the more notable actresses with whom Taylor was linked was Mabel Normand, who had distinguished herself as a comedian in Charlie Chaplin's films, and Mary Miles Minter, a popular performer. When police learned of Taylor's death and arrived at his home, they discovered pornographic photographs—some featuring Taylor—and catalogued lingerie, including Minter's robe. They also found Normand, who was upstairs searching the house for love letters, and the late Taylor, who lay on the floor with a bullet hole in his back, though a mysterious doctor had already pronounced him dead of natural causes.

In conducting his investigation forty-five years later, Vidor uncovered evidence of drug abuse, an abandoned family, sordid sexual practices, official corruption, and even another murder. By reexamining the evidence and conducting interviews with seemingly all living individuals tied to the murder, Vidor eventually managed to determine the likely killer, whose identity is disclosed in *A Cast of Killers.*

Upon publication in 1986, *A Cast of Killers* received widespread acclaim. *Washington Post Book World* reviewer Eliot Fremont-Smith hailed its readability, terming it a "perfect-for-summer, true-life whodunit" of "tingling suspense." Likewise, Anne Rice, writing in the *New York Times Book Review,* described Kirkpatrick's book as a "mesmerizing chronicle of greed, hypocrisy and misconstrued passion," and Toronto *Globe and Mail* reviewer Margaret Cannon called *A Cast of Killers* a "riveting account" and added that it is "one of those rare books . . . that has it all." Otto Friedrich, writing in *Time,* affirmed that "the story that [Kirkpatrick] has unearthed is a spellbinder."

Kirkpatrick once told *CA:* "Books and book publishing have long been an important part of my family. My grandfather and namesake, Sidney D. Kirkpatrick, Sr., was vice president and director of the McGraw-Hill Book Company. My mother published her first short story while I was in seventh grade. Katherine Kirkpatrick, my younger sister, is an editor at the Macmillan Publishing Company. My older sister, Jennifer Kirkpatrick, who gave me the idea for writing *Lords of Sipan,* is a researcher and writer for National Geographic magazine.

"At New York University I became interested in writing film scripts, and worked on numerous film projects with my classmates, among them Spike Lee. Another classmate and filmmaker whom I admire is Ken Burns, a Hampshire College alumnus, and the award-winning director of the PBS series *The Civil War.* A film that I wrote and directed as a student at NYU was *My Father the President,* which won best film in its category at the 1982 American Film Festival, and is a perennial favorite at over 350 libraries and museums across the country. This film can be seen daily in Manhattan at the Theodore Roosevelt Birthplace, at Twenty-eight West Twentieth Street.

"The success of *My Father the President* caught the attention of Hollywood film producer Harrison Engle, who hired me to work with George C. Scott on a two-hour television special titled *The Indomitable Theodore Roosevelt.* The program aired on CBS in 1984, and won a prestigious CINE Golden Eagle. In the course of making this movie I moved to Los Angeles, where I learned about Hollywood film director King Vidor's investigation of the William Desmond Taylor murder, which became the subject of my first book.

"*A Cast of Killers* stayed on the *New York Times* bestsellers list for sixteen weeks. Despite the book's commercial and critical success, I loved filmmaking too much to stay away from the medium for very long. I took a job at Paramount Studios in 1987 where I teamed up with Robert Towne, who wrote *Chinatown* and *The Two Jakes.* At the suggestion of Larry Ferguson, a Paramount Studios producer, Peter Abrahams and I wrote *Turning the Tide,* a book that was originally conceived as a movie. Filming of this true adventure story, about marine scientist Richard Novak's one-man war with Medellin drug lord Carlos Lehder, [took place] in the Bahamas in 1992, with *Sea of Love* director Harold Becker.

"My latest book, *Lords of Sipan,* will also be a film, with a screenplay by T. S. Cook, coauthor of Jane Fonda's *China Syndrome.* The idea for this book came to me over Thanksgiving dinner in 1989. My sister Jennifer, on vacation from *National Geographic,* told me about Dr. Walter Alva's extraordinary discoveries at Sipan, a pre-Inca excavation site that archaeologists were comparing in importance to Egypt's Valley of the Kings. With Jennifer's help and contacts I traveled to Sipan, where I began writing a story even richer than the one I had come to Peru to investigate. Not only had Alva and his excavators put their lives on the line to protect Sipan from armed thieves and assassins, but unscrupulous antiquities dealers had smuggled plundered treasures from the site out of Peru and into the homes of my Hollywood neighbors. Beyond my initial trip to Northern Peru, I could research the rest of the book right in my own backyard."

BIOGRAPHICAL/CRITICAL SOURCES:

PERIODICALS

Booklist, October 1, 1992, Donna Seaman, review of *Lords of Sipan,* p. 233; September 1, 2000, David Siegfried, review of *Edgar Cayce,* p. 33.

Chicago Tribune, June 23, 1986.
Entertainment Weekly, October 6, 2000, Charles Winecoff, review of *Edgar Cayce,* p. 80.
Globe and Mail (Toronto), August 16, 1986, Margaret Cannon, review of *A Cast of Killers.*
Kirkus Reviews, August 1, 2000, review of *Edgar Cayce,* pp. 1099-1100.
Library Journal, May 1, 1991, Gregor A. Preston, review of *Turning the Tide,* p. 89; November 15, 1992, Brian E. Coutts, review of *Lords of Sipan,* p. 87; September 15, 2000, Lucille M. Boone, review of *Edgar Cayce,* p. 125.
Los Angeles, January, 1987, Jim Seale, "A Cast of Liars?" p. 41.
Los Angeles Times Book Review, June 1, 1986, p. 9.
New York, June 9, 1986, Rhoda Koenig, review of *A Cast of Killers,* p. 127; June 29, 1987, Celia McGee, review of *A Cast of Killers,* p. 146.
New York Times, June 20, 1986; June 30, 1986.
New York Times Book Review, July 6, 1986, Anne Rice, review of *A Cast of Killers,* p. 9.
Playboy, June, 1991, Digby Diehl, review of *Turning the Tide,* p. 38.
Publishers Weekly, May 2, 1986, review of *A Cast of Killers,* p. 229; August 3, 1992, review of *Lords of Sipan,* p. 54; August 14, 2000, review of *Edgar Cayce,* p. 351.
Time, May 19, 1986, Otto Friedrich, review of *A Cast of Killers,* pp. 99-100.
Times Literary Supplement, August 8, 1986, p. 869.
Variety, July 9, 1986, review of *A Cast of Killers,* p. 93.
Wall Street Journal, September 17, 1986, Stanley Penn, review of *A Cast of Killers.*
Washington Post Book World, July 6, 1986, Eliot Fremont-Smith, review of *A Cast of Killers,* p. 9.

OTHER

Edgar Cayce Books, http://www.edgarcaycebooks.com/ (October 19, 2000).
Salon.com, http://www.salon.com/ (September 26, 2000).

* * *

KLEIN, Gerda Weissmann 1924-

PERSONAL: Born May 8, 1924, in Bielitz (now Bielsko), Poland; daughter of Julius (a business executive) and Helene (a homemaker; maiden name, Mueckenbrunn) Weissmann; married Kurt Klein (a printer), June 18, 1947; children: Vivian (Mrs. James Ullman), Leslie (Mrs. Roger Simon), James Arthur. *Education:* Attended secondary school in Bielsko, Poland. *Religion:* Jewish.

ADDRESSES: Home—Buffalo, NY, and Scottsdale, AZ. *Agent*—c/o St. Martin's Press, 175 Fifth Ave., New York, NY 10010.

CAREER: Writer and lecturer. Founder and honorary chairman of civic, educational, and philanthropic organizations, including Blue Rose Foundation, Silver Circle at Rosary Hill College (now Daemon College), and the Gerta and Kurt Klein Foundation; member of board of directors of United Jewish Appeal and Holocaust Commission.

AWARDS, HONORS: Woman of the Year Award from Council of Jewish Women, 1974; D.H.L. from Rosary Hill College (now Daemon College) and Our Lady of Holy Cross College, both 1974; Homanitaria Citation from Trocaire College; special award for Year of the Child from D'Youville College.

WRITINGS:

All but My Life (autobiography), Hill & Wang (New York, NY), 1957, expanded edition, 1995.
The Blue Rose (juvenile), Lawrence Hill (New York, NY), 1974.
Promise of a New Spring: The Holocaust and Renewal (juvenile), Rossel (Chappaqua, NY), 1981.
A Passion for Sharing: The Life of Edith Rosenwald Stern, Rossel (Chappaqua, NY), 1984.
(With Kurt Klein) *The Hours After: Letters of Love and Longing in the War's Aftermath,* St. Martin's (New York, NY), 2000.

Author of television scripts. Author of "Stories for Young Readers," a weekly column in *Buffalo Sunday News.*

ADAPTATIONS: Directed by Kary Antholis, *All but My Life* was adapted into the 1995 Home Box Office film *One Survivor Remembers,* winning an Academy Award for Best Documentary Short Subject. *All but My Life* has been recorded as a seven-cassette series by Blackstone Audio Books in 1997.

SIDELIGHTS: Gerda Weissmann Klein was a teenager when German Nazi forces invaded her native land of Poland during World War II. She and her family were among the millions of Jews deported to concentration camps. The bitter years of her struggle for survival are recounted in her first book, *All but My Life.* Published in 1957, the book was praised by critics who compared its sensitivity and compassion to *The Diary of Anne Frank.* The British War Museum uses Klein's autobiographical account as a reference work on European history, while parts of the book have appeared in a series of secondary school texts throughout the United States. The memoir was reissued in an expanded form in 1995; the new edition included "a wonderful epilog in which the author shares highlights of her new life in the United States and reflects upon the influence of her past," according to M. Anna Falbo in *Library Journal.* Falbo added: "Throughout this deeply moving narrative, Klein gives voice to the courage and dignity of the victims as well as to those who dared to help them by word or deed. . . . This unforgettable Holocaust narrative is highly recommended."

Klein met Kurt, her future husband, while she was hospitalized following a horrific period of slave labor and a 350-mile forced march at the hands of the Nazis. Kurt was a German Jew who had fled the Holocaust, reached the United States, joined the American army, and became an officer. The two had much in common, mostly of a horrible nature: the loss of their family, friends, and a whole way of life. They fell deeply in love, but their love was tested after Kurt was ordered back to the United States and Gerda found herself entangled in months of red tape as she attempted to win permission to immigrate to the United States and join him. Their correspondence is recorded in *The Hours After: Letters of Love and Longing in War's Aftermath.* Besides illuminating their personal struggles, Gerda's descriptions of her work at the Bavarian Aid Society offers moving insight into the problems of displaced people, including chronic illness, depression, and unrelenting psychic pain. "Gerda and Kurt . . . reveal their wonderful love story in this spell-binding series of missives," wrote *Library Journal* contributor Kay Dushek. The critic further observed that, "These wonderful letters reflect two very compassionate, schooled, and cultured students of life."

Klein's story was given another twist by filmmaker Kary Antholis, who used Klein's experiences in *All but My Life* as the basis for the film *One Survivor Remembers.* Jeff Dick, a contributor to *Booklist,* claimed that this documentary is much more than "just another awful Holocaust story . . . Antholis' deceptively simple yet inspired technique, combined with his subject's extraordinary eloquence, make this telling poetic. . . . This is one documentary viewers will always remember."

As a survivor of Hitler's concentration camps, Klein has assumed the task of explaining to children of succeeding generations this story of man's inhumanity to man. In *Promise of a New Spring,* she presents the horrors of the Holocaust to young readers by using the allegory of a forest fire that cruelly and completely destroys all in its path. With poetic images, Klein describes how it is possible for life to renew itself in the aftermath of destruction—be it plant, animal, or the human soul.

BIOGRAPHICAL/CRITICAL SOURCES:

PERIODICALS

Booklist, October 1, 1996, Jeff Dick, review of *One Survivor Remembers,* p. 362; March 1, 2000, review of *The Hours After: Letters of Love and Longing in War's Aftermath.*

English Journal, December, 1997, Harold Foster, review of *All but My Life,* p. 56.

Library Journal, October 1, 1997, M. Anna Falbo, review of sound recording of *All but My Life,* p. 146; April 15, 2000, Kay Dusheck, review of *The Hours After: Letters of Love and Longing in War's Aftermath,* p. 99.

New Orleans, review of *A Passion for Sharing: The Story of Edith Rosenwald Stern,* p. 12.

Publishers Weekly, March 26, 1982, review of *Promise of a New Spring,* p. 74.

Publishers Weekly, January 10, 2000, review of *The Hours After: Letters of Love and Longing in War's Aftermath,* p. 56.*

* * *

KOCH, Eric 1919-

PERSONAL: Born August 31, 1919, in Frankfurt, Germany; son of Otto (a jeweller) and Ida (Kahn) Koch; married Sonia Mecklenburg, May 11, 1948; children: Tony, Monica, Madeline. *Education:* Cambridge University, B.A., 1940; University of Toronto, LL.B., 1943.

ADDRESSES: *Home*—59 Standish Ave., Toronto, Ontario, M4W 3B2 Canada.

CAREER: Appleby College, Oakville, Ontario, teacher, 1943-44; Canadian Broadcasting Corporation (CBC), Montreal, Quebec, head of German section, 1944-53, program organizer for public affairs, 1953-60, television producer and executive producer, 1960-68, head of television arts and science programs, 1968-71, regional director for Quebec, 1971-77, associate general supervisor of policy, 1977-79; part-time professor, Division of Social Sciences, York University, Toronto, Ontario, 1985—.

WRITINGS:

(With Vincent Torell and John T. Saywell) *Success of a Mission: Lord Durham in Canada* (television play), Clarke, Irwin (Toronto, Ontario, Canada), 1961.

The French Kiss: A Tongue-in-Cheek Political Fantasy (novel), McClelland & Stewart (Toronto, Ontario, Canada), 1969.

The Leisure Riots (novel), Tundra Books (Plattsburgh, NY), 1973.

The Last Thing You'd Want to Know (novel), Tundra Books (Plattsburgh, NY), 1975.

Good Night, Little Spy (novel), Ram (Godalming, England), 1979.

Deemed Suspect: A Wartime Blunder (nonfiction), Methuen (New York, NY), 1980.

Hilmar and Odette (biography), McClelland & Stewart (Toronto, Ontario, Canada), 1995.

The Brothers Hambourg (biography), R. Brass (Toronto, Ontario, Canada), 1997.

Icon in Love: A Novel about Goethe, Mosaic Press (Niagara Falls, NY), 1998.

The Man Who Knew Charlie Chaplin: A Novel about the Weimar Republic, Mosaic Press (Niagara Falls, NY), 2000.

SIDELIGHTS: Eric Koch, whose writings encompass both fiction and biography, offers a fictional piece about a real person in *Icon in Love: A Novel about Goethe.* Koch imagines the great German Romantic writer Johann Wolfgang von Goethe as he might have been if born in 1919 (Koch's birth year) instead of 1749. The twentieth-century version of Goethe has to flee the Nazis for Switzerland, then returns to Germany after World War II; appears frequently on television; and counts rock operas among his body of work. In his seventies, he falls in love with a much younger woman, wins a Nobel Prize for literature, and becomes involved in investigating a murder that occurs at the prize ceremony. "Koch engages in witty chronological reversals," writes a *Publishers Weekly* critic, such as "tracing the influence of Thomas Mann's *Dr. Faustus* on *Faust.*" The critic, however, contends that Goethe never comes fully to life and that Koch's "cross-references and a thick plot overpower his characters' subtle romantic nuances and his ingenious historical recontextualization." *Library Journal* reviewer Mirela Roncevic thinks the book may be difficult for readers who know little about Goethe, but she nevertheless recommends it: "Any reader can learn much about Goethe's genius here, thanks to Koch's simple and eloquent writing."

The Man Who Knew Charlie Chaplin: A Novel about the Weimar Republic also mixes real and fictional figures as it follows a wealthy American, Peter Hammersmith, on a mission to investigate Adolf Hitler just as he is rising to prominence in Germany in the late 1920s. Along the way, Hammersmith falls in love with a young German actress to whom he promises an introduction to Charlie Chaplin. A *Publishers Weekly* commentator praises the book for its "ring of authenticity," but finds it weighed down by extensive exposition about the characters and about German politics, so that it "reads more like a thesis than a work of fiction." The critic concludes, "Although intelligently written and highly informative, this novel ultimately fails to capitalize on its premise."

BIOGRAPHICAL/CRITICAL SOURCES:

PERIODICALS

Library Journal, February 1, 1999, Mirela Roncevic, review of *Icon in Love,* p. 121.

Publishers Weekly, December 21, 1998, review of *Icon in Love,* p. 56; September 4, 2000, review of *The Man Who Knew Charlie Chaplin,* p. 84.

Quill and Quire (Toronto), October, 1995, p. 28; January, 1998, p. 28.

* * *

KRAUSS, Lawrence M. 1954-

PERSONAL: Born May 27, 1954, in New York, NY; son of Alfred Krauss (in sales) and Geraldine (Title) Appleton; married Katherine Anne Kelley, January 19, 1980; children: Lillian. *Education:* Carleton University, Ottawa, Ontario, B.Sc. (with first class honors), 1977; Massachusetts Institute of Technology, Ph.D., 1982.

ADDRESSES: Office—Department of Physics, Rockefeller Bldg., Case Western Reserve University, 10900 Euclid Ave., Cleveland, OH 44106-7079. *E-mail*—krauss@theory1.phys.cwru.edu.

CAREER: Yale University, New Haven, CT, assistant professor, 1985-88, junior and senior research fellow, both 1988, associate professor of physics and astronomy, 1988-93; Case Western Reserve University, Cleveland, OH, Ambrose Swasey Professor of physics and head of department, 1993—. Carleton University, Nesbitt Lecturer, 1988; lecturer at colleges and universities in the United States and abroad, including Stanford University, Massachusetts Institute of Technology, California Institute of Technology, Brigham Young University, and University of Toronto. Harvard University, research fellow, 1982-85, associate in physics, 1987—; visiting researcher at Institute for Theoretical Physics (Santa Barbara, CA), 1984, 1985, 1988, 1989, and 1992, and at University of Chicago, 1989; visiting scientist at Boston University and Smithsonian Astrophysical Observatory, both 1985-86, and Harvard-Smithsonian Center for Astrophysics, 1986-89; consultant to Ontario Science Centre. Cleveland School for the Arts, member of executive committee, board of trustees, and friends, 1994-96; Great Lakes Science Center, member of executive committee and board of trustees, 1999—.

MEMBER: American Physical Society (fellow), Canadian Association of Physicists (member of board of directors, 1977), American Association for the Advancement of Science, American Association of Physics Teachers, New York Academy of Science, Sigma Xi.

AWARDS, HONORS: Junior fellow, Harvard Society of Fellows, 1982-85; fellow of NSERC, 1982-83; awards from Gravity Research Foundation, 1984, 1989, and 1991; Presidential Young Investigator Award, 1986; *The Fifth Essence* was named Astronomy Book of the Year by Astronomical Society of the Pacific, 1990; *Fear of Physics* was named one of the "best science books of 1993" by *Library Journal;* Award for Public Understanding of Science, American Association for Advancement of Science, 2000; Julius Edgar Liliefield Prize, American Physical Society, for "a most outstanding contribution to physics," 2001.

WRITINGS:

(Editor with F. Accetta) *Cosmic Strings: The Current Status,* World Scientific (Singapore), 1988.

The Fifth Essence: The Search for Dark Matter in the Universe, Basic Books (New York, NY), 1989.

(Editor with S. J. Rey) *Baryon Number Violation at the Electroweak Scale,* World Scientific, 1992.

Fear of Physics: A Guide for the Perplexed, Basic Books (New York, NY), 1993.

(Editor) *Cosmic Microwave Background Anisotropies Two Years after COBE: Observations, Predictions, and the Future,* World Scientific, 1994.

The Physics of Star Trek, Basic Books (New York, NY), 1995.

Beyond Star Trek, Basic Books (New York, NY), 1997.

Quintessence: The Mystery of the Missing Mass in the Universe, Basic Books (New York, NY), 2000.

Atom: An Odyssey from the Big Bang to Life on Earth . . . and Beyond, Little, Brown (Boston, MA), 2001.

Contributor of articles and reviews to scientific journals and popular magazines, including *Scientific American, Science, Nature, American Scientist,* and *New York Times.*

WORK IN PROGRESS: Big Bang Nucleosynthesis, with D. Schramm, for World Scientific; a textbook for NOA-Science students for Prentice-Hall; research on particle physics, astrophysics, and cosmology.

SIDELIGHTS: Lawrence M. Krauss once told *CA:* "As one whose education has involved both science and the humanities, I have always had a strong interest in the connection between science and culture. In my writing, I strive to bridge the enormous gap between the two that seems to exist in our society.

"I have, at various times, been actively involved with arms control and disarmament, working within the physics community and outside. Besides some public lecturing and writing, I was an organizer and lecturer for the Union of Concerned Scientists' Convocation against Nuclear War in 1982, and I served as a regional coordinator for the International Physicists Petition for a Nuclear Freeze.

"I have maintained a strong interest in science education at all levels, and have extensive teaching experience from the university level to public lectures. I worked for several years with the Ontario Science Centre, where I gave public demonstrations and trained their staff. At Massachusetts Institute of Technology, I ran a live phone-in television program on physics for undergraduates, and I taught a science course for the Cambridge public school system. I regularly visit local public schools to give lectures or talk to students about science.

"In connection with my writing, I have given popular lectures at such places as the American Museum of Natural History in New York, and the Albert Einstein

Planetarium at the Smithsonian Air and Space Museum in Washington, D.C. I have also appeared on various radio and television programs in several countries, including a British Broadcasting Corporation documentary, which I narrated."

* * *

KUNITZ, Stanley (Jasspon) 1905-

PERSONAL: Born July 29, 1905, in Worcester, MA; son of Solomon Z. (a manufacturer) and Yetta Helen (Jasspon) Kunitz; married Helen Pearce, 1930 (divorced, 1937); married Eleanor Evans, November 21, 1939 (divorced, 1958); married Elise Asher (an artist), June 21, 1958; children: (second marriage) Gretchen. *Education:* Harvard University, A.B. (summa cum laude), 1926, A.M., 1927.

ADDRESSES: Home—37 West 12th St., New York, NY 10011-8502.

CAREER: Poet. *Wilson Library Bulletin,* New York City, editor, 1928-43; Bennington College, Bennington, VT, English faculty, 1946-49; Potsdam State Teachers College (now State University of New York College at Potsdam), Potsdam, NY, professor of English, 1949-50; New School for Social Research (now New School University), New York City, lecturer in English, 1950-57; Poetry Center, Young Men's Hebrew Association (YMHA), New York City, with poetry workshop, 1958-62; Columbia University, New York City, lecturer, 1963-66, adjunct professor of writing in School of the Arts, 1967-85. Member of staff of writing division, Fine Arts Work Center, Provincetown, MA, 1968—. Fellow, Yale University, 1969—; visiting senior fellow, Council of the Humanities, and Old Dominion Fellow in creative writing, Princeton University, 1978-79. Director of seminar, Potsdam Summer Workshop in Creative Arts, 1949-53; poet-in-residence, University of Washington, 1955-56, Queens College (now Queens College of the City University of New York), 1956-57, Brandeis University, 1958-59, and Princeton University, 1979. Danforth Visiting Lecturer at colleges and universities in the United States, 1961-63; visiting professor, Yale University, 1972, and Rutgers University, 1974. Lectured and gave poetry readings under cultural exchange program in USSR and Poland, 1967, in Senegal and Ghana, 1976, and in Israel and Egypt, 1980. Library of Congress, Washington, DC, consultant on poetry, 1974-76, honorary consultant in American letters, 1976-83. *Military service:* U.S. Army, Air Transport Command, 1943-45; became staff sergeant.

Stanley Kunitz

MEMBER: American Academy and Institute of Arts and Letters (secretary, 1985-88), Academy of American Poets (chancellor, 1970—), Poets House (founding president, 1985-90), Phi Beta Kappa.

AWARDS, HONORS: Garrison Medal for poetry, Harvard University, 1926; Oscar Blumenthal Prize, 1941; Guggenheim fellowship, 1945-46; Amy Lowell traveling fellowship, 1953-54; Levinson Prize, *Poetry* magazine, 1956; *Saturday Review* award, 1957; Harriet Monroe Poetry Award, University of Chicago, 1958; Ford Foundation grant, 1958-59; National Institute of Arts and Letters award, 1959; Pulitzer Prize, 1959, for *Selected Poems, 1928-1958;* Brandeis University creative arts award medal, 1964; Academy of American Poets fellowship, 1968; New England Poetry Club Golden Rose Trophy, 1970; American Library Association notable book citation, 1979, for *The Poems of Stanley Kunitz, 1928-1978;* Lenore Marshall Award for Poetry, 1980; National Endowment for the Arts senior fellowship, 1984; Bollingen Prize in Poetry, Yale University Library, 1987; Walt Whitman Award citation of merit, with designation as State Poet of New York, 1987; Montgomery Fellow, Dartmouth College, 1991; Centennial medal, Harvard University, 1992; National Medal of Arts, 1993; National Book Award, 1995, for *Passing Through: Later Poems, New and Selected;* Shelley Memorial Award, 1995; Courage of Conscience Award, 1998; Frost Medal, 1998; Jewish Cultural Achievement Award, 2000; named Poet Laureate of the United States, 2000. Litt.D., Clark University, 1961, Anna Maria College, 1977; L.H.D., Worcester State College, 1980, SUNY-Brockport, 1987, and Emerson College, 2001.

WRITINGS:

POETRY

Intellectual Things, Doubleday, Doran (New York City), 1930.
Passport to the War: A Selection of Poems, Holt (New York City), 1944.
Selected Poems, 1928-1958, Little, Brown (Boston), 1958.
The Testing-Tree: Poems, Little, Brown, 1971.
The Terrible Threshold: Selected Poems, 1940-70, Secker & Warburg (London), 1974.
The Coat without a Seam: Sixty Poems, 1930-1972, Gehenna Press (Northampton, MA), 1974.
The Lincoln Relics, Graywolf Press (Townsend, WA), 1978.
The Poems of Stanley Kunitz: 1928-1978, Little, Brown, 1979.
The Wellfleet Whale and Companion Poems, Sheep Meadow Press (Riverdale-on-Hudson, NY), 1983.
Next-to-Last Things: New Poems and Essays, Little, Brown, 1985.
Passing Through: Later Poems, New and Selected, Norton (New York City), 1995.
The Collected Poems, Norton, 2000.

NONFICTION

(Translator with Max Hayward) *Poems of Anna Akhmatova,* Little, Brown, 1973.
(Translator) Andrei Voznesensky, *Story under Full Sail,* Doubleday, 1974.
Robert Lowell: Poet of Terribilita, Pierpont Morgan Library (New York City), 1974.
A Kind of Order, a Kind of Folly: Essays and Conversations, Little, Brown, 1975.
Interviews and Encounters with Stanley Kunitz, edited by Stanley Moss, Sheep Meadow Press, 1993.

Also contributor of translations to: Andrei Voznesensky, *Antiworlds,* Basic Books (New York City), 1966; Voznesensky, *Antiworlds* [and] *The Fifth Ace,* Anchor Books (New York City), 1967; and Yevgeny Yevtushenko, *Stolen Apples,* Doubleday (Garden City, NY), 1971.

EDITOR

Living Authors: A Book of Biographies, H. W. Wilson (Bronx, New York), 1931.
(With Howard Haycraft) *Authors Today and Yesterday: A Companion Volume to "Living Authors,"* H. W. Wilson, 1933.
(With Haycraft) *The Junior Book of Authors: An Introduction to the Lives of Writers and Illustrators for Younger Readers,* H. W. Wilson, 1934, second revised edition, 1951.
(With Haycraft) *British Authors of the Nineteenth Century,* H. W. Wilson, 1936.
(With Haycraft) *American Authors, 1600-1900: A Biographical Dictionary of American Literature,* H. W. Wilson, 1938, 8th edition, 1971.
(With Haycraft) *Twentieth-Century Authors: A Biographical Dictionary,* H. W. Wilson, 1942, first supplement, 1955.
(With Haycraft) *British Authors before 1800: A Biographical Dictionary,* H. W. Wilson, 1952.
Poems of John Keats, Crowell (New York City), 1964.
(With Vineta Colby) *European Authors, 1000-1900: A Biographical Dictionary of European Literature,* H. W. Wilson, 1967.
(And author of introduction) Ivan Drach, *Orchard Lamps,* Sheep Meadow Press, 1978.
Selections: University and College Poetry Prizes, 1973-78, Academy of American Poets, 1980.
(Editor and author of introduction) *The Essential Blake,* Ecco Press, 1987.
(Editor, author of introduction, translator; with Max Hayward) *Poems of Akhmatova/Izbrannye stikhi,* Houghton Mifflin, 1997.
(Editor, with David Ignatow) *The Wild Card: Selected Poems, Early and Late,* by Karl Shapiro, University of Illinois Press (Champaign, IL), 1998.

CONTRIBUTOR

War Poets: An Anthology of the War Poetry of the Twentieth Century, edited by Oscar Williams, John Day (New York City), 1945.
The Criterion Book of Modern American Verse, edited by W. H. Auden, Criterion, 1956.
How Does a Poem Mean?, edited by John Ciardi, Houghton (Boston), 1959.
John Fischer and Robert B. Silvers, editors, *Writing in America,* Rutgers University Press (New Brunswick, NJ), 1960.
Modern American Poetry, edited by Louis Untermeyer, Harcourt (New York City), 1962.

American Lyric Poems: From Colonial Times to the Present, edited by Elder Olson, Appleton (New York City), 1964.

Anthony J. Ostroff, editor, *The Contemporary Poet as Artist and Critic,* Little, Brown, 1964.

Vineta Colby, editor, *American Culture in the Sixties,* H. W. Wilson, 1964.

The Distinctive Voice, edited by William J. Martz, Scott, Foresman (New York City), 1966.

Where Is Vietnam?: American Poets Respond, edited by Walter Lowenfels, Doubleday-Anchor (New York City), 1967.

Robert Lowell and others, editors, *Randall Jarrell, 1914-1965,* Farrar, Straus (New York City), 1967.

Norton Anthology of Modern Poetry, edited by Richard Ellmann and Robert O'Clair, Norton, 1973.

Fifty Years of American Poetry: Anniversary Volume for the Academy of American Poets, Abrams (New York City), 1984.

Contemporary American Poetry, edited by A. Poulin, Jr., Houghton, fourth edition, 1985.

Contributor to periodicals, including *Atlantic, New Republic, New Yorker, Antaeus, New York Review of Books, American Poetry Review,* and *Harper's.* General editor, "Yale Series of Younger Poets," Yale University Press (New Haven, CT), 1969-77.

SIDELIGHTS: Stanley Kunitz became the tenth Poet Laureate of the United States in the autumn of 2000. Kunitz was ninety-five years old at the time, still actively publishing and promoting poetry to new generations of readers. In the *New York Times Book Review,* Robert Campbell noted that Kunitz's selection as poet laureate—the highest literary honor in America—"affirms his stature as perhaps the most distinguished living American poet." *Atlantic Monthly* contributor David Barber likewise cited Kunitz as "not only one of the most widely admired figures in contemporary poetry but also, rarer still, a true ambassador for his art." Barber felt that Kunitz, having "continued to write poems of a startling richness at an advanced age . . . has arguably saved his best for last. . . . The venerable doyen of American poetry is still a poet in his prime."

Having published books throughout the greater part of the twentieth century, Kunitz has exerted a subtle but steady influence on such major poets as Theodore Roethke, W. H. Auden, and Robert Lowell. Through his teaching he has provided encouragement to hundreds of younger poets as well. His output has been modest but enduring: since 1930, he has published only a dozen volumes of poetry. "I think that explains why I am able to continue as a poet into my late years," Kunitz once explained in *Publishers Weekly.* "If I hadn't had an urgent impulse, if the poem didn't seem to me terribly important, I never wanted to write it and didn't. And that's persisted." While the complexity of Kunitz's initial works delayed critical attention, in 1959, he received a Pulitzer Prize for his third poetry collection, *Selected Poems, 1928-1958.* Since then, he has earned a high reputation for "work with a lifetime steeped in it," to quote Barber.

Some critics suggested that Kunitz's poetry has steadily increased in quality in the most recent decades. As *Virginia Quarterly Review* contributor Jay Parini observed: "The restraints of [Kunitz's] art combine with a fierce dedication to clarity and intellectual grace to assure him of a place among the essential poets of his generation, which includes Roethke, Lowell, Auden, and Eberhart." This place was confirmed in 1995, when Kunitz was honored with the National Book Award for *Passing Through: The Later Poems, New and Selected,* and again in 2000, when he assumed the mantle of poet laureate.

Kunitz's early poetry collections, *Intellectual Things* and *Passport to the War: A Selection of Poems,* earned him a reputation as an intellectual poet. Reflecting their author's admiration for English metaphysical poets like John Donne and George Herbert, the intricate metaphorical verses in these collections were recognized more for their craft than their substance. Thus, they were somewhat slow to garner widespread critical attention. "In my youth, as might be expected, I had little knowledge of the world to draw on," Kunitz once explained to *CA.* "But I had fallen in love with language and was excited by ideas, including the idea of being a poet. Early poetry is much more likely to be abstract because of the poverty of experience."

In his assessment of Kunitz's early work, Barber declared that the poems were "dense, fiercely wrought, intricately figured—and for their day rather beyond the pale. They gave the impression of owing more to the metaphysicals than to the moderns and of being nourished on a Yeatsian diet of eroticized mysticism. Formally accomplished, they were nonetheless humming with a cathartic energy that set them apart from the dominant strains of American lyric poetry."

Kunitz followed his Pulitzer Prize-winning *Selected Poems, 1928-1958,* with *The Testing-Tree: Poems,* a collection in which the author "ruthlessly prods wounds," according to Stanley Moss in the *Nation.* "His primordial curse is the suicide of his father before his birth. The poems take us into the sacred woods and houses of his 66 years, illuminate the images that have haunted him. . . . [Kunitz] searches for secret reality and the meaning of the unknown father. He moves from the known to the unknown to the unknowable—not necessarily in that order." And Robert Lowell commented in the *New York Times Book Review:* "One reads [*The Testing-Tree*] from cover to cover with the ease of reading good prose fiction. . . . I don't know of another in prose or verse that gives in a few pages the impression of a large autobiography." Discussing the self-revelatory nature of his work, Kunitz once told *CA:* "By its nature poetry is an intimate medium, . . . Perhaps that's why it is so dangerously seductive to the creative spirit. The transformation of individual experience—the transpersonalization of the persona, if you will—is work that the imagination has to do, its obligatory task. One of the problems with so much of what was called, in the '60s, confessional poetry was that it relied excessively on the exploitation of self, on the shock effect of raw experience. My conviction is that poetry is a legendary, not an anecdotal, art."

Published in 1971, *The Testing-Tree* was perceived by critics as a significant stylistic departure for its author. Lowell, for example, commented in the *New York Times Book Review* that the two volumes "are landmarks of the old and the new style. The smoke has blown off. The old Delphic voice has learned to speak 'words that cats and dogs can understand.'" *Dictionary of Literary Biography* contributor Marie Henault concurred: "*The Testing-Tree* [reveals] a new, freer poetry, looser forms, shorter lines, lowercase line beginnings. . . . Overall the Kunitz of this book is a 'new' Kunitz, one who has grown and changed in the thirteen years since *Selected Poems.*" Gregory Orr offered this view in *American Poetry Review:* "There *is* a stylistic shift, but more deeply than that there is a fundamental shift in Kunitz's relation to the world and to his life."

Asked to comment on this stylistic shift in *Publishers Weekly,* Kunitz noted that his early poems "were very intricate, dense and formal. . . . They were written in conventional metrics and had a very strong beat to the line. . . . In my late poems I've learned to depend on a simplicity that seems almost nonpoetic on the surface, but has reverberations within that keep it intense and alive. . . . I think that as a young poet I looked for what Keats called 'a fine excess,' but as an old poet I look for spareness and rigor and a world of compassion." If Kunitz's earlier poems were often intricately woven, intellectual, lyricized allegories about the transcendence of physical limitations, his later work can be seen as an emotive acceptance of those limitations.

While Kunitz's style has changed, his themes have not. One of Kunitz's most pervasive themes concerns the simultaneity of life and death. "It's the way things are: death and life inextricably bound to each other," he once explained to *CA.* "One of my feelings about working the land [as a gardener] is that I am celebrating a ritual of death and resurrection. Every spring I feel that. I am never closer to the miraculous than when I am grubbing in the soil." He once revealed in the *New York Times:* "The deepest thing I know is that I am living and dying at once, and my conviction is to report that dialogue. It is a rather terrifying thought that is at the root of much of my poetry." Other themes concern "rebirth, the quest, and the night journey (or descent into the underworld)," explained the poet in *Poetry.*

Kunitz's willingness to explore such serious themes has prompted critics to applaud his courage, and to describe him as a risk taker. Analyzing one of Kunitz's better-known poems, "King of the River," from *The Testing-Tree, New York Times Book Review* contributor Robert B. Shaw wrote: "Kunitz's willingness to risk bombast, platitude or bathos in his contemplation of what he calls 'mystery' is evident in [this poem]. Mystery—of the self, of time, of change and fate—is not facilely dispelled but approached with imaginative awe in his work; in our rationalistic century this is swimming against the stream. This is a form of artistic heroism; and when Kunitz's scorning of safety meshes firmly with his technical skills, the outcome is poetry of unusual power and depth." Mary Oliver similarly observed in *Kenyon Review* that "what is revealed, then, is courage. Not the courage of words only, but the intellectual courage that insists on the truth, which is never simple."

Kunitz reveals within his works an optimism that is apparent in *Next-to-Last Things: New Poems and Essays,* his celebration of rural life published in 1985. A collection of twelve poems, several prose essays, and an interview from the *Paris Review, Next-to-Last-Things* reflects the poet's love of nature, acts of conscience, and the loneliness that comes from both age and creativity. *New York Times Book Review* contributor R. W. Flint observed: "The sharp and seasoned good humor Stanley Kunitz brings to the poems, essays, interviews and aphorisms in *Next-to-Last Things* is a tonic in our literary life. . . . Paradox and complication entice him, and he now cheerfully discusses a body of poetry, his own, that he rightly finds to have been 'essentially dark and grieving—elegiac.'"

In *Next-to-Last Things,* critics found that both Kunitz's perception of the themes of life and death and his style had undergone further transitions. *Chicago Tribune Book World* contributor James Idema noted that Kunitz's poetry had become yet more austere: "The poems that open the book are leaner than those from the early and middle years, narrower on their pages. . . . Some of them are serene and melancholy, as you might expect. Most reflect the sky-and-weather environment of his Provincetown summer home, where he is most comfortable confronting 'the great simplicities.' But the best ones are full of action and vivid imagery."

Passing Through: The Later Poems, New and Selected encapsulates much of Kunitz's later oeuvre and includes nine new works of poetry. "The Wellfleet Whale," a nature poem that speaks to a finback whale run aground, is accompanied by "Touch Me," wherein the artist characteristically contemplates an earthbound immortality. The collection, which earned its ninety-year-old author the National Book Award for poetry, is considered to possess an assured poetic voice and a heightened vision, sensitive to subtleties and nuances of life filled with meaning. "In youth, poems come to you out of the blue," Kunitz told Mary B. W. Tabor in the *New York Times.* "They're delivered at your doorstep like the morning news. But at this age," he added, "one has to dig."

Barber felt that, in *Passing Through,* "one enters the presence of an indomitable elder spirit writing with alertness, tenacity, and finesse, still immersed in the life of the senses and persisting in the search for fugitive essences. Neither resigned nor becalmed, Kunitz's . . . poems are by turns contemplative, confiding, mythic, and elegiac. If they have the measured and worldly tone that befits an old master, they also have the ardent and questing air of one whose capacity for artless wonder seems inexhaustible."

Although Kunitz's style has changed over his seven decades as a poet, his methods have not. A notebook and a pen render a sketch; many late nights over a manual typewriter result in a finished poem. What he does not find satisfactory, he destroys. "I don't want my bad poems to be published after I'm not around to check them," he told Tabor.

"I don't try to preordain the form of a poem," Kunitz once revealed to *CA,* discussing his personal experience of the poetic craft. "There's a good deal of automatism in the beginning, as I try to give the poem its head. Most of all I am looking for a distinctive rhythm. . . . I want the poem to grow out of its own materials, to develop organically." The organic quality of a poem is of primary importance to Kunitz. "I write my poems for the ear," he explained. "In fact, my method of writing a poem is to say it. The pitch and tempo and tonalities of a poem are elements of its organic life. A poem is as much a voice as it is a system of verbal signs. I realize that ultimately the poet departs from the scene, and the poems that he abandons to the printed page must speak for themselves. But I can't help wondering about the influence on posterity of the technical revolution that will enable them to see and hear, on film and tape, the poets of our century. Suppose we had videotapes of Keats reading his ode 'To Autumn' or Blake declaiming 'The Marriage of Heaven and Hell'!"

BIOGRAPHICAL/CRITICAL SOURCES:

BOOKS

A Celebration for Stanley Kunitz on His Eightieth Birthday, Sheep Meadow Press (Riverdale-on-Hudson, NY), 1986.

Contemporary Literary Criticism, Gale (Detroit), Volume 6, 1976, Volume 11, 1979, Volume 14, 1980.

Dictionary of Literary Biography, Volume 48: *American Poets, 1880-1945, Second Series,* Gale, 1986.

Henault, Marie, *Stanley Kunitz,* Twayne (New York City), 1980.

Hungerford, Edward, editor, *Poets in Progress,* Northwestern University Press (Chicago), 1962, revised edition, 1967.

Kunitz, Stanley, *Interviews and Encounters with Stanley Kunitz,* Sheep Meadow Press, 1993.

Mills, Ralph J., Jr., *Contemporary American Poetry,* Random House (New York City), 1965.

Orr, Gregory, *Stanley Kunitz: An Introduction to the Poetry,* Columbia University Press (New York City), 1985.

Ostroff, Anthony J., editor, *The Contemporary Poet as a Critic and Artist,* Little, Brown (Boston), 1964.

Rodman, Selden, *Tongues of Fallen Angels,* New Directions (Newton, NJ), 1974.

Rosenthal, M. L., *The Modern Poets: A Critical Introduction,* Oxford University Press (New York City), 1960.

PERIODICALS

American Poetry Review, March/April, 1976; July, 1980; September-October, 1985.

Atlantic Monthly, June, 1996, David Barber, "A Visionary Poet at Ninety."

Boston Review, December 2000-January 2001, p. 53.

Chicago Tribune Book World, December 22, 1985.
Contemporary Literature, winter, 1974.
Harper's, February, 1986.
Houston Chronicle, December 24, 2000.
Iowa Review, spring, 1974.
Kenyon Review, summer, 1986, pp. 113-35.
Los Angeles Times Book Review, September 24, 2000, pg. 3.
Nation, September 20, 1971.
New Yorker, October 16, 1995, p. 50.
New York Quarterly, fall, 1970.
New York Review of Books, November 22, 1979.
New York Times, July 7, 1979; March 11, 1987; August 29, 1993, sec. 9, p. 3; November 30, 1995, p. B1, C18; August 2, 2000, Dinitia Smith, "The Laureate Distilled, to an Eau de Vie," p. B1.
New York Times Book Review, November 11, 1965; March 21, 1971; July 22, 1979; April 6, 1986, p. 11; October 1, 2000, Robert Campbell, "God, Man, and Whale," p. 16.
Paris Review, spring, 1982.
PeopleWeekly, October 30, 2000, p. 159.
Poetry, September, 1980.
Prairie Schooner, summer, 1980.
Publishers Weekly, December 20, 1985; November 20, 1995, pp. 17, 20; July 31, 2000, review of *Collected Poems,* p. 89.
San Francisco Examiner, October 4, 2000.
Saturday Review, September 27, 1958; December 18, 1971.
Sewanee Review, winter, 1988, pp. 137-49.
Times Literary Supplement, May 30, 1980.
USA Today, October 12, 2000, p. 15A.
Virginia Quarterly Review, spring, 1980.
Washington Post, May 12, 1987; July 29, 2000.
Washington Post Book World, September 30, 1979.
Yale Literary Magazine, May, 1968.
Yale Review, autumn, 1971.

OTHER

CNN.com, http://www.cnn.com/ (August 1, 2000), "Stanley Kunitz Named U.S. Poet Laureate."

L

LANDRUM, Gene N. 1935-

PERSONAL: Born July 13, 1935, in Covington, KY; son of Norman (a machinist and bar owner) and Charlotte Castle (a hostess; maiden name, Allen) Landrum; married Linda Barr, October 21, 1973 (divorced, 1981); married Diedra Gansloser (a counselor), June 6, 1987; children: Debbie (deceased), Sherry, Glen, Gene, Tammy. *Education:* Tulane University, B.A., 1965; West Virginia University, M.B.A., 1968; Walden University, Ph.D., 1991; attended various colleges in California. *Politics:* Libertarian. *Religion:* Agnostic. *Avocational interests:* Racquetball, tennis, golf, skiing.

ADDRESSES: Home—7065 Villa Lantana Way, Naples, FL 34108. *E-mail*—genelandrum@cs.com.

CAREER: Entrepreneur; started more than five businesses, including the Chuck E. Cheese pizza chain; real estate business broker in Florida; Condyne Technology, Orlando, FL, president, c1993—. Speaker at various colleges, universities, and organizations. International College, Naples, FL, professor of management.

AWARDS, HONORS: Ranked third in U.S. Racquetball for five years during the 1980s.

WRITINGS:

Profiles of Genius: Thirteen Creative Men Who Changed the World, Prometheus Books (Buffalo, NY), 1993.

Profiles of Female Genius: Thirteen Creative Women Who Changed the World, Prometheus Books (Buffalo, NY), 1994.

Profiles of Power: Success and Personality, Prometheus Books (Buffalo, NY), 1995.

Profiles of Black Success, Prometheus Books (Buffalo, NY), 1997.

Eight Keys to Greatness, Prometheus Books (Buffalo, NY), 1999.

Literary Genius, Prometheus Books (Buffalo, NY), 2000.

Sybaritic Genius, Prometheus Books (Buffalo, NY), 2001.

WORK IN PROGRESS: Profiles of athletic genius.

SIDELIGHTS: Entrepreneur and author Gene N. Landrum is perhaps best known for founding the Chuck E. Cheese family pizza parlor chain. But he has been involved in starting up several other businesses as well, and has been active in the field of high technology. Landrum's contacts in this area, which included Apple Computer founder Steven Jobs and Nolan Bushnell of Atari, led him to become interested in the psychological profiles of such people, whom he terms "geniuses." He discusses these men, along with eleven others, in his first book, 1993's *Profiles of Genius: Thirteen Creative Men Who Changed the World.*

In addition to Jobs and Bushnell, Landrum examines entrepreneurs such as broadcasting mogul Ted Turner, software giant William Gates III, and Akio Morita of the Sony Corporation. "Each of these individuals," Landrum told Claire M. Kingsley in *Mature Lifestyles,* "are innovative geniuses with a qualitative mentality, who are right-brain driven while living in a quantitatively driven left-brain world." He has also come up with several qualities that these men share, including optimism, intuitiveness, and a willingness to take risks.

The women of Landrum's follow-up effort, 1994's *Profiles of Female Genius: Thirteen Creative Women Who Changed the World,* share similar qualities. For the subjects of this work Landrum chose such diversely successful women as British Prime Minister Margaret Thatcher, talk-show host Oprah Winfrey, women's rights activist Gloria Steinem, philosopher Ayn Rand, and entertainer Madonna. He has been criticized for selecting the controversial performer, but he defended the choice to Kingsley, noting that Madonna has an IQ of 140 and stating: "I do not write about morals, and I do not judge by it. I write about extremely successful people who are driven, and that's the key."

Landrum told *CA:* "I am convinced most creative genius is learned via early imprinting and behavioral characteristics, which are the primary focus of my research and writing. 'What makes the great tick?' My 'Promethean Temperament' (Myers-Briggs) tends to seek knowledge and the opportunities and possibilities of life. This personality type dominates all great creative and innovative achievement. The power brokers, in contrast, tend to be manic-depressives and obsessive-compulsives.

"People tend to fulfill their own self-images. That is why great people tend to be egotistical, arrogant 'know-it-alls' who had mythological hero mentors as children. Great people have unrealistic self-images and impossible dreams which result in improbable success."

BIOGRAPHICAL/CRITICAL SOURCES:

PERIODICALS

Mature Lifestyles, February, 1994, pp. 8-9.

* * *

LARDNER, James 1948-

PERSONAL: Born September 15, 1948, in Los Angeles, CA; son of Ringgold Wilmer, Jr. (a writer) and Frances (an actress; maiden name, Chaney) Lardner; married Natalie Bider (a film editor), May 29, 1983; children: two. *Education:* Harvard University, B.A., 1969.

ADDRESSES: Home—New York, NY. *Agent*—Diane Cleaver, Inc., 55 Fifth Ave., New York, NY 10003.

CAREER: City of Washington, DC, police officer, 1970-72; freelance writer, 1972-77; *Washington Post,* Washington, DC, staff writer, 1977-79, theater critic, 1979-82; *New Yorker,* New York, NY, staff writer, beginning 1983.

WRITINGS:

Fast Forward: Hollywood, the Japanese, and the Onslaught of the VCR, Norton (New York, NY), 1987.

Crusader: The Hell-raising Police Career of Detective David Durk, Random House (New York, NY), 1996.

(With Thomas Reppetto) *NYPD: A City and Its Police,* Holt (New York, NY), 2000.

Contributor to periodicals, including *Atlantic Monthly* and *U.S. News & World Report.*

SIDELIGHTS: James Lardner, son of the screenwriter Ring Lardner, Jr., and grandson of the respected short-story writer Ring Lardner, has admitted to a fascination with the film business, something that plays a major role in his first book, *Fast Forward: Hollywood, the Japanese, and the Onslaught of the VCR.* Lardner, at the time a veteran writer for the *New Yorker* (which published excerpts from the book), details how moviemakers fought the development of the videocassette recorder (VCR), only to find it provided another outlet for their product, and reveals that the United States possessed pioneering VCR technology but mishandled it, allowing Japan to become the leader in VCR manufacturing. Lardner's tale includes explorations of copyright law, a history of Japan's technological expertise, and a comprehensive explanation of how the VCR became a common household item.

Lardner "writes with an appealingly dry wit" and "has an eye for extravagant characters and not easily imagined scenes," related Christopher Lehmann-Haupt in the *New York Times.* His prose, Lehmann-Haupt added, has "a dramatic verve that is not diminished in the least by such technological arcana as azimuth recording and transverse scanning, or by the sometimes perplexing history of America's copyright laws." *New York Times Book Review* contributor Peter Andrews praised Lardner's "prodigious research and clear writing," but offered a caveat. Observed Andrews: "The material has been thoroughly researched, with each element placed in its proper technological and historical context. . . . But within the strength of Mr. Lardner's reportorial thoroughness also lies his weakness. If he found out about something, he tells us about it. Details upon details continue to waft down upon the reader long after any reasonable desire for them has been slaked." Andrews concluded, "But it is nice to know that . . . nothing important has been left out of the story. Once having read this history of the introduction of the VCR, you will not have to read another within your lifetime."

Lardner's background also included a stint on the Washington, D.C., police force in the early 1970s, and this experience brought about his initial contact with New York City police officer David Durk in 1970. At that time, Lardner noted, the two did not discuss police corruption, but years later, Durk shared with Lardner the details of his role in exposing the unscrupulous practices of the New York Police Department in the late 1960s and early 1970s for the book *Crusader: The Hell-raising Police Career of Detective David Durk.* Lardner makes the point that Durk was responsible as much as—or perhaps more than—the better-known Frank Serpico for bringing to light police practices that included stealing, taking bribes, and giving special treatment to influential New Yorkers. Serpico left the department not long after the scandal broke, due to a severe wounding; Durk remained until the 1980s and retired reluctantly with a small pension. The two whistle-blowers also saw their friendship disintegrate.

"A movie made a hero out of Serpico (he was, and deserved it) and an unattractive minor figure out of Durk (to me, a horrible injustice—read Lardner's account and draw your own conclusions)," remarked Donald E. Graham in the *Washington Monthly. New York Times Book Review* contributor Craig Wolff reported, "Though the book clearly relies heavily on Mr. Durk's view of events, Mr. Lardner's account is compelling and, finally, poignant." Lardner shows Durk to be a difficult man in many ways. Wolff noted, "Mr. Lardner succeeds in staying with a character who first charmed and then wore out nearly every journalist with whom he dealt," and *New York Times* daily reviewer Richard Bernstein added that, "Mr. Lardner quotes some of those who knew Mr. Durk well, who rather politely say, in effect, that his obsessive zeal sometimes turned him into a pain in the neck." Graham lauded Lardner for maintaining his admiration of Durk while describing his faults. "In degree of difficulty," Graham continued, "this biography ranks near the top. I would have described Durk as, well, indescribable." Yet Lardner manages, Graham asserted, to remain "completely true to the reader while presenting Durk in his own terms." Bernstein suggested that the book suffers a bit from excessive detail about the New York Police Department, but allowed that "David Durk is an interesting subject who led an eventful and even edifying life." Graham's overall assessment was more enthusiastic. "This splendid book is a wonder of two kinds: It is a complete vindication of David Durk and a treat for any reader lucky enough to turn its pages."

Lardner collaborated with retired police officer Thomas Reppetto on a comprehensive chronicle of the New York City police force, *NYPD: A City and Its Police.* The book traces the department's history back to the mid-nineteenth century, when it "became a more-or-less-professional crime-fighting force," in the words of *New York Times Book Review* critic Jeffrey Goldberg. The authors detail the department's long-standing problems, including brutality and corruption in the ranks and poor relations with black New Yorkers, and also describe efforts, sometimes successful, to combat those problems. "Lardner and Reppetto make clear that outrageous graft is no longer an overwhelming problem of the N.Y.P.D.," Goldberg related. "But race, they suggest, is still its Achilles' heel." He suggested that "Lardner and Reppetto are at their most interesting when they talk about race and the N.Y.P.D. Unfortunately . . . they don't say enough about race, and this is an example of the book's greatest failure: they have simply decided to write about too much." In the final analysis, Goldberg wrote, the book "is immensely enjoyable to read, but quite unsatisfying as a work of definitive history."

BIOGRAPHICAL/CRITICAL SOURCES:

PERIODICALS

Booklist, July, 2000, Vernon Ford, review of *NYPD,* p. 1980.

Business Week, September 4, 2000, "Behind That Blue Wall of Silence," p. 22.

Library Journal, July, 2000, Tim Delaney, review of *NYPD,* p. 117.

New York Times, May 11, 1987, Christian Lehman-Haupt, review of *Fast Forward,* section C, p. 19; June 10, 1996, Richard Bernstein, "The Mournful Song of a Whistle-Blower."

New York Times Book Review, May 17, 1987, Peter Andrews, "How Tokyo Recovered the Fumble," p. 14; May 26, 1996, Craig Wolff, "Copping an Attitude;" September 17, 2000, Jeffrey Goldberg, "New York's Finest," p. 6.

Publishers Weekly, June 26, 2000, review of *NYPD,* p. 59.

Time, August 24, 1987, review of *Fast Forward,* p. 62.
Washington Monthly, May, 1987, Timothy Noah, review of *Fast Forward,* p. 57; May, 1996, Donald E. Graham, review of *Crusader,* p. 41.
Washington Post, August 29, 2000, Jabari Asim, "Police Record," p. C3.*

* * *

LAW, Janice
See TRECKER, Janice Law

* * *

LEEDER, Elaine J. 1944-

PERSONAL: Born July 7, 1944, in Lynn, MD; daughter of Samuel and Ida Sneierson; married David Leeder (divorced); children: Abigail. *Ethnicity:* "Jewish." *Education:* Northeastern University, B.A., 1967; Yeshiva University, M.S.W., 1969; University of California, Berkeley, M.P.H., 1975; Cornell University, Ph.D., 1985. *Politics:* "Anarchist feminist." *Religion:* "Atheist, returning to Judaism and thinking about spirituality."

ADDRESSES: Home—112 Bundy Rd., Ithaca, NY 14850. *Office*—Department of Sociology and Social Work, Muller 112, Ithaca College, Ithaca, NY 14850; fax: 607 274 3474. *E-mail*—leeder@ithaca.edu.

CAREER: Sheltering Arms Children's Service, New York, NY, caseworker, 1969-70; Elmira Psychiatric Center, Elmira, NY, psychiatric social worker, 1972-73; St. Joseph Hospital, Elmira, NY, intake worker and group leader for Southern Tier Alcoholism Rehabilitation Service, 1973-77; Ithaca College, Ithaca, NY, professor of sociology and social work, 1977—, coordinator of Social Work Program, 1977—, and head of department, also prior member of Hillel board of directors. Chemung County Mental Health Clinic, psychiatric social worker, 1973-80; private practice of psychotherapy, 1980-91; worker in refugee assistance programs. Lecturer at colleges and universities, including Tompkins Cortland Community College; public speaker. Economic Opportunities Corp., member of board of directors, 1980-83; Tompkins County Task Force for Battered Women, member of board of directors, 1986-91, head of board, 1989-91. U.S. Holocaust Memorial Museum, visiting professor, summer 2000.

AWARDS, HONORS: Community Achievement Awards from Greater Ithaca Activities Center, 1979, 1988, and Tompkins County Task Force for Battered Women, 1986-91. Research and teaching awards from Ithaca College.

WRITINGS:

The Gentle General: Rose Pesotta, Anarchist and Labor Organizer, State University of New York Press (Albany, NY), 1993.
Treating Abuse in Families: A Feminist and Community Approach, Springer Publishing (New York, NY), 1994.
We Are Family: A Global Journey into the Family, McGraw Hill (New York, NY), 2001.

Work represented in anthologies, including *Psychological Strategies,* edited by Mary Ballou, Praeger (New York, NY), 1995; and *Global Studies,* edited by Thomas O'Toole, Allyn & Bacon (Newton, MA), 1995. Contributor of articles and reviews to professional journals and popular journals, including *Sojourner: Journal of Feminist Opinion, Open Road, Off Our Backs,* and *Women and Therapy: A Feminist Quarterly.* Member of editorial board, *Social Anarchism: A Journal of Theory and Practice,* 1985—, and *Violence against Women: An Interdisciplinary and International Journal;* newsletter editor, New York State Social Work Education Association, 1987-88.

SIDELIGHTS: Elaine J. Leeder told *CA:* "Born and raised in a working-class suburb of Boston, I see myself as an 'outsider on the inside.' My books and articles all reflect my position of marginality and convey a critical commentary on contemporary society. Whether I am writing about anarchists, batterers, lesbians, refugees, working-class women in academia, children of Holocaust survivors, or infanticide in Africa, I raise questions from the left of center, suggesting the need for connection, communication, and responsibility for others. Raised orthodox Jewish, from Hasidic traditions, I went on to become a radical, feminist, atheist, anarchist, and lesbian. Now, at midlife, I am beginning to come back to my origins, trying to find a way to synthesize the ancient traditions with the visionary, spiritual, and political components of my identity. My writings reflect that attempt and often challenge the reader to think beyond the narrow confines of everyday ideas and ideologies."

* * *

LEIB, Franklin A(llen) 1944-

PERSONAL: Surname rhymes with "tribe"; born April 14, 1944, in Cincinnati, OH; son of Samuel Franklin (an airline executive) and Patricia (a painter; maiden name, Bigelow) Leib. *Education:* Stanford University,

A.B., 1966; Columbia University, M.B.A., 1971. *Avocational interests:* Sailing, scuba diving, collecting contemporary art.

ADDRESSES: Home—Westport, CT. *Office*—Nutmeg Group, 1 Morningside Dr. N., Westport, CT 06880. *Agent*—Chalfont Agency, 257 Water St., New York, NY 10038.

CAREER: Bankers Trust Co., New York, NY, vice-president and head of loan syndication, 1971-83; writer, 1985—. Mariner Capital Corp., president. *Military service:* U.S. Navy, 1966-69; became lieutenant.

MEMBER: Black Rock Yacht Club, Royal Hong Kong Yacht Club, Royal Ocean Racing Club (London, England).

WRITINGS:

NOVELS

Fire Arrow, Presidio Press (Novato, CA), 1988.
The Fire Dream, Presidio Press (Novato, CA), 1989.
Sea Lion, New American Library (New York, NY), 1990.
Valley of the Shadow (sequel to *The Fire Dream*), Presidio Press (Novato, CA), 1991.
The House of Pain, Forge (New York, NY), 1998.
Behold a Pale Horse, Forge (New York, NY), 2000.

SIDELIGHTS: After struggling to have his work accepted by New York publishers, Franklin A. Leib sold *Fire Arrow* to Presidio Press, a small California publisher. Although Presidio specialized in publishing nonfiction books on military history, the publisher bought his book and subsequently auctioned the rights to produce a paperback version of the novel for more than a half-million dollars. *Fire Arrow* was also optioned to the Book-of-the-Month Club as a possible main selection based on early positive reaction to the novel from club members. Such a sale was unprecedented for a first-time author. Colleen Murphy of the Book-of-the-Month Club admitted to the *New York Times,* "We have sometimes signed multiple contracts but only with big name commercial authors like Stephen King, Robert Ludlum and James Michener."

Fire Arrow concerns an international conflict sparked by the hijacking of an American airplane. The aircraft is forced to land in Libya, and the American military launches an assault on the captors. Leib's next effort, *The Fire Dream,* follows a group of young men serving in the Vietnam war. The soldiers are assigned to serve as on-land spotters for ships providing supplemental gunfire to U.S. troops from the water. Under the command of Blackjack Beaurive, an aggressive general, they learn about the hardship of war. A *Kirkus Reviews* contributor regarded *The Fire Dream* as "one of the finest military novels in many years—romantic, moving, and exciting. The battle scenes are hair-raising."

In *Sea Lion* Leib focuses on Holden Chambers, a financial expert involved in high-risk international banking. He has an affair with Barbara Ramsay, the wife of one of his biggest rivals. As the story progresses, an unknown informant, nicknamed the Sea Lion, begins to spread rumors designed to scare traders away from investing in Far East business interests. A *Publishers Weekly* reviewer noted, "Leib puts a clever twist on a timely thriller." Leib was also praised for his convincing depiction of life in settings such as Hong Kong and Singapore.

Returning to the setting of the Vietnam war, Leib wrote *Valley of the Shadow,* which includes characters first featured in *The Fire Dream.* Douglas MacArthur Moser, who is being held as a prisoner of war (POW) in Laos, writes a letter to his mother in Georgia that mentions his idol, William Stuart. After becoming aware of Moser's predicament, Stuart embarks on a mission to find the captured soldier. A reviewer for *Publishers Weekly* acknowledged that, in *Valley of the Shadow,* Leib "shows how the stark and tragic realities of war can be most powerfully conveyed in fiction."

The lasting trauma experienced by Vietnam veterans also forms the core of Leib's novel, *The House of Pain.* John Dietrich, a Vietnam veteran who specialized in rescue missions, is called upon to save his best friend's fifteen-year-old daughter, who has been abducted. The rescue is successful, but "Crazy Johnny" then faces criminal charges because he has killed the girl's captors. The bulk of the novel revolves around the trial—and some unexpected revelations that will affect Dietrich's fate. This "gripping courtroom drama," wrote a *Publishers Weekly* reviewer, reflects "a deep compassion for fellow Vietnam veterans;" in addition, "this solid legal thriller never loses contact with the moral questions that lie at its center."

Behold a Pale Horse is a thriller in which a Texas governor becomes president of the United States. The governor in question is a former evangelist named Rupert

Justice Tolliver, who became a clergyman in order to avoid serving in Vietnam, and whose political practices are seamy and touched with madness. The novel's other hero is a hit-man named Cobra, who comes out of retirement to assassinate the new president. A *Publishers Weekly* contributor called *Behold a Pale Horse* an "expertly layered thriller," adding that Leib's "juicy treatment of political chicanery, sexual promiscuity, media hijinks, international intrigue and atomic brinkmanship makes for a gripping read." In *Booklist,* Arthur Budd likewise deemed the novel "an entertaining thriller that projects a future just crazy enough to happen."

Leib once told *CA:* "I write on subjects of contemporary interest—terrorism, POWs and MIAs, Indochina, and international business practices. I believe popular fiction should be educational as well as entertaining. I have traveled extensively in Latin America, Europe, and Asia."

BIOGRAPHICAL/CRITICAL SOURCES:

PERIODICALS

Booklist, December 15, 1999, Arthur Budd, review of *Behold a Pale Horse,* p. 760.

Kirkus Reviews, April 15, 1989, p. 575.

New York Times, April 13, 1988; April 20, 1988.

Publishers Weekly, May 12, 1989, p. 279; May 3, 1991, p. 61; December 14, 1998, review of *The House of Pain,* p. 58; November 29, 1999, review of *Behold a Pale Horse,* p. 54.*

* * *

LeVAY, Simon 1943-

PERSONAL: Born August 28, 1943, in Oxford, England; son of David LeVay (an orthopedic surgeon) and Marjorie Cole (a psychiatrist); immigrated to United States, 1971; became a U.S. citizen. *Education:* Cambridge University, M.A., 1966; University of Göttingen, Ph.D., 1970. *Politics:* Democrat. *Religion:* Atheist.

ADDRESSES: Home—West Hollywood, CA. *Office*—Institute of Gay and Lesbian Education, 626 North Robertson Blvd., West Hollywood, CA 90069. *E-mail*—SLeVay@aol.com.

CAREER: Harvard Medical School, Boston, MA, 1971-84, began as an instructor, became assistant professor then associate professor of neurobiology; Salk Institute for Biological Studies, La Jolla, CA, associate professor, 1984-93; University of California, San Diego, adjunct associate professor of biology, 1985-93; freelance writer and speaker, 1992—. Co-founder and chair of board of directors, Institute for Gay and Lesbian Education, West Hollywood, CA, 1992-98; member of advisory board, School's Out!, Los Angeles Gay and Lesbian Center, 1996-98; member, NASA Astrobiology Roadmap Committee, 1998.

AWARDS, HONORS: Research Career Development Award, National Institutes of Health, 1976-98; Community Service Award, Southern California Physicians for Human Rights, 1993; Howard Brown Award, Christopher Street West, 1993.

WRITINGS:

The Sexual Brain, MIT Press (Cambridge, MA), 1993.

(With Elisabeth Nonas) *City of Friends: A Portrait of the Gay and Lesbian Community in America,* MIT Press (Cambridge, MA), 1995.

Queer Science: The Use and Abuse of Research into Homosexuality, MIT Press (Cambridge, MA), 1996.

Albrick's Gold (novel), Masquerade/Richard Kasak (New York, NY), 1997.

(With Kerry E. Sieh) *The Earth in Turmoil: Earthquakes, Volcanoes, and Their Impact on Humankind,* W. H. Freeman (New York, NY), 1998.

(With David Koerner) *Here Be Dragons: The Scientific Quest for Extraterrestrial Life,* Oxford University Press (New York, NY), 2000.

Author of newspaper columns, *Queer Science,* 1996-98, and *Simon Says,* 1999. Also author of a biweekly online column, "The Science of Sex," appearing on *Nerve.com,* February 8, 2000—. Contributor of articles to periodicals, including *Advocate, Guardian* (London), *Scientific American, Times Higher Education Supplement,* and *XY Magazine.*

SIDELIGHTS: Simon LeVay is a neurobiologist who has won renown for his landmark research on possible neurological causes of homosexuality. In his 1996 publication *Queer Science: The Use and Abuse of Research into Homosexuality,* LeVay presents a history of research on the causes of homosexuality, as well as the "anatomical, endocrinological, psychological, social, cultural, religious, and legal aspects," reported William Beatty in *Booklist.* LeVay gives particular attention to the work done in Berlin around the turn of the twetieth century by Magnus Hirschfield and Heinrich Ulrichs. Ulrichs was the first person to develop the idea of a "third sex," maintaining that homosexuals are a class of people entirely different from heterosexuals. Although Beatty found "occasional patches of difficult reading," he concluded that "readers who stick with the well-thought-out and documented text will learn much about science and humanity."

LeVay put his background to good use in his novel *Albrick's Gold.* In this medical thriller, Dr. Roger Cavendish, a doctor studying biological causes of homosexuality, is pitted against a colleague who is carrying on unethical research. Cavendish's foe, Dr. Guy Albrick, is determined to discover a surgical cure for homosexuality. To this end, he has secretly been transplanting fetal brain tissue into military cadets in order to alter their hypothalamus glands. He succeeds in making his subjects heterosexual, but their sexual behavior turns violent and aggressive. A subplot involves Cavendish's growing affection for Jeff Galatzin, a university student torn between embracing his homosexuality and his desire to be "cured" of it. A *Publishers Weekly* reviewer rated *Albrick's Gold* as "a well-plotted and imaginative, if none too subtle, biotech thriller." Robrt L. Pela, writing for *Advocate,* stated that "LeVay has done a fine job; his writing is well-paced and imaginative. But this book's real appeal is its creepy scientific inquiry into the implications of genetic engineering."

LeVay has also written *The Earth in Turmoil: Earthquakes, Volcanoes, and Their Impact on Humankind,* which focuses on the effects of natural disasters on human societies. His co-author for this volume was geologist Kerry Sieh, and in the opinion of Gloria Maxwell in *Library Journal,* they "skillfully incorporate human interest anecdotes and the latest scientific theories about volcanoes and earthquakes" as they look at the past and speculate about the future. Echoing that sentiment, Robert B. Olshansky declared in the *Quarterly Review of Biology:* "This is one of the most enjoyable, as well as substantive, scientific books I have read in recent years. . . . [It] is an enormously satisfying synthesis of the evolution of knowledge of seismology, tectonics, and vulcanism, and should be of great interest to both experts and novices."

LeVay and astronomer David W. Koerner tackled yet another subject in their collaboration *Here Be Dragons: The Scientific Quest for Extraterrestrial Life.* The co-authors present the thesis that many technologically advanced civilizations exist, in our galaxy and others. Their account of the many experiments and issues surrounding the search for extraterrestrial life is "clear, concise, and engaging," according to *Library Journal* reviewer H. James Birx. A *Publishers Weekly* writer added that the co-authors "have a gift for helping the uninitiated over technical terrain, aided by clear writing."

BIOGRAPHICAL/CRITICAL SOURCES:

PERIODICALS

Advocate, October 8, 1991, "Hypothalamus Study and Coverage of It Attract Many Barbs," p. 14; May 18, 1993, Lawrence D. Mass, review of *The Sexual Brain,* p. 74; June 1, 1993, Joe Dolce, "And How Big Is Yours?," p. 38; June 25, 1996, Gabriel Rotello, review of *Queer Science: The Use and Abuse of Research into Homosexuality,* p. 80; May 27, 1997, Robrt L. Pela, review of *Albrick's Gold,* p. 88.

Astronomy, August, 2000, review of *Here Be Dragons: The Scientific Quest for Extraterrestrial Life,* p. 106.

BioScience, February, 1994, Anne Fausto-Sterling, review of *The Sexual Brain,* p. 102.

Booklist, November 1, 1995, Ray Olson, review of *City of Friends: A Portrait of the Gay and Lesbian Community in America,* p. 441; June 1, 1996, William Beatty, review of *Queer Science: The Use and Abuse of Research into Homosexuality,* p. 1642; September 1, 1998, Gilbert Taylor, review of *The Earth in Turmoil: Earthquakes, Volcanoes, and Their Impact on Humankind,* p. 45.

Chronicle of Higher Education, September 4, 1991, "A Researcher's Claim of Finding a Biological Basis for Homosexuality Rekindles Debate over Link between Brain Morphology and Behavior," p. A9.

Discover, January, 1992, Denise Grady, "The Brains of Gay Men," p. 29; March, 1994, David Nimmons, "Sex and the Brain," p. 64.

Journal of the American Medical Association, September 11, 1996, Domeena C. Renshaw, review of *Queer Science: The Use and Abuse of Research into Homosexuality,* p. 836.

Jet, October 14, 1991, "Homosexuality: Is It by Birth or by Choice?," p. 28.

Library Journal, October 15, 1995, James E. Van Buskirk, review of *City of Friends: A Portrait of the Gay and Lesbian Community in America,* p. 79; July, 1996, Gregg Sapp, review of *Queer Science: The Use and Abuse of Research into Homosexual-*

ity, p. 150; October 15, 1998, Gloria Maxwell, review of *The Earth in Turmoil: Earthquakes, Volcanoes, and Their Impact on Humankind,* p. 94; January, 2000, H. James Birx, review of *Here Be Dragons: The Scientific Quest for Extraterrestrial Life,* p. 151.

Mademoiselle, January, 1992, Barbara Grizzuti Harrison, "Are Some Men Born to Be Gay?," p. 48.

National Catholic Reporter, September 13, 1991, Dawn Gibeau, "Study of Gay Men's Brains Raises New Questions; Theologians Differ on Implications for Church Teaching," p. 5.

Natural History, August, 1996, Mark Ridley, review of *Queer Science: The Use and Abuse of Research into Homosexuality,* p. 10; February, 2000, review of *Here Be Dragons: The Scientific Quest for Extraterrestrial Life,* p. 22.

New Statesman & Society, November 27, 1992, Marek Kohn, review of *The Sexual Brain,* p. 31; July 23, 1993, David Fernback, review of *The Sexual Brain,* p. 40.

Newsweek, September 9, 1991, Sharon Begley and David Gelman, "What Causes People to Be Homosexual? A Study Pinpoints a Difference in the Brain," p. 52.

New Yorker, April 3, 1995, Daniel J. Kevles, review of *The Sexual Brain,* p. 85.

New York Times Book Review, August 11, 1996, Roy Porter, review of *Queer Science: The Use and Abuse of Research into Homosexuality;* August 10, 1997, Martha E. Stone, review of *Albrick's Gold,* p. 16.

Publishers Weekly, May 10, 1993, review of *The Sexual Brain,* p. 60; October 30, 1995, review of *City of Friends: A Portrait of the Gay and Lesbian Community in America,* p. 54; May 20, 1996, review of *Queer Science: The Use and Abuse of Research into Homosexuality,* p. 249; February 3, 1997, review of *Albrick's Gold,* p. 97; January 24, 2000, review of *Here Be Dragons: The Scientific Quest for Extraterrestrial Life,* p. 303.

Quarterly Review of Biology, December, 2000, Robert B. Olshansky, review of *The Earth in Turmoil: Earthquakes, Volcanoes, and Their Impact on Humankind,* p. 484.

San Diego Business Journal, October 21, 1991, Bradley J. Fikes, "Salk Researcher Unleashes Torrent of Controversy," p. 8.

Science, August 30, 1991, Marcia Barinaga, "Is Homosexuality Biological?," p. 956; July 16, 1993, Katherine Livingston, review of *The Sexual Brain,* p. 370.

Science News, August 31, 1991, "Brain Feature Linked to Sexual Orientation," p. 134.

Scientific American, October, 1997, Tom Boellstorff and Lawrence Cohen, review of *Queer Science: The Use and Abuse of Research into Homosexuality,* p. 146.

Time, September 9, 1991, Christine Gorman, "Are Gay Men Born That Way?," p. 60.

U.S. News and World Report, September 9, 1991, "Are Some Men Born to Be Homosexual?," p. 58.

OTHER

Simon LeVay's Home Page, http://hometown.aol.com/ (May 17, 2001).*

*　*　*

LEWONTIN, Richard Charles 1929-

PERSONAL: Born March 29, 1929, in New York, NY; son of Max and Lillian (Wilson) Lewontin; married Mary Jane Christianson, April 10, 1947; children: David John, Stephen Paul, James Peter, Timothy Andrew. *Education:* Harvard University, A.B. (magna cum laude), 1951; Columbia University, M.A., 1952, Ph.D., 1954.

ADDRESSES: *Home*—Marlboro, VT. *Office*—Museum of Comparative Zoology, Harvard University, Cambridge, MA 02138. *E-mail*—dick@mcz.harvard.edu.

CAREER: North Carolina State University, Raleigh, assistant professor of genetics, 1954-58; University of Rochester, Rochester, NY, 1958-64, began as assistant professor, became professor of biology; University of Chicago, Chicago, IL, professor of zoology and mathematical biology, 1964-73, associate dean of biological sciences, 1966-69, Louis Block Professor of Biological Sciences, 1969-73; Harvard University, Cambridge, MA, Alexander Agassiz Professor of Zoology, 1973—, now emeritus professor, Department of Organismic and Evolutionary Biology; writer. Lecturer at Columbia University, 1959, associate of Seminar on Human Evolution, 1959-61.

MEMBER: American Academy of Arts and Sciences (fellow), American Association for the Advancement of Science (fellow), Genetics Society of America, American Eugenic Society (member of board of directors, 1966—), Society for the Study of Evolution (president, 1970), Biometric Society, National Academy of Sciences, Science for the People (founding member).

AWARDS, HONORS: National Science Foundation fellowship, 1954-55, senior fellowships, 1961-62, 1971-72; grants from National Science Foundation, 1958-59 and 1963—, Office of Naval Research, 1958-59, U.S. Public Health Service, 1958-63, and Atomic Energy Commission, 1960—; Fulbright fellowship, 1961-62.

WRITINGS:

(With Hans Ris and Herschel L. Roman) *Topics in Cell Biology, Inheritance, and Evolution,* Harper (New York, NY), 1971.

The Genetic Basis of Evolutionary Change, Columbia University Press (New York, NY), 1974.

(With Arthur Stanley Goldberger) *Jensen's Twin Fantasy,* University of Wisconsin—Madison (Madison, WI), 1976.

Human Diversity, Scientific American Library (New York, NY), 1982.

(With Steven Rose and Leon J. Kamin) *Not in Our Genes: Biology, Ideology, and Human Nature,* Pantheon (New York, NY), 1984.

(With Richard Levins) *The Dialectical Biologist* (essays), Harvard University Press (Cambridge, MA), 1985.

(With Michel Schiff) *Education and Class: The Irrelevance of IQ Genetic Studies,* Oxford University Press (New York, NY), 1986.

Biology as Ideology: The Doctrine of DNA, HarperPerennial (New York, NY), 1992.

Inside and Outside: Gene, Environment, and Organism, Clark University Press (Worcester, MA), 1994.

The Triple Helix: Gene, Organism, and Environment (essays), Harvard University Press (Cambridge, MA), 2000.

It Ain't Necessarily So: The Dream of the Human Genome, and Other Illusions (essays), New York Review of Books (New York, NY), 2000.

Also author of *Quantitative Zoology* and editor of *Population Biology and Evolution: Proceedings of the International Symposium, June 7-9, 1967, Syracuse University.*

Contributor to periodicals, including *New York Review of Books.* Associate editor of *Evolution,* 1959-63, and *Der Zuchter,* 1965—; co-editor of *American Naturalist,* 1964-70.

SIDELIGHTS: Richard Charles Lewontin is a world-renowned biologist whose research and teaching focuses on theoretical and experimental population genetics. Lewontin is described by author Kenan Malik as "one of the great unsung figures of postwar science. A brilliant geneticist, he invented in the 1960s a technique for measuring variation in genes, and used it to demonstrate that populations are much more variable than previously thought. Equally important have been his attempts to elucidate the philosophical and methodological problems of genetic research."

Lewontin was born in 1929 in New York City. He studied at Harvard University, from which he graduated in 1951, and Columbia University, where he earned a master's degree in 1952 and a doctorate two years later. He then joined the faculty of North Carolina State University, where he was assistant professor of genetics until 1958, when he departed for the University of Rochester. Lewontin taught at Rochester for six years, then left for the University of Chicago, where his teaching positions included Louis Block Professor of Biological Sciences. In 1973, Lewontin became Alexander Agassiz Professor of Zoology at Harvard University.

Lewontin collaborated with Hans Ris and Herschel L. Roman in writing *Topics in Cell Biology, Inheritance, and Evolution,* which appeared in 1971. He then wrote *The Genetic Basis of Evolutionary Change* and, with Arthur Stanley Goldberger,—*Jensen's Twin Fantasy.*

In 1982 Lewontin issued *Human Diversity,* where he argued against significant genetic distinctions between races. Danny Yee, at his *Danny Yee's Book Reviews* Web site, declared that the information provided in *Human Diversity* "must be high on any ranking of 'essential human knowledge.'"

Lewontin followed *Human Diversity* with *Not in Our Genes: Biology, Ideology, and Human Nature,* which he wrote with Steven Rose and Leon J. Kamin. This work further diminishes the notion of genetically distinctive races. In addition, the book refutes concepts of hereditary intelligence, and it examines genetic distinctions between the sexes. Yee commented that *Not in Our Genes* serves as "a brilliant attack on reductionist claims that there is a biologically determined 'human nature.'"

After completing *Not in Our Genes,* Lewontin joined Richard Levins in writing *The Dialectical Biologist,* a controversial book which rejects the Cartesian distinction between parts and the whole and between cause and effect. Lewontin and Levins contend that a dialectic approach—derived from Marxist analysis—would better serve scientists, and they apply their dialectical method in refuting Darwinian, as well as Cartesian, theory. Writing in the *New York Times Book Review,* Paul Thompson concluded, "The authors provide a sketch of an alternative method of analyzing the world. . . . As an initial attempt, [*The Dialectical Biologist*] is a rich source of understanding, and it will undoubtedly stimulate important discussion."

In Danny Yee's estimation, it is the authors' dialectical materialist viewpoint that "gives this book its unique perspective." Yee concluded, "The common feature of all the essays is a respect for the complexities of social processes, scientific practice and the interaction between them."

Lewontin's ensuing publications continue to address and analyze various aspects of genetics. *The Triple Helix: Gene, Organism, and Environment,* for example, decries the perception of genetics—and specifically the sequencing of human DNA—as the basis for understanding how the human being works. A writer for the *Complete Review* affirmed that "there is a complex interplay of gene, organism, and environment that determines eventual outcomes." The reviewer described *The Triple Helix* as a "penetrating book" and added that it is "clearly-written and rich in examples." Another critic, John R. G. Turner, wrote in the *New York Times Book Review* that *The Triple Helix* is "a tough, challenging and rewarding book. . . . The general reader will find here a constructive critique of the limitations of science by a very successful and accomplished scientist." In a *Library Journal* appraisal, Marit MacArthur deemed the book's essays "well worth reading for their brilliant, if sometimes partisan, criticisms." A *Publishers Weekly* critic, meanwhile, praised the book as "eloquent," and *Booklist* reviewer Ray Olson, observed that Lewontin's "remarks on biology studies couldn't be timelier."

Among Lewontin's other writings is *It Ain't Necessarily So: The Dream of the Human Genome, and Other Illusions,* a collection of essays on some of the most controversial subjects in the life sciences, such as heredity and natural selection, genetic determinism, and cloning. A *Publishers Weekly* critic hailed *It Ain't Necessarily So* as "a bracing, lucid collection" and concluded that it is "an illuminating forum of ideas." Reviewing the book for London's *Sunday Times,* John Cornwell commented: "The painstaking, highly accessible, but penetrating quality of his work is essential reading for anyone interested in or involved in biological science, particularly the science of genetics. . . . What is unusual about Lewontin and his eloquent critique is that, apart from being extremely subtle and intelligent, he is a working biologist and a wonderfully stylish writer. . . . If you read only one book on genetics this year, make sure it is this one."

BIOGRAPHICAL/CRITICAL SOURCES:

PERIODICALS

American Scientist, September, 2000, Rob Dorit, "Defying Genomania," reviews of *It Ain't Necessarily So: The Dream of the Human Genome, and Other Illusions* and *The Triple Helix: Gene, Organism, and Environment,* p. 448.

Booklist, March 15, 2000, Ray Olson, review of *The Triple Helix: Gene, Organism, and Environment,* p. 1304.

Library Journal, April 1, 2000, Marit MacArthur, review of *The Triple Helix: Gene, Organism, and Environment,* p. 126.

New England Journal of Medicine, August 31, 2000, Peter Parham, review of *The Triple Helix: Gene, Organism, and Environment,* p. 667.

New Statesman, July 3, 2000, Kenan Malik, "The Gene Genie," p. 53.

New York Times Book Review, September 29, 1985, Paul Thompson, "Science in the Style of Engels," review of *The Dialectical Biologist,* p. 14; April 16, 2000, John R. G. Turner, "What's the Forecast?," review of *The Triple Helix,* p. 24.

Publishers Weekly, April 10, 2000, reviews of *The Triple Helix: Gene, Organism, and Environment* and *It Ain't Necessarily So: The Dream of the Human Genome, and Other Illusions,* p. 81.

Sunday Times (London), June 11, 2000, John Cornwell, "The Limits of Genetics," review of *It Ain't Necessarily So: The Dream of the Human Genome, and Other Illusions. Technology Review Newsletter,* June 13, 2000, Wade Roush, "Genome, Schmenome," review of *It Ain't Necessarily So: The Dream of the Human Genome, and Other Illusions.*

OTHER

Complete Review, http://www.complete-review.com/ (May 19, 2001).

Danny Yee's Book Reviews, http://dannyreviews.com/ (May 4, 1992), review of *The Genetic Basis of Evolutionary Change;* (May 11, 1992), review of *Not in Our Genes;* (July 26, 1993), review of *The Dialectical Biologist;* (December 25, 1998), review of *Human Diversity.*

Salon, http://www.salon.com/ (January 1, 2001), Ralph Brave, review of *The Triple Helix: Gene, Organism, and Environment.**

* * *

LINDBERG, Carter (Harry) 1937-

PERSONAL: Born November 23, 1937, in Berwyn, IL; son of Harry and Esther (Bell) Lindberg; married Alice Knudsen, 1960; children: Anne, Erika, Matthew. *Education:* Augustana College, B.A., 1959; Lutheran School of Theology, Chicago, IL, M.Div., 1962; University of Iowa, Ph.D., 1965.

ADDRESSES: Home—113 Whitney St., Northboro, MA 01532. *Office*—School of Theology, Boston University, 745 Commonwealth Ave., Boston, MA 02215; fax: 617 353 3061. *E-mail*—clindber@bu.edu.

CAREER: Susquehanna University, Selinsgrove, PA, assistant professor of philosophy and religion, 1965-67; College of the Holy Cross, Worcester, MA, assistant professor of theology, 1967-72; Boston University, Boston, MA, assistant professor, 1972-76, associate professor, 1976-79, 1982-85, professor of theology, 1986—; Centre d'Etudes Oecumeniques, Strasbourg, France, research professor of theology, 1979-82. Lecturer at Assumption College, Worcester, MA, 1969-72; visiting lecturer at St. Francis Xavier University, Antigonish, Nova Scotia, summer, 1972; volunteer professor at Norfolk State Prison; lecturer at New England churches; member of New England Lutheran Social Ministry Committee, 1968-71, chair, 1971; member of Council of Theologians, 1972-79, and New England Lutheran-Catholic Dialogue, 1978-79.

MEMBER: American Society of Church History, American Society for Reformation Research, Luther-Gesellschaft, Society for Sixteenth-Century Studies (vice president, 1977-78; president, 1978-79).

WRITINGS:

(Editor, translator, and contributor) *Luther's Ecumenical Significance,* Fortress (Philadelphia, PA), 1983.

The Third Reformation?: Charismatic Renewal and Lutheran Tradition, Mercer University Press (Macon, GA), 1983.

(Editor) *Piety, Politics, and Ethics: Reformation Studies in Honor of George Wolfgang Forell,* Sixteenth Century Journal Publishers, Northeast Missouri State University (Kirksville, MS), 1984.

Martin Luther, Graded Press, 1988.

(With H. C. Kee, and others) *Christianity: A Social and Cultural History,* Macmillan (New York, NY), 1991, 2nd edition, Prentice-Hall, 1998.

Beyond Charity: Reformation Initiatives for the Poor, Fortress (Minneapolis, MN), 1993.

(Editor, with Emily Albu Hanawalt) *Through the Eye of a Needle: Judeo-Christian Roots of Social Welfare,* Thomas Jefferson University Press (Kirksville, MO), 1993.

The European Reformations, Blackwell (Cambridge, MA), 1996.

The European Reformations Sourcebook, Blackwell (Malden, MA), 2000.

(Editor) *The Reformation Theologians,* Blackwell, 2001.

Contributor to several books, including *Sixteenth-Century Essays and Studies,* edited by Carl Meyer, Foundation for Reformation Research, 1970; *Disguises of the Demonic,* edited by Alan Olsen, Association Press, 1975; *Les Dissidents du seizieme siecle entre l'humanisme et le catholicisme,* edited by Marc Lienhard, Koerner, 1983; *Oekumenische Erschliessung Martin Luthers,* edited by Peter Manns and Harding Meyer, Paderborn, 1983; and *Tainted Greatness: Anti-Semitism and Cultural Heroes,* edited by Nancy A. Harrowitz, Temple University Press (Philadelphia, PA), 1994. Also contributor of over eighty articles and reviews to various theology journals.

* * *

LOUVISH, Simon 1947-

PERSONAL: Born April 6, 1947, in Glasgow, Scotland; son of Misha (a translator) and Eva (a teacher; maiden name, Bersinski) Louvish; married Mairi Macdonald (a television programmer), October 12, 1979. *Education:* Attended London School of Film Technique. *Politics:* "Left." *Religion:* "No."

ADDRESSES: Home—London, England. *Agent*—David Grossman, 118B Holland Park Ave., London W11 4UA, England.

CAREER: Freelance documentary film producer and director, 1970-76; London International Film School, London, England, tutor and lecturer, 1978-86; writer/producer, motion pictures, 2000—.

WRITINGS:

FICTION

A Moment of Silence (autobiographical novel), Martin Brian & O'Keeffe (London, England), 1979.
The Therapy of Avram Blok, Stein & Day, 1985.
The Death of Moishe-Ganef, Heinemann (London, England), 1986.
City of Blok, Heinemann (London, England), 1988.
The Last Trump of Avram Blok, Heinemann (London, England), 1990.
Your Monkey's Schmuck, Flamingo (London, England), 1990.
The Silencer, Bloomsbury (London, England), 1991, Interlink Books (Brooklyn, NY), 1993.
Resurrections from the Dustbin of History, Bloomsbury (London, England), 1992, revised as *The Resurrections,* Four Walls Eight Windows (New York, NY), 1994.
What's Up God?, Gollancz (London, England), 1995.
The Days of Miracles and Wonders, Canongate (Edinburgh, Scotland), 1997.

Also author of the unpublished manuscripts *The Cosmic Follies, 1992-99; City of Mirrors,* and *The Governor's Show.*

NONFICTION

Man on the Flying Trapeze: The Life and Times of W. C. Fields, Norton (New York, NY), 1997.
Monkey Business: The Lives and Legends of the Marx Brothers: Groucho, Chico, Harpo, Zeppo with Added Gummo, Faber (London, England), 1999.

WORK IN PROGRESS: Stan and Ollie: The Roots of Comedy—The Double Life of Laurel and Hardy, Faber (London, England), 2002; *The Fundamental Blok,* fifth novel in the Blok saga.

SIDELIGHTS: Simon Louvish has written several novels of political satire as well as biographies of famed film comedians W. C. Fields and the Marx Brothers. He once told *CA* that his books on the modern State of Israel "reflect an unpopular (non-Zionist) point of view, mostly by the medium of satire. I feel that the breach of closed minds by means of jokes, rather than bombs, might be a contribution towards the alleviation of those conflicts. Is this the usual writer's delusion?"

A Moment of Silence was described by reviewer Edward Mortimer of the *Spectator* as "an account of [the author's] own progressive disillusionment" from the time he spent in Israel during the 1960s to his return some years later to a state "which has fallen ever further away from the socialist and humanist ideals of the original Zionists."

The Therapy of Avram Blok is the story of a young Israeli who wanders from dissidence through apathy into madness. In the *New York Times Book Review,* critic David Finkle called the novel "the hilarious wail of a stand-up comic delivering punch lines from the rubble." Finkle added: "Mr. Louvish has enough combustible talent linked with Jewish spiritual and kabbalistic compulsion to earn the comparisons with Joseph Heller, Kurt Vonnegut, and Swift that have come his way."

In *The Death of Moishe-Ganef,* asserted Jonathan Keates in the London *Observer,* Louvish means to "infuriate those for whom the Arab-Israeli conflict is a simple matter of trumpeting national loyalties or rubber-stamping magic peace formulas." During the course of the novel Louvish assaults Middle-Eastern politics while a television critic—a former intelligence agent—finds himself solving the mystery of his childhood friend and army comrade's death. Writing for the *Daily Telegraph,* Martyn Goff judged Louvish's descriptions of war-torn Lebanon "a thousand times more telling than any TV documentary." Praising Louvish as a "born story teller" with a "rare and rich" style, Gillian Reynolds of *Punch* assessed, "Simon Louvish has the talent and the stamina to set him in a place of his own." Concluded Keates, "Louvish comes into his own as a satirist rather than as a standup comedian, with an enviable gift for making hardened Zionists and PLO leaders squirm."

In *The Days of Miracles and Wonders* Louvish continues to deal with Lebanese and middle-eastern politics, this time via the tale of Petros Angelopoulos, a Greek doctor who is abducted by Syrian agents while visiting friends in the town of East Lothian. Reviewing this work for the *Literary Review,* John Murray remarked on Louvish's knowledge of Lebanese politics, noting that it is "impressive the way the author manages to incorporate lengthy political discussions" into the "fabric of the novel." Writing for the *Scotsman,* Ian Bell also commended Louvish's exuberant style of writing, categorizing this work as a "book . . . deserving high praise," a work in which Louvish "is at the height of his considerable powers."

A comedian, one of the most acclaimed ones of the twentieth century, is the subject of *Man on the Flying Trapeze: The Life and Times of W. C. Fields.* Fields, born William Claude Dunkinfield, was a former vaudeville performer who achieved film stardom in the 1930s with the persona of a lecherous, drunken curmudgeon who detested even dogs and children. Louvish debunks some myths that Fields promoted about himself; for instance, Fields claimed his early life was one of poverty and delinquency, but actually he was a fairly well-behaved boy from a middle-class family. Louvish also contrasts the real Fields with his screen personality. "Although Louvish claims that Fields's deficient personal life gave his characters their sting . . . he also reveals that Fields's miserable marriage had its soft side," related Katharine Whittemore in the *New York Times Book Review.* "Fields doted on his grandchildren, and once planned to open an orphanage." *Newsweek*'s Malcolm Jones, Jr., reported that Louvish shows Fields to be "much more mysterious than the fatuously bibulous clown. He was a great drinker, yes, but he was also a great gardener, a fact that he took great pains to hide." Whittemore lamented the dearth of information about Fields's films but liked the book's many Hollywood anecdotes, and she thought "Louvish does a heroic job of filling in Fields's life."

Monkey Business: The Lives and Legends of the Marx Brothers: Groucho, Chico, Harpo, Zeppo with Added Gummo traces the brothers' journey from impoverished children of immigrants to leading funnymen of stage and screen, with such films as *Animal Crackers, A Day at the Races, Monkey Business,* and *Duck Soup.* Louvish quotes many Marx Brothers routines and also details the difficulties the siblings faced in real life, including anti-Semitism, excessive gambling, and failed marriages. *Times Literary Supplement* reviewer Howard Jacobson thought Louvish treated the Marxes' personal problems a bit too lightly. "I am not sure whether Louvish cannot or will not take measure of his material, but throughout this book one is conscious of more cruelty—cruelty felt and cruelty given—more extremity of feeling, more harshness of behavior and more pain, than Louvish ever seems to register," Jacobson remarked. "I would have him consider the lives of the Marx Brothers as more tragically disarranged than he paints them." *Literary Review* contributor Humphrey Carpenter, however, was bored by the biographical detail. "The Marxes don't need deconstructing," he asserted, "and they don't need a biographer, because the 'real' Leo, Arthur and Julius seem to have done nothing other than become Chico, Harpo and Groucho. . . . The only proper way to celebrate them is to unearth forgotten Marx Brothers jokes. Fortunately, Louvish has plenty of these."

Louvish more recently told *CA:* "Delusions as to the contribution of fiction towards the alleviation of conflicts have been abandoned, in favor of art for art's sake."

BIOGRAPHICAL/CRITICAL SOURCES:

PERIODICALS

Daily Telegraph, June 27, 1986.
Globe and Mail (Toronto), April 19, 1997, Suanne Kelman, "Really Big Novel Takes It All On."
Guardian (London), May 15, 1986.
Literary Review, November, 1999, Humphrey Carpenter, "That's Them All Right"; John Murray, "All There."
London Standard, June 4, 1986.
Newsweek, October 13, 1997, Malcolm Jones, Jr., review of *Man on the Flying Trapeze,* p. 78.
New Yorker, September 8, 1997, p. 80.
New York Times Book Review, November 17, 1985; June 27, 1993; January 1, 1995; September 21, 1997, Katharine Whittemore, "Philadelphia Story."
Observer (London), June 8, 1986.
Punch, May 15, 1985; June 4, 1986.
Scotsman, April 12, 1997, Ian Bell, "Escaped Crusader."
Spectator, June 2, 1979.
Times Literary Supplement, January 21, 2000, Howard Jacobson, "Resignation Letters," p. 20.

* * *

LYON, David 1948-

PERSONAL: Born December 7, 1948, in Edinburgh, Scotland. *Education:* Attended Bristol College of Commerce, 1967-68; University of Bradford, B.Sc. (with honors), 1971, Ph.D., 1976. *Religion:* Christian.

ADDRESSES: *Office*—Department of Sociology, Queen's University, Kingston, Ontario, Canada K7L 3N6. *E-mail*—lyond@post.queensu.ca.

CAREER: High school English teacher in Surrey, England, 1972; lecturer at secondary schools in Bradford, England, 1972-74, and Bingley, England, 1975-78; senior lecturer in sociology at secondary schools in Ilkley, England, 1978-90; Queen's University, Kingston, Ontario, Canada, associate professor, 1991-94, professor of sociology and head of department, 1994—. Wilfrid Laurier University, visiting assistant professor, 1976-77, visiting professor, summer, 1984; Regent College, Vancouver, British Columbia, Canada, visiting lecturer, summer, 1976; Calvin College, research fellow, 1981-82; University of Leeds, visiting research fellow at Television Research Centre, 1984-85; London Institute for Contemporary Christianity, associate faculty member, 1985-90; New College, Berkeley, CA, visiting professor, summer, 1986; Open University, course tutor in sociology of technology, 1987-90; McGill University, Birks Lecturer, 1994; University of British Columbia, Murrin Lecturer, 1995; Ecole des Hautes Etudes en Sciences Sociales, Paris, professur invité, 1996; Monash University, Australia and the University of Melbourne, visiting research fellow, 1999; University of Auckland, New Zealand, visiting research fellow, 2000; University of Toyko, Japan, foreign research fellow. Consultant to Ottawa's Centre for Renewal in Public Policy and Toronto's Information and Privacy Commission.

MEMBER: International Sociological Association, Canadian Association for Sociology and Anthropology, British Sociological Association, Society for Philosophy and Technology, Association for Sociology of Religion, Research and Ethics Group on Information and Society.

AWARDS, HONORS: Grants from England's Social Science Research Council, 1972-76 and 1978-85, London's Community Projects Foundation, 1988-90, Social Science and Humanities Research Council of Canada, 1993-95, with Marguerite Van Die, Pew Charitable Trusts grant, 1996-99, Social Science and Humanities Research Council of Canada, 2000-03.

WRITINGS:

Christians and Sociology, Inter-Varsity Press (London, England), 1975, Inter-Varsity Press (Downers Grove, IL), 1976.

Karl Marx: An Assessment of His Life and Thought, Lion Publishing (Tring, England), 1979, Inter-Varsity Press (Downers Grove, IL), 1981.

Sociology and the Human Image, Inter-Varsity Press (Downers Grove, IL), 1983.

Future Society, Lion (Belleville, MI), 1984.

The Silicon Society: How Will Information Technology Change Our Lives?, Eerdmans (Grand Rapids, MI), 1986.

The Information Society: Issues and Illusions, Polity Press (Cambridge, England), 1988, Basil Blackwell (New York, NY), 1989.

Postmodernity, University of Minnesota Press (Minneapolis, MN), 1994, revised and expanded edition, 1999.

The Electronic Eye: The Rise of Surveillance Society, University of Minnesota Press (Minneapolis, MN), 1994.

Living Stones: St. James' Church, Kingston, 1845-1995: From Stuartville to Queen's Campus, Quarry Press (Kingston, Ontario, Canada), 1995.

(Editor with Elia Zureik) *Computers, Surveillance, and Privacy,* University of Minnesota Press (Minneapolis, MN), 1996.

Jesus in Disneyland: Religion in Postmodern Times, Polity/Blackwell, 2000.

(Co-editor with Marguerite Van Die) *Rethinking Church, State, and Modernity: Canada between Europe and America,* University of Toronto Press (Toronto, Ontario, Canada), 2000.

Surveillance Society: Monitoring Everyday Life, Open University Press (London, England), 2001.

Contributor to books, including *Norm and Context in the Social Sciences,* edited by S. Griffioen and J. Vergooht, University Press of America (Washington, DC), 1991; *Information, Ideology, and Utopia,* edited by Anthony Giddens, Polity Press, 1991; *Debates in Sociology,* edited by Liz Stanley and David Morgan, Manchester University Press (Manchester, England), 1992; *Post-Modernity, Religion, and Sociology,* edited by K. Flanagan and P. Jupp, Macmillan, 1996; and *Hermeneutics and a Christian Worldview,* edited by Roger Lundin, Eerdmans, 1997. Contributor of articles and reviews to scholarly journals and popular magazines, including *Christian Arena, New Society, Faith and Thought,* and *Third Way.*

Lyon's books have been translated into Korean, Italian, Portuguese, Japanese, Spanish, Danish, Romanian, Swedish, Chinese and Dutch.

SIDELIGHTS: David Lyon told *CA:* "I attempt to integrate radical Christian commitment with contemporary social analysis. From my earliest work, such as *Karl Marx* or *Sociology and the Human Image,* I have attempted dialogue between social thought and Christianity. More recently, work on the social and cultural aspects of information technology has led to books on major social change and its feared downside. I am working on a new book on cyberspace and another on how people negotiate and contest surveillance in everyday life."

M

MacDONOGH, Giles 1955-

PERSONAL: Surname is pronounced "mac-*don*-na"; born 1955; son of Redmond Joseph (an actor and playwright) and Elisabeth (a painter; maiden name, Zirner Bacon) MacDonogh. *Education:* Balliol College, Oxford, graduated (with honors), 1978; attended Ecole des Hautes Etudes Pratiques, Sorbonne, University of Paris, 1980-83. *Politics:* "None." *Religion:* Roman Catholic.

ADDRESSES: Home and office—London, England. *Agent*—David Miller, Ragers, Coleridge & White, 20 Powis Mews, London W11 1JN, England.

CAREER: Teacher of English as a foreign language in Paris, France, 1979-82; University of Paris II, Paris, *chargé de travaux dirigés* for legal English, 1982-83; Schiller International University, lecturer in history, 1983-84; public relations consultant, 1985-86; freelance journalist, 1986—. Occasional contributor to British Broadcasting Corp.

MEMBER: International PEN, Society for Court Studies, Biographers Club, Academy Club.

AWARDS, HONORS: Shortlisted for Andre Simon Prize, 1987; Glenfiddich Special Award, 1988, for *A Palate in Revolution: Grimod de La Reyniere and the Almanach des Gourmands.*

WRITINGS:

A Palate in Revolution: Grimod de La Reyniere and the Almanach des Gourmands, Robin Clark, 1987.

A Good German: Adam von Trott zu Solz, Quartet Books (New York, NY), 1990.

Brillat-Savarin: The Judge and His Stomach, J. Murray (London, England), 1991, I. R. Dee (Chicago, IL), 1992.

The Wine and Food of Austria, 1992.

Syrah, Grenache, and Mourvedre, 1992.

(Contributor) G. Garrier, editor, *Les rencontres de Dionysos,* Nîmes, 1993.

Prussia: The Perversion of an Idea, Sinclair-Stevenson, 1994.

(Contributor) Hartwig Hamer, *The Near and the Far,* Schwerin, 1996.

Berlin, St. Martin's Press (New York, NY), 1998.

The Wines of Austria: A Traveller's Guide, 1997.

Frederick the Great: A Life in Deed and Letters, St. Martin's Press (New York, NY), 2000.

(Contributor) S. Brook, *A Century of Wine,* 2000.

The Last Kaiser: William the Impetuous, Weidenfeld & Nicolson, 2000, St. Martin's Press (New York, NY), 2001.

Contributor to *Larousse Encyclopedia of Wine, Global Encyclopedia of Wine, Webster's Wine Guide,* and *The Faber Book of Food,* Faber. Wine correspondent, *Sunday Today,* 1986; food, drink, and travel correspondent and author of column "Food for Thought," *Financial Times,* 1989—. Contributor of articles and reviews to periodicals. Editor, *Made in France International,* 1984.

WORK IN PROGRESS: Wine of Portugal, for Grub Street; a biography of E. T. A. Hoffmann, completion expected in 2002.

SIDELIGHTS: Giles MacDonogh has written books on several subjects, including histories of wine and of French gastronomic writing, and on various aspects of

German history. In *A Good German: Adam von Trott zu Solz,* he gives readers an intimate look into the world of Nazi Germany through the biography of an anti-Nazi aristocrat. Adam von Trott zu Solz had a deep love for his country but was keenly aware of the corruption infecting it during Hitler's rise to power. He tried to do everything he could to remain loyal and yet principled, and to stop the Nazi cause while remaining on cordial terms with the leadership of the Third Reich. His twisted course and its ineffectiveness drew scorn and hatred from many, and Trott himself seemed poisoned by his choices. *A Good German* is "a fine biography and an evocative portrait of Trott's times," mused a contributor to *Kirkus Reviews.*

In 1998, MacDonogh published *Berlin,* a collection of personal and historical vignettes about the German capital. Moving from the first settlements to his own visit during the fall of communist rule in 1989, he focuses for the most part on the nineteenth century, when Berlin began to emerge as a great European city. Rather than approaching his subject in strictly chronological order, MacDonogh used a thematic approach, dividing his work into seven chapters with titles such as "Berlin Life," "Berlin Itineraries," and "Ich bin ein Berliner." *Berlin* is, in the words of Zachary T. Irwin in *Library Journal,* "less a history than a vast thematic tour that defies summary." Jay Freeman in *Booklist* praised MacDonogh's cultural review, "from art to architecture to beer drinking," as "both engaging and enlightening. This is a highly readable and informative survey."

MacDonogh next turned his attention to the king known as Frederick the Great—Frederick II of Prussia. An amazingly energetic, brilliant man, Frederick is comparable in some ways to America's Thomas Jefferson or Britain's William Gladstone. His intellectual and artistic interests were highly developed, yet he was also a renowned general. Liberals and authoritarians both find attributes to admire in Frederick. In *Frederick the Great: A Life in Deed and Letters,* MacDonogh's "wide-ranging and often compelling portrait, all of the varied facets of this complex man are examined," observed Jay Freeman in *Booklist.* Freeman praised the author's research as "excellent" and his style as able to "eloquently convey the conflicts and immense personal dynamism that lay behind his subject's ambitions and accomplishments." The book is a "gem," particularly for readers looking for a good introduction to Frederick the Great, wrote Randall L. Schroeder in *Library Journal,* and a *Kirkus Reviews* writer concluded that *Frederick the Great* was "a captivating, diverse study of an equally fascinating figure."

BIOGRAPHICAL/CRITICAL SOURCES:

PERIODICALS

American Historical Review, June, 1993, review of *A Good German,* p. 897.

Booklist, January 15, 1995, Gilbert Taylor, review of *Prussia,* p. 893; August 19, 1998, Jay Freeman, review of *Berlin,* p. 1957.

Bookwatch, July, 1993, review of *Syrah, Grenache, and Mourvedre,* p. 6.

Choice, January, 1993, review of *A Good German,* p. 861; May, 1995, review of *Prussia,* p. 1506.

Economist, April 15, 2000, David Fraser, review of *Frederick the Great,* p. 6.

Kirkus Reviews, February 15, 1992, review of *A Good German;* June 15, 1998, review of *Berlin,* p. 876; March 15, 2000, review of *Frederick the Great,* p. 360.

Library Journal, April 15, 2000, Randall L. Schroeder, review of *Frederick the Great,* p. 100; August, 1998, Zachary T. Irwin, review of *Berlin,* p. 109.

London Review of Books, November 24, 1994, review of *Prussia,* p. 18.

New York Review of Books, December 17, 1992, review of *A Good German,* p. 38.

Observer (London), June 8, 1997, review of *Berlin,* p. 15.

Publishers Weekly, June 29, 1998, review of *Berlin,* p. 44; March 27, 2000, review of *Frederick the Great,* p. 62.

Spectator, November 21, 1992, review of *Brillat-Savarin,* p. 40; September 3, 1994, review of *Prussia,* p. 39; April 17, 1999, review of *Frederick the Great,* p. 38.

Times Literary Supplement, June 29, 1990; October 23, 1992, review of *Brillat-Savarin,* p. 32; December 4, 1992, review of *Syrah, Grenache, and Mourvedre,* p. 23; December 2, 1994, review of *Prussia,* p. 26; October 10, 1997, review of *Berlin,* p. 33; April 16, 1999, review of *Berlin,* p. 7.

Washington Post Book World, February 5, 1995, review of *Prussia,* p. 13.

* * *

MAILLARD, Keith 1942-

PERSONAL: Surname is pronounced Muh-*lard;* born February 28, 1942, in Wheeling, WV; son of Eugene Charles and Aileen (a payroll office manager; maiden name, Sharp) Maillard; married; children: two daughters. *Education:* Attended West Virginia University, 1961-63.

ADDRESSES: Office—University of British Columbia, Creative Writing, Buch. E462-1866 Main Mall, Vancouver, British Columbia, Canada V6T 121. *Agent*—Felicia Eth, 555 Bryant St., Suite 350, Palo Alto, CA 94301.

CAREER: Writer in Boston, MA, 1967-70, and Vancouver, British Columbia, Canada, 1970—; University of British Columbia, Vancouver, British Columbia, Canada, sessional instructor, 1980-89, assistant professor, 1989-94, associate professor, 1994—. Worked as sessional instructor for screenwriting and dramatic direction, Praxis Film Development Workshop, Simon Fraser University, Centre for the Arts, 1986-89; worked variously as an editor, teacher, writer, and photographer, 1967-84.

MEMBER: Federation of British Columbia Writers.

AWARDS, HONORS: Ethen Wilson Fiction Prize, *Motet,* 1990; *Light in the Company of Women* was first runner-up for the Ethel Wilson Fiction Prize, B. C. Book Prizes, 1994; Gerald Lampert Prize for best first book of poetry, League of Canadian Poets, 1995, for *Dementia Americana; Hazard Zones* was short-listed for the Commonwealth Literary Prize, Canadian and Caribbean section, 1996; *Gloria* was nominated for the Governor General's Literary Award for fiction, 1999. Recipient of various grants, including Canada Council, 1974, 1977-78, 1978, and Ontario Arts Council, 1976, 1977.

WRITINGS:

(Contributor) Howard Reiter, editor, *Instead of Revolution,* Hawthorn, 1971.

Two Strand River (novel), Press Porcepic (Ontario, Canada), 1976, HarperCollins (New York, NY), 1996.

Alex Driving South (novel), Dial (New York, NY), 1980.

The Knife in My Hands, General Publishing (Toronto, Ontario, Canada), 1981, Beaufort Books (New York, NY), 1982.

Cutting Through, Stoddart (Toronto, Ontario, Canada), 1982, Beaufort Books (New York, NY), 1983.

Motet (novel), Random House (Toronto, Ontario, Canada), 1989.

Light in the Company of Women (novel), HarperCollins (Toronto, Ontario, Canada), 1993.

Dementia Americana (poems), Ronsdale Press (Vancouver, British Columbia, Canada), 1994.

Hazard Zones (novel), HarperPerennial (Toronto, Ontario, Canada), 1995.

Gloria (novel), HarperFlamingo Canada (Toronto, Ontario, Canada), 1999, Soho Press (New York, NY), 2000.

Writer for Canadian Broadcasting Corporation radio programs *This Country in the Morning, Our Native Land, Five Nights,* and *Ideas.* Contributor to periodicals, including *Fusion, Body Politic, Malahat Review, Books in Canada, Canadian Literature,* and newspapers.

WORK IN PROGRESS: The Clarinet Polka, a novel; *He Was a Good Dancer,* personal memoir and biography.

SIDELIGHTS: Keith Maillard worked his way through the United States (including Alaska) and Canada during the 1960s as a folk singer, photographer, music teacher, and writer. In 1970 he settled in Canada, becoming a Canadian citizen in 1976, and continued his work as writer, musician, and music teacher. Since 1989, he has taught creative writing at the University of British Columbia. He lives in Vancouver with his wife and two daughters.

Maillard's second published book was *Two Strand River,* a novel about a woman who feels she should have been a man and a man who feels he should have been a woman. Themes of breaking open and banishing conventions run through the book, which was described by a *Publishers Weekly* reviewer as one that "transcends the boundaries between the sexes, between humanity and nature, and between imagination and reality."

Hazard Zones, published in 1995, concerns a middle-aged man who reaches a certain state of contentment, only to be forced to look back at his past when his mother dies. As he makes arrangements for his mother's burial, an ex-wife, stepbrother, and assorted ghosts from the past rise up to haunt him. Michele Leber praised the book enthusiastically in *Booklist,* stating, "With its finely crafted prose, seamless narrative, wonderfully developed characters, and indelible vignettes, this is an exceptional novel, deserving to be read and reread."

Gloria is the coming-of-age story of an American country-club girl during the 1950s. Though she goes through all the motions of sorority and society life, Gloria Merriman Cotter is really an intelligent young woman who yearns to pursue life as a poetry scholar. Her marriage to a wealthy member of her family's social circle is a foregone conclusion, but one which is completely at odds with her desire to go on to graduate school. "With insight and clarity, Maillard illuminates the confused, complex, sometimes trivial but always heartfelt thoughts of a young woman trying to fathom her place in the world," asserted a *Publishers Weekly* writer, who added, "Maillard's precise prose weaves the long, meandering story together admirably." Other reviewers approved of the author's refusal to oversimplify his tale. A writer for *Kirkus Reviews* said, "Maillard makes us see the attraction of both worlds, as well as the alcoholism, infidelity, and misogyny that belie the outward complacency of the period." Michele Leber, a contributor to *Library Journal,* expressed the hope that *Gloria* might bring its author greater recognition: "Maillard invites comparison to John O'Hara for the time and place of this novel and its well-conceived characters and fluent narration; *Gloria* could be the breakthrough book for this deserving author."

BIOGRAPHICAL/CRITICAL SOURCES:

PERIODICALS

Booklist, June 1, 1996, Michele Leber, review of *Hazard Zones,* p. 1676; August, 2000, Grace Fill, review of *Gloria,* p. 2114.

Books in Canada, summer, 1993, review of *Light in the Company of Women,* p. 46; March, 1995, review of *Dementia Americana,* p. 45; March, 1996, review of *Hazard Zones,* p. 13.

Canadian Book Review Annual, 1994, review of *Dementia Americana,* p. 213.

Canadian Fiction, spring-summer, 1977.

Canadian Literature, summer, 1994, review of *Light in the Company of Women,* p. 115.

Globe & Mail, June 12, 1999, review of *Gloria,* p. D21.

Kirkus Reviews, April 15, 1996, review of *Hazard Zones,* p. 551; August 15, 1996, review of *Two Strand River,* p. 1178; July 1, 2000, review of *Gloria,* p. 909.

Library Journal, May 1, 1997, review of *Hazard Zones,* p. 164; August, 2000, Michele Leber, review of *Gloria,* p. 159.

Publishers Weekly, September 23, 1996, review of *Two Strand River,* p. 71; July 31, 2000, review of *Gloria,* p. 68.

Quill & Quire, March, 1993, review of *Light in the Company of Women,* p. 49; June, 1999, review of *Gloria,* p. 52.

* * *

MANCINI, Anthony 1939-

PERSONAL: Born January 17, 1939, in New York, NY; son of Ugo (a construction foreman) and Emma (Staniscia) Mancini; married Patricia McNees (a writer and editor), April 22, 1967 (divorced); married Maria Cellario (an actress), June 25, 1978; children: (first marriage) Romana; (second marriage) Nicholas. *Ethnicity:* "Italian." *Education:* Fordham University, B.A., 1961. *Politics:* "Humanist/skeptic." *Religion:* Roman Catholic. *Avocational interests:* Shooting pool, playing basketball, opera, reading.

ADDRESSES: Home—366 Broadway, Apt. 12-D, New York, NY 10013. *Office*—Journalism Program, Department of English, Brooklyn College of the City University of New York, Brooklyn, NY 11210; fax: 212-732-0096. *Agent*—Owen Laster, William Morris Agency, 1350 Avenue of the Americas, New York, NY 10019. *E-mail*—smith_carlo@hotmail.com.

CAREER: New York Post, New York, NY, reporter, 1959-76; Brooklyn College of the City University of New York, Brooklyn, NY, member of faculty, 1980—, professor of journalism, 1989—, and director of journalism program. New York University, adjunct professor, beginning in 1977. *Military service:* U.S. Army, 1961-63.

MEMBER: Authors Guild, Professional Staff Congress.

AWARDS, HONORS: First prize from Uniformed Firefighters Association, 1977, for newspaper feature "Inside a Hospital Burn Center."

WRITINGS:

(Contributor) *Kissinger: The Public and Private Story,* New American Library (New York, NY), 1974.

Minnie Santangelo's Mortal Sin (suspense novel), Coward (New York, NY), 1975.

Minnie Santangelo and the Evil Eye (suspense novel), Coward (New York, NY), 1977.

The Miracle of Pelham Bay Park, Dutton (New York, NY), 1982.

Menage, D. I. Fine (New York, NY), 1988.

The Yellow Gardenia (novel), D. I. Fine (New York, NY), 1990.

Talons (novel), D. I. Fine (New York, NY), 1991.

Godmother (novel), D. I. Fine (New York, NY), 1993.

Reporter and correspondent from Frankfurt, Germany, for *Overseas Weekly,* 1965-66. Contributor to popular magazines, including *Travel and Leisure, Self, Cosmopolitan, Penthouse,* and *Gentleman's Quarterly,* and to newspapers. Mancini's books have been published in Japan, Finland, Romania, Germany, France, Spain, and the Netherlands.

WORK IN PROGRESS: A novel, *The Death of Elma Sands.*

SIDELIGHTS: Anthony Mancini once told *CA:* "I am an identical twin. My brother Joseph is also a writer for the *New York Post.* I have lived in Germany and Italy."

Later, Mancini commented: "I write to fend off boredom. I write to earn money ('None but a blockhead,' said Sam Johnson). I write to learn. I write to suffer. I write to avoid suffering. I write to avoid working. I write to avoid playing. I write out of habit. I write because I can't sing arias or play the piano. I used to write to keep the wolf from the door; now I write out of some forlorn hope that I will find something to say. I write to keep off the streets.

"Everybody I read or have read influences my work. I steal from everybody. I don't plagiarize, but I 'pinch effects,' as Lawrence Durrell put it. Maybe someday I'll learn how to do it on my own. I doubt it.

"I have a simple writing process. I turn on the computer and wait for the beads of blood to form on my forehead.

"I have been inspired to write on the subjects I have chosen through some mysterious and probably dishonest process that will do until a better one comes along. The struggle is to go from word to word, phrase to phrase, clause to clause, sentence to sentence, paragraph to paragraph, chapter to chapter, book to book, and keep yourself from getting up from the chair, eating too much, drinking too much, or going absolutely nuts."

BIOGRAPHICAL/CRITICAL SOURCES:

PERIODICALS

Library Journal, January, 1989, Rex E. Klett, review of *Menage,* p. 105; August, 1991, Edwin B. Burgess, review of *Talons,* p. 146.

Publishers Weekly, November 27, 1981, Barbara A. Bannon, review of *The Miracle of Pelham Bay Park,* p. 80; November 18, 1988, Sybil Steinberg, review of *Menage,* p. 68; July 27, 1990, Steinberg, review of *The Yellow Gardenia,* p. 223; June 21, 1991, review of *Talons,* p. 51; September 13, 1993, review of *Godmother,* p. 92.

* * *

MARLING, Karal Ann 1943-

PERSONAL: Born November 5, 1943, in Rochester, NY; daughter of Raymond J. and Marjorie (Karal). *Education:* Bryn Mawr College, Ph.D., 1971.

ADDRESSES: *Office*—1920 South First St., Suite 1301, Minneapolis, MN 55454.

CAREER: University of Minnesota, Minneapolis, MN, professor of art history and American studies, 1977—. Visiting appointments at Carleton College, the Buffalo Bill Center, Cotnell University, University of Wyoming, Harvard University, University of Kansas, Catholic University of Lublin (Poland).

AWARDS, HONORS: Minnesota Humanities Commission Award, 1986; Minnesota Book Award-History, 1994; Robert C. Smith Award from the Decorative Arts Society, 1994; International Association of Art Critics award, 1998.

WRITINGS:

Federal Art in Cleveland, 1933-1943: An Exhibition, Cleveland Public Library (Cleveland, OH), 1974.

Wall-to-Wall America: A Cultural History of Post-Office Murals in the Great Depression, University of Minnesota Press (Minneapolis, MN), 1982.

The Colossus of Roads: Myth and Symbol along the American Highway, photographs by Liz Harrison and Bruce White, University of Minnesota Press, 1984.

Tom Benton and His Drawings: A Biographical Essay and a Collection of His Sketches, Studies, and Mural Cartoons, University of Missouri Press (Columbia, MS), 1985.

Frederic C. Knight (1898-1979), Everhart Museum (Scranton, PA), 1987.

George Washington Slept Here: Colonial Revivals and American Culture, 1876-1986, Harvard University Press (Cambridge, MA), 1988.

Looking Back: A Perspective on the 1913 Inaugural Exhibition, Memorial Art Gallery of the University of Rochester (Rochester, NY), 1988.

Blue Ribbon: A Social and Pictorial History of the Minnesota State Fair, Minnesota Historical Society Press (St. Paul, MN), 1990.

(With John Wetenhall) *Iwo Jima: Monuments, Memories, and the American Hero,* Harvard University Press, 1991.

Edward Hopper, Rizzoli (New York), 1992.

(Editor, with Jessica H. Foy) *The Arts and the American Home, 1890-1930,* University of Tennessee Press (Knoxville, TN), 1994.

As Seen on TV: The Visual Culture of Everyday Life in the 1950s, Harvard University Press, 1994.

In Search of the Corn Queen, National Museum of American Art, 1994.

Going Home with Elvis, Harvard University Press (Cambridge, MA), 1995.

The Architecture of Reassurance: Building the Disney Theme Parks, Flamarion (Paris), 1997.

Civil Rights in Oz: Images of Kansas in American Popular Art, Spencer Museum of Art (Lawrence, KS), 1997.

Norman Rockwell, Harry N. Abrams (New York), 1997.

L'architecture du Récomfort, Center Canadien d'Architecture (Montreal), 1997.

Merry Christmas! Celebrating America's Greatest Holiday, Harvard University Press, 2000.

Also author of the catalog essays for *Joe Jones and J. B. Turnbull: Visions of the Midwest in the 1930s,* Patrick and Beatrice Haggerty Museum of Art (Milwaukee, WI), 1987; *Niles Spencer,* Whitney Museum of American Art at Equitable Center (New York), 1990; *A Year from the Collection, circa 1952,* Whitney Museum of American Art (New York), 1994; *Double Trouble: The Patchett Collection,* Museum of Contemporary Art (San Diego), 1998; *Dateline Kenya: The Media Paintings of Joseph Bertiers,* Smart Ass Press (Santa Monica), 1998; Beth Venn and Adam P. Weinberg, *Frames of Reference: Looking at American Art, 1900-1950,* Whitney Museum of American Art/University of California Press (Berkeley), 1999; *Norman Rockwell: Pictures for the American People,* High Museum of Art, Norman Rockwell Museum, Harry N. Abrams, 1999; and *Illusions of Eden: Vision of the American Heartland,* Arts Midwest, Columbia Museum of Art, 2000; contributor of an essay, with Merry A. Foresta and Stephen Jay Gould, to *Between Home and Heaven: Contemporary American Landscape Photography from the Consolidated Natural Gas Company Collection of the National Museum of American Art,* Smithsonian Institution/ University of New Mexico Press (Albuquerque, NM), 1992.

SIDELIGHTS: Karal Ann Marling is a scholar of American popular culture and art. Her writings include exhibition catalogs, studies of individual artists as well as art movements, and historical surveys of American cultural icons and events. Marling's histories in particular have garnered praise for the clarity of her writing and the thoroughness of her research. Such titles as *Wall-to-Wall America: A Cultural History of Post-Office Murals in the Great Depression* and *As Seen on TV: The Visual Culture of Everyday Life in the 1950s* are viewed by critics as valuable contributions to twentieth-century art history and popular culture.

In *Wall-to-Wall America,* Marling examines the controversial result of an art contest sponsored by the U.S. Treasury Department's Section of Fine Arts in 1939. This contest, which was intended to supply one mural for a small-town post office in each state in the country, pitted government officials, citizens, and artists against each other in bitter disagreements about taste and propriety. *Wall-to-Wall America* includes illustrations of the murals under discussion along with sketches of proposed murals and quotes from letters, petitions, contracts, and government reports on works-in-progress from the voluminous official archives. Commenting on Marling's utilization of "an anecdotal, case-study approach" to her vast amount of research material, Le Anne Schreiber wrote in the *New York Times:* "The result is a book that is less rigorously analytical but more entertaining than might be expected."

Marling often focuses on long-standing, powerful American icons in her work. In *George Washington Slept Here,* she examines the emergence of myths surrounding the first president of the United States, how these myths have changed over the centuries, and what these changes reveal about the society as a whole. "Because the book is richly descriptive," remarked Michael Kammen in the *New York Times Book Review,* "readers will encounter many unfamiliar and enchanting tales" about the real people who surrounded Washington as well as those whose claim to fame rests in their obsession with a person some critics describe as our national patron saint. Although Marling was criticized for failing to cull her prodigious research materials to a more manageable size—"the author seems compelled to use all her notes," observed *Washington Post* critic Michael Kernan—*George Washington Slept Here* was also praised for its entertaining depiction of the trivialization and mythification of the first president. Kammen dubbed the book "a lively expose whose persuasiveness owes much to the banality, snobbery and ubiquity of the treasures turned up by Ms. Marling."

Like *George Washington Slept Here, Iwo Jima: Monuments, Memories, and the American Hero,* coauthored with John Wetenhall, exposes the myths that have grown up around a powerful American icon—in this case, a famous photograph and national monument of the raising of the American flag during one of the bloodiest battles of World War II. Marling and Wetenhall discuss the actual flag-raising event, which was an attempt to raise the spirits of the still-fighting American troops. A subsequent flag-raising, just hours later, yielded the famous photograph and, aided by a popular film, *The Sands of Iwo Jima,* helped sustain American support for the U.S. Marine Corps during the post-war years. However, the second flag-raising was also the source of some controversy and a subsequent government cover-up of its staging. John Bodnar remarked in the *American Historical Review:* "Marling and Wetenhall focus more on telling their story than analyzing its theoretical implications, but they clearly explain the role that the Marine Corps played in attempting to extract as much favorable public opinion from the episode as possible." Charles K. Piehl of *Library Journal* enthusiastically concluded: "This is popular culture at its best, thoroughly enjoyable to read."

Novelist John Updike termed Marling's book, *As Seen on TV: The Visual Culture of Everyday Life in the 1950s,* "an intellectual romp, a dizzying free fall through the exuberant 'visual culture' of that first post-World War II decade," in his review in the *New York Times Book Review.* In this work, Marling examines the influence of television on such signature aspects of the 1950s as the creation of Disneyland and huge, chrome-encrusted automobiles, Elvis Presley, Betty Crocker, vice president Richard Nixon and Soviet leader Nikita Khrushchev. Although the author was again criticized for providing less analysis than raw data, a *Kirkus Reviews* contributor nonetheless concluded: "This archaeology of our recent visual past is as important as any recent political history of the period, and far fresher in approach."

Marling is also the author of *Edward Hopper,* a brief, poster-size paperback that reproduces the American painter's most famous works, accompanied by an essay that describes and analyzes Hopper's contribution to American art.

Marling's popular culture treatises have garnered praise for their entertaining reflections on American society. While several critics expressed the desire for further analytical discussion of the topics her thorough researching has unearthed, many seemed fascinated by her accounts of such varied phenomena as the use of George Washington's image to sell consumer goods, the acrimony generated when people try to agree on matters of taste, and the influence of television on nearly every aspect of American society. According to Kammen in the *New York Times Book Review,* these works have justly contributed to Marling's "reputation as an energetic and observant practitioner of American studies."

Marling told *CA:* "I remain an art historian. That is, the object is more important to me than any theoretical construct into which it might be crammed. Things have stories to tell in a language of form, shape, and color: I try to tell these stories in the most accessible manner possible."

BIOGRAPHICAL/CRITICAL SOURCES:

PERIODICALS

American Historical Review, October, 1992, pp. 1305-1306.

Kirkus Reviews, July 15, 1994, p. 964.

Library Journal, June 15, 1991, p. 89; July, 1992, p. 80.

New York Times, November 12, 1982; October 1, 1991, p. C16.

New York Times Book Review, November 6, 1988, p. 26; August 25, 1991, p. 10; October 30, 1994, p. 31.

Publishers Weekly, June 21, 1991, pp. 46-47; September 5, 1994, p. 104.

School Library Journal, August, 1992, p. 182.

Washington Post, October 28, 1988.

* * *

MARRS, Jim 1943-

PERSONAL: Full name, James Farrell Marrs, Jr.; born December 5, 1943, in Fort Worth, TX; son of James F. and Pauline (an author; maiden name, Draper) Marrs; married Carol Worcester (a teacher), May 25, 1968; children: Cathryn Nova Ayn, Jayme Alistar. *Education:* North Texas State University, B.A., 1966; graduate studies at Texas Technological College (now Texas Tech University), 1967-68. *Politics:* Libertarian. *Religion:* Methodist.

ADDRESSES: Home and office—P.O. Box 189, Springtown, TX 76082.

CAREER: Magpie Magazine, editor and owner, 1963-64; reporter, cartoonist, and photographer for various Texas periodicals, including the *Denton Record*

Chronicle, the *Lubbock Avalanche-Journal,* the *Lubbock Sentinel,* and the *Fort Worth Star-Telegram,* 1965-80; freelance writer, 1970—; Jerre R. Todd & Associates, Fort Worth, TX, copywriter, public relations director, and cartoonist, 1972-74, director of special projects, account executive, public relations director, copywriter, and cartoonist, 1980-81; The Marketing Group, Dallas, TX, public relations consultant and copywriter, 1982-83; *Springtown Current,* Springtown, TX, publisher and co-owner, 1983-84; Innotech Energy Corporation, Las Collinas, TX, communications director, 1985-86; Northeast HealthCare Center, Hurst, TX, communications director, 1985-86; First Bank and Trust, Springtown, TX, communications director, 1985—. Chair of public information subcommittee for the Fort Worth Mayor's Committee on Employment of the Handicapped, 1979-82; community relations consultant for All Church Home for Children, 1984—; cochair of Springtown Centennial Committee, 1984. Teacher in Office of Continuing Education at University of Texas at Arlington, 1976—; workshop teacher for Operation CLASP under Community Development Block Grant, City of Fort Worth, 1984. Producer of cable television program *Texas Roundup,* on Sammons Cable TV, 1982-83; editor, publisher, and co-owner of monthly tourism magazine *Cowtown Trails,* 1983-84; arranged media publicity for Byte Computer Show, 1985. Various appearances as an expert on the assassination of President John F. Kennedy and the existence of UFOs, including the television programs *Geraldo, The Montell Williams Show, This Morning,* and *Today,* and the *Larry King* radio show, 1988—. *Military service:* Served in United States Army Reserve, 1969-70, 347th military intelligence platoon.

MEMBER: National Society of Professional Journalists (Sigma Delta Chi), North Texas Reenactment Society, Springtown Optimist Club, Delta Sigma Phi.

AWARDS, HONORS: White Helmet awards, Fort Worth Fire Department, 1969, 1971; various Associated Press writing awards, 1969-76; National Writing Award, Aviation/Aerospace Writers Association, 1972; Human Rights Leadership Award from *Freedom* magazine, 1993; national writing award from Aviation/Aerospace Writers' Association.

WRITINGS:

Crossfire: The Plot That Killed Kennedy (nonfiction), Carroll & Graf (New York, NY), 1989.

The Enigma Files: The True Story of America's Psychic Warfare Program, Harmony Books (New York, NY), 1995.

Alien Agenda: Investigating the Extraterrestrial Presence among Us, HarperCollins (New York, NY), 1997.

Rule by Secrecy: The Hidden History That Connects the Trilateral Commission, the Freemasons, and the Great Pyramids, HarperCollins (New York, NY), 2000.

PSI Spies, ebooksonthe.net/AlienZoo, 2000.

Author, with Robin Moore, of unpublished novel *The Man of the House,* 1982. Contributor to periodicals, including *Esprit* and *Freedom* magazines. Author of pieces for Texas Sesquicentennial Wagon Train publication.

SCRIPTS

Bucky Bunny (Dental Education Video Series), Spindletop Productions, 1982-83.

(And director) *Who Didn't Kill . . . JFK* (video; also known as *Fake*), 3-G Home Video, 1991.

Author and director of video *The Many Faces of Lee Harvey Oswald,* 1992.

ADAPTATIONS: Crossfire was one of two books adapted by Oliver Stone for the film *JFK,* 1991.

SIDELIGHTS: Jim Marrs is the author of books that seek to uncover truths he feels have been hidden by governments, both national and multi-national. Marrs does not see himself as a "conspiracy theorist," but rather as an investigative journalist who has unearthed contradictory information about such topics as the assassination of President John F. Kennedy, the aims of the Trilateral Commission, and visits by extraterrestrials. A former reporter for the *Fort Worth Star-Telegram* and a popular professor at the University of Texas at Arlington, Marrs has found his books on the bestseller list repeatedly, especially since director Oliver Stone used Marrs's *Crossfire: The Plot That Killed Kennedy* as a basis for the film *JFK.* According to Robert Wilonsky in the *Dallas Observer,* Marrs "would prefer you refer to him as a 'truth seeker.'" The reporter added: "Jim Marrs can't be ignored. Few in this country shout about The Truth louder than he."

Crossfire: The Plot That Killed Kennedy examines the numerous theories regarding the assassination of U.S. President John F. Kennedy. The book is based upon a decade of research, including interviews with Lee Harvey Oswald's family and a bystander who was struck by a bullet during the assassination. Marrs's coverage of the event is encyclopedic: He includes numerous theories on Kennedy's demise and voluminous evidence of a government cover-up conducted in lieu of a truthful investigation. His work does not make a definitive statement on who killed Kennedy or why, but it does demonstrate that the "single gunman theory" cannot account for the extent of Kennedy's wounds. Marrs once told *CA: "Crossfire* was largely ignored by the major media and Oliver Stone was viciously attacked by some because, for the first time, we presented a wealth of assassination information which had not been filtered first through those same major media."

The mainstream media has indeed tended to dismiss Marrs out of hand. The reading public feels otherwise, however. Marrs's books have found major publishers and have achieved bestseller status, and he is a frequent guest on television talk shows. Wilonsky called the author "a celebrity on the conspiracy circuit. . . . The curious seek his wisdom."

In 1997, Marrs released *Alien Agenda: Investigating the Extraterrestrial Presence among Us.* The book claims that the U.S. government knows about alien encounters and has sought to cover them up by belittling those who investigate them. The work also explores possible alien influences in the major world religions and in the dawn of organized civilization. It also hints that aliens have plans for Earth's future. *National Review* correspondent Andrew Stuttaford declared: "In a saner time, *Alien Agenda* would have been a crudely mimeographed pamphlet, pushed into your hand by a disheveled gentleman on a street corner. In the America of 1997 it will probably be a hit. And there is a sting in this campfire tale. The UFO myth mingles with and reinforces the other folk beliefs that increasingly shape a country where reason has gone quiet." Stuttaford was correct on one point: *Alien Agenda* did indeed become a hit that went into its third printing within a month of publication. A *Publishers Weekly* contributor called the work "the most entertaining and complete overview of flying saucers and their crew in years," and *Booklist* correspondent George Eberhart concluded: "The facts are mostly accurate, and the writing is crisp and journalistic."

Rule by Secrecy: The Hidden History That Connects the Trilateral Commission, the Freemasons, and the Great Pyramids finds a secret conspiracy of world domination behind one organization's public façade. According to Marrs, the world's wealthiest citizens exercise an undue influence over governments, with an eye toward a one-world ruling body. These manipulators, he believes, can trace their ancestry back through time in such secret societies as the Freemasons and the Illuminati. A *Publishers Weekly* reviewer observed of the book: "Conspiracy buffs will have a field day wading through this morass, but other readers will remain unpersuaded."

Marrs explained his methodology in the *Dallas Observer.* "This sounds kinda idealistic, but in journalism school . . . they taught you about trying to find the truth and telling the truth to the public and letting *them* decide," he said. "Look on both sides of the issue, look beyond the government's pronouncements—*all* this stuff. And, hey, I bought into it. I really bought into that. I thought that was what I was supposed to be doing." He added: "I've always gone for the unconventional and the different. But that's OK, because if you study something—*any* subject, I don't care whatever it is—and come to know the truth of what's going on in that subject, you've got the truth as a defense against everybody."

BIOGRAPHICAL/CRITICAL SOURCES:

PERIODICALS

Booklist, April 15, 1997, George Eberhart, review of *Alien Agenda: Investigating the Extraterrestrial Presence among Us,* p. 1363.

Dallas Observer, July 6, 2000, Robert Wilonsky, "The Truth Is Way out There."

Library Journal, November 15, 1989, Gary L. Malecha, review of *Crossfire: The Plot That Killed Kennedy,* p. 96.

National Review, July 28, 1997, Andrew Stuttaford, review of *Alien Agenda: Investigating the Extraterrestrial Presence among Us,* p. 56.

Publishers Weekly, October 20, 1989, Genevieve Stuttaford, review of *Crossfire: The Plot That Killed Kennedy,* p. 46; May 5, 1997, review of *Alien Agenda: Investigating the Extraterrestrial Presence among Us,* p. 188; March 27, 2000, review of *Rule by Secrecy: The Hidden History That Connects the Trilateral Commission, the Freemasons, and the Great Pyramids,* p. 65.

Wall Street Journal, July 25, 2000, Bill Kauffman, "Think You Know What's Going On? You Don't," p. A20.

Washington Post, December 24, 1989.

OTHER

AlienZoo, http://www.alienzoo.com/ (May 19, 2001).

Jim Marrs: The View from Marrs (author's web page), http://www.jimmarrs.com/ (May 19, 2001).

The Majestic Documents, http://www.majesticdocuments.com/ (May 19, 2001), "Investigation Team."*

* * *

MARSH, Jan 1942-

PERSONAL: Born October 5, 1942, in England. *Education:* Newnham College, Cambridge, B.A. (honors); London School of Economics, Diploma of Social Administration; University of Sussex, D.Phil.

ADDRESSES: *Agent*—Jennifer Kavanagh, 39 Camden Park Rd., London NW1, England.

CAREER: Writer and biographer.

AWARDS, HONORS: Gulbenkian Award for best museum publication, for *The Pre-Raphaelites.*

WRITINGS:

Edward Thomas: A Poet for His Country, Barnes and Noble (New York, NY), 1978.

Back to the Land: The Pastoral Impulse in Victorian England from 1880 to 1914, Quartet (New York, NY), 1982.

Against the Grain: The Sapperton Group (screenplay), Arts Council, 1983.

The Pre-Raphaelite Sisterhood, St. Martin's (New York, NY), 1985.

Jane and May Morris: A Biographical Story, 1839-1938, Pandora (New York, NY), 1986.

Pre-Raphaelite Women: Images of Femininity, Harmony (New York, NY), 1987.

May Morris and the Art of Embroidery (documentary film), Central Television, 1988.

(With Pamela Gerrish Nunn) *Women Artists and the Pre-Raphaelite Movement,* Virago (London, England), 1989.

The Legend of Elizabeth Siddal, Quartet, 1989.

(With Trevor Lummis) *The Woman's Domain: Women and the English Country House,* Viking (New York, NY), 1990.

The Pre-Raphaelites: Their Lives in Letters and Diaries, Collins & Brown (London, England), 1996.

Bloomsbury Women: Distinct Figures in Life and Art, Pavilion Books (London, England), 1995, Henry Holt (New York, NY), 1996.

Christina Rossetti: A Literary Biography, Jonathan Cape (London, England), 1994, published as *Christina Rossetti: A Writer's Life,* Viking (New York, NY), 1995.

The Pre-Raphaelites, National Portrait Gallery (London, England), 1998.

(With Nunn) *Pre-Raphaelite Women Artists,* Thames & Hudson (New York, NY), 1999.

Dante Gabriel Rossetti: Painter and Poet, Weidenfeld & Nicolson (London, England), 1999.

(Editor) Dante Gabriel Rossetti, *Collected Writings of Dante Gabriel Rossetti,* Dent (London, England), 1999, New Amsterdam Books (Chicago, IL), 2000.

Contributor to *Visions of Love and Life: Pre-Raphaelite Art from the Birmingham Collection,* by Stephen Wildman, Art Services International, 1995.

SIDELIGHTS: Jan Marsh has devoted much effort to bringing to light the achievements of nineteenth-century artists and muses. Her *Back to the Land: The Pastoral Impulse in Victorian England from 1880 to 1914* is a study of the pastoral nature of the late nineteenth century as seen through the works of art critic John Ruskin, writer and craftsman William Morris, and author Edward Carpenter. In it Marsh compares Victorian crazes and late twentieth-century fads. Calling Marsh "excellent" on the agrarian communes of that era, Deborah Singmaster of the *Times Literary Supplement* added, "I recommend [*Back to the Land*] to anyone who is not already thoroughly familiar with the period."

In many of her writings, including *Pre-Raphaelite Sisterhood, Pre-Raphaelite Women, Jane and May Morris,* and *The Legend of Elizabeth Siddal,* Marsh attempts to uncover the truth behind the images of pre-Raphaelite women, including Elizabeth Siddal, Annie Miller, Fanny Cornforth, Jane Burden, and Georgiana Macdonald—English women, who, because of their beauty, became models for the Pre-Raphaelite Brotherhood, a group of young English artists who eschewed what they considered the artificiality of the then-current style. Although their works were realistic in the depiction of the human figure, they were often based on subjects from ancient mythology and literature. A number of these models eventually married the artists for whom they posed. Marsh maintains that these women played roles that were much more involved than merely posing or fulfilling domestic activities.

While remarking that Marsh's subjects in *Pre-Raphaelite Sisterhood* are not unrecognized geniuses, John Russell Taylor of the London *Times* conceded that Marsh "does demonstrate without much difficulty that they were a lot more complex and individual, and a lot more independently minded, than their usual position in Pre-Raphaelite studies might lead one to suppose." Sarah Bradford, writing for the *Spectator,* found that despite the author's "painstaking research," Marsh cannot prove her thesis concerning several of her subjects. However, according to *Times Literary Supplement* critic Kate Flint, "*Pre-Raphaelite Sisterhood* is an important work of re-reading. It turns the familiar terrain of Pre-Raphaelitism on its axis, giving new history, new life to the previously silent subject of the paintings."

Written on the same subject is Marsh's *Pre-Raphaelite Women,* an introduction to Pre-Raphaelite art and a survey of the use of the female in these works. "This is not a study for scholars," wrote Sara Laschever in the *New York Times Book Review.* "But with its attractive color plates and clear text, the book provides a useful introduction to the work and lives of the Pre-Raphaelites."

In several of her books, Marsh focuses on specific individuals who were part of the Pre-Raphaelite movement—for example, Elizabeth Siddal and Jane and May Morris. *The Legend of Elizabeth Siddal* covers new ground in describing the relationship between Siddal and Dante Gabriel Rossetti. "Jan Marsh persuasively shows how Siddal's portrayal has depended on succeeding views of femininity and sexual politics," complimented Flint. While the critic faulted some of Marsh's historical generalizations and "summary treatments of historical periods," she noted that Marsh "uses her copious documentation judiciously." In *Jane and May Morris,* Marsh recounts the story of Jane Burden, the wife of William Morris, and their daughter May; women who were involved in the arts and crafts movement. Marsh "has done well to rescue these women's reputations and to establish them as historical figures in their own right," remarked an *Observer* critic.

With coauthor Trevor Lummis, Marsh detailed in *The Woman's Domain* the histories of seven English country houses, dating from the sixteenth to nineteenth centuries, and the powerful women who were the true masters there. In her review for the *Times Literary Supplement,* Caroline Bingham recommended *The Woman's Domain* as "popular history at its best: meticulously researched and elegantly written, attractively blending information and entertainment."

In *Bloomsbury Women: Distinct Figures in Life and Art,* Marsh offers an account of the group that included Virginia Woolf, Vanessa Bell, Dora Carrington, Vita Sackville-West, Lydia Lopokova, Katherine Mansfield, Frances Partridge, and Angelica Garnett. She draws from their diaries, letters, and writings to document their personal lives over a period of four decades. A *Kirkus Reviews* contributor felt that although all were involved with the arts, "with a few notable exceptions . . . most reserved their real talents for the art of living. . . . They lived the kind of lives that make for juicy reading."

Christina Rossetti: A Writer's Life is a biography of the fourth and youngest child of Gabriele Rossetti. Revolutionary Gabriele Rossetti left Italy to settle in England in 1824, where the Dante scholar became a professor of Italian. His children, influenced by their literary father, all became writers. His eldest child was his daughter Maria. His two sons, Dante Gabriel (a painter) and William Michael, became poets and founders of the Pre-Raphaelite Brotherhood, and Christina was also a poet.

Gabriele was anti-papal but respected the Gospel. The children were brought up as Anglicans, in accordance with their mother's religious beliefs. William described Christina as being Anglo-Catholic but opposed to Roman Catholicism. Dante rejected religion altogether. "But the household was a loving one," wrote Claude Rawson in the *New York Times Book Review,* and that Marsh's biography "brings out this lovingness very fully. The men contributed to it in various ways. . . . it is the mother and daughters who stand out, as real-life heroines of Victorian womanhood without the sentimentality or brainless sweetness evoked by the familiar fictional stereotypes." Rawson also commented that Marsh "writes with delicacy of the nature and limits of Christina's 'feminism,' its thoughtful ambivalence, and the difficulties of this issue for a literal believer in the Scriptures who expects that sexual inequalities will be transcended in eternity."

Marsh published two books that focus on Christina's brother Dante. *Collected Writings of Dante Gabriel Rossetti* and *Dante Gabriel Rossetti: Painter and Poet* were published simultaneously in 1999. Jerome McGann wrote in the *London Review of Books* that Rossetti "was, according to his age's two most imposing critics. . . . there were many whose imaginations were shifted or shaped by his ideas and practice." McGann said Marsh "is exact in writing that Rossetti's influence was 'denied and then erased by the critical dominance of Modernism in the twentieth century.' He would be drawn and quartered between the two poles of Modernist self-definition: on the one hand, tradition and Neoclassical standards; on the other, innovation and 'individual talent.' Rossetti came to seem lost on both sides of that division."

Vivien Allen, reviewing *Dante Gabriel Rossetti* for the *Richmond Review,* noted that the book is not typical of an academic book and added that Marsh "writes fluently and readably at great length." Allen praised the usefulness of the notes and bibliography. Marsh goes into detail about Rossetti's frugal lifestyle. He fell into debt, even though he often borrowed his brother's clothes and ate at home or from street stalls. Rossetti's wife, Elizabeth Siddal, died from a drug overdose, and Rossetti deposited the only copy of his poems in her coffin to be buried with her. Seven years later he had the coffin dug up in order to recover them. His own drug addiction led to his death at the age of fifty-three. Allen said Marsh's account of Rossetti's life "makes fascinating reading. . . . Her canvas is as big and as detailed as many Pre-Raphaelite paintings."

Marsh told *CA:* "I lecture widely in Britain, North America, and Japan, where three of my titles have been translated."

BIOGRAPHICAL/CRITICAL SOURCES:

PERIODICALS

Art Bulletin, December, 1998, Susan P. Casteras, review of *Pre-Raphaelite Women Artists,* pp. 750-752.

Journal of Pre-Raphaelite Studies, fall, 2000, Alicia Craig Faxon, review of *Dante Gabriel Rosetti,* pp. 116-117.

Kirkus Reviews, January 1, 1996, review of *Bloomsbury Women.*

Library Journal, September 1, 1995, Denise Sticha, review of *Christina Rossetti,* p. 177; May 1, 1999, Joseph C. Hewgley, review of *Pre-Raphaelite Women Artists,* p. 72.

London Review of Books, March 30, 2000, Jerome McGann, "Fundamental Brainwork," pp. 24-26.

Los Angeles Times Book Review, December 29, 1985, pp. 3, 10.

New Leader, December 4, 1995, Melissa Knox, review of *Christina Rossetti,* pp. 28-29.

New York Review of Books, November 2, 1995, Fiona MacCarthy, review of *Christina Rossetti,* pp. 35-38.

New York Times Book Review, October 27, 1985, p. 16; June 26, 1988, p. 39; July 30, 1995, Claude Rawson, "Victorian Heroine."

Observer (London), December 21, 1986, p. 20.

Publishers Weekly, January 8, 1996, review of *Bloomsbury Women,* p. 51.

Southern Humanities Review, winter, 1997, review of *Christina Rossetti,* pp. 74-77.

Spectator, October 5, 1985, pp. 38-39.

Times (London), November 7, 1985.

Times Literary Supplement, November 23, 1979, pp. 21-22; December 31, 1982, p. 1436; November 1, 1985, p. 1244; July 21, 1987, p. 816; February 19-25, 1988, p. 201; October 19, 1990; p. 1124; January 21, 2000, Clive Wilmer, review of *Dante Gabriel Rosetti,* pp. 12-13.

OTHER

Richmond Review, http://www.richmondreview.co.uk/ (November 24, 2000).*

* * *

MARTIN, Cort
See SHERMAN, Jory (Tecumseh)

* * *

MARTIN, Michael William 1946-
(Mike W. Martin)

PERSONAL: Born November 6, 1946, in Salt Lake City, UT; son of Theodore R. and Ruth (Lochhead) Martin; married Shannon Snow, August 1, 1968; children: Sonia Renee, Nicole Marie. *Education:* University of Utah, B.S. (magna cum laude), 1969, M.A., 1972; University of California, Irvine, Ph.D., 1977.

ADDRESSES: Home—22842 Via Octavo, Mission Viejo, CA 92691. *Office*—Department of Philosophy, Chapman University, One University Drive, Orange, CA 92866. *E-mail*—mwmartin@chapman.edu.

CAREER: Chapman College (now University), Orange, CA, instructor, 1976-78, assistant professor, 1978-82, associate professor, 1982-86, professor of philosophy, 1986—, chair of department, 1979-81, 1982-84, and 1989-91, chair of faculty, 1986-87. Member of graduate faculty, extension, California State Polytechnic University, Pomona, 1979 and 1981, and at University of California, Los Angeles, 1990-94; University of California, Irvine, visiting assistant professor, 1981, 1983, visiting scholar, 1981-82.

MEMBER: American Philosophical Association, Phi Beta Kappa, Phi Kappa Phi.

AWARDS, HONORS: National Endowment for the Humanities fellow, 1978-80, 1981-82; Graves Award, 1983, for outstanding teaching in the humanities; Association of American Colleges grant, 1986; Institute of Electrical and Electronics Engineers award, 1992, for "Distinguished Literary Contributions Furthering Engineering Professionalism"; Staley/Robeson/Ryan/St. Lawrence Research Prize, National Society of Fund Raising Executives, 1995.

WRITINGS:

UNDER NAME MIKE W. MARTIN

(With Roland Schinzinger) *Ethics in Engineering,* McGraw-Hill (New York, NY), 1983, new edition, 1996.

(Editor) *Self-Deception and Self-Understanding,* University Press of Kansas (Lawrence, KS), 1985, new edition, 1989.

Self-Deception and Morality, University Press of Kansas (Lawrence, KS), 1986.

Everyday Morality, Wadsworth (Belmont, CA), 1989, new edition, 2001.

Virtuous Giving: Philanthropy, Voluntary Service, and Caring, Indiana University Press (Bloomington, IN), 1994.

Love's Virtues, University Press of Kansas (Lawrence, KS), 1996.

(With Roland Schinzinger) *Introduction to Engineering Ethics,* McGraw-Hill, 2000.

Meaningful Work: Rethinking Professional Ethics, Oxford University Press (New York, NY), 2001.

Contributor to *Business and Professional Ethics,* edited by Wade L. Robison, Michael S. Pritchard, and Joseph Ellin, Humana, 1982; *The Contemporary Turn in Applied Philosophy,* edited by Michael Bradie, Thomas Attig, and Nicholar Rescher, Bowling Green State University Press, 1983; *The American Classics Revisited: Recent Studies in American Literature,* edited by P. C. Kar and D. Ramakrishna, American Studies Research Centre, 1985; *Wissen und Gewissen,* edited by Otto Neumaier, University of Salzburg, 1986; and *The Philosophy of Laughter and Humor,* edited by John Morreall, State University of New York Press, 1986.

Also contributor of more than fifty essays and articles to philosophy, engineering, and literature journals.

WORK IN PROGRESS: with Don Gabard, *Ethics in Physical Therapy; Moral Health: Ethics in a Therapeutic Culture.*

SIDELIGHTS: Michael William Martin told *CA:* "My primary interests are interdisciplinary—finding ways to link literatures and approaches of different fields as they jointly illuminate moral and intellectual issues that sprawl across any tidy academic boundaries, keeping in mind that interdisciplinary work is linking rather than dissolving disciplines. I have two favorite quotations about writing. One is from Ludwig Wittgenstein: 'It is only the attempt to write down your ideas that enables them to develop.' The other is Molière's counsel to 'humanize your talk, and speak to be understood.'"

* * *

MARTIN, Mike W.
See MARTIN, Michael William

* * *

MARX, Leo 1919-

PERSONAL: Born November 15, 1919, in New York, NY; married, 1943; children: Stephen, Andrew, Lucy. *Education:* Harvard University, B.A. (history and literature), 1941, Ph.D. (history of American civilization), 1950.

ADDRESSES: *Office*—c/o Massachusetts Institute of Technology, Cambridge, MA 02139. *E-mail*—leomarx@mit.edu.

CAREER: Educator and author. University of Minnesota—Twin Cities, Minneapolis, began as assistant professor, became associate professor of English, 1949-58;

Amherst College, Amherst, MA, professor of English and American studies, 1958-71, Kenan Professor, 1971-77; Massachusetts Institute of Technology, Cambridge, William R. Kenan Professor of American Cultural History, 1977-90, Program in Science, Technology, and Society, senior lecturer and professor emeritus, beginning 1990. Fulbright lecturer at University of Nottingham, 1956-57, and University of Rennes, 1965-66; visiting professor at Brandeis University, 1969-70; member of National Humanities Faculty, 1971-73.

MEMBER: American Academy of Arts and Sciences (fellow), American Studies Association (president, 1976-78), Modern Language Association (former chair, American literature section), American Council of Learned Societies (former member, board of directors).

AWARDS, HONORS: Guggenheim fellow, 1961, 1962; Rockefeller fellow; bicentennial fellow of Phi Beta Kappa, 1974-75. Leo Marx Career Development Professorship named in his honor in the Program in Science, Technology, and Society, Massachusetts Institute of Technology, 1998.

WRITINGS:

(Editor) *The Americanness of Walt Whitman* ("Problems in American Civilization" series), D. C. Heath (Boston, MA), 1960.

(Editor) Henry David Thoreau, *Excursions,* Corinth (New York, NY), 1962.

The Machine in the Garden: Technology and the Pastoral Ideal in America, Oxford University Press (New York, NY), 1964, revised, 2000.

(Editor) Mark Twain, *The Adventures of Huckleberry Finn,* Bobbs-Merrill (Indianapolis, IN), 1967.

(Editor, with Saul Friedländer and Eugene Skolnikoff) *The End of the World: Images of Apocalypse in Western Civilization,* Holmes & Meier (New York, NY), 1982.

(Editor, with Susan Danly) *The Railroad in American Art: Representations of Technological Change,* MIT Press (Cambridge, MA), 1987.

The Pilot and the Passenger: Essays on Literature, Technology, and Culture in the United States, Oxford University Press (New York, NY), 1988.

(Editor, with Merritt Roe Smith, and contributor) *Does Technology Drive History?: The Dilemma of Technological Determinism,* MIT Press (Cambridge, MA), 1994.

(Editor, with Bruce Mazlish) *Progress: Fact or Illusion?,* University of Michigan Press (Ann Arbor, MI), 1996.

(Editor, with Jill Ker Conway and Kenneth Keniston) *Earth, Air, Fire, Water: Humanistic Studies of the Environment,* University of Massachusetts Press (Amherst, MA), 1999.

(Contributor) John Loughery, editor, *The Eloquent Essay: An Anthology of Classic and Creative Nonfiction from the Twentieth Century,* Persea (New York, NY), 2000.

Also editor of *Anthology of American Literature,* 1974. Contributor of essay to *Three on Technology,* MIT List Center, and to *New Literary History,* 1969. Reviewer and contributor to academic journals and publications, including *Technology Review* and *New York Review of Books.*

SIDELIGHTS: Leo Marx's lifelong work has focused on the relationship between culture and technology in the United States during the nineteenth and twentieth centuries. His *The Machine in the Garden: Technology and the Pastoral Ideal in America* has been required reading for incoming freshman in the School of Humanities and Social Science at the Massachusetts Institute of Technology since its initial publication in 1964; a thirty-fifth-anniversary edition was published in 2000. In 1998 a chair at the Massachusetts Institute of Technology was named in Marx's honor, an acknowledgment of his contributions to the ongoing debate on the environment.

The Pilot and the Passenger: Essays on Literature, Technology, and Culture in the United States collects essays written by Marx over four decades which examine technology through the works of literary writers of the nineteenth and twentieth centuries. *New York Times Book Review* contributor Barney Pace noted that Marx's style is academic and his writing sometimes difficult for the general reader. "But his ideas are so well developed, illuminating, and richly illustrated," added Pace, "that his work repays the efforts of readers—experts and unlicenced lovers of literature alike."

Marx and Susan Danly, curator of the Pennsylvania Academy of Fine Arts, co-edited *The Railroad in American Art: Representations of Technological Change.* The volume includes photographs, paintings, and prints exhibited at the Wellesley College Museum in 1981. *New York Times Book Review* contributor Dolores Greenberg called the book an "elegant volume" and wrote that it "combines a remarkable collection of American railroad imagery with critical essays that explore the many cultural questions raised by the rendering of these artifacts of force and speed."

Does Technology Drive History?: The Dilemma of Technological Determinism, edited by Marx and historian Merritt Roe Smith, contains thirteen essays which consider the question of whether the nature of society is determined by technology. Smith looks back to the Industrial Revolution and the birth of the belief that technology, as it continued to develop, would deliver the idealized American life. "Technological determinism" became even more entrenched following the development of weapons of mass destruction toward the middle of the twentieth century. G. Pascal Zachary commented on Marx's essay contribution to the book in *Technology Review.* Zachary explained that Marx considers the 1960s "to be a watershed for technological determinists. . . . For many people, the Vietnam War, and the later miscalculations that produced acid rain, Chernobyl, Bhopal, and the possibility of global warming, have led to the conclusion that technology per se does not drive history after all. Rather, the driving force is seen to be the decisions people make about how to use technology. There has been a growing realization that 'high technical skills may serve to mask . . . the choice of ends,' Marx writes."

Progress: Fact or Illusion?, edited by Marx and fellow professor Bruce Mazlish, consists of essays from a 1991 conference held at the Massachusetts Institute of Technology. *Historian* reviewer Howard P. Segal commented that the essays of political theorist Alan Ryan, environmental historian Richard White, and technology historian John Staudenmaier were the most original in the collection. "All three offer broad historical perspectives on their fields that compare the past and the present without either romanticizing the past or damning the present," noted Segal.

Marx served as editor, with Jill Ker Conway and Kenneth Keniston, of *Earth, Air, Fire, Water: Humanistic Studies of the Environment,* which collects thirteen of the thirty-two "Humanities and the Environment" lectures presented at the Massachusetts Institute of Technology between 1992 and 1995. *Environment* reviewer Scott Slovic called the work "a rich miscellany of examples of humanistic environmental studies."

BIOGRAPHICAL/CRITICAL SOURCES:

BOOKS

Klingenstein, Susan, *Enlarging America: The Cultural Work of Jewish Literary Scholars,* Syracuse University Press (Syracuse, NY), 1998.

PERIODICALS

American Heritage, September-October, 1988, review of *The Pilot and the Passenger,* p. 124.

American Scholar, autumn, 1989, Paul Lukacs, review of *The Pilot and the Passenger,* p. 600.

Choice, February, 1995, W. K. Bauchspies, review of *Does Technology Drive History?,* p. 952.

Environment, July, 2000, Scott Slovic, review of *Earth, Air, Fire, Water,* p. 44.

Environmental Law, summer, 2000, review of *Earth, Air, Fire, Water,* p. 561.

Historian, spring, 1998, Howard P. Segal, review of *Progress,* p. 686.

History, January, 1996, Colin Chant, review of *Does Technology Drive History?. Isis,* September, 1990, Werner Sollors, review of *The Railroad in American Art,* p. 559.

Journal of Military History, October, 1995, Alex Roland, review of *Does Technology Drive History?,* p. 728.

Library Journal, December, 1987, C. Mark Hurlbert, review of *The Pilot and the Passenger,* p. 114.

Los Angeles Times, December 24, 1987.

New York Review of Books, February 16, 1989, Robert M. Adams, review of *The Pilot and the Passenger,* p. 33.

New York Times Book Review, April 24, 1988, Barney Pace, review of *The Pilot and the Passenger;* May 29, 1988, Dolores Greenberg, "The Culture and the Caboose," p. 14.

Publishers Weekly, December 18, 1987, Genevieve Stuttaford, review of *The Pilot and the Passenger,* p. 47.

Technology and Culture, October, 1989, Joseph W. Slade, review of *The Pilot and the Passenger,* p. 1050, Betsy Fahlman, review of *The Railroad in American Art,* p. 1052; October, 1998, Ulrich Wengenroth, review of *Does Technology Drive History?,* p. 755; January, 2000, Steven L. Goldman, review of *Progress,* p. 116.

Technology Review, October, 1988, Rebecca Nemser, review of *The Railroad in American Art,* p. 74; May-June, 1995, G. Pascal Zachary, review of *Does Technology Drive History?,* p. 74.

Times Literary Supplement, February 28, 1997, Fareed Zakaria, review of *Progress,* p. 26.*

* * *

MATHEWS, Harry 1930-

PERSONAL: Born February 14, 1930, in New York, NY. *Education:* Studied music at Princeton and Harvard Universities and at L'École Normale de Musique in Paris, France.

ADDRESSES: Home—619 Grinnell St., Key West, FL 33040; 67 rue de Grenelle, 75007 Paris, France. *Agent*—Maxine Groffsky, 2 Fifth Ave., New York, NY 10011.

CAREER: Poet, novelist, and translator. Has taught at Bennington College, Hamilton College, and Columbia University. Member of Ouvroir de Littérature Potentielle, Paris, France.

AWARDS, HONORS: National Endowment for the Arts grant for fiction writing, 1982; National Academy and Institute of Arts and Letters fiction writing award, 1991.

WRITINGS:

The Conversions (novel; also see below), Random House (New York, NY), 1962, Dalkey Archive Press (Normal, IL), 1997.

Tlooth (novel; also see below), Paris Review/Doubleday (New York, NY), 1966, Dalkey Archive Press (Normal, IL), 1998.

The Planisphere (poetry), Burning Deck (Providence, RI), 1974.

The Sinking of the Odradek Stadium and Other Novels (includes *The Conversions* and *Tlooth*), Harper (New York, NY), 1975.

Trial Impressions (poetry), Burning Deck (Providence, RI), 1977.

Selected Declarations of Dependence, 2 Press, 1977.

Country Cooking and Other Stories, Burning Deck (Providence, RI), 1980.

Armenian Papers (poetry), Princeton University Press (Princeton, NJ), 1987.

Cigarettes (novel), Weidenfeld & Nicolson (London, England), 1987, Dalkey Archive Press (Normal, IL), 1998.

The Orchard (memoirs), Bamberger Books, 1988.

Twenty Lines a Day (journal), Dalkey Archive Press (Normal, IL), 1988.

Singular Pleasures (fiction), Grenfell Press, 1988, Dalkey Archive Press (Normal, IL), 1993.

Out of Bounds (poetry), Burning Deck (Providence, RI), 1989.

The Way Home: Collected Longer Prose (contains *Singular Pleasures* and *Country Cooking*), Atlas Press (London, England), 1989.

The American Experience (fiction), Atlas Press (London, England), 1991.

Immeasurable Distances (criticism), Lapis Press, 1991.

The Journalist (novel), David Godine (Boston, MA), 1994.

(Coeditor) *Oulipo Compendium,* Atlas Press (London, England), 1998.

(Editor, with Jacques Roubaud) Georges Perec, *Fifty-Three Days* (novel), David Godine, 1999.

Sainte Catherine (in French), Éditions P.O.L. (Paris, France), 2000.

Contributor to *S.,* Lumen, 1997; *The Best American Poetry 1989* (anthology); *Postmodern American Poetry: A Norton Anthology;* and *The Best of American Poetry 1988-1997* (anthology). Contributor of criticism, fiction, and poetry to numerous periodicals, including *American Book Review, Bomb, Grand Street, New York Review of Books, Parnassus, Review of Contemporary Fiction, Shiny International, Times Literary Supplement, London Review of Books, Brick, Common Knowledge, Art and Literature, Grand Street, o.blek, Paris Review, Hudson Review, Partisan Review, Antaeus, Sub-Stance, Conjunctions, Grand Street, Voice Literary Supplement,* and *Boston Review.* Founding editor (with others) of *Locus Solus;* Paris editor, *Paris Review,* 1991—.

SIDELIGHTS: Harry Mathews's early experimental novels, *The Conversions, Tlooth,* and *The Sinking of the Odradek Stadium and Other Novels,* "have long been cult classics admired for their humor, linguistic inventiveness and narrative ingenuity," a *Washington Post Book World* reviewer commented. *The Conversions,* in which the narrator must possess a ritual golden adze and solve three riddles to inherit an enormous fortune, is "a kind of literary hopscotch, one foot in the air, always nearly off balance, but at no matter what cost abandoning one position speedily for another," according to a *New York Herald Tribune Book Review* contributor. A *Times Literary Supplement* critic found it "fertile in linguistic skylarkings and fantastic invention," and "as exhilarating to read as a fireworks set-piece is to watch."

Tlooth is an "elaborate game, a compound of absurd adventures, faked documents, diagrams and word puzzles," Peter Buitenhuis wrote in the *New York Times Book Review.* "There is little pretense of realism. Mathews has abandoned himself to an imagination full of strange lore and miscellaneous literary allusions. . . . The imagination of the artist projected into the work of art has taken the real and the fantastic as related, even interchangeable, perceptions of life." A *Tri-Quarterly* reviewer found *Tlooth's* "ingenious plot is that of travelogue-adventure in which all places are very much the same, even if they are called Afghanistan, Russia, India, Morocco; and in this respect *Tlooth* very much descends from Apollinaire's *Zone* (1913) with its unbounded sense of literary space and the higher nonsense fiction of Lewis Carroll and especially, the Frenchman Raymond Roussel." *The Conversions* and *Tlooth* are contained in *The Sinking of the Odradek Stadium and Other Novels;* the title story, described by Edmund White in the *New York Times Book Review* as "a comic masterpiece," relates a couple's search for treasure in a ship sunk in the sixteenth century off the coast of Florida. White observed, "As Mathews's art has matured he has moved away from pearls of exotic narration strung on a slender thread of continuity. In *The Sinking of the Odradek Stadium,* he has created a seamless fabric, as tense, light, and strong as stretched silk."

In *Cigarettes,* which appeared after a seven-year break in publication, the author follows thirteen characters through their contacts with Elizabeth, "who winds through the novel like a plume of smoke," Lisa Zeidner noted in the *New York Times Book Review. Partisan Review*'s Rachel Hadas commented that *Cigarettes* shows that "one reason complete happiness isn't possible . . . is that knowledge can be acquired but not lost." Hadas added, "Answers to many enigmas are teased out by the reader as well as the characters; the truth is like the seminal portrait of Elizabeth, which is cherished, stolen, forged, destroyed, bought, sold, restored—but about which we chiefly learn that it doesn't resemble her." Another enigmatic woman is at the center of *S.,* a collection of seven stories from seven authors about an alluring woman known variously as Suzanne, Susie, Suze, and Anna. Men desire her everywhere she goes, as she travels around the world. In Mathews's contribution, "The Quevedo Cipher," she is a character in an "encrypted tale of unrequited conjugal love," in the words of a *Publishers Weekly* reviewer, who credited this "kaleidoscopic chronicle" as having "its own heady appeal."

The Journalist is narrated by a middle-aged manic depressive who is advised to keep a journal as part of his therapy. This activity is apparently intended to ground him in practical reality by encouraging him to make careful observations about himself and the world around him. The opposite occurs, however; he withdraws increasingly from his wife, his best friend, his mistress, and his son. His meticulous charting of all their movements and possessions evokes his suspicion about all their activities, and he becomes increasingly obsessed with "categories and interpretations," advised Phoebe-Lou Adams in *Atlantic Monthly,* "the former increasingly intricate and the latter increasingly disturbing." Adams found the narrator an unappealing character, difficult to care about, and she concluded that the novel's chief interest is "the question of how Mr. Mathews will resolve the clever muddle he has devised." A *Publishers Weekly* reviewer believed *The Journalist* would have been a better book if Mathews had created "a more introspective narrator who could make the occasional astute perception about what it means to keep a journal," but concluded: "Yet it is by no means an unrewarding read, since Mathews depicts his forlorn protagonist with ironic humor."

BIOGRAPHICAL/CRITICAL SOURCES:

BOOKS

Contemporary Literary Criticism, Volume 6, Gale (Detroit, MI), 1976.

PERIODICALS

American Book Review, July, 1999, review of *Tlooth,* p. 1.

Atlantic Monthly, October, 1994, Phoebe-Lou Adams, review of *The Journalist,* p. 132.

Book Week, November 27, 1966.

Harper's, November, 1966.

Kirkus Reviews, March 1, 1993, review of *Singular Pleasures,* p. 266; July 1, 1994, review of *The Journalist,* p. 875.

Library Journal, June 1, 1962; December 1, 1966; August, 1994, review of *The Journalist,* p. 132; March 1, 2000, Michael Rogers, review of *The Sinking of the Odradek Stadium,* p. 129.

London Review of Books, April 29, 1999, review of *Oulipo Compendium,* p. 20.

Los Angeles Times, October 11, 1987.

Nation, September 29, 1962.

New Leader, October 14, 1963.

New Statesman & Society, July 30, 1993, review of *The Journalist,* p. 40.

New York, December 5, 1994, review of *The Journalist,* p. 150.

New York Herald Tribune Book Review, September 2, 1962.

New York Review of Books, August 7, 1975.

New York Times, May 18, 1975; November 29, 1987; January 21, 1988.

New York Times Book Review, October 30, 1966; May 18, 1975; November 29, 1987, p. 23; March 26, 1995, review of *The Journalist,* p. 18.

Observer (London), August 1, 1993, review of *Singular Pleasures,* p. 52.

Parnassus, volume 1, 1995, reviews of *Twenty Lines a Day, Armenian Papers, Cigarettes, The Conversions, Country Cooking and Other Stories, The Journalist, Out of Bounds, Selected Declarations of Dependence, Singular Pleasures, The Sinking of the Odradek Stadium and Other Novels, Tlooth, The Way Home,* and *Immeasurable Distances,* p. 338.

Partisan Review, February, 1989, p. 310.

Publishers Weekly, March 22, 1993, review of *Singular Pleasures,* p. 74; August 8, 1994, review of *The Journalist,* p. 382; August 11, 1997, review of *S.,* p. 386.

Review of Contemporary Fiction, fall, 1994, review of *The Journalist,* p. 205.

Saturday Review, November 12, 1966.

Time, June 15, 1962.

Times Literary Supplement, September 14, 1962; March 20, 1998, review of *The Conversions,* p. 24; September 15, 1989, p. 997; July 23, 1993, review of *A Mid-Season Sky,* p. 28; March 20, 1998, review of *The Journalist,* p. 24; April 16, 1999, review of *Oulipo Compendium,* p. 28.

Tribune Books (Chicago), January 8, 1995, review of *The Journalist,* p. 3.

Tri-Quarterly, winter, 1967.

Village Voice, January 26, 1967.

Washington Post Book World, December 29, 1991, p. 13.

Whole Earth Review, spring, 1993, Robert Rossney, review of *Tlooth,* p. 92.

OTHER

Oulipo, http://www.qsilver.queensu.ca (December 17, 1987), Alexander Laurence, "The Novels of Harry Mathews."

Sun & Moon Reviews, http://www.sunmoon.com (October 1, 2000), Eric Lorberer, review of *Selected Declarations of Dependence.*

*   *   *

McCLENDON, James William, Jr. 1924-

PERSONAL: Born March 6, 1924, in Shreveport, LA; son of James William and Mary (Drake) McClendon; married Marie Miles, 1949 (divorced, 1982); married Nancey Murphy (a professor of philosophy), 1983; children: (first marriage) James William III, Thomas Vernon. *Education:* University of Texas at Austin, B.A. (with high honors), 1947; Southwestern Baptist Theological Seminary, B.D., 1950, Th.D., 1953; Princeton Theological Seminary, Th.M., 1952; postdoctoral study at University of California, Berkeley, 1959-62, and Oxford University, 1962-63. *Avocational interests:* Outdoor activities, growing timber, world travel.

ADDRESSES: Home—Altadena, CA. *Office*—Fuller Theological Seminary, Pasadena, CA 91182.

CAREER: Ordained minister, Southern Baptist Convention; pastor in Austin, TX, 1946-47, and Keatchie, LA, 1948-50; Princeton University, Princeton, NJ, chaplain to Baptist students, 1950-51; interim pastor in Sydney, Australia, 1952; pastor in Ring-gold, LA, 1953-54; Golden Gate Baptist Seminary, Mill Valley, CA, assistant professor, 1954-57, associate professor, 1958-64, professor of theology, 1964-66; University of San Francisco, San Francisco, CA, associate professor of theology, 1966-69; Graduate Theological Union, Church Divinity School, Berkeley, CA, professor of theology, 1971-90, and Yom Ha Shoa Lecturer; Fuller Theological Seminary, Pasadena, CA, Distinguished Scholar in Residence, 1990—. Stanford University, visiting professor, 1967; Temple University, visiting associate professor, 1969; University of Pennsylvania, visiting lecturer, 1970; Goucher College, Jeffrey Lecturer in Religion, 1970-71; University of Notre Dame, visiting professor, 1976-77; Baylor University, visiting distinguished professor, 1995; Northern Baptist Theological Seminary, Browne Lecturer; Meredith College, Gullick Lecturer; Southeastern Baptist Theological Seminary, Carver-Barnes Lecturer; Houston Baptist University, Collins Lecturer; Southern Baptist Theological Seminary, Norton Lecturer; Bethany Theological Seminary, Huston Lecturer; Claremont Graduate School, Michalson Lecturer; University of Melbourne, Whitley Lecturer at Whitley Theological College. National Council of Churches, Member of National Faith and Order Colloquium, c. 1964-70; Institute for Ecumenical and Cultural Research, member of board of trustees, 1967-72. *Military service:* U.S. Naval Reserve, 1943-46; became lieutenant junior grade.

MEMBER: American Philosophical Association, American Academy of Religion (chair of Philosophy of Religion and Theology section, 1973-75), American Society of Church History, National Association of Baptist Professors of Religion (president, 1987-88), Pacific Coast Theological Society (executive secretary, 1978-80), United Nations Association of Marin County (president, 1967-69), Phi Beta Kappa.

AWARDS, HONORS: Grant for England, Rockefeller Brothers Fund, 1962-63.

WRITINGS:

Pacemakers of Christian Thought, Broadman (Nashville, TN), 1962.

(Contributor) W. Junker, editor, *What Can You Believe,* Broadman (Nashville, TN), 1966.

(Contributor) Michael Novak, editor, *American Philosophy and the Future,* Scribner (New York, NY), 1968.

Biography as Theology, Abingdon (Nashville, TN), 1974, new edition, Trinity Press International (Valley Forge, PA), 1990.

(With James M. Smith) *Understanding Religious Convictions,* University of Notre Dame Press (Notre Dame, IN), 1975, published as *Convictions: Defusing Religious Relativism,* Trinity Press International (Valley Forge, PA), 1994.

(Editor, with A. Stever) *Is God GOD?,* Abingdon (Nashville, TN), 1981.

Doctrine: Systematic Theology, Abingdon (Nashville, TN), Volume I: *Ethics: Systematic Theology Volume I,* 1986, Volume II: *Ethics: Systematic Theology Volume II,* 1994, Volume III: *Witness: Systematic Theology,* 2000.

(Contributor) D. W. Hardy and P. H. Sedgwick, editors, *The Weight of Glory: A Vision and Practice for Christian Faith: The Future of Liberal Theology; Essays for Peter Baelz,* T. and T. Clark (Edinburgh, Scotland), 1991.

(Contributor) Joseph Runzo, editor, *Ethics, Religion, and the Good Society: New Directions in a Pluralistic World,* Westminster/John Knox (Louisville, KY), 1992.

(Contributor) Donald W. Musser and Joseph L. Price, editors, *A New Handbook of Christian Theology,* Abingdon (Nashville, TN), 1992.

(Contributor) Paul Toews, editor, *Mennonites and Baptists: A Continuing Conversation,* Kindred Press (Hillsboro, NC), 1993.

(Contributor) Gary Furr and Curtis Freeman, editors, *Ties That Bind: Life Together in the Baptist Vision,* Smyth & Helwys (Macon, GA), 1994.

(Contributor) Stanley Hauerwas, Nancey Murphey, and Mark Nation, editors, *Theology without Foundations,* Abingdon (Nashville, TN), 1994.

Making Gospel Sense to a Troubled Church, Pilgrim Press (Cleveland, OH), 1995.

(Contributor) William H. Brackney, editor, *The Believers Church: A Voluntary Church,* Pandora Press (Kitchener, Ontario, Canada), 1998.

(Editor, with Curtis W. Freeman and Rosalee Velloso da Silva) *Baptist Roots: A Reader in the Theology of a Christian People,* Judson (Valley Forge, PA), 1999.

Contributor to religious journals, including *Baptist Student, Brethren in Christ History and Life, Concilium, Faith and Philosophy, Harvard Theological Review, Journal of Ecumenical Studies, Journal of Religious Ethics, Mennonite Quarterly Review, Modern Theology, Perspectives in Religious Studies, Religious Studies Review, Review and Expositor,* and *Theology Today.*

BIOGRAPHICAL/CRITICAL SOURCES:

PERIODICALS

Christianity Today, May 15, 1995, Rodney Clapp, review of *Doctrine: Systematic Theology,* Volume II, p. 65.

Pulpit Digest, May/June, 1994, David A. Thomas, "Narrative Theology and Communication."

* * *

McCOURT, James 1941-

PERSONAL: Born July 4, 1941, in New York, NY; son of James A. and Catherine (a teacher; maiden name, Moore) McCourt. *Education:* Manhattan College, B.A., 1962; graduate study at New York University, 1962-64, and Yale University, School of Drama, 1964-65. *Avocational interests:* Singing and directing opera, cooking, travel (Europe from Ireland to Czechoslovakia).

ADDRESSES: Home—New York, NY. *Agent*—Elaine Markson, 44 Greenwich Ave., New York, NY 10011.

CAREER: Has been employed as an actor in summer stock, 1962, and as a teacher of communication arts, 1968-69; writer.

WRITINGS:

NOVELS, EXCEPT AS INDICATED

Mawrdew Czgowchwz, Farrar, Straus (New York, NY), 1975.

Kaye Wayfaring in "Avenged": Four Stories, Knopf (New York, NY), 1984.

Time Remaining, Knopf (New York, NY), 1993.

Delancey's Way, Knopf (New York, NY), 2000.

Also author of *Panache,* a play. Contributor of stories to *The New Yorker, Paris Review, Grand Street,* and *Yale Review.*

WORK IN PROGRESS: Continuing the *Mawrdew Czgowchwz* saga; work in the theater.

SIDELIGHTS: Regarding his first book, the 1975 *Mawrdew Czgowchwz,* James McCourt once told the *New York Times Book Review:* "Nowhere on the book does it say it's a novel. In a novel, something is wrapped up, it finishes. But my stories just stop. Sure, *Mawrdew Czgowchwz* is an extended fiction, but it never wraps up. . . . A novel is something I don't get around to doing or don't want to do. I'm writing about this extended tribe of people, instead of writing about a family as J. D. Salinger does." In McCourt's next three "extended fictions," published over the following quarter century, this characterization of his own work holds true. McCourt's books return to the same overlapping and recurring cast of often bizarre characters and continue to explore their ongoing, unresolved adventures with one another and life.

The eponymous heroine of *Mawrdew Czgowchwz* is the ultimate operatic diva. She can sing any part from contralto to coloratura, and easily surpasses such real-life operatic icons as Renata Tebaldi and Maria Callas, not only with her vocal skills but with regard to the mania of her fans, mostly gay, who pack the Metropolitan Opera standing room only to see her perform. Christopher Lehmann-Haupt of the *New York Times* characterized the book as "a hilarious high-camp, low-comedy romp through New York City's high-culture melange." Susan Sontag compared it to work by Ronald Firbank and Vladimir Nabokov, while MacDonald Harris of the *New York Times Book Review* credited *Mawrdew Czgowchwz* with being "complicated and erudite."

Nearly a decade later, McCourt produced *Kaye Wayfaring in "Avenged": Four Stories.* This extended fiction attempts to do for the world of movies what *Mawrdew Czgowchwz* did for opera. Kaye is described as an overweight actress, pushing forty, and a previous Oscar contender. As the story opens, she is playing the lead in a film version of "Avenged," a short story by eighteenth-century French writer, François Diderot. The four stories in the book (two reprinted from *The New Yorker*) cover the filming of *Avenged,* both in Manhattan and Long Island, its premier at the Metropolitan Opera House, and a brief sojourn in Hollywood by way of Atlanta. MacDonald Harris of the *New York Times Book Review* commented: "As Kaye assumes the role in this book played by Mawrdew Czgowchwz in the earlier novel, she finds herself a kind of cinematographic reincarnation of that 'ultimate diva'—moving in Mawrdew's old circles, hungry for her celebrity, falling in love with her son, even proposing to make a picture of her life." Mawrdew also appears in the novel, both to throw the I Ching for Kaye and later to join her in singing a tune from *The Mikado.* "McCourt is at his best," Harris stated, "or most characteristic, in dialogue, and the voices are more or less interchangeable; the point is that they should be bright and brittle, heavy with allusions to chic matters, and they should attempt to titillate in every line." In sum, Harris viewed *Kaye Wayfaring in "Avenged"* as a sequel to *Mawrdew Czgowchwz,* and concluded: "It tends to fall into the same repetition, the same pallid fatigue, that all sequels do." Lehmann-Haupt felt that in the second book McCourt had made more of an effort to include sentiment and drama, yet nevertheless believed the effort runs aground on the author's excessive use of humor. According to Lehmann-Haupt, "as readers should be able to tell by now, it is difficult for Mr. McCourt to resist the wisecrack. After a while, not only does this tendency interrupt the emotional flow of the novel, but it also begins to irritate."

McCourt's next offering, the 1993 *Time Remaining,* was dubbed the first of his "explicitly gay fictions" by *New York Times Book Review* critic Bertha Harris. An admittedly serious fan of McCourt and his first two "novels," Harris was extravagant in her praise of his third. "On every page of *Time Remaining,*" she exclaimed, "his highest-camp wit retains its cutting edge. . . . ; his madcap Jesuiticisms are still traveling over the limit; the Celtic ascendancy over English prose holds fast." The book is composed of two stories told by two different, if not always distinct, narrative voices. The crew of eccentric hangers-on that circulated around Mawrdew in McCourt's previous outings has been decimated by AIDS, contracted as a result of what the author refers to as "kamikaze sex." The only two survivors, Delancey and Odette, both gay transsexuals, narrate *Time Remaining.* Much of the story concerns reminiscences by the two characters concerning recent events and their friends who have passed away. Harris contended: "Nearly every page of Odette's talks, with asides by Delancey, is thick with scandal, jokes, gossip, inspired literary criticism, good politics, mots as well as moues . . . you can let it fall open anywhere and, if you're so inclined, hear yourself laughing out loud." In a less partisan assessment, a reviewer for *Publishers Weekly* found in *Time Remaining* "frothy, entertaining evocations of New York's gay subculture. . . . To those who comprehend its nuances, this book will surely give pleasure; the rest of the reading public may be somewhat bewildered. A tour de force of high camp, Manhattan-style, this collection proves McCourt is a dazzling practitioner of the lost language of queens."

Both Delancey and Odette also play primary roles in McCourt's *Delancey's Way.* Times have changed and Delancey has abandoned his life as a female impersonator to become a reporter for the *East Hampton Star.* Sent south to the nation's capital to do a story on environmental legislation, Delancey is accompanied by Odette. The events that follow comprise what Michele Leber of *Booklist* referred to as "a dizzying, outrageous view of the puzzle palaces on the Potomac, with politics as pornography and Washington, D.C., as a city of nothingness." Robert E. Brown of *Library Journal* deemed it a book "dense with allusion—political, literary, filmic, operatic, mythological, and more—uncommon in today's watery literary scene," and Peter Donahue, writing in the *Review of Contemporary Fiction,* observed that *Delancey's Way* "derives its energy from its carnivalesque language . . . [as characters discourse] to one another in lively harangues . . . wild and virtuoso verbal performances." Some of the players include a gay Senator who was elected merely because his name is John Galt (the same as the protagonist of Ayn Rand's *Atlas Shrugged*), a cross-dressing ballerina, and an Italian diva. The plot, less than essential to the substance of the book, ultimately concerns an attempt on the president's life. A *Publishers Weekly* reviewer observed: "McCourt's colorful, if hardly three-dimensional, characters banter in continual conversations on everything from epistemology to opera to the mechanics of porn films," and concludes: "Readers who care for political theory, for Washington melodrama and for high camp . . . will likely find McCourt's work a scream and a half." However, Bill Goldstein of the *New York Times Book Review* was less convinced of the book's merits. Noting that *Delancey's Way* bears a "superficial resemblance" to *Mawrdew Czgowchwz,* Goldstein went on to draw a significant distinction between the two works. Whereas McCourt's first novel "successfully created an alternate universe from the familiar world of opera it nominally depicted," *Delancey's Way* "is a Washington novel that could not exist if there weren't other Washington novels to call upon as touchstones." In that context, Goldstein found the book's "supposedly witty talk" to be "artificial and uninspired," and viewed its many allusions as "a dangerously high level of cultural debris littering its pages." The *Washington Post*'s Michael Dirda, on the other hand, found *Delancey's Way* "quite marvelous, or even mahvelous. Like McCourt's other books, it's the sort of excessive novel that readily inspires a cult following. And deservedly so."

BIOGRAPHICAL/CRITICAL SOURCES:

BOOKS

Contemporary Literary Criticism, Volume 5, Gale (Detroit, MI), 1976.

PERIODICALS

Booklist, February 15, 2000, Michele Leber, review of *Delancey's Way,* p. 1083.

Gay & Lesbian Review, fall, 2000, Michael Schwartz, "Stand Still Talking," review of *Delancey's Way,* p. 43.

Lambda Book Report, July-August, 1993, Jim Marks, review of *Time Remaining,* p. 46; June, 2000, Reed V. Waller, "Deliciously Dishy," review of *Delancey's Way,* p. 17.

Library Journal, May 1, 1993, review of *Time Remaining,* p. 120; January, 2000, Robert E. Brown, review of *Delancey's Way,* p. 161.

Los Angeles Times, October 31, 1993, William Moses Hoffman, "The Interior Landscape of James McCourt," review of *Time Remaining,* p. MAG30.

New Yorker, July 26, 1993, review of *Time Remaining,* p. 89.

New York Review of Books, June 15, 2000, Garry Wills, review of *Delancey's Way,* p. 66.

New York Times, June 15, 1984, Christopher Lehmann-Haupt, review of *Kaye Wayfaring in "Avenged,"* Section C, p. 24.

New York Times Book Review, July 8, 1984, MacDonald Harris, "Czgowchwz! Simply Czgowchwz!," p. 12; June 13, 1993, Bertha Harris, "In a Pink Sequined Straitjacket," p. 27; February 27, 2000, Bill Goldstein, "Inside Politics," p. 27.

Partisan Review, winter, 1994, Pearl K. Bell, review of *Time Remaining,* p. 80.

Publishers Weekly, April 20, 1984, review of *Kaye Wayfaring in "Avenged,"* p. 80; March 29, 1993, review of *Time Remaining,* p. 37; January 3, 2000, review of *Delancey's Way,* p. 56.

Review of Contemporary Fiction, summer, 2000, Peter Donahue, review of *Delancey's Way,* p. 172.

Washington Post, February 27, 2000, Michael Dirda, review of *Delancey's Way,* p. X15.

Yale Review, October, 1993, Walter Kendrick, review of *Time Remaining,* p. 124.*

McCULLOUGH, Colleen 1937-

PERSONAL: Born 1937, in Wellington, New South Wales, Australia; married Ric Robinson, April 13, 1984. *Education:* University of Sydney and University of South Wales, B.S. (with honors); Institute of Child Health of London University, M.S. *Avocational interests:* Photography, music, chess, embroidery, painting, cooking, and writing the words side of stage musicals.

ADDRESSES: *Home*—Norfolk Island, Australia. *Office*—c/o Simon & Schuster, 1230 Avenue of the Americas, New York, NY 10020, or P.O. Box 333, Norfolk Island, Oceania via Australia.

CAREER: Founder of and worker at the Department of Neurophysiology at the Royal North Shore Hospital of Sydney, 1958-63; Yale University, School of Internal Medicine, New Haven, CT, associate in research neurology department, 1967-77; writer, 1976—. Has also worked as a teacher, a library worker, a bus driver in Australia's Outback, and in journalism.

MEMBER: Gerontology Foundation of Australia, Monash Medical Centre Literary Programme, Macquarie University, Foundation of the Study of Ancient Cultures, American Association for the Advancement of Science (fellow), New York Academy of Science, Board of Visitors of the International Programs Center at the University of Oklahoma.

AWARDS, HONORS: D. Litt., Macquarie University, Sydney, Australia, 1993; honorary founding governor of Prince of Wales Medical Research Institute; designated a "Living National Treasure" in Australia; Scanno Award for Literature, 2000.

WRITINGS:

NOVELS

Tim (also see below), Harper (New York City), 1974.
The Thorn Birds, Harper, 1977.
An Indecent Obsession (also see below), Harper, 1981.
A Creed for the Third Millennium, Harper, 1985.
The Ladies of Missalonghi (also see below), Harper, 1987.
The First Man in Rome, Morrow (New York City), 1990.
The Grass Crown, Morrow, 1991.

Colleen McCullough

Fortune's Favorites, Morrow, 1993.
Caesar's Women, Morrow, 1996.
Caesar: Let the Dice Fly, Morrow, 1998.
The Song of Troy, Orion (London, England), 1998.
Three Complete Novels (includes *Tim, An Indecent Obsession,* and *The Ladies of Missalonghi*), Wings Books (New York City), 1999.
Morgan's Run, Simon & Schuster (New York City), 2000.

OTHER

An Australian Cookbook, Harper, 1982.
Roden Cutler, V.C. (biography), Random House Australia (Milson's Point, New South Wales), 1998.

Contributor to magazines.

ADAPTATIONS: *Tim* was released as a film starring Piper Laurie and Mel Gibson, directed and produced by Michael Pate, in 1981. *The Thorn Birds* was broadcast as a ten-hour miniseries on ABC-TV in March, 1983, starring Rachel Ward and Richard Chamberlain.

SIDELIGHTS: "I always write books with peculiar themes: I don't like writing about boy meets girl, boy loses girl, boy gets girl," best-selling author Colleen

McCullough told Kay Cassill in a *Publishers Weekly* interview. The plots of McCullough's novels back her statement: in *Tim,* a middle-aged businesswoman becomes romantically linked with a twenty-five-year old, mentally retarded man; *The Thorn Birds* turns on a frustrated love between a young woman and a Roman Catholic cardinal; *An Indecent Obsession*'s heroine, a war nurse to battle-fatigued soldiers, is tacitly engaged to one of her patients and sexually attracted to another. Such ingenious story lines, combined with a talent for what Christopher Lehmann-Haupt called in the *New York Times* "good old-fashioned story telling," have made McCullough's books appeal to millions of readers.

McCullough, a native of Australia, first aspired to a career as a physician but could not afford the necessary tuition for a full medical education. She taught in the Outback, drove a school bus, worked as a librarian, and finally qualified as a medical technician specializing in neurophysiology. It was in this position that she eventually came to work at Yale University. In the evenings, she wrote—but not with an eye toward publication. "I always wrote to please myself," she told Cassill. "I was a little snobby about it—that way I could write entirely as I wished. To write for publication, I thought, was to prostitute myself." Once McCullough decided to approach writing commercially, however, she did so very systematically. "I sat down with six girls who were working for me. They were very dissimilar types, and not especially avid readers. Yet, they were all mad about Erich Segal's *Love Story.* I thought it was bloody awful and couldn't see what girls so basically intelligent could love about it. I asked them what they wanted most out of a book. First, they liked the idea that *Love Story* was about ordinary people. They didn't want to read about what was going on in Hollywood and all that codswallow, and they wanted something with touches of humor. Yet they enjoyed books that made them cry. . . . If you didn't cry the book wasn't worth reading. . . . So, I said, 'That's it, mate. No matter what else you do in a book, don't forget the buckets of tears.'"

McCullough had a story in mind that would conjure "buckets of tears," a grand romance set mostly on a sheep ranch. She knew, however, that this tale—which would eventually be published as *The Thorn Birds*—would be lengthy, and that "no one would publish such a long book as a first novel. So I wrote *Tim.*"

Tim is a "novel of awakenings," according to a *Publishers Weekly* writer, "a lovely and refreshing addition to tales of love." Its two central characters are Mary Horton and Tim Melville. In her climb from an orphanage to success as a mining executive, forty-five-year old Mary has developed her discipline and self-sufficiency to a high degree but has ignored her emotions. Tim arrives at her home one day to do some yard work. He catches her eye, for he is strikingly handsome. Eventually she learns that this attractive young man is "without the full quid"—that is, he is mentally retarded. First Tim's beauty, then his gentle innocence draw Mary to him, unsettling her rigidly ordered world. This unusual pair experience first love together. When Tim faces being left without a family to care for him, Mary realizes that marriage could be fulfilling and practical for both of them. She must then decide if she has the courage to take such an unconventional step.

Tim was well received by critics. A *New York Times Book Review* contributor praised the story's "delightful freshness," and Margaret Ferrari, writing in *America,* remarked upon McCullough's sensitive treatment of her subject matter: "There are many genuinely touching moments in the novel. . . . Its language is clear and direct, full of colorful Australian slang. McCullough's feeling for character, from major to minor, is compassionate yet concise. They are without exception well-rounded and believable. Her delicacy is perfectly suited to the story. . . . *Tim* is a warm book to read, reassuring about goodness in human nature and about the power of love to overcome worldly obstacles and to make us care more for another person's interests than for our own." A *Publishers Weekly* reviewer called McCullough's telling of the story "accomplished, sensitive, and wise." The author herself is less generous than most reviewers in describing her first novel. "It's an icky book," she told Cassill, "a saccharine-sweet book." In spite of this negative assessment, she was pleased by its success. "I made $50,000 out of *Tim,* which wasn't bad for a first novel, and I thought I'd always be a middle of the road, modest selling, respectable novelist," said McCullough to Phillipa Toomey in the London *Times.*

Having established herself as a good risk in the publishing world, she began to work intensely at getting that long novel she had already "written in her head" down on paper. It was *The Thorn Birds,* a multi-generational saga of the Cleary family and their life on an Australian sheep station named Drogheda. McCullough focuses on three Cleary women: Fiona, her daughter, Meggie, and Meggie's daughter, Justine. Meggie falls in love with Ralph de Bricassart, an ambitious Catholic priest who has known her since her childhood. When he leaves the Outback for the Vatican, Meggie enters into an unhappy marriage that produces one child, Justine. When Father Ralph visits Drogheda many years later, he and Meggie consummate their love. Her second child, a son named Dane, is born nine months later. Meggie keeps the knowledge that she has borne Ralph's son her secret, but it makes the boy especially beloved to her. When the child grows up, he, like his father, becomes a priest and leaves Drogheda for Rome; Justine goes to England to become the toast of the London stage.

McCullough was still working full-time at Yale while drafting this story and so had to confine her writing to the evenings. She spent such long hours sitting at the typewriter that her legs became swollen; she took to wearing elbow-length evening gloves to keep her fingers from blistering and her arms from chafing against her desk. These efforts paid off: she wrote the first two drafts of *The Thorn Birds* in three months, churning out 15,000-word blocks of prose nightly. After working at this pace for a year, the final draft was completed. It was 1,000 pages long and weighed ten pounds. McCullough felt that its hefty size was justified; in her interview with Cassill, she declared: "If an editor had seen *Thorn Birds* in manuscript and 'just loved it,' but suggested it would make a better book if I cut it to a nice 300-page story, I'd have simply said, 'Get stuffed, mate.'"

Her editors made no such suggestion. Sensing that *The Thorn Birds* had the potential to be a major bestseller, they prepared its release carefully and backed it with an extensive publicity campaign. By the time the book became available to the general public, the publishing industry was abuzz with excitement over its prospects; paperback rights had been sold for a then-record price of $1.9 million. This faith and investment in the book were rewarded, for *The Thorn Birds* has sold over a half million copies in hardcover and more than seven million copies in paperback.

Some reviewers quickly dismissed the popularity of *The Thorn Birds* as a tribute to marketing rather than a reflection of the book's worth. Amanda Heller denounced McCullough's novel as "awesomely bad" in the *Atlantic Monthly.* "The writing is amateurish, all adjectives and exclamation points. The dialogue is leaden. . . . The characters are mechanical contrivances that permit the plot to grind along without encountering much resistance." And Paul Gray, while admitting in *Time* that "McCullough knows how to stage convincing droughts, floods and fires," declared that she "has not made literature. For a season or so, her book will make commercial history."

Alice K. Turner countered negative assessments of *The Thorn Birds* with praise for the novel's value as entertainment. "To expect *The Thorn Birds* to be a Great Book would be unfair," she suggested in the *Washington Post.* "There are things wrong with it, stock characters, plot contrivances and so forth. But to dismiss it would also be wrong. On its own terms, it is a fine, long, absorbing popular book. It offers the best heartthrob since Rhett Butler, plenty of exotic color, plenty of Tolstoyan unhappiness and a good deal of connivance and action. Of its kind, it's an honest book." Eliot Fremont-Smith further praised McCullough's engaging style in the *Village Voice:* "Her prose, even when stately, owes little to any formula; it is driven by a curiosity of mind, a caring for the subject, and some other great energy within the author that in turn, at one remove, spurs the reader on. *The Thorn Birds* didn't make me laugh and weep, and I could put it down. It is, after all, a romance, and very long. But then I kept picking it up again, more times than can be accounted for by any sense of duty. A fine book."

Both Fremont-Smith and Turner expressed admiration for McCullough's vivid characterizations. "McCullough does make her characters and their concerns come alive," asserted Fremont-Smith. "She gives them (the leads particularly, and Ralph most of all) intelligence and complexity and dimension. Even the minor characters are not dull." Elaborating on the priest's role in the story, Turner wrote, "Very few novels spotlight a Roman Catholic priest as a sex symbol, but Father Ralph's bravura performance in this one rivals the landscape for originality. Father Ralph is simply yummy. . . . And, of course, he is out of the running, which gives the author plenty of opportunity to dangle him as an erotic tease." In her *Publishers Weekly* interview, McCullough said, "Actually, Ralph was supposed to be a minor character. Yet, when I was planning it in my head I was aware I didn't have a dominant male lead. The minute the priest walked into the book I said, 'Ah ha, this is it. This is the male character I've lacked!' But I had to keep him in the story and, logically, he didn't belong in it. The only way I could do it was to involve him emotionally with Meggie, the only woman available. It worked beautifully because again it made more interesting reading to have a love that couldn't be fulfilled. It kept the reader going."

The solid success of *The Thorn Birds* made it almost inevitable that McCullough's next books would be compared with it. "When you produce a book which is well loved—and people do love it—it's a very hard book to bury," noted the author in the London *Times.* Although she believes "a lot of writers keep feeding people the same book," McCullough stated in a *New York Times Book Review* interview with Edwin McDowell that she had "decided long ago . . . to have a bash at different kinds of books." Her third novel, *An Indecent Obsession,* certainly differs from its predecessor in many ways; while *The Thorn Birds* spanned three continents and most of a century, *An Indecent Obsession* is set entirely within the confines of a ward of a South Pacific army hospital near the end of World War II. The drama centers on the tension between Honour Langtry, Ward X's nurse, and her group of "troppo" patients—soldiers who have snapped under the strain of tropical jungle fighting. Many reviewers characterized *An Indecent Obsession* as a more serious work than *The Thorn Birds.*

Despite these differences, *Chicago Tribune Book World* reviewer Julia M. Ehresmann found that *An Indecent Obsession* "has McCullough's fingerprints all over it." Comparing the themes of *Tim, The Thorn Birds,* and *An Indecent Obsession,* Ehresmann observed that "in these times when personal gratification is valued so highly, Colleen McCullough is writing about old-time moral dilemmas and largely discarded qualities: self-denial, self-control, and notions of duty, honor, and love as self-displacing virtues." Joanne Greenberg similarly said in the *New York Times Book Review* that *An Indecent Obsession* is "a very old-fashioned novel, with its focus on the conflict between duty and love, a rare concern in contemporary fiction." McCullough's well-drawn characterizations and powerfully evoked setting once again gained praise from many critics, with Greenberg crediting the author's "attention to detail" as the factor that "makes one feel the discomfort of the sweltering tropical nights as well as appreciate the awesome beauty of the sea, the torrential rains and the sunsets." Finally, in his *Washington Post Book World* article, William A. Nolen addressed "the question a lot of potential readers will want answered: Is *An Indecent Obsession* as good as McCullough's *The Thorn Birds?* The question can't be answered. It's like asking if a nice, ripe orange is as tasty as a nice, ripe apple; it depends on your mood and your taste buds. I enjoyed both books, but I thought *An Indecent Obsession* was more intriguing, more thought provoking, than was *The Thorn Birds.*"

Christopher Lehmann-Haupt, however, found fault with the book in the *New York Times.* "We turn the pages," he acknowledged. "I do not mean to make light of Colleen McCullough's already best-selling successor to her gigantically successful *The Thorn Birds.* . . . Miss McCullough is a natural story-teller, more than merely clever at getting up a head of emotional steam. . . . But if [she] expects to be taken seriously as a novelist—and, to judge from the improvement of this book over *The Thorn Birds,* there's no reason why she shouldn't be—she's going to have to write just a little less slickly." McCullough's glibness, continued Lehmann-Haupt, "makes one want to say that *An Indecent Obsession* is merely a gilded version of what I believe teen-age readers used to refer to as a nurse book. It isn't really. But far too often, its faults reduce it to medical soap opera."

In 1990, after a decade of research, McCullough embarked on a series of novels set in ancient Rome. The first volume in the series, *The First Man in Rome,* focuses on Gaius Marius and his feud with his brother-in-law, Lucius Cornelius Sulla. The second volume, *The Grass Crown,* deals mainly with handsome and ambitious Sulla as he vies for control over Rome. *Fortune's Favorites,* the third installment, picks up Sulla's story as he grows old and dies; the story then turns to the rise of the younger generation of Roman power-seekers: Pompey, Crassus, and Julius Caesar. 1996's *Caesar's Women,* the fourth installment, focuses on Caesar's rise to power between 68 and 58 B.C., and *Caesar: Let the Dice Fly* takes the story to 48 B.C. All of the series' volumes feature meticulous details about life in ancient Rome. The works portray the timeless traits of men vying for power—lust, deception, and greed—and are offered in massive scope, with each volume typically comprising nine hundred pages.

Critics of McCullough's Roman series have praised her eye for detail, her research, and her storytelling powers, while noting that the sheer size and scope of the stories sometimes get in the way of character development. For instance, *Washington Post Book World* contributor Judith Tarr remarked that the author's ambition with the series is "laudable" but "a bit too ambitious. The result is often a loss of focus and a failure of Story in the face of History." Reviewing *Fortune's Favorites* in the Chicago *Tribune Books,* Geoffrey Johnson commented: "So intent is McCullough on including every iota of Roman history that occurred during the 14-year span of her novel that she relegates major events to a paragraph, and much of the novel seems to take place in the wings." However, Johnson praised the author for her handling of certain events and characters in the novel, calling it "artfully composed fiction." In his *New York Times Book Review* piece on *Caesar: Let the Dice Fly,* Allan Lincoln concluded that Julius Caesar "is essentially the same character one recalls from his . . . memoirs—brilliant, ambitious, ruthless and fascinating."

The true history of McCullough's husband's family serves as a basis for her 2000 novel *Morgan's Run.* The novel's hero, Richard Morgan, suffers a string of personal tragedies and then becomes the victim of a set-up, culminating in his deportation as one of the first prisoners sent to the Botany Bay penal colony. Though his many misfortunes would defeat a lesser man, Richard rises to the occasion as a leader and a man of principle under the most trying circumstances. Set in the late eighteenth century, the novel reveals how the vicissitudes of war and politics between England, America, and Australia affect one individual. "McCullough's narrative skills are fully displayed in this intricately researched, passionate epic," observed a *Publishers Weekly* reviewer. The reviewer added that the book unfolds "a complex, consistently entertaining narrative." In the *New York Times Book Review,* Peter Bricklebank voiced reservations about the "wholly noble" protagonist, feeling that Richard Morgan shows a "lack of compelling emotions." *Library Journal* correspondent Nancy Pearl also felt that Richard is "the major weakness of the novel."

McCullough responds to the occasional criticism of her work calmly. "Only time tells," she philosophized in her interview with Cassill. "If it lasts, it's good literature. If it dies, it's just another book. Very often the books the critics like today are gone tomorrow." She said that the greatest change that her phenomenal success has brought to her life has been a feeling of increased security and freedom. While working at Yale, she expected to "have to go home and look after mother when I was 50, and try to hold down a job at the same time—then at 70 I'd be living in a cold-water, walk-up apartment, just about able to afford a 60-watt light bulb." She now owns several homes, spending most of her time on tiny Norfolk Island, some one thousand miles off the east coast of Australia. This South Pacific island is inhabited mostly by descendants of the *Bounty* mutineers. Life there suits McCullough perfectly. "It isn't what you are, it's who you are in a place like this," she told Phillipa Toomey in the London *Times,* "It's incredibly beautiful and peaceful and remote. . . . I get a heck of a lot of work done because there is nothing much else to do."

BIOGRAPHICAL/CRITICAL SOURCES:

BOOKS

Contemporary Literary Criticism, Volume 27, Gale (Detroit), 1984.

DeMarr, Mary Jean, *Colleen McCullough: A Critical Companion,* Greenwood Press (Westport, CT), 1996.

Hjerter, Kathleen G., *Doubly Gifted: The Author as Visual Artist,* Harry N. Abrams (New York), 1986.

PERIODICALS

America, August 10, 1974, Margaret Ferrari, review of *Tim.*

Atlantic Monthly, June, 1977, Amanda Heller, review of *The Thorn Birds.*

Best Sellers, May 15, 1974.

Booklist, July, 2000, Diana Tixier Herald, review of *Morgan's Run,* p. 1975.

Chicago Tribune Book World, October 11, 1981, Julia M. Ehresmann, review of *An Indecent Obsession.*

Christian Century, March 31, 1982.

Library Journal, August, 2000, Nancy Pearl, review of *Morgan's Run,* p. 154.

Los Angeles Times Book Review, October 25, 1981.

National Observer, June 20, 1977.

New Leader, July 4, 1977.

Newsweek, April 25, 1977.

New York Times, May 2, 1977; March 25, 1979; September 17, 1981; October 29, 1981; March 26, 1983; March 27, 1983.

New York Times Book Review, April 21, 1974; May 8, 1977; October 25, 1981; November 15, 1981; February 1, 1998, Allen Lincoln, review of *Caesar Let the Dice Fly,* p. 18; October 22, 2000, Peter Bricklebank, review of *Morgan's Run.*

People, May 7, 1984; November 27, 2000.

Publishers Weekly, March 7, 1977; February 22, 1980; February 18, 1984; October 16, 1995, p. 42; July 24, 2000, review of *Morgan's Run,* p. 67.

Saturday Review, April 16, 1977.

Time, May 9, 1977; May 20, 1985, Paul Gray, review of *The Thorn Birds.*

Times (London), November 30, 1981.

Times Literary Supplement, October 7, 1977; December 11, 1981.

Tribune Books (Chicago), October 31, 1993, Geoffrey Johnson, review of *Fortune's Favorites,* p. 3.

Village Voice, March 28, 1977, Eliot Fremont-Smith, review of *The Thorn Birds.*

Washington Post, April 24, 1977; November 26, 1981; March 27, 1983.

Washington Post Book World, October 11, 1981; January 20, 1985; April 28, 1985; November 21, 1993, p. 4.

Writer's Digest, March, 1980.

McGRATH, Alister E(dgar) 1953-

PERSONAL: Born January 23, 1953, in Belfast, Northern Ireland; son of Edgar Parkinson (a physician) and Annie Jane (a nurse) McGrath; married Joanna Ruth Collicutt (a psychologist); children: Paul Alister, Elizabeth Joanna. *Education:* Attended Oxford University, 1971-78, and Cambridge University, 1978-80; earned B.A. (natural science; with first class honors), M.A., D.Phil., B.A. (theology; with first class honors), and B.D. *Religion:* Episcopalian.

ADDRESSES: Office—Wycliffe Hall, 54 Banbury Rd., Oxford OX2 6PW, England; fax: 01-86-527-4215. *E-mail*—Alister.McGrath@wycliffe.ox.ac.uk.

CAREER: Curate of parish church in Wollaton, Nottingham, England, 1980-83; Wycliffe Hall, Oxford, England, lecturer in historical and systematic theology, 1983-95, principal, 1995—. Oxford University, professor, 1983—; Drew University, Tipple Visiting Professor of Historical Theology, 1990; Regent College, Vancouver, British Columbia, Canada, research professor, 1993-97.

WRITINGS:

Luther's Theology of the Cross, Basil Blackwell (Cambridge, MA), 1985.

Iustitia Dei: A History of the Christian Doctrine of Justification, Cambridge University Press (New York, NY), 1986, 2nd edition, 1998.

The Intellectual Origins of the European Reformation, Basil Blackwell (Cambridge, MA), 1987.

Reformation Thought: An Introduction, Basil Blackwell (Cambridge, MA), 1988.

Explaining Your Faith without Losing Your Friends, 1989, revised edition published as *Explaining Your Faith,* Baker Book (Grand Rapids, MI), 1996.

A Life of John Calvin, Basil Blackwell (Cambridge, MA), 1990.

The Genesis of Doctrine, Basil Blackwell (Oxford, England), 1990, published as *The Genesis of Doctrine: A Study in the Foundations of Doctrinal Criticism,* Eerdmans (Grand Rapids, MI), 1997.

Making Sense of the Cross, Inter-Varsity Press (Leicester, England), 1992.

What Was God Doing on the Cross?, Zondervan (Grand Rapids, MI), 1992.

The Dilemma of Self-Esteem: The Cross and Christian Confidence, Crossway (Wheaton, IL), 1992.

Suffering, Hodder & Stoughton (London, England), 1992.

Understanding Doctrine: Its Relevance and Purpose for Today, Zondervan (Grand Rapids, MI), 1992.

(Editor) *The Blackwell Encyclopedia of Modern Christian Thought,* Basil Blackwell (Cambridge, MA), 1993.

The Renewal of Anglicanism, Morehouse (Harrisburg, PA), 1993.

Intellectuals Don't Need God and Other Modern Myths: Building Bridges to Faith through Apologetics, Zondervan (Grand Rapids, MI), 1993.

Reformation Thought: An Introduction, 2nd edition, Basil Blackwell (Cambridge, MA), 1993, 3rd edition, 2000.

The Making of Modern German Christology, 1750-1990, 2nd edition, Zondervan (Grand Rapids, MI), 1994.

Spirituality in an Age of Change: Rediscovering the Spirit of the Reformers, Zondervan (Grand Rapids, MI), 1994.

(Contributor) *Roman Catholicism: Evangelical Protestants Analyze What Divides and Unites Us,* Moody (Chicago, IL), 1994.

Christian Theology: An Introduction, Basil Blackwell (Cambridge, MA), 1994, 3rd edition, 2001.

(With Michael Green) *How Shall We Reach Them?,* Thomas Nelson (Nashville, TN), 1995.

Evangelicalism and the Future of Christianity, Inter-Varsity Press (Downers Grove, IL), 1995.

Beyond the Quiet Time: Practical Evangelical Spirituality, Baker Book (Grand Rapids, MI), 1995.

Suffering and God, Zondervan (Grand Rapids, MI), 1995.

(Editor) *The Christian Theology Reader,* Basil Blackwell (Cambridge, MA), 1995, 2nd edition, 2001.

A Passion for Truth: The Intellectual Coherence of Evangelicalism, Inter-Varsity Press (Downers Grove, IL), 1996.

An Introduction to Christianity, Basil Blackwell (Cambridge, MA), 1997.

Studies in Doctrine (contains *Understanding Doctrine, Understanding Jesus, Understanding the Trinity,* and *Justification by Faith*), Zondervan (Grand Rapids, MI), 1997.

The NIV Bible Companion: a Basic Commentary on the Old and New Testaments, Zondervan (Grand Rapids, MI), 1997.

J. I. Packer: A Biography, Baker Book (Grand Rapids, MI), 1997, published in England as *To Know and Serve God,* 1997.

The Foundations of Dialogue in Science and Religion, Basil Blackwell (Cambridge, MA), 1998.

Historical Theology: An Introduction to the History of Christian Thought, Basil Blackwell (Cambridge, MA), 1998.

"I Believe": Exploring the Apostles' Creed, Inter-Varsity Press (Downers Grove, IL), 1998.

Christian Spirituality: An Introduction, Basil Blackwell (Cambridge, MA), 1999.

The Unknown God: Searching for Spiritual Fulfillment, Eerdmans (Grand Rapids, MI), 1999.

Science and Religion: An Introduction, Basil Blackwell (Cambridge, MA), 1999.

(General editor) *The Hodder Dictionary of Bible Themes,* Hodder & Stoughton (London, England), 1999.

(General editor) *The NIV Thematic Reference Bible,* Zondervan (Grand Rapids, MI), 1999.

(Editor) *Christian Literature: An Anthology,* Basil Blackwell (Cambridge, MA), 2000.

(Editor) *The J. I. Packer Collection,* Inter-Varsity Press (Downers Grove, IL), 2000.

The Journey: A Pilgrim in the Lands of the Spirit, Doubleday (New York, NY), 2000.

In the Beginning: The Story of the King James Bible, Doubleday (New York, NY), 2001.

SIDELIGHTS: Alister E. McGrath has established a reputation as an expert in the field of historical theology. In addition to his work on historical subjects, he frequently addresses the challenges facing established religion in the modern world. In *The Journey: A Pilgrim in the Lands of the Spirit,* he uses the familiar metaphor of spiritual life as a journey, one which may have many frustrating setbacks, especially until one recognizes the need for navigational tools on that journey. In relating his own story, as Doris Donnelly stated in *America,* McGrath shows how he finally realized that he "needed a map, a compass, companionship and the willingness to try a new route to get out of the rut in which he found himself." He cautions against approaching Bible study as a purely intellectual exercise, urging readers to engage themselves emotionally as well. McGrath advises looking to great writers of the past for guidance, and provides words of wisdom from luminaries such as Jonathan Edwards, Martin Luther, J. I. Packer, and C. S. Lewis. McGrath does not try to "contemporize" the spiritual journey, advised Donnelly; instead, "his strength is to leave the wisdom of ages past intact for readers to make their own way and to find their own meaning and sustenance."

In *The Unknown God: Searching for Spiritual Fulfillment,* McGrath addresses the human longing for something that will fully satisfy the soul and concludes that the only thing that can accomplish this is God. Short chapters with vivid illustrations present ideas from great thinkers, ranging from Plato to Kierkegaard, all pointing to the Creator as the only real source of fulfillment. Reviewing the book for *Presbyterian Layman,* Robert P. Mills commented, "It is not without reason that McGrath has become one of today's most popular theologians. He has a keen appreciation of issues confronting contemporary Christians and a wonderful knack for deft turns of phrase." A *Publishers Weekly* writer declared, "McGrath's reflections are elegantly written defenses of the central elements of the Christian faith." Ray Olson's assessment in *Booklist* gave particular praise to McGrath's "graceful, limpid, beautiful language."

BIOGRAPHICAL/CRITICAL SOURCES:

PERIODICALS

America, September 30, 2000, Doris Donnelly, review of *The Journey,* p. 27.

Booklist, July, 1999, Ray Olson, review of *The Unknown God,* p. 1901.

Christian Century, July 19, 1995, Robert W. Patterson, review of *Evangelicalism and the Future of Christianity,* p. 719; July 15, 1998, David Stewart, review of *J. I. Packer,* p. 695.

Christianity Today, September 12, 1994, John Wilson, review of *Evangelicalism and the Future of Christianity* and *The Intellectual Origins of the European Reformation,* p. 76; April 6, 1998, review of *J. I. Packer,* p. 30; September 6, 1999, review of *The Unknown God,* p. 106.

History Today, March, 1995, Rosemary O'Day, review of *Reformation Thought,* p. 55.

Library Journal, July, 1999, Graham Christian, review of *The Unknown God,* p. 100; March 1, 2000, review of *The Journey,* p. 98.

New York Times Book Review, April 8, 2001, Simon Winchester, review of *In the Beginning,* p. 8.

Publishers Weekly, April 22, 1996, review of *A Passion for Truth,* p. 65; November 16, 1998, review of *Science and Christianity,* p. 68, review of *The Foundations of Dialogue in Science and Religion,* p. 522; June 14, 1999, review of *The Unknown God,* p. 66; March 13, 2000, review of *The Journey,* p. 78.

Religious Studies Review, January, 1998, review of *Christian Theology* (2nd edition), p. 17; January, 1999, review of *The Genesis of Doctrine,* p. 59.

Times Literary Supplement, May 5, 1989, p. 491; March 1, 1991, p. 24.

OTHER

Does God Exist, http://www.doesgodexist.org/ (October 8, 2000), review of *Intellectuals Don't Need God and Other Modern Myths.*

Presbyterian Layman, http://www.layman.org/ (October 8, 2000), Robert P. Mills, review of *The Unknown God.*

The Harvest, http://www.stmatts.com/ (October, 1995), Russell Reno, review of *The Renewal of Anglicanism.*

WebWorks, http://www.marietta.edu/ (October 8, 2000), Phillip A. Ross, review of *Evangelicalism and the Future of Christianity.*

* * *

McNEILL, J(ohn) R(obert)

PERSONAL: Male. *Education:* Swarthmore College, B.A., 1975; Duke University, M.A., 1977, Ph.D., 1981.

ADDRESSES: Office—Department of History, Georgetown University, Washington, DC 20057.

CAREER: Athens College, Athens, Greece, instructor in world geography, 1975-76; Duke University, Durham, NC, instructor, 1980-81, visiting assistant professor of history, 1982-83; Goucher College, Towson, MD, assistant professor of history, 1983-85; Georgetown University, Washington, DC, assistant professor, 1985-90, associate professor, 1990-93, professor of history, 1993—, member of executive committee of School of Foreign Service, 1989-91. Marine Biological Laboratory, researcher at Ecosystems Center, 1982-83; Maryland Area Coalition for Soviet-American Relations, lecturer, 1984-86.

MEMBER: World History Association, American Historical Association, American Society of Environmental History.

AWARDS, HONORS: Grant from National Endowment for the Humanities (for Columbia University), 1985; Fulbright grants for Greece, Italy, and Spain, 1987-88, and New Zealand, 1992; Guggenheim fellow, 1997-98; Canterbury fellow, 2000.

WRITINGS:

The Atlantic Empires of France and Spain: Louisbourg and Havana, 1700-1763, University of North Carolina Press (Chapel Hill, NC), 1985.

(Contributor) M. Ultee, editor, *Adapting to Conditions: War and Society in the Eighteenth Century,* University of Alabama Press (University, AL), 1985.

(Contributor) J. F. Richards and R. P. Tucker, editors, *World Deforestation in the Twentieth Century,* Duke University Press (Durham, NC), 1988.

(Contributor) Jill Jaeger, editor, *The Challenge of Sustainable Development in a Greenhouse World: Some Visions of the Future,* Stockholm Environmental Institute (Stockholm, Sweden), 1991.

(Editor, with Alan Karras, and contributor) *Atlantic American Societies from Columbus to Abolition,* Routledge, 1992.

The Mountains of the Mediterranean World: An Environmental History, Cambridge University Press (New York, NY), 1992.

Something New under the Sun: An Environmental History of the Twentieth-Century World, Norton (New York, NY), 2000.

Contributor of articles and reviews to professional journals.

SIDELIGHTS: J. R. McNeill takes a thorough look at the environmental events of the twentieth century in his book, *Something New under the Sun: An Environmental History of the Twentieth-Century World.* His perspective is fairly unique, according to a reviewer for *Business Week,* for he neither ignores the large-scale environmental damage that has been inflicted on the planet by human industry, nor does he forecast inevitable global disaster. Instead, "the author provides the reader with both fresh information and analysis. *Something New under the Sun* proves to be just that—an unusual look at a period we thought we know very well," stated the reviewer.

McNeill catalogs the economic, technological, and ideological changes of the twentieth century, which are already well-known to many readers. Newly developed chemicals, nuclear waste, and large-scale exploitation of natural resources are just some of the trends discussed by the author. His book takes an in-depth look at the sometimes surprising, long-term political consequences of some of these trends. For example, nickel mining in the French territory of New Caledonia led to displacement of native people, shifting of land, and the introduction of smoke and poisonous gas into the atmosphere. These events in turn led to political unrest and a fight for independence in the French territory. Many other instances of political consequences resulting from environmental changes are documented by the author.

McNeill also gives an evenhanded treatment to his subject. While not downplaying the potential—and in some cases actual—catastrophes brought about by human industry, he also points out the good that has come from technological advances: increased food production that provides food for billions of people, preservationist efforts that were spurred by overuse of natural resources, and various other improvements to the quality of life for millions of people. *Something New under the Sun* is a "scientifically informed survey" useful for "environmentalists, scholars, globalists, biologists, policy makers and concerned readers," wrote a *Publishers Weekly* reviewer. The *Business Week* writer summarized: "[McNeill] delivers nothing less than a history of the entire biosphere, giving a view that's rich in both anecdotes and data."

BIOGRAPHICAL/CRITICAL SOURCES:

PERIODICALS

Business Week, August 14, 2000, review of *Something New under the Sun,* p. 19.

Publishers Weekly, March 27, 2000, review of *Something New under the Sun,* p. 60.

* * *

MEADE, Marion 1934-
(Lee Morgan, a pseudonym)

PERSONAL: Born January 7, 1934, in Pittsburgh, PA; daughter of Surain (a physicist) and Mary (Homeny) Sidhu; children: Alison Linkhorn. *Education:* Northwestern University, B.S., 1955; Columbia University, M.S., 1956.

ADDRESSES: Agent—Julia Coopersmith Literary Agency, 10 West 15th St., New York, NY 10011.

CAREER: Novelist and biographer.

WRITINGS:

FICTION

Stealing Heaven: The Love Story of Heloise and Abelard, Morrow (New York, NY), 1979.

Sybille, Morrow (New York, NY), 1983.

NONFICTION

Bitching, Prentice-Hall (Englewood Cliffs, NJ), 1973.

Tennis (biographical sketches), Harvey House (New York, NY), 1975.

Eleanor of Aquitaine, Dutton (New York, NY), 1977.

Madame Blavatsky: The Woman behind the Myth, Putnam (New York, NY), 1980.

Dorothy Parker: What Fresh Hell Is This?, Villard (New York, NY), 1988.

Buster Keaton: Cut to the Chase, HarperCollins (New York, NY), 1995.

The Unruly Life of Woody Allen, Scribner (New York, NY), 2000.

Contributor to various periodicals, including the *New York Times, Village Voice, McCall's, Commonweal,* and *Cosmopolitan.*

JUVENILE NONFICTION

Free Woman: The Life and Times of Victoria Woodhull, Knopf (New York, NY), 1976.

Little Book of Big Riddles, illustrated by David Ross, Harvey House (New York, NY), 1976.

Little Book of Big Bad Jokes, illustrated by Chris Cummings, Harvey House (New York, NY), 1977.

(As Lee Morgan) *Abraham Lincoln,* illustrated by Piero Cattaneo, Silver Burdett (Morristown, NJ), 1990.

(As Lee Morgan) *Christopher Columbus,* illustrated by Claudio Solarino, Silver Burdett (Morristown, NJ), 1990.

SIDELIGHTS: According to *Spectator* critic David Wright, biographer and novelist Marion Meade's *Dorothy Parker: What Fresh Hell Is This?* is "a lively book, an entertaining read and a memorable portrait" of Parker, an author who ultimately became more famous for her cutting humor and wit than for her actual writings. Parker was a member of a New York City salon known as the Algonquin Round Table. Many of the members of this clíque, which flowered during the 1920s, were, like Parker, associated with the newly created *New Yorker* magazine, writers such as Robert Benchley, Robert Sherwood, Edmund Wilson, and Alexander Wolcott. Many members of the Algonquin Round Table would die young, burnt out from hard drinking and other excesses. Parker was as indulgent as any of them, but lived to a lonely old age. Her rapier wit, never tempered by kindness, was feared even by her friends; the subtitle to Meade's biography was Parker's standard response whenever her doorbell announced a visitor.

Parker's life was filled with dramatic events, including suicide attempts, failed marriages, long drinking binges, and misadventures with numerous notable literary figures. Reviewer Emily Toth praised Meade for avoiding a sensationalistic approach to her subject, writing in the *Women's Review of Books* that *Dorothy Parker* "does not build up to punch-lines (rising action, climax, falling action—a masculine approach). Rather, it follows what feminist theorists might call a feminine approach: moments of consciousness, a lyrical portrayal of the dailiness of life." As Meade herself once explained, "*Dorothy Parker* is a sad book: like many women's biographies, it concentrates on losses, and it would be dishonest to make Parker's disintegration anything but painful to read about."

Less impressed with *Dorothy Parker* was *New York Times* reviewer Michiko Kakutani, who complained that Meade did not penetrate deeply enough into her subject, demonstrating instead "a tendency to dwell on the details of Parker's and her friends' private lives, filling us in on their sexual predilections, their drinking habits and their continuing quarrels with one another. This makes for fast but not very illuminating reading; indeed, the reader ends with the feeling of having plowed through several decades worth of gossip columns." Still, other reviewers remained laudatory. Diana Eden, writing in *New Statesman,* declared that "Meade is to be congratulated upon a detailed and balanced reconstruction of a life based on interviews, insight, and research," while *Times Literary Supplement* contributor Shena Mackay credited the author with creating "a balanced and generally sympathetic study of an artist and her era, rich in detail and gossip." Meade was also given high marks for the scope of her work by Anne Chamberlin, who wrote in the *Washington Post Book World,* "Dorothy Parker . . . left no clues behind her when she died. No letters, no manuscripts, no memorabilia, no private papers of any kind. . . . Undismayed by this daunting void, biographer Marion Meade . . . has peered into every cranny that is left. No crumbling shard escaped her gaze."

Meade looked deeply into the background of another famous American in her 1995 biography, *Buster Keaton: Cut to the Chase.* First attaining fame as a star of silent film comedies, Keaton, according to Joseph McBride in the *New York Times Book Review,* "developed a stoicism that set him apart from the more sentimental comedy of his contemporaries." In her book, Meade reveals the macabre roots of Keaton's comic artistry. As a child, he was featured in his family's vaudeville act, the Three Keatons. Young Buster was billed as "the Human Mop," "the Little Boy Who Can't Be Damaged," and "Mr. Black and Blue." His part in the show was to remain stoic while his sadistic and frequently drunken father dragged, kicked, and threw him about the stage.

As an adult, Keaton became a famous silent film star, only to have his career go into a tailspin with the advent of talking pictures. According to McBride, Meade "chillingly details Keaton's headlong collapse with the coming of sound and gives a full and sympathetic account of his remaining decades as a dogged journeyman comic on television and in such movie potboilers as *Beach Blanket Bingo* and *How to Stuff a Wild Bikini.*" In the words of a *Publishers Weekly* reviewer, *Buster Keaton: Cut to the Chase* "is an engrossing portrait of a tormented comedic genius."

Meade's 2000 biography, *The Unruly Life of Woody Allen,* appeared in print as an "unauthorized" profile of the famous actor/writer/director a month after another major Allen biography, John Baxter's *Woody Allen.* Whereas Baxter devotes a considerable portion of his book dealing with Allen's movies and his other work as an entertainer, Meade concentrates on the personal aspects of Allen's life, with emphasis placed on what she considers the central event of that life: the 1992 scandal that began when Allen's then-long-time-lover Mia Farrow found nude Polaroid photographs of her adopted daughter Soon-Yi Previn on the mantle in Allen's Manhattan apartment. Meade's prologue to *The Unruly Life of Woody Allen* portrays Farrow's discovery of those photos in dramatic style, and more than half of the remaining text deals with that discovery and the events pertinent to it that followed, including the legal battles surrounding Allen's custody suit for his own son, Satchel, and Farrow's allegations of child abuse against her adopted daughter, Dylan.

Reviewers' estimation of Meade's approach to Allen varied widely. Iain Johnstone of the London *Sunday Times* noted: "Meade deals with . . . [the] initial part of Allen's career in an insightful fashion, bringing his family to life with a colorful pen, and pertinently integrating the roles of those who helped Allen on his way." This includes Allen's growing up a Jewish neighborhood in Brooklyn in a dysfunctional family, his frequent childhood retreats into movie theaters, his precocious comedic talents (selling jokes to newspapers while still a teenager), his failed marriage while in his early twenties, his relationships with Louise Lasser and Diane Keaton, and his dalliance with a teenager when he was forty-one, as well as the professional dealings and relationships that led to his worldwide success and acclaim as an independent film maker. Describing Meade's coverage of such events, Mim Udovitch commented in the *New York Times Book Review* that Allen's "basic biographical facts are handled with dispatch." "This is not a vile book," Udovitch added; "it is accurate to its sources; its presentation of the facts of Woody Allen's life, while highly selective, is not irresponsible." Still, the critic ended by characterizing Meade's treatment as a "triumph of the trash imperative." In contrast, L. S. Klepp of *Entertainment Weekly,* while observing that "Meade is often perfunctory about the movies and other work" created by Allen, still called *The Unruly Life of Woody Allen* "an evenhanded, prodigiously researched biography." A *Publishers Weekly* reviewer described the book as "a psychologically nuanced, tough-minded portrait," while Dade Hayes of *Variety* found Meade's biography to be an "exasperating read" because of its "sense of disappointment and disapproval in Allen." However, Hayes concluded, "Meade's attack fizzles, due to the lack of serious consideration about an artist's moral compass." Overall, the psychological portrait that emerges of Allen is not a favorable one.

BIOGRAPHICAL/CRITICAL SOURCES:

PERIODICALS

Belles Lettres, spring, 1995, p. 102.

Booklist, December 15, 1999, Bonnie Smothers, review of *The Unruly Life of Woody Allen,* p. 738.

Chicago Tribune, January 24, 1988, sec. 14, p. 6.

Christian Science Monitor, May 25, 1988, p. 20.

Entertainment Weekly, February 18, 2000, L. S. Klepp, "Scandal Sheets," p. 78.

Library Journal, July, 1994, p. 134; February 15, 2000, Stephen Rees, review of *The Unruly Life of Woody Allen,* p. 165.

Listener, April 21, 1988, p. 33.

Los Angeles Times Book Review, March 26, 1989, p. 10.

New Statesman, April 22, 1988, p. 28.

New Yorker, April 25, 1988, p. 109.

New York Times, January 9, 1988, p. A17; April 25, 1988, p. 109; February 26, 1995, section LI, p. 8.

New York Times Book Review, October 8, 1995, p. 12; March 5, 2000, Mim Udovitch, "Deconstructing Woody," p. 13.

Observer (London), February 27, 2000, Neil Mullarkey, "Misdemeanors and All."

Publishers Weekly, March 11, 1983, pp. 26-27; July 13, 1994, p. 466; September 4, 1995, p. 59; January 3, 2000, review of *The Unruly Life of Woody Allen,* p. 67.

Spectator, April 23, 1988, pp. 30-31.

Times (London), February 6, 2000, Iain Johnstone, "Woody and His Women," sec. 9, p. 39.

Times Literary Supplement, November 30, 1973, p. 1473; May 6, 1988, p. 497.

Variety, March 20, 2000, Dade Hayes, review of *The Unruly Life of Woody Allen,* p. 39.

Washington Post Book World, February 14, 1988, pp. 4, 7.

Women's Review of Books, May, 1988, p. 4.*

* * *

MESLE, C. Robert 1949-

PERSONAL: Born December 18, 1949, in Independence, MO; son of F. Carl and Kay A. (Sprague) Mesle; married Barbara Jalon Hiles, August 28, 1970; children: Sarah Elizabeth, Christopher Mark. *Education:* Graceland College, B.A., 1972 (Gold Seal); University of Chicago Divinity School, M.A., 1976; Northwestern University, Ph.D., 1980.

ADDRESSES: Home—RR1, Lamoni, IA 50140. *Office*—Department of Philosophy and Religion, Graceland University, 1 University Place, Lamoni, IA 50140. *E-mail*—bobmesle@graceland.edu.

CAREER: Graceland University (formerly Graceland College), Lamoni, IA, professor of philosophy of religion, head of Department of Philosophy and Religion, and director of honors program, 1980—. Elta University, member of faculty exchange program, 1991. Member of Center for Process Studies, Midwest Bioethics Center, and Hastings Center. Book review editor of *The American Journal of Theology and Philogophy.*

MEMBER: American Philosophical Association, American Academy of Religion, Center for Process Studies, Highlands Institute for American Religious and Philosophical Thought, Midwest Bioethics Center.

AWARDS, HONORS: Andrew Mellon fellow, Center for Humanistic Studies, University of Kansas, 1985; fellow of National Endowment for the Humanities, University of Santa Clara, 1986; Distinguished Author Award, Herald House Publishing Co., 1989; Excellence in Teaching Award, Graceland University, 1990; faculty exchange program, ELTA University, Budapest Hungary, 1991; *Process Theology: A Basic Introduction* was selected as the examination text, Newcastle Scholarship, Eton College, 1998; William E. Phipps Philosophy and Religion Interdisciplinary Lecturer, Davis & Elkins College, 2000.

WRITINGS:

Fire in My Bones: A Study in Faith and Belief, Herald House (Independence, MO), 1984.
The Bible as Story and Struggle, Herald House (Independence, MO), 1989.
(With John Hick) *John Hick's Theodicy,* St. Martin's Press (New York, NY), 1991.
(With John B. Cobb, Jr.) *Process Theology: A Basic Introduction,* Chalice Press, 1993.
(Editor) *Theology V: The Jesus Seminar,* Graceland/Park Press (Independence, MO), 1998.

Contributor of more than thirty book reviews and fifty essays, including *Our Caring Fellowship: A Program Resource for Church Groups,* Herald House (Independence, MO), 1983; *Problems in the Philosophy of Religion: Critical Studies of the Work of John Hick,* edited by Harold Hewitt, St. Martin's Press (New York, NY), 1991; and *With Equal Regard,* edited by Gail Mengel, Herald House (Independence, MO), 1992. Contributor to theology and philosophy journals and to religious magazines, including *Christian Century.* Abstracts editor, *Process Studies,* 1984—; member of editorial board, *American Journal of Theology and Philosophy,* 1987—; member of editorial review board, *Bioethics Forum,* 1993—.

SIDELIGHTS: C. Robert Mesle told *CA:* "I owe to Robert McAfee Brown the insight that 'we must put the welfare of children above the niceties of metaphysics.' I hope that the influence of my wife, Barbara, and children, Sarah and Mark, are clearly and increasingly woven into the pages of work. My mother's influence is evident in 'Sacred Fudge,' *The John Whitmer Historical Association Journal,* Vol. 8, 1998. My father taught me to ask of any theology, 'Would a loving God be like that?' This question has taken me down paths he would not have chosen, but for which I am grateful. Because the people I love, rather than transcendent realities, are central to my sense of sacredness, in my next book I plan to explore *Living without Eternity: Seeking the Welfare of Children within the Limits of Nature Alone.*"

BIOGRAPHICAL/CRITICAL SOURCES:

PERIODICALS

American Journal of Theology and Philosophy, January, 1993.
Journal of Religion, January, 1993; April, 1993.
Times Literary Supplement, May 8, 1992.

* * *

MICHOD, Richard E. 1951-

PERSONAL: Born May 11, 1951, in Chicago, IL; son of Charles Louis (a lawyer) and Florence (Wise) Michod; married Christina Megan Lawson, April 24, 1994; children: Kristin O., Katherine Anne Lawson. *Education:* Duke University, B.S. (cum laude), 1973; University of Georgia, M.A. and Ph.D., both 1978. *Religion:* "The possibilities of the wilderness." *Avocational interests:* Hiking, canoeing.

ADDRESSES: Home—Tucson, AZ. *Office*—Department of Ecology and Evolutionary Biology, University of Arizona, Tucson, AZ 85721.

CAREER: University of Arizona, Tucson, assistant professor, 1978-82, associate professor, 1982-87, professor of ecology and evolutionary biology, 1987—, department head, department of ecology and evolutionary biology, 2000—. Czechoslovak Academy of Sciences, lecturer, 1987; Georgetown University, Bicentennial Lecturer, 1989; University of Paris-Sud, visiting research professor, 1990-91; lecturer at colleges and universities in the United States and abroad. Rockefeller University, research fellow at Neurosciences Institute, 1984.

MEMBER: Society for the Study of Evolution, Genetics Society of America, American Society of Naturalists, Ecological Society of America, American Association for the Advancement of Science, American Microbiological Society.

AWARDS, HONORS: Grants from National Science Foundation, 1979-82, 1982-85, 1984-89, 1985-86, 1988, 1989-92, 1991-96, National Institutes of Health, 1984-89, 1985-90, 1986-89, 1990-95, 1995-2001, and American Cancer Society.

WRITINGS:

(Editor, with B. R. Levin, and contributor) *The Evolution of Sex: An Examination of Current Ideas,* Sinauer (Sunderland, MA), 1988.

(Editor, with M. Hechtor and L. Nadel, and contributor) *The Origin of Values,* Aldine de Gruyter (Hawthorne, NY), 1993.

Eros and Evolution: A Natural Philosophy of Sex, Addison-Wesley Longman (Reading, MA), 1995.

Darwinian Dynamics, Evolutionary Transitions in Fitness and Individuality, Princeton University Press, corrected paperback edition, 2000.

Work represented in anthologies, including *The Origin and Evolution of Sex,* edited by H. O. Halvorson, E. Adelberg, and N. Zinder, Alan Liss (New York, NY), 1985; *The Sociobiology of Reproductive Strategies in Animals and Man,* edited by Rasa, C. Vogel, and E. Voland, Chapman & Hall (London, England), 1989; and *The Natural History of Inbreeding and Outbreeding: Theoretical and Empirical Perspectives,* edited by N. Wilmsen Thornhill and W. M. Shields, University of Chicago Press (Chicago, IL), 1993. Contributor of more than sixty articles and reviews to scientific journals and newspapers. Special editor, *Evolution,* 1987-91.

WORK IN PROGRESS: A book on fitness and evolutionary explanation.

SIDELIGHTS: Richard E. Michod told *CA:* "In my writings I seek to understand the process by which living things evolve and create new life forms. I have been fascinated by evolution ever since I saw my first dinosaur bone at the Field Museum in Chicago, and I have devoted most of my professional life to understanding evolution and to teaching its principles. We learn from evolution that all living things, both past and present, are connected to each other. This gives me great inspiration and comfort; it makes me feel a part of something really big. In my recent book *Eros and Evolution,* I try to communicate this. I wrote the book because I believe that what we have discovered about the evolution of sex, death, and immortality speaks [of] issues of general concern to those who are curious about themselves and their place in the universe.

"My work also offers an explanation of one of the most curious features of life: that it is sexual. The world is male and female. Understanding this quite awkward arrangement is a universal problem in science, philosophy, literature, and art. In biology, the problem of sex can be traced back to Darwin and is generally regarded to be one of life's great mysteries. I think I know the answer."

* * *

MITCHUM, Hank
See SHERMAN, Jory (Tecumseh)

* * *

MORGAN
See MEADE, Marion

* * *

MORRIS, Christopher W. 1949-

PERSONAL: Born June 7, 1949, in Washington, DC. *Education:* Attended Trinity College, 1967-69; Vassar College, B.A., 1971; University of Toronto, M.A., 1974, Ph.D., 1977.

ADDRESSES: *Office*—Department of Philosophy, Bowling Green State University, Bowling Green, OH 43403.

CAREER: University of Ottawa, Ottawa, Ontario, Canada, assistant professor of philosophy, 1977-82; University of California, Los Angeles, visiting assistant professor of philosophy, 1982-85; University of California, Riverside, visiting lecturer in philosophy, 1985-86; Bowling Green State University, Bowling Green, OH, associate professor, 1986-94, professor of philosophy, 1986—, senior research fellow of Social Philosophy and Policy Center, 1990—, director of Philosophy and Public Policy Program for Central and Eastern European Scholars, 1993-94. CREA, Ecole Polytechnique, Paris, France, research associate, 1991—. Université du Québec a Montréal, visiting assistant professor, 1981 and 1985; University of California, Los Angeles, visiting scholar, 1981; University of Texas at Austin, visiting assistant professor of government, 1982; University of North Carolina at Chapel Hill, visiting associate professor, 1988-89.

WRITINGS:

(Editor, with R. G. Frey, and contributor) *Liability and Responsibility: Essays in Law and Morals,* Cambridge University Press (New York, NY), 1991.

(Editor, with Frey, and contributor) *Violence, Terrorism, and Justice,* Cambridge University Press (New York, NY), 1991.

(Editor, with Frey, and contributor) *Value, Welfare, and Morality,* Cambridge University Press (New York, NY), 1993.

(Editor, with Jules L. Coleman) *Rational Commitment and Social Justice: Essays for Gregory Kavka,* Cambridge University Press (New York, NY), 1998.

An Essay on the Modern State, Cambridge University Press (New York, NY), 1998, reprinted, 1999.

The Social Contract Theorists: Critical Essays on Hobbes, Locke, and Rousseau, Rowman & Littlefield (Lanham, MD), 1999.

(Editor, with Arthur Ripstein) *Practical Rationality and Preference: Essays for David Gauthier,* Cambridge University Press (New York, NY), 2001.

Editor (with Geoffrey Sayre-McCord) and contributor, *Contemporary Contractarianism,* Cornell University Press (Ithaca, NY). Contributor to books, including *The New Social Contract: Essays on Gauthier,* edited by Ellen Frankel Paul, Fred D. Miller, Jr., and others, Basil Blackwell (Oxford, England), 1988; *The State and Its Critics,* edited by Andrew Levine, Edward Elgar (Cheltenham, England), 1992; and *Moral Knowledge,* edited by Walter Sinnott-Armstrong and Mark Timmons, Oxford University Press (Oxford, England). Contributor of about fifty articles and reviews to philosophy journals. Member of editorial board, *Science(s) politique(s),* 1993—.

N-O

NESBITT, John D. 1948-

PERSONAL: Born December 14, 1948, in Lompoc, CA; son of A. D. (a farmer, rancher, and hired hand) and Elizabeth Margaret (an artist and writer; maiden name, Schneider) Nesbitt; married Laura Stokes, September 17, 1977 (marriage ended, February 14, 1983); married Liesa Jensen, January 4, 1988 (marriage ended, August 3, 1990); married Rocio Perez, July 21, 1995 (marriage ended, July 20, 2000). *Ethnicity:* "Caucasian." *Education:* University of California, Los Angeles, B.A. (magna cum laude), 1971; University of California, Davis, M.A., 1974, Ph.D., 1980; attended University of Wyoming, 1988; Instituto de Filologia Hispanica, Saltillo, Mexico, Diploma in Spanish Philology, 1994. *Avocational interests:* Hunting, camping, gardening.

ADDRESSES: *Office*—Eastern Wyoming College, 3200 West C St., Torrington, WY 82240. *E-mail*—jnesbitt@ewc.cc.wy.us.

CAREER: Eastern Wyoming College, Torrington, instructor in English and Spanish, 1981—.

MEMBER: Western Writers of America, Western Literature Association, Wyoming Writers, Phi Beta Kappa.

AWARDS, HONORS: Fellow of Wyoming Council for the Humanities and Wyoming Council on the Arts, both 1988; best short story award from *West Wind Review,* 1989; first place fiction awards from Wyoming Writers competitions, 1994 and 1995.

WRITINGS:

Adventures of the Ramrod Rider (3 stories), privately printed, 1991, expanded edition published as *Adventures of the Ramrod Rider: Gripping Tales, Augmented and Revised by the Author* (6 stories), Endeavor Books, 1999.

One-Eyed Cowboy Wild (novel), Walker and Co. (New York City), 1994.

Twin Rivers (novel), Walker and Co., 1995.

One Foot in the Stirrup: Western Stories, privately printed, 1995.

(Editor) *Wyoming Journeys* (poetry chapbook), WyoPoets, 1995.

I'll Tell You What: Fiction with Voice (stories), privately printed, 1996.

Blue Book of Basic Writing (textbook), Endeavor Books, 1996.

Antelope Sky: Stories of the Modern West (stories), privately printed, 1997.

Wild Rose of Ruby Canyon (novel), Walker and Co., 1997.

Seasons in the Fields: Stories of a Golden West (stories), privately printed, 1998.

Black Diamond Rendezvous (novel), Leisure Books (New York City), 1998.

Keep the Wind in Your Face (novel) Endeavor Books, 1998.

A Good Man to Have in Camp (novel) Endeavor Books, 1999.

Coyote Trail (novel) Leisure Books, 2000.

North of Cheyenne (novel) Leisure Books, 2000.

Writing for Real (textbook), Endeavor Books, 2000.

Man from Wolf River (novel) Leisure Books, 2001.

Work represented in anthologies, including *Critical Essays on the Western American Novel,* G. K. Hall (Boston, MA), 1980; *VeriTales: Note of Hope,* Fall Creek Press (Fall Creek, OR), 1993; and *New Trails,* edited by John Jakes and Martin H. Greenberg, Doubleday (New York City), 1994. Contributor of dozens of stories, poems, articles, and reviews to periodicals, including *Lines in the Sand, New Trails, American Literary Review, Western American Literature, South Dakota Review,* and *Wyoming Horizons.* Editor, *Westering,* 1986-92.

WORK IN PROGRESS: Contemporary and Old West fiction; research on western American fiction.

SIDELIGHTS: John D. Nesbitt told *CA:* "I grew up in a rural setting, in northern California, and I spent a large portion of my first thirty-three years working outdoors—at farm and ranch work, construction, landscaping, and gardening. I also developed a strong interest in camping and hunting. Since coming to Wyoming in 1981, I have continued my interests in hunting, camping, hiking, and working outdoors. I live in the plains country of Wyoming, where I do a variety of work on my own country place. I have a few animals of my own, and I have daily opportunities for observing wild plant and animal life.

"I write because I believe I have ideas and feelings that are worth expressing and that someone else might be interested in reading about. I write with the hope that other people will be interested in life as I see it. I write about human nature, human relationships, the Western outdoors, and the interplay between people and the environment. Most of my work is about people in the places where they live. Place is important in the lives of my characters, no doubt because it is important to me. I hope to communicate the importance of understanding the natural world and of not losing touch with it.

"I am influenced by the natural world around me, by narrative and lyrical works, and by relationships with people. When life is at its best for me, I have relationships with other people in which we share our interests in nature, literature, music, film, and language. At this point in my life, those interests intersect best in my relationship with a person named Cathy. Our shared experiences have contributed to my work more than any other single influence.

"When writing, I jot down notes, often without any specific sense of their destiny, and at some point or another, some notes end up in some folders. When I am ready to work on a particular piece, perhaps a story or an essay or a novel, I work those notes into some sort of an outline. Then I write a first draft by hand, in either blue or black ink, depending on the work I am writing. I don't mix colors. I type up the work on a word processor, revising at I type. Then I revise by hand, two or more times, until I think the work is ready for someone to see it.

"I am more particular than I used to be about writing in just one color of ink when I write a first draft. For example, I wrote *Black Diamond Rendezvous* in black ink, and I wrote *Man from Wolf River* in blue ink. The use of the word processor (in the last ten years) has made it much more convenient to revise. changing a word or a sentence used to be something which, I am ashamed to say, I was less likely to do if it meant retyping a page or re-typing the rest of a manuscript. Now, for the sake of a word, I am willing to re-do a page. I regret the use of so much paper, but I use a lot of it a second time (writing notes on the blank side), and I have always tried to conserve paper in other ways.

"I have done academic writing, and I expect to do more. I do not think that academic training or academic employment must be a detriment to one's creativity, but there are certainly competing demands on one's time and energy. I have heard many writers make snide remarks about academics, and I think that's too bad. It doesn't hurt to have had disciplined training and to have learned something in a field. I did have a professor in graduate school who told me that I would never get anywhere by studying Western American literature. I suppose he would have even less generous things to say about my having become a writer of traditional westerns, but I don't judge academic endeavor on the basis of people like him. Formal education, as a whole, is much greater than some of its parts.

"As a generalist in British and American literature, I have read widely. I like just about all the major fiction writers from Fielding onward, and it would be difficult to cite major influences. If pressed, I would say I feel the strongest affinities with Charles Dickens, A. B. Guthrie, Jr., and Alice Munro. I also feel some sort of artistic affinity with such songwriters and singers as Woody Guthrie, Merle Haggard, and Ian Tyson. Merely by mentioning these half-dozen, I feel I am slighting the hundreds of other writers and singers whose work has inspired me along the way."

* * *

NEWMAN, Debra Lynn
See HAM, Debra Newman

OLDS, Sharon 1942-

PERSONAL: Born November 19, 1942, in San Francisco, CA. *Education:* Stanford University, B.A. (with distinction), 1964; Columbia University, Ph.D., 1972.

ADDRESSES: *Home*—50 Riverside Drive, New York, NY, 10025-6146. *Office*—New York University, 19 University Pl. Rm. 200, New York, NY, 10003.

CAREER: Poet. Lecturer-in-residence on poetry at Theodor Herzl Institute, 1976-80; visiting teacher of poetry at Manhattan Theater Club, 1982, Nathan Mayhew Seminars of Martha's Vineyard, 1982, Poetry Center, Young Men's Christian Association of New York City, 1982, Poetry Society of America, 1983, New York University, 1983 and 1985, Sarah Lawrence College, 1984, Goldwater Hospital, Roosevelt Island, NY, 1985-90, Columbia University, 1985-86, and State University of New York College at Purchase, 1986. Holder of Fanny Hurst Chair, Brandeis University, 1986-87; New York University, New York City, associate professor of English, 1992—, acting director of graduate program in creative writing. Founding director, New York University workshop program at Goldwater Hospital, New York City.

MEMBER: Poetry Society of America, PEN, Author's Guild.

AWARDS, HONORS: Grants from Creative Artists Public Service, 1978, Guggenheim fellowship, 1981-82, and National Endowment for the Arts fellowship, 1982-83; Madeline Sadin Award, *New York Quarterly,* 1978; younger poets award from *Poetry Miscellany,* 1979; San Francisco Poetry Center Award, 1981, for *Satan Says;* Lamont Poetry Selection of the Academy of American Poets, 1984, and National Book Critics Circle Award, 1985, both for *The Dead and the Living;* Walt Whitman Citation of Merit, New York State Writers Institute, 1998; named New York State Poet, 1998-2000.

WRITINGS:

POETRY

Satan Says, University of Pittsburgh Press (Pittsburgh, PA), 1980.
The Dead and the Living, Knopf (New York City), 1984.
The Gold Cell, Knopf, 1987.

Sharon Olds

The Matter of This World, Slow Dancer Press, 1987.
The Sign of Saturn, Secker & Warburg, 1991.
The Father, Knopf, 1992.
The Wellspring: Poems, Knopf, 1996.
Blood, Tin, Straw, Knopf, 1999.

OTHER

(Author of foreword) *What Silence Equals,* Persea Books (New York City), 1993.

CONTRIBUTOR TO ANTHOLOGIES

The Norton Introduction to Poetry, 2nd edition, Norton (New York City), 1981.
The Bread Loaf Anthology of Contemporary American Poetry, edited by Robert Pack, Sydney Lea, and Jay Parini, University Press of New England (Hanover, NH), 1985.
Three Genres, The Writing of Poetry, Fiction, and Drama, edited by Stephen Minot, Prentice-Hall (Englewood Cliffs, NJ), 1988.
The Pushcart Prize, VIII: Best of the Small Presses, Wainscott, 1989.

Read to Write, Donald M. Murray, Holt (New York City), 1990.

The Longman Anthology of American Poetry: Colonial to Contemporary, edited by Hilary Russell, Longman (New York City), 1992.

Contributor to literary journals and magazines, including *New Yorker, Poetry, Atlantic Monthly, American Poetry Review, Nation, New Republic, Paris Review, Kayak, Massachusetts Review, Iowa Review, Poetry Northwest, Prairie Schooner, Ploughshares, Ms., Kenyon Review, Pequod, Mississippi Review, Yale Review,* and *Antioch Review.* Olds's works have been translated into Italian, Chinese, French, and Russian.

SIDELIGHTS: Sharon Olds's poetry, which graphically depicts personal family life as well as global political events, has won several prestigious prizes, including the National Book Critics Circle Award. "Sharon Olds is enormously self-aware," wrote David Leavitt in the *Voice Literary Supplement.* "Her poetry is remarkable for its candor, its eroticism, and its power to move." Discussing Olds's work in *Poetry,* Lisel Mueller noted: "By far the greater number of her poems are believable and touching, and their intensity does not interfere with craftsmanship. Listening to Olds, we hear a proud, urgent, human voice."

One of the constant characteristics of Olds's poetry is its accessibility. Her books appeal to a wide audience, and almost all of her work has undergone multiple printings. Her National Book Critics Circle Award-winning volume, *The Dead and the Living,* alone has sold more than 50,000 copies, ranking her as one of the most profitable of active poets. Her work is viewed in the tradition of Walt Whitman as a celebration of the body, in all its pleasures and pains, and it particularly resonates with women readers. As Charlie Powell put it in a *Salon* piece, "Domesticity, death, erotic love—the stark simplicity of Sharon Olds' subjects, and of her plain-spoken language, can sometimes make her seem like the brooding Earth Mother of American poetry."

Born in 1942 in San Francisco, Olds grew up in Berkeley, California. She attended Stanford University and earned her Ph.D. at Columbia in 1972. She was thirty-seven when she published her first book of poems, and she told *Salon* that her success was partly due to pure luck. "Anyone who can ever do anything is lucky," she said. "It means that there has been enough education, enough peace, enough time, enough whatever, that somebody can sit down and write. Many lives don't allow that, the good fortune of being able to work at it, and try, and keep trying."

Satan Says, Olds's first collection, explores "the roles in which she experiences herself, 'Daughter,' 'Woman,' and 'Mother,'" according to Mueller. In an article for the *American Book Review,* Joyce Peseroff claimed that throughout *Satan Says,* "the language often does 'turn neatly about.' In Olds's vocabulary ordinary objects, landscapes—even whole planets—are in constant motion. Using verbs which might seem, at first, almost grotesque, she manages to describe a violent, changing universe. . . . In a way, these poems describe a psychic world as turbulent, sensual, and strange as a world seen under water. . . . Sharon Olds convincingly, and with astonishing vigor, presents a world which, if not always hostile, is never clear about which face it will show her."

In a review for the *Nation,* Richard Tillinghast commented on *The Dead and the Living:* "While *Satan Says* was impossible to ignore because of its raw power, *The Dead and the Living* is a considerable step forward. . . . Olds is a keen and accurate observer of people." "I admire Sharon Olds's courage . . . ," declared Elizabeth Gaffney in *America.* "Out of private revelations she makes poems of universal truth, of sex, death, fear, love. Her poems are sometimes jarring, unexpected, bold, but always loving and deeply rewarding." Tillinghast felt, however, that Olds's attempts "to establish political analogies to private brutalization . . . are not very convincing. . . . This becomes a mannerism, representing political thinking only at the superficial level." Nevertheless, Tillinghast conceded that the book "has the chastening impact of a powerful documentary."

Olds's works were described by Sara Plath in *Booklist* as "poems of extreme emotions." Critics have found intense feelings of many sorts—humor, anger, pain, terror, and love. "Her poetry focuses on the primacy of the image rather than the 'issues' which surround it," observed Leavitt, "and her best work exhibits a lyrical acuity which is both purifying and redemptive."

Examples of this "primacy of the image" are displayed in *The Father,* a collection of poems about the death of Olds's father from cancer. While her alcoholic and distant father played a role in many of Olds's earlier poems, here he is the central concern. The author describes his illness, final days, and death in a series of graphic, narrowly focused poems. Writing in *Belles Lettres,* Lee Upton remarked that the collection "amounts to something close to a spiritual ordeal for the reader, for the poems are wrenching in their candor and detail." *American Book Review* contributor Steve

Kowit stated: "As a coherent sequence of poems, *The Father* has a most uncommon power—impelling the reader forward with the narrative and dramatic force of a stunning novel." Commenting on the collection's tight focus, Lisa Zeidner in the *New York Times Book Review* noted that "the deliberate tunnel vision is the book's originality and its liability." Clair Willis of the *Times Literary Supplement* came to a similar conclusion about the book, commenting: "The volume as a whole is a risky undertaking, nearly marred simply by offering us too much of the same. Yet finally it works." Upton concluded that *The Father* "is Olds's most important work to date."

Commenting on Olds's achievements in her several volumes of verse, Kowit noted that the poet "has become a central presence in American poetry, her narrative and dramatic power as well as the sheer imagistic panache of her work having won her a large following among that small portion of the general public that still reads verse." That popularity has not met with universal approval from the critics, some of whom have felt that her work lacks depth, revels in graphic images, and is narcissistic. "For a writer whose best poems evince strong powers of observation, Olds spends too much time taking her own emotional temperature," maintained Ken Tucker in the *New York Times Book Review.* ". . . Everything must return to the poet—her needs, her wants, her disappointments with the world and the people around her." In the *New Republic,* Adam Kirsch wrote: "Beneath all the surface agitation, all the vulgar language, the programmatically unfeminine sexual bravado, there is a deadening certainty that makes each poem unsurprising. And therefore ultimately consoling: Olds has a devoted and comparatively large following because no reader will ever be brought by any of her poems to question himself."

Other critics have been eager to champion Olds's work. In a *Seattle Times* review of *Blood, Tin, Straw,* Richard Wakefield noted that Olds writes "poetry more faithful to the felt truth of reality than any prose could be." Wakefield added: "Simply to say that Olds portrays a world suffused with love is to trivialize what these poems indisputably earn." *Poetry Flash* reviewer Richard Silberg commended Olds for "taking on subjects not written before, or not written in these ways . . . and the best of these poems have a density of inspiration line by line." In *Booklist,* Donna Seaman concluded that Olds's work is "blessed by the light that shines on each page from the entranced and grateful eyes of her readers."

In an interview with *Salon,* Olds addressed the aims of her poetry. "I think that my work is easy to understand because I am not a thinker. I am not a . . . How can I put it? I write the way I perceive, I guess. It's not really simple, I don't think, but it's about ordinary things—feeling about things, about people. I'm not an intellectual. I'm not an abstract thinker. And I'm interested in ordinary life." She added that she is "not asking a poem to carry a lot of rocks in its pockets. Just being an ordinary observer and liver and feeler and letting the experience get through you onto the notebook with the pen, through the arm, out of the body, onto the page, without distortion."

BIOGRAPHICAL/CRITICAL SOURCES:

BOOKS

Contemporary Literary Criticism, Gale (Detroit), Volume 32, 1985, Volume 39, 1986, Volume 85, 1995.

Contemporary Poets, 6th edition, St. James Press (Detroit), 1996.

Contemporary Women Poets, St. James Press, 1998.

Dictionary of Literary Biography, Volume 120: *American Poets since World War II,* Gale, 1992.

PERIODICALS

Albany Times Union, March 30, 1998.

America, June 30, 1984.

American Book Review, February, 1982; April, 1993, p. 24.

American Poetry Review, September, 1984; September-October, 1987, pp. 31-35; November/December, 1989.

Belles Lettres, fall, 1992, p. 30.

Booklist, October 1, 1999, Donna Seaman, review of *Blood, Tin, Straw,* p. 339.

Nation, October 13, 1984; December, 1992, p. 748.

New Criterion, December, 1999, William Logan, "No Mercy," p. 60.

New Republic, December 27, 1999, Adam Kirsch, "The Exhibitionist," p. 38.

New York Times Book Review, March 18, 1984; March 21, 1993, p. 14; November 14, 1999, Ken Tucker, "Family Ties."

Poetry, June, 1981; January, 1987, p. 231; April, 1994, pp. 39.

Publishers Weekly, November 8, 1993, p. 71; November 27, 1995, p. 65; September 27, 1999, review of *Blood, Tin, Straw,* p. 98.

Seattle Times, January 16, 2000, Richard Wakefield, "Olds' Poems Delve into Depths of Love."

Times Literary Supplement, May 31, 1991, pp. 11-12; July 16, 1993, p. 25.
Voice Literary Supplement, May, 1984.
Women's Review of Books, February, 1984, pp. 16-17.
Yale Review, autumn, 1987, p. 140.

OTHER

Gravity: A Journal of Online Writing, Music and Art, http://www.newtonsbaby.com/gravity/ (spring, 2000), Joy Yourcenar, review of *Blood, Tin, Straw.*
New York State Writer's Institute, http://www.albany.edu/writers-inst/ (November 28, 2000), "Sharon Olds: State Poet 1998-2000."
Poetry Flash, http://www.poetryflash.org/ (February-March, 2000), Richard Silberg, review of *Blood, Tin, Straw.*
Salon, http://www.salon.com/ (July 1, 1996), Charlie Powell, interview with Olds.*

* * *

OVERBYE, Dennis 1944-

PERSONAL: Born June 2, 1944, in Seattle, WA; son of Milan Robert (in business) and Olive (Eikum) Overbye. *Education:* Massachusetts Institute of Technology, B.S., 1966; attended University of California, Los Angeles, 1971.

ADDRESSES: Home—Woodstock, NY. *Agent*—c/o Viking, 375 Hudson St., New York, NY 10014.

CAREER: Essayist and science writer. *New York Times,* New York City, NY, deputy science editor; also worked as an editor for *Discover* and *Sky and Telescope* magazines. New York University, worked as journalism teacher. Also worked as a night watchman and an itinerant eclipse photographer.

AWARDS, HONORS: Science Writing Award, American Institute of Physics, and nominations for National Book Critics' Circle Award, nonfiction category, and *Los Angeles Times* Book Award, science category, all c. 1992, for *Lonely Hearts of the Cosmos.*

WRITINGS:

Lonely Hearts of the Cosmos, HarperCollins (New York, NY), 1991.
Einstein in Love: A Scientific Romance, Viking (New York, NY), 2000.

Contributor to periodicals, including *New York Times Magazine* and *Time.*

SIDELIGHTS: Dennis Overbye, science writer, former *Discover* magazine editor, and contributing essayist to *Time* magazine, told *New York Times Book Review* interviewer Sarah Boxer that he is "in love with hopeless quests and people who are on hopeless quests." Thus, it's not surprising that Overbye chose to write a book about cosmologists. For, as Overbye speculates in the preface to his book, *Lonely Hearts of the Cosmos,* cosmology—the study of the origin and structure of the universe—is a quest fraught with disappointments. "It is probably part of the human condition," Overbye writes, "that cosmologists (or the shamans of any age) always think they are knocking on eternity's door, that the final secret of the universe is in reach. It may also be part of the human condition that they are always wrong. Science, inching along by trial-and-error and by doubt, is a graveyard of final answers."

Lonely Hearts of the Cosmos, Overbye's exploration of the major figures in cosmology and their discoveries, has met with a host of positive reviews from critics. Hollywood has also expressed interest, with Touchstone Pictures purchasing an option to produce a movie based on the book. The positive response to *Lonely Hearts of the Cosmos* stems in part from Overbye's attempt to uncover the hidden appeal of the science. He does this, according to critics, because of his own enthusiasm for the subject and his ability to express this enthusiasm in the writing. "It is a vivid and passionate telling," wrote *New York Times Book Review* contributor James Gleick. Martin Gardner, writing in the *Washington Post Book World,* declared that "Overbye's book . . . is written with such wit and verve that it is hard not to zip through it at one sitting."

Another positive element cited by critics is Overbye's unique approach to the subject. Instead of concentrating solely on the details of the scientist's theories and interpretations, Overbye pays equal attention to the scientists themselves. Gardner noted that *Lonely Hearts of the Cosmos* derives part of its appeal "by stressing the appearances and personalities of the leading combatants" in the field of cosmology. The scientist who figures most prominently in the account is Allan Sandage, a man, Overbye writes in the book, who "has been doing cosmology, trying to solve the universe so much longer than anyone else." In order to depict Sandage and his peers, Overbye spent numerous years in the company of the scientists, attending conventions and observing their work. His portraits of the cosmologists often include elements of their everyday existence—snorkeling in Hawaii, for instance, or enjoying a cocktail—as well as their professional exploits and fierce rivalries. Gleick noted Overbye's relationship to the scientists in the *New York Times Book Review,* concluding that Overbye "likes them and admires them, and through their eyes he has assembled a mostly oral history of their enterprise."

Critics have found that the book, for all of its attention to personalities, also addresses the technical details of the cosmologists' work. *Business Week* reviewer John Carey, for instance, found that there was plenty of scientific substance to *Lonely Hearts of the Cosmos.* "Half of the book's appeal," Carey wrote, "lies in finally getting clear explanations of exotic theories, such as 'inflationary universe' and 'superstrings,' that try to describe why the universe is as it is today."

Summing up the book, Nancy M. Haegel of *Commonweal* declared that Overbye "does illuminate an area of mystery for many nonscientists, as he conveys the sense of wonder and 'wanting to know' that drives scientists." Gleick sounded a similar note. "For his sense of their culture of science," the critic wrote, "—the traditions, the slang, the rivalries, the unwritten rules—Mr. Overbye makes himself a wonderful tour guide."

BIOGRAPHICAL/CRITICAL SOURCES:

BOOKS

Overbye, Dennis, *Lonely Hearts of the Cosmos,* HarperCollins, 1991.

PERIODICALS

Business Week, February 25, 1991, John Carey, review of *Lonely Hearts of the Cosmos,* pp. 16-18.
Commonweal, May 17, 1991, Nancy M. Haegel, review of *Lonely Hearts of the Cosmos,* pp. 340-341.
Kirkus Reviews, August 1, 2000, review of *Einstein in Love,* p. 1103.
Los Angeles Times Book Review, January 13, 1991, p. 1.
New York Review of Books, May 16, 1991, p. 27.
New York Times Book Review, April 21, 1991, James Gleick, review of *Lonely Hearts of the Cosmos,* p. 8.
Publishers Weekly, November 9, 1990, p. 49; September 11, 2000, review of *Einstein in Love,* p. 76.
Washington Post Book World, January 20, 1991, Martin Gardner, review of *Lonely Hearts of the Cosmos,* p. 5.*

* * *

OWEN, Howard (Wayne) 1949-

PERSONAL: Born March 1, 1949, in Fayetteville, NC; son of E. F. and Roxie (Bulla) Owen; married Karen Van Neste (an editor), August 18, 1973. *Education:* University of North Carolina at Chapel Hill, A.B., 1971; Virginia Commonwealth University, M.A., 1981. *Politics:* Liberal. *Avocational interests:* Travel, cooking.

ADDRESSES: *Home*—612 West Franklin St., Apt. 6B, Richmond, VA 23220. *Office—Richmond Times-Dispatch,* P.O. Box 85333, Richmond, VA 23293. *Agent*—Max Gartenberg, 521 Fifth Ave., Suite 1700, New York, NY 10175.

CAREER: *Tallahassee Democrat,* Tallahassee, FL, executive sports editor, 1977-78; *Richmond Times-Dispatch,* Richmond, VA, assistant sports editor, 1978-86, sports news editor, 1986-92, sports editor, 1992-95, deputy managing editor, 1995—; writer. *Military service:* National Guard, 1971-77.

MEMBER: Associated Press Sports Editors Association, Virginia Press Association.

AWARDS, HONORS: Virginia Press Association, writing awards, 1972 and 1973, certificates of merit, 1988 and 1991; North Carolina Press Association, writing awards, 1975 and 1976.

WRITINGS:

Littlejohn, Permanent Press (Sag Harbor, NY), 1992.
Fat Lightning, Permanent Press (Sag Harbor, NY), 1994.
Answers to Lucky, HarperCollins (New York, NY), 1996.
The Measured Man, HarperCollins (New York, NY), 1997.
Harry and Ruth, Permanent Press (Sag Harbor, NY), 2000.

SIDELIGHTS: Howard Owen is a longtime newspaper editor who has also distinguished himself as a novelist. His five published novels—*Littlejohn, Fat Lightning,*

Answers to Lucky, The Measured Man, and *Harry and Ruth*—focus on the lives of ordinary characters in small Southern towns.

Owen's first work, *Littlejohn,* concerns the long, often hard life of a North Carolina farmer. Much of the narrative is composed of recollections as the hero, Littlejohn McCain, ponders his past. Additional narration is supplied by McCain's daughter, who is a professor, and his grandson, an unproductive malcontent. Robert P. Hilldrup, writing in the *Fredericksburg Free Lance-Star,* noted that Owen "sets a good scene and carries it off without beating it to death," and he praised *Littlejohn* as "a good first novel." Another positive response was posted by Ron Carter, who declared in the *Richmond Times-Dispatch* that with *Littlejohn* Owen had managed to produce "a sensitive, finely wrought tale filled with fully imagined characters and rich with the music of Southern speech." *New York Times Book Review* contributor Harry Middleton judged the book "quietly enchanting . . . a heartfelt celebration of the endurance of the human spirit."

In *Fat Lightning* Nancy Chastain is adjusting to life in her husband's hometown of Monacan, Virginia, and trying to deal with his eccentric family. Uncle Lot, for example, believes he has seen a vision of Jesus Christ on the side of his barn; a local black preacher wants to start a new church around his vision. Brian McCombie, reviewing the novel for *Booklist,* found that "heavy-handed symbols intrude, but a good read overall." The *Kirkus Reviews* contributor described *Fat Lightning* as "loopy and darkly comic, if sporadically out of control." Erik Esckilsen of *Entertainment Weekly* felt that Owen's "craftsmanship ignites interest in a place at once hospitable and unwelcoming." The critic for *Publishers Weekly* found the novel to be a "wise, warm and deeply satisfying story."

Answers to Lucky features a reconciliation between twin brothers who have been alienated due to their upraising. Lucky Sweatt contracts polio as a youth, moving his ambitious father to ignore the boy in favor of his healthy brother Tom Ed. When Tom Ed runs for governor years later, the brothers reunite. "The novel's strength," noted Linda Barrett Osborne in the *New York Times Book Review,* "lies in its moving portrait of Lucky and Tom Ed." The story of Lucky, according to the *Publishers Weekly* critic, "gains emotional resonance in Owen's sure evocation of Southern life." According to the critic for *Kirkus Reviews, Answers to Lucky* is "a completely engaging story about the family ties that bind—tight—and the ego-pricking legacy of growing up poor."

Owen's *The Measured Man* tells the story of Walker Fann, an editor at his father's small town newspaper. When local blacks propose construction of a slavery museum, Walker supports the idea while his father opposes it. But Walker is too weak to stand by his beliefs. Robin Nesbitt in *Library Journal* called *The Measured Man* a "well-plotted tale [about] race, family, and small-town dynamics." The critic for *Publishers Weekly* concluded that, in this novel, Owen "invites readers to hold up a yardstick to their own lives to calculate how far their adult behavior has strayed from the idealism of their youth."

An elderly couple is the focus of *Harry and Ruth,* Owen's fifth novel. Harry and Ruth fell in love in 1942, but Harry was unable to marry her because of their religious differences. He marries a Jewish girl instead, leaving Ruth pregnant with their daughter. Late in life, the couple try to tie up the loose ends of their lives and reconcile with their emotionally damaged daughter. The *Kirkus Reviews* critic found *Harry and Ruth* "a complicated drama, told with compassion and humor." The reviewer for *Publishers Weekly* explained that "Owen succeeds in capturing the yearnings of two people who are always aware that they belong together" and praised "Owen's old-fashioned storytelling skills."

Owen once told *CA* that his strengths as a writer are "a good imagination, the discipline and training of twenty-one years of newspapering, and a thorough knowledge of the settings and characters" he writes about. He also told *CA* that he hopes to impart to readers "a feeling that there is something mystical about my characters, even though those characters often have lived what seem to be 'ordinary' lives." In his writing Owen "seeks to celebrate the often-heroic, sometimes-tragic existence of these ordinary people."

BIOGRAPHICAL/CRITICAL SOURCES:

PERIODICALS

American Journal of Psychology, December, 1995, review of *Littlejohn,* p. 1822.

Booklist, June 1, 1994, Brian McCombie, review of *Fat Lightning,* p. 1772; March 1, 1996, Gilbert Taylor, review of *Answers to Lucky,* p. 1123; February 15, 1997, Jennifer Henderson, review of *The Measured Man,* p. 1005.

Entertainment Weekly, September 24, 1993, review of *Littlejohn,* p. 87; November 18, 1994, Erik Esckilsen, review of *Fat Lightning,* p. 101.

Fredericksburg Free Lance-Star, October 24, 1992, Robert P. Hilldrup, review of *Littlejohn.*

Kirkus Reviews, July 15, 1992, review of *Littlejohn;* July 1, 1994, review of *Fat Lightning,* p. 877; January 1, 1996, review of *Answers to Lucky,* p. 19; December 1, 1996, review of *The Measured Man,* p. 1697; June 15, 2000, review of *Harry and Ruth,* p. 825.

Library Journal, March 15, 1993, review of *Littlejohn,* p. 50; July 1, 1994, Thomas L. Kilpatrick, review of *Fat Lightning,* p. 129; February 1, 1997, Robin Nesbitt, review of *The Measured Man,* p. 107.

Los Angeles Times Book Review, October 9, 1994, review of *Littlejohn,* p. 10.

New York Times Book Review, January 17, 1993, Harry Middleton, review of *Littlejohn,* p. 24; September 4, 1994, Mason Buck, review of *Fat Lightning,* p. 16; May 5, 1996, Linda Barrett Osborne, review of *Answers to Lucky,* p. 22; April 27, 1997, David Murray, review of *The Measured Man,* p. 25.

Publishers Weekly, May 30, 1994, review of *Fat Lightning,* p. 34; July 11, 1994, review of *Littlejohn,* p. 76; January 1, 1996, review of *Answers to Lucky,* p. 56; December 9, 1996, review of *The Measured Man,* p. 59; June 26, 2000, review of *Harry and Ruth,* p. 50.

Richmond Times-Dispatch, October 4, 1992, Ron Carter, review of *Littlejohn.*

School Library Journal, August, 1997, Dottie Kraft, review of *The Measured Man,* p. 188.

Virginia Quarterly Review, summer, 1997, review of *The Measured Man,* p. 95.

Washington Post Book World, November 7, 1993, review of *Littlejohn,* p. 11.

P

PAGE, Benjamin I(ngrim) 1940-

PERSONAL: Born September 17, 1940, in Los Angeles, CA; son of Benjamin Markham (a geology professor) and Virginia (a lecturer on current events; maiden name, Ingrim) Page; married Mary Robertson (a teacher and curriculum writer), December 30, 1964; children: Benjamin R., Alexandra C., Timothy M., Eleanor St. J. *Education:* Stanford University, A.B., 1961, Ph.D., 1973; Harvard University, LL.B., 1965, postdoctoral study, 1972-73; postdoctoral study at Massachusetts Institute of Technology, 1972-73.

ADDRESSES: *Agent*—c/o University of Chicago Press, 1427 East 60th St., Chicago, IL 60637.

CAREER: Dartmouth College, Hanover, NH, assistant professor of political science, 1971-73; University of Chicago, Chicago, IL, assistant professor of political science, 1973-77; University of Wisconsin—Madison, associate professor of political science and staff member of Institute for Research on Poverty, 1977-78; University of Chicago, associate professor, 1978-82, professor of political science, 1982-83; University of Texas at Austin, Erwin Professor of Government, beginning in 1983; Northwestern University, Evanston, IL, member of political science faculty. National Opinion Research Center, Chicago, research associate, beginning in 1973; National Election Studies, member of board of overseers, 1975-80.

MEMBER: American Political Science Association, American Economic Association, American Association for the Advancement of Science, American Association for Public Opinion Research, Phi Beta Kappa.

AWARDS, HONORS: *Law Week* Award, Bureau of National Affairs, 1965; fellow, Social Science Research Council, 1972-73; national fellow, Hoover Institution on War, Revolution, and Peace, 1981-82.

WRITINGS:

(With Denis Sullivan and others) *The Politics of Representation,* St. Martin's Press (New York, NY), 1974.

Choices and Echoes in Presidential Elections: Rational Man and Electoral Democracy, University of Chicago Press (Chicago, IL), 1978.

Who Gets What from Government, University of California Press (Berkeley, CA), 1983.

(With Mark Petracca) *The American Presidency,* McGraw (New York, NY), 1983.

(Editor) David T. Canon, *Actors, Athletes, and Astronauts: Political Amateurs in the United States Congress,* University of Chicago Press (Chicago, IL), 1990.

(Editor) Cathie J. Martin, *Shifting the Burden: The Struggle over Growth and Corporate Taxation,* University of Chicago Press (Chicago, IL), 1991.

(With Robert Y. Shapiro) *The Rational Public: Fifty Years of Trends in Americans' Policy Preferences,* University of Chicago Press (Chicago, IL), 1992.

(Editor) Bryan D. Jones, *Reconceiving Decision-making in Democratic Politics: Attention, Choice and Public Policy,* University of Chicago Press (Chicago, IL), 1994.

(With Edward S. Greenberg) *The Struggle for Democracy,* HarperCollins (New York, NY), 1992, abridged edition, 1996.

Who Deliberates? Mass Media in Modern Democracy, University of Chicago Press (Chicago, IL), 1996.

(Editor) David C. King, *Turf Wars: How Congressional Committees Claim Jurisdiction,* University of Chicago Press (Chicago, IL), 1997.

(Editor) Susan Herbst, *Reading Public Opinion: How Political Actors View the Democratic Process,* University of Chicago Press (Chicago, IL), 1998.

(Editor) Elizabeth Sanders, *The Roots of Reform: Farmers, Workers, and the American State, 1877-1917,* University of Chicago Press (Chicago, IL), 1999.

(With James R. Simmons) *What Government Can Do: Dealing with Poverty and Inequality,* University of Chicago Press (Chicago, IL), 2000.

SIDELIGHTS: In *Choices and Echoes in Presidential Elections: Rational Man and Electoral Democracy,* Benjamin I. Page examines the foundations of the U.S. system of electoral politics and attempts to explain why it falls short in fulfilling its democratic promises. Supported by data providing information on the American electorate, political candidates, and political parties, the author "makes breathtakingly clear how extraordinarily narrow [the voters'] 'choices' really are," noted reviewer Dean Burnham in the *New Republic.* "All this reflects the underlying reality of American politics, past and present," the critic continued, "an uncontested hegemony of Lockian-liberal ideas in the political arena, and an uncontested hegemony of corporate capitalism as the dominant socioeconomic form of American life."

Burnham pronounced Page's study "a rich little book, . . . primarily written for a scholarly audience." "But it would be a mistake to assume that *Choices and Echoes* is of interest only to specialists," he added. "The use of data in this book is sound, the inferences and conclusions are shrewd, accurate and realistic. . . . This book is an important contribution to the existing literature on American electoral politics. There are too few studies that attempt seriously to think through the implications of empirical data on attitudes and campaigns for the state of democracy in the United States. Page's conclusions are profoundly disturbing, but not more so than the condition of the subjects supports."

In *Who Gets What from Government,* Page explores the U.S. tax system and federal spending programs. Condensing numerous studies that reveal the effect of government action on income distribution, the author presents a fiscal program that is "anti-poor," with a welfare system that provides a minimum level of existence for the needy without addressing the extreme inequalities in wealth that exist between citizens. Peter H. Schuck commented in the *Washington Post Book World* that Page "has somehow managed to extract useful and important insights, synthesizing them in ways that respect the subject's great complexity and uncertainty while being accessible to any serious reader."

Writing in a *New York Times Book Review* critique, Harold L. Wilensky observed that in *Who Gets What from Government* "Mr. Page's bias is certainly not hidden": he "brings to his debate a passion for equality." "[His] arguments for equality are traditional," the critic continued. "Extreme inequalities of income or wealth undermine the values of order and stability, communal harmony, liberty, self-fulfillment and equal opportunity. Extreme inequalities reduce the overall happiness of mankind." While Wilensky disagreed with some of Page's data interpretations and questioned many of his essential arguments, the reviewer did admit that the author's study "is ambitious, careful, clearly written and packed with provocative generalizations."

More convinced by the discussions in *Who Gets What from Government* was *New Republic* editor Jack Beatty, who called the book "a model of objective reasoning and tight argument; you couldn't put a communion wafer between the evidence and the conclusions." The critic noted particularly the author's assertion that "the narrower income gap between rich and poor prevailing in other industrial democracies shows that more equality is possible without sacrificing economic efficiency." "This book contains every economic fact and figure you are ever likely to want to know," he added. Schuck remarked that, while Page's arguments for greater equality in income distribution are "neither novel nor conclusive, his agenda for reform familiar," the author "makes an extremely valuable contribution" in bringing the discussion forward. "Perfect equality will always elude imperfect men and women," the critic reflected. "But surely it is not utopian to suggest that we can do better than we have done up until now."

Page once told *CA:* "My main aim is to learn and teach about how politics works, especially about relationships between government and ordinary citizens: what citizens get from government; how government does or doesn't respond to their desires; how those desires are formed. While enjoying this work, I hope to make a contribution to improving politics as well."

BIOGRAPHICAL/CRITICAL SOURCES:

PERIODICALS

American Political Science Review, December 1, 1997, review of *Who Deliberates?,* p. 972.

Annals of the American Academy of Political and Social Science, July, 1999, Gerald M. Kosicki, review of *Who Deliberates?,* p. 217.

Choice, May, 2001, D. R. Imig, review of *What Government Can Do,* p. 1693.

Commonweal, October 23, 1992, William G. Mayer, review of *The Rational Public,* p. 21; February 23, 2001, W. Shepherdson Abell, review of *In Government We Trust,* p. 22.

Critical Review, fall, 1998, review of *Who Deliberates?,* p. 529.

Journal of American History, September, 1993, Melvin Small, review of *The Rational Public,* p. 738.

Kirkus Reviews, August 15, 2000, review of *What Government Can Do,* p. 1175.

Library Journal, October 1, 2000, Stephen L. Hupp, review of *What Government Can Do,* p. 126.

New Republic, March 3, 1979; March 28, 1983.

New York Times Book Review, August 21, 1983.

Political Science Quarterly, spring, 1998, review of *Who Deliberates?,* p. 140.

Public Opinion Quarterly, winter, 1993, Stanley Feldman, review of *The Rational Public,* p. 612.

Washington Post Book World, August 7, 1983.*

* * *

PARRISH, Patt
See BUCHEISTER, Patt

* * *

PATENT, Dorothy Hinshaw 1940-

PERSONAL: Born April 30, 1940, in Rochester, MN; daughter of Horton Corwin (a physician) and Dorothy Kate (Youmans) Hinshaw; married Gregory Joseph Patent (a professor of zoology), March 21, 1964; children: David Gregory, Jason Daniel. *Education:* Stanford University, B.A., 1962; University of California, Berkeley, M.A., 1965, Ph.D., 1968; also studied at Friday Harbor Laboratories, University of Washington, 1965-67. *Avocational interests:* Gardening, cooking, hiking.

ADDRESSES: Home—5445 Skyway Dr., Missoula, MT 59804.

CAREER: Writer. Sinai Hospital, Detroit, MI, post-doctoral fellow, 1968-69; Stazione Zoologica, Naples, Italy, post-doctoral researcher, 1970-71; University of Montana, Missoula, faculty affiliate in department of zoology, 1975-90, acting assistant professor, 1977, faculty affiliate in environmental studies, 1995—.

MEMBER: American Institute of Biological Sciences, Authors Guild, Society of Children's Book Writers and Illustrators.

AWARDS, HONORS: The National Science Teachers Association has cited more than forty of Patent's books as outstanding science trade books; Golden Kite Honor Book, Society of Children's Book Writers, 1977, for *Evolution Goes on Every Day,* and Golden Kite Award, 1980, for *The Lives of Spiders;* Notable Book citation, American Library Association, 1982, for *Spider Magic;* Children's Books of the Year list, Library of Congress, 1985, for *Where the Bald Eagles Gather;* Best Books of the Year list, *School Library Journal,* 1986, for *Buffalo: The American Bison Today,* Best Book for Young Adults citation, American Library Association, 1986, for *The Quest for Artificial Intelligence;* Eva L. Gordon Award, American Nature Study Society, 1987, for the body of her work; Books for the Teenage citation, New York Public Library, 1990, for *How Smart Are Animals?;* Best Books of the Year list, *School Library Journal,* and Pick of the Lists, *American Bookseller,* both 1992, and both for *Feathers;* Children's Choice Award, 1994, for *Hugger to the Rescue;* Books for the Teenage citation, New York Public Library, 1994, for *The Vanishing Feast;* AAAS Best Science Books of 1996, for *Biodiversity;* Lud Browman Award for Science Writing, Friends of the Mansfield Library, University of Montana, 1994; Best Children's Books of the Year citations, Bank Street College of Education, 1997, for *Prairies, Children Save the Rainforests,* and *Biodiversity;* Books for Young People Award, *Scientific American,* 1997, for *Pigeons;* AAAS Best Science Books of 1998, for *Apple Trees;* Best Children's Books of the Year, Bank Street College of Education, 1998, for *Back to the Wild* and *Flashy Fantastic Rain Forest Frogs,* and 1999, for *Apple Trees* and *Fire: Friend or Foe;* CBC-IRA Children's Choices selection, 1999, for *Alex and Friends: Animal Talk, Animal Thinking.* Many of Patent's books have also received state nominations and awards and have been chosen as Outstanding Science Trade Books for Children by the National Science Teachers Association.

WRITINGS:

FOR CHILDREN

Weasels, Otters, Skunks, and Their Family, illustrations by Matthew Kalmenoff, Holiday House, 1973.

Microscopic Animals and Plants, Holiday House, 1974.

Frogs, Toads, Salamanders, and How They Reproduce, illustrations by M. Kalmenoff, Holiday House, 1975.

How Insects Communicate, Holiday House, 1975.

Fish and How They Reproduce, illustrations by M. Kalmenoff, Holiday House, 1976.

Plants and Insects Together, illustrations by M. Kalmenoff, Holiday House, 1976.

Evolution Goes on Every Day, illustrations by M. Kalmenoff, Holiday House, 1977.

Reptiles and How They Reproduce, illustrations by M. Kalmenoff, Holiday House, 1977.

The World of Worms, Holiday House, 1978.

Animal and Plant Mimicry, Holiday House, 1978.

(With Paul C. Schroeder) *Beetles and How They Live,* Holiday House, 1978.

Butterflies and Moths: How They Function, Holiday House, 1979.

Sizes and Shapes in Nature: What They Mean, Holiday House, 1979.

Raccoons, Coatimundis, and Their Family, Holiday House, 1979.

Bacteria: How They Affect Other Living Things, Holiday House, 1980.

The Lives of Spiders, Holiday House, 1980.

Bears of the World, Holiday House, 1980.

Horses and Their Wild Relatives, Holiday House, 1981.

Horses of America, Holiday House, 1981.

Hunters and the Hunted: Surviving in the Animal World, Holiday House, 1981.

Spider Magic, Holiday House, 1982.

A Picture Book of Cows, photographs by William Munoz, Holiday House, 1982.

Arabian Horses, Holiday House, 1982.

Germs!, Holiday House, 1983.

A Picture Book of Ponies, photographs by W. Munoz, Holiday House, 1983.

Whales: Giants of the Deep, Holiday House, 1984.

Farm Animals, photographs by W. Munoz, Holiday House, 1984.

Where the Bald Eagles Gather, photographs by W. Munoz, Clarion, 1984.

Baby Horses, photographs by W. Munoz, Dodd, 1985.

Quarter Horses, photographs by W. Munoz, Holiday House, 1985.

The Sheep Book, photographs by W. Munoz, Dodd, 1985.

Thoroughbred Horses, Holiday House, 1985.

Draft Horses, photographs by W. Munoz, Holiday House, 1986.

Buffalo: The American Bison Today, photographs by W. Munoz, Clarion, 1986.

Mosquitoes, Holiday House, 1986.

Maggie: A Sheep Dog, photographs by W. Munoz, Dodd, 1986.

The Quest for Artificial Intelligence, Harcourt, 1986.

Christmas Trees, Dodd, 1987.

All about Whales, Holiday House, 1987.

Dolphins and Porpoises, Holiday House, 1987.

The Way of the Grizzly, photographs by W. Munoz, Clarion, 1987.

Wheat: The Golden Harvest, photographs by W. Munoz, Dodd, 1987.

Appaloosa Horses, photographs by W. Munoz, Holiday House, 1988.

Babies!, Holiday House, 1988.

A Horse of a Different Color, photographs by W. Munoz, Dodd, 1988.

The Whooping Crane: A Comeback Story, photographs by W. Munoz, Clarion, 1988.

Humpback Whales, photographs by Mark J. Ferrari and Deborah A. Glockner-Ferrari, Holiday House, 1989.

Grandfather's Nose: Why We Look Alike or Different, illustrations by Diane Palmisciano, F. Watts, 1989.

Singing Birds and Flashing Fireflies: How Animals Talk to Each Other, illustrations by Mary Morgan, F. Watts, 1989.

Where the Wild Horses Roam, photographs by W. Munoz, Clarion, 1989.

Wild Turkey, Tame Turkey, photographs by W. Munoz, Clarion, 1989.

Looking at Dolphins and Porpoises, Holiday House, 1989.

Looking at Ants, Holiday House, 1989.

Seals, Sea Lions, and Walruses, Holiday House, 1990.

Yellowstone Fires: Flames and Rebirth, photographs by W. Munoz, Holiday House, 1990.

An Apple a Day: From Orchard to You, photographs by W. Munoz, Cobblehill, 1990.

Flowers for Everyone, photographs by W. Munoz, Cobblehill, 1990.

Gray Wolf, Red Wolf, photographs by W. Munoz, Clarion, 1990.

How Smart Are Animals?, Harcourt, 1990.

A Family Goes Hunting, photographs by W. Munoz, Clarion, 1991.

Miniature Horses, photographs by W. Munoz, Cobblehill, 1991.

The Challenge of Extinction, Enslow, 1991.

Where Food Comes From, photographs by W. Munoz, Holiday House, 1991.

African Elephants: Giants of the Land, photographs by Oria Douglas-Hamilton, Holiday House, 1991.

Feathers, photographs by W. Munoz, Cobblehill, 1992.

Places of Refuge: Our National Wildlife Refuge System, photographs by W. Munoz, Clarion, 1992.

Nutrition: What's in the Food We Eat, photographs by W. Munoz, Holiday, 1992.

Pelicans, photographs by W. Munoz, Clarion, 1992.

Cattle: Understanding Animals, photographs by W. Munoz, Carolrhoda, 1993.

Ospreys, photographs by W. Munoz, Clarion, 1993.

Prairie Dogs, photographs by W. Munoz, Clarion, 1993.

Habitats: Saving Wild Places, Enslow, 1993.

Killer Whales, photographs by John K. B. Ford, Holiday House, 1993.

Dogs: The Wolf Within, photographs by W. Munoz, Carolrhoda Books, 1993.

Looking at Penguins, photographs by Graham Robertson, Holiday House, 1993.

Looking at Bears, photographs by W. Munoz, Holiday House, 1994.

Horses: Understanding Animals, photographs by W. Munoz, Carolrhoda, 1994.

Deer and Elk, photographs by W. Munoz, Clarion, 1994.

Hugger to the Rescue, photographs by W. Munoz, Cobblehill, 1994.

The American Alligator, photographs by W. Munoz, Clarion, 1994.

The Vanishing Feast: How Dwindling Genetic Diversity Threatens the World's Food Supply, Harcourt Brace, 1994.

What Good Is a Tail?, photographs by W. Munoz, Cobblehill, 1994.

West by Covered Wagon: Retracing Pioneer Trails, photographs by W. Munoz, Walker, 1995.

Eagles of America, photographs by W. Munoz, Holiday House, 1995.

Return of the Wolf, illustrated by Hared T. Williams, Clarion, 1995.

Why Mammals Have Fur, photographs by W. Munoz, Cobblehill, 1995.

Prairies, photographs by W. Munoz, Holiday House, 1996.

Quetzal: Sacred Bird of the Cloud Forest, illustrated by Neil Waldman, Morrow, 1996.

Biodiversity, photographs by W. Munoz, Clarion, 1996.

Children Save the Rain Forest, photographs by Dan L. Perlman, Cobblehill Books, 1996.

Back to the Wild, photographs by W. Munoz, Harcourt Brace, 1997.

Pigeons, photographs by W. Munoz, Clarion, 1997.

Apple Trees, photographs by W. Munoz, Lerner, 1997.

Flashy Fantastic Rain Forest Frogs, illustrated by Kendahl Jan Jubb, Walker, 1997.

Homesteading: Settling America's Heartland, photographs by W. Munoz, Walker, 1998.

Fire: Friend or Foe, photographs by W. Munoz, Clarion, 1998.

Alex and Friends: Animal Talk, Animal Thinking, photographs by W. Munoz, Lerner, 1998.

Bold and Bright, Black-and-White Animals, illustrated by K. J. Jubb, Walker, 1998.

Mystery of the Lascaux Cave, Benchmark Books, 1998.

Secrets of the Ice Man, Benchmark Books, 1998.

Great Ice Bear: The Polar Bear and the Eskimo, illustrated by Anne Wertheim, Morrow, 1998.

Polar Bear: Sacred Bear of the Ice, illustrated by Anne Wertheim, Morrow, 1998.

In Search of Maiasaurs, Benchmark Books, 1999.

The Incredible Story of China's Buried Warriors, Benchmark Books, 1999.

Lost City of Pompeii, Benchmark Books, 1999.

Treasures of the Spanish Main, Benchmark Books, 1999.

Wild Turkeys, photographs by W. Munoz, Lerner, 1999.

Shaping the Earth, photographs by W. Munoz, Clarion, 2000.

The Bald Eagle Returns, photographs by W. Munoz, Clarion, 2000.

Polar Bears, photographs by W. Munoz, Carolrhoda, 2000.

Slinky, Scaly, Slithery Snakes, illustrated by K. J. Jubb, Walker, 2000.

Horses, photographs by W. Munoz, Lerner, 2001.

Charles Darwin: The Life of a Revolutionary Thinker, Holiday House, 2001.

A Polar Bear Biologist at Work, F. Watts, 2001.

Rescuing the Prairie Bandit, F. Watts, 2001.

FOR ADULTS

(With Diane E. Bilderback) *Garden Secrets,* Rodale Press, 1982, revised and expanded edition published as *The Harrowsmith Country Life Book of Garden Secrets: A Down-to-Earth Guide to the Art and Science of Growing Better Vegetables,* Camden House, 1991.

(With D. E. Bilderback) *Backyard Fruits and Berries,* Rodale Press, 1984.

(With Greg Patent), *A Is for Apple: More than 200 Recipes for Eating, Munching, and Cooking America's Favorite Fruit,* Broadway Books, 1999.

Contributor to gardening and farming magazines. Has also written for *Arizoo, Camas, Falcon, Spider, Storyworks, Horn Book, Writer, Cricket,* and *Missoulian* newspaper. Patent's photographs have appeared in *National Gardening Magazine, Missoulian,* and in many of her children's books.

SIDELIGHTS: Dorothy Hinshaw Patent is a highly acclaimed author of over one hundred science books for young readers. A trained zoologist, Patent has written books in the biological sciences about animals from the horse to the pelican, and has examined ecological challenges in such books as *Biodiversity, Back to the Wild,* and *The Vanishing Feast.* Patent's books are geared at readers from the elementary grades through high school, and are noted for their interpretation of complex topics in concise, spirited, and informal presentations. As Zena Sutherland and May Hill Arbuthnot noted in their *Children and Books,* "Dorothy Patent has become established as an author whose books are distinguished for their combination of authoritative knowledge, detached and objective attitude, and an ability to write for the lay person with fluency and clarity. . . . she communicates a sense of wonder at the complexity and beauty of animal life by her zest for her subject."

"Many writers have known for as long as they can remember that they wanted to write. Not me," Patent noted in *Something about the Author Autobiography Series* (*SAAS*). "I knew that I loved animals, the woods, and exploring, and I always wanted to learn everything possible about something that interested me. But I never yearned to be a writer." Patent remarked that she grew up a tomboy, exploring the terrain around her family's homes in Minnesota and later California with her older brother. She was always more interested in catching tadpoles, playing with toads, and collecting insects than in the more conventional interests shared by girls her age. In fact, Patent remembered having trouble making girl friends in school: "To this day I'm not sure why, but maybe it was because I'd never spent much time with girls and didn't know how to act around them."

When she was in elementary school, Patent received a gift from her mother that turned her general interest in nature into a firm resolve to know all that she could of a specific subject. As a reward for practicing the piano, her mother bought her a pair of golden guppies and she recalled in *SAAS:* "The morning after we bought the fish, I peered into the bowl to check on my new pets. To my surprise, the adult fish weren't alone—three new pairs of eyes stared out at me from among the plants. I couldn't believe this miracle—the female fish had given birth during the night, and now I had five fish instead of two!" Patent's enthusiasm led her to read every book she could about tropical fish and to frequent a special Japanese fish store to learn even more.

Patent's curiosity helped her to excel in school, as did the encouragement of her family. "Learning was highly valued in my family," she commented in *SAAS.* Despite her success academically, she felt like a misfit socially. "I wanted to be like the 'in' crowd . . . ," she recalled. "I admired the girls who became prom queens and cheerleaders. At the time, there was no way I could understand that some of them were living the best part of their lives during high school while the best parts of my life were yet to come and would last much longer." After high school Patent went to nearby Stanford University, one of the few highly rated schools in the nation that was coeducational at the time and had a strong science program. Patent blossomed in college, where her intelligence and intellectual curiosity were valued. Despite a tragedy during her freshman year—the suicide of her roommate—which put her "into a dark emotional frame of mind that lasted the entire four years," she wrote in her autobiographical sketch that she became involved with international folk dancing, made good friends, and had interesting, challenging classes. Many of her classes emphasized writing, and "by the end of my freshman year," she recollected, "I could set an internal switch for a paper of a certain length and write it. I'm sure this discipline and training has helped me in my writing career." After a trip to Europe with a friend, Patent enrolled in graduate school at the University of California at Berkeley, where she met the man she would marry, Greg Patent, a teaching assistant in her endocrinology class.

Patent and her new husband continued their graduate work and post-doctoral research in Friday Harbor, Washington; Detroit, Michigan; and Naples, Italy; settling for a while in North Carolina before moving to Montana. Searching for a job that would allow her to spend time with her two young boys, Patent decided to try writing and, following that age-old advice to write about what one knows best, she picked biology as her subject matter. Though her first two books were not published, one of them piqued the interest of an editor at Holiday House who eventually approached Patent with an idea for a book about the weasel family. Although she knew next to nothing about weasels, Patent agreed to write the book, *Weasels, Otters, Skunks and Their Family.* She spent hours doing research at the University of Montana library in Missoula, and received help from a professor at the university who happened to be one of the world's experts on weasels. Reviewing this debut volume in *Appraisal,* Heddie Kent found the book to be "fascinating and comprehensive." "[Patent's] style of writing is relaxed and enjoyable," noted a critic for *Science Books,* who also found *Weasels, Otters, Skunks, and Their Family* to be a "highly interesting, readable and informative book."

Patent soon developed a pattern of careful research and organization that allowed her to write first one, then two, then three books a year. "Each book was a review," she explained in *SAAS,* "in simple language, of everything known up to that time about the subject. I chose most of the subjects myself, and they were the things that had interested me as a child—frogs, tropical fish, reptiles, butterflies." Her 1977 title, *Evolution Goes on Every Day,* and her 1980 book, *The Lives of Spiders,* were both honored by the Society of Children's Book Writers; the former title received recognition as a Golden Kite Honor Book, and the latter won the Golden Kite Award. Reviewing *The Lives of Spiders* in *Science Books and Films,* Roy T. Cunningham called it "remarkable" for "retaining a high level of scholarship and breadth of coverage" with a "minimum of esoteric vocabulary."

In the early 1980s Patent began to work with photographer William Munoz, whose name she found in a Missoula newspaper. The two would travel together to photograph the animals for a book, and became a successful team. The first few books that Patent wrote with the help of Munoz allowed her to stay in Montana, but her desire to write books on grizzly bears, whooping cranes, and wolves soon took them to Alaska, New Mexico, Texas, and other states. *Pelicans,* a 1992 addition to Patent and Munoz's collaborative efforts, is exemplary of the tone and format of much of their work together. "The book has a well-organized text with clear, crisp, full-color photos and a thorough index," noted Susan Oliver in a *School Library Journal* review. Oliver called *Pelicans* a "high-quality nature-book on an endearing clown of a bird."

Dogs of all sorts get a similar treatment in several further titles. In *Dogs: The Wolf Within,* Patent "explores selective breeding," according to *Booklist*'s Deborah Abbott, "explaining how various types of dogs have been developed to accommodate people." From Greyhounds to Border collies, Patent explores a wide variety of such breeds in a "must" book for "dog lovers and science enthusiasts," Abbott wrote. Betsy Hearne, writing in *Bulletin of the Center for Children's Books,* commented that this "author-artist team's experience with books on various species makes for a smooth production as they coordinate appealing full-color photographs with facts on the origin, domestication, behavioral characteristics, and training potential of dogs." The Newfoundland breed came into focus in *Hugger to the Rescue,* another collaborative effort with Munoz that looks at the training of Newfoundlands as rescue dogs, and at one dog in particular, Hugger. Carol Kolb Phillips, reviewing the book in *School Library Journal,* paid special attention to Patent's "conversational, anecdote-filled narrative," and to Munoz's "attractive and informative" full-color photographs. A distant relative of dogs inspired Patent to create a work of fiction in *Return of the Wolf,* which tells the story of one lone wolf, Sedra, who is forced to leave her pack, then finds a mate, and has pups to begin to form a pack of her own. "Patent entirely resists anthropomorphism," commented Roger Sutton in *Bulletin of the Center for Children's Books,* "finding drama in the instinctive drives . . . that shape a wolf's life rather than in New Age sentimentality."

Horses are also dear to Patent's heart, and she has written about them in several volumes, including *Where the Wild Horses Roam* and *Horses.* Reviewing *Horses,* a contributor to *Appraisal* noted that "Patent has written a horse book that is a good read for pleasure or a source of information for reports." Deer, elk, eagles, bears, even pigeons and apples have received the collaborative treatment of Patent and Munoz. In *Looking at Bears* "Patent and Munoz have once again combined their talents to produce a stunning book about animals," wrote a reviewer for *Appraisal.* "The text is clear and straightforward, the format uncluttered, and on almost every page is a striking photograph of bears."

Reviewing *Pigeons* in *Booklist,* Carolyn Phelan noted, "This informative book offers a well-researched and readable text illustrated with clear, full-color photographs." Phelan found that the "most surprising chapter" dealt with studies of pigeon intelligence in which trained birds have been able to tell the difference between a Monet and a Picasso painting. "This excellent addition to science collections will make readers come away with a new respect for this common bird," Phelan concluded. Turning her skills to the plant kingdom, Patent has also written about America's most popular fruit in *Apple Trees,* a description of the life cycle of the apple from seed to fruit. A writer for *Kirkus Reviews* noted, "Crisp, full-color photographs highlight all phases of tree and apple growth, coupled with clear, detailed drawings that explain more difficult concepts and processes."

Working with Munoz and other illustrators, Patent has produced many books dealing with individual topics of evolutionary change and adaptation in animals. *Feathers* looks at the role of those quilled projections in flight, insulation, and camouflage in a "captivating volume" with "fact-filled pages" that is a "nonfiction bonanza," according to *Booklist*'s Abbott. Luvada Kuhn commented in *Voice of Youth Advocates,* "This small book with its handy little index will be a useful tool for the student in natural history or anyone with an interest in birds." In *What Good Is a Tail?,* Patent and Munoz teamed up "on another winning book . . . with a lively text, appealing color photographs, and intriguing science facts showing just how useful a tail can be," according to a writer for *Kirkus Reviews.* The two also worked together to determine *Why Mammals Have Fur,* an "eye-catching book . . . well designed with clear color photographs," according to a reviewer for *Appraisal.* Working with Kendahl Jan Jubb as illustrator, Patent has taken a look at animal adaptation in *Flashy Fantastic Rain Forest Frogs* and at coloration in *Bold and Bright, Black-and-White Animals.* Reviewing the former title, a writer for *Kirkus Reviews* called it a "beautiful concise look at a surprisingly varied subject." In the latter title, Patent turns her attention to fourteen animals, such as the skunk and zebra, that come in black and white and explains why. Reviewing *Bold and Bright* in *Booklist,* Shelley Townsend-Hudson noted, "There is so much to enjoy and learn in this beautiful book. . . . It's a standout and an outstanding book." And animal intelligence is explored in *Alex and Friends,* "a fascinating discussion," according to Elizabeth S. Watson writing in *Horn Book Guide.*

Becoming increasingly concerned with the plight of wildlife, Patent remarked in her autobiographical sketch that "wild things always seem to lose out in today's world. . . . We need to realize that we are part of nature, that without nature, we are not whole." To aid in such a realization, Patent has written a number of books dealing with issues of preservation, endangered species, and ecology. In *Places of Refuge* she takes a look at the National Wildlife Refuge System, while in *The Challenges of Extinction* she examines the impact of plant and animal extinction. Habitat preservation and restoration is the theme of *Habitats: Saving Wild Places,* a "brief but effective introduction," as a contributor to *Kirkus Reviews* noted, and in *The Vanishing Feast* Patent tackles the threat to the world's food supplies caused by the reduction of genetic diversity. This issue is further explored in her *Biodiversity,* a science book that is "both illuminating and inspiring," according to *Horn Book*'s Margaret A. Bush.

With *Back to the Wild,* Patent relates the successful return of animals to the wild, and in *Children Save the Rain Forest* she tells of the efforts of children around the world to raise enough money to buy a 42,000-acre tract of rain forest in Costa Rica.

Patent has also ventured into more historical and archaeological realms in such books as *West by Covered Wagon* and *Homesteading,* and also a group of books for the "Frozen in Time" series, including *In Search of Maiasaurs, Mystery of the Lascaux Cave, Secrets of the Ice Man, The Lost City of Pompeii,* and *The Incredible Story of China's Buried Warriors.* Reviewing the last two titles in *Booklist,* Hazel Rochman noted that the books "combine dramatic history with fascinating information." Such information comes in the form of text, time-lines, and a magazine-style design that "will encourage browsing," Rochman also remarked.

The majority of Patent's books, however, explain the history, breeding, growth, and habits of various groups of animals, and have been widely praised for their clarity, thoroughness, and readability. Whether she is describing worms or whales, Patent's works appeal to students of all ages, from the bright eight-year-old to the curious high school student. She may use difficult vocabulary, but she explains the words used and often supplies a helpful glossary. Also, humorous examples of strange animal behavior and vivid pictures frequently combine to make her books more interesting than the ordinary textbook.

Patent concluded in *SAAS:* "I hope that my writing can help children get in touch with the world of living things and realize how dependent we are on them, not just on the wild world but on domesticated plants and animals as well. We owe our existence to the earth, and it is the balance of nature that sustains all life; we upset that balance at our peril. I believe that well-informed children can grow up into responsible citizens capable of making the wise but difficult decisions necessary for the survival of a livable world. I plan to continue to write for those children, helping to provide them with the information they will need in the difficult but exciting times ahead."

BIOGRAPHICAL/CRITICAL SOURCES:

BOOKS

Authors of Books for Young People, 3rd edition, edited by Martha Ward and others, Scarecrow Press, 1990.

Children's Literature Review, Volume 19, Gale (Detroit, MI), 1990, pp. 147-166.

Sixth Book of Junior Authors and Illustrators, edited by Sally Holmes Holtze, H. W. Wilson, 1989.

Something about the Author Autobiography Series, Volume 13, Gale (Detroit, MI), 1991, pp. 137-154.

Sutherland, Zena, and May Hill Arbuthnot, *Children and Books,* seventh edition, Scott, Foresman (Chicago), 1986.

PERIODICALS

Appraisal: Science Books for Young People, fall, 1974, Heddie Kent, review of *Weasels, Otters, Skunks, and Their Family,* p. 33; winter, 1976, p. 33; spring, 1979, pp. 47-48; winter, 1980, pp. 45-46; winter, 1982, p. 52; fall, 1983, p. 52; spring, 1985, p. 32; winter, 1987, pp. 55-56; spring, 1988, p. 28; fall, 1989; winter, 1993, pp. 38-40; spring, 1994, review of *Horses,* pp. 76-77; spring, 1995, review of *Looking at Bears,* p. 46; autumn, 1995, review of *Why Mammals Have Fur,* p. 36; winter, 1996, pp. 46-47; summer, 1996, p. 27; spring, 1999, p. 44.

Booklist, June 15, 1987; May 15, 1989; March 15, 1990; June 1, 1991; May 15, 1992, Deborah Abbott, review of *Feathers,* p. 1680; June 1, 1993, D. Abbott, review of *Dogs: The Wolf Within,* p. 1826; February 1, 1997, p. 943; September 1, 1997, Carolyn Phelan, review of *Pigeons,* p. 120; September 1, 1998, Shelley Townsend-Hudson, review of *Bold and Bright, Black-and-White Animals,* pp. 122-23; November 15, 1998, pp. 488, 584; December 1, 1999, p. 699; February 1, 2000, Hazel Rochman, review of *The Incredible Story of China's Buried Warriors* and *Lost City of Pompeii;* March 15, 2000, Gillian Engberg, review of *Shaping the Earth,* p. 1373; October 15, 2000, Randy Meyer, review of *The Bald Eagle Returns,* p. 433; December 1, 2000, Carolyn Phelan, review of *Slinky, Scaly, Slithery Snakes,* p. 716.

Bulletin of the Center for Children's Books, November, 1991; February, 1993, p. 187; July-August, 1993, Betsy Hearne, review of *Dogs: The Wolf Within,* pp. 355-56; July, 1995, Roger Sutton, review of *Return of the Wolf,* p. 394; October, 1996, p. 71; September, 1997, p. 23; December, 1998, p. 141.

Horn Book, October, 1973; April, 1978; October, 1979; February, 1980; October, 1981, Sarah Gagne, review of *Horses and Their Wild Relatives,* pp. 558-559; January-February, 1995, p. 70; July-August, 1995, p. 481; January-February, 1997, Margaret A. Bush, review of *Biodiversity,* p. 78; January-February, 1999, p. 84.

Horn Book Guide, spring, 1999, Elizabeth S. Watson, review of *Alex and Friends,* p. 107.

Kirkus Reviews, February 15, 1993, review of *Habitats,* p. 233; January 1, 1994, review of *What Good Is a Tail?,* p. 73; January 15, 1997, review of *Flashy Fantastic Rain Forest Frogs,* p. 144; February 1, 1998, review of *Apple Trees,* pp. 199-200.

School Library Journal, February, 1977, p. 67; March, 1979, p. 150; February, 1980, p. 71; February, 1981, p. 77; November, 1984, p. 127; October, 1985, p. 186; August, 1987, p. 87; August, 1988, p. 91; January, 1989; March, 1990; December, 1992, Susan Oliver, review of *Pelicans,* p. 126; February, 1993, p. 102; July, 1993, p. 32; June, 1994, p. 141; July, 1994, Carol Kolb Phillips, review of *Hugger to the Rescue,* p. 97; July, 1995, p. 79; March, 1997, p. 180; April, 1998, p. 122; March, 1999, p. 226; October, 1999, p. 174; March, 2000, Andrew Medlar, review of *The Incredible Story of China's Buried Warriors,* p. 260; April, 2000, John Peters, review of *Shaping the Earth,* p. 154; July, 2000, Michele Snyder, review of *Polar Bears,* p. 96; November, 2000, Ellen Heath, review of *The Bald Eagle Returns,* p. 174; March, 2001, Karey Wehner, review of *Slinky, Scaly, Slithery Snakes,* p. 240.

Science Books: A Quarterly Review, May, 1974, review of *Weasels, Otters, Skunks, and Their Family,* p. 76.

Science Books and Films, September-October, 1981, Roy T. Cunningham, review of *The Lives of Spiders,* p. 21.

Voice of Youth Advocates, June, 1992, Luvada Kuhn, review of *Feathers,* pp. 131-32.

OTHER

Dorothy Hinshaw Patent Web site, http://www.dorothyhinshawpatent.com/ (May 24, 2001).

* * *

PAULIN, Thomas Neilson 1949-
(Tom Paulin)

PERSONAL: Born January 25, 1949, in Leeds, Yorkshire, England. *Education:* Hull University (first-class honors), B.A.; Lincoln College, Oxford University, B.Litt., 1973.

ADDRESSES: *Office*—Hertford College, Catte Street, Oxford OX1 2JD, England.

CAREER: Poet, biographer, and literary critic. University of Nottingham, Nottingham, England, lecturer in English, 1972—; Hertford College, Oxford University, Oxford, England, G. M. Young Lecturer in English Literature. Co-founder of Field Day Theatre Co., Londonderry, Northern Ireland.

AWARDS, HONORS: Eric Gregory Award, 1976, for poetry; Somerset Maugham Award, 1978, for poetry; Geoffrey Faber Memorial Prize, with Paul Muldoon, 1982; University of Virginia, Fulbright scholar, 1983-84.

Thomas Neilson Paulin

WRITINGS:

ALL UNDER NAME TOM PAULIN

POETRY

Theoretical Locations, Ulsterman (Belfast), c. 1975.
A State of Justice, Faber (London), 1977.
Personal Column, Ulsterman, 1978.
The Strange Museum, Faber (Boston), 1980.
The Book of Juniper, drawings by Noel Connor, Bloodaxe (Newcastle upon Tyne), 1981.
Liberty Tree, Faber, 1983.
Fivemiletown, Faber, 1987.
(Editor) *The Faber Book of Vernacular Verse,* Faber, 1990.
Seize the Fire: A Version of Aeschylus's Prometheus Bound, Faber, 1990.
Minotaur: Poetry and the Nation State, Harvard University Press, 1992.
Selected Poems, 1972-1990, Faber, 1993.
Walking a Line, Faber (London), 1994.
The Wind Dog, Faber, 1999.

EDITOR

(With Peter Messent) *Selected Tales: Henry James,* Biblio Distribution, 1982.
The Faber Book of Political Verse, Faber (Boston), 1986.
(With Ian Dury and Fanny Dubes) *Hard Lines Three,* Faber, 1987.
The Faber Book of Vernacular Verse, Faber, 1990.

OTHER

Thomas Hardy: The Poetry of Perception (criticism), Rowman Littlefield (Totowa, NJ), 1975.
A New Look at the Language Question (pamphlet) Field Day, 1983.
(With Seamus Heaney) *Seamus Heaney and Tom Paulin* (sound recording), Faber (London), 1983.
Ireland and the English Crisis (essays), Bloodaxe, 1984.
The Riot Act: A Version of Sophocles' Antigone (play; first produced in Belfast at Lyric Theater in 1984), Faber, 1985.
Minotaur: Poetry and the Nation State (criticism), Harvard University Press (Cambridge, MA), 1992.
Writing to the Moment: Selected Critical Essays, 1980-1996, Faber, 1996.
The Day-Star of Liberty: William Hazlitt's Radical Style (criticism), Faber, 1998.

WORK IN PROGRESS: A study of eighteenth-century British novelist Daniel Defoe.

SIDELIGHTS: Born in England but raised in Belfast, Northern Ireland, Tom Paulin "has emerged as one of the most interesting of an important group of Ulster poets whose work has been published against the background of political violence in Northern Ireland," according to P. R. King in his critical survey, *Nine Contemporary Poets.* Though often compared with other contemporary Irish poets, Paulin has distinguished himself with the forthright political inclination of his writings. "Distanced alike from the earth-dank pieties of a Seamus Heaney and the airy allusiveness of a Paul Muldoon," Terry Eagleton noted in the London *Observer,* "Tom Paulin's poetry embraces the austere, clear-eyed republican virtues of the Ulster enlightment."

In much of his poetry, included in such collections as *A State of Justice, The Strange Museum, Liberty Tree,* and *Fivemiletown,* Paulin laments the political separation of Northern Ireland—a part of the United Kingdom—from the independent Republic of Ireland to the south. Although he was raised a Protestant, Paulin supports religious freedom and tolerance for the oppressed Catholic population, and in his essay collection, *Ireland and the English Crisis,* Paulin envisions a unified, nonsectarian Irish republic.

Many of the poems in Paulin's first widely read volume, *A State of Justice,* concern the practice in Northern Ireland of retributive justice, which Paulin considers "terrifying, both as an idea and in practice," as John Haffenden quoted him in *Dictionary of Literary Biography.* "When it's institutionalized," Paulin explains, "it can seem to reproduce the cruel state of nature it's supposed to supersede." In *A State of Justice,* the poet wonders "whether it is possible to achieve a humane peace in a country like Ulster without the imposition of force by the state," wrote Anne Stevenson in the *Listener.* "His answer is mostly a grim 'no,' but still he keeps the question open."

Although the poems in *A State of Justice* are set mainly in Northern Ireland or the divided Irish province of Ulster, according to P. R. King, "the themes of the poems have a more universal significance than this localized subject matter might suggest." Commencing as simple descriptions, the poems "develop into an exploration of personal and social states of being, often ending in an image that expresses that state with almost symbolic force." While recognizing the powerful imagery, however, King described Paulin's writing style as "usually deliberately low-keyed." Stevenson likewise noted the poet's "laconic tone" and his "command of subtlety and allusion." Though admitting that Paulin's stylistic restraint renders some poems difficult to understand, she declared that it can also produce "masterpieces of understatement" like the poems "Provincial Narratives" and "A Traveller." Stevenson particularly commended Paulin's articulation of "the nuances of class distinction. His best poems suggest that the differences between the rich and poor in Ireland can be taken as an allegory of the relationship between England and Ireland itself." The reviewer concluded, "Perhaps a stoic, unrhetorical approach to the tragedy of Ireland is the right one for the temperament of a British audience."

Paulin's subtlety gives way to liveliness in *The Strange Museum* and *Liberty Tree.* "The poet's imagination has become more challenging, his language more energetic" than in previous works, Haffenden asserted. Although they continue to address the problems of political and religious tension in Northern Ireland, John Bayley explained in the *Times Literary Supplement,* the poems in *The Strange Museum* "make light of the darkness out of which they come; they are sardonic, even graceful." Such an attitude is, according to Bayley, "the tone that our culture adopts as it tries to extricate itself from an inextricable situation." Unable to accept Northern Ireland's political condition, wrote Andrew Motion in *New Statesman,* Paulin continually "tackles the vulnerability of idealism, the resilience of hope, and the danger to human nature of purely functional pragmatism. It's not often that contemporary British poets treat these things at all—let alone with such serious good sense." The reviewer added, "The scale of its ambitions, and the intelligence with which they are fulfilled, make [*The Strange Museum*] a continuously exciting book."

Liberty Tree, which includes selections from the earlier *Book of Juniper,* attempts to interpret Irish cultural identity through various analogies. In "What Kind of Formation Are the B Specials?" Paulin compares Northern Ireland's troubles with those of Poland, and in other poems he delineates a relationship between politics and art. "Paulin is not so much drawing parallels as identifying correspondences, seeking to use one situation to reach some kind of understanding of the other," explained Donald Campbell in *British Book News,* adding, "This kind of technique has almost endless possibilities, making for an absorbing, demanding poetry, never completely accessible, often infuriatingly difficult, but always more than worthy of attention."

Some critics complained that too much Irish dialect in *Liberty Tree* obscures the meaning of several poems. Denis Donoghue in the *London Review of Books,* for example, claimed that certain terms "require guesswork or a fairly big dictionary: 'fremd' means strange, unfriendly; I don't recognise 'glubbed', or 'glooby' . . . I didn't understand 'claggy' when Paulin used it in 'A New Look,' and I stumble over it in the poem 'Foot Patrol, Fermanagh' and as 'clagged' in the poem 'Trine.'" Other reviewers, however, agreed with the London *Observer* critic who found the book "wondrously bedecked with arcane words and phrases" and praised Paulin for being "willing to pack a glossary into each of his poems." Michael O'Neill in the *Times Literary Supplement* admired the language in *Liberty Tree* for transcending "compartmentalizing and rhetoric; it concocts an energizing brew of symbol and argument, attenuated lyricism and relished slang." And Donald Campbell, who considered the book "an immensely satisfying collection," maintained simply that "sometimes poetry needs to be obscure."

By contrast, Terry Eagleton in the London *Observer* thought that in Paulin's next book, *Fivemiletown,* "the masonic values of lucidity and crisp design . . . resonate through the pages of this vigorous new collection." Citing as an example the poem, "An Ulster Unionist Walks the Streets of London," Eagleton explained, "A poignant solitariness, the painful or sardonic alienation of the *emigre,* marks the collection all the way from its title." The topics in *Fivemiletown* range from politics and history to art and eroticism. "The book's major offering, 'The Caravans on Lueneberg Heath,'" noted the reviewer, compares the philosophies of seventeenth-century German writers with that of twentieth-century thinker Martin Heidegger. "The tone of this impressive piece, as of the collection as a whole," wrote Eagleton, "is sombre, elegiac, shorn of the brave utopian vision of the earlier 'A Liberty Tree.'"

In his "spirited" 1984 essay collection, *Ireland and the English Crisis,* Patricia Craig in her *Times Literary Supplement* review thought that "Tom Paulin is nothing if not forthright." Critic John Horgan agreed: "Paulin's voice—in poetry as in criticism—is informed, independent, argumentative." Reviewing *Ireland and the English Crisis* in the *London Review of Books,* Horgan noted the gradual evolution of Paulin's political thought as it is demonstrated in the series of essays. Although Paulin initially supported the union between Northern Ireland and England, during the 1980s he began to argue for an independent and nonsectarian Northern Irish republic. "Until that Utopian dream is realised," Mary Holland wrote in the London *Observer,* "he works for a 'fifth province' of the mind, a cultural sanctuary in which Irish artists must try to lay together foundations for a new political reality." Questioning the feasibility of such a state, Horgan commented, "The line between wishful thinking and hard analysis, even in Paulin's lucid and persuasive prose, is sometimes a bit difficult to draw."

Reviewers generally praised the ideas expressed in *Ireland and the English Crisis,* though many complained of incongruities among certain articles. In the essay, "English Now," for example, Paulin argues in favor of teaching only those literary works traditionally accepted in the English canon. "He sees those who would favour broadening the syllabus to include, for example, TV soap operas, as barbarians at the gates," Holland explained. Yet in his "riveting" article, "A New Look at the Language Question," Holland continued, Paulin protests the tradition of Irish and Scottish writers composing only in English, and he complains about how the English language "has been politically institutionalised and [of] the limitations this places on writers who are not English but write in that tongue." These two essays, according to Jennifer Fitzgerald in the *Irish Literary Supplement,* "make their own points validly enough, but they could go much further if their tantalizingly diverse perspectives were integrated and consolidated."

Of the collection as a whole, Fitzgerald wrote: "One receives the strong impression that in bringing together his writing of the last few years, Paulin is reviewing himself, beginning the process of sifting and self-arguing which will eventually lead to an acutely original thesis." The reviewer concluded, "The potential for a whole new cultural critique for Ireland lies within Paulin's reach if he would only reconcile his own contradictions and take a long, hard look at the realities of Irish experience, North and South."

New Statesman & Society contributor John Lucas reviewed Paulin's collection, *Walking a Line.* Lucas said, "His volume takes advantage of opportunities brought about by sophisticated machine typography." Lucas noted that Paulin uses no punctuation except for the parenthetic dash. "You have to read his poems. . . . listening for meaning to emerge through and as stress, intonation, cadence."

D. J. Taylor in *New Statesman* praised *The Day-Star of Liberty: William Hazlitt's Radical Style,* commenting that Paulin's achievement "is to show where the fluid, zestful immediacy of his subject's style came from. The roots are widely located: in 18th-century Unitarian dissent and its philosophers, in 'Irishness,' the Regency republican world of radical autodidacts such as William Hone." Taylor commended Paulin for his observations on Hazlitt's personal life, including his love affair with Sarah Walker that resulted in *Liber Amoris,* "and the interest in the destructive side of human behavior that resulted in some shrewd reflections on the psychology of capital punishment."

"One of the most recognizable features of Paulin's work in *The Wind Dog,* as elsewhere, is its onomatopoeic fizziness and excitability," wrote David Wheatley in *Irish Literary Supplement.* "This is a poetry which delights in refusing us the euphonies of lyric, as programmatically announced in one title, 'Not Musical.'" The art of Marc Chagall is a running theme throughout the collection. Poems that feature Chagall include "Marc Chagall, over the Town," and "The Quinn Brothers," about three brothers who die in a Loyalist bomb attack in 1998. Wheatley called the title poem "a cento made up of scraps of John Clare, Hopkins, MacNeice, and Joyce." Wheatley found the "most satisfying" of the poems to be "Bournemouth," "Odd Surname," "Le Crapaud," "The Utile as Fetish," and "A Naive Risk," describing them as poems "in which Paulin achieves freshness and bite rather than just invoking them from the style-sheet. In the last of these he evokes a 'condition of supremely unillusioned quietism,' to use a phrase he once applied to Derek Mahon, when he imagines 'the last bomb in the whole of Ireland' blowing up a shop but hurting no one."

BIOGRAPHICAL/CRITICAL SOURCES:

BOOKS

Contemporary Literary Criticism, Volume 37, Gale, 1986.

Dictionary of Literary Biography, Volume 40: *Poets of Great Britain and Ireland since 1960,* Gale, 1985.

King, P. R., *Nine Contemporary Poets: A Critical Introduction,* Methuen, 1979.

PERIODICALS

British Book News, October, 1983.

Choice, October, 1992, B. Wallenstein, review of *Minotaur,* p. 301.

Comparative Literature Studies, fall, 1995, Sanford Schwartz, review of *Minotaur,* p. 539.

Irish Literary Supplement, spring, 1985; spring, 2000, David Wheatley, "Billycan Campfire Tinniness," p. 7.

Listener, April 14, 1977, December 5, 1985.

London Review of Books, October 4, 1984; February 7, 1985.

New Statesman, April 4, 1980; November 11, 1983; June 5, 1998, D. J. Taylor, review of *The Day-Star of Liberty,* p. 48.

New Statesman & Society, February 14, 1992, Simon Carnell, review of *Minotaur,* p. 38; July 22, 1994, John Lucas, review of *Walking a Line,* p. 44.

Observer (London), July 3, 1983; January 20, 1985; October 25, 1987.

Spectator, February 1, 1992, Dudley Young, review of *Minotaur,* p. 29; November 23, 1996, James Simmons, review of *Writing to the Moment,* p. 52; July 11, 1998, Paul Foot, review of *The Day-Star of Liberty,* p. 31.

Times Higher Education Supplement, April 3, 1992, Ronald Hayman, review of *Minotaur,* p. 32; April 23, 1993, Martin Fagg, review of *Minotaur,* p. 10; June 17, 1994, John Davies, "Notes in the Margin," p. 19; September 18, 1998, Nick Groom, review of *The Day-Star of Liberty,* p. 23.

Times Literary Supplement, April 4, 1980; July 30, 1982; September 2, 1983; October 19, 1984; April 19, 1985; May 23, 1986; March 18, 1988, Hugh Kenner, review of *Fivemiletown,* p. 303; November 9, 1990, Tom Shippey, review of *The Faber Book of Vernacular Verse,* p. 1198; January 24, 1992, Claude Rawson, review of *Minotaur,* p. 19; May 7, 1993, Robert Potts, review of *Selected Poems,* p. 26; July 8, 1994, Lachlan Mackinnon, review of *Walking a Line,* p. 7; July 24, 1998, Paul Keegan, review of *The Day-Star of Liberty,* p. 3; February 25, 2000, Steven Matthews, review of *The Wind Dog,* p. 23.

Virginia Quarterly Review, summer, 1988, Sidney Burris, review of *The Faber Anthology of Political Verse,* p. 546.*

* * *

PAULIN, Tom
See PAULIN, Thomas Neilson

* * *

PAULY, Rebecca M. 1942-

PERSONAL: Born August 30, 1942, in Ashland, OH; daughter of Robert T. (a surgeon) and Virginia S. (a homemaker) Mehl; married Thomas H. Pauly (divorced, September, 1981); married Glenn P. Bentley (a land planner), March, 1985; children: (first marriage) Jeffrey T. Pauly. *Education:* Attended The Sorbonne, University of Paris, L'Institut de Sciences Politiques, and L'Ecole du Louvre, all 1961-62; Smith College, B.A. (cum laude), 1963; University of California, Berkeley, M.A., 1966, doctoral study, 1966-68; Middlebury College, D.M.L., 1984. *Politics:* Democrat. *Religion:* Presbyterian.

ADDRESSES: *Home*—163 East Avondale Rd., West Grove, PA 19390. *Office*—Department of Foreign Languages, 109 Main Hall, West Chester University, West Chester, PA 19383; fax: 610 436 3048. *E-mail*—rpauly@wcupa.edu.

CAREER: Teacher of French at schools in Palo Alto, CA, 1966-67, and Oakland, CA, 1967-70; Newark Center for Creative Learning, Newark, DE, curriculum developer, 1971-74 and 1975-78; Gruppo LePetit, Milan, Italy, teacher of English as a foreign language, 1974-75; French teacher at Tower Hill School in Wilmington,

DE, 1982; University of Delaware, Newark, lecturer, 1982-84, assistant professor of French and Italian, 1984-87; West Chester University, West Chester, PA, assistant professor, 1987-92, associate professor of French and Italian, 1992-96, professor of French and Italian, 1996—, coordinator of French section, 1989—, graduate advisor and coordinator, 1995—. Guest lecturer at Salisbury State University and University of North Carolina at Charlotte, both 1992. Winterthur Museum, senior guide, 1976-81.

MEMBER: American Association of Teachers of Italian (AATI), American Association of Teachers of French (AATF), Literature/Film Association (vice president, 1989-91, president, 1995-97), GKA Italian National Honor Society, Abbe Society (honorary member).

WRITINGS:

Le Berceau et la bibliothèque, Stanford French and Italian series, Volume 62, 1989.

The Transparent Illusion: Image and Ideology in French Text and Film, Peter Lang Publishing (New York, NY), 1993.

Also wrote "Impossible Dreams" in *The Cinema of Tony Richardson,* Suny Press, 1999. Author and producer of the documentary video series *La civilisation francophone dans le monde.* Contributor of articles and reviews to language, literature, film, and history journals. Editor of *Literature/Film Quarterly* and *College Literature,* both 1990—.

WORK IN PROGRESS: Painless French Grammar for People Who Hate Grammar; Painless Italian Grammar for People Who Hate Grammar; documentary video *Un mese in Italia.*

SIDELIGHTS: Rebecca M. Pauly told *CA:* "I have traveled to other countries all my life, and I have pursued a variety of interests in other peoples and their cultures during my professional career. First and foremost an anthropologist, I have studied material culture and art history, worked on a museum staff for a decade, and integrated my study and interest in art into my language research and teaching, combining literature, film, and art criticism. My articles on Sartre, Balzac, and Federico da Montefeltro (the fifteenth-century Duke of Urbino and fabled *condottiere*) demonstrate my ongoing research into the relationship between language and many types of icons, in a multicultural approach decoding the literal and pictorial. This type of interdisciplinary work led me to write on sources and structures of the autobiographic character in French literature in *Le Berceau et la bibliotheque* and on image and ideology in French text and film in *The Transparent Illusion.* This latter work pursues the evolution from the 'transparency' of documentary filmmaking to the 'opacity' of modernist self-reflexive works, ultimately connecting them through the production of artists like Resnais, Duras, and Robbe-Grillet. More recently, I produced my own documentary video series on francophone cultures around the globe and am preparing a second series on Italy. My primary concern is the relationship between the literary text, the film text, and other material icons of cultural identity, and the rapidly changing contexts of communication, particularly in technology."

* * *

PIERCE, Patricia Jobe 1943-

PERSONAL: Born May 18, 1943, in Seattle, WA; daughter of Leonard Carl (an oil executive) and Ruth H. (in real estate; maiden name, Baren) Jobe; married Marco Apollo (art consultant/musician); children: Christine Ruth, Matthew Jobe. *Education:* Boston University, B.F.A., 1965, and other studies; attended University of Connecticut, 1965-66; attended Harvard University, 1989-91. *Politics:* Independent. *Religion:* Protestant. *Avocational interests:* Public speaking, stage acting and directing, martial arts instruction, civil rights, environmental protection issues and AIDS research.

ADDRESSES: Office—721 Main St., Hingham, MA 02043. *Agent*—Ken Roberts, 306 West 100th St., New York, NY 10025. *E-mail*—piercegalleries@mediaone.net; fax: 781749-6685.

CAREER: Freelance writer, and owner and director of Pierce Galleries, Inc., 1968—. Has served as an art consultant, historian, and appraiser; a trainer and manager of martial arts world champions; and a public speaker. Literary agent for the Kahlil Gibran estate, 1978—; agent for impressionist painter E. Joseph Fontaine; estate representative for painters William S. Barrett, Anne Carleton, M. S. Pearson, C. F. Ryder, and J. W. S. Cox. Served on the advisory board for the Archives of American Art in New England; co-chair of the rules committee of the national karate championships; member of the Republican Presidential Task Force and the President's Citizen Advisory Committee, 1990-91.

MEMBER: International Society of Poets, National Writer's Union, National Writer's Club, American Film Institute Alumni Association, Appraisers Association of America, World of Poets, People for the American Way, Civil Rights Action Committee, Afro-American Center, Brockton Art Center, Boston Museum of Fine Arts, International Platform Committee, Smithsonian Associates, League of Women Voters, Audubon Society, National Federation for the Preservation of Wildlife, Hingham Historical Society, Karate Referees Association of New England, Massachusetts Chiefs of Police Association, Rock 'n' Roll Hall of Fame (charter member), National Indian Museum.

AWARDS, HONORS: Outstanding Young Woman of America, Washington, DC, 1974; World of Poets, gold and silver poet, 1987, 1988-91; Presidential Medal of Merit, 1990; Presidential Order of Merit awarded by senatorial committee, 1991; citation of historical documentary excellence, El Paso Museum of Art, 1991; Woman of the Year, Biographical Institute, 1991; Presidential Medal of Honor for Patriotism, 1992; Presidential Legion of Honor, 1992; World Peace Recognition Award, 1992, from the International Museum of Peace and Solidarity in the Republic of Uzbekistan, Commonwealth of Independent States.

WRITINGS:

"Tests" (avant-garde play), produced by the National Methodist Conference, 1968.

(With Rolf H. Kristiansen) *John Joseph Enneking: American Impressionist Painter,* Pierce Galleries (North Abington, MA), 1972.

The Ten: Frank W. Benson, Joseph R. DeCamp, Thomas W. Dewing, Childe Hassam, Willard L. Metcalf, Robert Reid, Edward Simmons, Edmund C. Tarbell, John H. Twachtman, J. Alden Weir, and William Merrit Chase (Who Replaced Twachtman, 1902), with introduction by Richard H. Love, Rumford Press (Concord, NH), 1976.

The Watercolored World of J. W. S. Cox, Pierce Galleries, 1981, *Edmund C. Tarbell and the Boston School of Painting, 1889-1980,* edited by John Douglas Ingraham, Pierce Galleries (Hingham, MA), c. 1980.

Richard Earl Thompson, American Impressionist: A Prophetic Odyssey in Paint, edited by Ingraham, Richard-James Publications (San Francisco, CA), 1982.

Edward Henry Potthast—More than One Man, (international art collection), San Bernadino, CA, 1990.

(And editor and director) *American Impressionist* (documentary film), Finley-Holiday Films, 1991.

The Ultimate Elvis: Elvis Presley Day by Day, Simon and Schuster (New York, NY), 1994.

Love (photographs and text), Fine Arts Books (Ronkonkoma, NY), 2000.

How to Invest and Collect Art in the twenty-first Century, 2001.

Author of art catalogue *The Master's Touch,* R. E. Thompson Gallery, San Francisco, CA, 1990; author of the screenplay *Heads* and the stage play *Secrets;* author of essay "Peace and Solidarity and the First Amendment," 1991; author of introduction, *Jane Peterson, American Impressionist,* J. Joseph (Boston, MA), 1982; contributor of articles to periodicals, including *Nantucket Beacon, Boston Post Gazette, Improper Bostonian, Winthrop News, Journal of the American Medical Association, Art and Antiques, Antique Monthly, Animals, Southwest Art, Karate Illustrated, Art U.S.A., Brockton Daily Enterprise, Patriot Ledger,* and *International Fine Arts Collector;* poetry published in the anthologies *Great Poems of Today,* 1987, and *Best Poems of 1994-95,* 1995.

SIDELIGHTS: Patricia Jobe Pierce is a public speaker, avid researcher, and art consultant-advisor. Her career has been focused on rediscovering and bringing to public attention masterful works executed by internationally recognized and lesser-known American and French painters and sculptors. She is the director of Pierce Galleries, Inc. of Hingham, Massachusetts (1968—), and a freelance writer and art appraiser. She tours the United States lecturing about art, environmental protection, endangered species, civil rights, and the life of Elvis Presley. She has managed the careers of martial artist Billy Blanks (1980s), sculptor Kahlil Gabran (b. 1922) and painters John Kilroy, J. W. S. Cos, Sergio Roffo, Thomas R. Dunlay, and Joseph Fontaine. Her art histories, biographies, plays, and screenplays focus on how past and present behavior and events effect current social, civil rights, and environmental issues. Her 2000 book, *Love,* and her environmental book *They Who Touch the Earth* include Pierce's artistic photography and poetic words of inspiration. In 2001 *How to Invest and Collect Art in the 21st Century* was published and a branch of Pierce Galleries, Inc., opened in Nantucket, Massachusetts.

Pierce showed signs early in life that she would have a distinguished career. She became the first female president of a Los Angeles-area junior high school in 1957. The following year, however, her family moved to

Greenwich, Connecticut; from there she matriculated at Boston University, where she earned a bachelor's degree in fine arts. Her concentration was in acting and directing, and she fully intended to pursue a career in the theater, having acted in various summer stock, off-Broadway, and television productions. Pierce was disillusioned, however, by the sexual harassment she experienced in this field, and abandoned it to start her art gallery in 1968. Previous to this career decision, Pierce had already begun her lifelong social activism, marching with civil rights leader Martin Luther King, Jr.

Pierce's interest in Elvis Presley stems from her social activism, because she sees the famed late singer as a pioneer of self-expression who faced a great deal of censorship at the beginning of his career. *The Ultimate Elvis* is considered to be an authoritative work, including everything from a lengthy discography to a list of Presley's girlfriends. *Publishers Weekly* hailed the book as "an astonishing compendium of factoids," while Ray Olson in *Booklist* blatantly urged his readers: "C'mon, you've got to get it."

BIOGRAPHICAL/CRITICAL SOURCES:

PERIODICALS

Booklist, July, 1994, p. 1913.
Boston Globe, October 27, 1977.
Los Angeles Times, June 20, 1994, p. A19.
Publishers Weekly, June 27, 1994, p. 64.

* * *

PODWAL, Mark 1945-

PERSONAL: Born June 8, 1945, in Brooklyn, NY; son of Milton (a restaurant owner) and Dorothy (a homemaker) Podwal; married Ayalah Siev-or (an artist and jeweler), March, 1977; children: Michael, Ariel. *Education:* Queens College of the City University of New York, B.A., 1967; New York University, M.D., 1970. *Religion:* Jewish.

ADDRESSES: Home—3 Cricklewood Ln., Harrison, NY 10528. *Office*—55 East 73 St., New York, NY 10021. *Agent*—Georges Borchardt, Georges Borchardt, Inc., 136 East 57th St., New York, NY 10022.

CAREER: New York University, New York City, clinical associate professor of dermatology, 1974—. Associate attending physician, Tisch University Hospital and Bellevue Hospital, both 1974—. Artist and illustrator, with work in solo and group exhibitions across the United States; work represented in permanent collections, including Metropolitan Museum of Art, Israel Museum, U.S. Library of Congress, Skirball Museum, and New York City's Jewish Museum. U.S. Memorial Holocaust Museum, member of Committee on Collections and Acquisitions and Committee on Art in Public Spaces. *Military service:* U.S. Army Reserve, 1970-76; became captain.

MEMBER: American Academy of Dermatology (fellow).

AWARDS, HONORS: Award of Excellence, Society of Newspaper Design, 1989, for a drawing in the *New York Times;* decorated chevalier, French Order of Arts and Letters, 1993; Sidney Taylor Award Honor Book, Association of Jewish Libraries, 1996, for *Dybbuk,* 1998, for *You Never Know;* Aesop Prize, American Folklore Society, 1999, Silver Medal, Society of Illustrators, 1999, both for *King Solomon and His Magic Ring;* Washington Irving Children's Choice Award Honor Book, Westchester Library Association, 2000, for *You Never Know.*

WRITINGS:

The Decline and Fall of the American Empire, Darien House, 1971.
Let My People Go: A Haggadah, Macmillan (New York, NY), 1972.
The Book of Lamentations, National Council on Art in Jewish Life, 1974.
Freud's da Vinci, Images Graphiques, 1977.
A Book of Hebrew Letters, Jewish Publication Society, 1977.
Leonardo di Freud, Sperling & Kupfer Editori (Milan, Italy), 1982.
A Jewish Bestiary, Jewish Publication Society, 1985.
The Book of Tens, Greenwillow, 1994.
Golem: A Giant Made of Mud, Greenwillow, 1995.
The Menorah Story, Greenwillow, 1998.

Contributor to periodicals.

ILLUSTRATOR

Paul Simon, *Paul Simon: New Songs,* Knopf (New York, NY), 1975.
Francine Klagsbrun, *Voices of Wisdom,* Pantheon (New York, NY), 1979.

Elie Wiesel, *The Golem,* Summit Books, 1983.

Howard Schwartz, *The Captive Soul of the Messiah,* Schocken (New York, NY), 1983.

The Elie Wiesel Collection, fourteen volumes, Bibliophile Library, 1985-88.

Wiesel, *Six Days of Destruction,* Paulist Press, 1988.

Wiesel, *A Passover Haggadah,* Simon & Schuster (New York, NY), 1993.

A Passover Seder Presented by Elie Wiesel (video), Time Warner (New York, NY), 1994.

Francine Prose, *Dybbuk: A Story Made in Heaven,* Greenwillow, 1993.

Klagsbrun, *Jewish Days,* Farrar, Straus (New York, NY), 1996.

Prose, *The Angel's Mistake: Stories of Chelm,* Greenwillow, 1997.

Prose, *You Never Know: A Legend of the Lamedvavniks,* Greenwillow, 1998.

Wiesel, *Le Golem: Legende d'une legende,* Bibliophane (Paris, France), 1998.

Ileene Smith Sobel, *Moses and the Angels,* introduction by Elie Wiesel, Delacorte Press (New York, NY), 1999.

Wiesel, *King Solomon and His Magic Ring,* Greenwillow, 1999.

Prose, *The Demons' Mistake: A Story from Chelm,* Greenwillow, 2000.

Contributor of illustrations to periodicals in the United States and abroad.

SIDELIGHTS: In addition to publishing several books focusing on Jewish themes, Mark Podwal has created artwork in a wide variety of media. He created a stage backdrop for a Simon and Garfunkel concert in Israel in 1981. A year later, he designed a gold medal for the U.S. Holocaust Memorial Council. In 1985 he designed the Congressional Gold Medal presented to author Elie Wiesel by President Ronald Reagan.

* * *

POTOK, Chaim 1929-

PERSONAL: Born Herman Harold Potok, February 17, 1929, in New York, NY; changed given name to Chaim, pronounced "*Hah*-yim"; son of Benjamin Max (in business) and Mollie (Friedman) Potok; married Adena Sarah Mosevitzky, June 8, 1958; children: Rena, Naama, Akiva. *Education:* Yeshiva University, B.A. (summa cum laude), 1950; Jewish Theological Seminary, M.H. L., 1954; University of Pennsylvania, Ph.D., 1965. *Avocational interests:* Oil painting, photography.

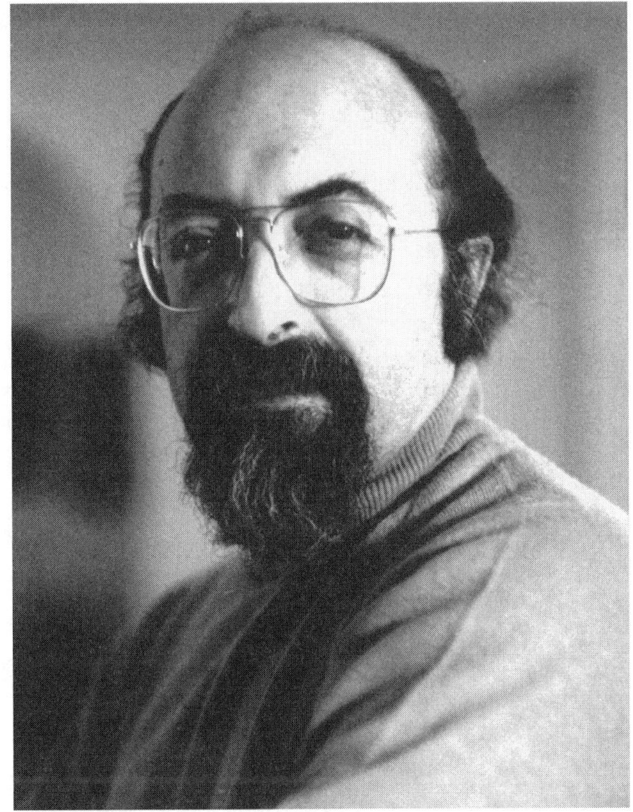

Chaim Potok

ADDRESSES: Home—20 Berwick St., Merion, PA 19066. *E-mail*—cpotok@sas.upenn.edu.

CAREER: Writer. Ordained rabbi (Conservative), Jewish Theological Seminary, New York City, national director, Leaders Training Fellowship, 1954-55; Camp Ramah, Ojai, CA, director, 1957-59; University of Judaism, Los Angeles, CA, instructor, 1957-59; Har Zion Temple, Philadelphia, PA, scholar-in-residence, 1959-63; Jewish Theological Seminary, member of faculty of Teachers' Institute, 1963-64; *Conservative Judaism,* New York City, managing editor, 1964-65; Jewish Publication Society, Philadelphia, editor-in-chief, 1965-74, special projects editor, 1974—. Visiting professor, University of Pennsylvania, 1983, 1992-98, Bryn Mawr College, 1985, and Johns Hopkins University, 1995-98. *Military service:* U.S. chaplain in Korea, 1956-57.

MEMBER: Authors Guild, Dramatists Guild, Authors League of America, Rabbinical Assembly, PEN, Artists Equity.

AWARDS, HONORS: Edward Lewis Wallant Award and National Book Award nomination, both for *The Chosen;* Athenaem Award for *The Promise;* Jewish National Book Award, 1997, for *The Gift of Asher Lev;* National Foundation for Jewish Culture Achievement Award.

WRITINGS:

NOVELS

The Chosen, Simon & Schuster (New York City), 1967.
The Promise (sequel to *The Chosen*), Knopf (New York City), 1969.
My Name Is Asher Lev, Knopf, 1972.
In the Beginning, Knopf, 1975.
The Book of Lights, Knopf, 1981.
Davita's Harp, Knopf, 1985.
The Gift of Asher Lev (sequel to *My Name Is Asher Lev*), Knopf, 1990.
I Am the Clay, Knopf, 1992.

CHILDREN'S LITERATURE

The Tree of Here, Knopf, 1993.
The Sky of Now, Knopf, 1995.
Zebra and Other Stories, Knopf, 1998.

OTHER

Jewish Ethics (pamphlet series), 14 volumes, Leaders Training Fellowship (New York City), 1964-69.
The Jew Confronts Himself in American Literature, Sacred Heart School of Theology (Hales Corners, WI), 1975.
Wanderings: Chaim Potok's History of the Jews (nonfiction), Knopf, 1978.
Ethical Living for a Modern World, Jewish Theological Seminary of America (New York City), 1985.
Theo Tobiasse: Artist in Exile, (nonfiction) Rizzoli International (New York City), 1986.
The Gates of November: Chronicles of the Slepak Family (nonfiction), Knopf, 1996.
(With Isaac Stern) *My First Seventy-nine Years,* Knopf, 1999.

Also contributor of short stories and articles to *TriQuarterly, Commentary, Reconstructionist, Moment, Esquire, American Judaism, Forward, Saturday Review, New York Times Book Review, Kenyon Review, American Voice, New England Review,* and other periodicals.

Selected holiday readings have been recorded and released on cassette by National Public Radio, 1995.

ADAPTATIONS: The Chosen, a Landau Productions movie based on Potok's novel of the same name, was distributed by Twentieth Century-Fox, written by Edwin Gordon, and starred Robbie Benson, Maximilian Schell, Rod Steiger, and Barry Miller, 1982; *The Chosen* was also adapted as a musical for the stage that first opened in New York City, December 17, 1987.

SIDELIGHTS: Chaim Potok is familiar to many readers as the author of best-selling novels like *The Chosen* and *The Promise.* Less well known, though equally important to Potok, is his devotion to Judaism: he is an ordained rabbi and scholar of Judaic texts. Potok's personal attempts to reconcile these disparate commitments have enriched his fiction, as many of his works explore the ways in which characters learn to deal with cultural conflict. Potok explained in the *Philadelphia Inquirer:* "While this tension is exhausting, . . . it is fuel for me. Without it, I would have nothing to say."

Because of his Jewish heritage, Potok is frequently called an American Jewish writer. Although he understands the need for such labels, he prefers to be described as "an American writer writing about a small and particular American world," as he put it in an essay for *Studies in American Jewish Literature.* His vision has attracted readers of many different religious faiths, due in part, according to *New York Times Book Review* contributor Hugh Nissenson, to Potok's "talent for evoking the physical details of this world: the tree-lined streets, the apartment filled with books, the cold radiators, the steaming glasses of coffee." Potok, however, attributes the success of his novels to the universality of his subject matter. Quoting James Joyce, he explained to Millie Ball in the *Times Picayune:* "'In the particular is contained the universal.' When you write about one person or set of people, if you dig deeply enough, you will ultimately uncover basic humanity."

Raised in an Orthodox Jewish family, Potok was drawn to the less restrictive doctrine of Conservative Judaism as a young adult and was eventually ordained a Conservative rabbi. His own life shows a smiliarity to that of some of his characters. Potok's interest in writing and literature, sparked in his youth by Evelyn Waugh's *Brideshead Revisited* and James Joyce's *A Portrait of the Artist as a Young Man,* was opposed by both his family and teachers. His mother, for example, when told of his aspiration to write, remarked, "'You want to be a writer? Fine. You be a brain surgeon, on the side [you'll write stories],'" Potok recalled in the *Fort Lauderdale News.* The teachers at his Jewish parochial school responded similarly, disappointed that Potok would want to take time away from studying the Talmud to read and write fiction. Potok discussed these reactions in an interview with S. Lillian Kremer in *Studies in American Jewish Literature:* "There was anger. There was rage. I still experience it. . . . [The] Jewish tradition . . . casts a very definite denigrating eye upon the whole enterprise of fiction. . . . Scholarship is what counts in the Jewish tradition, Talmudic scholarship, not the product of the imagination."

This conflict between religious and secular commitments is a recurring theme in Potok's novels. In his first book, *The Chosen,* Potok portrays Danny Saunders, a young man torn between fulfilling the expectations of his rabbi father and satisfying his own need for secular knowledge. The Saunders family belongs to the Jewish sect called Hasidim, whose members are "known for their mystical interpretation of Judaic sources and intense devotion to their spiritual leaders," according to S. Lillian Kremer in the *Dictionary of Literary Biography.* When Danny becomes an adult, he is expected to take on his father's role as *tzaddik,* which Nissenson described as "a teacher, spiritual adviser, mediator between his community of followers and God, and living sacrifice who takes the suffering of his people—of all Israel—upon himself." To strengthen Danny's soul and thus prepare him "to assume the burdens of his followers," wrote Kremer, Rabbi Saunders has raised Danny according to the unusual Hasidic tradition which dictates that under certain circumstances a father and son should speak only when discussing religious texts.

In direct contrast to the Saunders are the Malters: Reuven, who becomes Danny's close friend, and Reuven's father, who tutors Danny in secular subjects. As Orthodox Jews, the Malters "emphasize a rational, intellectual approach to Judaic law and theology," explained Kremer. Reuven's father recognizes the importance of Judaic scholarship, but he, unlike Rabbi Saunders, encourages his son to study secular subjects as well. Furthermore, Malter has built his relationship with Reuven on mutual love and respect, not suffering.

Though Danny's problems with his father are crucial to the narrative, *The Chosen* is more than a story of parental and religious conflict, according to Karl Shapiro in *Book Week—World Journal Tribune.* Shapiro stated: "The argument of the book concerns the level of survival of Judaism, whether it shall remain clothed in superstition and mysticism, or whether it shall convey the message of humanitarianism, with the secular Jew as the prophet of gentleness and understanding."

Like many first novels, *The Chosen* received mixed criticism from reviewers. *New York Times* contributing critic Eliot Fremont-Smith described the book as "a long, earnest, somewhat affecting and sporadically fascinating tale of religious conflict and generational confrontation in which the characters never come fully alive because they are kept subservient to theme: They don't have ideas so much as they represent ideas." While *New Republic* contributor Philip Toynbee observed that Potok's prose has "too many exhausted phrases and dead words," he maintained that *The Chosen* "is a fascinating book in its own right. Few Jewish writers have emerged from so deep in the heart of orthodoxy: fewer still have been able to write about their emergence with such an unforced sympathy for both sides and every participant." Concluded Nissenson: "The structural pattern of the novel, the beautifully wrought contrapuntal relationship of the boys, and their fathers, is complete. We rejoice, and we weep a little, at those haunting Hasidic melodies which transfigure their words."

Potok's novel *My Name Is Asher Lev* is a variation "on an almost classic theme: the isolation of the artist from society," according to Thomas Lask in the *New York Times.* Despite its conventional theme, *My Name Is Asher Lev* has what Lask called "a feeling of freshness, of something brand-new" that he attributed not to "the artist and his driving needs but [to] the society from which he is inexorably isolating himself: the intense, ingrown, passionate, mystical world of Hasidism." The protagonist, Asher Lev, lives in a familial and spiritual environment similar to that of Danny Saunders. Lev's parents are devout Hasidim, and his father is actively involved in rebuilding the Jewish community in Europe. Lev, however, is a gifted artist, and his father neither understands nor respects his artistry. While art is not expressly forbidden in the Hasidic tradition, it is considered "blasphemous at worst and mere indulgence of personal vanity at best," according to Kremer in the *Dictionary of Literary Biography.* The tenuous relationship between Lev and his father is strained further when Lev, as a part of his studies, learns to draw crucifixions and nudes.

Although Lev does not consciously reject his heritage, he finds it impossible to repress his artistic instinct. Lask observes that while both Lev and the Hasidic community do their "best to retain the old relationship, . . . there seems to be an artistic destiny greater than both of them." Lev's reluctance to abandon his religious tradition is a significant difference between Potok's characters and those of other American Jewish writers, according to Kremer. "They do not share the assimilationist goals of the Jews about whom Saul Bellow and Philip Roth write. . . . In the instances when Potok's characters enter the secular public world, they maintain orthodox private lives." Even after he has left his family and community, Lev identifies himself as an observant Jew. Thus, as John H. Timmerman observed in *Christian Century,* Lev "stands *not* in open rebellion against, but as a troubled seeker of, his place within a tradition."

Potok followed his fifth novel with his first nonfiction book, *Wanderings: Chaim Potok's Story of the Jews.* Although it is nonfiction, *Wanderings* is similar to Potok's novels, Jack Riemer suggested in *America.* "Just as there he really sought for his self in the guise of a story about a young man wrestling with modernity, so here he searches for his soul in the form of a confrontation with his roots and with his memories." Potok explained to Robert Dahlin in *Publishers Weekly:* "I went wandering inside my own tradition, its history. . . . And I didn't move on until I understood."

Wanderings, a lavishly illustrated book, was described by *Chicago Tribune Book World* contributor Dan Rottenberg as "a rare phenomenon: a coffee-table book with some real intellectual bite to it." Beginning with the family of Abraham, *Wanderings* traces 4,000 years of Jewish history. Potok portrays the Jews as a people who have cohabited with—and been persecuted by—many different civilizations throughout history, and who, despite their small population, have usually managed to survive their persecutors. According to Rottenberg, "what emerges from Potok's mixture of history, Scriptures, novelistic writing, and personal reminiscences is a portrait of Judaism as very much a living, breathing, kicking organism."

Several reviewers maintained that Potok's training as a novelist serves him well in his first foray into nonfiction. Rottenberg, for example, wrote: "The eye of the novelist can enhance our understanding of history, especially when the novelist is someone like Potok, whose fictitious work has always been firmly rooted in cultural and historical scholarship. . . . Potok is able to paint scenes for us, to put flesh on his characters, to speculate about their motives, without abandoning the detachment of the historian." *New York Times Book Review* contributor Alan Mintz described *Wanderings* as "a mixed performance. Mr. Potok can produce a good, strong narrative that also maintains a sense of historical proportion; and his occasional evocations of settings and feelings do contribute to a fuller sense of the past. But often the pursuit of drama gets him into trouble and the writing becomes stylized." Michael J. Bandler, however, suggested in the *Christian Science Monitor* that "one cannot resist the temptation to observe without being facetious that as a historian, Potok solidifies his reputation as a fine novelist."

Potok's next novels, *In the Beginning, The Book of Lights, Davita's Harp,* and *The Gift of Asher Lev,* continue to elaborate upon the theme of conflict between the religious and secular worlds. In *Davita's Harp,* however, the author tells this story from a female perspective. "That leap takes sensitivity and some daring, and Potok handles it well," stated *Detroit News* contributor Lisa Schwarzbaum. "*Davita's Harp* is a warm, decent, generous and patient exploration of important issues facing Jewish women today." When the novel opens, Davita is eight years old. She is the daughter of a Jewish mother and a Christian father who have abandoned their respective religions and are now devoted communists. Davita experiments with both faiths, but she is entranced by the Jewish rituals practiced by her neighbors and eventually embraces Orthodox Judaism. She soon realizes the limitations of her religion, however, when she is denied a prize as the best student in her parochial school graduating class solely because she is a girl.

A *Time* critic observed that "during the conflict between Davita's reverence for Hebraic tradition and her determination to make a place for herself, the narrative becomes far livelier and suggests possibilities for a worthier sequel." A similar opinion was expressed by Paul Cowan, who commented in the *New York Times Book Review* that the first quarter of *Davita's Harp,* which concerns the political activities of Davita's parents, contains "some of Mr. Potok's most disappointing pages," but that "as Davita comes to life, so does the book." *Chicago Tribune Book World* contributor George Cohen, however, maintained that the work provides "an engrossing plot—Potok is a master storyteller—but much of the pleasure in reading 'Davita's Harp' is the beauty of the language."

One of the harsher critical remarks about *Davita's Harp* was voiced by Andrew Weinberger, who commented in the *Los Angeles Times Book Review:* "The problem with this novel is that it is too predictable, too familiar. . . . Potok could do better, one feels, than to walk down this old road again." Nissenson claimed: "It is not a paucity of imagination, but rather an obsession that brings Potok back, again and again, to these kinds of characters, this milieu. However, he chooses a different theme for every book. And in each one he probes a little deeper in an attempt to get at some essential truth about the human condition which is hidden among the Biblical scholars, the explications of Rashi, the yeshivas and the nearsighted kids that haunt him."

In 1990, Potok published *The Gift of Asher Lev,* a sequel to *My Name Is Asher Lev.* The novel begins twenty years after the events in the author's earlier book. Lev has become a highly acclaimed artist living in southern France, has married, and has a son and a daughter. When he receives news that his uncle Yitzchok has died, Lev returns to Brooklyn for the funeral. Almost as soon as he arrives, he wishes to return to France, but his wife and children become attached to Lev's family and prefer the familial atmosphere of the Hasidic community to the relative isolation they experienced in France. Lev's father and the Rebbe, the spiritual leader of the Hasidim, want his family to stay as well, and it is not long before Lev discovers that their motive is to groom his son for leadership of the Rebbe's international movement. The novel concludes—in a manner reminiscent of the biblical story of Abraham and Isaac—with Lev "sacrificing" his son to God. He leaves his son and family in Brooklyn and returns to France to resume his artistic career, which, he discovers, has been revitalized by the whole experience.

Critical reaction to *The Gift of Asher Lev* was mixed. Chicago *Tribune Books* contributor Andy Solomon believed that "there is much about the book to admire," such as Potok's ability to add detail to his settings and portray the spirit of the Hasidic community. However, the critic also noted flaws in the narrative and complained that Lev is not the compelling character he was in the first book. "As Asher sleepwalks through these pages," wrote Solomon, "so too does the plot wander, despite some resolutions that form toward the end. The world of the Hasidim is intriguing, and Potok has knowledgeable insights to share about art. But Asher Lev casts far less spell in this revisit than he did two decades ago." Nikki Stiller similarly observed in the *New York Times Book Review* that Lev becomes a somewhat muted character in the sequel because he "never considers abandoning orthodoxy." Stiller added that Potok "does not wrestle with the angel of autonomy." Brian Morton, however, asserted in the *Times Literary Supplement* that when paired with the previous Asher Lev novel, *The Gift of Asher Lev* "covers much the same ground with considerable subtlety." Of Potok's writings, Morton also concluded that the author "has shown a marked awareness of the internal tensions of modern Judaism, which are prior to its conflicts and accommodations with the Gentile world. His Judaism has content, not just form; beliefs, not just abstract 'pieties'; an exact mentality that participates in a wider society at the same time as it belongs to a distinct enclave."

Set in Korea during the 1950s, Potok's 1992 novel, *I Am the Clay,* portrays the difficult journey of two aged peasants and a young orphaned boy from Seoul to a refugee camp. "Potok focuses in on the struggle for survival as the farmer, his wife and the boy battle hunger, sickness, cold, exhaustion and the land itself," observed Irving Abrahamson in the Chicago *Tribune Books.* Praised as "acutely moving" by a critic for *Kirkus Reviews,* and deemed "a modern myth" by Barbara Gold Zingman in the *New York Times Book Review,* the novel explores themes of human connection amid suffering and the confusion and hope associated with mystical and religious belief, as each of the characters is concerned in some way with a world of "spirits."

Potok has also written works for children and young adults. In *The Tree of Here,* the author introduces a young boy named Jason who is troubled by his family's frequent relocations. The "tree" of the title is a dogwood tree that serves as a symbol of rootedness and a feeling of being home. The work received mixed responses from critics, with Maria Posner of *School Library Journal* criticizing the sketchiness of its characterizations, and a reviewer for *Publishers Weekly* faulting the ambiguity of the main character's age and motivations. A subsequent children's story, *The Sky of Now,* depicts a glider flight experienced by ten-year-old Brian, who suffers from a fear of heights. The story generated similarly skeptical reviews: Susan Scheps of *School Library Journal* found the work "didactic," while *Publishers Weekly* deemed the plot "lifeless." Julie Corsaro of *Booklist,* in contrast, praised Potok's effective descriptions of the experience of flying and his rendering of the protagonist's doubts and fears.

Better reviews attended *Zebra and Other Stories,* a collection of coming-of-age tales suitable for both teens and adults. The characters in *Zebra* face the challenges of parental divorce and bullying, blended families and social consciousness, as they discover their places in an adult world. *Horn Book* contributor Nancy Vasilakis felt that the stories "carry layers of meaning, and teens will discover that one reading won't be enough." In *Booklist,* Stephanie Zvirin declared *Zebra* to be a "wonderful introduction" to Potok's work, adding that although the stories are written for younger readers, the author "respects his audience enough to allow them to draw from it what they will." A *Kirkus Reviews* critic likewise commented: "Readers sensitive to nuances of language and situation will be totally absorbed by these profound character studies."

Potok helped violinist Isaac Stern craft an autobiography titled *My First Seventy-nine Years.* The work detail's Stern's musical career as well as his role in saving Carnegie Hall from destruction and his devotion to the nation of Israel. Although the book is told from a first-person point of view and is purportedly Stern's voice, "Potok makes it flow beautifully, in a voice that is vital and exciting," according to Ray Olson in *Booklist. Library Journal* correspondent Carol J. Binkowski also deemed the book "a sensitive and engrossing history of a man and an era."

In a piece for the Web site *Jvibe,* Elizabeth Silver observed that Potok "remains a revered scholar in not only the Jewish and literary communities, but throughout the world. His philosophy of cultures transcends into all realms of humanity. Chaim Potok has spent the majority of his life silently mapping the territory of his Jewish past through his novels that have captivated people into is fictional worlds because of their universal truths." Silver concluded: "Chaim Potok has the ability to write novels that touch so many distinct people and also dive into the core of problems in today's society with such honesty and realism."

BIOGRAPHICAL/CRITICAL SOURCES:

BOOKS

Authors in the News, Gale (Detroit), Volume 1, 1976, Volume 2, 1976.

Contemporary Literary Criticism, Gale, Volume 2, 1974, Volume 7, 1977, Volume 14, 1980, Volume 26, 1983.

Dictionary of Literary Biography, Gale, Volume 28: *Twentieth-Century American-Jewish Fiction Writers,* 1984, Volume 152: *American Novelists since World War II, Fourth Series,* 1995.

Dictionary of Literary Biography Yearbook: 1984, Gale, 1985.

PERIODICALS

America, February 7, 1979.

Booklist, January 1 and 15, 1996, p. 848; July, 1998, Stephanie Zvirin, review of *Zebra and Other Stories,* p. 1878; September 15, 1999, Ray Olson, review of *My First Seventy-nine Years,* p. 96.

Book Week, April 23, 1967.

Chicago Tribune, December 1, 1987.

Chicago Tribune Book World, November 26, 1978; October 11, 1981; March 24, 1985.

Christian Century, February 17, 1982; May 16, 1984.

Christian Science Monitor, February 12, 1979.

CLA Journal, June, 1971.

Commentary, October, 1972; April, 1979; March, 1982.

Detroit News, March 17, 1985.

Fort Lauderdale News, March 22, 1976.

Horn Book Magazine, November, 1998, Nancy Vasilakis, review of *Zebra and Other Stories,* p. 739.

Kirkus Reviews, July 1, 1998, review of *Zebra and Other Stories.*

Library Journal, November 1, 1999, Carol J. Binkowski, review of *My First Seventy-nine Years,* p. 86.

Los Angeles Times Book Review, November 8, 1981; May 26, 1985.

Kirkus Reviews, April 1, 1992, p. 423.

New Republic, June 7, 1967.

New Yorker, November 17, 1975; November 9, 1981.

New York Times, April 24, 1967; September 12, 1969; April 21, 1972; December 3, 1975; November 2, 1986; July 24, 1987; January 3, 1988; January 7, 1988.

New York Times Book Review, May 7, 1967; September 14, 1969; April 16, 1972; October 19, 1975; December 17, 1978; October 11, 1981; March 31, 1985; May 13, 1990; June 28, 1992, p. 18; December 26, 1999, David Mermelstein, review of *My First Seventy-nine Years,* p. 14.

Philadelphia Bulletin, May 16, 1974.

Philadelphia Inquirer, April 27, 1976.

Publishers Weekly, May 22, 1978; December 12, 1986, p. 46; August 30, 1993, p. 96; November 27, 1995, p. 69.

Saturday Review, September 20, 1969; April 15, 1972.

School Library Journal, October, 1993, p. 108; January, 1996, p. 93.

Studies in American Jewish Literature, number 4, 1985.

Time, November 3, 1975; October 19, 1981; March 25, 1985.

Times (London), December 20, 1990.

Times Literary Supplement, March 5, 1970; October 6, 1972; April 9, 1976; May 28, 1982; November 2, 1990.

Times-Picayune (New Orleans), February 25, 1973.

Tribune Books (Chicago), May 6, 1990; May 17, 1992, p. 6.

Village Voice Literary Supplement, February, 1995.

Washington Post, November 27, 1981.

Washington Post Book World, December 13, 1978.

OTHER

Jvibe, http://www.jvibe.com/popculture/ (December, 1999), Elizabeth Silver, interview with Potok.

POWE, L. A. Scot
See POWE, Lucas A., Jr.

* * *

POWE, Lucas A., Jr. 1943-

PERSONAL: Born February 25, 1943, in Oakland, CA; son of Lucas A. (a lawyer) and Nellie (a homemaker; maiden name, Sheafe) Powe; married Carolyn McKenny (a homemaker), August 27, 1965; children: Monika Powe Nelson, Thomas Scott. *Ethnicity:* "Caucasian." *Education:* Yale University, B.A., 1965; University of Washington, Seattle, J.D., 1968. *Avocational interests:* Tennis.

ADDRESSES: *Office*—27 East Dean Keeton St., Austin, TX 78705. *E-mail*—spowe@mail.law.utexas.edu.

CAREER: University of British Columbia, Vancouver, assistant professor of law, 1968-70; law clerk to U.S. Supreme Court Justice William O. Douglas, Washington, DC, 1970-71; University of Texas at Austin, Anne Green Regents Professor of Law and Government, 1971—. History Book Club, reviewer, 1983—.

MEMBER: American Law Institute, American Bar Association.

AWARDS, HONORS: Electronic Media Book of the Year Award, Broadcast Education Association, 1987, and Silver Gavel Award, American Bar Association, 1988, both for *American Broadcasting and the First Amendment;* Scribes Book Award, American Society of Writers on Legal Subjects, and Certificate of Merit, American Bar Association, both 1992, for *The Fourth Estate and the Constitution.*

WRITINGS:

American Broadcasting and the First Amendment, University of California Press (Berkeley), 1987.

The Fourth Estate and the Constitution: Freedom of the Press in America, University of California Press (Berkeley), 1991.

(With Thomas G. Krattenmaker) *Regulating Broadcast Programming,* MIT Press (Cambridge, MA), AEI Press (Washington, DC), 1994.

The Warren Court and American Politics, Belknap Press of Harvard University Press (Cambridge), 2000.

SIDELIGHTS: Lucas A. Powe, Jr., is a law professor at the University of Texas, Austin, and the author of several books, including *American Broadcasting and the First Amendment.* In this study, Powe discusses the ways in which broadcasting and broadcast journalism are treated differently, under the law, than print journalism. Under a 1969 Supreme Court ruling, for example, broadcasters were required to offer time for opposing views or in response to an attack. In 1974, the Court ruled in a similar case involving the *Miami Herald,* saying the paper did not have to offer these options. The rulings in both cases were unanimous.

Powe writes that although broadcasting is supposedly protected under the First Amendment, it is treated differently under the law because of the idea that it must operate in the public interest. Herbert Dorfman wrote in the *New York Times Book Review,* that Powe states that "far from serving the public's best interests, the licensing and review powers of the Federal Communication Commission (FCC) have led to favoritism, the imposition of white middle-class ethics on listeners and viewers, the threat and sometime use of censorship, and political manipulation."

Powe points out that, although the public owns the airwaves, the government required the issuing of licenses beginning with the Radio Act of 1927. Congress felt that licenses should be awarded only to those radio stations that were necessary to the public interest, a standard to which newspapers have never been held. With the licensing of stations (also not required of newspapers) they faced the loss of their licenses if they failed to meet the standards of the regulators. When televison arrived, it fell under the same rules and restrictions. Dorfman noted that Congress insists on continued regulation, even when the FCC has tried to dismantle portions of it. Powe feels regulation has never worked. The Radio Act, now revised and titled the Communications Act, forbids censorship, but censorship is still carried out indirectly.

In Powe's opinion, print and broadcasting should be treated the same under the First Amendment. Dorfman called Powe's thesis "a good classical liberal position," but added that neither Congress nor communications analysts feel it is adequate to deal with the huge broadcasting industry of today. "In the end," wrote Dorfman, "Mr. Powe seems resigned that the differences in First Amendment protections afforded to broadcasting and print are here to stay, but voices like his will not be lost."

In *The Fourth Estate and the Constitution,* Powe addresses print journalism. He begins with an historical account of the First Amendment from the period of the framing of the Constitution. He discusses First Amendment repression during World War I, including the sentencing of Eugene V. Debs for his criticism of the war and the 1919 Schenck case, which ruled more liberally toward freedom of speech. Also reviewed is *New York Times v. Sullivan,* the 1964 case that limited the ability of public officials to sue for libel, and the Pentagon Papers ruling in 1971, which found that the government could not deny publication of information on the grounds of national security. Herman Schwartz wrote in the *New York Times Book Review* that the book "written in a lively, colloquial style by someone who knows how to tell a good story, is not only a thoughtful discussion of press freedom but also enjoyable to read."

In the second section, Powe addresses prior restraint, access to information, libel, and economic concentration. He demonstrates the difficulty in preserving press freedom. Schwartz said that "in libel cases, for example, he suggests that despite Sullivan, the press remains vulnerable to huge damages awarded by hostile and distrustful juries, and to crushingly expensive suits even when it wins."

Powe addresses the applicability and relevance of the "right to know" and "fourth estate" models of press protection as applied to the rights of the media. Elliot E. Slotnick wrote for the *Law and Politics Book Review* online that the analysis "illustrates that, ultimately, neither model fully justifies the full range of press freedom claims and that many such claims are, above all else, self-serving. Still, the fourth estate model, perhaps like judicial review itself, appears to win favor as an 'act of faith.'"

Powe fears the government could become involved with editorial decisions if the press received special constitutional privileges, and he does not see a need for reporters to keep their sources confidential. Schwartz wrote, "this seems too cautious and too optimistic." Schwartz also pointed out that some states and Federal courts have protected sources and that, because of this, the Supreme Court's decisions on confidentiality have not been as damaging as they could have been. Schwartz maintains that Powe also opposes offering response space to anyone who has been attacked in the press, but personally feels that an occasional letter would not infringe on editorial independence. Because of the continuing concentration of newspaper ownership, Powe suggests that a special antitrust law would guarantee competition. Schwartz called this "unrealistic. The current power of the press makes Congress more inclined to relax the antitrust laws than to tighten them."

The Warren Court and American Politics covers the Supreme Court under Chief Justice Earl Warren, from his appointment by President Dwight D. Eisenhower in 1953 until his resignation in 1969. The book is divided into four parts, with chapters on civil rights, domestic security, democratic representation, church/state, press freedom, obscenity, police procedures, and wealth and poverty. Powe discusses more than 200 significant rulings, including *Brown v. Board of Education* in which "separate but equal" and school segregation were repudiated. Other rulings resulted in criminal procedure reform (*Mapp, Gideon, Miranda*) and the ban on school-sponsored prayer. A.E. Dick Howard in the *Washington Post Book World* found the book "engaging and impressive, written in the grand tradition of such scholars as Edward S. Corwin and Walter F. Murphy."

The rulings of the Warren court that expanded civil liberties were handed down from 1962, when Justice Arthur, a liberal, replaced Frankfurter on the bench. Edward Lazarus wrote in the *Los Angeles Times Book Review* that, "despite the passage of more than three decades, the decisions of the Warren court remain at the heart of the often bitter legal debate within the Supreme Court and society at large. When abortion rights advocates and foes clash in protests on the court's front steps, when school principals defiantly post the Ten Commandments on classroom walls, when students hold sit-ins to save affirmative action, when the American Bar Association calls for a moratorium on executions, or when parents' groups protest pornography on the Internet, they are choosing sides in a war over the changes wrought by the Warren court." Lazarus said Powe "labors to bring dispassion to subject matter that stirs passion at every turn."

BIOGRAPHICAL/CRITICAL SOURCES:

PERIODICALS

American Political Science Review, June, 1992, Harold J. Spaeth, review of *The Fourth Estate and the Constitution,* p. 545.

Broadcasting, January 25, 1988, review of *American Broadcasting and the First Amendment,* p. 89.

Choice, September, 1995, A. P. Simonds, review of *Regulating Broadcast Programming,* p. 216.

Constitutional Commentary, summer, 1988, Henry Geller, review of *American Broadcasting and the First Amendment,* pp. 510-520; winter, 1992, Donald M. Gillmor, review of *The Fourth Estate and the Constitution,* pp. 119-125.

Editor & Publisher, June 22, 1991, Hiley Ward, review of *The Fourth Estate and the Constitution,* p. 28.

Federal Communications Law Journal, May, 1988, Diane S. Killory and Richard J. Bozzelli, review of *American Broadcasting and the First Amendment,* pp. 413-426.

Journalism Quarterly, spring, 1988, Jeffrey A. Smith, review of *American Broadcasting and the First Amendment,* p. 208.

Journal of American History, June, 1988, James L. Baughman, review of *American Broadcasting and the First Amendment,* p. 223; June, 1992, Norman Rosenberg, review of *The Fourth Estate and the Constitution,* p. 350.

Journal of Broadcasting & Electronic Media, fall, 1987, Theodore L. Glasser, review of *American Broadcasting and the First Amendment,* p. 477.

Journal of Communication, spring, 1988, Don R. Le Duc, review of *American Broadcasting and the First Amendment,* p. 157; spring, 1993, John Soloski, review of *The Fourth Estate and the Constitution,* p. 167.

Journal of Economic Literature, September, 1995, Timothy J. Brennan, review of *Regulating Broadcast Programming,* p. 1381.

Judicature, July-August, 1993, Michael P. Seng, review of *The Fourth Estate and the Constitution,* p. 50.

Law and Social Inquiry, spring, 1988, Ian Ayres, review of *American Broadcasting and the First Amendment,* pp. 413-427.

Legal Times, May 15, 2000, Otto G. Obermaier, "Canonize Earl Warren?" p. 31.

Library Journal, April 15, 1991, Kenneth F. Kister, review of *The Fourth Estate and the Constitution,* p. 102.

Los Angeles Times Book Review, June 11, 2000, Edward Lazarus, "What Warren Wrought."

New York Times Book Review, April 19, 1987, Herbert Dorfman, "Be Neutral—or Else," p. 19; July 28, 1991, Herman Schwartz, "Regarding the Press," p. 13.

Publishers Weekly, March 1, 1991, Genevieve Stuttaford, review of *The Fourth Estate and the Constitution,* p. 68.

Quarterly Journal of Speech, February, 1990, John M. Kittross, review of *American Broadcasting and the First Amendment,* p. 111.

Regulation, spring, 1995, Daniel D. Polsby, review of *Regulating Broadcast Programming,* p. 88.

Review of Politics, spring, 1988, Robert Schmuhl, review of *American Broadcasting and the First Amendment,* p. 304.

Reviews in American History, June, 1992, Thomas C. Leonard, review of *The Fourth Estate and the Constitution,* p. 247.

Urban Lawyer, winter, 1988, Tracey Plymell, review of *American Broadcasting and the First Amendment,* pp. 220-221.

Wall Street Journal, June 4, 1987, Thomas W. Hazlett, review of *American Broadcasting and the First Amendment,* p. 20; March 20, 2000, Jay P. Lefkowitz, "If the Legislature Won't Do It, We Will," p. A30.

Washington Post Book World, May 24, 2000, A. E. Dick Howard, review of *The Warren Court and American Politics.*

OTHER

Law and Politics Book Review, http://www.unt.edu/ (June 11, 2000), Elliot E. Slotnik, review of *The Fourth Estate and the Constitution.* (L. A. Scot Powe)

* * *

PRINCE, Peter (Alan) 1942-

PERSONAL: Born May 10, 1942, in Bromley, England; son of William John (a journalist) and Audrey (Kelley) Prince. *Education:* University of Pennsylvania, B.A., 1964; Columbia University, M.A., 1966.

ADDRESSES: *Home*—31 Meteor St., London SW11, England. *Agent*—Douglas Rae Management, 28 Charing Cross Rd., London WC2, England.

CAREER: Freelance writer. BPC Publishing Ltd., London, England, editor, 1969-71; Vauxhall Manor School, London, writer-in-residence, 1973-74.

AWARDS, HONORS: Somerset Maugham Award, Society of Authors, 1973, for *Play Things;* British Academy Award, best screenplay for a television series, British Academy of Film and Television Arts, for *Oppenheimer.*

WRITINGS:

NOVELS

Play Things (also see below), Gollancz (London, England), 1972.

Dogcatcher, Gollancz (London, England), 1974.

Agents of a Foreign Power, Gollancz (London, England), 1977.
The Good Father (also see below), J. Cape (London, England), 1983, Carroll & Graf (New York, NY), 1985.
Death of the Soap Queen, Bloomsbury (England), 1990.
The Great Circle, Random House (New York, NY), 1997.
Waterloo Story, Bloomsbury (England), 1999.

TELEVISION PLAYS

The Floater, British Broadcasting Corp. (BBC-TV), 1973.
Play Things (adapted from his novel), Thames TV, 1974.
Early Struggles, BBC-TV, 1975.
Last Summer, Thames TV, 1976.
Cold Harbour, Thames TV, 1978.
Oppenheimer (seven-part television drama), BBC-TV, 1980, Public Broadcasting Service (PBS), 1982.
Bright Eyes, BBC-TV, 1982.
(Adapter) *Mr. Right,* BBC-TV, 1983.
The Strange Case of Steven Dyer, Channel 4 (London, England)/ZDF (Germany), c. 1984.
Audubon (two-part television drama), BBC-TV, c. 1984.
A Song for Europe, 1985.

OTHER

The Hit (screenplay), Island Alive, 1984.
Waterland (screenplay; adapted from a novel by Graham Swift), Fine Line Features, c. 1992.

Also author of *Oh, Mischief,* Faber. Contributor of short stories and articles on television to periodicals, including *Riverside Writing.*

ADAPTATIONS: The Good Father was adapted into a motion picture by Christopher Hampton and released by Skouras Pictures, 1987.

SIDELIGHTS: Award-winning writer Peter Prince is noted for the unconventional prose style and realistic dialogue that he brings to his novels, short stories, and screenplays. In Prince's first novel, a disillusioned young architecture student gives up a promising career for a job managing an adventure playground frequented by gangs of London "toughs." *Play Things* discloses "a sharp mind and competent throwaway style," a reviewer for the *Times Literary Supplement* noted, while also commenting that Prince has "squandered, in what seems like an effort never to bore, never to overstate, the material for a very much longer book." Oswell Blakeston was enthusiastic in his praise of the novel, calling it "exciting [and] relevant" in *Books & Bookmen.* Blakeston went on to describe *Play Things* as "absolutely first class. [Prince's] short book grips as a story, and it manages to take all the modern problems into consideration: violence, drugs, colour, swastika and peace signs."

Prince followed the success of his first novel with *Dogcatcher,* which features an intelligence officer-turned-detective who abandons his native England to set up shop in Minnesota. The book was criticized by some reviewers for its stereotypical approach to the crime novel. "The danger in resorting to genre . . . is to assume that it is as easy as the best genre writers make it look," commented a reviewer for the *Times Literary Supplement.* Of interest to critics, however, was the novel's British perspective on American culture and the realistic portrayal of the story's protagonist.

In *The Good Father,* Prince introduces his readers to two men in their mid-thirties who suddenly find both their marriages and their families in the midst of breaking apart. Popular with both readers and critics, *The Good Father* was later filmed as a major motion picture. Prince's novel recounts the unique relationship which develops between the two men as they work to hang on to both their children and their self-respect through their support of one another. "Like any good treatment of the sex war, *The Good Father* is full of surprising reversals, as characters find themselves acting at variance with their declared principles or are tripped headlong into the mire of their motives," commented Lewis Jones in the *Times Literary Supplement.* Reviewer John Nicholson also gave the novel high marks in the London *Times:* "What makes [*The Good Father*] painfully fascinating to anyone in their thirties is Mr. Prince's attempt to answer two questions of great sociological interest: what happened to the Forever Young Generation when they realized that they weren't, and in the author's own words—will the men of the Class of '66 (or thereabouts) ever get over the burden of guilt and sense of their own inadequacy laid on them by their difficult, driven, ambivalent and astonishing women?"

Prince also wrote the screenplay for *Waterland,* a film of the early 1990s directed by Stephen Gyllenhaal that starred Jeremy Irons. As Richard Schickel informed in *Time,* it is a "knotty, curiously absorbing adaptation of

Graham Swift's novel." The story focuses on Tom Crick, a retiring high school teacher in Pittsburgh in 1974. Crick tells his students about "his marriage and his family—and a murder—back in the waterlands of eastern England," wrote Stanley Kauffmann in the *New Republic.* Through flashback sequences viewers are taken to England during the 1940s. "Madness, incest, something very close to fratricide and an abortion" are exposed as parts of Crick's past that have far-reaching affects in his personal and family life. "Through the metaphor of [its characters'] lives," analyzed Schickel, *Waterland* states that "our best hope lies in shedding [our histories] and finding our way back to a prelapsarian state." While Kauffmann was unimpressed with *Waterland,* denouncing it as "waterlogged and swollen," Schickel promoted the work, summarizing the story: "A tormented time traveler tries to make peace with his past in a challenging, absorbing film."

Prince's novel *The Great Circle* also travels back in time. Set in February of 1865, this story is staged on a paddle-steamer named *Laurentia.* A voyage of nearly two weeks takes passengers from Boston to London. Prince explores "mores both timely and timeless in this entertaining period piece," remarked Michele Leber, who, in a complimentary *Booklist* assessment, called *The Great Circle* a "well-fashioned tale . . . eminently satisfying for all." *Library Journal* contributor Barbara Maslekoff recommended the novel as "good reading," in which Prince creates "an interesting tale with some memorable characters and unpredictable outcomes." A *Publishers Weekly* reviewer commented: "While nothing is quite what it appears in this leisurely period piece . . . resolutions are predictably symmetrical, very much in the manner of the day."

Regarding Prince's 1999 novel, *Waterloo Story,* a *Publishers Weekly* reviewer praised the author for a "subtly brilliant story" with "energetic density," "unnerving frankness," and "utilitarian prose that leaps with spot-on dialogue . . . soberly observing the social and political upheavals that roiled Britain in the '60s and '70s."

BIOGRAPHICAL/CRITICAL SOURCES:

PERIODICALS

Booklist, July, 1997, Michele Leber, review of *The Great Circle,* p. 1800.

Books & Bookmen, January, 1973, Oswell Blakeston, review of *Play Things,* p. 85.

Chicago Tribune, July 5, 1985.

Library Journal, January, 1985, Shelley Cox, review of *The Good Father,* p. 101; July, 1997, Barbara Maslekoff, review of *The Great Circle,* p. 127.

Los Angeles Times, February 13, 1987.

New Republic, November 16, 1992, Stanley Kauffmann, review of *Waterland,* p. 28.

New Yorker, November 2, 1992, Terrence Rafferty, review of *Waterland,* p. 100.

New York Times Book Review, April 7, 1985, Karen Ray, review of *The Good Father,* p. 15; August 3, 1997, Joan Mooney, review of *The Great Circle,* p. 16.

Publishers Weekly, December 7, 1984, review of *The Good Father,* p. 64; June 23, 1997, review of *The Great Circle,* p. 71; January 17, 2000, review of *Waterloo Story,* p. 44.

Spectator, April 13, 1974, pp. 449-450; February 12, 1977, p. 23; April 21, 1990, p. 29.

Time, November 9, 1992, Richard Schickel, review of *Waterland,* p. 81.

Times (London), October 6, 1983, John Nicholson, review of *The Good Father.*

Times Literary Supplement, September 22, 1972, p. 1122; March 29, 1974, p. 313; November 4, 1983, Lewis Jones, review of *The Good Father,* p. 1227.*

* * *

PRISCO, Michele 1920-

PERSONAL: Born January 18, 1920, in Torre Annunziatia, Italy; son of Salvatore (a lawyer) and Annamaria Prisco; married Sarah Buonomo, October 6, 1951; children: Annella, Caterina. *Education:* University of Naples, Laurea in Giurisprudenza (law degree), 1942. *Politics:* Democratic. *Religion:* Roman Catholic. *Avocational interests:* Tennis, furniture, and antiques.

ADDRESSES: Home—Via Stazio n. 8, Naples, Italy 20123.

CAREER: Writer. Founder and director of magazine *Le Ragioni narrative,* 1961-62. *Military:* Scuola Allievi Ufficiali di Complemento, 1942-43.

MEMBER: Nazionale del Sindacato Scrittori (vice secretary), Lions Club di Napoli

AWARDS, HONORS: Prize Venezia, 1950; Prize Strega, 1966, for *A Spiral of Mist.*

WRITINGS:

IN ENGLISH TRANSLATION

Gli eredi del vento, Rizzoli (Milan), 1950, translation by Violet M. Macdonald published as *Heirs of the Wind: A Novel,* Verschoyle (London), 1953.

Una spirale di nebbia, Rizzoli, 1966, translation by Isabel Quigly published as *A Spiral of Mist,* Dutton (New York City), 1969.

UNTRANSLATED WORKS

La provincia addormentata: Racconti, Mondadori (Milan), 1949.

Figli difficili, Rizzoli, 1954.

Fuochi a mare, Rizzoli, 1957.

(Translator) Francois Mauriac, *Le Sagouin,* Mondadori (Milan), 1959.

La dama di piazza, Rizzoli, 1961.

Punto franco, Rizzoli, 1961.

Inventario della memoria, Rizzoli, 1970.

I cieli della sera, Rizzoli, 1970.

Gli ermellini neri, Rizzoli, 1975.

Il colore del cristallo, Rizzoli, 1977.

Le parole del silenzio, Rizzoli, 1981.

Il romanzo italiano contemporaneo, Cesati (Florence), 1983.

Lo specchio cieco, Rizzoli, 1984.

Ritratti incompiuti, I.P.S. (Rome), 1986.

I giorni della conchiglia, Rizzoli, 1989.

Terre basse: 25 racconti, Rizzoli, 1992.

Il cuore della vita, S.E.I (Turin), 1995.

Il pellicano di pietra, Rizzoli, 1996.

Una vita per il romanzo, Edizioni del Delfino (Naples, Italy), 1998.

Gli altri, Rizzoli, 1999.

Also contributor of articles to newspapers and journals, including *Il messaggero, Il Mattino, La feira letteraria, Mercurio, Tempo presente, Aretusa,* and *Risorgimento.*

WORK IN PROGRESS: Inventario della memoria, an autobiography.

SIDELIGHTS: Italian author Michele Prisco, after following through with family expectancies and educating himself as a lawyer, threw off the traditional means of labor and instead focused on writing. His complex styling—involving the search for the darkness that lies beneath the surface of the human mind—has given Prisco both his share of champions and critics.

Prisco was born in Torre Annunziatia, south of Naples, Italy, to lawyer Salvatore Prisco and Annamaria Prisco. Carrying on the family tradition, Prisco, the youngest of eleven children, studied law, graduating from the University of Naples in 1942. He attended Scuola Allievi Ufficiali di Complemento for his military service in 1942-43. On October 6, 1951, Prisco married Sarah Buonomo, and they have two daughters. But throughout his childhood and into his adulthood, Prisco harbored a love for writing. During his time in law school and military service, Prisco published short stories and wrote for newspapers and journals throughout Italy. After performing his family duty, Prisco abandoned convention and became a full-time writer.

Prisco began his examination of the human psyche through his first two works, *La provincia addormentata* (1949), a collection of eight stories set in Naples, and the novel *Gli eredi del vento* (1950). The latter tells the story of Mazzu, a police chief who marries a woman and upon her death proceeds to marry each of her five sisters over a period of time. Prisco's 1961 novel, *La dama di piazza,* scrutinizes the social status of a community and the way in which people try to achieve it. The main character, Aurora, marries an older man in order to gain a better social position. But because of her background, she is ridiculed and in the end is left alone. "Prisco's relentless probing of her aspirations, values, and desires evokes both sympathy and repulsion in the reader," comments Carmine Di Biase in the *Dictionary of Literary Biography.*

One of his most well-known works, *Una spirale di nebbia* (1966), also provided Prisco with his share of critics. Finding his wife dead under suspicious circumstances, the main character, Fabrizio, is subject to scrutiny by the townspeople. Over the course of several days, each town member's own baseness and motivations are probed into. A *Newsweek* contributor faulted the novel: "This is a blowfish of a novel. It tries to swim the depths only to puff itself up with false vanity and empty rhetoric, rising pathetically to the shallows to show itself off for the bloated creature that it is." However, the book won the Strega Prize in 1966.

Prisco's next book, *I cieli della sera* (1970), further explores the motives of the human mind. David's mother has died in an automobile accident and his father has committed suicide after murdering a friend. Fleeing from this violence in his past, David journeys to the south of Italy to try and make sense of the brutality that follows him. Alvaro, the narrator of Prisco's novel *Gli ermellini neri* (1975), is a wanderer like David. But while David is fleeing from evil produced externally, Alvaro tries to flee from evil that is created internally. Ironically, Alvaro becomes obsessed with evil while at a seminary. Prisco would again touch on this formula of one man's journey in 1989 with his book *I giorni della conchiglia.* Mauro, a forty-year-old married man and father of a son, searches for his past. Adopted at age six, through the course of the novel Mauro realizes that his older brother, who died, was in actuality his father. Like his previous characters, Mauro must confront his past in order to live in the future.

Prisco retraced his steps with his next two novels, *Le parole del silenzio* (1981) and *Lo specchio cieco,* by reexamining the female psyche and the effects of social position, as he had done with his previous novel, *La dama di piazza.* Like Aurora, the main character of *Le parole del silenzo,* Cristina, is alone at the end of the novel, remembering the steps that led her to that point. Margherita is almost two characters in *Lo specchio cieco.* In the beginning of the novel she is a dull woman, while at the end of the novel she is the exact opposite. Prisco's intention with Margherita was to show that depending on one's mindset, either of the "Margheritas" are the true character.

Il pellicano di pietra (1996) deals with not one but two unhappy and complex women. Maddalena is a bitter recluse, living with the memories of her dead lover Alfonso, whose body was found in a pine grove. Because her mother Giuseppina disliked Alfonso, Maddalena harbors intense resentment and anger toward her mother. When Maddalena meets Osvaldo, a potential suitor, she tricks her mother into believing that Osvaldo is in love with Giuseppina. The mother, upon learning of her daughter's treachery, kills Maddalena, and with her dead daughter's hands and feet tied, dumps her in the exact spot where her lover Alfonso's body was found. "Giuseppina personifies a pitiless and unredeeming vision of the feminine condition; in the context of the novel, life is tragic and it can be coped with only by living it or doing away with it," says Di Biase.

Many of Prisco's novels are set during the post-World War II era, when the brutality and violence of man was brought to the surface. By having his characters oftentimes trying to put themselves into a better social position with devastating results, he also uncovered the motives behind societal rituals and practices. Throughout the novels, his characters learn only to survive after confronting their own inner demons. Much of this is achieved through memories. Those characters that cannot confront their motivations end up tragically like Maddalena. For many in the literary world this probing of the inner mind, juxtaposed against societal positions, is Prisco's strong point. "While . . . [Prisco's] subsequent novels did show a gradual widening of the historical perspective, along with a new sense of the social reality of the postwar years, his main works of fiction—the novels *Una spirale di nebbia* (1966); *I cieli della sera* (1970); and *Gli ermellini neri* (1975)—focused again, with growing lucidity and slow but intense narrative pace, on the study of human nature as a consistent source for the portrayal of types and characters, on the complex world of family life, and on the moral decline of the provincial middle class," notes A. Illiano in *Encyclopedia of World Literature in the Twentieth Century.*

BIOGRAPHICAL/CRITICAL SOURCES:

BOOKS

Dictionary of Literary Biography, Volume 177: *Italian Novelists since World War II, 1945-1965,* Gale, 1997.

Encyclopedia of World Literature in the Twentieth Century, St. James, 1999.

PERIODICALS

Newsweek, August 18, 1969.

World Literature Today, autumn, 1990, Mario B. Mignone, review of *I giorni della conchiglia,* pp. 624-625; summer, 1997, Giovanni D'Angelo, review of *Il pellicano di pietra,* pp. 570-571.*

* * *

PURDY, Carol 1943-

PERSONAL: Born January 5, 1943, in Long Beach, CA; daughter of Melvin Boyce (a machinist) and Kathryn (a homemaker; maiden name, Wilbur) Slaughter; married John Purdy (a teacher), June 8, 1963; children: Laura, Mark, Sarah. *Education:* California State University, Long Beach, B.A., 1964; California State University, Sacramento, M.S.W., 1990. *Religion:* Church of Christ. *Avocational interests:* Music, gardening, aerobics, drawing, water-skiing, traveling.

ADDRESSES: Home—25310 68th Ave., Los Molinos, CA 96055. *Office*—Tehama County Mental Health, 1860 Walnut, Red Bluff, CA 96080. *Agent*—Faith Hamlin, Sanford J. Greenburger Associates, Inc., 55 Fifth Ave., New York, NY 10003.

CAREER: Orange Unified School District, Orange, CA, elementary school teacher, 1964-67; Kid Power Program, Red Bluff, CA, founder, 1988—; Tehama County Mental Health, Red Bluff, social worker, 1989—; writer.

MEMBER: Society of Children's Book Writers, National Association of Social Workers, American Art Therapy Association.

AWARDS, HONORS: School Library Journal voted *Mrs. Merriwether's Musical Cat* one of the best books of 1994; *Nesuya's Basket* was named *Smithsonian Magazine* Notable Book for Children, 1997.

WRITINGS:

Iva Dunnit and the Big Wind, illustrated by Steven Kellogg, Dial, 1985.
Least of All, illustrated by Tim Arnold, Macmillan, 1987.
Kid Power: Groups of High-Risk Children, Mill Creek Publishers, 1989.
Mrs. Merriwether's Musical Cat, illustrated by Petra Mathers, Putnam, 1994.
Nesuya's Basket, Robert Rinehart (Boulder, CO), 1997.

Also author of *Helping Them Heal, A Guide for Parents of Children in Play Therapy* and *Playing with Janet, A Child's Story about Play Therapy.*

SIDELIGHTS: Carol Purdy once commented: "I was not one of those children who took a flashlight to bed in order to write in my journal and knew from age three that my destiny was to be an author. While growing up in the big city of Long Beach, California, I had no idea that I would some day be a writer. My greatest interests as a child were art and music. I sang in the school choir, played several instruments, and took art classes.

"While in college I married a fellow student, and we both decided to become elementary school teachers. When we were expecting our first child, we wanted to find a country environment in which to raise a family. We moved to a seventy-five-year-old farmhouse near Red Bluff, California, and tried everything from raising pigs, horses, cattle and chickens to doing our own butchering, cheesemaking, and butter churning.

"After the birth of my third child, I thought of the advice of my high school English teacher who said I should become a writer. Six years later, after wearing out three typewriters, my book *Iva Dunnit and the Big Wind* was accepted for publication. . . .

"With the wealth of family stories and ever-changing events of my life, there are always ideas for children's books. Finding time to write is the continual problem. I have never been a writer who devotes a certain portion of each day to the written word. Rather, I have only written when an idea became enticing to the point that I couldn't keep from developing it into a story.

"My keen interest in the problems facing children today led me to learn skills to help with those problems. My primary activities today center around my work as a psychotherapist and counselor with children and families. In addition, I lecture and train on the subjects of high-risk children, art therapy, and the Kid Power Program, which I developed early in my career, to help children from troubled families.

"My enthusiasm for writing children's books has not dimmed, and one of the most delightful aspects of my life is doing author visits at elementary schools. I also continue to be alert for that compelling idea which will start me writing the next book."

Purdy's first book, *Iva Dunnit and the Big Wind,* warmed the hearts of reviewers who found in it a tall tale set in the American frontier west. Iva and her six children live by their wits and hard work and together they defeat a prairie fire and save the youngest child from hungry wolves. Then a big wind blows across the prairie and only the chickens are left outside to suffer it until Iva goes out to save them, knowing she has trained her children well to stay put out of danger when told. Unfortunately, the wind almost blows Iva away as she struggles to hold down the roof with four chickens tied to her corset strings, while her dependable children stay put inside the cabin. Iva ends up thankful when her children decide to disobey her and come to the rescue.

"Tall-tale heroes like Paul Bunyan may have met their match in Iva Dunnit and her six children," declared a reviewer for *Horn Book.* In addition, Steven Kellogg's illustrations "make the prairie a striking setting for a tongue-in-cheek pioneer story with built-in child appeal," averred a contributor to *Bulletin of the Center for Children's Books.*

Purdy's next story is set in turn-of-the-twentieth-century Vermont. In *Least of All* critics found a heartwarming story about the youngest child in a large farming family who is convinced she has little to contribute until the day she teaches herself to read. At seven, Little Raven Hannah is finally allowed to churn the butter and in that way contribute to the family's welfare, while her older brothers do all the other farm work. The girl decides to take the family Bible to keep her company while she performs her lonely chore and by reciting the verses she has memorized while following along with her finger, she teaches herself to read, something no one else in the family can do. Then Raven Hannah does an even better thing: she teaches her family to read too. "This is a quiet story, a fulfilling tale about the joy of accomplishment," remarked Christine Behrmann in *School Library Journal.* "The story is understated but warm," Betsy Hearne observed in *Bulletin of the Center for Children's Books.* "When the child's parents are moved by her reading, readers will be touched as well."

On a more whimsical note comes *Mrs. Merriwether's Musical Cat,* a gently humorous story about a stray cat whose metronomic tail saves Mrs. Merriwether's piano lessons from disaster until the day the cat disappears. When the cat returns with three similarly equipped kittens, joy and merriment are again restored to the houses on Mrs. Merriwether's street. "Music aficionados and cat lovers especially will find much to like here," declared a reviewer for *Publishers Weekly.*

BIOGRAPHICAL/CRITICAL SOURCES:

PERIODICALS

Booklist, May 1, 1986, review of *Iva Dunnit and the Big Wind,* p. 1321; March 1, 1987, Denise M. Wilms, review of *Least of All,* pp. 1055-56; November 15, 1994, Linda Ward-Callaghan, review of *Mrs. Merriwether's Musical Cat,* p. 613.

Bulletin of the Center for Children's Books, February, 1986, review of *Iva Dunnit and the Big Wind,* p. 116; March, 1987, Betsy Hearne, review of *Least of All,* pp. 133-34.

Horn Book, March-April, 1986, review of *Iva Dunnit and the Big Wind,* p. 196; March-April, 1995, Ann A. Flowers, review of *Mrs. Merriwether's Musical Cat,* p. 188.

Kliatt, September, 1997, Sherri Forgash Ginsberg, review of *Nesuya's Basket,* p. 14.

New York Times Book Review, September 20, 1987, Jane Yolen, review of *Least of All,* p. 32.

Publishers Weekly, August 1, 1994, review of *Mrs. Merriwether's Musical Cat,* p. 78.

School Library Journal, June-July, 1987, Christine Behrmann, review of *Least of All,* p. 88; December, 1994, review of *Mrs. Merriwether's Musical Cat,* p. 26.

West Coast Review of Books, November-December, 1985, review of *Iva Dunnit and the Big Wind,* p. 51.*

* * *

PUTNEY, Mary Jo

PERSONAL: Born in NY. *Education:* Syracuse University, B.A., B.I.D. (industrial design).

ADDRESSES: *Home*—P.O. Box 243, Riderwood, MD 21139-0243. *Agent*—c/o Topaz, 375 Hudson St., New York, NY 10014. *E-mail*—mjp624@aol.com.

CAREER: Writer, 1986—; industrial and graphic designer.

MEMBER: Romance Writers of America (RWA), Novelists, Inc., Author's Guild.

AWARDS, HONORS: Nominated six times for Golden Choice Award for best book of the year, RWA, for *The Rake and the Reformer, Dearly Beloved, Uncommon Vows, Silk and Shadows, Silk and Secrets,* and *Thunder and Roses;* Aphra Award for best book of the year, RWA Published Author Chapter, for *River of Fire;* Career Achievement Award, *Romantic Times,* 1990; Rita award for best Regency novel, RWA, 1991, for *The Rake and the Reformer;* Rita award for best long historical novel, RWA, 1994, for *Dancing on the Wind;* Golden Leaf awards for best historical novel, New Jersey Romance Writers, for *Uncommon Vows, Dearly Beloved, The Rake and the Reformer,* and *The Diabolical Baron;* Career Achievement Award for historical romance, New Jersey Romance Writers; second Career Achievement Award from *Romantic Times.*

WRITINGS:

The Diabolical Baron, Signet (New York, NY), 1987, Severn House (New York, NY), 1994, reprinted, Signet (New York, NY), 1999.
Lady of Fortune, New American Library (New York, NY), 1988.
The Controversial Countess, New American Library (New York, NY), 1989.
Carousel of Hearts, New American Library (New York, NY), 1989.
The Rogue and the Runaway, New American Library (New York, NY), 1990.
The Rake and the Reformer, Onyx (New York, NY), 1991, published as *The Rake,* Topaz (New York, NY), 1998.
Silk and Shadows, Onyx (New York, NY), 1991, Signet (New York, NY), 2000.
Uncommon Vows, Onyx (New York, NY), 1991.
Silk and Secrets, Onyx (New York, NY), 1992.
The Would Be Widow, Severn House (New York, NY), 1992, published as *The Bargain,* Signet (New York, NY), 1999.
Veils of Silk, Onyx (New York, NY), 1992.
Petals in the Storm, Topaz (New York, NY), 1993.
Thunder and Roses, Topaz (New York, NY), 1993.
Dancing on the Wind, Topaz (New York, NY), 1994.
Angel Rogue, Topaz (New York, NY), 1995.
River of Fire, Signet (New York, NY), 1996.
Shattered Rainbows, Topaz (New York, NY), 1996.
Dearly Beloved, Onyx (New York, NY), 1997.
One Perfect Rose, Fawcett (New York, NY), 1997.
The Wild Child, Ballantine (New York, NY), 1999.
The Burning Point, Berkley (New York, NY), 2000.
The China Bride, Ballantine (New York, NY), 2000.
Arco Iris Roto, Urano, 2000.

CONTRIBUTOR

A Regency Christmas II: Five Stories, Signet (New York, NY), 1993.
Promised Brides, Harlequin (New York, NY), 1994.
A Regency Christmas Carol: Five Stories, Signet (New York, NY), 1997.
A Stockingful of Joy, Onyx (New York, NY), 1997.
(And editor) *Faery Magic,* Kensington (San Diego, CA), 1998.
In Our Dreams, Zebra Books (New York, NY), 1998.
(And editor) *Captured Hearts: Five Favorite Love Stories,* Penguin (New York, NY), 1999.
(And editor) *Bride by Arrangement,* Harlequin (New York, NY), 2000.

SIDELIGHTS: Romance novelist Mary Jo Putney specializes in Regency period and Victorian tales featuring complex women characters. Her historical romances are generally respected for their strong characterizations, period detail, and solid writing. The winner of two Rita Awards and two lifetime achievement awards from *Romantic Times,* Putney has become "a favorite of romance fans," to quote *Booklist* contributor Diana Tixier Herald. As Ann Bouricius noted in another *Booklist* review, Putney's strengths "are her thoughtfulness and her well-drawn cast of compelling and very human characters."

Putney was born and raised in upstate New York and received her college education at Syracuse University. She completed a double major in English and industrial design, and commenced a career as a freelance graphic designer. In an online interview posted at *Romcom.com,* Putney explained how she became a writer. "I'd always been an addicted reader," she said, "but with terrible handwriting and vaguely dyslexic typing, the act of getting words down on paper legibly was so difficult that I never considered writing to be possible. Then I got a computer for my graphic design business and discovered the joys of word processing. Three months after starting my first Regency, *The Diabolical Baron,* I was offered a three-book contract, and I've never looked back. I'd finally found what I wanted to do when I grew up."

Most of Putney's novels are set in the Regency period, early nineteenth-century England. This particular era is so popular as a setting for romance novels that it has its own category contests and frequently a separate section on bookstore shelves. In another online interview, this one posted at *www.likesbooks.com,* Putney explained her own personal preference for Regencies. "I think the Regency is the most popular time period, as well as my personal favorite, because so many interesting currents cross then," she said. "It was the dawn of the modern age, where revolutions and industrial change were creating the society we recognize now. . . . At the same time, the Regency is distant enough to have glamour." Putney's mastery of the period is one reason why so many of her early books remain in print or have been issued in revised editions.

Critics have been generally receptive to Putney's novels. *Publishers Weekly* reviewer Peggy Kaganoff praised *Dearly Beloved*'s "spice and atmosphere," but suggested that *Uncommon Vows* relied too heavily on the plot device of amnesia. The same reviewer found 1992's *Silk and Secrets* too predictable, but admired its "spunky, happily flawed heroine." Kaganoff again noted compelling characters in *Thunder and Roses,* but found an "overload of extraneous historical detail." Maria Simson of *Publishers Weekly* commended *River of Fire* for its "strong romantic relationship, good writing, and memorable characters." *Library Journal* correspondent Kristin Ramsdell found *The Wild Child* to be "another gripping, well-crafted story that readers are sure to request."

In the late 1990s Putney began writing modern romances, the first of which was *The Burning Point.* Set in Baltimore and revolving around a demolition company, the novel explores the strained relationship between divorcees who are reunited in an effort to save the business. "This passionate love story unravels gradually, in trademark Putney style," maintained a *Publishers Weekly* reviewer. "The author has created a realistic, well-crafted story, laced with elements of suspense and mystery and featuring sympathetic protagonists."

In addition to her steady production of novels, Putney has also contributed short stories and novellas to several romance anthologies, including *Faery Magic,* a collection in which humans and faeries become entwined romantically. Several of her titles have made the bestseller lists, including the *New York Times, Wall Street Journal,* and *Publishers Weekly.*

Putney told *CA:* "Romance is a woman's genre, powerful and life affirming. It's a pleasure to write books that not only entertain, but sometimes heal."

BIOGRAPHICAL/CRITICAL SOURCES:

PERIODICALS

Booklist, June 1, 1999, Ann Bouricius, review of *The Wild Child,* p. 1802; May 1, 2000, Diana Tixier Herald, review of *The China Bride,* p. 1655.

Library Journal, February 15, 1997, p. 184; August, 1999, Kristin Ramsdell, review of *The Wild Child,* p. 72.

Publishers Weekly, January 26, 1990, p. 412; February 22, 1991, p. 215; June 1, 1992, p. 58; April 5, 1993, p. 71; March 6, 1995, p. 68; September 23, 1996, p. 74; February 15, 1997, p. 184; April 24, 2000, review of *The Burning Point,* p. 67; July 17, 2000, review of *The China Bride,* p. 174.

OTHER

Likesbooks Web site, http://www.likesbooks.com/quickie5.html/ (October 26, 2000), interview with Mary Jo Putney.

Light Street Book and Author Exchange, http://www.lightst.com/ (May 25, 2001).

Mary Jo Putney, http://www.maryjoputney.com/ (October 26, 2000).

Romcom, http://www.romcom.com/ (July, 2000), interview with Mary Jo Putney.*

* * *

PUTTERMAN, Louis (G.) 1952-

PERSONAL: Born April 27, 1952, in New York, NY; son of Milton and Eileen L. (Goldstein) Putterman; married second wife, Vivian Tseng, April 5, 1981; children: (first marriage) Laura Lee; (second marriage) Serena Rose, Mark Isaac. *Education:* Columbia University, B.A. (summa cum laude), 1976; Yale University, M.A. and M.Phil., both 1978, Ph.D. (with distinction), 1980.

ADDRESSES: *Home*—1128 Old Marlboro Rd., Concord, MA 01740. *Office*—Department of Economics, Brown University, 79 Waterman St., Providence, RI 02912-9000. *E-mail*—Louis_Putterman@brown.edu.

CAREER: Brown University, Providence, RI, assistant professor, 1980-82, associate professor, 1982-87, professor of economics, 1987—, associate director of Center for the Comparative Study of Development, 1989-97, acting director, 1990 and 1992, director, development studies program, 2000—, fellow of Wayland Collegium. Oxford University, St. Antony's College, visiting fellow at Centre for Chinese Studies, 1983; Yale University, visiting fellow at Institution for Social and Policy Studies, 1983-84; Harvard University, visiting scholar at John King Fairbank Center for East Asian Research, 1986-87, research associate, 1987-93.

MEMBER: American Economic Association, Association for Comparative Economic Studies, Phi Beta Kappa.

AWARDS, HONORS: Grants from Social Science Research Council and American Council of Learned Societies, 1981; Fulbright fellow in Africa, 1982-83; Lilly teaching fellow, 1982-83; grants from National Program for Advanced Study and Research in China, National Academy of Sciences, 1982-83 and 1985-86; honorary M.A. from Brown University, 1983; Mellon fellow in Chinese studies, 1983-84; fellow, Alfred P. Sloan Foundation, 1983-85; grants from Ford Foundation, 1984, 1985, and 1987; fellow in Chinese studies, Wang Institute, 1986-87; grants from National Science Foundation, 1986-88, and National Science Foundation, 1988-90; IRIS grant, University of Maryland at College Park, 1992-93.

WRITINGS:

Peasants, Collectives, and Choice: Economic Theory and Tanzania's Villages, JAI Press (Greenwich, CT), 1986.

(Editor and contributor) *The Economic Nature of the Firm: A Reader,* Cambridge University Press (New York City), 1986, 2nd edition, 1996.

(With John P. Bonin) *Economics of Cooperation and the Labor-managed Economy,* Harwood Academic (London), 1987.

The Division of Labor and Welfare: An Introduction to Economic Systems, Oxford University Press (New York City), 1990.

(Editor with Dietrich Rueschemeyer, and contributor) *State and Market in Development: Synergy or Rivalry?,* Lynne Rienner (Boulder, CO), 1992.

Continuity and Change in China's Rural Development: The Collective and Reform Eras in Perspective, Oxford University Press, 1993.

(Co-editor with Avner Ben-Ner) *Economics, Values and Organization,* Cambridge University Press, 1998.

Dollars and Change: Economics in Context, Yale University Press, 2001.

Contributor to books, including *Alienation, Society, and the Individual: Continuity and Change in Theory and Research,* Transaction Books (New Brunswick, NJ), 1992; *Market Socialism: The Current Debate,* edited by P. Bardhan and J. E. Roemer, Oxford University Press, 1993; and *China: A Reformable Socialism?,* edited by Yang Gan and Zhiyuan Cui, Oxford University Press (Hong Kong), 1994. *Modern China,* member of editorial board, 1990—, guest editor, 1992; member of editorial board, *Journal of Comparative Economics,* 1989-91, *Comparative Economic Studies,* 1991—, and *Annals of Public and Cooperative Economics,* 1992—. Contributor of more than seventy articles and reviews to economic and Chinese studies journals.

WORK IN PROGRESS: Research on aspects of Chinese industry; the effects of early history on modern economic growth; preferences and economic behavior in organizations.

BIOGRAPHICAL/CRITICAL SOURCES:

PERIODICALS

Contemporary Sociology, November, 1993, p. 833.

Journal of Comparative Economics, December, 1988, p. 622; March, 1992, p. 192.

Journal of Development Economics, February, 1988, p. 134.

Journal of Development Studies, July, 1988, p. 232.

Journal of Economic Literature, December, 1988, p. 1786.

Journal of Institutional and Theoretical Economics, September, 1990, p. 543.

Q-R

QUILTER, Deborah 1950-

PERSONAL: Born June 24, 1950, in San Diego, CA; daughter of Edward S. (a U.S. Navy captain) and Mary Ann Quilter. *Education:* San Francisco State University, B.A., 1973.

ADDRESSES: Home—108 West 73rd St., No. 2, New York, NY 10023.

CAREER: Freelance writer. *San Francisco Bay Guardian,* San Francisco, CA, consumer reporter, 1981-83; Andrews Publications, Westtown, PA, legal correspondent, 1982-85; *Better Health and Living,* New York City, travel and entertainment editor, 1985-87. Performs risk assessments, workstation evaluations, and computer technique training.

AWARDS, HONORS: San Francisco Press Club honorable mention for best news story, 1983.

WRITINGS:

(With Emil Pascarelli) *Repetitive Strain Injury: A Computer User's Guide,* Wiley (New York, NY), 1994.
The Repetitive Strain Injury Recovery Book, Walker (New York, NY), 1998.

Contributor to periodicals, including *Columbia Journalism Review, Woman's World, New York Times, Good Housekeeping, Woman's World, Computer Game Review, Woman,* and *Physician.* Former columnist, *Computer Currents* and *VDT News.* Contributing editor, *Dance Spirit* and *Stage Directions.*

WORK IN PROGRESS: Another book on her exercise program for people with repetitive strain injury.

BIOGRAPHICAL/CRITICAL SOURCES:

OTHER

Deborah Quilter's Web site, http://www.rsihelp.com/ (September 28, 2000).

* * *

RADCLIFFE, Donnie
See RADCLIFFE, Redonia

* * *

RADCLIFFE, Redonia
(Donnie Radcliffe)

PERSONAL: Born in Republican City, NE; daughter of Donnel F. and Lois (Woolman) Wheeler; married Robert Carter Radcliffe (a journalist), July 19, 1957; children: (first marriage) Melvyn Donnel Nunes. *Education:* San Jose State College (now University), B.A., 1951.

ADDRESSES: Agent—Gail E. Ross, Lichtman, Trister, Singer and Ross, 1666 Connecticut Ave., NW, Suite 501, Washington, DC 20009 (literary); Nancy Seis, Nancy Seis Presents, 408 East Duncan Ave., Alexandria, VA 22301 (speeches). *E-mail*—redrad@erols.com.

CAREER: Salinas Californian, Salinas, CA, reporter and editor, 1951-59; freelance journalist in Europe, 1959-66; *Washington Star,* Washington, DC, reporter, 1967-72; *Washington Post,* Washington, DC, reporter and columnist, 1972-95; freelance journalist, 1995—. Member of board of directors of National First Ladies Library, Canton, OH; trustee, Calvert County Public Library, Prince Frederick, MD.

WRITINGS:

(With *Washington Post* reporters and editors) *The Fall of a President,* Dell (New York, NY), 1974.

(As Donnie Radcliffe) *Simply Barbara Bush: A Portrait of America's Candid First Lady,* Warner Books (New York, NY), 1989.

(As Donnie Radcliffe) *Hillary Rodham Clinton: A First Lady for Our Time,* Warner Books (New York, NY), 1993, published as *Hillary Rodham Clinton: The Evolution of a First Lady,* 1999.

Also contributor to *The Washington Post Guide to Washington,* 1989, and to periodicals, including *McCall's, Ladies Home Journal, New York Times,* and *Town and Country.*

SIDELIGHTS: Redonia Radcliffe is a journalist who has covered first ladies for more than twenty-five years, most of them as a reporter, editor, and columnist for the Style section of the *Washington Post.* Radcliffe traveled with various first ladies as each pursued their personal causes in the United States and abroad.

Radcliffe is the author of biographies of Barbara Bush and Hillary Rodham Clinton. Frank Marafiote, who interviewed Radcliffe for the *Hillary Clinton Quarterly* online, asked her to talk about the differences in access she experienced in writing about the two first ladies. Radcliffe said she had "a great deal of access to Barbara Bush. . . . She was extremely cooperative after a while. . . . Hillary, on the other hand, had so many interviews during the campaign, that by the time they got to the White House, she's such a different person, she had such a different goal, that it was really difficult to nail her down." Radcliffe said Clinton "managed how she was going to talk to people. . . . Eventually, I got an interview with her toward the end of the book. As it turned out, the timing was very effective because it was the end chapter, and I could write about a sense of her evolution up to that point."

Marafiote wrote that Radcliffe "does bring some new details to light; a few are trivial, some are significant." Radcliffe offers insight into Rodham's childhood in Park Ridge, Illinois, and her political views—first as a Goldwater supporter, and then at Wellesley as a McGovern campaign worker and liberal Democrat. She writes of the First Lady's first meeting with Bill Clinton at Yale and her decision to relocate to Arkansas. Radcliffe also covered the first one hundred days of the Clinton presidency.

A *Kirkus Reviews* contributor called the biography "more a post-campaign bio than a probing assessment of a woman who doesn't need the White House to validate her." Michel McQueen said in the *New York Times Book Review* that the biography "offers a lot of nice little nuggets—for example, that in writing about herself for her high school paper, Hillary Rodham said her ambition was 'to marry a senator and settle down in Georgetown.' And in fact, the book is at its most poignant in describing Mrs. Clinton's decision to become Mrs. Clinton."

BIOGRAPHICAL/CRITICAL SOURCES:

PERIODICALS

Kirkus Reviews, August 1, 1993, review of *Hillary Rodham Clinton.*

New York Times Book Review, October 24, 1993, Michel McQueen, "First Lawyer."

Washington Post Book World, October 1, 1989, Liz Carpenter, review of *Simply Barbara Bush.*

OTHER

Hillary Clinton Quarterly, http://hillaryclintonquarterly.hypermart.net. (June 11, 2000).

* * *

RALPH, Margaret Nutting 1941-

PERSONAL: Born March 23, 1941, in Lincoln, NE; daughter of Charles B. (a professor of law) and Mary Agnes (a Latin teacher; maiden name, Flanagan) Nutting; married Donald E. Ralph (a psychologist), July 20, 1963; children: Daniel, John, Anthony, Kathleen. *Education:* St. Mary's College, Notre Dame, IN, B.A. (magna cum laude), 1963; University of Massachusetts at Amherst, M.A., 1970; University of Kentucky, Ph.D., 1980. *Religion:* Roman Catholic.

ADDRESSES: Home—431 Dudley Rd., Lexington, KY 40502. *Office*—Office of Catholic Education, 1310 West Main St., Lexington, KY 40508; fax: 859-254-6284. *E-mail*—mralph@cdlex.org.

CAREER: Teacher at Roman Catholic school in Hyattsville, MD, 1963-64; religion teacher at Roman Catholic high school in Lexington, KY, 1974-83; University of Kentucky, Lexington, instructor in English and religious studies, 1980—. Presenter of *The Bible as Literature,* a monthly program on WJMM Radio, 1976-79; Roman Catholic Diocese of Lexington, director of RCIA and Evangelization and secretary of educational ministries, 1988—; Lexington Theological Seminary, director of two master of arts tracks for Roman Catholics, 1988—; consultant in adult faith development to Office of Catholic Education.

WRITINGS:

"And God Said What?": An Introduction to Biblical Literary Forms for Bible Lovers, Paulist Press (Ramsey, NJ), 1986.
Willie of Church Street, Paulist Press (Ramsey, NJ), 1989.
Plain Words about Biblical Images, Paulist Press (Ramsey, NJ), 1989.
Discovering the Gospels: Four Accounts of the Good News, Paulist Press (Ramsey, NJ), 1990.
Discovering the First-Century Church: The Acts of the Apostles, Letters of Paul, and the Book of Revelation, Paulist Press (Ramsey, NJ), 1991.
Discovering Old Testament Origins, Paulist Press (Ramsey, NJ), 1992.
Discovering Prophecy and Wisdom, Paulist Press (Ramsey, NJ), 1993.
The Bible and the End of the World: Should We Be Afraid?, Paulist Press (Ramsey, NJ), 1997.
Nourished by the Word: Scripture, Logola Press, 1999.

"And God Said What?": An Introduction to Biblical Literary Forms for Bible Lovers was released on videocassette by American Video Cassette Educational Library, 1987. Contributor of articles to magazines, including *Christian Adulthood, Today's Parish, Living Light, Catechist Magazine,* and *Share the Word.*

Ralph's works have also been published in Italian and Portuguese.

SIDELIGHTS: Margaret Nutting Ralph told *CA:* "My primary goal is to enable adults to grow in their knowledge and love of Scripture. I see a gulf between the faith life of adults and the academic pursuits of Scripture scholars, but I find these two worlds are totally compatible. I would like to present the work of Scripture scholars to adults in such a way that the growth of knowledge and the growth in faith go hand in hand."

* * *

RIDGE, Martin 1923-

PERSONAL: Born May 7, 1923, in Chicago, IL; son of John and Ann (Lew) Ridge; married Marcella Jane VerHoef, March 17, 1948; children: John Andrew, Curtis Cordell, Wallace Karsten, Judith Lee. *Education:* Chicago Teacher's College (now Chicago State University), B.A., 1943; Northwestern University, M.A., 1949, Ph. D., 1951. *Politics:* Democrat.

ADDRESSES: Home—533 West Coolidge, San Gabriel, CA 91775. *Office*—Henry E. Huntington Library, San Marino, CA 91109; and Department of History, California Institute of Technology, 1201 East California Blvd., Pasadena, CA 91125.

CAREER: Westminster College, New Wilmington, PA, began as instructor, became assistant professor of American history, 1951-55; San Diego State College (now University), San Diego, CA, assistant professor of history, 1955-66; Indiana University, Bloomington, professor of history, 1966-77; Henry E. Huntington Library, San Marino, CA, senior research associate, 1977—; California Institute of Technology, Pasadena, CA, professor of history, 1981—. Visiting professor at Northwestern University, summer, 1959, and University of California, Los Angeles, summer, 1963. Member of board of directors of California Historical Landmarks Commission, 1954-64; consultant to San Diego City and County Schools, 1962-65, and Los Angeles County Museum, 1979—; member of Indiana Hospital and Health Planning Facilities Council, 1974-75; member of numerous prize committees, including Pulitzer Prize juries, 1978, 1979, 1981, and 1985. *Wartime service:* U.S. Merchant Marine, 1943-45.

MEMBER: American Historical Association, Organization of American Historians, Agricultural History Society, Pacific Coast Branch, American Historical Association (vice president, 1994-95; president, 1995-96), Social Science History Association, Southern Historical Association, Western History Association (vice president, 1985-86; president, 1986-87), Historical Society of Southern California (president, 1994-98), New Mexico Historical Association.

AWARDS, HONORS: Fellow of William Randolph Hearst Foundation, 1950, Social Science Research Council, 1950, American Council of Learned Societies, 1960, Newberry Library, 1962, Baker Library (Harvard School of Business), 1964, Guggenheim Foundation, 1965-66, Henry E. Huntington Library, 1973-74, American Antiquarian Society, 1982, and Historical Society of Southern California, 1992; Annenberg scholar at University of Southern California, 1979-80; Best Book awards, American Historical Association, and Phi Alpha Theta, both 1963, both for *Ignatius Donnelly: The Portrait of a Politician;* participant in British Academy Exchange, 1986; Gilberto Espinosa Prize, *New Mexico Historical Review,* 1989; Ray Allen Billington Prize for best article on western history, 1990-91.

WRITINGS:

Ignatius Donnelly: The Portrait of a Politician, University of Chicago Press (Chicago, IL), 1962, revised edition, Minnesota Historical Society (St. Paul, MN), 1991.

(With Vanza Devereau) *California Work and Workers,* Wagnar, Harr (San Francisco, CA), 1963.

(With Walker D. Wyman) *The American Adventure: A History,* Lyons & Carnahan (Chicago, IL), 1964.

(Editor, with Ray Allen Billington) *America's Frontier Story: A Documentary History of Western Expansion,* Holt (New York, NY), 1969.

(With Raymond J. Wilson and George Spiero) *Liberty and Union: A History of the United States* (juvenile), two volumes, Houghton (Boston, MA), 1973.

(With Billington) *American History after 1865,* 9th edition, Littlefield, (Totowa, NJ), 1981.

(Editor) *The New Bilingualism: An American Dilemma,* University of Southern California Press (Los Angeles, CA), 1981.

(With Billington) *Westward Expansion: A History of the American Frontier,* 5th edition, Macmillan (New York, NY), 1982.

Atlas of American Frontiers, Rand McNally (Chicago, IL), 1992.

(With Walter Nugent) *The American West,* Indiana University Press (Bloomington, IN), 1999.

EDITOR AND AUTHOR OF INTRODUCTION

Francis Parkman, *The Oregon Trail,* Folio Society (London, England), 1974.

Oliver Johnson, *A Home in the Woods,* Indiana University Press (Bloomington, IN), 1978.

Frederick Jackson Turner: Wisconsin's Historian of the Frontier, University of Wisconsin Press (Madison, WI), 1986.

Billy Bryant, *Children of Ol' Man River,* R. R. Donnelly (Chicago, IL), 1988.

Westward Journeys: Memoirs of Jesse A. Applegate and Vainia Honeywell Porter Who Traveled the Overland Trail, R. R. Donnelly (Chicago, IL), 1989.

Frederick Jackson Turner: Three Essays, University of New Mexico Press (Albuquerque, NM), 1993.

OTHER

Contributor to books, including *The Significance of the Frontier in American History,* by Francis Jackson Turner, University of Wisconsin Press, 1985; and *Incidents of a Voyage to California, 1849,* Arthur Clark (Glendale, CA), 1987. Member of editorial boards of *Encyclopedia Americana,* 1968—, and *Encyclopedia of the American West.* Coeditor of "Histories of the American Frontier" and "West in the Twentieth Century" series. *Southern California Quarterly,* associate editor, 1963-69, acting editor, 1964; *Journal of American History,* editor, 1966-77. Member of editorial boards, *Historian,* 1952-58, *Agricultural History,* 1957-75, *Pacific Historical Review,* 1961-64, *Southern California Quarterly,* 1962-65, *Prologue,* 1971-74, *America: History and Life,* 1973-93, *Arizona and the West,* 1977-81, *American West,* 1977-80, *New Mexico Historical Review,* 1987-92, and *Montana, the Magazine of Western History,* 1989—.

WORK IN PROGRESS: A social history of silver.

* * *

RITCHIE, Donald A(rthur) 1945-

PERSONAL: Born December 23, 1945, in New York, NY; son of Arthur V. and Jeannette (Kromm) Ritchie; married Patricia A. Cooper, July 14, 1973 (divorced, 1986); married Anne Glackin Campbell, June 20, 1988; children: (second marriage) Jennifer Campbell Hannon, Andrea Campbell (stepdaughters). *Education:* City College of the City University of New York, B.A., 1967; University of Maryland at College Park, M.A., 1969, Ph.D., 1975.

ADDRESSES: *Home*—6033 Avon Dr., Bethesda, MD 20814. *Office*—Senate Historical Office, U.S. Senate Building, Washington, DC 20510.

CAREER: University of Maryland at College Park, instructor in history, 1974-76; Northern Virginia Community College, Alexandria, VA, instructor in history, 1975; George Mason University, Fairfax, VA, instructor in history, 1976; U.S. Senate, Washington, DC, associate historian at Senate Historical Office, 1976—. Adjunct assistant professor, Cornell-in-Washington Program, 1990-2000. Letitia Woods Brown Memorial Lecturer, Historical Society of Washington, Washington, DC, 1990. *Military service:* U.S. Marine Corps, 1969-71.

MEMBER: American Historical Association (chair of congressional fellowship committee, 1982-84; council member, 1992-96), National Council on Public History (chair of nominating committee, 1994-95), Organization of American Historians (member of nominating committee, 1985-87; chair of committee on research and access to historical documentation, 1993), Oral History Association (president, 1986-87), Society for History in the Federal Government (council member, 1989-91).

AWARDS, HONORS: Forrest C. Pogue Award, Oral History in the Mid-Atlantic Region, 1984; Henry Adams Prize, Society for History in the Federal Government, 1992, for *Press Gallery;* Richard W. Leopold Prize, Organization of American Historians, 1992, for *Press Gallery.*

WRITINGS:

(Editor) *Executive Sessions of the Senate Foreign Relations Committee (Historical Series),* Volumes VIII-XV, U.S. Government Printing Office (Washington, DC), 1978-93.

James M. Landis: Dean of the Regulators, Harvard University Press (Cambridge, MA), 1980.

Press Gallery: Congress and the Washington Correspondents, Harvard University Press (Cambridge, MA), 1991.

The Young Oxford Companion to the Congress of the United States, Oxford University Press (New York, NY), 1993.

History of a Free Nation (high school textbook), Glencoe (New York, NY), 1994.

Doing Oral History, Twayne (Boston, MA), 1994.

American Journalists: Getting the Story, Oxford University Press (New York, NY), 1997.

The Oxford Essential Guide to the U.S. Government, Berkeley Books, 2000.

Contributor to history journals. Editor of *Maryland Historian,* 1972-73. Editor of "Oral History Series," Twayne (Boston, MA), 1988-98.

SIDELIGHTS: Donald A. Ritchie told *CA:* "While researching in the manuscript collection of James M. Landis, a leading regulatory adviser to presidents Franklin D. Roosevelt, Harry S Truman, and John F. Kennedy, I discovered the last thirty pages of an oral history interview that Landis had given shortly before his death. Further hunting located the complete seven-hundred-page manuscript at the Columbia Oral History Office. This was a magnificent find for a biographer: the subject's life in his own words. Even relatively well-known facts and incidents took on a new immediacy when presented in the first person, but, although the oral history illuminated Landis's long career as a lawyer, dean of the Harvard Law School, and government official, it revealed little about his private life. He made almost no mention of his two marriages, his children, or the income tax delinquency that eventually sent him to jail. I began to conduct my own interviews, with Landis's family, friends, colleagues, and even his psychiatrist. These oral histories significantly influenced my writing of the biography.

"I carried my interest in oral history to the Senate Historical Office, where I conduct interviews with former senators and members of the Senate staff. Oral history also influenced my writing of a high school textbook, *History of a Free Nation.* Using first-person accounts helped to enliven the narrative and to capture the attention of adolescents. After speaking about oral history at various conferences and workshops, I compiled my recommendations into an introductory guidebook, *Doing Oral History.*

"Conducting interviews raised my curiosity about other professional interviewers, particularly the journalists who regularly call the Senate Historical Office for information. Their requests made me aware of the working conditions under which journalists operate—particularly their reliance on oral rather than written sources. This led to *Press Gallery,* a study of how Washington correspondents historically gathered and reported news of the federal government to the general public."

In a review in the *New York Times,* George P. Will described *Press Gallery* as "sometimes startling, sometimes dismaying and constantly illuminating. . . . [Ritchie] is a scrupulous historian whose fine book brings back the powerful aroma of a past too raw to be romanticized. Thus does memory help reconcile us to current discontents."

BIOGRAPHICAL/CRITICAL SOURCES:

BOOKS

Howe, Barbara J., and Emory L. Kemp, editors, *Public History: An Introduction,* Robert E. Krieger, 1986.

PERIODICALS

Booknotes, July 7, 1991.
New York Times, June 30, 1991.
OHMAR Newsletter, fall, 1984.

* * *

ROBERTS, David S(tuart) 1943-

PERSONAL: Born May 29, 1943, in Denver, CO; son of Walter Orr (an astrophysicist) and Janet (Smock) Roberts; married Sharon Morris, October 29, 1967. *Education:* Harvard University, B.A., 1965; University of Denver, M.A., Ph.D., 1970. *Avocational interests:* Mountaineering (has made fourteen trips to Alaska).

ADDRESSES: *Office*—Department of Literature, Hampshire College, Amherst, MA 01002.

CAREER: Hampshire College, Amherst, MA, 1970—, began as assistant professor, currently associate professor of literature and mountaineering.

MEMBER: American Alpine Club.

WRITINGS:

Mountain of My Fear, Vanguard, 1968.
Deborah: A Wilderness Narrative, Vanguard, 1970.
Great Exploration Hoaxes, Sierra Club Books (San Francisco, CA), 1982.
Moments of Doubt and Other Mountaineering Writings, Mountaineers (Seattle, WA), 1986.
Jean Stafford: A Biography, Little, Brown (Boston, MA), 1988, published as *Jean Stafford: The Life of a Writer,* St. Martin's Press (New York, NY), 1989.
Iceland: Land of the Sagas, photographs by Jon Krakauer, Abrams (New York, NY), 1990.
Deborah; and, The Mountains of My Fear: The Early Climbs, foreword by Jon Krakauer, Mountaineers (Seattle, WA), 1991.
(With Bradford Washburn) *Mount McKinley: The Conquest of Denali,* preface by Ansel Adams, Abrams (New York, NY), 1991.
Once They Moved like the Wind: Cochise, Geronimo, and the Apache Wars, Simon & Schuster (New York, NY), 1993.
In Search of the Old Ones: Exploring the Anasazi World of the Southwest, Simon & Schuster (New York, NY), 1996.
Escape Routes: Further Adventure Writings of David Roberts, Mountaineers (Seattle, WA), 1997.
(With Conrad Anker) *The Lost Explorer: Finding Mallory on Mount Everest,* Simon & Schuster (New York, NY), 1999.
Points Unknown: A Century of Great Exploration, Norton (New York, NY), 2000.
A Newer World: Kit Carson, John C. Fremont, and the Claiming of the American West, Simon & Schuster (New York, NY), 2000.
True Summit: What Really Happened on the Legendary Ascent of Annapurna, Simon & Schuster (New York, NY), 2000.

Contributor to books, including *Earth and the Great Weather,* Friends of the Earth, 1971; *The Mountains of America,* edited by Franklin Russell, Abrams, 1975; and *Climb: Stories of Survival from Rock, Snow, and Ice,* edited by Clint Willis, Thunder's Mouth (New York, NY), 2000. Contributor of articles and reviews to mountaineering journals and national periodicals, including *Saturday Evening Post* and *New York Times Book Review.* Contributing editor to *Outside* Magazine.

SIDELIGHTS: A respected mountaineer and contributing editor for *Outside* magazine, David S. Roberts has written or contributed to several books on the themes of mountain climbing and wilderness adventure. He has also written three highly regarded histories of the American west, as well as a biography of writer Jean Stafford.

Mountain of My Fear and *Deborah: A Wilderness Narrative* are accounts of the author's early experiences climbing mountains in Alaska. These titles established Roberts's reputation as both a skilled mountaineer and a talented writer. He went on to contribute to several anthologies about mountain climbing and wilderness, collaborating with such esteemed figures as mountaineer and Boston Museum of Science founder Bradford Washburn, wilderness photographer Ansel Adams, and mountaineering writer Jon Krakauer, whose best-selling *Into Thin Air* documented the ill-fated 1996 Everest climb.

Among Roberts's mountaineering titles to attract significant critical attention was *True Summit: What Really Happened on the Legendary Ascent of Annapurna,* a book that challenges Maurice Herzog's account of the first successful ascent of Annapurna. Ironically,

Herzog's *Annapurna* was the book that inspired Roberts to become a mountain climber himself. First published in 1951, it has sold more than eleven million copies. Yet, after discovering new material about the famed climb, including an unedited diary of one of the team members, Roberts discovered that Herzog's heroically tinged story wasn't the whole truth. In *True Summit,* Roberts reveals discord and problems with the climb, suggesting that the expedition was, in the words of a *Publishers Weekly* reviewer, "a troublesome enterprise filled with doubt and peevishness and not a storybook triumph by valorous Frenchmen."

The Lost Explorer: Finding Mallory on Mount Everest, which Roberts wrote with Conrad Anker, also generated significant interest. The story of how Anker and his climbing team found the body of George Leigh Mallory, the renowned British climber who had disappeared on Everest in 1924, it "ranks with the best mountaineering literature," in the opinion of *New York Times Book Review* writer Susan Reed. Whether Mallory and his climbing partner had reached the summit—which would have made them the first to succeed in scaling the world's highest peak—and how they met their deaths on the mountain remained unclear until Anker's discovery. After identifying Mallory's body, Anker and a teammate attempted to reach the summit using the same course that Mallory had evidently tried. They succeeded, but concluded that Mallory and his partner had turned back before reaching the summit due to a storm and, slipping, had fallen to their deaths. Though Roberts did not accompany Anker's expedition, the alternate chapters he provided for *The Lost Explorer* on Mallory's life and climbing achievements impressed critics.

Roberts chose a different type of life to document in his only book-length biographical work, *Jean Stafford: A Biography.* Stafford (1919-1979) was a Pulitzer Prize-winning short story writer and author of the novels *Boston Adventure, The Mountain Lion,* and *The Catherine Wheel.* She endured an abusive marriage to poet Robert Lowell (as well as unhappy marriages to writers Oliver Jensen and A. J. Liebling) and battled severe alcoholism and chronic illness throughout much of her adult life, as well as being notorious for self-destructive and hostile behavior. Increasingly bitter, Stafford considered herself a failure and was unable to complete the novel on which she labored for the last twenty years of her life. In focusing on these sordid details, Joyce Carol Oates wrote in the *New York Times Book Review* that Roberts "has written a seemingly well-intentioned but numbingly repetitive and emetic [biography] . . . that falls into pathography's technique of emphasizing the sensational underside of its subject's life to the detriment of those more scattered, and less dramatic, periods of accomplishment and well being." Acknowledging that Roberts's account exhibits intelligence and compassion, Oates nevertheless found that the book fails to place Stafford's work in context and that its "intense focus upon the merely personal . . . leaves the account claustrophobic and airless." Many other judgments, however, were extremely favorable. According to a *Boston Globe* article, writer Walker Percy believed that Roberts "has done a remarkable job in re-creating the life of a remarkable woman—in all her beauty, her superb talent and the tragedy of her life." Merle Rubin, in the *Christian Science Monitor,* deemed the book "a vividly detailed account" that honors Stafford's artistry. And *Atlantic*'s Phoebe-Lou Adams observed that Roberts "brings his subject to life as a brilliant woman whom one would just as soon not have for a next-door neighbor."

His histories of the American west have also earned Roberts critical acclaim. *Once They Moved like the Wind: Cochise, Geronimo, and the Apache Wars,* a chronicle of the Apache Wars, which were waged from the early 1860s until Geronimo's surrender in 1886, was hailed by a *Publishers Weekly* writer as "history at its most engrossing." Fergus M. Bordewich, in *Smithsonian,* praised Roberts for striving to present both sides of the conflict, which was especially challenging because the Indians left no written histories of these events. In Bordewich's view, Roberts conveys sympathy for the Indians without ignoring the point of view among the Army troops dispatched to fight them. Another study of Southwestern Indians, *In Search of the Old Ones,* explores the culture of the Anasazi, the cave-dwelling ancestors of present-day Pueblo peoples. Roberts's "awe at the region's beauty . . . and at the testaments to an unknown culture," enthused a *Publishers Weekly* contributor, "will be contagious for readers."

A Newer World: Kit Carson, John C. Fremont, and the Claiming of the American West is a study of explorer John C. Fremont and his guide, Kit Carson, who mapped the eastern portion of the Oregon Trail in 1842 and played a significant role in seizing California from Mexico in 1846 and in joining U.S. Army forces against the Southwest Indians. In researching the book Roberts retraced, via automobile or on foot, all of Fremont and Carson's treks through New Mexico, Colorado, California, and Wyoming. He also used recent historical scholarship on Indians, as well as previous studies on Fremont and Carson, to provide what *New York Times Book Review* writer David Howard Bain considered a "remarkably well-balanced portrait of two major but still controversial figures of the Old West." Roberts presents evidence that links Fremont to an "unprovoked massacre" of California Indians "in every respect the equal of Wounded Knee or Aravaipa." He paints a grim picture of Fremont's 1848-49 Rockies campaign, which Fremont attempted without the help of Carson, and which resulted in a third of his party dying of cold or starvation. Cannibalism of the victims, Roberts writes, almost certainly occurred, and charges that Fremont left stragglers behind to die are probably true. Despite these unsavory facts, reviewers found *A Newer World* entertaining as well as informative. "Any fictitious adventurers would be hard put to compete with the real-life adventures of Fremont, Carson and their bands of hard mountain men," wrote Lyn Nofzier in *Insight on the News.* The book "captures the beauty and harshness of life on the frontier in a vivid and passionate style," observed a contributor to *Publishers Weekly,* who hailed it as "an engrossing story of a period in American history when explorers never knew what they would find around the next bend in the trail."

BIOGRAPHICAL/CRITICAL SOURCES:

PERIODICALS

Appalachia, December, 1974.

Atlantic, September, 1988, Phoebe-Lou Adams, review of *Jean Stafford,* p. 98.

Booklist, July, 1993, p. 1941; March 1, 1996, Donna Seaman, review of *In Search of the Old Ones,* p. 1120.

Boston Globe, October 9, 1988, Walker Percy, review of *Jean Stafford,* p. B93.

Christian Science Monitor, June 2, 1992, Merle Rubin, review of *Jean Stafford.*

Economist, July 15, 2000, review of *The Lost Explorer,* p. 81.

Insight on the News, March 6, 2000, Lyn Nofzier, review of *A Newer World,* p. 33.

Journal of American History, December, 1994, p. 1328; December, 1996, David J. Weber, review of *In Search of the Old Ones,* p. 994.

Library Journal, July, 1993, p. 97; March 1, 1996, Ken St. Andre, review of *In Search of the Old Ones,* p. 91; November 1, 1999, Grant A. Fredericksen, review of *A Newer World,* p. 109.

New Yorker, November 8, 1993, p. 139.

New York Times Book Review, August 28, 1988, Joyce Carol Oates, review of *Jean Stafford,* Section 7, p. 3; December 5, 1999, Susan Reed, review of *The Lost Explorer;* February 27, 2000, David Haward Bain, review of *A Newer World.*

Publishers Weekly, April 1, 1968; May 31, 1993, review of *Once They Moved like the Wind,* p. 38; January 1, 1996, review of *In Search of the Old Ones,* p. 61; December 6, 1999, review of *A Newer World,* p. 65; May 8, 2000, review of *True Summit,* p. 210.

School Library Journal, July, 1996, Pam Spencer, review of *In Search of the Old Ones,* p. 110.

Smithsonian, March, 1994, Fergus M. Bordewich, review of *Once They Moved like the Wind,* p. 125.

Sports Afield, winter, 1999, review of *The Lost Explorer,* p. 68.

Sports Illustrated, November 29, 1999, Ron Fimrite, review of *The Lost Explorer,* p. R22.

Time, September 19, 1988, review of *Jean Stafford,* p. 95.

Western Historical Quarterly, summer, 1996, p. 229.*

* * *

ROBERTS, Les 1937-

PERSONAL: Born Lester Roubert, July 18, 1937, in Chicago, IL; surname legally changed, 1968; son of Lester Nathaniel (a dentist) and Eleanor Sybil (Bauch) Roubert; married Gail Medland, September 19, 1957 (divorced, 1980); children: Valerie Lynne, Darren Jon. *Education:* Attended University of Illinois at Urbana-Champaign and Roosevelt University, 1954-56. *Avocational interests:* Gourmet cooking, theater, concerts, playing the piano, and reading.

ADDRESSES: *Office*—3244 Hyde Park Ave., Cleveland Heights, OH 44118. *Agent*—Dominick Abel, 146 West 82nd St., New York, NY 10024. *E-mail*—LESROBERTS6578@msn.com.

CAREER: Television writer and producer; jazz pianist and singer. Owner of Les Roberts Productions and Roberts Two, 1970-81; Delta Audio-Visual Services, director, 1984-85; creator and executive producer of *Cash Explosion* (weekly television game show for the Ohio Lottery), 1987, and for lottery programs in other states. Notre Dame College of Ohio, adjunct faculty member; Case Western Reserve University, lecturer; teacher of novel, screenplay, and mystery writing at Glendale Community College, Learning Tree, and Everywoman's Village. Producer of television programs, including *The Jackie Gleason Show, The Andy Griffith Show, The Man from U.N.C.L.E.,* and *The Lucy Show,* all 1967; and *When Things Were Rotten,* 1975. *Military service:* U.S. Army, Signal Corps, 1960-62.

MEMBER: Writers Guild of America, Private Eye Writers of America (president, 1992-94), American Crime Writers League.

AWARDS, HONORS: Best First Private Eye Novel Award, Private Eye Writers of America/St. Martin's Press, 1986, for *An Infinite Number of Monkeys;* Cleveland Arts Prize for Literature, 1992; grant from Ohio Arts Council, 1993.

WRITINGS:

DETECTIVE NOVELS; "SAXON" SERIES

An Infinite Number of Monkeys, St. Martin's Press (New York, NY), 1987.
Not Enough Horses, St. Martin's Press (New York, NY), 1988.
A Carrot for the Donkey, St. Martin's Press (New York, NY), 1989.
Snake Oil, St. Martin's Press (New York, NY), 1990.
Seeing the Elephant, St. Martin's Press (New York, NY), 1992.
The Lemon Chicken Jones, St. Martin's Press (New York, NY), 1994.

DETECTIVE NOVELS; "MILAN JACOVICH" SERIES

Pepper Pike (also see below), St. Martin's Press (New York, NY), 1988.
Full Cleveland, St. Martin's Press (New York, NY), 1989.
Deep Shaker, St. Martin's Press (New York, NY), 1991.
The Cleveland Connection, St. Martin's Press (New York, NY), 1993.
The Lake Effect, St. Martin's Press (New York, NY), 1994.
The Duke of Cleveland, St. Martin's Press (New York, NY), 1995.
Collision Bend, St. Martin's Press (New York, NY), 1996.
Cleveland Local, St. Martin's Press (New York, NY), 1997.
A Shoot in Cleveland, St. Martin's Press (New York, NY), 1998.
The Best-kept Secret, St. Martin's Press (New York, NY), 1999.
The Indian Sign, Thomas Dunne Books, 2000.
The Dutch, St. Martin's Press (New York, NY), 2001.

OTHER

Foxbat (screenplay), Bang Bang Films (Hong Kong, China), 1977.
Solar Plexus (screenplay), 1981.
(With Gail Roberts) *Those Little White Lies* (two-act play), produced in Los Angeles, CA, 1985.
A Carol for Cleveland (novella), Cobham-Hatherton (Cleveland, OH), 1991.
The Chinese Fire Drill, Thorndyke, 2001.

Author of the screenplay *Crooked River* (based on his novel *Pepper Pike*). Also author of an unproduced two-act play, *Writer's Block.* Producer of and writer for television programs, including *Hollywood Squares, It Takes Two, The Memory Game,* and *Runaround.* Restaurant reviewer for *Today,* 1984-86, and other local magazines; mystery book reviewer, *Cleveland Plain Dealer,* 1989—.

WORK IN PROGRESS: The Irish Sports Pages, publication by St. Martin's Press (New York, NY) expected in 2002; *"The Scent of Spiced Oranges" and Other Stories by Les Roberts,* Thorndyke, 2002.

SIDELIGHTS: The crime novels of Les Roberts fall naturally into two series, each of which reveals facets of the author's personal experience. One series follows the slick private eye Saxon through the entertainment world, where Roberts himself spent several years writing screenplays and television scripts. The other traces the adventures of private investigator Milan Jacovich through the streets of Cleveland, Ohio, where Roberts now lives. The author's evident affection for the Midwestern "city on the lake" is noted by several reviewers and acknowledged by the city itself, which in 1992 awarded Roberts the Cleveland Arts Prize for Literature. Based on this work, Barry W. Gardner called Roberts "one of the consistently best writers of private detective novels practicing today . . . [one whose work] has steadily improved over the course of his literary career, and one who will eventually attain the recognition he merits" in the *St. James Guide to Crime and Mystery Writers.*

The Saxon character emerged as an almost stereotypical Los Angeles investigator and sometime actor in *An Infinite Number of Monkeys,* which earned Roberts a "best first novel" award in 1986. His character deepened somewhat in *Not Enough Horses,* in which the detective adopts Marvel, a street kid who figures in a later novel, *The Lemon Chicken Jones.* In fact, wrote Gardner, "one of the most appealing aspects of the series is the evolution of Saxon's attitudes as he and Marvel both age and grow." Gardner's choice for "the deepest and best of the Saxon books" is *Seeing the Elephant,* which moves away from Los Angeles into the Midwest, where Saxon has gone to attend a funeral. Though Gardner praised the series for "novelistic strength," he also suggested that a potential weakness may be "Roberts's own ambivalence toward their [Hollywood-style] milieu," which nonetheless the author "brings sharply to life in all its grime and glory."

"The Jacovich books seem the darker of Roberts's two series," Gardner reported, "and the strongest." Milan Jacovich provides a genial, if somewhat straitlaced, contrast to Saxon. A detective of Slovenian descent with a master's degree in journalism, Milan plies his trade in Cleveland's variegated neighborhoods, on grimy city streets peopled with blue-collar laborers, organized crime bosses, and young people at risk. "Roberts is obviously at home in [Cleveland's] ethnic neighborhoods," Gardner commented, "and in his hands their inhabitants achieve a solid reality."

Beginning with *Pepper Pike,* Roberts reveals Jacovich as a man of what Gardner called "a stern and demanding *personal* morality . . . one of the best-characterized of today's P.I.'s." Whether Milan is chasing a scam artist who stole mob money in *Full Cleveland,* tackling a gang of drug dealers who target his friend's teenage son in *Deep Shaker,* or sleuthing among artists, art galleries, and his mob pals to locate a valuable ceramic vase in *The Duke of Cleveland,* Gardner found that "the broad themes of morality, of obligation and loyalty and responsibility, and what they cost and what they're worth, are the bones beneath the skin of all Roberts's fiction." Yet, he added, "they are never dealt with in a simplistic fashion . . . [or] allowed to become obtrusive." Commenting on *The Duke of Cleveland* in *Armchair Detective,* Don Sandstrom remarked that "Jacovich tells his story convincingly, smoothly, and interestingly. . . . He does it exceedingly well this time."

In *The Lake Effect* Jacovich finds himself reluctantly working for a mob boss, while acting as a bodyguard for a mayoral candidate in a local suburb. The political campaign proves to be an ugly and dangerous one, with Jacovich trying to determine who killed the opponent's wife. The novel received a cool reception in *Kirkus Reviews,* where a critic judged that the reading made for "A pleasant couple of hours—well, more hours than usual for Milan—but don't be fooled: This ragbag of subplots is untidy rather than complex."

In a subsequent novel, *Collision Bend,* Roberts blends his experiences as a television and film writer with his evident comfort in a Cleveland setting. In what Sybil S. Steinberg of *Publishers Weekly* called a "solid, keep-you-guessing mystery," Milan assists a former lover to save her current partner from arrest for the murder of a local television newscaster.

Similarly, movie-making is central to *A Shoot in Cleveland,* in which Jacovich is hired to protect and supervise the young movie star Darren Anderson. On Jacovich's day off, the young man rapes the daughter of a local man who is helping to finance the film. Milan quits in disgust, but when the actor is killed the next day, the detective has a murder to investigate. A *Publishers Weekly* reviewer called the novel part of an ever-improving series, in which Roberts's Cleveland provided much more than regional interest. "Roberts makes fine narrative use of the unlikely mix of Cleveland's blue-collar ethnic traditions with the fairy tale world of a movie shoot," the critic said. Emily Melton agreed in *Booklist,* when she wrote that Roberts's book "with its intriguing plot, provocative philosophical dilemmas, and strong Travis McGee-like hero—is his best yet." Conversely, a *Kirkus Reviews* critic found the novel lacking, and noted, "Roberts puts [his] story through its paces with vigor and heart, if without any real surprises."

The tenth book in the series is *The Best-kept Secret,* published some eleven years after the first Jacovich novel. It places Milan on the campus of Sherman College, where he is trying to exonerate Jason Crowell, a young man who is accused by a militant feminist group of raping an anonymous victim. Murder and drug dealing are later added to the charges against Jason, while Milan discovers that Jason's biggest secret is that he is gay. The story earned both praise and criticism, with *Publishers Weekly* declaring that despite his "enlightened intentions," Roberts is handcuffed by stereotypical feminist and academic characters and an "always moral" hero. The critic concluded that the book was "driven more by Milan's gruff voice than by any plot surprises or psychological exploration." In *Booklist,* however, Emily Melton continued to admire Roberts's hero, with his "pragmatic approach to life, . . . sometimes foolish bravado and quixotic attempts to save the world."

Jacovich's next installment, *The Indian Sign,* was published in 2000. In this story, Milan finds trouble virtually on his front step. An elderly Native American man is found dead in the river, the same man that the investigator had noticed sitting on a bench across from his apartment. Milan takes on the unpaid job of looking for a kidnapped baby, the dead man's great-granddaughter, while he is also employed by a toy manufacturer that itself needs investigating for making poisonous toys. *Publishers Weekly* suggested that the private investigator's personal comments on everything from cigarette brands to shopping in Cleveland were excessive: "These attempts at verisimilitude mostly get in the way of what could be two interesting storylines," and commented that the author "overrates readers' interest in his hero's personal life." In a *BookBrowser* review, Harriet Klausner agreed with this assessment: "Too much trivial characterization hurts an otherwise wonderful mystery." But other reviewers were pleased with Roberts's approach. In *Booklist,* Gary Niebuhr described *The Indian Sign* as "a solidly paced narrative that still allows for plenty of introspection and room to develop a cast of uniformly strong characters." Dawn Goldsmith also enjoyed the chance to learn more about the lead character and his home. She wrote in *Crescent Blues Book Views,* "This sense of place encourages readers to develop a closer affinity to Milan." And Goldsmith admired how "Roberts . . . knows how to tell a story that keeps readers moving toward the final 'Ah ha!' . . . He involves readers in the plot to the point where they find themselves shouting at Milan . . . because the readers figure out the clues just before the characters do."

Les Roberts once told *CA:* "I began writing books almost by accident. A producer asked me to come up with a private eye story for a film, and although he and the film's backers liked it, we couldn't come to terms. That story became *An Infinite Number of Monkeys* and changed the direction of my life. Although ninety-five percent of my income has come from writing or related fields, I have now realized, at a relatively advanced age, that writing novels is what I was born to do.

"My advice to aspiring writers is simple: read good writing. My own influences will surprise no one—John Steinbeck, for the raw emotion his work engenders; F. Scott Fitzgerald, for his glorious use of the language and his uncanny knack for describing the milieu in which he lived; Ernest Hemingway, who should be required reading for any writer tempted to use twelve overblown words where one perfect one will do; and the writers of the mystery genre: Raymond Chandler, Dashiell Hammett, Ross Macdonald, John D. McDonald. My second piece of advice is: write! 'Wannabees' talk about the book they are going to write; real writers do it!

"Writers of fiction, no matter what the genre, share a commonality. We write about people in crisis, in transition. I've chosen to deal with the greatest crisis of all—life or death. If along the way I can peel back a few layers of gunk and expose corruption, if I can comment on the human condition and provoke a thought, or give a reader a chuckle or two, why, so much the better. But I write because I have to—it's addictive, like heroin, beautiful women, or Big Macs.

"I plan to continue writing, at least two books a year, until (a) I get tired of them or (b) the public does." Roberts later added: "I was recently asked, on a television interview, what I would want to do with my life if I couldn't be a writer. I replied: 'I'd shine writers' shoes.' I meant that: Writers are God's angels."

BIOGRAPHICAL/CRITICAL SOURCES:

BOOKS

St. James Guide to Crime and Mystery Writers, 4th edition, St. James Press (Detroit, MI), 1996.

PERIODICALS

Armchair Detective, summer, 1990, p. 277; spring, 1996.

Booklist, November 1, 1989, p. 28; June 15, 1991, p. 1937; July 19, 1998, Emily Melton, review of *A Shoot in Cleveland;* June 1, 1999, Emily Melton, review of *The Best-kept Secret,* p. 1801; June 1, 2000, Gary Niebuhr, review of *The Indian Sign,* p. 1864.

Kirkus Reviews, May 1, 1991, pp. 568-569; October 15, 1994, review of *The Lake Effect;* September 1, 1995; August 1, 1996, p. 1103; May 15, 1998, review of *A Shoot in Cleveland.*

Library Journal, November 1, 1989, p. 114.

Los Angeles Times Book Review, August 9, 1987.

Mystery News, September-October, 1997, p. 29.

Publishers Weekly, July 29, 1996, p. 74; April 13, 1998, review of *A Shoot in Cleveland,* p. 55; July 26, 1999, review of *The Best-kept Secret,* p. 66; July 10, 2000, review of *The Indian Sign,* p. 48.

Romance Forever, June-July, 1997, pp. 64-65.

Washington Post, March 20, 1988.

OTHER

BookBrowser, http://www.bookbrowser.com/ (July 20, 2000), Harriet Klausner, review of *The Indian Sign.*

Crescent Blues Book Views, http://www.crescentblues.com/ (October 4, 2000), Dawn Goldsmith, "Les Roberts: *The Indian Sign.*"

* * *

ROBINSON, Jeffrey 1945-

PERSONAL: Born October 19, 1945, in Long Beach, NY; son of S. Jesse and Jessie (Roth) Robinson; married Aline Benayoun, 1985; children: Joshua Seth. *Education:* Temple University, B.S., 1967.

ADDRESSES: *Home*—39 Montagu Sq., London W1H 1TJ, England. *Agent*—Leslie Gardner, Artellus Ltd., 235 East 79th St., New York, NY 10021.

CAREER: Writer for television, radio, magazines, and newspapers, 1962—. *Military service:* U.S. Air Force, 1967-71; became captain.

MEMBER: International PEN.

WRITINGS:

Bette Davis: Her Stage and Film Career, Proteus, 1982.

Teamwork: Comedy Teams in the Movies, Proteus, 1983.

The Risk Takers: Portraits of Money, Ego, and Power, Allen & Unwin (Winchester, MA), 1985.

Pietrov and Other Games (novel), New English Library (Sevenoaks, England), 1985, published as *The Pietrov Game,* Pocket Books (New York City), 1987.

Minus Millionaires; or, How to Blow a Fortune, Unwin-Hyman, 1987.

The Ginger Jar (novel), New English Library (Sevenoaks, England), 1987.

Yamani: The Inside Story (biography), Simon & Schuster (London, England), 1987, Atlantic Monthly Press (New York, NY), 1989.

Rainier and Grace: An Intimate Portrait, Atlantic Monthly Press (New York, NY), 1989, published as *Rainier and Grace,* Simon & Schuster (London, England), 1989.

The Risk Takers: Five Years On, Mandarin (London, England), 1990.

The End of the American Century: Hidden Agendas of the Cold War, Hutchinson (London, England), 1992.

Bardot: An Intimate Portrait, D. I. Fine (New York, NY), 1994.

The Laundrymen: Inside Money Laundering, the World's Third-largest Business, Arcade Publishing (New York, NY), 1996.

The Hotel: Backstairs at the World's Most Exclusive Hotel, Arcade Publishing (New York, NY), 1997.

The Manipulators: The Conspiracy to Make Us Buy, Simon & Schuster (London, England), 1999.

A True and Perfect Knight (novel), Little, Brown (Boston, MA), 1999.

The Merger: How Organized Crime Is Taking over Canada and the World, McClelland & Stewart (Toronto, Ontario, Canada), 1999, published as *The Merger: The Conglomeration of International Organized Crime,* Overlook Press (Woodstock, NY), 2000.

Also author of the novels *The Margin of the Bulls* and *The Monk's Disciples.* Contributor of more than 600 articles and stories to U.S. and British periodicals.

SIDELIGHTS: Jeffrey Robinson is an American novelist as well as an author of nonfiction. His works include biographies of film legends such as Bette Davis and Brigitte Bardot, as well as nonfiction works on international business and history.

Robinson once told *CA* that he lived from 1971 to 1982 in southern France, where he supported himself by writing magazine features and short stories. He then moved to England to concentrate on writing books. One of these books, *The Risk Takers: Portraits of Money, Ego, and Power,* is a study of some of Britain's most controversial businessmen. The author makes no attempt in this work to whitewash the activities which led these figures to financial success, and he includes a wide variety of personalities in his seventeen commentaries. Many of his subjects have been scrutinized by national regulatory agencies or the police and castigated by the press. According to *Times Literary Supplement* reviewer J. H. C. Leach, Robinson "makes some pleasingly astringent comments on his risk-takers, whom he is far from viewing with starry eyes." *The Risk Takers* was a British bestseller in 1985 partly because, as Leach emphasized, Robinson "has clearly been at pains to get his facts right."

In some of his subsequent books, the author has taken a look at other wealthy, influential personalities. *Minus Millionaires; or, How to Blow a Fortune* is the off-beat sequel to the *Risk Takers.* Looking at the reverse side of the coin, Robinson studies the foibles and follies of men and women who have squandered fortunes. *Ya-*

mani: The Inside Story describes the former oil minister of Saudi Arabia, who for two dozen years was one of the most powerful men on earth. Zaki Yamani, sometimes called the man who ran OPEC, emerges in *Yamani* as a charming, charismatic, and brilliant leader, educated at Harvard University, politically moderate, comfortable at the highest levels of diplomacy and finance. However, Robinson contrasts this image with that of a man more closely akin to an old-fashioned Bedouin camel trader, a ruthless businessman capable of blackmailing the western world during the oil embargo in 1973 and ultimately responsible for astronomical rises in oil prices in 1979.

In *The Merger: How Organized Crime Is Taking over Canada and the World,* Robinson investigates the history of organized crime and its evolution into international crime syndicates. Covering such infamous organizations as the Sicilian Mafia, the Cosa Nostra, and the Chinese Triads, Robinson calls the conglomeration of organized crime syndicates the "'defining issue for the twenty-first century'" as quoted in *Kirkus Reviews.*

Critics were largely positive in their assessment of *The Merger.* "Robinson provides an exciting and unsettling glimpse of our future as a wired and globalized paradise for thieves," noted a critic for *Publishers Weekly.* A *Kirkus Reviews* critic concluded: "Robinson's prose is often breathless, urgent—even hyperbolic—but if only a modest moiety of his claims are accurate, the threats to the world's financial security are indeed ominous."

In addition to his bestselling nonfiction, Robinson is also the author of acclaimed novels, including *A True and Perfect Knight, The Monk's Disciples,* and *The Margin of the Bulls.*

BIOGRAPHICAL/CRITICAL SOURCES:

PERIODICALS

Booklist, July, 2000, David Rouse, review of *The Merger,* p. 1981.

Foreign Affairs, March-April, 1997, Richard N. Cooper, review of *The Laundrymen,* p. 177.

Globe and Mail (Toronto, Ontario), April 22, 1989.

Irish Independent (Dublin, Ireland), September 24, 1985; September 26, 1985.

Kirkus Reviews, June 1, 2000, review of *The Merger,* p. 778.

Library Journal, September 1, 1996, Bellinda Wise, review of *The Laundrymen,* p. 195; May 15, 1997, Jo-Anne Mary Benson, review of *The Hotel,* p. 91; June 15, 2000, Robert C. Jones, review of *The Merger,* p. 98.

Lloyds List, August 17, 1985; July 12, 1986.

Los Angeles Times, March 29, 1988.

Publishers Weekly, July 1, 1996, review of *The Laundrymen,* p. 51; March 31, 1997, review of *The Hotel,* p. 52; June 26, 2000, review of *The Merger,* p. 65.

Punch, December 11, 1985; September 24, 1986.

Security Management, August, 1997, Michael J. Koshel, review of *The Laundrymen,* p. 122; October, 2000, Michael J. Koshel, review of *The Merger,* p. 106.

Sunday Times (London, England), June 29, 1986.

Sunday Tribune (Dublin, Ireland), September 29, 1985.

Times Literary Supplement, September 6, 1985, J. H. C. Leach, review of *The Risk Takers.*

Today, July 17, 1986.

Wall Street Journal, August 27, 1985.

Washington Post Book World, July 2, 1989.*

* * *

ROBINSON, Ray(mond Kenneth) 1920-

PERSONAL: Born December 4, 1920, in New York, NY; son of Louis H. (a lawyer) and Lillian (Hoffman) Robinson; married Phyllis Cumins (a writer), September 18, 1949; children: Nancy, Stephen, Tad. Education: Columbia University, B.A., 1941, further study, 1941-42.

ADDRESSES: Home—530 East 90th St., New York, NY 10128.

CAREER: Real, New York City, editor, 1955-57; *Pageant,* New York City, managing editor, 1957-59; *Coronet,* New York City, senior editor, 1959-61; *Good Housekeeping,* New York City, articles editor, 1961-69; *Seventeen* magazine, New York City, executive editor, 1969—. Instructor at New York University, 1977. Trustee, Llewellyn Miller Trust Fund for Writers; member of board, Baseball Assistance Team. *Military service:* U.S. Army, 1942-46.

MEMBER: American Society of Magazine Editors (executive committee).

WRITINGS:

NONFICTION

(With Constantine Callinicos) *The Mario Lanza Story,* Coward (New York, NY), 1960.
(Editor) *Baseball Stars* (annual), Pyramid Books (New York, NY), 1961-75.
Ted Williams, Putnam (New York, NY), 1962.
Stan Musial: Baseball's Durable Man, Putnam (New York, NY), 1963.
Speed Kings of the Basepaths: Baseball's Greatest Runners, Putnam (New York, NY), 1964.
Greatest World Series Thrillers, Random House (New York, NY), 1965.
Baseball's Most Colorful Managers, Putnam (New York, NY), 1969.
The Greatest Yankees of Them All, Putnam (New York, NY), 1969.
(With Tim McCarver) *Oh, Baby, I Love It!,* Villard Books (New York, NY), 1987.
Iron Horse: Lou Gehrig in His Time, Norton (New York, NY), 1990.
The Home Run Heard 'round the World: The Dramatic Story of the 1951 Giants-Dodgers Pennant Race, HarperCollins (New York, NY), 1991.
Matty: An American Hero, Christy Mathewson of the New York Giants, Oxford University Press (New York, NY), 1993.
American Original: A Life of Will Rogers, Oxford University Press (New York, NY), 1996.
(With Christopher Jennison) *Yankee Stadium: Seventy-five Years of Drama, Glamour, and Glory,* Penguin (New York, NY), 1998.
Rockne of Notre Dame: The Making of a Football Legend, Oxford University Press (New York, NY), 1999.
New York Yankees: One hundred Years of Glory, Viking (New York, NY), in press.

Work represented in anthologies, including *Fireside Book of Baseball,* Simon & Schuster (New York, NY), 1956, *Second Fireside Book of Baseball,* Simon & Schuster (New York, NY), 1958; *Best Sport Stories of 1958,* Dutton (New York, NY), 1958, and *Best Sport Stories of 1959,* Dutton (New York, NY), 1959. Chairman, advisory board of *Columbia College Today.*

SIDELIGHTS: Ray Robinson is a veteran American journalist and nonfiction writer whose works focus on various sports figures, including Stan Musial and Lou Gehrig. He has also written accounts of sporting events such as his 1991 work, *The Home Run Heard 'round the World: The Dramatic Story of the 1951 Giants-Dodgers Pennant Race.* In addition to his sports writing, Robinson has also written biographies of entertainer Will Rogers and singer/film star Mario Lanza.

Robinson's 1999 work *Rockne of Notre Dame: The Making of a Football Legend,* focuses on the life of Notre Dame football coach Knute Rockne. From 1918-1930, Rockne coached Notre Dame to an astounding 105-12-5 record, including five undefeated seasons. Wes Lukowsky in *Booklist* found that, though the work does not break any significant new ground, "as a serious study of Rockne's place in football history and in American popular culture, it deserves a place in active sports collections." A *Publishers Weekly* critic argued that, though Robinson "does a good job of describing the football culture of the time and, to a lesser degree, American culture in general, Robinson never quite digs deep enough to reveal the man behind the coach." William Scheeren in *Library Journal* disagreed, calling the work "unchallenged as the definitive work on this icon of the Roaring Twenties."

BIOGRAPHICAL/CRITICAL SOURCES:

PERIODICALS

Booklist, June 1, 1998, GraceAnne A. DeCandido, review of *American Original,* p. 76; September 1, 1999, Wes Lukowsky, review of *Rockne of Notre Dame,* p. 63.
Kirkus Reviews, June 1, 1993, review of *Iron Horse;* February 15, 1996, review of *American Original.*
Library Journal, March 15, 1996, A. J. Anderson, review of *American Original,* p. 76; February 1, 1998, Paul Kaplan and Morey Berger, review of *Yankee Stadium,* p. 94; August, 1999, William Scheeren, review of *Rockne of Notre Dame,* p. 102.
New York Review of Books, February 24, 2000, Malcolm Gladwell, review of *Rockne of Notre Dame,* pp. 30-33.
Sports Illustrated, August 23, 1999, Ron Fimrite, review of *Rockne of Notre Dame,* p. R7.

* * *

RODOWSKY, Colby F. 1932-

PERSONAL: Born February 26, 1932, in Baltimore, MD; daughter of Frank M. Fossett and Mary C. Fitz-Townsend; married Lawrence Rodowsky (an appellate court judge), August 7, 1954; children: Laurie, Alice,

Emily, Sarah, Gregory, Katherine. *Education:* College of Notre Dame of Maryland, B.A., 1953. *Religion:* Roman Catholic.

ADDRESSES: Home and office—4306 Norwood Rd., Baltimore, MD 21218-1118. *Agent*—Gail Hochman, Brandt & Brandt, 1501 Broadway, NY 10036.

CAREER: Teacher in public schools in Baltimore, MD, 1953-55, and in a school for special education, 1955-56; Notre Dame Preparatory School, Baltimore, MD, librarian's assistant, 1974-79; children's book reviewer, *Baltimore Sunday Sun,* 1977-84.

AWARDS, HONORS: American Library Association Notable Book citation for *Not My Dog* and *The Gathering Room,* and Best Books for Young Adults citation for *Julie's Daughter, Hannah in Between,* and *Remembering Mog;* Hedda Seisler Mason Award, Enoch Pratt Library, for *Fitchett's Folly; School Library Journal* Best Books of the Year citations for *The Gathering Room, Julie's Daughter,* and *Sydney, Herself; Horn Book* Fanfare Award for *Not My Dog.*

WRITINGS:

FOR CHILDREN

What about Me?, F. Watts (New York, NY), 1976.
P.S. Write Soon, F. Watts (New York, NY), 1978.
Evy-Ivy-Over, F. Watts (New York, NY), 1978.
A Summer's Worth of Shame, F. Watts (New York, NY), 1980.
The Gathering Room, Farrar, Straus (New York, NY), 1981.
H, My Name Is Henley, Farrar, Straus (New York, NY), 1982.
Keeping Time, Farrar, Straus (New York, NY), 1983.
Fitchett's Folly, Farrar, Straus (New York, NY), 1987.
Dog Days, illustrated by Kathleen Collins Howell, Farrar, Straus (New York, NY), 1990.
Jenny and the Grand Old Great-Aunts, illustrated by Barbara Roman, Macmillan (New York, NY), 1992.
Hannah in Between, Farrar, Straus (New York, NY), 1994.
The Turnabout Shop, Farrar, Straus (New York, NY), 1998.
Not My Dog, illustrations by Thomas F. Yezerski, Farrar, Straus (New York, NY), 1999.
Spindrift, Farrar, Straus (New York, NY), 2000.
Jason Rat-a-Tat, illustrated by Beth Peck, Farrar, Straus (New York, NY), 2001.
Clay, Farrar, Straus (New York, NY), 2001.

FOR YOUNG ADULTS

Julie's Daughter (sequel to *Evy-Ivy-Over*), Farrar, Straus (New York, NY), 1985.
Sydney, Herself, Farrar, Straus (New York, NY), 1989.
Lucy Peale, Farrar, Straus (New York, NY), 1992.
Sydney Invincible, Farrar, Straus (New York, NY), 1995.
Remembering Mog, Farrar, Straus (New York, NY), 1996.

Rodowsky's young-adult short stories have been anthologized in *Visions,* edited by Donald Gallo, Delacorte, 1987, and in *Connections,* edited by Gallo, Delacorte, 1989.

OTHER

Contributor of fiction, essays, and reviews to periodicals, including *Christian Science Monitor, New York Times Book Review, Washington Post, McCall's,* and *Good Housekeeping.*

SIDELIGHTS: A former teacher, Colby F. Rodowsky turned to writing for children when she was forty years old. The author of such award-winning books as *The Gathering Room, Julie's Daughter,* and *Remembering Mog,* Rodowsky has earned praise from critics and readers alike for her likeable empathetic protagonists and true-to-life situations. While the young people who inhabit Rodowsky's fiction live in a tough world characterized by unpredictable events and undependable authority figures, their efforts to cope with parental abandonment, poverty, and even death, are aided by warm and loving individuals. As Carol Edwards noted in the *School Library Journal,* "Rodowsky makes her readers work, never patronizing or condescending, yet always revealing inner layers that poke through the surface."

Born in 1932, Rodowsky grew up in Baltimore, Maryland. As a child she wanted to become a writer, and her mother encouraged her. "I don't know whether it was because she was a doting mother or she really thought I could write, but she was very supportive," the author once told an interviewer. Due to her parents' rocky marriage, Rodowsky spent a great deal of time at the home of her grandmother in the Chesapeake Bay,

Virginia, town of Cape Charles, where she first discovered the library, and made many friends. That area, which Rodowsky recalled in an autobiographical essay for *Something about the Author Autobiography Series* (*SAAS*) was "a wonderful, almost magical place," would become the setting for several of her books.

Rodowsky's elementary-school education was completed in New York City, where she and her mother moved after her parents separated. Despite missing her friends, she loved the city; its energy inspired her to begin writing "'seriously'; pounding away on my mother's typewriter, dipping more often than not into an impassioned purple prose." She even completed her first long story, titled *The Strangons,* and confidently sent it off to a major New York publisher, although Rodowsky later recalled this childish first effort as "insignificant and forgotten."

Returning to Baltimore after her parents' divorce when she was fifteen, Rodowsky attended a prep school in Georgetown and lived with her father and his parents. After graduation, she enrolled at Maryland's College of Notre Dame, living at home and graduating with a degree in English. While there she edited the literary magazine, worked on the yearbook, and began to write vast quantities of poetry. She also met and fell in love with Lawrence Rodowsky, a history major and aspiring lawyer whom she would later marry. Colby established a career as an elementary school teacher and working with children with special needs; she left teaching before the births of the couple's six children. Meanwhile, Larry Rodowsky began a successful legal career that resulted in a seat on the State of Maryland's Court of Appeals. The Rodowsky family lived in "a very noisy house," as the author once said. "The house is quiet now—the children grown up and moved away," she later added. "But the family now includes five sons-in-law, one daughter-in-law, and *many* grandchildren, who all visit often (and only one dog and one cat)."

Rodowsky's writing career was inspired by a visit with one of her former teachers, Sister Maura Eichner, from Notre Dame. "We weren't talking about writing; we were just talking about books," the novelist noted. Sister Maura "finally stopped what she was saying and looked at me and said, 'Just think; you have all your writing still ahead of you.' It really kind of gives me cold chills even now when I think about it. I did not go home and write a book, but I went home thinking maybe I hadn't missed the boat on what I'd really wanted to do." She added, "I was about forty, and at that time I thought if you hadn't done anything by forty, you never would. Now I know a lot better."

In 1972 Rodowsky began a writing tutorial that forced her to return to a typewriter and, as she had done so many years before, start "banging" out a book-length manuscript. While her first effort was unsalable, it encouraged Rodowsky to attempt another . . . and then another. Finally, her third effort, about a fifteen-year-old girl who has a brother with Down's syndrome, was accepted by a publisher and released in 1976 as *What about Me?*

Drawing from her experience teaching mentally handicapped children, she once explained: "I kind of backed into [*What about Me?*] because I wanted to write about a child who had a younger brother or sister with a handicap. . . . I didn't set out to write about a retarded child." In the novel, Rodowsky's young protagonist resents her brother Fredlet, who has Down's syndrome. Although Rodowsky generally knows how a book will end, and often writes the last page first, Fredlet's death took her, as well as her fictional characters, by surprise. Reviewing the novel for *Publishers Weekly,* Jeane Mercier called it a "profoundly moving, honest and tightly controlled, important novel." With this praise echoed by other critics, Rodowsky was encouraged to continue her literary efforts. When the first of her children left home in the late 1970s, she took over a room in the house as an office.

Rodowsky's second published novel, *P.S. Write Soon,* concerns crippled Tanner McClean, who writes an idealized version of her life to her pen-pal Jessie Lee. Tanner glosses over her handicap and the unexpected marriage of her older brother. But although she dislikes her new sister-in-law, Cheryl, the older girl teaches Tanner how to face life realistically rather than hiding in fiction. *The Gathering Room* takes place in a Baltimore cemetery. Nine-year-old Mudge's father, Ned, moves his family from the inner city and takes a job as caretaker of the old cemetery after the death of a friend. Ned teaches his son in the room where mourners used to congregate, and the boy befriends the spirits of the dead, who "provide this simple, well-wrought story with a pleasant, if melancholy sense of time and mortality," according to Jane Langton in the *New York Times Book Review. School Library Journal* contributor Elizabeth Holtze noted that Rodowsky "writes clear narrative and convincing dialogue. . . . Despite the cemetery setting and the problem posed . . . this is a happy book."

A young girl with the unusual name of Slug connects three of Rodowsky's books that draw from several elements in the author's life. In *Evy-Ivy-Over,* which takes place in Rodowsky's childhood home of Cape Charles, she lives a carefree, if unorthodox, life with her grandmother, Gussie. But as Slug matures, she realizes her hand-me-down clothes are funny-looking and that Gussie herself is an odd character. She learns through contact with "normal" families, however, to appreciate Gussie. "I was very close to both of my grandmothers," Rodowsky once commented. "In *Evy-Ivy-Over* . . . I tried to describe the grandmother-grandchild relationship, though I must say neither of my grandmothers was at all like Gussie."

While not the main character, Slug also appears in *H, My Name Is Henley,* which deals with the plight of a young girl and her restless mother, Patti. Like Rodowsky's own mother, light-hearted, restless Patti is a bit of a dreamer; unable to stay in any one place for long, she stays until she quits her job and moves to another city. "Henley is probably the most mature and perceptive 12-year-old I've met in YA literature," stated *Voice of Youth Advocates* contributor Barbara Lenchitz Gottesman. "Rodowsky has created a masterpiece." While some reviewers pointed to some weak characterization, "The tension and conflict between mother and daughter, the strain on a child forced into adult responsibilities, and the characterization of Patti are intensely real," wrote Nancy C. Hammond in *Horn Book.*

Julie's Daughter, which won a Best Books for Young Adults award, unites Slug and her mother Julie, who abandoned her infant daughter at the bus station. Slug and Julie are brought together in caring for their neighbor, the artist Harper Tegges, who is dying of cancer. The story is seen through their three viewpoints. *Voice of Youth Advocates* contributor Debbie Earl maintained that "the differing narrations help us develop sympathy and understanding" for Rodowsky's protagonists; Earl found the novel "sensitively done and surprisingly humorous." Christine Jenkins in *Interracial Books for Children Bulletin* concluded that "*Julie's Daughter* succeeds in portraying strong women, both old and young."

Rodowsky teams adventure and comedy in *Fitchett's Folly,* which takes place on Maryland's Eastern shore. The novel focuses on a motherless girl, Sarey-Ann, whose father drowns while attempting to rescue another child. Sarey-Ann has to deal with her feelings of resentment toward the foundling, Faith, who comes to live with the girl, her little brother, and her aunt. A *Horn Book* contributor noted that "Sarey's prickly dislike is convincingly portrayed in her first-person recounting. . . . Scrapes and adventures add to the story of Sarey's eventual acceptance of Faith."

One of Rodowsky's best-known novels, *Sydney, Herself,* features another child who has lost a parent. Sydney's Australian father died a month before she was born; blocking out his death, in a school writing assignment, Sydney decides to reinvent herself as the daughter of a rock singer, a member of the group The Boomerangs. When Sydney gives her story to a local newspaper, events snowball. A *Horn Book* reviewer lauded the novel as "fresh, humorous, and believable. Sydney is interesting—bright, gritty, and sometimes sulky." And adds that the book is "funny, poignant, and appealing." *Sydney, Herself* would be followed by *Sydney, Invincible,* as Rodowsky's spunky heroine must deal with being a student in her mother's history class, working to resuscitate the school newspaper, and wait for her best friend Wally to return from boarding school in New Hampshire. Calling Sydney "a refreshingly realistic character" with problems that are "unique enough to be interesting" and solutions that are "plausible and endearing," *Voice of Youth Advocates* contributor Betsy Eubanks dubbed *Sydney, Invincible* a coming-of-age novel that shows its protagonist's "maturity evolv[ing] naturally as she deals with the accumulating stress. [Readers] are hopeful that she will succeed and gratified when she learns lessons that make her more sensitive and perceptive." "Rodowsky is an accomplished and sure-footed interpreter of what goes on in the mind of a teenaged girl," added *Washington Post Book World* critic Brigitte Weeks in praising both *Sydney, Herself* and its sequel.

In *Lucy Peale,* a love story for teens, a girl from a strict pastor's family is date-raped. Her father condemns her and she runs away to Ocean City, where she meets Jake, a kind young man, who invites her to stay with him. While the two eventually fall in love, Lucy realizes that she must find her own destiny. In the novel, Rodowsky alternates between Lucy's viewpoint and that of a narrator, a technique some reviewers found awkward. But in a starred review, a *Publishers Weekly* critic applauded the author's use of plot twists which keep Lucy and Jake's attention focused on their developing relationship, rather than on sex. *School Library Journal* contributor Jacqueline Rose appreciated "the moods created by descriptions of the sea town's atmosphere that mirror the characters' feelings." And a *Kirkus* reviewer concluded of *Lucy Peale* that Rodowsky had penned "a heartwarming story" that is "gentle and appealing [and] written with insight and skill."

Another troubled family is portrayed in 1994's *Hannah in Between,* as twelve-year-old Hannah Brant must cope with an alcoholic parent. Avoiding bringing friends over to her house is just one way of coping with her mother's erratic behavior. Hannah also attempts to solve the problem by hiding empty bottles and, along with a father in denial, pretending that everything is "normal" at home. When her mother is injured in a car accident as a result of her drinking, Hannah must deal with her situation. *Hannah in Between* is a book that "weaves a young teen's limited understanding of the disease with her gradual acceptance that only her mother can begin to reverse her illness," according to *Horn Book* contributor Elizabeth S. Watson. "Although Rodowsky may have us following a predictable path," added *Booklist* reviewer Stephanie Zvirin, "she guides us forward with sensitivity and a sure hand."

Coping with death is the theme of several of Rodowsky's novels for young teens, among them *Remembering Mog* and *The Turnabout Shop.* In *Remembering Mog,* Annie's high school graduation is overshadowed by memories of her older sister's death two years earlier, on the eve of her own graduation. As each of her family members deal with Mog's death in their own way, Annie takes the summer to realize that she must seek professional help in coming to terms with the loss of her sister so that she can move on in her own life. Counting *Remembering Mog* as among Rodowsky's "string of solid, real-life stories, without pretense or angst," *Voice of Youth Advocates* critic Patricia J. Morrow deemed the novel "a quiet book, whose characters and dialogue bring the reader along through insights and adjustments." In *Booklist,* Stephanie Zvirin added that the novel succeeds "as a poignant, crystalline rendering of death's legacy for a parent and child."

The Turnabout Shop features a fatherless fifth-grader named Livvy, whose mother, Althea, dies and leaves her in the care of Jessie Barnes, a single friend of Livvy's mother to whom Livvy's presence is as much a surprise and adjustment as her new home is to Livvy. Slowly, the two learn to live with one another, and Livvy adapts to a move to Baltimore, a new school, new friends, and being a part of Jessie's large, close-knit family. Noting that readers will immediately identify with Rodowsky's likeable characters, a *Kirkus* reviewer added that "Jessie . . . and Althea's characters burst forth from Livvy's narration as vividly as her own." A *Publishers Weekly* reviewer praised *The Turnabout Shop* as a "poignant, quiet story [that] offers a reassuring view of coming to terms with grief and unwelcome change."

In addition to her novels for older readers, Rodowsky has authored several novels for younger children. In 1990's *Dog Days,* a young girl discovers the author of her favorite dog stories is moving in next door . . . along with her famous dog. Dogs also figure prominently in *Not My Dog,* a story about a "sort of square, boring brown dog" that is inherited by nine-year-old Ellie in lieu of the bouncy puppy she had been promised by her parents—until Preston shows that he is truly the pick of the litter. 1992's *Jenny and the Grand Old Great-Aunts* is aimed at an even younger audience. In what *School Library Journal* reviewer Anna DeWind called an "appealing cross-generational story," Jenny is dropped off by herself to spend the afternoon with her great aunts in their terrifyingly quiet Victorian home. However, the home also reveals a wonderful magic, after one aunt introduces the little girl to a treasure cache in the attic. "This comforting story deftly conveys the strength of the bond that can exist between the old and the young," commented a *Publishers Weekly* contributor.

Rodowsky is perplexed by comments that imply that writing for children is easier than writing for adults. "I don't think when you write for children that you ever consciously decide you're going to make something simpler, that you ever write down in any way," she once commented. "It's a challenge—a kind of balancing act," she explained, "and I get irritated by people who think you write for children because that's where you start, and then you work up to writing for grownups. I don't think it's any easier to write for children than for adults, but the rewards are great—particularly when I get a letter from a child whose life has been touched by a book of mine."

BIOGRAPHICAL/CRITICAL SOURCES:

BOOKS

Authors and Artists for Young Adults, Volume 23, Gale (Detroit, MI), 1998, pp. 169-76.

Something about the Authors Autobiography Series, Volume 22, Gale (Detroit, MI), 1996, pp. 225-239.

PERIODICALS

Booklist, July, 1992, p. 1933; April 1, 1994, Stephanie Zvirin, review of *Hannah in Between,* p. 1437; April 15, 1995, S. Zvirin, review of *Sydney, Invincible,* p. 1493; February 1, 1996, S. Zvirin, review of *Remembering Mog,* p. 926; June 1, 1998, Kay Weisman, review of *The Turnabout Shop,* p. 1768; February 1, 1999, Carolyn Phelan, review of *Not My Dog,* p. 975; February 15, 2000, review of *Spindrift,* p. 1115.

Bulletin of the Center for Children's Books, February, 1984, p. 116.

Horn Book, October, 1981, p. 537; April, 1983, Nancy C. Hammond, review of *H, My Name is Henley,* p. 167; April, 1984, Mary M. Burns, review of *Keeping Time,* p. 203; July-August, 1987, review of *Fitchett's Folly,* p. 473; September-October, 1989, review of *Sydney, Herself,* p. 631; March-April, 1991, review of *Dog Days,* p. 202; May-June, 1992, p. 338; September-October, 1994, Elizabeth S. Watson, review of *Hannah in Between,* p. 601; March, 1999, Martha V. Parravano, review of *Not My Dog,* p. 212.

Interracial Books for Children Bulletin, Volume 17, number 1, 1986, Christine Jenkins, review of *Julie's Daughter,* p. 7.

Kirkus Reviews, June 15, 1992, review of *Lucy Peale,* p. 784; January 15, 1998, review of *The Turnabout Shop,* p. 117.

New York Times Book Review, October 25, 1981, Jane Langton, review of *The Gathering Room,* p. 47.

Publishers Weekly, January 22, 1979, review of *What about Me?,* p. 371; April 24, 1987, review of *Fitchett's Folly,* p. 70; June 9, 1989, p. 70; November 23, 1989, review of *Dog Days,* p. 65; January 6, 1992, review of *Jenny and the Grand Old Great-Aunts,* p. 66; May 4, 1992, review of *Lucy Peale,* p. 57; March 25, 1996, review of *Remembering Mog,* p. 85; January 5, 1998, review of *The Turnabout Shop,* p. 68; January 10, 2000, review of *Spindrift,* p. 69.

School Library Journal, October, 1981, Elizabeth Holtze, review of *The Gathering Room,* p. 146; January, 1983, p. 87; January, 1985, Barbara Jo McKee, review of *Keeping Time,* p. 88; September, 1985, p. 148; July, 1989, Carol A. Edwards, review of *Sidney, Herself,* p. 92; April, 1992, Anna DeWind, review of *Jenny and the Grand Old Great-Aunts,* p. 99; July, 1992, Jacqueline Rose, review of *Lucy Peale,* p. 91; August, 1995, review of *Sydney Invincible,* p. 164.

Voice of Youth Advocates, April, 1983, Barbara Lenchitz Gottesman, review of *H, My Name Is Henley,* p. 41; April, 1986, Debbie Earl, review of *Julie's Daughter,* p. 34; August, 1995, Betsy Eubanks, review of *Sydney, Invincible,* p. 164; June, 1996, Patricia J. Morrow, review of *Remembering Mog,* p. 100.

Washington Post Book World, July, 1995, Brigitte Weeks, review of *Sydney, Invincible,* pp. 16-17.

Wilson Library Bulletin, February, 1990, p. 84; May, 1990, p. 58.

ROORBACH, Bill 1953-

PERSONAL: Born August 18, 1953, in Chicago, IL; son of John E. and Reba (a horticulturist; maiden name, Burkhardt) Roorbach; married Juliet Brigitte Karelsen (an artist), June 23, 1990; children: Elysia Pearl. *Education:* Ithaca College, B.A., 1976; Columbia University, M.F.A., 1990.

ADDRESSES: Office—Department of English, Ohio State University, 164 West 17th Ave., Columbus, OH 43210. *Agent*—Betsy Lerner, The Gernert Co., 136 East 57th St., New York, NY 10021. *E-mail*—roorbach.1@osu.edu.

CAREER: University of Maine at Farmington, assistant professor of English, 1991-95; Ohio State University, Columbus, OH, assistant professor, 1995-98, associate professor of English, 1998—.

MEMBER: Associated Writing Programs, Authors Guild, Modern language Association, Maine Writers and Publishers Alliance.

AWARDS, HONORS: Flannery O'Connor Award in short fiction, 2001, for *Big Bend: Stories;* Ohio Arts Council grants in nonfiction and criticism.

WRITINGS:

Summers with Juliet, Houghton (Boston, MA), 1992, reprinted, Ohio State University Press (Columbus, OH), 2000.

Writing Life Stories: How to Make Memories into Memoirs, Ideas into Essays, and Life into Literature, Story Press (Cincinnati, OH), 1998.

(Editor) *The Art of Truth: A Contemporary Creative Nonfiction Reader,* Oxford University Press (New York, NY), 2000.

Big Bend: Stories, University of Georgia Press (Athens, GA), 2001.

The Smallest Color (novel), Counterpoint, 2001.

Work represented in anthologies, including *Turning Toward Home,* Franklin Square Press, 1995. Contributor to periodicals, including *Atlantic Monthly, New York Times Magazine, Harper's, Missouri Review, Granta, New York, Poets and Writers, Iowa Review, Witness, Philadelphia Inquirer,* and *Newsday.*

WORK IN PROGRESS: A novel; a natural history of Maine.

SIDELIGHTS: Bill Roorbach's *Summers with Juliet* is based on travels the author made with his wife, Juliet, before they were married. The book muses on nature, fishing, and the foundation blocks beneath a committed relationship. "Roorbach's debut provides pure enchantment," noted a reviewer in *Publishers Weekly.* The reviewer further commented that *Summers with Juliet* is "lyrical, earthy and suspenseful." *Cosmopolitan* writer Louise Bernikow called the book "touching," noting it provides "a really lovely love story." Harry Middleton, reviewing the book for *New York Newsday,* described *Summers with Juliet* as "an engaging love story" and praised Roorbach for writing "honestly, movingly, sometimes poetically."

Roorbach has also penned a "how-to" volume on creative nonfiction titled *Writing Life Stories: How to Make Memories into Memoirs, Ideas into Essays, and Life into Literature.* Lisa J. Cihlar, a *Library* Journal reviewer, praised Roorbach for his ability to encourage writers "with humor and a sense of fun."

Roorbach once told *CA:* "My writing is all dedicated to the preservation of this planet."

BIOGRAPHICAL/CRITICAL SOURCES:

PERIODICALS

Cosmopolitan, February, 1992, Louise Bernikow, review of *Summers with Juliet,* p. 18.

Library Journal, August, 1998, Lisa J. Cihlar, review of *Writing Life Stories: How to Make Memories into Memoirs, Ideas into Essays, and Life into Literature,* p. 104.

New York Newsday, February 2, 1992, Harry Middleton, "Splendor in the Grass."

Publishers Weekly, January 1, 1992, review of *Summers with Juliet,* p. 40.

* * *

ROSENBERG, Nathan 1927-

PERSONAL: Born November 22, 1927, in Passaic, NJ; son of Joseph and Mary (Kaplan) Rosenberg; married Rina Gordon, January 12, 1954; children: Karen, Gordon, Jonathan, David. *Education:* Rutgers University, B.A., 1950; University of Wisconsin, M.A., 1952, Ph. D., 1955. *Religion:* Jewish.

ADDRESSES: Office—Department of Economics, Encina Hall West, Stanford University, Stanford, CA 94305.

CAREER: Indiana University, Bloomington, lecturer, 1955-57; University of Pennsylvania, Philadelphia, assistant professor, 1957-61; Purdue University, West Lafayette, IN, associate professor, 1961-64, professor, 1964-67; University of Wisconsin, Madison, professor, 1969-74; Stanford University, Stanford, CA, professor of economics, 1974—. Visiting professor at Harvard University, 1967-69. *Military service:* U.S. Army, 1945-47.

MEMBER: American Economic Association, Economic History Association, Royal Economical Society (foreign member).

AWARDS, HONORS: Fellow of the American Academy of Arts and Sciences, and of the Royal Swedish Academy of Engineering; received honorary degrees from University of Lund, Sweden, and Bologna University, Italy. Leonardo da Vinci medal, Society for the History of Technology.

WRITINGS:

Economic Planning in the British Building Industry, 1945-1949, University of Pennsylvania Press, 1960.

(Editor and author of introduction) *The American System of Manufactures: The Report of the Committee on the Machinery of the United States, 1855, and the Special Reports of George Wallis and Joseph Whitworth, 1954,* Edinburgh University Press, 1969.

(Editor) *The Economics of Technological Change: Selected Readings,* Penguin, 1971.

Technology and American Economic Growth, Harper & Row, 1972.

Perspectives on Technology, Cambridge University Press, 1976.

(With Walter G. Vincenti) *The Britannia Bridge: The Generation and Diffusion of Technical Knowledge,* MIT Press, c. 1978.

Inside the Black Box: Technology and Economics, Cambridge University Press, 1983.

(Editor with Claudio Frischtak) *International Technology Transfer: Concepts, Measures, and Comparisons,* Praeger, 1985.

(Editor with Ralph Landau) *The Positive Sum Strategy: Harnessing Technology for Economic Growth,* National Academic Press, 1986.

(With L. E. Birdzell) *How the West Grew Rich: The Economic Transformation of the Industrial World,* Basic Books, 1986.

(With David C. Mowery) *Technology and the Pursuit of Economic Growth,* Cambridge University Press, 1989.

(Editor with Landau and Mowery), *Technology and the Wealth of Nations,* Stanford University Press, 1992.

Exploring the Black Box: Technology, Economics, and History, Cambridge University Press, 1994.

The Emergence of Economic Ideas: Essays in the History of Economics, Edward Edgar, 1994.

(With David Mowery) *Paths of Innovation: Technological Change in Twentieth-Century America,* Cambridge University Press, 1998.

(Editor with Ashish Arora, Ralph Landau) *Chemicals and Long-Term Economic Growth,* John Wiley & Sons, 1998.

Schumpete and the Endogenetics of Technology: Some American Perspectives, Routledge, 2000.

(With Magnus Henrekson) *Akakemisht entreprenörskap,* Universitet Och näringsliv, SNS Förlag, 2000.

Editor of the *Journal of Economic History,* 1972-74.

SIDELIGHTS: Nathan Rosenberg has been teaching economics for more than three decades at such universities as Purdue, Harvard, and Stanford. As an economic historian, most of his published works, including *Perspectives on Technology, Inside the Black Box: Technology and Economics,* and *How the West Grew Rich: The Economic Transformation of the Industrial World,* examine the ways in which innovations in technology have influenced economic history. One of Rosenberg's earlier works is a reprint of British Government reports about American industrial machinery dated from the 1850s; *Choice* magazine labeled the economist's introduction to these reports as "invaluable." Another of his efforts, a 1978 collaboration with Walter G. Vincenti titled *The Britannia Bridge: The Generation and Diffusion of Technical Knowledge,* takes the example of a bridge built in Wales between 1845 and 1850 and uses it to illustrate how innovations discovered in the course of its construction had important effects upon other areas, including shipbuilding and machine making. A *Choice* reviewer, impressed by *The Britannia Bridge,* declared: "No academic library can afford to be without it."

Rosenberg's *Perspectives on Technology* is a collection of essays that explores many aspects of technical development and their relationship to economic growth; Hillary D. Burton in the *Library Journal* determined that it is an "impressive effort." In 1983 the author issued his well-received *Inside the Black Box: Technology and Economics.* As Burton Klein explained in the *Journal of Economic Literature,* "when he says we must look inside of the black box to understand technological phenomena . . . Rosenberg means that we must try to understand, as best we can, the games being played by the players, and the rules they employ, rather than proceeding on the basis of a priori assumption."

Perhaps Rosenberg's best-known work is his 1986 collaboration with L. E. Birdzell, *How the West Grew Rich: The Economic Transformation of the Industrial World.* In this volume, the authors attempt to explain why the Western world (including Europe and the United States) has met with greater economic success than less developed nations, concluding that personal and economic freedom for individuals leads to financial prosperity. Eric J. Hobsbawn reported in the *Los Angeles Times Book Review* that the book "is a lengthy plea in favor of keeping government out of business and science, since the authors think that the separation of the political sphere from the economic is precisely what gave the West the secret of economic growth, and keeps it ahead of countries otherwise organized." Donald N. McCloskey in the *New York Times Book Review* proclaimed *How the West Grew Rich* "lively and intelligent," and went on to observe that "it is an essay of interpretation, not a tome. It carries on the project of historical research begun by Marx. And it contributes brilliantly to the argument in favor of [eighteenth-century economist] Adam Smith's deal—leave me alone and I'll make you rich."

Rosenberg told *CA:* "One of the main reasons that it is so difficult to come to grips with technological phenomena is that there is a strong tendency, especially among academics, to conceptualize it in overly simple ways. The essential point is that technology is not one thing. Rather, it is a great many things. Technological change in the pharmaceutical industry is very different from technological change in aircraft, agriculture, or semiconductors. What needs to be recognized is the extreme diversity not only of technologies themselves but also of the ways in which they are developed."

BIOGRAPHICAL/CRITICAL SOURCES:

PERIODICALS

Choice, November, 1969, p. 1268; March, 1979, pp. 100-101.

Economic History Review, February, 1995.

Journal of Economic Literature, June, 1984, p. 622.
Library Journal, September 15, 1976, p. 1870.
Los Angeles Times Book Review, January 12, 1986, pp. 1, 10.
New York Review of Books, May 29, 1986, pp. 46-49.
New York Times Book Review, February 9, 1986, p. 18.*

* * *

RUBIN, Larry (Jerome) 1930-

PERSONAL: Born February 14, 1930, in Bayonne, NJ; son of Abraham Joseph and Lillian (Strongin) Rubin. *Education:* Attended Columbia University, 1949-50; Emory University, B.A., 1951, M.A., 1952, Ph.D., 1956. *Religion:* Jewish.

ADDRESSES: *Home*—Box 15014, Druid Hills Branch, Atlanta, GA 30333. *Office*—Department of English, Georgia Institute of Technology, Atlanta, GA.

CAREER: Georgia Institute of Technology, Atlanta, instructor in English, 1956-58, assistant professor, 1958-65, associate professor, 1965-73, professor of English, 1973-99, professor emeritus, 1999—. Visiting professor, Jagiellonian University, Krakow, Poland, 1961-62, University of Bergen, Norway, 1966-67, Free University of West Berlin, 1969-70, and University of Innsbruck, Austria, 1971-72.

MEMBER: Poetry Society of America, College English Association, South Atlantic Modern Language Association, Phi Beta Kappa, Omicron Delta Kappa, Fulbright Association, Poetry Society of Georgia.

AWARDS, HONORS: Reynolds Lyric Award, Poetry Society of America, 1961, for "Instructions for Dying"; Georgia Writer's Association Literary Achievement Award, 1963, for *The World's Old Way;* Sidney Lanier Award, Oglethorpe University, 1964, for *The World's Old Way;* John Holmes Memorial Award, 1965, for "For Parents, Out of Sight"; Georgia Poet of the Year award, Dixie Council of Authors and Journalists, 1967, for *Lanced in Light,* and 1975, for *All My Mirrors Lie;* Poetry Society of America annual award, 1973, for "The Bachelor, as Professor."

WRITINGS:

POETRY

The World's Old Way, University of Nebraska Press (Lincoln, NE), 1962.
Lanced in Light, Harcourt (New York, NY), 1968.
All My Mirrors Lie, David Godine (Boston, MA), 1975.
Unanswered Calls: A Book of Poems, Kendall/Hunt (Dubuque, IA), 1997.

Poems also appear in anthologies, including *The Golden Year: The Poetry Society of America Anthology, 1910-1960,* Fine Editions, 1960; *La Poesie contemporaine aux Etats-Unis,* Editions de la Revue Moderne, 1962; *Southern Poetry Today,* Impetus Press, 1962; *The New Orlando Poetry Anthology,* Volume II, New Orlando Publications, 1963; *Anthology of Southern Writing,* edited by Miller Williams and John W. Carrington, Louisiana State University Press, 1967; *The Norton Introduction to Literature,* Norton, 1975, new edition, 1991; *A Geography of Poets,* Bantam, 1979; *Contemporary Southern Poetry,* Louisiana State University Press, 1979; and *The Made Thing: An Anthology of Contemporary Southern Poetry,* University of Arkansas Press, 1987, new edition, 1999; *Blood to Remember: American Poets on the Holocaust,* Texas Technological University, 1991; *Fathers,* St. Martin's Press, 1997; and *Georgia Voices: Poetry,* University of Georgia Press, 2000. Contributor to periodicals and poetry journals, including *American Scholar, Antioch Review, College English Commonweal, Epoch, Harper's, Kenyon Review, London Magazine, Nation, New Yorker, New York Times, Ontario Review Poetry, Prairie Schooner, Quarterly Review of Literature, Saturday Review, Sewanee Review, Transatlantic Quarterly, Virginia Quarterly Review,* and *Yale Review.*

WORK IN PROGRESS: New and Selected Poems.

SIDELIGHTS: A poet whose work has been published in a wide variety of anthologies and magazines, both popular and literary, Larry Rubin is known for writing structured poems that are influenced by formal conventions. On the dust jacket of Rubin's *Lanced in Light,* which was published in 1968, Emily Dickinson was said to be his mentor, and F. H. Griffin Taylor, writing in the *Sewanee Review,* noticed echoes of her work in Rubin's poems. In *Georgia Review,* Robert L. Hull commented: "It is not surprising that *Lanced in Light* succeeds as a fine collection of poetry. Mr. Rubin's first volume, *The World's Old Way* . . . clearly indicates the talent and promise of a gifted poet. The second collection provides even more evidence of that talent."

The virtues of *Lanced in Light,* according to Samuel French Morse's *Virginia Quarterly Review* article, are "those of a writer who is unintimidated by conventional structures." On the other hand, Morse found fault with the collection's "solemnity," and suggested that Rubin is more impressive in individual poems than in a book-length volume. Stanley Cooperman of *Prairie Schooner* lodged a similar complaint, stating that Rubin's reliance on poetic conventions too often renders his work "a *low-risk* poetry." However, Cooperman also pointed out that Rubin sometimes creates memorable verse with his conservative form. Wrote Cooperman: "There are, however, lyrics that do have a certain rolling nobility to them—a quality which many readers may find attractive precisely because so few contemporary poets attempt to achieve it. And there are moments when Mr. Rubin's insistence on careful shaping, and holding back, deliberately, seems at once old-fashioned and surprisingly new."

BIOGRAPHICAL/CRITICAL SOURCES:

PERIODICALS

Atlanta Journal-Constitution, April 28, 1963.

Chattahoochee Review, 1999.

Georgia Review, winter, 1968.

Georgia Tech Alumnus, March, 1961.

Prairie Schooner, fall, 1968.

Sewanee Review, April, 1969.

Southern Review, April, 1978.

Virginia Quarterly Review, summer, 1968; autumn, 1976.

S

SANDFORD, John
See CAMP, John (Roswell)

* * *

SANTE, Luc 1954-

PERSONAL: Name pronounced "luke sahnt"; born May 25, 1954, in Verviers, Belgium; immigrated to the United States, 1959; son of Lucien (a factory manager) and Denise (a secretary and homemaker; maiden name, Nandrin) Sante; married Melissa Holbrook Pierson, September 21, 1992; children: Raphael. *Education:* Attended Columbia University, 1972-76. *Politics:* "Crypto-anarchist." *Religion:* "Freethinker."

ADDRESSES: Home and office—283 Lapla Road, Kingston, NY 12401. *Agent*—Robert Lantz-Joy Harris Literary Agency, 156 Fifth Ave., New York, NY 10010. *E-mail*—melluc@earthlink.net; fax: 845-339-7997.

CAREER: Freelance journalist and critic. Strand Book Store, New York City, clerk, 1976-79; *New York Review of Books,* New York City, mail clerk and editorial assistant, 1980-84; *Sports Illustrated,* New York City, proofreader, 1987-90; Columbia University (School of the Arts), New York City, adjunct assistant professor of writing, 1994-97; New School, adjunct professor of writing, 1999; Bard College, visiting professor of writing, 1999—.

MEMBER: PEN.

AWARDS, HONORS: Whiting Writer's Award, Mrs. Giles Whiting Foundation, 1989, for literary and film criticism and nonfiction; Guggenheim fellowship, 1992-93, for work on the idea of nationality; literature award, American Academy of Arts and Letters, 1997; Grammy Award, 1998, for album notes.

WRITINGS:

Low Life: Lures and Snares of Old New York, Farrar, Straus (New York), 1991.

Evidence, Farrar, Straus, 1992.

The Factory of Facts, Pantheon Books, 1998.

(Co-edited with Melissa Holbrook Pierson) *O.K. You Mugs,* Pantheon Books, 1999.

Walker Evans, Phaidon, 2001.

Author of introductions for *How the Other Half Lives,* Jacob Riis, Penguin Classics, 1997; *New York Noir,* edited by Bill Hannigan, Rizzoli, 1999; *The Big Con,* edited by David Maurer, Doubleday, 1999; *Inferno,* edited by Vance Nachtwey, Phaidon, 2000; and *Classic Crime,* edited by William Roughead, New York Review Books, 2000. Contributor to periodicals, including *New York Review of Books* and *New York Times Magazine.*

WORK IN PROGRESS: A work of semi-fiction concerning New York City and its years of ruin.

SIDELIGHTS: Luc Sante, whose articles and criticism have appeared frequently in such periodicals as the *New York Review of Books,* is also the author of the books *Low Life: Lures and Snares of Old New York* and *Evidence,* which are both histories of New York City. Describing his research methods as unscientific, Sante approaches his subject matter by looking for the neglected, unusual aspects of times past. "I'm fascinated by the notion of lost history," he related to Karen Schoemer in the *New York Times.* "What is history, anyway? History is what happened to big, powerful people, and I'm really interested in what happened to obscure people about whom nothing is known. The more obscure and buried it is, the more it fascinates me." Sante brings to light many forgotten turn-of-the-twentieth-century personalities in *Low Life,* a volume which focuses on the low-rent districts of nineteenth- and early-twentieth-century New York City. In *Evidence,* he presents a collection of photographs and brief stories about New Yorkers who died, often mysteriously, around the time of World War I.

Born to a middle-class Belgian family, Sante moved back and forth between Belgium and the United States four times before his family settled in New York City. Because of the economic disparity between the two countries, Sante realized that his family, though comparatively well off by Belgian standards, did not have some of the things Americans took for granted, such as a refrigerator, central heating, a television, or a record player. "For me, going back and forth between Belgium and the United States when I was a kid, I had the feeling not only of traveling in space but also of traveling in time," he explained to Schoemer.

Sante commented that his work in the paperback department of a New York City book store enabled him to cultivate a penchant for obscure history. Part of his job involved sorting through boxes of dusty materials whenever the store would purchase a library. "It became almost an obsession with me," Sante told Schoemer in the *New York Times.* "It was a great thing to sort through this documentation and try to imagine what the lives behind all this junk had been. I'd find myself feeling rather intimate toward people I had never met and whom I could only speculate on, based on these assorted impedimenta and artifacts." Sante brought this love for obscure historical detail to his books on New York City.

In *Low Life,* Sante depicts the underside of New York from around 1840 to 1919, suggesting that any yearning for a return to a golden era is misguided. The social problems of present-day New York are not any worse than the problems of old New York, the author claims; this opinion is reinforced by Hanna Rubin in the *New York Times Book Review,* who stated that "Sante reclaims an essential piece of the city's past, one that should reassure contemporary New Yorkers. This is far from the worst of times." Basing his research on old newspapers, out-of-print books, and various other sources, Sante provides a detailed account of the prostitutes, thieves, drug dealers, tramps, thugs, corrupt police officers, and others who populated New York City, particularly the Lower East Side, where Sante lived for fourteen years after college.

The "saloon culture" of old New York is recounted in *Low Life,* including the various techniques used by gangs—often in league with tavern proprietors—of knocking out and robbing patrons. The drug chloral hydrate, mixed into a customer's beer, became a popular tool for thieves. As Sante notes in *Low Life,* "The taste was detectable by anyone of sound mind and body, so the victim needed to be thoroughly drunk before he could be thus clobbered. Then he would be robbed, perhaps stripped as well, and dumped in an obscure alley. Some dives maintained an arrangement with the police whereby knocked-out customers would be brought to a convenient location so that the cops could remove their lifeless bodies to the precinct house, where they would eventually be charged with public intoxication." Sante also describes the lives of the city's many anonymous "child gangsters": "There were boys' saloons, with three-cent whiskeys and little girls in the back rooms, and there were children's gambling houses, in which tots could bilk other tots at the usual menu of games." Most of these boys died at a premature age, according to Sante. "The whole adult order of high and low sensations had to be experienced in fifteen or twenty years at best before they succumbed to disease, malnutrition, exposure, stab wounds, or gunfire."

Low Life is divided into four parts, describing the poor sections of town, the rise of crime after the Civil War, the attempts—legal and otherwise—to control such vice, and the various characters and groups from New York's "low" culture. In one passage, the author reveals how the real New York comes alive after dark: "The night is the corridor of history, not the history of famous people or great events but that of the marginal, the ignored, the suppressed, the unacknowledged; the history of vice, of error, of confusion, of fear, of want; the history of intoxication, of vainglory, of delusion, of dissipation, of delirium. It strips off the city's veneer of progress and modernity and civilization and reveals the wilderness."

Low Life received both favorable and mixed reviews, with critics responding differently to Sante's detailed writing style. Sally S. Eckhoff in the *Village Voice* pointed out that "Sante's joy in his subject is obvious, as is the thoroughness of his research." A *Washington Post Book World* reviewer, however, charged that the author's "accumulation of trivial facts is more numbing than enlightening, and his attempts to find larger meaning in this raw material are only intermittently successful." *Times Literary Supplement* contributor David Rieff took a different view: "One may quarrel with the implicit argument of *Low Life,* about what both New York and low life represent, but as literature it is a *tour-de-force.* In fashioning it, Sante has developed a particular, lacquered Elizabeth Hardwick-like prose style, that serves his purposes magnificently." John Vernon, writing in the *Los Angeles Times Book Review,* also found considerable merit in the book, hailing it as "both an exuberant poem of praise for lost New York and an essential mine of information for anyone interested in New York's past."

In the course of researching *Low Life,* Sante came across an archive of fourteen hundred police photographs from 1914 to 1918 depicting people who had met with untimely deaths. Although he used some of these pictures for *Low Life,* he selected fifty-five of the most haunting images for his 1992 book, *Evidence.* The photographs in *Evidence* are accompanied by written accounts of the people pictured, whose deaths from gunshot wounds, stabbings, or other means—two fell down elevator shafts—were variously attributed to murder, suicide, or unknown reasons. Thomas Boyle noted in the *New York Times Book Review* that some may find the photographs too gruesome or object to the "hit-and-miss non-method of [the book's] editorial apparatus." Still, Boyle felt Sante's sparse writing does not indicate "any weakness but rather a shrewd strategy on the author's part. Mr. Sante has decided to rely on his strong suits: a talent for the striking, impressionistic insight and the ability to write transcendental prose."

Sante told *CA:* "I don't call myself a historian, but everything I do represents some kind of historical investigation. I'm fascinated by memory and forgetting, by records and what is not recorded in them, and by trajectories of lives, even those of the lives of objects. The older I get, the more I am drawn to archives, flea markets, and junkyards, the true memorials of whatever it is we call civilization."

BIOGRAPHICAL/CRITICAL SOURCES:

BOOKS

Sante, Luc, *Low Life: Lures and Snares of Old New York,* Farrar, Straus (New York, NY), 1991.

PERIODICALS

Chicago Tribune, September 27, 1991, sec. 5, p. 3.

Harper's, August 1991, pp. 30-34.

Library Journal, June 1, 1991, p. 163; November 1, 1992, p. 104.

Los Angeles Times Book Review, September 29, 1991, p. 4.

New Republic, March 2, 1992, pp. 41-42.

New York, August 12, 1991, pp. 26-36; September 14, 1992, p. 112.

New York Times, February 21, 1993, sec. 9, p. 8.

New York Times Book Review, August 12, 1991, p. 26; September 29, 1991, p. 14; January 10, 1993, p. 31.

Publishers Weekly, July 12, 1991, p. 59; October 19, 1992, p. 71.

Times Literary Supplement, September 18, 1992, p. 8.

Village Voice, October 15, 1991, p. 79.

Voice Literary Supplement, December 1991, p. 16.

Washington Post Book World, September 1, 1991, p. 3; November 22, 1992, p. 13.

* * *

SAUNDERS, George (W.) 1958-

PERSONAL: Born December 2, 1958, in Amarillo, TX; son of George Robert (a federal employee) and Joan (a federal employee; maiden name, Clarke) Saunders. *Ethnicity:* "Mongrel Caucasian." *Education:* Colorado School of Mines, B.Sc., 1981; Syracuse University, M.A., 1988. *Religion:* "Former Catholic, current Buddhist."

ADDRESSES: *Home*—Syracuse, NY. *Office*—Department of English, Syracuse University, Syracuse, NY 13244. *Agent*—Esther Newberg, International Creative Management, 40 West 57th St., New York, NY 10019.

CAREER: Radian International (environmental engineering firm), Rochester, NY, technical writer and geophysical engineer, 1989-96; Syracuse University, Syracuse, NY, visiting professor of creative writing, 1996-97.

AWARDS, HONORS: National Magazine Awards, 1994, for "The 400-Pound CEO," 1996, for "Bounty," and 1999, for "The Barber's Unhappiness"; *New York Times* Notable Book of the Year, and PEN/Hemingway Award finalist, both 1996, both for *CivilWarLand in Bad Decline;* named by *New Yorker* magazine as one of the Twenty Best American Fiction Writers under Forty, 1999; *Pastoralia* chosen as a *New York Times* Notable Book of the Year, 2000.

WRITINGS:

FICTION

CivilWarLand in Bad Decline (short stories and a novella), Random House (New York, NY), 1996.

Pastoralia: Stories (short stories), Riverhead Books (New York, NY), 2000.

The Very Persistent Gappers of Frip (fairy tale), illustrated by Lane Smith, Villard (New York, NY), 2000.

Work included in three O. Henry Award collections. Contributor of stories to periodicals, including *Harper's, Story, Kenyon Review, Quarterly West,* and *New Yorker.*

SIDELIGHTS: George Saunders is an acclaimed American author noted for his wisdom and wit. His works have been compared to those of Mark Twain, Thomas Pynchon, and Kurt Vonnegut. His first collection, *CivilWarLand in Bad Decline,* was critically lauded and was a *New York Times* "Notable Book of the Year" as well as a finalist for the 1996 PEN/Hemingway Award. Saunders teaches creative writing at Syracuse University in New York.

Saunders' 2000 collection, *Pastoralia,* contains short stories previously published in the *New Yorker* magazine. Saunders's stories portray contemporary life as both absurd and noble, according to Donna Seaman in *Booklist.* "Saunders' mordant wit and biting insights make his surreal stories crackle with alternating currents of humor and pathos." A *Business Week* reviewer concurred, arguing that "Saunders can make a reader laugh aloud, but his observations cut deeply." Lynne Tillman in the *New York Times Book Review* found that, compared to his first collection, the stories in *Pastoralia* "cover larger, more exciting territory, with an abundance of ideas, meanings and psychological nuance. Saunders can be brutally funny, and the better his stories are, the more melancholic, somber and subtle they are, too. Pathetic contradictions underlie the ruthless drive for success in love and work, and Saunders weaves them into artful and sophisticated narrative webs." A critic for *Publishers Weekly* concluded: "Saunders's extraordinary talent is in top form." Adrienne Miller in *Esquire* agreed, calling the stories in *Pastoralia* "a delight. We're very lucky to have them."

Saunders has also written *The Very Persistent Gappers of Frip,* a fairy tale for adults, illustrated by Lane Smith. It is set in a town inhabited by bright orange, multi-eyed "gappers" who, unless stopped, will cover goats until they stop giving milk. Three houses are the focus of the gappers' attack in this fable. Critics were largely positive in their assessment of the work, lauding both the illustrations and Saunders' wit. "The Saunders-Smith collaboration is inspired," concluded a critic for *Publishers Weekly.*

Saunders once told *CA:* "I was first introduced to the idea of being a writer by my father, who would bring home books like Machiavelli's *The Prince* and Upton Sinclair's *The Jungle* from his work as a salesman on the south side of Chicago and who would tell epic comic tales of the various hustlers and lunatics he ran into on his rounds. I had never met a writer, had no idea that one could just become a writer, but two high school teachers, Joe Lindbloom and Sheri Williams Lindbloom, made me feel that the world of ideas was the only vital world, and that if I worked hard enough, I could find a place in it. I will be forever grateful to them for their generosity and belief. My mother's role in all of this was continually to praise me to the skies and make me feel I was a person of talent, which would later get me through long periods where the external data indicated exactly the contrary.

"I graduated from the Colorado School of Mines in 1981 and went to work as a geophysical engineer in Sumatra, Indonesia. I traveled widely in Malaysia, Thailand, Russia, and Pakistan. I made various comical and unsuccessful attempts to get into Third World war zones so I could write the great Afghan or Cambodian novel and sell it to Hollywood, and so on, but instead I got a terrific Sumatran virus and began sleeping fifteen hours a night. I returned to the United States and worked as a doorman in Beverly Hills, roofer in Chicago, musician, slaughterhouse laborer, mover, and finally retreated to my parents' house in Amarillo, Texas, at about twenty-six year of age. I was admitted to the Syracuse creative writing program in 1986.

"I wrote *CivilWarLand in Bad Decline* while working as a technical writer and engineer at an environmental engineering company in Rochester, New York. In retrospect, I can see in that book a lot of what I was living through at the time as an underpaid, under-respected, aging lackey. My wife and I were broke, with bad cars and little babies at home and, though this certainly wasn't the gulag, it was perhaps my first hint that disaster was not only possible but probable, and that our country is not particularly kind to all of its citizens, and that this unkindness takes a toll on our grace and generosity and our collective peace of mind. At the time, these were just little shouts, written when I was supposed to be writing technical reports or on the bus or late at night. The darkness and satire come, I guess, from the prevailing mode of storytelling on the south side of Chicago where, if you want to tell someone you love him, you generally pretend to knee him in the groin, then throw him in the pool while guffawing.

"It seems to me that life is a dark proposition, or can be, and that we must bear this in mind as we construct our political and moral systems. The traits and abilities that allow some of us to become rich, remain healthy, travel, wallow in good food and drink, or enthusiastically sing the praises of life have been doled out in advance, and not equitably, and we can take no real credit for these. Capitalism is the systematic taking-of-credit for these and must, it seems to me, be tempered with great doses of kindness and empathy if it is to avoid being cruel."

BIOGRAPHICAL/CRITICAL SOURCES:

PERIODICALS

Booklist, April 15, 2000, Donna Seaman, review of *Pastoralia,* p. 1525.
Business Week, June 19, 2000, review of *Pastoralia,* p. E14.
Entertainment Weekly, November 19, 1999, review of *The Very Persistent Gappers of Frip,* p. 135.
Esquire, May, 2000, Adrienne Miller, review of *Pastoralia,* p. 36.
New York Review of Books, June 29, 2000, Joyce Carol Oates, review of *Pastoralia,* p. 38.
New York Times Book Review, May 28, 2000, Lynne Tillman, review of *Pastoralia.*
Publishers Weekly, March 13, 2000, review of *Pastoralia,* p. 62; July 10, 2000, review of *The Very Persistent Gappers of Frip,* p. 45.

OTHER

Atlantic, http://www.theatlantic.com/ (May 17, 2000).
LA Weekly, http://www.laweekly.com/ (May 19-25, 2000).
Wag, http://thewag.net/ (July 2000).

* * *

SCHNEEBAUM, Tobias 1921-

PERSONAL: Born March 25, 1921, in New York, NY; son of Jacob (a grocer) and Rebecca (Ehrenfreund) Schneebaum. *Education:* Attended City College (now City College of the City University of New York), 1939-41. *Politics:* Democrat.

ADDRESSES: Home—463 West St., Apt. 410A, New York, NY 10014. *Agent*—Don Congdon Associates, 177 East 70th St., New York, NY 10021.

CAREER: Writer and painter. Irma Jonas School of Painting, Ajijic, Mexico, teacher, 1949-50; cook and dishwasher on freighter traveling to Alaska, Japan, and Korea, 1951-52; affiliated with a greeting card company in New York City, beginning in 1954; Asmat Museum of Culture and Progress, Irian Jaya, Indonesia, served as director of research and documentation. Metropolitan Museum of Art, lecturer; guest on television programs, including *The Mike Douglas Show. Military service:* U.S. Army Air Forces, 1942-45.

AWARDS, HONORS: Fulbright fellow in Peru, 1955; grants from Creative Artists Public Service Program, 1974, John D. Rockefeller III Fund, 1975 and 1980, and Ingram Merrill Foundation, 1982; Rockefeller Foundation resident at Bellagia, Italy, 1984.

WRITINGS:

NONFICTION

Keep the River on Your Right, Grove (New York, NY), 1969.
Wild Man, Viking (New York, NY), 1979.
(With Gunter Konrad and Ursula Konrad) *Asmat: Life with the Ancestors,* Bruckner, 1981.
Asmat Images from the Collection of the Asmat Museum of Culture and Progress, Asmat Museum of Culture and Progress (Agats, Indonesia), 1985.
Where the Spirits Dwell: An Odyssey in the New Guinea Jungle, Grove (New York, NY), 1988.
Embodied Spirits: Ritual Carvings of the Asmat, Peabody Museum of Salem (Salem, MA), 1990.
Secret Places: My Life in New York and New Guinea, University of Wisconsin Press (Madison, WI), 2000.

Contributor to periodicals, including *Christopher Street.*

ILLUSTRATOR

Vance Bourjaily, *The Girl in the Abstract Bed,* Tiber Press, 1954.
Mary Britton Miller, *Jungle Journey* (juvenile nonfiction), Pantheon (New York, NY), 1964.

ADAPTATIONS: The author's life and work, as he described it in his books, is explored in an award-winning documentary film, *Keep the River on Your Right: A Modern Cannibal Tale,* released by New Wave Films.

SIDELIGHTS: Keep the River on Your Right is Tobias Schneebaum's memoir of a trip he made to Peru to study art in 1955. He traveled by himself through the jungle and lived for several months with primitive peoples, including a tribe of cannibals. He has painted on other trips in Central America, Asia, southern Europe, and Africa, and has also lived in Irian Jaya (formerly Netherlands New Guinea).

According to Nancy Naglin in the *Chicago Tribune,* Tobias Schneebaum "has repeatedly gone beyond the pale of civilization, seeking something in the wilds of desert and jungle that will reveal the key to himself." *Wild Man,* his account of some of his travels, is "a confusing, fascinating, occasionally mesmerizing sketch of his troubled, fanciful, erotic mindscape." Schneebaum "writes with a ruthless, unabashed candor," and his "language is mystical and compelling," continued Naglin. "He left me with the feeling that he was trying to describe important things that are so close to the heart it is disturbing to hear them try to be explained."

BIOGRAPHICAL/CRITICAL SOURCES:

PERIODICALS

Books, October, 1971.
Chicago Tribune, May 12, 1979, Nancy Naglin, review of *Wild Man.*
Commonweal, February 20, 1970.
Library Journal, February 1, 1988, Winifred Lambrecht, review of *Where the Spirits Dwell,* p. 72.
New Statesman & Society, June 17, 1988, Adam Kuper, review of *Where the Spirits Dwell,* p. 43.
New York, September 15, 1969.
New York Review of Books, April 28, 1988, Janet Malcolm, review of *Where the Spirits Dwell,* p. 26.
New York Times, September 12, 1969.
New York Times Book Review, November 16, 1969; March 11, 1979.
Publishers Weekly, December 11, 1987, Genevieve Stuttaford, review of *Where the Spirits Dwell,* p. 52.
Washington Post Book World, September 21, 1969.

OTHER

Next Wave Films, http://www.nextwavefilms.com/ (September 11, 2000).*

SCHWARZ, Daniel R(oger) 1941-

PERSONAL: Born May 12, 1941, in Rockville Centre, NY; son of Joseph A. (a certified public accountant) and Florence (a homemaker; maiden name, Rimler) Schwarz; divorced from first wife; married Marcia Jacobson, 1998; children: David, Jeffrey. *Education:* Attended Edinburgh University, 1961-62; Union College, B.A.(magna cum laude), 1963; Brown University, M.A., 1965, Ph.D., 1968.

ADDRESSES: Home—925 Mitchell St., Ithaca, NY 14850. *Office*—Department of English, 242 Goldwin Smith Hall, Cornell University, Ithaca, NY 14853. *E-mail*—drs6@cornell.edu.

CAREER: Cornell University, Ithaca, NY, assistant professor, 1968-74, associate professor, 1974-80, professor of English, 1980-99, professor of English and Stephen H. Weiss Presidential Fellow, 1999—, director of undergraduate studies, 1976-80, and served as acting chair, director, or member of various boards and committees. Director of nine National Endowment for the Humanities summer seminars for college teachers and for secondary school teachers, 1984-93. Distinguished Visiting Cooper Professor, University of Arkansas, Little Rock, AK, spring, 1988; Citizen's Chair in Literature, University of Hawaii, 1992-93; Visiting Eminent Scholar in the Humanities, University of Alabama, Huntsville, AL, spring, 1996. Visiting scholar at Oxford University and Cambridge University, and in the United States and Australia; served on the editorial boards of various academic journals, including *Conradiana,* 1983—; *Journal of Narrative Technique,* 1984—; *Weber Studies: An Interdisciplinary Humanities Journal,* 1991—; and *Narrative,* 1992—.

MEMBER: International Association of University Professors of English, Society for the Study of Narrative Literature (past vice president; president, 1990), Modern Language Association of America, Society for the Study of Narrative Literature (founding member), Phi Beta Kappa.

AWARDS, HONORS: Brown University scholarship, 1963-64; Wilbour fellowship, Brown University, 1965-66; grants from American Philosophical Society, 1981, and National Endowment for the Humanities, 1984-1991, 1993; *Narrative and Representation in the Poetry of Wallace Stevens* named an outstanding book by *Choice,* 1993; Institute for European Studies grant, 1994; Western Society travel grant, 1994; Stephen and

Margery Russell Distinguished Teaching Award, Cornell University, 1998; Stephen Weiss Presidential Fellowship for Distinguished Teaching lifetime award, Cornell University, 1999; various Cornell grants for research, travel, and course development.

WRITINGS:

Disraeli's Fiction, Barnes & Noble (New York, NY), 1979.

Conrad's Fiction: "Almayer's Folly" to "Under Western Eyes," Cornell University Press (Ithaca, NY), 1980.

Conrad: The Later Fiction, Humanities (Atlantic Highlands, NJ), 1982.

Humanistic Heritage: Critical Theories of the English Novel from James to Hillis Miller, University of Pennsylvania Press (Philadelphia, PA), 1986, revised, 1989.

Reading Joyce's "Ulysses," St. Martin's Press (New York, NY), 1989.

The Transformation of the English Novel, 1890-1930: Studies in Hardy, Conrad, Joyce, Lawrence, Forster, and Woolf, St. Martin's Press (New York, NY), 1989, revised, 1995.

The Case for a Humanistic Poetics, University of Pennsylvania Press (Philadelphia, PA), 1991.

Narrative and Representation in the Poetry of Wallace Stevens, St. Martin's Press (New York, NY), 1993.

Reconfiguring Modernism: Explorations in the Relationship between Modern Art and Modern Literature, St. Martin's Press (New York, NY), 1997.

Imagining the Holocaust, St. Martin's Press (New York, NY), 1999.

Rereading Conrad, University of Missouri Press (Columbia, MO), 2001.

EDITOR

(And contributor) James Joyce, *The Dead: Complete, Authoritative Text with Biographical Essays and Historical Contexts, Critical History, and Essays from Five Contemporary Critical Perspectives* ("Case Studies in Contemporary Criticism" series), Bedford Books/St. Martin's Press (Boston, MA), 1994.

(With Janice Carlisle) *Narrative and Culture,* University of Georgia Press (Athens, GA), 1994.

(And contributor) Joseph Conrad, *The Secret Sharer: Complete, Authoritative Text with Biographical Essays and Historical Contexts, Critical History, and Essays from Five Contemporary Critical Perspectives* ("Case Studies in Contemporary Criticism" series), Bedford Books/St. Martin's Press (Boston, MA), 1997.

Contributor of chapters to books, including *T. S. Eliot,* edited by Linda W. Wagner, McGraw, 1974; *Twentieth-Century Poetry, Fiction, Theory,* edited by Harry Garvin, Bucknell University Press, 1977; *Critical Approaches to Thomas Hardy,* edited by Dale Kramer, Barnes & Noble, 1979; *Sons and Lovers: A Critical Survey,* edited by J. N. R. Saunders, Macdonald & Evans; *Conrad Revisited: Essays of the Eighties,* edited by Ross Murfin, University of Alabama Press, 1985; *Encyclopedia of Literature and Criticism,* edited by Martin Coyle and others, Routledge, 1991; *Benet's Reader's Encyclopedia of American Literature,* edited by George and Barbara Perkins, HarperCollins, 1991; *A Companion to Henry James Studies,* edited by Daniel Fogel, Greenwood, 1993; and *Reference Guide to English Literature,* St. James, 1994. Contributor of articles, reviews, and poetry to publications and literary journals. Contributor to *Nineteenth-Century Literary Criticism,* Volume 2, Gale, 1982, *Victorian Novelists Before 1885,* Gale, 1983; and *Columbia History of the English Novel,* edited by John Richetti, Columbia University Press, 1994.

WORK IN PROGRESS: Under contract to write *Damon Runyon and the Making of Broadway,* St. Martin's Press (New York, NY); and *Reading the Modern British and Irish Novel: 1900-1950,* Blackwell (New York, NY). Also serving as general editor of *Reading the British and American Novel,* Blackwell (New York, NY).

SIDELIGHTS: Daniel R. Schwarz is a professor of English at Cornell University and the author and editor of many books of literary criticism and thought. Joseph Carroll reviewed Schwarz's *The Case for a Humanistic Poetics* in the *Journal of English and Germanic Philology.* Carroll noted that the book consists of essays formed from previously published conference papers and book reviews. The critic noted that Schwarz believes that literary texts are mimetic or representational and that readers can construe relatively determinate structures of meaning in a text. "Schwarz has no philosophical rationale for these beliefs, and he can thus only appeal stubbornly to common sense. I think this appeal is legitimate, particularly considering the flimsiness and arbitrariness of the poststructuralist theses that have superseded common-sense realism. But as Schwarz's case suggests, in order to mount an effective counter-attack to anti-realist argument like that of deconstruction, one needs a fully formulated realist argument."

The Dead: Complete, Authoritative Text with Biographical Essays and Historical Contexts, Critical History, and Essays from Five Contemporary Critical Perspectives is a volume in the Bedford Books "Case Studies in Contemporary Criticism" series written for college students. In reviewing the book for *Studies in Short Fiction,* Brian W. Shaffer called it a "splendid" addition and praised Schwarz for his selection of contributors. He said Peter J. Rabinowitz "approaches Joyce's final *Dubliners* story from the perspective of reader-response criticism; Michael Levinson from the perspective of New Historicism; Margot Norris from the perspective of feminism; and John Paul Riquelme from the perspective of deconstruction. Schwarz himself contributes a psychoanalytic reading of 'The Dead,' a balanced and wide-ranging discussion of the story's biographical and historical contexts, and a comprehensive and insightful critical history of the story's reception." Shaffer called the essays by Levinson and Norris "provocative and original."

Kathryn N. Benzel reviewed *Reconfiguring Modernism: Explorations in the Relationship between Modern Art and Modern Literature* in *Clio.* Benzel called Schwarz's book "useful in two important ways: as a commentary on the modernist aesthetic and as an exploration of the complex critical world of interdisciplinary study. Schwarz's analyses of such 'high modernists' as Henry James, Joseph Conrad, T. S. Eliot, James Joyce, and Wallace Stevens in terms of modern artistic movements (Impressionism, Post-Impressionism, and Cubism, with references to Dadaism, Fauvism, Futurism, and Surrealism) are provocative and introduce possibilities for further interdisciplinary discussion of modernists."

Diane Richard-Allerdyce noted in *Studies in the Novel,* that in *Reconfiguring Modernism,* Virginia Woolf is the single female whose works are featured. Richard-Allerdyce wrote that Schwarz's book doesn't "claim to provide a study of the Modernist period that takes the influence of male and female artists equally into account . . . and it leaves room for exploration of the implications of the African, Asian, and Pacific influences it demonstrates on European and American Modernism. But in its performing, as the best critical inquiry does, that which Cezanne and Eliot insisted was 'the function of art . . . to look at the world with fresh eyes and to cast aside assumptions about how the world was supposed to look' . . . , it points us in the direction of further study." Daniel Morris, writing in *Modern Fiction Studies,* praised, "His book should take its place within a larger meaningful pattern of cultural criticism that celebrates the work being discussed and, by doing so, reveals the author's deep affection for its sources and for the process of learning about them over a lifetime." In his book *Imagining the Holocaust,* Schwarz investigates how writers and filmmakers have portrayed the Holocaust through imaginative texts instead of strictly documentary ones. "Schwarz's book should be considered essential because of its purpose: to persuade readers that to vicariously experience the Holocaust means to address critical philosophical questions," noted Milton Goldin in *H-Holocaust. Jewish Currents* reviewer Joel Shatzky praised, "Schwarz's excellent analysis of so many [Holocaust texts] brings us closer to an understanding of the Holocaust." Schwarz's analysis includes Anne Frank's diary and Steven Spielberg's movie adaptation of *Schindler's List,* as well as works by such writers as Elie Wiesel, Primo Levi, and Cynthia Ozick. Daniel Morris, in *Studies in the Novel,* called *Imagining the Holocaust* a "valuable guide book," and Elliot H. Shapiro of the *Ithaca Times* wrote, "It is, moreover, satisfying to read the sensitive and intelligent readings of the works of many authors . . . by a literary critic of such wide experience and formidable intelligence."

Schwarz told *CA:* "My fields are the theory of the novel and the English novel from Daniel Defoe through James Joyce, especially from the late nineteenth century through Virginia Woolf. In my writing, I consider myself a teacher entering into a dialogue with advanced students, colleagues, and teachers at other universities. I am primarily a literary critic who is trying to create a dialogue between primary works and literary theory, as well as between traditional approaches and recent ones, such as Deconstruction. I always try to be true to the spirit of the author's original text, while realizing that literary works do have different meanings for different readers and eras."

BIOGRAPHICAL/CRITICAL SOURCES:

PERIODICALS

Choice, November, 1993, B. Galvin, review of *Narrative and Representation in the Poetry of Wallace Stevens,* p. 456; June, 1994, R. D. Newman, review of *The Dead,* p. 1579; May, 1998, S. Donovan, review of *Reconfiguring Modernism,* p. 1522.

Clio, fall, 1999, Kathryn N. Benzel, review of *Reconfiguring Modernism,* p. 69.

H-Holocaust, January 29, 2000, Milton Goldin, review of *Imagining the Holocaust.*

Ithaca Times, March 22, 2000, Elliot H. Shapiro, review of *Imagining the Holocaust,* p. 32.

James Joyce Quarterly, summer, 1996, John Whittier-Ferguson, review of *The Dead,* p. 641.

Jewish Currents, April, 2001, Joel Shatzky, "The Holocaust: Remembrance and Reflection, pp. 28-29.

Journal of English and Germanic Philology, October, 1995, Joseph Carroll, review of *The Case for a Humanistic Poetics,* p. 554.

Journal of Modern Literature, spring, 1999, Irving Malin, review of *Reconfiguring Modernism,* p. 429.

Library Journal, July, 1987, Keith Cushman, review of *Reading Joyce's "Ulysses,"* p. 79.

Modern Fiction Studies, winter, 1989, Monika Fludernik, "Monika Fludernik Responds," p. 722, Marvin Magalaner, review of *The Transformation of the English Novel, 1890-1930,* p. 849; summer, 1998, Daniel Morris, review of *Reconfiguring Modernism,* p. 438.

Review of Contemporary Fiction, fall, 1994, Irving Malin, review of *Narrative and Culture,* p. 237.

Southern Humanities Review, winter, 2000, Kim Moreland, review of *Reconfiguring Modernism,* p. 81.

Studies in Short Fiction, summer, 1995, Brian W. Shaffer, review of *The Dead,* p. 502.

Studies in the Novel, summer, 1989, Rosemarie A. Battaglia, review of *Reading Joyce's "Ulysses,"* p. 224; spring, 1990, Robinson Blann, review of *The Transformation of the English Novel, 1890-1930,* p. 109; spring, 2000, Diane Richard-Allerdyce, review of *Reconfiguring Modernism,* p. 97; summer, 2001, Daniel Morris, review of *Imagining the Holocaust,* pp. 243-245.

Times Higher Education Supplement, July 28, 1989.

Times Literary Supplement, April 13, 1980, September 26, 1980.

OTHER

Daniel R. Schwarz, http://www.people.cornell.edu/pages/drs6 (June 11, 2000).

* * *

SCOTT, Bonnie Kime 1944-

PERSONAL: Born December 28, 1944, in Philadelphia, PA; daughter of Roy Milford (an electrical engineer) and Sheila (a schoolteacher and homemaker; maiden name, Burton) Kime; married Thomas Russell Scott (an academic administrator and neuroscientist), June 17, 1967; children: Heather, Ethan, Heidi. *Education:* Wellesley College, B.A., 1967; University of North Carolina at Chapel Hill, M.A., 1969, Ph.D., 1973. *Politics:* Democrat. *Avocational interests:* "I derive personal satisfaction from everyday relationships with my husband, children, students, and colleagues, from international travel, reading, gardening, and excursions into nature."

ADDRESSES: Home—10758 Puebla Dr., La Mesa, CA 91941. *Office*—Department of Women's Studies, San Diego State University, San Diego, CA 92182-8138. *E-mail*—bkscott@mail,sdsu.edu.

CAREER: University of Delaware, Newark, assistant professor, 1975-80, associate professor, 1980-86, professor of English and Women's Studies, 1986-2001, coordinator of Women's Studies Interdisciplinary Program, 1980-81, acting director of Center for Teaching Effectiveness, 1980-81, president of faculty senate, 1994-95, director of graduate studies in English, 1998-2001; San Diego State University, San Diego, CA, professor of women's studies, 2001—. Delaware Humanities Council, chairperson of publicity and fundraising.

MEMBER: Modern Language Association of America, American Conference for Irish Studies (founding chairperson of mid-Atlantic region), James Joyce Foundation (founder of Women's Caucus, 1982; member of board of directors, 1990—), Virginia Woolf Society, Phi Beta Kappa.

AWARDS, HONORS: American Philosophical Society grant, 1981; National Endowment for the Humanities grant, 1984; Excellence in Teaching Grant, Mortar Board, 1984; University of Delaware Center for Advanced Study grant, 1991-92; named Outstanding Scholar, College of Arts and Sciences, University of Delaware, 1999.

WRITINGS:

NONFICTION; LITERARY CRITICISM

Joyce and Feminism, Indiana University Press (Bloomington), 1984.

James Joyce, Humanities Press International (Atlantic Highlands, NJ), 1987.

(Editor) *New Alliances in Joyce Studies: When It's Aped to Foul a Delfian,* University of Delaware Press (Newark), 1988.

(Editor) *The Gender of Modernism: A Critical Anthology,* Indiana University Press, 1990.

Refiguring Modernism, two volumes, Indiana University Press, 1995.

(Editor, with Ann Ardis) *Virginia Woolf: Turning the Centuries, Selected Papers from the Ninth Annual Conference on Virginia Woolf, University of Delaware, June 10-13, 1999,* Pace University Press (New York City), 2000.

(Author of introduction and editor, with Rebecca West) *Selected Letters of Rebecca West,* Yale University Press (New Haven, CT), 2000.

Also contributor to scholarly journals and to numerous anthologies of literary criticism, including *Classics of Joyce Criticism,* edited by Janet Egleson Dunleavy, University of Illinois Press, 1991; *Joyce in Context,* edited by Timothy P. Martin and Vincent Cheng, Cambridge University Press, 1992; *Irish Writing: Exile and Subversion,* edited by Paul Hyland and Neil Sammells, Macmillan, 1992; and *The Johns Hopkins Guide to Literary Criticism and Theory,* edited by Michael Groden and Martin Kreiswirth, Johns Hopkins University Press, 1993. Member of editorial board, *Joyce Studies Annual.*

WORK IN PROGRESS: A study of Virginia Woolf's uses of nature.

SIDELIGHTS: Literary critic and educator Bonnie Kime Scott was professor of English and women's studies at the University of Delaware from 1975 until 2001, when she moved to California to take a position as professor of women's studies at San Diego State University. Scott's works have typically focused on James Joyce and gender issues in literature, including *Joyce and Feminism, New Alliances in Joyce Studies, The Gender of Modernism,* and *Refiguring Modernism.*

In 2000 Scott edited a collection of the letters of Rebecca West. "In her ninety years," wrote Adam Kirsch in the *Washington Post,* "Rebecca West seemed to live half a dozen different lives. She first became known, barely out of her teens, as a polemicist for the British suffragette movement; after World War I she turned from politics to literature, establishing herself as a novelist and critic. In the 1930s she helped to sound the alarm against Hitler; in 1941 she was reborn as an expert on Yugoslavia, with the publication of her classic travelogue *Black Lamb and Grey Falcon;* in the 1950s she became a vocal anti-communist, much to the dismay of her friends on the Left. In her old age she was a sort of living link to the Modernist past, consulted by historians and biographers, always eager to set the record straight. And her life came full circle when she was in her late eighties and the women's movement rediscovered her as a forerunner."

Reviews of the work were largely positive. Francine Prose in *Lingua Franca* wrote: "Scott has judiciously culled more than two hundred letters from the ten thousand or so West wrote to friends, relatives, editors, and fellow writers." Though *New York Review of Books'* Hilary Mantel lauded the selection of letters with respect to West's interest in the Balkans, the critic faulted Scott as an unreliable guide to "the earthquake zones of West's political passions" and for not correcting mistakes in the letters and missing annotations of significant events referred to in the letters. In *Women's Review of Books,* Beth Carole Rosenberg praised Scott's selection of West's letters. Rosenberg found that "Scott has managed to choose those [letters] that create a full portrait of West's life and personality—her conflicts with family and lovers, her obsessions with her health, her involvement in politics and art, her sheer pleasure in travel and her wicked irony when writing to and about her peers." Frank Kermode argued in the *New Republic:* "Scott must have enjoyed her labor on this book. It is not quite flawless (there are corrigible slips in the text and corrigible faults in the notes), but she has done well to continue the work done by an earlier generation of feminists towards the restoration of Rebecca West to a place of honor among the writers of the twentieth century." Sarah Kerr, in a review for the *New York Times,* called the book, "majestic."

Scott once told *CA:* "As a student I had a bewildering array of profound interests, including astronomy and international politics. I decided that I could be most effective in probing human nature and contexts through literature. The advent of women's studies brought a new archive and a thorough revision of my view of the scope, politics, and possibilities of literature, including my two most valued authors, Virginia Woolf and James Joyce.

"Woolf offers methods of questioning and communicating with readers, of catching the atoms of experience, and of acknowledging the importance of female lives and perceptions. Joyce first attracted me with his rendering of sensual perception and human psychology; he retains my interest with his development of 'polylogue'—his evasion of monological language and philosophy. Modernist problems of disintegration and renewal, brought to the level of language itself, remain central to our postmodern world. The texts are demanding and thus stimulating to mental life, hence my satisfaction at studying and teaching them. Irish literature, which I entered via Joyce, offers other, decentered worlds to the modern imagination and reminds us of the constant merger of the political with the literary."

She later added, "Among the authors I have come to value recently are Rebecca West, for her amazing scope of history, and Djuna Barnes, for her ability to probe pain and sexual marginality. I look forward to better cross-cultural communication via writers such as Toni Morrison and Alice Walker."

BIOGRAPHICAL/CRITICAL SOURCES:

PERIODICALS

London Review of Books, June 22, 2000, Rosemary Dinnage, review of *Selected Letters of Rebecca West,* pp. 42-43.

Nation, April 24, 2000, Georgette Fleischer, review of *Selected Letters of Rebecca West,* p. 31.

New Criterion, May, 2000, Carl Rollyson, review of *Selected Letters of Rebecca West,* p. 78.

New Republic, March 20, 2000, Frank Kermode, review of *Selected Letters of Rebecca West,* p. 28.

New York Review of Books, June 29, 2000, Hilary Mantel, review of *Selected Letters of Rebecca West,* pp. 4-8.

New York Times, September 10, 2000, Sarah Kerr, review of *Selected Letters of Rebecca West,* pp. 10, 12.

Publishers Weekly, March 6, 2000, review of *Selected Letters of Rebecca West,* p. 96.

Times Literary Supplement, January 11, 1985.

Wall Street Journal, March 6, 2000, Merle Rubin, review of *Selected Letters of Rebecca West,* p. A28.

Women's Review of Books, July, 2000, Beth Carole Rosenberg, review of *Selected Letters of Rebecca West,* pp. 46-47.

OTHER

Lingua Franca, http://www.linguafranca.com/ (April 2000), Francine Prose, review of *Selected Letters of Rebecca West.*

Washington Post, http://www.washingtonpost.com/ (April 9, 2000), Adam Kirsch, review of *Selected Letters of Rebecca West.*

* * *

SEBALD, W(infried) G(eorg) 1944-

PERSONAL: Born 1944, in Wertach im Allgäu, Germany; immigrated to England, 1966. *Education:* University of Fribourg, Licence ès Lettres; University of Manchester, M.A.; University of East Anglia, Ph.D.; University of Hamburg, Dr.Phil.Habil.

ADDRESSES: Office—University of East Anglia, Norwich, Norfolk NR4 7TJ, England.

CAREER: Writer. University of East Anglia, Norwich, England, professor of European literature, 1970—. Director, British Center for Literary Translation, University of East Anglia, 1989-94.

AWARDS, HONORS: Berlin Literature Prize, Johannes Bobrowski Medal, Literature Nord Prize, and *Jewish Quarterly* Literary Prize for fiction, 1997, all for *The Emigrants;* International IMPAC Dublin Literary Award nomination, 1998, for *The Emigrants,* 2000, for *The Rings of Saturn; Los Angeles Times* Book Prize for Fiction for *The Rings of Saturn;* Heinrich Böll Preis, Cologne, Germany.

WRITINGS:

FICTION

Nach der Natur: Ein Elementardgedicht, photographs by Thomas Becker, Greno (Nördlingen, Germany), 1988.

Schwindel, Gefühle, Eichborn (Frankfurt am Main, Germany), 1990, English translation by Michael Hulse published as *Vertigo,* New Directions (New York, NY), 1999.

Die Ausgewanderten, Eichborn (Frankfurt am Main, Germany), 1992, English translation by Michael Hulse published as *The Emigrants,* New Directions (New York, NY), 1996.

Die Ringe des Saturn: Eine Englische Wallfahrt (title means "The Rings of Saturn: An English Pilgrimage"), Eichborn (Frankfurt am Main, Germany), 1995, English translation by Michael Hulse published as *The Rings of Saturn,* New Directions (New York, NY), 1998.

Austerlitz, Hanser (Munich, Germany), 2001, English translation by Anthea Bell published as *Austerlitz,* Random House (New York, NY), 2001.

Also author of poetry.

NONFICTION

Carl Sternheim: Kritiker und Opfer der Wilhelminschen Aera, Kohlhammer (Stuttgart, Germany), 1969.

Der Mythus der Zerstörung im Werk Döblins, Klett (Stuttgart, Germany), 1980.

Die Beschreibung des Unglücks: Zur Österreichischen Literatur von Stifter bis Handke, Residenz-Verlag (Salzburg, Austria), 1985.

(Editor and contributor) *A Radical Stage: Theatre in Germany in the 1970s and 1980s,* St. Martin's (New York, NY), 1988.

Unheimliche Heimat: Essays zur Österreichischen Literatur, Residenz-Verlag (Salzburg, Austria), 1991.

SIDELIGHTS: German-born literary and theatrical scholar W. G. Sebald, who immigrated to England in 1966, is widely known in the German-speaking world for his genre-crossing works of creative prose, as well as for his literary criticism. His novels, including *Vertigo, The Emigrants,* and *The Rings of Saturn,* were published in English during the 1990s to nearly universal acclaim. Joining that list is his novel *Austerlitz,* published in 2001. Sebald is a professor of European literature at the University of East Anglia, where he has taught since 1970.

In 1996 Sebald's *Die Ausgewanderten* was translated into English as *The Emigrants.* The novel, in the words of Lisa Cohen in the *Boston Review,* is a "complex attempt to track and dislodge the tenacious insanities of the Holocaust." Its four parts portray four different characters from Sebald's own past, all of whom were destroyed in one way or another during World War II. The book contains numerous old photographs that, according to reviewer Carole Angier in the *Spectator,* "are part of the artistry and originality of the text." Cohen also noted the unique format of Sebald's work, stating that the proper classification for *The Emigrants* is as "a novel-essay in the form of a scrapbook, a joint biography, an oral history, and a memoir." Sebald himself, Cohen reported, has disclaimed the status of novelist with the observation that "his 'medium is prose, not the novel.'" He has called *The Emigrants* "a metaphor or allegory" of historical experiences. Angier noted that the narratives "move like memory itself—not logically or openly, but mysteriously, through images, echoes and accidents."

Sebald's prose has been highly praised for its simplicity and lyrical qualities, as has its English translation by Michael Hulse. Angier found *The Emigrants* "exquisitely written and exquisitely translated" and declared, "I think it may be a masterpiece." *Washington Post Book World* critic Dennis Drabelle called the translation a "gem." "The brilliance of this book lies in the fact that Sebald never loses sight of either the power of metaphor or the viciousness of history," wrote Cohen, who appreciated the "uncanny vividness and specificity" of the stories Sebald tells. Martin Chalmers stated in the *New Statesman* that *The Emigrants* is "marvelous" and suggested that "we need stories like those of *The Emigrants*" to ensure that the lessons of history are not lost. A reviewer for the *New York Times Book Review,* Larry Wolff, wrote that "the impact of the Holocaust on the novel's emigrant survivors lies at the silent heart of the book, the suppressed tragedy they find so difficult to address directly." Andre Aciman described "Sebald's world" in *Commentary* as "haunting, hypnotic, and, at times, even hallucinatory."

The Emigrants' 1990 predecessor, *Schwindel, Gefühle,* translated in 1999 as *Vertigo,* is an autobiographical tale in which the narrator traverses four loosely related stories that occur at various times in European history. "Sebald attains a particularly fluid synthesis of intellect and sensation as the writer revisits the stunning scenery and complicated memories of his youth," claimed a critic in *Publishers Weekly.* "This extraordinary, unclassifiable book is a log of Sebald's inner life," argued W. S. Di Piero in the *New York Times Book Review.* Richard Eder, also writing in the *New York Times Book Review,* lauded the translation by Michael Hulse, but placed *Vertigo* behind Sebald's *The Emigrants* and *The Rings of Saturn.* "In this early book Mr. Sebald has not yet found a way to attach his melancholy and his oddly moving comedy to a convincing vision of history's fearful workings." Di Piero, on the other hand, concluded that "Sebald is a thrilling, original writer. He makes narration a state of investigative bliss. His narrative doesn't just tell stories; it offers itself as a model of consciousness, demonstrating that to be fully aware of oneself in time is to suffer incurable vertigo."

Pico Iyer, in his review of *Vertigo* for *Harper's Magazine,* pointed out that all of Sebald's "tales of memory and wandering [*The Emigrants, Vertigo,* and *The Rings of Saturn*]. . . are essentially part of the same ongoing life's work, which could be entitled *A la fuite du temps perdu.*" Iyer went on to explain that the procedure in all three books is much the same: "a narrator, in all ways indistinguishable from the author, goes on long haunted wanderings alone through shadowy European landscapes, driven by some private riddle that will not leave him alone. He crosscuts his journeys with enigmatic historical portraits of other curious misfits or wandering strangers from the past. And his text is broken up by reproductions of cryptic photographs, maps from old books, even photocopies of his passport, which uncaptioned and often bearing only the most oblique relation to the narrative, intensify the sense of placelessness and silence. . . . What terrifies in Sebald is . . . the disembodied calm, the sense of madness accepted. His is a world of which he can make nothing, and his prose, with its mortician's quiet, has, at its best, the spell-bound beauty of a frozen ship upon a frozen ocean."

Sebald's next novel, *Die Ringe des Saturn: Eine Englische Wallfahrt,* published in 1998 as *The Rings of Saturn,* is more linear in its narration than his earlier books; it uses a journey through Suffolk, England, as the central element in a work that features dreams, observations, and memories on a variety of topics. In the estimation of Matthew Roberson, writing in the *Review of Contemporary Fiction,* the book was a "map of the author's brilliantly wandering mind," as it takes flight into "biographical sketches of the famous, the eccentric, and the forgotten; into remembrances of momentous events and places . . . ; and into critical analyses of artworks . . . [and] the possible compulsions of their creators." *New York Times Book Review* contributor Roberta Silman compared the work to those of Zbigniew Herbert, Vladimir Nabokov, Italo Calvino, and Jonathan Swift, "yet by the end you know it is like none of these. For it is written in a voice so confident, so sympathetic and so much its own that it cannot be in any sense called derivative." A *Publishers Weekly* critic also lauded the work: "As he did so brilliantly in *The Emigrants,* German author Sebald once again blurs the boundaries between fact and fiction in this meditative work." The critic described the work as a "brooding, elegiac novel." *New Republic* reviewer James Wood called Sebald "one of the most mysteriously sublime of contemporary writers."

In his career as a scholar of German theater and literature, Sebald has also produced a number of nonfiction books. Some of his volumes have dealt with the works of individual playwrights, including Carl Sternheim and Alfred Döblin. In 1985 he published a collection of ten previously published essays on Austrian literature under the title *Die Beschreibung des Unglücks: Zur Österreichischen Literatur von Stifter bis Handke.* Martin Swales, reviewing the volume for *Modern Language Review,* stated that "Sebald writes well and there is a splendid urgency to every analysis that he offers." A second collection on the same subject, *Unheimliche Heimat: Essays zur Österreichischen Literatur,* appeared in 1991. Sebald "writes deftly and with clear inner involvement, all the while maintaining a salutary critical attitude towards the writers under view," commented Sidney Rosenfeld for *World Literature Today.* Readers were able to sample Sebald's critical writing in English in his contribution to the 1988 volume *A Radical Stage: Theatre in Germany in the 1970s and 1980s,* which he edited, and which John Brosnahan, a reviewer for *Booklist,* called "illuminating."

BIOGRAPHICAL/CRITICAL SOURCES:

PERIODICALS

Booklist, February 15, 1989, John Brosnahan, review of *A Radical Stage,* p. 972.

Boston Review, February/March, 1997, Lisa Cohen, review of *The Emigrants,* pp. 44-45.

Commentary, June, 1997, Andre Aciman, review of *The Emigrants.*

Economist, July 15, 2000, review of *Vertigo,* p. 12.

German Quarterly, March, 1983, pp. 341-343; winter, 1987, pp. 135-137.

Harper's Magazine, October, 2000, Pico Iyer, "The Strange, Haunted World of W. G. Sebald," review of *Vertigo,* p. 86.

Modern Language Review, April, 1972, pp. 471-472; January, 1987, pp. 248-250; July, 1993, pp. 803-805.

New Republic, July 6, 1998, James Wood, review of *The Rings of Saturn,* p. 38.

New Statesman, July 12, 1996, Martin Chalmers, review of *The Emigrants,* pp. 44-45.

New York Times Book Review, March 30, 1997, Larry Wolff, review of *The Emigrants;* July 26, 1998, Roberta Silman, review of *The Rings of Saturn;* May 22, 2000, Richard Eder, review of *Vertigo;* June 11, 2000, W. S. Di Piero, review of *Vertigo.*

Publishers Weekly, April 6, 1998, review of *The Rings of Saturn,* p. 60; April 24, 2000, review of *Vertigo,* p. 62.

Quadrant, November, 1998, Trudi Tate, review of *The Rings of Saturn,* p. 76.

Review of Contemporary Fiction, fall, 1998, Matthew Roberson, review of *The Rings of Saturn,* p. 241; fall, 2000, Philip Landon, review of *Vertigo,* p. 137.

Spectator, August 17, 1996, Carole Angier, review of *The Emigrants,* pp. 28-30.

Times Literary Supplement, July 12, 1996, p. 22.

Washington Post Book World, December 15, 1996, Dennis Drabelle, review of *The Emigrants,* p. X6; June 25, 2000, Michael Dirda, review of *Vertigo,* p. X15.

World Literature Today, winter, 1992, Sidney Rosenfeld, review of *Unheimliche Heimat,* pp. 127-128.*

* * *

SHERMAN, Charlotte A.
See SHERMAN, Jory (Tecumseh)

SHERMAN, Jory (Tecumseh) 1932-
(Frank Anvic, Walt Denver, Cort Martin, Hank Mitchum, Charlotte A. Sherman, Wilma Tarrant, pseudonyms)

PERSONAL: Born October 20, 1932, in St. Paul, MN; son of Keith Edward (a franchise consultant) and Mercedes (a stenographer; maiden name, Sheplee) Sherman; married Remy Montes Roxas, June 10, 1951 (deceased); married Felicia, August 15, 1958 (divorced December, 1967); married Charlotte Balcom (a writer), March 2, 1968; children: Francis Antonio, Jory Vittorio, Forrest Redmond, Gina Felice, Misty April, Marcus Tecumseh; stepchildren: Gerald LeRoy Wilhite, David Dean Wilhite, Janet Lynn Wilhite. *Education:* Attended San Francisco State College (now University) and University of Minnesota. *Politics:* Democrat. *Avocational interests:* Black powder guns, hunting, fishing, canoeing, computer programming, local and western history.

ADDRESSES: *Home*—Suite 642, 3044 Shepherd Hills Exp., Branson, MO 65616.

CAREER: Writer. Denver Dry Goods, Denver, CO, advertising copywriter, 1949-50; American President Lines, San Francisco, CA, computer programmer, 1953-54; Great Plays Co., Lethbridge, Alberta, Canada, actor, 1954-55; *San Francisco Examiner,* San Francisco, editor, 1960-61; American Art Enterprise, North Hollywood, CA, magazine editor, 1961-65; freelance editor, 1965-67; newspaper columnist, 1965—. San Bernardino County press chairperson for Gerald Brown; press chairperson for John Tunney and Jesse Unruh. Teacher of creative writing for adults at Southwest Missouri State University and elsewhere. President, MicroDramas Co., Rialto, CA, 1969-71. Editor, Academy Press, Chatsworth, CA, 1971-72. *Military service:* U.S. Navy, 1950-53.

MEMBER: Writers Guild of America, Authors League of America, Authors Guild, Western Writers of America, Ozark Writers League (co-founder), Missouri Writers Guild, Twin Counties Press Club (member of board of directors, 1966-70), Desert-Mountain Press Club, Baja California Writers Association.

AWARDS, HONORS: Best Newspaper Column Award, Twin Counties Press Club, 1970; Best Radio Station Public Service Program Award, Twin Counties Press Club, 1970 and 1971; Best Newspaper Column Award, 1985, Best Novel Award, 1985, Best Magazine Article Award, 1985, Best Major Work Award, 1988, for *Song of the Cheyenne,* Best Major Work Award, 1992, for *The Medicine Horn,* and award for best book, 1995, for *Trapper's Moon,* all from Missouri Writers Guild; Best Novel of the West Award, Western Writers of America, 1992, for *The Medicine Horn;* Pulitzer Prize in Letters nomination, 1994, for *Grass Kingdom.*

WRITINGS:

So Many Rooms, Galley Sail Publications, 1960.

My Face in Wax, introduction by Charles Bukowski, illustrated by Bobbie Blume, Windfall Press (Chicago), 1965.

Lust on Canvas, Anchor Publications, 1965.

The October Scarf, Challenge Books, 1966.

The Sculptor, Private Edition Books, 1966.

The Fires of Autumn, All Star Books, 1967.

Nightsong, All Star Books, 1968.

Blood Jungle, Triumph News, 1968.

(Under pseudonym Cort Martin) *The Star,* Dominion (San Marcos, CA), 1968.

(Under pseudonym Cort Martin) *Quest,* Powell Publications, 1969.

(Under pseudonym Cort Martin) *The Edge of Passion,* Saber Books, 1969.

The Love Rain, Tecumseh Press, 1971.

(Under pseudonym Frank Anvic) *The All Girl Crew,* Barclay, 1973.

(Under pseudonym Frank Anvic) *The Hard Riders,* Barclay, 1973.

There Are Ways of Making Love to You, Tecumseh Press, 1974.

(Under pseudonym Frank Anvic) *We Have Your Daughter,* Brandon Books, 1974.

(Under pseudonym Frank Anvic) *Bride of Satan,* Brandon Books, 1974.

Gun for Hire, Major (Canoga Park, CA), 1975.

(Under pseudonym Charlotte A. Sherman) *The Shuttered Room,* Major, 1975.

Ride Hard, Ride Fast, Major, 1976.

(Under pseudonym Wilma Tarrant) *Her Strange Needs,* Carlyle Communications, 1976.

(Under pseudonym Wilma Tarrant) *Trying Out Tricia,* Carlyle Communications, 1976.

Buzzard Bait, Major, 1977.

Satan's Seed, Pinnacle Books (New York City), 1978.

Chill, Pinnacle Books, 1978.

The Bamboo Demons, Pinnacle Books, 1979.

Hellfire Trail, Leisure Books (Norwalk, CT), 1979.

The Reincarnation of Jenny James, Carlyle Books, 1979.

The Fugitive Gun, Leisure Books, 1980.

Vegas Vampire, Pinnacle Books, 1980.

The Phoenix Man, Pinnacle Books, 1980.
House of Scorpions, Pinnacle Books, 1980.
Shadows, Pinnacle Books, 1980.
Dawn of Revenge, Zebra Books (New York City), 1980.
Mexican Showdown, Zebra Books, 1980.
Death's Head Trail, Zebra Books, 1980.
Blood Justice, Zebra Books, 1980.
Winter Hell, Zebra Books, 1980.
Bukowski: Friendship, Fame, and Bestial Myth, Blue Horse Publications (Augusta, GA), 1981.
Duel in Purgatory, Zebra Books, 1981.
Law of the Rope, Zebra Books, 1981.
Apache Arrows, Zebra Books, 1981.
Boothill Bounty, Zebra Books, 1981.
Hard Bullets, Zebra Books, 1981.
Trial by Sixgun, Zebra Books, 1981.
(Under pseudonym Cort Martin) *First Blood,* Zebra Books, 1981.
My Heart Is in the Ozarks, illustrated by Sherry Pettey, First Ozark (Harrison, AR), 1982.
The Widow Maker, Zebra Books, 1982.
Arizona Hardcase, Zebra Books, 1982.
The Buff Runners, Zebra Books, 1982.
Gunman's Curse, Pinnacle Books, 1983.
Dry-Gulched, Zebra Books, 1983.
Wyoming Wanton, Zebra Books, 1983.
Tucson Twosome, Zebra Books, 1983.
Blood Warriors, Zebra Books, 1983.
(Under pseudonym Walt Denver) *Pistolero,* Zebra Books, 1983.
(Under pseudonym Hank Mitchum) *Stagecoach Station 8: Fort Yuma,* Bantam (New York City), 1983.
Death Valley, Zebra Books, 1984.
Red Tomahawk, Zebra Books, 1984.
Blood Trail South, Zebra Books, 1984.
Song of the Cheyenne, Doubleday (New York City), 1987.
Winter of the Wolf, Walker & Co. (New York City), 1987.
Horne's Law, Walker & Co., 1988.
Eagles of Destiny, Zebra Books, 1990.
The Arkansas River, Bantam, 1991.
The Medicine Horn: Book One of the Buckskinners, Tom Doherty Associates (New York City), 1991.
An Early Frost, White Oak (Redwood City, CA), 1992.
Grass Kingdom, Forge (New York City), 1994.
Trapper's Moon, Tor (New York City), 1994.
The Rio Grande, Bantam, 1994.
The Columbia River, Bantam, 1996.
The Barons of Texas, Forge, 1997.
The Baron Range, Tom Doherty Associates, 1998.
The Baron Brand, Forge, 2000.
The Ballad of Pinewood Lake, Forge, 2001.

Also creator and producer of "Hellrider" series, Pinnacle Books, 1985, "Killsquad" series, Avon (New York City), 1986, "Remington" series, Avon, 1986, "Powell's Army" series, Zebra Books, 1986, "Brazo" series, Zebra Books, 1986, "Dateline" series, Paperjacks, 1987, and "Rivers West" series, Bantam, 1987—. Author of columns, "View on Living," *Grand Terrace Living,* 1966-67, "Ensenada at Bay," *Ensenada Hello,* 1966-67, "The New Notebook," *San Bernardino Independent,* 1970-71, "Baja Notebook," *Fiesta,* 1972-75, "Bear with Me," *Big Bear News,* 1972-75, and a column in *San Bernardino Mountain Highlander,* 1975-76. Author of two series of educational tapes for radio, "Youth and Drugs" and "Youth and Alcohol," distributed by Classroom World Productions. Contributor of poetry and articles to periodicals, including *Roundup, Branson Living, Ozarks Mountaineer,* and *Midwest Quarterly.* West Coast editor, *Outsider;* advisory editor, *Black Cat Review.*

WORK IN PROGRESS: Rendezvous, Greensleeves, and "The Way West" series, all for Tor Books; *The South Platte, The Brazos, The Mississippi River,* and the "Frontier Rivers" series, all for Bantam Books.

SIDELIGHTS: Jory Sherman once told *CA:* "My goal in writing novels of the West is to push the story of America's westward expansion into the mainstream of American literature. The category western novel has fallen by the wayside. Those of us still publishing have [dug] deeper into our history, producing books that rise above category. Women writers of the West are coming into their own, at last, and there is an entire new body of literature that should last for generations. In the vanguard of the new wave of novels of the West are my publishers, Bantam and Tor/Forge. There is some fine writing out there, and many of us are waiting for the general public to not only discover it, but to embrace it wholeheartedly. For the western is our only native literature and deserves much more respect than it has garnered in the past. This is an exciting time for me and my fellow novelists who are telling the story of America's push westward into new lands, unknown territories. It is a grand story, exclusive to us, and will never be fully told. I am proud to be among those writers who are forging new paths in western literature and to be associated with publishers who are not afraid to venture beyond the boundaries of category fiction. They, too, are among the pioneers who people the new literature of the West."

Among Sherman's numerous publications in the Western genre is the "Grass Kingdom" series, including *Grass Kingdom, The Barons of Texas, The Baron Range,* and *The Baron Brand.* In these books, Sherman recounts an epic saga of the Baron family, early North American settlers of Texas who battled Mexicans, Native Americans, and natural disasters to establish cattle ranches on the open range. *Grass Kingdom,* a 1994 Pulitzer Prize nominee, places the Baron ranch in a fairly contemporary setting, combining aspects of the traditional western with a world of ambulances, radio, and police cars. "Only a superabundance of characters . . . and a slightly disjointed plot line mar the fast-moving narrative spiced with salty dialogue," noted a *Publishers Weekly* reviewer.

In *The Baron Range,* Anson Baron and his father, Martin, are having a power struggle as the former strives to prove his manhood to the latter. Anson must fend off thieves and Apaches, as well as the usual dangers of a trail drive, after his father is driven off by the revelation of his wife's dreadful secret. Sherman's "real skill is in his gifted creation of gritty characters who must pay the price of greed and ambition," remarked a reviewer for *Publishers Weekly. Booklist* reviewer Budd Arthur praised the action-packed plot and the skill with which Sherman depicts frontier Texas. Arthur dubbed *The Baron Range* "outstanding western fiction from an ex-cowboy author who knows the territory."

Many of the characters from *The Baron Range,* which is set in the early 1800s, return in the next volume in the series, *The Baron Brand,* set in the middle of the nineteenth century. However, Sherman leaves behind the action of the earlier books for introspection in this book. Martin Baron has returned to the Box B Ranch, and in regaining control of the ranch must contend with his usual enemies as well as a syphilitic wife, a blind orphan, and a would-be murderer. Unfortunately, according to a reviewer for *Publishers Weekly,* "there's little action and less suspense" in this installment, and the author leaves the reader hanging on to the next volume to see the resolution of the "blazing showdown" depicted here.

In 2001, Sherman published *The Ballad of Pinewood Lake,* a departure from his epic westerns. A novel set in contemporary Southern California, *The Ballad of Pinewood Lake* tells the story of a hack writer, his alcoholic wife, and their young son, who flee the city in an attempt to escape from themselves. They settle at Pinewood Lake, a dysfunctional community full of people who are always petty and often drunk; instead of finding sanctuary, the relocation threatens to tear the family apart. "Sherman's characters and his powerful delivery grip the reader in an uncomfortable clinch until the final page," praised a *Publishers Weekly* reviewer, calling *The Ballad of Pinewood Lake* Sherman's "most ambitious novel to date."

BIOGRAPHICAL/CRITICAL SOURCES:

PERIODICALS

Booklist, September 1, 1998, Budd Arthur, review of *The Baron Range,* p. 68.

Listen, April, 1971.

Publishers Weekly, December 6, 1993, review of *Grass Kingdom,* p. 58; August 10, 1998, review of *The Baron Range,* p. 371; January 17, 2000, review of *The Baron Brand,* p. 45; January 15, 2001, review of *The Ballad of Pinewood Lake,* p. 54.*

* * *

SHIELDS, Carol 1935-

PERSONAL: Born June 2, 1935, in Oak Park, IL; daughter of Robert E. and Inez (Selgren) Warner; married Donald Hugh Shields (a professor), July 20, 1957; children: John, Anne, Catherine, Margaret, Sara. *Education:* Hanover College, B.A., 1957; University of Ottawa, M.A., 1975.

ADDRESSES: Agent—Bella Pomer, 22 Shallmar Blvd., PH2 Toronto, Ontario, M5N 2Z8 Canada.

CAREER: Canadian Slavonic Papers, Ottawa, Ontario, editorial assistant, 1972-74; writer, 1974—; University of Manitoba, professor, 1980-2000; Chancellor University of Winnipeg, 1996-2000.

MEMBER: Writers' Union of Canada, Writers Guild of Manitoba, PEN, Jane Austen Society, Royal Society of Canada.

AWARDS, HONORS: Winner of young writers' contest sponsored by Canadian Broadcasting Corp. (CBC), 1965; Canada Council grants, 1972, 1974, 1976; fiction prize from Canadian Authors Association, 1976, for *Small Ceremonies;* CBC Prize for Drama, 1983; National Magazine Award, 1984, 1985; Arthur Ellis Award, 1988; Marian Engel Award, 1990; Governor General's Award for English-language fiction, National Book Critics Circle Award for fiction, 1994, and Pulitzer Prize for

Carol Shields

fiction, 1995, all for *The Stone Diaries;* Orange Prize, 1998, for *Larry's Party;* Guggenheim fellow, 1999; Chevalier de l'Ordre des Arts et des Lettres (France), 2000. Honorary doctorates: University of Ottawa, 1995; Hanover College, 1996; University of Winnipeg, 1996; Queen's University, 1996; University of British Columbia, 1997; Concordia University, 1997; University of Toronto, 1998; University of Western Ontario, 1998; Carleton University, 2000; Mount St. Vincent University, 2000; and Wilfrid Laurier University, 2000.

WRITINGS:

Others (poetry), Borealis Press, 1972.
Intersect (poetry), Borealis Press, 1974.
Susanna Moodie: Voice and Vision (criticism), Borealis Press, 1976.
Small Ceremonies (novel), McGraw, 1976.
The Box Garden (novel), McGraw, 1977.
Happenstance (novel; also see below), McGraw, 1980.
A Fairly Conventional Woman (novel; also see below), Macmillan (Toronto, Canada), 1982.
Various Miracles (short stories), Stoddart (Don Mills, Canada), 1985, Penguin (New York City), 1989.
Swann: A Mystery (novel), General, 1987, Viking (New York City), 1989.
The Orange Fish (short stories), Random House (Toronto, Canada), 1989, Viking (New York City), 1990.
Departures and Arrivals, Blizzard, 1990.
(With Blanche Howard) *A Celibate Season* (novel), Coteau (Regina, Canada), 1991, Penguin (New York City), 1999.
The Republic of Love (novel), Viking (New York City), 1992.
Coming to Canada (poetry), Carleton University Press (Ottawa, Canada), 1992.
Happenstance (contains the novels *Happenstance* and *A Fairly Conventional Woman*), Random House, 1993, Viking, 1994.
The Stone Diaries (novel), Random House, 1993.
Thirteen Hands (drama), Blizzard (Winnipeg, Canada), 1993.
(With Catherine Shields) *Fashion, Power, Guilt, and the Charity of Families,* Blizzard, 1995.
Larry's Party (novel), Viking, 1997.
(With David Williamson) *Anniversary* (play), Blizzard, 1998.
(Editor) *Scribner's Best of the Fiction Workshops 1998,* Scribner, 1998.
Dressing Up for the Carnival (short stories), Viking, 2000.
Jane Austen (biography), Viking, 2001.

Author of *The View,* 1982, *Women Waiting,* 1983, and *Face Off,* 1987.

Some of the author's works have been translated to several languages, including Swedish, Italian, French, Chinese, Norwegian, German, Spanish, Danish, Korean, Japanese, and Polish.

ADAPTATIONS: Audio versions of *The Stone Diaries* and *Larry's Party; Swann: A Mystery* adapted for film, 1996.

WORK IN PROGRESS: Unless, a novel.

SIDELIGHTS: Pulitzer Prize-winning author Carol Shields was born in Oak Park, Illinois, the youngest of three children. Her mother was a former teacher, and her father managed a candy factory. After graduating from Hanover College, she met Donald Shields while they both studied in England. They married and moved to Vancouver a year later. Leslie Hughes interviewed her friend for a 1996 article published in *Chatelaine.*

Hughes called Shields "soft-spoken, a little mysterious—a woman you can talk to about men, childbirth, the universe, and the price of shoes."

Shields had a revelation when she read Betty Friedan's *Feminine Mystique,* as the family returned by boat from a three-year stint in England, where Don had been doing graduate work. Hughes said that before this time, in studying English literature, Shields hadn't noticed "the absence of women. Now she noticed. Enjoying the company of men, she had disregarded the anger of other women that had begun bubbling to the surface of the civilized world. Now, she was angry too." Shields wrote as she cared for her growing family, and in 1965 submitted a poem to a young writers' competition, which she won.

Don took a job at the University of Ottawa, and Shields enrolled to pursue a Master of Arts degree. Urged by professors who recognized her talent, she put together her first book of poems, which was published in 1972. Four years later she was offered an editing position with a small journal, the *Canadian Slavonic Papers.* Shields said "it was a jobette, really. I worked in a spare room upstairs. I became the Mother who Typed." Shields's first book *Small Ceremonies* was written, in part, from research she had done for her thesis on Susanna Moodie. With its publication, she began her long and distinguished writing and teaching career.

Hughes noted Shields's address to the 1995 graduating class of Balmoral Hall School for girls in Winnipeg. "She inverted the message she had received at her own graduation, which was: 'Tempus Fugit: Time Flies.' She told the young women: time does not fly. There is time to play, time to lose, time to slide backward. She told them not to be afraid of time. Just wake up and be yourselves, she said, even though it takes courage. The ancient (by their standard) woman brought them to their feet. As one who continues to reinvent herself, she has earned the right to say these things."

Shields has had two distinct phases in her writing career. Her first four novels, *Small Ceremonies* (1976), *The Box Garden* (1977), *Happenstance* (1980), and *A Fairly Conventional Woman* (1982), are portrayals of everyday life. Her heroes and heroines struggle to define themselves and make human connections in their close relationships. Kathy O'Shaughnessy wrote in *Observer Review* that "*Small Ceremonies* is a novel of ideas: about privacy, knowledge of others, about how we perceive each other, and are perceived by others," while *London Review of Books* writer Peter Campbell, in a review of *Happenstance,* stated that "Shields writes well about decent people, and her resolutions are shrewder than those in the self-help books."

The next phase of Shields's career is marked by risk taking. With her first short story collection, *Various Miracles* (1985), Shields began to experiment more with form by using a variety of voices. She continued, however, to portray ordinary people in everyday situations. *Books Magazine* writer Andrea Mynard asserted that Shields's "robust realism is typical of the growing sorority of Canadian writers, including Margaret Atwood and Alice Munro, who have been gaining a strong reputation. . . . In her accessibly simple and lucid style, Carol intelligently grasps the minutiae of everyday life and illuminates the quirks of human nature. Her observations of contemporary dilemmas are brilliant."

In *Swann: A Mystery* (1987), Shields continued her experimentation by using four distinct voices to tell the story. In this novel she also developed a theme seen in her other work, that of the mysterious nature of art and creation. *Swann,* noted Danny Karlin in *London Review of Books,* "is a clever book, self-conscious about literature, fashionably preoccupied with questions of deconstruction, of the 'textuality' of identity, of the powers and powerlessness of language. This impression is confirmed by its confident and playful manipulation of different narrative modes." Some critics, however, castigated what they considered Shields's simple characterizations. *New York Times Book Review* writer Josh Robins noted that "the characters remain too one-dimensional, often to the point of caricature, to support sporadic attempts at psychological portraiture." The book was adapted for film in 1996, and starred Miranda Richardson, Sean Hewitt, and Brenda Fricker.

Shields took another risk by attempting the genre of the romance novel in *The Republic of Love* (1992), but she made the form her own by making her main characters wade through the coldness and problems of the twentieth century before reaching the happy ending. "Shields has created a sophisticated [romance] story," stated *Books in Canada* writer Rita Donovan. "And the 'happy ending,' so traditional to the romance novel, is here refurbished, updated, and—most happily—earned."

Shields's early novels were popular but not taken seriously by critics. Some argued that in the early part of her career Shields was underestimated as a stylist and her works were dismissed as being naturalistic. Critics generally praised Shields when she began experimenting more with form. Some of her risks were originally considered failures, as in the case of the last section of *Swann,* in which she attempted to bring all four voices together in a screenplay form. However, contemporary critics no longer consider them so.

The Stone Diaries (1993) is the fictional biography of Daisy Goodwill Flett, whose life spans eight decades and includes time spent in both Canada and the United States. Written in both the first and third person, the story begins with her birth in 1905 in rural Manitoba, Canada. Daisy's mother, extremely obese and unaware that she is pregnant, dies moments later. Unable to care for his daughter, Cuyler Goodwill convinces his neighbor Clarentine Flett to raise the child. Soon afterward, Clarentine leaves her husband and, taking Daisy with her, travels to Winnipeg, where she moves in with her son, Barker. Cuyler later takes Daisy to Bloomington, Indiana, where he has become a highly successful stonecarver. There, Daisy marries a wealthy young man who dies during their honeymoon. In 1936 she marries Barker, who has become renowned for his agricultural research, and resettles in Canada. In her role as wife and mother, Daisy appears quiet and content, but after her husband dies, she takes over a gardening column for the *Ottawa Recorder,* writing as Mrs. Greenthumb. Her joy—she finds the work incredibly meaningful and fulfilling—is short-lived however, as the editor decides to give the column to a staff writer, despite Daisy's protests. She eventually recovers from the disappointment and lives the remainder of her life in Sarasota, Florida, where she amuses herself playing bridge.

Critical reaction to *The Stone Diaries,* which won the Governor General's Award, the National Book Critics Circle Award, and the Pulitzer Prize, and was also shortlisted for the Booker Prize, was overwhelmingly favorable. Commentators have praised Shields for exploring such universal problems as loneliness and lost opportunities and for demonstrating that all lives are significant and important no matter how banal and confined they appear. Others have lauded the novel as a brilliant examination of the divergence between one's inner and outer self, and of the relations between fiction, biography, and autobiography. Allyson F. McGill wrote in *Belles Lettres,* "Shields and Daisy challenge us to review our lives, to try and see life honestly, even while 'their' act of authorship only reveals how impossible it is to see and speak objective truth." A *Canadian Forum* reviewer noted that "Shields demonstrates there are no small lives, no lives out of which significance does not shine. She makes us aware that banality, ultimately, is in the eye of the beholder."

Shields's follow-up to *The Stone Diaries* was *Larry's Party,* published in 1997 and winner of the Orange Prize. Shields structured the novel thematically; each chapter covers a different area of Larry's life—his marriages and relationships, his friends, and his children. However, readers can follow Larry as he grows from an awkward adolescent to a somewhat settled, typical middle-aged white male. *Time* reviewer Paul Gray said Shields "captures an unremarkable man in a remarkable light."

What is not typical about Larry is his job. After working as a floral designer for twenty years, he develops an interest in, and becomes an expert at, building elaborate mazes out of shrubbery. And these, according to Michiko Kakutani of the *New York Times,* "become a metaphor for the path his own life has taken, full of twists and turns and digressions. They also become a metaphor for Ms. Shields's own looping narrative, a narrative that repeatedly folds back on itself to gradually disclose more and more details about Larry's past." Commentators have remarked that in *Larry's Party,* Shields portrays the Everyman, much as she portrayed the Everywoman in *The Stone Diaries.* Linnea Lannon wrote in the *Detroit Free Press,* "Shields gives us Larry Weller, a man who seems as average as any, but under her scrutiny, more fascinating than you might reasonably expect."

The "party" is one given by Larry and his girlfriend in honor of his forty-seventh birthday, and which is attended by both of his former wives. *Library Journal* reviewer Jo Carr wrote that the affair "is brilliantly described by Shields in a manner worthy of Virginia Woolf." Verlyn Klinkenborg, in reviewing *Larry's Party* for the *New York Times Book Review,* said of Shields that "the mood in which she writes is that of the final act of *A Midsummer Night's Dream*—a mood of complicity and withdrawal, affection and mockery. Like Larry, and like God, she sees the perfect sense that mazes make 'when you look down on them from above.'"

Shields began to attract an international following in the early 1990s, particularly after the American publication of *The Stone Diaries.* Many of her early novels have been reprinted in the United States and England to much popular and critical acclaim. *A Celibate Season,* written with Blanche Howard and originally published in 1991, is the story of Jocelyn (Jock) and Charles (Chas) Selby, a couple married for twenty years, who are separated when Jock takes a temporary government job. They make the decision not to communicate by telephone, but rather keep in touch with letters, in which they talk about their lives, children, and marriage. Shields wrote the letters from Chas, and Howard those from Jock. A *Publishers Weekly* reviewer called the authors "skillful writers, and the epistolary form adds dimension to their thoughtful novel of love, marriage, and forgiveness."

Dressing Up for the Carnival is a collection of twenty-two stories, many of which had previously appeared in various publications. "And yet," wrote Paul Gray in *Time,* "the result is not as random or eclectic as might be anticipated. Shields . . . displays in all her writing, long or short, a consistently whimsical ruefulness toward her characters and the dilemmas they face, some of which, in this collection, are engagingly bizarre." In the title story, eleven people choose clothing and accessories to take them through the day. *Maclean's* reviewer John Bemrose wrote that Shields "also specializes in a kind of breezy essay-story—call it Borges-lite—that wittily investigates such topics as keys, inventors, and the cooking habits of an imaginary kingdom. These pieces are heavily theme-driven." In "Dying for Love," three women, who are individually contemplating suicide over love gone wrong, decide that life is worth living. In "Windows" two artists cover their windows to keep daylight from entering when the government institutes a window tax.

"Many of the stories are light and breezy but not unsatisfying," said a *Publishers Weekly* contributor, "because the characters are winning even in their mostly cameo-like appearances." *Time International* reviewer Francine Prose wrote that for the couple in "Mirrors," "the decision not to put mirrors in their summer cottage becomes a metaphor for the shifting balance between partnership and solitude, contentment and dissatisfaction, intimacy and concealment." Prose said Shields "does a fine job of gauging and charting the subtle but volatile chemistry of domestic happiness, and of depicting the inner lives of her characters."

In another story, a writer finds that she has a malfunctioning letter "i" and tries to write without using that key. *New York Times Book Review* contributor David Willis McCullough wrote that "Absence" "could simply have been a virtuoso piece. Yet, with all its tricks of avoidance, the story is also a serious meditation on how writers write and readers read. Unfortunately, not all the ordinary moments in this collection are rendered extraordinary. The book has its clunkers. . . . But these weaker entries were probably included for variety's sake, and variety of setting, tone, sensibility, and subject is indeed one of the book's most obvious qualities." The final story, "Dressing Down," finds a boy spending the summer in a nudist camp founded by his grandfather. A contributor to *Kirkus Reviews* said that the ten-year-old discovers "how the battle over reticence and frankness has defined his grandparents' marriage—and learning also that nudity tends to dissolve possibility and mystery, making people more prosaic than alluring." Hilary Mantel wrote in the London Sunday *Times* that Shields's speciality is "to isolate moments that, because of some sensuous overkill they possess, remain distinct in the mind for years, perhaps for a lifetime."

BIOGRAPHICAL/CRITICAL SOURCES:

BOOKS

Contemporary Literary Criticism, Gale (Detroit), Volume 91, 1996, Volume 113, 1999.

PERIODICALS

Belles Lettres, spring, 1991, p. 56; summer, 1992, p. 20; fall, 1994, pp. 32, 34.

Booklist, July 1997, Donna Seaman, review of *Larry's Party,* p. 1777; April 15, 2000, Donna Seaman, review of *Dressing Up for the Carnival,* p. 1525.

Books in Canada, October, 1979, pp. 29-30; May, 1981, pp. 31-32; November, 1982, pp. 18-19; October, 1985, pp. 16-17; October, 1987, pp. 15-16; May, 1989, p. 32; January/February, 1991, pp. 30-31; April, 1992, p. 40; February, 1993, pp. 51-52; September, 1993, pp. 34-35; October, 1993, pp. 32-33.

Books in Review, summer, 1989, pp. 158-60.

Books Magazine, November-December, 1994, p. 12.

Canadian Forum, July, 1975, pp. 36-38; November, 1993, pp. 44-45; January-February, 1994, pp. 44-45; January, 1996, Christine Hamelin, "Coming to Canada," p. 46; November, 1997, Merna Summers, review of *Larry's Party,* p. 38.

Canadian Literature, summer, 1989, pp. 158-60; autumn, 1991, pp. 149-50; spring, 1995.

Chatelaine, April, 1996, Leslie Hughes, "The Shields Diaries," p. 110.

Christian Science Monitor, December 7, 1990, pp. 10-11.

Detroit Free Press, September 7, 1997.

Entertainment Weekly, September 19, 1997, Vanessa V. Friedman, review of *Larry's Party,* p. 78.

Kirkus Reviews, May 1, 1976, p. 559; March 15, 2000, review of *Dressing Up for the Carnival,* p. 328.

Library Journal, August, 1997, Ann Irvine, review of *Larry's Party,* p. 135; June 15, 1998, Jo Carr, review of *Larry's Party,* p. 122.

London Review of Books, September 27, 1990, pp. 20-21; March 21, 1991, p. 20; May 28, 1992, p. 22; September 9, 1993, p. 19.

Los Angeles Times Book Review, August 20, 1989, p. 2; April 17, 1994, pp. 3, 7.

Maclean's, October 11, 1993, p. 74; September 29, 1997, Diane Turbide, "The Masculine Maze: Carol Shields Gets Inside the Head of the Ordinary Guy," p. 82; March 20, 2000, John Bemrose, "Enriching a Fictional Universe: in Her New Collection of Short Stories, Carol Shields Proves Adept at Finding Wonder in the Unremarkable," p. 66.

Ms., January-February, 1996, Sandy M. Fernandez, reviews of *Small Ceremonies* and *The Box Garden,* p. 90.

New Statesman and Society, August 20, 1993, p. 40.

Newsweek, October 6, 1997, Laura Shapiro, review of *Larry's Party,* p. 76.

New York, March 7, 1994.

New York Review of Books, June 29, 2000, Joyce Carol Oates, review of *Dressing Up for the Carnival,* p. 38.

New York Times, July 17, 1989, p. C15; May 10, 1995.

New York Times Book Review, August 6, 1989, p. 11; August 12, 1990, p. 28; March 1, 1992, pp. 14, 16; March 14, 1992; March 27, 1994, pp. 3, 14; January 7, 1996, Claire Messud, "Why So Gloomy?," p. 12; August 26, 1997, Michiko Kakutani, "Br'er Rabbit, Ordinary in Nearly Every Way"; September 7, 1997, Verlyn Klinkenborg, "A Maze Makes Sense From Above," p. 7; June 20, 1999, Michael Porter, review of *A Celibate Season,* p. 16; June 11, 2000, David Willis McCullough, "Itemize This."

Observer Review, February 19, 1995, p. 19.

People Weekly, October 6, 1997, Paula Chin, review of *Larry's Party,* p. 43.

Performing Arts & Entertainment in Canada, winter, 1998, Karen Bell, "Carol Shields: All These Years Later, Still Digging," p. 4.

Publishers Weekly, February 28, 1994; August 11, 1997, review of *Larry's Party,* p. 383; April 26, 1999, review of *A Celibate Season,* p. 55; February 28, 2000, review of *Dressing Up for the Carnival,* p. 56.

Quill and Quire, January, 1981, p. 24; September, 1982, p. 59; August, 1985, p. 46; May, 1989, p. 20; August, 1993, p. 31.

Scrivener, spring, 1995.

Spectator, March 21, 1992, pp. 35-36; September 24, 1994, p. 41.

Time, September 29, 1997, Paul Gray, review of *Larry's Party,* p. 92; May 29, 2000, Paul Gray, "Fashion Statements: Carol Shields' *Dressing Up for the Carnival* Offers 22 Tales about the Costumes Life Requires Us to Wear," p. 82.

Time International, February 28, 2000, Francine Prose, "Acts of Redemption: Carol Shields' Book of Stories Brings a Master's Eye to the Transfiguring Aspects of the Everyday," p. 52.

Times (London), January 23, 2000, Hilary Mantel, "Full of domestic surprises," p. 44.

Times Literary Supplement, August 27, 1993, p. 22; February 17, 1995.

West Coast Review, winter, 1988, pp. 38-56, pp. 57-66.

Women's Review of Books, May, 1994, p. 20.

Writer, July, 1998, Carol Shields, "Framing the Structure of a Novel," p. 3.

[Entry reviewed by Bella Pomer, agent of Carol Shields.]

* * *

SHINN, Sharon 1957-

PERSONAL: Born April 28, 1957, in Wichita, KS; daughter of Raymond James, Jr. (a teacher) and Carol (a secretary; maiden name, Maile) Shinn. *Ethnicity:* "White." *Education:* Northwestern University, B.S.

ADDRESSES: Agent—Ethan Ellenberg, Ethan Ellenberg Literary Agency, 548 Broadway, Suite 5E, New York, NY 10012.

CAREER: Professional Photographer, Des Plaines, IL, associate editor, 1979-83; *Decor,* St. Louis, MO, managing editor, 1983-2001; American Assembly of Collegiate Schools of Business, 2001—.

AWARDS, HONORS: William Crawford Award, best first novel, International Association for the Fantastic in the Arts, 1996, for *The Shape-Changer's Wife;* nominated for the John W. Campbell Award for Best New Writer.

WRITINGS:

NOVELS

The Shape-Changer's Wife, Ace Books (New York City), 1995.

Archangel, Ace Books, 1996.

Jovah's Angel, Ace Books, 1997.

The Alleluia Files, Penguin (New York City), 1999.
Heart of Gold, Ace Books, 2000.
Wrapt in Crystal, Ace Books, 2000.
Summers at Castle Auburn, Ace Books, 2001.

SIDELIGHTS: Sharon Shinn combines such genres as fantasy, science fiction, romance, and mystery in her novels, which often focus on matters of faith and tolerance. In *Archangel, Jovah's Angel* and *The Alleluia Files,* Shinn sets her stories in Samaria, a world of angels. Speaking of *The Alleluia Files,* in which the elusive files of the title hold secrets which could change the angel society forever, Jackie Cassada in *Library Journal* found that Shinn "deftly combines mystery, high-tech sf, and romance with a layering of fantasy in a fresh and innovative tale full of surprising turns of plot." In his review of *Archangel,* the story of an angel's troubled marriage, Carl Hays in *Booklist* called it "an entertaining sf-fantasy blend that should please fans of both genres."

In *Wrapt in Crystal,* Interfed, a federation of planets, seeks to open the backwater world of Semay to trade but meets resistance from the planet's suspicious elders. When a serial killer begins stalking the planet's priestesses, however, an Interfed police officer is invited in to assist in the investigation. He falls in love with a Semay woman while tracking down the killer. The critic for *Publishers Weekly* especially praised "Shinn's flair for intriguing settings and sympathetic characters." Roberta Johnson in *Booklist* noted: "Shinn skillfully combines suspense, sf, and romance while posing thoughtful questions on worship, faith, and sacrifice."

Heart of Gold tells of a planet where a blue-skinned matriarchy vies with a golden-skinned people. A cross-racial romance leads to a struggle for justice and understanding between the two peoples as they war against each other with evermore deadly weapons. While the critic for *Publishers Weekly* found *Heart of Gold* a "flimsy attempt at crossing romance with sf," Cassada concluded that Shinn had written "an elegant and suspenseful tale."

BIOGRAPHICAL/CRITICAL SOURCES:

PERIODICALS

Booklist, May 1, 1996, Carl Hays, review of *Archangel,* p. 1492; May 15, 1999, Roberta Johnson, review of *Wrapt in Crystal,* p. 1684.

Library Journal, May 15, 1997, Susan Hamburger, review of *Jovah's Angel,* p. 106; April 15, 1998, Jackie Cassada, review of *The Alleluia Files,* p. 119; May 15, 1999, Jackie Cassada, review of *Wrapt in Crystal,* p. 130; April 15, 2000, Jackie Cassada, review of *Heart of Gold,* p. 126.

Publishers Weekly, April 12, 1999, review of *Wrapt in Crystal,* p. 59; March 20, 2000, review of *Heart of Gold,* p. 75.

* * *

SINGH, Simon 1964-

PERSONAL: Born September 19, 1964, in Somerset, England. *Ethnicity:* "Indian." *Education:* University of Cambridge, Ph.D. (particle physics), 1989.

ADDRESSES: Home—London, England. *Agent*—Patrick Walsh, Conville and Walsh Limited, 118-120 Wardour Street, London, W1V 3LA, England. *E-mail*—simonsingh@visto.com.

CAREER: Author and science journalist. British Broadcasting Company (BBC), producer, 1991-96.

AWARDS, HONORS: British Academy of Film and Television Arts Award for Best Documentary, 1996, for *Fermat's Last Theorem;* short listed for the Rhone-Poulenc Prize for Best Science Book, 1997, for *Fermat's Last Theorem.*

WRITINGS:

Fermat's Enigma: The Epic Quest to Solve the World's Greatest Mathematical Problem, Walker (New York, NY), 1997, published as *Fermat's Last Theorem: The Story of a Riddle That Confounded the World's Greatest Minds for 358 Years,* Fourth Estate (London, England), 1998.

The Code Book: The Evolution of Secrecy from Mary, Queen of Scots, to Quantum Cryptography, Doubleday (New York, NY), 1999, published as *The Code Book: The Evolution of Secrecy from Ancient Egypt to Quantum Cryptography,* Fourth Estate (London, England), 1999.

The Science of Secrecy, Fourth Estate (London, England), 2000.

SIDELIGHTS: Fermat's Enigma: The Epic Quest to Solve the World's Greatest Mathematical Problem by Simon Singh has been hailed as an appealing book for both a general audience and for mathematicians. Recounting the success of mathematician Andrew Wiles' proof of a theorem that had remained unproven for three hundred and fifty years, it is a dramatic tale that shows the personal side of such a quest. By detailing Wiles' nearly life-long interest in the theorem and the remarkable efforts of mathematicians before him, Singh provides a fascinating background to what is considered the most important mathematical event of the twentieth century.

The seventeenth-century judge and amateur mathematician Pierre de Fermat asserted that he had proven that the equation x to the nth power plus y to the nth power equals z to the nth power could not be solved using whole positive numbers when "n" is greater than 2. This theorem was penciled into the margin of one of Fermat's books, along with the comment that there was not enough space to write down the proof. The absence of this proof has intrigued mathematicians ever since, and many have devoted themselves to solving it. Indeed, amateur mathematician Paul Wolfskehl even claimed that the theorem saved his life, when having intended to commit suicide at a specific hour the puzzle distracted him and his decision to kill himself was abandoned.

Singh began researching the subject of Fermat's theorem for a 1996 BBC television documentary in the *Horizons* series, that he produced with John Lynch. Having spent many hours interviewing Wiles and gathering relevant mathematical history dating back to ancient Greece, Singh proceeded to turn his work into a more inclusive book. The result was a rare popular work on mathematics, one that *Library Journal* reviewer Gregg Sapp called a "mathematical page-turner." Sapp also compared *Fermat's Enigma* to another book, Amir Aczel's *Fermat's Last Theorem,* and found that "Singh's book has more perspective and builds to a truly engrossing climax." Likewise, Alan Clark noted in a *Lecturer* book review that "even though I knew the ending, I was captivated. This will join my (very small) collection of truly popular books on mathematics."

Other reviewers focused on the more academic merits of *Fermat's Enigma.* Richard Pinch, a mathematics lecturer writing for *New Scientist,* expressed some reservations regarding Singh's presentation of mathematical theory, and noted "Singh makes a worthy effort at explaining the highly technical theory of elliptic curves. . . . But there are some decisions in the exposition that seem ill-judged." Specifically, Singh chose to use some non-standard terms in his explanations that might ultimately confuse a reader who sought additional information elsewhere. Pinch, however, concluded that "overall the presentation succeeds in conveying some of the flavour." Writing for the *New York Times Book Review,* Roger Penrose asserted that the book was more than just an engaging story: "More important than Singh's accounts of individual mathematicians and particular mathematical events is his conveying of something of the mathematical ethos. . . . What motivates mathematicians is not the desire to solve practical problems, or even problems of science. The important drives are esthetic, coming from the internal appeal of mathematics itself." Penrose concluded, "I strongly recommend this book to anyone wishing to catch a glimpse of what is one of the most important and ill-understood, but oldest, cultural activities of humanity."

For his second book, Singh chose the subject of codes and secret languages, their impact on history and their implications for the future. Reviewing *The Code Book: The Evolution of Secrecy from Mary, Queen of Scots, to Quantum Cryptography* for the *London Review of Books,* Brian Rotman finds it to be "a very readable and skillfully told history of cryptography." Robert Osserman of the *New York Times Book Review* comments: "The almost universal fascination with codes undoubtedly derives from the extraordinary feats of ingenuity that have gone into devising and breaking them, as well as their enormous impact on world events. Singh's book offers more than its share of both."

Singh begins his discussion with one of the simplest codes or ciphers, know as Caesar's shift because Julius Caesar was one of the first to employ it. This monoalphabetic cipher shifts a letter of the alphabet a given number of places, three in Caesar's case, and replaces the first letter with the second. By the ninth century Arab philosopher-mathematicians al-Kindi discovered that codes such as this could be easily broken by recording the frequency of letters in a message. In English, the letter "e" occurs with greater frequency than any other letter, so it becomes the first key to deciphering an encrypted message. As Singh points out, the Caesar shift was used by Mary, Queen of Scots, and her co-conspirators in 1586 while plotting to overthrow Elizabeth I and seize the British throne. Due at least in part to the efforts of cryptanalyst Thomas Phelippes, who cracked the code using the frequency approach, the plot failed. The next advance in codes, a polyalphabetic cipher, was first formulated in the Renaissance and rediscovered in the sixteenth century by Blaise de Vigenere. Known popularly as the Vigenere cipher, this method varies the shifting factor by some prearranged method. Thus the first letter in a message might shift three letters in the alphabet, the second letter, seven, and so forth. Such codes were considered indecipherable until the nineteenth century when Prussian military officer Friedrich Kasiski and English inventor Charles Babbage hit upon a solution simultaneously.

Singh devotes a good deal of his discussion to the Enigma Code used by the Germans in World War II. This code, also considered unbreakable, was fashioned by a machine that changed the key to the code every day. The breaking of the Enigma Code, over a period of years, can be credited to the combined efforts of Polish mathematician Marian Rejewski and Englishman Alan Turing, who refined Rejewski's methods in response to a German refinement of the code.

In the last section of *The Code Book* Singh explores modern developments in cryptography that are derived in large part from the studies of the English mathematician G. H. Hardy and his work with the theory of numbers. Hardy felt that his mathematical research was pure abstraction in the sense that it would never find a practical application. Yet, as Singh notes, Hardy's theories paved the way for public-key cryptography. First posited in 1976 by Whitfield Diffie and Martin Hellman, and later refined by mathematicians at the Massachusetts Institute of Technology and patented as the RSA (Rivest-Shamir-Adelman) algorithm, public-key cryptography has evolved into a two-hundred-million-dollar per-year business that is responsible for keeping information of all sorts secure in computer network environments. Singh argues that RSA programs produce codes that are for the first time truly unbreakable. Reviewing *The Code Book* for the *New York Times,* Richard Bernstein remarks: "Mr Singh knows his subject and is a skillful popularizer of it. It would be hard to imagine a clearer or more fascinating presentation of cryptology and decryptology than nonspecialists will get in this book."

BIOGRAPHICAL/CRITICAL SOURCES:

PERIODICALS

Booklist, September 1, 1999, Gilbert Taylor, review of *The Code Book,* p. 5.

Economist (US), August 28, 1999, review of *The Code Book.*

Forbes, September 20, 1999, Susan Adams, "I've Got a Secret," p. 260.

Foreign Affairs, November-December, 1999, Eliot A. Cohen, "Recent Books on International Relations: Military, Scientific, and Technological."

Kirkus Reviews, September 1, 1997, p. 1372.

Library Journal, October 15, 1997, p. 88; October 15, 1999, Dayne Sherman, review of *The Code Book,* p. 102.

London Review of Books, June 1, 1999, Brian Rotman, "Pretty Good Privacy," p. 15.

Maclean's, October 18, 1999, Brian Bethune, "A History of Secrecy," p. A11.

Nature, June 26, 1997, p. 868.

New Scientist, May 17, 1997, p. 44-45.

New York Times, November 10, 1999, Richard Bernstein, "Crack a Communique, Shatter an Assumption."

New York Times Book Review, November 30, 1997, p. 12; November 7, 1999, Robert Osserman, "Cryptanalyze This."

Publishers Weekly, August 23, 1999, review of *The Code Book.*

* * *

SÍS, Peter 1949-

PERSONAL: Born May 11, 1949, in Brno, Czechoslovakia; immigrated to the United States, 1982, naturalized citizen, 1988; son of Vladimir (an artist and documentary filmmaker) and Alena (Petrvalsky) Sís; married Terry Ann Lajtha, October 23, 1990; children: Madeleine, Matej. *Education:* Academy of Fine Arts, Prague, Czechoslovakia, B.A., 1968, M.A., 1974; attended Royal College of Art, London, England, 1977-79.

ADDRESSES: Home—252 Lafayette St., Apt. 5E, New York, NY 10012-4064. *Office*—c/o Greenwillow Books, 1350 Avenue of the Americas, New York, NY 10019-4702.

CAREER: Writer and artist. Animator of the television series *Hexe Lakritze,* broadcast in Zurich, Switzerland, 1982, and of short films, including *Mimikry,* 1975; *Island for 6,000 Alarm Clocks,* 1977; *Heads,* 1979; *Players,* 1981; *You Gotta Serve Somebody,* 1983; *Aesop's Fables,* 1984; and *Twelve Months,* 1985. Oil paintings, prints, and illustrations exhibited at solo shows in London, Zurich, Delft, St. Gallen, and Prague, and at group shows in Los Angeles, San Diego, Portland, Montreal, London, Berlin, and Japan.

MEMBER: Association Internationale du Film d'Animation, American Institute of Graphic Arts, Graphic Artists Guild.

AWARDS, HONORS: Golden Bear Award from West Berlin Film Festival, 1980, for short film *Heads;* Grand Prix from Toronto Film Festival, 1981, for short film *Players;* CINE Golden Eagle from Council on International Non-Theatrical Events, 1983, for short film *You Gotta Serve Somebody;* Newbery Award, 1987, for illustrating *Whipping Boy;* Best Illustrated Book of the Year awards from *New York Times,* for *Rainbow Rhino, Beach Ball, Follow the Dream: The Story of Christopher Columbus, Komodo!,* and *The Three Golden Keys;* Gold Medal from Society of Illustrators, 1993, for *Komodo!; Horn Book* Honor Book Awards, 1993, for *Komodo!,* and 1994, for *A Small Tall Tale from the Far Far North;* Silver Medal from Society of Illustrators, 1994, for *The Three Golden Keys;* Caldecott Honor Award, 1997, for *Starry Messenger: Galileo Galilei;* Caldecott Honor Award for *Tibet: Through the Red Box.*

WRITINGS:

SELF-ILLUSTRATED CHILDREN'S BOOKS

Rainbow Rhino, Random House (New York, NY), 1987.
Waving, Greenwillow (New York, NY), 1988.
Going Up, Greenwillow (New York, NY), 1989.
Beach Ball, Greenwillow (New York, NY), 1990.
Follow the Dream: The Story of Christopher Columbus, Knopf (New York, NY), 1991.
An Ocean World, Greenwillow (New York, NY), 1992.
A Small Tall Tale from the Far Far North, Knopf (New York, NY), 1993.
Komodo!, Greenwillow (New York, NY), 1993.
The Three Golden Keys, Doubleday (New York, NY), 1994.
Starry Messenger: Galileo Galilei, Farrar, Straus (New York, NY), 1996.
Fire Truck, Greenwillow (New York, NY), 1998.
Tibet: Through the Red Box, Farrar, Straus (New York, NY), 1998.
Ship Ahoy!, Greenwillow (New York, NY), 1999.
Trucks, Trucks, Trucks, Greenwillow (New York, NY), 1999.
Dinosaur!, Greenwillow (New York, NY), 2000.
Ballerina!, Greenwillow (New York, NY), 2000.
An Ocean World, Mulberry, 2000.
Madlenka, Frances Foster Books (New York, NY), 2000.
Madlenka's Dog, Frances Foster Books (New York, NY), in press.

ILLUSTRATOR

Fairy Tales of the Brothers Grimm, Albatros (Prague, Czechoslovakia), Volume I, 1976, Volume II, 1977.
Hexe Lakritze and Buchstabenkonig (title means "Witch Licorice and King of the Letters"), Benziger (Zurich, Switzerland), 1977.
Zizkov Romances, Ceskoslovensky Spisovatel (Prague, Czechoslovakia), 1978.
Hexe Lakritze and Rhino Rhinoceros, Benziger (Zurich, Switzerland), 1979.
Poetry, Ceskoslovensky Spisovatel (Prague, Czechoslovakia), 1980.
Baltic Fairy Tales, Orbis, 1981.
Max Bolliger, *Little Singer,* Bohem (Zurich, Switzerland), 1982.
George Shannon, *Bean Boy,* Greenwillow (New York, NY), 1983.
Shannon, *Stories to Solve,* Greenwillow (New York, NY), 1984.
Sid Fleischmann, *Whipping Boy,* Greenwillow (New York, NY), 1985.
Julia Cunningham, *Oaf,* Knopf (New York, NY), 1986.
Caron Lee Cohen, *Three Yellow Dogs,* Greenwillow (New York, NY), 1986.
Myra Cohn Livingston, *Higgledy Piggledy,* Atheneum (New York, NY), 1986.
Jean Marzollo and Claudio Marzollo, *Jed and the Space Bandits,* Dutton (New York, NY), 1987.
Monica Mayper, *After Good-Night,* Harper (New York, NY), 1987.
Eve Rice, *City Lights,* Greenwillow (New York, NY), 1987.
Fleischmann, *Scarebird,* Greenwillow (New York, NY), 1988.
Kate Banks, *Alphabet Soup,* Knopf (New York, NY), 1988.
Halloween, Lippincott (New York, NY), 1989.
Fleischmann, *The Ghost in the Noonday Sun,* Greenwillow (New York, NY), 1989.
Fleischmann, *The Midnight Horse,* Greenwillow (New York, NY), 1990.
Shannon, *More Stories to Solve,* Greenwillow (New York, NY), 1990.
Jack Prelutsky, *The Dragons Are Singing Tonight,* Greenwillow (New York, NY), 1993.
Shannon, *Still More Stories to Solve,* Greenwillow (New York, NY), 1994.
Fleischman, *The 13th Floor: A Ghost Story,* Greenwillow (New York, NY), 1995.
Christopher Noel, *Rumpelstiltskin,* Simon & Schuster (New York, NY), 1995.

Jack Prelutsky, *Monday's Troll,* Greenwillow (New York, NY), 1996.

Miriam Schlein, *Sleep Safe, Little Whale: A Little Lullaby,* Greenwillow (New York, NY), 1997.

Madeleine L'Engle, *Many Waters,* Laurel Leaf (New York, NY), 1998.

Jack Prelutsky, *The Gargoyle on the Roof,* Greenwillow (New York, NY), 1999.

José Saramago, *The Tale of the Unknown Island,* translated by Margaret Jull Costa, Harcourt (New York, NY), 1999.

Diane Ackerman, *The Senses of Animals,* Knopf (New York, NY), 2000.

Johann Wolfgang von Goethe, *Faust, Part I,* translated by Randall Jarrell, Farrar, Straus (New York, NY), 2000.

William Nicholson, *The Wind Singer: An Adventure,* Hyperion (New York, NY), 2000.

Ackerman, *Deep Play,* Vintage, 2000.

Nicholson, *Slaves of the Mastery,* Hyperion (New York, NY), 2001.

Jacques Taravant, *The Little Wing Giver,* translated by Nina Ignatowicz, Holt (New York, NY), 2001.

Prelutsky, *Scranimals,* Greenwillow (New York, NY), in press.

OTHER

Contributor of more than 1000 illustrations to *New York Times Book Review* and *New York Times Magazine.* Contributor of articles and illustrations to other periodicals, including *American Illustration, Atlantic Monthly, Boston Globe, Esquire, Forbes, House and Garden, Nation, Newsweek, Time,* and *Travel and Leisure.* Sís's works have been translated into German.

WORK IN PROGRESS: Various film-animation projects.

SIDELIGHTS: Peter Sís is an artist, filmmaker, and highly acclaimed illustrator and author of children's books. Many of his books have very few words, but are notable for their ability to create a solid story with innovative illustrative techniques. Critics agree that his style is deceptively simple, using spare lines and well-thought-out color schemes to develop complex concepts. In *Fire Truck,* for example, the simplicity of a small boy's world is evoked through black lines and lots of white space, while generous use of red suggests his obsession with fire trucks. In the course of the book, he imagines himself to be a kind of fire-truck centaur—until lunch time, when he "parks" himself at the kitchen table to eat. *Trucks, Trucks, Trucks* shows the same boy being asked to put his toys away. He complies with the request, but as he does so, he imagines himself driving around a fantastic construction site. When he finishes his task, his mother takes him to see some real construction vehicles. "By cleverly evoking the way a child uses creativity to construct his own fantasy world, the author gets readers all revved up too," claimed a reviewer for *Publishers Weekly.*

Ballerina! offers girls the same playful delights that *Trucks, Trucks, Trucks* has brought to boys. Simple line drawings feature little Terry, trying on her ballet recital costumes; on facing pages, reflected in an imaginary mirror, a grownup Terry poses in what Gillian Engberg described in *Booklist* as "elaborately rendered magical scenes" worthy of an aspiring dancer's most fanciful dreams. Little Terry (and the more austere line drawings) returns to reality when the imaginary recital ends and she is embraced by her parents' hugs. In *School Library Journal,* Patricia Pearl Dole wrote that *Ballerina!* is "sure to feed young dancers' dreams and encourage them to step a little higher."

Madlenka is another story about a little girl, one that may reflect Sís's own international background and experience. When Madlenka discovers a loose tooth, she travels through her multicultural New York City neighborhood to announce the big news. Critics praised this book for the profuse visual detail that characterizes Sís's work. In typical Sís style, a shift from the modest, colorless line drawings of the city-scape give way to what Wendy Lukehart called in *School Library Journal* "a fanciful dreamscape" full of "mystical creatures and magical symbols" as Madlenka enters each cultural microcosm that she encounters. An added feature is a series of die-cut windows that allow the reader to peek into storefronts to view Madlenka's adventures indoors. *Booklist* reviewer Engberg complimented the "visually stunning spreads" that accompany Sís's exciting "surreal, wordless stories-within-the-story." A *Horn Book* critic observed that "journeys have long been one of Peter Sís's most potent and allusive themes," and that *Madlenka* is not only "luscious with visual imagery" but also "wondrously playful and resonant with meaning."

Sís creates a unique biography with *Starry Messenger: Galileo Galilei,* which "takes the essentials of Galileo's life and discoveries to frame a rich galaxy of paintings that recall both the scientist's [life] and the persistence of wonder," asserted Roger Sutton in *Horn Book.* Intricate borders, miniature portraits and vignettes set into the main pictures, and other unique decorations create a "detailed and delicate, ingeniously conceived" tribute to the great astronomer, in the opinion of a *Publishers Weekly* writer.

The artist's childhood in Prague formed the inspiration for *The Three Golden Keys,* a fanciful tale about a balloonist who, blown off his course by high winds, finds himself carried back to his boyhood home. It features "elegantly crafted, breathtaking fine line illustrations, marvelous to behold," in the words of *Horn Book* contributor Mary M. Burns. "There is no more enticing remembrance of things past than this enigmatic, haunting evocation of childhood. . . . Its images resonate and fascinate." Burns noted that *The Three Golden Keys* was, perhaps, "less a picture book than an illustrated memoir" and suggested that it might have more appeal to adults than children; it incorporates quotes from the likes of Andre Gide and Albert Camus.

Sís again drew on his past and created a book with appeal to all ages with *Tibet: Through the Red Box.* His father, who was also an artist, spent much time in Tibet during the 1950s. His experiences there were the raw material for countless wonderful tales he told his son. In 1994, the elder Sís entrusted his diary from those years to his son, who found that he was almost afraid to read it because of the possibility the reality would distort those wonderful stories. In his book, Sís recreates the diary with parchment-like backgrounds full of jotted notes and pencil sketches; this facsimile of the actual diary is intertwined with Sís's own story. "The guileless prose of both father and son makes Sís's juxtaposition of the journal records with his own childhood memories all the more poignant," stated a *Publishers Weekly* writer. "The luminous colors of the artwork, the panoramas of Tibetan topography and the meticulous intermingling of captivating details and the mystical aspects of Tibetan culture make this an extraordinary volume that will appeal to readers of all ages." Roger Sutton of *Horn Book* deemed the artwork "transcendental, with cryptic and maze-like wheels of life, double-spread renditions of the Tibetan landscape that seem to breathe with life, and pictures of the room in which Sís reads the diary that reveal an internal, emotional landscape. . . . This book will have audiences of all ages completely involved in this Lost Horizon of the imagination."

Sís once told *CA:* "I guess my father's stories and films about his extensive travels and encounters (with the Dalai Lama in Lhasa, Dajaks on Borneo, jazz musician Louis Armstrong in New York, or Greek fishermen) made me want to explore the unknown horizons. Pictures seemed to be the answer. Thanks to my professor and great artist, illustrator, filmmaker, and human being, Jiri Trnka, I have found that film and books seem to be the solution. The picture book, or the animated film based on the book, can be real art and can influence young people all around the world. With my illustrations I am participating in the future in a world that is in desperate need of feelings, consideration, love, and education.

"Growing up in Prague, Czechoslovakia, amidst towers, streets, palaces, bridges, Kafka, Emperor Rudolf II, surrealism, and dada was useful, but now I become homesick sometimes. Not having grown up in America makes me curious about lots of things from peanut butter sandwiches to waving at cabs. I hope this curiosity won't wear out and that I will have a chance to see many new things in many places, since people in this part of the world can come and go as they please. I would like to contribute—with my art, books, films, and whatever may come—to that fundamental yet privileged right."

BIOGRAPHICAL/CRITICAL SOURCES:

BOOKS

Host, Michel, *Peter Sís, ou L'imagier du temps,* Grasset (Paris, France), 1996.

PERIODICALS

Booklist, December 1, 1994, Carolyn Phelan, review of *The Three Golden Keys,* p. 687; January 15, 1995, Michael Cart, "How Memory Looks," p. 907; October 1, 1995, Ilene Cooper, review of *The 13th Floor,* p. 314; April 15, 1996, Janice Del Negro, review of *Monday's Troll,* p. 1437; October 15, 1996, Carolyn Phelan, review of *Starry Messenger,* p. 423; November 15, 1997, Susan Dove Lempke, review of *Sleep Safe, Little Whale,* p. 567; March 15, 1999, review of *Tibet,* p. 1310; September 1, 1999, Lauren Peterson, review of *Ship Ahoy!,* p. 143; October 1, 1999, Susan Dove Lempke, review of *The Gargoyle on the Roof,* p. 355; March 15, 2000, Gillian Engberg, review of *Dinosaur!,* p. 1389; September 1, 2000, Gillian Engberg, review of *Madlenka,* p. 126; April 1, 2001, Gillian Engberg, review of *Ballerina!,* p. 1480.

Horn Book, May, 1993, review of *Komodo!,* p. 325; September, 1993, Mary M. Burns, review of *The Dragons Are Singing Tonight,* p. 615; January,

1994, Ellen Fader, review of *A Small Tall Tale from the Far Far North,* p. 66; March, 1995, Mary M. Burns, review of *The Three Golden Keys,* p. 189; May, 1996, Ann A. Flowers, review of *Monday's Troll,* p. 345; January, 1997, Roger Sutton, review of *Starry Messenger,* p. 79; September, 1998, Marilyn Bousquin, review of *Fire Truck,* p. 601; November, 1998, Roger Sutton, review of *Tibet,* p. 719; September, 1999, Lolly Robinson, review of *Ship Ahoy!,* p. 601; January, 2000, review of *Tibet,* p. 53; July, 2000, review of *Dinosaur!,* p. 445; September, 2000, review of *Madlenka,* p. 558.

Mothering, September, 1999, Peter Neumeyer, review of *Tibet,* p. 81.

New York Times Book Review, February 22, 1987, Martha Saxton, review of *The Whipping Boy,* p. 23; November 8, 1987, review of *Rainbow Rhino;* May 8, 1988, review of *Waving;* November 13, 1988, review of *The Scarebird;* November 14, 1993, David Small, "Gentle Giants," and Cynthia Zarin, "It's Easy Being Green;" June 2, 1996, Zack Rogow, review of *Monday's Troll;* December 13, 1998; April 11, 1999, Scott Veale, "Through Prague to Lhasa," and Heather Vogel Frederick, review of *Fire Truck.*

Publishers Weekly, February 26, 1988; August 10, 1990, Diane Roback and Richard Donahue, reviews of *Beach Ball* and *The Midnight Horse,* pp. 443, 445; June 28, 1991, review of *Follow the Dream,* p. 101; October 12, 1992, review of *An Ocean World,* p. 78; May 24, 1993, review of *Komodo!,* p. 87; October 11, 1993, review of *The Dragons Are Singing Tonight,* p. 88; September 20, 1993, review of *A Small Tall Tale in the Far Far North,* p. 72; November 7, 1994, review of *The Three Golden Keys,* p. 76; November 4, 1996, review of *Starry Messenger,* p. 76; October 9, 1995, review of *The 13th Floor,* p. 86; March 11, 1996, review of *Monday's Troll,* p. 64; April 29, 1996, Paul Nathan, "Special Handling," p. 25; August 10, 1998, review of *Tibet,* p. 365; August 17, 1998, Heather Vogel Frederick, "Peter Sís's Red Box Diaries: A Glimpse [of] Old Tibet," p. 13; April 26, 1999, review of *Trucks, Trucks, Trucks,* p. 81; July 5, 1999, review of *The Gargoyle on the Roof,* p. 71; July 19, 1999, review of *Ship Ahoy!,* p. 193.

School Arts, October, 1999, Ken Marantz, review of *Tibet,* p. 62.

School Library Journal, September, 1998, review of *Fire Truck;* May 1, 1999, review of *Trucks, Trucks, Trucks;* September, 1999, Rosie Peasley, review of *Ship Ahoy!,* p. 206; June, 2000, JoAnn Jonas, review of *Dinosaur!,* p. 125; October, 2000, Wendy Lukehart, review of *Madlenka,* p. 137; April, 2001, Patricia Pearl Dole, review of *Ballerina!,* p. 122.

Scientific American, December, 1998, review of *Fire Truck.*

Teaching K-8, April, 1988.

Time, December 14, 1987, Stefan Kanfer, review of *Rainbow Rhino,* p. 78.

OTHER

Tibet: Through the Red Box, http://www.petersistibet.com/ (May 19, 1999).*

* * *

SMITH, Sally Bedell 1948-

PERSONAL: Born 1948; married Stephen G. Smith (an executive editor at *Newsweek*); children: three. *Education:* Attended Wheaton College; M.A., Columbia Journalism School.

ADDRESSES: Home—Washington, DC. *Agent*—c/o Times Books, 201 East 50th St., New York, NY 10022.

CAREER: Journalist and author. Reported for several publications, including coverage of the media for the *New York Times* and *TV Guide.*

AWARDS, HONORS: Sigma Delta Chi Award for magazine reporting, Society of Professional Journalists, 1982; Fellow, Freedom Forum Media Studies Center, 1986.

WRITINGS:

In All His Glory: The Life of William S. Paley, the Legendary Tycoon and His Brilliant Circle, Simon & Schuster (New York, NY), 1990, reissued as *In All His Glory: The Life and Times of William S. Paley and the Birth of Modern Broadcasting,* 1991.

Reflected Glory: The Life of Pamela Churchill, Simon & Schuster (New York, NY), 1996.

Diana in Search of Herself: Portrait of a Troubled Princess, Times Books (New York, NY), 1999.

Also wrote *Up the Tube: Prime Time TV and the Silverman Years.* Contributor to numerous periodicals.

SIDELIGHTS: Journalist Sally Bedell Smith began her career covering network television for the *New York Times* and *TV Guide* for several years before establishing herself as a respected celebrity biographer. She had already written one book, *Up the Tube: Prime Time TV and the Silverman Years,* before penning her highly regarded biography, *In All His Glory: The Life of William S. Paley, the Legendary Tycoon and His Brilliant Circle.* Published in 1990 by Simon & Schuster, *In All His Glory* chronicles the life of Paley, who owned and managed the Columbia Broadcasting System, Inc. (CBS) network for many years. Smith gives a detailed account of both Paley's business dealings and his lavish personal life; as Christopher Buckley surmised in his commentary on the biography in the *New York Times Book Review,* "her superb and thorough reporting uncovered all the unpleasantness along with the greatness."

In All His Glory narrates how Paley became involved with CBS as a young man, while it was still a struggling radio network centered in Philadelphia, Pennsylvania. He produced a half-hour program called *The La Palina Smoker* that featured a husky-voiced woman. The show proved so popular that the sponsor, La Palina Cigars, saw sales of its products skyrocket. It was the first of many successes in which Paley demonstrated that programming was the key to becoming tops among the networks. Under his direction, CBS became a major network and made a smooth transition to television, though Paley initially resisted the new technology.

While not minimizing his true triumphs, Smith suggests in her book that Paley sometimes took credit for the creative ideas of others, such as longtime CBS president Frank Stanton. She also discusses Paley's two marriages, his numerous affairs, and his extravagant lifestyle. Smith also includes commentary on many of Paley's friends and acquaintances, including pioneer news reporter Edward R. Murrow and writer Truman Capote. Reviewer Leah Rozen in *People* concluded that Smith's work "is thoroughly researched and crammed with telling details, killer quotes and rousing anecdotes."

Smith's next subject was Pamela Churchill Harriman (1920-1997), whom she scrutinized in her 1996 unauthorized biography, *Reflected Glory* (1996). Described by *New York Times Book Review* critic Ben Macintrye as an "upper-class English party girl and gold digger," "globe-trotting mistress of rich men," "show-biz socialite," and "queen of the American Embassy in Paris," Harriman was a prominent figure whose first husband was the son of Winston Churchill. She became notorious for her many adulterous affairs with millionaires, aristocrats, and powerful politicians—among them Averell Harriman, heir to a railroad fortune and a prominent diplomat, who eventually become her third husband. Despite her racy reputation, Pamela Harriman, in later life, became a philanthropist and lent highly publicized support to the Clinton-Gore campaign. She was appointed ambassador to France in 1993. Smith's biography of the courtesan-diplomat, according to Macintyre, is distinguished by research so thorough that it "leaves no stone unturned and no layers of slung mud unexcavated," and "occasionally veers from biography into vivisection as she slices away at the myth." Smith spent five years researching her subject and conducted more than four hundred interviews, creating a portrait the reviewer found unflattering yet "finely balanced." "The biographer's dislike for her subject boils on the page," Macintyre wrote, "but she is too honest to disguise the grudging admiration that goes with it." *Reflected Glory,* he concluded, is the "fullest [portrait of Harriman] we are likely to get."

With her 1999 biography of Diana, Princess of Wales, Smith again garnered critical attention. In *Diana in Search of Herself,* which became a best-seller, Smith argues that the princess suffered from "borderline personality," a serious psychological disorder seemingly at the root of such destructive behaviors as her eating disorders, self-mutilation, and painful romances. *New York Times Book Review* critic Frank Kermode maintained that the book reveals a strong bias in favor of Diana's husband, Prince Charles, and "raises questions that people of ordinary experience are quite unqualified to answer." While Kermode acknowledged that Smith had conducted considerable research and presents an account of Diana's life "as full as any sane person could wish, and even a shade fuller," he found that her portrait lacked insight as to why the princess was so loved by the public. Several other reviewers, however, considered *Diana in Search of Herself* convincing, fair, and intelligent. Laura Shapiro, in *Newsweek,* called the book "an evenhanded analysis" of the princess, and commended Smith's prodigious research and "careful assessment" of her subject. "If you're going to read one Diana book," she advised, "this should be it." *Time* writer Elizabeth Gleick called the biography a "well-written, evenhanded work" that "sympathetically documents Diana's precarious mental state and her need for sustained professional help." *Entertainment Weekly*'s Lisa Schwarzbaum found the work an "unusual and mournful" contribution to the Diana industry, and a "calmly persuasive" account of the princess's troubled life. And a reviewer for *Publishers Weekly* called *Diana in Search of Herself* "a sharply etched and engrossing study."

BIOGRAPHICAL/CRITICAL SOURCES:

PERIODICALS

Boston Globe, October 3, 1999, p. C2.
Business Week, December 10, 1990, p. 10.
Entertainment Weekly, August 20, 1999, p. 117.
Library Journal, September 1, 1999, p. 202.
Newsweek, December 10, 1990, p. 88; August 23, 1999, p. 60.
New Yorker, February 18, 1991, pp. 79-84.
New York Times Book Review, November 4, 1990, pp. 1, 40-41; November 10, 1996; August 22, 1999.
People, January 14, 1991, pp. 31-32.
Publishers Weekly, July 5, 1999, p. 46; August 30, 1999, p. 18.
Time, September 13, 1999, p. 76.
Vanity Fair, September 1999, p. 268.
W., November 1999, p. 68.
Women's Review of Books, January 2000, p. 17.*

* * *

SMITH, Sarah (Winthrop) 1947-

PERSONAL: Born December 9, 1947, in Boston, MA; daughter of Owen Roger and Mary French (Buck) Smith; married David Lee Robbins, January 6, 1974 (divorced, 1977); married Frederick Sayward Perry, Jr. (an electronics company president), August 26, 1979; children: Mariah Contant Nóbrega, Justus Raymond Owen Perry, Frederick, III (deceased), Elizabeth (stepdaughter). *Education:* Radcliffe College, B.A., 1968; attended University College, London, and Queen Mary College, London, 1968-69; Harvard University, Ph.D., 1975. *Politics:* Congenital Democrat, pacifist. *Religion:* Quaker. *Avocational interests:* Chinese cooking, movies, sports, exercise.

ADDRESSES: Home and office—32 Bowker St., Brookline, MA 02445-6955. *Agent*—Christopher Schelling, Ralph Vicinanza Literary Agency, 111 8th Ave., Suite 1501, New York, NY 10011. *E-mail*—swrs@world.std.com.

CAREER: Northeastern University, Boston, MA, assistant professor of English, 1975-76; Tufts University, Medford, MA, assistant professor of English, 1976-82; G. K. Hall, Boston, MA, field editor, 1977-83; LISP Machine, Cambridge, MA, director of documentation, 1982-86; Bachman Information Systems, Cambridge, MA, director of documentation, 1986-88; ITP Systems, Inc., Cambridge, MA, manager of training and documentation, 1988-90; independent multimedia consultant and writer, 1990—.

MEMBER: Amnesty International, National Peace Foundation, Science Fiction Writers of America, Mystery Writers of America (webmaster, 1999—), Sisters in Crime (New England regional steering committee; past New England president), Signet Society, Habitat for Humanity, Cambridge Science Fiction Workshop, Hi-Pitched Voices.

AWARDS, HONORS: Fulbright fellowship, 1968-69; graduate fellowship from Harvard University, 1969-74; Frank Knox fellowship from Harvard University, 1972-73; Bowdoin Prize from Harvard University, 1975; Mellon fellowship from Tufts University, 1977; listing among year's notable books from *New York Times,* 1992, for *The Vanished Child,* 1996, for *The Knowledge of Water.*

WRITINGS:

NOVELS

King of Space (science fiction), Eastgate (Watertown, MA), 1991.
The Vanished Child (historical mystery; first book in trilogy), Ballantine (New York, NY), 1992.
(Co-author; edited by David A. Smith) *Future Boston,* Tor (New York, NY), 1994.
The Knowledge of Water (historical mystery; second book in trilogy), Ballantine (New York, NY), 1996.
The Dolls (children's fantasy novella), Tribune Media Services, 1996.
Mindriders (serial), Tribune Media Services, 1996-97.
A Citizen of the Country (historical mystery; third book in trilogy), Ballantine (New York, NY), 2000.

OTHER

(Translator) *Colette at the Movies,* Ungar (New York, NY), 1980.
Samuel Richardson: A Critical Bibliography, G. K. Hall (Thorndike, ME), 1984.

Work represented in anthologies, including *Shudder Again,* edited by Michele Slung, NAL-Dutton, 1993; *Christmas Forever,* edited by David Hartwell, Tor

Books, 1993; *Best New Horror #5,* edited by Stephen Jones and Ramsey Campbell, Carroll & Graf, 1994; *A Taste of Murder, The Bakery Men Don't See,* and *Her Smoke Rose Up from Supper.* Contributor to periodicals, including *Aboriginal SF, Fantasy and Science Fiction, New York Review of Science Fiction,* and *Friends Journal.* Also author of technical publications about computers.

WORK IN PROGRESS: Will Shakespeare, modern novel with Elizabethan elements; *Treasures Upon Earth,* a mystery.

SIDELIGHTS: Sarah Smith is a versatile writer whose accomplishments include publications in numerous genres. Her first novel, *King of Space,* is a computer-based dark fantasy of death and regeneration set in a deserted space station. The three novels following *King of Space—The Vanished Child, The Knowledge of Water,* and *A Citizen of the Country*—comprise a best-selling trilogy of historical mysteries that some reviewers have dubbed "neo-Victorian." All three books have as their protagonist the Austrian Baron Alexander Von Reisden. A young biochemist, Reisden suffers from a partial amnesia concerning his childhood. He remembers nothing prior to his tenth birthday and as a result harbors doubts about his true identity. As *The Vanished Child* opens in 1905, Reisden encounters an old man at a train station who insists that Von Reisden is actually Richard Knight, who disappeared as a child after witnessing his own grandfather's murder in New England in 1897. The murder has remained unsolved and Reisden becomes involved in tracking down the killer. In Boston, he meets and falls in love with would-be concert pianist Perdita Halley, a young woman whose eyes have been injured and who is legally blind. Alexander moves into the Knight household and assumes the identity of the missing Richard Knight to pursue the murder investigation. A critic for *Kirkus Reviews* commented that some "riddles . . . are still floating unresolved at the final John Fowles-ish curtain," adding that "Smith . . . paints a canvas reminiscent of Robert Goddard's period thrillers, though more . . . inconclusive at every stage." An online reviewer for *http://www.wenet.net* stated: "The characters of Alexander Von Reisden and Perdita are richly drawn and complex, the language Edwardian, the history painstakingly researched. . . . The mystery of finding the murderer is not nearly as satisfying as the mystery of how Alexander and Perdita define their relationship to one another."

In the second volume of the trilogy, *The Knowledge of Water,* the action shifts to Paris in 1910. A number of famous historical personages, such as Gertrude Stein, Picasso, and Colette, appear in the course of the narrative, as well as the calamitous flood that swept through Paris that year. The mystery centers on painter Claude Maillais and the fact that after his death new paintings by him continue to appear. The relationship between Perdita and Alexander has deepened, and Perdita continues to pursue her dream to become a concert pianist despite the prejudices of the era against women. Another central character, writer and theater artist Milly Xico, urges Perdita to abandon her love for Alexander in favor of her career. A *Publishers Weekly* reviewer described *The Knowledge of Water* as "a sprawling baroque tale of budding feminism, murder, and art forgery . . . with a subtle eroticism and luxuriant atmosphere." On the down side, this same reviewer noted that "the writing can be awkward, and the plot is slow to cohere." Liz Rifkin of *Booklist* stated: "Although Smith transports the reader back almost a century, her capability for posing ageless questions about love, subterfuge, and reality creates an absorbing contemporary climate."

A Citizen of the Country, the concluding volume of the trilogy, is also set in France, in both Paris and Flanders on the eve of World War I. Alexander, who runs the Jouvet Institute for medical research, takes on the task of curing the mentally disturbed André du Monde, Count of Montfort. André, both a playwright and theater owner, is a man obsessed with the darker sides of reality. Much of the action of the novel takes place at Castle Montfort where André is producing a silent-film version of *Macbeth* starring his wife Sabine, a woman who is rumored to have taken a demon lover. Alexander, while still experiencing the doubts about his own past introduced in *The Vanished Child,* must placate André's stepfather, who had hoped for a military career for his son, and also Perdita, now Alexander's wife, who wants to return to America to renew her aspirations as a concert pianist. A reviewer for *Publishers Weekly* observed: "In addition to providing fascinating background on early filmmaking, the author adds French military secrets, murder, blackmail and witchcraft. Though the buildup to the revelation of Reisden's dilemma seems unnecessarily complicated, readers will care about the splendidly realized characters, whose fates are decided in an eminently satisfying conclusion." A critic for *Kirkus Reviews* found *A Citizen of the Country* even more praiseworthy, suggesting that the novel "evokes fond memories of Poe, Agatha Christie, Dicken's *A Tale of Two Cities,* and Polanski's *Chinatown,*" concluding: "Fiction just doesn't get any more entertaining and satisfying than this. A bloody triumph."

Smith told *CA:* "Mysteries, science fiction, and thrillers show real people in hyper-real situations. In mysteries the detective has to find, not only the killer, but the truth and a remedy. In science fiction, the protagonist deals with the human effects of society and technology. These are big, serious genres where you can have a lot of fun and tell a fascinating story.

"The Internet has completely transformed entertainment for me. As a writer, I talk with my readers all the time over the Net. I've read interesting new people published by print-on-demand, online publication, and small presses. I love the novel, and Lord willing, I'll always write them. But somewhere out there is a new medium, a Web-based story, with pictures and text, with input from readers—with characters, story, ideas, beauty, passion, another kind of storytelling.

"What a playground that kind of story will be! I keep hoping that I'll write one that's as good as what I want to read. But if I don't, I hope you do."

BIOGRAPHICAL/CRITICAL SOURCES:

PERIODICALS

Booklist, August, 1996, Liz Rifkin, review of *The Knowledge of Water,* p. 1888; June 1, 2000, Connie Fletcher, review of *A Citizen of the Country,* p. 1865.

Bookselling This Week, August 29, 1994, p. 1.

Kirkus Reviews, January 1, 1992, review of *The Vanished Child;* July 15, 1996, review of *The Knowledge of Water;* June 1, 2000, review of *A Citizen of the Country,* p. 745.

Library Journal, August, 1996, Mary Ellen Rutledge, review of *The Knowledge of Water,* p. 114.

New York Times Book Review, June 7, 1992, p. 19; August 29, 1992, p. 11.

Publishers Weekly, January 13, 1992, p. 48, January 16, 1995, p. 319; August 5, 1996, review of *The Knowledge of Water,* p. 431; July 17, 2000, review of *A Citizen of the Country,* p. 176.

OTHER

Sarah Smith, http://www.sarahsmith.com/ (July 19, 2000).

* * *

SOUEIF, Ahdaf 1950-

PERSONAL: Born 1950, in Cairo, Egypt; married Ian Hamilton (a writer), March, 1981; children: two sons. *Education:* Cairo University, B.A. (literature), 1971; American University, M.A. (literature), 1973; University of Lancaster, Ph.D. (linguistics), 1978.

ADDRESSES: Home—London, England. *Agent*—Wyley Agency, 4-8 Rodney St., London N1 9JH, England.

CAREER: Fiction writer. Lecturer at colleges and universities, including University of Cairo and Riyadh University. Birmingham University, member of the board of the Center for Study of Christian-Muslim Relations.

MEMBER: Egyptian Writers' Union, PEN Egypt, London International Festival of Theatre (board member), Council for Advancement of Arab British Understanding (CAABU), Arts Council of England (literature advisory board member), Arts Council of Britain (translation advisory group member), Egyptian-British Society.

AWARDS, HONORS: Shortlist, *Guardian* Fiction Award, 1983, for *Aisha;* Cairo Book Fair Award for Best Short Stories of the Year, for *Zinat al-Hayah wa Qisas Ukhra;* shortlist, Booker Prize, 1999, for *The Map of Love;* Radio South Africa Book of the Week designation, 2000, for *The Map of Love.*

WRITINGS:

Aisha (short stories), J. Cape (London, England), 1983.

In the Eye of the Sun (novel), Bloomsbury (London, England), 1992.

Sandpiper (novel), Bloomsbury (London, England), 1996.

Zinat al-Hayah wa Qisas Ukhra (short stories), Kitab al-Hilal, 1996.

Ahdaf Suwayf: Mukhtarat min A'maliha (collection), General Egyptian Book Organisation (Cairo, Egypt), 1998.

(Translator) *In Deepest Night* (play for al-Warsha Theatre Group), produced at the Kennedy Centre in Washington, DC, 1998.

The Map of Love (novel), Bloomsbury (London, England), 1999.

(Translator) Mourid al-Barghouti, *I Saw Ramallah* (memoir), AUC Press (Cairo, Egypt), 2000.

Contributor of critical essays, short stories, and reviews to periodicals, including *Times Literary Supplement, Washington Post, Cosmopolitan, New Society, Sunday Telegraph, Akhbar al-Adab,* and *London Review of Books;* some of Soueif's works have been translated to Dutch, French, German, Greek, Italian, Spanish, and Swedish.

WORK IN PROGRESS: Translating *The Map of Love* into Arabic, with her mother.

SIDELIGHTS: Like her protagonists, Egyptian writer Ahdaf Soueif is a bit of a hybrid. Born into a Muslim family in Cairo, Egypt, Soueif was educated in both England and Egypt, eventually going abroad to earn her Ph.D. at the University of Lancaster. Growing up and maturing in such diverse cultures was a constant challenge for Soueif, one she addresses through many of her characters in such works as *Aisha, In the Eye of the Sun, Sandpiper,* and *The Map of Love.* Because she has an insider's view of both cultures, Soueif has a heightened awareness of the stereotypes that often cloud relations between the two worlds. Through a poetic narrative style and descriptive settings, as well as through characters who, like herself, are fundamentally touched by both the English and the Egyptian worlds, Soueif exposes these stereotypes as her characters tread the landscapes of both worlds.

Though Soueif writes in English, much of her work is set in Egypt or elsewhere in the Middle East, giving Western readers an insider's glimpse into a world they would seldom otherwise see. Through detailed descriptions, Soueif creates a realistic view of everyday life in these exotic places. Through her characters, she is able to offer first-hand glimpses into the sexual politics of both the Eastern and Western worlds.

Soueif's first work was *Aisha,* a collection of short stories that focuses almost exclusively on Egyptian culture and life. Her aim in writing the book was to dispel some of the myths that Westerners attribute to the Arab world, particularly the belief that it is a barbaric culture. However, Soueif also reinforces some of these stereotypes, especially those concerning the interactions between men and women. The eight short stories, although seemingly unconnected, each feature an Egyptian girl named Aisha who is caught between two worlds and having a difficult time fitting into either.

Like Soueif herself, Aisha is Egyptian with an English education. Throughout the different stories, Aisha finds herself more and more isolated. In each episode, different stages of Aisha's rebellious life are explored. In the first episode, we are introduced to her character as she revisits the dwelling where she had a "Western" marriage to an Egyptian intellectual. The marriage becomes a burden for Aisha, largely due to a breakdown in communication between the two, and she realizes she has no love for the man. While she is imaginative and passionate, he is very practical and distant. In the second segment of the book, the setting switches to England where, as a schoolgirl, Aisha spends much of her time reading Western literature and connecting with many of the characters contained within the pages. Because she is Egyptian, she is isolated from the more boastful English school girls. Still, she believes herself more sexually liberated than her classmates, which makes her feel superior to them. In the next sequence, Aisha's nanny, Zeina, recounts with sadness the story of her forced marriage in a tale that highlights Egyptian matchmaking and the jousting that takes place between mothers and daughters during the process. The following episode finds Zeina completely submissive and content with her brutish husband and his aggressive sexual antics. In the final episode, entitled "Nativity," by far the most sexually revealing, Aisha travels to a working-class section of Cairo where she enters a tent in which several women are dancing frenetically. Aisha has become desperate to conceive a child, and the dancing women are part of a folk ritual known as *zars,* which is a way of invoking certain saints to help in making the participants fertile. Aisha's frustration with Western practices has led her to this ceremony, in which she becomes a player in her own rape.

Aisha was well received by critics. Thomas Blaikie in *Books & Bookmen* called *Aisha* a "remarkable first novel." Each of the sections was "evoked with truthful and moving simplicity," this critic continued. Issa Peters, reviewing the book in *World Literature Today,* wrote that "Soueif is masterful in creating atmosphere and mood through graphic description." Peters called Soueif "a budding talent of the highest order." Likewise, John Mellors in *Listener* lauded the vivid descriptions of Cairo and other Middle Eastern locations. Mellors predicted that readers would look forward to further installments of Soueif's "penetrating exploration of . . . bilingual culture."

In her highly acclaimed novel, *In the Eye of the Sun,* Soueif creates another remarkable heroine named Asya. Reminiscent of the lead character from *Aisha,* Asya is an Egyptian girl who has been educated in the English language and its literature. After graduating from Cairo University, she heads off to England to earn her Ph.D. in English literature. Set in Cairo in the 1960s, Soueif recreates what it was like to live in the Middle East at the time of the Arab-Israeli War, the rise and fall of pan-Arabic leader Gamal Abdel Nasser, and the beginning of the presidency of Anwar Sadat and his despised pro-Western government. It is during these tumultuous times that Asya comes of age, but while many of her peers are fully aware of the political environment, Asya digs herself deeper into a secluded world of books and Western popular music. She reads the novels and stories of Dickens, Tolstoy, and Louisa May Alcott, and listens to the songs of Motown. "I just think that if we could manage to look at real people and real actions with the same interest, the same generous detachment, that we give to a novel or play we should—we should understand things better," Asya says at one point in the novel.

The beautiful Asya falls in love with Saif Madi and marries him. But their union leaves her unfulfilled both emotionally and sexually, so she decides to leave Cairo to earn her Ph.D. at a British university. While in England, she loses some of her passion for the literature and music that once so enthralled her. She also takes on an English lover who gives her sexual pleasure but little else. When Saif learns of the affair, he angrily shouts at her: "In life people—real people—suffer as a consequence of action, or inaction, on the part of others, while in a novel you can spin things out as much as you like." Feeling somewhat nostalgic, Asya returns to Egypt, where she educates a poor village on the benefits of birth control. Ironically, she longs for her own child. As the story closes, Asya happens upon the statue of an ancient female pharaoh. In the statue, she sees some of herself; an Egyptian woman who has withstood the trials of time.

In the Eye of the Sun received a great deal of critical praise after it was published. Writing in *New Statesman,* Kathryn Hughes found Soueif's descriptive settings appealing, particularly her detailed picture of everyday life in Middle Eastern cities. "By the end, we know which university departments have most prestige, how much you get on social security, the cost of a plane ticket to Syria," Hughes wrote. Frank Kermode, reviewing the novel in the *London Review of Books,* was also impressed with Soueif's writing. "It is the combination of scrupulous deliberation and formidable narrative energy that makes this such an impressive work," Kermode wrote. "The extraordinary thing about *In the Eye of the Sun* is that Soueif writes of both England and Egypt from within," wrote Edward Said in *Time Literary Supplement.* Said added that "Soueif renders the experience of crossing over from one side to the other, and then back again, indefinitely, without rancour or preachiness."

In her third book, Soueif again created a sequence of related short stories, as she had in *Aisha. Sandpiper* is a series of seven stories that center on an array of women from different cultures: Arab, American, English, and Greek. With *Sandpiper,* Soueif goes to her greatest lengths to expose the views each culture has of the others, as well as how they see themselves. In one of the more intriguing sequences, entitled "Melody," a narrator tells the story of the title character. Melody is the daughter of a Turkish Muslim woman who cannot speak any English, and the narrator is a woman from North America living in the Arab world, who, as the story unfolds, exposes her xenophobia and feelings of superiority over the other women in the story. In telling Melody's story, the North American woman often insults what she calls "the Muslim way" in such matters as family life and dealing with death. She often condemns this way of life, especially the submissiveness of Arab women to their husbands. Yet, as the story unfolds, the woman must confront her own oppression by a professional husband, who is distant but commanding.

Other episodes in *Sandpiper* also explore the sexual politics that exist within different cultures. Andrea Ashworth in *Times Literary Supplement* believed the book's message was encumbering at times and confusing to the reader. Ashworth admitted that it was a worthy message, however. "Across divergences in nationality, ethnicity, class and idiosyncrasy, Soueif's writing both draws and blurs boundaries . . . to demonstrate that skin-deep differences can conceal profound affinities and continuities."

With *The Map of Love,* Soueif abandoned the structure of the related short story for that of the romantic saga that spans generations. Garnering comparisons to A. S. Byatt's literary detective story, *Possession,* and to Michael Ondaatje's *The English Patient,* Soueif intertwines two love stories set one hundred years and a continent apart, but connected by the ties of blood and coincidence. In 1900 Anna Winterbourne travels to Egypt to start a new life after the death of her husband, and finds herself falling in love with Sharif Pasha-al-Barudi, a leader in the fight against the British colonizers. In 1997, newly divorced Isabel Parkman travels to Egypt to seek the advice of a woman who may be able to translate the documents found in a trunk which was bequeathed to Isabel on her mother's death. What Isabel and her new friend find is that they are distant cousins, both descendants of Anna and Sharif. The contents of the trunk recount the progress of the affair a century earlier, which Soueif intersperses with details of Isabel's ongoing love affair with another Egyptian, her translator's brother.

"Soueif writes simply and, on occasion, beautifully," remarked a reviewer for *Publishers Weekly,* who nonetheless faulted the author for relying a bit too heavily on coincidence for plot movement. For a reviewer for *African Business,* however, Soueif's characters are drawn too closely to the popular romance model, and thus lack nuance or subtlety. "I found it a pity," this reviewer concluded, "that the book's interesting and demanding structure, with the many complex political and religious questions it raises, is let down by the author's formulaic approach to character creation." Like many other reviewers, *Booklist* contributor Danise Hoover called *The Map of Love* "a very romantic book," but found the juxtaposition of Egypt and England at either end of the twentieth century to be edifying. And *Library Journal* contributor Ann H. Fisher said, "This colorful, involving story offers a good dose of history of the struggle for Egyptian independence from British rule."

BIOGRAPHICAL/CRITICAL SOURCES:

BOOKS

Soueif, Ahdaf, *In the Eye of the Sun,* Bloomsbury (London, England), 1992.

PERIODICALS

African Business, January, 2000, review of *The Map of Love,* p. 42.
Al-Hayat, May 1, 1996, review of *Sandpiper,* p. 16.
Al-Yom, October 16, 1996, interview with the author.
Asharq al-Awsat, June 15, 1995, interview with the author, p. 19.
Booklist, September 1, 2000, Danise Hoover, review of *The Map of Love,* p. 67.
Books & Bookmen, September, 1983, pp. 32-33.
Boston Sunday Globe, June 13, 1993, review of *In the Eye of the Sun,* p. B43.
Christian Science Monitor, August 3, 1993, review of *In the Eye of the Sun.*
Globe & Mail (Toronto), November 13, 1999, review of *The Map of Love,* p. D22.
Independent, August 8, 1992, review of *In the Eye of the Sun,* p. 26.
Kirkus Reviews, March 1, 1993, review of *In the Eye of the Sun.*
Library Journal, May 1, 1993, review of *In the Eye of the Sun;* November 15, 2000, Ann H. Fisher, review of *The Map of Love,* p. 98.
Listener, July 21, 1983, pp. 27-28.
London Magazine, April, 1996, review of *Sandpiper.*
London Review of Books, June 25, 1992, pp. 19-20; July 15, 1999, review of *The Map of Love,* p. 28.
Los Angeles Times, September 26, 1993, review of *In the Eye of the Sun.*
New Statesman, July 10, 1992, p. 35.
New York Review of Books, September 23, 1993, review of *In the Eye of the Sun,* pp. 27-29.
New York Times, September 22, 1999, "Booker Prize Nominees," p. B8.
New York Times Book Review, October 23, 1994, review of *In the Eye of the Sun,* p. 36; October 1, 2000, Annette Kobak, "Out of the Trunk: A Novel of Egypt Interweaves the Lives of Three Women, One Long Dead," p. 30.
Observer, March 3, 1996, review of *Sandpiper,* p. 15; June 20, 1999, review of *The Map of Love,* p. 13.
Publishers Weekly, April 12, 1993, review of *In the Eye of the Sun,* p. 45; August 14, 2000, review of *The Map of Love,* p. 326.
Sunday Times, April 7, 1996, review of *Sandpiper.*
Times Literary Supplement, June 19, 1992, p. 19; March 1, 1996, p. 22; June 4, 1999, review of *The Map of Love,* p. 22.
Vogue, July, 1992, review of *In the Eye of the Sun,* p. 30.
Washington Post Book World, October 8, 2000, Laura Miller, "Desert Hearts," p. X08.
World Literature Today, spring, 1984, p. 318.

OTHER

Arab View, http://www.arab.net/ (May 17, 2000), Asim Hamdan, "Zionist Denies Soueif the Booker Prize."

* * *

SOWELL, Thomas 1930-

PERSONAL: Born June 30, 1930, in Gastonia, NC; married Alma Jean Parr (divorced); current wife's name, Mary; children: two. *Education:* Harvard University, A.B. (magna cum laude), 1958; Columbia University, A.M., 1959; University of Chicago, Ph.D. (economics), 1968.

ADDRESSES: *Office*—Hoover Institution, Stanford University, Stanford, CA 94305-6010.

CAREER: U.S. Department of Labor, Washington, DC, labor economist, 1961-62; Douglass College, Rutgers University, New Brunswick, NJ, instructor in economics, 1962-63; Howard University, Washington, DC, lecturer in economics, 1963-64; American Telephone &

Telegraph Co., New York, NY, economic analyst, 1964-65; Cornell University, Ithaca, NY, assistant professor of economics, 1965-69, director of Summer Intensive Training Program in Economic Theory, 1968; Brandeis University, Waltham, MA, associate professor of economics, 1969-70; University of California, Los Angeles, associate professor, 1970-74, professor of economics, 1974-80; Hoover Institution, Stanford University, Stanford, CA, senior fellow, 1977, Rose and Milton Friedman Senior Fellow in Public Policy, 1980—. Urban Institute, Washington, DC, project director, 1972-74; American Enterprise Institute, adjunct scholar, 1975-76; Center for Advanced Study in the Behavioral Sciences, Stanford, CA, fellow, 1976-77; visiting professor, Amherst College, 1977. *Military Service:* U.S. Marine Corps, 1951-53.

WRITINGS:

Economics: Analysis and Issues, Scott, Foresman (Glenview, IL), 1971.

Black Education: Myths and Tragedies, McKay (New York, NY), 1972.

Say's Law: An Historical Analysis, Princeton University Press (Princeton, NJ), 1972.

Classical Economics Reconsidered, Princeton University Press (Princeton, NJ), 1974.

Affirmative Action: Was It Necessary in Academia?, American Enterprise Institute for Public Policy Research (Washington, DC), 1975.

Race and Economics, McKay (New York, NY), 1975.

Patterns of Black Excellence, Ethics and Public Policy Center, Georgetown University (Washington, DC), 1977.

(Editor) *American Ethnic Groups,* Urban Institute (Washington, DC), 1978.

(Editor) *Essays and Data on American Ethnic Groups,* Urban Institute (Washington, DC), 1978.

Markets and Minorities, Basic Books (New York, NY), 1981.

(Editor, with others) *The Fairmont Papers: Black Alternatives Conference, December, 1980,* ICS Press (San Francisco, CA), 1981.

Pink and Brown People, and Other Controversial Essays, Hoover Institution (Stanford, CA), 1981.

Knowledge and Decision, Basic Books (New York, NY), 1983.

Ethnic America: A History, Basic Books (New York, NY), 1983.

The Economics and Politics of Race: An International Perspective, Morrow (New York, NY), 1983.

Compassion versus Guilt, and Other Essays, Quill (New York, NY), 1984.

Marxism: Philosophy and Economics, Morrow (New York, NY), 1985.

Civil Rights: Rhetoric or Reality?, Morrow (New York, NY), 1985.

Education: Assumptions versus History (essays), Hoover Institution (Stanford, CA), 1986.

A Conflict of Visions: Ideological Origins of Political Struggles, Morrow (New York, NY), 1987.

Judicial Activism Reconsidered (essays), Hoover Institution (Stanford, CA), 1989.

Choosing a College: A Guide for Parents and Students, Perennial Library (New York, NY), 1989.

Preferential Policies: An International Perspective, Morrow (New York, NY), 1990.

Inside American Education: The Decline, the Deception, the Dogmas, Free Press (New York, NY), 1992.

Race and Culture: A World View (part one of "Cultural Trilogy"), Pennsylvania State University Press (University Park, PA), 1992.

Is Reality Optional?: and Other Essays, Hoover Institution (Stanford, CA), 1993.

The Vision of the Anointed: Self-Congratulation as a Basis for Social Policy, Basic Books (New York, NY), 1995.

Migrations and Cultures: A World View (part two of "Cultural Trilogy"), Basic Books (New York, NY), 1996.

Late-talking Children, Basic Books (New York, NY), 1997, published as *The Einstein Syndrome: Bright Children Who Talk Late,* 2001.

Conquests and Cultures: An International History (part three of "Cultural Trilogy"), Basic Books (New York, NY), 1998.

Race, Culture, and Equality, Hoover Institution (Stanford, CA), 1998.

Barbarians inside the Gates—and Other Controversial Essays, Hoover Institution (Stanford, CA), 1999.

The Quest for Cosmic Justice, Free Press (New York, NY), 1999.

A Personal Odyssey, Free Press (New York, NY), 2000.

Basic Economics: A Citizen's Guide to the Economy, Basic Books (New York, NY), 2001.

Some Thoughts about Writing, Hoover Institution (Stanford, CA), 2001.

Work represented in anthologies, including *Readings in the History of Economic Thought,* edited by I. H. Rima, Holt (New York, NY), 1970; and *Discrimination, Affirmative Action, and Equal Opportunity: An Economic and Social Perspective,* edited by W. E. Block and M. A. Walker, Fraser Institute, 1982. Columnist for *Los Angeles Herald-Examiner,* 1978-80, for syndication, 1984-90, for *Forbes,* 1991-99, and for syndication,

1991—. Contributor to numerous periodicals, including *American Economic Review, American Spectator, Commentary, Economica, Education Digest, Ethics, Fortune, New York Times Magazine, Oxford Economic Papers, Social Research, Western Review,* and *University of Chicago Magazine.*

SIDELIGHTS: Called "a free-market economist and perhaps the leading black scholar among conservatives" by Fred Barnes of the *New York Times Book Review,* Thomas Sowell has written numerous controversial books about economics, race, and ethnic groups. His support for a laissez-faire economic system with few government constraints and his vocal opposition to most of the social programs and judicial actions favored by other black spokespersons have made him a target for much criticism. Yet Steven E. Plaut of *Commentary* called Sowell "one of America's most trenchant and perceptive commentators on the subject of race relations and ethnicity." Davis Holmstrom, writing in the *Los Angeles Times,* maintained that "in the writing of economist Thomas Sowell, scholarship, clarity and genuine information come together as nicely and perfectly as a timeless quote." Because of his "insights on some of the most pressing social-science concerns of our times," according to the *Wall Street Journal* contributor Joel Kotkin, Sowell is "in a very real sense, a modern successor to the kind of acute, culture-based social science epitomized by Max Weber."

A senior fellow at Stanford University's Hoover Institution on War, Revolution, and Peace since 1980, Sowell has done extensive research into the economic performance of racial and ethnic groups throughout the world, trying to determine the factors which make some groups more successful than others. He has presented both his research and his conclusions in such books as *Ethnic America: A History, The Economics and Politics of Race: An International Perspective,* and *Civil Rights: Rhetoric or Reality?.* These and other of Sowell's books have attempted to disprove a number of popularly held beliefs while bringing new and potentially valuable information to light. As George M. Fredrickson noted in the *New York Times Book Review,* "Sowell is engaged in a continuing polemic against the basic assumptions of liberals, radicals and civil rights leaders. But the quality of his evidence and reasoning requires that he be taken seriously. His ideological opponents will have to meet his arguments squarely and incisively to justify the kind of policies currently identified with the pursuit of racial equality and social justice."

Sowell's own life story seems to illustrate many of the values he now expounds. Born in North Carolina, Sowell attended a segregated high school where he graduated at the top of his class. "We never wondered why there weren't any white kids there," he told Joseph Sobran in the *National Review.* "We never thought we'd be learning more if there *had* been white kids there. In fact, we never *thought* about white kids." A graduate of Harvard University, Columbia University, and the University of Chicago, Sowell went on to hold a number of positions in government and academia before joining the Hoover Institution in 1980. Through it all, Sobran remarked, Sowell has been "matter-of-fact about his race and its bearing on his intellectual life."

At least one critic perceived personal influences in some of Sowell's writing. Scott McConnell of the *Wall Street Journal* found *The Vision of the Anointed: Self-Congratulation as a Basis for Social Policy* to be an "uncompromising and often angry book." McConnell explained: "Mr. Sowell—a black intellectual whose prose seldom sends out even the faintest glint of ethnic references—draws from a well of both sorrow and anger when he reflects on some remarkable facts"; these facts point out that blacks either were bettering their own lives without the help of twentieth-century social policy or have actually suffered more under the auspices of social changes designed to help people, such as the pro-defendant *Miranda* decision.

One of Sowell's most controversial contentions is that a racial or ethnic group's economic success is not seriously hindered by discrimination from society at large. The economist believes that immigrants bring to their new homelands a collection of habits and beliefs—what he terms "cultural capital"—and it is this cultural capital that is the determining factor in their future economic success or failure. "This is a theory," wrote Thurston Clarke in the *New York Times Book Review,* "that deflates any windbag oratory about the United States being a unique land of opportunity, where migrants succeed by discarding their former culture and leaping naked into the great melting pot."

In his 1983 work, *The Economics and Politics of Race,* Sowell cites several examples of minority groups around the world which have fared well despite prejudice against them in their adopted country, as well as groups faced with little discrimination who have done poorly. The Chinese minorities in Southeast Asian countries, despite intense resistance from the native populations, have done very well economically, and often dominate their local economies. European Jews have faced long-term opposition from majority population groups, yet they too have performed outstandingly well and enjoy a high level of economic success. On the other hand,

Plaut explained, in *The Economics and Politics of Race* Sowell shows that "In Brazil and other parts of South America blacks face less racism than do American blacks. . . . Yet for all this tolerance, Brazil shows a larger gap in black-white earnings, social position, and education than does the United States."

The key factor in an ethnic group's economic success, Sowell argues, is "something economists refer to as human capital—values, attitudes and skills embodied in a culture," as Stanley O. Williford outlined in the *Los Angeles Times Book Review.* An ethnic or racial group that emphasizes hard work, saving money, and acquiring an education will generally do well regardless of the political or social climate. *Newsweek* contributor David Gelman, dubbing Sowell's approach "conservative," explained: "Essentially, it is that diligence, discipline and entrepreneurial drive can overthrow the most formidable barriers of poverty and bigotry." Thurston Clarke, writing in the *New York Times Book Review,* pointed out that Sowell's assertions "will unsettle multiculturalists who believe that all cultures make equivalent contributions to human progress." Yet, according to *National Review* contributor Jacob Cohen, in *Race and Culture* Sowell "has produced a book that will compel every careful reader, and not just those on the Left, to rethink their most confident views on matters of race and culture"; *Race and Culture* challenges both sides to rethink the effect of individual effort on economic performance.

Because of his belief in human capital, Sowell argues against continued efforts by the federal government to end racial discrimination, a problem he believes was largely eliminated during the civil rights struggle. Instead he calls for a greater emphasis on free-market economics. A healthy, growing economy, Sowell believes, does the most good for minority groups who suffer from poverty. As Aaron Wildavsky opined in the *National Review,* "When labor is scarce and the markets for it are competitive, wages go up regardless of the prejudices of employers." Sowell points out in *Civil Rights: Rhetoric or Reality?* that "the economic rise of minorities preceded by many years [the] passage of the Civil Rights Act. . . . [and] this trend was not accelerated either by that legislation or by the quotas introduced during the seventies." According to Chris Wall in the *Los Angeles Times Book Review,* Sowell believes that minority groups are "crying racism at every turn to divert attention from the fact that their cultures or subcultures may be economically unproductive."

Sowell dismisses much of what black civil rights leaders believe necessary for the betterment of American blacks. He questions, for example, the value for black students of integrated public schools, called for by the Warren court in *Brown vs. Board of Education.* Sobran reported that Sowell finds the court's contention "that segregated schools produced inferior black education . . . expresses and justifies a destructively paternalistic attitude, according to which a black child can't learn anything except in close proximity to a white one. With forced busing . . . the white man's burden has become 'the white *child's* burden—to go forth and civilize the heathen.'"

Sowell, in fact, finds grave fault with the U.S. educational system in terms of what it offers to many children other than black children. According to *New Republic* reviewer Alan Wolfe, "American students, like their textbooks, have been 'dumbed down.'" In *Inside American Education,* Sowell makes the claim that "It is not merely that Johnny can't read, or even that Johnny can't think. Johnny doesn't even know what thinking is." As explained by Wolfe, Sowell further rails against the "therapeutic" ideology in education today—that "All should be taught to appreciate themselves, even if they don't know a thing." Sowell claims that, to protect their jobs, educators simply advance "unprepared children" through the system.

Students who diverge from the academic norm are particularly at risk, according to Sowell. In *Inside American Education he* enumerates two such groups: bilingual students and athletes. Bilingual students cause an inflow of federal money for special-education classes, a situation that, in the opinion of *Wall Street Journal* contributor Michael Schwartz, "creates an incentive for keeping as many students as possible in such programs for as long as possible." In the case of athletes, the demands of the game may be what prevents learning. Combined with his or her already "sub-standard academic background," the athlete, writes Sowell, "usually finds himself out on the street with no skills, no degrees, and perhaps no character."

Government programs such as affirmative action racial quotas and public welfare also come under Sowell's fire, particularly in his 1992 work *Inside American Education: The Decline, The Deception, the Dogmas.* Here the economist maintains that African American students who would excel at second-tier educational institutions such as many state universities may instead find themselves near the bottom of the class at Harvard, or even become a college dropout. In analyzing this problem, Schwartz explained: "the administrators of these institutions . . . can cheerfully pat themselves on the back for having proved numerically that they provided educational 'opportunity' to minority students." Sowell quotes a Harvard dean as saying: "if we're driven exclusively by academic qualities, we would have a much less interesting student body." As Schwartz termed it, "It is a case of ideology over education."

Some critics of Sowell's position on education have protested that his rhetoric is overinflated. John Brademas, in a review for the *New York Times Book Review,* maintained that in *Inside American Education,* the author's "generalizations are so extravagant and his tone so self-righteous and bombastic that he undermines his case. He is his own worst enemy." With regard to the challenges facing American education, Sowell "offers little constructive counsel on how to deal with them," according to Brademas. Peter Schrag, writing in *Nation,* called this same book "a near-perfect inventory of what the far right is saying about our schools and colleges, some of it true enough but much of it exaggerated."

Many others, however, found this same work coherent and exact. Michael Schwartz in the *Wall Street Journal* found that *Inside American Education* "demonstrates an impressive range of knowledge and acuity of observation." Chester E. Finn Jr. in the *National Review* called it a "splendid new book." Some of these contradictions in interpretation of the book's effectiveness come from an inherent difference between conservatives and liberals on what the role of public education should, in fact, be. Conservatives such as Sowell believe, according to *New Republic* contributor Alan Wolfe, that "the education of children is a secondary goal: serving some larger political purpose comes first." Wolfe continued, "When the schools take on so many functions other than the transmission of knowledge they inevitably become battlegrounds in ideological wars, and all who fight in these wars have a panacea, not a well-thought-out solution to the educational crisis in America."

In *Preferential Policies: An International Perspective,* Sowell argues against equal opportunity hiring and admissions policies, which mandate that employers and school officials judge minority applicants by different, more relaxed, criteria than they use to judge other applicants. Sowell believes such policies result in less-qualified candidates gaining preferential treatment over better-qualified candidates and eventually lower the standards by which all individuals are measured. Citing examples from such countries as Sri Lanka, Nigeria, and India, as well as the United States, he contends that preferential policies can be found around the globe.

Adolph L. Reed Jr., reviewing *Preferential Policies* in the *Washington Post Book World,* found Sowell's thesis unconvincing, stating that "the relation between his examples and his underlying argument—that preferential policies undermine their own objectives and cause more problems then they resolve—is tortured and unconvincing." Andrew Hacker disagreed in the *New York Times Book Review,* noting that Sowell does make an important point about the effects of these policies, namely that "those who lose out [to preferential policies] are generally lower-middle-class candidates, who adhered to the rules and find themselves displaced by others deemed entitled to exemptions." "Whether in fire departments or on campuses," Hacker added, "groups at the end of the queue are being played off against one another—hardly the best way to promote racial amity."

In fact, Nathan Glazer wrote in *New Republic,* Sowell is convinced "that hardly anything government will do can help blacks and other minorities with high levels of poverty and low levels of educational and economic achievement, and that almost anything government will do will only make matters worse." In a *Choice* review of 1985's *Civil Rights,* R. J. Steamer noted that "Sowell's revolutionary view—that government programs such as affirmative action, forced busing, and food stamps will not bring the disadvantaged black minority into the economic and social mainstream and might better be abandoned—will anger many." One such angered critic was Gelman, who claimed that Sowell "seems to fault blacks for resting on their grievances instead of climbing aboard the success wagon." Sowell states the view that government programs and those who advocate them are part of a self-destructive mindset. The black civil rights establishment, he contends, "represents a thin layer of privileged blacks who have risen socially by echoing liberal ideology, with its view of blacks in general as helpless victims who depend on political favors for whatever gains they can make," according to Sobran.

The impasse between Sowell and many other African American commentators—as well as the differences between the political left and right—moved the economist to examine the underlying assumptions creating this dichotomy. In 1987's *A Conflict of Visions: Ideological Origins of Political Struggle* he describes "two divergent views of man and society that he convincingly contends underlie many of the political, economic and social clashes of the last two centuries and remain very much with us today," according to *New York Times* contributor Walter Goodman. Sowell posits the unconstrained and the constrained views of man. "The unconstrained see human beings as perfectible," Otto

Friedrich wrote in *Time,* "the constrained as forever flawed." Sowell writes in the book that "the constrained vision is a tragic vision of the human condition. The unconstrained vision is a moral vision of human intentions."

Daniel Seligman wrote in *Fortune* that these two visions are "the mind-sets that originally made [intellectuals] gravitate to some ideas instead of others." Those with an unconstrained view of man, for example, tend to believe that social problems can be ultimately solved, and that man will usually act rationally. Such beliefs lead to social engineering efforts to correct perceived societal ills. Those with a constrained view of man see him as imperfect and human nature as unchanging. They often call for a limited government, a strong defense, and strict criminal penalties.

Sowell admits that not all people hold to one or the other vision consistently; for example, ideologies like as Marxism and fascism are compounds of both constrained and unconstrained visions. Yet critics saw much of value in Sowell's thinking. "Right or wrong in his main thesis," Sobran stated, "he is full of stunning insights." "The split between the constrained and the unconstrained," Barnes noted, "works as a framework for understanding social theories and politics." Goodman found that *A Conflict of Visions* "does lay out styles of thinking that we can readily recognize today in the divisions between left and right." And Michael Harrington, who in his *Washington Post Book World* review rejected "the basic assumptions and the very intellectual framework" of Sowell's book, nonetheless concluded that "its insights and *apercus* reveal a serious mind honestly and fairly . . . trying to grapple with those visionary premises on which our supposedly objective data are so often based and ordered."

Sowell further expands upon the idea of the liberal vision in *The Vision of the Anointed.* The "anointed," Sowell here argues, are those who view the world as a place where "criminals can be 'rehabilitated', irresponsible mothers taught 'parenting skills,' and where all sorts of other social problems can be 'solved'." Sowell contrasts this liberal vision with the view of conservatives "that liberal schemes to eradicate these evils a) never work, and b) inevitably impose huge social costs of their own," noted Robert P. George in his *National Review* article. Sowell maintains that the anointed have, in fact, caused damage to the social fabric of America, in particular because their "*prevailing* vision" is taken as true without empirical evidence to prove it so.

Richard Epstein, writing in the *New York Times Book Review,* pointed out that *The Vision of the Anointed* was published in 1995, prior to political shifts occurring during the Clinton presidency that appeared to draw power away from the liberals. "Sowell . . . surely has given voice to many of [the new American political majority's] longstanding frustration," wrote Epstein. "It is too bad that he has overstated his case and failed to suppress his obvious enmity toward his intellectual and political targets. Mr. Sowell has written an important and incisive book, even with its flaws. But with a bit more moderation at the margin, he could have written a better one still."

In *Conquests and Cultures: Military Expansion and the Making of Civilization,* Sowell concludes a trilogy that began with *Race and Culture: A World View* and continued in *Migrations and Cultures: A World View.* As in the earlier volumes, *Conquests and Cultures* makes the case that, throughout history, certain nations have successfully conquered others by virtue of the excellence of their cultures, rather than merely through oppression or theft of foreign ideas or technology. Sowell uses examples that range from ancient China and Islam to nineteenth-century England and France, as well as the Plains Indians of North America. *National Review* contributor John Keegan admitted that "This is a thesis with which it is difficult to disagree," but added that Sowell's thesis nonetheless offers no illumination on why England surpassed France economically in the nineteenth century, when material factors would seem to have made them contenders and, indeed, when France was the undisputed cultural, if not economic, capital of the world. "It is at this point that one begins to doubt whether Thomas Sowell's painstaking geographical and economic analysis really provides answers to the questions he raises," Keegan concluded. *Booklist* reviewer Philip Herbst similarly found that the path of Sowell's argument occasionally took unorthodox turns in order to support one or another of his conservative ideals. "Thoughtful history, if you don't mind it slanted," was this critic's conclusion. For others, however, Sowell's insights into the mysterious give-and-take relationship between conquered and conqueror nations, in which both sides gain and lose in the exchange, was enlightening. For *Library Journal* contributor Norman Malwitz, the "readable style and impressive scope [of *Conquests and Conquerors*] make it suitable for all libraries."

In 1999's *The Quest for Cosmic Justice* Sowell attacks what he considers to be one of the most dangerous liberal convictions: the idea that the causes of inequality must be addressed in pursuit of justice, a notion the author dubs "cosmic justice." Against this ideal Sowell posits the rectitude of "traditional justice," the idea that laws should be clearly written and applied equally to all citizens. The author bolsters his complaints against the liberal pursuit of "cosmic justice" with cautionaries about the costs of pursuing it, even for the intended beneficiaries. He cites as an example the implementation of bilingual education, which he argues has irrevocably damaged a generation of Latino students in the United States. Underlying his argument is the conservative's mistrust of big government, and reviewers have noted that Sowell's most extreme statements in *The Quest for Cosmic Justice* concern the dire consequences of continuing to pursue this ideal at the expense of traditional justice. "Sowell is undoubtedly correct that the utopian agenda of a major strand of contemporary liberalism has been misguided and antidemocratic, and has had and continues to have deleterious consequences for American society across the board," opined Arch Puddington in *Commentary.* However, Puddington continued, the economist himself seems to doubt the American people and the ability of democracy itself to right the wrongs committed by the liberals. "If conservatives have learned anything from recent history," the critic continued, "it is that success requires confidence in the American people and in the functioning of American democracy, a lesson that applies to the war of ideas no less than to electoral politics." For a *Kirkus* reviewer Sowell's dubious accomplishment in *The Quest for Cosmic Justice* is the vanquishing of "a cosmic straw man . . . in the fight against dangerous ideals such as social justice and equality." On the other hand, Jack Forman, a reviewer for *Library Journal,* declared: "As Sowell does so well in his other books . . . he presents his case in clear, convincing, and accessible language."

In 2000 Sowell published his autobiography, *A Personal Odyssey,* in which he recounts incidents from his own life that exemplify how the conservative values of hard work and self-determination brought him success. A reviewer for *Publishers Weekly* noted that although Sowell is "known for his attention to detail and the nuance of his theoretical writings," his memoir does not always display these same attributes, for he skips over large periods in his life, "offering only a controlled, muted look at the author's inner world." A contributor to *Kirkus Reviews* similarly noted that "this is not a personal memoir, but rather an account of a philosophical and professional evolution shaped by a lifetime of challenging experiences." For James W. Michaels of *Forbes, A Personal Odyssey* offers an opportunity to get to know "this splendid, witty character. . . . It's a warm memoir, tinged with humor and considerable indignation. Do yourself a favor: Read it."

During his career as a leading African American economist, Sowell "has spoken out often, with considerable force and eloquence, against many of the assumptions about black life in the United States that are widely held by the black leadership and its white allies," Jonathan Yardley reported in the *Washington Post Book World.* Over his career, Sowell's arguments increasingly attracted converts in the black community. As Glazer noted, "One has the impression that increasingly he is heeded, that this unbending analyst is having a greater influence on the discussion of matters of race and ethnicity than any other writer of the past ten years." *Commentary* contributor Arch Puddington remarked of Sowell's effect on U.S. conservatism: "After all, it is thanks in no small measure to Thomas Sowell's carefully reasoned and impassioned arguments over the years that we have made as much progress as we have." Harrington, a socialist who admits he is "utterly at odds" with Sowell's political beliefs, nevertheless dubbed him "one of the few conservative thinkers in America today who is interesting as a theorist."

BIOGRAPHICAL/CRITICAL SOURCES:

BOOKS

Sowell, Thomas, *Civil Rights: Rhetoric or Reality?* Morrow (New York, NY), 1985.

Sowell, Thomas, *A Conflict of Visions: Ideological Origins of Political Struggles,* Morrow (New York, NY), 1987.

Sowell, Thomas, *A Personal Odyssey,* Free Press (New York, NY), 2000.

PERIODICALS

American Political Science Review, June, 1991.

American Spectator, July 1984; November, 1990; October, 1995, p. 75; February, 2000, Joseph Shattan, "Tocquevillian Sowell," p. 71.

Annals of the American Academy of Political and Social Science, July, 2000, Jean W. Sedlar, review of *Conquests and Cultures,* p. 212.

Booklist, August, 1997, review of *Late-talking Children,* p. 1863; April 15, 1998, Philip Herbst, review of *Conquests and Cultures,* p. 1401; September 1, 1999, Ray Olson, review of *The Quest for Cosmic Justice,* p. 46.

Business Library Review, no. 4, 1997, review of *The Vision of the Anointed,* p. 335.

Change, January, 1990.

Choice, September, 1984; November, 1990; January, 1999, review of *Conquests and Cultures,* p. 944.

Commentary, December, 1983; September, 1996, p. 78; January, 2000, Arch Puddington, review of *The Quest for Cosmic Justice,* p. 77.
Commonweal, January 13, 1995, p. 22.
Economic Geography, October, 1997, review of *Migrations and Cultures,* p. 445.
Forbes, October 2, 2000, James W. Michaels, "Practicing What He Preaches," p. 216.
Foreign Affairs, Vol. 70, no. 3, 1991; July-August, 1998, Francis Fukuyama, review of *Conquests and Cultures,* p. 122.
Fortune, March 16, 1987; February 13, 1989.
Journal of Social History, fall, 1999, review of *Migrations and Cultures,* p. 209.
Kirkus Reviews, June 1, 1997, review of *Late-talking Children,* p. 862; April 1, 1998, review of *Conquests and Culture,* p. 482; September 1, 1999, review of *The Quest for Cosmic Justice,* p. 1397.
Library Journal, March 1, 1996, p. 91; May 1, 1998, Norman Malwitz, review of *Conquests and Cultures,* p. 116; October 15, 1999, Jack Forman, review of *The Quest for Cosmic Justice,* p. 88.
Los Angeles Times, March 22, 1985.
Los Angeles Times Book Review, September 6, 1981; January 8, 1984.
Nation, May 10, 1993, p. 638.
National Review, October 16, 1981; February 13, 1987; June 25, 1990; February 15, 1993, p. 49; November 7, 1994, p. 69; October 23, 1995, p. 52; November 25, 1996, p. 65; June 2, 1998, John Keegan, review of *Conquests and Cultures,* p. 50; October 25, 1999, Jay Nordlinger, "Sowell's Plain Truths," p. 62.
New Republic, November 21, 1983; June 11, 1984; February 8, 1993, p. 25; November 16, 1998, review of *Conquests and Cultures,* p. 36.
Newsweek, August 24, 1981.
New York Review of Books, October 12, 1989; January 12, 1995, p. 29.
New York Times, January 24, 1987.
New York Times Book Review, October 16, 1983; January 25, 1987; July 1, 1990; March 28, 1993, p. 11; November 27, 1994, p. 28; July 30, 1995, p. 6; June 2, 1996, p. 9; January 16, 2000, Allen D. Boyer, review of *The Quest for Cosmic Justice,* p. 20.
Publishers Weekly, April 27, 1990; February 19, 1996, p. 195; July 21, 1997, review of *Late-talking Children,* p. 198; April 6, 1998, review of *Conquests and Cultures,* p. 68; September 20, 1999, review of *The Quest for Cosmic Justice,* p. 61; August 14, 2000, review of *A Personal Odyssey,* p. 335.
Reason, December, 1998, review of *Conquests and Cultures,* p. 70.
Research and Reference Book News, November, 1998, review of *Conquests and Cultures,* p. 22.
Society, May, 1997, review of *The Vision of the Anointed,* p. 84; September, 1997, review of *Migrations and Cultures,* p. 92.
Time, March 16, 1987.
Times Literary Supplement, September 22, 1995, p. 10.
Voice Quarterly Review, summer, 1998, review of *Migrations and Cultures,* p. 564.
Wall Street Journal, September 25, 1989; February 12, 1993; July 22, 1994; July 28, 1995, p. A9; October 20, 1000, Jason L. Riley, review of *A Personal Odyssey,* p. W10; August 25, 1997, review of *Late-talking Children,* p. A16; May 19, 1998, John Lehman, review of *Conquests and Cultures,* p. A20; October 6, 1999, Donald J. Silver, review of *The Quest for Cosmic Justice,* p. A20.
Washington Monthly, June, 1990.
Washington Post Book World, April 29, 1984; January 4, 1987; September 9, 1990; April 7, 1996, p. 4; August 17, 1997, review of *Late-talking Children,* p. 9; September 5, 1999, review of *The Quest for Cosmic Justice,* p. 5; October 10, 1999, review of *The Quest for Cosmic Justice,* p. 6.
Wilson Quarterly, Vol. 14, no. 3, 1990.

OTHER

Salon, http://www.salon.com/ (November 10, 1999), Ray Sawhill, "Black and Right."
Thomas Sowell Home Page, http://www.tsowell.com/ (May 19, 2001).*

* * *

STABENOW, Dana 1952-

PERSONAL: Born March 27, 1952, in Anchorage, AK; father, a pilot; mother, an aviation service bookkeeper and ground crew assistant. *Education:* University of Alaska, B.A., 1973, M.F.A., 1985.

ADDRESSES: *Agent*—Richard Henshaw Group, 132 West 22nd St., New York, NY 10023.

CAREER: Science fiction and mystery writer. Cook Inlet Aviation, Seldovia, AK, worked as assistant; Whitney-Fidalgo Seafoods, Anchorage, AK, worked as egg grader, bookkeeper, and expediter; also worked for Alyeska Pipeline, Galbraith Lake, AK; and for British Petroleum, Prudhoe Bay, AK.

AWARDS, HONORS: Edgar Allan Poe Award, Mystery Writers of America, 1992, for *A Cold Day for Murder.*

WRITINGS:

NOVELS; "STAR SVENSDOTTER" SERIES

Second Star, Berkley Publishing/Ace Books (New York, NY), 1991.
A Handful of Stars, Ace Books (New York, NY), 1991.
Red Planet Run, Berkley Publishing/Ace Books (New York, NY), 1995.

NOVELS; "KATE SHUGAK" SERIES

A Cold Day for Murder, Berkley Publishing (New York, NY), 1992.
Dead in the Water, Berkley Publishing (New York, NY), 1993.
A Fatal Thaw, Berkley Publishing (New York, NY), 1993.
A Cold-Blooded Business, Berkley Publishing (New York, NY), 1994.
Play with Fire, Berkley Publishing (New York, NY), 1995.
Blood Will Tell, Putnam (New York, NY), 1996.
Breakup, Putnam (New York, NY), 1997.
Killing Grounds: A Kate Shugak Mystery, Putnam (New York, NY), 1998.
Hunter's Moon: A Kate Shugak Mystery, Putnam (New York, NY), 1999.
Midnight Come Again, St. Martin's Minotaur (New York, NY), 2000.
The Singing of the Dead: A Kate Shugak Novel, St. Martin's Minotaur (New York, NY), 2001.

NOVELS; "LIAM CAMPBELL/WYANET CHOUINARD" SERIES

Fire and Ice: A Liam Campbell Mystery, Dutton (New York, NY), 1998.
So Sure of Death: A Liam Campbell Mystery, Dutton (New York, NY), 1999.
Nothing Gold Can Stay: A Liam Campbell Mystery, Dutton (New York, NY), 2000.

SIDELIGHTS: Dana Stabenow is the author of two fiction series that feature courageous, independent women: a mystery series that follows the exploits of Alaskan detective Kate Shugak and a science fiction series about space pioneer Star Svensdotter. The Svensdotter stories appeared first, in 1991, but books about Shugak have surpassed them in number. Both series are generally characterized by the lavish use of detail and fast-spinning plots. A new mystery series featuring protagonists Liam Campbell, an Alaska state trooper, and his romantic partner, bush pilot Wyanet Chouinard, debuted in 1998.

Second Star was Stabenow's first novel, introducing readers to Svensdotter, who is in charge of building a space station in the face of such obstacles as terrorists, an attempted military takeover, and aliens. Writing for *Booklist,* Roland Green praised the author's "almost cinematic vividness" in describing the book's setting and recommended the book as "entirely respectable." *Second Star*'s sequel, *A Handful of Stars,* finds Star trying to colonize an asteroid belt. *Voice of Youth Advocates* reviewer Vicky Burckholder found this book less satisfying than the first, reading "more like a diary than a novel." *Red Planet Run,* the next book in the series, is set in part on Mars, where Star is studying a new weapon. Reviewers Green and Burckholder expressed contradictory opinions on this story; the former wrote in *Booklist* that "the action is brisk" while Burckholder called the book "tame," with "very little action."

Stabenow's first Kate Shugak mystery was the Edgar Award-winner, *A Cold Day for Murder.* Shugak, a thirty-something Aleut, has previously worked for the Anchorage district attorney and now lives in the Alaskan wilderness. When two people go missing in a multi-million-acre (fictitious) national park, her investigative prowess, survival skills, and knowledge of the landscape are pressed into service. This story line allowed Stabenow to examine Aleutian culture and the pressure that Native Americans feel to assimilate into white society. The author was herself born in Alaska and raised on a fishing boat in the Gulf of Alaska, and critics found her familiarity with the beauty of the Alaskan wilderness evident in her descriptive passages. Subsequent books in the series use related settings and topics, including crab fishing, the oil fields, mushroom picking, and logging. Such elements often reflect the author's experiences living and working in Alaska, including a series of jobs held before she became a full-time writer.

With a total of eight Kate Shugak mysteries published by 1998, Stabenow has offered readers an alternative to the ubiquitous urban crime novel. Claire Rosser of *Kliatt* reviewed the second book in the series, *A Fatal Thaw,* noting, "the greatest appeal of these mysteries is the setting. . . . [and] the exotic way of life there."

Other elements of the series also drew praise from Emily Melton in a *Booklist* review of the author's hardcover debut, *A Cold-Blooded Business.* According to Melton, "Shugak is an uncommonly charismatic heroine . . . and Stabenow is a splendid writer who knows how to hook her readers with an exciting blend of thrills, danger, humor, pathos, fact, and fable."

According to reviewers, Stabenow has managed to keep her characters and plots fresh throughout an extended series. In *Killing Grounds,* the author was given credit for seamlessly interweaving information about Native Alaskan lifestyles with a compelling murder mystery set in an impressively detailed Alaska fishing village. Here, an abusive salmon fisher is brutally murdered and Kate's own aunts are among the numerous suspects. Among the many enjoyable aspects of the book, according to *Booklist* reviewer John Rowen, are "the passages on women hunters and on fishing," which "compare favorably" to nonfiction efforts by the likes of Mary Stange and Holly Morris. As in her earlier mysteries, using "powerful prose, Stabenow evokes Alaska's rugged physical splendors and the toll taken on the humans who live there," a reviewer remarked in *Publishers Weekly.* Indeed, a *Kirkus Reviews* critic reported that, in *Killing Grounds,* "crime and punishment take a backseat" to "a leisurely guided tour of still another unexpected corner of the Yukon State."

Killing Grounds was followed by *Hunter's Moon,* in which Kate and her lover, Jack Morgan, agree to act as guides for a friend who has a group of German computer company executives coming out for a big-game hunt. Kate's experience in sleuthing comes in handy, however, when the Germans begin showing up dead. A reviewer for *Publishers Weekly* dubbed this installment "gripping and adrenaline-charged, punctuated with extreme violence . . . all delivered with Stabenow's razor-sharp suspense and gritty prose." The stunning climax of this novel, in which Kate's lover is killed and she herself barely escapes with her life, sets the stage for Stabenow's next Kate Shugat mystery, *Midnight Come Again,* in which a grieving Kate is living under an assumed name in a fishing village in western Alaska. There she is sought out by friend and state trooper, Chopper Jim Chopin, to help out on a case that already includes several FBI agents in what appears to be an international banking scandal. *Publishers Weekly* called this an unevenly paced book that begins slowly, with the grieving Kate, and ends "in a heart-stopping climax aboard a hijacked airplane."

The background for *The Singing of the Dead* is both political and historical. A hard-boiled election campaign results in murder that may be connected to a family scandal which originated during the Alaskan gold rush a century earlier. The story in the foreground is about Kate's murder investigation, surrounded by the relentless thrust and parry of regional politics, and Kate's evolving life as she recovers from the death of her lover in *Midnight Come Again* and collaborates once more with state police officer Jim Chopin. As the murder investigation deepens, Kate is drawn toward the backgrounds of the political candidates, where she encounters the colorful history of a gold rush entertainer known as the "Dawson Darling." Alternating smoothly between the contemporary political setting and the primitive wilderness of miners and their companions, Stabenow treats her readers to what a *Publishers Weekly* contributor called a "fine novel," featuring complex characters amidst the scenic splendor for which Stabenow's work is routinely praised, and a mystery of "even greater depth than usual." The reviewer particularly noted the vivid image that Stabenow presents of the hard lives that women like Angel Beecham, the Dawson Darling, had to face in a land where alternatives were few and far between. *The Singing of the Dead* is marketed as "a Kate Shugak novel," unlike the previous "Kate Shugak mystery" titles; *Publishers Weekly* suggested that the appeal of this novel, "one of Stabenow's best," could expand beyond the mystery genre and the regional niche that have defined her writings to date.

With *Fire and Ice,* Stabenow introduced a new protagonist: Liam Campbell, a reformed drunkard and Alaskan state trooper reeling from aftershocks of a car accident that killed his son and left his wife in a coma. At the start of *Fire and Ice,* Campbell has been bumped from duty in Anchorage to the small town of Newenham, where things quickly heat up when a bush pilot is killed by his own propeller, someone shoots up a jukebox playing "Margaritaville," and Campbell's first true love, Wy Chouinard, turns up. Reviewers noted that, as in the Kate Shugak books, this series promises a richly detailed backdrop of Alaskan landscapes and lifestyles, and Stabenow's experienced hand at writing solid mysteries is shown to advantage. "Happily, this much mayhem has rarely been in surer literary hands," commented a reviewer for *Publishers Weekly. Booklist* reviewer John Rowen enumerated the assets of this first installment: "The mystery is hard to solve, the plot fast moving and well organized, the Arctic landscape stunning, and the characters vivid and sympathetic."

Rowen praised the second Campbell novel, *So Sure of Death,* even more highly than the first, calling it "among the best of the year." In this mystery, Liam is ferried about by Wy Chouinard in her air taxi while he pursues two murderers, the first having killed an entire family and two deckhands aboard a fishing boat, and the second having stabbed an archaeologist's assistant on a nearby dig using a native knife. "Nonstop incident and matchless local color keep you from noticing that you don't get to spend enough time with them to make the real perps as vivid as the Alaska scenery," noted a reviewer for *Kirkus Reviews.* Rowen too found that the pleasures of *So Sure of Death* are not the ones usually found in a mystery. "Best of all," Rowen wrote in *Booklist,* "are the fully realized, multidimensional characters." The reviewer concluded, "Clearly, Stabenow's is a star on the rise."

In the third installment of the series, *Nothing Gold Can Stay,* Stabenow's protagonist investigates two seemingly unrelated killings, one of the local postmistress and the other of a gold prospector. The solution of the mystery becomes crucial in ensuring the safety of Wy's adopted son. Although a critic in *Publishers Weekly* complained that in this mystery, "the sense of place overwhelms everything else," Rowen compared Stabenow's writings favorably to those of other women writing about the experience of women in the modern wilderness, women such as Margaret Coel and Sue Henry: "Stabenow has a gift for describing native cultures and the nature of contemporary life in the wilderness."

BIOGRAPHICAL/CRITICAL SOURCES:

PERIODICALS

Alaska, September, 1996, p. 70; October, 1998, Jill Shepard, "Growing up Alaskan," p. 18.

Analog, December, 1991, p. 159.

Armchair Detective, fall, 1992, p. 433; summer, 1994, p. 373; fall, 1995, p. 456; fall, 1996, p. 495; summer, 1997, review of *Blood Will Tell,* p. 343, review of *Breakup,* p. 345.

Booklist, June 1, 1991, p. 1861; March 1, 1994, pp. 1183, 1188; January 1, 1995, pp. 1312, 1317; March 15, 1995, pp. 1312, 1317; April 15, 1996, pp. 1424, 1428; May 15, 1997, p. 1567; February 15, 1998, John Rowen, review of *Killing Grounds,* p. 989; September 1, 1998, John Rowen, review of *Fire and Ice,* p. 72; September 1, 1999, John Rowen, review of *So Sure of Death,* p. 74; September 1, 2000, John Rowen, review of *Nothing Gold Can Stay,* p. 70.

Kirkus Reviews, January 1, 1994, p. 22; February 15, 1995, p. 186; April 1, 1996, p. 492; February 1, 1998, review of *Killing Grounds,* p. 158; April 1, 1999, review of *Hunter's Moon,* p. 492; September 1, 1999, review of *So Sure of Death,* p. 1350.

Kliatt, September, 1992, p. 16; March, 1993, p. 10; September, 1993, p. 14; May, 1995, p. 11; September, 1999, review of *A Cold Day for Murder,* p. 52.

Library Journal, March 1, 1994, p. 123; February 1, 1995, p. 103; September 1, 1995, p. 236; May 1, 1996, p. 137; June 1, 1997, review of *Breakup,* p. 156; March 1, 1998, Rex E. Klett, review of *Killing Grounds,* p. 131; September 1, 1998, Rex E. Klett, review of *Fire and Ice,* p. 219; April 1, 1999, Rex E. Klett, review of *Hunter's Moon,* p. 133.

Locus, June, 1991, p. 27; July, 1991, p. 48; November, 1991, p. 27; January, 1992, p. 60; February, 1995, p. 58.

New York Times Book Review, April 3, 1994, p. 22; May 23, 1999, Marilyn Stasio, review of *Hunter's Moon,* p. 33.

Publishers Weekly, May 18, 1992, p. 64; June 14, 1993, p. 64; January 17, 1994, p. 410; February 6, 1995, p. 79; April 1, 1996, p. 59; April 21, 1997, p. 64; January 19, 1998, review of *Killing Grounds,* p. 374; August 3, 1998, review of *Fire and Ice,* p. 77; April 19, 1999, review of *Hunter's Moon,* p. 64; October 4, 1999, review of *So Sure of Death,* p. 68; April 10, 2000, review of *Midnight Come Again,* p. 78; September 4, 2000, review of *Nothing Gold Can Stay,* p. 89; April 2, 2001, review of *The Singing of the Dead,* p. 42.

School Library Journal, November, 1992, p. 147; September, 1994, p. 256; June, 2000, Pam Spencer, review of *So Sure of Death,* p. 174.

Science Fiction Chronicles, January, 1995, p. 37.

Voice of Youth Advocates, August, 1991, p. 182; February, 1992, p. 387; April, 1992, p. 11; June, 1995, p. 110; December, 1997, review of *A Cold Day for Murder,* p. 295.

Washington Post Book World, July 26, 1992, p. 1; July 20, 1997, review of *Breakup,* p. 10.

Wilson Library Bulletin, November, 1993, p. 86; June, 1995, p. 98.

OTHER

Dana Stabenow Web site, http://www.stabenow.com/ (May 16, 2001).*

* * *

STEBBINS, Theodore E(llis), Jr. 1938-

PERSONAL: Born August 11, 1938, in New York, NY. *Education:* Yale University, B.A. (political science), 1960; Harvard University, J.D. (with honors), 1964, M.A. (art history), 1966, Ph.D., 1971.

ADDRESSES: Home—57 Hedge Rd., Brookline, MA 02146. *Office*—Fogg Art Museum, 32 Quincy St., Cambridge, MA 02138.

CAREER: Smith College, Northampton, MA, instructor in art history, 1967-68; Yale University, New Haven, CT, lecturer, 1968-71, assistant professor, 1971-75, associate professor of art history and American studies, 1975-77, associate curator of Garvan Collections of American Art, 1968-77, curator of American painting and sculpture, 1971-77, acting director of art gallery, 1975; Museum of Fine Arts, Boston, MA, curator of American painting, beginning 1977, John Moors Cabot Curator of American Paintings, 1981-99, chair of Art of the Americas department, 1999; Fogg Art Museum, Harvard University, Cambridge, MA, consultative curator of American art, 2000—. Visiting professor at Boston University, 1978; lecturer at museums, galleries, and scholarly meetings. Member of board of trustees of Wyeth Endowment for the American Arts and American Federation of the Arts.

MEMBER: Friends of American Art at Yale (chairperson).

WRITINGS:

(Editor and contributor) *Martin Johnson Heade,* Museum of Fine Arts (Boston, MA), 1969.

The Life and Works of Martin Johnson Heade (monograph and catalog), Yale University Press (New Haven, CT), 1975, expanded edition, with Janet L. Comey and Karen E. Quinn, published as *The Life and Works of Martin Johnson Heade: A Critical Analysis and Catalogue Raisonne,* 2000.

(With John Caldwell and Carol Troyen) *American Master Drawings and Watercolors: A History of Works on Paper from Colonial Times to the Present,* Harper (New York, NY), 1976.

(Author of introduction) *Dennis Miller Bunker Rediscovered,* New Britain Museum of American Art (New Britain, CT), 1978.

Close Observation: Selected Oil Sketches by Frederic Edwin Church, Museum of Fine Arts (Boston, MA), 1978.

(With William H. Gerdts) *"A Man of Genius": The Art of Washington Allston (1779-1843),* Museum of Fine Arts (Boston, MA), 1979.

(With Galina Gorokhoff) *A Checklist of American Paintings at Yale University,* Yale University Art Gallery (New Haven, CT), 1982.

(With Carol Troyen) *The Lane Collection: Twentieth-Century Paintings in the American Tradition,* Museum of Fine Arts (Boston, MA), 1983.

(With Troyen and Trevor J. Fairbrother) *A New World: Masterpieces of American Painting, 1760-1910,* essays by Pierre Rosenberg and H. Barbara Weinberg, Museum of Fine Arts (Boston, MA), 1983.

(With Judith Hoos Fox) *Boston Collects: Contemporary Painting and Sculpture,* Museum of Fine Arts (Boston, MA), 1986.

(With Norman Keyes Jr.) *Charles Sheeler: The Photographs,* Little, Brown (Boston, MA), 1987.

Weston's Westons: Portraits and Nudes, Museum of Fine Arts (Boston, MA), 1989.

(With Karen E. Quinn) *Ansel Adams: The Early Years,* Museum of Fine Arts (Boston, MA), 1991.

(With William H. Gerdts) *Lure of Italy: American Artists and the Italian Experience, 1760-1914,* Museum of Fine Arts (Boston, MA), 1992.

(With Joel Sternfeld and Richard Brilliant) *Campagna Romana: The Countryside of Ancient Rome,* Knopf (New York, NY), 1992.

(Editor with Annette Blaugrund) *John James Audubon: Watercolors for "The Birds of America,"* Villard (New York, NY), 1993.

(With Karen E. Quinn) *Weston's Westons: California and the West,* Museum of Fine Arts/Little, Brown (Boston, MA), 1994.

(With others) *John Singleton Copley in America,* Metropolitan Museum of Art (New York, NY), 1995.

(With Janet L. Comey) *Martin Johnson Heade* (exhibition catalog), Yale University Press (New Haven, CT), 1999.

(With Karen E. Quinn and Leslie Furth) *Edward Weston: Photography and Modernism,* Museum of Fine Arts/Bulfinch Press (Boston, MA), 1999.

Masterpiece Paintings from the Museum of Fine Arts, photographs by Peter C. Sutton, Abrams (New York, NY), 2000.

Also author of *William Rimmer: A Yankee Michelangelo,* 1986. Author of exhibition catalogs. Contributor to *Art Works: Law, Policy, Practice,* edited by Stephen Weil and Franklin Feldman, 1974, and *The Hudson River School: Nineteenth-Century American Landscapes in the Wadsworth Atheneum,* Wadsworth Atheneum (Hartford, CT), 1976. Contributor to *Britannica Encyclopedia of American Art;* contributor of articles and reviews to art and art history journals. Member of editorial board, *American Art Journal.*

WORK IN PROGRESS: A book on American landscape painting.

SIDELIGHTS: During his twenty-two-year tenure at Boston's Museum of Fine Arts, Theodore Ellis Stebbins Jr. organized many major exhibitions and oversaw important acquisitions in his position as the museum's curator of American art. Among Stebbins' most important scholarly writings are two books written on the nineteenth-century American landscape artist Martin Johnson Heade. As Kathryn Wekselman noted in *Library Journal,* Heade "has gained recognition as a major contributor to American representational art—owing in part to Stebbins's efforts to reawaken interest" in the artist. In late 2000 Stebbins left the Museum of Fine Arts and accepted a position at Harvard University's Fogg Art Museum, where he serves as consultative curator of the museum's extensive collection of American Art.

Stebbins first wrote about Heade in his 1975 book, *The Life and Works of Martin Johnson Heade.* In 2000, Stebbins updated the book with the assistance of Janet L. Comey and Karen E. Quinn, adding information from newly available archives of Heade's letters and diaries. The resulting work contains a catalogue of some six hundred of Heade's paintings, as well as an analysis of the artist's life and career. The book, according to Jack Perry Brown in *Library Journal,* is "a substantial rewriting and massive expansion" of the earlier text that "brings Heade to life." In the 1999 book *Martin Johnson Heade,* co-written with Comey, Stebbins "argues convincingly that Heade's vision was Darwinian, and that his work's magnetism resides in its dynamic depiction of nature's conflicts, interconnectedness, and perpetual change," according to Donna Seaman in *Booklist.*

BIOGRAPHICAL/CRITICAL SOURCES:

PERIODICALS

Booklist, December 15, 1999, Donna Seaman, review of *Martin Johnson Heade,* p. 751.

Choice, February, 1993, review of *The Lure of Italy,* p. 954.

Entertainment Weekly, December 10, 1993, Rebecca Ascher-Walsh, review of *John James Audubon,* p. 69.

Library Journal, January, 1986, Raymond L. Wilson, review of *William Rimmer,* p. 75; June 15, 1987, Lynell A. Morr, review of *Masterpiece Paintings from the Museum of Fine Arts,* p. 65; December, 1999, Kathryn Wekselman, review of *Martin Johnson Heade,* p. 127; March 1, 2000, Jack Perry Brown, review of *The Life and Works of Martin Johnson Heade,* p. 89.

New York Times Book Review, December 12, 1993, Alan Fern, review of *John James Audubon.*

Publishers Weekly, September 18, 1995, review of *John Singleton Copley in America,* p. 120.

Sculpture Review, Volume 42, number 4, 1993, review of *The Lure of Italy,* p. 30.

Wall Street Journal, December 8, 1987, Jack Flam, review of *Charles Sheeler,* p. 34.*

* * *

STEELE, James B(ruce, Jr.) 1943-

PERSONAL: Born January 3, 1943, in Hutchinson, KS; son of James Bruce and Mary (Peoples) Steele; married Nancy Saunders, June 25, 1966; children: Allison. *Education:* University of Missouri at Kansas City, B.A. (journalism), 1967.

ADDRESSES: Office—c/o Time, Inc., Time & Life Building, Rockefeller Center, New York, NY 10020-1393.

CAREER: Kansas City Times, Kansas City, MO, copy boy, 1962, reporter, 1962-67; Laborers' International Union of North America, Washington, DC, director of information, 1968-70; *Philadelphia Inquirer,* Philadelphia, PA, investigative reporter, 1970-96; Time, Inc., New York City, editor-at-large, 1997—. Has appeared on numerous television talk shows, including *Good Morning America, Today Show,* and *Larry King Live.*

AWARDS, HONORS: (All with Donald L. Barlett) American Political Science Association award for distinguished reporting of public affairs, 1971, for a series on abandoned housing; George Polk Memorial awards for metropolitan reporting, Long Island University, 1971, 1973, 1991, 1999, 2000, 2001; Sigma Delta Chi Distinguished Service in Journalism award, 1971, for newspaper series on the Federal Housing Authority; Heywood Broun Award for public interest reporting, and Sidney Hillman Foundation Award, both 1973, both for newspaper series "Crime and Injustice"; American Bar Association Gavel Award, John Hancock Award for business reporting, and Business Journalism award from the University of Missouri at Columbia, all 1973, all for newspaper series "Oil: The Created Crisis"; Pulitzer prizes for national reporting, 1975, for newspaper series "Auditing the IRS," and 1989, for work on the Tax Reform Act of 1986; Honor Award for Distinguished Service in Journalism, University of Missouri, 1983; George Orwell Award for Distinguished Contributions to Honesty and Clarity in Public Language, National Council of Teachers of English, 1988 and 1992; inclusion among the top hundred works of American journalism, New York University, 1999, for *America: What Went Wrong?;* Goldmith Prize for investigative reporting, Harvard University, 2000, for series "What Corporate Welfare Costs."

WRITINGS:

NONFICTION; WITH DONALD L. BARLETT

Oil: The Created Crisis (pamphlet), Philadelphia Inquirer (Philadelphia, PA), 1973.
Empire: The Life, Legend, and Madness of Howard Hughes, Norton (New York, NY), 1979.
Forevermore: Nuclear Waste in America, Norton (New York, NY), 1985.
America: What Went Wrong?, Andrews & McMeel (Kansas City, MO), 1992.
America: Who Really Pays the Taxes?, Simon & Schuster (New York, NY), 1994.
America: Who Stole the Dream?, Andrews & McMeel (Kansas City, MO), 1996.
The Great American Tax Dodge: How Spiraling Fraud and Avoidance are Killing Fairness, Destroying the Income Tax, and Costing You, Little, Brown (Boston, MA), 2000.

Contributor to periodicals, including *New Republic* and *Nation.*

SIDELIGHTS: As one half of what James H. Dygert described in his *The Investigative Journalist* as "perhaps the most systematic and thorough investigative reporting team in the U.S. today," James B. Steele is well known for his work with fellow journalist Donald L. Barlett. Since teaming up in 1970, the pair have uncovered fraud in the Federal Housing Administration's (FHA) subsidy program for rehabilitating and selling slum houses, disclosed inequities in Philadelphia's criminal courts, and, in a Pulitzer Prize-winning series of articles, demonstrated that the Internal Revenue Service enforces tax laws more stringently on middle-income and poor taxpayers than on the wealthy. Two-time Pulitzer Prize-winners Barlett and Steele remained at the Philadelphia *Inquirer* for almost three decades before assuming positions as editors-at-large at *Time* magazine.

Prior to collaborating with Barlett at the *Inquirer,* Steele worked as a reporter for Missouri's *Kansas City Times* and then as an information director of a labor union in Washington, D.C. These jobs taught him the skills needed by investigative journalists. According to Leonard Downie Jr. in *The New Muckrakers,* at the Kansas City daily Steele was, in his own words, "schooled in the use of records to verify facts for stories like obituaries [and] taught respect for facts and shown how they could be found in records of all kinds." Lessons from this early training were reinforced during his tenure in Washington, D.C., where, according to Downie, "he learned in detail just where information could be found in the federal bureaucracy."

The two men began working at the *Inquirer* on the same day in 1970, and since their first joint assignment (documenting abuses in the FHA subsidy program) reliance on the facts has been their trademark. They are among a "new breed of muckraker," contended Downie, who rely on the public record for evidence rather than solely on stories from informants. According to Steele, "the challenge is to gather, marshal, and organize vast amounts of data already in the public domain and see what it adds up to." He insists that investigative reporters must be systematic and review their assumptions as they go; they must constantly evaluate the evidence they turn up and determine if it is adequate to prove their thesis.

Overall, Steele takes satisfaction, he told Downie, in "spending months on a subject and having it all come together at the end. . . . No matter how much you know, there is always more to find out." One of his favorite projects was investigating billionaire Howard Hughes's dealings with the U.S. government. After months of reviewing contracts, trial records, partnership agreements, financial statements, and the like, Barlett and Steele had amassed ten thousand pages of notes and documents. They published their initial findings in a series of articles for the *Inquirer* in 1975, but when more material became available after Hughes's death, the reporters took the opportunity to collaborate on their first book, *Empire: The Life, Legend, and Madness of Howard Hughes.* It is "the best big business-big government biography of 1979, maybe of the decade," declared a *Washington Post Book World* reviewer, while a critic for the *New York Times Book Review* opined, "Of all the books written about Howard Hughes, 'Empire' is easily the best. . . . From the mountain of subpoenaed files and depositions, and from interviews, the authors have assembled the first fully documented, cradle-to-grave account of a unique American life."

Steele and Barlett also received praise for their 1985 work, *Forevermore: Nuclear Waste in America.* Evolving from a 1983 investigative series for the Philadelphia *Inquirer,* the book discusses failed attempts to safely store nuclear waste. According to Victor Gilinsky's critique in the *Los Angeles Times Book Review,* "the authors have dug up interesting material" for their "important" story.

In the 1990s, Barlett and Steele published their "America" series: *America: What Went Wrong?, America: Who Really Pays the Taxes?,* and *America: Who Stole the Dream? America: What Went Wrong?* investigates the increasing hardships faced by America's middle class, hardships caused, according to Barlett and Steele, by the advantages given to the upper class. Originally published as a series in the *Philadelphia Inquirer* (a series that generated the largest response to a story in the paper's history), the work, which garnered the duo the first of several George Polk awards for economic reporting, was published in an expanded form in the three volumes of the "America" trilogy.

Many critics joined the reading public in its enthusiastic response to the America trilogy. "Mr. Barlett and Mr. Steele don't patronize readers by oversimplifying these matters," claimed James D. Atwater in a *New York Times Book Review* critique of 1992's *America: What Went Wrong?* "The good news is," Atwater concluded, "that Mr. Barlett and Mr. Steele have incisively and vividly defined the problem facing the nation, and proved again that there is an audience for a message that cannot be captured by sound bite, a photo opportunity or even a bumper sticker."

America: Who Really Pays the Taxes? and *America: Who Stole the Dream?* were also well received by a number of critics upon their release in the mid-1990s, though some disagreed with the authors' proffered solution to the problem of tax inequity. "Barlett and Steele's greatest achievement," wrote a critic for *Publishers Weekly,* "is to have painstakingly translated mountains of often deliberately obscure material, thereby making their book a dream for those who've never quite grasped what government, corporations and the wealthiest few are doing—and a nightmare for those who have and want to keep that knowledge to themselves." Ray Olson in *Booklist* called the work "Superb investigative journalism." Andy Apathy, writing in *National Catholic Reporter,* faulted *America: Who Stole the Dream?* for failing to include a discussion of the role U.S. military involvement plays in developing countries for the benefit of multinationals and also for "failing to point out our own complicity." Apathy, however, concluded, "This book offers a solid opportunity to realize the connection between the 'good buys' we demand as consumers and the 'goodbyes' we fear as employees. It might also be a good time to say goodbye to all of our sentimental, romanticized notions of the American Dream for which we seem to feel so much nostalgia and—God help us—defensiveness."

While most critical reaction to their America series was positive, a negative response came from several in the journalism world, who viewed Steele and Barlett's factoid-based analysis with suspicion. Charges were made that the pair started with a hypothesis, and then sifted among the relevant facts for those supporting their position. Defending what he terms the pair's "expert journalism" technique, *Columbia Journalism Review* essayist Steve Weinberg commented: "Have their critics analyzed seventy years of income tax data, as Barlett and Steele did? Have they visited factories in dozens of states, documenting the broken careers and families of thousands of workers? Have they read corporate filings at the Securities and Exchange Commission from every business [they mention in their books]? Such research does not guarantee truth, but it certainly gives a reporter the authority to challenge conventional wisdom."

In 2000 Steele and Barlett published *The Great American Tax Dodge: How Spiraling Fraud and Avoidance Are Killing Fairness, Destroying the Income Tax, and Costing You.* The work focuses on wide-spread tax fraud and the complicity of the government in taxation inequity between the rich and the middle and lower classes. This work was also well received by critics. *Library Journal* reviewer Patrick J. Brunet called the work a "responsible and well-argued effort on a topic of great civic importance." A *Publishers Weekly* critic concurred, concluding of *The Great American Tax Dodge* that "This important, incendiary book may spark a national debate."

Steele has joined Barlett in attributing much of his success to the support he received from the *Inquirer.* There the two men were free to investigate whatever subject seemed pertinent to them, had open-ended work schedules, could travel if necessary, and had access to computers and other resources. In addition, the paper never killed one of their stories under pressure, even when it meant losing advertisements. This being the case, Downie reported that Steele claims not to tire of his work. And regarding the future Steele has said: "There are always more records and more in them to find out. . . . The work is never done."

BIOGRAPHICAL/CRITICAL SOURCES:

BOOKS

Downie, Leonard, Jr., *The New Muckrakers,* New Republic (New York, NY), 1976.

Dygert, James H., *The Investigative Journalist,* Prentice-Hall (New York, NY), 1976.

PERIODICALS

Booklist, March 1, 1994, Ray Olson, review of *America: Who Really Pays the Taxes?,* p. 1138.

Columbia Journalism Review, January-February, 1997, Steve Weinberg, "In Defense of 'Expert Journalism,'" p. 18.

Christian Science Monitor, May 21, 1979.

Fortune, May 2, 1994, Rob Norton, review of *America: Who Really Pays the Taxes?,* p. 124.

Library Journal, July, 2000, Patrick J. Brunet, review of *The Great American Tax Dodge,* p. 111.

Los Angeles Times Book Review, March 24, 1985, Victor Gilinsky, review of *Forevermore: Nuclear Waste in America.*

Maclean's, June 4, 1979.

Mother Jones, September, 2000, Steve Weinberg, review of *The Great American Tax Dodge,* p. 81.

Nation, May 5, 1979.

National Catholic Reporter, February 7, 1997, Andy Apathy, review of *America: Who Stole the Dream?,* p. 34.

National Review, April 27, 1979.

Newsweek, December 30, 1974; April 23, 1979.

New West, May 21, 1979.

New York, May 7, 1979.

New York Review of Books, May 31, 1979.

New York Times Book Review, May 6, 1979; November 25, 1979; March 22, 1981; March 17, 1985, Allen L. Hammond, review of *Forevermore,* p. 9; April 5, 1992, James D. Atwater, review of *America: What Went Wrong?,* p. 9.

Publishers Weekly, April 26, 1976; February 10, 1992, Connie Goddard, review of *America: What Went Wrong?,* p. 22; February 21, 1994, review of *America: Who Really Pays the Taxes?,* p. 247; July 31, 2000, review of *Great American Tax Dodge,* p. 83.

Technology Review, February-March, 1995, Jonathan Schlefer, review of *America: Who Pays the Taxes?,* p. 75.

Washington Monthly, April, 1979.

Washington Post Book World, December 2, 1979, review of *Empire.*

West Coast Review of Books, July, 1979.

OTHER

Philadelphia Inquirer: Bartlett and Steele: AMERICA: Who Stole the Dream?, http://www.philly.com (May 19, 2001), "About Bartlett & Steele."*

* * *

STEWART, Kenneth L. 1949-

PERSONAL: Born April 2, 1949, in Weiser, ID; son of Lawrence L. (a plumber) and Juanita (a homemaker) Stewart; married Susan W. Carpenter (a consultant in education), September 7, 1984. *Ethnicity:* "White-American-Scottish Descent." *Education:* Boise State University, B.A., 1971; Colorado State University, M.A., 1973; Western Michigan University, Ph.D., 1975. *Politics:* Liberal Democrat. *Religion:* Methodist.

ADDRESSES: *Home*—5205 Beverly Dr., San Angelo, TX 76904. *Office*—Department of Psychology and Sociology, Angelo State University, San Angelo, TX 76909; fax: 915-223-0721. *E-mail*—kenneth.stewart@angelo.edu.

CAREER: Angelo State University, San Angelo, TX, assistant professor, 1975-80, associate professor, 1980-93, professor of sociology and university studies, 1993—, department head, 1984-93.

MEMBER: American Sociological Association, Population Institute, Pi Gamma Mu, National Campaign for Tolerance.

WRITINGS:

(With Arnoldo De Leon) *Tejanos and the Numbers Game: A Socio-Historical Interpretation from the Federal Censuses, 1850-1900,* University of New Mexico Press (Albuquerque, NM), 1989.

(With De Leon) *Not Room Enough: Mexicans, Anglos, and Socio-Economic Change in Texas, 1850-1900,* University of New Mexico Press (Albuquerque, NM), 1993.

Race and Ethnic Relations in America: An Introduction Using MicroCase, MicroCase Corp. (Bellevue, WA), 1997.

(Editor) *The Angelo State University Symposium on American Values,* Angelo State University (San Angelo, TX), 1998, electronic edition: http://www.angelo.edu/events/university_symposium.

Contributor to books, including *The Tejano Community, 1836-1900,* edited by De Leon, University of New Mexico Press (Albuquerque, NM), 1982. Contributor to sociology, history, and education journals.

SIDELIGHTS: Kenneth L. Stewart once told *CA:* "The topic of racial, ethnic, and gender diversity has a magnetic pull for me as an academic writer. I can think of no more important sociological force affecting American society and the world today. Issues, conflicts, and controversies involving these human differences daily grab headlines and enter passionately into public discourse.

"It is the passion that people attach to differences of race, ethnicity, and gender that draws me to research and writing in this field. Such passions are deeply human and fully contradictory. Anger and fear are aroused, yet people are hopeful. Many responses are shamefully degrading, yet there is a continuous struggle for dignity. Most people readily admit limitations in their understanding of other races and cultural groups, and of the other sex, and yet passions lead most of us to reach conclusions, pass judgment, and often condemn. The central purpose of my writing is to help expand understandings of human diversity, not in the hope of eliminating passions, but to help collapse some of the contradictions.

"This, to me, has been the main point of my jointly authored writings with my friend and colleague, Arnoldo De Leon. Together, we have written about the history of *Tejanos* (Mexicans in Texas). What makes our writing different from other histories is that we strive to see the Mexican past in Texas as interlocked with the history of other Texas peoples. It is my hope that seeing *Tejano* history, not as a separate past, but as an intertwining thread in the fiber of Texas history helps to collapse some of the ambivalent passions that divide Mexicans and Anglos.

"Another of my writing projects is wider in scope, but similar in purpose. *Race and Ethnic Relations in America* is aimed at college students nationwide. It seeks to engage undergraduate students in courses dealing with human diversity in active and thoughtful analysis of both scholarly and public issues. The book provides a format, not only for reading about issues, but also for conducting realistic statistical analysis with actual data from national social surveys and other types of national and international data sources. This writing is particularly unique, I believe, because it gives students a framework for investigating important issues, but also lets them 'own' the results and conclusions they reach."

Stewart later told *CA:* "My most recent editorial work on the collected papers of *The Angelo State University Symposium on American Values* is both preparing and pointing me toward a more ambitious project. Any serious intellectual inquiry into 'American Values' leads quickly into what some analysts have called America's 'culture wars.' Many fine scholars have written highly rational critiques and defenses of 'traditional' American culture and 'multiculturalism.' My next ambition is to write about the passions underlying America's culture wars. It is here, in our passions more than in rational argument, that I believe it is possible to reveal the real contradictions of American culture, as well as the 'common ground' for the future."

* * *

STOLTZFUS, Ben Franklin 1927-

PERSONAL: Born September 15, 1927, in Sofia, Bulgaria; U.S. citizen born abroad; son of B. Frank (a professor) and Esther (a teacher; maiden name, Johnson) Stoltzfus; married Elizabeth Burton, August 20, 1955 (divorced, October 20, 1975); married Judith Palmer (an artist), November 8, 1975; children: Jan, Celia, Andrew. *Ethnicity:* "Caucasian." *Education:* Amherst College, B.A., 1949; Middlebury College, M.A., 1954; attended University of Paris, 1955-56; University of Wisconsin (now University of Wisconsin—Madison), Ph.D., 1959. *Politics:* Democrat. *Avocational interests:* Travel, skiing, fishing.

ADDRESSES: Home—2040 Arroyo Dr., Riverside, CA 92506. *Office*—c/o Department of Comparative Literature and Foreign Languages, University of California, Riverside, CA 92521.

CAREER: Smith College, Northampton, MA, instructor in French, 1958-60; University of California, Riverside, assistant professor, 1960-65, associate professor, 1965-66, professor of French, comparative literature, and creative writing, 1967-93, professor emeritus,

1993—, vice-chair of Division of Humanities, 1962, chair of humanities interdisciplinary program, 1973-76, chair of education abroad program, 1976-78.

MEMBER: American Association of Teachers of French, Modern Language Association of America, New Novel Association, Albert Camus Society, Ernest Hemingway Association, American Literature Association, American Comparative Literature Association, Associated Writers, Poets and Writers, Association des amis d'André Gide, Southern Comparative Literature Association.

AWARDS, HONORS: Fulbright scholarships for France, 1955-56, 1963-64; University of California, awards from Creative Arts Institute, 1968 and 1975, Humanities Institute, 1969 and 1972, and Center for Ideas and Society, 1992; H.D.L., Amherst College, 1974; Camargo Foundation grants for France, 1983 and 1985; NAAP Gradiva Award, 1997, for *Lacan and Literature.*

WRITINGS:

Alain Robbe-Grillet and the New French Novel, Southern Illinois University Press (Carbondale, IL), 1964.
Georges Chenneviere et l'unanimisme, Minard (Paris, France), 1965.
The Eye of the Needle (novel), Viking (New York, NY), 1967.
Gide's Eagles, Southern Illinois University Press (Carbondale, IL), 1969.
Black Lazarus (novel), Winter House (New York, NY), 1972.
Gide and Hemingway: Rebels against God, Kennikat (Port Washington, NY), 1978.
Alain Robbe-Grillet: The Body of the Text, Fairleigh Dickinson University Press (Cranbury, NJ), 1985.
Alain Robbe-Grillet: Life, Work, and Criticism, York (Fredericton, New Brunswick), 1987.
Postmodern Poetics: Nouveau Roman and Innovative Fiction, 1987.
Red, White, and Blue (novel), York (Fredericton, New Brunswick), 1989.
(Translator and author of introduction and essay) Robbe-Grillet and René Magritte, *La Belle Captive* (novel), illustrated by Magritte, University of California Press (Berkeley, CA), 1995.
(Editor) *Lacan and Literature: Purloined Pretexts,* State University of New York Press (Albany, NY), 1996.

Contributor of stories, poems, and essays to literature and language journals and literary magazines, including *Modern Fiction Studies, North Dakota Quarterly, Comparative Literature, Chelsea, Kayak,* and *Mosaic.* Guest editor, *New Novel Review,* 1996 and 2000.

WORK IN PROGRESS: A novel, *Dumpster;* a "pictonovel," *Romoland,* with wife, Judith Palmer; *The Target,* a study of Jasper Johns and Alain Robbe-Grillet; research on "Ernest Hemingway and the French."

SIDELIGHTS: Ben Franklin Stoltzfus once told *CA:* "Men frequently walk a thin line between passion and intellect. In situations of conflict, often out of ignorance, passion dictates responses that are sometimes violent. The role of intellect, out of respect for life and stable, long-term goals, is to soothe the passions, nudging and coaxing them onward toward nonviolent solutions.

"There need not be a difference, though there all too frequently is, between life and art. They can be one and the same, and the artist's responsibility is to both, constantly transforming one into the other. The work of art is not only a reflexive voice dealing with love and death and violence, and the meaning of art itself; it is also a place of mirrors and distortions. The artist must be like a thorn in the side of the establishment, reminding it that all forms of 'ideology' are oppressive, demonstrating by his life and his art that in spite of television, advertising, slogans, and coercions of all kinds, it is possible to resist the 'tyranny' of the system by playing with, hence exposing, the terrible seriousness of the cliche and the ready-made. To create is to play with contemporary myths, assembling fragments of reality into an artistic whole that challenges every callous, monolithic, and inhumane aspect of establishment 'ideology.' Art is also a theater of play which mimes the great cosmic game. The work of art is thus always a personal signature attesting to man's passion, his rebellion, and his freedom."

Stoltzfus later added: "My primary motivation for writing must be an incestual longing for the mother tongue. I am probably influenced by an unconscious desire to play with language and to explore new literary venues. Half of me writes fiction and half writes criticism. The two complement each other. My interest in art produced *La Belle Captive* and *Romoland.* I write metafiction (most of the time) because the only character in fiction I like is language: its play, its sound, its opaqueness."

BIOGRAPHICAL/CRITICAL SOURCES:

PERIODICALS

French Review, October, 1999, review of *Lacan and Literature,* p. 137.
Library Journal, June 1, 1985, review of *Alain Robbe-Grillet,* p. 128; March 1, 1995, Ann Irvine, review of *La Belle Captive,* p. 103.
Publishers Weekly, February 6, 1995, review of *La Belle Captive,* p. 78.

T

TARRANT, Wilma
See SHERMAN, Jory (Tecumseh)

* * *

TRACY, James D. 1938-

PERSONAL: Born February 14, 1938, in St. Louis, MO; son of Leo W. (an accountant) and Marguerite (Meehan) Tracy; married Nancy Ann McBride, September 6, 1968; children: Patrick, Samuel, Mary Ann. *Education:* St. Louis University, B.A., 1959; Johns Hopkins University, M.A., 1960; University of Notre Dame, M.A., 1961; Princeton University, Ph.D., 1967. *Politics:* Democrat. *Religion:* Roman Catholic.

ADDRESSES: *Home*—757 Osceoloa Ave., Apt. 2, St. Paul, MN 55105. *Office*—Department of History, University of Minnesota—Twin Cities, 267 19th Ave. S., Minneapolis, MN 55455. *E-mail*—tracy001@umn.edu.

CAREER: University of Michigan, Ann Arbor, instructor in history, 1964-66; University of Minnesota, Minneapolis, associate professor, 1966-77, professor of history, 1977—, chair of department. Organized international conference on "The Rise of Merchant Empires," University of Minnesota, October, 1987.

WRITINGS:

Erasmus: The Growth of a Mind, Droz (Geneva, Switzerland), 1972.
(Editor) *Early Modern European History, 1500-1715,* 1976.
The Politics of Erasmus: A Pacifist Intellectual and His Political Milieu, University of Toronto Press (Toronto, Ontario, Canada), 1979.
True Ocean Found: Paludanus's Letters on Dutch Voyages to the Kara Sea, 1595-1596, University of Minnesota Press (Minneapolis, MN), 1980.
A Financial Revolution in the Habsburg Netherlands: Renten and Renteniers in the Country of Holland, 1515-1565, University of California Press (Berkeley, CA), 1985.
Holland under Habsburg Rule, 1506-1566: The Formation of a Body Politic, University of California Press (Berkeley, CA), 1990.
(Editor) *The Rise of Merchant Empires: Long-Distance Trade in the Early Modern World, 1350-1750,* Cambridge University Press (New York, NY), 1990.
(Editor) *The Political Economy of Merchant Empires: State Power and World Trade, 1350-1750,* Cambridge University Press (New York, NY), 1991.
(Editor with Thomas A. Brady and Heiko A. Oberman) *Handbook of European History, 1400-1600: Late Middle Ages, Renaissance, and Reformation,* Eerdmans (Grand Rapids, WI), 1996.
Erasmus of the Low Countries, University of California Press (Berkeley, CA), 1996.
Europe's Reformations, 1450-1650, Rowman & Littlefield (Lanham, MD), 1999.
(Editor) *City Wall: The Urban Enceinte in Global Perspective,* Cambridge University Press (New York, NY), 2000.

Managing editor, *Journal of Early Modern History,* 1995—.

WORK IN PROGRESS: A book on the finances of the Dutch revolts; research into the Dutch influence in South Asia.

SIDELIGHTS: Educator and historian James D. Tracy's field of expertise is Europe during the fourteenth through eighteenth centuries. In addition to editing and publishing numerous books on the politics and economics of this era, he has also written extensively about the scholar and philosopher Erasmus of Rotterdam (1469-1536). In 1987 Tracy organized an international conference at the University of Minnesota focusing on the rise of merchant empires throughout the world, primarily in the period before 1750. He later edited two volumes of papers presented at the conference, *The Rise of Merchant Empires: Long-Distance Trade in the Early Modern World, 1350-1750,* and *The Political Economy of Merchant Empires: State Power and World Trade, 1350-1750.* Reviewing the first volume for *Business History,* Donald Woodward remarked: "This is an important book, a significant staging-post in the historiography of world integration." Woodward commented that the thirteen essays selected for the volume present "a truly exotic diet" in that they cover trade development not only in Europe but throughout the entire world. Singling out articles on caravan routes across the Sahara, trade in pre-colonial India, the Atlantic slave trade, and migrant Chinese merchant communities, Woodward observed that "like the product of any worthwhile academic conference, this volume contains both important retrospective surveys and an agenda for future research." Constance Jones Mathers, writing in *Business History Review,* took a more critical approach to *The Rise of Merchant Empires.* Noting that the collection lacks a central thesis, Mathers went on to remark upon Tracy's tendency to be descriptive rather than explanatory in his prose, and also pointed out the book's failure "to dwell on the fate of non-European peoples who were touched by Europe's expanding commercial empires."

Commenting on *The Political Economy of Merchant Empires,* the second collection of essays drawn from Tracy's 1987 conference, Henry G. Roseveare noted in *Business History* that although the contributors maintain a commendable dialogue with the entries in the first compilation, the emphasis in this book is on "the mercantile and military success of European structures in dominating world trade by the mid-eighteenth century." Roseveare credited the work with "a high degree of coherence" and "an unusual sharpness of focus upon the fundamental question [Why Europe?] confronting all students of early-modern world trade."

Published in 1997, *Erasmus of the Low Countries* is Tracy's third book on the Dutch scholar. In it, Tracy portrays Erasmus as both a humanist and would-be reformer, a man who used his writings to further Christian morality and religious doctrine. Erasmus's ideal was a Christian republic composed of individuals that were both devout and well educated. Finding the roots of such values in Erasmus's Low Country origins, Tracy also depicts Erasmus as a writer conflicted by both the controversies of the Reformation and the dichotomy between creating works of depth and works which would have a beneficial effect upon the moral character of those who read them.

According to Diarmaid MacCulloch of *History Today,* "Tracy brings a lifetime of study of Erasmus and the Netherlands to a wise and useful survey of the Reformation" in *Europe's Reformations, 1450-1650.* On the negative side, MacCulloch found that Tracy's "treatment is sometimes impressionistic or gappy, and there are rather too many slips or imprecisions in the material which I know best, on the English Reformation." He also faulted the study for its "problematic . . . threefold division into doctrine, politics and society," and its failure to move on from the Reformation movement to examine the question of why the European Enlightenment should have followed it. However, MacCulloch credited the survey with being "an attractively and sensitively illustrated book."

BIOGRAPHICAL/CRITICAL SOURCES:

PERIODICALS

American Historical Review, April, 1987, John H. Munro, review of *A Financial Revolution,* p. 434; February, 1989, p. 160; February, 1992, review of *Holland under Habsburg Rule,* p. 222; April, 1998, Bruce E. Mansfield, review of *Erasmus of the Low Countries,* p. 534.

Business History, January, 1992, Donald Woodward, review of *The Rise of Merchant Empires,* p. 211; January, 1993, Henry G. Roseveare, review of *The Political Economy of Merchant Empires,* p. 80.

Business History Review, spring, 1991, Constance Jones Mathers, review of *The Rise of Merchant Empires,* p. 201.

Historian, spring, 1992, Richard G. Kyle, review of *Holland under Habsburg Rule,* p. 532.

History Today, July, 2000, Diarmaid MacCulloch, review of *Europe's Reformations,* p. 59.

Journal of Modern History, June, 1994, A. T. Van Deursen, review of *Holland under Habsburg Rule, 1506-1566,* June, 1995, p. 376; December, 1998, Derk Visser, review of *Erasmus of the Low Countries,* p. 956.

New York Times Book Review, Felipe Fernan, review of *Europe's Reformations,* p. 28.

OTHER

University of California Press Web site, http://www.ucpress.edu/ (August 8, 2000), press releases on *Erasmus of the Low Countries* and *Holland under Habsburg Rule, 1506-1566.*

University of Minnesota Web site, http://www.hist.umn.edu/ (August 8, 2000), online faculty directory.*

* * *

TRECKER, Janice Law 1941-
(Janice Law)

PERSONAL: Born June 10, 1941, in Sharon, CT; daughter of James Ord and Janet (Galloway) Law; married Jerrold B. Trecker (a teacher and sportswriter), June 9, 1962; children: James. *Education:* Syracuse University, B.A., 1962; University of Connecticut, M.A., 1967, Ph. D., 1992. *Avocational interests:* Art, philosophy, music, bird-watching.

ADDRESSES: Home and office—408 North Bigelow Rd., Hampton, CT 06247. *E-mail*—halfyank@aol.com.

CAREER: Junior high school English teacher in Windsor, CT, 1962-66; elementary school mathematics teacher in West Hartford, CT, 1967; writer, 1967—. University of Hartford, writing instructor, 1981-83; University of Connecticut, instructor, 1992—.

MEMBER: Authors Guild, Authors League of America, National Organization for Women, Phi Beta Kappa.

AWARDS, HONORS: Edgar Allan Poe Award nomination, Mystery Writers of America, for *The Big Payoff.*

WRITINGS:

UNDER NAME JANICE LAW TRECKER

Women on the Move, Macmillan (New York, NY), 1975.

Preachers, Rebels, and Traders, Pequot Press, 1975.

Discovering Hampton: A Guide with History, Hampton Historical Society (Hampton, CT), 2000.

FICTION; UNDER NAME JANICE LAW

The Big Payoff, Houghton (Boston, MA), 1975.

Gemini Trip, Houghton (Boston, MA), 1976.

Under Orion, Houghton (Boston, MA), 1978.

The Shadow of the Palms, Houghton (Boston, MA), 1979.

Death under Par, Houghton (Boston, MA), 1981.

All the King's Ladies, St. Martin's Press (New York, NY), 1986.

Infected Be the Air, Walker and Co. (New York, NY), 1991.

Time Lapse, Walker and Co. (New York, NY), 1992.

A Safe Place to Die, St. Martin's Press (New York, NY), 1993.

Backfire, St. Martin's Press (New York, NY), 1994.

Cross-Check, St. Martin's Press (New York, NY), 1997.

The Night Bus, Forge (New York, NY), 2000.

OTHER

Author of "Women's Work in America" (filmstrip series), Schloat Productions, 1974. Film reviewer, *West Hartford News,* 1967-85. Contributor of short stories to mystery magazines, including *Ellery Queen's Mystery* and *Alfred Hitchcock Mystery.* Contributor to academic journals and popular magazines, including *Saturday Review, Michigan Quarterly, Northeast Magazine,* and *Take One.*

WORK IN PROGRESS: A novel, *The Lost Diaries of Iris Weed,* for Forge (New York, NY), completion expected in 2002; *Voices,* Forge (New York, NY), c. 2003.

SIDELIGHTS: When Janice Law Trecker introduced the character of Anna Peters in the 1975 novel *The Big Payoff,* there were few other female detectives featured in crime fiction. The Edgar Award-nominated novel would serve as the introduction to a long line of novels about Peters, as well as other suspense fiction that Trecker has published under the name Janice Law. Among her other works are *All the King's Ladies,* a mystery set in the court of King Louis XIV of France, and the contemporary novels *Infected Be the Air* and *Night Bus.*

The creation of Anna Peters took place amidst the drama of the White House scandal that resulted in the Watergate investigation. As Trecker explained on the *Janice Law Home Page, The Big Payoff* sprang from her assumption that "some underpaid and overlooked secretary knew all about what was going on. I moved my secretary to an oil company, gave her a shady background, and cooked up malfeasance in the executive suite." The author had written nine Anna Peters novels by the year 2000, including *Death under Par,* in which Peters travels with husband Harry to the British Open golf tournament.

By 1992 Trecker had penned her sixth novel in the series, *Time Lapse.* This story centers on the death of actor Henry Brooks, a skilled swimmer who drowns while shooting a film in a small town in upstate New York. The production's insurer hires Peters to investigate, hoping to prove that Brooks committed suicide. Peters, a longtime fan of the actor, discovers that the two women in his life each had opportunity and motive to kill him, one being an underage girlfriend. His wife had been a frequent victim of verbal abuse by the egotistical star, even though she controlled his finances. During the investigation both Peters and a possible witness to Brooks's death are violently attacked. A critic for *Publishers Weekly* called the novel a "crisp, cinematic mystery" in which the question of the actor's true fate is "resolved in a neat twist." The reviewer concluded that it was "sophisticated and believable entertainment."

Time Lapse was followed by *A Safe Place to Die.* In this story Peters becomes involved in a murder investigation in Branch Hill, Connecticut. She has traveled to the wealthy residential community with husband Harry because his art is being exhibited at a local gallery. When a teenage girl is found murdered, Peters uncovers the unsavory activities hidden behind the town's genteel veneer, including adultery and drug use. In *Publishers Weekly* a reviewer noted the "palpable sense of rural claustrophobia" that pervades the novel and called Peters "a sharp-eyed, pleasant guide" to the psychological peculiarities of the place, albeit one who has "precious few eccentricities of her own."

In the novel *Backfire* Peters takes on a case after being contacted by an anonymous figure. She is enlisted in the defense of an immigrant housekeeper who has been charged with the arson-murder of her wealthy employer. Peters is persuaded that the woman may be innocent because she has not spoken since the incident. The investigation will require Peters to travel from Washington, D.C., to Tucson, Arizona. Her discovery of the employer's family secrets puts both detective and client in further danger. In a review for *Booklist,* Stuart Miller admired the Anna Peters character as being "intelligent, observant, low key, but tenacious and with nerves of steel" and complimented the book's "brisk pace, appealing characters, and good plotting." Miller concluded that the author had made yet another successful installment in the series.

The novel *Cross-Check* puts Peters in a setting that is unfamiliar to her: the world of professional hockey. She is hired by Jurgen Parkes, a star player for an Orlando expansion team, when he is implicated in the death of teammate Alf Rene. When Peters learns more about the case, she becomes less enamored of her client and the environment in which he operates. Shady business dealings combine with personal and professional intrigue, and make a dangerous climate for all. At story's end, it appears that Peters may be thinking of retirement, having sold her share of the business. In a review for *Booklist,* Wes Lukowsky found, however, that she remains a vital figure, commenting, "Peters remains among the most complex, fully drawn female series leads in crime fiction."

Another work of fiction in Trecker's repertoire is *Infected Be the Air.* This novel focuses on the mystery-solving abilities of a Connecticut homemaker and farmer. Alice Bertram finds herself unraveling the facts behind the mysterious death of her ex-husband Max, whom the police believe was part of a murder-suicide involving his girlfriend and her son. Alice, however, thinks it was triple murder; soon she is digging up sordid facts about the family of a Connecticut senator, the subject of a book Max had been commissioned to write. Mob involvement and illegal disposal of medical waste are among the crimes she uncovers with the help of the local plumber, Sam, who also provides romantic interest. In a *Publishers Weekly* review, a critic judged that the story "rolls along with some charm but never makes much of an impact" and that "Stock villains . . . fail to spice up standard fare."

A very different heroine figures in Trecker's *The Night Bus.* Amnesia victim Cath Tolland wakes up in a Florida hospital, where she is greeted by her sister-in-law, Yvonne. Cath knows that she fears Yvonne and her husband, with whom she is reunited at home in Connecticut, and she doesn't understand why the three live together. It turns out that Cath is a church singer, while her husband is the parish music instructor. She learns that their marriage has been a rocky one, and that she had been fleeing from something when knocked out by a purse-snatcher. Her life is further complicated when investments made with her own money yield a small fortune and she discovers that a number of her husband's young female singing students are dead. Reviews of *The Night Bus* did not quite meet high grades earned by

Trecker for her earlier works. Critic Ellie Barta-Moran wrote in *Booklist* that answers to Cath's questions about her life were "disappointingly obvious" but that "Cath's rediscovery of herself and her inner monologues keep the story afloat." A *Publishers Weekly* reviewer judged the book to be a "smoothly written yet intermittently overwrought romantic thriller." Yet *Kirkus Reviews* awarded the novel a "starred" review, and the conclusion of the *Publishers Weekly* critic was that the author had succeeded "in delineating deliciously plotted revenge and in granting Cath an enlightening and redemptive concluding insight."

BIOGRAPHICAL/CRITICAL SOURCES:

PERIODICALS

Booklist, November 1, 1994, Stuart Miller, review of *Backfire,* p. 480; May 1, 1997, Wes Lukowsky, review of *Cross-Check,* p. 1482; May 1, 2000, Ellie Barta-Moran, review of *The Night Bus,* p. 1652.

Chicago Tribune Book World, February 15, 1981.

Los Angeles Times Book Review, May 18, 1980.

New York Times Book Review, March 8, 1981.

Publishers Weekly, September 27, 1991, review of *Infected Be the Air,* p. 46; June 8, 1992, review of *Time Lapse,* p. 55; March 29, 1993, review of *A Safe Place to Die,* p. 38; April 24, 2000, review of *The Night Bus,* p. 58.

Washington Post Book World, January 18, 1981.

OTHER

Janice Law Home Page, http://virtual.class.uconn.edu/ (October 19, 2000).

* * *

TRIPP, Miles (Barton) 1923-2000
(John Michael Brett, Michael Brett, pseudonyms)

PERSONAL: Born May 5, 1923, in Ganwick Corner, near Barnet, England; died September 2, 2000; son of Cecil Lewis and Brena Mary (Yells) Tripp. *Education:* Attended county school in Hertfordshire, England.

CAREER: Freelance writer. Admitted as solicitor, 1950; private law practice, Stamford, England, 1950-52; Charity Commission, London, England, member of legal staff, 1953-83. *Military service:* Royal Air Force, served in bomber command, 1942-46.

MEMBER: Society of Authors (England), Crime Writers Association (England; chair, 1968-69).

WRITINGS:

Faith Is a Windsock, P. Davies (London, England), 1952.

The Image of Man, Darwen Finlayson (London, England), 1955.

A Glass of Red Wine, Macdonald (London, England), 1960.

Kilo Forty, Macmillan (London, England), 1963, Holt (New York, NY), 1964.

(Under pseudonym Michael Brett) *Diecast,* Fawcett (New York, NY), 1963, published under pseudonym John Michael Brett, Pan Books (London, England), 1966.

The Skin Dealer, Macmillan (London, England), 1964, Holt (New York, NY), 1965.

(Under pseudonym Michael Brett) *A Plague of Dragons,* Arthur Barker (London, England), 1965, published under pseudonym John Michael Brett, Pan Books (London, England), 1966.

A Quartet of Three, Macmillan (London, England), 1965.

The Chicken (also see below), Macmillan (London, England), 1966.

(Under pseudonym John Michael Brett) *A Cargo of Spent Evil,* Arthur Barker (London, England), 1966.

The Fifth Point of the Compass, Macmillan (London, England), 1967.

One Is One, Macmillan (London, England), 1968.

The Chicken [and] *Zilla,* Pan Books (London, England), 1968.

Malice and the Maternal Instinct, Macmillan (London, England), 1969.

The Eighth Passenger: A Flight of Recollection and Discovery, Heinemann (London, England), 1969.

A Man without Friends (also see below), Macmillan (London, England), 1970.

Five Minutes with a Stranger, Macmillan (London, England), 1971.

The Claws of God, Macmillan (London, England), 1972.

Obsession, Macmillan (London, England), 1973.

Woman at Risk, Macmillan (London, England), 1974.

A Woman in Bed, Macmillan (London, England), 1976, State Mutual (New York, NY), 1982.

The Once a Year Man, Macmillan (London, England), 1977.

The Wife-Smuggler, Macmillan (London, England), 1978.

Cruel Victim, Macmillan (London, England), 1979, St. Martin's Press (New York, NY), 1985.

High Heels, Macmillan (London, England), 1980, State Mutual (New York, NY), 1982.

Going Solo, Macmillan (London, England), 1981.

One Lover Too Many, Macmillan (London, England), 1983.

A Charmed Death, Macmillan (London, England), 1984, St. Martin's Press (New York, NY), 1985.

Some Predators Are Male, Macmillan (London, England), 1985, St. Martin's Press (New York, NY), 1986.

Death of a Man-Tamer, St. Martin's Press (New York, NY), 1987.

The Frightened Wife, Macmillan (London, England), 1987, St. Martin's Press (New York, NY), 1988.

The Cords of Vanity, Macmillan (London, England), 1989, St. Martin's Press (New York, NY), 1990.

Video Vengeance, Macmillan (London, England), 1990, St. Martin's Press (New York, NY), 1991.

The Dimensions of Deceit, Macmillan (London, England), 1993.

A Woman of Conscience, Macmillan (London, England), 1994.

Extreme Provocation, Macmillan (London, England), 1995.

Samson and the Greek Delilah, Severn House (Sutton, England), 1995, Severn House (New York, NY), 1996.

The Suitcase Killings, Severn House (New York, NY), 1998.

Deadly Ordeal, Severn House (New York, NY), 2000.

Also author of television adaptation of *A Man without Friends* (based on his novel), broadcast in England, 1972.

SIDELIGHTS: Don Cole in the *St. James Guide to Crime and Mystery Writers* called Miles Tripp "an outstanding practitioner of the disturbing art of creating psychological suspense." In Tripp's best work, Cole remarked, "the writing is brilliant and always witty; the reader does not so much ask himself 'who done it?' as 'who could have expected that to happen?'"

Tripp's fiction is often praised for its smooth writing and reliable ability to generate suspense. In his review of *Kilo Forty,* D. B. Hughes in *Book Week* noted "the intensity which generates compulsive suspense." Speaking of the same novel, the critic for the *Times Literary Supplement* explained that it "is curiously disturbing; it holds the attention in an Ancient Mariner grip." Reviewing the novel *The Wife-Smuggler,* in which an English journalist becomes involved in a plot to smuggle a woman from behind the Iron Curtain, *Times Literary Supplement* reviewer opined: "This is not a conventional thriller, but it is an absorbing and well-written one."

Tripp's books range widely in character and background. *A Man without Friends* concerns a charming, high-living con-man who enjoys graphology and is accused of murdering his wife; *Woman at Risk* follows a barrister entangled in the murder of his mistress; and *Kilo Forty* tells of a fishing party of British tourists off the Egyptian coast who suffer a murder within their ranks. Whatever the subject, Cole found that "in reading Tripp's books you get the feeling that he could have been a regular contributor to the great Alfred Hitchcock movies: Tripp's style fits the old master to a T."

Tripp's series of novels about London private investigator John Samson have won him special praise. As Sybil Steinberg noted in *Publishers Weekly,* "Samson is no run-of-the-mill detective-series hero: he collects antique clocks and eats quiche during stakeouts." Samson trails a philandering husband in *The Cords of Vanity* only to discover an unusual menage-a-trois; in *Video Vengeance* he must investigate a woman's husband, long believed dead, after he reappears when she receives an inheritance; and in *The Suitcase Killings,* Samson finds that a wealthy surgeon's dead son was involved with a group of deadly drug smugglers. Mary Frances Wilkens, reviewing *The Suitcase Killings* for *Booklist,* found that "Tripp effectively evokes both the high and low ends of his London setting, complete with dreary weather, pub crawls, and gentleman-speak."

BIOGRAPHICAL/CRITICAL SOURCES:

BOOKS

St. James Guide to Crime and Mystery Writers, 4th edition, St. James Press (Detroit, MI), 1996.

PERIODICALS

Best Sellers, May 1, 1964, p. 58.

Booklist, April 15, 1998, review of *The Suitcase Killings,* p. 1395.

Book Week, May 3, 1964, D. B. Hughes, review of *Kilo Forty,* p. 11.

Books and Bookmen, December, 1965, p. 48; October, 1973, p. 139; May, 1984, p. 30.

Kirkus Reviews, April 15, 1990, p. 539; December 1, 1990, p. 1643; June 1, 1996, review of *Samson and the Greek Delilah,* p. 790; February 1, 1998, review of *The Suitcase Killings,* p. 159.

Observer, May 10, 1970, p. 31; February 24, 1980, p. 39; January 23, 1983; April 8, 1984.

Publishers Weekly, March 1, 1985, review of *Cruel Victim,* p. 73; December 13, 1985, review of *Some Predators Are Male,* p. 46; July 3, 1987, Sybil Steinberg, review of *Death of a Man-Tamer,* p. 55; April 6, 1990, Sybil Steinberg, review of *The Cords of Vanity,* p. 104; December 14, 1990, Sybil Steinberg, review of *Video Vengeance,* p. 56; February 9, 1998, review of *The Suitcase Killings,* p. 78.

Punch, May 1, 1968, p. 653; February 16, 1977, p. 294.

Times Literary Supplement, June 21, 1963, review of *Kilo Forty,* p. 465; June 11, 1970, p. 642; February 17, 1978, p. 185.*

* * *

TROW, M(eirion) J(ames) 1949-

PERSONAL: Surname rhymes with "crow"; born October 16, 1949, in Ferndale, South Wales; son of Edward Charles and Glenys (Evans) Trow; married Carol Mary Long (an operator of an authors' support agency), July 14, 1973; children: Taliesin James. *Education:* King's College, London, B.A. (with honors), 1971; Jesus College, Cambridge, Postgraduate Certificate of Education, 1972. *Politics:* "Slightly right of center."

ADDRESSES: *Home*—Nonsuch, Church Rd., Havenstreet, Ryde, Isle of Wight, England. *Office*—Ryde High School, Pell Lane, Ryde, Isle of Wight, England.

CAREER: History teacher at school in Welwyn Garden City, England, 1972-76; Ryde High School, Ryde, England, history teacher, 1976—, head of department, 1976-80, head of Sixth Form, 1980-93, community and publicity officer, 1993—.

MEMBER: Society of Authors.

WRITINGS:

"LESTRADE" SERIES; MYSTERY NOVELS

The Supreme Adventure of Inspector Lestrade, Stein & Day (New York, NY), 1985, published as *The Adventures of Inspector Lestrade,* Macmillan (London, England), 1985.

Brigade: Further Adventures of Inspector Lestrade, Macmillan (London, England), 1986.

Lestrade and the Hallowed House, Macmillan (London, England), 1987.

Lestrade and the Brother of Death, Regnery (Washington, DC), 1999.

Lestrade and the Deadly Game, Regnery (Washington, DC), 1999.

Lestrade and the Ripper, Regnery (Washington, DC), 1999.

Lestrade and the Guardian Angel, Regnery (Washington, DC), 1999.

Lestrade and the Leviathan, Regnery (Washington, DC), 1999.

Lestrade and the Magpie, Regnery (Washington, DC), 2000.

Lestrade and the Gift of the Prince, Regnery (Washington, DC), 2000.

Lestrade and the Dead Man's Hand, Regnery (Washington, DC), 2000.

Lestrade and the Sawdust Ring, Regnery (Washington, DC), 2000.

Lestrade and the Sign of Nine, Regnery (Washington, DC), 2000.

Lestrade and the Mirror of Murder, Regnery (Washington, DC), 2001.

Lestrade and the Kiss of Horus, Regnery (Washington, DC), 2001.

Lestrade and the Devil's Own, Regnery (Washington, DC), 2001.

"PETER MAXWELL" SERIES; MYSTERY NOVELS

Maxwell's House, Chivers, 1996.

Maxwell's Flame, New English Library (London, England), 1998.

Maxwell's Movie, Hodder & Stoughton (London, England), 1998.

Maxwell's War, New English Library (London, England), 1999.

Maxwell's Ride, New English Library (London, England), 2000.

Maxwell's Curse, Hodder & Stoughton (London, England), 2000.

OTHER

The Wigwam Murder, Constable, 1994.

The Many Faces of Jack the Ripper, Summersdale, 1997.

(With John Harris) *Hess: The British Conspiracy,* Deutsch (London, England), 1998.

Who Killed Kit Marlowe?, Sutton, 2001.

SIDELIGHTS: M. J. Trow's lighthearted mystery novels feature Sholto Lestrade, a Scotland Yard police inspector who first appeared as a supporting character in the Sherlock Holmes stories of Arthur Conan Doyle. Trow has borrowed the character and stars him as a detective in his own right, solving crimes in London of the 1890s. Lestrade's adventures involve him in such famous cases as the Jack the Ripper murders and introduce him to such leading figures of the time as George Bernard Shaw, Oscar Wilde, Aubrey Beardsley, and Bram Stoker. A critic for *Publishers Weekly* stated, "Trow, having appropriated Conan Doyle's ferret-faced inspector to good advantage, has created a delightful series."

The Lestrade series has pitted the good inspector against such varied villains as a serial killer targeting women on the London Underground, a killer bent on poisoning the remaining participants in the Charge of the Light Brigade, and a murderer who is tracking down British athletes at the Olympic games. As the series develops, Lestrade ages, moves up the ranks at Scotland Yard, and eventually retires. A *Publishers Weekly* reviewer opined that "among the charms of Trow's Lestrade novels . . . are tight historical detail, an unusual mix of slapstick and literate humor, and unpredictable plots."

The humor found in the Lestrade mysteries include wordplay, puns, self-referential jokes, and parodic character names. Sherlock Holmes and Dr. Watson often appear as comical figures—Holmes as a neurotic cocaine user and Watson as a pompous would-be writer. Maureen O'Connor, writing for the *Book Browser* Web site, recommended the Lestrade books "if you like the kind of mystery that emphasizes the humor over the whodunit." *Over My Dead Body* Web site writer J. Ashley explained that "the Lestrade series is funny, well-written, thoughtful, and wonderfully characterized."

Trow once told *CA:* "I always wanted to make historical films. Brought up as I was on the Heston epics of the 1960s, I wanted to share in the glory of all that. At the same time, first as an amateur and later as a professional historian, I was aware that there was a huge gulf between reality and celluloid fiction. British films like *Zulu, The Charge of the Light Brigade,* and *A Man for All Seasons* came closest to the truth—or what approximates it in the eyes of the public.

"My series of Lestrade novels stemmed from a sense of fury at the arrogance of the characterization of Sherlock Holmes, not by Conan Doyle, but by Basil Rathbone in the films of the 1940s shown for the umpteenth time on British television in 1982. A humorous style comes naturally to me, although I intend to branch out. Grisly death, or the description of it, is also easy. Indeed, one of my reviewers was rather disturbed by the ingenious deaths in my first novel!

"My first love, outside my family, is the British cavalry and the collection of officers' uniforms. Sadly, such a hobby is increasingly expensive, and my job as a teacher leaves me unable to afford such items or even to attend auctions. I sell my art work, usually on military subjects, I lecture to history societies and other groups, and, when time permits, I dabble in amateur dramatics, both as actor and producer.

"I suppose I still have the film ambition at heart and long to have the opportunity to write film scripts. At the moment I am in a weird limbo between teaching and writing, unable to leave the former for financial reasons. One way or the other, the next few months or years will, I hope, resolve this one for me."

BIOGRAPHICAL/CRITICAL SOURCES:

PERIODICALS

Armchair Detective, fall, 1993, review of *The Supreme Adventure of Inspector Lestrade,* p. 70.

Booklist, May 15, 1998, Mike Tribby, review of *The Many Faces of Jack the Ripper,* p. 1572.

Kirkus Reviews, June 1, 1995, review of *Maxwell's House,* p. 744; March 15, 2000, review of *Lestrade and the Magpie,* p. 342.

Library Journal, May 1, 1998, Michael Rogers, review of *The Many Faces of Jack the Ripper,* p. 118; August, 1999, Rex. E. Klett, reviews of *Lestrade and the Ripper* and *Lestrade and the Deadly Game,* p. 146.

New Statesman & Society, September 21, 1990, Bill Breenwell, "Let Him Have It, Chris," p. 44.

Publishers Weekly, June 26, 1995, review of *Maxwell's House,* p. 93; August 3, 1998, review of *The Adventures of Inspector Lestrade,* p. 78; October 26, 1998, review of *Brigade,* p. 47; July 5, 1999, review of *Lestrade and the Ripper,* p. 61; July 19, 1999, review of *Lestrade and the Deadly Game,* p. 188; December 6, 1999, review of *Lestrade and the Brother of Death,* p. 67; March 6, 2000, review of *Lestrade and the Magpie,* p. 86; July 17, 2000, review of *Lestrade and the Dead Man's Hand,* p. 178.

OTHER

BookBrowser, http://www.bookbrowser.com/ (March 17, 2000), Maureen O'Connor, review of *Lestrade and the Magpie;* (April 26, 2000) Sharon Galligar Chance, review of *Lestrade and the Gift of the Prince.*

Over My Dead Body, http://www.overmydeadbody.com/ (November, 1999), J. Ashley, reviews of *Lestrade and the Brother of Death, Lestrade and the Deadly Game, Lestrade and the Guardian Angel,* and *Lestrade and the Ripper.*

* * *

TYGIEL, Jules 1949-

PERSONAL: Born March 9, 1949, in Brooklyn, NY; son of Gustave (a retailer) and Rose (a retailer; maiden name, Gross) Tygiel; married Luise Custer (a teacher of English as a second language), October 10, 1982; children: Charles, Sam. *Education:* Brooklyn College of the City University of New York, B.A., 1969; University of California, Los Angeles, M.A., 1973, Ph.D., 1977.

ADDRESSES: Office—Department of History, San Francisco State University, 1600 Holloway Ave., San Francisco, CA 94132. *Agent*—Peter Ginsberg, Curtis Brown Ltd., 10 Astor Pl., New York, NY 10003. *E-mail*—tygiel@sfsu.edu.

CAREER: University of Tennessee, Knoxville, assistant professor of history, 1976-77; University of Virginia, Charlottesville, assistant professor of history, 1977-78; San Francisco State University, San Francisco, CA, assistant professor, 1978-82, associate professor, 1982-83, professor of history, 1983—.

MEMBER: North American Society for Sports History, American Historical Association, Organization of American Historians, Society for American Baseball Research, California Historical Society.

AWARDS, HONORS: Second prize, Robert F. Kennedy Book Awards, and Ambassador of Honor Award, English Speaking Union, both 1985, for *Baseball's Great Experiment: Jackie Robinson and His Legacy;* Seymour Medal best book on baseball history, Society for American Baseball Research, 2000, for *Past Time: Baseball as History.*

WRITINGS:

Baseball's Great Experiment: Jackie Robinson and His Legacy, Oxford University Press (New York, NY), 1983.

Workingmen in San Francisco, 1880-1901, Garland Publishing (New York, NY), 1992.

The Great Los Angeles Swindle: Oil, Stocks, and Scandal during the Roaring Twenties, Oxford University Press (New York, NY), 1994.

(Editor) *The Jackie Robinson Reader: Perspectives on an American Hero,* Dutton (New York, NY), 1997.

Past Time: Baseball as History, Oxford University Press (New York, NY), 2000.

SIDELIGHTS: Jules Tygiel is best known for his works on the history of baseball. Rather than merely offering accounts of the sport, however, Tygiel's books use baseball as a barometer that reflects changes in the wider American society. In *Baseball's Great Experiment: Jackie Robinson and His Legacy,* for instance, Tygiel uses the experiences of Jackie Robinson and other African-American baseball players to demonstrate the emotional issues surrounding integration in the United States. As Christopher Lehmann-Haupt noted in the *New York Times,* the book "puts the baseball story on a bigger canvas . . . and lets the reader draw his own conclusions." Lehmann-Haupt characterized *Baseball's Great Experiment* as a "rich, intelligent cultural history . . . fascinating even for baseball fans without the faintest trace of social conscience."

Past Time: Baseball as History not only uses baseball as an entrée into racism and integration, it also explores suburban flight, marketing trends, and computer technology as they relate to the sport. *Sports Illustrated* reviewer Ron Fimrite observed: "In these nine chapters . . . Tygiel accomplishes what many baseball scholars have promised but rarely delivered. . . . He shows how the game has adapted to larger changes in the world around it." Styling the work as an "extraordinary collection," Roberto Gonzalez Echevarria in the *New York Times Book Review* commended Tygiel for "his eye for what may appear nugatory or marginal but, when focused upon, illuminates the temper of a given moment." *Booklist* correspondent Wes Lukowsky also praised the book as "a unique perspective on the game, its fans, and their partnership in American sporting history."

BIOGRAPHICAL/CRITICAL SOURCES:

PERIODICALS

Booklist, April 1, 2000, Wes Lukowsky, review of *Past Time,* p. 1425.

New York Times, July 13, 1983, Christopher Lehmann-Haupt, review of *Baseball's Great Experiment,* p. C22.

New York Times Book Review, August 7, 1983; July 2, 2000, Roberto Gonzalez Echevarria, "From Ruth to Rotisserie."

Publishers Weekly, February 24, 1997, review of *The Jackie Robinson Reader,* p. 78; March 27, 2000, review of *Past Time,* p. 68.

Sports Illustrated, April 7, 1997, Ron Fimrite, review of *The Jackie Robinson Reader,* p. 1; April 24, 2000, Ron Fimrite, "Doubleheader: Two Views of the Grand Old Game through the Prism of History," p. R8.

U-V

UNDERDOWN, David (Edward) 1925-

PERSONAL: Born August 19, 1925, in Wells, Somerset, England; son of John Percival and Ethel (Gell) Underdown; married Mary Ebba Ingholt, 1954 (divorced, 1985); children: Harold D., Peter C., Philip J. *Education:* Exeter College, Oxford, B.A., 1950, M.A., 1951, B.Litt., 1953; Yale University, M.A., 1952.

ADDRESSES: *E-mail*—dunderd@attglobal.net.

CAREER: Royal Holloway College, London, England, tutorial fellow, 1952-53; University of the South, Sewanee, TN, assistant professor, 1953-58, associate professor of history, 1958-62; University of Virginia, Charlottesville, associate professor of history, 1962-68; Brown University, Providence, RI, professor of history, 1968-85; Yale University, New Haven, CT, professor of history, beginning 1986, director, Yale Center for Parliamentary History, currently professor emeritus. Visiting Mellon Professor, Institute for Advanced Study, 1988-89; fellow, Exeter College, Oxford, beginning 1990; visiting fellow, All Souls College, Oxford, 1992. *Military service:* Royal Air Force, 1944-47; became sergeant.

MEMBER: American Historical Association, Conference on British Studies, Royal Historical Society (fellow), British Academy (corresponding fellow).

AWARDS, HONORS: Guggenheim fellow, 1964-65 and 1992-93; American Council of Learned Societies fellow, 1973-74; National Endowment for the Humanities fellow, 1980-81; D.Litt., University of the South, 1981; John Ben Snow Prize, North American Conference on British Studies, and New England Historical Association Book Prize, both 1993, both for *Fire from Heaven: Life in an English Town in the Seventeenth Century.*

WRITINGS:

Royalist Conspiracy in England, 1649-1660, Yale University Press (New Haven, CT), 1960.

Pride's Purge: Politics in the Puritan Revolution, Oxford University Press (New York, NY), 1971.

Somerset in the Civil War and Interregnum, Shoe String Press (Hamden, CT), 1973.

Revel, Riot, and Rebellion: Popular Politics and Culture in England, 1603-1660, Oxford University Press (New York, NY), 1985.

Fire from Heaven: Life in an English Town in the Seventeenth Century, Yale University Press (New Haven, CT), 1992.

A Freeborn People: Politics and the Nation in Seventeenth-Century England, Clarendon Press (Oxford, England), 1996.

Start of Play: Cricket and Culture in Eighteenth-Century England, Allen Lane (London, England), 2000.

Contributor of articles and reviews to professional journals.

SIDELIGHTS: David Underdown is a highly respected historian of early modern England. His 1992 Ford lectures, given at Oxford University, are the source for *A Freeborn People: Politics and the Nation in Seventeenth-Century England,* in which Underdown argues that there were more affinities in the political arena between the social classes than was previously recognized by historians. In that sense, remarked Blair Worden in *History Today,* Underdown's thesis is anti-revisionist; where historical revisionism finds the political interests of the economic elites at odds with those of the rest of the voting populace, Underdown contends that prior to the civil war that put the Puritans in power in the 1640s the two political forces generally cooperated. Underdown's discussion sheds light on the rise of witch-hunting in the 1620s and "redeems the Court/Country model," according to Connie S. Evans on the Web site for the Arkansas Technical University Social Science and Philosophy department. This model explains how elites and commoners shared interests by virtue of locality and Parliamentary representation; thus, people from the same locality but different classes might share more political interests than people from the same class who lived in different areas. "Drawing on decades of work, at both a national and a regional level, on the seventeenth-century relationship between political and social change, the book suggests and stimulates even when it does not persuade," Worden commented. Evans likewise praised Underdown's evident expertise in this area: "He clearly demonstrates a thorough mastery of the parliamentary records, but it is his impressive command and analysis of the secondary literature that makes the study invaluable to specialists and the general reader alike."

Underdown next turned to the history of the British national pastime, cricket. In *Start of Play: Cricket and Culture in Eighteenth-Century England,* the author traces the evolution of the game from its birth after the Restoration of the British monarchy through its consolidation in the second half of the eighteenth century, to its corruption by London elites and bookies in the nineteenth. As in *A Freeborn People,* Underdown's narrative captures occasions when elites mixed with commoners, focusing on both the nobility and gentry, and the ordinary folk who made up the remainder of the teams and the tentative democracy that reigned as the teams became a more genuine mixture of the classes. Rural teams were the losers as the money and the prestige moved to London and its environs—a sore point for the author, according to John Sturrock in *London Review of Books.* "Underdown's lingering resentment about this surfaces from time to time in his book and puts a bracingly keen edge on its argument that the dukes and other notables who got involved in cricket did so more to advance their own glory and political influence than the welfare or fun of the working men who played it." Throughout, Underdown places the players and the history of the game in context. "In a mere double century of pages, *Start of Play* roots cricket more firmly and knowledgeably within its social, economic and cultural matrix than any other book known to me," Sturrock concluded.

BIOGRAPHICAL/CRITICAL SOURCES:

PERIODICALS

Albion, spring, 1998, review of *A Freeborn People,* p. 110.

American Historical Review, December, 1987; April, 1999, Johann P. Sommerville, review of *A Freeborn People,* p. 632.

English Historical Review, January, 1987; June, 1998, review of *A Freeborn People,* p. 733.

History Today, August, 1987; January, 1998, Blair Worden, review of *A Freeborn People,* p. 53.

Journal of Interdisciplinary History, summer, 1987.

London Review of Books, September 7, 2000, John Sturrock, "6/4 He Won't Score 20," pp. 23-24.

New York Review of Books, February 26, 1987.

Renaissance Quarterly, winter, 1998, review of *A Freeborn People,* p. 1372.

Seventeenth-Century News, spring, 1987.

Sewanee Review, October, 1987.

Sixteenth-Century Journal, spring, 1998, review of *A Freeborn People,* p. 245.

Times Literary Supplement, July 18, 1986; May 2, 1997, review of *A Freeborn People,* p. 10.

OTHER

Arkansas Technical University Social Science and Philosophy Department, http://lfa.atu.edu.ssphil/publications/ Connie S. Evans, review of *A Freeborn People,* (November 10, 2000).

* * *

URRY, John 1946-

PERSONAL: Born June 1, 1946, in London, England; son of Richard James (an accountant) and Wilga (a secretary; maiden name, Smith) Urry; children: Thomas, Amy. *Ethnicity:* "White." *Education:* Christ's College, Cambridge, B.A. (with first class honors), 1967, M.A., 1970, Ph.D., 1972.

ADDRESSES: Home—Lancaster, England. *Office*—Department of Sociology, Lancaster University, Lancaster LA1 4YL, England. *E-mail*—j.urry@lancaster.ac.uk.

CAREER: Lancaster University, Lancaster, England, lecturer, 1970-81, senior lecturer, 1981-84, professor of sociology, 1985—, dean of social sciences faculty, 1989-94.

MEMBER: Royal Society of Arts (fellow), Academy of Learned Societies in the Social Sciences.

WRITINGS:

Reference Groups and the Theory of Revolution, Routledge & Kegan Paul (London, England), 1973.

(Editor with John Wakeford) *Power in Britain,* Heinemann (London, England), 1973.

(With Russell Keat) *Social Theory as Science,* Routledge & Kegan Paul (London, England), 1975, 2nd edition, 1982.

The Anatomy of Capitalist Societies, Macmillan (London, England), 1981.

(With Nicholas Abercrombie) *Capital, Labour, and the Middle Classes,* Allen & Unwin (London, England), 1983.

(Editor with Derek Gregory) *Social Relations and Spatial Structures,* Macmillan (London, England), 1985.

(With Linda Murgatroyd, Michael Savage, Dan Shapiro, and others) *Localities, Class, and Gender,* Pion (London, England), 1985.

(With Scott Lash) *The End of Organized Capitalism,* Polity Press (Oxford, England), 1987.

(With Abercrombie, Alan Warde, and others) *Contemporary British Society,* Polity Press (Oxford, England), 1987.

The Tourist Gaze, Sage, 1990.

(With Paul Bagguley and others) *Restructuring Place, Class, and Gender,* Sage, 1990.

(With Scott Lash) *Economies of Signs and Space,* Sage, 1990.

Consuming Places, Routledge & Kegan Paul (London, England), 1995.

(With Phil MacNaghten) *Contested Natures,* Sage, 1998.

Sociology beyond Societies, Routledge (London, England), 2000.

WORK IN PROGRESS: Research on travel, leisure, and tourism, environmental issues, class, urban change, and social theory.

* * *

VALENTINE, Jean 1934-

PERSONAL: Born April 27, 1934, in Chicago, IL; daughter of John W. and Jean (Purcell) Valentine; married James Chace (divorced); children: Sarah, Rebecca. *Education:* Radcliffe College, B.A., 1956.

ADDRESSES: *Home*—527 West 110th St., No. 81, New York, NY 10025. *Office*—Department of Writing, Sarah Lawrence College, Bronxville, NY 10708.

CAREER: Poet. Swarthmore College, Swarthmore, PA, poetry workshop teacher, 1968-70; Hunter College, staff member, 1970-75; Sarah Lawrence College, Bronxville, NY, staff member in Department of Writing, 1974—. Instructor at Barnard College, New York University graduate writing program, and 92nd Street Y, New York, NY. Has read poetry at numerous institutions, including Yale University, Brown University, Sarah Lawrence College, and the YMHA.

AWARDS, HONORS: Yale Series Younger Poets Award, 1965, for *Dream Barker;* Guggenheim fellowship, 1976; Shelley Memorial Award, Poetry Society of America, 2000; received grants from New York State Council for the Arts, New York Foundation for the Arts, National Endowment for the Arts, Rockefeller Foundation, and Bunting Institute.

WRITINGS:

POETRY

Dream Barker, and Other Poems (Volume 61 of the "Yale Series of Younger Poets"), foreword by Dudley Fitts, Yale University Press (New Haven, CT), 1965, second edition, Carnegie Mellon University Press (Pittsburgh, PA), 1995.

Pilgrims, Farrar, Straus (New York, NY), 1969, second edition, Carnegie Mellon University Press (Pittsburgh, PA), 1995.

Ordinary Things, Farrar, Straus (New York, NY), 1974.

The Messenger, Farrar, Straus (New York, NY), 1979.

Home, Deep, Blue: New and Selected Poems, Alice James (Cambridge, MA), 1989.

The River at Wolf, Alice James (Cambridge, MA), 1992.

The Under Voice: Selected Poems, Salmon Poetry (Galway, Ireland), 1995.

Growing Darkness, Growing Light, Carnegie Mellon University Press (Pittsburgh, PA), 1997.

The Cradle of the Real Life, Wesleyan University Press (Middletown, CT), 2000.

Valentine's poetry also appears on the recording, *Jean Valentine and Cornelius Eady Reading Their Poems with Comment,* Library of Congress (Washington, DC), 2001.

SIDELIGHTS: Jean Valentine's poetry career began inauspiciously. For ten years she submitted her writing to publications, but each time met with rejection, perhaps due to what *Times Literary Supplement* reviewer Jay Parini described as "the stripped, unyielding quality" of her work, a quality Parini maintained "will admit few and discourage most of her readers." Finally, in 1965, Valentine's last-minute entry in Yale University's Younger Poets award won her both the prize and publication of her first book, *Dream Barker, and Other Poems.* She has since established herself with the same obscure, suggestive style that characterized her first volume. "Valentine's audience has always been small but enthusiastic," wrote Parini, "which is the sort of response one expects for a poet whose work is dense, almost hermetic, yet striking and intense." According to *Praxis* contributor Crystal Koch, who reported on a 1997 poetry reading attended by Valentine that was held at University of California-Davis, Valentine's audience found her work to be appealing and thought-provoking; they appeared to feel connected to the "vivid images" that she presented in "a simple manner."

Koch also commented of Valentine's work that one of the poet's strengths is "her ability to portray the down-to-earth quality of [her subjects]." The people and life on Saint Lucia Island and in rural Ireland are among the subjects she profiles in *Growing Darkness, Growing Light,* her 1997 collection. Koch related: "The poet expressed an empathy toward her subjects and a desire to convey their struggles, their attitudes and their feelings." The pieces in the volume "are marked by moments of brief intensity," stated a *Publishers Weekly* reviewer, who went on to declare Valentine "a commanding poet" and *Growing Darkness, Growing Light* "one of [her] best collections." Do not read Valentine's work as "straightforward logic," warned Barbara Hoffert in a *Library Journal* assessment of *Growing Darkness, Growing Light,* for her "poems are like little drops of pure, unfiltered feeling."

In the *New York Times Book Review* David Kalstone described Valentine's unique language: "Miss Valentine has a gift for tough strangeness, but also a dreamlike syntax and manner of arranging the lines of . . . short poems so as to draw us into the doubleness and fluency of feelings." Paul Zweig claimed in the *Village Voice* that one problem with Valentine's dreamy style is "diffuseness. The impressionistic play of images tends, now and then, simply to trail away; to unravel, without any underpinning of form. When this happens, poems become flat, indecisive." However, Zweig had praise for Valentine's ability "to unresolve the reader's mind, to peel away its armor of opinions; to make it solitary, vulnerable and attentive." Kalstone admitted a similar reactive response to Valentine's poetry: "She does not 'see and take' so much as initiate the reader into very private feelings."

"Valentine's lifelong identification with poets like Rilke and Mandelstain is a key to understanding her own dreamlike but fierce stance," explained Carol Muske, reviewing *Growing Darkness, Growing Light* in *Nation.* Valentine, who deserves to be given more considerable and considered attention according to Muske, is "a writer of deep-image, projective verse." Muske added: "What has distinguished her verse in the past is its refusal to be anything other than what the 'conscience' of her poetic vision has sanctioned. Thus, her poems are brief, unswervingly drawn to the oracular. Yet nothing is 'enhanced' or self-consciously mythic. . . . There are no unessential details, everything is given equal moral and aesthetic weight, as in a dream." Muske concluded that "the poems in [*Growing Darkness, Growing Light*] are indeed dreams, but precise dreams of waking: startling junctures of the abstract and the carnal."

Referring to Valentine's "dizzying, elliptical but seemingly effortless coincidence of emotion and idea within the confines of the pared-down lyric," Muske acknowledged that "Valentine's style definitely leans to the cryptic." However, declared the critic, "[her] mastery of the form, the deep image, [is what] keeps these unlikely barks afloat." Despite such an assessment, in a review of Valentine's 2000 poetry collection, *The Cradle of the Real Life,* a *Publishers Weekly* critic remarked that Valentine's "command of form can't always equal her feeling." As such, concluded the reviewer, *The Cradle of the Real Life* is both "harrowing and frustrating." In her quest to compress, commented the critic, she creates "ostensibly completed poems and series read like notes for poems not yet written." Ellen Kaufman more optimistically promoted Valentine's 2000 volume in *Library Journal,* praising *The Cradle of the Real Life* as a "mature collection from an important writer" who gives "spare form imbued with spirituality." Although "filled with sadness," remarked Kaufman, *The Cradle of the Real Life* "is a book of much joy."

BIOGRAPHICAL/CRITICAL SOURCES:

PERIODICALS

American Poetry Review, July-August, 1991, interview with Michael Klein, pp. 39-41.

Field, spring, 1989.

Harper's, January, 1980, Hayden Carruth, review of *The Messenger,* p. 76.

Library Journal, February 1, 1989, review of *Home, Deep, Blue,* p. 66; May 1, 1997, Barbara Hoffert, review of *Growing Darkness, Growing Light,* p. 109; March 1, 2000, Ellen Kaufman, review of *The Cradle of the Real Life,* p. 96.

Los Angeles Times Book Review, August 10, 1980.

Nation, July 21, 1997, Carol Muske, review of *Growing Darkness, Growing Light,* p. 36.

Newsweek, March 1, 1965.

New York Times Book Review, August 2, 1970; October 21, 1979.

Ploughshares, fall, 1993, David Rivard, review of *The River at Wolf,* p. 246.

Poetry, December, 1970; August, 1980, William H. Pritchard, review of *The Messenger,* p. 296; December, 1992, Steven Cramer, review of *The River at Wolf,* p. 159.

Publishers Weekly, March 31, 1997, review of *Growing Darkness, Growing Light,* p. 70; February 7, 2000, review of *The Cradle of the Real Life,* p. 70.

Times Literary Supplement, March 20, 1981, review by Jay Parini.

Village Voice, January 13, 1975; May 23, 1989.

Washington Post Book World, August 19, 1979.

OTHER

Praxis, http://www.californiaaggie.com/ (October 16, 1997), Crystal Koch, "Jean Valentine Poetically Enchants Audience.*

* * *

VILLARI, Rosario 1925-

PERSONAL: Born July 12, 1925, in Bagnara, Italy; son of Francesco and Isaia Anna Villari; married Degioannis Aldina, 1948 (died, 1972); married Arcidiacono Elvira, 1976 (marriage ended); married Santi Anna Rosa, 1994; children: Francesco, Antonella. *Ethnicity:* "Italian." *Education:* Earned fine arts degree, 1947.

ADDRESSES: *Home*—Via Giovanni Lanza 154, 00184 Rome, Italy. *E-mail*—r.villari@tiscalinet.it.

CAREER: University of Messina, Messina, Italy, teacher, 1959-70; University of Florence, Florence, Italy, teacher, 1971-78; University of Rome "La Saprienza", Rome, Italy, teacher of early modern history, 1979-95, director of Department of Medieval and Modern History, 1992-94, professor emeritus, 1996—. Visiting professor at St. Antony's College, Oxford, 1974, Newbery Library, 1980, and Institute for Advanced Study, Princeton, NJ, 1981-82. Italian Parliament, member, 1976-79.

MEMBER: Accademia dei Lincei, Accademia Pontaniana, Bureau of the International Commitee of Historical Science (1998-2000), Siunta Centrale per gli Studi Storici, Italy, (1996-2000, president).

WRITINGS:

La rivolta antispagnola a Napoli, Laterza (Bari-Rome), 1967, translation published as *The Revolt of Naples,* Polity Press, 1993.

(Editor) *L'Uomo barocco,* Laterza (Bari-Rome), 1991, translation published as *Baroque Personae,* Chicago University Press, 1995.

UNTRANSLATED WORKS

Il Sud nella storia d'Italia, Laterza (Bari-Rome), 1961.

Mezzogiorno e contadini nell'eta moderna, Laterza (Bari-Rome), 1961.

Conservatori e democratici nell'Italia liberale, Laterza (Bari-Rome), 1964.

Storia dell'Europa contemporanea, Laterza (Bari-Rome), 1971.

Ribelli e riformatori dal XVI al XVIII secolo, Editions Riuniti (Rome), 1979.

Mezzogiorno e democrazia, Laterza (Bari-Rome), 1979.

Elogio della dissumulazione: la lotta politica nel Seicento, Laterza (Bari-Rome), 1987.

Com'e nata l'Italia: il Risorgimento, Editions la Repubblica (Rome), 1991.

Per il re o per la patria: la fedelta nel Seicento, Laterza (Bari-Rome), 1994.

Mille ami di Noria: della citta 'medievale all' vinta dell'Europa, Laterza (Bari-Rome), 2000.

Napoli e la Spagna nel XVII secolo, Mondadori, in press.

Author of the textbook *Storia medievale, Storia moderna, Storia contemporanea,* Laterza.

SIDELIGHTS: Rosario Villari once told *CA:* "I began my research with a contribution to the revived discussion on the 'question meridionale' and to the study of political debate in Italy from the *Risorgimento* to the rise of fascism. During the early years of my research, I also took an interest in the social history of eighteenth-century Italy, particularly in the crisis of feudal regime. I then developed interests in the early modern relations between Italy and Spain, the Neapolitan revolution of 1647 and the seventeenth-century European revolutions. While working on these subjects, I continued to analyze and discuss historical problems relating to socialist movements and democratic systems in Europe and Italy."

W

WALKER, Martin 1947-

PERSONAL: Born January 23, 1947 (some sources say 1949), in Durham, England; son of Tom and Dorothy (McNeill) Walker; married Julia Watson (a writer), May 6, 1978. *Education:* Balliol College, Oxford, M.A. (with first class honors), 1969; graduate study at Harvard University. *Politics:* "Libertarian anti-fascist." *Religion:* "Vague."

ADDRESSES: *Office*—c/o 3462 Macomb St., N.W., Washington, DC 20016. *E-mail*—martwalker@aol.com.

CAREER: Affiliated with *Johannesburg Star* and *Newscheck,* both in South Africa; speechwriter for U.S. Senator Edmund Muskie, 1970-71; *Guardian,* Manchester, England, reporter, columnist, and foreign correspondent, beginning 1972, Moscow bureau chief 1983-88, U.S. bureau chief, Washington, DC., 1989-98. European Policy Institute, associate director, London and Geneva; European Institute, vice-chairperson, Washington, DC. Broadcaster for BBC-TV and BBC-Radio; Washington commentator for Radio Telefeis Eiran, Radio and TV New Zealand, and for Australia's ABC-TV and ABC-Radio; commentator for CNN, CBC, C-Span, CBS-TV, and National Public Radio. Harvard University, Harkness fellow and resident tutor at Kirkland House, 1969-70; New School for Social Research (now New School University), New York, senior fellow of World Policy Institute; Loyola College, Baltimore, H. L. Menken Lecturer, 1994; lecturer at colleges and universities in Moscow, Pittsburgh, Toronto, Chicago, and New York City, and at National War College. *Military service:* Royal Air Force cadet, pilot, 1960-65.

MEMBER: National Union of Journalists.

AWARDS, HONORS: Congressional fellow of American Political Science Association, 1970-71; Public Policy Fellow, Woodrow Wilson International Center for Scholars, 2000-01.

WRITINGS:

The National Front, Collins, 1977, revised edition, 1979.

Daily Sketches (history of political cartoons), Muller, 1978.

The Infiltrators (novel), Dial, 1978.

(Editor and translator from Arabic) *Poems on the Glass of Windows,* OCPD, 1979.

A Mercenary Calling (novel), Doubleday, 1980.

The Eastern Question (novel), Hart-Davis, 1981.

The President We Deserve: Bill Clinton: His Rise, Falls, and Comebacks, Crown (New York), 1996.

America Reborn: A Twentieth-Century Narrative in Twenty-six Lives, Knopf (New York), 2000.

Publications include *Daily Sketches: A History of Political Cartoons,* 1978; *Powers of the Press: A Comparative Study of the World's Leading Newspapers,* 1981; *The Waking Giant: Gorbachev and Perestroika,* 1987; *Martin Walker's Russia,* 1989; *The Independent Traveler's Guide to the Soviet Union,* 1990; *The Insight Guide to Washington, D.C.,* 1992; and *The Cold War: A History,* 1993. Work also represented in anthologies, including *The Young Unicorns,* Sidgwick & Jackson, 1973. Writer for British Broadcasting Corp. World Service. Contributor to *Encyclopaedia Britannica.* Contributor to periodicals in the United States and abroad, including a weekly column for the *Moscow Times* and essays for the *Los Angeles Times* "Opinion" section.

WORK IN PROGRESS: The Great Papers, nonfiction, a study of the world's twelve top newspapers, with comparative analysis of their 1979-80 Iranian coverage; *Stechkin,* a novel on modern Russia.

SIDELIGHTS: British journalist Martin Walker is a multi-talented writer who has branched out into a variety of genres including fiction, travel, politics, and history. He has also worked extensively as a commentator on radio and television, and taught at numerous colleges and universities. Walker's long career as a writer and editor for the Manchester *Guardian* has included stints as bureau chief in Moscow and Washington, D.C.; both assignments resulted in books written on the places, people, and politics he encountered. Walker's biography of President Bill Clinton, *The President We Deserve: Bill Clinton: His Rise, Falls, and Comebacks,* and a collection of narrative biographies, *America Reborn: A Twentieth-Century Narrative in Twenty-six Lives,* have received considerable critical praise.

Walker's earlier work included assignments as a foreign correspondent. He commented to *CA* that during the 1960s he "reported on and suffered wars in the Congo, the Spanish Sahara, Iran, and Afghanistan." During the 1970s his work as a journalist included an interview with Idi Amin, then president of Uganda, and an exposé that halted the sale to South Africa (by Jordan) of modern tanks, anti-aircraft missiles, and jet fighter aircraft. He also noted: "My wife and I spent a year traveling around the world, and were on the last civilian convoy down the Khyber Pass from Afghanistan."

Regarding his some of his early books, Walker wrote: "*The National Front,* on fascist movements in modern Britain, was in response to an emerging political crisis in Britain. My first novel, *The Infiltrators,* was written while I was covering the Portuguese revolution for the *Guardian,* to tell of the political machinations I knew to be happening, but could not prove adequately for a newspaper. My other novels follow a similar pattern."

The book that ties together Walker's work in the Soviet Union and the United States is *The Cold War: A History.* Originally published in Great Britain in 1993, the book presents the Cold War from a global perspective and includes research using newly available information from the Kremlin archives. In *Kirkus Reviews,* a critic described the work as an "Absorbing history spanning five complex decades of geopolitics and economics with clarity and panache" and credited Walker with "combin[ing] a broad awareness of history with a journalist's magpie eye for the telling anecdote."

In 1996 Walker published *The President We Deserve: Bill Clinton: His Rise, Falls, and Comebacks,* which covers events in the politician's life from birth to early 1996. While some critics saw the book as a decidedly Clinton-friendly presentation, it was also regularly judged to be a superior biography of the president. In the *New York Times* Douglas Brinkley said that Walker had written "a shrewd, stylishly conceived narrative that distinguishes itself as the most comprehensive book on Mr. Clinton to date," although he felt it lacked the documentary background to make it of lasting interest. Brinkley found that Walker focused heavily on the Clinton administration's role in global free-trade developments and identified his "overall thesis" as being "that Bill Clinton is the archetypal postwar American . . . [and] the perfect symbol of the great American meritocracy." *Booklist*'s Gilbert Taylor characterized *The President We Deserve* as a "policy-oriented biography" that was "strong on domestic politics."

Continuing in the biographical vein, Walker next penned *America Reborn: A Twentieth-Century Narrative in Twenty-six Lives.* In this narrative, he offers chapters on twenty-six famous Americans who played important roles in their country's history or who otherwise illustrate an important aspect of their society. Among those treated in the book are Theodore Roosevelt, Babe Ruth, Henry Ford, Duke Ellington, Betty Friedan, William Boeing, Richard Nixon, Walter Reuther, Frank Lloyd Wright, Katharine Hepburn, and John Steinbeck. Again, critics were pleased with Walkers' perceptive, if not scholarly, approach to his subject. In his review of *America Reborn* for *Booklist,* Gilbert Taylor enjoyed Walker's "impressive command over a range of topics" and noted how he "teases out the larger meanings of figures many highbrows hate" such as Walt Disney. In *Library Journal,* Edward Gibson suggested that the author "uses an almost novelistic approach to the telling of America's story." Gibson felt that among similar books "none [are] as sweeping or as well written." Milder praise came from a *Publishers Weekly* critic, who remarked "the early chapters are essentially recapitulations of received wisdom"; however, starting with figures from the 1970s, the narrative was considered greatly improved, especially in the chapter on Richard Nixon. And *New York Times* critic Adam Hochschild complimented Walker as being among those "literate Britons who didn't stop thinking about history when they took up daily journalism." While he considered the absence of a strong theme to be a possible fault in the book, Hochschild identified Walker's "shrewd eye for the significance of people and events we otherwise take for granted, and a consistent undertone of gentle demythologizing." He concluded that *America Reborn* was "a quirky, readable and thoughtful look at the American century by an outsider who knows us very well indeed."

BIOGRAPHICAL/CRITICAL SOURCES:

PERIODICALS

Booklist, October 15, 1998, Gilbert Taylor, review of *The President We Deserve,* p. 396; May 1, 2000, Gilbert Taylor, review of *America Reborn,* p. 1648.

Kirkus Reviews, April 15, 1994, review of *The Cold War: A History.*

Library Journal, May 1, 2000, Edward Gibson, review of *America Reborn,* p. 134.

New York Times, September 22, 1996, Douglas Brinkley, "A Postrevolutionary Man"; August 20, 2000, Adam Hochschild, "The Way We Were."

Publishers Weekly, July 1, 1996, review of *The President We Deserve,* p. 48; May 1, 2000, review of *America Reborn,* p. 60.

* * *

WALKER, Paul E(rnest) 1941-

PERSONAL: Born 1941, in Salt Lake City, UT; son of Don D. and Marjorie F. Walker; married Karen L. Wilson; children: Adam, Katrina, Jeremy. *Education:* University of Utah, B.A., 1964; American University in Cairo, M.A., 1966; doctoral study at Harvard University, 1966-67; University of Chicago, Ph.D., 1974.

ADDRESSES: Home—5761 South Blackstone, Chicago, IL 60637. *E-mail*—pwalker@midway.uchicago.edu.

CAREER: Teacher at a private school in Milton, MA, 1967-68; Smithsonian Institution, Washington, DC, historian at National Museum of History and Technology, 1973-76; American Research Center in Egypt, Inc., Cairo, director, 1976-80, executive director, 1980-86; McGill University, Montreal, Quebec, Canada, associate professor at Institute of Islamic Studies, 1987-90; independent scholar, 1990-93; University of Michigan, Ann Arbor, visiting associate professor of Islamic studies, 1993-94, visiting professor of Islamic studies, 1997; independent scholar, 1994—. Columbia University, part-time lecturer, 1981-86; McGill University, visiting assistant professor, 1984-86; University of Chicago, Center for Middle Eastern Studies, visiting scholar, 1998—. National Endowment for Humanities fellow, 1999-2000.

WRITINGS:

Early Philosophical Shiism: The Ismaili Neoplatonism of Abu Ya'qub al-Sijistani, Cambridge University Press (New York, NY), 1993.

The Wellsprings of Wisdom, University of Utah Press (Salt Lake City, UT), 1994.

Abu Ya'qub al-Sijistani: Intellectual Missionary, I.B. Tauris and the Institute of Ismaili Studies (London, England), 1996, translated into Persian, 1998.

An Ismaili Heresiography: The "Bab al-Shaytan" from Abu Tammam's Kitab al-Shajara, Brill (Leiden), 1998.

Hamid al-Din al-Kirmani: Ismaili Thought in the Age of al-Hakim, I. B. Tauris (London, England), 1999.

(With Wilferd Madelung) *The Advent of the Fatimids: A Contemporary Shi'i Witness,* I. B. Tauris (London, England), 2000.

(Translator) Imam al-Haramayn al-Juwayni, *A Guide to Conclusive Proofs for the Principles of Belief: Kitab al-irshad ila qawati'al-adilla fi usul al-i'tiqad,* Garnet Publishing (Reading), 2000.

Exploring an Islamic Empire: Fatimid History and Its Sources, I. B. Tauris and the Institute of Ismaili Studies (London, England), 2001.

Work represented in anthologies, including *Studies in Neoplatonism: Ancient and Modern,* edited by R. Baine Harris, State University of New York Press (Albany, NY), 1992; *The Political Aspects of Islamic Philosophy,* edited by C. Butterworth, Harvard University Press (Cambridge, MA), 1992; and *Religion and Practical Reason: New Essays in the Comparative Philosophy of Religion,* edited by Frank Reynolds and David Tracy, State University of New York Press (Albany, NY), 1994. Contributor of about fifty articles and reviews to Islamic studies and religious studies journals. Islamic Near East Editor, *Journal of the American Oriental Society,* 1998—.

* * *

WATKINS, Paul 1964-

PERSONAL: Born February 23, 1964, in Redwood City, CA; son of Norman David (a geophysicist) and Patricia (de Luly) Watkins; married, wife's name, Cath; children: Emma. *Education:* Attended Eton College, 1977-82; Yale University, B.A., 1986; graduate study at Syracuse University, 1986-88.

ADDRESSES: Home—New Jersey. *Agent*—Amanda Urban, International Creative Management, 40 West 57th St., New York, NY 10019.

CAREER: Writer. Teaches fiction writing and participates in drama productions at The Peddie School, Hightstown, New Jersey.

AWARDS, HONORS: Calm at Sunset, Calm at Dawn won the 1989 Encore Award.

WRITINGS:

NOVELS

Night over Day over Night, Knopf (New York, NY), 1988.
Calm at Sunset, Calm at Dawn, Houghton (Boston, MA), 1989.
In the Blue Light of African Dreams, Houghton (Boston, MA), 1990.
The Promise of Light, Faber (London), 1992, Random House (New York, NY), 1993.
Archangel, Random House (New York, NY), 1995.
The Story of My Disappearance, Picador (New York, NY), 1998.
The Forger, Picador (New York, NY), 2000.

OTHER

Stand before Your God (memoir), Random House (New York, NY), 1994.

SIDELIGHTS: American author Paul Watkins has quickly gained a reputation for his dedication to research and for his vivid, detailed prose. His first novel, *Night over Day over Night,* tells the story of Sebastian Westland, a seventeen-year-old German who enlists in the Nazi SS in 1944 and witnesses the horrors of the Third Reich's last, frenzied assaults on the Allied forces at the close of World War II. Michiko Kakutani wrote in the *New York Times* that "Watkins's orchestration of the combat scenes attests to a remarkably assured command of narrative and a journalistic instinct for the telling detail." In a *Chicago Tribune* review, John Blades praised the book's "crystalline prose" and compared it to the works of Stephen Crane and Ernest Hemingway. "The similarities are real," wrote Blades, "but Watkins has a style and angle of vision that are distinctly his own, and . . . his virtuosic first novel won't easily be forgotten."

In preparation for writing *Night over Day over Night* Watkins studied German army equipment both in museums and at flea markets, read long-out-of-print volumes on the Ardennes Campaign, toured the battle area near Rockerath, and spoke with both German and American war veterans. Inspiration for the book came from Watkins's stay in Germany as a student at age sixteen. "I stayed with a family of old Prussian aristocrats," the novelist explained in *Contemporary Literary Criticism,* "who fled the Russians at the end of [World War II]. The father of the family found himself, in the closing stages of the war, in a similar situation to the book's main character."

Watkins's second novel, *Calm at Sunset, Calm at Dawn,* is the result of his experiences working for several seasons on a New England scallop trawler. The story centers on twenty-year-old James Pfeiffer—the restless son of a scallop trawler captain—who, after being expelled from college, decides to go to sea, despite his father's protests. The novel follows Pfeiffer, first to a run-down Portuguese ship, then to a better trawler, as he experiences the difficulties of life at sea and learns that life on the ocean is not immune to the problems which drove him from the land. Reviews of the book were generally favorable. In the *Los Angeles Times,* Carolyn See noted that sections of the plot seemed "contrived and artificial" but added that the author's evocations of life on the sea "are dazzlingly rendered." See concluded, "Paul Watkins is not a dilettante but a human being who takes life seriously, an author whose work should be read with great respect." John Casey in Chicago *Tribune Books* called *Calm at Sunset, Calm at Dawn* "a book that will have value and appeal for more than sea-story lovers," adding "it is written out of acute feeling and experience, in the voice of an artful storyteller."

In *The Promise of Light,* Watkins created Ben Sheridan, a young man who, on the eve of his college graduation, sees his father seriously injured while fighting a fire. The trauma of his father's accident causes Ben to abandon his promising job as a bank teller and go instead to Ireland, where he eventually joins that country's struggle for independence. James Hynes, writing in *Washington Post Book World,* noted that the plot was a bit melodramatic, but he added that it was "melodrama done with such conviction and such a light touch that it is noticeable only in the retelling. . . . Watkins's evocation of a small Irish town at war with itself is so skillfully and unsentimentally rendered. He captures the rage and bitter wit of men and women who have known each other all their lives, but are ready at a moment's notice to slit each other's throats over politics." Hynes concluded that *The Promise of Light* was "part coming-of-age story, part political thriller, part historical novel, and part blood-and-thunder adventure tale."

In the novel *Archangel,* Watkins created another dramatic adventure tale, this time set in the woods of

Maine. Jonah Mackenzie, one of the central characters, chainsaws his own leg off after being trapped beneath a tree deep in the woods. The incident leaves him with a hatred for the forces of nature, and later in life he arranges a government contract that will allow him to clear-cut the forest of his youth. He is opposed by Adam Gabriel, a young environmental activist who resorts to extreme means to protect the trees he loves. Writing in *Spectator,* D. J. Taylor noted that Watkins's style "looks unforced while intermittently hinting that a great deal of care and attention has been lavished on it." Donna Seaman, a reviewer for *Booklist,* noted that "Watkins adeptly orchestrates a thoroughly believable escalation of tension, madness, and violence, all conveyed with bone-chilling accuracy. As taut and expressive as a violin string, this is an outstandingly intelligent and significant novel." And a *Publishers Weekly* writer remarked, "Watkins evokes the grandeur of the woods as well as the wild unpredictability of both natural and social violence. His vision of rural New England refracts through the interactions of multifaceted characters, most notably of the willful Mackenzie, who is no stock villain but a wonderfully complex and often sympathetic creation." The writer concluded that in addition to creating a multitude of memorable characters, Watkins had also captured "the tortured spirit of a place."

In *The Story of My Disappearance,* Watkins provides a thrilling spy adventure tale with a postmodern twist in which the main character, East German spy for the KGB Paul Wedekind is eventually transformed into the American Paul Watkins. Related in the first person, the story takes Paul from days as an engineering student to membership in the East German secret police, where he's recruited to spy on a friend, a suspected drug dealer. From there he is transferred to the KGB which sends him to Afghanistan. Rescued from the torturers who killed his compatriot but decreed officially dead, Paul ends up in Newport, Rhode Island, helping smuggle Russian spies into the United States and falling in love with Suleika, his accomplice. *Kirkus Reviews* was less than enthusiastic about Watkin's chronological narrative interspersed with flashbacks to the horrors of Paul's past, seeing *Story of My Disappearance* as merely "another step in Watkins's carefully calculated progress toward becoming our contemporary Hemingway." A reviewer for *Publishers Weekly* found more to praise in Watkins's ambitious tale: "Subtly evocative prose and a convincing first-person narrative may have readers wondering if this tense and absorbing tale . . . could actually be true."

In *The Forger* a young American painter receives a scholarship to travel to Paris in the late 1930s and becomes embroiled in Resistance efforts to rescue works of art from destruction by the Nazis. "Watkins appears to be fascinated with the way fictional worlds can be made to resemble the real world, and thereby give rise to unexpected continuities between otherwise loosely connected lives," remarked Sam Gilpin in a *London Review of Books* review of Watkins's latest novel, continuing: "The parallel between a believable historical fiction and a successful counterfeit painting is obvious." Thus, whereas in *Story of My Disappearance* Watkins created a sort of counterfeit autobiography of a character called "Paul Watkins," in *The Forger* the author muses on the nature of artistic production and the line between original art and derivative copy. For Gilpin, "The best and most intense moments in the novel have to do with the process of forgery itself: the attempt to enter someone else's consciousness, the minute attention to detail, the techniques required by different styles of painting." A reviewer in *Publishers Weekly* praised the author's ability to seamlessly weave period details of wartime Paris into his suspenseful plot. "While Watkins's themes are familiar, they are deftly handled, the writer's painterly eye for detail matching that of his protagonist," this critic remarked. *Library Journal* contributor David Keymer praised *The Forger* for its "full-fleshed personalities, dramatically visual prose, and . . . strong narrative thrust."

In *Publishers Weekly,* contributor Gary M. Kramer called the author "an expert in creating characters burdened by their pasts" who "describes his protagonists as men who must confront their demons before they can move on with their lives. Typically, his heroes are driven by deep-rooted obsessions, from which Watkins creates what he calls 'a sense of urgency' in his works. His characters' emotional crusades . . . make his fiction convincing and compelling." Speaking on his own behalf in an interview in *Peddie Life,* Watkins remarked: "Basically, I try to portray people who are jarred out of their daily lives and who are faced with a challenge that will define their character through action. People have to do things to define themselves, not just talk about them."

"The work of Paul Watkins is refreshingly old fashioned," mused Hynes. "Watkins is not fixated upon the minutiae of the contemporary 20-something experience but ranges farther afield than most young writers. . . . There's nothing self-indulgent about [his protagonists]; they are passionate and engaged, defining themselves by action rather than by narcissistic introspection. . . . Watkins appears to have immersed himself in the work of Hemingway, Remarque and Stephen Crane. As a result, his books are lucid, intelligent and shamelessly entertaining, written in lean, evocative prose and displaying an uncommon delight in storytelling."

BIOGRAPHICAL/CRITICAL SOURCES:

BOOKS

Contemporary Literary Criticism, Volume 55, Gale (Detroit), 1989.

PERIODICALS

Atlanta Journal-Constitution, February 7, 1993, p. N12.
Booklist, December 1, 1995, p. 610.
Christian Science Monitor, September 12, 1989, p. 12.
Entertainment Weekly, January 26, 1996, p. 50.
Esquire, March, 1994, p. 57.
Kirkus Reviews, February 1, 1988, pp. 157-158; October 15, 1995, p. 1455; February 1, 1998, review of *Story of My Disappearance,* p. 148.
Kliatt, September, 1997, review of *Stand before Your God,* p. 4; January, 1998, review of *Archangel,* p. 40.
Library Journal, November 1, 1995, p. 108; December, 1997, review of *The Story of My Disappearance,* p. 157; August, 2000, review of *The Forger,* p. 163.
London Review of Books, September 24, 1992, pp. 18-20; October 7, 1993, pp. 18-19; August 10, 2000, Sam Gilpin, "Faking It," p. 39.
Los Angeles Times, September 25, 1989, section IV, p. 1; March 10, 1994, p. E4.
Los Angeles Times Book Review, December 30, 1990, p. 8; February 28, 1993, p. 8.
New Statesman & Society, August 20, 1993.
New York, January 25, 1993.
New York Times, March 26, 1988, p. 18.
New York Times Book Review, December 23, 1990, p. 7; April 11, 1993, p. 29; March 6, 1994, p. 8; February 18, 1996, p. 17.
Observer, September 13, 1992, p. 54; August 22, 1993, p. 47; September 7, 1997, review of *The Story of My Disappearance,* p. 16; February 14, 1999, review of *The Story of My Disappearance,* p. 16.
Publishers Weekly, February 12, 1988, p. 72; January 4, 1993, p. 55; October 23, 1995, p. 58; January 19, 1998, review of *The Story of My Disappearance,* p. 368; September 25, 2000, review of *The Forger,* p. 84.
Sewanee Review, fall, 1990.
Spectator, September 4, 1993, p. 30; July 8, 1995, p. 37; August 23, 1997, review of *The Story of My Disappearance,* p. 34.
Times Literary Supplement, August 10, 1990; September 4, 1992, p. 19; September 17, 1993, p. 24; August 29, 1997, review of *The Story of My Disappearance,* p. 22.
Tribune Books (Chicago), March 20, 1988, p. 3; September 10, 1989, p. 6; September 9, 1990, p. 6.
Vogue, March, 1994, p. 282.
Wall Street Journal, April 4, 1994, p. A10.
Washington Post, September 25, 1990, p. C2; March 2, 1994, p. B2.
Washington Post Book World, April 24, 1988, pp. 5, 14; September 3, 1989, p. 10; January 24, 1993, p. 5; March 21, 1996, p. D2.*

* * *

WEBER, Bruce 1942-

PERSONAL: Born November 20, 1942, in Brooklyn, NY; son of Paul Karl (an educator) and Miriam Lillian (a homemaker; maiden name, Goldstein) Weber; married Annette Katz (in sales), May 30, 1968; children: Allison Emma, Jonathan Russell. *Education:* University of Maryland, B.S., 1964; Pace University, M.B.A., 1968. *Politics:* Democrat. *Religion:* Jewish. *Avocational interests:* Sports, music.

ADDRESSES: Home—511 Marion Ln., Paramus, NJ 07652. *Office*—Scholastic Inc., 730 Broadway, New York, NY 10003.

CAREER: University of Maryland, College Park, MD, assistant director of sports information, 1962-64; *Scholastic Coach* magazine, New York City, assistant editor, 1965-70, associate editor, 1970-81, publisher, 1981—; New York City Board of Education, Brooklyn, NY, music teacher, 1968-72; writer. *Scholastic Sports Academy* (television series), writer, 1981-84. Paramus, New Jersey Board of Education, member, 1978-87, president, 1981-83; Devonshire School Board of Governors, president, 1988-90. Director of Paramus Run, 1979—; director of Athletic Institute, 1991-93.

MEMBER: National Soccer Coaches Association of America, Football Writers Association of America, American Football Coaches Association.

AWARDS, HONORS: Action for Children's Television (ACT) Award, 1982, for *Scholastic Sports Academy;* award from Sports in America, 1987, for his work for the Athletic Institute; honorary member, American Football Coaches Association, 1995.

WRITINGS:

(With William Hongash) *Questions and Answers about Baseball,* Scholastic Book Services (New York, NY), 1974.

The Funniest Moments in School, illustrated by Kevin Callahan, M. Evans & Company (New York, NY), 1973, reprinted as *School Is a Funny Place,* Scholastic Book Services (New York, NY), 1977.

Weird Moments in Sports, Scholastic Book Services (New York, NY), 1975.

The Pro Football Quiz Book, Scholastic Book Services (New York, NY), 1976.

The Pro Basketball Reading Kit, Bowmar, 1976.

All-Pro Basketball Stars, annual editions, Scholastic Book Services (New York, NY), 1976-81, Scholastic, Inc. (New York, NY), 1982-83.

The Quest for Camelot, Scholastic, Inc. (New York, NY), 1979.

The Dynamite Animal Hall of Fame, Scholastic Book Services (New York, NY), 1979.

The T.V. Olympic Program Guide, Scholastic Book Services (New York, NY), 1980.

More Weird Moments in Sports, Scholastic, Inc. (New York, NY), 1983.

Bruce Weber's Inside Pro Football, annual editions, Scholastic, Inc. (New York, NY), 1983-92.

Bruce Weber's Inside Baseball, annual editions, Scholastic, Inc. (New York, NY), 1984-92.

Athletes: Photographs by Bruce Weber, Twelvetrees, 1985.

Magic Johnson and Larry Bird, Morrow/Avon, 1986.

Sparky Anderson, edited by Michael E. Goodman, Crestwood (Mankato, MN), 1988.

The Indianapolis 500, The Creative Company (Minneapolis, MN), 1990.

Mickey Mantle: Classic Sports Shots, Scholastic, Inc. (New York, NY), 1993.

Lou Gehrig: Classic Sports Shots, Scholastic, Inc. (New York, NY), 1993.

Jackie Robinson: Classic Sports Shots, Scholastic, Inc. (New York, NY), 1993.

Ted Williams: Classic Sports Shots, Scholastic, Inc. (New York, NY), 1993.

Babe Ruth: Classic Sports Shots, Scholastic, Inc. (New York, NY), 1993.

Willie Mays: Classic Sports Shots, Scholastic, Inc. (New York, NY), 1993.

Baseball Trivia and Fun Book, Scholastic, Inc. (New York, NY), 1993.

Pro-Football Megastars, 1993, 1994, 1995, and *1997,* Scholastic, Inc. (New York, NY), 1993, 1994, 1995, 1997.

Pro-Basketball Megastars, 1994, 1995, and *1996,* Scholastic, Inc. (New York, NY), 1994, 1995, 1996.

Sport Shots: Barry Bonds, Scholastic, Inc. (New York, NY), 1994.

Baseball Megastars, 1994, 1995, and *1996,1998,* Scholastic, Inc. (New York, NY), 1994, 1995, 1996, 1998.

NBA Megastars, 1997, 1998, 1999, Scholastic, Inc. (New York, NY), 1997, 1998, 1999.

You Can Yo-Yo!, Scholastic, Inc. (New York, NY), 1998.

Mark McGwire: The Home-Run King, illustrated by Thomas La Padula, Scholastic, Inc. (New York, NY), 1999.

Advanced Yo-Yo Tricks, Scholastic, Inc. (New York, NY), 1999.

Greatest Moments of the NBA, Scholastic, Inc. (New York, NY), 2000.

(With Savion Glover) *Savion: My Life in Tap,* Morrow/Avon, 2000.

Also author of sixty-five half-hour instructional programs for the USA Network television series *Scholastic Sports Academy,* 1981-84. Contributor to *Modern Encyclopedia of Basketball,* edited by Zander Hollander, Doubleday, 1979, and *Evetec, The McGregor Solution,* Houghton-Mifflin, 1985. Columnist for *Junior Scholastic, Science World, Voice, Scope, Dynamite, Scholastic Math, Sprint,* and *Action.* Contributor to *Teen Age* and other magazines for young people; additional writings published under a pseudonym.

SIDELIGHTS: Bruce Weber once commented: "When I found myself sitting farther and farther away from the coach on the bench, it didn't take a genius to figure out that if I wanted to stay in sports, I'd have to find some other route than the locker-room door. I found my entrance at the press gate and I've been working my way in there every since.

"It has been wonderful. I know a great many adults who are fed up with their professional lives, doing something every day that they hate. Not me. As Garrett Morris used to say on *Saturday Night Live,* 'Baseball been very, very good to me.' The same goes for football and soccer and track and field, among other things. There is a genuine fraternity of sports, and most of my professional relationships, many of which are a quarter-century or more old, begin with sports."

Weber is an avid sports fan who has turned his avocation into his profession through writing. He has written numerous books assessing the annual performance of the nation's football, basketball, and baseball teams, and several biographies of sports figures. In Weber's annual *Inside Baseball* books, the author provides brief profiles of individual players and teams, enumerating trades, injuries, and strengths and weaknesses for each, and concludes with his choice for an all-star team, and the requisite statistics. Weber's "breezy conversational style suits baseball," contended Sherry Palmitier in her *Voice of Youth Advocates* piece on *Inside Baseball 1989,* which she dubbed "a thorough review of an exciting season." Similarly, William E. Littlefield recommended the following year's edition, *Inside Baseball 1990* in *Kliatt,* as "an easy-to-use book for the younger fan."

Among Weber's several sports biographies is the dual *Magic Johnson and Larry Bird,* which focuses on the longstanding comparisons between the two professional basketball players—one black, the other white—that reached its height when their teams competed for the NCAA championship in 1979. Weber grounds his discussion of the two players in detailed examinations of the pivotal games in the career of each, necessitating a good familiarity on the part of his audience, as Raymond L. Puffer pointed out in *Kliatt.* But Puffer noted that Weber's account of Johnson and Bird's high school playing experiences, emphasizing how each made up his mind about college and heading off for the pros, would be of particular interest to the young adult audience. As in his annual sports round-ups, *Magic Johnson and Larry Bird* contains plenty of statistics and photographs, noted a reviewer for *Booklist,* who contended that "Basketball buffs will welcome Weber's brisk-paced style."

Weber's other great love is music: he has a degree in instrumental music education and early in his career taught music at a school in Brooklyn. Weber once commented: "How have I managed to combine the two seemingly distant interests? My favorite response is: 'I'm probably the only sports writer in New York who can cover both the football game and the half-time show with equal facility.' My critics might debate my ability to do either well, but I'm more than willing to go one-on-one with any of them."

Weber drew upon his musical background in his biography of dancer Savion Glover, co-written by its subject, in *Savion: My Life in Tap.* Glover is a performer who first came to public attention at the age of eleven, and whose success is attributed in part to his wise choice of mentors, among them tap dance legends Honi Coles and Jimmy Slyde. *Booklist* reviewer Randy Meyer articulated his appreciation for the "deep respect and reverence Glover shows for his 'uncles' and their advice," which went far beyond the realm of the dance floor. The book's text alternates between Glover's own words and those of Weber, who, among other things, provides a concise history of the evolution of tap. He helps put in context the young dancer's phenomenal success by age twenty-six—Glover's accomplishments include the creation of the show *Bring in 'da Noise, Bring in 'da Funk,* for which he won a Tony Award for choreography. Aspiring performers will be inspired by Glover's "life, work and words," noted a reviewer in *Publishers Weekly.*

BIOGRAPHICAL/CRITICAL SOURCES:

PERIODICALS

Booklist, April, 1986, review of *Magic Johnson and Larry Bird,* p. 1147; January 1, 2000, Randy Meyer, review of *Savion: My Life in Tap,* p. 896.

Kliatt, spring, 1986, Raymond L. Puffer, review of *Magic Johnson and Larry Bird,* p. 56; September, 1990, William E. Littlefield, review of *Inside Baseball 1990,* p. 52.

Publishers Weekly, December 6, 1999, review of *Savion: My Life in Tap,* p. 78.

School Library Journal, February, 1989, p. 93.

Voice of Youth Advocates, August, 1989, Sherry Palmitier, review of *Inside Baseball 1989,* pp. 181-182.*

* * *

WELLS, Martha 1964-

PERSONAL: Born September 1, 1964, in Fort Worth, TX; daughter of Irvin E. (a contractor) and Mary Wells. *Education:* Texas A&M University, B.A., 1986. *Avocational interests:* History, antiques, folklore.

ADDRESSES: *Home*—College Station, TX. *Agent*—Matt Bialer, Trident Media Group, 488 Madison Ave., 17th Floor, New York, NY 10022.

CAREER: Texas A&M University, College Station, systems operator and research assistant for Ocean Drilling Program, beginning 1989; part-time computer programmer.

MEMBER: Science Fiction Writers of America.

AWARDS, HONORS: Nebula Award nomination, Science Fiction Writers of America, 1998, for *The Death of the Necromancer.*

WRITINGS:

The Element of Fire (novel), Tor Books (New York, NY), 1993.

Charisat, Tor Books (New York, NY), 1994.

City of Bones (novel), Tor Books (New York, NY), 1995.
The Death of the Necromancer (novel), Avon Eos (New York, NY), 1998.
Wheel of the Infinite (novel), Avon Eos (New York, NY), 2000.

Contributor of short stories to *Realms of Fantasy.*

WORK IN PROGRESS: A three-volume series of novels, set approximately thirty years after the end of *The Death of the Necromancer,* for HarperCollins Eos (New York, NY), publication of volume one expected in 2002.

SIDELIGHTS: Fantasy writer Martha Wells has become a popular and critically respected contributor to the genre. Her first novel, *The Element of Fire,* which a reviewer for *Publishers Weekly* called "a rich fantasy debut," was a runner-up for the 1994 Crawford Award and a finalist for the 1993 Compton Crook/Stephen Tall Award. Set in a vaguely medieval time and place, the book tells the story of Thomas Boniface, who must protect the kingdom of Ile-Rien from several threats, including evil sorcerer Urban Grandier and political interloper Denzil, while falling in love with Kade, daughter of the late King Fulstan and Moire, Queen of Air and Darkness. Shira Daemon, in the *St. James Guide to Fantasy Writers,* considered *The Element of Fire* a "really fine first work" despite some minor flaws. Daemon especially admired Wells's skill at creating fully developed characters, her fast pace, and her entertaining approach to sometimes clichéd material.

Wells's next novel, *City of Bones,* was likewise well received; Dorman T. Shindler, in the *Dallas Morning News,* hailed it and its predecessor as "minor classics." Yet Wells's third novel, *The Death of the Necromancer,* is the book that established her critical reputation. Nominated for a prestigious Nebula Award, the novel returns to Ile-Rien two centuries after the events of *The Element of Fire,* making the setting suggestive of nineteenth-century Europe but with distinct elements of magic. Its plot centers on disgraced nobleman and thief Nicholas Valiarde and his conflict with the infamous necromancer of the book's title. To escape the necromancer's clutches, Nicholas must cooperate, however uneasily, with detective extraordinaire Ronsarde. Reviewer Jackie Cassada, in *Library Journal,* hailed the book as an "enchanting blend of detection and sorcery," and Karen Simonetti of *Booklist* deemed it "a chillingly convincing fantasy that will entrap genre readers." A contributor to *Publishers Weekly* observed that "In her third novel, Wells . . . continues to demonstrate an impressive gift for creating finely detailed fantasy worlds rife with many-layered intrigues and immensely personable characters."

In *Wheel of the Infinite,* Wells places her characters and action in a setting reminiscent of India and South Asia. Maskelle, the Voice of the Adversary, has been exiled from the city of Duvalpore but is called back to help defeat the mysterious evil that threatens to destroy the Wheel of the Infinite before the religious rite associated with it can be completed. Roland Green, in *Booklist,* found the novel "an intelligent variation of the standard quest tale," and especially admired Wells's ability to create a convincingly detailed system of religion in the book. A *Publishers Weekly* reviewer considered the novel "fast-paced, witty and inventive," and appreciated its believable characterizations. "There is real reading pleasure here," the critic concluded.

An anthropology graduate of Texas A&M University, Wells has said that she enjoys the kind of research that makes her fiction distinctive. In an interview on the *Martha Wells* Web site, she tells readers: "I always discover a lot of historical detail that is far stranger than anything you would believe in fiction." As she explained to *Insite* magazine interviewer Elizabeth Todd, she considers a novel's context to be very important and pays attentive care to historical details. "It's obvious to me when fantasy writers are in it for the money," she commented. "Some stories have an old feel to them. To me, this is like fraud."

Wells once told *CA:* "*The Element of Fire* is my first professional sale, and my first try at a novel. I was encouraged to consider writing as a serious career by author Steven Gould during a writing workshop he taught in 1984. I work slowly. It took me slightly over a year and a half to write the book, and I have been working on my current novel for over a year.

"Research is very important to me. While the world in *The Element of Fire* is entirely imaginary, it is based heavily on seventeenth-century France. I find that a grounding in the real world, an understanding of how society and culture function and how they are affected by their environment, are essential to the creation of imaginary worlds. Giving attention to the material culture is a serious concern. What level of technology has it attained? What is the effect of literacy? Do the people have printing presses, or are they still struggling to invent the stirrup? These things have an impact on how characters view their world and themselves, and can make the difference between whether those characters seem to the reader like people from another time and place, or like modern Americans in funny clothes. Fantasy novels that reflect this concern are the kind that I most enjoy reading."

BIOGRAPHICAL/CRITICAL SOURCES:

BOOKS

St. James Guide to Fantasy Writers, St. James Press (Detroit, MI), 1996, pp. 601-602.

PERIODICALS

Booklist, June 1, 1995, Roland Green, review of *City of Bones,* p. 1737; May 15, 1998, Karen Simonetti, review of *The Death of the Necromancer,* p. 1608; June 1, 2000, Roland Green, review of *Wheel of the Infinite,* p. 1866.

Dallas Morning News, May 21, 2000, Dorman T. Shindler, review of *City of Bones.*

Library Journal, June 15, 1998, Jackie Cassada, review of *The Death of the Necromancer,* p. 100; June 15, 2000, Jackie Cassada, review of *Wheel of the Infinite,* p. 120.

Publishers Weekly, June 7, 1993, review of *The Element of Fire,* p. 57; May 15, 1995, review of *City of Bones,* p. 59; May 25, 1998, review of *The Death of the Necromancer,* p. 70; May 22, 2000, review of *Wheel of the Infinite,* p. 78.

OTHER

Insite, http://www.rtis.com/mwells/insite/ (March 19, 1998), Elizabeth Todd, "The Fantasy Life."

Martha Wells Web site, http://www.rtis.com/mwells/ (May 17, 2001).*

* * *

WOLLHEIM, Richard Arthur 1923-

PERSONAL: Born May 5, 1923, in London, England; son of Eric and Constance (Baker) Wollheim; married Anne Powell, 1950 (divorced, 1967); married Mary Day Lanier (a potter), 1969; children: (first marriage) Rupert Daniel, Bruno Richard; (second marriage) one daughter. *Education:* Balliol College, Oxford, M.A., 1948.

ADDRESSES: Home—20 Ashchurch Park Villas, London W12 9SP, England; and 1814 Marin Ave., Berkeley, CA 94707. *Office*—Department of Philosophy, University of California, Berkeley, CA 94720.

CAREER: University of London, University College, London, England, assistant lecturer, 1949-51, lecturer, 1951-60, reader, 1960-63, Grote Professor of Philosophy of Mind and Logic, 1963-82, Emeritus Grote Professor, 1982—; Columbia University, New York, NY, professor of philosophy, 1982-84; University of California, Berkeley, professor of philosophy, beginning 1985; University of California, Davis, professor of philosophy and humanities, 1989-95, later professor-in-residence and department head. Columbia University, visiting professor, 1959-60 and 1970; Visva-Bharati University, visiting professor, 1968; University of Minnesota, visiting professor, 1972; University of Sydney, Power Lecturer, 1972; City University of New York, visiting professor, 1975; University of California, Berkeley, visiting professor, 1981; Harvard University, William James Lecturer, 1982; Yale University, Ernst Cassirer Lecturer, 1991; National Gallery of Art, Mellon Lecturer. *Military service:* British Army, 1942-45; served in northern Europe; became captain.

MEMBER: American Academy of Arts and Sciences (fellow), British Academy (fellow), British Society of Aesthetics (vice president, beginning 1969), Aristotelian Society (president, 1967-68).

WRITINGS:

F. H. Bradley, Penguin Books (New York, NY), 1959, 2nd edition, 1969.

Art and Its Objects: An Introduction to Aesthetics, Harper (New York, NY), 1968, 2nd edition published as *Art and Its Objects: Six Supplementary Essays,* Cambridge University Press (New York, NY), 1980.

A Family Romance (novel), Farrar, Straus (New York, NY), 1969.

Sigmund Freud, Viking (New York, NY), 1971, published in England as *Freud,* Fontana, 1971.

On Art and the Mind (essays and lectures), Allen Lane, 1973, Harvard University Press (Cambridge, MA), 1974.

The Good Self and the Bad Self, British Academy, 1976.

The Sheep and the Ceremony, Cambridge University Press (New York, NY), 1979.

The Thread of Life (lectures), Harvard University Press (Cambridge, MA), 1984.

Painting as an Art (lectures), 1987.

The Mind and Its Depths (essays and lectures), 1993.

(Author of introduction) Sigmund Freud, *The Case of the Wolf-Man: From the History of an Infantile Neurosis,* illustrated by Jim Dine, Arion (San Francisco, CA), 1993.

Formalism and Its Kinds, Tapies Foundation, 1995.

On the Emotions, Yale University Press (New Haven, CT), 1999.

Richard Wollheim on the Art of Painting: Art as Representation and Expression, edited by Rob van Gerwen, Cambridge University Press (New York, NY), 2001.

Contributor of articles to periodicals.

EDITOR

(And author of introduction) Francis Herbert Bradley, *Ethical Studies,* 2nd revised edition, Oxford University Press (New York, NY), 1962.

David Hume, *Hume on Religion,* Collins, 1963.

(And author of introduction) Bradley, *Appearance and Reality: A Metaphysical Essay,* Oxford University Press (New York, NY), 1969.

Adrian Durham Stokes, *The Image in Form: Selected Writings,* Harper (New York, NY), 1972.

Freud: A Collection of Critical Essays, Anchor Books (New York, NY), 1974.

John Stuart Mill, *Three Essays,* Oxford University Press (New York, NY), 1975.

SIDELIGHTS: Richard Wollheim is a philosophy professor and writer whose books include philosophical analysis, biography, and fiction. One of these books is *Art and Its Objects: An Introduction to Aesthetics.* Michael Podro, writing in *New Statesman,* described the work as "perhaps the first really important and fertilising book by a modern analytical philosopher on aesthetics," and he added that "the sheer inventiveness of its arguments makes most recent discussion from the side of professional philosophy look mechanical." *Listener* reviewer Anthony Quinto was likewise impressed, noting, "To say that [*Art and Its Objects*] is the best modern book on philosophical aesthetics is fainter praise than it deserves." Quinto acknowledged "the engaging elegance of [Wollheim's] style and . . . the authority with which he handles a large number of complex disciplines," and he observed that *Art and Its Objects* "covers a wide range of problems with great verve and originality."

The next year, Wollheim published a novel, *A Family Romance.* The novel is presented as a diary in which a man reflects on his relationships with his wife, his lover, and his father. A critic wrote in the *New York Times Book Review* that the novel "is old fashioned in a refreshing way—post Freudian and pre-war." The critic added: "Peering backward into memory and forward into illusion, the narrator keeps returning to the increasingly unbearable present. The effect is to produce a sequence of Proustian variations, in which the sins of the son are visited on the father."

Wollheim's more recent publications include *On the Emotions,* a collection of essays and lectures examining the nature of emotions and their moral and social implications. Writing in the *New York Times Book Review,* Paul Mattick dismissed Wollheim's writing as "ponderous and humorless," but *Library Journal* reviewer Francisca Goldsmith concluded that "specialists will find this book provocative and engaging." Elizabeth Spelman, meanwhile, wrote in the *London Review of Books* that "*On the Emotions* invites questions for which it only provides the sketch of an answer, perhaps because its author thinks that anything more would require a kind of speculation improper in a work of philosophy."

BIOGRAPHICAL/CRITICAL SOURCES:

PERIODICALS

Library Journal, November 1, 1999, Francisca Goldsmith, review of *On the Emotions,* p. 88.

Listener, Anthony Quinto, review of *Art and Its Objects,* November 7, 1968.

London Review of Books, March 30, 2000, Elizabeth Spelman, "Plumping up Philosophy with the Lipids of Desire," pp. 9-10.

Nation, October 13, 1969; February 26, 1973.

New Statesman, December 6, 1968; May 2, 1969; February 1, 1974.

New York Times Book Review, September 7, 1969, review of *A Family Romance;* March 26, 2000, Paul Mattick, "You've Got an Attitude," p. 28.

Times Literary Supplement, May 22, 1969.*

* * *

WRIGHT, Eric 1929-

PERSONAL: Born 1929, in London, England; immigrated to Canada, 1951; son of Joseph and Caroline (Curnow) Wright; married, 1958 (wife's name, Valerie); children: Victoria, Jessica. *Education:* University of

Manitoba, Winnipeg, B.A. (with honors), 1957; University of Toronto, Ontario, M.A., 1960.

ADDRESSES: Home—65 Gormley Ave., Toronto, Ontario, Canada M4V 1T9. *Agent*—Bella Pomer, 22 Shallmar Boulevard, Toronto, Ontario, Canada.

CAREER: Writer. Ryerson Polytechnic, Toronto, Ontario, teacher of English. Worked briefly as a freelance writer for television.

AWARDS, HONORS: Crime Writers Association John Creasey Award and City of Toronto Book Award, both 1983, both for *The Night the Gods Smiled;* Arthur Ellis awards, Crime Writers of Canada, 1983, for *The Night the Gods Smiled,* and 1985, 1987, and 1991; fellow of Ryerson Polytechnic University, Toronto, 1993.

WRITINGS:

DETECTIVE NOVELS; "CHARLIE SALTER" SERIES

The Night the Gods Smiled, Scribner (New York, NY), 1983.
Smoke Detector, Scribner (New York, NY), 1984.
Death in the Old Country, Scribner (New York, NY), 1985.
The Man Who Changed His Name, 1986, published as *A Single Death,* Collins (London, England), 1986.
A Body Surrounded by Water, Scribner (New York, NY), 1987.
A Question of Murder, Scribner (New York, NY), 1988.
A Sensitive Case, Scribner (New York, NY), 1990.
Final Cut, Scribner (New York, NY), 1991.
A Fine Italian Hand, Scribner (New York, NY), 1992.
Death by Degrees, Scribner (New York, NY), 1993.

"LUCY TRIMBLE" SERIES

Death of a Sunday Writer, St. Martin's Press (New York, NY), 1998.
Death on the Rocks, St. Martin's Press (New York, NY), 1999.

OTHER

(Contributor) Beverly Beetham-Endersby, editor, *Fingerprints,* Irwin, 1984.
Moodies's Tale (novel), Key Porter (Toronto, Ontario, Canada), 1994.
Buried in Stone (detective novel), Scribner (New York, NY), 1996.
The Kidnapping of Rosie Dawn, J. Daniel, 2000.
Death of a Hired Man (detective novel), Thomas Dunne Books, 2001.

Contributor of short stories to periodicals.

SIDELIGHTS: "On any list of the best crime fiction writers in Canada, you find Eric Wright," declared Margaret Cannon in the Toronto *Globe and Mail.* Critics have extolled Wright's detective novels for their depth of characterization, elegant prose, dry humor, and faithful depictions of Canadian settings. In the *St. James Guide to Crime and Mystery Writers,* Bernard A. Drew wrote, "Wright's soft-boiled police procedurals featuring Inspector Charlie Salter involve murders with middle-class victims: aspiring actors, local historians, college professors. The investigations are low-tech: he specializes in unusual cases but is not a homicide detective. The novels are low on graphic violence: Salter is seldom in physical danger. And they're big on personal background: Charlie's a family man with family joys and sorrows." One of the best-loved features of the series is Wright's protagonist, Charlie Salter, "whose life and times the author observes with both humor and insight," according to *New York Times Book Review* contributor Jeanne MacFarlane Wright. Reviewers sometimes refer to Salter as if he were a real person—and a likeable man whom you would prize as a friend.

A Toronto police inspector in his late forties, Salter is down-to-earth, happily married to his independent-minded wife, Annie, and the father of two teen-aged sons, Angus and Seth. The relationships between Annie's more well-to-do family and Charlie's testy working-class father add a bit of tension to Charlie's otherwise quiet personal life. When asked about the origin of Charlie Salter, Wright told *CA:* "Once I decided to start writing, I sat down and thought, I want an absolutely typical Canadian. And that's always a big question in Canada: What is a Canadian? He isn't American, he isn't English, but what is he? To solve that problem for myself, I remembered a plumbing foreman who had worked on a construction crew that I'd been on thirty years ago. That man seemed to me the essence of decency and the essence of Canadianism too. I kept him in mind from the start. I moved him about; I gave him a different background. But Salter talks as that man would have talked had he had Salter's kind of training. That man was someone I admired very much when I was young. He looked after me when I was a kid on a construction crew, and that's really the sense I have of Charlie Salter—he's a man who looks after people."

Wright introduced readers to the Salter family in his enthusiastically received first novel, *The Night the Gods Smiled,* winner of Canada's John Creasey Award in 1983. This novel finds the detective investigating the murder of a professor at an academic conference in Montreal. The world of academe is well known to Wright, who has taught English for many years, and the novel garnered praise for its satiric, behind-the-scenes view of university life. In successive novels the reader learns not only the solution of each crime or mystery, but more and more about Charlie's family and its foibles. Wright's 1986 novel, *The Man Who Changed His Name* (also published as *A Single Death*), for example, acquaints readers with Charlie's ex-wife, Gerry, an activist and former flower child who pushes Charlie to uncover the truth about a woman's murder. In other novels Charlie can be seen engaged in fatherly talks and fishing trips with his sons during lulls in his crime cases.

All of Wright's books have won praise for characterization, which takes precedence over intricate plotting or quick-paced action. The author's success in creating believable characters, some critics contend, results from his ability to write dialogue that is appropriate to each character, whether the speaker is a member of the upper class or a street-wise cop. "One of the pleasures of reading Mr. Wright's books is his deft delineation of minor characters, often with just a few lines of dialogue or description," remarked Jeanne MacFarlane Wright in the *New York Times Book Review.* The reviewer cited as an example, "'a recruit whose near baldness only emphasized his shining newness . . . and whose eagerness to be of service made him hard to look at directly.'" Similarly, in a review of *A Single Death,* Cannon stated that "while the murder plot is good, Wright's well-drawn characters, as usual, steal the book. . . . [They] emerge as decent, interesting people whom most of us would like to meet." Another *Globe and Mail* critic, reviewing *A Body Surrounded by Water,* had high praise for the author: "Wright's style is easy and elegant . . . and the setting beautifully rendered. . . . As always, he's at home outlining the ins and outs of male-female relationships and the human condition in general." Reviewers also appreciated Wright's amusing, astute portrayals of Canadians and the British, particularly in *Death in the Old Country,* in which Salter aids British police after a murder occurs at the inn where he and Annie are vacationing. "In this particularly gentle mystery, Wright's humor shines," remarked Drew.

The protagonist of *Buried in Stone,* Mel Pickett, is a retired policeman who appeared with Salter in Wright's earlier novel, *A Sensitive Case.* "Pickett is an equally comfortable character," noted Drew. A *Publishers Weekly* reviewer praised *Buried in Stone* for maintaining Wright's "distinguish[ed]" writing characteristic—"the wry sensitivity with which he explores the uncertainties that dog his older characters" and "his sure way with a murder plot." Conversely, a *Publishers Weekly* reviewer of *A Fine Italian Hand* stated that the "contrived plot falters due to undeveloped characters and a notable lack of suspense."

Calling the entire Salter series "first-rate," *Washington Post Book World* contributor Jean M. White credited the novelist with "provid[ing] some of the brighter moments in the mystery field in the last few years." Drew contended, "While perhaps modest on innovation, the Salter and Pickett novels are strong on character, setting, and subtle psychology. The personal backgrounds and interplay of the heroes, and of the victims, suspects, and other players are as enjoyable as the puzzles."

In the late 1990s Wright introduced a new series protagonist, divorcee-turned-sleuth Lucy Trimble. Following her debut in *Death of a Sunday Writer,* Trimble turns up again in *Death on the Rocks.* In this tale Trimble, who has left her domineering husband to find a new life running her distant cousin's detective agency in Toronto, is retained by successful Greta Golden to identify a stranger who has been stalking Golden. What seems at first to be a simple case mushrooms into intrigue when Trimble discovers that the ominous figure is in fact another detective. The action shifts to Cornwall, England, to piece together the details of Trimble's now-mysterious client's life. While a *Publishers Weekly* reviewer found Wright's depictions of Canada and England unexceptional, the critic did go on to praise the author's "well-rounded characters, lyric if low-key prose and subtle humor." Likewise, *Booklist*'s Emily Melton recommended *Death on the Rocks* for readers who would eschew graphic action and suspense for a dose of "British cozies."

In 2001 Wright reintroduced Mel Pickett in *Death of a Hired Man.* When a dead body is found in Pickett's cabin, he has to investigate whether the man was murdered by scheming relatives, or whether, in fact, Pickett himself was the intended target. A *Kirkus Reviews* reviewer described *Death of a Hired Man* as "a bare-boned plot with cozy overtones," while a reviewer in *Publishers Weekly* wrote that it "demonstrate[s] Canadian author Wright's versatility and excellence."

For an interview with Wright, see entry in *Contemporary Authors,* Volume 132.

BIOGRAPHICAL/CRITICAL SOURCES:

BOOKS

St. James Guide to Crime and Mystery Writers, fourth edition, St. James (Detroit, MI), 1996.

PERIODICALS

Booklist, May 15, 1999, review of *Death on the Rocks.*

Books in Canada, October, 1994.

Boston Globe, October 27, 1996.

Globe and Mail (Toronto), May 4, 1985; September 27, 1986; July 18, 1987; October 1, 1988; October 15, 1994.

Kirkus Reviews, November 15, 2000, review of *Death of a Hired Man,* p. 1581.

Library Journal, June 1, 1999, review of *Death on the Rocks,* p. 186.

New York Times Book Review, October 9, 1988.

Publishers Weekly, August 10, 1992; February 5, 1996; May 17, 1999, review of *Death on the Rocks,* p. 60; February 5, 2001, review of *Death of a Hired Man,* p. 71.

Washington Post Book World, December 16, 1984; August 17, 1986; December 20, 1987.*

Y-Z

YANCEY, Philip D(avid) 1949-

PERSONAL: Born November 4, 1949, in Atlanta, GA; son of Marshall Watts and Mildred (a teacher; maiden name, Diem) Yancey; married Janet Norwood (a social work director), June 2, 1970. *Education:* Columbia Bible College, Columbia, B.A., 1970; Wheaton College, Wheaton, M.A., 1972; University of Chicago, M.A., 1990. *Religion:* Protestant.

ADDRESSES: Office—c/o *Christianity Today,* 465 Gundersen Dr., Carol Stream, IL 60188.

CAREER: Campus Life, Wheaton, IL, editor, 1971-77, publisher, 1978-79; freelance writer, 1980—.

AWARDS, HONORS: Eleven Golden Medallion Awards, Evangelical Christian Publishers Association, including awards, 1978, for *Where Is God When It Hurts?,* 1980, for *Fearfully and Wonderfully Made,* 1985, for *In His Image,* 1989, for *The Student Bible,* 1990, for *Disappointment with God: Questions Nobody Asks Aloud,* 1996, for *The Jesus I Never Knew,* and 1998, for *What's So Amazing about Grace?*

WRITINGS:

After the Wedding, Word Inc. (Waco, TX), 1976.

Where Is God When It Hurts?, Zondervan (Grand Rapids, MI), 1977, revised edition, Walker and Co. (New York, NY), 1996.

(With Tim Stafford) *Unhappy Secrets of the Christian Life,* Zondervan (Grand Rapids, MI), 1979.

(With Paul Brand) *Fearfully and Wonderfully Made,* Zondervan (Grand Rapids, MI), 1980.

Open Windows, Thomas Nelson (Nashville, TN), 1982.

(With Brand) *In His Image,* Zondervan (Grand Rapids, MI), 1984.

(With Stafford) *The Student Bible,* Zondervan (Grand Rapids, MI), 1988, published as *The Student Bible: New International Version,* 1996, revised edition published as *The Student Bible: Updated New American Standard,* 1999.

Disappointment with God: Questions Nobody Asks Aloud, Zondervan (Grand Rapids, MI), 1989.

A Guided Tour of the Bible: Six Months of Daily Readings, Zondervan (Grand Rapids, MI), 1990.

I Was Just Wondering, Eerdmans (Grand Rapids, MI), 1990, revised edition, 1998.

Reality and the Vision, Word Inc. (Waco, TX), 1990.

(With Brand) *Pain: The Gift Nobody Wants,* HarperCollins (New York, NY), 1993.

Discovering God: A Devotional Journey through the Bible, Zondervan (Grand Rapids, MI), 1993.

Finding God in Unexpected Places, Moorings (Nashville, TN), 1995.

The Jesus I Never Knew, Walker and Co. (New York, NY), 1996.

(With Brenda Quinn) *The Jesus I Never Knew Study Guide,* Zondervan (Grand Rapids, MI), 1997.

What's So Amazing about Grace?, Zondervan (Grand Rapids, MI), 1997.

(Contributor) *Destiny and Deliverance* (companion volume to film *The Prince of Egypt*), Thomas Nelson (Nashville, TN), 1998.

Church, Why Bother? My Personal Pilgrimage, Zondervan (Grand Rapids, MI), 1998.

The Bible Jesus Read, Zondervan (Grand Rapids, MI), 1999.

When Life Hurts: Understanding God's Place in Your Pain, Multnomah (Sisters, OR), 1999.

(With Quinn) *Meet the Bible: A Panorama of God's Word in 366 Readings and Reflections,* Zondervan (Grand Rapids, MI), 2000.

Reaching for the Invisible God: What Can We Expect to Find?, Zondervan (Grand Rapids, MI), 2000.

Contributor of about 800 articles to magazines, including *Reader's Digest* and *Saturday Evening Post.* Editor at large, *Christianity Today.*

SIDELIGHTS: Philip D. Yancey's books are "fast becoming classics of the evangelical literature," according to a *Publishers Weekly* article by Miriam Berkley. Using many of the same techniques Jesus employed in his own ministry, Yancey tackles tough theological questions in a style that general readers can easily understand. He uses anecdotes from the modern world and from his own spiritual search to highlight the issues facing Christians today, such as how to find a relationship with God in an increasingly hectic and secular world. A number of Yancey's books have been bestsellers in the Christian market, and a few—including *The Jesus I Never Knew* and *What's So Amazing about Grace?*—have sold well enough to find places on the mainstream bestseller lists. *Booklist* correspondent June Sawyers called Yancey "one of the most approachable evangelical Christian writers."

Yancey was raised in Georgia, in an atmosphere of strict Christian fundamentalism, where "anything you could think of that was fun was wrong." He remarked to Berkley: "You cannot imagine, unless you've been in a background like that, how narrow it is." He eventually rejected the fundamentalist tradition, in part because of exposure to Orwellian literature, which he says "shattered my airtight framework of what the world was like. That's probably one of the main reasons why I'm a writer today: because there are millions of people in a [closed] world like [the one in which I was raised]. Literature for me . . . opened the cage door that let me fly out."

Despite his renunciation of strict fundamentalism, Yancey remained religiously active and, after college, he began writing for the Christian magazine *Campus Life.* He told Berkley that many of his assignments were "'drama in real life' articles, where people have been involved in tragedy, and as a Christian I was puzzled by this problem of pain. Why would God allow it? Why does He let us suffer?" His musings on these questions eventually formed the basis for his book, *Where Is God When It Hurts?,* an award-winning volume that has currently sold over 500,000 copies.

Yancey's books offer "no facile solutions, no panacea to suffering and misery," to quote Sawyers. Instead he shows how ordinary people, himself included, conduct their daily lives in a way that best magnifies God's grace. Having himself undergone crises of faith, Yancey understands the varying degrees of belief amongst his readers, and he challenges Christians to become less judgmental and more childlike in their faith. "Yancey considers honestly the predicaments of human existence," declared a *Publishers Weekly* reviewer. "With common sense and a poetic sensibility, Yancey poses fruitful questions and offers real insights."

BIOGRAPHICAL/CRITICAL SOURCES:

PERIODICALS

Booklist, October 15, 1995, Steve Schroeder, review of *The Jesus I Never Knew,* p. 368; July, 1997, Ray Olson, review of *What's So Amazing about Grace?,* p. 1772; August, 1999, Ray Olson, review of *The Bible Jesus Read,* p. 1995; September 1, 2000, June Sawyers, review of *Reaching for the Invisible God,* p. 36.

Christian Century, May 18, 1994, Frank Ramirez, review of *Pain,* p. 545.

Journal of the American Medical Association (JAMA), April 27, 1994, Bashir Qureshi, review of *Pain,* p. 1294.

Publishers Weekly, March 9, 1984; September 29, 1997, review of *What's So Amazing about Grace?,* p. 85; August 16, 1999, review of *The Bible Jesus Read,* p. 76; July 24, 2000, review of *Reaching for the Invisible God,* p. 88; July 31, 2000, review of *Reaching for the Invisible God,* p. 55.

* * *

YOSHIMOTO, Banana
See YOSHIMOTO, Mahoko

* * *

YOSHIMOTO, Mahoko 1964-
(Banana Yoshimoto)

PERSONAL: Born July 24, 1964, in Tokyo, Japan; daughter of Takaaki "Ryumei" (a literary critic) and Kazuko Yoshimoto. *Education:* Graduated from Nihon University. *Politics:* Nonpolitical. *Religion:* "No particular one." *Avocational interests:* "To take a walk with my two dogs."

ADDRESSES: Agent—Japan Foreign-Rights Centre, 27-18-804, Naka Ochiai 2-chome, Shinjuku-ku, Tokyo 161, Japan.

CAREER: Writer. Former waitress in Tokyo, Japan.

MEMBER: Japan Writers' Association.

AWARDS, HONORS: Izumi Kyoka Prize, 1986, for "Moonlight Shadow"; New Writers Prize, *Kaien* magazine, 1987, for *Kitchen;* Izumi Kyoka Literary Prize, Kanazawa City Council, Cultural Affairs Department, 1988, for *Kitchen;* Geijutsu Sensho, Japan Ministry of Education, 1988, for *Kitchen* and *Utakata/Sanctuary;* Shugoro Yamamoto Award, Shincho-sha Publishing Company, 1989, for *Tugumi;* Literary Prize Scanno, 1993, for *NP;* Murasakishikibu Prize for *Amurita.*

WRITINGS:

FICTION; UNLESS OTHERWISE NOTED

Kitchin (contains the novella *Kitchen* and the short story "Moonlight Shadow"), Fukutake Shoten (Tokyo, Japan), 1988, translation by Megan Backus published as *Kitchen,* Grove (New York, NY), 1993.

Shirakawa yofune, Fukutake Shoten (Tokyo, Japan), 1989.

Tsugumi/Yoshimoto Banana = Tugumi (novel), Chuo Koronsha (Tokyo, Japan), 1989.

Fruits Basket: taidanshu (literary criticism), Fukutake Shoten (Tokyo, Japan), 1990.

N. P. (novel), Kadokawa Shoten (Tokyo, Japan), 1990, translation by Ann Sherif published as *N.P.: A Novel,* Grove (New York, NY), 1994.

Tokage (short stories), Shinchosa, 1993, translation by Ann Sherif published as *Lizard,* Grove (New York, NY), 1995.

Amurita (novel), Fukutake Shoten (Tokyo, Japan), 1994, translation by Russell F. Wasden published as *Amrita,* Grove (New York, NY), 1997.

Asleep (novellas), translated by Michael Emmerich, Grove (New York, NY), 2000.

Author of novels *Kanashii, Yokan, Honeymoon,* and *SLY;* also author of *Utakata/Sanctuary, Pineapple Pudding,* and *Song from Banana.*

ADAPTATIONS: Kitchen has been adapted twice into film, once as a Japanese television feature and the second produced in Hong Kong, 1997.

SIDELIGHTS: Banana Yoshimoto took Japan by storm in 1988 with her premier work, *Kitchen,* two short works of fiction about life and death in contemporary Japan. *Kitchen* sold over two million copies in Japan and won several literary awards. Four years later Yoshimoto's audience expanded to the United States when an English translation of *Kitchen* made its way onto best-seller lists. Yoshimoto believes that *Kitchen*'s success is a result of its appeal to a young audience, particularly women in their twenties. "I think that young people would meditate the essence of life at least once. My novel happened to have something to win the sympathy of such young people who are in deep thought about life," Yoshimoto explained to David J. Morrow of the *Detroit Free Press.*

The title novella revolves around the life of a female college student, Mikage, who struggles to cope with the death of her grandmother, with whom she has lived for years. Mikage is invited to live with a friend of her grandmother, Yuichi, and Yuichi's father, who has undergone a sex change operation. When Yuichi's father/mother, in turn, is killed, the two college students console each other, a process that leads them toward a more intimate relationship. Like "Kitchen," the accompanying novella, "Moonlight Shadow," deals with the themes of love, death, and the confusion of reality. It portrays two college students, a woman and a man, both of whom lose their loves to death and cope in varying ways.

American reviewers were split over Yoshimoto's accomplishment. "'Kitchen' is light as an invisible pancake, charming and forgettable," scoffed Todd Grimson in the *Los Angeles Times Book Review.* "The release of information to the reader seems unskilled, or immature," Grimson continued, "weak in narrative or plot." In the *New York Times Book Review,* Elizabeth Hanson criticized the overall effect of the book, writing that "the endearing characters and amusing scenes in Ms. Yoshimoto's work do not compensate for frequent bouts of sentimentality." Other reviewers were more taken with Yoshimoto's debut. *Detroit Free Press* reviewer Georgea Kovanis found that there was more to the book's appeal than the story elements suggest. "It's not the off-beat soap opera plot that makes Banana Yoshimoto's 'Kitchen' . . . so compelling," Kovanis wrote. "Instead, it's Yoshimoto's observation and rich detail. . . . 'Kitchen' is sad and witty and introspective and observant and dreamy. And a wonderful read." *New York Times* reviewer Michiko Kakutani called the book "oddly lyrical" and compared Yoshimoto's prose favorably to that of American authors Jane Smiley and Anne Tyler. Kakutani sounded one reservation in noting that

"Ms. Yoshimoto occasionally allows her narrator to meditate at length about suffering and death, and these interludes have a way of growing maudlin. . . . Fortunately," Kakutani pointed out, "such passages are relatively rare, and they are offset by Ms. Yoshimoto's wit, her clarity of observation and her firm control of her story. She has a wonderful tactile ability to convey a mood or a sensation through her description of light and sound and touch, as well as an effortless ability to penetrate her characters' hearts."

Yoshimoto followed *Kitchen* with the novel *N. P.,* published in the United States in 1994. The book centers around an author, Sarao Takase, who committed suicide after completing a collection of stories, and this fate is also shared by three people who attempt to translate Takase's book. Several years after the last of these suicides, the book's narrator, Kazami Kano, the ex-girlfriend of one of the unfortunate translators, becomes involved with the author's children. Their investigation of the story collection leads to startling discoveries for all involved.

Critics were mixed in their assessment of the novel. A critic for *Publishers Weekly* found the book "off-beat, intriguing, but ultimately unsatisfying." Donna Seaman in *Booklist,* on the other hand, was more positive, arguing that "Yoshimoto's fans won't be disappointed." David Galef in the *New York Times Book Review,* faulted the work for lack of depth and banal prose. Meg Cohen in *Harper's Bazaar,* however, lauded the work's "insightful prose," concluding, "*N. P.,* with its eccentric plot twists and charming superstition, proves not only that Yoshimoto has broken the language barrier but also that there's plenty more where this came from."

Yoshimoto's *Amrita* is the story of actress Sakumi, who, after the death of her younger sister, falls down some steps and loses her memory. The novel then follows Sakumi on an emotional journey wherein she "tries to replace her lost, pre-fall self, seeking some connection between dream and reality, past and present, the dead and the living," summarized Yoji Yamaguchi in the *New York Times Book Review.*

Critical reception to the work was again mixed. Margot Mifflin in *Womenswire* argued that the work has "all the guileless zeal and intimate detail of Yoshimoto's earlier books—and none of the concision. . . . With more plot and fewer epiphanies, *Amrita* might have soared; as it is, it reads like a running commentary on a story that never quite happens." Donna Seaman, in *Booklist,* commented, "Yoshimoto 'tells' instead of dramatizes, but even so, she spins a mesmerizing and haunting tale."

Yoshimoto's 2000 novel *Asleep* is a collection of three novellas, "each telling a somewhat mystical tale of haunted slumber," noted Kathleen Hughes in *Booklist.* The first novella is the story of a woman mourning the death of her lover; the second involves a woman who is in love with a man whose wife is in a coma; the last involves a woman who is haunted by the ghost of a woman with whom she had previously shared a lover. Each "woman sees herself as an incidental or supporting character, in refreshing contrast to Western self-involvement," wrote a critic for *Publishers Weekly.*

"The writing is introspective and, although simple, extremely thought-provoking as Yoshimoto takes her readers on a journey in search of absolution for each of her characters," found Shirley N. Quan in *Library Journal.* Other critics were also positive in their reviews of the work. "This collection," concluded Hughes, "is delicately tinged with sadness and lovely to read, and Yoshimoto's fervent American fan base will clamor for it."

BIOGRAPHICAL/CRITICAL SOURCES:

BOOKS

Contemporary Literary Criticism, Volume 84, Gale (Detroit, MI), 1995.

Furuhashi, Nobuyoshi, *Yoshimoto Banana to Tawara Machi,* Chikuma Shobo (Tokyo, Japan), 1990.

Yoshimoto, Banana, *Banana no banana* (interviews), Metarogu (Tokyo, Japan), 1994.

Yoshimoto, Takaaki, *Yoshimoto Takaaki x Yoshimoto Banana* (interviews), Rokkingu On (Tokyo, Japan), 1997.

PERIODICALS

Booklist, February 1, 1994, Donna Seaman, review of *N. P.,* p. 996; July, 1997, Donna Seaman, review of *Amrita,* p. 1801; April 15, 2000, Kathleen Hughes, review of *Asleep,* p. 1501.

Detroit Free Press, April 2, 1993, pp. 1G-2G.

Economist, February 20, 1993.

Entertainment Weekly, July 25, 1997, A. J. Jacobs, review of *Amrita,* p. 67.

Harper's Bazaar, March, 1994, Meg Cohen, review of *N. P.,* p. 170.

Library Journal, June 15, 1997, Janet Ingraham, review of *Amrita,* p. 100; May 1, 2000, Shirley N. Quan, review of *Asleep,* p. 156.

Los Angeles Times Book Review, January 10, 1993, pp. 3, 7.

Nation, August 11, 1997, Diane Simon, review of *Amrita,* p. 30.

New York Times, January 12, 1993.

New York Times Book Review, January 17, 1993, p. 18; February 27, 1994, David Galef, review of *N. P.,* p. 23; August 17, 1997, Yoji Yamaguchi, review of *Amrita.*

Publishers Weekly, December 13, 1993, review of *N. P.,* p. 61; May 8, 2000, review of *Asleep,* p. 206.

Times Literary Supplement, January 8, 1993, p. 18.

Washington Post Book World, January 10, 1993.

OTHER

Women's Wire, http://www.womenswire.com/ (July 2, 2000).*

* * *

ZACK, Naomi 1944-

PERSONAL: Born July 21, 1944, in Brooklyn, NY; children: Alexander Erdmann, Bradford Mahon. *Ethnicity:* "Multiracial." *Education:* New York University, B.A.; Columbia University, Ph.D., 1970.

ADDRESSES: Office—Philosophy HV 257, State University of New York at Albany, Albany, NY 12222. *E-mail*—nzack@albany.edu.

CAREER: State University of New York at Albany, assistant professor, 1991-2000, professor of philosophy, 2000—, director, doctor of arts program in humanistic studies.

MEMBER: American Philosophical Association, Phi Beta Kappa.

AWARDS, HONORS: Two Woodrow Wilson fellowships.

WRITINGS:

(With Jack Henry Abbott) *My Return,* 1987.

Race and Mixed Race, Temple University Press (Philadelphia, PA), 1993.

(Editor) *American Mixed Race and Comparing Sex and Race,* Rowman & Littlefield (Totowa, NJ), 1995.

Bachelors of Science: Seventeenth-Century Identity, Then and Now, Temple University Press (Philadelphia, PA), 1996.

(Editor) *Race/Sex: Their Sameness, Difference, and Interplay,* Routledge, 1997.

(Editor with Crispin Sartwell and Laurie Shrage) *Race, Class, Gender, and Sexuality: The Big Questions,* Blackwell Publishers, 1998.

Thinking about Race, Wadsworth, 1998.

(Editor) *Women of Color and Philosophy: A Critical Reader,* Blackwell Publishers, 2000.

* * *

ZALBEN, Jane Breskin 1950-

PERSONAL: Born April 21, 1950, in New York, NY; daughter of Murry (a certified public accountant) and Mae (a librarian; maiden name, Kirshbloom) Breskin; married Steven Zalben (an architect), December 25, 1969; children: Jonathan, Alexander. *Education:* Queens College of the City University of New York, B.A., 1971; Pratt Institute Graphic Center, graduate study in lithography, 1971-72. *Religion:* Jewish. *Avocational interests:* Travel, gardening, gourmet cooking, pets.

ADDRESSES: Home—Port Washington, NY. *Agent*—Marilyn Marlow, Curtis Brown Ltd., 10 Astor Pl., New York, NY 10003. *E-mail*—janezalben@hotmail.com.

CAREER: Dial Press, New York City, assistant to art director of children's book department, 1971-72; Holt, Rinehart & Winston, Inc., New York City, freelance book designer, 1973-74; Thomas Y. Crowell Co., New York City, senior designer of children's books, 1974-75; Scribner's, New York City, art director of children's books, 1975-76; writer and illustrator of children's books and novels, 1973—. School of Visual Arts, New York City, instructor of illustration, design, and writing of children's books, 1976-93; Vassar Publishing Institute, Poughkeepsie, NY, writer/artist-in-residence, 1988. *Exhibitions:* Exhibitor at individual and group shows at various institutions, including Metropolitan Museum of Art, Justin Schiller Gallery, and the American Institute of Graphics Art Show, all New York City; Every Picture Tells a Story, Los Angeles, CA; Bush Gallery, Vermont; Books of Wonder, Beverly Hills, CA; Elizabeth Stone Gallery, Michigan; Port Washington Library; Hecksher Museum, Long Island, NY; Vassar College; and Findlay College.

MEMBER: Society of Children's Book Writers and Illustrators (judge of Golden Kite award).

AWARDS, HONORS: AIGA award, 1978 and 1979; *Beni's First Chanukah* was named an *American Bookseller* Pick of the Lists, 1988, and a Sidney Taylor Honor Book, 1989; *Parents* magazine award, 1993; IRA Teachers' Choice award, 1993.

WRITINGS:

SELF-ILLUSTRATED

Cecilia's Older Brother, Macmillan (New York, NY), 1973.
Lyle and Humus, Macmillan (New York, NY), 1974.
Basil and Hillary, Macmillan (New York, NY), 1975.
Penny and the Captain, Collins (New York, NY), 1977.
Norton's Nighttime, Collins (New York, NY), 1979.
Will You Count the Stars without Me?, Farrar, Straus (New York, NY), 1979.
"Oh, Simple!", Farrar, Straus (New York, NY), 1981.
Porcupine's Christmas Blues, Philomel/Putnam, 1982.
Beni's First Chanukah, Holt (New York, NY), 1988.
Happy Passover, Rosie, Holt (New York, NY), 1990.
Leo and Blossom's Sukkah, Holt (New York, NY), 1990.
Goldie's Purim, Holt (New York, NY), 1991.
Beni's Little Library (Jewish holiday boxed set), Holt (New York, NY), 1991.
Buster Gets Braces, Holt (New York, NY), 1992.
Happy New Year, Beni, Holt (New York, NY), 1993.
Papa's Latkes, Holt (New York, NY), 1994.
Miss Violet's Shining Day, Boyds Mills Press, 1995.
Pearl Plants a Tree, Simon & Schuster (New York, NY), 1995.
Beni's Family Cookbook for the Jewish Holidays, Holt (New York, NY), 1996.
Pearl's Marigolds for Grandpa, Simon & Schuster (New York, NY), 1997.
Beni's Family Treasury: Stories for the Jewish Holidays, Holt (New York, NY), 1998.
Beni's First Wedding, Holt (New York, NY), 1998.
Pearl's Eight Days of Chanukah, Simon & Schuster (New York, NY), 1998.
To Every Season: A Family Holiday Cookbook, Simon & Schuster (New York, NY), 1999.
Don't Go!, Clarion Books (New York, NY), 2001.
Pearl's Passover: A Family Celebration through Stories, Recipes, Crafts, and Songs, Simon & Schuster (New York, NY), in press.

YOUNG ADULT NOVELS

Maybe It Will Rain Tomorrow, Farrar, Straus (New York, NY), 1982.
Here's Looking at You, Kid, Farrar, Straus (New York, NY), 1984.
Water from the Moon, Farrar, Straus (New York, NY), 1987.
Earth to Andrew O. Blechman, Farrar, Straus (New York, NY), 1989.
The Fortuneteller in 5B, Holt (New York, NY), 1991.
Unfinished Dreams, Simon & Schuster (New York, NY), 1996.

ILLUSTRATOR

Jan Wahl, *Jeremiah Knucklebones,* Holt (New York, NY), 1974.
Jane Yolen, *An Invitation to the Butterfly Ball: A Counting Rhyme,* Parents Magazine Press, 1976.
Lewis Carroll, *Jabberwocky,* F. Warne, 1977.
Yolen, *All in the Woodland Early: An ABC Book,* Collins (New York, NY), 1979.
Carroll, *The Walrus and the Carpenter,* Holt (New York, NY), 1986.
Inner Chimes: Poems on Poetry, selected by Bobbye S. Goldstein, Wordsong/Boyds Mills Press, 1992.

OTHER

Oliver and Alison's Week, illustrated by Emily Arnold McCully, Farrar, Straus (New York, NY), 1980.
A Perfect Nose for Ralph, illustrated by John Wallner, Philomel, 1980.
The Magic Menorah: A Modern Chanukah Tale, illustrated by Donna Diamond, Simon & Schuster (New York, NY), 2001.

SIDELIGHTS: Jane Breskin Zalben is an author and illustrator with numerous books to her credit, from simple counting and ABC picture books for preschoolers to young adult novels dealing with the death of a parent, Holocaust survivors, and AIDS. Since the 1983 publication of *Beni's First Chanukah,* she has become best known as the creator of several series of picture books about the Jewish holidays that feature lovable animal characters. As an illustrator, Zalben is lauded for her warm, finely detailed watercolor renderings of anthropomorphic animals—squirrels, monkeys, penguins, and bears. Alice Digilio noted in a *Washington Post Book*

World review of *"Oh, Simple!"* that stories "can seem too precious when small animal characters are substituted for small human ones" and praised Zalben for avoiding this problem in her "excellent tale" about two chipmunk characters. Marcia Posner, in a *School Library Journal* appraisal of *Goldie's Purim,* found the pictures "totally charming and accomplished," lauding the author-illustrator's "tiny, intricate patterns and . . . attention to detail."

Born in 1950 in New York City, Zalben was drawing from the time she could hold a crayon. "Formal" art study began at age five when her mother took her for weekly arts lessons at the Metropolitan Museum of Art in New York City. "I just loved it," Zalben once recalled of her time at the museum school, saying in an interview that "it became like a comfortable second home." In sixth grade Zalben decided that when she reached the ninth grade she would apply to the High School of Music and Art; soon after she began building her portfolio.

After graduating from high school, Zalben went on to major in art at Queens College, where she was fortunate to study under several inspiring teachers. One was Marvin Bileck, a Caldecott Honor runner-up for his book *Rain Makes Applesauce.* "I still have parchment and Japanese rice paper from when I was in one of his classes," she once recalled. Bileck would talk about "the importance of the brushes and papers you use. It changed my life. I started thinking, gee, this would be interesting to do for a living." Another fond memory from Zalben's college years is the barn that was converted into studios for the art students. "I had my own big space," she once recalled, "so it was the first time in my life I could paint until three in the morning."

Her first job after college was as a part-time assistant in the art department at New York City's Dial Press. One advantage of the job was being in the office only "three days a week, so I could do my own work the other two." But it was during this time that Zalben began to really learn about book design, and her passion for the entire process of creating children's books was developing. "I was getting advice and knowledge from people who were really the best in the field," she once explained.

Nine months after finishing college, Zalben met Susan Hirschman, then editor-in-chief of children's publishing at Macmillan. Zalben credits Hirschman with having a great effect on her career. "She said certain things to me," Zalben once recalled, "about writing—the clarity, the simplicity, the whole architectural concept of less is more."

A month after meeting Hirschman, Zalben published her first book, *Cecilia's Older Brother,* a tale of sibling rivalry with a twist. In this story about a family of mice, Cecilia is constantly being teased and bullied by her older brother Timothy—that is, until "something better" comes along. That something better is a baby brother, and now both Timothy and Cecilia have someone new to fight with. Zalben drew on personal memories of growing up with an older brother to create the book, which, according to a *Times Literary Supplement* critic, "has its funny moments," and is "neatly and wittily illustrated." Ethel L. Heins in *Horn Book* praised *Cecilia's Older Brother* for its "crisply detailed pictures."

With her first three books published, Zalben found herself drawn toward a different style; what she once called "the elf-and-details direction of *Butterfly Ball.*" Zalben has been developing and refining this warm, sometimes offbeat and whimsical, and, above all, richly detailed style of watercolor and pencil drawing in the more than thirty picture books she has illustrated since.

Reviewers are frequently charmed by Zalben's drawings. For example, Kristi L. Thomas's review of *"Oh, Simple!"* in *School Library Journal* praised Zalben's "exquisite tableaux of anthropomorphic animals." Carolyn K. Jenks, in her *School Library Journal* critique of *Norton's Nighttime,* commented favorably on the way "the soft, dark watercolor illustrations reflect the nighttime atmosphere of the text."

After contributing to some thirteen picture books over ten years' time, Zalben also began writing young adult novels. She recalled that Sandra Jordan, then editor-in-chief at Farrar, Straus & Giroux, helped encourage this change by suggesting, "I think there's more you need to say than you're able to say in a thirty-two-page picture book." Zalben was then raising a baby and a toddler, and although she had little extra energy, she decided that naptimes would provide her the opportunity to start working on a longer story.

Her first novel, *Maybe It Will Rain Tomorrow,* was published in 1982. It is the story of Beth, a sixteen-year-old girl who must go to live with her father and his second wife after her mother's suicide. The story focuses on growing up, loss, first love, and most of all about the difficult relationship between Beth and her stepmother. Symme J. Benoff, writing in *School Library Journal,* called the book "touching" and the relationship between Beth and Linda "real [and] understandable."

Zalben went on to write three novels in a row, inspired by her experiences as a parent of teenagers. In *Water from the Moon,* teen Nicole Bernstein seems to have it all, except a love interest, which causes her to misinterpret the friendly overtures of a young man working in her father's office. The young woman's efforts to establish a secure friendship with a fellow art student are also frustrated when her friend announces her plans to leave the area when her mother changes jobs. *The Fortune-teller in 5B,* which Zalben published in 1991, focuses on Alexandria Pilaf, a teen whose anguish over the death of her own father is transferred into paranoia about an elderly woman in her apartment building. Alexandria begins to spread rumors that the woman is a vampire, because she is rarely seen during the day. Finally the truth is learned—the woman is a survivor of the concentration camps where she lost much of her family—and Alexandria finds a way to deal with her own loss. "Readers will be moved by the author's note about the concentration camp at Terezin," noted Kathy Peihl in *St. James Guide to Young Adult Writers,* "where thousands of children were sent during World War II."

The 1980s were a time of transition for Zalben. She had left the city in which she had been born and raised, and moved to the Long Island suburbs, where she felt lonely. "I hated it for the first three years," she once explained, "and my first novel starts out like that about suburbia and all the houses looking the same." Although it was a difficult adjustment, her new life in the suburbs inspired her work on the "Beni" books, her illustrated series about the Jewish holidays. Zalben once recalled in an interview the story of driving down the main street of town with her family. The streets were decorated for Christmas and her younger son Alexander wanted to know where the Chanukah decorations were. "He wanted to have a Christmas tree and the holly trailing down the banister," Zalben explained. "I said, 'Alexander, we're not going to do that, we're Jewish.' And he said, 'Well, if you don't do that then I'm going to marry a girl who's not Jewish when I grow up.'" Zalben was amused at the strong reaction she had to this situation, but it encouraged her to do a Chanukah book.

"The more I thought about it, the more I wanted to give my children, and Jewish children, a gift—something they could cuddle up with during their holiday that wasn't moralistic, pedantic and preachy," Zalben wrote in an essay in the *Miami Jewish Tribune.* She presented the idea of a picture book featuring a cuddly family of bears to her publisher, and the next six months were filled with meetings and discussions trying to answer the question, "How would Jewish people take to animals?" As Zalben wrote in her essay, the response to her idea was generally that "cute little mice were okay for Christmas books, but Jewish children shouldn't have animals."

Ultimately Zalben prevailed. She wrote the book as she had envisioned it, and the first printing of *Beni's First Chanukah*—12,500 copies—sold out in three weeks. A *Publishers Weekly* reviewer called *Beni's First Chanukah* "enchanting . . . a gentle reminder that children take pleasure in simple things and that holidays need not be elaborate to be memorable." A *School Library Journal* critic termed the book "a pleasant celebration" and "a quiet story of family holiday togetherness."

The critical and popular success of *Beni's First Chanukah* led to books celebrating Passover, Sukkot, Purim, and thc Jewish New Year, all featuring Beni's bear family. Zalben once commented that it wasn't until the fifth book, *Happy New Year, Beni,* that she really started to feel like she "knew" the characters. *Happy New Year* was inspired by her own experience of "Tashlikh," the ritual of throwing bits of bread into a river, symbolizing the casting away of past wrongdoing to start the new year afresh. "It was so spiritual and wonderful," she remembered, "that after the holidays were over, I went home and wrote the book." A review of *Happy New Year, Beni* in *Publishers Weekly* pointed to "Zalben's sweet-natured watercolor-and-pencil illustrations" that "portray the festivities in inviting detail, from the table set with lace cloth and candles to the Torah scrolls and prayer shawls in the synagogue." Hazel Rochman, writing in *Booklist,* noted how the "sweetness is nicely undercut by pesky cousin Max, whose practical jokes and wet plastic spiders spoil Beni's fun."

Other Beni books include *Beni's Family Cookbook,* which collects recipes organized around each of the Jewish holidays. While the recipes are designed for cooks who know their way around the kitchen, the layout of the book, and its engaging illustrations, will be sure to captivate younger helpers. The young bear experiences yet another first when he hears Uncle Izzy announce his wedding plans. In *Beni's First Wedding,* readers share Beni's excitement at being a part of the wedding party, and learn about Jewish customs. Writing in *School Library Journal,* Elizabeth Palmer Abarbanel called *Beni's First Wedding* "a wonderful selection for children anticipating a family wedding, and a must for libraries serving Jewish communities."

In addition to her Beni character, Zalben has introduced a young sheep named Pearl who, with her little brother Avi in tow, explores the Jewish tradition from a female perspective. In *Pearl's Eight Days of Chanukah,* published in 1998, Pearl's twin cousins, Sophie and Harry, come to spend the holidays, allowing readers to share in the crafts, ceremonies, and festivities that comprise Chanukah. Noting that the book's strength "lies in the depiction of Chanukah as a time to celebrate and enjoy the company of friends and family," a *School Library Journal* contributor praised the colored pencil and watercolor illustrations as "warm and appealing." While noting that Zalben's "cozy, finely detailed" illustrations are the strength of this book, a *Publishers Weekly* contributor warned that the crafts described in *Pearl's Eight Days of Chanukah* required more craft supplies than are readily available in the average home.

Pearl Plants a Tree describes the "environmental" holiday of Tu B'shvat, as Pearl and her grandfather discuss his first home in America and the tree he once planted there. Pearl decides to follow the tradition by raising an apple tree seedling; the following spring she and her grandfather celebrate the tree-planting holiday together. In the poignant *Pearl's Marigolds for Grandpa,* the young sheep must cope with the loss of her beloved grandfather, in a story that *School Library Journal* contributor Susan Scheps noted "will be comfortably reassuring to children who have lost a beloved grandparent." The book also contains information on the mourning customs for six major religious traditions.

Although Zalben's primary fame rests on her "Beni" books, she continues exploring the many different projects that have allowed her to express herself. A young adult novel, 1996's *Unfinished Dreams,* focuses on sixth grade student Jason Glass and his relationship with his middle school principal, Mr. Carr, who ultimately dies of AIDS. It is also about music—Mr. Carr had inspired Jason to learn to play the violin—and Zalben's story explores the healing power of art. "Zalben has written an introspective novel, with real people who have real conversations," commented *Voice of Youth Advocates* contributor Ann Bouricius. The critic added that the book "will be savored by those who enjoy a subtly rich and quiet read."

In addition to writing books about friendship, feelings, warmth, and family, Zalben travels around the world, speaking to young fans about her writing and her art. Her experiences with her readers, her family, and others in her life, continue to fuel her passion for her work. "Sometimes you need to rewrite things that you haven't had, and you also need to duplicate things you have had. If I've had bad times in my life, I don't stop my art. I get closer to it and go into it more. The art is a friend."

BIOGRAPHICAL/CRITICAL SOURCES:

BOOKS

St. James Guide to Young Adult Writers, St. James Press (Detroit, MI), 1997.

PERIODICALS

Booklist, December 15, 1975, p. 583; December 15, 1988; March 15, 1990, p. 1464; September 15, 1990; January 1, 1992; July, 1993, Hazel Rochman, review of *Happy New Year, Beni;* August, 1995, Kathy Broderick, review of *Miss Violet's Shining Day,* p. 1958; November 15, 1995, Stephanie Zvirin, review of *Pearl Plants a Tree,* p. 566; June 1, 1996, Susan Dove Lempke, review of *Unfinished Dreams,* p. 1704; September 15, 1996, Stephanie Zvirin, review of *Beni's Family Cookbook,* p. 236; November 1, 1997, Ilene Cooper, review of *Pearl's Marigolds for Grandpa,* p. 485.

Bulletin of the Center for Children's Books, November, 1973; February, 1979; November, 1982; October, 1984; December, 1991, p. 111.

Hadassah Magazine, August-September, 1993, Rahel Musleah, "Love Pictures," pp. 38-39.

Horn Book, June, 1973, Ethel L. Heins, review of *Cecilia's Older Brother,* pp. 263-264; October, 1978, p. 511; March-April, 1990, p. 197; January-February, 1992, p. 77; September-October, 1996, Elizabeth Watson, review of *Unfinished Dreams,* p. 603.

Miami Jewish Tribune, December 22, 1989, Jane Breskin Zalben, "Chanukah Story."

Publishers Weekly, November 3, 1975, p. 72; June 26, 1978, p. 117; October 15, 1979, p. 67; December 12, 1980, p. 47; July 3, 1981, p. 146; April 30, 1982; October 15, 1982; April 10, 1987, p. 95; November 11, 1988, review of *Beni's First Chanukah,* p. 55; October 27, 1989, p. 70; January 19, 1990; October 26, 1990, p. 69; January 18, 1991, p. 57; September 20, 1991, p. 135; May 18, 1992, p. 68; August 16, 1993, p. 49; September 20, 1993, review of *Happy New Year, Beni;* October 14, 1996, review of *Beni's Family Cookbook,* p. 85; September 28, 1998, review of *Pearl's Eight Days of Chanukah,* p. 52.

School Library Journal, December, 1975, p. 65; September, 1979, Carolyn K. Jenks, review of *Norton's Nighttime,* p. 125; November, 1981, Kristi L. Thomas, review of *"Oh, Simple!,"* p. 84; May, 1982, Symme J. Bennoff, review of *Maybe It Will Rain*

Tomorrow, p. 76; October, 1988, review of *Beni's First Chanukah;* November, 1989, p. 116; April, 1990, p. 101; February, 1991, p. 77; May, 1991, Marcia Posner, review of *Goldie's Purim,* p. 86; December, 1991, p. 120; April, 1992, p. 102; December, 1993, p. 97; January 1, 1996, Marcia W. Posner, review of *Pearl Plants a Tree,* p. 99; February, 1997, Susan Scheps, review of *Beni's Family Cookbook,* p. 126; September, 1997, Susan Scheps, review of *Pearl's Marigolds for Grandpa,* p. 198; May, 1998, Elizabeth Palmer Abarbanel, review of *Beni's First Wedding,* pp. 128-29; October, 1998, review of *Pearl's Eight Days of Chanukah,* p. 39; February, 2000, Augusta R. Malvagno, review of *To Every Season,* p. 116.

Times Literary Supplement, November 23, 1973, review of *Cecilia's Older Brother,* p. 1436.

Voice of Youth Advocates, August, 1996, Ann Bouricius, review of *Unfinished Dreams,* p. 164.

Washington Post Book World, August 9, 1981, Alice Digilio, "Young Bookshelf."*